LITERATURE FOR TODAY'S YOUNG ADULTS

SECOND EDITION

Alleen Pace Nilsen   Kenneth L. Donelson
Arizona State University

SCOTT, FORESMAN AND COMPANY
Glenview, Illinois   London, England

To Bob Carlsen,

partly for what he has done in a lifetime of service to young adult
literature, but mostly for what he has done for each of us

Cover and Part Opener Art by Mike Muir

Photographs by John P. Vergis

The authors and publishers would like to thank all sources for the use of their material. The
credit lines for copyrighted materials appearing in this work appear in the Acknowledgments
section beginning on page 631. This section is to be considered an extension of the
copyright page.

Library of Congress Cataloging in Publication Data

Donelson, Kenneth L.
    Literature for today's young adults.

    Includes bibliographies and indexes.
    1. Young adults—Books and reading.   2. Young
adult literature—History and criticism.   3. Young
adult literature—Bibliography.   I. Nilsen, Alleen Pace.
II. Title.
Z1037.A1D578   1985   823'.009'9283   84-23633
ISBN 0-673-15933-7

    5 6 7 - KPF - 90 89 88 87

PREFACE

Thanks to the generosity of a publisher at a national meeting, we were having dinner with Robert Cormier and his family. When we mentioned that we were beginning to work on this second edition of *Literature for Today's Young Adults*, Cormier's eyes lit up and he sounded almost envious that our kind of writer gets a second chance at a book while with novelists—notwithstanding the 5,000 corrections recently made on James Joyce's *Ulysses*—once a book is published it belongs to the ages. As the months dragged on and the work seemed never-ending, we kept reminding each other that Cormier looked on what we were doing as an opportunity rather than an obligation. Actually it was both.

One of the things we said in the first edition was that the field of young adult literature changes quickly. We hardly realized the truthfulness of this statement until we came back five years later and saw how many changes had occurred. For example, in the first edition, we lamented a shortage of modern romances for young readers, and now we are lamenting how the romances seem to overshadow everything else. Readers who are interested in making other comparisons should look especially at Chapter 8 on informative books and at Chapter 11 on issues and concerns where we added sections on books with religious themes and influences from the mass marketing of paperbacks. Censorship has increased so much that it merits its own Chapter 12 this time. In Chapter 9, we also included completely new sections on poetry, drama, and humor. And in answer to teachers who wanted help in breaking down the isolation of young adult books from literature in general, in Chapter 9 we tie it in with video games and rock music and in Chapter 10 we tie it in with significant adult books.

We had many reasons for writing this book, but chief among them was our belief that it was needed and worth doing. When in the late 1970s we surveyed teachers of young adult literature in library science, English, and education departments, an overwhelming majority expressed a need for a scholarly and readable textbook to provide history and background of the field. One teacher wrote that her major problem "in establishing and promoting the work of the course was the sometimes skeptical view of colleagues about the worth of this literature," and added she would welcome a book to educate professionals in related fields about the growing body of good young adult books. We hope our book answers some of these needs, not only for academic classes in young adult literature but also for librarians, teachers, counselors, and others working with young people between the ages of twelve and twenty.

For our purposes, we define "young adult literature" as any book freely chosen for reading by someone in this age group. We say "young adult" rather than "adolescent" because many people, particularly students, find the word "adolescent" condescending. We do not make a distinction between books distributed by juvenile divisions and adult divisions of publishing houses because teenagers read both. We estimate that 80 percent of the books read by younger teenagers will have been distributed as juvenile titles while most of the books read by older teenagers will have been published as adult books—those shelved in libraries and bookstores under no specific age designation.

We organized our book much as we teach our courses: first, an introduction to young adults and to their literature, then a look at contemporary books followed by a view of the professional's role in relation to books and young readers. For this edition, we moved the history of the field to the final three chapters, not because we thought it any less important but because teachers told us their students were better able to appreciate the historical background when they knew what it was leading up to. There is obviously nothing sacred about the organization, and, depending on the background of the students in your class and their needs and interests, you may wish to rearrange chapters and to give more or less attention to particular sections.

At various points we present criteria for evaluating different kinds of books. Evaluation is complex, and one sports novel, for example, is so different from other sports novels that any list of definitive criteria would be foolish, if not impossible. These criteria, then, are not Mosaic Law and should be considered starting places. Developing skill in evaluation comes only with practice and wide reading.

Because so many excellent new books are written each year, lists of suggested or recommended titles are doomed to be dated almost before they are printed. You can supplement the lists here with the help of current reviewing sources and annual lists of recommended titles compiled by *School Library Journal, Booklist,* the Young Adult Services Division of the American Library Association, the *New York Times,* and the University of Iowa Books for Young Adults Poll published in the *English Journal.*

Although we realize that in most classes and in many libraries it is the paperback editions of books that are usually read by young adults, in our book lists we show the original hardback publishers where we are able to identify them. We do this for two reasons. First, we want to give credit to the companies who found the authors and did the editorial work and the initial promotions on each book. Second, by relying on the hardback editions we are able to achieve a greater degree of consistency and accuracy than if we relied on the paperback editions. The paperback publishing industry is relatively fluid and a title may be published and then go out of print within only a few months. To find whether there is a paperback edition of a book available, we suggest you refer to the most recent issue of *Paperbound Books in Print* published annually (with frequent supplements) by R. R. Bowker Company and purchased by practically every library in the country.

The subject of young adult literature is vast and we were not always able to mention books and authors that we might have liked, some of them our personal favorites. The historical chapters needed to cover so much so rapidly that the compression of material became breathless at times. We wanted to keep the book short enough that students could read it and still have time for the most important part of the course, the reading of young adult books. Charles Weingartner ended one of his talks at a National Council of Teachers of English convention by relating an argument he had had with a colleague over a book. They couldn't come to any agreement, not even on details, much less on the basic idea of the book. Finally, in exasperation, Weingartner asked, "Have you read the book?" "Certainly!" came the reply and then, almost as an afterthought, "Well, not personally."

We hope students—and their instructors—will not let our words about books substitute for reading them "personally." It is the personal reading that brings understanding of what young adult literature is all about and enables people to develop skills for both evaluation and promotion of young adult books.

A small change in this second edition is that Nilsen's name comes first. This does not reflect a change in our working relationship, it's simply that we are taking turns—our apologies to librarians who will have to recatalogue the book. As with any partnership as complex as this one, it's impossible to say exactly who did what, but basically Nilsen was responsible for Chapters 1, 2, 3, 4, 8, 10, and 11 while Donelson was responsible for Chapters 5, 6, 7, 12, 13, 14, and 15. In Chapter 9, Nilsen did the poetry and drama sections while Donelson did the humor section.

For help in preparing this edition, we need to again acknowledge the support of the Departments of English and of Educational Technology and Library Science at Arizona State University. We thank Betty Whetton and Annette Donelson for help with the chapter on science fiction and fantasy; secretaries Liz Outcault, Dorris Moloso, and Pat Peterson for patience in typing and retyping the manuscript, and photographer John Vergis for skill and care both behind the camera and in the darkroom. Other colleagues whose ideas and words we respect so much that they have probably found their way onto these pages more than we realize include the *English Journal* YA book review editors Dick Abrahamson and Ben and Beth Nelms, YA librarian Christy Tyson, fellow teacher Karen Beyard-Tyler, and graduate students Margaret Ferry, Nel Ward, Don Melichar, Chris Crowe, and Ric Alpers. We are grateful to our Scott, Foresman editors Chris Jennison and Anita Portugal and to the readers of the manuscript who saved us from making more errors than we might have otherwise: Edward R. Fagan,

Carolyn Baggett, Nevada Thomason, Edwyna Gilbert, Pat Sullivan, and Elizabeth Wahlquist.

We are also grateful to the authors, editors, teachers, critics, and librarians who wrote the statements on the future of young adult literature which appear in boxes throughout the fifteen chapters. When we sat down to draw up an invitation list for these predictions, we were surprised and pleased to realize that many more people deserved inclusion than we had space for. We settled on what we hope is a representative sampling of those who share our faith in young adults and our belief that the books they read, whether written for them or for adults, deserve thoughtful attention.

Ninety-five years ago, Edward Salmon defended his work in children's literature by writing:

> It is no uncommon thing to hear children's literature condemned as wholly bad, and some people are good enough to commiserate with me on having waded through so much ephemeral matter. It may be my fault or my misfortune not to be able to see my loss. I have spent many pleasant and I may say not unprofitable hours in company with the printed thoughts of Mr. Kingston, Mr. Ballantyne, Mr. Henty, Jules Verne, Miss Alcott, Miss Meade, Miss Molesworth, Miss Doudney, Miss Yonge, and a dozen others, and hope to spend as many more in the time to come as a busy life will permit.*

Today it is heartening to consider how many talented people share Edward Salmon's feelings, and like us, feel joy in spending their lives working in a world of literature that is always changing, exciting, and alive.

Alleen Pace Nilsen
Kenneth L. Donelson

*"Should Children Have a Special Literature?" *The Parents' Review* 1 (June 1890): 339.

CONTENTS

P·A·R·T O·N·E

UNDERSTANDING
YOUNG ADULTS AND BOOKS

YOUNG ADULTS
AND THEIR READING

An optimist might describe the field of young adult literature as "dynamic," while a pessimist would be more apt to say it is "unstable." Until 1868 when Louisa May Alcott wrote *Little Women* and her contemporary Oliver Optic began publishing his endless series of books, there was almost nothing written specifically for adolescents. Shortly afterwards—to the joy of the young and the anguish of the old—dime novels were published in the millions. But still "young adult literature," "teenage books," and "adolescent literature" would have been strange, even meaningless, terms because only within the last half of the twentieth century has literature for young adults developed as a distinct unit of book publishing and promotion.

Because of the newness of the concept and practice, there are no long-standing traditions as in children's literature. No major prizes are given and opinions vary tremendously on whether or not there is even a need for a specialized approach to teenage books. The development of such books coincided with the development of the concept of adolescence as a specific and unique period of life. Puberty is a universal experience, but adolescence is not. Even today, in nontechnological societies the transition from childhood to adulthood may be quite rapid, but in the United States it begins at about age twelve or thirteen and continues through the early twenties. This stretching out of the transition between childhood and adulthood came about after the Civil War. Until then, people were simply considered either children or adults. The turning point took place at about age fourteen or fifteen when children could go to work and become economic assets to the family and the community. But as the predominantly agricultural society in which children worked with their families gave way to a technological society in which people worked in factories, offices, schools, hospitals, research centers, and think-tanks, the jobs that were available required specialized training. The more complex society became, the longer children had to go to school to prepare for their eventual adulthood. These children, waiting to be accepted as full-fledged members of society, developed their own unique society. They became "teenagers" and "young adults," or as the psychologists prefer to call them, "adolescents."

Any change that affects this many people in such a major way demands adjustments and a reshuffling of priorities and roles. Such changes do not come automatically and few of us would venture the opinion that all the adjustments have been made.

◈ A PLEA FOR THE STUDY OF ADOLESCENT PSYCHOLOGY

When the Nilsens' first baby was born, they proudly sent out announcements and received from a revered professor a check for $5.00 with the terse note, "Congratulations on your future teenage problem." Although stated in more "scientific" terms, a similar message appears in much psychological writing on adolescence, for example in G. Stanley Hall's "sturm und drang" (storm and stress) theory,[1] A. L. Gesell's alternating cycles of conflict and calm,[2] Erik H. Erikson's "identity crisis,"[3] and Robert J. Havighurst's description of developmental tasks.[4] Fortunately for the Nilsens the professor's ominous congratulatory note proved to be overly pessimistic, and fortunately for many other parents so do the dire sounding names of many psychological theories.

But parents, teachers, librarians, social workers, and young people themselves agree that during the teenage years, tremendous changes take place—physically, intellectually, and emotionally. Of course such changes necessitate adjustments that often result in friction between young people and their associates. For this reason, we encourage you to take a solid course in adolescent psychology.

Cognitive or intellectual development has a tremendous influence on reading interests at all stages from early childhood through adolescence. Jean Piaget theorized that at about the age of twelve, the "formal operational" stage of thinking begins to develop.[5] This gives young people the power to consider the hypothetical. Teenagers differ from children in being able to imagine actions and their results even though there is no way to actually try them out. Boyd McCandless and Richard Coop describe this stage as an ability to "adopt several different viewpoints for considering a given act: a policeman's view, a parent's view, even the views of a dog, a Martian, society in general, or God. In short, [the young person] has gained possession of all the powers of If."[6] When reading imaginative literature, there is probably no intellectual quality more important than possessing "the powers of If." This is true not only of fantasy and science fiction, but also of any literature dealing with subjects and viewpoints beyond the reader's actual experience. Even in realistic novels, for example, we are asked to enter into the being and viewpoint of other characters where we must think as if we are someone else.

Our original plan in preparing this second edition was to include a section on adolescent psychology, but the more we worked on it, the more convinced we became that the kind of superficial treatment that we could pack into the few pages available would do more harm than good by encouraging you to overgeneralize and expect all teenagers to fit into textbook categories. And so rather than trying to provide you with an introduction to adolescent psychology, we will show some of the ways it relates to adolescent literature and will hope that in doing so, we will convince you to embark upon your own study of a very interesting field.

When we were still thinking of doing a summary, we turned to several textbooks[7] to determine just what parts would most closely relate to literature and should therefore be included here. In the table of contents of just one of the books,[8] we found the following headings or subheadings, all of which we could imagine illustrating through discussions of particular young adult books:

◇*Adolescence Here and Elsewhere, The Universality of Adolescence, Why Initiation Rites, Modern Rites, The Immense Journey: Biological Changes, The Growth Spurt, Early and Late Maturing, Operant Conditioning, Social Learning, Effects of Imitation, Theories of Adolescent Development, Developmental Tasks, Psychosexual Stages, Abnormal Development, Defense Mechanisms, Identity and Crises, Cognitive Theory, Creativity and Adolescence, Factors Affecting Self-Concept, The Contemporary Family, Changes in Adolescent-Parent Relationships, Affection and Control, Family versus Peers, Who Are Friends, Cliques and Crowds, Attitudes toward School, Theories of Moral Development, Who Is Delinquent, Adolescent Sexual Outlets, Social Disapproval, Peace? Love? Drugs, Sources of Frustration, Rebellious and Nonrebellious Groups,* and *Alienated Adolescents.*

What this listing makes clear is that adolescent psychology and adolescent literature are complementary fields. Specialists in either one should read widely in the other because while psychology provides the overall picture, adolescent literature—at least that which is honest—provides the individual portrait. Psychologists and writers are both people watchers. Back in the days before we had college degrees, accreditation boards, and professional associations, it was the storytellers—such writers as Chaucer, Shakespeare, and even Mark Twain—who served the roles that today are played by the sociologists, the psychologists, the textbook writers, and the performers on television talk shows.

But of course today's writers also have the advantage of the knowledge that has been gained through formal study. Judith Guest, author of *Ordinary People,* the story of seventeen-year-old Conrad Jarrett's psychological recovery, confessed in an interview to finding it "damn flattering" that the American Psychiatric Association invited her to address its 1981 annual meeting after the film version of her powerful book won four Academy Awards. When asked if she had done formal research in preparation for creating Berger, the unusual but appealing therapist in her book, she said she hadn't, but that people are doing research on their preoccupations all the time. "If you kept a list of the newspaper and magazine articles that you choose to read, they'd probably pretty much be the same kinds of articles. Psychiatry, psychology, all the behavioral sciences—why people act the way they do and what motivates them—have been preoccupations of mine throughout my life."[9]

There's ample evidence that other writers share Guest's preoccupation with psychological matters, and that the interest in her book which prompted the psychiatrists to invite her to speak was just one aspect of a broad interest that social scientists have in literature. Two literary collections edited by Thomas West Gregory are used as supplementary textbooks. *Adolescence in Literature* is used in adolescent psychology classes, and *Juvenile Delinquency in Literature* is used in criminal justice classes.[10] And it's fairly common in psychological writings to find references such as this one to literature, "An enormous literature documents the sexual initiation of boys. It has been said that almost every first novel is such a document."[11]

Going the other direction, Judith Guest's Dr. Berger is only one of a whole array of counselors, psychologists, and psychiatrists in contemporary novels that young adults are reading. They range from the cold and calculating Brint in Robert Cormier's *I Am the Cheese* to the efficient and brilliant Dr. Fried in Hannah Green's *I Never Promised You a Rose Garden*. In between are the more typical counselors such as the one in Judy Blume's *Then Again, Maybe I Won't* who helps Tony Miglioni adjust to his family's new wealth and the behavior of his friends as well as his social-climbing parents. In Sandra Scoppettone's *Trying Hard to Hear You*, Camilla's mother conveniently happens to be a psychoanalyst who can answer Camilla's questions when she discovers that two boys—including one she has a crush on—are lovers.

All of this points to another reason for studying adolescent psychology, and that is that it will help you to understand and appreciate what is being written about and why particular books speak forcefully to young readers, while others that are just as well written from a literary standpoint do not seem to touch kids "where they live." It's not that authors—at least not the good ones—sit down and peruse psychology books searching for case histories or symptoms of teenage problems they can envision making into a good story. This would be as unlikely—and as unproductive—as for a writer to study a book on literary devices and make a list: "First, I will use a metaphor, and then a bit of alliteration and some imagery followed by personification." But just as being able to recognize the way an author has brought about a particular effect whether through imagery or metaphor or allusion will bring you an extra degree of pleasure and understanding, so will being able to recognize the psychological underpinnings of fictional treatments of human problems. For example, the knowledgeable adult reader will recognize that there is a common thread running through the three quotes below, which touch on the problem of finding one's identity. Some psychologists label this as the major challenge of adolescence. Teenage readers do not necessarily have to know this to be interested, but it helps for adults who are selecting books to recognize what readers and characters might have in common. The quotes range from a light and relatively superficial comment made by

Marcy in Paula Danziger's junior novel *The Cat Ate My Gymsuit* to the questioning observation that Alex makes in Philip Roth's *Portnoy's Complaint,* and then to the explanation of the mental hospital patients in Ken Kesey's *One Flew Over the Cuckoo's Nest.*

> ◇ Getting dressed was a real trip. I got nervous about the color of the outfit. Purple was a pretty color, but what if I looked like a large grape in it? I was sure that everyone at the party was going to say "Joe, who is that grape you're dragging around?" Or "Marcy, Halloween is over." When I put on the earrings, necklace, and ring, I felt better. I mean, grapes don't wear jewelry. People would know it was me.   [Danziger]

> ◇ I am something called "a weekend guest"? I am something called "a friend from school"? What tongue is she speaking? I am "the bonditt," "the vantz," I am the insurance man's son. I am Warsaw's ambassador.   [Roth]

> ◇ All of us here are rabbits of varying ages and degrees, hippity-hopping through our Walt Disney world. Oh, don't misunderstand me, we're not in here *because* we are rabbits—we'd be rabbits wherever we were—we're all in here because we can't *adjust* to our rabbithood. We need a good strong wolf like the nurse to teach us our place.   [Kesey]

Although the latter two books were published for adults rather than teenagers, they have been popular with mature high school students partially because they deal with the problems of achieving independence and establishing one's identity.

Simply by reading adolescent literature, you will learn many things about adolescent psychology. But it will be helpful if you have a frame on which to hang what you learn and to fill in the gaps. It sometimes seems that there is an adolescent novel about every conceivable problem (see Chapter 4 for a discussion), but you won't be able to read them all because more good books are published than any one person has time to read. And if you are going to be successful in bringing young people and books together, you won't want to devote all your reading time to problem novels. You will want to read all kinds of books—fantasy, trivia, biography, humor, suspense, science fiction, and true accounts of people and events. A good background in adolescent psychology will enable you to appreciate all of these books from a teenager's viewpoint. It will also enable you to discuss the problems in many more books than you have time to read.

◈ WHAT IS YOUNG ADULT LITERATURE?

Even now, although most of us are quite sure we know what a teenager is, no hard and fast rules have developed for defining *teenage books, adolescent literature,* or *books for young adults.* The terms are vague and in professional literature are used interchangeably although some individuals do make distinctions. In 1981 we took a survey to see how much agreement we could find among a sampling of people working with books and young readers.[12] We chose twenty books reflecting a wide range of reading matur-

THE PEOPLE BEHIND THE BOOKS

When we drew up a list of people whose work we admired—publishing house editors, book reviewers, editors of periodicals, librarians, teachers of young adult literature, and of course those authors whose books we find ourselves returning to over and over again, we were happily surprised at how long the list was. Our intent was to ask these people to help us predict the future of young adult literature, but we soon realized that space limitations precluded asking everyone on the list. Our compromise was to invite a sampling of some forty people to either describe what they

envision for their own work or for the future of young adult literature as a whole. Their comments appear throughout this text under the heading, "The People Behind the Books." The titles listed by the individuals' names indicate the kinds of work they do, but the lists are by no means complete.

Our hope is that these forty statements will present a composite picture that is both more accurate and complete than one that could be arrived at in any other way. Additionally, the statements serve as introductions to some very interesting people. ◆

ity. We divided the books into groups of five that we perceived as belonging to each of the following categories: *juvenile fiction* (books for preteens such as Judy Blume's *Are You There God? It's Me, Margaret* and a Nancy Drew book), *junior (or teen) novel* (books for slightly older readers such as S. E. Hinton's *The Outsiders* and Richard Peck's *The Ghost Belonged to Me*), *adolescent literature* (books with more substance for older high school students such as M. E. Kerr's *Dinky Hocker Shoots Smack* and Robert Cormier's *I Am the Cheese*), and finally *young adult literature* (books published as adult books but often read by good high school readers such as Judith Guest's *Ordinary People* and Chaim Potok's *My Name Is Asher Lev*). We alphabetized our list of twenty books and sent it off to 100 nationally recognized people asking them to identify each book as belonging to one of the four categories or to mark it as "other." Responses came back from 14 editors and authors, 15 high school English or reading teachers, 18 university instructors, and 31 librarians. Not one of these 78 people classified the books exactly as we did. From the comments that were made, it became obvious that much more than the age of the reader is implied by these terms.

Part of the disagreement comes from the fact that people working with books and young readers have different training and different perspectives. Editors and authors commented that *adolescent literature* has "academic overtones"; English teachers said that *juvenile fiction* was "a publisher's term"; librarians said that *"adolescent literature* is what English teachers (or educators) use for *young adult literature."* One English teacher said she was trying to switch over to *young adult literature* while another one said she hesitated to use this "library term" because she wasn't sure of all the ramifications.

The term that proved to be the most popular was *young adult literature.*

On the survey form it was marked as the preferred term 496 times, while *adolescent literature* was marked 248 times, *junior (or teen) novel* 211 times, and *juvenile fiction* 189 times.

The terms that have been around the longest seem to have developed the most negative connotations, perhaps because these were the terms used in the kinds of negative criticism quoted later in this chapter. For example, one respondent said that "I suspect many folks think, as I am inclined, *juvenile fiction* is a pejorative term and may include what Bob Carlsen referred to in the first edition of *Books and the Teenage Reader* as 'sub-literature.'" Another one said that to her the term *junior novel* meant "light, insignificant, innocuous books like Nurse Barton . . . written specifically for teenagers following certain established formulas and not particularly well written from a literary point of view." The confusion that people feel was reflected in a note from an English teacher who identified *The Man Without a Face* as a junior novel but then questioned her decision by adding, "I have often used *junior novel* derogatorily although I think this is a good book."

The term *adolescent literature* gains some prestige from the word *literature*. For example, one person noted that her reason for classifying Nancy Drew books as *juvenile fiction* or something else is because "I don't think they deserve the respect which I give to *literature*." However, the *adolescent* part of the term is much more troublesome as shown by these comments:

◇ *Adolescent lit* sounds analytical—like a conference about young adults with none present.
◇ The term often suggests *immature* in a derogatory sense—hence could turn away people.
◇ It has the ugly ring of pimples and puberty.
◇ There is a strong bent on the part of some English teachers to view adolescent literature as if it were dirty laundry. If the word *adolescent* is to be used at all, it should be phrased "*Literature for Adolescents*."

The person making this last comment is apparently not the only one holding this opinion as shown by the fact that in 1976, three years after its founding, the Adolescent Literature Assembly of NCTE (ALAN) officially changed its name to the Assembly on Literature for Adolescents—National Council of Teachers of English.

Another potential problem with the term was indicated by a woman's statement to the effect that she considers the term as being in reference to literature *about* adolescence. "The problems/traumas/developments of moving *out* of childhood *into* a different stage—usually that of a teenager—like a first boyfriend, getting a motorcycle, a girl getting her period, etc."

Young adult literature was not only chosen as the preferred term twice as often as any of the others, it also received the most positive comments:

◇ Well-written material (as opposed to junior novels) with more lasting value—primarily for high school.

◇ Lends more a sense of dignity to the book.

◇ It makes young adults feel respected.

◇ A more general term—anything a YA might read, which is anything. It can also include nonfiction.

◇ It is becoming the umbrella term for anything teens read.

It is this latter comment which most closely reflects the way we're using the term throughout this text. When we say *young adult literature*, we mean anything that readers between the ages of twelve and twenty choose to read (as opposed to what they may be coerced to read for class assignments). We realize that the age range is broad, but we did not want to exclude teachers or librarians working with readers in middle schools or junior high schools nor with those young people who are out of high school but have not yet found their way into mainstream adult books.

In our survey there was no clear-cut agreement as to just who should be considered a young adult. Ages mentioned were "14 and up," "11 or 12 and up," "13 to 18 group," "12 to 19," "teenagers over 16," and "tenth to twelfth grades." One respondent made a note praising this kind of flexibility, "not just with the terms in a particular library system but nationwide, thus allowing each community to set up what's good for its youth."

We settled on *young adult literature* as our cover term because we have positive feelings toward our subject matter and want to use whatever term will be the most apt to encourage others to share our positive feelings. But we do confess to feeling a bit pretentious or false when referring to a twelve- or thirteen-year-old as a "young adult." Nevertheless, we shy away from using such terms as *juvenile literature, junior novel, teen novel,* and *juvie* because they have become so weighed down with connotations about quality—or lack of quality—that they no longer serve as neutral designators of the probable age of the reader. It's unfortunate that this happened because there's often a need for communicating that a particular book is more likely to appeal to a thirteen-year-old than to a nineteen-year-old. With adults a six-year-age difference may not affect choice of subject matter and intellectual and emotional response, but for teenagers even two or three years can make a tremendous difference.

When we talk about *children's literature*, we will be referring to books released by the juvenile or junior division of a publisher and intended for children from pre-kindergarten to about sixth grade. For variety we will sometimes use the terms *teenage books* and *adolescent literature.* This latter term reflects our English-teacher training where nearly all college courses offered by English departments were (or are) labelled *adolescent literature.* Technically, these courses deal only with books released by juvenile divisions of publishing houses. Hence we try to avoid using *adolescent literature* to refer to either today's or yesterday's best sellers that are popular with teenagers, for example *Rabbit Run, Ordinary People,* and *The World According to Garp,* or *Gone with the Wind, A Tree Grows in Brooklyn,* and *The Catcher in the Rye.*

It wasn't until the 1920s and 1930s that most publishers divided their

◆ The Honor Sampling does not accurately reflect the popularity of informative nonfiction because these books usually have shorter life spans and are aimed at more specific audiences than is fiction.
Courtesy of the Instructional Resources Library, Arizona State University.

offerings into adult and juvenile categories. And today it is sometimes little more than chance whether an adult or juvenile editor happens to get a manuscript. Robert Cormier had never thought of himself as a writer for young people, but when his agent submitted *The Chocolate War* to Pantheon, the editor convinced Cormier that, good as the book was, it would be simply one more in a catalog of adult books. On the other hand, if it were published for teenagers, it might sell well, and it certainly would not be one more in a long string of available adolescent novels. The editor's predictions came true, and Cormier later acknowledged that although his initial reaction to becoming a "young adult" author was one of shock followed by a month-long writer's block, he now feels grateful for what he considers to be stronger editorial help and more attention from reviewers at the juvenile level. Although he had already published several stories and three novels, it was *The Chocolate War* that brought him his first real financial gain.

Until very recently an author who had a choice of a book coming out as an adult title or a juvenile title probably would have automatically selected the adult division in hopes of receiving greater respect, acclaim, and financial rewards. This is less true today because of several breakthroughs. One is financial. Because of the base of support from school libraries, the YA market remained relatively strong during the economic recession of the early 1980s. Because we have a youth oriented society, teenage books are popular choices for general audience movies and television specials (see

Chapter 9), and as the book industry discovered that teenagers were willing to spend their own money for paperbacks in shopping mall bookstores (see Chapter 11), the whole financial base began to change. Developments in the 1970s had already brought considerable financial success to the YA book business. Reading came into the high school curriculum as a regular class taken for at least one semester by many students. In such classes there had to be something for students to read and in many cases this something was teenage fiction. During the late 1960s students and teachers turned away from the "classics" and the standard, required four years of English. English departments began offering electives, and courses in modern literature that included both adult and teenage fiction were popular with students. Many teachers who had previously scorned teenage books found themselves being forced to take a new look and to conclude that it was better to teach adolescent literature than no literature at all.

All of the interest has had a circular effect. The more important books for teenagers have become, the more respect the field has gained, and the better talent it has attracted. For example, on the basis of his Pulitzer Prize-winning play, *The Effect of Gamma Rays on Man-in-the-Moon Marigolds*, Paul Zindel was invited by Harper and Row to try writing teenage fiction. His first book was the well received *The Pigman*. Both M. E. Kerr and Robert Cormier, who are currently two of the most respected writers for this age group, have acknowledged taking positive note of this book as they pondered the effect that writing books for teenagers might have on their own careers.

◈ A BRIEF, UNSETTLED HERITAGE

The whole field of young adult literature is one some writers, teachers, and other interested parties have many questions about. It is, after all, a relatively new area. Teenage books have not always enjoyed the best reputation. An article in the *Louisville Courier-Journal* in 1951 indicates no great fondness for adolescent literature:

> ◇The blame for the vulgarity, the dull conformity and the tastelessness of much in American life cannot be laid altogether at the doors of radio, television, and the movies as long as book publishers hawk these books for young people. Flabby in content, mediocre in style, narrowly directed at the most trivial of adolescent interests, they pander to a vast debilitation of tastes, to intolerance for the demanding, rewarding and ennobling exercise which serious reading can be. . . . Like a diet of cheap candies, they vitiate the appetite for sturdier food— for that bracing, ennobling and refining experience, immersion in the great stream of the English classics.[13]

Fourteen years later, J. Donald Adams, editor of the "Speaking of Books" page in *The New York Times Book Review* wrote:

◇ If I were asked for a list of symptoms pointing to what is wrong with American education and American culture, or to the causes for the prolongation of American adolescence, I should place high on the list the multiplication of books designed for readers in their teens. The teen-age book, it seems to me, is a phenomenon which belongs properly only to a society of morons. I have nothing but respect for the writers of good books for children; they perform one of the most admirable functions of which a writer is capable. One proof of their value is the fact that the greatest books which children can enjoy are read with equal delight by their elders. But what person of mature years and reasonably mature understanding (for there is often a wide disparity) can read without impatience a book written for adolescents?[14]

As recently as 1977, John Goldthwaite writing in *Harper's* gave as one of his nine suggestions for improving literature for young readers in particular and the world in general:

◇ *The termination of teen-age fiction.* No one has ever satisfactorily explained why there is or ought to be such a thing as teen-age fiction at all. In the case of science fiction and fantasy, for example, there is little being written for adults that could not be understood by any literate twelve-year-old. Conversely, some prize winning fantasies for teen-agers have a turgidity of style the worst SF hack would be hard put to achieve. As for all that novelized stuff about alienation, drugs, and pregnancy, the great bulk of it might be more enjoyable presented in comic books. There are any number of very good underground cartoonists on the West Coast who need the money and might be willing to make something halfway real of such material.[15]

Those of us who have more positive attitudes toward teenage books can argue that these critics were writing about books that are far different from the good adolescent literature being published today. We can also conjecture that they were making observations based on a biased or inadequate sampling. Teenage books were never as hopelessly bad as such statements imply. Criticism of any field, young adult literature or ornithology or submarine designing, begins with first-hand experience of the subject. Critics who decide to do a cursory piece on young adult literature once a year or so seldom have the reading background necessary to choose representative titles. People who make generalizations about an entire field of writing based on reading only five or ten books are not merely unreliable sources, they are intellectual frauds. Wide knowledge surely implies a background of at least several hundred books.

Although we have grounds for rejecting the kind of negative criticism quoted above, we need to be aware that it still exists, though to a lesser extent than in years previous. This pessimistic view of teenage books is an unfortunate literary heritage that may very well be influencing the attitudes of school boards, library directors, parents, teachers, and anyone else who has had no particular reason actually to read and examine the best of the new teenage literature. Besides, so many new books for young readers appear each year (approximately 2,000 with about one third of these aimed at teenagers) that people who have already made up their minds about adolescent literature can probably find titles to support their beliefs no matter what they are. In an area as new as young adult literature, we can look at much of the disagreement and the conflicting views as inevitable. They are signs of a lively and interesting field.

◈ SOME MYTHS ABOUT YOUNG ADULT LITERATURE

Many of the old—and a few new—beliefs about teenagers and books have taken on the characteristics of myths. Some of the myths grew out of attempts to explain apparent contradictions; others are true in certain circumstances but have been overgeneralized and exaggerated; others have been used in such a way that they have become self-fulfilling prophecies. It seems appropriate at the beginning of a survey of young adult literature to examine some of these myths and to test them out against what we know about teenage reading and the best young adult literature. Your own wide and continued reading will help you form your own opinions.

We did some research to come up with a body of books that would be representative of what both young adults and professionals working in the field consider the best books. But we should caution you that books are selected as "the best" on the basis of many different criteria, and someone else's "best" will not necessarily be yours or that of the young people with whom you work. We hope that you will read many books so that you can recommend them, not because you saw them on a list, but because you personally enjoyed them and judge them to contain qualities that will appeal to a particular student.

In drawing up our list of "best books," we started with 1967, because in looking back this seemed to be a milestone year in which writers and publishers turned in new directions. We went to several different groups to see what books they recommend as the best in each of the succeeding years. The groups included the Young Adult Services Division of the American Library Association which each January issues a list containing between 30 and 50 titles considered the best of the previous year. Every December the editors of *School Library Journal* compile a list of the year's best juvenile books, plus a list of adult titles recommended as the best for young adults. From the children's list we took any title recommended for grade six and above. The editors of *The New York Times Book Review* also do an annual list of "best books," and again we noted any children's book recommended for readers 12 and up. To get the opinions of English teachers we went to the *English Journal*, which until recently has reviewed relatively few contemporary YA books and noted any book recommended either in a feature article, a young adult literature review column, or in the yearly poll prepared by the Books for Young Adults program founded by G. Robert Carlsen at the University of Iowa. For our last source, we took a survey of approximately 100 college instructors of young adult literature asking them what contemporary titles they assigned their students to read. Any book that

◆ The variety on the Honor Sampling contradicts the myths that teenage books are all the same. The honored books include historical fiction, nonfiction, short story collections, humor, new journalism, fantasy, love stories, poetry, and realistic problem novels.

was named by three out of these five sources was put on a master list and studied in some detail. This master list, hereafter referred to as the "Honor Sampling" is reprinted in this chapter for your convenience. A table with more complete information appears in Appendix A.

1983
Beyond the Divide. Kathryn Lasky. Macmillan
The Bumblebee Flies Anyway. Robert Cormier. Pantheon
A Gathering of Old Men. Ernest J. Gaines. Knopf
Poetspeak: In Their Work, About Their Work. Paul Janeczko, ed. Bradbury
The Sign of the Beaver. Elizabeth Speare. Houghton Mifflin
Solitary Blue. Cynthia Voigt. Atheneum
The Tempering. Gloria Skurzynski. Clarion
The Wild Children. Felice Holman. Scribner

1982
Annie on My Mind. Nancy Garden. Farrar, Straus & Giroux
The Blue Sword. Robin McKinley. Greenwillow
Class Dismissed! High School Poems. Mel Glenn. Clarion
The Darkangel. Meredith Ann Pierce. Atlantic
A Formal Feeling. Zibby Oneal. Viking
Homesick. Jean Fritz. Putnam

A Midnight Clear. William Wharton. Knopf
Sweet Whispers, Brother Rush. Virginia Hamilton. Philomel

1981
The Battle Horse. Harry Kullman. Bradbury
Dont forget to fly. Paul Janeczko, ed. Bradbury
Let the Circle Be Unbroken. Mildred D. Taylor. Dial
Little Little. M. E. Kerr. Harper & Row
Mazes and Monsters. Rona Jaffe. Delacorte
Notes for Another Life. Sue Ellen Bridgers. Knopf
Pack of Wolves. Vasil Bykov. Crowell
Rainbow Jordan. Alice Childress. Coward, McCann
Stranger with My Face. Lois Duncan. Little, Brown
Tiger Eyes. Judy Blume. Bradbury
Westmark. Lloyd Alexander. Dutton

1980
The Beginning Place. Ursula K. Le Guin. Harper & Row
Jacob Have I Loved. Katherine Paterson. Crowell
A Matter of Feeling. Janine Boissard. Little, Brown
One Child. Torey Hayden. Putnam
The Pigman's Legacy. Paul Zindel. Harper & Row
The Quartzsite Trip. William Hogan. Atheneum
When No One Was Looking. Rosemary Wells. Dial

1979
After the First Death. Robert Cormier. Pantheon
All Together Now. Sue Ellen Bridgers. Knopf
Birdy. William Wharton, Knopf
The Disappearance. Rosa Guy. Delacorte
The Last Mission. Harry Mazer. Delacorte
Tex. S. E. Hinton. Delacorte
Words by Heart. Ouida Sebestyen. Little, Brown

1978
Beauty: A Retelling of the Story of Beauty and the Beast. Robin
   McKinley. Harper & Row
The Book of the Dun Cow. Walter Wangerin, Jr. Harper & Row
Dreamsnake. Vonda N. McIntyre. Houghton Mifflin
Father Figure. Richard Peck. Viking
Gentlehands. M. E. Kerr. Harper & Row

1977
Hard Feelings. Don Bredes, Atheneum
I Am the Cheese. Robert Cormier. Knopf

I'll Love You When You're More Like Me. M. E. Kerr. Harper & Row
Ludell & Willie. Brenda Wilkinson. Harper & Row
One Fat Summer. Robert Lipsyte. Harper & Row
Trial Valley. Vera and Bill Cleaver. Lippincott
Winning. Robin Brancato. Knopf

1976

Are You in the House Alone? Richard Peck. Viking
Dear Bill, Remember Me? Norma Fox Mazer. Delacorte
The Distant Summer. Sarah Patterson. Simon and Schuster
Home Before Dark. Sue Ellen Bridgers. Knopf
Never to Forget. Milton Meltzer. Harper & Row
Ordinary People. Judith Guest. Viking
Pardon Me, You're Stepping on My Eyeball! Paul Zindel. Harper & Row
Roots. Alex Haley. Doubleday
Tunes for a Small Harmonica. Barbara Wersba. Harper & Row
Very Far Away from Anywhere Else. Ursula Le Guin. Atheneum

1975

Dragonwings. Laurence Yep. Harper & Row
Feral. Berton Roueche. Harper & Row
Is That You Miss Blue? M. E. Kerr. Harper & Row
The Lion's Paw. D. R. Sherman. Doubleday
The Massacre at Fall Creek. Jessamyn West. Harper & Row
Rumble Fish. S. E. Hinton. Delacorte
Z for Zachariah. Robert C. O'Brien. Atheneum

1974

The Chocolate War. Robert Cormier. Pantheon
House of Stairs. William Sleator. Dutton
If Beale Street Could Talk. James Baldwin. Dial
M. C. Higgins, the Great. Virginia Hamilton. Macmillan
Watership Down. Richard Adams. Macmillan

1973

A Day No Pigs Would Die. Robert Newton Peck. Knopf
The Friends. Rosa Guy. Holt, Rinehart and Winston
A Hero Ain't Nothin' But a Sandwich. Alice Childress. Coward,
  McCann
The Slave Dancer. Paula Fox. Bradbury
Summer of My German Soldier. Bette Greene. Dial

1972

Deathwatch. Robb White. Doubleday
Dinky Hocker Shoots Smack! M. E. Kerr. Harper & Row

Dove. Robin L. Graham. Harper & Row
The Man Without a Face. Isabelle Holland. Lippincott
My Name Is Asher Lev. Chaim Potok. Knopf
Report from Engine Co. 82. Dennis E. Smith. McCall
Soul Catcher. Frank Herbert. Putnam
Sticks and Stones. Lynn Hall. Follett
Teacup Full of Roses. Sharon Bell Mathis. Viking

1971
The Autobiography of Miss Jane Pittman. Ernest Gaines. Dial
The Bell Jar. Sylvia Plath. Harper & Row
Go Ask Alice. Anonymous. Prentice-Hall
His Own Where. June Jordan. Crowell
Wild in the World. John Donovan. Harper & Row

1970
Bless the Beasts and Children. Glendon Swarthout. Doubleday
I Know Why the Caged Bird Sings. Maya Angelou. Random House
Love Story. Erich Segal. Harper & Row
Run Softly, Go Fast. Barbara Wersba. Atheneum

1969
I'll Get There. It Better Be Worth the Trip. John Donovan.
    Harper & Row
My Darling, My Hamburger. Paul Zindel. Harper & Row
Sounder. William H. Armstrong. Harper & Row
Where the Lilies Bloom. Vera and Bill Cleaver. Lippincott

1968
The Pigman. Paul Zindel. Harper & Row
Red Sky at Morning. Richard Bradford. Lippincott
Soul on Ice. Eldridge Cleaver. McGraw-Hill
True Grit. Charles Portis. Simon and Schuster

1967
The Chosen. Chaim Potok. Simon and Schuster
Mr. and Mrs. Bo Jo Jones. Ann Head. Putnam
The Outsiders. S. E. Hinton. Viking
Reflections on a Gift of Watermelon Pickle. Stephen Dunning and
    others, eds. Scott, Foresman

If a book is included on this honor sampling, then obviously it is in some
way an outstanding book, but the reasons might differ considerably. One
book may be here because of its originality, another its popularity, and
another its literary quality. And we should warn that just because a book has

not found its way to this list, it should not be dismissed as mediocre. The list covers seventeen years during which there were many more outstanding books published than the 109 included here. Whenever such lists are drawn up, there's a degree of luck involved. For example, some of the books that were on the honor sampling in the first edition of this text do not appear here because the professors we wrote to did not happen to recommend them this particular semester. Also books from adult divisions of publishing houses were at a disadvantage because one of the sources (the children's book section of the *New York Times Book Review*) considers only juvenile titles.

The strength and value of this list is that it draws upon the judgment of a widely read group of adults and that it also represents the actual reading tastes of young adults. Most of the books recommended in the *English Journal* were selected as favorites by individualized reading students who in their high schools were participating in the University of Iowa's young adult literature program which was designed to measure the appeal of selected new books to high school students. Also the librarians who draw up the best book lists of the Young Adult Services Division of ALA try to incorporate the reactions of the young readers they work with.

Many of these books will be described in more detail in the following chapters. Here they will simply be cited as the evidence we used to assess the following generalizations or myths as they relate to the best of modern young adult literature. By dispelling some of the myths, we will establish a clearer view of what young adult literature is and can be. But we should caution that we too are using a biased sampling. Whereas some critics use the worst books as examples, we have restricted ourselves to the best. You should, therefore, realize that some of the myths that we reject in relation to the Honor Sampling may very well be true of other books.

Myth No. 1: Teenagers Today Cannot Read

During the past few years, newspapers and magazines have trumpeted forth to a waiting world the news that "Teenagers Can't Read" and "Illiteracy Rate Rising" and "Tests Prove That Schools Not Doing Job." Ever since 1955, when Rudolf Flesch made such a stir with his book *Why Johnny Can't Read*, journalists, politicians, and general critics have found that as prophets of doom, they can easily gain a large and sympathetic audience. Of course parents want their youngsters to learn to read and are concerned about whether or not schools are succeeding. But few people look for the facts behind the stories of falling test scores and widespread illiteracy. There are seldom enough facts to support the claims.

In 1976 Jaap Tuinman, Michael Rowls, and Roger Farr conducted an extensive study to measure the validity of such claims. They found fifty studies that in some way measured education achievement spanning 102 years. Thirteen studies focused specifically on reading, and twelve of these showed that reading skills were improving. They concluded with, "We are convinced that anyone who says that he *knows* that literacy is decreasing is

THE PEOPLE BEHIND THE BOOKS

JEAN KARL, Editor

Children's Books, Atheneum Publishers

Do books written specifically for adolescents have a future? Yes, they do. There has always been a debate about just who reads them. Some say it is the ten- and eleven-year-olds, and others say that these books are read not only by junior high school age young people but high school people as well. I suspect that everyone is right. There is a time in the life of each growing individual when he or she is balanced on the edge of becoming an adult in outlook and attitudes, but is not quite there. For some it comes young, for others much later. But at that point, while some adult books are just what readers want, there is also a need for books that help them explore the world they are about to enter from the point of view of characters near their own age, in other words, adolescent literature. These days such reading may be spurred on by movies and television programs based on such books. But film or not, the books exist and will continue to exist because they give readers experiences of the world that no other books can give in quite the same way. And they will continue to be written because there will always be authors sensitive to the special problems experienced by young people in those growing years when they are moving away from family patterns into an acceptance of themselves as distinct individuals with lives of their own to plan. Such books may now be read more often in paper than in hardback and may explore areas of living and thought that shock some adults; but well done, they provide a needed bridge between the concerns of childhood and children's books and the concerns and books of the mature adult. ◆

ignoring the data. Such a person is at best unscholarly and at worst dishonest."[16]

Miles Myers writing in the *English Journal* under the title "Shifting Standards of Literacy—the Teacher's *Catch-22*,"[17] explained that while conventional illiteracy—the inability to read a simple message in any language—has virtually disappeared in the United States, functional illiteracy—the inability to read and write at a level required to function in society—appears to be increasing. During World War I only about 45 percent of 17- and 18-year-old recruits could read at what is now identified as a fourth-grade level. By World War II the figure had risen to about 65 percent, while during the Vietnam War it was 80 percent. The problem, as Myers sees it, is that reading at a fourth-grade level is no longer sufficient. When Defense Secretary Caspar Weinberger said that scientific and technical illiteracy could jeopardize the nation's ability to defend itself, he was talking about a kind of literacy that was never expected in the "good old days," but indeed may be quite necessary for modern life—civilian as well as military. For example in industry, such trends as automation, shared decision making, and more free time for workers mean that people need to be able to read at higher levels in which they interpret, criticize, and solve problems. The 1980 National Assessment of Educational Progress[18] showed that while the ability of high school students to read and comprehend on a literal or basic level was "fairly well under control, higher order skills are not."

What all this means is that as educators we do not need to believe—in fact should not believe—everything we read in the newspapers about students not being able to read. However, we should realize that a problem exists, which though not of our own making, has nevertheless been given to us to solve. Part of the solution lies in doing whatever we can to encourage students to select reading as one of their leisure time activities and to guide them to books that will not only entertain but will also be challenging and thought provoking.

Myth No. 2: Young Adult Literature Is Simplified to Accommodate Low Reading Skills

This myth has more truth to it than some of the other myths, but it is still overgeneralizing to think, as some people do, that the reason for the rise in popularity of young adult literature over the last few years is that teenagers are incapable of reading regular adult books or "great literature." None of the books on the honor list is of the controlled vocabulary or the easy-to-read variety. However, one of the characteristics of juvenile books as compared to adult books is that they are shorter. The average length of the juvenile titles in the honor list is 192 pages while the average length of the adult titles is 271 pages. Only one of the juvenile titles, Mildred Taylor's *Let the Circle Be Unbroken*, has over 300 pages. Four of them, Mel Glenn's *Class Dismissed! High School Poems*, Ursula Le Guin's *Very Far Away from Anywhere Else*, June Jordan's *His Own Where*, and John Donovan's *Wild in the World*, have fewer than 100 pages, while another eight have fewer than 150 pages.

Young adults, teachers, librarians, and editors have come to expect teenage books to be compact. In 1964, when the British author, Leon Garfield, submitted his first novel to a publishing house it was turned down "after three or four agonizing months, when they said they couldn't quite decide whether it was adult or junior." He next submitted it to an editor who was just beginning to develop a juvenile line. Garfield said, "She suggested that, if I would be willing to cut it, then she'd publish it as a juvenile book. And of course, though I'd vowed I'd never alter a word, once the possibility of its being published became real, I cut it in about a week."[19]

We should point out that reading difficulty and level of literary sophistication do not always correlate with length. Furthermore, teenagers will read longer books, as is shown by the length of some of the adult titles on the list. For example, Alex Haley's *Roots* has 587 pages, Chaim Potok's *My Name Is Asher Lev* has 369 pages, Jessamyn West's *The Massacre at Fall Creek* has 373 pages, Don Bredes' *Hard Feelings* has 377 pages, and Richard Adams' *Watership Down* has 429 pages. (Quite possibly, it was the length of *Watership Down* that influenced American publishers to release it as an adult book rather than as a juvenile title, as it was originally published in England.)

It has often been said that teenage books are stylistically simple and that the plot moves forward without subplots or deviations. Again, this is not so much a myth as it is an overgeneralization. It is true of the majority of books that teenagers read, but there are certainly exceptions. Robert Cormier's *I Am the Cheese*, for example, has a very complex plot, and June Jordan's *His Own Where* is far from being stylistically simple. In both William Wharton's *Birdy* and Alice Childress' *A Hero Ain't Nothin' But a Sandwich* readers must draw together and sort out the alternating viewpoints and chronology. And it is obvious from perusing some of the adult titles that are popular with teenagers, Judith Guest's *Ordinary People* and Chaim Potok's *My Name Is Asher Lev*, for example, that their appeal is based on something other than an easy reading level.

Myth No. 3: Teenage Books Are All the Same

The existence of this myth says more about the reading patterns of the people who believe it than about the state of young adult literature. There is a tremendous variety of types, subjects, and themes represented in the Honor Sampling. In addition, teenagers read informative nonfiction—trivia, health, history, sports, and how-to books—which we did not include because the way we compiled the Honor Sampling over a seventeen-year period does not accurately reflect the popularity of these books. See Chapter 8 for a discussion of informative books which by their nature usually have shorter life spans and are aimed at more specific audiences than fiction.

Four collections of poetry and one collection of short stories are on the list. Seven of the books are written in a form which we call *new journalism*. They are based on true events, but the authors have used the techniques of fiction such as character development, the building of suspense, and the creation of dialogue to make their stories more than purely informative accounts. Books of this type include Dennis Smith's *Report from Engine Co. 82*, Milton Meltzer's *Never to Forget: The Jews of the Holocaust*, Alex Haley's *Roots*, and Torey Hayden's *One Child*, which is about a teacher discovering that a brilliant child was hidden under six years of abuse and neglect.

Eleven of the books are either science fiction or fantasy. They are as old as the oldest folk tales (Walter Wangerin's *The Book of the Dun Cow* and Robin McKinley's *Beauty: A Retelling of the Story of Beauty and the Beast*) and as new as a nuclear war (Robert C. O'Brien's *Z for Zachariah*) and Skinnerian experiments on human guinea pigs (William Sleator's *House of Stairs* and Robert Cormier's *The Bumblebee Flies Anyway*). Touches of the occult enter into a couple of the stories including Virginia Hamilton's compelling *Sweet Whispers, Brother Rush*.

A little over half of the books are contemporary realistic fiction, and they too are far from being "all the same." They range from tightly plotted suspense stories such as Robb White's *Deathwatch* and Robert Cormier's *After the First Death* to serious treatments of what it means to be a star football player who in just one play is turned into a paraplegic (Robin

Brancato's *Winning*), the precarious position of a foster child in a family (Rosa Guy's *The Disappearance*), and how it's possible to forget where fantasy ends and reality begins (Rona Jaffe's *Mazes and Monsters*).

Twenty-two of the books are historical, and in these readers meet a group of Russian soldiers who manage to save the new baby born to their female radio operator (Vasil Bykov's *Pack of Wolves*), a Chinese immigrant in the early 1900s who came to San Francisco as a laborer but prefers to fly kites and eventually builds an airplane (Lawrence Yep's *Dragonwings*), and a fife-playing boy who is kidnapped and taken on a slave ship so that on the way back from Africa he can use his musical talent to encourage the captives to dance and get exercise (Paula Fox's *The Slave Dancer*).

Not all the books are deadly serious. *True Grit* by Charles Portis is as one reviewer said "pure, beautiful corn." It's the story of a 14-year-old Arkansas girl who in the 1880s sets out to avenge the murder of her father. M. E. Kerr's books are also likely to bring smiles, if not outright giggles, for example, *Little Little* about a PF (perfectly formed) dwarf and a most unlikely group of acquaintances.

The theme that most commonly appears in young adult literature regardless of the format is one of change and growth which suggests either directly or symbolically the gaining of maturity, i.e., the passage from childhood to adulthood. Such stories communicate a sense of time and change, a sense of becoming something and catching glimpses of possibilities, some that are fearful, others that are awesome, odd, funny, perplexing, or wondrous. A related theme is that of the quest which is common in fantasy and science fiction, and on the Honor Sampling is seen in Robin McKinley's *The Blue Sword* and Lloyd Alexander's *Westmark*.

Other themes include alienation and loneliness as seen in John Donovan's *Wild in the World* and Eldridge Cleaver's *Soul on Ice*. The need for a hero is seen in Robert Newton Peck's *A Day No Pigs Would Die* and Glendon Swarthout's *Bless the Beasts and Children*. Threats to the social order are explored in William Sleator's *House of Stairs*, Robert C. O'Brien's *Z for Zachariah*, and Robert Cormier's *I Am the Cheese*. A search for values is shown in Richard Bradford's *Red Sky at Morning* and S. E. Hinton's *That Was Then, This Is Now*. What it means to care for others is examined in Isabelle Holland's *Man Without a Face*, Paul Zindel's *The Pigman*, and Ann Head's *Mr. and Mrs. Bo Jo Jones*. Our need for others and our eternal need for laughter are shown in M. E. Kerr's *Dinky Hocker Shoots Smack*. First love is explored in Brenda Wilkinson's *Ludell & Willie*, Barbara Wersba's *Tunes for a Small Harmonica*, Sarah Patterson's *The Distant Summer*, and June Jordan's *His Own Where*.

Myth No. 4: Teenage Books Avoid Taboo Topics and Feature White, Middle-Class Protagonists

In 1959, when Stephen Dunning wrote his dissertation on the adolescent novel, he observed that "junior novels insistently avoid taboo concerns," and that "junior novels are typically concerned with socially and economically fortunate families."[20] This was undoubtedly true then, when the popular books were *Going on Sixteen, Practically Seventeen, Class Ring,* and *Prom Trouble.* Anyone familiar with bookselling trends in the early 1980s (see Chapter 4 for a discussion of romances) will recognize the similarity between these titles and those of the currently popular paperback romances. The contents are also similar and the observations that Dunning made in his dissertation about 1950s "junior novels" are probably quite true for "Wildfire" and "Sweet Dream" romances, but they are not true for the books on the Honor Sampling. The mid-1960s witnessed a striking change in attitudes. One by one, taboos on profanity, divorce, sexuality, drinking, racial unrest, abortion, pregnancy, and drugs disappeared.

Books became painfully honest about the reality of young people and their frequently cold and cruel world. Some critics have suggested, in fact, that modern young adult literature is exclusively pessimistic or cynical. This is as much of an overgeneralization as the counterclaim that teenage books present a romanticized and frivolous view of life. What has happened in recent years is that restrictions have been lifted so that writers can explore a variety of topics and concerns. One of the things that the Honor Sampling shows is a steady increase in the number of popular and respected books coming from the juvenile divisions of publishing houses. This is because as publishers were given more freedom to publish controversial material, books that formerly appeared as adult books, for example Ann Head's 1967 *Mr. and Mrs. Bo Jo Jones* about the pregnancy of an unwed girl, today will probably come from a publisher's juvenile division, as did Nancy Garden's 1982 *Annie on My Mind,* the love story of two young lesbians.

But even though restrictions have been lifted, juvenile publishers have not cast them aside completely, especially in regard to sexually explicit material. Note that in 1977, Don Bredes' *Hard Feelings,* which graphically desribes the sexual awakening of a sixteen-year-old boy, came out as an adult rather than a juvenile title. And when Bradbury Press decided to publish Judy Blume's *Forever* (which is not on the Honor Sampling), they created an adult division, which they had never had before, probably hoping to forestall adverse criticism for presenting to teenagers a warm and positive story about premarital sex.

The Honor Sampling strongly refutes the idea that the protagonists in young adult literature are mainly white and middle class. Probably because there was such a void in good books about non-middle-class protagonists and also because this is where some very interesting things were happening, many writers during the 1970s focused their attention in this direction. Thirty-one of the books on the Honor Sampling feature protagonists who are members of minority groups. Blacks are shown more often than any other group, but there appears to be a slowing down of the trend. Of the 62 books on the Honor Sampling published in 1976 or later, only seven feature black protagonists, while of the 47 books published in 1975 or earlier, 12 feature black protagonists. One book features Chinese Americans, four Jewish Americans, three Native Americans, two Mexican Americans, and four isolated, rural families who, although white, are certainly not in the American mainstream.

An encouraging fact is that on the Honor Sampling in the last edition only D. R. Sherman's *The Lion's Paw* was set outside the United States, but the new list contains Harry Kullman's *The Battle Horse* translated from Swedish, Vasil Bykov's *Pack of Wolves* translated from Russian, and Janine Boissard's *A Matter of Feeling* translated from French. Maybe American teenagers are becoming a little less parochial, or perhaps it's that the publishers are getting translators able to write in more natural sounding American English. Either way it is refreshing to see a broadening of horizons.

Myth No. 5: Teenage Books are Didactic or Preachy

In this list of myths, this is the one that comes closest to being true. Of course adults want to teach young people what they have learned about life, so when they set out to write a book they probably want to share with their readers some kind of insight, an understanding, or a lesson. This might be said of everyone who writes for readers of any age, but writers for young people have often had more confidence in doing this because of the greater distance between the experience of writer and reader. The major difference between the books on the Honor Sampling and those published in earlier years is the subtlety with which the messages are presented. In earlier books there was a direct hard sell, but today's writers tell stories that point the reader in specific directions and then leave it to the reader to arrive at a final conclusion.

Writing in 1977 about British young adult literature and a smattering of American young adult novels, Sheila Ray observed that "despite their outspoken coverage of a wide range of controversial topics, the majority of teenage novels tend to reinforce conventional and establishment attitudes."[21] Books on the Honor Sampling support her observation. They are clearly on the side of the angels. Even when the subject is sexuality, alcoholism, divorce, or drugs, the books support conventional middle-class standards. This is to be expected because many writers came from the middle class or aspired to it when young. Also it is the middle-class value system that supports schools and libraries. But in reality this is not so different from adult books, most of which promote the same attitudes and values.

Myth No 6: Teenage Books Are Anti-Adult, Especially Anti-Parent

Another common belief is that as part of their desire to achieve independence from their parents, teenagers are resentful of adults and, at least in fiction, could as easily do without them. But such books as Mildred Taylor's *Let the Circle Be Unbroken*, Kathryn Lasky's *Beyond the Divide*, Lois Duncan's *Stranger with My Face*, Ouida Sebestyen's *Words by Heart*, Robert Cormier's *I Am the Cheese*, Virginia Hamilton's *M. C. Higgins the Great*, Alice Childress' *A Hero Ain't Nothin' But a Sandwich*, and William

Armstrong's *Sounder* do not support this view. In each of these books at least one parent is presented as a strong, positive character who plays an important role in the teenage protagonist's development. In Robert Newton Peck's *A Day No Pigs Would Die* the boy has a great love for his father, and a main point in *Dinky Hocker Shoots Smack* is that Dinky wants attention from her mother.

However, it is true that young adult readers want the protagonists in their stories to be young. In trying to discover why, of the hundreds of popular adult books appearing in recent years, approximately thirty titles on the Honor Sampling rose to the top as favorites of teenagers, we found that one common denominator was that the protagonists were young adults probably not over thirty. It was not as easy to judge the ages of these protagonists because while within the first few pages of juvenile books the authors mention the ages of their protagonists, authors of the adult titles are more likely to simply imply a general age category.

But chronological age does not seem to be as important as life-style in determining the kinds of protagonists with whom young adults can identify. Apparently in the eyes of teenagers, the big dividing line—the final rite of passage—between youth and adulthood is having children of one's own, becoming a parent. Young adiults easily identify with adults and think of them as just slightly older than themselves as long as little or no mention is made of family responsibilities as in Berton Roueche's *Feral*, William Wharton's *Birdy* and *A Midnight Clear*, and Eldridge Cleaver's *Soul on Ice*. Even though *Mr. and Mrs. Bo Jo Jones* is about pregnancy, none of the young fictional protagonists are parents. Practically the only books on the Honor List which present people whose lives have spanned the whole cycle of life-experiences, including parenthood, are Ernest J. Gaines' *The Autobiography of Miss Jane Pittman* and *A Gathering of Old Men*. Young readers are probably attracted to these books because of the strength shown by the persecuted blacks whose stories are told so eloquently.

Myth No 7: Girls Read About Girls and Boys; Boys Read Only About Boys

Of all the myths, this is the one that has the most potential of becoming a self-fulfilling prophecy. Studies done in the early 1950s indicated that starting with fourth or fifth grade, boys showed a slight preference for reading stories about males. This kind of information was widely publicized especially in the education explosion that followed the launching of Russia's Sputnik. During this period, there was great emphasis on teaching boys to read and enouraging them in academic endeavors in the hope that they would grow up and become the engineers and the scientists who would help Americans compete successfully with the Russians. Teachers, librarians, publishers, and authors often heard or read statements to the effect that whereas girls will read books about both boys and girls, boys will read only those books that feature males. This led authors and publishers to concentrate on stories about males because they naturally wanted the largest possible market for their books. For example, Scott O'Dell tells how he was asked to change Karana, the heroine in *Island of the Blue Dolphins*, to a boy so that it would be read by more people. He refused since it was a true story and much of its value rested on the fact that Karana was a female who in order to survive had to break her tribal male/female restrictions.

O'Dell's experience was typical of a publishing world that considered males to be the reading audience to be wooed. Then, as now, young girls read more than did boys, so there was always a market for so-called girls' books. But the kind of books produced with females as the intended audience were the kind of lopsided romances that tended not to be read by boys.

Such books are still not read by boys as shown by their lack of interest in the paperback romances now being marketed under such logos as "Sweet Dreams," "First Love," and "Wildfire." However good authors can write love stories that will be read by both sexes if they make a special effort to include male and female viewpoints as do M. E. Kerr and Paul Zindel.

The juvenile titles on the Honor Sampling are almost equally divided between male and female protagonists. It's true that few boys are reading such "feminine" books as Sarah Patterson's *The Distant Summer*, Zibby Oneal's *A Formal Feeling*, Sue Ellen Bridgers' *All Together Now*, and Robin McKinley's *Beauty*. But this has to be viewed in perspective. Boys don't read nearly as much fiction as do girls, especially the kind that explores inner feelings. A Los Angeles bookstore owner estimated that her committed teenage readers were female in a ratio of fifty-to-one. Nevertheless, boys do read books about girls if the girls are involved in doing something the boys perceive as interesting or exciting as in Robert C. O'Brien's *Z for Zachariah*, M. E. Kerr's *Dinky Hocker Shoots Smack*, Vera and Bill Cleaver's *Where the Lilies Bloom*, Lois Duncan's *Stranger with My Face*, Bette Greene's *Summer of My German Soldier*, and M. E. Kerr's *Little Little*.

And certainly boys have no qualms about reading the numbers of good, new books which feature both males and females in more or less equal roles, for example Rona Jaffe's *Mazes and Monsters*, Ursula Le Guin's *Very Far Away from Anywhere Else* and *The Beginning Place*, William Sleator's *House of Stairs*, and Jessamyn West's *The Massacre at Fall Creek*. Perhaps the literary level at which these books are written has something to do with their contradiction of this myth about "sex appeal." After all, they were chosen as "best" books by many knowledgeable people. The segregation of books by sex may occur more with poorly written, exaggerated romances, adventure stories, and pornography. The implication here seems to be that the topic and the theme have just as much to do with reader choice as the sex of the protagonist. When the plot is one that is equally interesting to males and females, and the book is written honestly enough to represent real life, then it can be appreciated by all readers regardless of their sex or the sex of the protagonist.

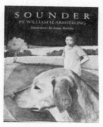

◆ These Honor Sampling books from the 1960s are now being read and appreciated by a second generation of teenagers.

From *Red Sky at Morning* by Richard Bradford. Copyright © 1968 by Richard Bradford. Reprinted by permission of J. B. Lippincott Company. From *Sounder* by William H. Armstrong. Text Copyright © 1969 by William H. Armstrong. Illustrations Copyright © 1969 by James Barkley. Reprinted by permission of Harper & Row.

Myth No. 8: If Teenagers See the Movie, They Won't Read the Book

This is a myth that time has proved unfounded. Although people used to worry about it, today the idea is fairly well accepted that the existence of a well-done media piece increases the number of readers that a book has. If they've enjoyed the film version, they're likely to want their pleasure reinforced by encountering the familiar characters and situations again in the book.

In the Honor Sampling, a large percentage of the early books have probably been kept alive both in libraries and on the reading lists of literature professors because interest is renewed each time a movie is rereleased or shown on television, for example, the 1967 *Mr. and Mrs. Bo Jo Jones* and *The Chosen*, 1968 *Red Sky at Morning*, 1969 *Sounder* and *Where the Lilies Bloom*, 1970 *Love Story* and *Bless the Beasts and Children*, and 1971 *Go Ask Alice* and *The Autobiography of Miss Jane Pittman*. More recently several books including *Summer of My German Soldier* and *Dinky Hocker Shoots Smack* have been ABC After School Specials, while several of S. E. Hinton's books have been made into full-length movies.

Throughout the industry media and book people are beginning to work more closely together so that when books are adapted for television, either the opening or closing credits encourage viewers to read the book. But sometimes producers will use a different title for their media production. For example, when Robb White's *Deathwatch* was adapted for television, the title was changed to *Savages* because two other movies already had similar-sounding titles. Unfortunately, a different name does not do as much to boost a book's readership.

Myth No. 9:
Young Adult Literature Is Less Enduring—There Are No Classics

A junior high reader brought what she considered a bad book into the library, shared her opinion with the librarian, and then with admirable forthrightness demanded to know "Why do they publish bad books?" The librarian tried to explain that what was bad to one person might seem good to someone else and that obviously the author must have thought it was good or changes would have been made.

All of us who struggle to read each year's new crop of books probably share the frustration that the girl expressed. We think how much easier our jobs would be if only the best twenty or thirty books were published each year or if we had a group of proven classics we could offer. Where's the *Charlotte's Web*, the *Winnie the Pooh*, the *Alice in Wonderland* of YA lit? Or for that matter, the *Moby Dick* or *Crime and Punishment*?

A great work by definition is individual and rare. Considering how new the phenomenon of young adult literature is, it would be astonishing indeed if there were a teenage book with the stature and enduring quality of *Moby Dick*. Books for young adults range from truly fine and imaginative works to outright trash. And although young adult literature includes books of widely varying quality, certainly the field has no monopoly on mediocrity or hack writing, which can be found in any area. It probably is fair to say, though, that as more freedom has been given to the writers and publishers of teenage books, this freedom has been used by good writers to produce better books, but poor writers have used it to hang themselves on every social ill they could find. The result has been a widening of the gap between the talented and the hack.

Admittedly many of the young adult books published today are ephemeral, but the same can be said for most of what is published whether intended for adults, children, or teenagers. People read some books for information and others for their significance, but they also read for entertainment and relaxation. There's nothing wrong with this. And although young adult literature may not yet have what could undeniably be labelled a classic, it does have some truly outstanding writers. All the authors with three or more books on the Honor Sampling—Sue Ellen Bridgers, Robert Cormier, S. E. Hinton, M. E. Kerr, and Paul Zindel—surely deserve to be called stars whether or not they have produced any classics. Those with two honored books include Alice Childress, Vera and Bill Cleaver, John Donovan, Ernest J. Gaines, Rosa Guy, Virginia Hamilton, Ursula Le Guin, Robin McKinley, Richard Peck, Chaim Potok, Barbara Wersba, and William Wharton.

Myth No. 10:
Any Book Worth Its Ink Will Come Out in Hardback First

Ever since peddlers hawked their chapbooks on the streets of London, the attitude among book people has been that the poorer the quality of the paper, the poorer the quality of the writing. The dime novels of the late

1800s added to this feeling as did the mass production of escapist paperbacks during World War II. For these and other reasons, paperback books have been treated like poor country cousins. We know one English teacher who won't let her student give book reports on paperbacks. Her students read them anyway, but before they give their reports they take the paperback into the school librarian who either finds them the hardback edition to carry to class or shows them how to cite the bibliographic information from the hard rather than the soft cover.

This prejudice against paperback books has influenced publishing and book promotion in several ways, one of which is that books coming out only in paperback have not received as much attention from reviewers. For a book to be taken seriously, it was mandatory that it come out as a hardback even though we all know that teenagers much prefer to carry around paperbacks. But the increased costs of publishing may turn this procedure around. Speaking at a workshop of the 1983 Young Adult Services Division of the American Library Association, George Nicholson, Editor-in-Chief of Dell Publishing Company, predicted that within five years a large percentage of young adult books will come out first in paperback and then if they prove successful enough will be brought out in hardback. This has already happened with Norma Fox Mazer's *Taking Terri Mueller* which came out as an Avon Flare original in 1981 and then was brought out by William Morrow as a hardback in 1983.

Although none of the books on our Honor Sampling came out first in paperback, it's not inconceivable that by the next revision several of them could have. Joyce Carol Thomas' *Marked by Fire* (Avon Flare Original, 1982) came close to making it this year by being on *The New York Times* and the YASD/ALA best books lists. *The Popularity Plan* by Rosemary Vernon (Bantam/Sweet Dreams Romance, 1981) made its way to the 1982 University of Iowa Young Adults Poll of favorites, and *The Grounding of Group Six* by Julian F. Thompson (Avon Flare Original, 1983) received prepublication endorsements from Robert Cormier and several other well-known YA writers.

See Chapter 11 for a further discussion of changes in marketing practices, but the point here is that even though reviewing sources receive more books than their reviewers have time to read or there is space to write about, and even though none of us has time to read all the young adult literature published each season, it is professionally unenlightened to make initial evaluative judgments based on the outside cover rather than the inside pages of a book.

The rejection, either in whole or in part, of these ten myths has shown what the best of young adult literature is not, but it seems appropriate to try turning these statements around and ending with a positive statement about what the best young adult literature is. First, it is written in a natural, flowing kind of language very much like that which young adults use orally. Although it is not simplified for easy reading, writers do avoid the long, drawn-out descriptions, the interweaving of multiple, complex plots, and the kind of pedantic or overblown language that is sometimes found in

THE PEOPLE BEHIND THE BOOKS

BARBARA J. DUREE, Editor

Books for Young Adults
ALA *Booklist*

By defining young adult literature in the narrow sense as that written especially for teenagers and by looking to the immediate future, i.e., the next few years, one can make some reasonable though not very startling predictions. Both teenage preference and the economics of publishing would seem to indicate an increasing number of paperbacks, with a corresponding decrease in hardcover editions. Series publications, which began with the "new wave" romances, followed by mysteries and stories of the occult, will proliferate, especially in genres of current YA interest, because of their recognition impact in direct marketing. Original paperback publishing will probably become the norm, with hardcover reprints reserved for those books with more permanent literary value. With the escalation of publishing costs, hardcover books may indeed become artistic possessions for the aesthetic enjoyment of the affluent rather than utilitarian vehicles for the conveyance of factual information. In this atmosphere, some of today's competent but less dedicated and inspired YA authors may be-

writing for adults. In the Honor Sampling the quality of the writing varies from good to excellent, but, in young adult literature as a whole, it varies from poor to excellent just as it does in writing aimed at any other audience.

Writers treat a wide variety of subject matter and themes, including many controversial ideas. And they choose their protagonists from minority groups as well as from the white middle-class majority. Like most adult and children's books, young adult literature usually supports the middle-class value system. And though recent books may push the boundaries out a little, they still point young readers toward the moral values and the behaviors deemed desirable by society. The protagonists, who can be either male or female, are relatively young (in their teens or early twenties) and are virtually free from family responsibilities. And, finally, the production of a well-done media piece seems to promote the popularity of the book on which it is based, and there is no longer a definite correlation between the quality of a book and whether it appears first in a hardback or a paperback edition.

Has contemporary young adult literature anything to offer teachers, librarians, or—most of all—students? Is young adult literature worth studying, given the multitudinous responsibilities we all have?

We believe the answer to both questions is an unqualified yes. Young adult literature was never intended to replace other forms of literature. It provides enjoyment, satisfaction, and literary quality while it brings life and hope and reality to young people. Some students may find it beyond their come discouraged by the lack of publishing outlets and turn to other less frustrating, more remunerative fields. And regrettably but conceivably, there may be fewer teenage readers.

Defining young adult literature in the broader sense as that read by, rather than written for, adolescents and looking ahead to the twenty-first century—or even to the star-distant future—who can say? Some prognosticators are already predicting the ascendancy of video communications and electronic data banks in a paperless society. On the basis of past history, however, it seems justifiable to believe that the survival of the book, in whatever form (whether one turns a page or changes the image on a screen), will be tied to the survival of the human race—since communication by way of the written word remains the province of our particular species. So long as human life endures, thinking people will attempt to communicate to others their vision of the world and their perception of the human condition. Likewise, individual young people will continue to seek in literature not only the meaning of existence but also what author Natalie Babbitt has called the "soul's own country." ◆

abilities, unfortunately, whereas other young people will have passed beyond it. Pigeon-holing has always been tempting for teachers and librarians. It would be so easy if we could place students in neat categories but reality doesn't work that way. Teachers or librarians who force-feed a steady diet of either great literature or teenage books, or any other particular kind of book, down the gullets of young readers prove that they know nothing about them and care as little about finding out. Susan Sontag reported in an interview in the *New York Times* for January 30, 1978, that she remembered all too well attending a "dreadful high school" where she was reprimanded for reading Immanuel Kant's *Critique of Pure Reason* instead of the assigned portion of the *Reader's Digest*. Responsible teachers and librarians individualize their work, recommending particular books to students, not because they are classics or because everyone else has liked them, but because the student's own personality and interests are respected.

In order to fill this leadership role, adults must first understand what and who and where young adults are, and second they must know the books. There's only one way to know the books and that is to read them in their entirety, not just the dust jackets or the reviews.

Young adult literature is not the whole of literature, but it is an increasingly important part. The future teacher or librarian unfamiliar with young adult literature begins disadvantaged and, given the flow of the presses, is likely to remain so. This would be professionally irresponsible, but it would be a disaster for the students who will thus miss out on being introduced to the delights of reading for pleasure.

◆ ACTIVITIES ◆

1. Interview four adults who are in some way connected with education. Ask them to describe for you what young adult literature is. Write a report on their opinions. Which, if any, of the myths appear in their descriptions? What evidence do they seem to be using for their opinions? Is there a correlation between how closely your informants work with young adult literature and how positive their feelings are about it? For example, does a high school reading teacher know more and feel more optimistic about young adult books than a college student preparing to teach history or a parent with children in high school? What terminology are they familiar with? Do they think that *young adult literature, juvenile literature, teen novel,* and *adolescent literature* are synonomous terms? If not, what are the differences?

2. Read two of the books on the Honor Sampling. In making your selection, show the list to a high school student and ask for recommendations of books that the student has read and enjoyed or that friends have talked about. As you read the books, see if you enjoy them for the same reasons that the high school students did.

3. Check the card catalog of a local high school or public library to see how many of the books on the Honor Sampling are in the collection. Are there particular gaps that would reveal the personal preferences of those who do the purchasing? For example, are the adventure stories missing? Or the books about ethnic groups? Or the ones that treat controversial topics? If the library is a general public library, does it have a young adult section? If so, are some of the books double-shelved in both the children's and the young adult sections? Are others shelved in both the young adult and the adult sections? Does it appear that the decision to shelve a book in a young people's section or in an adult section is made on the basis of which division of a publishing house it came from or is made because of the nature of the topic and language?

This activity may be done as a class project with students responsible for visiting different libraries and reporting on books of designated years. Some interesting observations and comparisons can then be made about local public or school libraries.

◆ NOTES ◆

[1]G. Stanley Hall, *Adolescence: Its Psychology and Its Relations to Physiology, Anthropology, Sociology, Sex, Crime, Religion and Education* (New York: Appleton, 1904).

[2]A. L. Gesell, F. L. Ilg, and L. B. Ames, *Youth: the Years from Ten to Sixteen* (New York: Harper, 1956).

[3]E. H. Erikson, *Identity: Youth and Crisis* (New York: W. W. Norton, 1968).

[4]Robert J. Havighurst, *Developmental Tasks and Education* (New York: Longman, Green, 1951).

[5]Jean Piaget, *The Origins of Intellect* (San Francisco: W. H. Freeman, 1969).

[6]Boyd R. McCandless and Richard H. Coop, *Adolescents: Behavior and Development,* 2nd ed. (New York: Holt, Rinehart and Winston, Inc., 1979), p. 160.

[7]Glen H. Elder, Jr., ed., *Adolescence in the Life Cycle* (Washington, D.C.: Hemisphere Publishing Corporation, 1975); Boyd R. McCandless and Ellis D. Evans, *Children and Youth: Psychosocial Development* (Hinsdale, Illinois: Dryden Press, 1973); Barbara M. Newman and Philip R. Newman, *An Introduction to the Psychology of Adolescence* (Homewood, Illinois: Dorsey Press, 1979); Robert E. Grinder, *Adolescence* (New York: John Wiley and Sons, 1978); Peter Blos, *The Adolescent Passage: Developmental Issues* (New York: International Universities Press, 1979).

[8]Guy R. Lefrancois, *Adolescents* (Belmont, California: Wadsworth, 1976).

[9]"Judith Guest on *Ordinary People,*" Karen Beyard-Tyler, *English Journal* 79 (September 1981): 22–25.

[10]Thomas West Gregory, *Adolescence in Literature* (New York: Longman, 1978); and *Juvenile Delinquency in Literature* (New York: Longman, 1979).

[11]Jessie Bernard, "Adolescence and Socialization for Motherhood," in *Adolescence in the Life Cycle*, edited by Glen H. Elder (Washington, D.C.: Hemisphere Publishing Corp., 1975), p. 244.

[12]Alleen Pace Nilsen, "Rating, Ranking, Labeling Adolescent Literature," *School Library Journal* 28 (December 1981): 24–27.

[13]"Trash for Teen-Agers: Or Escape from Thackeray, the Brontës, and the Incomparable Jane," *Louisville Courier-Journal*, June 17, 1951, quoted in Stephen Dunning, "Junior Book Roundup," *English Journal* 53 (December 1964): 702–3.

[14]J. Donald Adams, *Speaking of Books—and Life* (New York: Holt, Rinehart and Winston, 1965), pp. 250–52.

[15]John Goldthwaite, "Notes on the Children's Book Trade," *Harper's* 254 (January 1977): 76, 78, 80, 84–86.

[16]Jaap Tuinman, Michael Rowls, and Roger Farr, "Reading Achievement in the United States: Then and Now," *Journal of Reading* 19 (March 1976): 455–63.

[17]Miles Myers, *English Journal* 73 (April 1984): 26–32.

[18]National Assessment of Educational Progress *Newsletter*, Fall 1982.

[19]Justin Wintle and Emma Fisher, eds., *The Pied Pipers: Interviews with the Influential Creators of Children's Literature* (New York: Paddington Press, 1974), p. 194.

[20]Stephen Dunning, "A Definition of the Role of the Junior Novel Based on Analyses of Thirty Selected Novels" (Ph.D. diss., Florida State University, 1959), pp. 317–18.

[21]Sheila Ray, "The Development of the Teenage Novel," in *Reluctant to Read?* ed. John L. Foster (London: Ward Lock Educational Publishers, 1977), p. 63.

◆ TITLES MENTIONED IN CHAPTER 1 IN ADDITION TO THE HONOR SAMPLING ◆

Alcott, Louisa May. *Little Women: Meg, Joe, Beth, and Amy. The Story of Their Lives. A Girl's Book.* Roberts Brothers, 1868.

Blume, Judy. *Are You There God? It's Me, Margaret.* Bradbury, 1970.

———. *Forever.* Bradbury, 1976.

———. *Then Again Maybe I Won't.* Bradbury, 1971.

Danziger, Paula. *The Cat Ate My Gymsuit.* Delacorte, 1974.

Flesch, Rudolf. *Why Johnny Can't Read and What You Can Do About It.* Harper & Row, 1966.

Green, Hannah. *I Never Promised You a Rose Garden.* Holt, Rinehart and Winston, 1964.

Hinton, S. E. *That Was Then, This Is Now.* Viking, 1971.

Kant, Immanuel. *Critique of Pure Reason.* St. Martin, 1929, written in 1781.

Kesey, Ken. *One Flew Over the Cockoo's Nest.* Viking, 1962.

Mazer, Norma Fox. *Taking Terri Mueller.* Avon, 1981; Morrow, 1983.

O'Dell, Scott. *Island of the Blue Dolphins.* Houghton Mifflin, 1960.

Peck, Richard. *The Ghost Belonged to Me.* Viking, 1975.

Roth, Phillip. *Portnoy's Complaint.* Random House, 1969.

Scoppettone, Sandra. *Trying Hard to Hear You.* Harper & Row, 1974.

Thomas, Carol. *Marked by Fire.* Avon, 1982.

Thompson, Julian F. *The Grounding of Group Six.* Avon, 1983.

Vernon, Rosemary. *The Popularity Plan.* Bantam, 1981.

LITERARY ASPECTS OF YOUNG ADULT BOOKS

In beginning the systematic study of young adult literature, we quickly discover many of the same questions and considerations we face in studying any body of literature. Writers of books for young readers work in much the same way as writers of other sorts of books. They have the same tools available to them, and largely the same intent: to evoke a response in a reader through words on a page. And young adult readers read with the same range of responses as any other group of readers.

One of the reasons that within any group of readers there may be many different responses to the same piece of literature is that individuals may be at quite different levels in their appreciation of literature. We will therefore begin this chapter with a metaphorical description of stages that most people experience as they grow into mature readers. We have chosen to call it "The Birthday Cake Theory." It is based on work done in the 1950s by Margaret Early and in the 1960s by G. Robert Carlsen. It has been altered by our own studies of the reading autobiographies shared by those college students who have voluntarily chosen to take our classes because somewhere, somehow, they learned to love reading. Since we seldom get to meet students who do not like to read, we have not been able to test it out on nonreaders. But with book lovers, we have had its soundness verified over and over again. One caution we should mention is that the age/grade levels indicated on the left of the illustration are the earliest at which a level is reached. Even for many book lovers, the stages come later.

◈ THE BIRTHDAY CAKE THEORY OF READING DEVELOPMENT

Alvin Schwartz tells a story about a house-building crew which arrived on the job before their foreman did. They went ahead without him and had the frame up by the time he arrived. "Did the owner want us to start from the bottom up or the top down?" called one of the men. The foreman consulted the plans and replied, "The top down!" "Whoops!" said the man. "Tear it down, boys. We've got to start over!"

Regardless of this story, houses are not built from the top down. Neither are birthday cakes, and that is one of the reasons that we have chosen to illustrate the stages of reading development that most people experience by comparing them to a birthday cake. Another reason that a birthday cake makes a good metaphor is that there are all different sizes of birthday cakes, but regardless of the number of layers each layer must be supported by the one below. Some people will have a two-layer cake, others a three-layer cake, and still others will go on to have a six-layer cake. But when someone has a six-layer cake, this doesn't mean that the other layers will have lost their appeal and value. Readers continue to partake of and enjoy each layer.

Likewise, we do not *go through* stages of reading development; instead we *add on*. With each additional level we have all that we had before, plus a new way to gain pleasure and understanding. The *bottom* layer of the birthday cake should not be thought of in the negative sense of being lower or less important, but in the positive sense of being the foundation, the underpinning and support, which holds up all the rest. Lucky children begin building this layer when they are still infants. These are the children who have songs, nursery rhymes, and jingles woven into the fabric of everyday life, go to the library for story hour and checking out books, and are fortunate enough to have bedtime stories.

Jim Trelease in his highly successful *Read-Aloud Handbook* explained that he was not writing a book to help parents teach their children to read, but to help them teach their children to *want to read*. This building of desire is the first crucial layer of the birthday cake. Without it, the rest of the cake will fail to rise.

The ages shown on the accompanying illustration are the earliest ages at which readers can be expected to concentrate on developing each layer. They were drawn from studies of successful readers. Many people will begin later or not at all in developing each layer. The challenge for teachers and librarians is to find where a particular reader is and then provide the kind of support that will be most beneficial. For example, a child who has been introduced to literature in the loving arms of parents or others has an advantage over the child who first meets the printed page under the stressful situation of school. Teachers of children in this latter situation need to concentrate on providing the kind of pleasure and fun that will show children what they have to gain from learning to read. If they see no benefit, they can hardly be expected to put forth the tremendous intellectual effort

◆ **FIGURE 2.1   The Birthday Cake Theory of Reading Development**

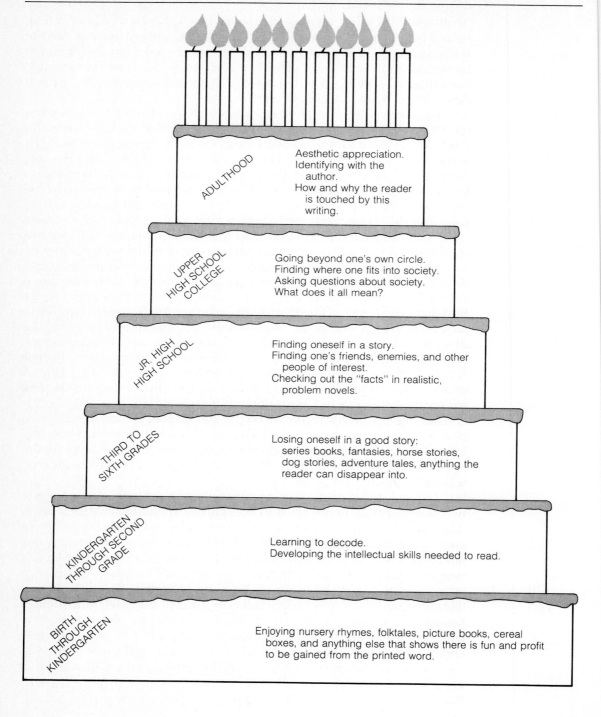

ADULTHOOD

Aesthetic appreciation.
Identifying with the
   author.
How and why the reader
   is touched by this
   writing.

UPPER
HIGH SCHOOL
COLLEGE

Going beyond one's own circle.
Finding where one fits into society.
Asking questions about society.
What does it all mean?

JR. HIGH
HIGH SCHOOL

Finding oneself in a story.
Finding one's friends, enemies, and other
   people of interest.
Checking out the "facts" in realistic,
   problem novels.

THIRD TO
SIXTH GRADES

Losing oneself in a good story:
   series books, fantasies, horse stories,
   dog stories, adventure tales, anything the
   reader can disappear into.

KINDERGARTEN
THROUGH SECOND
GRADE

Learning to decode.
Developing the intellectual skills needed to read.

BIRTH
THROUGH
KINDERGARTEN

Enjoying nursery rhymes, folktales, picture books, cereal
   boxes, and anything else that shows there is fun and profit
   to be gained from the printed word.

needed to develop the second layer of the birthday cake, which is that of actually learning to read.

For most children, the benefit they perceive is that of enjoyment, but in today's increasingly print-oriented society, preschool children may also develop an awareness of concrete benefits to be gained. For example, there's hardly a four-year-old—at least in United States metropolitan areas—who doesn't recognize the golden arches of a McDonald's restaurant. And toddlers too young to walk around grocery stores reach out from their seats in grocery carts to grab favorite brands of cereal. We know one child who by the time he entered first grade had taught himself to read from the *TV Guide*. The format of *TV Guide* breaks almost every rule any good textbook writer would follow in designing a primer for clear and easy reading, but it did have one overpowering advantage. The child could get immediate feedback. If he made a correct guess he was rewarded by getting to watch the program he wanted. If he made a mistake, he knew immediately that he had to return to the printed page and try again.

Developing the first layer of the birthday cake used to be called "reading readiness," and to a large extent this was what kindergarten was devoted to. But now with increased worry over declining reading interest and ability, there is widespread pressure to push children ahead. Many school districts expect children to come to kindergarten with the first layer well in place so that instruction in decoding can begin immediately. And many ambitious parents who are caught up in the "Super Baby" syndrome[1] are teaching their two-and three-year-olds the names and sounds of the letters of the alphabet. The bright children who are able to learn these do so for the reward of their parents' approval, not because they have an understanding of the value of the printed word. This may mean that educators will need to continue to help children in developing the bottom layer of the birthday cake long after they are in school, lest we end up with even greater numbers of young people who can, but do not want to, read.

The second layer of the cake, that of learning to read, gets maximum attention during the primary grades where as much as 70 percent of the school day is devoted to various aspects of language arts. But developing literacy is a never-ending task at least for anyone who is intellectually active. Even at a mundane level, adults continue working to develop their reading skills. The parent, who on Christmas Eve is faced with playing Santa Claus and getting the bicycle put together before dawn, and the person who rereads several tax guides in preparation for an audit, exhibit the same symptoms of concentrated effort as do children first learning to read: they point with their fingers, move their lips, return to reread difficult parts, let their minds wander to more interesting daydreams, and perhaps in frustration slam the offending booklet to the floor. But in each case, they are motivated by a vision of some benefit to be gained and so they increase their efforts.

It's been so long since most of us learned the basic skills of decoding that we have probably forgotten the work involved. And since we are among those who have chosen literature as our life's work, we were probably more successful at it than some children. If it came easily to us, we may lack empathy for those children who must struggle to read. In our impatience as we wait for them to add the third layer of the birthday cake, we are in danger of forgetting to help them find pleasure and enjoyment.

Those children who make it successfully to the third level find their own reward in the books they read. This is the girl who sits in the backseat of the car and reads all through the family vacation and the boy who reads a book while delivering the neighborhood newspapers. For children like this, the years between seven and twelve are golden. This is when they can read the great body of literature that the world has saved for them: *Charlotte's Web, The Little House* Books, *The Borrowers, The Chronicles of Narnia, The Wizard of Oz, Where the Red Fern Grows,* and books by Beverly Cleary, Judy Blume, John Fitzgerald, and hundreds of other good writers.

At this level children are undemanding. They are in what Margaret Early has described as a stage of unconscious enjoyment.[2] With help, they may enjoy such classics as *Alice in Wonderland, The Wind in the Willows, Treasure Island,* and *Little Women,* but by themselves they are far more likely to turn to less challenging material. This is the age when children have traditionally gobbled up series books such as *The Hardy Boys, The Bobbsey Twins, Nancy Drew,* and *Tom Swift.* Parents who are more aware than are children of how brief childhood is worry that their children are wasting time reading what some people have labelled subliterature. We hear such complaints as, "My daughter is reading her twenty-seventh book about horses. What could she possibly be learning?" and "What's the matter with the librarian? My child never brings home anything but junky little books."

Parents who worry in this way have taken seriously the often quoted "Only the rarest kind of best is good enough for children." This is a noble sentiment, but there's a problem in interpretation. Best from whose viewpoint? Children will most likely tell you that the funnier (or the grosser or the more extreme) is the best while adults are more likely to judge on the basis of subtlety, the lesson being taught, the literary skill displayed, or the author's reputation.

When parents consult us about their children reading "trash," the only comfort we can give them is that when our college students write their reading histories, nearly 100 percent of the ones who say they love to read went through childhood stages of being addicted for months at a time to one particular kind of book. Today it may be *Encyclopedia Brown* books or *Choose Your Own Adventure* paperbacks or "everything" by a particular author. Apparently readers find comfort in knowing the characters in a book and what to expect. They develop speed and skill which stand them in good stead when they tire of a particular kind of book—which they always do sooner or later—and go on to reading some of the books parents and teachers wished they had been reading all along.

It's during this stage that differences in reading abilities stretch out across the wide spectrum that high school teachers are accustomed to meeting. Those children who love to read may check out a book a day from their school library or go once a week to a public library where they take out the maximum allowed. It's not unusual for such children to spend a couple of hours a night reading at home. In contrast those who don't like to read, do it only for the assigned time in school, perhaps a half-hour or an hour, much of which may be devoted to "skills development," the filling in of worksheets rather than reading.

The difference, of course, is going to be noticeable. Many of these school-only readers will never lose themselves in a book. And if they do, it is likely to happen much later than the ages shown on the birthday cake. For example, in this segment from *The Car Thief* by Theodore Weesner, Alex Housman, who is being kept in a detention home, is seventeen years old when he first has the experience of losing himself in a story.[3]

◇ After breakfast they did not return immediately upstairs but followed Mr. Kelly to his office. There on the floor was a long wooden crate filled with books, and Mr. Kelly was saying that someone had donated them to the home and they could have them upstairs if they liked, as long as the books were not mistreated, were not torn or mutilated. No one said much of anything. They carried the box upstairs, Red Eye taking one end, Billy Noname the other. Placing it on the picnic table, they waited without touching for Mr. Kelly to leave, to see what they had.

Their disappointment was calm. They expected little. There were no photographs, no drawings, nothing but words packed on each fanned page as thickly as leaves on a tree. The first book grabbed—it had the only dust jacket, the only color—was called *The Egyptian*. It was dropped at once, by Leonard, and picked up by Thomas, who said, "The *what?*" Red Eye said, "Oh, man, *The Egyptian*, mummy stuff—man, you so dumb!"

The other books were old novels, books with pale and faded covers by authors named A. J. Cronin, Hans Hellmut Kirst, Virgil Scott, Jan Struther, Vincent Carr.

Alex was the only one who read, perhaps the only one who could read, although Thomas sat with *The Egyptian* for a while before he pitched it back into the box.

Alex started to read a book called *Gunner Asch*, starting it mainly because he knew how to read, although he was intimidated by the mass of words. He had never read anything but the lessons in schoolbooks—assignments in history or science spaced with water colors of Washington crossing the Delaware or Thomas Edison working under candlelight. But the novel was simply written and fairly easy to understand, and he soon became interested enough in what was happening to stop reminding himself page after page that he was reading a book, to turn the pages to see what was going to happen next.

He sat on the floor reading until he grew sleepy. When his eyelids began to slide down and his head began to cloud, he lay over on his side on the floor to sleep awhile, pulling up his knees, resting his head on his arm. When he woke he got up and carried the book with him to the bathroom . . . reading the book again, he became so involved in the story that his legs fell asleep. He kept reading, intending to get up at the end of this page, then at the end of this page, if only because he would feel more comfortable with his pants up and buttoned, but he read on. He rose finally at the end of a chapter, although he read a little into the next chapter before he made himself stop. His legs were buoyant with saws and needles as he buttoned up, and he had to hold a hand against the wall not to sway from balance. Then he checked the thickness of pages he had read between his fingers, and experienced something he had never experienced before. Some of it was pride—he was reading a book—and some of it was a preciousness the book had assumed. Feeling relaxed, unthreatened, he wanted to keep the book in his hands, for what it offered. He did not want to turn the pages, for then they would be gone and spent; nor did he want to do anything but turn the pages.

He stepped over legs again and sat down to read, as far from anyone as he could get, some fifteen feet, to be alone with the book. He read on. Something was happening to him, something as pleasantly strange as the feeling he had had for Irene Sheaffer. By now, if he knew a way, he would prolong the book the distance his mind could see, and he rose again, quietly, to sustain the pleasant sensation, the escape he seemed already to have made from the scarred and unlighted corridor. Within this shadowed space there were now other things— war and food and a worry over cigarettes and rations, leaving and returning, dying and escaping. The corridor itself, and his own life, were less present. (pp. 98–100)

The more experience children have with reading, the more discriminating they become. The rest of their lives they will be on the lookout for "a good read" and will anticipate the kind of pleasure in a book that surprised Alex in *The Car Thief,* but to receive this kind of pleasure they have to respect the book. In reminiscing about his childhood fondness for both *The Hardy Boys* and motorcycles, the late John Gardner remarked that his development as a literary critic took a step forward when he lost patience with the leisurely conversations that the Hardy boys were supposed to have as they roared down country roads, side-by-side on their motorcycles.

Good readers begin developing this critical sense in literature at about the same time they develop it in real life—at the end of childhood and the beginning of their teen years. They move away from a simple interest in what happened in a story to ask *why.* They want logical development. They are no longer satisfied with stereotypes. They want characters controlled by believable human motives. They are more demanding in what they read because now their reading has a real purpose to it. They are reading to find out about themselves, not simply to escape into someone else's experiences for a few pleasurable hours. They have attained the fourth level of reading development.

The egocentric way that some teenagers read was shown by an incident at our local high school. A fifteen-year-old girl went to her counselor and asked that she please inform the librarian she was not "that kind of a girl." When the counselor questioned why she was to deliver this message, she found that the girl had been going to the librarian all year for reading suggestions. The girl read and identified strongly with everything the librarian gave her. She apparently used the reading suggestions much the way some people use newspaper horoscopes. But now she was upset because the librarian had handed her *Mr. and Mrs. Bo Jo Jones,* which is about a young couple who have to get married when the girl becomes pregnant.

Fortunately this kind of egocentric reading is not an end in itself. It's the basis from which teachers and librarians can help young readers go beyond their narrow concerns to think about society as a whole. As they anticipate leaving their parents' homes and protection, teenagers are understandably curious about the world and so on one hand they read dozens of contemporary, teenage novels. They are looking for lives as much like their own as possible. But on the other hand they are curious about the flip side of life too and so they seek out books which present lives totally different from their own. They look for anything bizarre, unbelievable, weird, or grotesque: stories of occult happenings, trivia books, and horror stories. But whatever it is they are reading, the purpose is largely one of finding themselves and their places in society, which moves readers up to the fifth layer of the birthday cake.

Senior high school English teachers have some of their best teaching experiences with books by such writers as Ernest Hemingway, John Steinbeck, Harper Lee, F. Scott Fitzgerald, Carson McCullers, William Faulkner, Arthur Miller, and Flannery O'Connor. Students respond to the way these books raise questions about conformity, social pressures, justice, and all the other aspects of human frailties as well as strengths. It is at this level that students are ready to begin looking at shades of gray rather than black and white. Book discussions can have real meat to them because readers make different interpretations as they bring their own experiences into play against those in the books.

Obviously, getting to this level of literary appreciation is more than a matter of developing an advanced set of decoding skills. It is closely tied in with the kind of intellectual development that Jean Piaget described when he observed that it is not until the teenage years that normal children develop the "formal operational" stage of thinking in which they become able to handle abstract ideas. It also relates to the teenage identity crisis as described by Erik H. Erikson, the developmental tasks outlined by R. J. Havighurst, and the stages of moral development outlined by Lawrence Kohlberg. Teenagers are faced with the tremendous responsibility of assessing the world around them and deciding where they might best fit in. Reading at this fifth level of the birthday cake allows teenagers to focus on their own psychological needs in relation to society. The more directly they can do this the more efficient they feel, which probably explains the popularity of contemporary problem novels featuring young protagonists as in the books by Robert Cormier, Alice Childress, Sue Ellen Bridgers, and Richard Peck.

While many people read fantasy and science fiction at the third level, that is, losing themselves in a good story, others may read such books as William Sleator's *House of Stairs*, Virginia Hamilton's *Sweet Whispers, Brother Rush*, and Robin McKinley's *The Blue Sword* at this fifth level. They come back from spending a few hours in the imagined society with new ideas about their own society.

The top layer of the birthday cake is that of literary or aesthetic appreciation. This is where the bright lights are: where the authors, critics, and literary scholars live—but only on their best days. As rewarding as it is, this layer is so demanding that most people partake of it only a nibble at a time.

The professor who teaches Shakespeare all day goes home at night and loses himself in a televised rerun of *Charlie's Angels*, and the author who writes for four hours in the morning might read herself to sleep that night with an Agatha Christie mystery.

The reason that the top layer is so demanding is that readers' minds must work at each of the lower levels of finding enjoyment, developing and exercising reading skills, losing and/or finding themselves in the story, relating the story to society, and then adding to all this the conscious awareness and analysis of the literary techniques through which authors perform their magic. In writing about this level of literary appreciation, Margaret Early described a *New Yorker* cartoon in which an aggressive character, with martini in hand and chip on shoulder, accosts a guest at a literary cocktail party and says, "So you write? Well, I read!"

This cartoon makes the same point that author Mark Harris made when he said, "I write; let the reader learn to read."

The implication is that at the highest level, reading is an active, rather than a passive endeavor and that to get the maximum good out of a piece, readers must do half of the work. Reading at this top level is being a literary critic, a creative act much like being an author.

In a 1983 article entitled, "Finally Only the Love of the Art,"[4] poet Donald Hall wrote about his own ascent up to the top layer of the birthday cake. Of course he didn't call it that, but it nevertheless matches the theory so well—except for the accelerated speed befitting his giftedness—that excerpts are printed below as a concrete example of the metaphor. The Hall family lived in a variety of homes until, during his early school years in the 1930s, his family assumed a mortgage on a house that a bank had re-possessed because of the Depression.

◇ When I was in my snooty teens I would have denied it, but these houses were bookish. Because the Book-of-the-Month Club supplied 13 masterpieces a year, because the Reader's Digest and Collier's lay beside easy chairs, I felt superior. My father read Kenneth Roberts, not Gerard Manley Hopkins, but he read *books*—which means that I grew up un-American. An only child, I lived with people who continually gazed at print. My mother even read poems and read them aloud to me when I was little. My favorite was Vachel Lindsay's "The Moon's the North Wind's Cooky."

My grandfather said poems all day long without repeating himself, recited not Keats or Henry King or Vachel Lindsay but (without ascription) "Casey at the Bat" and "Lawyer Green" and "What the Deacon Said"—long poems, usually narrative, either comic or melodramatic. I sat in the tie-up on a three-legged stool watching him milk his Holsteins as his dear voice kept time with his hands and he crooned wonderful bad poems with the elocutionary zeal of another century.

By the time I was 12 I spent all summer there. I got up at 6 and fed the chicks and read and wrote all morning; in the afternoon I hayed with my grandfather, absorbing his stories and poems. . . . There was also a great-uncle, Luther the retired minister, born in 1856, who had taught himself Greek and who wrote verses mainly devotional; we sat on the porch as he recollected his boyhood during the Civil War. There was my literary Aunt Caroline, English teacher in

Massachusetts, who amused herself writing light verse and rhymes for greeting cards; we went on long walks and she told me about a seafaring adventurer trapped by a cruel one-eyed giant.

And in Hamden from September to June I dreamed of returning to the farm. I did not enjoy the company of other children; I wanted to grow up, even to be old, like the people I loved the most. Alone after school I took pleasure in books—in the Bobbsey Twins, in the Hardy Boys, later in Roy Helton's "Jimmy Sharswood," then gradually in grown-up books. And in movies of werewolves and vampires, which when I was 12 prompted a boy next door (bless you, wherever you are) to recommend the works of Edgar Allan Poe.

I swallowed Poe whole. Then I swallowed Hervey Allen's biography of Poe, "Israfel," and discovered for myself the thrilling role of *poete maudit*. . . . From 12 to 14 I wrote poems and short stories. I started novels and five-act tragedies in verse. But I had not yet committed myself wholly to writing; I entertained occasional notions of becoming an actor, or President. ("Nothing is so common-place," Oliver Wendell Holmes said, "as to wish to be remarkable.")

When he was fourteen, Hall went to a Boy Scout meeting and happened to tell another boy that he had written a poem that day in study hall. The boy confessed that writing poems was "his profession" and he took Hall with him on poetic excursions into New Haven where he introduced him to "Yale freshmen—18-year-olds!—who were literary geniuses."

It was during this "heady time" that Donald Hall first began to get poems accepted by "little" magazines and eventually bigger ones. And now in his fifties, he's still aspiring for the top layer. He concluded his article:

◇ If you continue to write, you go past the place where praise, publication or admiration sustains you. The more praise the better—but it does not sustain you. You arrive at a point where only the possibilities of poetry provide food for your desires, possibilities glimpsed in great poems that you love. What began perhaps as the north wind's cooky—what continued variously as affectation and self-love; what zaps crazily up and down in public recognition—finds repose only in love of the art, and in the desire, if not precisely the hope, that you may make something fit to endure with the old ones.

◈ BECOMING A LITERARY CRITIC

As Hall indicates, the top level is not something that a writer reaches effortlessly, or that once reached requires no further effort. Reaching the top level as a reader means becoming a literary critic, not necessarily for other people but at least for oneself. The difference between being a critic and a reviewer is that a reviewer evaluates and makes recommendations as to who would most like to read which book. Critics do more than that. Besides evaluating and recommending books, they give guidance. They explicate. The good critic makes observations that, when shared, help others to read with understanding and insight.

Developing into the kind of reader who is able to derive nourishment at the highest level of literary response is a lifelong task, one which continues to challenge all of us. The information presented in this chapter is basic to identifying with a story through the eyes of the author as well as through the eyes of the characters. We are presenting it at the beginning of this textbook for three reasons. First, it will help you get more out of the reading you do throughout this course. Second, when you enjoy the books you read in this way and when you sharpen your insights into authors' working methods, then you will be in a good position to share your insights with those young readers who are ready for them. You will also be better able to evaluate new books and to help young readers move along in developing their own abilities to evaluate and to receive pleasure at higher levels of reading appreciation. A third advantage to understanding literary terms and concepts is that they will provide you with a handle for discussion. Without appropriate terminology, it will be hard for you to carry discussions beyond the "I-like-it" and "I don't-like-it" stage. It is much easier to appreciate and to understand what an author has done when you are acquainted with the techniques and can give them names. Knowing and using literary terms correctly will enable you to get maximum benefits from book discussions with both students and colleagues. It will also help you to read reviews, articles, and other books with greater understanding.

Some people speak of literature with a capital *L* to identify the kind of literature that is set apart from, or has a degree of excellence not found in, the masses of printed material that roll from the presses of the world each day. This type of literature rewards study, not only because of its content, but because of its style, the literary devices and techniques that are used, and the universality, permanence, and congeniality of the ideas expressed.

It is on the question of universality and permanence that some critics have asked whether stories written specifically for young readers can be considered Literature. Their feeling is that if a story speaks only to readers of a certain age, then it cannot really have the kind of universality required in true literature. However, every adult has lived through an adolescence and continues to experience many of the doubts, leave-takings, embarkings on new roles, and sudden flashes of joy and wonder that are written about in books with protagonists between the ages of twelve and twenty-five. Books that show the uniqueness and at the same time the universality of such experiences—*The Adventures of Huckleberry Finn*, *The Catcher in the Rye*, *Little Women*, and *Lord of the Flies*, for example, are often referred to as classics. They have proven themselves with different readers across different time periods. And they are the books that readers return to for a second and third reading, each time feeling rewarded.

In contrast to literature with a capital *L*, there is formula literature and escape literature. In truth, all stories consist of variations on a limited number of plots and themes, but the difference between what is referred to simply as literature and what is referred to as formula literature is one of degree. Formula literature is almost entirely predictable. Many of the situation comedies, westerns, and adventure shows on television are formula pieces. So are many of the books that young people enjoy reading.

Because formula literature is highly predictable, the reader can relax and enjoy a story while expending a minimum of intellectual energy. For

LOIS LOWRY, Author

Autumn Street
Find a Stranger, Say Goodbye
A Summer to Die
Taking Care of Terrific

In one book of mine, a mother stitches together a patchwork quilt, using bits and pieces from her two daughters' clothing, outgrown as they journeyed from childhood to maturity: a flower-sprigged gingham here, with memories of a birthday party; a sturdy plaid there, recalling summer backyard afternoons. In much the same way, for me, the writing of fiction is a patchwork craft. I sit alone at a typewriter, sorting, arranging, and piecing together scraps: a bit of a dream, a fragment of a memory, trying to create a pattern which will speak to the private emotions of the audience. Hopes, hungers, and humor; innocence, integrity, and love—the patchwork secrets of the human heart—these things form the fabric of our lives. So it is from these unchanging elements of human relationships that I try to fashion something warm and colorful for young readers. ◆

Autumn Street. Houghton Mifflin, 1980.
Find a Stranger, Say Goodbye. Houghton Mifflin, 1978.
A Summer to Die. Houghton Mifflin, 1977.
Taking Care of Terrific. Houghton Mifflin, 1983.

---

this reason, formula literature is often used as escape literature—something people read only for entertainment and relaxation with little or no hope of gaining insights or learning new information. Many of the paperbacks sold in airports and hospital waiting rooms were written as escape literature. Some people prefer to escape for a few hours with a murder mystery, others with a gothic, others with science fiction, and still others with a Harlequin romance. Much television programming meets many of the same needs as escape literature.

A difference between "significant" and "formula" fiction is that while some significant literature will have an exciting enough plot that it can be read at the level of escapism and fun, the reverse isn't true. There simply isn't enough content in formula fiction to make it worthy of the kind of reading done at the upper levels. Because of this, many "literary" people are prone to look down their noses at it. But when viewed in perspective as only part of the world's literature, there is nothing wrong with young people enjoying formula or escape literature either in books or on film.

However, it is understandable that the goal of most educators who work with young readers is to help them develop enough skill that they are not limited only to this kind of reading. We want them to be able to receive pleasure from all kinds of literature, including that which offers much more than escape or amusement.

Authors of the best young adult books use the same literary techniques—though perhaps to a different degree—as the authors of the best books for adults. As will be seen in the following chapters, these literary techniques can be discussed in many different ways. Two approaches that have proven useful include classification by genre and the analysis of such essential literary elements as plot, theme, character, point of view, tone, setting, and style.

Interrelationships exist between genres and literary elements in that some genres are more apt than others to rely on or to emphasize particular literary elements. For example, setting is usually a more important part of a historical novel than of a romance, and an exciting plot is crucial to an adventure story, whereas good character development is crucial to a story of personal achievement. Figurative language is essential to poetry and good dialogue to drama, and so on. Because of these interrelationships, the following discussion of literary elements touches on genres as well.

◈ PLOT

In examining the books that become popular with young adults as compared to those that do not, a crucial difference often appears in the plotting. The plot of a story is the sequence of events in which the characters play out their roles in some kind of conflict. Plot is what happens.

Elements of Plot

For most young readers, there needs to be a promise within the first few pages that something exciting is going to happen, that there is going to be a believable conflict. Authors use various techniques to get this message across to their readers, or to "hook" them.

Joan D. Vinge needed only the first three paragraphs of *Psion* to set an "other" world scene and at the same time hook readers into wanting to find out what is going to happen to "the kid":

> ◇ The gem-colored dream shattered, and left the kid gaping on the street. Jarred by passers-by and stunned by ugliness, he gulped humid night air. The dream-time he had paid his last marker for was over, and somewhere in the street voices sang, "Reality is no one's dream . . ."
>
> A richly robed customer of the Last Chance suicide gaming house knocked him against a pitted wall, not even seeing him. He cursed wearily and fumbled his way to the end of the building. Pressure-sensitive lighting flickered beneath the heavy translucent pavement squares, trailing him as he stepped into the funnel of an alleyway. Aching with more than one kind of hunger, he crept into the darkness to sleep it off.
>
> And one of the three Contract Labor recruiters who had been watching nodded, and said, "Now."

Other authors use catchy titles as narrative hooks, for example, Alice Bach's *Waiting for Johnny Miracle* and Robin Brancato's *Sweet Bells Jangled Out of Tune*. Titles that are questions, such as Richard Peck's *Are You in the House Alone?* M. E. Kerr's *If I Love You, Am I Trapped Forever?* and Nat Hentoff's *Does This School Have Capital Punishment?* trigger other questions in readers' minds and make them pick up the book to find the answers.

Asking questions like this works much the same as *in medias res*, Latin for "in the midst." It's a technique that authors use to bring the reader directly into the middle of the story. This will usually be followed by a flashback to fill in the missing details. Paul Zindel did this in *The Pigman*. Few readers put the book down after they get acquainted with two likable teenagers and then read John's statement:

◇ Now Lorraine can blame all the other things on me, but she was the one who picked out the Pigman's phone number. If you ask me, I think he would have died anyway. Maybe we speeded things up a little, but you really can't say we murdered him.
Not murdered him.

An exciting plot is generally essential in adventure stories, fantasy, science fiction, and mysteries, less important in biographies, memoirs, and romances. The most exciting plots are the ones in which the action is continually rising, building suspense, and finally leading to some sort of climax.

In contrast to plots with rising action are those that are episodic as in Theodore Kazimiroff's true account, *The Last Algonquin*. The chapters, for example, "A Clay Pot," "On the Hudson River," "The Red-Haired Woman," and "The Hardest Winter" are all more or less of equal interest. The title of the book, as well as the dust jacket design, removes any vestige of suspense about whether Joe Two Trees will be able to find and join others of his tribe. Although the chapters are related chronologically, they do not build on each other in such a way that the reader's excitement is brought to a peak because everything is falling into place. This is typical of memoirs such as James Herriot's *All Creatures Great and Small*, Maya Angelou's *I Know Why the Caged Bird Sings*, and Margaret Mead's *Blackberry Winter*.

The endings for episodic books may resemble chapter endings, but when a book has built to a climax, something more is needed. Readers need to be let down gently. This brief subsiding and wrapping up of details is called the *denouement*. For example, in the climax of Lloyd Alexander's *Westmark*, readers find that the waif, Mickle, is really the princess, who was thought dead. In the denouement, they get the explanation of how she both literally and figuratively fell from the highest to the lowest position in her father's medieval kingdom. And furthermore, they get the satisfaction of seeing the wicked prime minister, Cabbarus, punished for his crimes; the wily Las Bombas humbled; and Theo, the worthy young protagonist, given a position of honor and trust. It is hinted that a time of justice and peace is ahead for the entire kingdom. But the revolutionaries have not given up the idea of overthrowing the monarchy, so the political question is left up in the air.

It would have been unrealistic for something so pervasive as that to have been answered in the denouement where readers are looking only for the details to the answers they have pretty much figured out. The denouement is not a place to add surprises or new twists to the plot.

Sometimes the denouement will be formally set apart. In *The Quartzsite Trip*, William Hogan tells the story of a wonderfully eccentric high school

English teacher, P. J. Corbett, who for seven springs, ending in 1962, took a group of carefully chosen seniors from the John Muir High School in Los Angeles on a desert camping trip near Quartzsite, Arizona. The body of the book tells about this trip, day-by-day, chapter-by-chapter.

On the sixth day, the students are back in Los Angeles to attend their teacher's funeral at the Herrick Memorial Chapel at Occidental College. Essentially this is the end of the story, but Hogan gives his readers a denouement in three parts. First there is a three-page "Epilogue" which briefly details the remaining seven weeks of school and what became of several of the students after they graduate. Then as a bonus, there's a two-and-a-half page "Afterword" set "Many years later, long after 1962 and the Quartzsite Trip," in which readers are privileged to witness the chance meeting of two of the most likable of the students. And then finally, there is a seven-sentence "The End" to tie up loose philosophical ends.

The fact that something dreadful happened to their teacher was more of a surprise to the students in the story than it was to the readers because author William Hogan had carefully laid out hints foreshadowing the disaster. For example:

◇ On Wednesday morning, P. J. Cooper rose early, with the first light of dawn, to watch the sun rise in solitude and build up the fire for breakfast. He had slept in the cab of his pickup truck. He awoke with the first light, sat up and stretched, and quietly opened the cab door and swung his legs out. He was just about to step down, sink his bare feet in the cool morning alkaline soil, when he saw the tracks, the interlocking J tracks of the sidewinder, diagonal curves, in the loose sand.

P. J. Cooper froze. He had never been afraid of snakes. The sidewinder was the smaller and faster of the desert rattlesnakes, he knew; and its venom less powerful. But it had passed right next to his pickup in the night, between his truck and the fire, where he had earlier stood talking with the graduates, where he had earlier stood telling his ghost story to the students. He froze. He had not heard the rattles in the night as the snake passed by. Where had it come from, where had it gone, why had it come his way?

"The Great Equalizer," he said automatically, spontaneously. The Great Equalizer had always been an amusement to him. P. J. Cooper looked at the silent rattlesnake tracks next to his truck in the dawn, then he looked at his bare feet and wiggled his toes. He smiled at how calmly he had reassured the students the day before against the danger of snakes.

Then he held his breath and jumped to the ground and stood still, listening for the buzzing rattle of the sidewinder. Silence. He rubbed out a section of the snake tracks with his bare foot, then bent down and pulled some kindling from under the truck and started the fire. When it was built up and blazing, he went back to the cab of his pickup and put on his socks and boots.

His barefoot jump had been a dare to the Great Equalizer. It was dawn, April 18th, on the Quartzsite Trip, in 1962.

The effect of this foreshadowing was not to give away the ending, but to increase excitement and suspense and prepare the reader for the shock. If authors fail to prepare readers—at least on a subconscious level—their stories may lack verisimilitude or believability. Readers want interesting and exciting plots, but they don't want to feel manipulated. Authors must therefore keep themselves and their efforts out of sight. They write as omniscient observers recounting events that appear to be under the control of some greater power than that of a poor, working writer.

Traditionally readers have expected to know all the answers by the end of the book, to have the plot come to a tidy close. But with some of the new stories authors feel this is an unrealistic expectation and so they leave it up to the reader to imagine the ending. In *A Hero Ain't Nothin' But a Sandwich*, Alice Childress didn't think it fair to predict either that Benjie would become a confirmed drug addict or that he would go straight. Boys in his situation turn either way and Childress wanted readers to think about this. Although stories with open-ended plots are sometimes frustrating, they are interesting to read and discuss as a group because they force readers to ponder the story and come to conclusions.

Another modern trend that is frustrating to some readers and critics is that as authors strive for realism, they forget about plot. Instead of writing stories, some critics say, they write case histories. Such books often have to do with a young person's struggle with drug or alcohol addiction, mental or physical illness, conflict with parents, sexual problems, or problems with the law. When an author has not planned an exciting plot, it seems that the temptation is greater to rely on unsavory details. These are the books that are often criticized for their sensationalism.

To have an interesting plot, a story must have a problem of some sort. In adult books, several problems may be treated simultaneously, but in most of the books written specifically for young adults, as well as in those that they respond to from the adult list, the focus is generally on one problem. However, authors may include a secondary or minor problem to appeal to specific readers. For example, in most of Paul Zindel's books, the primary problem is one of personal growth and development on the part of either one or two protagonists. But he tucks in an unobtrusive element of love that will bring satisfaction to romantically inclined readers without being bothersome to the rest of his audience.

Types of Plots

Basically the problems around which plots are developed are of four types: protagonist against self, protagonist against society, protagonist against another person, and protagonist against nature.

Protagonist against self. A large portion of the rites-of-passage stories popular with young adults are of the protagonist-against-self type. Through the happenings in the book, the protagonist comes to some new understanding or level of maturity. For example, in Robin Brancato's *Winning*, paralyzed Gary Madden's struggle is in his own mind. Can he cope with his limitations and make the decision to build a fulfilling life? In the title story of Norma Fox Mazer's *Dear Bill, Remember Me?* the girl comes to an honest appraisal of the relationship that she had with her big sister's boyfriend, and in Katherine Paterson's *The Great Gilly Hopkins*, rebellious eleven-year-old Gilly must give up her dreams about her flower-child mother and accept the fact that we maneuver life best in forward, not reverse gear.

Protagonist against society. Protagonist-against-self stories are often, in part, protagonist-against-society stories. For example, in Sylvia Plath's *The Bell Jar*, Esther Greenwood is struggling to understand herself, but the depression and the fears and doubts that she feels are brought on by her experience in New York as a college intern on a fashion magazine. Getting accepted for this position had been an important goal of hers, and she is disappointed because, when she achieves this goal, she finds that the work and the life that go with it seem frivolous and hollow.

Sue Ellen Bridgers' *Home Before Dark* is another book in which the protagonist struggles both against herself and against society. Fourteen-year-old Stella has lived most of the life she can remember in the old white station wagon which her family used for traveling from one crop to the next. When finally Stella's father returns to the family farm that he had abandoned years before, Stella does not want to leave—ever. She refuses to leave even after her mother dies and her father remarries. As she explains:

> ◇ None of us ever owned anything until we came back to Daddy's home and Newton gave us the little house. But, somehow, I felt like it had always been ours. That land out there belonged to us no matter what anyone said. Daddy was born to it, and I was born to Daddy; so the land and the house were mine. They truly belonged to me, and I belonged to them, like I had known the house and land long before and had somehow forgotten about them for a while.

Finally Stella accepts the little house and the farm as being only one part of her life. They will always be there and she can come back to them, but she must go from them too, unless she wants to be trapped at a standstill while the rest of her family moves forward.

Several books that feature characters from "disadvantaged" homes and neighborhoods are also combinations of the protagonist-against-self and protagonist-against-society patterns. In these, the individuals' self-concepts as well as the problems they face are directly related to the society around them as in Nicholasa Mohr's *Nilda*, Rosa Guy's *The Friends*, and Sharon Bell Mathis' *Teacup Full of Roses*. Chaim Potok's *My Name Is Asher Lev* and *The Chosen* show boys who are trying to reach understandings of themselves, but these understandings are greatly affected by the Hasidic Jewish societies in which the boys were born and raised.

Robert Cormier's *The Chocolate War*, *I Am the Cheese*, *After the First Death*, and *The Bumblebee Flies Anyway* all come close to being pure examples of plots in which the protagonists are in conflict with society. In *The Chocolate War*, almost everyone in the school—faculty and students alike—go along with the evil plan to force Jerry to conform. In *I Am the Cheese*, Adam is left friendless and vulnerable in an institution as the result of organized crime combined with government corruption. In *After the First Death*, one young boy is betrayed by his father who is a military psychologist, while another is kept by his father in a terrible state of innocence in which he is trained as a terrorist and never allowed to experience human feelings of compassion, love, or fear. But the blame for the tragic consequences cannot be laid on the fathers' shoulders because each of them is a victim in his own way of the society to which he belongs. *The Bumblebee Flies Anyway* is in some ways a person-against-nature story in that the boys are fighting against their terminal illnesses. But that they have been placed in an experimental hospital where they are at the mercy of "the Handyman" is the fault of society, not just the one doctor.

In a similar way, it is not a single individual, but a whole interrelated system that causes the conflicts in Glendon Swarthout's *Bless the Beasts and Children*, which is about cruelty to both animals and to young boys who don't quite fit the standard mold, and in Peter Maas' *Serpico*, which is about corruption on the New York City police force.

Protagonist against another. Sometimes there is a combination in which the protagonist struggles with self, and also with another person or persons. For example, in Judith Guest's *Ordinary People*, Conrad is struggling to gain his mental health after he attempts suicide, but this struggle is tied to the sibling rivalry that he felt with his older brother who was accidentally killed. And the sibling rivalry is tied to the relationship that exists between him and his parents. Because nearly everyone has experienced conflicts with family members, they can identify with the sibling rivalry in Katherine Paterson's *Jacob Have I Loved*, the father/son conflict in Barbara Wersba's *Run Softly, Go Fast*, and the family/foster child conflict in Rosa Guy's *The Disappearance*.

Another example of protagonist-against-another-person is Richard Peck's *Are You in the House Alone?* A high school girl is harassed and finally raped by a classmate, but even here society enters in because one of the points being made is that society lets the rapist go and punishes the victim. Suspenseful adventure stories are often of the person-against-person type. David Morrell's *First Blood* is a violent account of what happens when the antagonisms of a Vietnam veteran are pitted against the antagonisms of the small town sheriff whom he challenges. Lois Duncan's occult story *Stranger with My Face* is about identical twins, one evil and one good. Through astral projection the evil twin tries to inhabit the body of her sister.

Protagonist against nature. Among the most exciting of the protagonist-against-nature stories are accounts of true adventures, such as Piers Paul Read's *Alive: The Story of the Andes Survivors*, Thor Heyerdahl's *The "RA" Expeditions*, and Dougal Robertson's *Survive the Savage Sea*.

Within recent years, several authors have done a reverse twist on the person-against-nature plot and have made nature the protagonist and people the antagonists. This is the beginning situation in Richard Adams'

Watership Down and throughout *The Plague Dogs.* It is also what underlies the story in John Donovan's *Family* and in Robert C. O'Brien's *Z for Zachariah.*

◈ THEME AND MODE

Closely related to plot is theme. Theme in a book is what ties it all together and answers the questions: What does the story mean? What is it about? Theme should not be confused with a didactic moral tagged on at the end of a story, nor should it be confused with plot. Instead it is something that pervades the story and stays with the reader long after details of plot, setting, and even character have faded. Linguistic scholars talk about the deep structure of a sentence as compared to its surface structure. The surface structure is the exact words that are used, whereas the deep structure is the underlying meaning. Dozens of different surface structures could communicate the same idea, a message of love, for example. Plot and theme are related in the same way. A plot relates to a single story, whereas a theme is applicable to hundreds of stories.

Sometimes an author will be very explicit in developing a theme, even expressing part of it in the title as with John Knowles' *A Separate Peace* and S. E. Hinton's *The Outsiders.* At other times the theme is almost hidden so that young readers need help in finding it through discussion of the book with others who have read it. A book can have more than one theme, but usually the secondary themes will be less important to the story. However, because of the experiences that a reader brings to a book, it may be a secondary theme that happens to impress a particular reader. A theme must be discovered by the reader. It can't simply be told or else it is reduced to a moral.

The kinds of themes treated in stories are closely correlated with the mode in which they are written. Mode is most commonly divided into comedy, romance, irony/satire, and tragedy. Together these make up the story of everyone's life, and in literature as in life they are interrelated, flowing one into the other. Comedy might be compared to spring, childhood, innocence, and happiness. Romance also connotes happiness and is often associated with summer, the teen years, young love, and growth. Irony and satire correlate symbolically with fall, middle-age, the existence of problems, and unhappiness. Tragedy is correlated with winter, old-age, suffering, and sadness.[5]

Books for children and young people have most often been written in the comic and romantic modes because as Annie Gottlieb pointed out in "A New Cycle in 'YA' Books," "An unwritten commandment of YA fiction had always been, 'Thou shalt leave the young reader with hope.'" She credited Robert Cormier with shattering this rule in 1974 when he published *The Chocolate War,* and "The American Library Association's *Booklist* gave it a black-bordered review, suggesting an obituary for youthful optimism."[6] Throughout the 1970s the books that got the most attention from teachers, librarians, reviewers, and young readers were books in the darker modes of irony/satire and even tragedy. These included such books as the anonymous *Go Ask Alice,* John Donovan's *Wild in the World,* and Jean Renvoize's *A Wild Thing.* The protagonists in these books are helpless to change the forces of the world that gather against them.

Some critics would argue that such books are tragedies rather than ironies. The reader of a tragedy is usually filled with pity and fear—pity for the hero and fear for oneself that the same thing might happen. The intensity of this involvement causes the reader to undergo an emotional release or catharsis which drains away subconscious fears leaving the reader filled with pride in what the human spirit is able to undergo and still survive.

Robert Cormier's books, including his more recent *After the First Death* and *The Bumblebee Flies Anyway,* stand out as being among a very small number of YA books that come close to being tragedies. However, as shown in Chapter 3, "The New Realism," numerous books are written in the ironic mode. Marilyn Sach's *The Fat Girl* is a good example. High school seniors Jeff Lyons and Norma Jenkins are an attractive and happy teenage couple, but in their ceramics class is "the fat girl," Ellen DeLuca, who is obviously attracted to Jeff. When Ellen overhears Jeff make a snide remark about her, she is devastated; in fact she becomes suicidal. In trying to make amends, Jeff becomes obsessed with helping Ellen. All goes well at first, but then when Ellen begins to assert herself, Jeff is hurt and resentful, and by the end of the book he is the one that readers should worry about.

Two other examples of recent well-written books in the ironic mode include John Wain's *The Free Zone Starts Here* and Suzanne Newton's *I Will Call It Georgie's Blues.* In Wain's book, 17-year-old Paul Waterford finds through the trauma of his sister's death in an aircrash and his trip to her memorial service in Lisbon that he is not as morally and emotionally superior to those around him as he thought he was. In Newton's book, the family of a small town preacher—perfect from outward appearances—is actually disintegrating from the inside strain of appearing to be something they're not.

In the mid-1980s, it is easy to find examples of books written in the happier modes, those of comedy and romance. In these optimistic books, there are challenges to be met, but the stories have happy endings. Chapter 4, "The Old Romanticism" explores the romantic mode in two senses, that of a love story and that of an adventure/accomplishment story. Romances are characterized not only by happy endings, but also by exaggeration and wish-fulfillment.

In popular culture, the term *comedy* is most often used in reference to something funny, something that makes people laugh. But in literary criticism, *comedy* or *the comic mode* are terms that can be used as descriptors for stories that are mostly serious, or even grim. What is necessary is that the events in the story move from ironic chaos to a renewal of human hope and spirit. An example is Felice Holman's *The Wild Children* set in the post-revolutionary Russia of the 1920s. Twelve-year-old Alex comes downstairs from his attic bedroom to find that his family has been taken away. He is alone in the world, as are thousands of young Russians who make up the *bezprizorni*—the unsheltered ones. Most of the story is about Alex's terrible fear, his loneliness, and the hardships endured by these children of war. He becomes part of a gang who aid each other in the hard business of survival and at the end of the book escape to Finland. The closing line is a brief sentence which is almost a literal fulfillment of the definition of the comic mode, "Once again, life began." But it is important to the symbolic nature of the story that it wasn't only Alex's life, but also the lives of the other ten children who escaped with him, that could begin again. And hope for the future is made even bigger by the decision of the gang's leader, fourteen-year-old Peter, to stay behind as a helper in the underground bringing more of the orphans to freedom.

◈ CHARACTER

The popularity of many books that do not have exciting or even interesting plots is a testament to the power of good characterization. When, through a writer's skill, readers identify closely with the protagonist, they feel as if they are living the experience. They become more interested in what is going on in the character's mind than they may be in what is happening to the character from the outside. Young adult authors who do an especially good job of developing memorable characters include Virginia Hamilton, Sue Ellen Bridgers, Katherine Paterson, Robert Cormier, Lawrence Yep, and Rosa Guy.

Character Development and Types

Because of the shorter length of most adolescent books, the author does not have space to develop fully more than a small cast of characters. There is usually a protagonist, an antagonist, and various supporting characters. The protagonist is usually the central character, the one with whom the reader identifies. Most commonly, this will be a young adult, perhaps a bit older than the reader, but not always. After reading a book with a fully developed protagonist, readers should know the character so well that if a situation outside of the book were described, they could predict how this character would feel and act in the new situation. The reason they would be able to do this is that the author has developed a round character. Many sides—many different aspects—of the character have been shown. A major character can undergo changes in personality in ways a minor character cannot. Such changes are often the heart of the story, but unless the character is well developed, the changes have no meaning. Readers cannot rejoice in the arrival of a character unless they know where the character started.

In contrast, many characters in literature are flat or stereotyped. As books (not just books for teenagers but for all ages) have gotten shorter and shorter, the literary element most affected has been characterization. For the sake of efficiency, authors have begun to rely more heavily on character types than on unique individuals.

THE PEOPLE BEHIND THE BOOKS

KEVIN MAJOR, Author

Far from Shore

Hold Fast

Thirty-Six Exposures

My novels to date have been set in Newfoundland, an area of North America for the most part removed from the urban mainstream. I have tried to show a young people beset by change, as the traditional way of life faces and assimilates external cultural influences. At the same time I have attempted to create characters who, although they bear the marks of being raised in this environment, share the universal confusions and joys of adolescence.

The books were not written for one particular audience, although I knew they would have special appeal to teenagers because of the ages of the main characters. I despair of writers who formulate their writing to eliminate elements of a situation because they fear burdening their established readership. Life, after all, is complex; there is not a one-dimensional answer to its difficulties. I feel adolescent literature must become more diverse and challenging. While its readers must still be able to see themselves in the characters portrayed, they should be offered a greater variety of styles, of techniques, of insights into their place in the world. ◆

Far from Shore: A Novel. Delacorte, 1981.
Hold Fast. Delacorte, 1980.
Thirty-Six Exposures. Delacorte, 1984.

Of course this is not entirely new. Since the beginning of literature, there have been archetypes that appear again and again. Archetypal characters include the wise and helpful older person who befriends and teaches a young protagonist, the villain or enemy, and the wicked or unsympathetic parent or stepparent. Archetypes differ from stereotypes in that they are usually main characters in the story. Stereotyped characters will be in the background with very little attention given to their development. The absent-minded professor, the nagging mother, and the "jock" are stereotypes. The hero who leaves home on a danger-fraught mission and returns as a stronger and better person is an archetype seen in stories as divergent as the biblical story of Joseph, Robin Graham's true-life *Dove*, Robin McKinley's fantasy *The Blue Sword*, and Sue Ellen Bridgers' realistic *Home Before Dark*. It is because this particular archetype is a part of most readers' backgrounds that we can have a good feeling at the end of Robert C. O'Brien's *Z for Zachariah*. As Ann Burden leaves the "safety" of Hidden Valley and ventures out into the radioactive world, readers feel confident that she will safely complete her quest and find other people with whom she can live and build a new society.

A reviewer is probably making a negative comment in saying that an author's characters are stereotyped, but, in reality, the conventions of writing make it necessary that at least some characters in nearly every story be stereotyped. The word "stereotyped" comes from the printer's world where it is used to mean the process by which an image is created over and over again. It would be too ponderous for an author to have to build a unique personality for every background character. And it would be too demanding for a reader to respond to a large number of fully developed characters. For example, the Newbery Award winner *The Westing Game* by Ellen Raskin, is too difficult for many junior high school readers because they can't keep the thirteen characters straight.

The use of stock characters was always accepted as part of the art of storytelling, but in the late 1960s and 1970s, as people's social consciousness grew, so did their dislike for stereotyping. Minority groups complained that their members were stereotyped in menial roles, feminists complained that women and girls always took a back seat to men and boys, and parents complained that they were presented as unimportant or even damaging to their children's lives. Justified as these complaints were (or are), it doesn't mean that writers can get along without relying on stock characters or stereotypes. But what they can do is feature as main characters members of those groups who have previously been ignored or relegated to stereotypes. Since the early 1970s, authors and publishers have been responsive to the need to present fully developed characters who are members of racial minority groups (see Chapter 11). When these characters are playing main roles in a story, then the author can take the necessary space to delineate individual qualities. Doing this well is always a challenge, but especially when the character is someone that most young readers are not accustomed to identifying with, for example, a boy with cerebral palsy as in *The Alfred Summer* by Jan Slepian, a lesbian as in *Annie on My Mind* by Nancy Garden, and the single mother of a teenage son as in *IOU's* by Ouida Sebestyen.

When an author is very successful at developing the characters in a book, readers get the feeling that the characters are real. They identify with them as friends and find it hard to believe that these "friends" live only between the covers of a book. Because of this involvement, readers often write to authors and request more information. This, along with financial success, sometimes inspires authors to write one or more sequels about the same characters.

However, a sequel for some reason is rarely as good as the original. Bette Greene says she hates sequels and swore she would never write one even when she received hundreds of letters asking her to continue the story of Patty Bergen and Ruth from *Summer of My German Soldier*. Even though she had no intention of doing a sequel, every time she sat down to write she found herself writing about Patty and Ruth. She finally gave in and wrote *Morning Is a Long Time Coming*, which was published in 1978, five years after the original story.

It took Scott O'Dell much longer to do a sequel to his 1960 *Island of the Blue Dolphins*. The book, which won the American Library Association's Newbery Award, was based on the true story of Karana, an Indian girl, left on an island off the coast of California when in the mid-1800s her tribe was relocated by the United States government. The story ended with her rescue and arrival at a California mission. Many readers wanted to know what happened to Karana, but the real story would not have made a very good sequel because Karana died within a few months of her rescue. Finally

O'Dell came up with an idea. He focused on Zia, a distant relative of Karana's. In this way he could be faithful to the historical fact of Karana's death and yet have a character with whom readers could identify. *Zia* appeared in 1976, sixteen years after the original. In the first book Karana is the main character, but in the sequel she is a foil. Her role in the story is to illuminate the personality and the struggles of Zia, the new protagonist.

Sequels differ from trilogies or other preconceived sets in that they are usually not planned when the original book is written. When a set is preplanned, as with Susan Cooper's *The Dark Is Rising* or Anne McCaffrey's *Dragon* books, the author will have plotted out the whole series. These sets of books grow out of interesting plots, whereas sequels are more apt to develop from interesting characterization.

Communicating Character

Authors use various techniques to achieve characterization. For example, they tell us what the characters do, what they say, what others say about them, what they think, and how they feel. In developing minor characters, authors are more likely to rely on communicating the physical qualities of a person (or an animal) because these can be written about with relative ease. One stereotype that people have complained about, justifiably, is a wicked or villainous characterization achieved through an ugly or deformed appearance, for example, Long John Silver in Robert Louis Stevenson's *Treasure Island*. Critics have pointed out that such characterization extends people's inclination to think in terms of "the good and the beautiful" and "the bad and the ugly."

The way people speak, aside from what they say, can be very revealing. Sometimes authors will have certain characters speak with a dialect or will have them use "different" words as Richard Adams did with the rabbits in *Watership Down*. This sets them apart, shows that they are somewhat different from the reader and therefore of special interest.

The writers of ethnic books often use touches of dialectal speech to communicate something about the background of their characters. But, because of difficulties in spelling, printing, and reading, few writers will do a whole book in dialect. Instead they will give only a hint. Native American speech is most often shown through loan translations (English words used in place of Native American ones) as in this sentence from *When the Legends Die* by Hal Borland: "The Ute people have lived many generations, many grandmothers, in that land."

Black dialects are shown through vocabulary and grammatical constructions that are peculiar to black English. Black speech may also be shown through what is called eye dialect. A writer gives nonstandard spelling to words to show the reader that a dialect is being spoken. Many such spellings are actually phonetically accurate representations of standard speech as much as of nonstandard speech. The use of black dialect in fiction has increased in recent years as a reflection of black pride. June Jordan, Brenda Wilkinson, Maya Angelou, and Alice Childress are among black writers who code shift between standard and dialectal English. For example, in Childress' *A Hero Ain't Nothin' But a Sandwich*, Benjie talks about his parents' asking him if he wants to "go to the show, too?"

◇ They always say "too," and when they say it, I'm thinkin that me as the one more would be one too many. I always say, "No, I got me a TV thing I wanta see." But, dig it, who wanta be the extra one goin along to eyeball some picture bout Black people bein poor? I dig movies where people got high-rise hotels and where they be international spies wearin they fine suits and hoppin big planes from one airport to nother.

One of the advantages of books over movies and plays is that an author can more easily get inside the characters' minds and tell what they are thinking in greater detail. This is much harder to do when almost everything has to be communicated through dialogue. Characters often think things that they would not say to another person. A literary technique that is sometimes used to get around this problem both in stories and plays is the dramatic monologue. In this, the author has the character speak out in a direct way revealing things about both the speaker and the situation. If it is done in the form of a soliloquy, the speaker seems to be unaware of the audience. It is a kind of interior monologue, also called stream-of-consciousness, in which the words are written down as if they were not prepared for an outside reader. Sometimes they tumble out as disjointed or random thoughts, but at other times they may make coherent sense. They give the reader the feeling of coming into the middle of something. The beginning of Robert Cormier's *I Am the Cheese* is a good example of this kind of monologue:

◇ I am riding the bicycle and I am on Route 31 in Monument, Massachusetts, on my way to Rutterburg, Vermont, and I'm pedaling furiously because this is an old-fashioned bike, no speeds, no fenders, only the warped tires and the brakes that don't always work and the handlebars with cracked rubber grips to steer with. A plain bike—the kind my father rode as a kid years ago. It's cold as I pedal along, the wind like a snake slithering up my sleeves and into my jacket and my pants legs, too. But I keep pedaling, I keep pedaling.

This monologue serves as a narrative hook. It draws the reader into the midst of an intriguing story. The monologues most often seen in young adult literature are first-person stories in which this technique allows protagonists to speak frankly about their most intimate feelings. In Judy Blume's *Are You There God? It's Me, Margaret*, the monologues are in the form of nighttime prayers. In S. E. Hinton's *The Outsiders*, Ponyboy is writing his term paper; and in Paul Zindel's *The Pigman*, Lorraine and John take turns writing what they call their "memorial epic":

◇ It's just that some very strange things have happened to us during the last few months, and we feel we should write them down while they're still fresh in our minds. It's got to be written now before John and I mature and repress the whole thing.

Having characters do their own speaking is a forceful means of characterization, but the technique of having the protagonist tell the story through letters or a diary has been used so much in recent years that it is becoming trite. A better and less self-conscious technique that is growing in popularity is simply to have the protagonist tell the story in the first person with no apologies.

◈ POINT OF VIEW

Point of view is expressed largely through the person who tells the story. A story has to be told from a consistent viewpoint. The storyteller has to decide just how far from the characters to stand, from which direction to illuminate their actions with sympathy, and when and if it is time to speak from inside one of them. The viewpoint that gives the storyteller the most freedom is the one called omniscient or "all knowing." With this viewpoint it is as if the writer is present in all the characters, knowing what is inside their minds. This was the viewpoint that Joanne Greenberg, writing under the pseudonym of Hannah Green, used when she wrote *I Never Promised You a Rose Garden*. It would hardly have been believable for the girl Deborah to tell the story since throughout most of the book she is psychotic. Yet it is necessary that the readers be told what she is thinking since the real story takes place in her mind. Also, by using the third person omniscient viewpoint, Green could share the thoughts of the other patients, Deborah's psychiatrist, and her parents.

Writers have much less freedom if they decide to enter into the mind and body of one of the characters and stay there, that is, to write the book in the first person. It takes real skill on the writer's part to tell the story without slipping in facts or attitudes that would be unknown to the character whose voice is being used. First person narrators can describe other characters in an objective manner; that is, they can tell about whatever can be seen from the outside, but they cannot tell what is going on inside the minds of the other characters. One way to get around the limitation of having a first person book come all from the same viewpoint is to have first person chapters coming alternately from different people. M. E. Kerr used this technique in *I'll Love You When You're More Like Me* and so did Alice Childress in *A Hero Ain't Nothin' But a Sandwich*. William Wharton began *Birdy* by having Birdy's friend Al visit him in a veterans' hospital where he alternates between talking to the unresponsive Birdy and thinking his own thoughts. Birdy's thoughts—at first just fragments and pieces—are given in a slightly different style of type. By the end of the book, Birdy's thoughts have grown to whole chapters.

This technique was very satisfying to readers because it put them in a better position to understand Birdy than either his friend or his psychiatrist. It also let them know things about Birdy's childhood and his family that Birdy would never have told, for example:

◇ Birdy's old lady'd keep any baseballs that went over the fence into their yard. Ball players didn't even try anymore. Semi-pros, everybody, gave up. Hit a homer over that fence, into Birdy's yard; good-bye, ball. Nothing to do but throw in a new one. It got to be expensive playing in that ball park if you were a long-ball-hitting right-hander.

What the hell could she've done with all those baseballs? Birdy and I used to look for those baseballs everywhere around his place. Maybe she buried them, or she could've sold them; big black market source for used baseballs.

In a similar way to how William Wharton told most of Birdy's story through the eyes of his best friend, authors may look around for a relatively minor character to tell the story. Richard Peck has explained that he chooses to do this because the interesting stories are at the extreme ends of the normal curve. The exciting things are happening to the brilliant and successful students such as those that Ursula Le Guin wrote about in *Very Far Away from Anywhere Else.* Or they are happening to the kids at the other end of the scale as in Fran Arrick's *Steffie Can't Come Out to Play* and S. E. Hinton's *That Was Then, This Is Now.* Peck says that these extreme characters are wonderful to write about, but they aren't the ones who will read his books. They are too busy, too involved in their own lives. Readers are most likely to come from the large group of students in between whose lives aren't full of such highs and lows. Therefore, what Peck does is to choose for a narrator someone from the middle group with whom readers can identify. He then tells the story through this person's eyes. For example in *Don't Look and It Won't Hurt,* it is the fifteen-year-old sister who tells the story of the pregnant and unmarried Ellen who goes to Chicago to have her baby. And in *Representing Super Doll,* it is the beauty queen's friend Verna who relates the story and who, in an example of wish fulfillment, is shown to be the real winner.

◈ TONE

The tone of a book is determined by the author's attitude toward subject, characters, and readers. It is difficult to pick out the exact elements that contribute to the tone of a book because many times the author is not even aware of them. Some people think that the most distinctive thing about young adult literature is its tone. They say they can pick up two books treating protagonists of the same age who are faced with similar problems, and, by reading a few pages, can tell that one has been written for a general adult audience while the other has been written for teenagers. If an author were speaking directly to you, tone would simply be communicated through the lilt of the voice, the lifting of an eyebrow, a twinkle in the eye, or a crease in the forehead. But when tone has to be communicated exclusively through the written word, then it is more complex.

Sometimes language reminiscent of church hymns or the Bible is used to lend weight and dignity to a book as in the titles *All Creatures Great and*

Small by James Herriot, *The People Therein* by Mildred Lee, *Jacob Have I Loved* by Katherine Paterson, and *Manchild in the Promised Land* by Claude Brown.

The tone in these books contrasts sharply with the humorous and irreverent tone that appears in many of the popular new books. Americans have always been fond of exaggeration or hyperbole and its use is one way of establishing a light, humorous tone. When writers use hyperbole, readers know that what they say is not true, but they nevertheless enjoy the far-fetched overstatement as in Ellen Conford's title, *If This Is Love, I'll Take Spaghetti* and Paul Zindel's title, *Pardon Me, You're Stepping on My Eyeball!*

Another literary technique that authors rely on when they are establishing the tone they desire is euphemistic wording. Euphemisms are words or phrases carefully chosen to avoid harsh or unpleasant concepts. In general, modern writers think it better to speak directly than to make the vague kinds of circumlocutions that used to be fashionable in writing. But still there are euphemisms that have literary impact. For example, Margaret Craven's title *I Heard the Owl Call My Name* is more intriguing than a bald statement such as, "I knew I was going to die." And Hemingway's title *For Whom the Bell Tolls* is both more euphemistic and euphonious than "the one who has died."

A semantic area more susceptible to euphemism in adolescent than in adult literature is that of sex. Authors are constantly looking for ways to communicate sexual information without setting up a tone that would arouse "prurient interests"—or censors. This is why it is likely that in adolescent literature you will read about such parts of the body as the "fork of the thighs" as in Renvoize's *A Wild Thing*, "my special place" as in Blume's *Deenie*, and the "posterior fornix" as in Peck's *Are You in the House Alone?*

Euphemisms can be created because there are so many ways to denote or communicate the same basic information, but each variation will have a different connotation. It will trigger a different emotional response in the reader. In establishing tone, a skilled writer will take advantage of the connotations of words, but, because connotations are somewhat vague and will probably be interpreted differently by different readers, the author may not always be in total control of the message that reaches the readers. For example, some, but not all, readers who see the titles of R. R. Knudson's books: *Zanballer, Zanbanger, Zanboomer,* and *Fox Running* will think that sexual connotations were intended. Perhaps they were, but the books do not fulfill the promise as many readers would interpret it.

For certain kinds of books a reverent tone is appropriate, as, for example, a memoir about someone who has died. They are usually written in a loving tone by someone who was close to the person who died and who wants to pay tribute to or honor the person's memory. John Gunther's *Death Be Not Proud: A Memoir* telling about Gunther's teenage son's struggle against a fatal brain tumor has remained popular for three decades. Doris Lund's *Eric*, which tells about her seventeen-year-old son's four-year battle with leukemia, is, like Gunther's book, a sad but inspiring memoir. For memoirs to be successful the tone cannot be so worshipful that it becomes too sentimental.

The tone of a biography is equally important in attracting an audience. Part of the appeal of *Geri*, the autobiography of Geri Jewell, the young actress/comedienne who has cerebral palsy, is its upbeat approach and the candor with which the author discusses her disability. But if throughout the book the tone had been one of feeling sorry for herself, then readers could never have forgotten about the disability and gotten to know the woman behind it. It would have defeated the purpose of the book, which Jewell summed up as being "to show the hardness and usefulness of the disabled."

Another pitfall that young adult authors must try to avoid is an overly didactic tone. Certainly it is the goal—conscious or unconscious—of most adults to teach worthwhile values to young people. Nevertheless, in literary criticism, calling a work "didactic" usually implies that the tone comes across as preachy. The story has been created around a message instead of having a message or a theme grow naturally out of the story. For example, Gertrude Samuels' book *Run, Shelley, Run!* appears to have been written for the didactic purpose of bringing the plight of homeless girls to the public's attention, and Gloria D. Miklowitz' *Close to the Edge* is a plea for involvement and service to others as a key to good mental health.

Great literature always leaves the reader with something to think about. Lessons are taught, but they are subtle lessons, and the reader is left with the responsibility of analyzing what the writer has presented and of coming to a conclusion. *Lord of the Flies* is a book from which people learn a great deal, but it is not usually considered a didactic book because the author, William Golding, does not spell out the lesson for the reader. We might contrast Golding's nondidactic tone with the didactic message that appears in an introduction written by E. M. Forster to a 1962 edition of the same book:

> ◇ It is certainly not a comforting book. But it may help a few grownups to be less complacent and more compassionate, to support Ralph, respect Piggy, control Jack, and lighten a little the darkness of man's heart. At the present moment (if I may speak personally) it is respect for Piggy that seems needed most. I do not find it in our leaders.

Forster's comments could also be described as *editorializing*. Notice how he asked permission to express his personal opinion. Sometimes authors will editorialize, or give their own opinions, through the voice of a character as S. E. Hinton did in *The Outsiders* when Ponyboy explains why he wrote his story:

> ◇ I could see boys going down under street lights because they were mean and tough and hated the world, and it was too late to tell them that there was still good in it, and they wouldn't believe you if you did. It was too vast a problem to be just a personal thing. There should be some help. Someone should tell their side of the story, and maybe people would understand then and wouldn't be so quick to judge a boy by the amount of hair oil he wore.

In reality, it is probably not so much that we dislike didactic tone as it is that we dislike that tone when the message is something with which we do not agree. If the message is reaffirming one of our beliefs, then we identify with it and enjoy the feeling that other people are going to be convinced of the "truth." It is partly because it is their message that teenagers respond so warmly to Hinton's book.

A nostalgic tone is a potential problem in much young adult literature. Nearly all books with teenage protagonists are of potential interest to young adult readers. But one of the things that keeps some of them from reaching a large young adult audience is that the authors have looked back at their own adolescence and have romanticized it. They are nostalgic about the good old days. But to a sixteen-year-old, "sweet sixteen" is nothing about which to be nostalgic. The tone comes through as condescension, which is unappealing to readers of any age.

◈ SETTING

Setting—the context of time and place—is more important in some genres than in others. For example, it is often the setting, a time in the future or the far past or some place where people now living on this earth have never actually been, that lets readers know they are embarking on reading a fantasy. The special quality in J. R. R. Tolkien's *The Lord of the Rings* would not be possible were it not set in the mythical world of Middle Earth. Nor would many popular pieces of science fiction be possible without their outer space or futuristic settings.

Historical fiction is another genre in which the setting is important to the story. Bette Greene's *Summer of My German Soldier* could not have happened at any time other than during World War II. Without the war, there would not have been German prisoners in this country, nor would there have been the peculiar combination of public and private hysteria that worked on Patty Bergen's southern Christian community and her Jewish family. All of this makes it easy to think of *Summer of My German Soldier* as a historical novel. In contrast, Maureen Daly's *Seventeenth Summer* was set in approximately the same time period, but the crux of the story does not center around the war. It centers around a young girl's feelings toward the adult role that she is growing into and toward her first experience with love. Many girls who read *Seventeenth Summer* come away with the feeling that they are reading a slightly old-fashioned, but contemporary, novel.

For our purposes, we have rather arbitrarily chosen to label any book that is set during or prior to World War II as historical fiction. Often-read books whose settings make them fall clearly into the category of historical fiction are Jack Schaefer's *Shane*, Mark Twain's *The Adventures of Huckleberry Finn*, and Fred Gipson's *Old Yeller*. Of recent pieces of popular young adult fiction, good examples of how a story is controlled by its historical setting are Robert Newton Peck's *A Day No Pigs Would Die*, a 1920s family story set in a rural Vermont community of Shakers, and Jean

Fritz' *Homesick: My Own Story*, the true account of Fritz' growing up in China with her American parents and then coming "home" to the United States in 1927.

Kinds of Settings

There are basically two kinds of settings in stories: one is integral and the other is backdrop. When the setting is a part of the plot, then obviously it is integral as in the historical books and fantasies mentioned earlier. It is also integral in stories—whether fictional or true—in which the plot or problem is person against nature. In accounts of mountain climbing, survival, exploring, and other sorts of adventuring, the setting is actually the antagonist. It is interesting in and of itself just as a character would be.

Another kind of story in which the setting is integral is the regional story. For example, after reading James Michener's *Hawaii*, we want to visit Hawaii, or, if we live there, we want to learn more about it, and after reading *Caravans*, we have a new interest in Afghanistan. This is similar to the way we develop feelings for particular characters and want to get to know them better in a sequel or in a movie taken from the book. In some degree, nearly all realistic fiction is regional since the setting influences the story, but the term is usually applied to stories where the setting plays an unusually important part. For example, Hal Borland's *When the Legends Die* and Frank Herbert's *Soul Catcher* are both regional stories about young Native American men whose searches for their own identities cannot be separated from the regions in which they grew up. Vera and Bill Cleaver also wrote regional stories including *Where the Lilies Bloom*, which is set in backwoods Appalachia, and *Dust of the Earth*, which is set in the Dakotas during the Depression.

Traditionally most regional stories have had rural settings in which the protagonists are close to nature, but as the United States has changed to an urban society and realism has become more fashionable, cities also appear as important background settings as in Nicholasa Mohr's *El Bronx Remembered* and *In Nuevo York*. These are both collections of short stories that are held together by their common setting. Mohr communicates the Puerto Rican background of her stories through the touch of Spanish in the titles.

In contrast to stories with integral settings are those with backdrop settings. Stories of this type are set in a small town, an inner-city neighborhood, a modern suburb, or a high school. When authors establish this kind of setting, they are not particularly anxious to make it so clear-cut that it would be identifiable as only one place. They want to give enough details so that it comes alive, but to leave it vague enough that readers can imagine the story happening, for example, in their own town or at least in one they know.

The most common backdrop setting in young adult literature is that of a high school. Since school is the business—the everyday life—of teenagers, many of the books relate to school just as many adult books somehow relate to jobs and work. However, there is a difference in that adult jobs are extremely varied, but schools are pretty much the same. There may be

◆ Traditionally most regional stories have had rural settings in which the protagonists are close to nature, but as the United States has changed to an urban society and realism has become more fashionable, cities also appear as important background settings as in Nicholasa Mohr's *El Bronx Remembered* and *In Nueva York.*

From EL BRONX REMEMBERED by Nicholasa Mohr. Copyright © 1975 by Nicholasa Mohr. Jacket art by Nicholasa Mohr. Reprinted by permission of Harper & Row, Publishers. From IN NEUVA YORK by Nicholasa Mohr. Copyright © 1977 by Nicholasa Mohr. Jacket art by Leo and Diane Dillon. Reprinted by permission of The Dial Press.

boarding schools, exclusive day schools, military schools, and religious schools, as well as the "typical" public high school, but a school is still a school with its stairways, restrooms, lockers, cafeteria, classrooms, and parking lot. There are only so many ways to describe such places, which is one of the things that gives a sameness to books for this age group.

How Setting Works

But even in school-related stories in which the setting is pretty much a matter of backdrop, it is more important than many readers realize. Because of the length restrictions in books for this age group, setting is usually established quickly and efficiently. It continues to be developed throughout the story and to affect readers' reactions. A good example is Lois Duncan's *Killing Mr. Griffin,* which is about a group of high-school students who want to get even with a demanding teacher who has publicly humiliated them. They kidnap him, planning only to frighten and humble him, but he has a heart condition and dies.

The first line of the book establishes both the setting and the seriousness of the matter: "It was a wild, windy, southwestern spring when the idea of killing Mr. Griffin occurred to them." From here, Duncan goes on to describe the protagonist's walk across a playing field to the school building:

◇ Susan McConnell leaned into the wind and cupped her hands around the edges of her glasses to keep the blowing red dust from filling her eyes. Tumbleweeds swept past her like small, furry animals, rushing to pile in drifts against the fence that separated the field from the parking lot. The parked cars all had their windows up as though against a rainstorm. In the distance the rugged Sandia Mountains rose in faint outline, almost obscured by the pinkish haze.

I hate spring, Susan told herself vehemently. I hate dust and wind. I wish we lived somewhere else. Someday—

It was a word she used often—*someday*.

In less than half a page setting has already served three purposes. First, it has established a troubled mood; second, it has given basic information about where and who is going to be in the story; and, third, it has revealed something about the character of the protagonist. It has let readers know that she is dissatisifed with her life and will therefore be vulnerable to suggestions or opportunities to bring about changes.

Later in the book, setting serves other important purposes. We are shown Mr. Griffin at home offering to make breakfast for his pregnant wife, and we see a different side of his personality so that we can feel truly sorry about his death. It would have been less credible if Duncan had tried to show us this different side of Mr. Griffin in the school setting where his students also could have seen it. By showing different characters in different settings, authors are able to reveal things to readers in such a way that the readers get the feeling of being in control of the situation because they know more than some of the characters do.

Settings can also act as symbols. They can provide a visible way to describe feelings that are very real even though they cannot be seen. For example, while the other boys are burying Mr. Griffin, David walks back to the two cars:

◇ He started first for Jeff's car and then, on impulse, opened instead the door of the Chevrolet and climbed in behind the steering wheel. In times past he had sometimes amused himself by contemplating how cars often seemed extensions of the people who owned them. There was Jeff's car, large and loud and flashy, and David's mother's, compact, economical and serviceable. Betsy's mother's Volkswagen was small and fitful, a nervous little automobile, painted bright yellow.

Now, in Brian Griffin's car, he closed his eyes and tried to feel the presence of the man who had driven it, hoping for one last image of warmth and life. It did not come. The car was as cold and devoid of personality as the thing in the grave by the waterfall.

Mr. Griffin's car brings home to David the fact that Mr. Griffin is indeed dead. Sitting in the car he offers a prayer which is half a defense of himself and half a prayer for forgiveness, but hardly a blessing on the grave or the man whose body lies in it.

Even when the setting is a backdrop through most of the book, there may be places where it becomes integral as a part of the plot. This happens in Duncan's book in relation to the secret waterfall up in the mountains. One of the boys had found it with his former girlfriend. They were the only ones who ever went there so it seems an excellent place to take Mr. Griffin, and, when he dies, it also seems to be an excellent place to bury him. But the former girlfriend also remembers the place and just happens to go on a spring picnic with her new boyfriend. The two of them discover the evidence that leads the police to Mr. Griffin's body.

A setting does not really have to exist to play a part in a story. It might be just a dream of one of the characters, as when David and Sue imagine getting out of the whole problem by driving straight west to California and taking a ship to an uninhabited island. At one point, Sue confides that she has always had a dream of living by herself in a forest cabin by a peaceful lake instead of in a noisy, family household located in a dry and windy desert.

Setting may also serve as foreshadowing. For example, the night that everything comes to a climax (which incidentally is a bit overdone and melodramatic for our tastes), readers are prepared for something awful by the description of the weather:

> ◇ The wind began in the early afternoon. It rose slowly at first, but increased steadily . . . The Sunday twilight was muted and pink, as the sun's last rays slanted through the thick, red air, and when dark came the wind did not drop but seemed to grow stronger, whining around the corners of houses and stripping the first new leaf buds from trees.

Being able to establish settings so that they accomplish multiple purposes is one of the most important skills a writer can develop. Successful writers use settings not only as parts of plot, but also to make the story live for readers, to help them visualize exactly what is happening, to illuminate character, to symbolize important feelings, and to establish moods.

◈ STYLE

Style is the way a story is written as contrasted to what the story is about. It is the result or effect of combining the literary aspects we have already talked about.

An Individual Matter

No two authors have exactly the same style because with writing, just as with appearance, behavior, and personal belongings, style consists of the unique blending of all the choices each individual makes. From situation to situation, these choices may differ, but they are enough alike that the styles of particular authors such as Kurt Vonnegut, Jr., Richard Brautigan, and E. L. Doctorow will be recognizable from book to book. But style is also influenced by the nature of the story being told. For example, Ursula K. Le Guin used a different style when she wrote the realistic *Very Far Away from Anywhere Else* from the one she used when she wrote her science-fiction *A Wizard of Earthsea*. Nevertheless, in both books she relied on the particular writing techniques that she likes and is skilled at using.

Virginia Hamilton is another author whose sense of style is evident throughout her writing which ranges from the realistic *M. C. Higgins, the Great* to the romantic *A Little Love,* the occult *Sweet Whispers, Brother*

◆ Virginia Hamilton is an author whose distinctive style comes through whether she's writing fantasy as in *Justice and Her Brothers* or romance as in *A Little Love.*

Rush, and the science-fictional Justice trilogy beginning with *Justice and Her Brothers.*

Authors' styles are influenced by such factors as their intended audience and their purpose in writing. For example, a nonfiction informative book will have a different style from that of an informative book that is written to persuade readers to a belief or an action. And, even after an author has made the decision to write a persuasive book, the style will be affected by whether the author chooses to persuade through humor, through a dramatic fictional account, or through a logical display of evidence.

The fact that the protagonists are young in most books for this age group also influences style. Probably the book that has had the greatest influence on writing style is J. D. Salinger's *The Catcher in the Rye.* Nearly every year, promotional materials or reviews compare five or six new young adult books to *Catcher.* Some of these comparisons are made on the basis of the subject matter, but the theme of a boy wavering between the innocence of childhood and the acceptance of the adult world—imperfect as it is—is not all that unusual. It is the style of the writing that makes Salinger's book so memorable, indeed such a milestone, and has inspired other authors to imitate the colloquial speech, the candid revelations of feelings, the short snappy dialogues, the instant judgments, and the emotional extremes ranging from hostility to great tenderness.

One of the most memorable scenes in the book is the one in which the young prostitute comes to Holden's hotel room, and he is so touched by her youth and innocence that he gives up the whole idea:

◇ She was very nervous, for a prostitute. She really was. I think it was because she was young as hell. She was around my age. I sat down in the big chair, next to her, and offered her a cigarette. "I don't smoke," she said. She had a tiny little wheeny-whiny voice. You could hardly hear her. She never said thank you, either, when you offered her something. She just didn't know any better.

"Allow me to introduce myself. My name is Jim Steele," I said.

"Ya got a watch on ya?" she said. She didn't care what the hell my name was, naturally. "Hey how old are you, anyways?"

"Me? Twenty-two."

"Like fun you are."

It was a funny thing to say. It sounded like a real kid. You'd think a prostitute and all would say, "Like hell you are" or "Cut the crap" instead of "Like fun you are."

As the girl gets ready to leave, Holden observes that, "If she'd been a big old prostitute, with a lot of makeup on her face and all, she wouldn't have been half as spooky."

It is possible to describe the literary devices that are the basic ingredients of an author's style. But there is more to literary style than these various devices. Before a writer can be said to have a distinctive style, something has to click so that the devices blend together into a unified whole.

Figurative Language

Much of what determines writers' styles is how they use figurative language. This is language that is interesting and important above and beyond the literal information it communicates. Writers use figurative language to set a mood, to surprise the reader, to create imagery, to make a passage memorable, and sometimes to show off their skill. Words used figuratively have different, or at least additional, meanings from those they have in standard usage. One type of figurative language—metaphors, symbols, allegories, and similes—stimulates the reader's mind to make comparisons. A second type appeals to the sense of sight or hearing. Examples include alliteration, assonance, rhyme, euphony, rhythm, and cadence. In the following sentence from Harold Brodkey's story, "Sentimental Education," both kinds of figurative language occur:

> ◇ Dimitri had a car, which Elgin borrowed—an old, weak-lunged Ford—and they could wheeze up to Marblehead and rent a dinghy and be blown around the bay, with the sunlight bright on Caroline's hair and the salt air making them hungry and the wind whipping up small whitecaps to make the day exciting.

The personification of the "weak-lunged Ford" that "wheezes" up to Marblehead helps the reader visualize the old car while the alliteration in "be blown around the bay" and "wind whipping up small whitecaps" and the rhyme in "sunlight bright" and "Caroline's hair and the salt air" affect the reader more subtly in establishing mood. The word "wheeze" is also an example of onomatopoeia in which the sound of a word gives a hint of its meaning.

Metaphors are among the most common kinds of figurative language. In a metaphor basically dissimilar things are likened to one another so that the reader gets a new insight. A fresh metaphor can be an effective device for making readers active instead of passive participants. Readers have to become mentally involved in order to make associations that they have not thought of before.

THE PEOPLE BEHIND THE BOOKS

SUE ELLEN BRIDGERS, Author

All Together Now
Home Before Dark
Notes for Another Life

Because my first novel appealed to young adults, I have been classified as a young adult author. However, I have never given much thought to what might or might not be appropriate for a particular group of readers. So far I have tried to write books that I like and I expect to continue to work to please myself,

hoping to please other readers, both young and old, along the way.

Having come to young adult literature without scholarship or experience, I find I have ambivalent feelings about such a classification of books. I am not sure there needs to be a category of young adult literature at all, and I don't understand the criteria for its classification. If it means that, because of their style or subject matter, beautifully written, accomplished stories that stretch the reader's understanding of life are eliminated, then I hope young adult literature as a category dies

---

A metaphor can be very simple consisting of only a word or a phrase as when in Sue Ellen Bridgers' *Notes for Another Life*, Jolene grasps "at the last thread of romance floating by." Or they might be more fully developed as when Kevin falls during practice for a tennis tournament and breaks his wrist. After coming home from having it set, he lies on the couch waiting for his grandmother, his sister, and his mother "to attempt a miracle, a feeble gesture he could deride and toss back at them with his anger." Later, Kevin visits his schizophrenic father who is hospitalized for treatment. His father seems to be unusually happy and in control of himself and then Kevin mentions something about the divorce proceedings that Kevin's mother is planning. The father had not been told and he suffered a relapse, which Kevin feels terribly guilty about. Bridgers used a powerful metaphor to explain this when she wrote that Kevin at last told Wren, his sister, "Told her and left her with it, a grenade of guilt and remorse clutched in her hand to prevent its exploding in his own."

Similes, like metaphors, make comparisons between basically dissimilar things, but they are literally true, while metaphors are true only figuratively. The creator of a simile hedges by putting in such words as *like, as, similar,* or *resembles* to indicate that a comparison is being made. Still using Bridgers' *Notes for Another Life* as an example, when Kevin breaks his wrist and is taken to the hospital, his girlfriend:

◇ . . . watched the car go and already was thinking how he'd look in a cast, what she'd write on it, how at first he wouldn't be able to use his fingers. She would tie his shoes, cut his meat, button his shirts. She would be there every day, just in case he needed her. The fantasy was as blinding as the sun, as heady as Christmas punch, as impossible as any midnight dream.

quickly. If it means that young people are given access to good books that might otherwise go unpublished for lack of a market, then I have warm wishes for its future.

The placement of a book in libraries and book stores is not in the hands of the writer, and from where I sit, the dilemma of dual marketing looks like an insurmountable problem unless publishers, librarians, and store managers engage in cooperative and creative thinking on the subject. One thing I know for certain. Young people deserve the best the community of writers has to offer. The quality of writing should carry the same weight as subject matter in the decision to classify a book. Young adult literature is transitional literature. By its nature, it should not only move the reader closer to maturity by its subject matter and philosophy, but also by its inventiveness of style, its characterization, sensitivity and discovery, and most of all, by the commitment of its writers to do their best work. ◆

This concluding simile is especially effective because of the way Bridgers set up three parallel clauses with the surprise letdown at the end.

In Zibby Oneal's *A Formal Feeling,* sixteen-year-old Anne Cameron must let go of the dream of perfection in which she had wrapped the memories of her deceased mother. Near the end of the book, she was able at least to form the question that had bothered her since she was eight years old and her mother temporarily left the family, "If she loved me, why did she leave me?"

◇ That was one of the questions, but it was only one. Beneath it there was another. It had been swimming at the edges of her mind for days, darting away as a fish does, startled by a movement that comes too close. She thought she could not avoid it any more, and so she pushed herself down one more time, like a diver. She knew the question had always been there, unspeakable, at the bottom of all she remembered and had chosen to forget. And she made herself ask: Did I ever love my mother at all?

Being able to ask this question is in effect the climax of the book, but without the interesting simile readers would have been less likely to recognize its importance. Also, since it was something that occurred only in Anne's mind, the only interesting way to make readers visualize it was through some sort of figurative language.

Allegories are extended comparisons or metaphors. They can be enjoyed on at least two levels. One is the literal or surface level on which the story is enjoyed simply for itself. On the second or deeper level, we can interpret and extend the meaning of the story, and it thereby becomes more interesting. It is in part the challenge of interpreting the allegory in William

Golding's *Lord of the Flies* that makes it a good piece to read and discuss in a group.

An allegorical device that authors sometimes use is giving their characters symbolic names as Robert C. O'Brien did in *Z for Zachariah*. The title is taken from a Bible ABC book in which the first letter of the alphabet stands for Adam and the last for Zachariah. The symbolism suggests that if Adam were the first man on earth, Zachariah must be the last. The girl in the book who carries a tremendous responsibility and at the end is left with the task of rebuilding a civilization is symbolically named Ann Burden. These names may influence readers' attitudes and enhance their pleasure without their being aware of it.

Allusions work in the same way. They are an efficient way to communicate a great deal of information because one reference in a word or a phrase triggers the readers' minds to think of the whole story or idea behind the allusion. Robert Cormier's title *I Am the Cheese* is an allusion to the old nursery song and game, "The Farmer in the Dell." Besides being efficient, allusions, like metaphors, are effective in forcing readers to become actively involved in making connections. A lazy or uninterested reader might not see any allusion in Cormier's title. Someone else, especially when discovering that the family's name is Farmer, would connect the title to the nursery rhyme and perhaps think of the last line, "And the cheese stands alone!" An even more thoughtful reader might carry it back one more step and think of the next to last line, "The rat takes the cheese." It is this type of reader who may discover the most in Cormier's writing.

Harry Kullman in *The Battle Horse* makes a more obvious allusion. The book, set in 1930s Stockholm, Sweden, is a story of resentments and competition between upper and lower class youth and between boys and girls. Their hostilities are acted out in a neighborhood jousting tournament. A large, ungainly lower class girl serves as the horse for one of the upper class preppies. So that no one will know that she is a girl, the boys make her a costume.

> ◇ When she'd been wearing the horse costume and she'd adjusted the horse head so that it merged into her brown-covered arms, there was something familiar about her, something I'd seen before. Suddenly it dawned on me what it was—she looked like one of the pictures in *Gulliver's Travels* when Gulliver is in the Kingdom of the Horses—a Houyhnhnm who stood on his back legs and held both his front hooves in front of his face as he threaded a needle.

From this reference, the comparison is made to "The Kingdom of the Horses! Oh, yes! That's where the horses are the crown of creation and the Yahoos are dumb animals even though they look like human beings." The allusion is repeated with added significance at the very end of the book.

Although in literature, symbols are communicated through words, they are more than words, which is why their meanings cannot be looked up in dictionaries. Also, they are more complex than metaphors. For example, the semantic feature or meaning common to the word *thunder* and the metaphorical phrase *thunderous applause* is that of a big noise. But in Mildred Taylor's title *Roll of Thunder, Hear My Cry* there is no such simple explanation. The idea of noise is still there, but added to it is the idea of size and relativity. It is the power of all nature contrasted to the smallness of one human voice. Additionally, there's the negativeness, the ominous feeling that is communicated through the mention of a storm and the word *cry* which has a negative or at least a serious connotation as compared, for example, with *shout* or *yell*. Yet, in spite of this, the title has an optimistic ring to it, probably because the reader intuitively recognizes the strength of the voice behind the *my*. Weak characters hide under the bedcovers during a thunderstorm. Only the strong stand in the storm and yell back.

Symbolism can be a good subject for discussion because what one reader will miss, another might find. It is almost like hunting for clues in a game. When all the clues are filled in, the total picture is much more meaningful than the separate pieces.

This chapter has been little more than an introduction to—or perhaps for some of you simply a review of—the basics of literary criticism and appreciation. The concepts and the terminology will reappear throughout the rest of this textbook as well as in much of whatever else you read about books written for any age of reader.

We placed this discussion early in the textbook for two reasons. First, we wanted to make it clear that authors for young adults make use of the same literary techniques as used by all good writers. And second, we wanted to lay a foundation for the way you approach the reading you will do throughout this course. We want you to lose yourselves—and also find yourselves—in some very good stories. But at the same time we want to encourage you to keep a part of your mind open for looking at literature from the pleasure-giving top of the birthday cake.

◆ ACTIVITIES ◆

1. Write your own reading autobiography. Tell about your first memories of receiving pleasure from books. Do you remember the first book you really liked? If so, what was it? When you started to choose books for yourself, did you read series books? How about books of a particular type, such as sports stories, horse stories, or dog stories? What about informative books? Did you have one or more influential adults who encouraged you? If so, what did they do? Finally, analyze how your own stages of reading development measure up with those described by the birthday cake theory.

2. Read a book from the Honor Sampling. Write a one or two sentence description of each of the following: plot, theme, character, point of view, tone, setting, and style.

3. Choose one of the young adult books you have read and analyze the author's style. What makes it distinctive? Is it the dialogue? The descriptions? The figurative language? The tone? Or something else? Cite specific examples to support your generalizations.

◆ NOTES ◆

[1]"Bringing Up Superbaby," *Newsweek* 101 (March 28, 1983): 62–68.

[2]Margaret Early, "Stages of Growth in Literary Appreciation," *English Journal* 49 (March 1960): 163–66.

[3]First cited by G. Robert Carlsen in an article exploring stages of reading development similar to those illustrated by the birthday cake theory. "Literature IS," *English Journal* 63 (February 1974): 23–27

[4]Donald Hall, "Finally Only the Love of the Art," *New York Times Book Review*, January 16, 1983, pp. 7, 25.

[5]Glenna Davis Sloan, *The Child as Critic* (New York: Teachers College Press, 1975).

[6]Annie Gottlieb, "A New Cycle in 'YA' Books," *New York Times Book Review*, June 17, 1984, pp. 24–25.

◆ TITLES MENTIONED IN CHAPTER 2 ◆

For information on the availability of paperback editions of these titles, please consult the most recent edition of *Paperbound Books in Print*, published annually by R. R. Bowker Company.

Adams, Richard. *The Plague Dogs*. Knopf, 1978.
————. *Watership Down*. Macmillan, 1974.
Alexander, Lloyd. *Westmark*. Dutton, 1981.
Angelou, Maya. *I Know Why the Caged Bird Sings*. Random House, 1970.
Arrick, Fran. *Steffie Can't Come Out to Play*. Bradbury, 1978.
Bach, Alice. *Waiting for Johnny Miracle*. Harper & Row, 1980.
Blume, Judy. *Are You There God? It's Me, Margaret*. Bradbury, 1970.
————. *Deenie*. Bradbury, 1973.
Borland, Hal. *When the Legends Die*. Harper & Row, 1963.
Brancato, Robin. *Sweet Bells Jangled Out of Tune*. Knopf, 1982.
————. *Winning*. Knopf, 1977.
Bridgers, Sue Ellen. *All Together Now*. Knopf, 1979.
————. *Home Before Dark*. Knopf, 1976.
————. *Notes for Another Life*. Knopf, 1981.
Brown, Claude. *Manchild in the Promised Land*. Macmillan, 1965.
Childress, Alice. *A Hero Ain't Nothin' But a Sandwich*. Coward, 1973.
Cleaver, Vera and Bill Cleaver. *Dust of the Earth*. Harper & Row, 1975.
————. *Where the Lilies Bloom*. Harper & Row, 1969.
Conford, Ellen. *If This Is Love, I'll Take Spaghetti*. Four Winds, 1983.

Cooper, Susan. *The Dark Is Rising*. Atheneum, 1973.
Cormier, Robert. *After the First Death*. Pantheon, 1979.
————. *The Bumblebee Flies Anyway*. Pantheon, 1983.
————. *The Chocolate War*. Pantheon, 1974.
————. *I Am the Cheese*. Pantheon, 1977.
Craven, Margaret. *I Heard the Owl Call My Name*. Doubleday, 1973.
Daly, Maureen. *Seventeenth Summer*. Dodd, 1942.
Donovan, John. *Family*. Harper & Row, 1976.
Duncan, Lois. *Killing Mr. Griffin*. Little, Brown, 1978.
————. *Stranger with My Face*. Little, Brown, 1981.
Fritz, Jean. *Homesick: My Own Story*. Putnam, 1982.
Garden, Nancy. *Annie on My Mind*. Farrar, Straus & Giroux, 1982.
Gipson, Fred. *Old Yeller*. Harper & Row, 1964.
Golding, William. *Lord of the Flies*. Coward, McCann & Geoghegan, 1955.
Graham, Robin. *Dove*. Harper & Row, 1972.
Green, Hannah. *I Never Promised You a Rose Garden*. Holt, Rinehart and Winston, 1964.
Greene, Bette. *Morning Is a Long Time Coming*. Dial, 1978.
————. *Summer of My German Soldier*. Dial, 1973.
Guest, Judith. *Ordinary People*. Viking Press, 1976.
Gunther, John. *Death Be Not Proud: A Memoir*. Modern Library, 1953.

Guy, Rosa. *The Disappearance*. Delacorte, 1979.

————. *The Friends*. Holt, Rinehart and Winston, 1973.

Hamilton, Virginia. *Justice and Her Brothers*. Geenwillow, 1978.

————. *A Little Love*. Philomel, 1984.

————. *M. C. Higgins, the Great*. Macmillan, 1974.

————. *Sweet Whispers, Brother Rush*. Philomel, 1982.

Hemingway, Ernest. *For Whom the Bell Tolls*. Scribner, 1940.

Hentoff, Nat. *Does This School Have Capital Punishment?* Delacorte, 1981.

Herbert, Frank. *Soul Catcher*. Putnam, 1972.

Herriot, James. *All Creatures Great and Small*. St. Martin, 1972.

Heyerdahl, Thor. *The "RA" Expeditions*. New American Library, 1972.

Hinton, S. E. *The Outsiders*. Viking, 1967.

————. *That Was Then, This Is Now*. Viking, 1971.

Hogan, William. *The Quartzsite Trip*. Atheneum, 1980.

Holman, Felice. *The Wild Children*. Scribner's, 1983.

Jewell, Geri with Stewart Weiner. *Geri*. Morrow, 1984.

Kazimiroff, Theodore. *The Last Algonquin*. Walker, 1982.

Kerr, M. E. *If I Love You, Am I Trapped Forever?* Harper & Row, 1973.

————. *I'll Love You When You're More Like Me*. Harper & Row, 1977.

Knowles, John. *A Separate Peace*. Macmillan, 1960.

Knudson, R. R. *Fox Running*. Harper & Row, 1975.

————. *Zanballer*. Delacorte, 1972.

————. *Zanbanger*. Harper & Row, 1977.

————. *Zanboomer*. Harper & Row, 1978.

Kullman, Harry. *The Battle Horse*. Bradbury, 1981.

Lee, Mildred. *The People Therein*. Houghton Mifflin, 1980.

Le Guin, Ursula. *Very Far Away from Anywhere Else*. Atheneum, 1976.

————. *A Wizard of Earthsea*. Parnassus, 1968.

Lund, Doris. *Eric*. Harper & Row, 1974.

Maas, Peter. *Serpico*. Viking, 1973.

Mathis, Sharon Bell. *Teacup Full of Roses*. Viking, 1972.

Mazer, Norma Fox. *Dear Bill, Remember Me?* Delacorte, 1976.

McCaffrey, Anne. *Dragon* (series). Atheneum.

McKinley, Robin. *The Blue Sword*. Greenwillow, 1982.

Mead, Margaret. *Blackberry Winter*. Morrow, 1972.

Michener, James. *Caravans*. Random House, 1963.

————. *Hawaii*. Random House, 1959.

Miklowitz, Gloria D. *Close to the Edge*. Delacorte, 1983.

Mohr, Nicholasa. *El Bronx Remembered*. Harper & Row, 1975.

————. *Nilda*. Harper & Row, 1973.

————. *In Nuevo York*. Dial, 1977.

Morrell, David. *First Blood*. M. Evans, 1972.

Newton, Suzanne. *I Will Call It Georgie's Blues*. Viking, 1983.

O'Brien, Robert C. *Z for Zachariah*. Atheneum, 1975.

O'Dell, Scott. *Island of the Blue Dolphins*. Houghton Mifflin, 1960.

————. *Zia*. Houghton Mifflin, 1976.

Oneal, Zibby. *A Formal Feeling*. Viking, 1982.

Paterson, Katherine. *The Great Gilly Hopkins*. Harper & Row, 1978.

————. *Jacob Have I Loved*, Harper & Row, 1980.

Peck, Richard. *Are You in the House Alone?* Viking, 1976.

————. *Don't Look and It Won't Hurt*. Holt, Rinehart and Winston, 1972.

————. *Representing Super Doll*. Viking. 1974.

Peck, Robert Newton. *A Day No Pigs Would Die*. Knopf, 1972.

Plath, Sylvia. *The Bell Jar*. Harper & Row, 1971.

Potok, Chaim. *The Chosen*. Simon and Schuster, 1967.

————. *My Name Is Asher Lev*. Knopf, 1972.

Raskin, Ellen. *The Westing Game*. Dutton, 1978.

Read, Piers Paul. *Alive: The Story of the Andes Survivors*. Harper & Row, 1974.

Renvoize, Jean. *A Wild Thing*. Little, Brown, 1971.

Robertson, Dougal. *Survive the Savage Sea*. G. K. Hall, 1974.

Sachs, Marilyn. *The Fat Girl*. Dutton, 1984.

Salinger, J. D. *The Catcher in the Rye*. Little, Brown, 1951.

Samuels, Gertrude. *Run, Shelley, Run!* Harper & Row, 1974.

Schaefer, Jack. *Shane*. Houghton Mifflin, 1949.

Sebestyen, Ouida. *IOU's*. Little, Brown, 1982.

Sleator, William. *House of Stairs*. Dutton, 1974.

Slepian, Jan. *The Alfred Summer*. Macmillan, 1980.

Stevenson, Robert Louis. *Treasure Island*. 1882.

Swarthout, Glendon. *Bless the Beasts and Children*. Doubleday, 1970.

Taylor, Mildred. *Roll of Thunder, Hear My Cry*. Dial, 1976.

Tolkien, J. R. R. *The Lord of the Rings*. Houghton Mifflin, 1974.

Trelease, Jim. *Read-Aloud Handbook*. Penguin, 1982.

Twain, Mark. *The Adventures of Huckleberry Finn*. Harper, 1884.

Vinge, Joan D. *Psion*. Delacorte, 1982.

Wain, John. *The Free Zone Starts Here*. Delacorte, 1984.

Weesner, Theodore. *The Car Thief*. Random House, 1972.

Wersba, Barbara. *Run Softly, Go Fast*. Atheneum, 1970.

Wharton, William. *Birdy*. Knopf, 1978.

Zindel, Paul. *Pardon Me, You're Stepping on My Eyeball!* Harper & Row, 1976.

————. *The Pigman*. Harper & Row, 1968.

P·A·R·T T·W·O

MODERN YOUNG ADULT READING

THE NEW REALISM

◇

OF LIFE AND OTHER SAD SONGS

When critic Northrop Frye used the term *realism* in his *Anatomy of Criticism*, he put it in quotation marks because with literature the term doesn't—or shouldn't—mean the same thing that it does in other contexts. Frye argues that expecting literature to simply portray real life is a mistaken notion. The artist who can paint grapes so realistically that a bird will fly up and peck at the canvas is not the most highly acclaimed artist. Nor would people want to listen to a symphony in which all the instruments imitated "real" sounds from nature—the cooing of doves, the rushing of a waterfall, a clap of thunder, and the wind whistling through trees.

In arguing this point, G. Robert Carlsen wrote:

◇ —a painting, a sculpture, a drama, a piece of literature is never real. It is an object created out of the imagination from the inner life of the artist. . . . Art is part of the mind set that we term intellectualism, that interest in manipulating ideas rather than things. Literature, as with all art, considers and clothes concepts in symbolic patterns that produce aesthetic satisfaction.

Carlsen went on to say that a piece of literature first exists in the mind of its creator and then in the minds of its readers. And because it was never anything "real," it cannot be tested against an external reality as can the plans for a building, chemical formulas, case studies, etc.

◇ If we evaluate literature by its realism alone, we should be forced to abandon most of the truly great literature of the world: certainly most of tragedy, much of comedy, and all of romance. We would be forced to discard the Greek plays, the great epics, Shakespeare, Molière. They succeed because they go beyond the externals of living and instead reach out and touch that imaginative life deep down inside where we live.[1]

When two highly respected critics both argue against "realism" as a literary concept, we owe at least an explanation of why we are using the term in our chapter title.

The main reason is that we can't think of a better word. Besides, so many people use it to describe the kinds of books that are being discussed in this chapter that we would be at a communication disadvantage if we tried to invent a new term. We might call the books *problem novels*, but every novel includes a "problem." If it didn't, there wouldn't be a plot. And so even though we can't give a foolproof definition of "the new realism," and we're not even sure that it's the best term, that's what this chapter is about. By the end of the chapter, you should have a good idea of what such books have in common, but for now we will start by saying that realism is experientially true. It is an author's honest attempt to depict people in ordinary situations without sentimentalizing or glossing over anything.

Such books make up what many people consider to be the main body of modern young adult literature. Anyone really looking at the field or even browsing through this textbook will realize that young adults are reading many other kinds of books. But the new realism receives the lion's share of attention because it is new and different and sometimes controversial.

What is distinctive about the new realism is that the best of it treats candidly and with respect problems that belong specifically to young adults in today's world. As we pointed out in Chapter 1, adolescence as a unique period of life is a fairly recent development coinciding with the development of complex industrial societies. The problems that go along with modern adolescence did not exist in the nineteenth century, so, of course, they were not written about. At least in this one area, there is ample justification for books directed specifically to a young adult audience because there is a difference in the kinds of real-life problems that concern adults and teenagers.

Many critics are pleased that juvenile literature has "come of age," but others are not so enthusiastic. Sheila Egoff, in the 1979 May Hill Arbuthnot lecture, quoted from the Book of Matthew: "What profiteth a man if he shall gain the whole world and lose his own soul?" Then she stated, "I am very much afraid that in contemporary children's literature, when it gained the whole world of adult freedom and power and vast expansion of subject matter, it lost some of its soul—its identity as a separate and distinctive branch of writing."[2]

She outlined four reasons for the appeal of the problem novel. "One explanation—or perhaps claim is the more accurate word—is that the problem novel has therapeutic value." Today many young people have severe problems, she reasoned, and perhaps by reading about similar cases they are helped to find solutions to their own problems. Or at least they find comfort in the fact that they are not alone. Second, for those children whose lives are not filled with such problems there is the appeal of the exotic. Said Egoff: "Just as adult, upper-class suburbanites find *The God-father* absorbing, so well brought up girls may find a kind of romance and excitement in the 'hard-boiled' naturalism of the problem novels." (Girls far outnumber boys in this reading audience.) A third theory Egoff developed was that "the problem novel wins its audience by flattery. Children want to feel grown-up and problem novels offer to youngsters—in simple language that they can perfectly well follow—the implication that they are ready to deal with issues and themes that are indisputably 'adult.'" She cited the movie makers who have long attracted juvenile audiences by labeling movies "for mature viewers." As the fourth reason, she explained "the appeals of the p's—prurience and peer pressure":

> ◇ How welcome it must be to find between the covers of a book both words and subjects that have been considered taboo and may still be so in an individual child's home or school environment. While they may give the child a delicious *frisson*, they also spell respectability. . . . Not to have read Judy Blume seems as socially unacceptable as not being familiar with the latest "in" television show.

Egoff worried that the trend toward realism was so exaggerated that young readers would turn away from it just as they turned away from the didacticism of earlier years. She conjectured that the late 1970s surge of popularity in the Hardy Boys and the Nancy Drew books was a result of readers not being able to find enough escape entertainment in new realistic books. The 1980s popularity of the escapist romances (discussed in Chapter 4) lends credence to her observation.

◈ WHAT ARE THE PROBLEMS?

What are some of the problems faced by today's youth? A look at any newspaper can provide clues, but if all we knew of teenagers came from newspapers, we might well think that all young people drink heavily, run away from home, expect contraceptives on demand, commit crimes, and kill themselves. We know this isn't true, but it is true that young people today find themselves having to make decisions regarding their own values and behavior in a bewilderingly complex society. Choices exist that didn't exist even a few years ago: psychoactive drugs are readily available; abortions are legal under many circumstances; a college education is no longer considered the panacea it once was; the traditional structure of marriage and family is being challenged as never before. This is not to say that these are the first teenagers in history with difficult decisions to make, just that every generation of young people has a special set of problems unique to the age. The teenagers of this decade are no exception.

A rather common observation about adolescent reading has been that young people are looking for mirror images of themselves. In relation to realistic fiction, this may be only partially true. A more accurate analogy could be made to the wedding custom in Afghanistan where the bride and groom say their vows while facing a large mirror, rather than each other.

Traditionally at the age of twelve a girl begins wearing a *chaderi* so that her face is covered to everyone outside her immediate family. Marriages are arranged and when the *mullah* declares the couple husband and wife, the girl removes her *chaderi*. But instead of looking at each other, the bride and groom satisfy their curiosity by staring intensely in the mirror. Of course they see themselves in the mirror, but what they are really examining is the other person. This does not mean that they are above egocentricity. On the contrary they are being understandably selfish in trying to answer such questions as, "What is this person like?" "How do I look in relation to this person?" "How should I act toward him (or her)?" and "How will my life be affected?"

Being blatantly curious and openly staring face-to-face would not be culturally acceptable, so the mirror (which, incidentally, is given to the couple as their first piece of household furniture) serves a purpose similar to that of books in the lives of adolescent readers. It puts a frame around someone who, in relation to the viewer, is of intense interest, and it makes it acceptable to stare.

Young readers use books as the Afghans use their wedding mirrors. The author acts as the mirror, absorbing directly from life what is of importance and then reflecting this information back to the viewer so that it can be openly examined as true life never could be. What teenagers are interested in examining through this mirroring of life are all those people and forces that stand between them and the finding of their own identities.

This sounds like a relatively simple task, but a discussion of the books and the various alternatives that they explore will illustrate that the matter is not so simple after all, nor is it easy to write high quality books that can serve this purpose. In order to understand the nature of the problem novel, it is necessary to look not only at the subject matter, but also at how the subject matter influences writing styles and at how one book lays the groundwork for others. Suggestions for evaluating the problem novel are listed in Table 3.1 (p. 82).

◈ THE GROUND-BREAKING BOOKS

If we were to try to pinpoint the birth of the new realism, the year would probably be 1967, when S. E. Hinton's *The Outsiders*, Ann Head's *Mr. and Mrs. Bo Jo Jones*, and Jean Thompson's *House of Tomorrow* appeared. These were followed in 1968 by Paul Zindel's *The Pigman* and Richard Bradford's *Red Sky at Morning*. In the next year came William Armstrong's *Sounder*, Vera and Bill Cleaver's *Where the Lilies Bloom*, and John Donovan's *I'll Get There, It Better Be Worth the Trip*.

These books had a new candor to them. Hinton wrote about the Socs and the Greasers, and it was the Greasers whose story she told. Prior to this, it had nearly always been stories about the society kids in their white middle-class neighborhoods that found their way into adolescent fiction. Both Head and Thompson wrote about unmarried girls who were pregnant. In Head's

◆ **TABLE 3.1   Suggestions for Evaluating the Problem Novel**

A good problem novel usually has:	A poor problem novel may have:
A strong, interesting, and believable plot centering around a problem that a young person might really have.	A totally predictable plot with nothing new and interesting to entice the reader.
	Characters that are cardboardlike exaggerations of people who are too good or too bad to be believed.
The power to transport the reader into another person's thoughts and feelings.	More characters than the reader can comfortably keep straight.
Rich characterization. The characters "come alive" as believable with a balance of good and negative qualities.	Many stereotypes.
	Lengthy chapters or descriptive paragraphs that add bulk but not substance to the book.
A setting that enhances the story and is described so that the reader can get the intended picture.	A preachy message. The author spells out the attitudes and conclusions with which he or she wants each reader to leave the book.
A worthwhile theme. The reader is left with something to think about.	Nothing that stays with the reader after the book has been put down.
A smoothness of style that flows steadily and easily, carrying the reader along.	A subject that is of interest only because it is topical or trendy.
A universal appeal so that it speaks to more than a single group of readers.	Inconsistent points of view. The author's sympathies change with no justification.
	Dialogue that sounds forced and/or inappropriate to the characters.
A subtlety that stimulates the reader to think about the various aspects of the story.	"Facts" that do not jibe with those of the real world.
	Unlikely coincidences or changes in characters' personalities for the sake of the plot.
A way of dealing with the problems so that the reader is left with insights into either society or individuals or both.	Exaggerations which result in sensationalism.

book, the girl marries the father, but in Thompson's book the father is already married and the girl goes to a home for unwed mothers.

In Zindel's *The Pigman* an alienated boy and girl make friends with a lonely old man who can't admit that his wife has died. The three of them share true feelings of love and carefree playfulness, but in the end the old man dies tragically, and the boy and girl are left to ponder their role in his death and what it all means. In *Red Sky at Morning*, southerner Josh Arnold and his mother go to a little town in New Mexico where they are to wait out the Second World War. While living there, Josh gains at least a partial understanding not only of his Mexican American neighbors but also of himself. Some people—mostly adults—were shocked by the language in this book.

The next three books continued the trend of pushing away from safe, middle-class settings. *Sounder* is a grim historical piece about a poverty-stricken black family of tenant farmers. In *Where the Lilies Bloom,* which is set in the Tennessee mountains, fourteen-year-old Mary Call struggles to keep her orphaned brothers and sisters together after they secretly bury their father. And in *I'll Get There. It Better Be Worth the Trip,* Davy, who has been raised by his grandmother, has to move to New York to live with an alcoholic mother that he hardly knows and certainly does not understand.

These eight books of the late 1960s exemplify several of the characteristics that during the 1970s came to be associated with the problem novel for young adults. There are basically four ways, besides the subject matter, in which these books differ from earlier books. First, there is the choice of *characters.* Unlike previous books for young people, the protagonists come mostly from lower-class families. This ties in with the second major difference, which is that of *setting.* Whereas most earlier books are set in idyllic and pleasant suburban homes, the settings in these books are often portrayed as harsh, difficult places to live. In order to get the point across about the characters and where and how they live, authors used colloquial *language,* which is the third major difference. Authors began to write the way people really talked. For example, in dialogue, they used profanity and ungrammatical constructions. That the general public allowed this change in language in most cases is significant. It shows that people were drawing away from the idea that the main purpose of fictional books for young readers is to set an example of proper, middle-class behavior.

The fourth difference also relates to this change in attitude, and that is the change in *mode.* As more and more people began to think that the educational value of fiction is to extend young readers' experiences and to give them opportunities to participate vicariously in more roles and activities than would be either desirable or possible in real life, the possibility arose for a change in the mode of the stories. In the old days most of the books—at least most of the books approved of by educators—were written in the comic and romantic modes. These were the books with upbeat, happy endings. As long as people believed that children would model their lives after what they read, then of course they wanted young people to read happy stories because a happy life is what all of us want for our children. But the problem novel is based on a different philosophy, which is that young people will have a better chance to be happy if they have realistic expectations, if they know both the bad and the good about the society in which they live. This changed attitude opened the door to writers of irony and even tragedy for young people.

Irony differs from tragedy in that it may be less intense, and instead of having heroic qualities, the protagonist is an ordinary person, much like the reader. One definition of irony is "a tennis serve that you can't return." You can admire its perfection, its appropriateness, and even the inevitability of the outcome, but you just can't cope with it.

There's a refreshing honesty to stories that show readers they aren't the only ones who get served that kind of ball and that the human spirit, though totally devastated in this particular set, may rise again to play another match. Robin Brancato's *Winning*, Richard Peck's *Are You in the House Alone?* and Robert C. O'Brien's *Z for Zachariah* are books of this sort.

Robert Cormier's books come closer to being tragedies. In traditional literary criticism, tragedies have three distinct elements. First, there is a noble character who, no matter what happens, maintains the qualities that the society considers praiseworthy. Second, there is an inevitable force that works against the character, and, third, there is a struggle and an outcome. In Cormier's *I Am the Cheese*, the boy being interrogated throughout the book is the tragic hero. The inevitable force is corruption and government duplicity. And the outcome—in which the best that the boy can hope for is to live his life in a drugged and incoherent state—is indeed a tragedy. Yet the reader is left with some satisfaction and pride because there is a resiliency in the boy that keeps him, even when he is drugged, from totally surrendering to his highly skilled interrogators.

Another tradition sometimes considered essential in tragedy holds that the hero—worthy and admirable as he or she may be—has nevertheless contributed to the unfolding of the terrible events through some tragic flaw of character. With Cormier's book, the reader has the nagging feeling that maybe if the boy had not been so bright and so inquisitive (which were the characteristics that first brought trouble to his father) and had not found out his family's history, then maybe life could have gone on as before and Mr. Grey wouldn't have bothered with him. But at the same time, it is this brightness and persistence that keeps him from surrendering at the end.

The reader of a tragedy is usually filled with pity and fear—pity for the hero and fear for oneself that the same thing might happen. The intensity of this involvement causes the reader to undergo an emotional release as the outcome of the story unfolds. This release is known as catharsis and it has the effect of draining away dangerous human emotions, and it also fills the reader with a sense of exaltation or amazed pride in what the human spirit is called upon to undergo.[3]

◈ *THE CHOCOLATE WAR* AS A PROBLEM NOVEL

The book that we have chosen as an example of the best of modern realism for young adults is Cormier's *The Chocolate War* (1974). It contains the kind of realism that many other books had been leading up to. Its message about conformity and human manipulation is all the more powerful because the young protagonist is so vulnerable. The religious symbolism that pervades the book serves as a contrasting backdrop to the terrible evil that pervades Trinity High School where the protagonist is a freshman. The opening paragraph is the simple line: "They murdered him." Readers, who at first might think the reference is to Jesus, soon find that it is to fourteen-year-old Jerry Renault who is being "tested" to see if he has enough guts to get on the football team.

 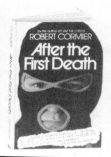  

◆ Robert Cormier dared to "disturb the upbeat universe of juvenile Books" with *The Chocolate War*. His other YA books include *After the First Death, The Bumblebee Flies Anyway*, and *I Am the Cheese*.

The story begins and ends on the athletic field where the shadows of the goal posts resemble "a network of crosses, empty crucifixes." On Jerry's third play at Trinity High he is "hit simultaneously by three of them." He blinks himself back to consciousness and jumps to his feet:

◇ intact, bobbing like one of those toy novelties dangling from car windows, but erect.

"For Christ's sake," the coach bellowed, his voice juicy with contempt. A spurt of saliva hit Jerry's cheek.

Hey, coach, you spit on me, Jerry protested. Stop the spitting, coach. What he said aloud was, "I'm all right, coach," because he was a coward about stuff like that, thinking one thing and saying another, planning one thing and doing another—he had been Peter a thousand times and a thousand cocks had crowed in his lifetime.

What happens is that in the course of the book Jerry gets the courage to think and do the same thing. He refuses to sell fifty boxes of chocolates that the corrupt teacher, Brother Leon, has assigned to each student. For the first ten days of the candy campaign, he simply follows the orders of the Vigils, a gang who in the words of their head man, Archie Costello, "were the school." But when the ten days are up and the Vigils order Jerry to do a reversal and to participate in the selling campaign, he dares to say no.

At first Jerry is a hero, but because this threatens the power of the Vigils, Archie uses his full potential in people management to turn the student body against Jerry. When all the chocolates except Jerry's are sold, Archie arranges a boxing match between Jerry and a bully who is trying to work his way into the Vigils. It is supposed to be set up "with rules. Fair and square," but what Archie really masterminds is a physical and psychological battering much worse than anything Jerry underwent at football practice.

The last chapter of the book could have begun with the same line as the first chapter—"They murdered him"—only this time it would have been more than a metaphor. Although Jerry is probably going to recover physically from a fractured jaw and internal injuries, his spirit has been murdered. In the midst of the fight:

◇ a new sickness invaded Jerry, the sickness of knowing what he had become, another animal, another beast, another violent person in a violent world, inflicting damage, not disturbing the universe but damaging it. He had allowed Archie to do this to him.

And after the fight when the pain—"Jesus, the pain"—brings Jerry back to consciousness, the reader sees how changed he is because of what he tries to tell his friend Goober:

◇ They don't want you to do your thing, not unless it happens to be their thing, too. It's a laugh, Goober, a fake. Don't disturb the universe, Goober, no matter what the posters say.

In selecting *The Chocolate War* as a touchstone example, we asked ourselves several questions about the book. These same or similar questions could be asked when evaluating almost any problem novel. First, does the book make a distinctive contribution? Does it say something new or does it convey something old in a new way? And if so, is it something of value?

Robert Cormier was praised by *The Kirkus Reviews* because he dared to "disturb the upbeat universe of juvenile books" with *The Chocolate War*. He did not compromise by providing a falsely hopeful conclusion, nor did he sidestep the issue by leaving it open for readers to imagine their own happy ending. Until Cormier, most writers for young readers had chosen one of these two approaches. Yet Cormier was not being "difficult" just for the sake of being different. When he was questioned at a National Council of Teachers of English convention about his motives in writing such a pessimistic book for young readers, he answered that he had written three other novels and numerous short stories all with upbeat endings and that in *The Chocolate War* he was simply providing a balance. He then went on to say that today's young readers are a television generation. They have grown up thinking that every problem can be solved within a half-hour or an hour at the most, with time out for commercials. It's important for people to realize that all problems are not that easily solved. In real life there are some problems that may never be solved and others whose solutions will demand the utmost efforts of the most capable people in the world.

The plot of a book must be examined to see how closely it grows out of the characters' actions and attitudes. Is it an idea that could easily have been dropped into another setting or onto other characters? With Cormier's book, there wouldn't have been a story without the unique but believable personalities of both Jerry and Archie, as well as of Brother Leon. The problem was not so bizarre or unusual that it overshadowed the characters, nor were the characters such unusual people that readers could not identify with them or imagine themselves having to deal with people like them. It is because the characters at first appear to be such ordinary people that readers are drawn into the story. The theme is similar to that in Golding's *Lord of the Flies*, but because Golding's book is set on a deserted island in the midst of a war it could be dismissed as unrealistic. Cormier's book has an immediacy that is hard to deny. The problem is a real one that teenagers can identify with on the first or literal level, yet it has implications far beyond

THE PEOPLE BEHIND THE BOOKS

ROBERT CORMIER, Author

After the First Death
The Bumblebee Flies Anyway
The Chocolate War
I Am the Cheese
Beyond the Chocolate War

I have always been interested in the plight of the individual versus the system, whether the system is the family, the school, the government or society in general. I hope to pursue this theme on an increasingly broader and more penetrating level. However, I am really more interested in creating credible human beings in situations that provide shocks of recognition for the reader. And I'm willing to let these characters take me where they will, even if I have to abandon preconceived notions about a particular theme. What's beautiful about this is that I can deal with character and theme in a manner that satisfies me as an author and have my work accepted in the field of adolescent literature. ◆

one beaten-up fourteen-year-old and 20,000 boxes of stale Mother's Day candy.

In looking at the setting, we might ask, is it just there or does it contribute something to the mood or the action or to revealing characterization? In *The Chocolate War* the story would not have been nearly so chilling without the religious setting which provided contrast. In some ways the evil in Archie is less hideous than that in Brother Leon, the corrupt teacher who enlists Archie's help in making his unauthorized investment pay off. The brother hides behind his clerical collar and his role of teacher and assistant headmaster, whereas Archie only identifies himself as a nonbeliever in the so-called "Christian ethic." For example, when his stooge Obie asks him how he can do the things he does and still take communion, he responds, "When you march down to the rail, you're receiving the Body, man. Me, I'm just chewing a wafer they buy by the pound in Worcester."

Another question especially relevant in respect to books for young readers is the respect the author has for the intended audience. Cormier showed a great deal of respect for his readers: nowhere did he write down to them. The proof of his respect for them is in some of the subtle symbolization that he worked into the story and the care with which he developed his style. For example, the irony of the whole situation is exemplified in the gang's name the *Vigils*. He chose the name as a shortened form of *vigilante*, an accurate description of the way the gang worked. But in response to an interview question about whether or not the name was an ironic reference to vigil lights, the candles placed devotionally before a shrine or image, he agreed that the religious connotation, the image of the boys in the gang standing like vigil lights before Archie, who basked in the glow of their admiration, "was also very much a part of my choice."[4] Another example of Cormier's subtlety is the fact that Archie's name has such meanings as "principal or chief" as in archvillain, "cleverly sly and alert," and "at the extreme, that is, someone or something most fully embodying the qualities of its kind."

A question that has to be asked somewhere in the evaluation process is whether or not anyone is reading the book. G. Robert Carlsen said that if he were giving prizes for the best book published each year for young adult readers, in 1974 he would have given first place to James Baldwin's *If Beale Street Could Talk* and second place to *The Chocolate War* even though *The Chocolate War* is really the better book. His reasoning for putting it second instead of first was that teenagers were not reading it in large enough numbers. In his experience it was a book better loved by critics than by teenagers. Lou Willett Stanek also reported that the teenage readers with whom she visited were uncomfortable with the portrayal of the boys in the school as basically evil. Her sample readers could accept the evil in Brother Leon and maybe in Archie, but not in the whole student body. In spite of these reactions, it is obvious that someone is reading *The Chocolate War*. In its first year as a paperback (1975) it went through three printings, and when in 1977, and again in 1982, we took surveys to see what novels college professors were assigning students in adolescent literature classes to read, it was at the top of the list.

Nearly all writers for teenagers make certain adjustments to attract a reading audience. Some authors will say that they write strictly for themselves and it's immaterial to them whether or not anyone reads their books. This is probably either an exaggeration or an ego-defense mechanism. The physical act of typing up a manuscript and mailing it off to an editor is so demanding that someone writing only for personal fulfillment would not be likely to go through the effort. Besides, literature consists of a two-way process in which the reader brings thoughts and feelings to be intertwined with those of the author. If no one is reading a book, then only half the process is taking place. Reader reactions are important, especially when it is mainly adults who purchase the books that will be offered to youngsters.

But how far an author bends to attract an audience usually affects the quality and the honesty of a book. Richard Peck says that young readers do not really want realism. Instead they want romance masked as realism. They want to identify with teenage protagonists who accomplish something that in real life teenagers probably couldn't do on their own.

Betsy Byars, in a speech at the University of Iowa, said that the first thing she does when planning a book is to get rid of all the parents so that the children can feel they are accomplishing things on their own. This seems to be a commonly agreed upon convention and one which Cormier followed. Jerry's mother had died of cancer and his father is preoccupied, "sleepwalking through life." With the other characters there is simply no mention of parents or family. It could be argued that this isn't realism, especially in view of the fact that Robert Cormier got the inspiration for his book when he casually gave his own son a ride back to his private high school to return, without incident, a carton full of chocolates that he did not want to sell. For most of the teenage protagonists who appear in modern fiction to live their lives "untouched" by parental influence may not be "realistic," but it is nevertheless a commonly accepted convention in the problem novel.

CATEGORIES OF CONCERN IN PROBLEM NOVELS

Family Relationships

A look at mythology, folklore, and classical and religious literature shows that the subject of parent/child relationships is not what's new about the new realism. One could find virtually thousands of stories touching on the theme. And although in Chapter 1, we identified the idea that books for teenagers are anti-parent or anti-adult as a "myth," it's true that in many of the problem novels, one or both of the parents is the problem.

This is one of the most noticeable changes brought by the new realism. Imperfect parents previously appeared in books featuring youth, but these were books written for adults rather than for teenagers. Beginning in the late 1960s and continuing through today, it's fairly easy to find parents in adolescent literature who are more than a little flawed. They give immoral advice, as in Paul Zindel's *My Darling, My Hamburger*; they are cruel, as in Bette Greene's *Summer of My German Soldier*; they desert their children, as in Richard Peck's *Father Figure*; they abuse their children, as in Virginia Hamilton's *Sweet Whispers, Brother Rush*; they sacrifice their children for political ends, as in Robert Cormier's *After the First Death*; and they are preoccupied and unobservant, as in Zibby Oneal's *The Language of Goldfish*. This negatively impressive list doesn't even include those parents who are so unable to cope with life that they are institutionalized, as in Sue Ellen Bridgers' *Notes for Another Life*, Cynthia Voigt's *Dicey's Song*, and Jocelyn Riley's *Only My Mouth Is Smiling*. The appearance of parents like these in juvenile novels made it easier for adult novels featuring imperfect parents to find their way into young adult collections, for example, Judith Guest's *Ordinary People* and *Second Heaven* and William Wharton's *Birdy*.

There are two reasons for the preponderance of these negative portrayals of parents. The first reason relates to the real life challenge facing all young adults. They are at the age when they must somehow make the switch from being daughters and sons to being individuals in their own right. Because of the tremendous adjustments involved, children and parents have disagreements and when young people read about the encounters of others, they identify with the young protagonists, often against the parents.

The second reason relates, but it's basically literary. By creating obviously flawed parents, authors can provide believable situations which push protagonists from the family nest and thereby force them to embark on quests in which they establish their own identities. In Mary Ann Gray's *The Truth About Fathers*, 14-year-old Stevie watches her professor father go through a midlife crisis changing him from her best friend into her enemy. The eventual collision helps them both grow. In Lynn Hall's *The Leaving*, eighteen-year-old Roxanne observes the hopelessness of her parents' marriage, and decides that she wants more from life than to work on the family farm, just waiting until some boy decides to marry her. She has lived a sheltered life, and her decision to move to Des Moines and get a job is momentous. One of the most powerful explorations of a child breaking free from a parent is Barbara Wersba's *Run Softly, Go Fast*. Dave Marks writes the book just after his father has died. In it he explores their love-hate relationship and what it has meant to his own values and beliefs. Paula Fox's *Blowfish Live in the Sea* treats a similar theme except for younger readers. Also for younger readers is Walter Dean Myers' *It Ain't All for Nothing* which is set in an inner city. A young boy whose grandmother has grown too old and sick to care for him must go and live with his father, a two-bit criminal who welcomes the boy chiefly for his welfare check. The main interest in the story is the boy's growing awareness of what his father is and the realization that he does not need to be the same.

The absence of a fulfilling relationship between a parent and child sometimes opens the way for the young protagonist to establish a friendship with a surrogate parent. In Alice Childress' *Rainbow Jordan*, 14-year-old Rainbow is periodically abandoned by her 29-year-old mother who leaves to live with new boyfriends or to find work as a go-go dancer. One of the strongest parts of the book is the role played by 57-year-old Josephine, a dressmaker who serves as an "interim guardian," and takes Rainbow in even when her own heart is breaking. In Katherine Paterson's *The Great Gilly Hopkins*, readers feel little for Gilly's flower-child mother, but they can't forget Trotter, the foster-mother that even Katherine Paterson describes as "bigger than real life." In Kin Platt's *The Boy Who Could Make Himself Disappear*, 12-year-old Roger lapses into schizophrenia. One doctor says about him: "This boy is suffering from the condition, not too unusual today, of having two highly intelligent, busily preoccupied, unconditionally detached people for parents." Actually, the extent to which Roger's parents ignore him is far more extreme than the diagnosis makes it sound. In the end, Roger begins to make his way back to sanity through the help of a speech therapist and the fiancé of a woman who lives in his New York apartment house. In Judith Guest's *Second Heaven*, the whole story is centered around the development of a family-like relationship between a 16-year-old abused boy, a 40-year-old woman whose doctor husband left her, and the woman's divorce lawyer, who is suffering from the aftermath of his own divorce.

Sometimes the surrogate parent friendship will skip over a generation so that it's a surrogate grandparent who is found, as in Paul Zindel's *The Pigman* and *The Pigman's Legacy* where John and Lorraine in each book make friends with a lonely, old man. In John Donovan's *Remove Protective*

Coating a Little at a Time, 14-year-old cynical Harry makes friends with 72-year-old rebellious Amelia. And in Lois Lowry's *A Summer to Die*, 13-year-old Meg, who has wonderful parents, nevertheless benefits greatly from the friendship of 70-year-old landlord, handyman, and photographer, Will Banks. The family needs all the help it can get the year that Meg's older sister, Molly, develops leukemia.

With extended families no longer living in close proximity of each other, true grandparent/grandchild relationships may develop almost as between strangers. This is the situation in Robin Brancato's *Sweet Bells Jangled Out of Tune* and M. E. Kerr's *Gentlehands*. In both books, the grandparents are far removed from the Norman Rockwell type of "Home, Sweet Home" family members. In Brancato's book, 15-year-old Ellen is drawn to the eccentric old lady that she used to know as her wealthy and elegant grandmother. Now the woman scrounges through trash containers and picks up leftovers (including money) from restaurant tables. In the end, Ellen realizes that her grandmother needs psychiatric help.

In Kerr's book, Grandpa Trenker is the model of elegance, sophistication, and culture—all the upper-class things that Buddy Boyle's middle-class parents are not. He "uses" his grandfather to help him impress Skye Pennington, a wealthy girl that he's courting. But in the end, it backfires when mounting evidence shows Grandpa Trenker to be a Nazi war criminal.

Another thing that the absence of parents does is to clear space for fully developed sibling relationships. For example, Cynthia Voigt's Newbery Award-winning *Dicey's Song* begins with:

◇ AND THEY LIVED HAPPILY EVER AFTER.
Not the Tillermans. Dicey thought. That wasn't the way things went for the Tillermans, ever. She wasn't about to let that get her down. She couldn't let it get her down—that was what had happened to Momma.

Dicey's attitude that when parents are weak the children have to be that much stronger is a theme often illustrated through the way brothers and sisters pull together to close gaps in the family circle. This is the way it is in *Dicey's Song* as well as in the earlier *Homecoming*, where 13-year-old Dicey and her younger sister and two brothers are abandoned by their mother in a shopping mall parking lot. Their father had left six years earlier. They eventually learn that their mother has lost touch with reality and is in a mental hospital. By this time they have set out on a determined quest to find a home where they can stay together as a family. They make it to the rundown farm that their eccentric grandmother owns on the Chesapeake Bay. *Dicey's Song* chronicles what it takes to make this new unit into a family. Dicey reminds readers of Vera and Bill Cleaver's Mary Call Luther who in *Where the Lilies Bloom* and its sequel *Trial Valley* works with the same kind of ingenuity and dedication to keep her family together.

One of the best parts of S. E. Hinton's *Tex* is the relationship between the two brothers who are left to fend for themselves when "Pop" forgets to come home or to send money from the rodeo circuit. And although Virginia Hamilton's *Sweet Whispers, Brother Rush* contains a wonderful fantasy

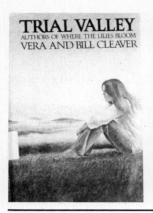
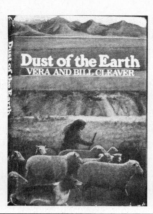

◆ Vera and the late Bill Cleaver have produced an unusually fine set of realistic stories. Their strong heroines face offbeat, but believable, problems.

element, what many readers will remember the longest is the devotion that 14-year-old Teresa, or Tree, had for her older brother, Dab. Dab is retarded, but their relationship is not one-sided, and when at the end of the book he dies from porphyria, a rare genetic abnormality, Tree is truly devastated. But because of the strength she has developed while she and Dab took care of each other in the absence of their mother, she is able to take tentative steps toward a life without Dab.

The main problem in Richard Peck's *Father Figure* is that 17-year-old Jim has developed such a close relationship thinking of himself as a substitute father for his little brother, that when circumstances change bringing the two boys back in touch with their father, Jim feels competitive. He is jealous and hurt when his little brother chooses the real father over the "father figure."

Of course not all sibling relationships are mutually supportive. When Katherine Paterson gave her Newbery Award acceptance speech for *Jacob Have I Loved*, she said that the conflict at the core of the book:

◇ began east of Eden, in the earliest stories of my heritage. "Cain was jealous of his brother and slew him." If, in our Freudian orientation, we speak of the basic conflict as that between parent and child, the Bible—which is the earth from which I spring—is much more concerned with the relationships among brothers and sisters. "A friend loveth at all times," says the writer of Proverbs, "but a brother is born for adversity." They never taught us the second half of that verse in Sunday School.[5]

She went on to cite the numerous fairy tales in which the youngest brother or sister must surpass the supposedly more clever elders or outwit the wicked ones, and she argued with Bruno Bettelheim's suggestion that the rivalry between brothers and sisters is actually an Oedipal conflict or is about the split self. "I do not think," she said, "we can avoid the most obvious meaning of the stories, which is that among children who grow up together in a family there run depths of feeling that will permeate their souls for both good and ill as long as they live."

The title *Jacob Have I Loved* alludes to the biblical story of Jacob and Esau. It's an appropriate choice because the protagonist, Louise, feels that it's her younger twin, Caroline, who receives all the blessings.

Probably because it intensifies the sibling relationship, several writers in addition to Paterson have featured twins as in Lois Duncan's *Stranger with My Face*, Robert Cormier's *The Bumblebee Flies Anyway*, and Natalie Babbitt's *Herbert Rowbarge*. This latter book is especially recommended to all those who are tired of "typical" YA fare. Each of these three books goes beyond the purely "realistic," in that the twins are drawn to each other in mysterious ways.

It's a mark of progress that in young adult literature we now have some exceptionally well written books exploring positive family relationships. Madeleine L'Engle's *Ring of Endless Light* focuses on the Austin family and their experiences during the summer that they come to live with their grandfather who is dying of leukemia. Her *Wrinkle in Time*, *A Wind in the Door*, and *A Swiftly Tilting Planet*, although labelled fantasy, have some realistic portrayals of the loves and strengths of the Murry family.

Mildred Taylor's historical *Roll of Thunder, Hear My Cry* and its sequel, *Let the Circle Be Unbroken*, are powerful accounts of the Logan family and its united struggle to make it through the depression while maintaining their dignity and playing a leadership role to other black families.

Ouida Sebestyen is another writer who does not "do away" with the parents. In her first book, *Words by Heart*, there was a wonderful father/daughter relationship between young and ambitious Lena and her father, who in 1910 dared to move his family from a relatively secure black community into an all-white southwestern town where he thought their opportunities would be greater. In her 1920s *Far from Home*, the parent/child relationship is more complex. Thirteen-year-old Salty Yeager lives with his great grandmother and his mother, who is mute. His mother dies, but leaves him a note telling him to go into town to the boarding house run by Tom Buckley. Tom takes Salty in and gives him a job and a strange, new life. Salty eventually figures out that Tom is really his father, but he's a father who prefers an incomplete relationship because he's not willing to reveal the information to his wife or the community.

In Sebestyen's *IOU's*, 13-year-old Stowe Garrett and his single mother, Annie, are actually good friends. Their relationship contrasts sharply with that of Annie and her own alienated father, who in the course of the book dies without a reconciliation. Stowe's coming-of-age, as well as his mother's love for him, is shown by his resolve at the end of the book to seek out his own father and break the pattern of negative family relationships.

Sue Ellen Bridgers is another writer who includes whole families in her books. *Home Before Dark* was powerful in its portrayal of love and respect

THE PEOPLE BEHIND THE BOOKS

BETTE GREENE, Author

I've Already Forgotten Your Name
Philip Hall Likes Me. I Reckon Maybe
Summer of My German Soldier
Them That Glitter and Them That Don't

Becoming real is both my major personal problem and my major occupational problem. Being real, which would have to include a willingness to be intimate, is the problem and the challenge because I know of no way to be any more dimensional as an artist than I already am as a person.

If it is my job (and I believe that it is) to examine life, the only little grain of life that I know, then I should have no concerns with being either heroine or clown, but only with being real.

I only write about those things that make me burst out into song . . . or into tears because I believe that that's where all the good writing hides. But to strike at it, I must teach myself to have all the instincts of a kamikaze pilot. No more fears about seeing myself in print looking like so much exposed flesh.

Since intimacy is my greatest fear, I have discovered quite by accident that confronting that fear has led to my most compelling writing: writing which I hope is populated with real breathing people who though painfully struggling toward new insights will offer vitality and truth to my work. ◆

---

between a father and a daughter. And although the parents were basically out of the picture in *All Together Now* and *Notes for Another Life*, there were other wonderful family attachments between brother and sister, grandparent and grandchild, and aunts, uncles, and cousins.

As Sheila Egoff said at the beginning of this chapter, girls far outnumber boys as readers of problem novels, especially those dealing with close personal relationships. However, boys may be attracted to the following books which focus on sports but also have a strong father/son relationship as a bonus: Richard Blessing's *A Passing Season* and David Guy's *Football Dreams*, Robert Lehrman's soccer story *Juggling*, and Steve Tesich's powerful story of a young wrestler, *Summer Crossing*.

The mother/daughter relationship is probably the most neglected in YA literature, but it is well developed in Norma Klein's *Mom, The Wolfman and Me*, and in some of Norma Fox Mazer's stories published in *Dear Bill, Remember Me?* In Mazer's *Taking Terri Mueller*, a divorced father steals his 4-year-old daughter and raises her. But when she figures out that something is strange she sets out to find her mother and reestablish contact.

In Paula Fox's *A Place Apart* and in Judy Blume's *Tiger Eyes*, the father of the family dies unexpectedly (a heart attack and a shooting, respectively) and the mothers and daughters move to new locales, almost as if they are embarking on dual quests in search of a way to put their lives back together. In neither book is it easy, as shown by the climax of *Tiger Eyes*, when Davey's mother invites her out to a special dinner.

◇ "This is nice," I say. What I mean is that it is nice to be alone with my mother. This is the first time since we came to Los Alamos that it is just the two of us.

"Yes," Mom says. "It's very nice."

"It's been a long time."

"Yes," Mom says. "And I've wanted to explain that to you, Davey." She is arranging and rearranging her silverware, moving the spoon into the fork's place, then the fork into the spoon's. "Up until now, I've been afraid to be alone with you."

"Afraid?"

"Yes."

"But why?"

"I was afraid you'd ask me questions and I wouldn't have any answers. I've been afraid you'd want to talk about Daddy . . . and the night he was killed . . . and the pain would be too much for me."

"I did want to talk about it," I tell her. "For a long time . . . and it hurt me that you wouldn't."

"I know," she says, reaching across the table and touching my hand. "But I had to come to terms with it myself, first. Now I think I'm ready . . . now I can talk about it with you."

"But now I don't need to," I say.

◈ FRIENDS AND SOCIETY

Social problems treated in "problem books" vary from a disregard for nature as explored in Virginia Hamilton's *M. C. Higgins, the Great*, D. R. Sherman's *The Lion's Paw*, and Robb White's *Deathwatch* to questions about institutions designed to "control" young people's lives. The protagonists in June Jordan's *His Own Where* and Vera and Bill Cleaver's *Where the Lilies Bloom* are trying desperately to stay free from such control, and in Sue Ellen Bridgers' *All Together Now*, one of the issues is whether a thirty-year-old retarded man should be institutionalized.

Religion as an institution is a subject that should probably be treated in more young adult books (see Chapter 11 for a discussion). As one librarian was overheard saying, "What we need is a Christian *The Chosen*." It wasn't that she had anything against all students, regardless of their religious backgrounds, reading Chaim Potok's book; she just wanted some other books written with power equal to that of *The Chosen, In the Beginning*, and *My Name Is Asher Lev*, all of which are about Hasidic Jews.

Many writers and publishers shy away from treating religious topics for fear of offending believers of one faith or another, but with people's increasing willingness to publicly discuss their feelings about religious matters, authors are no longer quite so hesitant as shown by such books as Phyllis Reynolds Naylor's *A String of Chances*; Fran Arrick's *Tunnel Vision*; M. E. Kerr's *What I Really Think of You, Little Little*, and *Is That You Miss Blue?*; Katherine Paterson's *Jacob Have I Loved*; Ouida Sebestyen's *Words by Heart*; Gloria D. Miklowitz' *The Love Bombers*, and Robin Brancato's *Blinded by the Light*.

Peer groups become increasingly important to teenagers as they move beyond a social and emotional dependence on their parents. By becoming part of a group, clique, or gang which they can rely on for decisions about such social conventions as clothing, language, and entertainment, teenagers take a step toward emotional independence because even though they aren't making such decisions for themselves, it's no longer their parents who are deciding on and enforcing their behavior. Another benefit of belonging to a group is that teenagers can try out various roles ranging from conformist to nonconformist, from follower to leader. These roles can be acted out by individuals within the group or they can be acted out by the group as a whole, as, for example, when one gang challenges another gang. Group members in such a situation are caught up in a kind of emotional commitment that they would seldom feel as individuals.

But it isn't automatic that all teenagers find groups to belong to, and even if they do, they are still curious about other groups. This is where young adult literature comes in. It extends the peer group, giving teenagers a chance to participate vicariously in many more personal relationships than are possible for most kids in the relatively short time that they spend in high school. By reading about other individuals trying to find places for themselves, teenagers begin answering such questions as: Who is making "the right" decisions? What values and attitudes are "best"? How will they be judged by other groups? By other individuals? What are the possible results of certain choices? And what are attractive and reasonable alternatives?

The whole area of making friends is a challenge to teenagers. When they were very young, it was a simple matter of playing with whoever happened to be nearby. Parents were responsible for locating in the "right" neighborhood near "good" schools, so that children had no reason to give particular thought to differences in social and economic classes or ethnic backgrounds. But the older children get, the more they own the responsibility for making their friends. Quite suddenly their environments are expanded not only through larger, more diverse schools, but also through jobs, extracurricular activities, public entertainment programs, and just plain living. In Nancy Garden's *Annie on My Mind*, private school student Liza Winthrop meets public school student Annie Kenyon in the New York Metropolitan Museum of Art. In Todd Strasser's *Workin' for Peanuts*, stadium vendor Jeff Mead meets and falls in love with the daugher of his boss, five levels up, when he gets scolded for bypassing the Stott's private box. And in M. E. Kerr's *I'll Love You When You're More Like Me*, Wally Witherspoon, the son of the town undertaker, meets teenage soap opera star Sabra St. Amour when she asks him for a match at the beach.

In social studies and American history classes, young people are taught that America is a democracy and that we do not have a "caste" system. Any boy—and maybe today, any girl—can grow up to be president. But real-life observations don't support this, and that may be why books exploring differences in social classes are especially popular with young adults who, as they emerge from childhood, are in a position to begin making observations about social class structures.

One of the most perceptive and at the same time humorous explorations of the topic is E. L. Konigsburg's *Journey to an 800 Number*. When Maximillian Stubbs' divorced mother remarries and leaves for a long honeymoon, he takes his prep school jacket and fifty dollars and heads off to spend time with his father. Woody, the father, makes a living by travelling around to tourist and convention centers where he sells rides on the camel he keeps. Max is horrified at what he perceives as a difference in class between his father and himself, but in the words of one reviewer, he gradually learns "to separate the outward, lavish trappings of class from the simple meaning of the word."[6]

In Judy Blume's *Tiger Eyes*, the protagonist Davey, makes some observations about the class structure of her new high school in Los Alamos, New Mexico:

◇ I have learned plenty about the dynamics of this school in just two weeks. For one thing, everyone is classified by groups. There are Coneheads, Loadies, Jocks, and Stomps. Coneheads are into computers and wear calculators strapped to their belts. They are carbon copies of their fathers, grinding away for the best grades so that they can go to the best colleges. Loadies are into booze and drugs and there is plenty available. You can buy whatever you want out of the trunk of a car in the parking lot. Jocks are jocks. Every group makes fun of every other group. Coneheads laugh at Jocks. Jocks laugh at Loadies. Loadies laugh at Stomps. Stomps dress in ten gallon hats and cowboy boots. They chew tobacco and spit and ride around in pickup trucks, looking for fights.

I know that I will never fit in here. Of course, there are other kids like me, other kids who don't fit in either. There is a girl, Ann, who screams in the hallways. I can't figure her out. Maybe she realizes the futility of trying to fit in, just as I do.

There are guys who aren't really Coneheads, but who aren't anything else either. And it's tough on them. Because the kids here are very into putting down anybody and anything that is not exactly like they are. I sometimes think it would be terrific if all of us who don't fit in formed a group called the Leftovers. Then we could get together and laugh our heads off at the Stomps, Loadies, Jocks and Coneheads.   (pp. 94–95)

Naturally school is a common topic for teenage books since this is what young people are involved in on a daily basis, and fortunately some writers are looking beyond high school. W. E. Butterworth's *Flunking Out*, Rona Jaffe's *Mazes and Monsters*, and Jacob Epstein's *Wild Oats* all provide glimpses into college life.

There are some compassionate teachers in books, for example Ann Treer in Robin Brancato's *Winning*, Nigeria Greene and Bernard Cohen in Alice Childress' *A Hero Ain't Nothin' But a Sandwich*, Miss Stevenson and Miss Widmer in Nancy Garden's *Annie on My Mind*, and P. J. Cooper in William Hogan's *The Quartzsite Trip*, but these are the exceptions. Society forces young people to treat authority figures—teachers, librarians, ministers, housemothers, coaches, parole officers, etc.—with respect. Because young people aren't allowed to discuss differences of opinion or "quarrel" with these adults as they might with their parents, hostilities undoubtedly build up. It's therefore easy for authors to tap into this reservoir of resentment and bring understanding smiles to young readers. M. E. Kerr does it with names, for example in *Me, Me, Me, Me, Me* she has a teacher named Miss Lackbrest, who is also known as *No Tits* and a housemother named Mrs. Needleman but called *Needle Eye, the Nazi Spy*.

Paul Zindel uses a similar technique. For example early in *The Pigman*, John explains why the students call Miss Reillen *the Cricket*:

> ◇ Anyway, Miss Reillen is a little on the fat side, but that doesn't stop her from wearing these tight skirts which make her nylon stockings rub together when she walks so she makes this scraaaaaaatch sound. That's why the kids call her the Cricket. If she taught woodshop or gym, nobody'd really know she makes that sound—but she's the librarian, and it's so quiet you can hear every move she makes.

In Zindel's *Confessions of a Teenage Baboon*, fatherless Chris relates his conversation with a solicitous police officer:

> ◇ "What you need is the PAL or a Big Brother," he advised, squeezing my shoulder. "If you were my kid you'd be playing football." "If I were your kid I'd be playing horse," I said. "Horse?" he asked, looking a little puzzled as he opened the patrol-car door. "You know," I clarified. "I'd be the front end—and you could just be yourself."

Although this kind of humor is both unfair and irritating to adults, it serves as a respite, a refreshing change of pace, in the problem books which without such light moments might be too depressing.

The problem of group identification is a part of all of S. E. Hinton's books, especially *The Outsiders* where the *greasers*, i.e., *the dirt heads*, are in conflict with the *socs*, i.e., *the society kids*. Myron Levoy's *A Shadow Like a Leopard* is a grim, but at the same time upbeat, story of fourteen-year-old Ramon Santiago who makes friends with an old man who is a painter. Ramon is a Puerto Rican living in the slums of New York and in one scene when people stare at him as he walks through a hotel lobby, he feels ashamed of "his clothing, of his face, of his very bones. Ashamed to be Puerto Rican."

Harry Kullman's *The Battle Horse* gives a different twist to the theme of the outsider because it is set in 1930s Stockholm. Here the private school kids fight out their aggressions with the public school kids through their own kind of jousting tournament. In Glendon Swarthout's *Bless the Beasts and Children*, the outsiders are five leftover problem boys at a summer camp in Arizona. They are known as "the bedwetters," and they end up aligning with a herd of buffaloes.

It's a mark of maturity in the field of young adult literature that it's no longer just the big group distinctions that are being made. In *Tiger Eyes*, Blume includes more subtle observations and leads readers to inductively see and judge various status symbols in the high tech, scientific community of Los Alamos, for example Bathtub Row, gunracks in pickup trucks, and tell-tale comments about Native Americans and Chicanos.

THE PEOPLE BEHIND THE BOOKS

ROSA GUY, Author

The Friends
Ruby
Edith Jackson
The Disappearance

In this world growing ever smaller and more vulnerable to the holocaust that might mean its end, it is of the utmost importance for young adults to break with prejudices—that value system which creates the socio-economic pressures that mangle the minds of minorities and create the dangers of world annihilation. A more profound understanding, a broader vision of those with whom we must share space between shore and sea can only make a coming together easier for the battle in which we all must engage if the world as we know it is to survive. This, I suggest, is the theme of most of my novels for young adults. ◆

In *The Friends*, Rosa Guy does a masterful job in leading her readers to see how Phyllisia is taught that she's too good for the neighborhood. Her family has immigrated to Harlem from the West Indies, and her overly strict, restaurant-owner father constantly instills in her a feeling of superiority. He is horrified when Phyllisia brings home poor "ragamuffin" Edith with her ragged coat, holey socks, turned-over shoes, and matted hair. In *The Disappearance*, Guy explores the mistrust between a "respectable" middle-class black family and 16-year-old Imamu, a street kid from Harlem that they take in as a foster child.

M. E. Kerr's *Little Little* shows prejudices among handicapped people through the story of a PF (perfectly formed) dwarf, Little Little LaBelle, who to her mother's dismay picks humped-back Sydney Cinnamon for her boyfriend. *Little Little* also touches on other kinds of prejudices as when she explains that she and Calpurnia Dove are the best writers in their English class. The teacher always reads aloud something one or the other of them has written. They are "neck and neck in the race," but Little Little explains:

> ◇ When something Calpurnia wrote is read, I decide Miss Grossman is only being nice to her because Calpurnia is black, and mine is really better. Something tells me that when what I wrote is read, Calpurnia Dove decides Miss Grossman is only being nice to me because I'm a dwarf, and hers is really better.

Kerr is consistent in putting little reminders about prejudice in most of her books, but she keeps it at a fairly light level. More serious treatments showing how minorities are victimized include James Baldwin's love story, *If Beale Street Could Talk*, Louise Meriwether's *Daddy Was a Number Run-*

ner, Ernest Gaines' *The Autobiography of Miss Jane Pittman,* Mildred Taylor's *Let the Circle Be Unbroken,* William Armstrong's *Sounder,* and Jessamyn West's *The Massacre at Fall Creek.* Two haunting and powerful stories of doomed individuals are Frank Herbert's *Soul Catcher* and Marilyn Harris' *Hatter Fox.* The books are microcosms of the disastrous relationships and misunderstandings which have occurred between European immigrants and Native Americans.

Adolescence is commonly said to end when a young person marries, becomes a parent, or gains financial independence, which usually means having full-time employment. Affluent parents are able to provide their children with a longer adolescence so that they can go about establishing their identities in a more leisurely fashion. They can take longer to choose and prepare for their life's work which gives them alternatives not open to the youngster who must be self-supporting at age sixteen, eighteen, or even twenty. Also, if a middle-class teenager gets into some kind of trouble, chances are that the parents will be able to cushion the blow and provide a second chance, while youngsters without an adult support system may prematurely brand themselves as losers.

By gaining vicarious experiences through reading, young people can in effect lengthen the time, or at least make better use of what they have, before they commit themselves to lifelong decisions. This is one of the reasons for encouraging wide reading including reading about lifestyles far different from that of the reader. For example, it's probably not juvenile delinquents who get the most out of reading such books as Frank Bonham's *Durango Street,* Kin Platt's *Headman,* and S. E. Hinton's *Rumble Fish.* Instead it's more "typical" students who are curious about, and perhaps afraid of, kids like Emmett Sundback in Fran Arrick's *Chernowitz!* Emmett is a high school bully who over a two-year period torments Bob Cherno because he's Jewish. A number of events lead to a show-down and an all-school assembly where anti-Semitism is treated openly, and movies of the holocaust are shown. Most of the students are stunned, but Emmett is not like the others. As Bob observes, " . . . nothing happened on Emmett's insides, nothing. Emmett would go on and on . . ."

He's the same kind of character as is Urek, the antagonist in Sol Stein's *The Magician.* In this book, the protagonist is 16-year-old Ed Japhet who "could be fairly called an accomplished magician." But after he provides the intermission entertainment at a school dance, Urek and his followers beat him severely because Urek is jealous of Ed's success. The close of the book is ironic because Ed ends up killing Urek and Ed's schoolteacher father phones the same unethical lawyer who had gotten Urek off in the beginning.

In a slightly different kind of book about delinquency, authors lead readers to identify with the lawbreaker, not as an encouragement toward imitation, but toward understanding. In Todd Strasser's *Angel Dust Blues,* readers see how a lonely high school student with well-to-do parents can end up getting busted for selling drugs to an undercover agent. And in Robert McKay's *The Running Back*, readers are on the side of 18-year-old Jack Delaney who after being released from reform school, works to find acceptance on the football team at Holbrook High School.

A less disturbing aspect of fitting into society is that of gaining financial independence. For young people this is a two-pronged issue. First, they must get enough money to achieve the degree of independence that in their peer groups is considered appropriate. It may be only enough money to buy soda pop and an occasional ticket to the movies, or with other kids the goal may be to acquire enough money to pay for clothing, entertainment, and transportation, or even to take themselves away from parental control by moving out. Achieving this kind of immediate financial independence usually means having a job. Books that touch on this aspect of teenagers' lives include Todd Strasser's *Rock 'n' Roll Nights* and *Workin' for Peanuts*, Robert Lipsyte's *Summer Rules* and *The Summerboy*, Lynn Hall's *The Leaving*, and Kristin Hunter's *The Soul Brothers and Sister Lou*.

The second and probably more significant aspect of gaining financial independence has to do with the future. Young adults must choose and prepare for the way they will earn their living in years to come. Making this choice can bring conflicts and problems as, for example, in Chaim Potok's *My Name Is Asher Lev* in which a young Jewish boy persists in his dream to be an artist in spite of the great disappointment this brings to his traditional father who views art as superfluous. In most realistic fiction, the choice of a future career will appear as a subtheme as in Ursula Le Guin's *Very Far Away from Anywhere Else* and in Anne Tyler's *Dinner at the Homesick Restaurant*. Readers wishing to focus directly on the problem of choosing a career will more likely turn to the kinds of informative books presented in Chapter 8 or to the biographical-career type of book discussed in Chapter 7. Books that take a broader look at the whole question of what "success" means include Rosemary Wells' *When No One Was Looking*, the story of a young tennis player with the chance of national ranking. She is forced by the death of a competitor to question her future as well as the ethics of the adults in her life. A book for older readers is Joyce Carol Thomas' *Marked by Fire*, which one reviewer compared to Maya Angelou's *I Know Why the Caged Bird Sings* and said: " . . . many will be moved by the story of a girl who achieves recognition not through individual career or relationship with a man, but as leader and healer of her community."[7]

Body and Self

Books that treat problems related to accepting and effectively using one's physical body will be treated in several sections of this text. When the physical problem is relatively minor, or is at least one that can be solved, then it might be treated as an accomplishment-romance, as is Robert Lipsyte's *One Fat Summer* in Chapter 4. Informative books, sports books, and biographies may also deal with physical problems. And in many pieces of modern realistic fiction, physical problems are a secondary part of the plot. Their real purpose is to serve as a concrete or visible symbol for mental growth, which is harder to show. It has almost become an obligatory element in realistic fiction for young protagonists to express dissatisfaction with their appearance. Part of this is because hardly anyone has a perfect body or hasn't envied others for their appearance or physical skill. A bigger part is that adolescent bodies are changing so fast that their owners have not yet had time to adjust. The reason they spend so much time looking in mirrors is to reassure themselves that, "Yes, this is me!"

In 1970, Judy Blume surprised the world of juvenile fiction by writing a book that gave major attention to physical aspects of growing up. Margaret Simon in *Are You There God? It's Me, Margaret* worries because her breasts are small and because she's afraid she will be the last one in her crowd to begin menstruating. A later Blume book, *Then Again, Maybe I Won't* features Tony Miglione and his newly affluent family. He too worries about his developing body. In fact, he carries a jacket even on the warmest days so that he will have something to hide behind in case he has an erection. These books are read mostly by younger adolescents. But Blume's *Deenie* is read by both junior and senior high students. It is about a pretty teenager whose mother wants her to be a model, but then it's discovered that she has scoliosis and must wear an unsightly back brace. A minor point which goes unnoticed by some readers (but not by censors), is that Deenie worries that her back problem might be related to the fact that she masturbates.

What has made Blume's books so popular is their refreshing candor about worries that young people really do have. Another plus is that physical development is not treated separately from emotional and social development. This is why Blume's books are more fun to read (and more controversial) than are factual books about the development of the human body.

But the problem novel does not stop with treating the more or less typical problems of growing up. It has gone on to explore such physical problems as epilepsy in Barbara Girion's *A Handful of Stars* and cerebral palsy in Jan Slepian's *The Alfred Summer*, drug abuse in Sharon Bell Mathis' *Teacup Full of Roses* and Alice Childress' *A Hero Ain't Nothin' But a Sandwich*, anorexia nervosa in Steven Levenkron's *The Best Little Girl in the World*, Deborah Hautzig's *Second Star to the Right*, and Margaret Willey's *The Bigger Book of Lydia*, teenage alcoholism in Shep Greene's *The Boy Who Drank Too Much* and James Trivers' *I Can Stop Anytime I Want*, suicide in Fran Arrick's *Tunnel Vision* and Susan Beth Pfeffer's *About David*, and serious, perhaps terminal, illness in Alice Bach's *Waiting for Johnny Miracle* and Susan Sallis' *Only Love*.

The openness with which such a subject as death is discussed is shown in Gunnel Beckman's *Admission to the Feast*. In it, 19-year-old Annika Hallin accidentally learns from a substitute doctor that she has leukemia. She flees by herself to her family's summer cottage where she tries to sort out her reactions:

◇I don't think I understood it until last night . . . that I, Annika, . . . will just be put away, wiped out, obliterated. . . . And here on earth everything will just go on. . . . I shall never have more than this little scrap of life.

Zibby Oneal's A *Formal Feeling* is about 16-year-old Anne Cameron's adjustment to the death of her mother and the remarriage of her father. It was refreshing for a contemporary author to find some other way to write about an adjustment to death than simply doing a fictionalized version of the stages of acceptance described by Elisabeth Kübler-Ross. Oneal's title is taken from the beginning line of an Emily Dickinson poem, "After great pain, a formal feeling comes—."

Although Katherine Paterson's *Bridge to Terabithia* is considered a children's book because it's about two fifth-graders, we know several young adults who have read it and wept, just as have many adults.

It's almost harder to write a believable and yet not totally depressing story about someone who is not going to die but who has a severe physical problem that cannot be cured. Robin Brancato succeeded in doing this in *Winning*, the story of English teacher Ann Treer and an injured high school football player, Gary Madden. When the book opens, he has not been told that he is permanently paralyzed. Ann has reluctantly agreed to tutor him at the hospital, and she is surprised when he asks her to bring him some books from the library:

◇"Which ones?"
"Books—that I could read—that we could read when you're here."
"O.K. What books?"
"Books about what's wrong with me. You know, about spine injuries."

She protests that surely he ought to ask his doctor who would not only know what books to recommend but could also give him whatever information he needs. But Gary doesn't want to ask the doctor; in fact, he doesn't want anyone to know that he is curious so Ann agrees:

◇"I'll do what I can," she said. "You mustn't count on me, though. I don't know what books I can get."
Gary smiled ironically. "Just get one that widens my view of the world."
"So you do see the value of books!" Ann said.
"Yeah. They tell us about ourselves."

As Ann Treer leaves, she ponders why Gary has chosen her to be his agent in confirming his suspicions and concludes that it is:

◇because she wasn't as likely to judge him as the doctor was, probably. Not about to measure his manhood as his friends might. Because she hadn't borne him, with all the pain and expectations surrounding that. Because she didn't worship him and hanker for him, as Diane did.

The value of such fictional treatments as the ones cited in this section is that they involve the reader in the problem from many different viewpoints. A relationship is shown between physical and emotional problems. For example, one of the strong points of Brancato's book is that it shows the ripple effect of Gary's accident: how it changes his friends, his parents, his girlfriend, and his teacher. In one brief moment their definition of winning is changed forever. In the new situation, surviving—just wanting to survive—means winning, and readers cheer with Gary when he makes it through the depression that causes some of his hospital mates to commit suicide.

Sexual Relationships

In this chapter, we will give some examples of different kinds of sexual relationships which might be treated in problem novels, but lest we leave the impression that we look at sex only as a problem, we will hasten to add that discussions of the matter also appear in Chapter 4 ("The Love Romances"), Chapter 8 ("Informational Books"), and Chapter 11 where both sexuality and the establishment of sex-related roles are discussed as controversial issues.

In trying to satisfy their curiosity, teenagers seek out and read the vivid descriptions of sexual activity in such books as Scott Spencer's *Endless Love* and William Hogan's *The Quartzsite Trip*, both published for adults but featuring young protagonists. Male and female readers have also been intrigued by Don Bredes' *Hard Feelings*, Terry Davis' *Vision Quest*, Jay Daly's *Walls*, and Aidan Chambers' *Breaktime*, all coming-of-age stories which focus on young men's sexual desires. "Equivalent" books about young women's sexual desires are much more likely to be less direct. The sexuality is hidden under a love story, or else it is shown as a "problem" to be overcome.

Books with sexual themes vary from Richard Peck's *Are You in the House Alone?* and Patricia Dizenzo's *Why Me?* both treating the physical, emotional, and societal aspects of rape to Fran Arrick's *Steffie Can't Come Out to Play*, which is a sympathetic portrayal of a teenage prostitute. One of the most unusual of the problem books is Allen Hannay's *Love and Other Natural Disasters*. It was chosen as a favorite by young readers participating in the University of Iowa's 1983 Books for Young Adults Poll, but as shown by the description, opinions were sharply divided:

> ◇ "Some discoveries set you free, but most just complicate your life," begins 19-year-old Bubber Drumm as he relates his story of his love affair with Rose Butts, the 35-year-old divorced mother of his ex-girlfriend, Shirley. Shirley gets her revenge by poking holes in her mother's diaphragm and the resulting pregnancy complicates all their lives. Bubber tells his story with humor and exaggeration. This novel, read by many, received mixed reactions. Some described it as "fast-moving," "interesting," "weird," "never boring," and "humorous." Others felt the characters were "totally unbelievable" and "didn't think the subject should be treated so lightly."[8]

The three main problems treated in sex-related realistic books for teenagers are rape, homosexuality, and premarital sex resulting in pregnancy. That the whole subject of sexuality is treated so negatively is one of the criticisms of the new realism. For example, when W. Keith Kraus analyzed several books about premarital pregnancy including Ann Head's *Mr. and Mrs. Bo Jo Jones*, Zoa Sherburne's *Too Bad About the Haines Girl*, Jean Thompson's *House of Tomorrow*, Margaret Maze Craig's *It Could Happen to Anyone*, Nora Stirling's *You Would if You Loved Me*, Jeannette Eyerly's *A Girl Like Me*, Paul Zindel's *My Darling, My Hamburger*, and John Neufeld's *For All the Wrong Reasons*, he concluded that "the old double standard is reinforced by the so-called new realism." He compared the wish fulfilling nature of the stories to the old romances in which the girl is at the beginning an outsider who is discovered by a popular athlete. As she begins to date, a whole new social world opens up to her. But the dating leads to petting, and then to sex, and finally pregnancy and unhappiness. He lamented that "the sexual act itself is never depicted as joyful, and any show of intimacy carries a warning of future danger."[9]

In these problem books, the emphasis is usually on the physical aspect of the problem, but it's really the emotional aspects that most readers are interested in. When Paul Zindel was speaking in Arizona in the late 1970s, he commented on the fact that next to *The Pigman*, his most popular book was *My Darling, My Hamburger*, which is about pregnancy and abortion. Soon after the book was published in 1969, a Supreme Court decision made most abortions legal, and Zindel thought that would be the end of all sales because his book would seem terribly old fashioned. However, this didn't turn out to be the case because rather than settling the issue, the legalization of abortions served to increase interest in the moral and psychological aspects of the problem. Decision making was passed from the courts to every female with an unwanted pregnancy. And it isn't just the woman herself who is involved. For example, Jeannette Eyerly wrote about a teenage father who wanted to keep the baby in *It's My Baby Now* while Blossom Elfman showed an entire support system in *A House for Jonnie O.*

In Rosa Guy's *Edith Jackson*, Edith has grown up from the ragamuffin child readers first met when Phyllisia brought her home in *The Friends*. She is now looking forward to her eighteenth birthday in hopes of being free of foster homes and the Institution so that she can try again to set up a home for her younger sisters. But, by the end of the book, the girls are scattered, and Edith realizes that it is her own life she must plan. She has had a brief love affair with a handsome Harlem playboy almost twice her age and is excited at finding herself pregnant. But in the end of the book, she decides that the mature thing to do is to have an abortion.

Even in books where the main focus is not on whether someone is going to have an abortion, it may be mentioned as a possibility. For example in Judy Blume's *Forever*, one of Katherine's friends has an abortion. In *Love Is One of the Choices*, Norma Klein tells the story of two close friends and their first sexual loves. One of them chooses to marry and become pregnant right away while the other one gets pregnant, refuses to marry, and has an abortion.

Three landmark books opened the door to the treatment of homosexuality in books for young readers. They were John Donovan's *I'll Get There. It Better Be Worth the Trip* in 1969, Isabelle Holland's *The Man Without a*

Face, and Lynn Hall's *Sticks and Stones*, both in 1972. The protagonists are male and in all three books an important character dies. In none of them can a direct cause-and-effect relationship be charted between the death and the homosexual behavior, but possibilities for blame are there. And because of the coincidence of the three books appearing relatively close in time, critics were quick to object to the cumulative implications that homosexual behavior will be punished with some dreadful event. In spite of this criticism, Sandra Scoppettone's *Trying Hard to Hear You* published in 1974 was surprisingly similar, ending in an automobile accident which kills one of the teenage male lovers.

In 1976, Rosa Guy published *Ruby*, which was a sequel to *The Friends*. Ruby is Phyllisia's older sister and in the book she had a lesbian relationship with a beautiful classmate. *Publishers Weekly* described the book as "a sensitive novel in which adolescent homosexuality is viewed as nothing so frightening, but perhaps just a way-step toward maturity." This relaxed attitude toward female homosexuality was reflected in Deborah Hautzig's 1978 *Hey Dollface*, and in Nancy Garden's 1982 *Annie on My Mind*, which is on the Honor Sampling, and was described by Zena Sutherland as "candid, dignified, perceptive and touching; although the crux of the story line is the encounter that makes a physical relationship clear, it is the romantic element that dominates the book, with its strong characters and its tender love story."

In actuality, the three big problems—rape, homosexuality, and unwanted pregnancy—are experienced by few teenagers while nearly all young people wonder about the moral and social implications of experimenting with sexual activity whether or not it leads to intercourse. Norma Fox Mazer's *Up in Seth's Room* does a good job of showing the magnitude of teenagers' concerns. It's the story of 15-year-old Finn, who loves 19-year-old Seth, but doesn't think she's ready to give up her virginity. As Jean Fritz said when she reviewed the book for the *New York Times Book Review*:

> ◇ The questions we follow relentlessly from beginning to end are the perennial ones of adolescence: Will she or won't she? And what's it like? . . . Everyone should be pleased with the outcome. Finn sticks to her guns, although the fact that she "doesn't" is hardly more than a technicality. There are enough explicit scenes to give young readers, who don't know, a good idea of "what it's like."[10]

Mazer's description of the sexual activities of Finn and Seth have been criticized as being overly specific, but the fact that Finn and Seth don't actually go "all the way" probably appeases at least some of the potential censors. Mazer wrote the book as an antidote to all the "realistic" books implying that having sexual relationships is the norm for high school kids. As Mazer said in a speech at the 1979 NCTE convention in San Diego, statistics show that half of the kids in high school are not sexually intimate, and even the half that are have dozens of unanswered questions and worries.

To get direct answers to their questions, young readers can turn to the informational books discussed in Chapter 8. But because the questions they are the most concerned with are about moral, emotional, and psychological issues, the fuller kinds of fictional treatments described here will continue to be popular.

◆ ACTIVITIES ◆

1. Psychologist R. J. Havighurst outlined a teen-ager's developmental tasks as achieving new and more mature relations with agemates of both sexes, achieving a masculine or feminine social role, accepting one's physique and using the body effectively, achieving emotional independence of parents and other adults, achieving assurance of economic independence, selecting and preparing for an occupation, preparing for marriage and family life, developing intellectual skills and concepts necessary for civic competence, desiring and achieving socially responsible behavior, and acquiring a set of values and an ethical system as a guide to behavior. Read *The Chocolate War* and write an analysis of it based on the developmental tasks listed above. How many of them appear somewhere in the book? How are they treated? Which ones get the most attention? Are any of them totally ignored?

2. Read one of the problem novels and analyze the degree to which it is realistic, that is, true to life. You might interview a counselor, a social worker, or a young adult who has had experience with this particular problem. If the book differs from reality, tell how and conjecture on why. Is the author trying to teach a lesson? Make the story more exciting? Simplify it for the sake of brevity? Or something else?

3. Read several books that treat a similar theme, for example, drugs, pregnancy, handicaps (either mental or physical), gangs, or parent-child relationships. Write a paper showing what the books have in common. Some of the questions that you might try to answer include: Are there new stereotypes that have developed? Does each book offer something distinctive? Would you recommend that young adults read all of them, some of them, or none of them? Which is written at the highest level of literary quality? Which at the highest level of popular appeal? Which book is likely to last the longest, and which is the most trendy?

◆ NOTES ◆

[1]G. Robert Carlsen, "Bait/Rebait: Literature Isn't Supposed to Be Realistic," *English Journal* 70 (January 1981): 8–12.

[2]Sheila Egoff, "May Hill Arbuthnot Honor Lecture: Beyond the Garden Wall," *Top of the News* 35 (Spring 1979): 257–71.

[3]Glenna Davis Sloan, *The Child as Critic* (New York: Teachers College Press, 1975), pp. 19–21.

[4]Alleen Pace Nilsen, "The Poetry of Naming in Young Adult Books," *ALAN Review* 7 (Spring 1980): 3–4, 31.

[5]Katherine Paterson, "Newbery Medal Acceptance," *Horn Book Magazine* 57 (August 1981): 385–93.

[6]Dick Abrahamson and Betty Carter, "Positive Young Adult Novels," *English Journal* 71 (December 1982): 66–68.

[7]Hazel Rochman, Review of *Marked by Fire*, *School Library Journal* 28 (March 1982): 162.

[8]Elizabeth A. Belden, Agnes D. Stahlschmidt, David P. Lass, Alyce J. Toloui, "1983 Books for Young Adults Poll," *English Journal* 72 (December 1983): 66–70.

[9]W. Keith Kraus, "Cinderella in Trouble: Still Dreaming and Losing," *School Library Journal* 21 (January 1975): 18–22.

[10]Jean Fritz, Review of *Up in Seth's Room*, *New York Times Book Review*, January 20, 1980, p. 30.

◆ TITLES MENTIONED IN CHAPTER 3 ◆

For information on the availability of paperback editions of these titles, please consult the most recent edition of *Paperbound Books in Print*, published annually by R. R. Bowker Company.

Introductory Material

Baldwin, James. *If Beale Street Could Talk*. Dial, 1974.

Brancato, Robin. *Winning*. Knopf, 1977.

Cormier, Robert. *The Chocolate War*. Pantheon, 1974.

_____. *I Am the Cheese*. Pantheon, 1977.

Donovan, John. *I'll Get There. It Better Be Worth the Trip*. Harper & Row, 1969.

Golding, William. *Lord of the Flies*. Putnam's, 1955.

Greene, Bette. *Morning Is a Long Time Coming*. Dial, 1978.

_____. *Philip Hall Likes Me. I Reckon Maybe*. Dial, 1974.

_____. *Them That Glitter and Them That Don't*. Knopf, 1983.

O'Brien, Robert C. *Z for Zachariah*. Atheneum, 1975.

Peck, Richard. *Are You in the House Alone?* Viking, 1976.

Family Relationships

Babbitt, Natalie. *Herbert Rowbarge*. Farrar, Straus & Giroux, 1981.

Blessing, Richard. *A Passing Season*. Little, Brown, 1982.

Blume, Judy. *Tiger Eyes*. Bradbury, 1981.

Brancato, Robin. *Sweet Bells Jangled Out of Tune*. Knopf, 1982.

Bridgers, Sue Ellen. *All Together Now*. Knopf, 1979.

_____. *Home Before Dark*. Knopf, 1976.

_____. *Notes for Another Life*. Knopf, 1981.

Childress, Alice. *Rainbow Jordan*. Putnam's, 1981.

Cleaver, Vera and Bill. *Trial Valley*. Lippincott, 1977.

_____. *Where the Lilies Bloom*. Harper & Row, 1969.

Cormier, Robert. *After the First Death*. Pantheon, 1979.

_____. *The Bumblebee Flies Anyway*. Pantheon, 1983.

Donovan, John. *Remove Protective Coating a Little at a Time*. Harper & Row, 1973.

Duncan, Lois. *Stranger with My Face*. Little, Brown, 1981.

Fox, Paula. *Blowfish Live in the Sea*. Bradbury, 1970.

_____. *A Place Apart*. Farrar, Straus & Giroux, 1980.

Gray, Mary Ann. *The Truth About Fathers*. Bradbury, 1982.

Greene, Bette. *Summer of My German Soldier*. Dial, 1973.

Guest, Judith. *Ordinary People*. Viking, 1975.

_____. *Second Heaven*. Viking, 1982.

Guy, David. *Football Dreams*. Seaview Books, 1980.

Hall, Lynn. *The Leaving*. Scribner's, 1980.

Hamilton, Virginia. *Sweet Whispers, Brother Rush*. Putnam's, 1982.

Hinton, S. E. *Tex*. Delacorte, 1979.

Kerr, M. E. *Gentlehands*. Harper & Row, 1978.

Klein, Norma. *Mom, the Wolfman, and Me*. Pantheon, 1972.

Lehrman, Robert. *Juggling*. Harper & Row, 1982.

L'Engle, Madeleine. *Ring of Endless Light*. Farrar, Straus & Giroux, 1980.

_____. *A Swiftly Tilting Planet*. Farrar, Straus & Giroux, 1973.

_____. *A Wind in the Door*. Farrar, Straus & Giroux, 1973.

_____. *A Wrinkle in Time*. Farrar, Straus & Giroux, 1962.

Lowry, Lois. *A Summer to Die*. Houghton Mifflin, 1977.

Mazer, Norma Fox. *Dear Bill, Remember Me?* Delacorte, 1976.

_____. *Taking Terri Mueller*. Avon, 1981. Morrow, 1983.

Myers, Walter Dean. *It Ain't All for Nothing*. Viking, 1978.

Oneal, Zibby. *The Language of Goldfish*. Viking, 1980.

Paterson, Katherine. *The Great Gilly Hopkins*. Crowell, 1978.

_____. *Jacob Have I Loved*. Crowell, 1980.

Peck, Richard. *Father Figure*. Viking, 1978.

Platt, Kin. *The Boy Who Could Make Himself Disappear*. Dell, 1971.

Riley, Jocelyn. *Only My Mouth Is Smiling*. Morrow, 1982.

Sebestyen, Ouida. *IOU's*. Little, Brown, 1982.

————. *Words by Heart*, Little, Brown, 1979.

Taylor, Mildred. *Let the Circle Be Unbroken*. Dial, 1981.

————. *Roll of Thunder, Hear My Cry*. Dial, 1976.

Tesich, Steve. *Summer Crossing*. Random House, 1982.

Voigt, Cynthia. *Dicey's Song*. Atheneum, 1982.

————. *Homecoming*. Atheneum, 1981.

Wersba, Barbara. *Run Softly, Go Fast*. Atheneum, 1970.

Wharton, William. *Birdy*. Knopf, 1978.

Zindel, Paul. *My Darling, My Hamburger*. Harper & Row, 1969.

————. *The Pigman*. Harper & Row, 1968.

————. *The Pigman's Legacy*. Harper & Row, 1980.

Friends and Society

Angelou, Maya. *I Know Why the Caged Bird Sings*. Random House, 1970.

Armstrong, William. *Sounder*. Harper & Row, 1969.

Arrick, Fran. *Chernowitz!* Bradbury, 1981.

————. *Tunnel Vision*. Bradbury, 1980.

Baldwin, James. *If Beale Street Could Talk*. Dial, 1974.

Blume, Judy. *Tiger Eyes*. Bradbury, 1981.

Bonham, Frank. *Durango Street*. Dutton, 1967.

Brancato, Robin. *Blinded by the Light*. Knopf, 1978.

————. *Winning*. Knopf, 1977.

Bridgers, Sue Ellen. *All Together Now*. Knopf, 1979.

Butterworth, W. E. *Flunking Out*. Four Winds, 1981.

Childress, Alice. *A Hero Ain't Nothin' But a Sandwich*. Coward, McCann & Geoghegan, 1973.

Cleaver, Vera and Bill. *Where the Lilies Bloom*. Harper & Row, 1969.

Epstein, Jacob. *Wild Oats*. Little, Brown, 1979.

Gaines, Ernest. *The Autobiography of Miss Jane Pittman*. Dial, 1971.

Garden, Nancy. *Annie on My Mind*. Farrar, Straus & Giroux, 1982.

Guy, Rosa. *The Disappearance*. Delacorte, 1979.

————. *The Friends*. Holt, Rinehart and Winston, 1973.

Hall, Lynn. *The Leaving*. Scribner's, 1980.

Hamilton, Virginia. *M. C. Higgins, the Great*. Macmillan, 1974.

Harris, Marilyn. *Hatter Fox*. Random House, 1973.

Herbert, Frank. *Soul Catcher*. Putnam's, 1972.

Hinton, S. E. *The Outsiders*. Viking, 1967.

————. *Rumble Fish*. Delacorte, 1979.

Hogan, William. *The Quartzsite Trip*. Atheneum, 1980.

Hunter, Kristin. *The Soul Brothers and Sister Lou*. Scribner's, 1968.

Jaffe, Rona. *Mazes and Monsters*. G. K. Hall, 1981.

Jordan, June. *His Own Where*. Crowell, 1971.

Kerr, M. E. *I'll Love You When You're More Like Me*. Harper & Row, 1977.

————. *Is That You, Miss Blue?* Harper & Row, 1975.

————. *Little Little*. Harper & Row, 1981.

————. *Me, Me, Me, Me, Me*. Harper & Row, 1983.

————. *What I Really Think of You*. Harper & Row, 1983.

Konigsburg, E. L. *Journey to an 800 Number*. Atheneum, 1982.

Kullman, Harry. *The Battle Horse*. Bradbury, 1981.

Le Guin, Ursula. *Very Far Away from Anywhere Else*. Atheneum, 1976.

Levoy, Myron. *A Shadow Like a Leopard*. Harper & Row, 1981.

Lipsyte, Robert. *The Summer Boy*. Harper & Row, 1982.

————. *Summer Rules*. Harper & Row, 1981.

McKay, Robert. *The Running Back*. Harcourt Brace Jovanovich, 1979.

Meriwether, Louise. *Daddy Was a Number Runner*. Prentice-Hall, 1970.

Miklowitz, Gloria D. *The Love Bombers*. Delacorte, 1980.

Naylor, Phyllis Reynolds. *A String of Chances*. Atheneum, 1982.

Paterson, Katherine. *Jacob Have I Loved*. Crowell, 1980.

Platt, Kin. *Headman*. Greenwillow, 1975.

Potok, Chaim. *The Chosen*. Simon & Schuster, 1967.

————. *In the Beginning*. Knopf, 1975.

————. *My Name Is Asher Lev*. Knopf, 1972.

Sherman, D. R. *The Lion's Paw*. Doubleday, 1975.

Stein, Sol. *The Magician*. Delacorte, 1971.

Strasser, Todd. *Angel Dust Blues*. Coward, McCann & Geoghegan, 1979.

_____. *Rock 'n' Roll Nights*. Delacorte, 1982.

_____. *Workin' for Peanuts*. Delacorte, 1983.

Swarthout, Glendon. *Bless the Beasts and Children*. Doubleday, 1970.

Taylor, Mildred. *Let the Circle Be Unbroken*. Dial, 1981.

Thomas, Joyce Carol. *Marked by Fire*. Avon, 1982.

Tyler, Anne. *Dinner at the Homesick Restaurant*. G. K. Hall, 1982.

Wells, Rosemary. *When No One Was Looking*. Dial, 1980.

West, Jessamyn. *The Massacre at Fall Creek*. Harcourt Brace Jovanovich, 1975.

White, Robb. *Deathwatch*. Doubleday, 1972.

Zindel, Paul. *Confessions of a Teenage Baboon*. Harper & Row, 1977.

_____. *The Pigman*. Harper & Row, 1968.

Body and Self

Arrick, Fran. *Tunnel Vision*. Bradbury, 1980.

Bach, Alice. *Waiting for Johnny Miracle*. Harper & Row, 1980.

Beckman, Gunnell. *Admission to the Feast*. Holt, Rinehart and Winston, 1972.

Blume, Judy. *Are You There God? It's Me, Margaret*. Bradbury, 1970.

_____. *Deenie*. Bradbury, 1973.

_____. *Then Again, Maybe I Won't*. Bradbury, 1971.

Brancato, Robin. *Winning*. Knopf, 1978.

Childress, Alice. *A Hero Ain't Nothin' But a Sandwich*. Coward, McCann & Geoghegan, 1973.

Girion, Barbara. *A Handful of Stars*. Scribner's, 1981.

Greene, Shep. *The Boy Who Drank Too Much*. Viking, 1979.

Hautzig, Deborah. *Second Star to the Right*. Greenwillow, 1981.

Levenkron, Steven. *The Best Little Girl in the World*. Contemporary Books, 1978.

Lipsyte, Robert. *One Fat Summer*. Harper & Row, 1977.

Mathis, Sharon Bell. *Teacup Full of Roses*. Viking, 1975.

Oneal, Zibby. *A Formal Feeling*. Viking, 1982.

Paterson, Katherine. *Bridge to Terabithia*. Crowell, 1977.

Pfeffer, Susan Beth. *About David*. Delacorte, 1980.

Sallis, Susan. *Only Love*. Harper & Row, 1980.

Slepian, Jan. *The Alfred Summer*. Macmillan, 1980.

Trivers, James. *I Can Stop Anytime I Want*. Prentice-Hall, 1974.

Willey, Margaret. *The Bigger Book of Lydia*. Harper & Row, 1983.

Sexual Relationships

Arrick, Fran. *Steffie Can't Come Out to Play*. Bradbury, 1978.

Blume, Judy. *Forever*. Bradbury, 1975.

Bredes, Don. *Hard Feelings*. Atheneum, 1977.

Chambers, Aidan. *Breaktime*. Harper & Row, 1979.

Craig, Margaret Maze. *It Could Happen to Anyone*. Berkley, 1970.

Daly, Jay. *Walls*. Harper & Row, 1980.

Davis, Terry. *Vision Quest*. Viking, 1979.

Dizenzo, Patricia. *Why Me? The Story of Jenny*. Avon, 1976.

Donovan, John. *I'll Get There. It Better Be Worth the Trip*. Harper & Row, 1969.

Elfman, Blossom. *A House for Jonnie O*. Houghton Mifflin, 1977.

Eyerly, Jeannette. *A Girl Like Me*. Lippincott, 1966.

_____. *He's My Baby Now*. Archway, 1978.

Garden, Nancy. *Annie on My Mind*. Farrar, Straus & Giroux, 1982.

Guy, Rosa. *Edith Jackson*. Viking, 1978.

_____. *The Friends*. Holt, Rinehart and Winston, 1973.

_____. *Ruby*. Viking, 1976.

Hall, Lynn. *Sticks and Stones*. Follett, 1972.

Hannay, Allen. *Love and Other Natural Disasters*. Little, Brown, 1982.

Hautzig, Deborah. *Hey Dollface*. Morrow, 1978.

Head, Ann. *Mr. and Mrs. Bo Jo Jones*. Putnam's, 1967.

Hogan, William. *The Quartzsite Trip*. Atheneum, 1980.

Holland, Isabelle. *The Man Without a Face*. Lippincott, 1972.

Klein, Norma. *Love Is One of the Choices*. Dial, 1979.

Mazer, Norma Fox. *Up in Seth's Room*. Delacorte, 1979.

Neufeld, John. *For All the Wrong Reasons*. New American Library, 1980.

Peck, Richard. *Are You in the House Alone?* Viking, 1976.

Scoppettone, Sandra. *Trying Hard to Hear You.* Harper & Row, 1974.

Sherburne, Zoa. *Too Bad About the Haines Girl.* Morrow, 1967.

Spencer, Scott. *Endless Love.* Knopf, 1979.

Stirling, Nora. *You Would If You Loved Me.* Evans, 1969.

Thompson, Jean. *House of Tomorrow.* Harper & Row, 1967.

Zindel, Paul. *My Darling, My Hamburger.* Harper & Row, 1969.

————. *The Pigman.* Harper & Row, 1968.

THE OLD ROMANTICISM

◊

OF WISHING AND WINNING

A kind of story that serves as a counterbalance to the depressing realism of the problem novel is the romance. Romances were among the first stories to be told. People like to hear them because they have happy endings, and the tellers of romances are willing to exaggerate just enough to make the stories more interesting than real life. A basic part of the romance is a quest of some sort. In the course of the quest, the protagonist will experience doubts and will undergo severe trials, but he or she will be successful in the end. This success will be all the more appreciated because of the difficulties that the protagonist has suffered. The extremes of suffering and succeeding are characteristic of the romance. In good moments, it is like a happy daydream, but in bad moments it resembles a nightmare.

The word *romance* comes from the Latin adverb *romanice* which means "in the Latin manner." It is with this meaning that Latin, Italian, Spanish, and French are described as romance languages. The literary meaning of *romance* grew out of its use by English speakers to refer to French dialects, which were much closer to Latin than was their own Germanic language of English. Later it was used to refer to Old French and finally to anything written in French.

Many of the French stories that were read by English speakers were tales about knights who set out on such bold adventures as slaying dragons, rescuing princesses from ogres, and defeating the wicked enemies of a righteous king. Love was often an element in these stories, for the knight was striving to win the hand of a beloved maiden. So, today, when a literary piece is referred to as a romance, it usually contains either or both adventure and love.

The romance is appealing to teenagers because it is matched in several ways to their roles in life. The symbols that are used often relate to youthfulness and hope, and, in keeping with this, many of the protagonists even in the traditional and classic tales, are in their teens. Modern young adults are at an age when they leave home or anticipate leaving to embark on a new way of life. It is more likely to be called "moving out" than "going on a romantic quest," but the results are much the same. And seeking and securing a "true love" usually—but not always—takes up a greater proportion of the time and energy of the young than of middle-aged adults. And the exaggeration that is part of the romantic mode is quite honestly felt by young people. Never at any other stage of life do people feel their emotions quite so intensely. It was noticing this intensity about his own children that led Robert Cormier to begin writing about young protagonists. He observed that in one afternoon at the beach, they could emotionally go through what to an adult would be a whole month of experience.

Another teenage characteristic particularly appropriate to the romantic mode is the optimism of youth. Whether or not young people, either as a group or as individuals, are really more optimistic than their elders, they are presumed to be so, and a writer doing the same story for adults might be more tempted to present it as irony than as romance.

◈ THE ADVENTURE/ACCOMPLISHMENT ROMANCE

The great satisfaction of the adventure or the accomplishment romance lies in its wish fulfillment, as when David slays Goliath, when Cinderella is united with the noble prince and given the fitting role of queen, and when Dorothy and Toto find their way back to Kansas. In every culture there are legends, myths, and folk and fairy tales which follow the pattern of the adventure/accomplishment romance. In the Judeo-Christian culture, the biblical story of Joseph is a prime example. Early in life, he is chosen and marked as a special person. When his brothers sell him as a slave to the Egyptian traders, he embarks on his quest for wisdom and knowledge. Just when all seems lost, he receives divine help in being blessed with the ability to interpret dreams. This gets him out of prison and into Pharaoh's court. The climax of the story comes years later during the famine that brings his brothers to Egypt and the royal palace. Without recognizing Joseph, they beg for food. His forgiveness and his generosity is final proof of his worthiness.

It is a distinguishing feature of such romances that the happy ending is achieved only after the hero's worth is proven through a crisis or an ordeal. Usually as part of the ordeal the hero must make a sacrifice, must be wounded, or must leave some part of his or her body, even if it is only sweat or tears. The real loss is that of innocence, but it is usually symbolized by a physical loss as in Norse mythology when Odin gives one of his eyes to pay for gaining knowledge, or in J. R. R. Tolkien's *The Lord of the Rings* when Frodo, who has already suffered many wounds, finds that he cannot throw

THE PEOPLE BEHIND THE BOOKS

MARILYN KAYE

Library Science Professor, St. John's University

Editor, *Top of the News*

When I read *The Catcher in the Rye*, at age 12, I can't say that I consciously identified with Holden Caulfield; after all, he was the wrong sex and age, and he was a product of a class and an environment of which I knew little. But it was a revelation to me to follow an emotional quest in literature. It may not have replicated my own personal quest, but I could certainly recognize the confusion and turmoil that accompanies any adolescent attempt to make some sense of the world. We need more literature which addresses these themes, novels that do not readily lend themselves to subject headings like "Drugs—Fiction." Adolescents are still asking themselves "Who am I?" I doubt that they purposely turn to literature for answers. But literature can raise the questions that serve as catalysts to aid their search, to suggest a new approach, an expanded awareness. Certainly there is room in this vaguely defined body of literature for every conceivable genre and literary form, from topical problem-solving fiction to escapist romance. But there are also young people out there who want novels which are philosophical, contemplative, and—dare I suggest?—profound. We have yet to develop a real body of serious literature for these readers. But then, the whole concept of a literature for young adults is in its infancy. Perhaps, as the concept gains maturity and respect, the literature can become more provocative, more open-minded in its assessment of adolescent concerns. I think we've got something to look forward to. ◆

the ring back and so must let Gollum take his finger along with the ring. What is purchased with the suffering of the hero is nearly always some kind of wisdom, even though wisdom is not what the hero set out to find.

The adventure/accomplishment romance has elements applicable to the task of entering the adult world, which all young people anticipate. The story pattern includes the three stages of formal initiation as practiced in many cultures. First, the young and innocent person is separated both physically and spiritually from the nurturing love of friends and family. Then, during this separation, the hero, who embodies noble qualities, undergoes a test of courage and stamina that may be either mental, psychological, or physical. In the final stage the young person is reunited with former friends and family in a new role of increased status.

One Fat Summer as Adventure/Accomplishment Romance

How this archetypal initiation rite can be translated into a modern, somewhat realistic story for young adults is shown through Robert Lipsyte's *One Fat Summer*. It is the story of a quest for self-respect. When the protagonist begins it, he is quite unaware of the magnitude of his undertaking. As part of the quest, he is isolated from his family. The suffering that he undergoes is something that no one else could do for him, but it makes the victory that much sweeter.

The story begins on the Fourth of July with fourteen-year-old Bobby Marks feeling sorry for himself at the Rumson Lake Community Association Carnival. He hates summertime because that is when his family moves out to Rumson Lake where everyone goes around in a swimming suit so the other kids can see "your thick legs and your wobbly backside and your big belly and your soft arms. And they laugh." Bobby weighs more than 200 pounds. He doesn't know how much more because he always bails out when the pointer on the bathroom scale starts to climb past the 200 pound mark.

What happens in the book is that Bobby takes a job as an underpaid and overworked yard boy. He does it only so he won't have to be a camp counselor or a mother's helper on the beach where he would have to wear a swimming suit. By the end of the summer, Bobby weighs 175 pounds, which isn't exactly thin, but it isn't what anyone would call fat either. His loss of weight is his tangible reward, but, more important than this is his coming to know himself and to understand, at least partially, the motives of the half-dozen people who play significant roles in his life that summer. This understanding brings him relief from the fears that had haunted him during all the summers his family had spent at Rumson Lake.

Bobby does not lose weight or come to these understandings without the central struggle or ordeal that is at the heart of all romances. His physical ordeal is the task of keeping Dr. Kahn's huge hillside lawn immaculate. In the eyes of the world cutting a lawn may not seem like the kind of Herculean task that would qualify for a romantic quest, but for Bobby it was such:

> ◇ The longer I cut, the bigger the lawn seemed to get. A friend of my father's once showed us his color movies of a mule trip down into the Grand Canyon. He said that the farther down he went, the bigger the canyon seemed to get. From the top, it looked like just a huge hole, but as he descended, the walls of the canyon seemed to flatten back and the hole became another world. It was something like that with the lawn.
>
> I tried to go faster, but then I went over a stone. Clang. The blade batted it against a tree. Thud. I got panicky. The rest of the afternoon was a blur. The heat was pounding into the ground and my clothes stuck to me. My underwear was strangling me. Sweat pouring down my forehead stung my eyes and blinded me. My hands and feet were burning. My lungs were bursting.

As befits the mode of romance, the place that Bobby works is both idyllic and far removed from the small houses and cottages that make up the middle-class beach community that he is accustomed to. Dr. Kahn's house is on the other side of the lake, and at first Bobby's family and friends do not know that he is working. When Bobby first looks at Dr. Kahn's lawn it is "like a velvet sea, a green velvet sea that flowed up from the gray shore of the county road to surround a great white house with white columns. The house looked like a proud clipper ship riding the crest of the ocean."

A more important challenge than that of the lawn is the one that Bobby meets in the ex-Marine Willie Rumson who is the kind of villain that appears in nearly all romances. It is in keeping with the romance pattern that the characters, other than the protagonist, are one-sided. They are either villains or angels. Since a romance is essentially the story of one person's achievement and development, everything else is a condensation. For the sake of efficiency, the personalities of the supporting characters are shown through symbols, metaphors, and significant details, all of which highlight the qualities that are important to the story. (Dr. Kahn, Bobby's Jewish employer, is presented as such a negative stereotype, though, that some readers have been offended.)

It is not usually the villain whom the hero has to defeat ultimately, but the villain stands in the way of the real accomplishment and gives the hero an enemy upon whom to focus. Without some scary, nightmarish, and usually life-threatening incident, the happy ending could not be appreciated. At first, Willie and his friends just tease Bobby calling him "The Crisco Kid" because he's "fat in the can," and asking him if he has a license to drag that trailer behind him. But then Willie can't get a job, and he decides that he wants to be Dr. Kahn's yard boy. He demands that Bobby quit the job and, when it becomes apparent that he won't, Willie and his buddies get mean.

In keeping with the form of the romance it is significant in the ordeal that follows that Bobby experiences something similar to what in the traditional romance would have been a vision or a visit from a divine being. He has been stripped of his clothes and left on an island in the lake. Symbolically the peaceful setting of the lake has changed into something fearsome. The night "exploded with thunder and lightning and the wind drove nails of rain" into his naked body. Bobby is lying in the mud and puddles where they dumped him and he thinks he's going to drown, but then he hears a voice:

◇ "On your feet, Marks."
I looked around. I saw no one in the darkness.
"Stand up."
The voice was familiar.
"Up. Get up."
Lightning hit the water, the black sky parted like curtains at high noon, flooding the island with light. But there was no one there.
"I SAID GET UP. YOU CAN DO IT, BIG FELLA."
The water touched my lips. Be so easy now to relax into the soft mud, get it over with.
"ON YOUR FEET. YOU'RE NOT GONNA LET THOSE BASTARDS KILL YOU. YOU BEAT THE LAWN, YOU CAN BEAT THEM. YOU'RE TOUGH. YOU RAN, YOU FOUGHT, YOU'LL DO IT AGAIN. YOU'LL DO IT TILL YOU WIN."
I recognized the voice.
Captain Marks, Commander Marks, Big Bob Marks.
It was me.
I stood up.

Another element of the romance is that the protagonists put forth efforts on their own behalf. By standing up, Bobby proves that he is willing to do this and is, therefore, worthy of outside help. As it often does in the romance, outside help comes from an unexpected source. A cousin of Willie's arrives in a canoe and takes Bobby back to Rumson Beach. All that Bobby loses in the ordeal is a sock. What he finds is a new kind of confidence. This prepares him for the final confrontation with Willie Rumson, which, fortunately for Bobby, turns out to be an underwater fight. Bobby has the advantage because all his life he has swum underwater to keep people from seeing how fat he is. Bobby wins the fight, but this physical act is only a symbolic way of showing the emotional victory that Bobby achieves over his own misunderstandings and fears.

The whole experience gives him enough confidence to face Dr. Kahn at last and ask him for the pay that was originally advertised for the job:

> ◇ He stared at me. Just like he did the very first time, a lifetime ago. But those shotgun eyes didn't scare me anymore.
> "You should pay me for this summer," said Dr. Kahn. "I've watched you change from a miserable fat boy into a fairly presentable young man. On my lawn. On my time."
> "You didn't do it, Dr. Kahn. I did it."

This last statement sums up a prime requisite for a modern young adult romance. The hero has to accomplish the task and it has to be one that readers can respect and at the same time imagine themselves accomplishing.

Other Stories of Accomplishment

Isabelle Holland's story *Heads You Win, Tails I Lose* has a similar theme to *One Fat Summer*, only it is not as believable. With the help of pills stolen from her mother's dresser drawer, the protagonist loses enough weight within six weeks to transform her from a pudgy, unpopular adolescent into a thin, pretty girl who for the first time is being asked on more dates than she can accept.

Despite the lack of believability, the wish-fulfillment nature of the story is so powerful that Holland says it outsells several of her better books including the highly acclaimed *Man Without a Face*. Some adults have objected to this kind of portrayal of the romantic quest. They understand the need to show in some tangible way that the young person has made an accomplishment, but they fear that young readers will interpret the physical achievement literally rather than figuratively. Teenagers are already overly concerned about their physical bodies and any defects that they might have. Most physical defects—even many cases of obesity—cannot be changed. They would therefore prefer stories in which the protagonist comes to terms with the problem and adjusts to it or compensates for it. Mildred Lee's *The Skating Rink* is such a story. Tuck Faraday stutters, and, because of this, he withdraws into such a shell that everyone assumes that he is stupid. Then Pete Degley comes to town and builds a roller skating rink. He likes the shy Tuck, who hardly ever speaks, and recognizes his need to do something special. He trains Tuck as a skater, and, on opening night, Tuck's dreams are fulfilled as he performs with Pete Degley's wife in front of the whole community.

Anne Eliot Crompton's *The Sorcerer* is another story where the young protagonist compensates for, rather than overcomes, a disability. It is the story of Lefthand, a boy who has been injured by a bear so that he cannot hunt. In his tribe, this is a serious problem because hunting is what the men do. There is no miraculous cure for his disability, but he gains both his own and his tribe's respect when he develops enough skill as an artist to draw the pictures of animals needed for the tribe's hunting rituals.

In referring to the genre, we use the dual term adventure/accomplishment romance because the stories don't always involve an adventure or a trip, but they do involve an accomplishment of some kind. The significant accomplishment is usually a mental one even if, for the sake of the story, it is dramatized as a physical one. When there is no symbolization, then it is more likely that the author will have to show the protagonist suffering actual defeat or death. This would result in irony or tragedy rather than romance. The tone an author uses might also change a story from romance to irony or tragedy. Although romance has its share of somber moments, the overall tone must be relatively light and optimistic. For example, Holden Caulfield sets out on a quest, but J. D. Salinger's *The Catcher in the Rye* does not qualify as a romance. It is too grim. The same could be said for Hannah Green's *I Never Promised You a Rose Garden* and Judith Guest's *Ordinary People*. These three books contain many of the elements of the traditional romance including worthy young heroes who set out to find wisdom and understanding. In the course of the stories, they make physical sacrifices but these are real rather than symbolic, for example, the suicide attempts in the latter two titles. The wise and kindly psychiatrists are modern realistic counterparts to the white witches, the wizards, and the helpful gods and goddesses who in the traditional romances have always been there to aid and instruct worthy young heroes much as Merlin did with young Arthur. The difference between the traditional helpers in romances and the modern ones in realistic stories is that the realistic ones lack magic; they must rely on hard painstaking work. This is what is communicated by the title *I Never Promised You a Rose Garden*. Deborah Blau's psychiatrist says this to her when she wants to warn the young girl that even when she is "cured" and has left the mental institution, life will still be full of problems. If Green's book had been a romance, then there would have been no mention of this fact. Readers could have pictured Deborah leaving the institution and living "happily ever after."

The important role of physical effort and danger in the romantic mode has caused people to assume falsely that the adventure-romance is an exclusively male story. But, of course, in real life it isn't only males who experience physical danger, even though cultural expectations have caused society to place males, more than females, in dangerous situations. This has naturally affected the genre and readers' expectations. For example, Irene

Hunt wrote two stories, one about a boy and one about a girl traveling the route to maturity. One was a war story (*Across Five Aprils*) and the other one was the story of an orphan raised by an unmarried schoolteacher (*Up a Road Slowly*). It is to be expected that she would put the male protagonist in the war story and the female protagonist in the gentler home-oriented story.

As a counterbalance to the many adventure stories featuring males, Harry Mazer wrote *The Island Keeper*, a story of fat and awkward sixteen-year-old Cleo Murphy. Cleo runs away from expensive clothes, exclusive boarding schools, and a family whose members are incapable of love. She goes to a deserted island in the north woods, which is owned by her father. Her plans are vague, but she intends to leave before winter. However, winter comes early, her boat is gone, and what started out as a mild adventure turns into a struggle for existence. In managing to survive she finds a new person within herself and learns the valuable lesson that self-respect precedes respect from others.

The story seemed believable and exciting to us and to the few teenagers we know who have read it, but when we gave it to an adult who is a specialist in outdoor survival, he had a credibility problem. In his opinion, there is no way that an untrained young person, male or female, could survive a winter on such an island.

In fairness to Mazer, we should point out that the majority of adventure-romances would probably not pass this kind of reality test. It is the nature of the genre that they are exaggerated. The question in evaluation is the degree of exaggeration and whether or not it stands between readers and their ability to identify with the story.

An unusual war-related story in which a thirteen-year-old girl achieves personal maturity by going on a quest is T. Degens' *Transport 7-41-R*. The story is set in Germany one year after the end of World War II. The girl's parents, who for physical and/or psychological reasons can no longer afford to have her at home, arrange papers saying that she is a former resident of Cologne so that she will be given a place on the train as a returning refugee. Her parents are supposedly sending her to a school, but she's not even sure it exists, and her own goal is to find her older brother Jochen. She imagines that once she is with him, everything will be wonderful. During the train trip she grows close to an elderly couple, the Lauritzens. Midway, the wife dies and the girl assists the old man in keeping his wife's death a secret because the whole reason for his trip was to take her "home" and give her a real burial. The girl helps the old man to succeed in his promise to his wife, but in the process she has to give as a bribe to the cemetery attendant her leather boots, which were the only things of value she owns. This is her symbolic sacrifice.

The story doesn't have a totally happy ending, but the girl is nevertheless in a far better position than at the beginning of the journey. She is no longer all alone. She has a companion and a purpose in life. She is not going to give up her independence or her search for her brother, but neither is she going to live in limbo waiting for him to come and make everything

THE PEOPLE BEHIND THE BOOKS

WELDON HILL, Author

The Iceman
Lonesome Traveler
Onionhead
Rafe

My agent, fellow writers, and various people from Back East keep telling me the publishing business is in dire straits, a real disaster area. And here I thought it was just me.

The cost of publishing a fiction book nowadays is reflected in the outrageous prices asked for the finished products, like $17.50, $18.50, $22, for hardcovers. It is also reflected in budget-cutting in the advertising and promoting departments. All of which is very confusing to writers. Also disheartening.

Aside from our wistful dreams of achieving modest wealth and fame, I think authors of young adult books yearn most just to be widely read, to touch the minds and maybe the hearts of people all over the U.S.A., not to mention Canada, England, and Japan. We can always earn a living doing something else, but there is no panacea for the sad frustration of not being read. And having a book accepted for publication is no guarantee it will reach its intended audience. In these parlous times awful things happen to a lot of pretty good books. Cost-conscious publishers don't advertise or promote them, critics ignore them, lo-

wonderful. She has come to the realization that it is up to her. And the story ends with her and the old man leaving the cemetery knowing that they have a lot of work to do.

This acceptance of the compromised dream is another element of the romance pattern that is particularly meaningful to young adults. Many of them are just beginning to achieve some of their lifelong goals, and they are finding that the end of the rainbow, which is a symbolic way of saying such things as "When I graduate," "When we get married," "When I'm eighteen," or "When I have my own apartment," is illusory. Like the characters in the romances, they are not sorry that they have ventured for they have indeed found something worthwhile, but it is seldom the pot of gold that they had imagined.

Jean George's *Julie of the Wolves*, which is read by younger adolescents, is a classic example of the romantic quest ending in a compromised dream. Julie's separation from her Eskimo family and friends is a result of her running away from the retarded Daniel who was planning to make her his wife in fact as well as in name. She sets out with the vague and unrealistic goal of running away to her pen pal in San Francisco. As she gains wisdom this changes to a decision to live in the old ways. Amaroq, the great wolf, lends "miraculous" help to her struggle for survival on the Arctic tundra. The climax comes when she learns that her father still lives and that she has arrived at his village. But she is disillusioned when she finds that he has married a "gussack" and pilots planes for hunters. She slips away to return to the tundra, but that night when the temperature falls far below zero and cal reviewers don't get their free copies, and nobody hears about them so they don't get read and authors go around feeling unhappy about all of those tens of thousands of potentially satisfied customers who are deprived of the opportunity to read those pretty good books. It's enough to make a writer wonder if it's too late to kick the habit and become a rich and arrogant plumber or TV repairman or something.

Unless, as happens to me four or five times a year, he gets a fan letter like the one the mailman brought me the other day from a lady in Redwood City, California, who is still a young adult at seventy. She wrote about the warm feeling she gets from reading one of my books and ended with "You may have another book in the works but until it is finished it isn't going to do me any good. I can't wait forever you know!"

Okay, the hell with plumbing. Forget that stuff about kicking the writing habit. As long as I hear from a satisfied reader once in a while I will continue to battle the odds and the current economic ills afflicting the publishing industry, and keep on trying to give someone out there somewhere that warm feeling we can only get from the private pleasure of reading books. ◆

The Iceman. Morrow, 1976.
Lonesome Traveler. McKay, 1970.
Onionhead. McKay, 1957.
Rafe (c. 1966). M + H, 1980.

"the ice thundered and boomed, roaring like drumbeats across the Arctic," Tornait, Julie's golden plover who has been her faithful companion, dies in spite of all that Julie does to save him.

Tornait is the last symbol of Julie's innocence and as she mourns his death she comes to accept the fact that the life of both the wolf and the Eskimo is changing and she points her boots toward her father and the life that he now leads. Through her quest, she gains the understanding that her life must change, but she also gains something unexpected. She learns a great deal about her native land and the animals whose home it is. Readers are optimistic that Julie will not forget what she has experienced and that she will have some part in protecting it, though perhaps not to the degree that she would have desired.

Virginia Hamilton's *M. C. Higgins, the Great* is another example of the compromised dream. A young boy must settle for less than he wants because of the selfishness of adults who pay little heed to ecology. Strip miners have threatened the security of M. C.'s Appalachian family by taking the coal from the top of the mountain on which their home is located. A great spoil is gradually creeping toward the house. M. C. thinks the family should leave and move to the city. He envisions his mother becoming a famous singer, but a young woman who is travelling through helps M. C. to get a more realistic view of the family's chances of being transformed through his mother's singing. M. C. decides that there is something worth saving in his family heritage and their third-generation home on the mountain. He begins building a retaining wall behind the house.

A part of the book that makes it especially interesting as a romance is the role played by M. C.'s steel pole with the bicycle seat mounted on top. It is while sitting on the pole and contemplating the surrounding countryside that M. C. comes to his realization. In traditional romances, the protagonist usually receives the vision or insight "in a high or isolated place like a mountain top, an island, or a tower."[1] M. C.'s pole fills these qualifications and is at the same time unique and intriguing. It is also significant that M. C. earned his pole through his own physical efforts. His father gave it to him for swimming the Ohio River.

Since the pattern of the romance has been so clearly outlined by critics, and since its popularity has passed the test of time with honors, it would seem to be a very easy story to write. The plot has already been worked out. All an author needs to do is develop a likable protagonist, figure out a quest, fill in the supporting roles with stock characters, and then supply a few interesting details. But it is far from being this simple. Sometimes, as in dance, the things that look the simplest are in fact the hardest to execute. The plot must not be so obvious that a reader will recognize it as "the same old thing." The really good author will develop a unique situation that on the surface will appear to be simply a good story. Its appeal as a romantic quest should be at a deep almost subconscious level, with readers experiencing a sense of *déjà vu*. It is as if their own life story is being told because the romantic quest is everyone's story. We are all searching for answers to the great questions of life.

Characterization is especially important in relation to the protagonist in an accomplishment- or adventure-romance. Readers must be able to identify with the hero. As *Julie of the Wolves* proves, this does not mean that the hero has to live in the same life-style or even have the same conflicts as the reader. But it does mean that the emotions must be ones that the reader can understand, and the author has to present them in such a way as to create empathy.

In spite of the fact that the adventure-romance is one of the most common patterns in books for young adults, relatively few titles are listed in this chapter because the motif of a worthy young hero embarking on a quest in which wisdom is gained is most often worked into other genres. For example, Cynthia Voigt's *Homecoming* and Judy Blume's *Tiger Eyes* are written about as realistic problem novels; Lloyd Alexander's *Westmark* and Kathryn Lasky's *Beyond the Divide* as historical fiction; Robin McKinley's *The Blue Sword* and Jane Yolen's *Dragon's Blood* and its sequel *Heart's Blood* as fantasy; Joan Vinge's *Psion* and Madeleine L'Engle's *A Wrinkle in Time* as science fiction; and Harry Mazer's *The Last Mission* and Peter Dickinson's *Tulku* as adventure.

◈ THE LOVE-ROMANCE

The love-romance is of a slightly different nature, but it shares many characteristics with the adventure-romance. They are symbolically associated with youth and with springtime. There is an ordeal or a problem to be overcome followed by a happy ending. The "problem" is invariably the successful pairing of a likable young couple. An old definition of the love-romance pattern is, "Boy meets girl, boy loses girl, boy wins girl." This is a fairly accurate summary except that with teenage literature it is the other way around. Most of the romances are told from the girl's point of view. She is the one who meets, loses, and finally wins a boy.

The tone of the love-romance is lighter than that of the adventure-romance. In a love story the protagonist neither risks nor gains as much as in an adventure. Notwithstanding *Romeo and Juliet*, people seldom die, emotionally or physically, because of young love. For this reason, the love-romance tends to be less serious in its message. Its power lies in its wish fulfillment.

Romance as Big Business

How quickly the field of adolescent literature can change is shown by a statement from the first edition of this text where we said that few love-romances were currently being published for young adults. Five years later, a more accurate statement would be that few books are being published for young adults that do not include at least some aspects of a love story.

In the book business, the runaway popularity of paperback love-romances written especially for teenagers was the big marketing surprise of the early 1980s. It began when Scholastic book club editors noticed that their best-selling books, especially in junior highs, were those that treated boy/girl relationships. They decided to launch a clearly identifiable line of "squeaky clean" young love stories. They called the line Wildfire, and within the first year, sold 1.8 million titles. Bantam soon followed with Sweet Dreams and Simon and Schuster with Silhouette First Love, Dell combed through its Yearling and Laurel Leaf reprints to pull out romances which could be packaged under a Young Love insignia. Other companies joined in, even ones which had never marketed books to teenagers.

The international popularity of paperback, formula romances was recently brought home when in a 48-hour period we happened to read that the Harlequin company in Canada—the publishers who perhaps started the whole thing—were going to come out with a line of romances specifically for teenagers; a student brought in an article from *The* (London) *Times Educational Supplement*, July 1, 1983, "Oh, Boy! My Guy" in which Mary Harron wrote about weekly romance magazines put out for teenage girls in England; and a colleague wandered into the office with a stack of paperbacks from Spain. They were Spanish translations of some of the more sensationalized American problem novels and romances. Her question was whether she needed to read all this "trash" to maintain her place as an authority on books in Spanish for young readers in the United States. We assured her that if she read two or three of each type she would probably know what the rest were like. Her question aroused a sense of *déjà vu* because we had asked ourselves a similar question about the same books when they were originally printed in English. But along with the *déjà vu*, we experienced a degree of pleasure in seeing a pile of books that had made a

◆ This publicity photo was part of the press pack announcing *First Love from Silhouette*. According to the accompanying release, advertising expenditures would total $1,400,000.

round-trip from New York to Spain and had come home dressed in a new language and a new format. Perhaps big business will be able to do what librarians, teachers, councils, and associations have tried but failed at, which is to make the teenage book world truly international and cross-cultural.

Told from the girl's point of view, the romances most often feature girls 15, 16, or 17 years old with boyfriends who are slightly older. The target audience is supposedly girls between the ages of twelve and sixteen although some ten- and eleven-year-olds are also finding them. The typical setting is a small town or suburb. There is no explicit sex or profanity. As one editor told us, "If there are problems, they have to be normal ones—no drugs, no sex, no alcohol, no bad parents, etc."

The kinds of problems featured are ones that most girls dream of coping with. For example in Jill Ross Klevin's *That's My Girl*, ice skater Becky has to fight off getting ulcers while worrying about the upcoming Nationals, her chance at the Olympics. Her biggest worry is whether she will lose her boyfriend who feels ignored. Janet Quin-Harkin's *California Girl* has an almost identical plot except that Jennie is competing for the Olympics as a swimmer. In Rosemary Vernon's *The Popularity Plan*, Frannie is too shy to talk to boys but her friends draw up a plan in which she is assigned certain ways to relate to a boy each day. Sure enough, she is soon asked for so many dates she has to buy a wall calendar to keep from getting mixed up. But by the end of the story she is happy to "give it all up" and settle for Ronnie, the boy she really liked all along. When this book was chosen as a favorite by sample readers in the University of Iowa's Young Adult Poll, the adult researchers felt the need to add an apology to the effect that they were not the ones doing the choosing.

Women of all ages enjoy reading romances for the same reasons that people have always enjoyed either hearing or reading wish-fulfilling fantasies. The "Open Sesame" door to prosperity and the transformation of a cindermaid into a queen, a frog into a prince, and a Scrooge into a kindly old man are all examples of the same satisfying theme that is the key to the appeal of love-romances. In the teen romances an ugly duckling girl is transformed by the love of a boy into a swan. In her new role as swan she is not only popular and successful; she is happy.

Critics, of which there are many, worry that young girls take the books seriously, that they fail to recognize them as fantasy, and that they therefore will model their behavior and attitudes after those portrayed in the books. A sampling of quotations illustrates the flavor of concern:

> ◇ The real power of the Wildfire books is that they purport to depict the real lives and problems of U.S. teenagers. Playing on the insecurities and self-doubt which plague most teenaged girls, the Wildfire romances come just close enough to real life to be convincing to young readers. But implicit in these hygienic stories are the old, damaging and limiting stereotypes from which we've struggled so hard to free ourselves and our children: that the real world is white and middle-class; that motherhood is women's only work; that a man is the ultimate prize and a woman is incomplete without one; and that in the battle for that prize, the weapons are good looks and charm, intelligence is a liability, and the enemy is other women.[2]

> ◇ Absence is, in fact, at the heart of the criticism of these books. Third World people are absent, disabled people are absent, lesbians and gay men are absent, poor people are absent, elderly people are absent. . . . The First Love series from Silhouette clearly makes its claim that one way of life is morally superior to others. To allow that claim to go unchallenged is to give it a credence it does not deserve. As teachers, parents and librarians we have choices to make. We can validate, by our silence, the prejudicial implications and omissions endorsed by the First Love world, or we can encourage young people to learn to read critically, to become aware of underlying messages, and to appreciate the value of a pluralistic world that supports, rather than denies, diversity.[3]

> ◇ By taking popular culture seriously, we often forget how lightly it is received by the audience themselves, who use it quite knowingly for cheap thrills. The teenagers who read *My Guy* and *Blue Jeans* laugh at their stories even as they identify with them.
> And yet escapism is a serious business. The teen photo magazines, like all romances, operate on a level that goes deeper than common sense, in the realm of fantasy and expectation. There is an eternal paradox here. We read such romantic stories as an escape from reality and yet they form our ideals of what reality should be. Hence that frustration, that vague sense of failure and disappointment when a night out at the disco doesn't turn out the way it does in the magazines.[4]

◇The future of the teenage romance lines is very much an open question. Although enormous publishing investments are being made, they could peak, fade, and go the way of the Gothic and Sweet Savage adult genres of the seventies. If librarians purchase these books at all, it will be for the same reasons that they've bought Nancy Drew books—as literary loss leaders.[5]

Defenders of the romances most often focus on their popularity and the fact that they are recreational reading freely chosen by young girls who would most likely be watching TV. Vermont Royster, writing in the *Wall Street Journal*, compared the romances to the reading of books his mother considered trash—Tom Swift, the Rover Boys, Detective Nick Carter, and Wild Bill Hickok. He acknowledged that the plotting was banal and monotonous and that writers could probably turn them out wholesale, but at least, "The spelling is correct and they do manage mostly to abide by the rules of English grammar." He welcomes the books as an aid in helping a generation of television oriented kids acquire the habit of reading. Once they are hooked, "Call it an addiction if you will . . . young people can be led by good teachers to enlarge their reach."[6]

The idea that students "can be led by good teachers to enlarge their reach," is crucial to this line of reasoning. In relation to the birthday cake theory presented in Chapter 2, the question is whether the romances are the same kinds of books that young readers turn to at Level 3 when they are just beginning to lose themselves in a good story, or whether they perceive them as the kind they read at Level 4 when they are trying to find themselves and their acquaintances in good stories. Either way, teachers and librarians have the challenge of making sure that readers do not get stuck at one of these levels. The romances are so appealing that the danger of never going beyond them may be especially strong. For example, librarians and book sellers report that they see the same women coming in year after year for their weekly "fix" of romance novels. They do not automatically progress to Ernest Hemingway or even John Irving.

Going Beyond Formula Romances

Several factors contribute to the popularity of the paperback romances, and there may be some book promotional lessons in their success story which can be transferred to work with a larger body of books. For example, they are easily available. They are being marketed in shopping center bookstores in their own attractive display cases. Prices are less than the cost of a movie or about the same as that of a magazine. Many of them are purchased as a result of impulse buying. Readers literally stumble over the display racks which are usually near the fronts of bookstores and clearly labelled "Young Adult." Attention is grabbed by the appealing cover photos. As Pamela Pollack observed about the *Seventeen Magazine* models whose photos appear on the covers, "They are nineteen-year-olds who are a thirteen-year-old's ideal image of a sixteen-year-old."[7]

And in general the romances have the same qualities that publishers have developed for high interest/low vocabulary books. They are short books divided into short chapters. They have quick beginnings, more action than description, considerable use of dialogue, a straightforward point of view, and a reading level not much above fifth grade. And perhaps most important of all, the books are clearly labelled so that readers know what they will be getting into. As shown by the popularity of movie sequels, television serials and reruns, and continuing columns in newspapers, although viewers and readers do not want to see or read the exact same thing over and over again they are nevertheless comforted by knowing that a particular piece is going to be very similar to something they have previously enjoyed.

If we want to help young readers go beyond superficial romances, we must approach the task cautiously. Young readers are as sensitive as anyone else to hints about a lack of taste and refinement. So rather than making fun of romances, it is better to approach the matter from a positive angle offering romance buffs a wide variety of reading materials including books that treat boy/girl relationships but offer a little something in addition as do Virginia Hamilton's *A Little Love* and Myron Levoy's *Three Friends*.

The something extra may be an especially interesting historical setting as in Sarah Patterson's *The Distant Summer* where World War II threatens to keep the young lovers apart. Kathie is the sixteen-year-old daughter of an English rector, and Johnny is an American pilot who wanders into her father's church to play the organ. The surprise ending is that their love survives through incredible odds even as Johnny flies daily bombing raids, and then through the next thirty years of what is apparently quite ordinary living. The characterization is excellent, but the bonus for readers is that they can vicariously live not just the love story but also a part of World War II that they probably have never thought about.

A different look at the same war is provided in Irving Korschunow's moving *A Night in Distant Motion*, translated from the German by Leigh Hafrey. It is the story of 17-year-old Regine who in the summer of 1944 briefly loved a Polish boy named Jan. In the eyes of the Gestapo, this was an act of treason and Regine must hide in the Henning family's attic where she has many months in which to ponder her "crime." As Isabel Soffer said in a *School Library Journal* review:

> ◇ At the end of this sad tale Regine realizes that one rebuilds, one searches for joy because there is life still. Her growth from despair to a quiet reaffirmation of life elevates this work to its place of dignity.[8]

Interesting historical details will not save a weak story, but they will add interest to a strong one as with Jessamyn West's *The Massacre at Fall Creek*. It illustrates how a love story that is integrated into a larger story can be better because of the dual plot. Readers get to know the young couple through the part they play in the first American court case (Fall Creek, Indiana, 1824) in which white men were tried, convicted, and executed for killing Indians.

Mildred Lee's *The People Therein* also has a frontier, or pioneer, setting. But what stays in the mind after reading the book is not the setting as much as the characterization of the physically lame Lanthy and her lover, a travelling botanist/scholar who comes to the backwoods from Boston in hopes of curing his own kind of lameness. Other recommended love stories with interesting historical settings are Mollie Hunter's *Hold On to Love*, the romantic sequel to *A Sound of Chariots*, and Ilse Koehn's *Tilla*, which is set in postwar Germany.

For the writer of a love story, there is probably no talent more important than the ability to create believable characters. If readers do not feel that they know the boy and girl or the man and woman as individuals, then they can't identify with them and consequently won't care whether they make it or not. It's the effective characterization that makes the following books stand out in readers' memories: Joyce Carol Thomas' *Bright Shadow*, Ursula K. Le Guin's *Very Far Away from Anywhere Else*, James Baldwin's *If Beale Street Could Talk*, Katie Letcher Lyle's *Fair Day and Another Step Begun*, and Katherine Paterson's *Rebels of the Heavenly Kingdom*.

Included in "the something extra" that readers might get from love stories are glimpses into complex social issues. M. E. Kerr does a good job of illustrating social class differences in both *Gentlehands* and *I'll Love You When You're More Like Me*. Also in *Gentlehands* she touches on the nature of evil and the fact that there are more shades of gray than either black or white.

Robert Cormier always leaves his readers with lots to think about. The gentle love story that's a subplot in *The Bumblebee Flies Anyway* serves as a balance to the more ominous subject of the book which is medical experimentation on young patients who are terminally ill.

Katie Letcher Lyle's *Dark But Full of Diamonds* explores a whole range of emotions experienced by 16-year-old Scott Dabney. Four years after his mother's death, he is still lonely and bitter. He develops a crush on his high school drama teacher but then his father begins taking her out, and this makes Scott feel even more betrayed. A similar subplot of father/son competition runs through Richard Peck's *Father Figure*.

Who Reads the Romances and Why

It is impossible to evaluate the love-romance without taking into consideration the purpose for which someone chooses to read a particular title. If it is as escape fantasy, then the best book is the one with the happiest ending and the most idealized characters. The titles of current formula romances reveal their wish-fulfilling nature, for example, *Ten Boy Summer*, *Teach Me to Love*, *Love Match*, *That's My Girl*, and *Portrait of Love*. In such books as these there are several time-honored conventions which are quite unrealistic. For example, when a romance flounders, there is always another boy, or the promise of another boy, waiting nearby as was Danny in Irene Hunt's *Up a Road Slowly*. Julie, the protagonist, had already rejected him. Nevertheless he hung around doggedly, and sure enough, Julie comes to understand what the reader knew all along. The second boy is far superior to the first.

Another unrealistic convention is that, for some unexplained reason, a popular boy will suddenly take a look at a shy and previously unnoticed girl and fall in love with her. The impression given is that this happens at least once to everyone, and that, when it happens, the couple will live happily ever after.

Perhaps the most unrealistic convention of all is the way in which the writers tend to gloss over the part that sex plays in such relationships. Ironically it's love at first sight, which must imply a physical attraction, that is, a sexual attraction, yet the boys are portrayed as being almost platonically interested in the girl's thoughts and feelings. As Rainbow Jordan, the protagonist in Alice Childress' book of the same name complained:

> ◇ *True* love is mostly featured in fairy tales. Sleepin Beauty put off sex for a hundred years. When a prince finally did find her . . . he kiss her *gently*, then they gallop off on a pretty horse so they could enjoy the happy-ever-after. They never mentioned sex.

Another unrealistic convention is for authors to treat love as if it is the brass ring on the merry-go-round of life—something guaranteed to bring success and happiness to whoever is lucky enough to grab it. For example, when Patty Campbell reviewed four books about disturbed teenagers, Frank Bonham's *Gimme an H, Gimme an E, Gimme an L, Gimme a P*, Anne Snyder's *Goodbye, Paper Doll*, Mary Alexander Walker's *Maggot*, and Kin Platt's *Flames Going Out*, she concluded that the salvation of the female characters came "through the transforming effect of admitting their love, a not-unfamiliar literary theme but an unfortunate example for young women just learning to stand on their own feet. The message is clear: nutty girls should look around for a stalwart boy to save them."[9]

The love-as-a-cure-all kind of wish fulfillment runs through the pages of much young adult fiction. An extreme example is Crescent Dragonwagon's and Paul Zindel's *To Take a Dare* in which a sixteen-year-old runaway gets her own elegant guest house to live in, becomes the assistant manager of a resort kitchen at a salary of $1,000 a month, is paid expenses plus $600 a month to go to vocational school in the off-season, and is promised the full manager's job the next summer at $1,500 a month. This is all tied in with the fact that nineteen-year-old folksinger/psychology student Luke Beauford falls in love with her. He thinks she's twenty-four.

A Touch of Realism

For those who want to read romances to find out what having a boy- or girlfriend is really like, the better books are going to be the ones with a touch of realism—the ones that present both the happy and the sad and even the plain old boring parts of love and commitment. Barbara Robinson tried to do this for young teens in *Temporary Times, Temporary Places*. It's the dual story of Janet whose summer crush is foiled by a case of poison ivy and Janet's Aunt May who comes home to recover from a broken heart. Robinson did a good job of presenting revealing details showing how relationships change but how what they have meant to individuals remains a part of their total life experience.

Norma Fox Mazer's *Up in Seth's Room* explores the tremendous ambiguity that fifteen-year-old Finn feels about the should-we/shouldn't-we-have-sex conflict that creates tension between her and her nineteen-year-old boyfriend. In Mazer's *Someone to Love*, seventeen-year-old college sophomore Nina falls in love with a school drop-out. They live together for seven months before Nina realizes that emotionally the two are far apart and she moves out.

We could go on and list other books here, but the result would be to circle around into the same books that have already been discussed under the category of realistic problem novels.

◈ ROMANCES FOR OR ABOUT BOYS

In 1977, Robert Unsworth writing in *School Library Journal* decried the dearth of books giving an unbiased treatment to the part that male sexuality plays in the growing-up process of all boys. As an example, he quoted Alan Bennett's statement in M. E. Kerr's *If I Love You, Am I Trapped Forever?* "I'm not going to describe in detail the very personal things that take place between me and Leah. I'm not writing this book for a bunch of voyeurs." In Unsworth's view:

> ◇ It is fear of censorship, not voyeurism, which plagues too many young adult novels to a degree where the image of the male in the juvenile novel is woefully incomplete. Leaving sex out of a novel that purports to examine male maturation and growth is like writing a cookbook without mentioning food.[10]

He went on to say that "We do not need explicit sex in teenage fiction any more than we need the head-in-the-sand approach to sexuality that seems to be the current norm. There is a middle ground." Books he commended for including at least some honest mention of male sexual development were Judy Blume's *Then Again, Maybe I Won't*, Robert Cormier's *The Chocolate War*, Mildred Lee's *Fog*, and Don Moser's *A Heart to the Hawks*.

Today Unsworth's list could be much longer because of the development of a new type of "boys' book" far different from the sports, adventure, and mystery stories traditionally thought of as "boys' books." Hazel Rochman described such books as "'domestic' novels about boys in which heroes stay home and struggle with their feelings and their conscience rather than with tumultuous external events." Many such books are love stories, and as Rochman observed:

> ◇ The theme of so many girls' books—finding that you love the boy next door after all—has a new vitality from the male perspective, as in [Harry] Mazer's *I Love You, Stupid!* Sex is treated with honesty: in [Chris] Crutcher's *Running Loose*, after a long romantic buildup in which the couple drive and then ski to an isolated cabin for a weekend of lovemaking, the jock hero finds that he cannot perform. In [Richard] Peck's *Father Figure* and [Katie Letcher] Lyle's *Dark But Full of Diamonds*, the love for an older woman, in rivalry with the boy's own

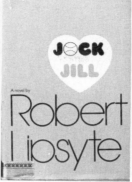

◆ A new kind of romance is what Hazel Rochman describes as "'domestic' novels about boys in which heroes stay home and struggle with their feelings and their consciences rather than with tumultuous external events."

father is movingly handled. And in YA novels about girls in love, romantic stereotypes of the attractive male are also being undercut (even while "Sweet Dreams" romances flourish): in *The Course of True Love Never Did Run Smooth*, [Marilyn] Singer's heroine finds strong and sexy a boy who is short, funny, and vulnerable.[11]

The most obvious difference between these "boy" books and the larger body of love stories written from a girl's point of view is that their authors, who are mostly males, tend to put less emphasis on courtship and romance and more on sexuality. Rather than relying on the discreet fadeouts of the "squeaky clean" romances, they allow their readers to remain for the grand finale. For the most part, the descriptions are neither pornographic nor lovingly romantic, but in such books as Robert Lipsyte's *Jock and Jill*, Todd Strasser's *Workin' for Peanuts*, Chris Crutcher's *Running Loose*, Robert Lehrman's *Juggling*, Terry Davis' *Vision Quest*, and Thomas Rogers' *At the Shores* there is little doubt about the abundance of sexual feelings that the characters experience.

◈ BOOKS OF FRIENDSHIP

As an antidote to the current emphasis on either romance or sexuality, some adult critics suggest offering books where boys and girls are as much friends as lovers. Friendship stories include significant boy/girl relationships, but they differ from the more traditional romances in several ways. First, there is something more to the story than the relationship, which despite its

THE PEOPLE BEHIND THE BOOKS

TODD STRASSER, Author

Angel Dust Blues
Rock 'n' Roll Nights
Turn It Up!
Workin' for Peanuts

I am particularly interested in writing books for teenaged boys. By that I mean contemporary fiction and not sci fi or war stories. There are some very good writers writing for boys, but generally I'd say that most YA literature for the teenaged male is still in the Dark Ages. Many writers seem to have ignored the idea that a teenaged boy can be just as sensitive, just as mixed-up, just as curious as a teenaged girl. Well, I think he can (at least I know I was).

I also think that books for teenagers today have to be very entertaining. We are dealing with kids who have been fed entertainment by the shovel-full, whether it comes from television, video games, or whatever the next fad will be. Books for teenagers have to compete or they simply will not get read. So when I write about an important subject like drug abuse or disease, I try to write a compelling story with humor and romance as well as serious matters. ◆

emotional importance is only part of a bigger story. Second, the story is not told exclusively from the girl's point of view. As a ploy to attract male readers, since authors already feel confident that girls will read love stories, the narrator may be the boy, or there may be a mix with alternate chapters coming from the boy and the girl as in Paul Zindel's *The Pigman* and M. E. Kerr's *I'll Love You When You're More Like Me*. A third difference is that there is no indication of either partner exploiting or manipulating the other as often happens in exaggerated romances or in pornographic or sex-oriented stories. In the friendship stories that appeal to both sexes, no one is out to "make a catch." Instead the couple works together to solve some kind of mutual problem or to achieve a goal of some sort.

An example is Ronald Kidd's funny but compelling mystery *Sizzle and Splat*. It is the story of the friendship of Prudence Szyznowski and Arthur Hadley Reavis Pauling III, who fortunately go by the shorter nicknames of Sizzle and Splat. They are true opposites who are accustomed to combining their musical talents for the sake of a youth orchestra, but then they find that they also have to learn to combine their unique intellectual talents to solve a mystery. Someone does not want them to play the benefit performance of an original concerto created for them by a famous composer prior to his death from cancer. There's a happy, but surprising, ending.

Other good books of the friendship type include: Lawrence Yep's *Sea Glass*, Katherine Paterson's *Bridge to Terabithia*, Myron Levoy's *Alan and Naomi*, and Jan Slepian's *The Alfred Summer*.

Both the adventure-romance and the love-romance are psychologically very satisfying. More than any other genre, they are especially well matched to the particular stage of life that is young adulthood. The stories are optimistic and wish fulfilling. Their basic pattern resembles the real-life activities of young people who are moving from childhood into adulthood. Romances incorporate the successful completion of a quest in which the protagonist is elevated in status. But usually more important than the respect earned from others is the feeling of self-respect and self-confidence that the young hero gains in the course of the story. All of these things work together to ensure that the books treated in this chapter will be among the most popular in the young adult section of any library.

◆ ACTIVITIES ◆

1. Read a modern adventure-romance and see how many of the following elements from traditional romances that you can find: (a) a worthy young hero; (b) a journey (literal or symbolic); (c) a villain; (d) physical danger; (e) a sacrifice symbolized by some physical damage to the protagonist's body or to something valued by the protagonist; (f) an older, wiser person who lends assistance; (g) an idyllic setting near the end of the story; (h) a sudden insight or realization that comes in this idyllic setting; (i) an accomplishment that gives the protagonist new status with both adults and peers.

2. Read one of the formula love-romances published for teenagers. In an attempt to empathize with young readers, engage in a "willing suspension of disbelief" and note the incidents of wish fulfillment that are incorporated in the story. As a class, discuss whether or not adults should try to lead young readers to recognize the unrealistic wish fulfillment nature of these stories. Are these stories just something that young teens will outgrow? Is it worth running the risk of insulting readers' taste and therefore destroying a desirable rapport? And is it fair to attack these elements in romance novels when they appear daily in television commercials, advertisements, movies, songs, and human interest newspaper stories? You might compare the wish fulfillment seen in romances to that seen in the headlines of tabloid newspapers. What does this show about human nature?

3. Read one of the friendship books or one of the boy-oriented stories and write a one-page paper in which you show how the book differs from the more common love-romances written to be read mainly by girls.

◆ NOTES ◆

[1]Glenna Davis Sloan, *The Child as Critic* (New York: Teachers College Press, 1975), p. 33.

[2]Brett Harvey, "Wildfire: Tame but Deadly," *Interracial Books for Children Bulletin* 12:4 and 5 (1981): 10.

[3]Sharon Wigutoff, "First Love: Morality Tales Thinly Veiled," *Interracial Books for Children Bulletin* 12:4 and 5 (1981): 17.

[4]Mary Harron, "Oh Boy! My Guy," (London) *Times Educational Supplement*, July 1, 1983, p. 22.

[5]Pamela D. Pollack, "The Business of Popularity: The Surge of Teenage Paperbacks," *School Library Journal* 28 (November 1981): 28.

[6]Vermont Royster, "Thinking Things Over: The Reading Addiction," *Wall Street Journal*, June 24, 1981, p. 30.

[7]Pollack, p. 28.

[8]Isabel Soffer, *School Library Journal* 30 (December 1983): 75.

[9]Patty Campbell, "The Young Adult Perplex," *Wilson Library Bulletin* 55 (February 1981): 454–55.

[10]Robert Unsworth, "Holden Caulfield, Where Are You?" *School Library Journal* 23 (January 1977): 40–41.

[11]Hazel Rochman, "Bringing Boys' Books Home," *School Library Journal* 29 (August 1983): 26–27.

◆ TITLES MENTIONED IN CHAPTER 4 ◆

For information on the availability of paperback editions of these titles, please consult the most recent edition of *Paperbound Books in Print*, published annually by R. R. Bowker Company.

Adventure/Accomplishment Romances

Alexander, Lloyd. *Westmark*. Dutton, 1981.

Blume, Judy. *Tiger Eyes*. Bradbury, 1981.

Crompton, Anne Eliot. *The Sorcerer*. Second Chance, 1982.

Degens, T. *Transport 7-41-R*. Viking, 1974.

Dickinson, Peter. *Tulku*. E. P. Dutton, 1979.

George, Jean. *Julie of the Wolves*. Harper & Row, 1972.

Green, Hannah. *I Never Promised You a Rose Garden*. Holt, Rinehart and Winston, 1964.

Guest, Judith. *Ordinary People*. Viking, 1975.

Hamilton, Virginia. *M. C. Higgins, the Great*. Macmillan, 1974.

Holland, Isabelle. *Heads You Win, Tails I Lose*. Lippincott, 1973.

———. *Man Without a Face*. Lippincott, 1972.

Hunt, Irene. *Across Five Aprils*. Follett, 1964.

———. *Up a Road Slowly*. Follett, 1966.

Lasky, Kathryn. *Beyond the Divide*. Macmillan, 1983.

Lee, Mildred. *The Skating Rink*. Houghton Mifflin, 1969.

L'Engle, Madeleine. *A Wrinkle in Time*. Farrar, Straus & Giroux, 1962.

Lipsyte, Robert. *One Fat Summer*. Harper & Row, 1977.

Mazer, Harry. *The Island Keeper*. Delacorte, 1981.

———. *The Last Mission*. Delacorte, 1979.

McKinley, Robin. *The Blue Sword*. Greenwillow, 1982.

Salinger, J. D. *The Catcher in the Rye*. Little, Brown, 1951.

Vinge, Joan. *Psion*. Delacorte, 1982.

Voigt, Cynthia. *Homecoming*. Atheneum, 1981.

Yolen, Jane. *Dragon's Blood*. Delacorte, 1982.

———. *Heart's Blood*. Delacorte, 1984.

Love-Romances

Baldwin, James. *If Beale Street Could Talk*. Doubleday, 1974.

Blume, Judy. *Then Again, Maybe I Won't*. Bradbury, 1971.

Bonham, Frank. *Gimme an H, Gimme an E, Gimme an L, Gimme a P*. Scribner's, 1980.

Cormier, Robert. *The Chocolate War*. Pantheon, 1974.

———. *The Bumblebee Flies Anyway*. Pantheon, 1983.

Crutcher, Chris. *Running Loose*. Greenwillow, 1983.

Davis, Terry. *Vision Quest*. Viking, 1979.

Dragonwagon, Crescent and Paul Zindel. *To Take a Dare*. Harper & Row, 1982.

Hamilton, Virginia. *A Little Love*. Philomel, 1984.

Hunt, Irene. *Up a Road Slowly*. Follett, 1966.

Hunter, Mollie. *Hold On to Love*. Harper & Row, 1984.

————. *A Sound of Chariots*. Harper & Row, 1982.

Kerr, M. E. *Gentlehands*. Harper & Row, 1978.

————. *If I Love You, Am I Trapped Forever?* Harper & Row, 1973.

————. *I'll Love You When You're More Like Me*. Harper & Row, 1977.

Kidd, Ronald. *Sizzle and Splat*. Lodestar, 1983.

Koehn, Ilse. *Tilla*. Greenwillow, 1981.

Klevin, Jill Ross. *That's My Girl*. Scholastic, 1981.

Korschunow, Irina. *A Night in Distant Motion*. Godine, 1983.

Lee, Mildred. *Fog*. Houghton Mifflin, 1972.

————. *The People Therein*. Houghton Mifflin, 1980.

Le Guin, Ursula K. *Very Far Away from Anywhere Else*. Atheneum, 1976.

Lehrman, Robert. *Juggling*. Harper & Row, 1982.

Levoy, Myron. *Alan and Naomi*. Harper & Row, 1977.

————. *Three Friends*. Harper & Row, 1984.

Lipsyte, Robert. *Jock and Jill*. Harper & Row, 1982.

Lyle, Katie Letcher. *Dark But Full of Diamonds*. Putnam's, 1981.

————. *Fair Day and Another Step Begun*. Lippincott, 1974.

Mazer, Harry. *I Love You, Stupid!* Harper & Row, 1981.

Mazer, Norma Fox. *Someone to Love*. Delacorte, 1983.

————. *Up in Seth's Room*. Delacorte, 1979.

Moser, Don. *A Heart to the Hawks*. Atheneum, 1975.

Paterson, Katherine. *Bridge to Terabithia*. Harper & Row, 1977.

————. *Rebels of the Heavenly Kingdom*. Lodestar, 1983.

Patterson, Sarah. *The Distant Summer*. Archway, 1977.

Peck, Richard. *Father Figure*. Viking, 1978.

Platt, Kin. *Flames Going Out*. Methuen, 1980.

Quin-Harkin, Janet. *California Girl*. Bantam, 1981.

Robinson, Barbara. *Temporary Times, Temporary Places*. Harper & Row, 1982.

Rogers, Thomas. *At the Shores*. Simon & Schuster, 1980.

Singer, Marilyn. *The Course of True Love Never Did Run Smooth*. Harper & Row, 1983.

Slepian, Jan. *The Alfred Summer*. Macmillan, 1980.

Snyder, Anne. *Goodbye, Paper Doll*. New American Library, 1980.

Strasser, Todd. *Angel Dust Blues*. Putnam's, 1979.

————. *Rock 'n' Roll Nights*. Delacorte, 1982.

————. *Turn It Up!* Delacorte, 1984.

————. *Workin' for Peanuts*. Delacorte, 1983.

Thomas, Joyce Carol. *Bright Shadow*. Avon, 1983.

Vernon, Rosemary. *The Popularity Plan*. Bantam, 1981.

Walker, Mary Alexander. *Maggot*. Atheneum, 1980.

West, Jessamyn. *The Massacre at Fall Creek*. Harcourt Brace Jovanovich, 1975.

Yep, Lawrence. *Sea Glass*. Harper & Row, 1979.

Zindel, Paul. *The Pigman*. Harper & Row, 1968.

EXCITEMENT AND SUSPENSE

OF SUDDEN SHADOWS

Something within us does not love our quiet lives. Something within us demands vicarious thrills, suspense, danger, the unknown. When we are young, we love to frighten others with stories of bogeymen and murderers and spooks, anything to make friends' blood chill and hands sweat. Tales of horror and danger and mystery allow us the delicious luxury of knowing fear without living it.

As we grow older, our need for vicarious danger hardly lessens though we pretend that it becomes more sophisticated. Instead of simple tales, we read the latest thriller by Stephen King to learn again the eternal fear of the unknown. We read a historical novel by Rosemary Sutcliff to learn the dangers of living in Roman Britain. We read a new mystery by P. D. James to remind us that in the midst of life there is death.

We go to amusement parks, not to sit sedately on a merry-go-round but to head for the latest thrill-a-minute, guaranteed-to-cause-a-heart-attack ride. We go to car races knowing that danger and death are always present. We stay up till the wee hours to watch a favorite old horror film and feel cheated if nothing terrifies us. We watch reruns of old movies like Charles Laughton's *The Night of the Hunter* (1955), Jules Dassin's *Topkapi,* and almost anything by the master of suspense, Alfred Hitchcock, *The Thirty-Nine Steps* (1935), *The Lady Vanishes* (1938), *Strangers on a Train* (1951), or *North by Northwest* (1959). And if we needed proof that contemporary Americans love to feel danger, the popularity of *Halloween* (1978) and its ilk and that finest of modern pure adventure films, *Raiders of the Lost Ark* (1981), should dispel doubts.

Why are we so eager to be in the midst of danger? Why do we need to feel fear? Perhaps it is because our lives are so mundane and uneventful and dull that vicarious danger is all we will ever know. Perhaps we fear death so much that we need to tempt and cheat it for the moment. Certainly, every culture has its folktales and stories well-calculated to make goosebumps rise and bad children behave—tales embodying terror, mystery, death, the unknown, the impossible, the deadly—in short, all that we fear. Perhaps adventure stories allow us a catharsis, if not an Aristotelian purging of emotions, at least a purging of primeval fears, of monsters and enemies we might eons ago have faced in bloody battle. Denied those outlets today, we gladly pay others to provide them for our reading and viewing pleasure.

In tales of adventure and stories from the past, we can revel in times and places when evil was evil, good was good, and each was easily distinguishable. Such stories allow us to believe that humanity will not merely survive but that our courage makes us worthy of surviving.

◈ ADVENTURE STORIES

"Once upon a time" are magic words. Stated directly or implied, they open every adventure tale and suggest action and excitement to follow. We may care about the people, but the action and violence are all-important. And the greatest of these is implied violence, things we fear may happen. Pace and tempo force action to move faster and faster and speed us into the tale.

The most common of all stories of pure adventure, largely devoid of characterization, pits one human against another. Richard Connell's "The Most Dangerous Game," perhaps *the* classic adventure short story, reduces the cast of characters to two people, the big game hunter Sanger Rainsford and General Zaroff, in a simple setting, an apparently deserted island with an evil reputation. Before he is accidentally cast ashore on the island, Rainsford and a friend talk about the nature of hunting and debate whether an animal can feel fear and impending death. Rainsford says, "Be a realist. The world is made up of two classes—the hunter and the huntee," words he will soon regret. When he meets the apparently highly civilized Zaroff, Rainsford soon learns that Zaroff is a hunter gone sour and mad through lack of game worth hunting, and Zaroff lives "for danger." Once Zaroff implies that only one animal—a human—is worth hunting, few readers could stop reading.

The better adventure stories demand more than mere excitement and action. Writers must provide believable characters, at the very least a likable and imperfect (and young) protagonist and a wily and dangerous antagonist (or villain). But because we are primarily interested in action, we are likely to be irritated by the intrusion of long descriptive or meditative passages. Writers must reveal characterization through the plot—what could happen, what has happened, what might happen, and how do all these tie together?

We want surprises and turns of the screw. Heroes become entrapped, and the way to safety lies only through greater jeopardy. Of the three basic conflicts, adventure tales will usually center on person against person, though person against nature and person against self will often become important as the tale unfolds and the protagonist faces frustration and possible failure.

The most significant literary device found in adventure stories is verisimilitude. With so much emphasis on danger, writers must provide realistic details galore to reassure us, despite our inner misgivings, that the tale is possible. We want to believe that the hero's frustrations and the cliffhanging episodes really could have happened. Without that, the story is a cheat, and that we cannot tolerate, no matter how we try.

A love interest is possible but unlikely. Perhaps there is a love left behind, but none during the tribulations. A girl and boy may flee together, and sex is possible—some writers would have us believe that sex is inevitable—but only as a momentary diversion.

Robb White's *Deathwatch* epitomizes the elements of adventure novels—person versus person, person versus nature, person versus self, conflicts, tension, thrills, chills, a hero frustrated at every turn by an inventive, devious, and cruel villain.

The first paragraph forces us into the action and introduces the two actors:

> ◇ "There he is!" Madec whispered. "Keep still!"
> There had been a movement up on the ridge of the mountain. For a moment something had appeared between the two rock outcrops.
> "I didn't see any horns," Ben said.
> "Keep quiet!" Madec whispered fiercely.

We know from those few words that *Deathwatch* has something to do with hunting, though we have no reason yet to believe that hunting will become an ominous metaphor. We recognize that the name Madec has a harsh sound and that it seems vaguely related to the word *mad*, again without recognizing how prescient we are. Within the next few pages, we learn how carefully White has placed the clues before us. Ben crouches with his little .22 Hornet and watches Madec with his "beautifully made .358 Magnum Mauser action on a Winchester 70 stock with enough power to knock down an elephant—or turn a sleeping Gila monster into a splatter" and remembers that Madec had been willing to shoot anything that moved.

> ◇ Madec huddled over his gun. There was an intensity in his eyes far beyond that of just hunting a sheep. It was the look of murder.

And murder is there. Before long, Madec takes a shot at a bighorn sheep, which turns out to be an old desert prospector—now quite dead—and he asks Ben to quash the incident and forget it ever happened. Ben refuses, and the book is off and running. So is Ben, running for his life, without gun, water, or food, amid hostile desert mountains and sand and a killing sun.

Madec personifies the maddened but crafty villain, able to read Ben's mind and forestall his attempts to get clothes or weapons or water. We are almost certain Ben will win but we wonder, for Madec is a worthy opponent. And at each of Madec's devious turns to stop Ben from escape, we doubt that sanity and the right will win, just as we should in a good adventure novel. Ben changes from a calm and rational young man to a frightened, desperate animal and then to a cold and dangerous person who must think as Madec thinks to win out over the villain. Madec begins with all the power on his side—guns, water, food, and wealth. Given reality, we know that Madec must win, but given our sense of rightness and justice, he cannot be allowed to win. Ben has little interest in right or wrong after the first few pages. His interest is more elemental and believable, simple survival until he can escape.

Three recent adventure stories emphasizing person versus person should prove popular with young adults. P. J. Petersen's *Nobody Else Can Walk It for You* concerns a group of backpackers mercilessly harassed by three motorcycle hoods and fighting their way back to safety. In Michael French's *Pursuit*, a sadistic leader on a hiking trip deliberately causes the death of a young boy, and the dead boy's brother goes for help. Most intriguing of the three, yet the most improbable, is Julian F. Thompson's *The Grounding of Group 6*. A group of admittedly misfit teenagers, hated by their parents who have paid to have them killed, survive against heavy odds in a rough forest. Unlikely or not, Thompson's novel succeeds, partly because we begin to care about the young people and their developing skills at survival, partly because the book is often quite intentionally funny.

Many adventure stories focus on person versus nature. Harry Mazer's *Snow Bound* shows us two young people caught in a blizzard who survive despite cold, wild dogs, and no food. How they change makes a fine story despite poor characterization.

Far better is Mazer's *The Island Keeper*. Cleo Murphy is an overweight sixteen-year-old who wilfully decides to run away from her unhappy home and return to her father's isolated island in Canada. She discovers that the cabin she had assumed would shelter her has burned down, and when the lovely weather turns miserable, Cleo learns that she must find shelter and she must learn to kill if she is to survive:

> ◇ "What do I do now?" she cried out. Then she listened, as if someone would answer. She heard the wind and water—nothing else. The island didn't care. It wouldn't cheer if she struggled. It wouldn't cry if she lost. The island was indifferent to her tears and cries. It had always been indifferent to her, to her self-pity and self-loathing, to the masks and disguises she hid behind; indifferent, too, to her conceit that she was herself at last, one with nature. All vanity, foolishness, stupidity. She was alone, isolated, and forgotten, with no expectations except the one nature forced on her.

She knows that the doe she had so admired must die if she is to live. And she learns how to live.

> ◇ The deer was standing directly over the snare. Cleo leaned forward. The sapling whipped into the air. The deer recoiled, one of its hind legs caught by the rope. Cleo darted forward. The deer leaped up. A hoof caught Cleo in the shoulder as she drove the knife into its body. The animal cried out. She drove the knife in again. The deer grunted, sighed quietly, died. Cleo looked around.

She was acutely aware of every single thing, of the silence, of her aloneness. The two other deer had disappeared. She shuddered. A black smear spread across the velvet fur.

Other fine survival stories are Elizabeth George Speare's *The Sign of the Beaver* with twelve-year-old Matt forced to take care of the family cabin in the late 1760s while his father goes off to get the rest of the family, and Dennis J. Reader's *Coming Back Alive* with two emotionally hurt young adults seeking to find themselves and learn to survive in the Trinity Mountains of northern California. A lovely and moving account of a young sailor stranded on an Antarctic island in 1818 can be found in Marie Herbert's *Winter of the White Seal*.

Piers Paul Read's *Alive: The Story of the Andes Survivors* has become something of a modern classic. The story of sixteen athletes who survived a plane crash in the Andes raises questions about our moral right to do what must be done to survive that continue to puzzle and intrigue young people. A similar, if simpler story, is Peter Gzowski's *The Sacrament: A True Story of Survival* in which these moral issues are raised about two young people who survive a plane crash that kills the pilot of the plane.

A few adventure stories focus on initiation rites. Peter Dickinson's *Tulku* is filled with the adventures of a young survivor of the Boxer Rebellion in China picked up by the worldly-wise Mrs. Jones. The sensory details so well handled by Dickinson and the initiations of young boys are also found in his other powerful books, among them *The Seventh Raven* and *Annerton Pit*. Though the later novels of Bruce Clements have been disappointing, his early books, notably the *Face of Abraham Candle* and *I Tell a Lie Every So Often*, are adventure-packed, and the portraits of young people in search of themselves and a better life are rewarding. And D. R. Sherman's *The Lion's Paw* is a fine adventure tale mixed with initiation rites mixed with problems of modern-day Africa.

Terrorism is very much a part of our modern world. It is hardly surprising that the theme has been used in several adventure stories. John Godey's (real name, Morton Freedgood) *The Taking of Pelham One Two Three*, with its story of five hijackers capturing a New York City subway train and holding it for ransom, continues to be popular reading. Libyan terrorists plant a thermonuclear bomb in New York City in Larry Collins and Dominique Lapierre's *The Fifth Horseman*. Proof that New York City is not the sole seat of all terrorism, Ambrose Clancy's *Blind Plot* shows us the chilling side of the Irish Republican Army, and Robert Littell's *The Amateur* pictures a man driven to revenge when his fiancée is executed by terrorists.

Far more popular are the many spy thrillers. John Buchan's *The Thirty-Nine Steps* and *Greenmantle*, both in 1915, and Geoffrey Household's *Rogue Male* in 1939 established the ground rules of international intrigue and one good man determined to stop the forces of evil. Eric Ambler's many thrillers, notably *A Coffin for Dimitrios* and *The Light of Day* (filmed as *Topkapi*) and Helen MacInnes' delightful books, especially *Above Suspicion, Assignment in Brittany, The Salzburg Connection,* and the more recent *The Hidden Target* continued the genre and maintained its popularity.

Ian Fleming's Number 007 has become for many readers the prototype of the modern spy, and films made from Fleming's books have done much to perpetuate the myth. More realistic, if slower moving—sometimes to the point of hardly moving at all—are the thrillers of John Le Carré (real name, David John Moore Cornwell). The world of George Smiley, who binds a number of the books together, is hardly a happy or settled one, but it is a world in which people rarely are what they appear to be, and betrayal is a fact of life. *Tinker, Tailor, Soldier, Spy* focuses on George Smiley, retired agent, who is asked to return to the Circus, the code word for the British Intelligence Agency, to seek out the mole—an enemy agent—who has infiltrated the Agency. *The Honorable Schoolboy* takes Smiley to Hong Kong to undo the work of Karla, the master Russian agent, and *Smiley's People* takes Smiley to Switzerland and Paris and ultimately to Berlin to a final meeting with Karla. The lonely, personally unfulfilled life of the spy is, perhaps, best illustrated by Le Carré in his earlier novel, *The Spy Who Came In from the Cold*, but his more recent *The Little Drummer Girl* has much to recommend it.

Other fine spy thrillers include Jack Higgins' (real name, Harry Patterson) *Touch the Devil* in which British agents must kill a psychopathic assassin; Gerald Seymour's *Archangel* in which a retired British businessman is recruited for a mission that fails; and Gerald Green's *Karpov's Brain* in which a brilliant KGB agent begins to suffer epileptic seizures. Anyone curious about more amusing spy thrillers should try William F. Buckley's *Who's on First* or *The Story of Henri Tod* with master spy (and master of almost everything else) Blackford Oakes doing all the derring-do that any reader could ask for. A delightful spoof on the genre is Scott C. S. Stone's *Spies*—the American agent is equipped with a cyanide pen, a briefcase that easily becomes a rifle, bifocals that become binoculars, luggage that becomes a raft, and more.

David Morrell's *Blood Oath* is not precisely a spy story, but it is certainly a thriller. Peter Houston visits France to see his father's grave in a World War II memorial cemetery, and that simple visit turns into a nightmare as he learns that his father's body is missing, his wife murdered, and an international band of killers is determined to eliminate him.

Mountains have figured in a number of adventure stories, real and fictional. The abiding fascination with mountains has been part of our lives for centuries, and William Blake's lines from "Gnomic Verses" aptly describes their appeal:

> ◇ Great things are done when men and mountains meet;
> This is not done by jostling in the street.

True accounts of mountain climbing differ slightly from the usual person versus nature story. A person goes forth to seek adventure, to challenge nature, and to find himself or herself. Few acts of courage (or foolhardiness) appeal more to young adults. Why does the climber go on against snow, ice, rocks, cold, uncertainty, and loneliness? The classic answer, "Because it's there," is enough for most climbers, though they might add, somewhat self-consciously, "Because I am there, too, the real me."

◆ **TABLE 5.1   Suggestions for Evaluating Adventure Stories**

A good adventure story has most of the positive qualities generally associated with good fiction. In addition it usually has:	A poor adventure story may have the negative qualities generally associated with poor fiction. It is particularly prone to have:
A likable protagonist with whom young readers can identify.	A protagonist who is too exaggerated or too stereotyped to be believable.
An adventure that readers can imagine happening to themselves.	Nothing really exciting about the adventure.
Efficient characterization.	Only stereotyped characters.
An interesting setting that enhances the story without getting in the way of the plot.	A long drawn-out conclusion after the climax has been reached.
Action that draws readers into the plot within the first page or so of the story.	

Maurice Herzog's *Annapurna: First Conquest of an 8000 Meter Peak* was, for many readers, their first book to introduce them to this unusual, sometimes unreal, world. It still reads well.

The best introduction to the world of mountaineering is Allen Steck and Steve Roper's collection, *Ascent: The Mountaineering Experience*, particularly David Roberts' "Slouching Toward Everest: A Critique of Exploration Narratives." Roberts' two books, *The Mountain of My Fear* and *Deborah: A Wilderness Narrative* come close to letting outsiders see what drives people to climb mountains.

Excellent accounts of mountain climbing can be found in Galen Rowell's *High and Wild: A Mountaineer's World*, Steve Roper and Allen Steck's *Fifty Classic Climbs of North America*, Tom King's *In the Shadow of the Giants: Mountain Ascents Past and Present*, George B. Schaller's *Stones of Silence: Journeys in the Himalayas*, Reinhold Messner and Alessandro Gogna's *K2: Mountain of Mountains*, and Arthur Roth's *Eiger: Wall of Death*.

Chris Bonington's *Annapurna: South Face* describes the 1970 ascent, and its photographs are worth the price alone. More important, Bonington details the politicking and nitpicking and antagonisms among the climbers without in any way detracting from the adventure or the ultimate achievement.

The finest recent book on mountain climbing is Arlene Blum's *Annapurna—A Woman's Place*. The story, in grueling and often unpleasant detail, of thirteen women who set out to scale Annapurna is powerful reading. That the two women in the second summit party died makes the book even more moving. *Annapurna—A Woman's Place* is a gallant story of adventure and quest about people who did not always get along well. Elizabeth Arthur's *Beyond the Mountain* sensitively describes a similar climb in a beautifully written novel.

Another kind of climbing, more lunatic yet, is described in George Willig and Drew Bergman's *Going It Alone*. Willig was the climber—more properly the "builderer"—who scaled New York City's World Trade Center.

◈ MYSTERIES

Daniel's detection of the guilty Elders in *The Story of Susanna* in the *Apocrypha* may be the world's first detective story, but the modern mystery begins with Edgar Allan Poe's "The Murders in the Rue Morgue" though the tale of detection in his later "The Purloined Letter" is certainly more satisfying. Dime Novel detectives soon appeared, notably Old King Brady, Old Sleuth, Young Sleuth, Cap Collier, and—best known of them all—Nick Carter. Surely the world's first great detective appeared in 1887 when Sherlock Holmes strode out of the pages of Arthur Conan Doyle's *A Study in Scarlet* accompanied by the ever-faithful and always befuddled Dr. Watson.

Holmes was soon followed by some almost as distinctive detectives. Jacques Futrelle's Professor S. F. X. Van Deusen (*The Thinking Machine*) and G. K. Chesterton's Father Brown in several collections of short stories, most notably *The Innocence of Father Brown* which contains "The Secret Garden" and "The Blue Cross." And after Father Brown came the deluge.

Why are mysteries so popular? Basically they are unrealistic and have almost nothing to do with real-life detection by police or private agents as mystery writers cheerfully admit. They demand deep suspension of our disbelief yet the faithful gladly give it. Mysteries are mere games, but we love games. We hope, or so many of us claim, to beat the detective to the murderer, but we rarely do, and when it does happen, we feel cheated.

The characteristics of the traditional murder mystery are well known and relatively fixed. Devotees are more interested in variations on the theme than in violations of the rule, and variations are apparently endless.

There must be a crime. A short story may settle for blackmail or robbery, but a novel demands a murder; whatever lesser crimes the writer chooses to toss in are fine as long as there is at least one murder. The murder normally takes place after a few chapters introduce the characters, including the victim and those who might pray for his or her death. Soon after the murder, perhaps before, a detective enters, though he or she may not be a part of the official police force. Clues are scattered, the investigation proceeds, and the detective solves the case and explains the solution. The plot is an intricate interweaving of suspicion, motives, clues, red herrings, but the characters are often undeveloped stick-figures save in the best of the genre. The average reader of mysteries simply cares more about the puzzle than the people.

The hard-boiled mystery differs in significant ways. The detective is usually male. He is privately employed and has no altruistic motives. He enters the case for pay, not for love of the chase or the intellectual love of a puzzle. The traditional detective/solver of crimes is cheerful and optimistic, sometimes painfully so. Not so the private detective. Working out of a cheerless office and around even less cheerful people, he is tired, cynical, having seen too much of the seamy side of life to feel hope for anything. He often has a quiet dignity that he covers by wisecracks. He believes in justice, but he is not above going outside the law to do the job. He is cynical about the courts, the police, the system, class distinctions, and the establishment generally. The traditional detective is bright and sees what others fail to see. The private eye knows that detective work is hard and routine, and any bright person could find what he will find had he or she the patience. The traditional mystery may have some violence after the murder, but in the private eye's world, violence comes with the territory.

The quite arbitrary rules of the traditional mystery were itemized by Hillary Waugh:

◇ Rule One: All clues discovered by the detective must be made available to the reader.

Rule Two: Early introduction of the murderer.

Rule Three: The crime must be significant.

Rule Four: There must be detection.

Rule Five: The number of suspects must be known and the murderer must be among them.

Rule Six: Nothing extraneous must be introduced.[1]

An elderly female tutor in Michael Innes' *Appleby and Honeybath* neatly summarized the traditional mystery when she said, "An unresolved fatality is an unsatisfactory thing to leave behind one after a quiet weekend in the country."

The traditional mystery flourished in the 1920s and 1930s, novels read even today. Earl Derr Biggers' Charlie Chan books were almost as popular as the later filmed versions proved, especially *The House Without a Key*, *Behind That Curtain*, and *The Black Camel*. Frederic Dannay and Manfred Lee's Ellery Queen mysteries were models of fair play, and often included a "Challenge to the Reader" in which Queen announced that he now had all the clues needed to point to one and only one culprit. *The French Powder Mystery*, *The Dutch Shoe Mystery*, *The Egyptian Cross Mystery*, and especially *The Greek Coffin Mystery* among the early Queens are most readable even today. Among Queen's later books, *Calamity Town* stands out. Rex Stout's Nero Wolfe books, notably *Fer-de-Lance*, *The League of Frightened Men*, *Too Many Cooks*, *Black Orchids*, and *The Black Mountain*, continue to be read with enthusiasm.

Erle Stanley Gardner's courtroom pyrotechnics enliven most of his Perry Mason mysteries. Among the best are *The Case of the Velvet Claws*—which sold 28,000,000 copies in fifteen years—*The Case of the Stuttering Bishop*, *The Case of the Howling Dog*, *The Case of the Perjured Parrot*, and *The Case of the Counterfeit Eye*. The prolific Gardner also wrote as A. A. Fair.

Perhaps less lively but far purer traditional mysteries are John Dickson Carr's books, notably *The Three Coffins* with detective Dr. Gideon Fell. Carr used the pen name of Carter Dickson for his Sir Henry Merrivale mysteries. Carr's best book is *The Burning Court* although whether it is a mystery at all is open to interpretation.

Two exponents of the fair play, traditional school of mystery writing are Dorothy Sayers with her Lord Peter Wimsey and his butler Bunter (there are even those who claim to have read Sayers' books with pleasure) and Agatha Christie with her two detectives, Hercule Poirot and Miss Jane Marple who have given hours of pleasure to an incredible number of addicts. Poirot, the pompous little detective from Belgium, is at his very best in *The Mysterious Affair at Styles*, *The Murder of Roger Ackroyd*—which broke an unwritten rule of mysteries and caused a furor when it appeared— *The A. B. C. Murders*, *Sad Cypress*—and probably Christie's best book featuring Poirot—*The Hollow*. The somewhat prissy Miss Marple is at her cleverest in *A Murder Is Announced* and *What Mrs. McGillicuddy Saw*. Christie's often tiresome Tuppence and Tommy Beresford appear to advantage in one of Christie's best mysteries, *By the Pricking of My Thumbs*. Christie's best book is *Ten Little Indians* (a.k.a. *And Then There Were None*) though it is not strictly speaking a mystery.

The hard-boiled private eye came alive with Dashiell Hammett's Continental Op in *Red Harvest* and *The Dain Curse*, Sam Spade in *The Maltese Falcon*, Nick and Nora Charles in *The Thin Man*, and Ned Beaumont in *The Glass Key*, Hammett's finest novel. Ten years later, Raymond Chandler's Philip Marlowe appeared in *The Big Sleep*—arguably Chandler's finest work and the prototype of the private eye novel—followed by *Farewell, My Lovely*, *The High Window*, *The Lady in the Lake*, *The Little Sister*, and *The Long Goodbye*, all worth reading today. Mickey Spillane's Mike Hammer mysteries followed in *I, the Jury*. The book, written in nine days and reading almost that well, presented a new private eye, a one-man detective-prosecutor-judge-jury-executioner, an exercise in sadism difficult to equal in the field.

Modern private eyes include Ross Macdonald's (real name, Kenneth Millar) Lew Archer books, often beautifully written and highly literate. *The Moving Target*, *The Drowning Pool*, *The Galton Case*, *The Zebra-Striped Hearse*, *The Far Side of the Dollar*, and *The Blue Hammer* merit reading. John D. MacDonald's Travis McGee books have been almost equally popular, but *The Deep Blue Good-Bye* and *Bright Orange for a Shroud* betray McGee as avenger more than detective. Stuart Kaminsky's Toby Peters' mysteries, all set in a 1940s Hollywood, are affectionately modeled after Chandler's books, and are all worth reading, both for their re-creation of a time and a place and for their ingenious puzzles. *Murder on the Yellow Brick Road* concerns the murder of one of *The Wizard of Oz* munchkins with Judy Garland and Clark Gable among the bystanders. *You Bet Your Life* includes the Marx Brothers, Ian Fleming, and Al Capone. *He Done Her Wrong* includes Mae West. And *Never Cross a Vampire* includes Bela Lugosi.

Mark Schorr's *Red Diamond: Private Eye* is a funny take-off on private eye stories. A New York City cabbie lives in a world of fantasy and tough-guy pulp magazines and assumes the role of a private eye.

The police procedural novel is a relatively new addition to the genre. Ed

McBain's (real name, Evan Hunter) 87th Precinct series featuring detective Steve Carella shows the plodding character of most murder cases with detectives walking endlessly and interviewing people interminably, much as real life crime is handled. *Cop Hater, 'Til Death, Lady Killer*, and *Long Time No See* are good introductions to McBain's world. Joseph Wambaugh was a policeman and his sense of authenticity comes across in *The New Centurions, The Choirboys, The Onion Field*, and *The Glitter Dome*. Wambaugh's world is grimy, bloody, frustrating, and endless.

Nicholas Freeling's Inspector Van de Valk books allow readers to compare the American police world with this Dutch world of cops and crime. *Love in Amsterdam, Criminal Conversation, The King of Rainy Country*, and *Auprès de Ma Blonde* are among his most popular books. Per Wahlöö's Chief Inspector Peter Jensen Swedish police stories are well liked, notably *The Thirty-First Floor*. With his wife, poet Maj Sjowall, Wahlöö has written Inspector Martin Beck mysteries such as *The Man on the Balcony, The Man Who Went Up in Smoke*, and *The Laughing Policeman*.

One of the more unusual settings for a police novel is a New Mexico Indian Reservation, but Tony Hillerman creates fascinating mysteries set in cultures most of us will never know in *Dance Hall of the Dead, The Blessing Way, The Listening Woman*, and *The Dark Wind*.

A number of excellent writers have continued to write traditional puzzle mysteries. Edmund Crispin's (real name, Bruce Montgomery) Gervase Fen, the Oxford don, delighted fans for years with *The Case of the Gilded Fly*, murder and wit at the Oxford Repertory Theatre; *Love Lies Bleeding*, murder surrounds a lost Shakespearian play; and *The Long Divorce*, poison-pen letters lead to murder in a small English village. His most delightful book is *Buried for Pleasure* in which Fen comes to an English village to stand as an independent candidate for Parliament and finds a loyal pig, a lunatic, two murders, and wit aplenty. Dick Francis, a former Welsh jockey, sets most of his fine mysteries at the racetrack, and *Enquiry, For Kicks, Slayride, Banker*, and *Odds Against* show his expertise at both the world of the turf and constructing intricate and delightful puzzles. Patricia Moyes' Chief Inspector Henry Tibbetts is always fun to watch, especially in *Down Among the Dead Men, Many Deadly Returns*, and *A Six-Letter Word for Death*.

Many addicts believe that Ruth Rendell is the logical successor to Agatha Christie as the Queen of English Mystery Writers. Rendell's Chief Inspector Wexford may be less flashy than other detectives, but his steady work in *Murder Being Once Done, Make Death Love Me, Death Notes*, and *Master of the Moor* impresses most readers. Rendell's recent *Speaker of Mandarin* deserves special notice. Wexford travels to China for business, and when he returns to England he finds that one of his fellow travelers has been murdered. When the chief suspect commits suicide, Wexford feels that the solution is a little too pat. All in all, a most satisfying case.

One of the great joys in reading mysteries is running into all sorts of unusual detectives. Arthur William Upfield's Australian Aborigine detective, Napoleon Bonaparte, is well educated but his ability to blend into the background helps him unravel the puzzles in *The Lure of the Bush, Winds of*

Evil, Death of a Swagman, and *Death of a Lake.* Even better written are H. R. F. Keating's Inspector Ganesh Ghote's books. Ghote is a naive but hardworking member of the Bombay Police, and *The Perfect Murder, Inspector Ghote Hunts the Peacock,* and *Go West, Inspector Ghote* are extraordinarily satisfying reading. Less recent but still worth reading are Harry Kemelman's Rabbi David Small books, notably *Friday the Rabbi Slept Late, Saturday the Rabbi Went Hungry, Sunday the Rabbi Stayed Home,* and *Monday the Rabbi Took Off.*

Two unusual detectives deserve particular notice. Lillian de la Torre's (real name, Lillian Bueno McCue) use of Dr. Samuel Johnson, of eighteenth-century dictionary fame, as a detective may seem curious at first, but the stories work. *Dr. Sam: Johnson, Detector* and *The Detections of Dr. Sam: Johnson* introduce readers to a time and place and provide good mysteries to boot. Robert Van Gulik's Judge Dee mysteries introduce readers to seventh century China, a world foreign to most of us. The world of court and political intrigue and ancient Chinese law are at the heart of *The Chinese Bell Murders,* The *Chinese Gold Murders,* and *Murder in Canton,* the best of some fine offbeat mysteries.

The wackiest murder mystery must be Gary Wolf's *Who Censored Roger Rabbit?* Eddie Valiant, tough-guy private eye, lives in a Hollywood of real people and 'toons, cartoon characters who speak in balloons above their heads. It is a strange world, but Wolf makes us believe in it.

A marvelous book which is a mystery and far more is Umberto Eco's *The Name of the Rose.* Eco, an Italian critic and semiotician, sets his story in a fourteenth-century monastery where six monks have been murdered. William of Baskerville, an English clergyman schooled in the philosophies of Roger Bacon and William of Occam, comes to solve a mystery which involves the deaths and the second book of Aristotle's *Poetics* which someone desperately hopes to stop anyone from reading. Eco's book demands some background in theology and ecclesiastical conventions, but those willing to work will find this intellectually engaging.

The two wittiest writers in the field are Amanda Cross (real name, Carolyn Heilbrun) and P. D. James. Cross' Kate Fansler books have been consistent delights. Fansler, a professor of English—like her creator, is reasonably wealthy, happily astute, and actively feminist. Her ability to unravel mysteries and to be clever, generally without being cute, is demonstrated in *In the Last Analysis, The Theban Mysteries, The Question of Max,* and *Death in a Tenured Position.* P. D. James gets better and better with almost each book. While *The Skull Beneath the Skin, Death of an Expert Witness, The Black Tower,* and *Shroud for a Nightingale* are fine, her best book remains *An Unsuitable Job for a Woman* in which Cordelia Gray, partner in a detective agency, learns that her partner has killed himself and she becomes the agency. She is hired to find out why a young man has hanged himself. It is a leisurely book—the author clearly wants to do more than provide a fast puzzle and a faster solution for readers—but it is rewardingly literate and often quite amusing.

Georges Simenon is far more interested in psychological probings than

THE PEOPLE BEHIND THE BOOKS

ROBERT WESTALL, Author

Break of Dark
The Devil on the Road
Futuretrack 5
The Haunting of Chas McGill and Others

For me, in adolescence, there were two burning questions. "Help, something horrible's getting at me, using me, twisting my life. How do I cope?" and "I know there's something absolutely marvelous out there, but how do I find it?"

Trouble is, these twin dilemmas seem to have followed me into middle-age, getting stronger all the time. Frankly, I don't like the way the world's moving. Until about four years ago, I envied my students their youth.

Now, I don't any more. I envied one the other day; a brilliant mathematician who was going up to Cambridge. I realized he was the first I'd envied in a long, long, time. Perhaps the trouble is that at college, I teach careers. Suddenly I find that every year I have to sing a different song, and the tune seems constantly to get worse. I feel almost a hypocrite when I face my students today; how do I tell them the truth, without destroying hope? I feel we have to send each of them out like an astronaut, into the unknown; it's my job as a teacher and writer to make sure they have survival equipment that really works and doesn't let them down. That's what my books are about.

So I have to keep my own survival equipment in order. What keeps me sane? Well, I live in a very solid old house, where families

in the mysteries themselves, though the puzzles are pleasing enough. No writer of the genre does a better job of developing character or establishing a sense of time and place. Amazingly prolific, Simenon is worth reading on many levels. His detective, Jules Maigret, has appeared in more than a hundred books, among them *The Madman of Bergerac, Inspector Maigret and the Strangled Stripper, Maigret and the Headless Corpse,* and *Maigret on the Defensive.*

For short stories (and one novelette) about the law and some puzzles, readers should thoroughly enjoy John Mortimer's stories about Horace Rumpole, a rumpled old English barrister, featured in *Rumpole of the Bailey, The Trials of Rumpole,* and *Rumpole's Return.* Witty, often very, very funny, masterfully told stories.

While most young adults who enjoy mysteries will rapidly turn away from YA detective stories and head toward better written adult mysteries, a few writers for young adults deserve brief attention.

Jay Bennett's books are the most popular of the lot. *Deathman, Do Not Follow Me,* his first book, opened with a brilliant character study of a loner, but the introduction of the mystery did nothing to advance characterization and proved disappointing in the long run. *The Executioner, The Birthday Murder,* and *The Pigeon* are well-constructed, run-of-the-mill thrillers. Probably the best of the bunch is *Say Hello to the Hit Man,* a good study of a young man chosen for death.

Three mystery writers deserve more readers than they have found. Charlotte MacLeod writes good, if hardly outstanding adult mysteries, but have been happy for well over a hundred years. It seems full of happy ghosts. I live with six cats, and a lot of plants, to remind me I'm part of nature. I see some homes with no plants or animals, not even a canary, and I think, "God, how do they *survive?*" In my office at college, I have a 7th century Celtic Crucifix and a modern Indian brass Buddha that cost me fifty dollars (and I'll bet the guy who made it didn't get ten). My Crucifix cares about everything, and my Buddha lets nothing bother him, and between them they get me by. And my father and my son are such that any man would thank God for them, and they keep cropping up in my books. These are my roots that keep me upright when the wind is blowing.

I read a lot of history. How did *they* cope with *their* times? It's like looking back over the stern of a ship, watching its wake. If I can see where people have been, maybe I can guess where they're going. A lot of my books are about the past. Why don't you write about the future, they said? I did. The book upset my editor so much she wouldn't publish it. Thank God I got a new editor who did.

But the future has to be lived, with care and concentration, hope and prayer. If your roots are strong enough in the past, the future won't blow you over. One day, our future will be some others' pasts and they'll be looking back to find out how *we* coped. For we shall cope; if we don't let people sell us things we never knew we wanted. ◆

two YA books, *We Dare Not Go A-Hunting* and *Cirak's Daughter*, particularly the latter, are fine mysteries. Joan Lowery Nixon's books are less mysteries than out-and-out thrillers. *A Deadly Game of Magic* and *The Seance* are well done, but *Specter* is better, a superior YA thriller though the puzzle is likely to be solved by most readers fairly early. Teachers and librarians may easily underrate T. Ernesto Bethancourt's Doris Fein mysteries. They seem at first reading little more than advanced Nancy Drew books, but if the mysteries are nothing much, the humor and the attractive heroine make *Dr. Doom: Superstar*, *Doris Fein: Superspy*, *Doris Fein: Quartz Boyar*, *Doris Fein: Phantom of the Casino*, and all that follow great fun to read.

Anyone looking for books somewhat below Nancy Drew in perception and literary quality will find them in Kate Chambers' Diana Winthrop mysteries. *The Secret of the Singing Strings*, *Danger in the Old Fort*, and *The Case of the Dog-Lover's Legacy* are embarrassingly stupid, obviously plotted, noncharacterized, dull books. Doubtless, Bantam will keep cranking them out for sale to the unsuspecting.

◈ STORIES OF THE SUPERNATURAL

The supernatural has been an important part of our conscious fascination and our subconscious fear ever since humanity learned to communicate. That ambivalence may go back to prehistoric times when cave shadows and lightning and darkness mystified and frightened us. We have demanded answers to the unknown but have rarely found them, and the answers we found have provided myths and legends about superior and unseen beings. Such explanations may have satisfied legendary heroes out to best the unknown—fighting the inexplicable and unbeatable must appeal to any hero. Winning would be more pleasing, losing more acceptable.

Amidst all our modern knowledge and sophistication, we hold onto our fascination with the unknowable. We delight in chambers of horrors, tunnels of terror, haunted houses. We claim to be rational beings, yet we read astrology charts. We mock superstitions of others yet hold a pet one or two ourselves, joking all the time that we don't take them seriously when we toss salt over our shoulder, refuse to walk under a ladder, avoid black cats, and knock on wood. We follow customs without wondering why the custom came about. Black is assumed to be the appropriate dress for funerals since it is dark and gloomy and demonstrates solemnity. We may not know that black was worn at some time lost in history because spirits, sometimes malignant or perhaps indignant, were thought to linger near a corpse for a year. Wearing black made the living difficult for the evil spirits to see. As long as spirits were around, danger lurked. Hence, long mourning periods.

Greek and Roman literature abounds with supernatural elements. So does Elizabethan literature. Whether Shakespeare believed in ghosts or witches or things that go bump in the night is anyone's guess. Certainly, his audiences often did.

The Gothic novel of unexplained terror began with Horace Walpole's *The Castle of Otranto* in 1764. Success breeds imitators and Clara Reeves' *The Old English Baron* appeared in 1780 and William Beckford's *Vathek* in 1786. The two greatest of the Gothics appeared in the 1790s, Ann Radcliffe's *The Mysteries of Udolpho* and Matthew Gregory Lewis' *The Monk*. Though Jane Austen did much to demolish the fad with *Northanger Abbey* in 1818, that posthumously published novel did not prevent Mary Shelley's *Frankenstein, or the Modern Prometheus*, the apotheosis of the genre, from winning admirers. The Romantic poets and prose writers continued to be half in love with the dark and the unknown as much of Coleridge and Keats and the novels of the Brontë sisters illustrate.

Television never capitalized on the supernatural, perhaps because it is too literal a medium. Radio shows did far better, as anyone old enough to have enjoyed "Inner Sanctum" or "The Whistler" will testify. Horror movies, such as Carl Mayer's *The Cabinet of Dr. Caligari* (1919), F. W. Murnau's *Nosferatu* (1922), Carl Dreyer's *Vampyr* (1932), Val Lewton's *Cat People* (1942), and Robert Wise's *The Haunting* (1963), have sometimes produced masterpieces of our internal struggles against the evil of the unknown. And anyone who saw the episode with Michael Redgrave playing a schizophrenic ventriloquist in *Dead of Night* (1945) knows how intensely powerful such movies can be.

Michael Armstrong noted the power of these movies:

◇ With the exception of love, fear must rate as the most potent emotion in Man. No religion and no mythology has been completely without it—the playing upon Man's fear of the unknown. . . . one of the three primary emotions in Art (laughter and sadness being the other two).[2]

That power has been equally apparent in the best literature in the genre, particularly the short story where brevity allows for intensity without letting up. H. P. Lovecraft, *the* master, wrote much that is still highly readable, but nothing surpasses two stories, "The Rats in the Wall" and "The Dunwich Horror." M. R. James' "The Mezzotint" and "Oh, Whistle, and I'll Come to You, My Lad," Walter de la Mare's "A Recluse" and "What Dreams May Come," Arthur Machen's "The White People," and H. G. Wells' "The Pollock and the Porroh Man" are still read with horror. Saki's "The Open Window" is both a fine story and a send-up of the type. The best collection of such stories is Herbert A. Wise and Phyllis Fraser's *Great Tales of Terror and the Supernatural.* Joan Kahn's three collections, *Some Things Dark and Dangerous, Some Things Fierce and Fatal,* and *Some Things Strange and Sinister,* should be in every collector's library, as should Peter Haining's two collections, *Gothic Tales of Terror: Classic Horror Stories from Great Britain* and *Gothic Tales of Terror: Classic Horror Stories from Europe and the United States.* Seon Manley and Gogo Lewis' *Ladies of Horror: Two Centuries of Supernatural Stories by the Gentle Sex* has much to recommend it.

Supernatural novels have well-established ground rules. Settings are usually in some eerie or haunted house or in a place where a mysterious event occurred years ago. Some thrillers are set in more mundane places, perhaps a brownstone in New York City or a hotel shut down for the season, but readers know the mundane will remain calm only for a short time as frightening events begin and strange people come out to play. Darkness is essential, usually but not always physical darkness. The protagonist, male or female, will be oblivious to evil for a time but ultimately will recognize the pervasive power of the darkness of the soul. Sometimes, the wife or husband will sell out to evil and entice the spouse to join in a black mass. Rituals or ceremonies are essential. Family curses or pacts with the Devil have become commonplaces of the genre.

Among YA novelists, Lois Duncan has proved consistently popular. In *Summer of Fear,* Rachael Bryant's family is notified that relatives have died in a car crash leaving a seventeen-year-old daughter, Julia, behind. The girl, who looks surprisingly mature, soon arrives and changes the lives of everyone around her. Rachael, the narrator, knows, without knowing quite how or why, that Julia is different, somehow sinister, particularly because Julia has "the strangest eyes." The family dog, Trickel, clearly distrusts Julia— according to legend, animals have insight about the forces of evil. Trickel does not last long, but then neither does anyone who gets in Julia's way. A burned wax image, Julia's inability to be photographed, and more contribute to her downfall, but not before Duncan has told a fine story. *Down a Dark Hall* is worth reading, and *Stranger With My Face* is almost as good as *Summer of Fear.*

British novelist Robert Westall is the best YA writer in the field, but since his novels have not appeared in paperback in the United States, they

THE PEOPLE BEHIND THE BOOKS

LOIS DUNCAN, Author

Summer of Fear
Stranger With My Face
The Third Eye
Down a Dark Hall

The juvenile book field has changed tremendously since I was twenty and wrote my first teen novel which was returned to me for revisions because I had a nineteen-year-old drink a beer. The subject matter of today's youth novels has no boundaries. The only taboo seems to be sex discrimination. When I wrote *Down a Dark Hall*, a wild teenage gothic, my editor's concern was that the ghosts in the story were male and their victims female. When I changed the ghost of poet Alan Seeger to Emily Brontë, he felt better.

I can only guess about where we're going, but I think we have come about as far as we can in the direction of "let-it-all-hang-out" realism. My reader-mail indicates that kids are beginning to feel bogged down with so much depressing slice-of-life. My own most successful books have been those that were high in entertainment value, especially those touching on the supernatural. My newest Y.A. novel, *Stranger With My Face*, is about a girl with a talent for astral projection. One of my most popular books, *Summer of Fear*, is about Ozark witchcraft, and *Killing Mr. Griffin*, also popular, is a tightly plotted suspense story.

My prediction is that the next few years will show an increase in the demand for such escape literature. There may even be a swing back toward fantasy, which to my way of thinking would be wonderful. The most valuable thing an author can do for today's teenagers is to help them realize it's as much fun to read a book as to turn on the television. ◆

have not yet found their audience. Violence in *The Wind Eye* is powerfully implied as three youngsters find an old boat, with strange designs, which they learn can take them back to St. Cuthbert's time and place. *The Watch House* carries on the theme of time shifts. A young girl's imagination is captured by an old and crumbling watch house on the coast. *The Devil on the Road* is the best of Westall's supernatural tales. A university student on a holiday travels north and finds temporary employment as a caretaker of an old barn, once the home of a witch hanged 300 years before. *Break of Dark* is a fine series of chilling short stories.

The house where evil lurks continues to find readers. Jay Anson's *The Amityville Horror* and its sequel, *666*, and Gerald Sullivan and Harvey Aronson's *High Hopes: The Amityville Murders* still have their appeal. Far better is Herman Raucher's *Maynard's House* in which a Vietnam veteran claims a house in northern Maine bequeathed to him by a war buddy. Anyone who expects a warm house and a toasty fire simply has no idea of the evil forces that propel the supernatural novel.

Marlys Millhiser and Peter Straub deservedly appear frequently on the best-seller lists. Millhiser's *The Mirror* concerns a young woman who stands before a mirror on her wedding eve and is pulled back into a nineteenth century mining camp by unknown powers. *Nightmare Country*, though advertised as equal to Stephen King's best, was something of a disappointment to fans. Straub's *Ghost Story*, made into a disappointing movie, may become one of the genre's classics. Four old friends are reunited, a young novelist in California is obsessed with a young woman, and these stories, and more, are intertwined in a fine horror tale. *Floating Dragon* and *Shadowland* are almost equally good.

Tales of exorcism and devil worship remain popular with young adults, notably William Blatty's *The Exorcist* and Ira Levin's *Rosemary's Baby*, perhaps as much because of the reshowings of the movie versions as anything else. John Coyne's *The Piercing* and *The Searing* are both superior to Blatty's or Levin's books, though Coyne remains less well known for some reason.

Unquestionably, V. C. Andrews is much read, by adults and young adults, though precisely why mystifies many others. Her tales of incest and general family ghoulishness in *If There Be Thorns, Flowers in the Attic* (the best known), and *My Sweet Audrina* are badly written but the piling up of horrors apparently finds readers. Some things about the supernatural clearly defy rational explanation.

Leading all the writers in the field is Stephen King. *Carrie* appeared in 1974, sold well for a then unknown writer, and from that point on, King maintained his place as *the* writer of the genre. Carrie is a young outsider, the daughter of religious fanatics, and the brunt of cruel jokes. She possesses the power of telekinesis, and she uses it to destroy the school, the students, and the town in a fit of justified rage. *Salem's Lot*, though better characterized, is something of a letdown after *Carrie* as are *The Shining*, possibly better known through its filmed version than as a novel, and *The Stand*. *Firestarter* is far better with its portrait of an eight-year-old girl with the power to start fires merely by looking at an object. A government agency, "The Shop," learns about the child and launches a search for her while King effectively indicts bureaucracy gone evil. *Firestarter* may not be King's best book, but it is his most penetrating study of character and our country.

His last four books added to his sales without adding to his reputation. *Different Seasons* is four generally effective novelettes. *Cujo* is a messy and disappointingly obvious horror tale of a lovable St. Bernard dog gone mad. *Christine* is a 1958 Plymouth Fury gone equally mad. Only *Pet Sematary* has some of the old King about it. A variation of W. W. Jacobs' "The Monkey's Paw"—and so acknowledged by King—*Pet Sematary* has a power that cannot be ignored although it remains something of a prolonged ghastly joke.

Supernatural books usually ignore the comic, so it is a relief occasionally to turn to Richard Peck's *The Ghost Belonged to Me, Ghosts I Have Been*, and *The Dreadful Future of Blossom Culp*. In the first book, Alexander Armsworth uses his gift of second sight to contact a young ghost. In the second, Blossom Culp, one of the spunkiest characters in American fiction, uses her talents with the supernatural to become more and more compassionate, not to hurt others. The last book is the least satisfying, but a slightly older Blossom who projects herself into a 1980s world of video games is still entertaining.

Dixie Tenny's recent *Call the Darkness Down* is an impressive first novel about the spirit world in modern Wales. Morfa Owen is anxious to study in Wales, partly because of her Welsh ancestry, partly because her mother has created a family mystery by refusing to tell anyone why she and her sister fled Wales when they were teenagers. Despite some clichés, the feeling that is Wales and the convincing characters make for a fine ghost story.

Because young adults are curious and relatively open about exploring new ideas, the supernatural has a natural appeal to them. Treading on spooky ground is a social experience—one not always approved by censorious parents—and teenagers delight in rounding up friends to see a scary movie or discussing the possibilities of ghosts and goblins and more.

◈ HISTORICAL NOVELS

Most of us read historical novels because we are curious about other times and other places and other peoples, and, most important, because we want adventure and suspense and mystery. Movies as old as *Captain Blood* or *Gone with the Wind* or *The Scarlet Pimpernel* continue to pique our interest, however ignorant we may be of the times and places described.

Certainly, best-selling historical fiction has provided excitement. Adventures galore can be found in historical novels as good and as popular as Sir Walter Scott's *Ivanhoe* (1819), Alexandre Dumas' *The Count of Monte Cristo* (1844), Mary Johnston's *To Have and to Hold* (1900), Rafael Sabatini's *Scaramouche* (1921), Helen Waddell's *Peter Abelard* (1933), Elizabeth Goudge's *Green Dolphin Street* (1944), or Margaret Walker's *Jubilee* (1966). Indeed, all these novels remain readable today, a claim impossible to make for novels of the same time written about contemporary issues.

As in any literary form, historical novels have their conventions. They should be historically accurate and steeped in the sense of time and place. We should recognize totems and taboos, food, clothing, vocations, pleasures, customs, smells, religions, literature, all that goes to make one time and one place unique from another. Enthusiasts will forgive no anachronism, no matter how slight. Historical novels should give a sense of history's continuity, a feeling of the flow of history from one time unto another that will, for good reason, be different from the period before. But as writers allow us to feel that flow of history, they should particularize their portraits of one time and one place. Historical novels should tell a lively story with a sense of impending danger, mystery, suspense, or romance that impels action, and action aplenty there must be. That is what we must have, and an enormous demand it is.

Historical novels allow us—at their best they force us—to make connections to realize that despair is as old, and new, as hope, that loyalty and treachery, love and hatred, compassion and cruelty, were and are inherent in humanity whether it be in ancient Greece or Elizabethan England or Post-World War I Germany.

That poses a problem. Interested as we may be in the past, we are always more concerned about the present, and we find ourselves comparing the past with today, perhaps even imposing present-day values on the past. Historians can pretend to be objective, but historical novelists, concerned about people they have created and those they address, may find such objectivity harder to come by. What Henry Seidel Canby wrote in 1927 concerns anyone working with history:

> ◇ Historical fiction, like history, is more likely to register an exact truth about the writer's present than the exact truth of the past.[3]

And sometimes, the historical novelist may be grinding an axe. How hidden the axe may be is for the reader to determine. Christopher Collier, for example, makes no pretense why he and his brother write about the American Revolution in their fine historical novels:

> ◇ . . . the books I write with my brother are written with a didactic purpose—to teach about ideals and values that have been important in shaping the course of American history. This is in no way intended to denigrate the importance of the dramatic and literary elements of historical novels. Nothing will be taught, and certainly nothing learned, if no one reads the books.[4]

Since people are at the heart of what makes history, historical novels usually focus on one major character, following this person from birth or early childhood through marriage or some major historical crisis. The major figure will be involved with real historical figures and will be caught up in real historical events. The hero presents a picture of the time and place better than any schoolbook text could. In effect, the hero serves as a mediator between us and the history we do not know or have forgotten.

Historical novels can take us places where no historian can go. Jean M. Auel's *The Clan of the Cave Bear* and *The Valley of Horses* move us back to Cro-Magnon times as we see what Ayla sees and feels about this harsh ice-age world. Perhaps less well known, Bjorn Kurten's *Dance of the Tiger: a Novel of the Ice Age* takes us to an equally intriguing world 35,000 years back.

Or we can visit ancient Greece and Persia with Mary Renault (real name, Mary Challans). A masterful writer—any of her novels are worth reading by even the most discriminating reader—her *Funeral Games* completed the Alexander cycle begun with *Fire from Heaven* and continued in *The Persian Boy*. It tells of the dying Alexander, only 35, and the contenders who battle for his empire, a stirring introduction to a world most of us know only slightly. Not quite so good but still fine are the novels of Mary Ray, set in Rome. The trilogy of *The Ides of April*, *Sword Sleep*, and *Beyond the Desert Gate* will open the eyes of anyone who believes early history lacked intrigue and thrills. And Gore Vidal's *Creation*, though calling for some maturity on the reader's part, brings fifth century B.C. Greece before us.

THE PEOPLE BEHIND THE BOOKS

KATHERINE PATERSON, Author

Jacob Have I Loved
Rebels of the Heavenly Kingdom
The Sign of the Chrysanthemum
Bridge to Terabithia

Nearly everywhere I have spoken during the last two years, someone has told me how glad she was that I had given up writing historical fiction. "Young people don't like historical novels," she'd say. "They only like books about people like themselves." I would nod and grimace, knowing that waiting at home on my desk was the most demanding piece of historical fiction I had ever attempted. One way I examine the problems of today is by looking at another time and place. The novels I wrote set in feudal Japan were written against the background of war and civil unrest which we were experiencing in the United States in the late '60s and early '70s. In the same way, *Rebels of the Heavenly Kingdom*, is set in 19th-century China, a period that speaks to me because of what is happening now in our country.

Actually, any true novel becomes historical fiction by the time it is published. Stories have to take place in definite settings at particular points in history. To attempt to make a story timeless by leaving out concrete historical details, is to rob it of life. Moreover, if we give the young only what they think they want, we are condemning them to adolescence forever. I believe our chief task whether we are writers or teachers is the care and feeding of the imagination. ◆

Feudal Japan with formalized code and all its color marches past us in James Clavell's *Shōgun*. Students unable, or unwilling, to face the length of that book will find Lensey Namioka's novels good introductions to the time, whether in *Village of the Vampire Cat* or *Valley of the Broken Cherry Trees* or *The Samurai and the Long-Nosed Devils*.

A much later time in China, the 1850s and the Taiping Rebellion, is brilliantly handled in Katherine Paterson's *Rebels of the Heavenly Kingdom*. Wang Lee, a fifteen-year-old peasant, is caught up in a bloody series of battles when he becomes part of a Christian army, the God-Worshiping Society. He watches as ideals and people are sacrificed for what was supposedly a greater and eternal good.

Sixteenth-century Aztec society can be visited, thankfully from a safe distance, in three books, Jamake Highwater's *The Sun, He Dies*, Daniel Peters' *The Luck of Huemac: A Novel About the Aztecs*, and Gary Jennings' *Aztec*. The last is the superior novel.

But then so can England be visited from the fourteenth century through the nineteenth. Ann Warren Turner's *The Way Home* is the story of the Black Plague as it strikes a small English village. In Elizabeth Marie Pope's fine *The Perilous Gard*, Kathryn Sutton, one of Princess Elizabeth's ladies, is banished to Elvenwood Hall, and there she becomes part of a world she has never known. *Kate Ryder*, by Hester Burton, shows the English Civil

War with many of its political repercussions. Even better is Barbara Willard's five-volume Middlemass Chronicles. *Harrow and Harvest*, last of the series, lets us see the living conditions during the Civil War. It might serve as an introduction to a writer who deserves far more readers.

Jill Paton Walsh's *A Parcel of Patterns* takes place in the village of Eyam in 1665 when the plague hits. Young Mall Percival loses her intended husband, and the villagers panic as death seems everywhere. Erick Christian Haugaard's *A Messenger for Parliament* and *Cromwell's Boy* are good novels about political intrigue and warfare.

Two novels about the nineteenth century are Ann Schlee's *Ask Me No Questions*, a powerful story of child abuse and a cholera epidemic in 1847, and K. M. Peyton's *The Right-Hand Man*, set in Georgian England and more specifically in Newgate Prison, a boxing ring, and the world of carriage racing. Schlee is a fine writer, for this and anything else she has written. Peyton has a loyal following in England. Why teachers and librarians and students in the United States have not found her remains something of a mystery.

Mollie Hunter's novels set in Scotland have proved popular with American young adults. *The Stronghold* presents the world of the Iron Age people who once lived in the Orkney Islands off the northern tip of Scotland. *A Pistol in Greenyards* is the story of Scottish Highland tenant farmers who, in 1854, were dispossessed to make way for sheep grazing. *You Never Knew Her as I Did* retells the romance of Mary, Queen of Scots.

Good historical novels about our country are not difficult to find. Patricia Clapp's *Witches' Children* would serve as a fine fictional introduction to the 1692 hysteria which culminated in the Salem witch trials. Even better on early American history is Norma Farber's remarkable journal-novel, *Mercy Short: A Winter Journal, North Boston, 1692–93*. Based on fact, Mercy is a young girl, recently released from captivity by the Indians, forced by Cotton Mather to redeem her soul by keeping a journal. Perhaps Mercy writes more lucidly than perceptive readers may accept—she has, after all, undergone incredible misfortunes and she writes with humor and great perception—but the novel is almost totally convincing and moving.

James and Christopher Collier have written several fine, admittedly didactic, novels about the Revolutionary War, any of which would let students see the nature of the cause that led to the War and understand the people behind the cause. Because the protagonists of *My Brother Sam Is Dead*, *The Bloody Country*, and *The Winter Hero* are young, young adults may find a point of contact that may lead them to understand that the War involved everyone, not just the heroes they have read about in schoolbooks. *Jump Ship to Freedom* and *War Comes to Willy Freeman* tells of black former slaves involved in the Revolution, an even more appealing theme.

Two English historical novelists lead all the rest, though two Americans follow soon behind.

Rosemary Sutcliff won admirers and readers with her first books. The books that followed further enhanced her reputation as the finest historical novelist for young adults. She is a born storyteller whose tales are intense

THE PEOPLE BEHIND THE BOOKS

ROSEMARY SUTCLIFF, Author

Frontier Wolf
Blue Remembered Hills
Song for a Dark Queen
The Lantern Bearers

Adults have done their growing up. They have arrived (more or less) at the people they are going to be for the rest of their lives, and are not likely to suffer a real change as a result of the books they read. But the adolescent is still in the making, and books can play a big part in that process, since they are still young enough to identify strongly with the characters, and even wish to be like them, for good or ill.

Therefore the writer for the young has certain aims, duties, obligations which do not apply to the writer for a completely adult readership, and most writers above the hack level are fully aware of these.

Speaking for myself, I try to put over a set of values beyond the material kind. I deal in the big basic themes of life, love and hate, friendship, treachery, loyalty and divided loyalties, courage, kindness; the raw materials of the western and the hero myth alike; both of which seem to wake a deep seated response in the young. The characters in my books generally find that the only reward for doing the right/honest/brave/difficult thing lies in having done it; in the knowledge of having kept

and fast-moving and poetic. Her novels have ranged in time from the Bronze Age to the Iron Age, as in *Warrior Scarlet* and *Sun Horse, Moon Horse*. She has touched on many periods of English history in *Blood Feud* (tenth century), *The Shield Ring* (Normans and Saxons), *Dawn Wind* (Saxons), *Knight's Fee* (William the Conquerer), and *Simon* (English Civil War).

But she is almost certainly best known for her novels set in Roman-Britain, particularly *The Mark of the Horse Lord, Outcast, The Capricorn Bracelet, Song for a Dark Queen*, and *Frontier Wolf*.

Her favorite novel, and probably her best, opens the trilogy completed by *The Silver Branch* and *The Lantern Bearers*. *The Eagle of the Ninth* is set in Roman Britain, and, as is true in most Sutcliff novels, the protagonist must face up to problems inherent in different kinds of handicaps. Marcus, a young Roman centurion, is forced by a leg wound to leave the legions and make his home in Britain. There he learns that the eagle standard of the Ninth Legion, the Lost Legion once led by his father who is presumed dead, may have fallen into the hands of a tribe beyond Hadrian's Wall to the north. Marcus deeply believes in honor—deep convictions typify Sutcliff's books—and along with his British slave, he sets out on this personal quest, for himself, for his father, for Rome, for honor.

Leon Garfield's world is the eighteenth century, with an occasional detour into early nineteenth-century England. Beginning with *Jack Holborn* in 1965, Garfield set a standard for historical writing that few can match.

Garfield's eighteenth century is the world of Fielding and Smollett, lusty and squalid and ugly and bustling and swollen, full of life and adventure and the faith with some integrity deep within themselves—and often a harder job to do next time.

I try to provide my readers with the gift of langauge; not just technically good English, but a feel for the shape of sentences and the colors and texture and power of words and the things that one can do with them. This I feel to be desperately important, for not only is language a means of communication, but at a deeper level, words are what make people able to harness and give shape to their thoughts, and without them it is very difficult to think clearly beyond a very rudimentary level.

I try to teach history. Not the history book kind, but the flesh-and-blood kind, as true to the spirit as to the facts of place and period and event as I can make it; because I believe strongly that the understanding of what has gone before helps one to understand and cope with the world of today.

When I receive a letter from a 25-year-old telling me that as a result of reading my books he is studying archaeology instead of medicine, it frightens me! We who write for the young wield considerable power. We should be careful how we use it. ◆

the certainty that being born an orphan may lead you ultimately to fame and fortune. Typically, eighteenth-century novels open with an orphan searching for identity. Garfield does not fear conventions, but his stories also play with reality versus illusion, daylight versus dreams, flesh versus fantasy. His ability to sketch out minor characters in a line or two and make them come alive is impressive. Of a man in *The Sound of Coaches*, he writes, "He was one of those gentlemen who affect great gallantry to all the fair sex except their wives." Of a prostitute, he writes, "A face full of beauty spots, with graveyard dust between." And of the protagonist we are told, "although jealousy was ordinarily foreign to Sam's nature, they did, on occasion, talk the same language." Garfield's epigrams are often most effective, for example, "Many a man is made good by being thought so."

Garfield's best book is *The Sound of Coaches* with an opening that catches the sights and sounds and feeling of the time:

> ◇ Once upon a winter's night when the wind blew its guts out and a fishy piece of moon scuttled among the clouds, a coach came thundering down the long hill outside of Dorking. Its progress was wild and the coachman and his guard rocked from side to side as if the maddened vehicle was struggling to rid itself of them before going on to hell without the benefit of further advice. Even the passing landscape conspired to increase the terror of the journey, and the fleeting sight of a gibbet—its iron cage swinging desolately against the sky— turned the five passengers' thoughts towards the next world . . . of which destination there'd been no mention in Chichester where they'd booked their passage.

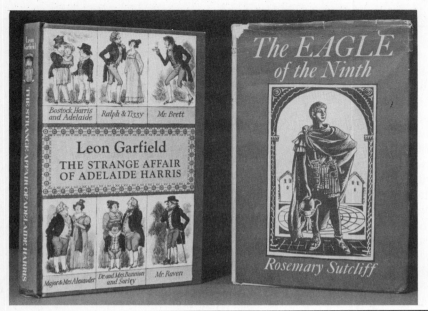

◆ Two English historical novelists, Rosemary Sutcliff and Leon Garfield, lead all the rest.

Once the five passengers, the coachman and the guard (who is the coachman's wife) reach Dorking, a young girl has a baby, dies, and leaves the orphan behind without any identity. The passengers, though at first annoyed by the irregularity of all that has happened, become parents of sorts to the baby, while the coachman and his wife raise the child. When Sam, our hero, grows up, he heads for London searching for his father.

Wit and humor and liveliness permeate Garfield's books. Perhaps the funniest are *The Strange Affair of Adelaide Harris* and its sequel *The Night of the Comet*. In *Adelaide*, Bostock and Harris, two nasty pupils in Dr. Bunnion's Academy become so entranced with stories of Spartan babies abandoned on mountain tops, there to be suckled by wolves, that they borrow Harris' baby sister to determine for themselves the truth of the old tales. Therein begins a wild comedy of errors and an even wilder series of coincidences and near-duels and wild threats which hardly lets up until the last lines.

If Scott O'Dell and Claudia Von Canon fall slightly behind the standards set by Sutcliff and Garfield, they are very good nonetheless.

O'Dell's *Island of the Blue Dolphins* (and to a considerably lesser degree its sequel, *Zia*) has already become a classic of young adult literature. Based on fact, the story of a young girl, accidentally abandoned by her tribe on an island for many years, powerfully attunes us to the problems of survival and the need for companionship. His finest book is *The King's Fifth*, a story of sixteenth-century Spanish conquest. Fifteen-year-old cartographer Estaban accompanies Captain Mendoza on the search for gold, a search that becomes as much Estaban's search to understand himself.

O'Dell's recent trilogy, *The Captive, The Feathered Serpent*, and *The*

◆ **TABLE 5.2 Suggestions for Evaluating Historical Fiction**

A good historical novel usually has:	A poor historical novel may have:
A setting that is integral to the story.	A story that could have happened any time or any place. The historical setting is for visual appeal and to compensate for a weak story.
An authentic rendition of the time, place, and people being featured.	
An author who is so thoroughly steeped in the history of the period that he or she can be comfortably creative without making mistakes.	Anachronisms in which the author illogically mixes up people, events, speaking styles, social values, or technological developments from different time periods.
Believable characters with whom young readers can identify.	
Evidence that even across great time spans people share similar emotions.	Awkward narration and exposition as the author tries to teach history through the characters' conversations.
References to well-known events or people, or other clues through which the reader can place the happenings in their correct historical framework.	Oversimplification of the historical issues and a stereotyping of the "bad" and the "good" guys.
Readers who come away with the feeling that they know a time or place better. It is as if they have lived in it for at least a few hours.	Characters who fail to come alive as individuals who have something in common with the readers. They are just stereotyped representatives of a particular period.

Amethyst Ring, chronicle Julian Escobar's attempt to impersonate the anticipated Mayan messiah, Kukulcan. If none of the books are outstanding, they are all highly readable.

Claudia Von Canon has written only two historical novels, but both effectively convey the feeling of worlds foreign to most readers, *The Moonclock* set in late seventeenth-century Vienna as Turkish invaders threaten, and an even better book, *The Inheritance*, set in Inquisition Spain. It is too early to know whether Von Canon will become a major figure in young adult literature, but these two books are impressive starts.

◈ WESTERNS

The appeal of the American West is as old as the first explorer who saw it and marveled. Dime novelists of the 1870s and 1880s glorified the wildness and vitality of miners and cowboys and mountain men and soldiers and outlaws. Ned Buntline was particularly effective in his tall stories—amidst some out-and-out lies—about Buffalo Bill and his supposed exploits.

If anything else were needed to make the West the heartland of adventure, movies provided rootin-tootin-shootin cowboys and rustlers, good guys and bad guys—always easy to separate depending on who wore white and who wore black. Edwin S. Porter's *The Great Train Robbery* in 1903, though filmed in New Jersey, helped develop the Western myth, but later films like James Cruze's *The Covered Wagon* (1923), John Ford's *Stagecoach* (1939), and Fred Zinnemann's *High Noon* (1952) helped mightily.

Perhaps films were not needed, for Owen Wister's *The Virginian* (1902) had already established the central characters of too many Westerns, the quiet and noble hero, the schoolmarm heroine, the hero's weak friend, the villain, and rustlers, along with some basic plot devices, cattle drives, the inevitable showdown between good guys and bad guys, violence aplenty, and revenge-revenge-revenge. Andy Adams' *The Log of a Cowboy: A Narrative of the Old Trail Days* (1903) brought a semblance of honesty to the field, and that was heightened by the honest and fine novels of Eugene Manlove Rhodes, *Stepsons of Light* (1921), *Paso Por Aqui* (1927), and *The Proud Sheriff* (1935).

For the most part, realism was rare in Westerns; note the romanticized but highly popular novels of Zane Grey, *The Heritage of the Desert* (1910), *Riders of the Purple Sage* (1912)—his best-known book—and *The Thundering Herd* (1925).

But an amazing number of fine writers lived and breathed the real West and wrote accurate, nonromantic novels, for example Oliver LaFarge with *Laughing Boy* (1929), A. B. Guthrie with *The Way West* (1949), and Charles L. McNichols with *Crazy Weather* (1944). The prototype of the Western came with Jack Schaefer's *Shane* (1949), much overrated but certainly consistently praised. Frank Waters, one of the best writers of the West—or the East—wrote a lovely and loving novel of a young man caught between two cultures in *The Man Who Killed the Deer* (1942). Two of his nonfiction books that convey Indian ways and beliefs sensitively are *Masked Gods* (1950) and *Book of the Hopi* (1963).

Conventions of the Western are so well established for commercial books that any writer who ignored them would be laughed out of bookstores. The setting is obviously the West, preferably some time between 1880 and 1895, the high point of cowboy life. Excitement pervades the novel— attacks, rustlers, the cavalry, lynchings, bank holdups, jailbreaks, goldfields, ladies of the evening (and night), crooked lawyers, and on and on. Violence is far more likely to be gaudily portrayed rather than implied. Nostalgia permeates everything in this best of all the old times when men were rugged and life was cheap. The hero (a marshal, cowboy, drifter, ex-gunfighter, wagonmaster, mountain man) will be moral, though that may have come after a reformation which he rarely will be willing to talk about with anyone save the heroine in one tender moment. And morality will ultimately triumph as the hero plays Hamlet and puts the world aright.

The villain could be a crooked lawyer (or banker), owner of the biggest spread in the territory, a gunfighter looking to nick one more notch on his gun, or a political boss.

Others in the cast are likely to include the hero's sidekick, a trail boss or ranch owner, a saloon girl or two, one oh-so-decent woman (the heroine), several second-string bad guys, and assorted townspeople or rovers to make all the appropriate crowd noises.

Action will come fast on the open range (or in a mine, in a showdown on Front or Main Street or some corral or other, or in a saloon).

Fortunately, some good Westerns either ignore these hackneyed conventions or freshen them up. Louis L'Amour is unquestionably the most famous of all living Western writers. He is also a far better novelist than most teachers and librarians realize, hardly a surprise since all too many ignore L'Amour and practically all of Western literature. L'Amour loves the West, but more important, he knows Western literature and Western history. His readers know that details will be true and history will be accurate. Among his books, the one most likely to appeal to beginners in the field is one of his best, *Down the Long Hills*. Seven-year-old Hardy wakes up one morning to find his horse missing. He leaves the wagon train, followed by his little sister, and when he returns he finds everyone massacred. Hardy and sister head west facing starvation and blizzards and wild animals.

Kathryn Lasky's *Beyond the Divide* is a remarkable novel, a record of the coming of age of a young girl in journal form from April 1, 1849, until June 1, 1850. Meribad Simon and her father question their Amish community and head West after her father is shunned for attending the funeral of a friend who had not strictly observed Amish custom. What they encounter is anything but a storybook delight—cruel emigrants, death everywhere, selfishness and miserliness, rape, and finally the father's death. It is an engrossing book, surehanded throughout, and a strong portrait of a most determined and believable young woman who is a survivor.

The quest for the golden future of the West is also treated in Amelia Bean's *The Fancher Train*, and Ferol Egan's *The Taste of Time*, the latter a delightful picture of an old man, presumably near death, who finds life and love and his youth in the West. Vardis Fisher's *The Mothers: An American Saga of Courage* tells the story of the Donner Party, trapped in the mountains of California as snows begin and reduced to horrors almost beyond belief.

The best accounts of mountain men can be found in Fisher's *Mountain Men* and Bill Hotchkiss' *The Medicine Calf*. Cowboy tales abound, but among the most honest and the best written are William Decker's *To Be a Man* and Robert Flynn's *North to Yesterday*, the latter a somewhat tall tale about a group of misfits who gather to ride the cattle trails long after they have dried up. Clair Huffaker's *The Cowboy and the Cossack* concerns fifteen Montana cowboys and fifteen Russian Cossacks who ride herd on a 4,000 mile cattle drive across Siberia.

E. L. Doctorow's *Welcome to Hard Times*, Charles O. Locke's *The Hell Bent Kid*, and Glendon Swarthout's *The Shootist* are fine novels about the gunman. Locke's novel, particularly, despite the melodramatic title, is well written, and it handles a trite theme most effectively.

Among the many novels about the cultural clash between whites and Indians, these stand out. Will Henry (real name, Henry Wilson Allen) is always sensitive and satisfying, no more so than in *From Where the Sun Now Stands*, his slightly fictionalized heroic tale of Chief Joseph. The usually dependable James Forman is at his best in *People of the Dream*, the story of Chief Joseph, and *The Life and Death of Yellowbird*, fact mixed with fiction about a mystical Indian.

Modern Indian life, or existence, is the subject of James Welch's *Winter in the Blood* and *The Death of Jim Loney*, both bitter studies of cultural

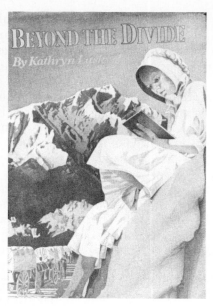

◆ These two strong Western novels portray young people who are survivors.

death in life. Leslie Silko's monumental *Ceremony* is somewhat more hopeful than Welch's novels. For anyone who wants to understand what Indians feel about whites, no better source can be found than Vine Deloria's *Custer Died for Your Sins*, still the most biting and often the funniest attack on the market.

The modern cowboy, facing a West that no longer exists and still searching for his identity and a job, is the subject of Edward Abbey's *The Brave Cowboy* and *Fire on the Mountain*, two books difficult to overrate, J. P. S. Brown's *Jim Kane*, Robert Day's *The Last Cattle Drive*, and Larry McMurtry's *Horseman, Pass By* (better known under its filmed title, *Hud*).

Westerns are often so serious, so mythic, so desolate, that it is pleasant to read a few that are genuinely funny, deliberately so. David Wagoner's *The Road to Many a Wonder* is, simply put, one of the funniest books in English. Ike Bender, age twenty, leaves home to find gold and is soon followed by his younger soon-to-be bride, though he hardly suspects that earlier. Their struggles to get to Colorado and find the pot at the end of their rainbow are believable, generally, and utterly delightful.

Other books for anyone searching for a bit of laughter among the blood-soaked trails of the West are Andrew Dequasie's *Thirsty*—a mule kicks up a gold nugget and starts the town booming—Bill Gulick's *The Liveliest Town in the West*—the editor of the town paper starts a rumor to make a dead town sound exciting to tourists; and Gary Jenning's *The Terrible Teague Bunch*—an inept band of train robbers find it is all more trouble than it is worth.

As the books mentioned in this chapter illustrate, adventure and suspense stories provide opportunities for sharing others' lives. Readers feel emotions they can get in few other ways whether it is the joy of reaching a mountain top, the satisfaction of winning out against great odds, or just the weak-kneed relief that comes from living through a harrowing experience.

With some recent stories, authors offer a bonus, the opportunity to think about something after the story is over. The bonus may be about cultural clashes or ecological concerns. It may be about prejudice and the unfairness of things that seems to strike minorities. Whatever the problem, the mark of success in these stories is the degree to which the authors have involved the reader's emotions.

◆ ACTIVITIES ◆

1. Select an adventure, mystery, or supernatural novel that is popular with young adults. Analyze the book to determine what makes the book popular. Ask three or four students who enjoy the book to talk to you (and possibly your class) about their reactions to the book and why they like it.
2. Because of the excitement and suspense, books mentioned in this chapter are excellent material for book talks. Read three books mentioned and prepare book talks on them aimed at specific grade levels. If you need help, look ahead to Chapter 10 for ideas and suggestions about book talks.
3. Select one of the books mentioned in this chapter that has not yet been made into a movie that you think would be effective on the screen. Describe why you believe it should be filmed and what changes would be necessary in writing a film script from the novel.

4. Read a historical novel and write an evaluation of it. What historic or literary criteria did you use, and how did you use them in evaluating the novel? How historically accurate must a historical novel be? Ask a few students to read and comment to you on their interest in historical novels. Ask students who read Rosemary Sutcliff's or Leon Garfield's books what appeal these novels have.
5. Compare a Western novel that has not been filmed with one of your favorite Western films. Why have Western films been so popular over the years? Why are they currently difficult to find at the box office (or hard to find in the schedule of network television)? Why are Western novels often regarded as subliterature? Is that term valid as literary commentary about the Westerns cited in this chapter?

◆ NOTES ◆

[1]"The Mystery Versus the Novel" in *The Mystery Story*, ed., John Ball (New York: Penguin, 1978), pp. 71–73.

[2]Michael Armstrong, "Some Like It Chilled," *Films and Filming* 17 (February 1971): 28.

[3]Henry Seidel Canby, "What Is Truth?" *Saturday Review of Literature* 4 (December 31, 1927): 481.

[4]Christopher Collier, "Criteria for Historical Fiction," *School Library Journal* 29 (August 1982): 32.

◆ TITLES MENTIONED IN CHAPTER 5 ◆

For information on the availability of paperback editions of these titles, please consult the most recent edition of *Paperbound Books in Print*, published annually by R. R. Bowker Company.

Adventure Stories

Ambler, Eric. *A Coffin for Dimitrios*. Knopf, 1937.

————. *The Light of Day*. Knopf, 1962.

Arthur, Elizabeth. *Beyond the Mountain*. Harper & Row, 1983.

Blum, Arlene. *Annapurna—A Woman's Place*. Sierra Club, 1983.

Bonington, Chris. *Annapurna: South Face*. McGraw-Hill, 1971.

Buchan, John. *The Thirty-Nine Steps*. Doran, 1915.

————. *Greenmantle*. Doran, 1915.

Buckley, William F., Jr. *The Story of Henri Tod*. Doubleday, 1983.

————. *Who's on First*. Doubleday, 1980.

Clancy, Ambrose. *Blind Pilot*. Morrow, 1980.

Clements, Bruce. *The Face of Abraham Candle*. Farrar, Straus & Giroux, 1969.

————. *I Tell a Lie Every So Often*. Farrar, Straus & Giroux, 1969.

Collins, Larry and Dominique Lapierre. *The Fifth Horseman*. Simon and Schuster, 1980.

Dickinson, Peter. *Annerton Pit*. Little, Brown, 1977.

————. *The Seventh Raven*. E. P. Dutton, 1981.

————. *Tulku*. E. P. Dutton, 1979.

French, Michael. *Pursuit*. Delacorte, 1982.

Godey, John. *The Taking of Pelham One Two Three*. Putnam's, 1973.

Green, Gerald. *Karpov's Brain*. William Morrow, 1983.

Gzowski, Peter. *The Sacrament: A True Story of Survival*. Atheneum, 1980.

Herbert Marie. *Winter of the White Seal*. William Morrow, 1982.

Herzog, Maurice. *Annapurna: First Conquest of an 8000 Meter Peak*. E. P. Dutton, 1952.

Higgins, Jack. *Touch the Devil*. Stein and Day, 1982.

Household, Geoffrey. *Rogue Male*. Little, Brown, 1939.

King, Tom. *In the Shadow of the Giants: Mountain Ascents Past and Present*. A. S. Barnes, 1981.

Le Carré, John. *The Honorable Schoolboy*. Knopf, 1977.

————. *The Little Drummer Girl*. Knopf, 1983.

————. *Smiley's People*. Knopf, 1980.

————. *The Spy Who Came in from the Cold*. Coward, McCann & Geoghegan, 1964.

————. *Tinker, Tailor, Soldier, Spy*. Knopf, 1974.

Littell, Robert. *The Amateur*. Simon and Schuster, 1981.

MacInnes, Helen. *Above Suspicion*. Little, Brown, 1941.

————. *Assignment in Brittany*. Little, Brown, 1942.

————. *The Salzburg Connection*. Harcourt Brace Jovanovich, 1968.

————. *The Hidden Target*. Harcourt Brace Jovanovich, 1981.

Mazer, Harry. *The Island Keeper*. Delacorte, 1981.

————. *Snow Bound*. Delacorte, 1973.

Messner, Reinhold and Alessandro Gogna. *K2: Mountain of Mountains*. Oxford University Press, 1982.

Morell, David. *Blood Oath*. St. Martin's, 1982.

Petersen, P. J. *Nobody Else Can Walk It for You*. Delacorte, 1982.

Read, Piers Paul. *Alive: The Story of the Andes Survivors*. Lippincott, 1974.

Reader, Dennis J. *Coming Back Alive*. Random House, 1981.

Roberts, David. *Deborah: My Wilderness Narrative*. Vanguard, 1970.

————. *The Mountain of My Fear*. Vanguard, 1968.

Roper, Steve and Allen Steck. *Fifty Classic Climbs of North America*. Sierra Club, 1979.

Roth, Arthur. *Eiger: Wall of Death*. W. W. Norton, 1982.

Rowell, Galen. *High and Wild: A Mountaineer's World*. Sierra Club, 1979.

Schaller, George B. *Stones of Silence: Journeys in the Himalayas*. Viking, 1980.

Seymour, Gerald. *Archangel*. E. P. Dutton, 1982.

Sherman, D. R. *The Lion's Paw*. Doubleday, 1975.

Speare, Elizabeth George. *The Sign of the Beaver*. Houghton Mifflin, 1983.

Steck, Allen and Steve Roper, eds. *Ascent: The Mountaineering Experience in Word and Image*. Sierra Club, 1980.

Stone, Scott C. S. *Spies*. St. Martin's, 1980.

Thompson, Julian F. *The Grounding of Group 6*. Avon, 1983.

White, Robb. *Deathwatch*. Doubleday, 1972.

Willig, George and Drew Bergman. *Going It Alone*. Doubleday, 1979.

Mysteries

Bennett, Jay. *The Birthday Murderer*. Delacorte, 1977.

————. *Deathman, Do Not Follow Me.* Hawthorne, 1968.

————. *The Executioner.* Avon, 1982.

————. *The Pigeon.* Avon, 1981.

————. *Say Hello to the Hit Man.* Delacorte, 1976.

Bethancourt, T. Ernesto. *Doris Fein: Phantom of the Casino.* Holiday House, 1981.

————. *Doris Fein: Quartz Boyar.* Holiday House, 1980.

————. *Doris Fein: Superspy.* Holiday House, 1980.

————. *Dr. Doom: Superstar.* Holiday House, 1978.

Biggers, Earl Derr. *Behind That Curtain.* Bobbs-Merrill, 1928.

————. *The Black Camel.* Bobbs-Merrill, 1929.

————. *The House Without a Key.* Bobbs-Merrill, 1925.

Carr, John Dickson. *The Burning Court.* Harper, 1937.

————. *The Three Coffins.* Harper, 1935.

Chambers, Kate. *The Case of the Dog-Lover's Legacy.* Bantam, 1983.

————. *Danger in the Old Fort.* Bantam, 1983.

————. *The Secret of the Singing Strings.* Bantam, 1983.

Chandler, Raymond. *The Big Sleep.* Knopf, 1939.

————. *Farewell, My Lovely.* Knopf, 1940.

————. *The High Window.* Knopf, 1942.

————. *The Lady in the Lake.* Knopf, 1943.

————. *The Little Sister.* Houghton Mifflin, 1949.

————. *The Long Goodbye.* Houghton Mifflin, 1954.

Chesterton, G. K. *The Innocence of Father Brown.* Lane, 1911.

Christie, Agatha. *The A.B.C. Murders.* Dodd, Mead, 1935.

————. *By the Pricking of My Thumbs.* Dodd, Mead, 1968.

————. *The Hollow.* Dodd, Mead, 1946.

————. *A Murder Is Announced.* Dodd, Mead, 1950.

————. *The Murder of Roger Ackroyd.* Dodd, Mead, 1926.

————. *The Mysterious Affair at Styles.* Dodd, Mead, 1920.

————. *Sad Cypress.* Dodd, Mead, 1940.

————. *Ten Little Indians.* Dodd, Mead, 1940.

————. *What Mrs. McGillicuddy Saw.* Dodd, Mead, 1954.

Crispin, Edmund. *Buried for Pleasure.* Lippincott, 1949.

————. *The Case of the Gilded Fly.* Lippincott, 1945.

————. *The Long Divorce.* Dodd, Mead, 1951.

————. *Love Lies Bleeding.* Lippincott, 1948.

Cross, Amanda. *Death in a Tenured Position.* E. P. Dutton, 1981.

————. *In the Last Analysis.* Macmillan, 1964.

————. *The Question of Max.* Knopf, 1976.

————. *The Theban Mysteries.* Knopf, 1971.

de la Torre, Lillian. *The Detections of Dr. Sam: Johnson.* Doubleday, 1960.

————. *Dr. Sam: Johnson, Detector.* Knopf, 1946.

Eco, Umberto. *The Name of the Rose.* Harcourt Brace Jovanovich, 1983.

Francis, Dick. *Banker.* Harper & Row, 1983.

————. *Enquiry.* Harper & Row, 1969.

————. *For Kicks.* Harper & Row, 1965.

————. *Odds Against.* Harper & Row, 1965.

————. *Slayride.* Harper & Row, 1973.

Freeling, Nicholas. *Auprès de Ma Blonde.* Harper & Row, 1972.

————. *Criminal Conversations.* Harper & Row, 1966.

————. *The King of Rainy Country.* Harper & Row, 1966.

————. *Love in Amsterdam.* Harper & Row, 1963.

Futrelle, Jacques. *The Thinking Machine.* Dodd, Mead, 1907.

Gardner, Erle Stanley. *The Case of the Counterfeit Eye.* Morrow, 1935.

————. *The Case of the Howling Dog.* Morrow, 1934.

————. *The Case of the Perjured Parrot.* Morrow, 1939.

————. *The Case of the Stuttering Bishop.* Morrow, 1936.

————. *The Case of the Velvet Claws.* Morrow, 1933.

Hammett, Dashiell. *The Dain Curse.* Knopf, 1929.

————. *The Glass Key.* Knopf, 1931.

————. *The Maltese Falcon.* Knopf, 1930.

————. *Red Harvest.* Knopf, 1929.

————. *The Thin Man.* Knopf, 1934.

Hillerman, Tony. *The Blessing Way.* Harper & Row, 1970.

————. *Dance Hall of the Dead.* Harper & Row, 1973.

————. *The Dark Wind*. Harper & Row, 1982.

————. *The Listening Woman*. Harper & Row, 1978.

Innes, Michael. *Appelby and Honeybath*. Dodd, Mead, 1983.

James, P. D. *The Black Tower*. Scribner's, 1975.

————. *Death of an Expert Witness*. Scribner's, 1977.

————. *A Mind to Murder*. Scribner's, 1967.

————. *Shroud for a Nightingale*. Scribner's, 1971.

————. *The Skull Beneath the Skin*. Scribner's, 1982.

————. *An Unsuitable Job for a Woman*. Scribner's, 1972.

Kaminsky, Stuart. *He Done Her Wrong*. St. Martin's, 1983.

————. *Murder on the Yellow Brick Road*. St. Martin's, 1977.

————. *Never Cross a Vampire*. St. Martin's, 1980.

————. *You Bet Your Life*. St. Martin's, 1978.

Keating, H. R. F. *Go West, Inspector Ghote*. Doubleday, 1981.

————. *Inspector Ghote Hunts the Peacock*. E. P. Dutton, 1968.

————. *The Perfect Murder*. E. P. Dutton, 1961.

Kemelman, Harry. *Friday the Rabbi Slept Late*. Crown, 1964.

————. *Monday the Rabbi Took Off*. Putnam's, 1972.

————. *Saturday the Rabbi Went Hungry*. Crown, 1966.

————. *Sunday the Rabbi Stayed Home*. Putnam's, 1969.

MacDonald, John D. *Bright Orange for a Shroud*. Gold Medal, 1966.

————. *The Deep Blue Good-Bye*. Gold Medal, 1964.

Macdonald, Ross. *The Blue Hammer*. Knopf, 1976.

————. *The Drowning Pool*. Knopf, 1950.

————. *The Far Side of the Dollar*. Knopf, 1964.

————. *The Galton Case*. Knopf, 1959.

————. *The Moving Target*. Knopf, 1949.

————. *The Zebra-Striped Hearse*. Knopf, 1962.

MacLeod, Charlotte. *Cirak's Daughter*. Atheneum, 1982.

————. *We Dare Not Go A-Hunting*. Atheneum, 1980.

McBain, Ed. *Cop Hater*. Permabooks, 1956.

————. *Lady Killer*. Simon and Schuster, 1950.

————. *Long Time No See*. Random House, 1977.

————. *'Til Death*. Simon and Schuster, 1958.

Mortimer, John. *Rumpole of the Bailey*. Penguin, 1979.

————. *Rumpole's Return*. Penguin, 1982.

————. *The Trials of Rumpole*. Penguin, 1980.

Moyes, Patricia. *Down Among the Dead Men*. Holt, Rinehart and Winston, 1961.

————. *Many Deadly Returns*. Holt, Rinehart and Winston, 1970.

————. *A Six-Letter Word for Death*. Holt, Rinehart and Winston, 1983.

Nixon, Joan Lowery. *A Deadly Game of Magic*. Harcourt Brace Jovanovich, 1983.

————. *The Seance*. Harcourt Brace Jovanovich, 1980.

————. *Specter*. Delacorte, 1982.

Queen, Ellery. *Calamity Town*. Little, Brown, 1942.

————. *The Egyptian Cross Mystery*. Stokes, 1932.

————. *The French Powder Mystery*. Stokes, 1930.

————. *The Greek Coffin Mystery*. Stokes, 1932.

Rendell, Ruth. *Death Notes*. Pantheon, 1981.

————. *Make Death Love Me*. Doubleday, 1979.

————. *Master of the Moor*. Pantheon, 1982.

————. *Murder Being Once Done*. Doubleday, 1972.

————. *Speaker of Mandarin*. Pantheon, 1983.

Schorr, Mark. *Red Diamond: Private Eye*. St. Martin's, 1983.

Simenon, Georges. *Inspector Maigret and the Strangled Stripper*. Doubleday, 1955.

————. *The Madman of Bergerac*. Harcourt, Brace, 1940.

————. *Maigret and the Headless Corpse*. Doubleday, 1968.

————. *Maigret on the Defensive*. Harcourt Brace Jovanovich, 1981.

Spillane, Mickey. *I, The Jury*. E. P. Dutton, 1947.

Stout, Rex. *The Black Mountain*. Viking, 1954.
———. *Black Orchids*. Farrar, Straus & Giroux, 1942.
———. *Fer-de-Lance*. Farrar, Straus & Giroux, 1934.
———. *The League of Frightened Men*. Farrar, Straus & Giroux, 1935.
———. *Too Many Cooks*. Farrar, Straus & Giroux, 1938.
Upfield, Arthur William. *Death of a Lake*. Doubleday, 1954.
———. *Death of a Swagman*. Doubleday, 1945.
———. *The Lure of the Bush*. Doubleday, 1965.
———. *The Winds of Evil*. Doubleday, 1944.
Van Gulik, Robert. *The Chinese Bell Murders*. Harper & Row, 1959.
———. *The Chinese Gold Murders*. Harper & Row, 1961.
———. *Murder in Canton*. Scribner's, 1967.
Wahlöö, Per. *The Laughing Policeman*. Pantheon, 1970.
———. *The Man on the Balcony*. Pantheon, 1968.
———. *The Man Who Went Up in Smoke*. Pantheon, 1969.
———. *The Thirty-First Floor*. Knopf, 1967.
Wambaugh, Joseph. *The Choirboys*. Delacorte, 1975.
———. *The Glitter Dome*. Morrow, 1981.
———. *The New Centurions*. Little, Brown, 1970.
———. *The Onion Field*. Delacorte, 1973.
Wolf, Gary. *Who Censored Roger Rabbit?* St. Martin's, 1981.

Stories of the Supernatural

Andrews, V. C. *Flowers in the Attic*. Simon and Schuster, 1979.
———. *If There Be Thorns*. Simon and Schuster, 1981.
———. *My Sweet Audrina*. Poseidon, 1982.
Anson, Jay. *The Amityville Horror*. Prentice-Hall, 1977.
———. *666*. Simon and Schuster, 1981.
Blatty, William. *The Exorcist*. Harper & Row, 1971.
Coyne, John. *The Piercing*. Putnam's, 1979.
———. *The Searing*. Putnam's, 1980.

Duncan, Lois. *Down a Dark Hall*. Little, Brown, 1974.
———. *Stranger with My Face*. Little, Brown, 1981.
———. *Summer of Fear*. Little, Brown, 1976.
———. *The Third Eye*. Little, Brown, 1984.
Haining, Peter, ed. *Gothic Tales of Terror: Classic Horror Stories from Europe and the United States*. Taplinger, 1972.
———, ed., *Gothic Tales of Terror: Classic Horror Stories from Great Britain*. Taplinger, 1972.
Kahn, Joan, ed. *Some Things Dark and Dangerous*. Harper & Row, 1970.
———, ed. *Some Things Fierce and Fatal*. Harper & Row, 1971.
———, ed. *Some Things Strange and Sinister*. Harper & Row, 1973.
King, Stephen. *Carrie*. Doubleday, 1974.
———. *Christine*. Viking, 1983.
———. *Cujo*. Viking, 1981.
———. *Different Seasons*. Viking, 1982.
———. *Firestarter*. Viking, 1980.
———. *Salem's Lot*. Doubleday, 1975.
———. *Pet Sematary*. Doubleday, 1983.
———. *The Shining*. Doubleday, 1977.
———. *The Stand*. Doubleday, 1978.
Levin, Ira. *Rosemary's Baby*. Random House, 1967.
Manley, Seon and Gogo Lewis, eds. *Ladies of Horror: Two Centuries of Supernatural Stories by the Gentle Sex*. Lothrop, Lee and Shepard, 1971.
Millhiser, Marlys. *The Mirror*. Putnam's, 1979.
———. *Nightmare Country*. Putnam's 1981.
Peck, Richard. *The Dreadful Future of Blossom Culp*. Delacorte, 1983.
———. *The Ghost Belonged to Me*. Viking, 1975.
———. *Ghosts I Have Been*. Viking, 1977.
Raucher, Herman. *Maynard's House*. Putnam's, 1981.
Straub, Peter. *Floating Dragon*. Putnam's, 1981.
———. *Ghost Story*. Coward, McCann & Geoghegan, 1979.
———. *Shadowland*. Coward, McCann & Geoghegan, 1981.
Sullivan, Gerard and Harvey Aronson. *High Hopes: The Amityville Murders*. Coward, McCann & Geoghegan, 1981.

Tenny, Dixie. *Call the Darkness Down*. Atheneum, 1984.

Westall, Robert. *Break of Dark*. Greenwillow, 1982.

————. *The Devil on the Road*. Greenwillow, 1979.

————. *Futuretrack 5*. Greenwillow, 1984.

————. *The Haunting of Chas McGill and Others*. Greenwillow, 1983.

————. *The Watch House*. Greenwillow, 1978.

————. *The Wind Eye*. Greenwillow, 1977.

Wise, Herbert A. and Phyllis Fraser, eds. *Great Tales of Terror and the Supernatural*. Modern Library, 1944.

Historical Novels

Auel, Jean M. *The Clan of the Cave Bear*. Crown, 1980.

————. *The Valley of Horses*. Crown, 1982.

Burton, Hester. *Kate Ryder*. Crowell, 1975.

Clapp, Patricia. *Witches' Children*. Lothrop, Lee and Shepard, 1982.

Clavell, James. *Shōgun*. Atheneum, 1975.

Collier, James Lincoln and Christopher Collier. *The Bloody Country*. Four Winds, 1976.

————. *Jump Ship to Freedom*. Delacorte, 1981.

————. *My Brother Sam Is Dead*. Four Winds, 1974.

————. *War Comes to Willy Freeman*. Delacorte, 1983.

————. *The Winter Hero*. Four Winds, 1978.

Farber, Norma. *Mercy Short: A Winter Journal, North Boston, 1692–93*. E. P. Dutton, 1982.

Garfield, Leon. *Jack Holburn*. Pantheon, 1965.

————. *The Night of the Comet*. Delacorte, 1979.

————. *The Sound of Coaches*. Viking, 1974.

————. *The Strange Affair of Adelaide Harris*. Pantheon, 1971.

Haugaard, Erik Christian. *Cromwell's Boy*. Houghton Mifflin, 1978.

————. *A Messenger for Parliament*. Houghton Mifflin, 1976.

Highwater, Jamake. *The Sun, He Dies*. Lippincott, 1980.

Hunter, Mollie. *A Pistol in Greenyards*. Funk and Wagnalls, 1968.

————. *The Stronghold*. Harper & Row, 1974.

————. *You Never Knew Her as I Did*. Harper & Row, 1982.

Jennings, Gary. *Aztec*. Atheneum, 1980.

Kurten, Bjorn. *Dance of the Tiger: A Novel of the Ice Age*. Pantheon, 1980.

Namioka, Lensey. *The Samurai and the Long-Nosed-Devils*. McKay, 1976.

————. *Valley of the Broken Cherry Trees*. Delacorte, 1980.

————. *Village of the Vampire Cat*. Delacorte, 1981.

O'Dell, Scott. *The Amethyst Ring*. Houghton Mifflin, 1983.

————. *The Captive*. Houghton Mifflin, 1979.

————. *The Feathered Serpent*. Houghton Mifflin, 1982.

————. *Island of the Blue Dolphins*. Houghton Mifflin, 1960.

————. *The King's Fifth*. Houghton Mifflin, 1966.

————. *Zia*. Houghton Mifflin, 1976.

Paterson, Katherine. *Bridge to Terabithia*. Crowell, 1977.

————. *Jacob Have I Loved*. Crowell, 1980.

————. *Rebels of the Heavenly Kingdom*. E. P. Dutton, 1983.

————. *The Sign of the Chrysanthemum*. Crowell, 1973.

Peters, Daniel. *The Luck of the Huemac: A Novel About the Aztecs*. Random House, 1981.

Peyton, K. M. *The Right-Hand Man*. Oxford University Press, 1980.

Pope, Elizabeth Mary. *The Perilous Gard*. Houghton Mifflin, 1974.

Ray, Mary. *Beyond the Desert Gate*. Faber, 1977.

————. *Sword Sleep*. Faber, 1976.

Renault, Mary. *Fire from Heaven*. Pantheon, 1969.

————. *Funeral Games*. Pantheon, 1982.

————. *The Persian Boy*. Pantheon, 1972.

Schlee, Ann. *Ask Me No Questions*. Holt, Rinehart and Winston, 1982.

Sutcliff, Rosemary. *Blood Feud*. E. P. Dutton, 1977.

————. *Blue Remembered Hills*. Morrow, 1984.

————. *The Capricorn Bracelet*. Walck, 1973.

————. *Dawn Wind*. Walck, 1961.

————. *The Eagle of the Ninth*. Walck, 1954.

————. *Frontier Wolf*. E. P. Dutton, 1981.

————. *Knight's Fee*. Walck, 1960.

————. *The Lantern Bearers*. Walck, 1959.

————. *The Mark of the Horse Lord*. Walck, 1965.

————. *Outcast*. Oxford University Press, 1955.

————. *The Shield Ring*. Oxford University Press, 1957.

————. *The Silver Branch*. Oxford University Press, 1958.

————. *Simon*. Oxford University Press, 1954.

————. *Song for a Dark Queen*. Crowell, 1979.

————. *Sun Horse, Moon Horse*. E. P. Dutton, 1978.

————. *Warrior Scarlet*. Walck, 1958.

Turner, Ann Warren. *The Way Home*. Crown, 1982.

Vidal, Gore. *Creation*. Random House, 1981.

Von Canon, Claudia. *The Inheritance*. Houghton Mifflin, 1983.

————. *The Moonclock*. Houghton Mifflin, 1979.

Walsh, Jill Paton. *A Parcel of Patterns*. Farrar, Straus & Giroux, 1983.

Willard, Barbara. *Harrow and Harvest*. E. P. Dutton, 1976.

Westerns

Abbey, Edward. *The Brave Cowboy: An Old Tale in a New Time*. Dodd, Mead, 1956.

————. *Fire on the Mountain*. Dial, 1962.

Bean, Amelia. *The Fancher Train*. Doubleday, 1959.

Brown, J. P. S. *Jim Kane*. Dial, 1970.

Day, Robert. *The Last Cattle Drive*. Putnam's, 1977.

Decker, William. *To Be a Man*. Little, Brown, 1967.

Deloria, Vine. *Custer Died for Your Sins: An Indian Manifesto*. Macmillan, 1969.

Dequasie, Andrew. *Thirsty*. Walker, 1983.

Doctorow, E. L. *Welcome to Hard Times*. Simon and Schuster, 1960.

Egan, Ferol. *The Taste of Time*. McGraw-Hill, 1977.

Fisher, Vardis. *The Mothers: An American Saga of Courage*. Vanguard, 1943.

————. *Mountain Men*. Morrow, 1965.

Flynn, Robert. *North to Yesterday*. Knopf, 1967.

Forman, James. *The Life and Death of Yellowbird*. Farrar, Straus & Giroux, 1973.

————. *People of the Dream*. Farrar, Straus & Giroux, 1972.

Gulick, Bill. *The Liveliest Town in the West*. Doubleday, 1968.

Henry, Will. *From Where the Sun Now Stands*. Random House, 1960.

Hotchkiss, Bill. *The Medicine Calf*. W. W. Norton, 1981.

Huffaker, Clair. *The Cowboy and the Cossack*. Simon and Schuster, 1973.

Jennings, Gary. *The Terrible Teague Bunch*. W. W. Norton, 1975.

L'Amour, Louis. *Down the Long Hills*. Bantam, 1968.

Lasky, Kathryn. *Beyond the Divide*. Macmillan, 1983.

Locke, Charles O. *The Hell Bent Kid*. W. W. Norton, 1957.

McMurtry, Larry. *Horseman, Pass By*. Harper, 1961.

Silko, Leslie Marmon. *Ceremony*. Viking, 1977.

Swarthout, Glendon. *The Shootist*. Doubleday, 1974.

Wagoner, David. *The Road to Many a Wonder*. Farrar, Straus & Giroux, 1974.

Waters, Frank. *The Man Who Killed the Deer*. Farrar, Straus & Giroux, 1942.

Welch, James. *The Death of Jim Loney*. Harcourt Brace Jovanovich, 1979.

————. *Winter in the Blood*. Harcourt Brace Jovanovich, 1974.

SCIENCE FICTION, FANTASY, AND UTOPIAS

OF WONDROUS WORLDS

All of us, save the most exactingly literal-minded, need occasionally to go outside ourselves, to dream old and new dreams about the strange and impossible and dangerous and exacting, to travel to lands that lie beyond our mundane and limited worlds and exist only in the imaginations of other people. We may even create a new world for ourselves, peopled with creations fashioned in our own image or in the images of people and animals and things we love. The works we create often derive from favorite authors. Thousands of young people have loved *The Wizard of Oz* so much that they borrowed from Frank Baum to create their own Oz books or became wrapped in the wonderful world of Kenneth Grahame's *The Wind in the Willows* and have written amazingly parallel stories.

That need hardly diminishes as we grow older, and that helps to account for the continuing popularity of science fiction, fantasy, and utopian books. Fantasy and science fiction allow us to see the golden worlds of the past and future, and utopias permit us to see an imperfect society made attainable. Without dreams, we die. But we worry about becoming too preoccupied with our dreams. To live permanently in science fiction, fantasy, and utopia is to divorce ourselves from the very real concerns of our very real world. On the other hand, to accept the real world we know as the only possible world is to damn ourselves to a stifling and deadly existence. Perhaps because young adults are not entirely squelched by society, they respond openly to the kinds of books presented in this chapter. Many young adults are still examining the life-styles and the society around them, and they are keenly interested in looking at the alternatives in science fiction, fantasy, and utopias.

◈ SCIENCE FICTION

Science fiction enjoys tremendous popularity today, but that was not always the case. A visit to the paperback racks in a bookstore only a few years ago would likely have revealed no section devoted to science fiction, though some science fiction might have been found in the fiction department. Today's science fiction fans have no trouble finding the large section for science fiction alone, though the books are sometimes mixed in with fantasy. Publishers, both hardback and paperback, recognize the size of the market, and several—Ballantine, for example—have developed separate divisions for science fiction.

Proof, if more were needed, for science fiction's popularity is easy to find. If a serious science fiction film like *Things to Come* in 1936 was a rarity—most filmgoers still thought of "Buck Rogers" or "Flash Gordon" serials if they thought of science fiction at all—that is not true today. *Invasion of the Body Snatchers* in 1956 (and its remake in 1978), *Village of the Damned* and *The Time Machine* in 1960, *2001: A Space Odyssey* in 1968, *Close Encounters of the Third Kind* in 1977, and the trilogy by George Lucas, *Star Wars* in 1977, *The Empire Strikes Back* in 1980, and *Return of the Jedi* in 1983, were popular and/or critically well received. In fact, *Return of the Jedi* set a new record for first-day box office receipts when it opened in May 1983: $6,219,629 from more than a million and a half people. And the record it broke had been set eleven months earlier by *Star Trek II: The Wrath of Khan*.

Books written from or about science fiction movies or television continue to sell. *Star Trek* spawned A. E. Crispin's *Yesterday's Son* and Vonda N. McIntyre's *Star Trek: The Wrath of Khan*. George Lucas' work led to Donald F. Glut's *Star Wars: The Empire Strikes Back*. Jim Henson and Gary Kurtz's *The Dark Crystal* generated A. C. H. Smith's *The Dark Crystal* and Brian Froud's *The World of the Dark Crystal*. Disney Production's *Dragonslayer* led to Wayland Drew's book of the same title. And television's less popular "Battlestar Galactica" series became a book with the same title by Glen A. Larson and Robert Thurston.

Science fiction's increasing popularity can be traced by the attendance at the World Con meetings of sci-fi buffs. The first was held in conjunction with the 1939 New York World's Fair which celebrated "the world of tomorrow." Two hundred fans appeared, most of them in their teens or early twenties. In 1950, 400 showed up for the meeting in Portland, 568 for the 1960 meeting in Pittsburgh, 620 in 1970 in Heidelberg, West Germany, but more than 3000 in Brighton, England, in 1979, more than 4000 in Chicago in 1982, and 6500 people in 1983 in Baltimore.

And anyone who looks even casually at an issue of *Locus*,[1] best of all the science fiction fanzines, recognizes how very popular this literary form has become.

Ray Bradbury argues that the appeal of science fiction is understandable because science fiction is important literature, not merely popular stuff. Opening his essay on "Science Fiction: Why Bother?" he compares himself to a fourth-rate George Bernard Shaw who makes an outrageous statement and then tries to prove it. Bradbury's statement is that "Science fiction is the most important fiction being written today." He adds that it is not "*part* of the Main Stream. It *is* the Main Stream."[2]

Carl Sagan, the Cornell University astonomer-author, has added his testimony, writing that it was science fiction that brought him to science. Kurt Vonnegut, Jr., also applauded science fiction through his character Eliot Rosewater in *God Bless You, Mr. Rosewater, or Pearls Before Swine.* Stumbling into a convention of science fiction writers, Rosewater drunkenly tells them that he loves them because they are the only ones who:

> ◇ know that life is a space voyage, and not a short one either, but one that'll last for billions of years. You're the only ones with guts enough to really care about the future, who really notice what machines do to us, what wars do to us, what cities do to us, what big, simple ideas do to us, what tremendous misunderstandings, mistakes, accidents and catastrophes do to us.

He goes on to praise them for being "zany enough to agonize over time and distances without limit, over mysteries that will never die, over the fact that we are right now determining whether the space voyage for the next billion years or so is going to be Heaven or Hell."

Science fiction writer and scientist Arthur C. Clarke agrees with Rosewater on the admittedly limited but still impressive power of science fiction to scan the future. In his introduction to *Profiles of the Future*, Clarke writes:

> ◇ A critical—the adjective is important—reading of science-fiction is essential training for anyone wishing to look more than ten years ahead. The facts of the future can hardly be imagined *ab initio* by those who are unfamiliar with the fantasies of the past.
>
> This claim may produce indignation, especially among those second-rate scientists who sometimes make fun of science-fiction (I have never known a first-rate one to do so—and I know several who write it). But the simple fact is that anyone with sufficient imagination to assess the future realistically would, inevitably, be attracted to this form of literature. I do not for a moment suggest that more than one per cent of science-fiction readers would be reliable prophets; but I do suggest that almost a hundred per cent of reliable prophets will be science-fiction readers—or writers.[3]

Why does science fiction appeal to young adults, and to adults? First and probably most important, it is exciting. Science fiction may have begun with the "rah-rah-we're-off-to-Venus-with-Buck-Rogers" kind of book, and while it has gone far beyond that, the thrill of adventure is still there in most science fiction. Science fiction writers refuse to write down to their audience, the highest praise they can give to their readers, and that is recognized and admired. Science fiction allows anyone to read imaginative fiction without feeling the material is kid stuff. Science fiction presents real heroes to readers who find their own world often devoid of anyone worth admiring, heroes doing something brave, going to the ultimate frontiers, even pushing these frontiers further back, particularly important at a time when many young people wonder if any new frontiers exist. Most important, science fiction writers see their readers as intellectually curious, praise of the highest order, and that is repaid by readers who often venerate the best of science fiction writers.

Science fiction has a heritage of fine writers and important works. Some critics argue that Mary Godwin Shelley's *Frankenstein* (1817) was the first work in the field. Others argue for Swift's *Gulliver's Travels* (1726) or Lucian's *The True History* (first century A.D.). No matter, for nearly everyone agrees that the first popular writer of science fiction was Jules Verne whose *A Voyage to the Center of the Earth* (1864) and *Twenty Thousand Leagues under the Sea* (1870) pleased readers for years thereafter. The first American science fiction short story was Edgar Allan Poe's "The Unparalleled Adventure of One Hans Pfaall" which he published in the June 1835 *Southern Literary Messenger* and included in *Tales of the Grotesque and Arabesque* in 1840. The tale of Hans Pfaall's balloon trip to the moon in a nineteen-day voyage is a hoax, as Poe added in a concluding note, but the early trappings of science fiction are present. Dime novel science fiction appeared in Edward S. Ellis's *The Huge Hunter, or The Steam Man of the Plains* in 1869. *Frank Reade, Jr. and His Steam Wonder* (a locomotive that needed no rails) appeared in 1879, the first of 187 science fiction dime novels written by Louis Senarens who signed his books, "Noname." He was not quite eighteen when he wrote the first one.

Edward Stratemeyer's Literary Syndicate produced thirty-eight books in the "Tom Swift" series though they were more adventure than science. The Syndicate also produced the nine-volume "Great Marvel" series. Written by Howard Garis under the pen-name of Roy Rockwood, the books were far-fetched, but they provided adventures in strange and new places, witness titles like *Lost on the Moon, or In Quest of the Field of Diamonds* (1911) and *By Air Express to Venus, or Captives of a Strange Planet* (1929).

The development of modern science fiction began with Hugo H. Gernsback. (The Hugo Awards given each year for excellence in science fiction honor his name.) An electrical engineer, in 1908 he began publishing *Modern Electrics*, the first magazine devoted to radio. In 1911 after finding a few extra pages, he wrote a serialized story, *Ralph 124C/41 + : A Romance of the Year 2660*, a utopian vision about the inventions and innovations of the future. It was successful, and Gernsback included more stories about the future thereafter. In 1926, he began *Amazing Stories*, the first issue containing stories by Poe, Verne, and H. G. Wells. By 1929 he had lost control of that magazine so he began *Science Wonder Stories* and coined the term, "science fiction." His demands for a too-literal and sterile scientific accuracy in stories made his work formula-ridden and repetitive, but he did offer a market for a kind of science fiction story. When the title of *Amazing Stories* was changed to *Amazing Science Fiction* and when two new magazines appeared, *Fantasy and Science Fiction* and *Analog*, writers now had a much wider market for their science fiction. As stories appeared, these magazines became increasingly liberal and willing to accept new ideas and new writers and different approaches. Many of today's major science fiction writers first appeared in these magazines.

Other writers appeared during this time who were to influence later writers. H. G. Wells' *The Time Machine* (1895), *The Invisible Man* (1897), and *The First Men in the Moon* (1901) were read and admired. *The War of the Worlds* (1898) became even better known forty years later when Orson Welles dramatized it for radio's Mercury Theater for a Halloween production on October 30, 1938. The nationwide hysteria that followed as many listeners heard and believed that Martians were indeed taking over the Earth created a furor that many people still remember. Sir Arthur Conan Doyle, better known for his Sherlock Holmes stories, wrote a tale about scientists investigating a South American plateau where a prehistoric world with deadly animals still existed in *The Lost World* (1912). Edgar Rice Burroughs, already popular for his Tarzan stories, wrote some bad but very popular stories of Mars including *A Princess of Mars* (1917), *The Warlord of Mars* (1919), *The Chessmen of Mars* (1922), and another story of a lost world with prehistoric animals, *The Land That Time Forgot* (1924).

Much better were the works of Karel Capek and Olaf Stapledon. Capek's *War with the Newts* (first published in Czechoslovakia in 1926 and in America in 1939) describes the evolution of a nonhuman race, the Newts, which is gentle and intelligent. Humans use them for profit until the Newts revolt. Better known is Capek's drama, *R. U. R.* (first produced in Prague on January 26, 1921). Rossum's Universal Robots also revolt against the mistreatment of humans, and as the play ends, the human race may be beginning all over again. Stapledon's intelligent if now unfashionable novels deserve rereading. *Last and First Men* (1930) describes a time from 1930 to two billion years into the future when humanity is destroyed in a cosmic accident. *Odd John* (1935), in which a human mutant is far superior to ordinary humanity, may be his best book, but *Star Maker* (1937) and *Sirius: A Fantasy of Love and Discord* (1944) are not without admirers.

Science fiction took vast strides toward greater respectability as literature and prophecy after World War II, partly because science fiction writers had predicted both the atomic age and the computer revolution. People seemed more willing to consider alternatives and to reappraise society. The paperback revolution flourished, and that made science fiction easily available to many new readers.

Sure proof that science fiction had become mature and respectable came in December 1959 when the prestigious and often stuffy Modern Language Association began its science fiction newsletter, *Extrapolation*. Colleges and secondary schools offered courses in science fiction. Major publishers and significant magazines recognized and even published science fiction writers.

Robert A. Heinlein, one of science fiction's big four writers, defined science fiction in 1953:

> ◇ But what, under rational definition, is *science* fiction? There is an easy touchstone; science fiction is speculative fiction in which the author takes as his first postulate the real world as we know it, including all established facts and natural laws. The result can be extremely fantastic in content, but it is not fantasy; it is legitimate—and often very tightly reasoned—speculation about the possibilities of the real world.[4]

Heinlein's definition distinguishes science fiction from fantasy without in any way denigrating the latter, and as any fan of either literature knows—and many readers read and love both science fiction and fantasy—fine writers like Ursula Le Guin and Anne McCaffrey and many others write in both fields. But science fiction must adhere to natural law. A novel can use quite different laws of another planet, but those laws must be scientifically clear and consistent. No dragons need apply for work in science fiction—they are the province of fantasy. The limitation has rarely proved onerous to science fiction writers, many of whom are engineers or scientists or had their early training in the sciences.

There are other conventions though none so important as Heinlein's. Characters voyage into space facing all sorts of dangers—science fiction is, after all, more adventure than philosophy though the latter is often present. Other planets have intelligent and/or frightening life forms though they may differ drastically from Earth's humans. Contemporary problems are projected hundreds or thousands of years into the future, and those new views of overpopulation, pollution, religious bickering, political machinations, and sexual disharmony often give readers a quite different perspective of our world and our problems today. Prophecies are not required in science fiction, but some of the richest books of Isaac Asimov and Arthur C. Clarke have been prophetic. Occasionally a scientifically untenable premise may be used. On the August 15, 1983, "Nightcap" talk show on Arts Cable Television, Isaac Asimov said, "The best kind of sci-fi involves science" and then agreed that "Time travel is theoretically impossible but I wouldn't want to give it up as a plot gimmick." Essentially, he was agreeing with Heinlein but adding that the plot and excitement counted even more. The internal consistency and plausibility of a postulated imaginary society creates its own reality.

Ballantine editor Judy Del Rey said, "Defining science fiction is simply saying three names—Isaac Asimov, Robert A. Heinlein, and Arthur C. Clarke, one could almost add Bradbury. The four of them established touchstones for those who are to come."[5]

Bradbury's *The Martian Chronicles* is widely known and taught in secondary schools, though whether the work is science fiction is open to argument. Bradbury has no interest in science, except that humans use science to destroy one another. He certainly pays no attention to the way in which passengers get to Mars. They get on a rocket, and somehow it takes them where they want to go. The novel, really a collection of some good, some excellent, short stories loosely tied together, is an important work, whether science fiction or not. In a prefatory note to Bantam's 1954 paperback edition of *The Martian Chronicles*, Clifton Fadiman perceptively writes that Bradbury:

> ◇ has caught hold of a simple, obvious but overwhelmingly important moral idea, and, quite properly, he will not let it go. That idea . . . is that we are in the grip of a psychosis, a technology-mania, the final consequence of which can only be universal murder and quite conceivably the destruction of our planet.
>
> His colonizers—not all, but the majority—cannot help destroying the mag-

nificent civilization of Mars, any more than they could help destroying their own earth civilization.

And Bradbury has said, "I don't try to predict the future—I try to prevent it."

Bradbury's only true science fiction novel (or novelette) is *Fahrenheit 451,* a warning about a world to come so anti-intellectual that firemen are trained to burn books, not protect the world from fires. *Where Robot Mice and Robot Men Run Round in Robot Towns: New Poems, Both Light and Dark* is worth anyone's time. He may not be a great poet, but he is a fine writer.

Arthur C. Clarke is a more important science fiction writer, and *Childhood's End* is frequently listed among the great science fiction novels though more readers begin rather than finish it. The story of aliens who take over the Earth's problems and ultimately the Earth itself is utopian science fiction. Under the guidance of Chief Orverlord Karellen, aliens develop what seems to be a perfect society for humans. "For the first time in human history, no one worked at tasks they did not like . . . Ignorance, disease, poverty, and fear had virtually ceased to be." More approachable are *The City and the Stars* set a billion years from now with the last people living in a sand-surrounded city, and *Rendezvous with Rama* set in 2130 as humans investigate a hollow, fifty-kilometer long cylindrical alien spaceship called Rama and inhabited by robots.

Isaac Asimov remains one of the most popular writers in the field, more for what he has done in the past than what he has done recently. Author of an incredible number of books, all revealing a curious and perceptive mind, he is best known for his *Foundation* trilogy. *Foundation* prophesies the doom of the Empire. Mathematician Hari Selden establishes two Foundations to survive the coming crisis, one on the planet Terminus for hard science, one on the other end of the galaxy for purposes unclear. *Foundation and Empire* describes the destruction of the imperial planet with much about the first foundation and a genetic mutant, Mule, who hopes to take over the fallen empire. *Second Foundation* tells of the Mule who seeks to destroy the first foundation. The second foundation psychically challenges the mutant. Twenty-nine years later, in 1982, Asimov wrote a fourth in the series, *Foundation's Edge.* Set 498 years since the reestablishment of the First Foundation, the book carries the story further.

Far better than the last of the Foundation series are *The Caves of Steel* about a human and a robot detective who join forces to solve a crime and *I, Robot,* short stories reprinted from the science fiction magazine *Astounding* in the 1940s and among the best writing Asimov has done. A great recent collection contains Asimov's short story "Runaround" along with Asimov's best known contribution to science fiction, his Three Laws of Robotics:

1. A robot may not injure a human being, nor through inaction allow a human being to come to harm.
2. A robot must obey the orders given it by human beings except where such orders would conflict with the First Law.

◆ Defining science fiction is simply saying three names— Robert A. Heinlein, Arthur C. Clarke, and Isaac Asimov.

3. A robot must protect its own existence as long as such protection does not conflict with the First or Second Law.[6]

Asimov's autobiography covering the years before he became a well-known writer, *In Memory Yet Green: The Autobiography of Isaac Asimov, 1920–1954,* tells of his early interest in science fiction, but the book is such that almost anyone curious about an interesting life will enjoy it.

The giant of science fiction writers is Robert A. Heinlein. Prolific and consistently fine, his novels range from relatively unsophisticated thrillers for young readers from the 1940s through the early 1960s, *Rocket Ship Galileo, Space Cadet, Red Planet, Starman Jones, Tunnel in the Sky, Have Space Suit—Will Travel,* and *Podkayne of Mars* to later adult works. The YA books were not without distinction, and *Have Space Suit—Will Travel,* despite the hokey title, is still an exciting novel. *Podkayne of Mars* was a rarity for its time, for the hero is female. But if Heinlein had done little more than continue to mine the science fiction vein for young readers he would not be considered important.

Stranger in a Strange Land in 1961 marked the change in Heinlein's work. One of the most widely read novels during the revolting 1970s, *Stranger* became something of a bible to many college students and was used to justify everything from total sexual freedom to humanity's eternal need for spiritual love, though most readers seemed to lean more toward the sexual than the spiritual. Valentine Michael Smith feels and thinks like a Martian, but when he is brought to Earth, he finds human feelings coming out as he meets and travels with Jill. He learns about sex—an un-Martian quality—and religion as he founds his church, "The Church of All Worlds." When his church is destroyed, Smith escapes with Jill, only to be stoned by a crowd who calls Smith a heretic.

The Moon Is a Harsh Mistress appeared five years later, and it is a far more satisfying, if simpler, novel than *Stranger.* Three people and a humanized computer lead a revolt in Luna, a penal colony in the twenty-first century. The story parallels our own Revolution against the British—the Declaration of Independence is dated July 4, 2076. *The Number of the Beast* in 1980, Heinlein's first novel in seven years, was more self-indulgent, a fascinating failure but worth reading because it was by Heinlein. Four people zip around the universe finding universe after universe, some of them already familiar to readers—Lewis Carroll's Wonderland and Frank Baum's Oz.

Friday, far more successful, wastes no words getting started:

> ◇ As I left the Kenya Beanstalk capsule, he was right on my heels. He followed me through the door leading to Customs, Health, and Immigration. As the door contracted behind him I killed him.

Friday is an A.P. (artificial person) who acts as courier for someone she knows only as Boss. Earth has become some 400 territorial states, and intrigue and death are everywhere. As usual, Heinlein attacks common humanity and praises the military, savages organized religion and praises rugged individualism. And once more, his female characters are weakly developed. But *Friday* is an important book, one that is likely to be read for years to come.

Certain themes run through much of science fiction—the love of exploration; alien invasions; the future, promising or frightening; sex and sexism; technology; and religion. Many books, of course, combine or play with several of these themes.

Exploration is celebrated in A. E. Van Vogt's *The Voyage of the Space Beagle*, obviously a play on Darwin's trip aboard the *Beagle* in the nineteenth century. The Space Beagle is on a scientific survey for new planets and new life-forms. James Tiptree, Jr.'s (real name, Alice Sheldon) *10,000 Light Years from Home* and *Up the Walls of the World* are explorations of Earth, the planet Tyree, and deep space with three sets of characters free to exchange bodies and planets.

Ever since H. G. Wells' *The War of the Worlds*, the-aliens-are-coming theme has been a favorite with science fiction writers. Although it borders dangerously on being a cliché, some writers have used it intelligently. It is, after all, a provocative idea. As anthropologist Loren Eiseley said, "One does not meet oneself until one catches the reflection from an eye other than human."

In John Rowe Townsend's *The Visitors*, three travelers from the twenty-second century come to present-day Cambridge, England, to record the "bad old days." Townsend has a finely tuned sense of irony, and this is one of his better books. Louise Lawrence's *Star Lord* is about an alien who crashes into the Earth and is saved by Rhys Williams and his dog. Lawrence's *Calling B for Butterfly* shows a benevolent alien presence which protects six young people when they are isolated in space. Larry Niven and Jerry Pournelle's *The Mote in God's Eye* tells of a first contact with another galaxy. When the alien dies, Earth must send an emissary speeding to avert war and destruction.

Less kindly aliens are the subjects of two science fiction classics. John

Wyndham's *The Midwich Cuckoos* focuses on one quiet, almost idyllic, English village. During one September night and a day-long blackout that follows, every woman in the village becomes pregnant. Nine months later, sixty children are born, all quiet and odd, all with strange eyes. It was filmed under the title, *Village of the Damned*. In Jack Finney's *The Body Snatchers* (better known under its film title, *Invasion of the Body Snatchers*), alien forces use pods to replace the population of a small town. The novel ends with the main character trying vainly to convince others that something sinister is afoot.

Worry about the future ahead of us is a common theme in science fiction. John Christopher's books present a gloomy view though each has a hero who valiantly works to change the world around him. *The White Mountains, The City of Gold and Lead*, and *The Pool of Fire* form one such trilogy. Better is another trilogy, *The Prince in Waiting, Beyond the Burning Lands*, and *The Sword of the Spirits*, set after the Disaster in England when machines and technology are feared and banned. Luke Perry, the Prince in Waiting, learns about a secret society of seers, literally an underground group who understand and can control machines. Robert C. O'Brien's (real name, Robert Leslie Conly) *Z for Zachariah* takes place after the nuclear holocaust. Ann Burden believes she is the sole survivor until another survivor appears, the cruel and selfish John Loomis.

Pollution and cloning are central to Kate Wilhelm's *Where Late the Sweet Birds Sang*. The Sumner family lives in an isolated valley in Virginia. When the collapse of civilization comes, the family believes that its experiments with cloning are essential to humanity's survival. But the clones are hopelessly unlike humans—the clones fear individualism. The experiment fails, and barbarism threatens. The savagery that follows the death of our world is brilliantly described in Russell Hoban's *Riddley Walker*. About 1997, cataclysms wipe out the world. Two thousand years later, the landscape is monotonous and the remnants of life are grim. Packs of wild dogs live off the dead land, and traveling puppet shows dramatize versions of the events of the past. The language of the book is English, but the words are garbled, but understandable—*masheans* is machines, *weals* is wheels. Riddley Walker is one of many commentators who try to make sense of the puppet shows to leave a record of the past's events for the future. And at one point, Riddley breaks into tears as he realizes that there was once a lovely world that is now dead:

> ◇O what we ben! And what we come to! How cud any 1 not want to get that shyning Power back from time back way back? How cud any 1 not want to be like them what had boats in the air and picters on the wind. How cud any 1 not want to see them shyning weals terning?

The book is not easy going, but it is a book worth struggling over.

Two novelists have written of overpopulation in the future. Lester Del Rey's *The Eleventh Commandment* takes the biblical edict, be fruitful and multiply, to its logical and horrifying conclusion. John Brunner's *Stand on Zanzibar* concerns the world of 2010 with its incredible overpopulation.

Ursula Le Guin's *The Left Hand of Darkness* describes a race neither male nor female, neither asexual or bisexual, on the planet Gethen. The Gethenians' sexual cycle is twenty-six days; for four-fifths of the period they are sexually inactive, and then about the twenty-first or twenty-second day, they become sexually active, either female or male hormones dominating. Individuals have neither choice nor interest in which sex they will be this time. It is possible to be pregnant and bear a child, and then father a child at another time. Le Guin's *The Dispossessed* also attacks the conventional-traditional view of women and men. Joanna Russ' *And Chaos Died* and *The Female Man* also deal with the theme of sex and sexism.

Technology run wild is a common theme. Walter Tevis' *Mockingbird* portrays a world where humans are subservient to robots, and where robots wish only to die but must wait for the death of the last human. David Gerrold's *When Harlie Was One* has as its hero a superhuman computer with the emotional temperament of a child, a dangerous and powerful child. Frederik Pohl's *Midas World* is both a spoof of robot novels and a commentary on humanity's love of the easy life. A far more touching work is Anne McCaffrey's *The Ship Who Sang*. A brain from a hopelessly crippled body (Helva) is taken to become the brain of a spaceship.

John Brunner's *The Shockwave Rider* shows us a twenty-first century America where data processing has made life so easy that an earthquake in San Francisco totally immobilizes life and leads to a government which uses drugs to modify behavior. Yevgeny Zamyatin's *We*, written in 1920, first published in 1924, and never published in the author's native Russia, is set in a totalitarian society in the twenty-sixth century. People are forced to live in glass apartments to do away with privacy, and people have numbers, not names.

Perhaps the strangest of all, Maureen Duffy's *Gor Saga* is about an inhuman scientist who uses his own sperm to breed a gorilla. Gor is the result, but what is Gor? Neither animal nor human, Gor tries to find an answer but religion and science have none.

Religion has been less widely treated in science fiction than readers might suppose, but several important writers have focused on it. C. S. Lewis's *Out of the Silent Planet* features Weston, a scientist gone bad, and a heroic man, Ransom, off to Malacandra (Mars). There Ransom learns of four races who live harmoniously. He lives with one of the races, the hrossa, and learns the truth of many myths. Through that knowledge, Ransom meets the eldila, ethereal spirits of the place. In *Perelandra*, Random travels to Perelandra (Venus) with its one inhabitant, the Green Lady. Weston arrives on a spaceship, determined to destroy the Eden of Perelandra. Ransom engages in battle to save the innocence of the planet. *That Hideous Strength* disappointingly concludes the trilogy, with a battle between Ransom and N.I.C.E. (the National Institute of Coordinated Experiments). Ransom is aided by Merlin.

More contemporary, in time of writing if not in spirit, than Lewis are Frank Herbert's several books about the planet Dune. The first, and still the best of the books, is *Dune* about the inhabitants of the planet; *Dune* is loosely based on the life of Mohammed. *Dune Messiah, The Children of*

Dune, and *God Emperor Dune* followed, not one being the equal of the earlier book. Vonda N. McIntyre's *Dreamsnake* is about Healer Snake and her friend Arevin. Snake comes to Arevin's clan to heal a child with her dreamsnake. It is killed, and she must go on a quest to find another dreamsnake.

Walter H. Miller, Jr.'s *A Canticle for Leibowitz* is three related novels about the United States after the nuclear holocaust as an area moves through three generations of barbarism toward destruction. In "Fiat Homo," the engineer Leibowitz joins the Catholic Church and discovers it means to destroy all knowledge. He founds an abbey to preserve ancient science. Six centuries later, Leibowitz is gone, but monks copy his memorabilia meaninglessly. When a novice discovers some new documents left by Leibowitz, Leibowitz is canonized.

Lighter by far, Frederick Pohl's *The Cool War* is set in 2020 when the Reverend Hornswell (Horny) Hake is forced to become part of the Team— something like the old C.I.A. The Team moves about the world, trying desperately to make life in other countries as miserable as it is in the United States—pollution, clogged waterways, and no gas. Hake is a believable human, horrified by what he is told to do—some of it hopelessly outrageous—yet caught up in his work, trying hard to make sense out of the world and having little luck doing so.

Readers asked to describe science fiction might easily come up with several adjectives—*thrilling, compelling, startling, frightening.* But rarely would a reader come up with *amusing* and for good reason. Science fiction is rarely funny. That is why a few books are so refreshing. The perfect child turns out to be dangerous to other children in Christine Nostlinger's *Konrad,* a pleasant spoof on technology gone wacky. Mrs. Bartolotti receives a package containing a factory-created son, Konrad, perfect in every way.

Frederick Pohl and C. M. Kornbluth's *The Space Merchants* is a delightfully nasty attack on Madison Avenue hucksters. Mitchell Courtenay is assigned the job of persuading people to emigrate to Venus, and his methods form the basis of this social satire. A satirical view of social engineers is seen in Stanislaw Lem's *The Futurological Congress: The Memoirs of Ijon Tichy.* The catastrophes of human absurdity and dreams gone mad are continued in *Memoirs of a Space Traveler: Further Reminiscences of Ijon Tichy* and *More Tales of Pirx the Pilot.* Funniest of all are three books by Douglas Adams, all send-ups of science fiction yet delightful to those who like or hate the field. *The Hitchhiker's Guide to the Galaxy, The Restaurant at the End of the Universe,* and *Life, the Universe and Everything* are discussed in the section on humor in Chapter 9.

◈ FANTASY

In the November 4, 1972, *Saturday Review,* Patrick Merla argued that as young adults' literature became more realistic, adult literature grew more fantastic.

◇ The paradox of "reality" for children versus "fantasy" for adults may be double-edged—children looking for facts to help them cope with an abrasive environment while adults probe a deeper, archetypal reality that can transform society altogether. A paradox not merely bemusing or amusing, but one that betokens a renascence of the wish to live humanely: a wealth of profound possibilities for mankind.[7]

What Merla wrote about adult reading remains true. But he overestimated the power of realistic literature and badly underestimated the power of fantasy on young people. Fantasy now is popular with readers of all ages.

Testimony to the therapeutic value of fantasy is easy to find. Folklorist and fantasy writer J. R. R. Tolkien wrote:

◇ Fantasy is a natural human activity. It certainly does not destroy or even insult Reason; and it does not either blunt the appetite for, nor obscure the perception of, scientific verity. On the contrary, the keener and the clearer is the reason, the better fantasy it will make. If men were ever in a state in which they did not want to know or could not perceive truth (facts or evidence) then Fantasy would languish until they were cured.[8]

Theologian Harvey Cox maintains that fantasy is essential and allows humanity to relive and anticipate, to remake the past and create new futures:

◇ Fantasy is the richest source of human creativity. Theologically speaking, it is the image of the creator God in man. Like God, man in fantasy creates whole worlds *ex nihilo*, out of nothing.

   Yet despite its importance, our era has dealt shabbily with fantasy. In many other cultures fantasy has been carefully nurtured and those with unusual abilities in fantasy honored. In ours, we have ignored fantasy, deprecated it, or tried to pretend it wasn't really there. Above all, we pride ourselves on being "realists."[9]

But Ray Bradbury agreed that fantasy is essential to our lives today:

◇ The ability to "fantasize" is the ability to survive. It's wonderful to speak about this subject because there have been so many wrong-headed people dealing with it. We're going through a terrible period in art, in literature and living, in psychiatry and psychology. The so-called realists are trying to drive us insane, and I refuse to be driven insane. . . . We survive by fantasizing. Take that away from us and the whole damned race goes down the drain.[10]

The appeal of fantasy may come from a simple fact with complex underlyings. The world of fantasy is both greater and seemingly simpler than our mechanistic, technological, absurd, mad world. Most of us are— or will be—bounded by making a living, paying taxes, trying desperately to find a bit of satisfaction in our jobs and in our lives. We will never have the opportunity to battle for pure good against total evil, as happens in fantasy, or so we think. But we can fight that battle and journey on fabulous quests in strange lands against frightening beasts by reading Tolkien or Ursula Le Guin or Anne McCaffrey or Walter Wangerin, Jr. The rational is important, but it is not all of life.

Fantasy allows—or forces—us to become greater than we had hoped we

◆ Fantasy is now popular with readers of all ages. The librarian who made this promotional display apologized because so many of the books had already been borrowed.

Courtesy of the Instructional Resources Library, Arizona State University

were. Fantasy confronts us with the major ambiguities and dualities of life—evil and good, guilt and innocence, appearance and reality, baseness and nobility, weakness and strength, life and death, negligence and responsibility, the cowardly and the heroic, indolence and hard work, vacillation and determination, affectation and openness, anarchy and order, dark and light, confusion and discipline. And the multitudinous shadings in between these linked pairs must be considered and thought through, by adults and young adults.

Two attacks have been leveled against fantasy.

It is sometimes said to be childishly easy reading, but only nonreaders of fantasy could long persist in that nonsense. Fantasies are often very long, and they are almost always more difficult and require closer reading than most other literature, filled as they are with strange beings and mythical overtones and ambiguities.

Fantasy is often labeled escapist literature, and, of course, it is, in several ways. Fantasy allows readers to escape the mundane reality that surrounds all of us and to revel in glorious adventures. For some readers, that is quite enough to ask of books. For other readers, venturing into possibly endless quests (for the books often come in series), discovering incredible obstacles, and facing apparently unbeatable antagonists, all to defend good and defeat evil, transitory though the defeat will prove, leads to more than mere reading. The escape from reality sends them back into their own limited and literal worlds to face many of the same problems they found in fantasy. Fantasy in many ways parallels life. The quest is the long journey we all set out on, seeking the good and fighting the bad, facing obstacles and barriers throughout, and ultimately hoping that we will find satisfaction and meaning during and after the quest. Our emotional and intellectual wrestling with life's dualities and ambiguities may not be as earth-shaking as those of fantasy heroes, but it may shake our own personal worlds.

In the December 1971 *Horn Book Magazine*, Lloyd Alexander drew the parallel between the fantasy hero and the lives of readers:

> ◇ The fantasy hero is not only a doer of deeds, but he also operates within a framework of morality. His compassion is as great as his courage—greater, in fact. We might consider that his humane qualities, more than any other, are what the hero is really all about. I wonder if this reminds us of the best parts of ourselves?[11]

In his brilliant and often difficult *After Babel: Aspects of Language and Translation*, George Steiner wrote:

> ◇ *Language is the main instrument of man's refusal to accept the world as it is. . . . Ours is the ability, the need, to gainsay or "unsay" the world, to image and speak it otherwise.*[12]

Fantasy comes from a Greek word meaning "a making visible." Perhaps more than any other form of literature, fantasy is a way of refusing to "accept the world as it is," a way of making experience visible so readers can see what could have been—and could be—rather than merely what was or must be. Certainly, fantasy gives hope where much literature denies the right to hope.

In an article on teaching science fiction, Ursula Le Guin distinguished fantasy from science fiction:

> ◇ The basic concept of fantasy, of course, is this: you get to make up the rules, but then you've got to follow them. Science fiction refines the canon: you get to make up the rules, but within limits. A science-fiction story must not flout the evidence of science, must not, as Chip Delaney puts it, deny what is known to be known.[13]

But no matter what the definition, or who propounds it, the boundaries between the two are often fuzzy, witness a Science Fiction Book Club ad in the September 1983 *Discover*. Dust jackets of thirty books were shown. The first four in the top line were Douglas Adams' *Life, the Universe and Everything*, a spoof of science fiction, Jean M. Auel's *The Valley of Horses*, something of a historical novel set in prehistoric times, Terry Brooks' *The Elfstones of Shannara*, out-and-out-fantasy, and Robert A. Heinlein's *Friday*, out-and-out-science fiction.

The conventions of fantasy are well-established, though any clever writer is encouraged to create new ones. First and most important, there must be a quest. Someone, probably a young person, alone or accompanied by friends goes on a quest to protect someone or some country from the powers of evil. The quest may be ordained or required or may, occasionally, be self-determined. Good and evil may be confused briefly by the hero, but the protagonist will ultimately recognize the distinction. The obligatory battle between the powers of good and evil will result in victory for the side of good, though the struggle may be in doubt and may be prolonged. But the victory is always transitory.

Heroes must prove worthy of their quests though they may early be fumbling or stumbling or unsure about both themselves and their quests. Heroes in fantasy are young, but the quests hasten maturity, and the striplings we first saw soon prove wise and courageous.

Fantasy is clearly related to mythology, either creating new myths with hobbits or dragons or using old myths many readers will recognize, particularly from Arthurian legend or the Welsh *Mabinogion*. Fantasy is a world of magic. Colors may be important symbols, but light and dark are always symbolic.

And to aid readers, the author will usually preface the book with a map which will introduce readers to the new world and aid them in following the hero's quest.

A few forerunners of today's fantasy are still widely read. Edwin A. Abbott's *Flatland, A Romance of Many Dimensions* features a narrator, "A square," who discovers a third dimension in his two-dimensional world and feels the fury of his fellow Flatlanders because he writes about it. The novel, revised in 1884, is a clever and still readable blend of mathematics and science fiction and fantasy and social satire. (The recent *Planiverse: Computer Contact with a Two-Dimensional World* by R. T. Dembard is a take-off on Abbott's book.) E. R. Eddison's *The Worm Ouroboros* attracted readers in 1922 with its account of Lessingham's dream-flight in a chariot drawn by a hippogriff to Mercury, a planet inhabited by demons, witches, goblins, imps, and ghouls.

Better known by far are the novels by J. R. R. Tolkien, for many people *the* beginnings of fantasy. *The Hobbit, or There and Back Again* began in 1933 as a series of stories Tolkien told his children about the strange little being known as Bilbo, the Hobbit. Even more famous is his trilogy, *The Lord of the Rings*. His love of language led him to create a language, Elfish, for his own amusement and for the book. Appendices to *The Lord of the Rings* are devoted to the history of Middle-Earth, its language, and its geography. An extension of Tolkien's work, *The Silmarillion* led the *New York Times* best-seller list for several weeks in 1977, amazing for a fantasy, though the work proved disappointing to many Tolkien fans. Tolkien created many of the conventions of fantasy. For that alone, he would be important. But his greatest importance lies in the excellence of *The Hobbit* and *The Lord of the Rings* which can be—and for many people are—read again and again for delight and insight.

A new Time-Life series of books, "The Enchanted World," should serve as a fine introduction to fantasy for either adults or young adults. Brendan Lehane's *Wizards and Witches*, the first volume, is beautifully illustrated, and if it is any indication of books to follow, the volumes on *Dragons, Fairies and Elves, Ghosts, Legends of Valor*, and *Fabled Kingdoms*, will be enjoyed by thousands of fantasy buffs.

Two writers dominate contemporary fantasy—Ursula Le Guin and Anne McCaffrey.

Le Guin's early books, *The Left Hand of Darkness* and *The Dispossessed*, were intelligent mixtures of science fiction and fantasy, but her finest three books, "The Earthsea Trilogy," are the purest of fantasies. The setting of A

THE PEOPLE BEHIND THE BOOKS

URSULA K. LE GUIN, Author

A Wizard of Earthsea
The Tombs of Atuan
The Dispossessed
The Farthest Shore

To tell you the direction my own work is taking would be to tell you a great deal more than I know myself. Might I ask you to consider the fact that though we writers use words as our artistic medium, we are usually no more articulate, no more able to say what we are doing and why, than the most typically tongue-tied sculptor or composer. Words used by the intellect are a very different lot from words used by the daimon. And words used about daimons are generally inadequate if not downright lies. Particularly when people announce what they're going to do next. Your guess is absolutely as good as mine. ◆

Wizard of Earthsea is, of course, Earthsea, a world of vast oceans and multitudinous islands. Duny demonstrates early that he is capable of becoming a wizard, is given his true name, Ged, and learns the names of all things—word magic binds the worlds of fantasy and fairy tales together. Childishly showing off in a forbidden duel of sorcery at his school on Roke Island "where all high arts are taught," he uses his powers to call a woman from the dead and accidentally releases an evil Power, a Shadow that follows him thereafter. That capricious and childish act causes Ged to become deaf, blind, and mute for four weeks in a hot summer. The Archmage Gensher comes to Ged and says:

◇ You have great power inborn in you, and you used that power wrongly, not knowing how that spell affects the balance of light and dark, life and death, good and evil. And you were moved to do this by pride and by hate. Is it any wonder the result was ruin?

Ged completes his training and leaves a certified wizard, but with Ged goes the shadow, of what he knows not except that it is evil.

The remaining two-thirds of the novel consists of many adventures, but always, at the center of Ged's existence, is his quest for the meaning of the shadow. Ged ultimately recognizes that his quest is not to undo what he has done but to finish what he has started. On a lonely shore, Ged meets the shadow, and as if they were one—and they are—they speak the shadow's name, "Ged," and "Light and darkness met, and joined, and were one."

Vetch, Ged's friend, believes that Ged has been overcome by his foe, and he runs to help Ged. When Vetch finds Ged safe:

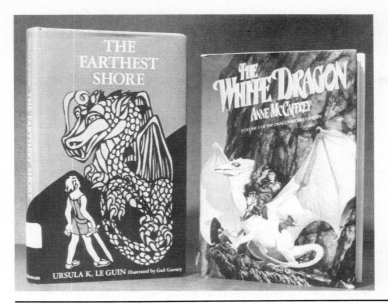

◆ These are books of two writers who dominate contemporary fantasy: Ursula K. Le Guin and Anne McCaffrey.

◇ he began to see the truth, that Ged had neither lost nor won but, naming the shadow of his death with his own name, had made himself a whole: a man who, knowing his whole true self cannot be used or possessed by any other power other than himself, and whose life therefore is lived for life's sake and never in the service of ruin, or pain, or hatred, or the dark.

A short work less than two hundred pages long, A *Wizard of Earthsea* is rich in characters and suspense and meaning. Ged's quest is an initiation rite which leads him to understand the nature of responsibility and who and what he is.

Ged reappears in *The Tombs of Atuan*, but the chief character is Tenar, dedicated from youth to the Powers of the Earth. In the final book of the trilogy, *The Farthest Shore*, Ged, now Archmage and the most powerful of wizards, accompanies a young man on a quest to seek out the evil that threatens to destroy the lands and the powers of the wizards. The evil is Cob, one of the living dead who seeks the peace of death but cannot find it. Ged helps to find death for Cob, but it costs Ged dearly. Even that is not too much, for earlier Ged had told the young man:

◇ You will die. You will not live forever. Nor will any man nor any thing. Nothing is immortal. But only to us is it given to know that we must die. And that is a great gift: the gift of selfhood. For we have only what we know we must lose, what we are willing to lose.

"The Earthsea Trilogy" entertains—above all it is a remarkable and long adventure tale—as it poses unanswerable and eternal questions to readers. What is the purpose of life? Of death? Of balance and equilibrium? What is the nature of evil? Of good? Of humanity? Le Guin's work rarely disappoints and in these three books, she satisfies readers, not by offering easy, pat answers but by respecting her readers and offering truths in all their richness and complexities and frustrations. Her books are not merely based on myths and magic. Her books *are* myths. Her books *are* magic.

Anne McCaffrey's fantasy world is set on Pern. In her trilogy of *Dragonsong, Dragonsinger,* and *Dragondrums,* Pern is threatened every two hundred years by shimmering threadlike spores. Inhabitants protect themselves through the great Pern dragons who destroy the threads as they fall. In *Dragonsong,* Menolly is forced by her father to give up music and her dream of becoming a Harper though at the book's conclusion, she is known to the Master Harper and well on her way to a life of music. In the lesser second volume, Menolly trains to become a Harper and meets the sweet-voiced young boy, Piemur. In this fantasy version of an old-fashioned school story, Menolly has trouble with envious students and faces demanding teachers. *Dragondrums* gets back on track in an exciting finale to the series. Pern is again threatened by the deadly Threadfall, and Piemur, whose voice has changed and made him doubt his future as a singer, is sent off as a drum apprentice and then is stranded along with a stolen firedragon. A bit rambling, *Dragondrums* is a satisfying portrait of a troubled boy who learns about responsibility and survival.

McCaffrey tells fine stories of adventure and young people in the throes of initiation rites, but rarely does she approach the complexity of thought or the mythic qualities of Le Guin's work, not even in *The White Dragon* or *Moreta: Dragon Lady of Pern,* satisfying fantasies though they are.

While most fantasies will follow the basic conventions, they tend to fall into these categories: those set in new worlds, as with Le Guin and McCaffrey; those following myths from the Welsh *Mabinogion;* those celebrating Arthurian legends; those with one foot in contemporary reality and one foot in a fantasy world; those employing animals and often aiming moral barbs at humans; and those using fantasy to amuse. Obviously, some overlapping occurs in many fantasies.

Marion Zimmer Bradley's "Darkover" books are among the most popular of the fantasies set in a new world. Colonists from Earth come to the planet, Darkover, with its one sun and four multicolored moons. Over two thousand years, they lose contact with their home planet and evolve new cultures and new myths alongside the psi-gifted natives. *Darkover Landfall* is a good introduction to the series. A recent book, *Thendara House,* is set on Darkover, but it is less fantasy than feminist tract. Katherine Kurtz's "Deryni" series features a race of extrasensory-powered people in *Deryni Rising, Deryni Checkmate,* and *High Deryni.* Her "Camber" series takes place two hundred years before the "Deryni" books. Closer to a Tolkien world, in spirit if not in performance, are Terry Brooks' *The Sword of Shannara* and *The Elfstones of Shannara.*

Three highly satisfying writers of other-worlds fantasies for young adults are Meredith Ann Pierce, Patricia McKillip, and Jane Yolen. Meredith Pierce's *The Darkangel* conveys a fine sense of evil as a vampyre carries off his thirteenth bride from a small village. A servant girl, Aeriel, sets out to

THE PEOPLE BEHIND THE BOOKS

ANNE McCAFFREY, Author

Dragondrums
Dragonsong
The Ship Who Sang
The White Dragon

As to predictions about the field, or my part in it, I'm not good at such critical analysis. I'm a story teller, basically, and unconsciously reflect in my stories the pressures, the problems, and the ambiance which beset me and our world while I am writing a story. I can't predict what those pressures, problems, and vibrations will be: I haven't lived through and with them yet. I say I write love stories, and that is the truth. I also write xenophilic stories, rather than xenophobic since I do feel that we shall, one day or another, encounter other sentient beings: I can devoutly hope that our species will greet them with tolerance and an overwhelming desire to understand alien minds and mores. Alexander Pope said, "Man must when he can, / Vindicate ways of God to man." I would paraphrase this . . . "Man must, when he can, / Vindicate the ways of Science to man." And, with that science, contact other sentient beings. I think educators are learning that the genre of science fiction is considerably more complex than has been thought: that good science fiction can be a teaching aid on many levels. This position and acceptance is bound to be strengthened since more top writers in the field are turning their attention to the young adult field as an audience, a vital and inspiring audience well worth cultivating. ◆

destroy the power of evil in a beautifully realized epic struggle. In four books, *The Forgotten Beasts of Eld*, *The Riddle-Master of Hed*, *Heir of Sea and Fire*, and *Harpist in the Wind*, McKillip successfully re-creates lands of witches and magic and riddles and music and great adventures. The most successful of the three, Yolen creates believable worlds of witch-mermaids and wizards in *The Magic Three of Solatia*, and her *Dragon's Blood* and *Heart's Blood* portrays an unsure but noble young hero and one of the best developed strong females in recent fiction.

Robert Silverberg's *Lord Valentine's Castle* proved popular with young adults, and the two completing volumes of the trilogy, *The Majipoor Chronicles* and *Valentine Pontifex*, will likely prove equally and magically potent. Roger Zelazny's "Amber" series began with *Nine Princes in Amber*. That story of two co-existing worlds, Amber and the Shadow Earth, was followed by *The Guns of Avalon*, *Sign of the Unicorn*, *The Hand of Oberon*, and *Courts of Chaos*.

The Mabinogion is a collection of medieval Welsh tales, first published in English in 1838–1849 by Lady Charlotte Guest. The eleven stories fall into three parts: the four branches of the Mabinogi (tales to instruct young bards) deal with Celtic legends and myths dealing with (1) Pywll, prince of Dyved, (2) Branwen, daughter of Llyr, (3) Manawyddan, son of Llyr, and (4) Math, son of Mathonwy; four independent tales; and four Arthurian romances. Several writers have used the Mabinogi myths and legends as a basis for their books.

Lloyd Alexander's "Prydain Chronicles" consists of five volumes about Taran, the young Assistant Pig-Keeper. The opening book of this rich fantasy, *The Book of Three*, introduces the main characters, especially Taran, and sends him on his quest to save his land, Prydain, from evil. He seeks his own identity as well, for none know his heritage. Taran's early impatience is understandable but vexing to his master, Dalben, who counsels patience "for the time being."

> ◇ "For the time being," Taran burst out. "I think it will always be for the time being, and it will be vegetables and horseshoes all my life."
>
> "Tut," said Dalben, "there are worse things. Do you set yourself to be a glorious hero? Do you believe it is all flashing swords and galloping about on horses? As for being glorious . . ."
>
> "What of Prince Gwydion?" cried Taran. "Yes, I wish I might be like him."
>
> "I fear," Dablen said, "that is entirely out of the question."
>
> "But why?" Taran sprang to his feet. "I know if I had the chance . . ."
>
> "Why?" Dalben interrupted. "In some cases," he said, "we learn more by looking for the answer to a question and not finding it than we do from learning the answer itself."

Taran, youthful impetuousness and righteous indignation aglow, is bored by Dalben's thoughts and wants action, and that he finds soon enough.

In *The Black Cauldron*, Taran faces the evil Arawn, and in *The Castle of Llyr*, he and his friends rescue Princess Eilonwy from an evil enchantress. In *Taran Wanderer*, he searches for his heritage and learns something about accepting that most dreadful of events, failure. In the last book, *The High King*, the Sword of Dyrnwyn falls into the hands of Arawn, and once more Taran and Prince Gwydion and friends march against evil. Taran learns what all other heroes of fantasy learn, that evil is difficult to conquer even temporarily and impossible to conquer permanently.

Taran's quest allows Alexander to portray a young man stumbling into maturity. From a child who admires heroes for their derring-do, Taran grows into a man who recognizes heroes as symbols of good. From a child who idealizes and idolizes Princess Eilonwy, he grows into a man who can woo and win her. (One of the appeals of fantasy for young males may be that they can read high adventure stories and real love stories at the same time.) From a child who sees the quest as an adventure leading to heroism, Taran grows into a man who recognizes that heroism requires making choices between good and evil and continuing the quest though it takes a lifetime if necessary. Late in the series when Dalben warns Taran that the tasks he has set for himself are difficult and without certainty of attainment, Taran responds:

> ◇ So be it. . . . Long ago I yearned to be a hero without knowing, in truth, what a hero was. Now, perhaps, I understand it a little better. A grower of turnips or a shaper of clay, a common farmer or a king—every man is a hero if he strives more for others than for himself alone. Once . . . you told me that the seeking

counts more than the finding. So, too, must the striving count more than the gain.

Far more difficult than Alexander and aimed at an older audience, Alan Garner's earlier books force his young protagonists to face the problem of good versus evil in *The Weirdstone of Brisingamen, The Moon of Gomrath,* and *Elidor.* Though Garner maintains they are less successful than his later work, the three books have proved popular in England while they are almost entirely ignored in America, mostly because of teacher and librarian ignorance. His two best works are *The Owl Service* and *Red Shift,* both complex—perhaps unduly so—and rewarding. *The Owl Service* has been praised by Mary Cardogan and Patricia Craig:

> ◊ *The Owl Service* is perhaps the first really adult children's book; the first book, that is, in which childish sensibilities are not deferred to, in which the author has not felt that his audience needs, above all, to be protected.[14]

Based on the legend of Blodenweddin in "Math, son of Mathonwy" in the *Mabinogion, The Owl Service* tells of three young people who find a set of old dishes in an attic and learn that the pattern in the dishes is related to an old Welsh legend involving love and jealousy and hatred. *Red Shift* uses three parallel narratives about love—contemporary, seventeenth century, and second century—intertwining them to make connections about love and about our relationships with the past.

Among other writers who have used the *Mabinogion* as a basis for fantasy, Evangeline Walton (real name, Evangeline Walton Ensley) stands out. Her four-part series, *Prince of Annwn: The First Branch of the Mabinogion, The Children of Llyr: The Second Branch of the Mabinogion, The Song of Rhiannon: The Third Branch of the Mabinogion,* and *The Virgin and the Swine: The Fourth Branch of the Mabinogion* (the last volume was reprinted in 1970 as *The Island of the Mighty: The Fourth Branch of the Mabinogion*) are among the best of direct retellings of the old Welsh legends. Walton's quartet is both mythology and ecology, for the author makes the earth a divinity which must not be despoiled by humanity. In an afterword to the first book, Walton writes:

> ◊ When we were superstitious enough to hold the earth sacred and worship her, we did nothing to endanger our future upon her, as we do now.

Two writers for young adults have used the *Mabinogion.* Louise Lawrence's *The Earth Witch* tells of young Owen Jones and his attempts to help and then become the lover of an old Earth Witch. In Nancy Bond's *A String in the Harp,* a young boy finds the harp key of a sixth-century Welsh bard. The key sings to the boy and forces him into a mission.

Arthurian legends have long been staples of fantasy. T. H. White's *The Once and Future King* (a source, for which it can hardly be blamed, for that most dismal of musicals, *Camelot*) is basic to any reading of fantasy. In four books, *The Sword in the Stone, The Witch in the Wood, The Ill-Made King,* and *The Candle in the Wind,* White retells the story of Arthur—his boyhood, his prolonged education at the hands of Merlin, his seduction by Queen Morgause, his love for Guinivere and her affair with Lancelot, and Mordred's revenge and Arthur's fall. A later work, *The Book of Merlyn: The Unpublished Conclusion to The Once and Future King* should, like most work left unpublished at an author's death, have been allowed to remain unpublished and largely unknown.

Among the shorter retellings of the legends, no one has surpassed the three-part series by Rosemary Sutcliff. *The Sword and the Circle: King Arthur and the Knights of the Round Table*, *The Light Beyond the Forest: The Quest for the Holy Grail*, and *The Road to Camlann: The Death of King Arthur* are masterfully written by a writer who loves the legends and has a firm grasp on the materials and the meanings.

Mary Stewart, author of several fine suspense novels, focuses more on Merlin than Arthur in *The Crystal Cave, The Hollow Hills*, and *The Last Enchantment* and on Mordred rather than Arthur in the last book, *The Wicked Day*. Even better are Gillian Bradshaw's three books: *Hawk of May, Kingdom of Summer*, and *In Winter's Shadow* may puzzle a few readers at first—the author writes about Medraut instead of Mordred, Gwynhwyfar rather than Guinivere, Gwalchmai rather than Gawain—but readers who stay with the books will find them readable and most satisfying. Marion Zimmer Bradley's *The Mists of Avalon* takes a different approach, the conflict between the old religion of the Celtics, represented by Morgan Le Fay (here called Morgaine), and the new religion of Christianity, represented by Guinivere (here called Gwenhwyfar). Among recent books, Roderick MacLeish's *Prince Ombra* is particularly exciting. Set in Maine and about the periodic inevitable battle between good and evil, the hero and his teacher have clear parallels with Arthur and Merlin.

Anyone curious about these legends will find interesting background in John Darrah's *The Real Camelot: Paganism and the Arthurian Romances*. For those who enjoy spoofs of legends, Arthur Berger's *Arthur Rex* will provide several delightful hours.

Virginia Hamilton's "Justice" cycle is set both in contemporary reality and in fantasy. In her most ambitious if not always successful work, *Justice and her Brothers, Dustland*, and *The Gathering*, Hamilton writes of eleven-year-old Justice and her older twin brothers, ESP, a future land (an "endless, gritty" world), a computerized humanoid, and evil in a richly symbolic language. Whether Hamilton's difficult series will find its intended readers is yet unclear.

Australian writer Patricia Wrightson has written excellent fiction about mythology of her native land from *The Nargun and the Stars* to *A Little Fear*. A young Aborigine, Wirrun, struggles against ice-spirits who plan to cover the continent with a new ice age in *The Ice Is Coming*. He battles other spirits in *The Dark Bright Water* and *Journey Behind the Wind*.

In her best books, Phyllis Reynolds Naylor tells of the Roberts family and its sudden decision to go to England, Dan Roberts' explorations of the York Roman ruins, and what his discoveries led to in *Shadows on the Wall, Faces in the Water*, and *Footprints at the Window*.

Two exceptional talents handle humanity's obsession with flying in books that go back and forth between reality and fantasy. William Wharton's *Birdy* tells of two boyhood friends, reunited in a World War II psychiatric ward. Always worried about his parents and life generally, Birdy invents another self who can fly away, becomes fascinated by canaries, and tries to dream himself into the soul and body of a bird. Jane Langton's *The Fledgling* is transcendental in tone and setting. Uncle Freddy Hall, founder of the Concord College of Transcendental Knowledge, asks, "Why should we not have been born with wings?" His young niece yearns to fly and, helped by a wild goose, she does, in this warm and delicious novel.

Animal stories aimed at instructing humans are as old as Aesop and almost as recent as yesterday's book review. One of the most beloved is Kenneth Grahame's *The Wind in the Willows* about Toad, Rat, and Mole, just as it is about Toad Hall, fast driving, medieval dungeons, pantheism, and delights fondly remembered by thousands.

The finest of all recent animal fables about humanity's foibles is Walter Wangerin, Jr.'s *The Book of the Dun Cow*, a delightfully funny theological thriller retelling the story of Chauntecleer the Rooster. Nominally the leader of good against evil (the half-snake, half-cock Cockatrice, and the black serpent, Wyrm), Chauntecleer is beset by personal doubts. He is aided by the humble Mundo Cani, the dog, some hilariously pouting turkeys, and other assorted barnyard animals. If the cast sounds cute, Wangerin's novel is not, and the battle scenes are bloody and horrifying.

More famous by far, but less successful, Richard Adams' *Watership Down* was published in England as a children's book and in the United States as an adult novel. The saga of a band of rabbits led by Hazel from a home doomed to become a housing development to Watership Down is exciting and is still occasionally read.

Other animalistic books include William Horwood's *Duncton Wood* about a divided and tyrannical kingdom of moles, Diana Wynne Jones' *Dogsbody* about a Dog Star convicted of murder at a galactic trial and doomed to live on earth until he can find the guilty party, and Allen Andrews' delightful *The Pig Plantagenet* about a war between forest animals and humans.

Two works deal with humans who become animals—William Rayner's *Stag Boy* and Ronald Lockley's *Seal-Woman*.

Two seemingly simple children's books deserve more young adult readers than they have found. Alan Arkin's *The Lemming Condition* tells of a young lemming, Bubber, who questions the mythic force that leads lemmings to march on to the sea and die suicidally by leaping into the water. Russell Hoban's *The Mouse and His Child* seems, at first glance, to be easy reading. It is not. The search for home and security and personal territory is told through two wind-up mouse toys who stay toys and thankfully never become cute and cuddly real animals. The toys find their longed-for home despite the totalitarian gangster, Manny Rat, being left in a trash heap, and watching murder and a bloody battle. Hoban's book is one of the great books of our time.

 **THE PEOPLE BEHIND THE BOOKS**

DIANA WYNNE JONES, Author

Archer's Goon
The Homeward Bounders
Dogsbody

There are three main things about my writing. First and foremost and above all else what I enjoy is telling a story. Writing a story is like reading one that you remember reading before. When I began writing, doing this was not respectable: most books were boring and heavy with Message, and my children complained of them bitterly. Nowadays, this is not so, largely because of the efforts and talents of the hundreds of good writers in this field, most of whom awe me with their inventiveness and general excellence. But I wouldn't wish to leave the field. Young people use their heads as they read, and you never have to tell them a thing twice. I am far too impatient to get on and tell a story to keep stopping and repeating explanations, the way you have to do for older readers. On the other hand, I am bad at just writing: I always end up saying something. That is why—and this is my second thing—I think I shall always write fantasy. It is not only infinitely fascinating in itself, but you can say so much with it. I have only begun to scratch its rich surface and can't wait to go on. A fantasy situation, by the very fact of not being anybody's actual situation, will mean more, to more people, than something specific from the everyday world. Who does not identify with Cinderella? And if the situation is funny—and I intend to go on writing funny books—people can see all around it without being hurt. This brings me to my third thing: young people, as a group, spend a lot of time hurting. They are a prey to the neurosis of any parent, teacher, relative or friend who happens to be ordering them around at the time. By presenting my stories with real people in them, albeit in strange situations, I hope to help a bit. I always put my friends—and even oftener, my enemies—in my books. If you happen to recognize yourself in one, be sure it is no accident. ◆

Most readers of fantasy associate the form with high seriousness, but a number of writers have used the conventions of fantasy to spoof the literature or simply to be amusing. William Goldman's *The Princess Bride*, a parody of heroic fantasy, is supposedly an abridgment of an old work, "S. Morgenstern's Satiric History of His Country" sans the dull parts. Set in the Kingdom of Florin (Guilder is the enemy country), the novel tells of heroic Westley's efforts to rescue his beloved Buttercup from the dastardly Prince Humperdink with an equally silly subplot. Less obviously funny but witty throughout is John Gardner's *Grendel*, a retelling of "Beowulf," and the unheroic efforts of the Anglo-Saxons to defeat the monster.

Peter Beagle's quiet and amusing *A Fine and Private Place* and *The Last Unicorn* will appeal to many readers willing to look for more than the usual fantasy. The title of *A Fine and Private Place* comes from Andrew Marvell's "To His Coy Mistress":

◇ The Grave's a fine and private place,
But none, I think, do there embrace.

The grave is also a lively and frequently funny place in Beagle's fantasy. A living human talks to a delightfully tough old raven. In *The Last Unicorn*, a lonely unicorn seeks the company of others of its kind, helped by the magician Schmendrick who is incapable of telling any story without wild elaboration. Stopping at a town early in the quest, Schmendrick tells of his adventures:

> ◇ During the meal Schmendrick told stories of his life as an errant enchanter, filling it with kings and dragons and noble ladies. He was not lying, merely organizing events more sensibly.

Two much-admired fantasies deserve special attention. Robin McKinley's *Beauty* is another retelling of the "Beauty and the Beast" legend, differing from earlier versions in few significant details. McKinley's Beauty is strong and unafraid and loving. When her father tells her that he has been condemned to death by the Beast for stealing a rose, Beauty gladly agrees to change places with her father:

> ◇ "He cannot be so bad if he loves roses so much."
> "But he is a Beast," said Father helplessly.
> I saw that he was weakening, and wishing only to comfort him, I said, "Cannot a Beast be tamed?"

McKinley's version lacks the surrealistic quality of Jean Cocteau's magnificent film, but in most important ways, McKinley's novel compares favorably with any other retelling.

Antoine de Saint-Exupery's *The Little Prince* has been popular with discerning readers for years, and every generation adds to its share of fans. An airplane pilot, forced down in the Sahara Desert from engine problems, encounters a little boy who asks him, "If you please—draw me a sheep." The Little Prince, from a planet no larger than a house, wanders from planet to planet seeking friendship and love. On Earth, he meets a fox who shares his secret: "It is only with the heart that one can see rightly; what is essential is invisible to the eye." But what is essential can be learned from *The Little Prince*, as multitudes of readers have found.

◈ UTOPIAS

Utopias are never likely to be popular with the masses. Utopias lack excitement and fast-moving plots needed for fast reading and easy appeal. Writers of adventure or fantasy or science fiction begin with a story, the more thrilling the better, and later, if at all, add a message. Writers of utopias think first of the message, and then devise a story to carry the weight of the message.

And utopias are usually about dissatisfaction with contemporary society. Many readers have no wish to think seriously about societal issues, much less to read about them. Readers often do not share the anger or irritation of utopian writers, and they will easily miss the allusions needed to follow the story or find the message.

◆ **TABLE 6.1   Suggestions for Evaluating Imaginative Literature**

A good piece of imaginative literature has most of the positive qualities generally associated with good fiction. In addition it usually has:	A poor piece of imaginative literature has the negative qualities generally associated with poor fiction. In addition it may have:
A smooth, unhackneyed way of establishing the imaginative world.	An awkward transition between reality and fantasy.
An originality of concept. Without this originality, it cannot accurately be labelled *fantasy*.	A reliance on trite stereotypes already created by other writers of science fiction or fantasy.
Enough relationship to the real world so that the reader is led to look at the world in a new way or from a new viewpoint.	No relationship to the real world or to human nature.
Something that stimulates readers to participate in the author's creative thinking and to carry the story further in their own minds.	Inconsistencies within the story. The author unpredictably changes the behavior of the characters or relies on unexpected magical solutions to solve problems.
A rigorous adherence to the "rules" of the imaginative world so that the story is internally consistent even though it may break with the physical laws of this world as they are now known.	

For these reasons, utopian literature is likely to appeal only to more thoughtful and intellectual readers. Young adults may not share all the anger of the writer, but given their idealism, they share the writer's concerns about society and humanity.

The centuries-old fascination with utopias is suggested by the Greek origin of the word which includes two meanings, "no place" and "good place." Most of us, in idle moments, dream of a perfect land, a perfect society, a place that would solve all our personal problems and, if we are altruistic enough, all the world's problems as well. Few of us do more than dream. That may explain why some people are so intrigued with others who take the dream onto the printed page.

In his *Republic* in the fifth century B.C., Plato presented his vision of the ideal world, offering suggestions for educating the ruling class. With wise philosopher-kings, or so Plato maintains, the people would prosper, intellectual joys would flourish (along with censorship for Plato would ban poets and dramatists from his perfect society), and the land would be permanently safe.

Later utopias were geared less to a ruling class and more to a society that would preserve its peace and create harmony and happiness for the people. Sir Thomas More's *Utopia* (1516) argued for mental equality of the sexes, simple laws understandable to all, and common ownership of everything. Whether More intended his book as a practical solution to society's problems is doubtful, but he probably did mean it as a criticism of contemporary English life. Utopias, after all, are personal and reflect an author's enthusiasm for (or abhorrence of) certain ideas. That was clearly true of two other early utopias, Francis Bacon's *The New Atlantis* (1626) and Tommaso Campanella's *City in the Sun* (1623).

During the 1800s, utopias were popular, notably Samuel Butler's *Erewhon* (1872) and *Erewhon Revisited* (1901); William Morris' *News from Nowhere, or an Epoch of Rest* (1891); William Dean Howells' *A Traveler from Altruria* (1894); and the most famous of them all, Edward Bellamy's *Looking Backward* (1888) and its less well-known sequel, *Equality* (1897). In the United States, people sought for better societies through various utopian schemes, rarely more than temporarily satisfactory, in places like Harmony, Pennsylvania; New Harmony, Indiana; Brook Farm, Massachusetts; Fruitlands, Massachusetts; Oneida, New York; Nauvoo, Illinois; and Corning, Iowa.

Twentieth-century writers produced more dystopias (diseased or bad lands) than perfect lands and perfect societies. Dystopias warn us of society's drift toward a particularly horrifying or sick world lying just over the horizon. They are sometimes misinterpreted as prophecies alone, but books like Aldous Huxley's *Brave New World* and George Orwell's *1984* and *Animal Farm* are part prophecy, part warning.

A utopia first serialized in an obscure magazine, *The Forerunner*, in 1915 and seemingly forgotten was reprinted in 1979 and emerged as a book deserving wide attention. Charlotte Perkins Gilman's *Herland* has clear and obvious appeal to feminists. But its importance is broader than merely for that group, for it is about real equality for all people. Three male adventurers stumble onto an all-female society. Sociologist Vandyck Jennings announces, "This is a civilized country! There must be men." Inhabitants of the land frustrate the three men by making clear that the women have no understanding of words such as *lover* or *wife* or *home*:

> ◇ We are not like the women of your country. We are not Mothers, and we are People, but we have not specialized in this line.

The men learn how very strange it is to be treated as people, not men, and how odd it is that the land has no sexual tension. They recognize that sex is often a practice used by males to subjugate females. They learn that this world is based on love and reason with ideals being "Beauty, Health, Strength, Intellect, and Goodness."

Actual utopian communities have been used in several novels. Elizabeth Howard's *Out of Step with the Dancers* shows a celibate Shaker community in 1853 through the eyes of Damaris as she accompanies her converted father to a strange new life. Religious pacifism facing the Civil War is the subject of Janet Hickman's *Zoar Blue* about the German separatist community of Zoar, Ohio. Lynn Hall's excellent *Too Near the Sun* focuses on sixteen-year-old Armel Dupree and his Icarian community near Corning, Iowa. To the shame of his family, Armel's older brother has sought life in the outside world. Armel now wonders if he should follow his brother as he views an ideal community composed of less than ideal people. The world outside and inside the Oneida, New York, community where love is everywhere and sex is to be shared with all proves something other than a heaven to the Berger family in Blossom Elfman's *The Strawberry Fields of Heaven*.

Two novels set in older utopias stand out. Jane Yolen's *The Gift of Sarah*

Barker is set in the Shaker village of New Vale. Taken there by her psychotic mother, Sarah learns that whatever happiness she can find with her beloved Abel, it cannot be in New Vale. Benjamin Capps' *The Brothers of Uterica* deserves far more readers than it has found. Brother Jean Charles Bossereau leads a group into Texas to establish a utopian community predicated on religious freedom, universal suffrage, community-owned land, care of the old, and reward for hard work. The premise of the community is stated in item eleven of the "Goals of Our Common Faith" in the New Socialist Colonization Company. "We seek a life ordered by reason and good will; we expect to find such a life amid the beauties and common virtues of nature." Nature refuses to cooperate, and the people inside and outside the community lack reason and good will as well as common sense, and the venture fails.

Among the novels set in contemporary utopias, Ernest Callenbach's *Ecotopia: The Notebooks and Reports of William Weston* has proved popular with more than a few readers. His novel assumes that the northwest part of the United States has seceded. In 1999, reporter William Weston is the first outsider allowed to visit. As Callenbach's title suggests, the new country is based on ecology and 1960s communal ideas. *Ecotopia Emerging* continues the tale. Joyce Rockwood's *Enoch's Place* tells of a Southern mountain community founded, in part, by Enoch's parents. When he realizes it is time for him to find his own way, he tries the outside world before he knows that home is where he lived and loved his life.

Communes so popular in the 1960s and early 1970s persist even today. Raymond Mungo's *Total Loss Farm: A Year in the Life* and Richard Wizansky's *Home Comfort: Life on Total Loss Farm* extol the virtues and joys of the Vermont farm and why many have tried the life, why some have left, but why many find peace and comfort. Psychologist B. F. Skinner's utopian suggestions and criticisms of our society in *Walden Two* served as a basis for the Twin Oaks community in Virginia described in Kathleen Kinkade's *A Walden Two Experiment: The First Five Years of Twin Oaks Community*.

Yearnings for a simpler life where we can become part of something greater, more important than ourselves are natural. But for many young people, the search led to religious groups less like communes than like cults. Robert Coover examined the power and madness of a cult in *The Origin of the Brunists*. In this novel, a mining explosion kills ninety-seven people, but one man survives and decides that God has saved him to proclaim the approaching end of the world. The death of the mind and the dangers of cults are portrayed in several young adult novels: Robin F. Brancato's *Blinded by the Light*, Gloria D. Miklowitz's *The Love Bombers*, Nancy J. Veglahn's *Fellowship of the Seven Stars*, and Ronni Sandroff's *Fighting Back*. A fine discussion of cults, and humanity's ambivalent fear of and need for them, can be found in David Bromley and Anson D. Shupe, Jr.'s *Strange Gods: The Great American Cult Scare*.

Though its early publicity ranged from good to nonexistent, Jim Jones' People's Temple Sect ultimately received more publicity and attention than all the other cults combined. In San Francisco, Jones was seen as a well-meaning crank, no worse, but when his financial empire and the torture and sexual perversions and brainwashings were exposed in 1977, he and his people fled to Guyana. Jones was perpetually paranoid about the United States and its interference with his grandiose plans, and he believed in grand gestures. On November 18, 1978, he announced, "The best testimony we can make is to leave the goddamn world" and led his followers into death. More than nine hundred died in a frenzy of cyanide suicide. Ugly as the story is, it cannot be ignored. One of the best, and perhaps the most complete, books on the subject is Marshall Kildruff and Ron Javers' *The Suicide Cult: The Inside Story of the People's Temple Sect and the Massacre in Guyana.* James Reston, Jr.'s *Our Father Who Art in Hell* is especially well written. A more agonized story by a family split by Jones is Min S. Yee and Thomas N. Layton's *In My Father's House.* And even more poignant, for obvious reasons, is Kenneth Wooden's *The Children of Jonestown.* More details can be found in George Klineman, Sherman Butler, and David Conn's *The Cult That Died: The Tragedy of Jim Jones and the People's Temple.*

With a few exceptions, young adults are basically optimistic and imaginative. They have not yet lived long enough to lose their natural curiosity, nor have they yet been weighed down with adult problems such as failing health, heavy family responsibilities, expenses far surpassing income, and dreams gone bankrupt.

The three types of books in this chapter are generally optimistic. Even the visions of a world gone mad or the books about cults gone insane leave readers grateful for the world as it usually is. These books start with life as we know it and attempt to stretch the readers' imaginations.

We need to dream, all of us, not to waste our lives but to enrich them. To dream is to recognize humanity's possibilities. In a world hardly characterized by undue optimism, the three genres treated in this chapter offer us hope, not the sappy sentimentalism of "everything always works out for the best"—for it often does not—but realistic hope based on our noblest dreams of surviving. If we go down, we do it knowing that we have cared and dreamed and found something for which we are willing to struggle.

◆ ACTIVITIES ◆

1. "Science fiction presents real heroes to readers who find their own world often devoid of anyone worth admiring, heroes doing something important and brave." Read a novel by Heinlein or Clarke or Asimov looking carefully at the heroism of the main character or characters. What kind of heroism is exemplified? Is the heroism admirable and worth emulating for young adults today?

2. Read an early science fiction novel by Jules Verne or H. G. Wells *and* one by a contemporary science fiction writer. Compare the two books and their attitudes toward heroes and life. What ideas or characteristics of modern science fiction have their roots in Verne or Wells? What changes have taken place as science fiction developed? Why?

3. Take a reading interest survey of your classes (or your school). What kinds of people enjoy reading science fiction or fantasy? How do they differ in any way from those who claim no enthusiasm for either of these forms of literature? Talk with a few science fiction or fantasy buffs about their interests. What do

they believe makes either form of literature particularly appealing? Who do they believe are the most enjoyable writers today in either field? Why?

4. Interview one or two young adults asking them what their visions are of a perfect society or a perfect way of life. Read a utopian novel or two and compare the life presented there with the life described by the young adults. How are they similar? Different? Do you believe the young adults would have enjoyed the books you read?

5. Read a science fiction, fantasy, *and* a utopian novel. Examine the techniques the three authors use to establish the fact that the novels are not real but the worlds portrayed are worth examining and considering. Write an evaluation explaining how the three authors handled the same problems in different ways. Which of the three books did you find most convincing or interesting? Why?

6. Given the current popularity of filmed fantasy or science fiction (for example, *Dragonslayer, Return of the Jedi, Star Trek*), which fantasy or science fiction work not yet filmed would you most recommend as a good choice for future filming? Why? What difficulties would the filmmaker face in planning a film of your choice? Why do you believe it would be a box office success?

◆ NOTES ◆

[1]*Locus*, 34 Ridgewood Lane, Oakland, CA 94611.

[2]Ray Bradbury, "Science Fiction: Why Bother?" *Teacher's Guide: Science Fiction* (New York: Bantam, n.d.), p. 1.

[3]Arthur Clarke, *Profiles of the Future* (New York: Holt, Rinehart and Winston, 1984), p. 9.

[4]Robert Heinlein, "Ray Guns and Rocket Ships," *Library Journal* 78 (July 1953): 1188.

[5]Aljean Harmetz, "Filming a Ray Bradbury Fantasy," *New York Times*, April 24, 1983, p. 17-H (National Edition).

[6]Introduction to "Runaround" in *Machines That Think: The Best Science Fiction Stories about Robots and Computers*, eds., Isaac Asimov, Patricia S. Warrick, and Martin H. Greenberg (New York: Holt, Rinehart and Winston, 1984), p. 209.

[7]Patrick Merla, "'What Is Real?' Asked the Rabbit One Day," *Saturday Review* 55 (November 4, 1972): 49.

[8]J. R. R. Tolkien, *The Tolkien Reader* (New York: Ballantine, 1966), pp. 74–75.

[9]Harvey Cox, *The Feast of Fools: A Theological Essay on Festivity and Fantasy* (Cambridge: Harvard University Press, 1969), p. 59.

[10]Mary Harrington Hall, "A Conversation with Ray Bradbury and Chuck Jones," *Psychology Today* 1 (April 1968): 28–29.

[11]Lloyd Alexander, "High Fantasy and Heroic Romance," *Horn Book Magazine* 47 (December 1971): 583.

[12]George Steiner, *After Babel: Aspects of Language and Translation* (New York: Oxford University Press, 1975), pp. 217–18.

[13]Ursula K. Le Guin, "On Teaching Science Fiction" in *Teaching Science Fiction: Education for Tomorrow*, ed., Jack Williamson (Philadelphia: Oswick Press, 1980), p. 22.

[14]Mary Cadogan and Patricia Craig, *You're a Brick, Angela! A New Look at Girls' Fiction from 1839 to 1975* (London: Gollancz, 1976), p. 371.

◆ TITLES MENTIONED IN CHAPTER 6 ◆

For information on the availability of paperback editions of these titles, please consult the most recent edition of *Paperbound Books in Print*, which is published annually by R. R. Bowker Company.

Science Fiction

Adams, Douglas. *The Hitchhiker's Guide to the Galaxy*. Harmony, 1980.

————. *The Restaurant at the End of the Universe*. Harmony, 1982.

————. *Life, the Universe and Everything.* Harmony, 1982.

Asimov, Isaac. *The Caves of Steel.* Doubleday, 1954.

————. *Foundation.* Doubleday, 1951.

————. *Foundation and Empire.* Doubleday, 1952.

————. *Foundation's Edge.* Doubleday, 1982.

————. *In Memory Yet Green: The Autobiography of Isaac Asimov, 1920–1954.* Doubleday, 1979.

————. *I, Robot.* Doubleday, 1950.

————. *Second Foundation.* Doubleday, 1953.

Bradbury, Ray. *Farenheit 451.* Ballantine, 1953.

————. *The Martian Chronicles.* Doubleday, 1950.

————. *Where Robot Mice and Robot Men Run Round in Robot Towns: New Poems, Both Light and Dark.* Knopf, 1978.

Brunner, John. *The Shockwave Rider.* Harper & Row, 1975.

————. *Stand on Zanzibar.* Doubleday, 1968.

Capek, Karel. *War with the Newts.* Putnam's, 1939.

Christopher, John. *Beyond the Burning Lands.* Macmillan, 1971.

————. *The City of Gold and Lead.* Macmillan, 1967.

————. *The Pool of Fire.* Macmillan, 1968.

————. *The Prince in Waiting.* Macmillan, 1970.

————. *The Sword of the Spirits.* Macmillan, 1972.

————. *The White Mountain.* Macmillan, 1967.

Clarke, Arthur. *Childhood's End.* Houghton Mifflin, 1953.

————. *The City and the Stars.* Harcourt, Brace, and World, 1956.

————. *Rendezvous with Rama.* Harcourt Brace Jovanovich, 1973.

Crispin, A. E. *Yesterday's Son.* Pocket Books, 1983.

Del Rey, Lester. *The Eleventh Commandment.* Regency, 1962.

Doyle, Arthur Conan. *The Lost World.* Doran, 1912.

Drew, Wayland. *Dragonslayer.* Ballantine, 1981.

Duffy, Maureen. *Gor Saga.* Viking, 1982.

Finney, Jack. *The Body Snatchers.* Dell, 1955.

Froud, Brian. *The World of the Dark Crystal.* Knopf, 1982.

Gerrold, David. *When Harlie Was One.* Ballantine, 1972.

Glut, Donald F. *Star Wars: The Empire Strikes Back.* Ballantine, 1980.

Heinlein, Robert. *Friday.* Holt, Rinehart and Winston, 1982.

————. *Have Space Suit—Will Travel.* Scribner's, 1958.

————. *The Moon Is a Harsh Mistress.* Putnam's, 1966.

————. *The Number of the Beast.* Fawcett, 1980.

————. *Podkayne of Mars: Her Life and Times.* Putnam's, 1963.

————. *Red Planet.* Scribner's, 1949.

————. *Rocket Ship Galileo.* Scribner's, 1947.

————. *Space Cadet.* Scribner's, 1948.

————. *Starman Jones.* Scribner's, 1953.

————. *Stranger in a Strange Land.* Putnam's, 1961.

————. *Tunnel in the Sky.* Scribner's, 1955.

Herbert, Frank. *The Children of Dune.* Berkley, 1976.

————. *Dune.* Chilton, 1965.

————. *Dune Messiah.* Putnam's, 1969.

————. *God Emperor of Dune.* Putnam's, 1981.

Hoban, Russell. *Riddley Walker.* Summit, 1981.

Larson, Glen A. and Robert Thurston. *Battle Star Galactica.* Berkley, 1979.

Lawrence, Louise. *Calling B for Butterfly.* Harper & Row, 1982.

————. *Star Lord.* Harper & Row, 1978.

Le Guin, Ursula. *The Dispossessed: An Ambiguous Utopia.* Harper & Row, 1974.

————. *The Left Hand of Darkness.* Walker, 1969.

Lem, Stanislaw. *The Futurological Congress: The Memoirs of Ijon Tichy.* Harcourt Brace Jovanovich, 1971.

————. *Memoirs of a Space Traveler; Further Reminiscences of Ijon Tichy.* Harcourt Brace Jovanovich, 1982.

————. *Tales of Pirx the Pilot.* Harcourt Brace Jovanovich, 1979.

Lewis, C. S. *Out of the Silent Planet.* London: Lane, 1938.

————. *Perelandra*. London: Lane, 1943.

————. *That Hideous Strength*. London: Lane, 1945.

McCaffrey, Anne. *The Ship Who Sang*. Walker, 1969.

McIntyre, Vonda N. *Dreamsnake*. Houghton Mifflin, 1978.

————. *Star Trek: The Wrath of Khan*. Pocket Books, 1982.

Miller, Walter H., Jr. *A Canticle for Leibowitz*. Lippincott, 1959.

Niven, Larry and Jerry Pournelle. *The Mote in God's Eye*. Simon and Schuster, 1974.

Nostlinger, Christine. *Konrad*. Watts, 1977.

O'Brien, Robert C. *Z for Zachariah*. Atheneum, 1975.

Pohl, Frederick. *The Cool War*. Ballantine, 1981.

————. *Midas World*. St. Martin's, 1983.

Pohl, Frederick and C. M. Kornbluth. *The Space Merchants*. Ballantine, 1953.

Russ, Joanna. *And Chaos Died*. Avon, 1970.

————. *The Female Man*. Bantam, 1975.

Shelley, Mary Godwin. *Frankenstein, or the Modern Prometheus*. 1818.

Smith, A. C. H. *The Dark Crystal*. Holt, Rinehart and Winston, 1982.

Stapledon, Olaf. *Last and First Men*. London: Methuen, 1930.

————. *Odd John*. London: Methuen, 1935.

————. *Sirius: A Fantasy of Love and Discord*. London: Secker and Warburg, 1944.

————. *Star Maker*. London: Methuen, 1937.

Tevis, Walter. *Mockingbird*. Doubleday, 1980.

Tiptree, James, Jr. *10,000 Light Years from Home*. Ace, 1973.

————. *Up the Walls of the World*. Berkley, 1978.

Townsend, John. *The Creatures*. Lippincott, 1980.

————. *The Visitors*. Lippincott, 1977.

Van Vogt, A. E. *The Voyage of the Space Beagle*. Simon and Schuster, 1939.

Verne, Jules. *Twenty Thousand Leagues Under the Sea*. 1870.

————. *Voyage to the Center of the Earth*. 1864.

Wells, H. G. *The First Men in the Moon*. 1901.

————. *The Invisible Man*. 1897.

————. *The Time Machine*. 1895.

————. *The War of the Worlds*. 1898.

Wilhelm, Kate. *Where Late the Sweet Birds Sang*. Harper & Row, 1976.

Wyndham, John. *The Midwich Cuckoos*. Random House, 1957.

Zamyatin, Yevgeny. *We*. E. P. Dutton, 1924.

Science Fiction Anthologies

Asimov, Isaac, ed. *100 Great Science Fiction Short Stories*. Doubleday, 1978.

Asimov, Isaac; Patricia S. Warrick; and Martin H. Greenberg, eds. *Machines That Think: The Best Science Fiction Stories about Robots and Computers*. Holt, Rinehart and Winston, 1983.

Laurence, Alice, ed. *Cassandra Rising*. Doubleday, 1978.

Sargeant, Pamela, ed. *More Women of Wonder: Science Fiction Novelettes by Women about Women*. Random House, 1976.

————. *The New Women of Wonder: Recent Science Fiction Stories by Women about Women*. Random House, 1978.

————. *Women of Wonder: Science Fiction Stories by Women about Women*. Random House, 1974.

Silverberg, Robert, ed. *The Science Fiction Hall of Fame: The Greatest Science Fiction Stories of All Time*. Doubleday, 1970.

Fantasy

Adams, Richard. *Watership Down*. Macmillan, 1974.

Alexander, Lloyd. *The Black Cauldron*. Holt, Rinehart and Winston, 1965.

————. *The Book of Three*. Holt, Rinehart and Winston, 1964.

————. *The Castle of Llyr*. Holt, Rinehart and Winston, 1966.

————. *The High King*. Holt, Rinehart and Winston, 1968.

————. *Taran Wanderer*. Holt, Rinehart and Winston, 1967.

Andrews, Allen. *The Pig Plantagenet*. Viking, 1981.

Arkin, Alan. *The Lemming Condition*. Harper & Row, 1976.

Beagle, Peter. *A Fine and Private Place*. Viking, 1960.

————. *The Last Unicorn*. Viking, 1968.

Berger, Thomas. *Arthur Rex*. Delacorte, 1978.

Bond, Nancy. *A String in the Harp*. Atheneum, 1976.

Bradley, Marion Zimmer. *Darkover Landfall*. Daw, 1972.

————. *The Mists of Avalon.* Knopf, 1983.

————. *Thendara House.* Daw, 1983.

Bradshaw, Gillian. *Hawk of May.* Simon and Schuster, 1980.

————. *In Winter's Shadow.* Simon and Schuster, 1982.

————. *Kingdom of Summer.* Simon and Schuster, 1981.

Brooks, Terry. *The Elfstones of Shannara.* Ballantine, 1982.

————. *The Sword of Shannara.* Random House, 1977.

Darrah, John. *The Real Camelot: Paganism and the Arthurian Romances.* Thames and Hudson, 1981.

Dembard, R. T. *Planiverse: Computer Contact with a Two-Dimensional World.* Poseidon, 1984.

Eddison, E. R. *The Worm Ouroboros.* London: Cape, 1922.

Gardner, John. *Grendel.* Knopf, 1971.

Garner, Alan. *Elidor.* London: Collins, 1965.

————. *The Moon of Gomrath.* London: Collins, 1963.

————. *The Owl Service.* Walck, 1967.

————. *Red Shift.* Macmillan, 1973.

————. *The Weirdstone of Brisingamen.* London: Collins, 1960.

Goldman, William. *The Princess Bride.* Harcourt Brace Jovanovich, 1973.

Grahame, Kenneth. *The Wind in the Willows.* Scribner's, 1908.

Hamilton, Virginia. *Dustland.* Greenwillow, 1980.

————. *The Gathering.* Greenwillow, 1981.

————. *Justice and Her Brothers.* Greenwillow, 1978.

Hoban, Russell. *The Mouse and His Child.* Harper & Row, 1967.

Horwood, William. *Duncton Wood.* McGraw-Hill, 1980.

Jones, Diana Wynne. *Archer's Goon.* Greenwillow, 1984.

————. *Dogsbody.* Greenwillow, 1977.

————. *The Homeward Bounders.* Greenwillow, 1981.

Kurtz, Katherine. *Deryni Checkmate.* Ballantine, 1972.

————. *Deryni Rising.* Ballantine, 1970.

————. *High Deryni.* Ballantine, 1973.

Langton, Jane. *The Fledgling.* Harper & Row, 1980.

Lawrence, Louise. *The Earth Witch.* Harper & Row, 1981.

Le Guin, Ursula. *The Farthest Shore.* Atheneum, 1972.

————. *The Tombs of Atuan.* Atheneum, 1971.

————. *A Wizard of Earthsea.* Parnassus, 1968.

Lehane, Brendan, and the editors of Time-Life Books. *Wizards and Witches.* Time-Life Books, 1984.

Lockley, Ronald. *Seal-Woman.* Bradbury, 1974.

MacLeish, Roderick. *Prince Ombra.* Congdon and Weed, 1983.

McCaffrey, Anne. *Crystal Singer,* Ballantine, 1982.

————. *Dragondrums.* Atheneum, 1979.

————. *Dragonsinger.* Atheneum, 1977.

————. *Dragonsong.* Atheneum, 1976.

————. *Moreta: Dragon Lady of Pern.* Ballantine, 1983.

————. *The White Dragon.* Ballantine, 1978.

McKillip, Patricia. *The Forgotten Beasts of Eld.* Atheneum, 1974.

————. *Harpist in the Wind.* Atheneum, 1979.

————. *Heir of Sea and Fire.* Atheneum, 1977.

————. *The Riddle-Master of Hed.* Atheneum, 1976.

McKinley, Robin. *Beauty: A Retelling of the Story of Beauty and the Beast.* Harper & Row, 1978.

Naylor, Phyllis Reynolds. *Faces in the Water: The York Trilogy, Book Two.* Atheneum, 1981.

————. *Footprints at the Window: The York Trilogy, Book Three.* Atheneum, 1981.

————. *Shadows on the Wall: The York Trilogy, Book One.* Atheneum, 1980.

Pierce, Meredith Ann. *The Darkangel.* Little, Brown, 1982.

Rayner, William. *Stag Boy.* Harcourt Brace Jovanovich, 1973.

Saint-Exupery, Antoine de. *The Little Prince.* Harcourt, Brace, and World, 1943.

Silverberg, Robert. *Lord Valentine's Castle.* Harper & Row, 1980.

————. *The Majipoor Chronicles.* Arbor House, 1982.

————. *Valentine Pontifex.* Arbor House, 1983.

Stewart, Mary. *The Crystal Cave.* Morrow, 1970.

————. *The Hollow Hills.* Morrow, 1973.

————. *The Last Enchantment.* Morrow, 1979.

————. *The Wicked Day.* Morrow, 1984.

Sutcliff, Rosemary. *The Light Beyond the Forest:*

The Quest for the Holy Grail. E. P. Dutton, 1980.

————. *The Road to Camlann: The Death of King Arthur.* E. P. Dutton, 1981.

————. *The Sword in the Circle: King Arthur and the Knights of the Round Table.* E. P. Dutton, 1981.

Tolkien, J. R. R. *The Fellowship of the Ring.* Houghton Mifflin, 1954. Revised edition, 1967.

————. *The Hobbit: Or There and Back Again.* Houghton Mifflin, 1938.

————. *The Return of the King.* Houghton Mifflin, 1956. Revised edition, 1967.

————. *The Silmarillion.* Houghton Mifflin, 1977.

————. *The Two Towers.* Houghton Mifflin, 1955. Revised edition, 1967.

Walton, Evangeline. *The Children of Llyr.* Ballantine, 1971.

————. *The Prince of Annwn.* Ballantine, 1974.

————. *The Song of Rhiannon.* Ballantine, 1972.

————. *The Virgin and the Swine.* Willett, Clark, 1936. Reprinted as *The Island of the Mighty.* Ballantine, 1970.

Wangerin, Walter, Jr. *The Book of the Dun Cow.* Harper & Row, 1978.

Wharton, William. *Birdy.* Knopf, 1979.

White, T. H. *The Book of Merlyn: The Unpublished Conclusion to The Once and Future King.* University of Texas Press, 1977.

————. *The Once and Future King.* Putnam's, 1958.

Wrightson, Patricia. *The Dark Bright Water.* Atheneum, 1979.

————. *The Ice Is Coming.* Atheneum, 1977.

————. *Journey Behind the Wind.* Atheneum, 1981.

————. *A Little Fear.* Atheneum, 1983.

————. *The Nargun and the Stars.* Atheneum, 1974.

Yolen, Jane. *Dragon's Blood.* Delacorte, 1982.

————. *Heart's Blood.* Delacorte, 1984.

————. *The Magic Three of Solatia.* Crowell, 1974.

Zelazny, Roger. *Courts of Chaos.* Doubleday, 1978.

————. *The Guns of Avalon.* Doubleday, 1972.

————. *The Hand of Oberon.* Doubleday, 1976.

————. *Nine Princes in Amber.* Doubleday, 1970.

————. *Sign of the Unicorn.* Doubleday, 1975.

Utopias

Brancato, Robin F. *Blinded by the Light.* Knopf, 1978.

Bromley, David G. and Anson D. Shupe, Jr. *Strange Gods: The Great American Cult Scare.* Beacon Press, 1982.

Callenbach, Ernest. *Ecotopia Emerging.* Bantam, 1982.

————. *Ecotopia: The Notebooks and Reports of William Weston.* Bantam, 1975.

Capps, Benjamin. *The Brothers of Uterica.* Meredith, 1967.

Coover, Robert. *The Origin of the Brunists.* Viking, 1977.

Elfman, Blossom. *The Strawberry Fields of Heaven.* Crown, 1983.

Gilman, Charlotte Perkins. *Herland.* Pantheon, 1979.

Hall, Lynn. *Too Near the Sun.* Follett, 1970.

Hickman, Janet. *Zoar Blue.* Macmillan, 1978.

Howard, Elizabeth. *Out of Step with the Dancers.* Morrow, 1978.

Kilduff, Marshall and Ron Javers. *The Suicide Cult: The Inside Story of the People's Temple Sect and the Massacre in Guyana.* Bantam, 1979.

Kinkade, Kathleen. *A Walden Two Experiment: The First Five Years of Twin Oaks Community.* Morrow, 1974.

Klineman, George, Sherman Butler, and David Conn. *The Cult That Died: The Tragedy of Jim Jones and the People's Temple.* Putnam's, 1980.

Miklowitz, Gloria. *The Love Bombers.* Delacorte, 1980.

Mungo, Raymond. *Total Loss Farm: A Year in the Life.* E. P. Dutton, 1971.

Reston, James. *Our Father Who Art in Hell.* New York Times Books, 1981.

Rockwood, Joyce. *Enoch's Place.* Holt, Rinehart and Winston, 1980.

Sandroff, Ronni. *Fighting Back.* Knopf, 1978.

Skinner, B. F. *Walden Two.* Macmillan, 1948.

Veglahn, Nancy T. *Fellowship of the Seven Stars.* Abingdon, 1981.

Wizansky, Richard. *Home Comfort: Stories and Scenes of Life on Total Loss Farm.* Saturday Review Press, 1973.

Wooden, Kenneth. *The Children of Jonestown.* McGraw-Hill, 1980.

Yee, Min S. and Thomas N. Layton. *In My Father's House.* Holt, Rinehart and Winston, 1981.

Yolen, Jane. *The Gift of Sarah Barker.* Viking, 1981.

LIFE MODELS

OF HEROES AND HOPES

The word *hero* may conjure up a picture of King Arthur and his Knights of the Round Table seeking the Holy Grail or John Wayne charging up a hill ahead of a company of marines. All societies and cultures have had their heroes who embodied the proper virtues and values of that culture. Prior to the beginning of writing, storytellers kept legends of heroes alive—and likely embroidered and magnified heroes and legends with each retelling. As writing and then printing appeared, these tales were permanently recorded so new generations would remember the deeds of great heroes of old. The Greeks gave us their gods and heroes who confronted the gods, Prometheus, Oedipus, and Antigone. Writers provided fictional heroes as different as Shakespeare's Portia, Dostoevsky's Prince Myshkin, Ibsen's Dr. Stockmann, and Shaw's St. Joan. These characters have always competed for readers' attention with historical heroes like Ruth, Muhammad, Galileo, Eleanor of Aquitaine, Thomas Jefferson, Helen Keller, Chief Joseph, Margaret Sanger, John Kennedy, and on and on.

◈ WHO ARE THE HEROES? WHO NEEDS THEM?

Joe McGinnis wrote in *Heroes*:

◇ I had a theory: America no longer had national heroes as it once did because the traditional sources of heroes had dried up. The sources had dried up, I believed, because the values and ideals that traditional heroes once had personified no longer were dominant in American society. My theory was that after a long period of erosion, they had ceased to be dominant in the 1960s.[1]

And he concluded the chapter,

> ◇ The truth was, we did not have heroes any more because *there were no heroic acts left to be performed*.[2]

Is McGinnis right? Certainly, we needed heroes at one time. In 1941, Dixon Wector argued, "Hero-worship answers an urgent American need."[3] Seventeen years later, Arthur Schlesinger worried that if our need for hero-worship was no longer a national need, "then our instinct for admiration is likely to end by settling on ourselves. The one thing worse for democracy than hero-worship is self-worship."[4] And in 1978, Henry Fairlie agreed with Schlesinger when he wrote, "A society that has no heroes will soon grow enfeebled."[5]

We need heroes today even more desperately than we did only a few years ago. Writer Mollie Hunter reflects what many of us believe when she began a *Horn Book Magazine* article, "There is a need for heroes in children's books."[6] Only a few months later, a Reuters' dispatch from Moscow made clear that heroes are needed today in other cultures:

> ◇ The Communist Party instructed Soviet artists and writers today to create positive heroes and to increase their vigilance against Western imperialist reaction.[7]

The dispatch went further to call for the "positive hero" in Soviet writing.

Why do we need heroes? Noel Annan explained one ever-present reason for heroes in his introduction to Isaiah Berlin's *Personal Impressions*:

> ◇ Heroes enhance life, the world expands and becomes less menacing and more hopeful by their very existence. To know a great man is to change one's notions of what a human being can do or be.[8]

We need, all of us, young and old, to find people worth looking up to, worth admiring. We all need reassurance, especially given our unsettled and warlike world, that if we are mortal, a few of us find ways of transcending earthly mortality to leave a record of noble and brave acts. We need the records of people pushed to the brink of psychological or physical disaster who fight back and do not give up. We need constant reminders that we are not merely likely to survive but that we are worth surviving. We need to be reminded that some people are willing to stand up for their beliefs no matter what the pressures.

A character in Jerzy Kosinski's *The Devil Tree* sums up a faith that there are the few who will stand no matter what:

> ◇ Of all mammals, only a human being can say "no." A cow cannot imagine itself apart from the herd. That's why one cow is like any other. To say "yes" is to follow the mass, to do what is commonly expected. To say "no" is to deny the crowd, to be set apart, to reaffirm yourself.

Henry James said that life is a slow, reluctant march into enemy territory. Maybe being a hero means marching onward without making peace with the enemy, no matter what or who that is.

To have heroes means that we must accept ourselves and even like what we stand for. If some people seem to have no heroes, or strange heroes, perhaps it is because they find little of the hero within themselves. People who have contempt for themselves and their beliefs, who seem to have few roots and no future, and who flounder trying to find something and someone to believe in may resist the heroic impulse in others. Or they may try to share the reflected glory of the apparently heroic without making any effort to understand what is truly heroic.

In M. E. Kerr's *Gentlehands*, the rather unlikable Buddy Boyle loves wealthy Skye Pennington. Buddy takes Skye to his Grandfather Trenker's home to show off the culture Buddy feels is lacking in his own home. Trenker sees through Buddy's actions:

◇ "Do you think you impressed her, Buddy?"

"Well, *you* did," I mumbled, and his remark had made my face red.

He didn't say anything, so I said, "It was borrowed glory, I guess."

"I'm happy to lend it to you," he said.

"Thanks."

"You know, Buddy," my grandfather finally said, "you can get there on your own once you're pointed in the right direction."

"Get where?" I said, but I knew what he was talking about. He knew I knew, too, and didn't even bother explaining where.

"I'd be happy to point you, if that's what you want," he said.

And a few minutes later, Trenker tries to show his grandson that winning what he wants, whatever it is, is possible. "Obstacles are challenges for winners, and excuses for losers."

We may all of us be diverted in our search for heroes and attracted to the temporarily charismatic entertainer or politician. We may for a time seek someone who talks and acts and thinks the way we do. But what we need to seek out—and we do in our better moments—are the heroes with dignity who are above the crowd and who are admirable though not necessarily immediately likable. Looking up to the heroes in the sections that follow is needed to allow us to survive and to make that survival worthwhile.

One theory holds that storytelling began when cavemen came back from a hunt and told about the day's exploits. If they had nothing better to do, they made up stories and the art of fiction was born. When an exceptionally brave storyteller confessed that he had been frightened and had called out for help from a superior being, religious elements entered into the storytelling. And when a hunter or warrior showed particular bravery or skill, his fellows bragged about him and perhaps exaggerated his experience in their tales. In this way, the heroic legends needed for every tribe developed. And these stories took place in predominantly masculine groups.

Women, who gave birth to children and provided the child's first nourishment, had the primary responsibility for the care of the young. Throughout the ages, they stayed home while men went off to battle the elements, animals, or other humans. When they returned home, women and children provided the audience for any new tales of heroism.

That heritage made people think of heroic activity as inherently male.

Proof that people have thought it unusual for females to play the role is the coinage of the word *heroine* to refer to a female doing something unexpected. Today the word *hero* has changed to include both males and females. There is nothing new about heroic women but in the past they have largely been admired for how well they raised their children, all well and good, but raising children rarely makes an exciting story. Besides, a mother's success in raising children is usually judged by her children's accomplishments, not by her own.

Some stories about women doing exciting, physical things were created, for example, the Greek legends about Amazons and the German folktale about Molly Whuppie who outwitted the giants, but they were exceptions. Today, we are far more likely to find many heroic tales about women who have done something admirable, even incredible by anyone's standards.

When we wrote the first edition, we said that it would have been difficult only a few years earlier to present a balanced chapter about male and female heroes. We added that we hoped it would soon be nothing out of the ordinary. That hope may not yet be realized, but it comes closer every year.

◈ HEROES IN BIOGRAPHIES AND AUTOBIOGRAPHIES

Humanity's need for the life stories of important and admirable people is much older than the word *biography* first used by John Dryden in his 1683 edition of Plutarch's *Parallel Lives*. Indeed, Plutarch's first century A.D. account of fifty famous Greeks and Romans, usually paired to make a moral or historical point, has served for fifteen hundred years as a source of heroes and heroic tales.

But other life stories, perhaps less famous today, also served as models. Bishop Asser's *The Life of Alfred the Great* in the late ninth century, William Roper's fine biography of his father-in-law, *Life of Sir Thomas More*, about 1557, and Samuel Clarke's compilation of ecclesiastical biographies, *Collection of the Lives of Ten Eminent Divines*, in 1662, provided many lives worth emulating. Indeed, that presents a problem for those of us today who try to read Clarke's book, for he early declares about his divines:

> ◇We must eye them, as we look into Glasses, to dress and adorn ourselves thereby. We must eye them for imitation: We must look upon the best, and the best in the best.

As we seek someone admirable, we also seek someone human, someone who might understand us because the hero has suffered the problems of being human and being imperfect. Clarke's figures are divine and glorious but they lack the common touch. We may admire them, but they are too much above us, impossible to emulate.

Pepys' *Diary*, though never intended for publication, is the first life story which lets us see the subject, warts and all. From the first entry on January 1, 1660, until the last on May 31, 1669, we are allowed to see an important man—he was both the Secretary of the Admiralty and President of the

Royal Society—who writes about the politics of the time amidst the London Fire of 1666 and the plague of 1665, but also writes of love and music and life. Pepys celebrates life, all of it, and what makes his autobiography so incredible is his honesty.

James Boswell's *The Life of Samuel Johnson*, published in two volumes in 1791, is usually considered to be the first modern biography. Boswell revered his friend, but the tone is not entirely reverential, and Boswell clearly is writing more than simply the record of deeds done in one man's life. Boswell set out to give an accurate history of Johnson, Johnson's thoughts as best Boswell knew them, the people Johnson had known and what he thought of them, how the times influenced Johnson and how Johnson influenced the times; in short the cultural and historical milieu. The book was not a series of moral lessons nor was it so laudatory that a reader could model a life after Samuel Johnson.

A modern biography aims at catching the spirit of the subject, the passions and fears, the essence that made the subject distinctive and memorable. It attempts to make the subject's time come alive and place the subject within that time. It attempts to make the subject come alive, not to present a perfect, wholly admirable person without defects. Authenticity and objectivity are the guides to the biographer. And, as Iris Origo wrote in "Biography, True and False" the modern biographer tries to avoid three insidious temptations, "to suppress, to invent, and to sit in judgment, and of these, the earliest and most frequent is suppression."9

Biographies and autobiographies often remain popular with young adults for several years. One reason is that the genre often fills in details about the past that we recognize, at least vaguely, at the same time letting us in on parts of a life we admire yet know only superficially.

Why do young adults read biography or autobiography?

They may read to learn more about people who have interesting careers and in reading, young adults may find that these famous people have often been as troubled as humans who lack glamorous jobs. Sid Caesar's *Where Have I Been?* is both the life of an apparently incredibly successful comedian and the life of a confused man who found that success rarely brought him happiness or satisfaction. Reading about his life will give readers some chuckles and much to think about.

Young adults fascinated by the entertainment world might enjoy reading about movie stars and all the thrills of being famous. If they read Ingrid Bergman's *My Story*, they will find an honest woman telling an honest and not always happy story about what fame means. *Fonda: My Life* by Henry Fonda will give readers another view of what the life of a famous stage and screen star has been like. Kitty Kelley's often unpleasant *Elizabeth Taylor: The Last Star* may throw an even greater damper on those sure that success and stardom are synonymous. One of the most honest and refreshing of the movie star biographies is Anne Baxter's *Intermission: A True Story*, a frank and amusing story of an Oscar-winning actress who married and moved to Australia.

Young adults curious about the life of the stage actor will find little revealing about the actors but much that is magic in Laurence Olivier's *Confessions of an Actor: An Autobiography* and Garry O'Connor's *Ralph Richardson*. Far better is John Gielgud's *Gielgud: An Actor and His Time,* not because Gielgud gives copious secret revelations but because he seems to have known almost everyone who was important or interesting on the stage of his time, and he writes interestingly about actors like Orson Welles, Ralph Richardson, Laurence Olivier, Sarah Bernhardt, and Edith Evans; and of writers like T. S. Eliot, Isak Dinesen, Samuel Beckett, and Edward Albee.

Claire Bloom's *Limelight and After: The Education of an Actress* is delightful throughout, both for the picture of the stage and the actors and its portrait of a very decent human being. Born in England of a Jewish immigrant family, Bloom found no easy path to fame or fortune, but her life has been easier and less traumatic than many other actors convinced, apparently, that fame and personal success were one and the same.

Less happy but perhaps more intriguing thereby is Susan Strasberg's *Bittersweet.* Daughter of the famous director of the Actors Studio, Susan Strasberg had all the brains and talent and beauty she needed for glory, but after an early successful performance as Anne in *The Diary of Anne Frank,* everything went downhill with drugs, a violent and miserable marriage, hatred of her mother and father, and psychoanalysis that was worse than merely unsuccessful.

Lives of popular singers often reveal more turmoil than pleasure. Jerry Hopkins and Daniel Sugarman's *No One Gets out of Here Alive* presents the late Jim Morrison in all his drugged and alcoholic glory. Country music is the subject of Robert Cain's *Whole Lotta Shakin' Goin' On: Jerry Lee Lewis.* A much happier story is the delightful *Minnie Pearl: An Autobiography* by Minnie Pearl with Joan Dew. Her life may have lacked the drama and conflict that makes other biographies so intense, but her life has been full and, fortunately for us, it has been very funny.

Two folk singers have been the subject of important biographies. Joe Klein's *Woody Guthrie, A Life* is a fine recounting of the travails of one of the founders of modern folk singing. Guthrie doubtlessly lacks some essential characters of the hero, but his slow death by Huntington's Disease and his wandering the face of America creating songs born of the American Depression make him a fascinating person. David King Dunaway's *How Can I Keep from Singing: Pete Seeger* presents a man who has become a popular folk singer and who—despite his running battle with the U.S. House Un-American Activities Committee—has had a relatively easy life. But the portrait of Seeger that emerges is somehow bloodless and ambiguous, almost as if Dunaway had been unable to make up his own mind about his subject.

The world of jazz music is well handled in Anita O'Day's *High Times, Hard Times,* and the title is a fair summary of O'Day's life. After starring with Gene Krupa's band, O'Day accompanied her success with a fourteen-year heroin habit. Friends like Charlie Parker, Judy Garland, Lenny Bruce, and Billie Holiday, all with stories equally unhappy, fill her book. Alexis De

THE PEOPLE BEHIND THE BOOKS

SHARON BELL MATHIS, Author

Listen for the Fig Tree
Ray Charles
Teacup Full of Roses

I do hope my writing nourishes young people, salutes them—portrays them in transition, examining their own adolescence, exploring their pursuit of independence. This pursuit—so natural for all of us—is often horrifying, but always triumphant. The field of adolescent literature is also in transition, as is any literature—constantly evolving, signaling and welcoming fresh insights—while continuing to be a storehouse filled with the treasures of wonder and enchantment. ◆

Listen for the Fig Tree. Viking, 1974.
Ray Charles. Harper & Row, 1973.
Teacup Full of Roses. Viking, 1972.

Veaux's *Don't Explain: A Song for Billie Holiday* provides readers with greater detail about an illegitimate child who grew up to musical fame and personal misery.

Two black musical geniuses with good biographies are *Miles Davis* by Ian Carr and *Louis Armstrong* by James Lincoln Collier. Ted Fox's *Showtime at the Apollo* is a fine portrayal of Harlem's great Apollo Theater in its heyday of the 1930s with fine brief portraits of Ella Fitzgerald, Duke Ellington, Count Basie, Sara Vaughan, and many many others.

The world of the dance is covered by Robert Maiorano's *Worlds Apart: The Autobiography of a Dancer,* the story of Bobby Maiorano who joined the American Ballet when he was eight, entering a world incredibly different from his Brooklyn coldwater flat. John Percival's *Nureyev: Aspects of a Dancer* is more conventional, but its study of a ballet superstar would delight anyone who dances. More human is Toni Bentley's *Winter Season,* the story of a member of the New York City Ballet corps who slowly realizes that she is good enough for the corps, just as she lacks the excellence to become a soloist. The book is painful, for in having much, she knows she will always be denied what she most wants. James Haskins' *Katherine Dunham* is a fine, brief life of the important black dancer, choreographer, and anthropologist.

Young adults may seek biographies to learn something about historically important people that does not appear in too-frequently dull history texts. Or they want to learn about contemporary important or controversial figures.

While the medieval world may not seem likely to attract many young adults, one of the best recent biographies is Polly Schoyer Brooks' *Queen Eleanor: Independent Spirit of the Medieval World.* Eleanor, first a queen of

France and later of England, rode with her husband on a crusade to save Jerusalem, raised a ransom to save her son, Richard the Lion Heart, and is an altogether fascinating and heroic person. Readers wanting more might enjoy the scholarly and highly readable biography by Amy Kelly, *Eleanor of Aquitaine and the Four Kings*.

Collective biographies provide multiple viewpoints on history, Joanna L. Stratton's *Pioneer Women: Voices from the Kansas Frontier* lets us know Lilla Day Monroe, first woman admitted to practice before the Kansas Supreme Court, who collected an incredible amount of material on Kansas pioneer women "of warmth and grit," all of them survivors, most of them worth knowing. Linda Peavy and Ursula Smith's *Women Who Changed Things* has nine brief biographies, among them Kate Barnard, who fought to protect Indian orphans at the turn of the last century, Williamina Fleming, pioneer astronomer, and Annie Peck, the first person to climb Peru's Mt. Huascaran. Bernice Selden's *The Mill Girls* is the story of three mill workers, Lucy Larcom, Harriet Robinson, and Sarah Bagley, who affected the lives of their time and place.

The most impressive of this brief lot is Doris Faber's *Love and Rivalry*. Faber's study of three nineteenth-century women writers *and* their sisters contains much information certain to be new to young adults (and adults as well). The stories of Harriet Beecher Stowe and her sister Catharine Beecher and Charlotte Cushman and her sister Susan Cushman Spratt are well done, but the section given to Emily Dickinson and her sister Lavinia is superb. No fictionalized conversation is used, but the material is lively and convincing and often highly moving.

Still, it is probable that many young people using biographies to search out information will be more attracted to contemporary figures. Merle Miller's warm and often salty oral biographies of two late presidents, *Plain Speaking: An Oral Biography of Harry S. Truman* and *Lyndon: An Oral Biography*, should intrigue anyone curious about recent politics.

The late and persistently controversial Senator Joseph McCarthy has been the subject of two recent biographies, Robert Ingalls' *Point of Order: A Profile of Senator Joe McCarthy* aimed at young adults and a longer and far better book, Thomas C. Reeves' *The Life and Times of Joseph McCarthy*. Neither book makes much pretense of objectivity, but then McCarthy was someone difficult for anyone to be objective about.

The Sweetheart of the Silent Majority: The Biography of Phyllis Schlafly by Carol Felsenthal deserves reading if for no more reason than Schlafly's stand on the E.R.A. and women's rights generally. That she is not beloved by everyone is obvious, but that she is a heroic figure to many others makes the book significant reading for everyone, no matter what the political stripe.

Young adults may read biographies to learn about important people who have tried to make the world a better place. Linda Atkinson's *Mother Jones: The Most Dangerous Woman in America* portrays an American legend of the 1890s and 1900s, a union organizer in the coal mines who was jailed and worked all her life to improve the lot of others. She died when she was

◆ **TABLE 7.1   Suggestions for Evaluating Biographies**

A good biography usually has:	A poor biography may have:
A subject of interest with whom the author and, therefore, the readers feel intimately acquainted.	A subject who happens to be of current interest but whose life the author has no real commitment to or knowledge of beyond that available in any good public library.
Documentation of sources and suggestions for further reading—both done inconspicuously so as not to interfere with the story.	An adulatory tone which makes the person too good to be true.
New and/or unusual sources of original information.	Sensationalism, that is, a focus on the negative aspects of the subject's life. A debunking of a historically respected character without adequate documentation of the reasons that the author's viewpoint differs from history's perception.
Accurate facts about setting and characters.	
A central theme or a focus point that has been honestly developed from the author's research.	
In-depth development of the character so that readers understand the way in which the subject shaped his or her own life. Things did not just happen to the person.	None of the interesting detail that makes the story of a person's life unique.
Use of language that is appropriate to the historical period and the literary style of the book.	A disproportionate emphasis on the history and the circumstances surrounding this subject's life so that the reader does not get acquainted with the person. E.g., one biography of Golda Meir is really the story of modern Israel using Mrs. Meir as an attention-getting device and a selling point for libraries looking for biographies of strong women.
Information showing how the subject was thought about by contemporaries.	

100, only three years before the federal government passed legislation guaranteeing the rights of workers to form unions and forcing employers to deal with unions.

Roy Wilkins and Tom Mathew's *Standing Fast: The Autobiography of Roy Wilkins* conveys much of what it must have been like to be present in the early days of the Civil Rights Movement. Wilkins' passion for real freedom for blacks and his lifelong work with the N.A.A.C.P. is the focus of the book and Wilkins' life. But the vignettes of fascinating people like Fiorello La Guardia, Thurgood Marshall, Martin Luther King, Jr., Adam Clayton Powell, and Whitney Young enliven a fine story.

Young adults often read biographies for the same reason they read fiction, to people their seemingly dull and narrow lives with characters who lead lives that are not commonplace. Sometimes those other lives are admirable and dedicated to good. Sometimes they are selfish and dedicated to evil. Sometimes they are simply curious and different.

We may have no personal desire to lead a life dedicated solely to God, but we are curious about those who do. What is it like to be a nun? Find out by reading Karen Armstrong's *Through the Narrow Gate* which tells of her seven years as a nun, and the difficulties she had in renouncing the world and undergoing the rule of silence. Or we might read Mary Gillian Wong's *Nun: A Memoir*, virtually a diary of a young girl who entered the convent and ultimately left it. Paul Hendrickson's *Seminary: A Search* is a wistful, almost wish-it-could-have-lasted look at the life of a priest by the author who entered the Trinitarian seminary at fourteen and left it much later to seek another world. Hendrickson's description of seminary life, particularly the attempts to scourge away sexual desire, will fascinate many young readers. Thomas Merton, the modern prototype of the thoughtful, analytical, meditative priest-writer, is well served by his biographer, Monica Furlong, in *Merton: A Biography*. Furlong does not sentimentalize seminary or Trappist life, and she does make an important modern man come alive.

What would it be like to be a surgeon, particularly a woman trying to enter a male-dominated profession? Elizabeth Morgan recounts her story in *The Making of a Woman Surgeon*, a detailed and frank account of her fight against admission practices and the rigors of the intern's life. The rivalries, the sexual prejudices, the pettiness, and the wonders of medicine are remarkably well described.

What would it be like to be a woman trying to enter the world of science? Vivian Gornick provides a wide view in *Women in Science: Portraits from a World in Transition*. She interviewed more than one hundred women scientists who do basic research in cell biology and biophysics, from ages twenty-four to seventy-eight, and recorded their intellectual highpoints and lowpoints, most of the latter coming from sexual prejudice. Far more enjoyable is Evelyn Fox Keller's *A Feeling for the Organism: The Life and Work of Barbara McClintock*. McClintock, winner of a 1983 Nobel Award, enrolled in Cornell's College of Agriculture despite the opposition of her mother who questioned whether women should be allowed a college education and became a botanist. Fascinated by genetics, she has worked at the Carnegie Institute's laboratory at Cold Spring Harbor on Long Island since 1942. Though her work was often dismissed by male molecular scientists, in her 80s McClintock had her work vindicated.

What would it be like to enter the male world of journalism? Margo Howard's *Eppie: The Story of Ann Landers* is delightfully gossipy and great fun for anyone who starts the day (or ends it) with Ann Landers' column. Jean E. Collins' *She Was There: Stories of Pioneering Women Journalists* describes the battles of several women to be respected and equal journalists. Kathleen McLaughlin of the *New York Times*, for example, said that when she first arrived in the news room, she was the only woman there "and you could have cut the ice with a hatchet." Good stories about pioneer journalists like Emma Bugbee (*New York Herald Tribune* and also a YA writer of the 1930s); Mildred Gilman (*Washington Herald*); Carolyn Anspacher (*San Francisco Chronicle*); and Mary Garber (*Winston-Salem Journal-Sentinel*). And for any readers curious about the world of television news, *This Is Judy Woodruff at the White House* by Judy Woodruff and Kathy Maxa and *Anchorwoman* by Jessica Savitch should answer some questions and raise others. Woodruff has more to say about sexual prejudice, but Savitch's is the most poignant, given her recent death.

Young adults curious about the world of the defense lawyer will enjoy Robert Pack's *Edward Bennett Williams for the Defense*. Reputedly worth more than fifty million dollars, owner of the Baltimore Orioles, and attorney for clients as varied as John Connally, Jimmy Hoffa, Adam Clayton Powell, Frank Costello, and Senator Joseph McCarthy, Williams is a success by most American standards. Pack introduces readers to a world most of them, happily, will never know first hand.

Some biographies introduce us to a more shadowy, less acceptable, and for that reason an even more fascinating world. Ted Conover left college and spent several months riding the rails and living as a hobo. *Rolling Nowhere* begins as Conover outfits himself in a secondhand clothing store and boards a freight bound for St. Louis. Fortunately, he runs into Lonny who gives him some rudimentary lessons, especially in what tramps cannot stand—marriage, regular jobs, responsibility, and stability. Conover learns how to hustle daily for food and drink, how to go without shaving or washing, how to survive fights, and how to forget who and what he is, temporarily.

Few of us are immune from the ambivalent fascination-horror we feel about murders. Murders may be games in a well-written mystery story, but we *know* that we are reading fiction, and that reassures us. No such outlet is possible when we read true stories of mass killings. That disturbs us, but it certainly does not keep us from reading.

Truman Capote's *In Cold Blood* has been a favorite with young readers ever since its first printing. We watch the planning of the killing and the brutal details come alive for us, and we are alternately horrified by the account and horrified that we are fascinated by the tale of butchery. An even more graphic, if less well-written, account of mass murder is Vincent Bugliosi and Curt Gentry's *Helter Skelter: The True Story of the Manson Murders*. Clara Livsey analyzed the murders in even greater detail in *The Manson Women: "A Family" Portrait*. Some adults worry that young readers may be attracted to Manson and his ilk and find something heroic in murder, but reading about someone does not imply that the reader will find anything heroic or admirable in what society condemns. More likely, the reader reads out of curiosity, just as we all do at times. As humans, we are fascinated by the duality of our. natures. We peer into the evil nature of something horrible just as we peer into a chasm or look momentarily at an automobile accident as the highway patrol waves us by. We have no intention of jumping into the chasm, we have no intention of killing ourselves on the highway, yet murders and accidents and suicides make us queasy, for we recognize the possibility in our own natures. Adults read the sleazy headlines in the *National Enquirer*, watch reports of killings and rapes and suicides on televised news, and read lurid details about adultery and scandals in the newspapers, all without worrying that their own morals will be corrupted. Young adults are almost equally able to read about the seamy side of life without being corrupted. These books should be discussed by adults with their children, but banning the books is hardly the answer unless, of course, adults wish to ensure that their children will read the books.

Some biographies deserve wide readership because they are extraordinarily well written. Among the best is Maxine Hong Kingston's *China*

Men, a collective biography of the men in her family, a mixture of myth and history. At first she tells how her father was smuggled to New York in a crate, but then she adds, "of course, my father could not have come that way," and she describes how he came to Angel Island, across from San Francisco, and persuaded immigration officials that his father was a naturalized citizen. Her book is rich and mythic, and at the same time is detailed and concrete. It is also sometimes an angry book, for Kingston re-creates the suffering the Chinese who built the railroads underwent. *China Men* is one of those rare and satisfying books that can be read on many levels by many different kinds of students.

Autobiographies often prove satisfying to young adults. After all, no one should know a person's life better than that person. An excellent recent book is Russell Baker's *Growing Up*. A columnist for *The New York Times*, Baker writes of his Depression childhood and his iron-willed mother who was determined to make something of him and did, sometimes with his help. The story of warm and loving relatives and Baker's unwillingness to overdramatize Depression life makes for a highly satisfying and often quite touching book. Some scenes, notably Baker's spectacularly unsuccessful campaigns to sell copies of the *Saturday Evening Post* while his sister Doris sells them as if they were soon to become collectors' items and the burial of the local bootlegger in a glass coffin, "the fanciest Mason Jar in Loudoun County," are likely to stay with readers for some time.

Mary Mebane's *Mary* and *Mary, Wayfarer* are autobiographies of a black woman growing up in the South. From an impoverished background and surrounded by violence and people who fought for a time and then gave up and became whatever they could become to survive for an even shorter time, Mary Mebane was both a survivor and an achiever who went to college and eventually became a college teacher.

Best of them all are the autobiographies by Maya Angelou. *I Know Why the Caged Bird Sings*, *Gather Together in My Name*, *Singin' and Swingin' and Gettin' Merry Like Christmas*, and *The Heart of a Woman* may be tough going for some young adults, for they pull no punches about the life Angelou has led. After what seemed like an almost idyllic childhood, she sees white prejudice close at hand, sees and experiences violence, and learns more about the cruelty of life than any child should. Angelou becomes pregnant, works to support herself and her son, gets involved in the Civil Rights Movement, meets Malcolm X and Godfrey Cambridge and Rosa Guy, marries an African freedom fighter, and travels throughout the world. Her books are sometimes angry, often humorous, and always frank commentaries on herself and the people and world she knows. All four books, and all that we hope will follow, are worth any reader's time.

Young adults sometimes become fans of a writer, usually in fiction, almost never in biography. An exception is James Haskins whose many books are consistently well written and entertaining accounts of the lives of important black people. *Fighting Shirley Chisholm* is about the first black woman to serve in the U.S. Congress. *James Van DerZee: The Picture-Takin' Man* is about the Harlem photographer who recorded black life and, in 1968, was given a one-person exhibit at the Metropolitan Museum of Art. *I'm Gonna Make You Love Me: The Story of Diana Ross* is less satisfying, perhaps because Haskins has little to offer that hasn't been said elsewhere about this pop singer. Better is *Lena Horne,* partly because she has been too little written about, partly because her battle with blacklisting made her more controversial. *Katherine Dunham* is satisfying, especially for Haskins' account of her work with the East St. Louis Performing Arts Training Center. Haskins' most exciting book is essentially a series of short biographies. *Black Theatre in America* is a history of black actors and comics and entertainers, but as with all good history, it is a story of people like Ira Aldridge, a nineteenth-century American actor who had to travel to London and Europe to do *Othello* and *Macbeth* and *King Lear;* dancers like Bert Williams, musicians like Eubie Blake and Ethel Waters, writers like Langston Hughes and Ntozake Shange, and modern actors like Canada Lee, Paul Robeson, Ruby Dee, Ossie Davis, and James Earl Jones.

To summarize, biographies and autobiographies are popular with many young adults. If the genre once concentrated on the lives of men, often told didactically as models for readers, many current biographies are about heroic women and minorities. Although most biographies are written about someone who is admired, and often famous, authors present balanced material to give both the positive and the negative sides of the subjects. As with modern fiction, many readers prefer realism over romanticism. And most biographies provide young adults today with models worth emulating, people who are frank and spirited and compassionate.

◈ QUIET HEROES

Fiction abounds with quiet heroes worth admiring and emulating. They reassure us that although we are mortal, a few individuals find ways to transcend their mortality to leave behind a record. In these books, attention is paid to character development, especially of the quiet hero. Other characters may reflect or comment on the hero. The works are often episodic, and particular episodes focus on problems confronting the heroes and forcing them into decisions that will clarify their values or beliefs. Heroes are often pushed to physical or psychological precipices to establish their beliefs and their quiet, but obvious, superiority to other people. Quiet heroes carry burdens, but they do so quietly, not dramatically. What the magician Schmendrick said in Peter Beagle's *The Last Unicorn* about great heroes applies almost equally to quiet heroes: "Great heroes need great sorrows and burdens, or half their greatness goes unnoticed." With quiet heroes, greatness often goes unnoticed by friends and neighbors but not by readers. If quiet heroes have a tragic flaw, it is not Aristotelian but akin to that described by Arthur Miller, the unwillingness to remain passive when one's dignity is challenged, "those who act against the scheme of things that degrades them."[10]

Papa in Robert Newton Peck's *A Day No Pigs Would Die* has great dignity. Poor in money he may be but rich in spirit he is. The narrator in this novel-autobiography sometimes does not understand his father, but he always respects him, knowing instinctively that Papa has stature and dignity.

Two crucial and bloody scenes establish Papa's humanity, his willingness to admit error, and his dignity. The first is for many readers the ugliest episode in the book. A weasel has been caught and Papa puts the weasel and a dog, Hussy, in a barrel to teach the dog to hate and kill weasels, an age-old if cruel way to educate a dog. Rob protests, but the weasel is killed, the dog nearly so, and Pa knows he was wrong.

The second episode is near the end of the book when Rob and Papa discover that Pinky, Rob's pet pig, is sterile. Given the Depression setting and the sad state of the family's finances, Pinky must die to give the family food for the coming winter. Rob cannot, for a moment, accept the necessity of Pinky's death:

◇ "Oh, Papa. My heart's broke."

"So is mine," said Papa. "But I'm thankful you're a man."

I just broke down, and Papa let me cry it all out. I just sobbed and sobbed with my head up toward the sky and my eyes closed, hoping God would hear it.

"That's what being a man is all about. It's just doing what's got to be done."

A Day No Pigs Would Die is not about the "cult of kill," as Jean McClure Kelty maintains in a muddle-headed argument in the February 1975 *English Journal*. The book is about a quiet hero and a boy who reveres his father. Papa has no wish to kill, but he knows when killing has to be done, and he knows what being responsible is all about.

Two of Alice Childress' novels are studies in loneliness and quiet heroism. *A Hero Ain't Nothin' But a Sandwich* could have easily been a sociological treatise about a young drug user, but Benjie is no sociological specimen. Neither is his would-be stepfather, Butler Craig, one of the noblest creations of modern young adult fiction. Butler saves Benjie's life, and later, when Benjie admits his mistakes and apologizes, Butler makes clear what the quiet hero is, though Butler would never have admitted he was in any way heroic:

◇ I say, "I'm sorry, Butler."

"Look here," he say. "Square your shoulders, admit you been a junkie, but now gonna stay clean and report to daytime center for your followups. If you don't do right, Butler gonna have to knuckle you down, you hear?"

"I can do it," I say, "long as somebody believe in me."

"Dammit, Benjie," he say, "you gotta do it even if *nobody* believe in you, gotta be your own man, the supervisor of your veins, the night watchman, and day shift foreman in charge-a your own affairs."

In *Rainbow Jordan*, Rainbow is a fourteen-year-old girl who lives some of the time with her immature mother, Kathie, and when her mother leaves for places unknown, Rainbow lives with Miss Josie who runs a temporary way-station for children with problems. Although the adults should serve as hero-models for Rainbow, in a reversal of normal roles, Rainbow emerges as the strongest of the three, the most admirable, the most deserving of emulation by readers.

Paula Fox's *The Slave Dancer* offers more proof that quiet heroes need not be hoary with age. The novel is a first person narrative of young Jessie Bollier, kidnapped to play the fife aboard a slave ship and thus keep the slaves physically fit and more likely to bring better prices at slave auctions. Fox's novel grimly demonstrates the depths of our inhumanity to our fellows in an undertone of rage that would be difficult to handle by an author less able than Fox. By the close of the book, Jessie has grown and learned the stupidities and horrors of prejudice and the cowardice that underlies doing nothing at all to alter an evil situation. The book could easily have become another heavyhanded polemic about brotherhood. In Fox's hands, it becomes a believable, well-told story of human beings, some of them permanently warped by prejudice; one of them, Jessie, a reluctant and quiet hero freed from prejudice and able to move on to another part of his life.

Three black novelists present the young and the old facing prejudice and ignorance. Ernest Gaines' *The Autobiography of Miss Jane Pittman* shows the tenacity of a woman who has lived 110 years first as slave and then free woman and who faces black militancy of the 1960s fearlessly and quietly. Mildred D. Taylor's *Roll of Thunder, Hear My Cry* and its sequel, *Let the Circle Be Unbroken*, introduce readers to a rural Mississippi loving family during some frightening Depression years when families either came apart or held together. The Logan family is a model of one family that became closer, and young Cassie should serve many readers as a model of the quiet hero who, despite the chaos and cruel initiation rites, endures, but then so should her father and the Logan clan. The family, like all quiet heroes, stood for life despite "humiliations and loss, tragedies and death." Alex Haley's *Roots*, perhaps even more successful as a television series, presents a number of quiet heroes, from Kunta Kinte brought to America in 1767 as a slave to Haley's grandmother who told Haley stories about his roots in Henning, Tennessee, and started Haley on his way toward Africa to discover his sources.

Some quiet heroes are rugged individualists, unafraid to be different and almost certainly misunderstood. Alan Sillitoe's *The Loneliness of the Long-Distance Runner* has as its reluctant hero a Borstal (reform school) boy forced to run a long distance race to win respect for an institution and warden the boy despises. He loves to run, but at the end of the book he is forced to decide what is right for him and what is required by society. Sillitoe's book has long been popular with young adults who recognize the magnitude of the boy's decision and the need to be honest with oneself.

Edward Abbey also deeply believes in fighting back at the establishment. *The Brave Cowboy* shows the last of a dying breed, a living anachronism. John Burns rides his horse, Whisky, into Duke City to free a friend from jail. Failing that—his friend is willing to serve his term—Burns flees and faces modern technology, cars, and high-powered rifles. Probably better known under its movie title, *Lonely Are the Brave*, Abbey shows us one side of the lonely and quiet hero, forced to do what he must to be honest with himself.

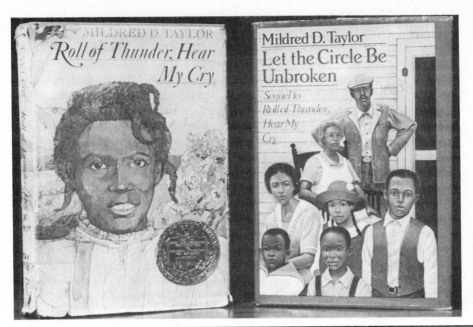

◆ In these books, Mildred Taylor introduces readers to young Cassie, who should serve as a model of the quiet hero.

Another Abbey novel, *Fire on the Mountain*, is about old rancher Joe Vogelin who, with his twelve-year-old grandson, temporarily stands off the United States Air Force who wants his land for a missile range.

Bernard Malamud's *The Assistant* is a modern classic about redemption and the reluctant, quiet hero. Frank Alpine hurts small-time grocer Morris Bober in an abortive robbery and returns to the store, and to Bober's life, out of guilt. There, Alpine finds a new life, partly because of Bober's saintliness—or foolishness—partly because of Helen, Bober's daughter, partly because of Bober's Jewishness. Redemption through guilt and pain also comes to John Proctor in Arthur Miller's *The Crucible*. Set during the witch-hunting hysteria in seventeenth-century Salem, and paralleling the McCarthy induced witch-hunts in the 1950s, Miller characterizes John Proctor as a good man once seduced by Abigail, a ringleader among the girls inciting the hysteria, now trying to save his wife who has been accused of witchcraft. But he implicates himself. Then offered a way out devoid of honor, he refuses to take it. His wife weeps and says she cannot judge him for his sins, and John Proctor responds:

> ◇ Then who will judge me? God in Heaven, what is John Proctor, what is John Proctor? I think it is honest, I think so; I am no saint. Let Rebecca go like a saint; for me it is a fraud.

Proctor is no saint, but he is an honest man, a quiet hero for us.

Some quiet heroes have walked the country seeking identity and a reason to believe in themselves and their country. Peter Jenkins' *A Walk Across America* and *The Walk West: A Walk Across America 2* shows a young man who has lost faith in his country and himself. Tempted to flee America by his own disillusionment, he decides instead to walk, and on October 15, 1973, he leaves Alfred, New York, headed out for nowhere. He never found that, but by April 11, 1975, he had found New Orleans and people worth knowing and a woman he loved. In a sequel, he and his wife leave New Orleans on July 5, 1976, and eventually come to the Pacific Ocean on January 18, 1979, again discovering America and its people and reasons aplenty for being contented with our country.

Warm as Jenkins' two books are, William Least Heat Moon's *Blue Highways: A Journey into America* is even better. Least Heat Moon's love affair with America and its people begins:

> ◇ Beware thoughts that come in the night. They aren't turned properly; they come in askew, free of sense and restriction, deriving from the most remote of sources. Take the idea of February 17, a day of canceled expectations, the day I learned my job teaching English was finished because of declining enrollment at the college, the day I called my wife from whom I'd been separated for nine months to give her the news, the day she let slip about her "friend"—Rick or Dick or Chick. Something like that.[11]

Least Heat Moon is not concerned about finding himself, but he has little to do, and that little might as well be spent on the open road finding out about America so he travels to Nameless, Tennessee, and Swamp Guinea's Fish Lodge where you can eat all you want.

> ◇ I was watching everyone else and didn't see the waitress standing quietly by. Her voice was deep and soft like water moving in a cavern. I ordered the $4.50 special. In a few minutes she wheeled up a cart and began off-loading dinner: ham and eggs, fried catfish, fried perch fingerlings, fried shrimp, chunks of barbecued beef, fried chicken, French fries, hush puppies, a broad bowl of cole slaw, another of lemon, a quart of ice tea, a quart of ice, and an entire loaf of factory-wrapped white bread. The table was covered.[12]

Blue Highways is not entirely about food, though much of it is, but it is about people in Dime Box, Texas, and the Trappist monks in a monastery near Conyers, Georgia, and Othello, New Jersey, and how it got its name, and much more. Least Heat Moon celebrates the essential goodness of others, the many quiet heroes we should admire and do not since they are too close to us.

There are many other books about quiet heroes. Wendell Berry's *The Memory of Old Jack* about an old man worth our time and admiration, Virginia Hamilton's *Zeely* about a young girl and her need for a hero, Rumer Godden's *In This House of Brede* about a successful modern businesswoman who finds little in the modern world to admire and finds peace and heroes in a convent, Christopher Hope's *A Separate Development* about a young South African caught between color lines and searching for a hero who, in an often funny and sometimes bitter novel, becomes something of a hero to us, Studs Terkel's *American Dreams: Lost and Found* describes Terkel's interviews with many Americans about their need for heroes and a place in the sun. Glendon Swarthout's *Bless the Beasts and Children* is

◈ THE PEOPLE BEHIND THE BOOKS

COLIN THIELE, Author

Blue Fin

Fight Against Albatross Two

Fire in the Stone

The Hammerhead Light

I have always believed that human beings as a whole have not changed down the centuries—not fundamentally. Some biologists tell me they are unlikely to change for another million years, if they survive.

The essential characteristics of human beings—love and hate, wisdom and stupidity, cruelty and compassion, generosity and greed—are there today as they have always been. The story of the Good Samaritan is re-enacted on the streets of New York every year. The story of the three robbers and the bag of gold keeps reappearing in the daily press, in its modern form. For of course the society in which children and adolescents exist, the social milieu in which they have to live and grow, keeps changing beyond all recognition, especially as humanity destroys its environment more and more quickly.

I therefore like to explore this process of growth in different circumstances that impinge on the age-old verities of human character—the influence of endurance, love, solitude, malice, rejection, loneliness, success, responsibility and personal loss.

I think I am likely to go on examining these things in the future, whether with historical events set in the past or present day stories set in contemporary Australia. ◆

Blue Fin. Harper & Row, 1974.
Fight Against Albatross Two. Harper & Row, 1976.
Fire in the Stone. Harper & Row, 1974.
The Hammerhead Light. Harper & Row, 1977.

---

about misfits searching for goodness and finding it in themselves, and *The Shootist* is about a dying gunman in the West, the last of a type, who finds a reason for dying.

Quiet heroes would probably laugh at the notion that someone might pattern a life after them, but they do offer general patterns worth examining and considering. They have something unique in their lives that makes them admirable. Their lives demonstrate the worth and individuality of the human spirit. Their lives share a passion for life, for they are fighters for their beliefs, their goals, their dreams.

Books about quiet heroes are a relatively new kind of book, but they appeal to young adults who have enough experience with life to become somewhat skeptical of flamboyant and empty heroes. The need for this kind of skepticism is itself, sometimes, the subject of young adult novels. The protagonist finds a hero but is disillusioned to learn that the hero has clay feet. Rafael Yglesias' *The Game Player* is one of the more distinguished of these books. Howard Cohen is shy and fascinated by Brian Stoppard's ability to win every game, no matter what—baseball, football, acting, chess, sex, poker, bridge. But Brian is the game player who derives no joy from any game, only the intense and cold satisfaction of winning every game by psyching out opponents. The denouement of Yglesias' novel is a bit anticlimactic, but Brian Stoppard serves as a prototype of people for whom all life is a game that must be won without happiness. The quiet hero of the book is Howard Cohen who slowly recognizes that there is more to heroism than winning.

◈ HEROES IN SPORTS

Adults and young adults alike have been fascinated by sports and sports heroes as far back as the Olympic Games in ancient Greece. Today, spectator and participation sports are highly popular activities across the world. Everyday, millions of people go jogging or play tennis or swim or golf. Even more people watch basketball or football or baseball on television. Others play in organized softball or soccer leagues sponsored by churches, city recreation departments, or private clubs. Sports play an incredibly important part in our lives, and in our language, witness the clichés of adults—playing for the team, go for broke, red-dogging the opponents, win at all costs, and on and on. Given our national mania, most of us would be shocked if the current president of Cornell University repeated what his predecessor said in 1873 about a proposed football game with the University of Michigan: "I will not permit 30 men to travel 400 miles merely to agitate a bag of wind."

More than any other important facet of American life, sports are youth oriented. Athletes reach their peak in their teens or their twenties, and that leads to a powerful identification between sports heroes and young adults. Other than in sports, could young adults dream of the fame and adulation heaped upon Nadia Comaneci or Mark Spitz or Tracy Austin so early in their lives? Sports are emphasized so much in the maturation of young adults that it would be an unusual American child who has not been pressured, by parents or peers, to try out for some sort of team.

Parents and schools encourage young people to engage in sports because, in addition to providing good physical exercise, sports are thought to be one way to teach the principles of competition. Sports provide, so people think, an outlet for young adults to play out conflicts within the security of the rules of the game. And the game, so people think, is a microcosm of the great American system of competition.

Sports books, fiction or nonfiction, have common elements. A description of the game itself—rules, training, crowds, thrills, appeal—has increasingly been expanded to include the players and what the game does to them. Rather than being simply an account, as some older books seemed to be too much of the time, of one inning or one quarter after another, emphasis is now on the toughening, the character-changing aspects of the sport. At the heart of most contemporary sports fiction is an examination of the price of fame, the worth of the game, the transitory nature of glory, and the temptation, always doomed, to make temporary glory permanent.

Early sports writers taught the same kinds of things that they had learned through idealized participation in sports. The purity of sports at the turn of the last century was preached by Ralph Henry Barbour who devoutly believed in hard play, fair play, and the amateur spirit and dedicated his 1900 novel, *For the Honor of the School*, "To That School, Wherever It May Be, Whose Athletics Are Purest." Dated though this fine novel now seems, Barbour was deadly serious in his belief that school spirit was inextricably coupled with athletic *and* academic excellence. He and other writers for young adults preached this doctrine until the 1940s.

Despite the American love affair with sports, surprisingly little serious fiction about sports emerged until recent times. Barring an occasional boxing story by Hemingway, some outlandish and amusing stories by Damon Runyon, and some savagely ironic yet uproarious stories by Ring Lardner, only a few major writers wrote about sports: Bernard Malamud in his mythic and underrated *The Natural*, Mark Harris' touching story of baseball and death *Bang the Drum Slowly*, Robert Coover's strange and compelling tale of baseball as the counterpart of American life *The Universal Baseball Association, Inc., J. Henry Waugh, Prop.*, and Jason Miller's fine play about lost dreams *That Championship Season*. But in the last few years, two excellent films have demonstrated that sports deserve to be the province of serious writers. *Chariots of Fire* in 1981 was a moving story of Jewish Oxford university student Harold Abrahams and Scottish missionary Eric Liddell and their love of running and competing in the 1924 Olympics. Not quite as successful, *Personal Best* in 1982 demonstrated the joy of running by an established runner and a neophyte, though the lesbianism may have unfortunately and unfairly turned some viewers away from a fine film.

The traditional sport novels for young adults go unread and largely unwritten. John Tunis' many excellent novels filled with heroes who reek of sweat sit sedately on library shelves, and books of the late 1950s and early 1960s written by John F. Carson and H. D. Francis are going out of print. Perhaps kindly old Pop Dugout, wily with his sports wisdom and remembered for his warm and genial backpatting, was never very real, but somehow sentimental fiction of the past had a charm that we have lost and with it many sports heroes for young readers.

To attract young adults, sports fiction must now provide something not present in either the old sports fiction or in nonfiction stories in current media. It must, essentially, bring a sense of reality about sports, a sense of the joy in sports, that the St. Johns' basketball coach recently said of his star, Chris Mullin: "Basketball is nourishment for Chris. He is a dancer who loves to dance. He is in love with the game."[13] Or the high of sports that cycling champion John Howard talked about in an interview with Jonathan Goodman:

> ◇ There is nothing quite so impressive as plain old gut-wrenching determination. I enjoy going out there and finding out just how much self-determination I have stored in me.
>
> The thing that most people have never learned is how to suffer, to push back their pain. The feeling of self-accomplishment after having done just that— that's a high you won't experience any other way. I find that surprisingly few people really know what that is about.[14]

But a few writers for young adults know about the joy and the pain and have tried to convey it to their readers.

In Michael French's *The Throwing Season*, Henry Chevrolet, nick-named Indian, wants to be the best shot-putter in America, and he is being scouted by big universities. But he has no idea how much pressure being a winner can put upon himself, nor the gamblers that sometimes taint big-time athletics. Robert McKay wrote two good novels in *The Running Back* about Jack Delaney who leaves reform school, returns to high school, and tries out for the football team, and *The Girl Who Wanted to Run the Boston Marathon*, a fine book for its scenes of running and training. Thomas J. Dygard wrote pleasant if undistinguished sports novels like *Outside Shooter*, *Soccer Duel*, and *Winning Kicker* and two quite good books, *Rebound Caper* about a boy who joins a girls' basketball team for kicks and learns about life and sports and himself, and the better *Quarterback Walk-on* which uses a cliché-ridden football plot about a player who yearns to play and comes in when three players (count them) ahead of him cannot play and leads his team to victory making readers believe it all in a funny and enjoyable book.

Somewhat better is Douglas Terry's *The Last Texas Hero* which explores sexism and the dubious virtues of winning at all costs. Martin Quigley's *The Original Colored House of David* is about small town life in the 1920s and a young boy who talks the Colored House of David team into taking him along on a barnstorming trip. Otto R. Salassi writes a very funny story about professional wrestling and initiation rites in *On the Ropes*. Walter Dean Myers writes a more serious novel than his usual in *Hoops* about Lonnie Jackson and his desire to use his basketball ability to flee the slums.

Sports and the nearness of death is the subject of Robin Brancato's *Winning* about Gary Madden, paralyzed in a football accident. In Barbara Stretton's *You Never Lose*, a young football player begins his senior year unaware that his beloved football coach-father is dying of cancer. Even better is Todd Strasser's *Friends Till the End* with its story of soccer star David Gilbert and newcomer Howie Jamison who is dying of leukemia.

Until recently, sports fiction was largely male turf, but women are the heroes of several good books. When R. R. Knudson published *Zanballer* in 1972, little fanfare greeted it, but high school girls soon found it, and its popularity grew. Zan Hagen attends Lee High School and is appalled to learn that girls' P.E. classes have been shifted to the old Home Ec room while the gym is remodeled for the coming boys' basketball season. The girls are expected to folk dance, dodging around sinks and gas stove outlets. Zan finally manages to convince the football coach to let her and her friend train in the same way as the football team. But Zan is not willing to settle for mere training—she wants real football competition, with the boys. Unhappily, as the reputation of *Zanballer* grew, Knudson wrote more books, all dismal imitations. *Zanbanger*, *Zanboomer*, and *Rinehart Lifting*. Her latest book, *Zan Hagen's Marathon*, suggests that Knudson is once more capable of writing a good book.

Far superior to any of Knudson's books are Don Meredith's *Home Movies* about gifted middle-distance runner Sherry Kincaid who loves her

father-trainer but who questions his ambitions for her, and Rosemary Wells'
When No One Was Looking about Kathy Bardy, twelfth-ranked tennis player
in her class who learns how desperate and humiliating competition can be.
Best of them all is Jenifer Levin's *Water Dancer*. Dorey Thomas, long
distance swimmer, is trained by Sarge Olssen and his wife Ilana, both of
whom become entangled with her and her dreams and her body.

The best recent sports fiction for young adults would also interest
adults. Terry Davis' *Vision Quest* is a quiet book about eighteen-year-old
Loudon Swain preparing for a wrestling match. Loudon's friends and lover
and family are attractive people, and his quest for manhood and perfection
in wrestling are impressive. Robert Lehrman's *Juggling* introduces readers
to soccer and to Howie Berger who learns about the sport, the teammates
who disdain him, his education, his father, and a strange but believable girl,
and far more in a fine novel.

The finest recent sports novels are all, strangely enough, first novels.

David Guy's *Football Dreams* is a bit reminiscent of F. Scott Fitzgerald's
stories of the long thoughts and dreams of youth. Dan Keith returns to
Arnold Prep fifteen years after his graduation and remembers his life there
and the football he played and the big game and the emptiness of too much
of it. Especially he remembers Sarah, her pale blue eyes and her blond hair
and her flawless face and all she meant to him and how he ruined any
chance he had with her.

Poet Richard Blessing's A *Passing Season* portrays the desperation of
anyone who lives in Oiltown, Pennsylvania, to flee the town. Craig Warren
is a third-string quarterback with ability to do better but he plays scared and
indifferently, as his coach recognizes. Craig is known by his teammates as
"Artsy-Craftsy" because he loves books and English class and poetry. Blessing brilliantly describes a young man who does not know precisely what he
wants and who struggles to find it and himself. Blessing also conveys the
feeling of small town life and its need to find excellence and myth in football
for it has nothing else and never will.

Chris Crutcher's *Running Loose* is about far more than sports, though
the sports scenes are well done. Louie Banks, age seventeen, finds himself
booked off the football team when he objects to the way his coach wants the
game played, and he falls in love with Becky. When she dies, his life comes
apart. His hatred of the school principal and his love of running bring him
back to life. *Running Loose* is a surprisingly funny book at times, and it is
always a paean to life and love and the joy of sports.

The finest of all the 1970s adult sports novels, and one certain to be
controversial given the homosexual major characters, is Patricia Nell Warren's *The Front Runner*. Harlan Brown, track coach at small Prescott College in New York state, inherits three fine runners who left the University of
Oregon because they are gay. A former coach at Penn State who left the job
when rumors of his own homosexuality circulated around campus, Brown
wonders whether he ought to take another chance, but the three runners,
especially long distance runner Billy Sive appeal to him, in at least two ways,
and they stay. The racing scenes and the prejudice the characters face make

◆ The best of the new sports books will be read by adults as well as teenagers. They include *Juggling* by Robert Lehrman, *A Passing Season* by Richard Blessing, and *Running Loose* by Chris Crutcher.

for a beautifully written novel, one most young adults would benefit from reading.

And where would sports lovers be without well-written biographies of sports heroes? Good ones include Robert Lipsyte's *Free to Be Muhammad Ali*; Alan Goldstein's *A Fistful of Sugar: The Sugar Ray Leonard Story* and James Haskins' *Sugar Ray Leonard*; Joe Louis with Edna and Art Rust, Jrs.'s *Joe Louis: My Life*; Pele with Robert L. Fish's *My Life and the Beautiful Game*; Earvin (Magic) Johnson and Richard Levin's *Magic*; and Nancy Lieberman's *Basketball My Way*. The best of the lot are Kareem Abdul-Jabbar and Peter Knobler's *Giant Steps* for their honest looks at one of the great basketball players of all time and his life outside the game, and Bill Bradley's *Life on the Run*, the story of a great player from an Ivy League school who played pro basketball and was a scholar at Oxford University. *Life on the Run* conveys the love of the game and the team camaraderie amidst the boredom of waiting at hotels and air terminals. What emerges from the book is not simply one game after another but the sweat and pain and anxiety and the talk of the players and the delight in playing.

Jim Bouton's *Ball Four* was not the first, nor certainly the last, of the debunking books about the horrors and stupidities and foolishness and duplicity of players and managers. The book unquestionably put sports mania in some sort of perspective, but with our need for heroes—real heroes—Bouton may have offered us more honesty—if that is what Bouton wrote—than we wanted or needed. Honesty, like most virtues, may easily be overrated. That heroes are human is a truism. That the public needs or wants to know all their sins and warts may be open to question. Other iconoclastic books of the last few years include Tom Hardy's expose of the corruption that underlies much of college football in *Unsportsmanlike Conduct* and Peter Gent's attack on pro football in *The Franchise*. Books like these are antidotes for too much hero-worship. Not to read an occasional debunking book is to miss one facet of humanity. To read only debunking books is to produce only debunkers, and that we already have in abundance.

The mania for running has produced several appealing books—Jim Fixx's *The Complete Book of Running* and *Jim Fixx's Second Book of Running*; Jim Shapiro's *On the Road—The Marathon: The Joys and Techniques of Marathon Running*; and the uncommonly fine *Healing Journey: The Odyssey of an Uncommon Athlete* by David Smith and Franklin Russell. A fine novel about the marathon and three runners, an East German, a Japanese, and an American, is Mark Kram's *Miles to Go*.

The two best nonfiction studies of transitory fame are Martin Ralbovsky's *Destiny's Darlings: A World Championship Little League Team Twenty Years Later* and Jay Acton's *The Forgettables*. Ralbovsky describes the Little League team from Schenectady, New York, and their World Championship game on August 27, 1954, and his interviews with the players twenty years later. The contrast is hardly surprising, but it stays with readers long after the book is closed. Acton's book features a group of nearly-great football players now playing for the Pottstown, Pennsylvania, Firebirds. A few players are doomed to play a little longer, most are on their way down, and one or two have promise.

Sports enthusiasts are insatiable readers about their teams and their heroes and their sports. Luckily, a few sportswriters are fine stylists and deserve to be read by sports nuts or anyone who likes good writing. Thomas Boswell's *How Life Imitates the World Series* reflects Boswell's affection for the Orioles and the nicely turned phrase. Pat Jordan's several fine books betray his own enthusiasm for baseball—he was a minor league prospect— and anything he writes is authoritative and well written.

The best two sportswriters, by consensus of other sportswriters, are Roger Angell and Red Smith. Angell's *Five Seasons: A Baseball Companion* is a study of love, of baseball, and of writing. But then so are *The Summer Game* and *Late Innings*. Red Smith deserved to win a Pulitzer Prize, and did, and his books are about the participants and the games and his love of sports. *To Absent Friends from Red Smith* is a fine introduction to a gentleman, a scholar (about far more than merely sports), and a great writer. He was capable of quoting from Ambrose Bierce and Sam Johnson and John Donne to make a point about a sport, and he was incapable of writing bad prose.

◈ HEROES IN DEATH

In the mid-1970s when young adults were surveyed about their favorite nonfiction books, the ten favorites were accounts of the struggle for survival. In the order of their popularity, they were *Alive: The Story of the Andes Survivors*; *Eric*; *Brian's Song*; *Bermuda Triangle*; *Go Ask Alice*; *I Am Third*; Anne Frank's *The Diary of a Young Girl*; *Death Be Not Proud*; *Dove*; and *Brian Piccolo: A Short Season*.

The list was hardly a surprise. Indeed, many of these books remain favorites into the 1980s. What seemed surprising to some adults after they considered the titles was that nine of the ten are about death. It may seem ironic that young people, supposedly on the threshold of their lives, are so interested in death. Perhaps some of the interest comes from the fact that survival stories always imply the presence of death, just as mystery stories do.

But an interest in death in these books is not an oddity. Only a few years ago when electives were the rage in secondary schools, electives on death were highly popular. The "Education" section of the March 14, 1977, *Newsweek* reported that "death, a topic most people would prefer to ignore, is an increasingly popular subject among U.S. high-school students."[15] It was true in Florida, Illinois, Montana, and other states across the country.

Parents, and some teachers and librarians, are worried about the interest in death. Some argue it is a morbid subject for otherwise healthy young people to be concerned with. Other see the sinister hand of the international Communist party at work. Others thought and remembered that they, too, had been preoccupied with "easeful death" when they were young, not because they were unduly morbid or nigh unto death, but because death is an eternal mystery, as anyone who has read *Hamlet* or Dickinson's poetry or Edgar Lee Masters' *Spoon River Anthology* knows full well. And anyone who even casually glances at the recent anthology by D. J. Enright, *The Oxford Book of Death*, will find it rich and fascinating and representative of more writers than most of us would have guessed.

Another explanation by Roger Rosenblatt may be close to the mark:

◇ Death is one of the things that children take most seriously. Not that adults take death lightly, but they do try to tame it. This is done, it is said, in order to prove that death is a continuous part of life, to make death easier to deal with by facing it squarely. Children are all for facing death squarely, but they do not regard it as a continuous part of life. To a child death is the archenemy of life, an absolute calamity. It is the beginning of nothing but emptiness and absence, prolonged and lengthening absence, and with the increasing distance all the pain of acknowledging that fact doubling and redoubling.[16]

Young adults sometimes complain bitterly about the "morbid" and "sick" literature adults foist off on the young, *Macbeth*, Romantic poetry, "Thanatopsis," *Death of a Salesman*, *Oedipus Rex*, and "A Rose for Emily." What is equally clear is that young adults are every bit as preoccupied with death, but they prefer to choose their own literature. Surely reading such literature helps young adults begin to develop their own code of values to hold dear in the dread times to come, to take a closer look at adults and young adults who face death in the midst of life, and to develop an even greater appreciation of the life that flies by so very soon.

For a few young people that may lead to reading books like Robert Jay Lifton's *The Broken Connection* or Jill Krementz's *How It Feels When a Parent Dies*. A few may read one of Elisabeth Kübler-Ross' excellent studies,

On Death and Dying, Questions and Answers on Death and Dying, Death: The Final Stage of Growth, or *Coping with Death and Dying.* Some may become involved with a local chapter of the Hospice movement.

Others will want to read true stories of people who fought death, who may even have died but in dying proved their personal heroism. *Eric* by Eric's mother, Doris Lund, has long been popular with young people who see Eric as a real hero. Eric did not give in to his leukemia, which he prolonged two years beyond any doctor's prediction. He also captained a soccer team, had a love affair, went scuba diving, and traveled with a close friend across America in an old van.

Three books that maintain their appeal deal with the cancer death of football player Brian Piccolo. The favorite of the three is usually William Blinn's *Brian's Song,* created from the television script. The television movie came from a chapter, "Pick," in Gayle Sayers' *I Am Third.* The most complete story is Jeannie Morris' *Brian Piccolo: A Short Season.*

Other true stories about death fought valiantly include William Buchanan's *A Shining Season* which tells how a twenty-four-year-old runner spent the last eighteen months of his life. *Hope: A Loss Survived* by Richard Merryman is about the two years his doomed wife and he and their children spent coming alive and celebrating life, not death; Victor and Rosemary Zorza's *A Way to Die* about the slow death of their daughter; and Joie Harrison McGrail's *Fighting Back* about a brave woman fighting cancer. Three fine autobiographies may appear depressing, but their accounts of mighty battles by brave people are heroic, not sad. Violet Weingarten's *Intimations of Mortality* ends with her death, but her meditations about her approaching death and her fighting spirit impress rather than depress. Even better and more perceptive are Cornelius and Kathryn Morgan Ryan's *A Private Battle* about the death of the historian in 1974 and Stewart Alsop's *Stay of Execution* consisting of notes and diaries as the columnist prepared to die.

The death of a child frightens and saddens us even more than the death of an adult. Two moving and legitimately tearful accounts are Elaine Ipswitch's *Scott Was Here,* a story of a five-year battle with Hodgkin's Disease, and Frank Deford's *Alex, The Life of a Child* in which the sportswriter watches his daughter die slowly and painfully and bravely.

Among the very best books on the subject are John Gunther's *Death Be Not Proud* and Mark and Dan Jury's *Gramp.* At sixteen, Gunther's son developed a cancerous brain tumor. *Death Be Not Proud* is both an account of the death and an account of Gunther's long struggle to retain his sanity in handling his loss. *Gramp* tells of the obviously lovable and delightful grandfather who, finding that he is slowly and inevitably going senile, decides with his family's approval to die by starvation. *Gramp* is a lovingly illustrated memorial to a brave and good man.

Many young people, perhaps most of them, would prefer to read about fictional deaths, finding them real enough, perhaps even more real and moving than the most striking nonfiction. Some of these novels are about the death of the central character, some about the effects of a death on those left behind, and some few about suicide.

Four fine books focus on the death of the central character, Gunnel Beckman's *Admission to the Feast*, Monica Hughes' *Hunter in the Dark*, Margaret Craven's *I Heard the Owl Call My Name*, and John Donovan's *Wild in the World*.

When Annika Hall learns that she is dying of leukemia in *Admission to the Feast*, she panics and runs away to a country cottage to sort out her thoughts and feelings. She is alone, her father dead, her mother halfway around the world, and her best friend is thousands of miles away. She dreads telling her fiancé, for she fears that whatever love he has for her will easily become pity. And so she begins to write to her best friend, and what she writes is the book we read. She wonders why her parents divorced, about becoming "nothing, nothing in the infinity of infinity," about the beauty of the world she will miss so much, about her ability to face death with dignity.

Mike Rankin in Monica Hughes' *Hunter in the Dark* has even more reason to be bitter, for his parents, wanting only to protect him from reality, keep him in the dark about his illness. Knowing that he is getting no better, Mike uses the name of his medicine, vincristine, to discover his disease in a medical book in the local library.

He knows he is going to die, but first he must shoot a white-tail buck deer, to get the antlered head that will prove his manhood. At the close of the novel, Mike has the buck in his rifle sights, a buck "better than his dreams," and then he finds that he cannot pull the trigger, and with that comes his own resignation to his impending death.

When the Bishop in *I Heard the Owl Call My Name* learns that twenty-seven-year-old Mark Brian has a terminal illness with less than two years to live, he says to the doctor:

◇ So short a time to learn so much? It leaves me no choice. I shall send him to my hardest parish. I shall send him to Kingcome on patrol of the Indian villages.

And off Mark goes, there supposedly to help but actually, as the Bishop knows, to learn how to live and how to die. He approaches the Indians both fearfully and thankfully, fitting his ambivalent view of the world. Craven's book is filled with ambivalence, life and death, success and failure, sympathy and cruelty, pride and resentment, giving and begging, keeping and releasing, destroying and honoring, all there to help readers recognize the ambivalence of life.

And, of course, the greatest ambivalence in the novel is reserved for Mark's death. Sent to an obscure village to prepare for death by learning about life, Mark succeeds in learning about life and death. Then prepared for his end, the end comes suddenly, capriously, almost like the jest of some maniac gods determined to prove that whatever mortals plan for, even death, the gods will rip asunder. This is a remarkably mature book young adults will admire, just as they will admire the heroism of Mark and others in the book.

John Donovan's *Wild in the World* puzzles many readers. It seems simple, too simple, and direct, too direct. John Gridley relates how his father and mother, and his many brothers and sisters died in Spartan-cold diction, not because he is without feeling but because life *and* death are cold facts of life in his isolated New Hampshire mountain home. There is no mention of grief or fear or loneliness, for death is a commonplace to John. Then Son, half-dog, half-wolf, comes to live with John, and where life and death had been equally sterile, there is now reason to live. And that is the pain of *Wild in the World*, for as John learns about living, he dies of pneumonia. John's death is more moving than all the deaths that have gone before. Yet it is appropriate that the book ends, not with John's death, but with the discovery of it and the lack of understanding by the outside world of the relationship that was most important in all of John's short life. "Son taught me a lot," he told his dead brothers. "Human critters hold back."

Many more novels deal with the effect a death has on people left behind. The classic is James Agee's *A Death in the Family*. After the quiet opening of the prose-poem "Knoxville: Summer 1915" with its quiet affirmation of the dignity of the family and the need for love, the novel reaffirms the love of Jay Follett for his wife Mary and his children Rufus and Catherine. When Jay leaves early of a morning to see Grandfather Follett who has been taken ill, he is too rushed to wake the children to say goodbye. Tragically, he is killed in a car accident, and his wife and children, especially Rufus, try to make sense out of his death and his life. Agee's work is vastly superior to a work with which it is sometimes compared, Judith Guest's *Ordinary People*. Agee's people are ordinary at the first of the book and extraordinary by the close. Guest's people stay ordinary and hardly worth knowing.

As David Marks returns from his father's funeral, he announces the theme of Barbara Wersba's *Run Softly, Go Fast,* the ambivalent love-hatred David feels for his father:

> ◇ The funeral was such a farce. The rabbi didn't even know Dad. Just hired for the occasion like an entertainer. . . . Why did he seem so different when I was little? I looked at him in that hospital bed, high on morphine and babbling about the office, the business, and I had a sudden memory of being five. The bungalow in the Catskills . . . I don't want to think about it. He said I was a bum to let a girl support me. As if painting wasn't work. . . . "At least get engaged," he kept saying. "Did I raise you for this? To live like a degenerate in the East Village?" . . . He was so crude . . . But the summers in the Catskills . . .
>
> I wish Maggie would get home. I want to make love. Which would shock Ben—right after the funeral. But sex is life and tonight I want life very much. My life, not his. . . . There weren't any real friends at the funeral. It's funny, but that was the only part that bothered me.
>
> Be honest. He was a bastard and you hated him.

David sets out to put the record about him and his father straight, the good times, the bad times. The stream of consciousness in this complex young adult novel is not always easy to follow, but ultimately David works through

THE PEOPLE BEHIND THE BOOKS

ZIBBY ONEAL, Author

A Formal Feeling
The Language of Goldfish

The field of adolescent literature has, I think, increasingly in recent years become a territory rich in opportunity for a writer. One might once have felt uncomfortably limited by what were believed to be the interests and requirements of the adolescent audience. No longer. We have discovered that few ideas are too complicated, few emotions too foreign, few subjects too "adult" for this audience. The challenge now becomes dealing with this open frontier. How well can we do it? How thoughtfully, skillfully, honestly can we handle this material? The challenge interests me.

Adolescents interest me—intensely. All that the individual will become is nascent in these years. How a particular individual negotiates this brief but intense passage between childhood and adult life is something that I want to continue to explore. ◆

A Formal Feeling. Viking, 1982.
The Language of Goldfish. Viking, 1980.

the tangle of love and hate until he makes a truce with his dead father and finds peace within himself.

The death of a parent or grandparent can be traumatic, as David knows and as the major characters in other novels learn. A father's death devastates Bridie McShane in Mollie Hunter's *A Sound of Chariots* and becomes almost obssessive and the impetus to her becoming a writer in the sequel, *Hold On to Love.* It also becomes the central problem in Carol Farley's *The Garden Is Doing Fine,* Ann Rinaldi's *Term Paper,* and Jane Gardam's fine novel, *The Summer After the Funeral.* A mother's death causes expected and unexpected problems for the protagonists on Barbara Girion's *A Tangle of Roots,* Alice Bach's *Mollie Make-Believe,* and Zibby Oneal's *A Formal Feeling.* The death of a beloved grandfather hits hard at characters in Madeleine L'Engle's *A Ring of Endless Light* and even harder in the superb *A Figure of Speech* by Norma Fox Mazer.

Although written for younger readers, Katherine Paterson's *Bridge to Terabithia* is a warm and wise book for any reader, child, young adult, or adult. Ten-year-old Jess Aarons runs to impress his father who detests the artistic side of his son. But Jess, to his surprise, is beaten in a race by Leslie Burke, new girl at school. Drawn to each other because both are loners, they create the magic kingdom of Terabithia. While Jess is away, Leslie dies in a tragic accident. Jess' reaction is self-pity, feeling that she has betrayed him by leaving, but as others help to comfort him, he begins to feel a more honest grief and an awareness that he has learned about himself and his needs through Leslie and their mutual love for Terabithia. Jess is, above all else, a survivor.

Paterson's novel set impossibly high standards that no other such book about the death of a friend has equalled, but two other works deserve readers. In Richard Peck's *Close Enough to Touch,* Matt Moran suffers through a void when his girlfriend dies. Then he meets another girl who is not impressed with his self-pity. Chris Crutcher's *Running Loose*, mentioned earlier in the section on sports heroes, is a fine first novel about a sensitive young man and the torments he goes through after his girlfriend dies in a car accident. Lois Lowry's *A Summer to Die* is the story of two sisters, cheerleader Molly and younger and quieter Meg Chalmers. Meg is worried when Molly becomes sick much of the time, but she is also jealous that Molly is, as usual, getting all the attention. Then Meg learns that Molly has incurable leukemia. A fine book about loneliness and despair and ultimate acceptance.

For many adults, books about suicide are even more worrisome than other books about death. For these adults, reading about suicide is to be morbidly preoccupied with a subject best left alone by healthy young people. But young adults know about the reality of suicide, many at first hand in schools where suicides are omnipresent. It has been for years the second leading cause of teenage deaths surpassed in numbers only by accidents, and some accidents may have been suicides.

Headlines banner the news across the country. The June 18, 1978, *Chicago Tribune* used "Suicide: No. 3 Killer of Teens" as its major headline on the first page. More recently, the May 27, 1982, *Los Angeles Times* headlined "Shaken by Teen Suicides, School District Seeks a Cure for the Hidden Epidemic," and the same paper on August 14 announced, "Teen-Age Suicides on the Increase—Officials Struggle to Cope with a 'Devastating Problem.'" *The New York Times* during March 1984 alone had three stories on young adult suicides. "The Haunting Specter of Teen-Age Suicide" by Jane E. Brody on March 4, "Seeking to Prevent Teen-Age Suicide" by the same author on March 7, and "Suicide in New York Suburbs" on March 14. Brody's March 4 article noted:

> ◇ Since the 1950s, the suicide rate among young people in the United States has increased by about 300 percent while the rates among other age groups have not changed markedly. Suicide is the second leading cause of death, after accidents, among teenagers. For every successful adolescent suicide, there are reported to be at least 50 and probably as many as 200 suicide attempts. [17]

Perhaps young people sometimes want to read about suicide because it is omnipresent in their world, perhaps because it has an ambivalent appeal to them—many adults when they were young contemplated suicide, not necessarily seriously, wondering what it might be like to end all their problems so easily—perhaps because they are curious as to what would drive another person to want to end life. Nonfiction like Francis Klagsbrun's *Too Young to Die: Youth and Suicide*, Peter Giovacchini's *The Urge to Die: Why Young People Commit Suicide*, and John E. Mack and Holly Hickler's *Vivienne: The Life and Suicide of an Adolescent Girl* will help young people to understand why suicide happens and adults to recognize some of the danger signs that precede suicide.

Sylvia Plath's *The Bell Jar* is a fictionalized autobiography about her own life and her own death-wish. Esther is preoccupied by the execution of the

Rosenbergs, and throughout her story she reads constantly about death and suicide. At one point, Esther says, "I am an observer," and later she withdraws more and more from reality:

> ◇ I slunk down on the middle of my spine, my nose level with the rim of the window, and watched the houses of outer Boston glide by.
> As the houses grew more familiar, I slunk still lower.

Esther dreams of a wonderful career in exciting and glamorous New York City and a perfect marriage.

> ◇ I was supposed to be having the time of my life. I was supposed to be the envy of thousands of other college girls just like me all over America. . . . Look what can happen in this country, they'd say. A girl lives in some out-of-the-way town for nineteen years . . . then gets a scholarship to college and wins a prize here and a prize there and ends up steering New York like her own private car. *Only I wasn't steering anything, not even myself.*

Fans of *The Bell Jar* will also want to read Plath's poetry and journals.

Of the two good young adult novels about suicide, A. E. Johnson's (Annabel and Edgar Johnson) *A Blues I Can Whistle* is the better. Young Cody sets out to kill himself and fails. His doctors want to know why, but he will not tell them but he will tell his best friend, Barney:

> ◇ They were here again just now, pestering. The doctors—they keep asking, "Why?" Why this, why that, when all the time the real question is: why should I tell them why? Trying to discontinue my life was a very personal decision; they never thought of it that way. They act as if I owe it to science, somehow, to explain.
> For them, I wouldn't do it—spill the whole thing. And for my own sake I certainly wouldn't bother, But, as Barney once said, there are other sakes.

And with that, Cody starts to work through his greatest puzzle, himself, to find some answers.

Fran Arrick's *Tunnel Vision* is about the people fifteen-year-old Anthony Hamil left behind when he hanged himself in his bedroom, apparently without reason. Two fine dramas will interest more mature young people. Marsha Norman's *'night, Mother* slowly reveals the plans of a woman to kill herself as she spends a last evening with her mother. She is not seeking pity nor anyone to stop her, but she does want her mother to know so that her mother will not blame herself.

The right to choose one's own way out of life is made by Ken Harrison, an artist now totally paralyzed by a car accident, in Brian Clark's play, *Whose Life Is It, Anyway?* Harrison could hardly have demanded better treatment than that accorded him at the hospital, but the doctors fight to keep him alive when all he wants is to be allowed to die with dignity. His lawyer sues for Harrison's simple right to die. In a moving scene, Harrison explains his reasoning:

> ◇ *Ken:* I choose to acknowledge the fact that I am in fact dead and I find the hospital's persistent effort to maintain this shadow of life an indignity and it's inhumane.

Judge: But wouldn't you agree that many people with appalling physical handicaps have overcome them and lived essentially creative, dignified lives?

Ken: Yes, I would, but the dignity starts with their choice. If I choose to live, it would be appalling if society killed me. If I choose to die, it is equally appalling if society keeps me alive.

Judge: I cannot accept that it is undignified for society to devote resources to keeping someone alive. Surely it enhances that society.

Ken: It is not undignified if the man wants to stay alive, but I must restate that the dignity starts with his choice. Without it, it is degrading because technology has taken over from human will. My Lord, if I cannot be a man, I do not wish to be a medical achievement.

The moral question is not easily solved in this play, or in life, but the issues and arguments for both sides are well and fairly presented in Clark's play.

◈ HEROES IN WAR

War is a constant in our lives. Old war movies abound on the late show. Newspapers and magazines banner the headlines of this new or that old war. Television news programs barrage us with the latest atrocities.

Why are we so continually preoccupied with war, bloodshed, and death? Perhaps because war is inherently frightening and evil, and in the minds of too many of us, horribly inevitable. The Bible is full of battles, but then so are the *Iliad* and the *Odyssey*. War serves as background for *Antigone* just as it does for *The Red Badge of Courage* and *A Farewell to Arms* and *The Naked and the Dead*. War has influenced artists and musicians, or, perhaps, it would be fairer to say that it has left its indelible mark on them.

Young adults are painfully aware of the nearness of war, though they may know little about the realities of war and even less about the details of past wars. Reading war literature, fiction or not, serves to acquaint young people with some of war's horrors and how easily people forget, or ignore, their humanity in the midst of war. War novels must, of course, have a war at the center, but authors are almost always more interested in what war does to humans than in a mere historic recounting of battles and campaigns and casualties. War books are likely to center on physical and psychological suffering. Death lurks on every doorstep, or it did once, and it still may emotionally for the characters. Often the war seems to happen in slow motion, focusing on one person engaged in one act. Or the reverse may be true, events being telescoped to eliminate the trivial or nonessential to force readers (and sometimes characters) to see the realities and horrors of war even more intensely. At one time, we might have accepted romantic war stories, but a romanticized picture of war today would seem dishonest and offensive to most readers.

Five novelists have written particularly effective war novels.

Harry Mazer's *The Last Mission* is set in the last months of World War II. Jack Raab uses his older brother's identification to lie his way into the Air Force to destroy Hitler and save democracy, all by himself. That dream lasts only a short time before Jack learns that the Air Force is more training and boredom than fighting. When Jack does go to war, his first twenty-four bombing raids go well, but on the last mission, his plane is hit, all his buddies die, and he is captured. When he returns home, the principal at his old school asks him to talk:

> ◇ "I'm glad we won," he said. "We couldn't let Hitler keep going. We had to stop him. But most of all, I'm glad it's over." Had he said enough? There was a silence . . . a waiting silence. There was something more he had to say.
>
> "I don't like war. I thought I'd like it before. But war is stupid. War is one stupid thing after another. I saw my best friend killed. His name was Chuckie O'Brien. My whole crew was killed." Now he was talking, it was coming out, all the things he'd thought about for so long. "A lot of people were killed. Millions of people. Ordinary people. Not only by Hitler. Not only on our side. War isn't like the movies. It's not fun and songs. It's not about heroes. It's about awful, sad things, like my friend Chuckie that I'm never going to see again." His voice faltered.
>
> "I hope war never happens again," he said after a moment. "That's all I've got to say."
>
> He sat down. He hardly heard the applause. The floor of the radio room was still slippery with Chuckie's blood. . . . Dave was still fumbling with his chute . . . the plane was still falling through the sky.

Six high-I.Q. soldiers in an intelligence and reconnaissance platoon are sent to find if any Germans are near a French chateau during World War II in *A Midnight Clear* by William Wharton (a pseudonym of a writer who refuses to identify himself publicly). The six play bridge, chess, and word games and refuse to admit they have anything to do with the war. Then the Germans show up, but instead of warfare, both Americans and the supposed enemy engage in a snowball fight. A meeting is arranged, they fraternize, they sing Christmas carols and set up a Christmas tree, and then as peace reigns, war starts up again and the killing begins. Wharton tells a powerful story which is as much about humanity's goals being above its ability as it is about war. A powerful story no reader will forget.

English novelist Robert Westall writes about young people who refuse to stay outside the war in *The Machine Gunners* and its sequel, *Fathom Five*. The first novel is set in an English coastal town during 1940–1941. Rumors of a German invasion are rife, and Chas McGill wants to help win the war. Westall is superb at catching some of the humor of the time. Bombs drop, Chas' family heads for the shelter, and his mother remembers insurance policies they must have with them. They turn back toward home.

> ◇ A body fell through. It was Mrs. Spalding.
>
> "Is she dead?" said Mrs. McGill.
>
> "No, but she's got her knickers round her ankles," said Mr. McGill.
>
> "Aah had tey hop aal the way," gasped Mrs. Spalding. "I was on the outside lav and I couldn't finish. The buggers blew the lav door off, and they've hit the Rex Cinema as well. Is there a spot of brandy?"
>
> "Aah pulled the chain, Mam. It flushed all right." It was Colin, with a self-satisfied smirk on his face.
>
> "You'll get the Victoria Cross for that," said Chas with a wild giggle.

Chas and his friends locate a downed German plane, find the machine gun in working order, and hide it. When his school is hit by another plane a bit later, Chas steals sandbags to create a fortress, a safe place to display the machine gun. Then the rear gunner of the downed plane stumbles onto their fortress and becomes the boys' prisoner. The end of childish innocence comes when adults discover the fortress, the German is shot, and the young people are rounded up by their parents. *Fathom Five* is a rousing spy story set a little later in the war and is a story of Chas' lost love. Westall has amazing ability to portray the ambivalence of young people, the alienation they feel mixed with love and duty.

Howard Fast's *April Morning* with its Revolutionary War setting has sometimes been favorably compared with *The Red Badge of Courage*. Fast's novel focuses on fifteen-year-old Adam Cooper, no hero but only a frightened mortal. He knows the rightness of war until he is thrust into the midst of it, and then he wonders more about the carnage and stupidity than the heroism. In eight sections which take readers from the afternoon of April 18, 1775, through the evening of April 19, *April Morning* explores the family relationships of Adam and his father, his mother, his beloved Granny, and the girl he loves.

It would be unfair and inaccurate to call Adam a hero, at least in the usual sense. But Adam is a hero in other important ways. He survives, he does what has to be done, and he tries to make sense out of the horror, to understand what the war is all about. It is about him, whether he wants it to be or not.

James Forman has written widely about war: *The Cow Neck Rebels* about the American Revolution, *The Skies of Crete* about Nazi-occupied Greece, *Horses of Anger* about a young German soldier in World War II, *My Enemy, My Brother* about a survivor of the Warsaw Ghetto who goes to Israel, *Ring the Judas Bell* about Greece after the Nazis when Communist partisans try to take over the government, *The Shield of Achilles* about the Cypriot revolt after World War II, *A Fine, Soft Day* about the I.R.A., and *That Mad Game: War and the Chances of Peace*, a history of the motives for war throughout humanity's history.

But Forman's finest work, too little known, is *Ceremony of Innocence*. Hans and Sophie Scholl, brother and sister in Nazi Germany, print and distribute literature attacking Hitler. Arrested by the Gestapo, they are urged to escape by friends and to plead insanity by a lawyer Hans suspects is a Nazi. They refuse, endure the mock trial, are found guilty, and are taken away to be executed. Hans is the last to die by the guillotine.

> ◇ Hans heard the sound of rollers, and at last there burst from his throat a cry, uttered in a great voice, a voice that combined anger, reproof, and an overwhelming conviction for which he was willing to die.
> "Long live freedom!"
> Then the greased blade fell. His teeth met through his tongue, and it was over.

Forman's novel is powerful, terrifying, and heroic, but no more so than the true story of Hans and Sophie—and their work as members of the "White Rose," an underground group of Munich University teachers and students opposed to Hitler—in Richard Hanser's *A Noble Treason: The Revolt of the Munich Students against Hitler*. In May 1983, a film, *The White Rose*, directed and written by Michael Verhoeven opened in New York City—another retelling of the brave story of Hans and Sophie Scholl. Herman Vinke's *The Short Life of Sophie Scholl* provides additional details.

Several novels about World War I deserve readers. Ernest Hemingway's *A Farewell to Arms* and Erich Maria Remarque's *All Quiet on the Western Front* are well known. Less so are Dalton Trumbo's *Johnny Got His Gun*, about a literal basket-case soldier trying to communicate to others, one of the most violently anti-war books of this or any time, and William March's (real name, William Edward March Campbell) *Company K*, episodic and the best novel about the war.

A few nonfiction books are equally good, though fewer readers know of them. Kit Denton's *The Breaker* is based on the true story of the Australian soldier executed for killing a civilian, certainly better known in the film *Breaker Morant* (1979). Gordon Brook-Shepherd's *November 1918* is a fine history of its time. Vera Brittain's *Testament of Youth* and *Chronicle of Youth: The War Diary 1913–1917* are eloquent statements about a war Brittain detested and a war that devastated her entire existence.

There have been a number of young adult novels written about World War II. Nathaniel Benchley's *A Necessary End* is the diary of seventeen-year-old Ralph Bowers' navy life; Milton Dank's *The Dangerous Game* is about a young French Resistance agent—its sequel is *Game's End*; and John Tunis' superb *His Enemy, His Friend* is about a German sergeant in occupied France forced by his superiors to execute some hostages. Later, after serving a war-crimes sentence, he returns to the French town after the war to play a soccer match. Then hostilities begin again.

The plight of English refugee children moved from London to the countryside is told in Nina Bawden's *Carrie's War* and Michelle Magorian's too little known *Good Night, Mr. Tom*. David Rees' *The Exeter Blitz* should give any reader an understanding of what it was like to endure nightly bombing attacks.

Alki Zei's *Petros' War* and *Wildcat Under Glass* tell of Greece before and during the Nazi rule. Jan Terlouw's *Winter in Wartime* and Els Pelgrom's *The Winter When Time Was Frozen* focus on Holland and the Dutch Resistance. Life in Germany during World War II is the subject of Frank Baer's *Max's Gang* and Ilse Koehn's *Tilla*.

Norman Mailer's *The Naked and the Dead* was certainly *the* American novel of the war although some readers might argue that James Jones' *The Thin Red Line* or *The Pistol* were as good. Among the best selling pictures of men at war during the time was Harry Brown's *A Walk in the Sun*.

Two unusual books about the war, both published long after the war ended, were Daniel Panger's *Search in Gomorrah* and John Hammond Moore's *The Faustball Tunnel*. Panger's novel calls for maturity in its readers, because of a couple of explicit love scenes and details of the atrocities at Treblinka. It is about an American soldier left to guard five captured SS Germans in 1945. Later, he is deeply troubled by his act and travels through post-war Germany to find who is guilty. *The Faustball Tunnel* is a true story of the attempt of German prisoners of war, most of them naval personnel, to escape from their prison camp in Phoenix. It is, surprisingly, a quite funny book.

Richard Tregaskis' *Guadalcanal Diary* was widely read for its depiction of American heroes in the Pacific Theater. The attack on Pearl Harbor is the subject of Walter Lord's *Day of Infamy* as is the more recent and more scholarly *At Dawn We Slept: The Untold Story of Pearl Harbor* by Gordon W. Prange.

The war in Europe is told in Walter Lord's *The Miracle of Dunkirk*, David Shoenbrun's *Soldiers of the Night: The Story of the French Resistance*, and John Keegan's *Six Armies in Normandy: From D-Day to the Liberation of Paris*. For readers curious about the life of the footsoldier during the war, there is nothing better than Bill Mauldin's *Up Front*, a narrative accompanied by cartoons of common soldiers Willie and Joe.

The pain of civilians caught up in a war that they do not understand is well described in the much read *I Am Fifteen—And I Don't Want to Die* by Christine Arnothy. The author and her Hungarian parents were trapped in a cellar of their apartment complex as the war raged over and around them.

The most shameful American wartime act during World War II began in February 1942 when, under orders of President Roosevelt, the government rounded up 120,000 people of Japanese ancestry living in the United States and held them in detention camps for the duration of the war. The racial prejudice lingered on the West Coast for years. *Farewell to Manzanar* by Jeanne Wakatsuki Houston and James D. Houston describes the first author's life in a camp ringed by barbed wire and guardtowers and open latrines. The three years' ordeal destroyed the family unity and left a heritage of personal self-inadequacy that took years to remove. Yoshiko Uchida's *Journey Home* recalls the camps and the family's return to life after the war. Daniel S. Davis' *Behind Barbed Wire: The Imprisonment of Japanese Americans During World War II* is a history of those bleak times.

For several years after the end of our involvement in Vietnam, it seemed that few novels about the war were likely to come forth. Histories and political accounts were not hard to find—Frances FitzGerald's *Fire in the Lake: The Vietnamese and Americans in Vietnam* in 1973 was the best of the lot although the insanity of the war somehow came across better in C. D. B. Bryan's *Friendly Fire* and Ronald J. Glasser's *365 Days*. Nonfiction continues to pour forth in the last few years. Mark Baker's *Nam: The Vietnam War in the Words of the Men and Women Who Fought There*; Al Santoli's *Everything We Had: An Oral History of the Vietnam War by Thirty-Three American Soldiers Who Fought It*; Lynda Van Devanter's *Home Before Morning*; Peter Goldman and Tony Fuller's *Charlie Company: What Vietnam Did to Us*; Robert Mason's *Chickenhawk*; Stanley Karnow's *Vietnam: A History*; Winston Groom and Duncan Spencer's *Conversations with the Enemy: The Story of PFC Robert Garwood*; and Frederick Downs' *After-*

math: *A Soldier's Return from Vietnam* all tell horrors that most of us would prefer to forget, horrors we had better remember or we will repeat them. George Esper's *The Eyewitness History of the Vietnam War, 1961–1975* and *Tim Page's Nam* are pictorial records of the tragedies and the stupidities and the horrors.

Publishers and public alike assumed that this was a war to be reported on, not fictionalized, for few novels of consequence appeared early. Perhaps this was to be a war we would prefer to forget.

Then in 1978 Tim O'Brien's *Going After Cacciato* was published. Private Cacciato decides, one fine day, that he has had enough of Vietnam so he begins his march out of the jungles and on for another 8600 miles to Paris. Treating his march as just another mission, his squad follows to bring him back. Jack Anderson and Bill Pronzini's *The Cambodia File*, far less known, concerns 1975–1976 and David Foxworth, political liaison with the U.S. Embassy. John M. Del Vecchio's *The 13th Valley* shows soldiers inching their way up formidable terrain to win battles no one understands. Best of them all is the frighteningly wacky *Meditations in Green* by Stephen Wright. James Griffin, now living in a squalid apartment, returns in his mind to Vietnam where he is part of Military Intelligence Group 1069 and watches as all the people he knows are destroyed in one way or another by the madness of the events they witness. Wright's novel is complex and often difficult and rewarding.

Of all the many books on war, there is no greater indictment of the absurdity and cruelty of war than Roger Rosenblatt's *Children of War*. Rosenblatt circled the globe seeking out children in Belfast, Ireland, in Israel, in Cambodia, in Hong Kong, and in Lebanon and asking them about themselves and what war had done to them. A nine-year-old girl in Cambodia made a drawing, and after a year of help by an American psychologist, she was able to explain how the instrument in the drawing worked. Rosenblatt writes:

> ◇ The children harvesting rice include Peov. She is the largest of the three. Whenever a child refused to work, he was punished with the circular device. The soldiers would place it over the child's head. Three people would hold it steady by means of ropes. . . . A fourth would grab hold of the ring at the end of the other rope. . . . When the rope with the ring was pulled . . . the child would be decapitated. A portable guillotine.
>
> But it wasn't the soldiers who worked the device. It was the children.[18]

◈ HEROES OF THE HOLOCAUST

Only a few years back, anyone wishing to read about the Holocaust would begin by reading Anne Frank's *Diary of a Young Girl*, then move on to the 1955 play, *The Diary of Anne Frank* by Frances Goodrich and Albert Hackett, and wrap up the study by looking at the 1959 film, *The Diary of Anne Frank*, directed by George Stevens and starring a hopelessly inadequate Millie Perkins. Advanced students might find a few other sources, mostly historical, and the most mature might view Alain Resnais' short and powerful film, "Night and Fog."

Times have changed. Anyone now wishing to read about the Holocaust would still be advised to begin with Anne Frank's *Diary*—it is still that moving and poignant—but a world of books opens after Frank. Heroes of the Holocaust are now celebrated in young adult books, in more histories, in interviews with Holocaust victims, in plays, in every literary form.

Good introductions to the horrors of that time and place are in Alvin H. Rosenfeld's *A Double Dying: Reflections on Holocaust Literature*, David A. Altschuler's *Hitler's War Against the Jews*, Milton Meltzer's *Never to Forget: The Jews of the Holocaust*, Lawrence L. Langer's *Versions of Survival: The Holocaust and the Human Spirit*, Sidra DeKoven Ezrahi's *By Words Alone: The Holocaust in Literature*, Charles Patterson's *Anti-Semitism: The Road to the Holocaust and Beyond*, Yehuda Bauer's *A History of the Holocaust*, Martin S. Bergmann and Milton E. Jucovy's *Generations of the Holocaust*, and Annette Insdorf's *Indelible Shadows: Film and the Holocaust*. The two most readable introductions, though not always easy and frequently anguishing, are Lucy S. Dawidowicz's *The Holocaust and the Historians* and Helen Epstein's *Children of the Holocaust: Conversations with Sons and Daughters of Survivors*.

For the milieu that fostered the Holocaust, two plays are essential—Rolf Hochhuth's *The Deputy* and Peter Weiss' *The Investigation*. The latter play is quietly terrifying as it portrays a war crimes trial of minor officials, all of whom deny responsibility for their acts since they did only what they were told to do.

Most young adults will seek out books about young people caught in the Holocaust because they are better able to identify with people their own age or slightly older. Anne Frank's *Diary of a Young Girl* is, as noted above, still one of the best starting points, and recently more material about Anne Frank has been published. Anne Frank's *Tales from the Secret Annex* is a collection of personal essays and stories and fables she wrote during her time hiding from the Germans. She writes about elves and flower girls and dreams and fears and happiness, all youthful, all saddened by what we know will happen to Anne all too soon.

For those seeking similar accounts, Etty Hillesum's *An Interrupted Life: The Diaries of Etty Hillesum, 1941–1943* is the answer. Hillesum's record is not better or worse than Anne Frank's; it is the product of a twenty-seven year-old woman who knows precisely what her fate is certain to be. She begins her first entry, "Here goes, then," and she writes of her love affairs, her graduate study at the University of Amsterdam, and her friends and ideas. She seems to have had little interest in politics until Jews were required to wear the yellow star. That jolted her, but she never sought to escape. In her last days, she volunteered to go with a group of condemned Jews to Westerbork Camp. She must have known that Westerbork was the usual first step before Auschwitz. Her journal complements Anne's *Diary*; Etty's irony and sophistication neatly counterpointing Anne's simplicity and innocence.

There are several other autobiographical accounts of the time that young adults should read. Hana Demetz's autobiographical novel, *The House on Prague Street*, is about a young girl who summers in her grandfather's beautiful house on Prague Street while Naziism waits to pounce on her and her family. That sense of a wonderful time soon to be destroyed is the theme of George Clare's *Last Waltz in Vienna: The Destruction of a Family, 1842–1942* and Emma Macalik Butterworth's *As the Waltz Was Ending*. Jack Eisner's *The Survivor* is an almost unbearable story of what it meant to be a thirteen-year-old Jew when the Holocaust erupted. Ilse Koehn's *Mischling, Second Degree* is a quieter but no less effective reminder of what it meant to be a Jew in the 1930s. Ilse was six when she was classified as a "Mischling, Second Degree," meaning that she was a person with one Jewish grandmother. Her parents divorced to save her, and she spent the war as a "Hitler Youth." Johanna Reiss' *The Upstairs Room* and *The Journey Back* and Judith Kerr's *When Hitler Stole Pink Rabbit, The Other Way Round*, and *A Small Person Far Away* are aimed at slightly younger readers, but any young adult would learn about a time and a place and a people by reading them.

Wendelgard Von Staden's *Darkness over the Valley, Growing Up in Nazi Germany* describes the times but from a quite different perspective. She grew up in economically tight conditions, but when Hitler came to power, she gladly joined the "Hitler Youth." It was not until the family doctor showed her mother snapshots of Nazi atrocities in Russia and told her of the Jewish purge that the family knew the evil of Naziism. When their valley became the site of a concentration camp, mother and daughter knew they must do something, and they worked to alleviate the conditions of the camp. Two other German autobiographies of slightly less interest are Ingeborg Day's *Ghost Waltz* and Crista Wolf's *A Model Childhood*.

Of the many young adult novels about the time, two stand out. Hans Peter Richter's *Friedrich* and Fred Uhlman's *Reunion*. Richter's narrator and Jewish Friedrich Schneider remain friends though the narrator's father is a Nazi. When Friedrich's mother dies and his father is arrested, Friedrich becomes an outcast and is eventually expelled from school. He dies in a bombing raid when he is denied a place in an air raid shelter. Fred Uhlman's *Reunion* begins in 1932 in a Stuttgart school. Hans Schwartz, the Jewish narrator, strikes up a friendship with Konradin Von Hohenfels. Konradin's mother detests Jews, and the friendship is shaken but not destroyed. Hans is sent for safety to relatives in New York, and his parents stay behind, sure that Germany will regain its sanity. A few other novels young adults would like are Edith Baer's *A Frost in the Night*, Mara Kay's *In Face of Danger*, Marilyn Sachs' *A Pocket Full of Seeds*, Hilda van Stockum's *The Borrowed House*, and Doris Orgel's *The Devil in Vienna*.

Joseph Ziemian's *The Cigarette Sellers of Three Crosses Square* and Joseph Joffo's *A Bag of Marbles* reflect the fighting spirit of Jews unwilling to go quietly to their graves. A Jewish Resistance fighter himself, Ziemian's group of Jewish boys and girls escape the Warsaw Ghetto and survive by hiding and begging and seeking sympathy wherever they could find it. In

Joffo's book, two Jewish brothers hide and run, run and hide, to escape the Gestapo, one time by "proving" that they were Catholics. Other nonfiction on the topic are Leonard Gross' *The Last Jews in Berlin* and Jan Nowak's *Courier from Warsaw*. Two heroes are celebrated in Hannah Senesh's *Hannah Senesh: Her Life and Diary* and Frederick E. Werbell and Thurston Clarke's *Lost Hero: The Mystery of Raoul Wallenberg*. Senesh was tortured and killed by Nazis when she was only twenty-three for her work rescuing Jews. Wallenberg was a thirty-one-year-old Swede who arrived in Budapest in 1944, "The only American agent sent into an Axis country for the sole and express purpose of saving the last remnant of European Jewry," as the authors note. Wallenberg used his diplomatic skills, and some well-placed bribes, to save 40,000 Jews. In 1945, Russian troops entered Hungary and Wallenberg disappeared. Peter Hellman's *Avenue of the Righteous* tells of four people who spent their lives helping to save Jews at this horrible time. The title comes from an avenue in Jerusalem which honors seven hundred Christians who helped to save Jews from the Nazis.

An outstanding novel by Thomas Keneally tells of a man with no pretensions to heroism who becomes a hero to thousands of Jews. *Schindler's List* is based on facts so disturbingly unbelievable that only a novel could make the truth into a reality. Oskar Schindler was one of many opportunists who followed the German invasion into Poland to make quick and easy money. After carefully bribing and fawning to the right people, he raked in the money, and then discovered he had a problem—his Jewish workers were harried by soldiers who forced them to live in a crowded ghetto. Schindler became so obsessed with saving his workers that he fed them with his own money and stole medicine and supplies to help others. As the slaughter of Jews increased later in the war, Schindler recognized that his workers were increasingly likely to be shipped to concentration camps so he bribed high-placed people in Berlin to relocate his camp to Czechoslovakia. And this most unlikely of heroes saved 1300 Jews from death. Keneally makes us believe the story of a man who wanted only to make money but who captained a tiny ship to life for as many victims as he could.

The barbarism of the concentration camps is adequately described in Marietta Moskin's *I Am Rosemarie,* a simple and honest introduction for younger adolescents to the anguish and pain. Far better are Tadeusz Borowski's *This Way to the Gas, Ladies and Gentlemen; and Other Stories,* Aharon Appelfeld's riveting *Badenheim 1939,* and the widely read *Night* by Elie Wiesel. Isabella Leitner's *Fragments of Isabella—A Memoir of Auschwitz* is a series of nightmares from the camp. Kitty Hart, author of *Return to Auschwitz,* agreed to return to the camp to film a British television documentary, largely to refute the lies that have circulated for years by anti-Semites that the Holocaust was a hoax. Much of the book takes place in the Birkenau section known as Auschwitz II where Hart and her mother kept each other alive.

Sylvia Rothchild's *Voices from the Holocaust* and Azriel Eisenberg's *Witness to the Holocaust* portray life before and during the concentration camps. Both are celebrations of life that honor the dead. More moving yet

THE PEOPLE BEHIND THE BOOKS

MYRON LEVOY, Author

Alan and Naomi
A Shadow Like a Leopard
Three Friends

The teenagers I'm drawn to and have explored in my work are generally sensitive, offbeat, in conflict with the mainstream. They want to belong, to be part of a group or scene, but must face the reality of their own strangeness. They will always be the outsider; their friends will be outsiders, too. Their struggles for identity are doubly difficult, for their acceptance must come from within: the ghetto boy who carries a knife but writes poetry, the bisexual girl who feels rejected, the sensitive Jewish boy facing anti-Semitism. Though these cases may be special, I believe young adults must confront their selves and the world, sooner or later, in order to make one of the great decisions of their lives: whether to conform to outside pressures, or be their own persons.

This seems to be the central theme of my work, yet the characters, in each case, tug and pull at their problems in their own ways, often with humor—that indispensable tool for living—and come up with answers that leave the future open-ended, to be continued, to be discovered further. I think life's like that; few of us solve everything with one mighty stroke. I like to end my books feeling there's another book which I most likely will never write, but which is there for readers to imagine, or half-create, for themselves. ◆

Alan and Naomi. Harper & Row, 1977.
A Shadow Like a Leopard. Harper & Row, 1981.
Three Friends. Harper & Row, 1984.

---

are two works that relate extraordinary musical events in the camps. Josef Bor's *The Terezin Requiem* is about a conductor who recruited an orchestra to perform Verdi's *Requiem* in the Terezin camp, a performance so incredible that even German officers were moved. Fania Fenelon's *Playing for Time* is better known from its television version, but the book is still stirring as we see the development of a women's orchestra in the Birkenau extermination camp.

Pictures from the camps are distressing and necessary to remind us of what others endured. Lili Meier's photographs and Peter Hellman's text in *The Auschwitz Album* makes us newly aware that these were real people who died, not historical objects. Janet Blatter and Sybil Milton's *Art of the Holocaust* presents loveliness and horror intermixed, a record of people who managed to do what they had to do despite their nearness to death.

Most touching of all is Hana Volavkova's *I Never Saw Another Butterfly: Children's Drawings and Poems from Terezin Concentration Camp.* Nearly 15,000 children came to the camp. About 100 survived. Some of the poems or drawings are childish scribblings, some reveal real talent, but all touch the readers.

After the war was done, the Holocaust was ended, except for its victims. The dead could rest but rarely could the living. Elisha, a young Israeli freedom fighter haunted by memories of the camps, is told he must kill a young British officer in Elie Wiesel's memorable *Dawn*. Two of James Forman's novels show the effects of the Holocaust on the survivors. *The Survivor*'s protagonist is David Ullman, the only one of his family to live through the terror of concentration camps and fighting in the underground. His struggle to stay alive, physically and mentally, is dramatic and honest. *My Enemy, My Brother* is about Daniel Baratz who barely survives the camp. He meets Hanna who convinces him that Israel is the answer. He finds brief happiness before war erupts and he finds that he must again kill or be killed.

In America, the Holocaust lingers on as Fran Arrick's *Chernowitz* eloquently proves. Ninth-grader Bobby Cherno finds his classmates turning against him, and when his best friend calls him a "Jew Bastard," Bobby cannot believe what he hears. When the local bully, Emmett Sundback, throws a burning cross on the Chernos' lawn, many people get involved in the anti-Semitism. The book has a tough dose of reality for all readers, and the bully changes not a whit by the end, discomforting but realistic. Myron Levoy's *Alan and Naomi* and M. E. Kerr's *Gentlehands* also concern the remnants of the Holocaust in our country.

T. Degens' *The Visit* is an exceptionally satisfying novel about the continuing effects of the Nazi era. Kate Hofman, a young contemporary German girl, loves to visit her Aunt Sylvia in Berlin. Then she discovers a diary written by her namesake aunt, long-dead, which reveals that Sylvia may have caused Kate's death when both were members of the Hitler Youth. Told in chapters which alternate between the summer of 1943 and the present, this is a fine study of betrayal and disillusionment.

Heroes exist in real life and in fiction. We read about quiet heroes, sports heroes, war heroes, heroes in death, heroes of the Holocaust. They do not parade forth their heroism, except to the sound of their own drummers.

In Sam Peckinpah's film, *Ride the High Country*, two aging former U.S. Marshals down on their luck are hired to bring a gold shipment down from a mountain mining town. Gil Westrum wants to take the money and run. Steve Judd refuses to go along with his old friend, and when Westrum asks him why, Judd answers simply, "All I want is to enter my house justified."

That is all any hero could ask, to live a life of integrity, humanity, and dignity based upon what she or he believes in. That's all but it is everything. To our eternal gratitude, heroes do exist, heroes willing to die for what they believe in, but more important, willing to live to fight for their beliefs. We all need heroes to help us stumble through the darkness of our lives to help us find the light, as they have, to falter and fail and fight and maybe even win sometimes. We do not need those grandiose heroes of old so much as we need heroes like ourselves who achieve an immortality within a family or a community. As teachers and librarians, we have both the responsibility and the opportunity to bring books to young adults that tell them about heroes and the possibility of becoming heroes.

◆ ACTIVITIES ◆

1. Do young adults need heroes? Poll (or interview) several young adults to find who their heroes are and what characteristics are most admired today. Read one or two biographies (or autobiographies) of one of the people most admired by young adults. What heroic (or anti-heroic) qualities/characteristics emerge from the portraits? What does that say about the world of young adults today?

2. Read a biography (or autobiography) of someone you admire. Write an evaluation of the book pointing out in what ways the book heightened (or lessened) your admiration. Is it the biographer's (or autobiographer's) responsibility to leave readers with a belief that the subject is admirable in some way?

3. Select one of the novels about sports mentioned in this chapter along with another nonfiction account of the sport. Read both and compare and contrast the portrayal of the excitement and thrill of the sport. Which do you believe did the better job of getting the excitement across? Why and how? What does the novel offer that is less likely with nonfic-

tion? What does nonfiction offer that is less likely with a novel?

4. Why are young adults continually fascinated with books about death? Poll a group of readers (or interview several) to find what books on the subject are currently popular. Why are they popular? Read one or two. What do these books say about our lives today? Why are tearjerkers popular with television audiences? Are these novels tearjerkers?

5. Are war novels inherently and inevitably anti-war? Read a young adult war novel and compare it with an adult war novel. How do the two differ in their attitudes toward war and people caught in the midst of war? Are both anti-war? How so?

6. More books are published about the Holocaust now than in the several years following World War II. Why do you suppose that is true? Read one of the YA Holocaust novels and a nonfiction account of the same period and place. What do these works have in common? How do they differ? Which is better for a young reader? Why?

◆ NOTES ◆

[1]Joe McGinnis, *Heroes* (New York: Viking, 1976), p. 16.

[2]McGinnis, p. 21.

[3]Dixon Wector, *The Hero in America: A Chronicle of Hero-Worship* (New York: Charles Scribner's Sons, 1941), p. 1.

[4]Arthur Schlesinger, Jr., "The Decline of Greatness," *Saturday Evening Post* 231 (November 1, 1958): 70.

[5]Henry Fairlie, "Too Rich for Heroes," *Harpers Magazine* 257 (November 1978): 33.

[6]Mollie Hunter, "A Need for Heroes," *Horn Book Magazine* 59 (April 1983): 146.

[7]*New York Times*, June 27, 1983, p. 5 (National Edition).

[8]Isaiah Berlin, *Personal Impressions* (New York: Viking, 1981), p. xiv.

[9]Iris Origo, "Biography, True and False," *Atlantic* 203 (February 1959): 39.

[10]Arthur Miller, "Tragedy and the Common Man" in *Aspects of the Drama*, eds., Sylvan

Barnet, Morton Berman, and William Burto (Boston: Little, Brown, 1962), p. 65.

[11]William Least Heat Moon, *Blue Highways: A Journey into America* (Boston: Little, Brown, 1982), p. 3.

[12]Moon, p. 79.

[13]Peter Alfano, "Chris Mullin Drives to Excel as Preparation for the Pros," *New York Times*, March 5, 1984, p. 34 (National Edition).

[14]Jonathan Goodman, "Athletes Chasing after Their Potential," *Los Angeles Times*, September 6, 1983, p. V-1.

[15]Merill Sheils, "Studying Death," *Newsweek* 89 (March 14, 1977): 43.

[16]Roger Rosenblatt, *Children of War* (Garden City, NY: Anchor Press/Doubleday, 1983), p. 22.

[17]"The Haunting Specter of Teen-Age Suicide," *New York Times*, March 4, 1984, p. 8-E (National Edition).

[18]Rosenblatt, p. 148.

◆ TITLES MENTIONED IN CHAPTER 7 ◆

For information on the availability of paperback editions of these titles, please consult the most recent edition of *Paperbound Books in Print,* published annually by R. R. Bowker Company.

Heroes in Biographies and Autobiographies

Angelou, Maya. *Gather Together in My Name.* Random House, 1974.

————. *The Heart of a Woman.* Random House, 1981.

————. *I Know Why the Caged Bird Sings.* Random House, 1970.

————. *Singin' and Swingin' and Gettin' Merry like Christmas.* Random House, 1976.

Armstrong, Karen. *Through the Narrow Gate.* St. Martin's, 1981.

Atkinson, Linda. *Mother Jones: The Most Dangerous Woman in America.* Crown, 1978.

Baker, Russell. *Growing Up.* Congdon and Weed, 1982.

Baxter, Anne. *Intermission: A True Story.* Putnam's, 1976.

Bentley, Toni. *Winter Season.* Random House, 1983.

Bergman, Ingrid and Alan Burgess. *My Story.* Delacorte, 1980.

Bloom, Claire. *Limelight and After: The Education of an Actress.* Harper & Row,1982.

Brooks, Polly Schoyer. *Queen Eleanor: Independent Spirit of the Medieval World.* Lippincott, 1983.

Bugliosi, Vincent and Curt Gentry. *Helter Skelter. The True Story of the Manson Murders.* W. W. Norton, 1974.

Caesar, Sid with Bill Davidson. *Where Have I Been? An Autobiography.* Crown, 1982.

Cain, Robert. *Whole Lotta Shakin' Goin' On: Jerry Lee Lewis.* Dial, 1981.

Capote, Truman. *In Cold Blood.* Random House, 1966.

Carr, Ian. *Miles Davis.* Morrow, 1982.

Collier, James Lincoln. *Louis Armstrong: An American Genius.* Oxford University Press, 1983.

Collins, Jean. *She Was There: Stories of Pioneering Women Journalists.* Messner, 1980.

Conover, Ted. *Rolling Nowhere.* Viking, 1983.

De Veaux, Alexis. *Don't Explain: A Song for Billie Holiday.* Harper & Row, 1980.

Dunaway, David King. *How Can I Keep from Singing: Pete Seeger.* McGraw-Hill, 1981.

Faber, Doris. *Love and Rivalry.* Viking, 1983.

Felsenthal, Carol. *The Sweetheart of the Silent Majority: The Biography of Phyllis Schlafly.* Doubleday, 1981.

Fonda, Henry with Howard Teichmann. *Fonda: My Life.* New American Library, 1981.

Fox, Ted. *Showtime at the Apollo.* Holt, Rinehart and Winston, 1983.

Furlong, Monica. *Merton: A Biography.* Harper & Row, 1980.

Gielgud, John with John Miller and John Powell. *Gielgud: An Actor and His Time.* Clarkson N. Potter, 1980.

Gornick, Vivian. *Women in Science: Portraits from a World in Transition.* Simon and Schuster, 1983.

Haskins, James. *Black Theatre in America.* Crowell, 1982.

————. *Fighting Shirley Chisholm.* Dial, 1975.

————. *I'm Gonna Make You Love Me: The Story of Diana Ross.* Dial, 1980.

————. *James Van DerZee: The Picture-Takin' Man.* Dodd, Mead, 1979.

————. *Katherine Dunham.* Coward, McCann & Geoghegan, 1982.

————. *Lena Horne.* Coward, McCann & Geoghegan, 1983.

Hendrickson, Paul. *Seminary: A Search.* Summit, 1983.

Hopkins, Jerry and Daniel Sugarman. *No One Gets Out of Here Alive.* Warner, 1980.

Howard, Margo. *Eppie: The Story of Ann Landers.* Putnam's, 1982.

Ingalls, Robert P. *Point of Order: A Profile of Senator Joe McCarthy.* Putnam's, 1981.

Keller, Evelyn Fox. *A Feeling for the Organism: The Life and Work of Barbara McClintock.* Freedman, 1983.

Kelley, Kitty. *Elizabeth Taylor: The Last Star.* Simon and Schuster, 1981.

Kelly, Amy. *Eleanor of Aquitaine and the Four Kings.* Harvard University Press, 1950.

Kingston, Maxine Hong. *China Men.* Knopf, 1980.

Klein, Joe. *Woody Guthrie, A Life.* Knopf, 1981.

Livsey, Clara. *The Manson Women: A "Family" Portrait.* Marek, 1980.

Maiorano, Robert. *Worlds Apart: The Autobiography of a Dancer from Brooklyn*. Coward, McCann & Geoghegan, 1980.

Mebane, Mary. *Mary*. Viking, 1981.

————. *Mary, Wayfarer*. Viking, 1983.

Miller, Merle. *Lyndon: An Oral Biography*. Putnam's, 1980.

————. *Plain Speaking: An Oral Biography of Harry S. Truman*. Berkley, 1974.

Morgan, Elizabeth. *The Making of a Woman Surgeon*. Putnam's, 1980.

O'Connor, Garry. *Ralph Richardson: An Actor's Life*. Atheneum, 1982.

O'Day, Anita with George Eels. *High Times, Hard Times*. Putnam's, 1981.

Olivier, Laurence. *Confessions of an Actor*. Simon and Schuster, 1982.

Pack, Robert. *Edward Bennett Williams for the Defense*. Harper & Row, 1983.

Pearl, Minnie with Joan Dew. *Minnie Pearl: An Autobiography*. Simon and Schuster, 1981.

Peavy, Linda and Ursula Smith. *Women Who Changed Things*. Scribner's, 1983.

Percival, John. *Nureyev: Aspects of a Dancer*. Putnam's, 1975.

Reeves, Thomas C. *The Life and Times of Joseph McCarthy: A Biography*. Stein and Day, 1982.

Savitch, Jessica. *Anchorwoman*. Putnam's, 1982.

Selden, Bernice. *The Mill Girls*. Atheneum, 1983.

Strasberg, Susan. *Bittersweet*. Putnam's, 1980.

Stratton, Joanna L. *Pioneer Women: Voices from the Kansas Frontier*. Simon and Schuster, 1981.

Wilkins, Roy with Tom Mathews. *Standing Fast: The Autobiography of Roy Wilkins*, Viking, 1982.

Wong, Mary Gillian. *Nun: A Memoir*. Harcourt Brace Jovanovich, 1983.

Woodruff, Judy and Kathy Maxa. *This Is Judy Woodruff at the White House*. Addison-Wesley, 1982.

Quiet Heroes

Abbey, Edward. *The Brave Cowboy*. Dodd, Mead, 1956.

————. *Fire on the Mountain*. Dial, 1962.

Berry, Wendell. *The Memory of Old Jack*. Harcourt Brace Jovanovich, 1973.

Childress, Alice. *A Hero Ain't Nothin' But a Sandwich*. Coward, McCann & Geoghegan, 1973.

————. *Rainbow Jordan*. Coward, McCann & Geoghegan, 1981.

Fox, Paula. *The Slave Dancer*. Bradbury, 1973.

Gaines, Ernest J. *The Autobiography of Miss Jane Pittman*. Dial, 1971.

Godden, Rumer. *In This House of Brede*. Random House,1969.

Haley, Alex. *Roots*. Doubleday, 1976.

Hamilton, Virginia. *Zeely*. Macmillan, 1967.

Hope, Christopher. *A Separate Development*, Scribner's, 1981.

Jenkins, Peter. *A Walk Across America*. Morrow, 1979.

————. *The Walk West: A Walk Across America 2*. Morrow, 1981.

Least Heat Moon, William. *Blue Highways: A Journey into America*. Little, Brown, 1982.

Malamud, Bernard. *The Assistant*. Farrar, Straus & Cudahy, 1957.

McGinnis, Joe. *Heroes*. Viking, 1976.

Miller, Arthur. *The Crucible*. Viking, 1954.

Peck, Robert Newton. *A Day No Pigs Would Die*. Knopf, 1973.

Sillitoe, Alan. *The Loneliness of the Long-Distance Runner*. Knopf, 1959.

Swarthout, Glendon. *Bless the Beasts and Children*. Doubleday, 1970.

————. *The Shootist*. Doubleday, 1975.

Taylor, Mildred. *Let the Circle Be Unbroken*. Dial, 1981.

————. *Roll of Thunder, Hear My Cry*. Dial, 1976.

Terkel, Studs. *American Dreams: Lost and Found*. Pantheon, 1980.

Yglesias, Rafael. *The Game Player*. Doubleday, 1978.

Heroes in Sports

Abdul-Jabbar, Kareem and Peter Knobler. *Giant Steps*. Bantam, 1983.

Acton, Jay. *The Unforgettables*. Crowell, 1973.

Angell, Roger. *Five Seasons: A Baseball Companion*. Simon and Schuster, 1977.

————. *Late Innings*. Simon and Schuster, 1982.

————. *The Summer Game*. Viking, 1972.

Blessing, Richard. *A Passing Season*. Little, Brown, 1982.

Boswell, Thomas. *How Life Imitates the World Series*. Doubleday, 1982.

Bouton, Jim. *Ball Four: My Life and Hard Times Throwing the Knuckleball in the Big Leagues*. World, 1970.

Bradley, Bill. *Life on the Run*. Quadrangle, 1976.

Brancato, Robin F. *Winning*. Knopf, 1977.

Buchanan, William J. *A Shining Season*. Coward, McCann & Geoghegan, 1978.

Coover, Robert. *The Universal Baseball Association, Inc., J. Henry Waugh, Prop.* Random House, 1968.

Crutcher, Chris. *Running Loose*. Greenwillow, 1983.

Davis, Terry. *Vision Quest*. Viking, 1979.

Dygard, Thomas J. *Outside Shooter*. Morrow, 1979.

————. *Quarterback Walk-On*. Morrow, 1982.

————. *Rebound Caper*. Morrow, 1983.

————. *Soccer Duel*. Morrow, 1981.

————. *Winning Kicker*. Morrow, 1978.

Fixx, James F. *The Complete Book of Running*. Random House, 1977.

————. *Jim Fixx's Second Book of Running*. Random House, 1980.

French, Michael. *The Throwing Season*. Delacorte, 1980.

Gent, Peter. *The Franchise*. Villard, 1983.

Goldstein, Alan. *A Fistful of Sugar: The Sugar Ray Leonard Story*. Coward, McCann & Geoghegan, 1981.

Guy, David. *Football Dreams*. Seaview, 1980.

Hardy, Tom. *Unsportsmanlike Conduct*. Dodd, Mead, 1983.

Harris, Mark. *Bang the Drum Slowly*. Knopf, 1956.

Haskins, James. *Sugar Ray Leonard*. Lothrop, Lee & Shepard, 1982.

Johnson, Earvin (Magic) and Richard Levin. *Magic*. Viking, 1983.

Knudson, R. R. *Rinehart Lifting*. Farrar, Straus & Giroux, 1980.

————. *Zanballer*. Delacorte, 1972.

————. *Zanbanger*. Harper & Row, 1977.

————. *Zanboomer*. Harper & Row, 1978.

————. *Zan Hagen's Marathon*. Farrar, Straus & Giroux, 1984.

Kram, Mark. *Miles to Go*. Morrow, 1982.

Lehrman, Robert. *Juggling*. Harper & Row, 1982.

Levin, Jenifer. *Water Dancer*. Poseidon, 1982.

Lieberman, Nancy. *Basketball My Way*. Scribner's, 1982.

Lipsyte, Robert. *Free to Be Muhammed Ali*. Harper & Row, 1979.

Louis, Joe with Edna and Art Rust. *Joe Louis: My Life*. Harcourt Brace Jovanovich, 1978.

Malamud, Bernard. *The Natural*. Harcourt Brace Jovanovich, 1952.

McKay, Robert. *The Girl Who Wanted to Run the Boston Marathon*. Elsevier/Nelson, 1980.

————. *The Running Back*. Harcourt Brace Jovanovich, 1979.

Meredith, Don. *Home Movies*. Avon, 1982.

Miller, Jason. *That Championship Season*. Atheneum, 1972.

Pele and Robert L. Fish. *My Life and the Beautiful Game*. Doubleday, 1977.

Quigley, Martin. *The Original Colored House of David*. Houghton Mifflin, 1981.

Ralbovsky, Martin. *Destiny's Darlings: A World Championship Little League Team Twenty Years Later*. Hawthorn, 1974.

Salassi, Otto R. *On the Ropes*. Greenwillow, 1981.

Shapiro, Jim. *On the Road—The Marathon: The Joys and Techniques of Marathon Running*. Crown, 1978.

Smith, David and Franklin Russell. *Healing Journey: The Odyssey of an Uncommon Athlete*. Sierra Club, 1983.

Smith, Red. *To Absent Friends from Red Smith*. Atheneum, 1982.

Strasser, Todd. *Friends Till the End*. Delacorte, 1981.

Stretton, Barbara. *You Never Lose*. Knopf, 1982.

Terry, Douglas. *The Last Texas Hero*. Doubleday, 1982.

Warren, Patricia Nell. *The Front Runner*. Morrow, 1974.

Wells, Rosemary. *When No One Was Looking*. Dial, 1981.

Heroes in Death

Agee, James. *A Death in the Family*. McDowell, Obolensky, 1957.

Alsop, Stewart. *Stay of Execution*. Lippincott, 1973.

Arrick, Fran. *Tunnel Vision*. Bradbury, 1980.

Bach, Alice. *Mollie Make-Believe*. Harper & Row, 1974.

Beckman, Gunnel. *Admission to the Feast*. Holt, Rinehart and Winston, 1972.

Blinn, William, *Brian's Song*. Bantam, 1972.

Buchanan, William. *A Shining Season*. Coward, McCann & Geoghegan, 1978.

Clark, Brian. *Whose Life Is It Anyway?* Dodd, Mead, 1979. First televised on Granada (British) television on March 12, 1972. First staged in London, March 6, 1978. First staged in New York, April 17, 1979.

Craven, Margaret. *I Heard the Owl Call My Name*. Doubleday, 1973.

Deford, Frank. *Alex, The Life of a Child*. Viking, 1983.

Donovan, John. *Wild in the World*. Harper & Row, 1971.

Enright, D. J., ed. *The Oxford Book of Death*. Oxford University Press, 1983.

Farley, Carol. *The Garden Is Doing Fine*. Atheneum, 1975.

Gardam, Jane. *The Summer After the Funeral*. Macmillan, 1973.

Giovacchini, Peter. *The Urge to Die: Why Young People Commit Suicide*. Macmillan, 1981.

Girion, Barbara. *A Tangle of Roots*. Scribner's, 1979.

Guest, Judith. *Ordinary People*. Viking, 1976.

Gunther, John. *Death Be Not Proud*. Random House, 1953.

Harris, Mark. *Bang the Drum Slowly*. Knopf, 1956.

Housman, A. E. *The Shropshire Lad*. London: K. Paul, Trench, Trübner, 1896.

Hughes, Monica. *Hunter in the Dark*. Atheneum, 1983.

Hunter, Mollie. *A Sound of Chariots*. Harper & Row, 1972.

———. *Hold On to Love*. Harper & Row, 1984.

Ipswitch, Elaine. *Scott Was Here*. Delacorte, 1979.

Johnson, A. E. *A Blues I Can Whistle*. Four Winds, 1969.

Jury, Mark and Dan Jury. *Gramp*. Grossman, 1976.

Klagsbrun, Francine. *Too Young to Die: Youth and Suicide*. Houghton Mifflin, 1976.

Krementz, Jill. *How It Feels When a Parent Dies*. Knopf, 1981.

Kübler-Ross, Elisabeth. *Coping with Death and Dying*. Macmillan, 1981.

———. *Death: The Final Stage of Growth*. Prentice-Hall, 1975.

———. *On Death and Dying*. Macmillan, 1969.

———. *Questions and Answers on Death and Dying*. Macmillan, 1974.

L'Engle, Madeleine. *A Ring of Endless Light*. Farrar, Straus & Giroux, 1980.

Lifton, Robert Jay. *The Broken Connection*. Simon and Schuster, 1979.

Lowry, Lois. *A Summer to Die*. Houghton Mifflin, 1977.

Lund, Doris. *Eric*. Lippincott, 1974.

Mack, John E. and Holly Hickler. *Vivienne: The Life and Suicide of an Adolescent Girl*. Little, Brown, 1981.

Matson, Katinka. *Short Lives: Portraits in Creativity and Self-Destruction*. Morrow, 1980.

Mazer, Norma Fox. *A Figure of Speech*. Delacorte, 1973.

McGrail, Joie Harrison. *Fighting Back: One Woman's Struggle Against Cancer*. Harper & Row, 1978.

Merryman, Richard. *Hope: A Loss Survived*. Little, Brown, 1978.

Morris, Jeannie. *Brian Piccolo: A Short Season*. Rand McNally, 1972.

Norman, Marsha. *'night, Mother*. Hill and Wang, 1983.

Oneal, Zibby. *A Formal Feeling*. Viking, 1982.

Paterson, Katherine. *Bridge to Terabithia*. Crowell, 1977.

Peck, Richard. *Close Enough to Touch*. Delacorte, 1981.

Plath, Sylvia. *The Bell Jar*. Harper & Row, 1971.

———. *The Collected Poems*. Harper & Row, 1981.

———. *The Journals of Sylvia Plath*. Dial, 1982.

Rinaldi, Ann. *Term Paper*. Walker, 1980.

Rosenblatt, Roger. *Children of War*. Anchor Press/Doubleday, 1983.

Ryan, Cornelius and Kathryn Morgan Ryan. *A Private Battle*. Simon and Schuster, 1979.

Sayers, Gale. *I Am Third*. Viking, 1970.

Weingarten, Violet. *Intimations of Mortality*. Knopf, 1978.

Wersba, Barbara. *Run Softly, Go Fast*. Atheneum, 1970.

Zorza, Victor and Rosemary Zorza. *A Way to Die*. Seabury, 1980.

Heroes in War

Anderson, Jack and Bill Pronzini. *The Cambodia File*. Doubleday, 1981.

Arnothy, Christine. *I Am Fifteen—And I Don't Want to Die*. E. P. Dutton, 1956.

Baer, Frank. *Max's Gang*. Little, Brown, 1983.

Baker, Mark. *Nam: The Vietnam War in the Words of the Men and Women Who Fought There*. Morrow, 1981.

Bawden, Nina. *Carrie's War*. Lippincott, 1973.

Benchley, Nathaniel. *A Necessary End*. Harper & Row, 1976.

Brittain, Vera. *Chronicle of Youth: The War Diary 1913–1917*. Morrow, 1982.

———. *Testament of Youth*. London: Victor Gollancz, 1933.

Brook-Shepherd, Gordon. *November 1918*. Little, Brown, 1982.

Brown, Harry. *A Walk in the Sun*. Knopf, 1944.

Bryan, C. D. B. *Friendly Fire*. Putnam's, 1976.

Dank, Milton. *The Dangerous Game*. Lippincott, 1977.

———. *Game's End*. Lippincott, 1979.

Davis, Daniel S. *Behind Barbed Wire: The Imprisonment of Japanese Americans During World War II*. E. P. Dutton, 1982.

Del Vecchio, John M. *The 13th Valley*. Bantam, 1982.

Denton, Kit. *The Breaker*. St. Martin's, 1973.

Downs, Frederick. *Aftermath: A Soldier's Return from Vietnam, 1968*. Norton, 1984.

Esper, George and the Associated Press. *The Eyewitness History of the Vietnam War, 1961–1975*. Villard Books, 1983.

Fast, Howard. *April Morning*. Crown, 1961.

FitzGerald, Frances. *Fire in the Lake: The Vietnamese and Americans in Vietnam*. Vintage, 1973.

Forman, James. *Ceremony of Innocence*. Hawthorn, 1970.

———. *The Cow Neck Rebels*. Farrar, Straus & Giroux, 1969.

———. *A Fine, Soft Day*. Farrar, Straus & Giroux, 1978.

———. *Horses of Anger*. Farrar, Straus & Giroux, 1967.

———. *My Enemy, My Brother*. Hawthorn, 1969.

———. *Ring the Judas Bell*. Farrar, Straus & Giroux, 1965.

———. *The Shield of Achilles*. Farrar, Straus & Giroux, 1966.

———. *The Skies of Crete*. Farrar, Straus & Giroux, 1963.

———. *That Mad Game: War and the Chances for Peace*. Scribner's, 1980.

Glasser, Ronald J. *365 Days*. Braziller, 1971.

Goldman, Peter and Tony Fuller. *Charlie Company: What Vietnam Did to Us*. Morrow, 1983.

Groom, Winston and Duncan Spencer. *Conversations with the Enemy: The Story of PFC Robert Garwood*. Putnam's, 1983.

Hanser, Richard. *A Noble Treason: The Revolt of the Munich Students Against Hitler*. Putnam's, 1979.

Hemingway, Ernest. *A Farewell to Arms*. Scribner's, 1929.

Houston, Jeanne Wakatsuki and James D. Houston. *Farewell to Manzanar*. Houghton Mifflin, 1973.

Jones, James. *The Pistol*. Scribner's, 1959.

———. *The Thin Red Line*. Scribner's, 1962.

Karnow, Stanley. *Vietnam: A History*. Viking, 1983.

Keegan, John. *Six Armies in Normandy: From D-Day to the Liberation of Paris. June 6th–August 25th, 1944*. Viking, 1982.

Koehn, Ilse. *Tilla*. Greenwillow, 1981.

Lord, Walter. *Day of Infamy*. Holt, Rinehart and Winston, 1957.

———. *The Miracle of Dunkirk*. Viking, 1983.

Magorian, Michelle. *Good Night, Mr. Tom*. Harper & Row, 1982.

Mailer, Norman. *The Naked and the Dead*. Holt, Rinehart and Winston, 1948.

March, William. *Company K*. H. Smith and R. Haas, 1933.

Mason, Robert. *Chickenhawk*. Viking, 1983.

Mauldin, Bill. *Up Front*. Holt, 1944.

Mazer, Harry. *The Last Mission*. Delacorte, 1979.

Moore, John Hammond. *The Faustball Tunnel*. Random House, 1978.

O'Brien, Tim. *Going After Cacciato*. Delacorte, 1978.

Page, Tim. *Tim Page's Nam*. Knopf, 1983.

Panger, Daniel. *Search in Gomorrah*. Dembner, 1982.

Pelgrom, Els. *The Winter When Time Was Frozen*. Morrow, 1980.

Prange, Gordon W. *At Dawn We Slept: The Untold Story of Pearl Harbor*. McGraw-Hill, 1981.

Rees, David. *The Exeter Blitz.* Elsevier, 1980.

Remarque, Erich Marie. *All Quiet on the Western Front.* Little, Brown, 1929.

Rosenblatt, Roger. *Children of War.* Doubleday, 1983.

Santoli, Al, ed. *Everything We Had; An Oral History of the Vietnamese War by Thirty-Three American Soldiers Who Fought It.* Random House, 1981.

Schoenbrun, David. *Soldiers of the Night: The Story of the French Resistance.* E. P. Dutton, 1980.

Terlouw, Jan. *Winter in Wartime.* McGraw-Hill, 1976.

Tregaskis, Richard. *Guadalcanal Diary.* Random House, 1943.

Trumbo, Dalton. *Johnny Got His Gun.* Lippincott, 1939.

Tunis, John A. *His Enemy, His Friend.* Morrow, 1967.

Uchida, Yoshiko. *Journey Home.* Atheneum, 1978.

Van Devanter, Lynda. *Home Before Morning.* Beaufort, 1983.

Vinke, Herman. *The Short Life of Sophie Scholl* (Trans. Hedwig Pachter). Harper & Row, 1984.

Westall, Robert. *Fathom Five.* Greenwillow, 1980.

————. *The Machine Gunners.* Greenwillow, 1976.

Wharton, William. *A Midnight Clear.* Knopf, 1982.

Wright, Stephen. *Meditations in Green.* Scribner's, 1983.

Zei, Alki. *Petros' War.* E. P. Dutton, 1972.

————. *Wildcat Under Glass.* Holt, Rinehart and Winston, 1968.

Heroes of the Holocaust

Altschuler, David A. *Hitler's War Against the Jews.* Behrman, 1978.

Appelfeld, Aharon. *Badenheim, 1939.* Godine, 1980.

Arrick, Fran. *Chernowitz.* Bradbury, 1981.

Baer, Edith. *A Frost in the Night.* Pantheon, 1980.

Bauer, Yehuda. *A History of the Holocaust.* Watts, 1982.

Bergmann, Martin S. and Milton E. Jucovy, eds. *Generations of the Holocaust.* Basic Books, 1982.

Blatter, Janet and Sybil Milton. *Art of the Holocaust.* Rutledge, 1982.

Bor, Josef. *The Terezin Requiem.* Knopf, 1963.

Borowski, Tadeusz. *This Way to the Gas, Ladies and Gentlemen; and Other Stories.* Viking, 1967.

Butterworth, Emma Macalik. *As the Waltz Was Ending.* Four Winds, 1983.

Clare, George. *Last Waltz in Vienna: The Destruction of a Family, 1842–1942.* Holt, Rinehart and Winston, 1982.

Dawidowicz, Lucy S. *The Holocaust and the Historians.* Harvard University Press, 1981.

Day, Ingeborg. *Ghost Waltz: A Memoir.* Viking, 1980.

Degens, T. *The Visit.* Viking, 1982.

Demetz, Hana. *The House on Prague Street.* St. Martin's, 1980.

Eisenberg, Azriel, ed. *Witness to the Holocaust.* Pilgrim Press, 1981.

Eisner, Jack. *The Survivor.* Morrow, 1980.

Epstein, Helen. *Children of the Holocaust: Conversations with Sons and Daughters of Survivors.* Putnam's, 1979.

Ezrahi, Sidra DeKoven. *By Words Alone: The Holocaust in Literature.* University of Chicago Press, 1980.

Fenelon, Fania. *Playing for Time.* Atheneum, 1977.

Forman, James. *My Enemy, My Brother.* Hawthorn, 1969.

————. *The Survivor.* Farrar, Straus & Giroux, 1976.

Frank, Anne. *Anne Frank's Tales from the Secret Annex.* Doubleday, 1984.

————. *The Diary of a Young Girl.* Norton, 1957.

Gross, Leonard. *The Last Jews in Berlin.* Simon and Schuster, 1982.

Hart, Kitty. *Return to Auschwitz.* Atheneum, 1982.

Hellman, Peter. *Avenue of the Righteous.* Atheneum, 1981.

Hillesum, Etty. *An Interrupted Life: The Diaries of Etty Hillesum, 1941–1943.* Pantheon, 1984.

Hochhuth, Rolf. *The Deputy.* Grove, 1963.

Insdorf, Annette. *Indelible Shadows: Film and the Holocaust.* Random House, 1983.

Joffo, Joseph. *A Bag of Marbles*. Houghton Mifflin, 1974.

Kay, Mara. *In Face of Danger*. Crown, 1977.

Keneally, Thomas. *Schindler's List*. Simon and Schuster, 1982.

Kerr, Judith. *The Other Way Round*. Coward, McCann & Geoghegan, 1975.

———. *A Small Person Far Away*. Coward, McCann & Geoghegan, 1979.

———. *When Hitler Stole Pink Rabbit*. Coward, McCann & Geoghegan, 1972.

Kerr, M. E. *Gentlehands*. Harper & Row, 1978.

Koehn, Ilse. *Mischling, Second Degree: My Childhood in Nazi Germany*. Greenwillow, 1977.

Langer, Lawrence. *Versions of Survival: The Holocaust and the Human Spirit*. State University of New York Press, 1982.

Leitner, Isabella. *Fragments of Isabella—A Memoir of Auschwitz*. Crowell, 1978.

Levoy, Myron. *Alan and Naomi*. Harper & Row, 1977.

Meier, Lili and Peter Hellman. *The Auschwitz Album*. Random House, 1982.

Meltzer, Milton. *Never to Forget: The Jews of the Holocaust*. Harper & Row, 1976.

Moskin, Marietta. *I Am Rosemarie*. John Day, 1972.

Nowak, Jan. *Courier from Warsaw*. Wayne State University Press, 1982.

Orgel, Doris. *The Devil in Vienna*. Dial, 1978.

Patterson, Charles. *Anti-Semitism: The Road to the Holocaust and Beyond*. Walker, 1982.

Reiss, Johanna. *The Journey Back*. Crowell, 1976.

———. *The Upstairs Room*. Crowell, 1972.

Richter, Hans Peter. *Friedrich*. Holt, Rinehart and Winston, 1970.

Rosenfeld, Alvin H. *A Double Dying: Reflections on Holocaust Literature*. Indiana University Press, 1980.

Rothchild, Sylvia, ed. *Voices from the Holocaust*. New American Library, 1981.

Sachs, Marilyn. *A Pocket Full of Seeds*. Doubleday, 1973.

Senesh, Hannah. *Hannah Senesh: Her Life and Diary*. Schocken, 1972.

Uhlman, Fred. *Reunion*. Farrar, Straus & Giroux, 1977.

Van Stockum, Hilda. *The Borrowed House*. Farrar, Straus & Giroux, 1975.

Volavkova, Hana, ed. *I Never Saw Another Butterfly: Children's Drawings and Poems from Terezin Concentration Camp, 1942–1944*. Schocken, 1978.

Von Staden, Wendlegard. *Darkness over the Valley*. Ticknor and Fields, 1981.

Weiss, Peter. *The Investigation*. Atheneum, 1966.

Werbell, Frederick E. and Thurston Clarke. *Lost Hero: The Mystery of Raoul Wallenberg*. McGraw-Hill, 1982.

Wiesel, Elie. *Dawn*. Hill and Wang, 1961.

———. *Night*. Farrar, Straus & Giroux, 1960.

Wolf, Christa. *A Model Childhood*. Farrar, Straus & Giroux, 1980.

Ziemian, Joseph. *The Cigarette Sellers of Three Crosses Square*. Lerner, 1975.

INFORMATIONAL
BOOKS

OF TANTALIZING TOPICS

When E. L. Doctorow, the author of *Ragtime*, made his acceptance speech for the best novel of 1975 before the National Book Critics Circle, he said, "There is no more fiction or nonfiction—only narrative." Some critics think that this blending of fiction and nonfiction which Doctorow alluded to may be the most significant literary development of the century. Certainly today it is harder than it was seventy-five or a hundred years ago to make a clear-cut distinction between novels and informational books that are based on real events. How closely fiction and nonfiction have blended together in the minds of teachers was shown by a survey in which 300 English teachers responded to a request to list ten adolescent novels and ten adult novels as worthy of recommending to teenagers for reading. The following nonfiction titles were recommended as novels by one or more teachers: Piers Paul Read's *Alive*, James Herriot's *All Creatures Great and Small*, Robin Graham's *Dove*, Peter Maas' *Serpico*, Doris Lund's *Eric*, Alvin Toffler's *Future Shock*, Maya Angelou's *I Know Why the Caged Bird Sings*, Dee Brown's *Bury My Heart At Wounded Knee*, Claude Brown's *Manchild in the Promised Land*, Eldridge Cleaver's *Soul on Ice*, John H. Griffin's *Black Like Me*, Carlos Castaneda's *Journey to Ixtlan*, Vincent Bugliosi and Curt Gentry's *Helter Skelter*, Studs Terkel's *Working*, Pat Conroy's *The Water Is Wide*, Henry David Thoreau's *Walden*, Eliot Wigginton's *Foxfire* books, N. Scott Momaday's *The Way to Rainy Mountain*, Lorraine Hansberry's *A Raisin in the Sun*, and Annie Dillard's *Pilgrim at Tinker Creek*.

◈ BLENDING FICTION AND NONFICTION

The blending has occurred from both directions. On one side are all the nonfiction writers who use the techniques of fiction including suspense, careful development of plot and characterization, and literary devices such as symbolism and metaphor. On the other side are the novelists who collect data as an investigative reporter would. For example, when Richard Peck wrote *Are You in the House Alone?* he gathered current statistics on rape and then fashioned his story around the most typical case, that is, a young girl in a familiar setting being raped by someone she knows who is not prosecuted for the crime. When Robin Brancato wrote *Winning*, she did a similar kind of investigation. She visited hospitals and rehabilitation centers and interviewed patients and their families and friends. And when she wrote *Blinded by the Light*, she not only gathered statistics and interviewed people whose lives had been affected by a religious cult, she temporarily joined a group in one of its weekend retreats. The books that resulted from these investigations are fiction in the sense that fictional names are used and also that they combine bits and pieces of many individual stories. Nevertheless, in another sense, these stories are more real and actually present a more honest portrayal than some pieces labeled nonfiction that are true accounts of bizarre or strange happenings.

In relation to these changing styles of writing, it is interesting to ponder just what we mean by "real." What is true (nonfiction) and what is untrue (fiction)? The question in this context might be compared to the one Margery Williams asked in her children's classic *The Velveteen Rabbit*. The answer in her book was that when something had lived a long time and was well loved and well worn through use, then it became real. According to this definition, Louisa May Alcott's *Little Women* is real. A mental image of the warm supportive family portrayed in the book is a real part of the psyches of literally millions of readers around the world who believe that the book is a true presentation of the Alcott family. Actually, the genteel poverty that Alcott wrote about is a far cry from the facts. It was not so much a question of the girls' not having matching gloves on their hands as it was a question of their not having food on the table. We can say, then, that the "reality" of *Little Women* exists quite apart from verifiable facts.

Literature—fiction and nonfiction—is more than a simple recounting or replaying of the life that surrounds the writer. It is a distillation and a crystallization. Only when an author skillfully chooses descriptive details and develops believable dialogue does an account of an actual event become "real" to the reader. Certainly Alex Haley's *Roots* became real to millions of television viewers as well as to millions of readers, yet the book contains many fictional elements in both subject matter and presentation. It is these elements that make the book stand out as "literature," whereas the histories of other families are nothing more than dreary records read on special occasions by dutiful family members. Although dozens of reasons could be given for the success of Haley's book, many of them would probably relate to the matter of choice. Alex Haley was a master at selecting the incidents and the details he wanted to include. Good writers of nonfiction do not simply record everything they know or can uncover. For example, with Haley's book, people's imaginations were captured by the fact that on September 29, 1967, he "stood on the dock in Annapolis where his great-great-great-great-great grandfather was taken ashore on September 29, 1767," and sold as a slave to a Virginia plantation owner. From this point, Haley set out to trace backwards the six generations that connected him to a sixteen-year-old "prince" newly arrived from Africa.

What the public might not stop to consider as they read about this dramatic incident is that it is setting the stage for only a small portion of Haley's "roots." In 1767 there were people living all around the world in all kinds of situations whose bloodlines are related to Haley's. It would almost be an impossible task of research to connect all of them. In the generation in which Haley started his story with the young couple Omoro and Binta Kinte and the birth of their first son, Kunta, there were 256 parents giving birth to 128 children, each one of whom is also a great-great-great-great-great grand-father or grandmother to Alex Haley.

The point is that even though Haley was writing nonfiction he had an almost unlimited range of possibilities from which to choose. With the instincts of a good storyteller he chose to trace the family line that could be presented in the most dramatic fashion. At each stage of the writing, he made similar choices. Part of the reason that his book is literature, rather than only a family record, is that he made the choices as a storyteller instead of as a clerk.

Because of the mass media, today's readers are so accustomed to strange facts and hard-to-believe stories that they have begun consistently to ask such questions as "Is it true?" "Is that for real?" and "Honestly?" This emphasis on "truth" has put some writers of fiction in a peculiar situation. One of the most striking examples is the case of Clifford Irving, a successful novelist who early in the 1970s wrote a perfectly good piece of fiction about an eccentric billionaire. The book would have probably reached a modicum of success and then slipped unobtrusively into oblivion except that Irving said the story was true. He claimed that it was a biography of Howard Hughes and ended up serving a jail term for fraud.

A much less dramatic case was reported to the fourth annual conference of the Children's Literature Association. Alfred Slote, who writes sports stories, told how his publishers, in an attempt to make his fiction look more like true stories, which sell better, have begun to use photographs rather than drawings for illustrations. Slote is a photographer as well as a writer, so he offered to take the pictures. It was an interesting experience for him to discover that photographs are considered more "real" or persuasive than his own storytelling and that his writing was being influenced by whether or not he would be able to get an actual photograph. He wasn't sure that he liked what was happening, and he concluded his speech by questioning whether or not he could build castles in the sky if he had to produce a photograph of each one.

Several authors are probably asking themselves similar questions. The public wants "true" stories, yet expects them to be as well crafted and as exciting as the best of fiction. Beatrice Sparks, who seven years after the publication of the "anonymous" *Go Ask Alice*, came forward and announced herself on the covers of two other books (*Voices* and *Jay's Journal*) as "the author who brought you *Go Ask Alice*," said that the reason she published the story, which was "based on" a girl's actual diary, anonymously, was to make it seem more authentic. She thought that having the story appear to come directly from a young girl who died of an overdose would make its anti-drug message more acceptable to the target audience.[1]

When the book *Go Ask Alice* came out in the early 1970s and climbed teenage popularity lists, a few adult readers muttered doubts about its authenticity. They pointed out that the book was more like a collage of practically every possible drug-related incident and they questioned the likelihood of all these things happening to the same girl in such a short period of time. If the book were fiction, critics could have accused the author of crowding too much into a single story, but the fact that it was considered to be the diary of a deceased girl made book reviewers hesitant to criticize.

◇ THE NEW JOURNALISM

Several factors have contributed to the development of what Truman Capote called, "the most avant-garde form of writing existent today." He was the one who coined the term "nonfiction novel" in reference to *In Cold Blood*, an account of an especially brutal murder and the subsequent trial. Tom Wolfe prefers the term "new journalism" and wrote a book by that name in which he proposes that it is the dominant form of writing in contemporary America. Other terms that are used include "creative nonfiction," "literary journalism," "journalistic fiction," and "advocacy journalism." Although its roots were growing right along with journalism in general, it did not really begin to flower until the 1950s and 1960s. Part of the reason for its development is the increased educational level of the American public. Newspaper readers, including young adults, are no longer satisfied with simplistic explanations in which people and issues are either all good or all bad. Readers recognize not just black and white but many shades of gray, which they are curious to read about.

Our affluence, combined with modern technology, helps make the new journalism possible. Compare similar incidents that happened 126 years apart. In 1846 a group of travelers who came to be known as the Donner party were trapped in the high Sierras by an early snow. They had to stay there all winter without food except for the flesh of their dead companions. After they were rescued, word of their ordeal gradually trickled back East so that for years afterward sensationalized accounts were being made up by newspaper reporters who had no chance to actually come to the scene or interview the survivors.

Contrast that with what happened in 1972 when a planeload of Uruguayan travelers crashed in the Andes mountains. Just as in the Donner

◆ **TABLE 8.1   Suggestions for Evaluating Journalistic Fiction**

A good piece of journalistic fiction usually has:	A poor piece of journalistic fiction may have:
An authentic story that is individual and unique but also representative of human experience as a whole.	A stacking of the evidence to prove a sensational idea. The author set out not to find the truth but to collect evidence on only one side of an issue.
Information that is accurate and carefully researched. This is extremely important because, with most of these stories, readers will have heard news accounts and will lose faith in the story if there are inconsistencies.	A trite or worn subject that is not worthy of book-length attention from either writer or reader.
A central thesis that has grown out of the author's research.	Evidence of sloppy research and little or no documentation of sources.
Enough development to show the relationship between the characters' actions and what happens. People's motives are explored, and cause and effect are tied together.	Conversations and other accessory literary devices that contradict straight news accounts.
An author with all the writing skills of a good novelist so that, for example, the characters reveal themselves through their speech and actions, rather than through the author's descriptions.	Inclusion of extraneous information that does not help the story build toward a central idea or thesis.
A dramatic style of writing that draws readers into the story.	A pedestrian style of writing that lacks drama.

party, some of the people knew each other before the trip but others were strangers. During the terrible weeks of waiting they all got to know each other and to develop intense relationships revolving around leadership roles and roles of rebellion and/or giving up. They endured unspeakable hardships. Many died; those who lived did so because they ate the flesh of those who died. But in this situation, the people were rescued by helicopters after two of the men made their way out of the mountains. Word of their two-and-a-half month ordeal was flashed around the world and by the time the sixteen men, mostly members of a rugby team, had been flown back to Uruguay, reporters from many nations were there. A press conference was held, and the journalists were all told about the cannibalism at the same time.

This was the second big surprise in the story. The first had been their survival. The drama of the situation naturally fired imaginations all around the world. Lippincott suggested to writer Piers Paul Read that this was the kind of story that would make a good book. He went to Uruguay where he stayed for several months interviewing survivors, rescuers, family, and friends of both the deceased and the survivors, and government officials who had been in charge of the search. More than a year later he came out with *Alive: The Story of the Andes Survivors*, which was on the *New York*

Times best seller list for seven months, and which will probably continue to be read by young adults for the next several years both in their English classes and in their free time.

The fact that the survivors were barely older than most young adult readers undoubtedly helps teenagers to identify with the story, but so do the literary techniques that Read used. He focused on certain individuals, presenting miniature character sketches of some and fully developed portraits of others. The setting was crucial to the story and he described it vividly. He was also careful to write in such a way that the natural suspense of the situation came through. His tone was consistent throughout the book. He respected and admired the survivors but he did not shy away from showing the negative aspects of human nature when it is sorely tried. In a foreword he says that the only liberty he allowed himself was the creation of dialogue between the characters, although, whenever possible, he relied on diaries and on remembered comments and quarrels as well as on his acquaintance with the speaking styles of the survivors.

The influence of the new journalism is seen in many aspects of books promoted for young readers. Theodore Taylor's *Battle in the Arctic Seas*, for example, is described as a "re-creation . . . drawn from naval records and a personal diary" and Colin Stuart's *Shoot an Arrow to Stop the Wind* is described as an "autobiographical novel." M. E. Kerr's *Me, Me, Me, Me, Me, Not a Novel* has too much truth in it to be a novel, but it also has too much creative exaggeration in it to be accurately classed as an autobiography. Likewise Jean Fritz hesitated to claim that *Homesick: My Own Story* was an autobiography. In the foreword she explained:

> ◇ When I started to write about my childhood in China, I found that my memory came out in lumps. Although I could for the most part arrange them in the proper sequence, I discovered that my preoccupation with time and literal accuracy was squeezing the life out of what I had to say. So I decided to forget about sequence and just get on with it.
>
> Since my childhood feels like a story, I decided to tell it that way, letting the events fall as they would into the shape of a story, lacing them together with fictional bits, adding a piece here and there when memory didn't give me all I needed. I would use conversation freely, for I cannot think of my childhood without hearing voices. So although this book takes place within two years— from October 1925 to September 1927—the events are drawn from the entire period of my childhood, but they are all, except in minor details, basically true. The people are real people; the places are dear to me. But most important, the form I have used has given me the freedom to recreate the emotions that I remember so vividly. Strictly speaking, I have to call this book *fiction*, but it does not feel like fiction to me. It is my story, told as truly as I can tell it.[2]

Jamake Highwater used the careful research endemic to the new journalism when he wrote *The Sun, He Dies*, which is described as a "cultural autobiography" giving an American Indian's version of how the Europeans conquered the Aztecs and decimated their culture. Kim Chernin used her own experience to prepare *In My Mother's House: A Daughter's Story*, which is a history of the political turmoil in the 1950s when Chernin's mother was an active Communist.

Many books of the type treated in Chapter 7 on heroes are written by authors using the techniques of the new journalism, for example, Tom Wolfe's *The Right Stuff*, the story of the astronauts; Elaine Ipswitch's *Scott Was Here*, the story of her fifteen-year-old son's losing battle with Hodgkin's disease, and Cherry Boone O'Neill's *Starving for Attention*, the story of O'Neill's victory over anorexia nervosa. Teacher Mary McCracken wrote successfully about her experiences in working with unusual children in *City Kid*, *A Circle of Children*, and *Lovey*. Therapist Torey Hayden's *One Child* is the story of abused and abandoned six-year-old Sheila, who underneath pain and suffering is a remarkably gifted and determined little girl. His 1983 *Murphy's Boy* is the true account of a struggle between a mute teenager and therapist Murphy. In the end, they both win.

What all of these books have in common is a combination of factual information and emotional appeal. They are stories of real people with whom readers can identify. Technically they might be classified under many different genres: biography, history, drama, essay, and personal philosophy. But regardless of classification, they are among those books that are likely to serve young adults as a bridge between childhood and adult reading. They have this power because of the straightforward, noncondescending manner of writing which is a characteristic of good journalism.

Because of the popularity of nonfiction writing, "best seller" lists now come in fiction and nonfiction categories. On television, producers know they can add millions of viewers if they advertise a program as "a documentary" rather than "a drama," and even some of the most popular movies are done in "nonfiction" style, for example, *Reds*, *Ghandi*, *Silkwood*, and *The Right Stuff*.

But in young adult literature, we sometimes treat informational books as unwelcome or at least unrecognized cousins of "real" literature. Aidan Chambers has pointed out how the term *nonfiction* is "curiously negative and off-putting" and how information books get "pushed to the back" as though they are "socially inferior to the upper crust stuff we call literature." It's almost as if the same twenty-year lag that is said to exist between research findings at the university level and their being put into practice at the local school level exists between what is being published in New York and what is being promoted for young readers in local schools and libraries as well as in our professional classes.

When we took a survey of books studied in 200 adolescent literature classes, very few informational books appeared on the combined list of assigned books. And on the Honor Listing discussed in Chapter 1 there are only a half-dozen nonfiction books.

Starting in 1976, the *Boston Globe–Hornbook* Awards program added to its categories of writing and illustration a prize for excellence in nonfiction, but still most of us do not give the same respect and reverance to nonfiction that we do to fiction. Milton Meltzer has written a sterling defense of nonfiction under the title "Where Do All the Prizes Go?: The Case for Nonfiction" in which he states:

◈ THE PEOPLE BEHIND THE BOOKS

MILTON MELTZER, Author

All Times, All Peoples:
   A World History of Slavery
The Jewish Americans:
   A History in Their Own Words
Never to Forget:
   The Jews of the Holocaust
The Terrorists

I will continue to write about the struggle for freedom and justice. Our need of them never disappears; it is only the form the struggle takes that changes. But that change offers the nonfiction writer an unlimited range of opportunity—not only in subject, but in the imaginative use of mind and heart to recreate the men and women and the times and trials which measure their humanity. I think critics, librarians, and teachers are coming to realize that nonfiction for children or adolescents, when it is honest and artful, can offer the reader as much reward in pleasure and expansion of the spirit as any other form of writing.

◇ Librarians, teachers, reviewers—the three groups who usually administer the awards or serve as judges—seem confident that only fiction can be considered literature. But what is Henry David Thoreau's *Walden*? What is James Boswell's *Life of Samuel Johnson*? What is Tom Paine's *Common Sense*? Not one of them literature? All merely nonfiction?

He took to task several critics and writers about children's literature who ignored nonfiction and then argued:

◇ But I say that the best writers of nonfiction put their hearts and minds into their work. Their concern is not only with what they have to say but with how they say it. Lillian Smith, like so many others, is guilty of bearing in mind only the finest writers of fiction when she discusses children's literature and thinking only of run-of-the-mill writers when she discusses information books.[3]

The Evaluation of Nonfiction

As we prepared this chapter, Meltzer's implied question of why nonfiction is less honored than fiction kept coming back to us and giving us the feeling that if we could answer his question we would learn something important about a kind of book that is moving up in the literary hierarchy.

The first contributing factor that we uncovered is that there is less agreement about what makes a good nonfiction book. For books to be included on our Honor Sampling they had to have been recommended as a "best book" by three out of the five sources we consulted. Several nonfiction titles appeared on each of the five lists, but when the lists were combined such books as Ruth Bell's *Changing Bodies, Changing Lives* and Jill Krementz's *How It Feels When a Parent Dies* were squeezed out because they received only two votes. On many of the individual lists, numerous nonfiction titles were included, for example the 1983 "Best Books for Young Adults" list published in *School Library Journal* was more than half (11 out of 20 titles) nonfiction.

English teachers generally pay less attention to nonfiction than do reading teachers and librarians, and this was shown in the University of Iowa poll published in the *English Journal* in December of 1983 where only three out of 21 titles were nonfiction. But even this is a higher percentage than appeared on the final Honor Listing. What happens is that individuals select informational books primarily on the basis of the subject matter and since there is such incredible variety the choices may differ widely. For example, we were working in a classroom where high school students were helping us evaluate some new books. One boy was tremendously impressed with a book we had on finding foods from nature. When we asked him if he thought it should be put on our recommended list for library purchase throughout the state, he responded negatively and explained that he was a backpacker and had been looking for such a book for several years but he was quite sure that he was the only person within 100 square miles who would be interested.

A second contributing factor is that nonfiction books become dated more quickly than do fiction books. This transitory nature discourages teachers from giving them serious consideration as teaching materials.

For a variety of reasons, many of the nonfiction titles that teachers were recommending to students a decade ago are no longer being read. Advances in technology have made the 1970s books on such topics as computers and car repair obsolete. And if someone wants to prepare for taking the SAT tests or read advice on handling money, or selecting a college, or planning for a career, obviously recent information is going to be more valuable than older information. Also styles and interests change. Even crafts as time-honored as those described in Jean Young's *The Woodstock Craftsman's Manual* suffer from Americans' tendency to chase a fad into the ground and then leave it lying while we run off in pursuit of something else that has caught our collective eye. We treat social issues and questions about history in this same all-or-nothing fashion.

The lack of staying power in nonfiction books was reflected in the choice of books included on ALA's Young Adult Services "The Best of the Best Books 1970–1983" list. Out of 85 books, only 15 were nonfiction. On the yearly lists, between one-third and one-half of the titles are nonfiction. Those that made it to this cumulative list include Maya Angelou's *I Know Why the Caged Bird Sings*; Ruth Bell's *Changing Bodies, Changing Lives: A Book for Teens on Sex and Relationships*; The Boston Women's Health Book Collective's *Our Bodies, Ourselves*; Dee Brown's *Bury My Heart at Wounded Knee: An Indian History of the American West*; Lauren Elder's *And I Alone Survived*; Torey L. Hayden's *One Child*; Kathy McCoy and Charles Wibbelsman's *The Teenage Body Book*; Mary MacCracken's *A Circle of Children*; Milton Meltzer's *Never to Forget: The Jews of the Holocaust*; Muhammad Ali and Richard Durham's *The Greatest: My Own Story*; John Powers' *The Last Catholic in America*; Dougal Robertson's *Survive the*

Savage Sea; Al Santoli's *Everything We Had: An Oral History of the Vietnam War as Told by 33 American Soldiers Who Fought It*; Flip Schulke's *Martin Luther King, Jr.: A Documentary*; and Isabella Leitner's *Fragments of Isabella: A Memoir of Auschwitz*.

Notice how many of these books are accounts of personal adventures or experiences; they are not the kinds of books that instruct people on how to do something or provide back-up for school subjects such as math, science, art, music, etc. It is these latter types of books that most people think of when they hear the term nonfiction, and so the long-lasting success of biographies or other accounts of personal experiences does little to help change the image that comes to most of our minds when we hear the term *informative nonfiction*.

A third reason that nonfiction books are not given the same chance at awards is that the typical reviewer may not have the expertise to judge the accuracy of the information presented in such books as Leonard Lubin's history of costume, *The Elegant Beast*; Graham Wade's *The Shape of Music: An Introduction to Form in Classical Music*; or Patrick Moore's *The Unfolding Universe* which recounts recent discoveries in astronomy.

With children's books, the information is usually not so complex as to intimidate reviewers, but authors of informative books for teenagers probably spend at least a year—maybe a lifetime—researching their subjects and few reviewers come with an equivalent academic background. They therefore may feel hesitant about reviewing an informational book, and since there are always more books to be reviewed than space to print the reviews, many such books never get reviewed. If when reviewers are making choices, each one shows a slight preference for fiction, then the cumulative effect is that fiction will receive the lion's share of attention.

This lopsidedness is aggravated further by the fact that many reviewers, especially those working with educational journals, come from the English literature or English teacher tradition, and they naturally tend to focus their attention on books that would be used in conjunction with literature classes rather than biology, home economics, social studies, industrial arts, or business classes.

A fourth reason for problems in evaluating nonfiction is that there is no generally agreed-upon theory of criticism or criteria for judgment. With fiction, it's always possible to start with a summary and an evaluation of plot, then to go on to discuss characterization, setting, theme, point of view, style, and tone, but because there are no plots in nonfiction (if it has a plot, that means it's fiction), people don't know quite how to get a handle on informational books. But if evaluators can replace the idea of looking at plot and characterization with looking at the contents of the book (What is it about? What information does it present?), then they can go from there and use much the same criteria as they are accustomed to using in evaluating fiction.

Informative books have settings. For example they may be contemporary as is Doug McClelland's *Hollywood on Ronald Reagan: Friends and Enemies Discuss Our President, the Actor*. Or they may be historical as is

Lillian Schlissel's *Women's Diaries of the Westward Journey*. They may be restricted to local interests as is S. Allen Chambers' *Discovering Historical America: Mid-Atlantic States*. They may include information on the whole world as does Ellen Switzer's *Our Urban Planet*.

Informational books also have themes or purposes which are closely tied to the author's point of view. Authors may write in hopes of persuading someone to a particular belief as did Hope Ryden when she wrote *God's Dog* as a defense of the coyote. Or the purpose may be to inspire thoughtfulness as Michio Kaku and Jennifer Trainer tried to do in *Nuclear Power: Both Sides*. When Margaret Hyde wrote *Is the Cat Dreaming Your Dream?* her purpose was probably to stimulate interest in a subject that most teenagers are close to (their dreams) but haven't given a lot of thought to. Some authors shout out their themes so no potential reader could possibly miss the point, for example the title of Nissa Simon's *Don't Worry, You're Normal: A Teenager's Guide to Self-Health*, Arlene Kramer Richards and Irene Willis' *What to Do if You or Someone You Know Is Under 18 and Pregnant*, and Harvey R. Greenberg's *Hanging In: What You Should Know about Psychotherapy*.

The manner in which an author goes about achieving a desired goal, whether it is to persuade, inform, inspire, or amuse, sets the tone of a book. Is it hard-sell, strident, one-sided, humorous, loving, sympathetic, adulatory, scholarly, pedantic, energetic, or leisurely? Authors of informative books for children used to lean more toward a leisurely style because they were thinking of children as empty vessels waiting to be filled with information. They considered it their task to trick children into becoming interested in their subject and so they tried to be as entertaining as possible. But today's young readers are just as busy as their parents and most likely go to informative books, not for leisure time entertainment but to get quick information. A boy who wants to repair a bicycle doesn't want to start out by reading about the Wright brothers and their bicycle shop before getting to the part on how gears and brakes work.

The best informative books also have style. When Meltzer questioned author Jane Langton who was serving as a judge for the *Boston Globe–Hornbook* Awards about what her criteria for judging nonfiction was, she said that for a book to be worthy of recognition, it has to "exude some kind of passion or love or caring." It has to have literary quality and the potential for leaving a mark on the readers, changing them in some way.[4]

George A. Woods, children's book review editor of the *New York Times Book Review* said that he selects the informational books to be featured in his reviews mostly on his own "gut-level" reactions. "What I respond to as being new or far better than what we have had before, what has a majesty of language, is unique, aids a child's understanding, makes him an eyewitness to history."[5]

What these people are talking about is style. A problem in examining an author's style is that the author's style in each book must be judged according to the purpose that the author had in mind. From book to book, purposes are so different that it is like the old problem of comparing apples and oranges. Some books will be successful simply because they are different—more like a mango than either an apple or an orange.

David Macaulay's *Unbuilding* is such a book. Technically it should probably be classed as fiction because it's the make-believe story of an Arab oil magnate who in 1989 purchases the Empire State Building and has it dismantled and crated up for shipment to his Arab desert to be reconstructed as his company's office building. In the fictional part of the book, Macaulay makes snide jokes about big money, historical preservationists, and people's gullibility. The nonfiction, informative part of the book is the accuracy of the detailed architectural drawings which show how the building was created.

Cutaways and double-page spreads emphasize the building's beauty as well as the magnificent accomplishment of its 1930s construction. From a purely informational stand, Macaulay could have used the same drawings and entitled the book something like *Construction of the Empire State Building*. That's really what readers learn, but the effect of the clever reversal—turning the book into what one reviewer called "an urban fairytale"—was to take it out of the "ordinary" category and to make it a book that in Jane Langton's words exudes "some kind of passion or love or caring."

A fifth way that the kind of information books we're talking about suffers from bad PR relates to their target audience of teenagers. When young adult librarian Patty Campbell spoke at the 1983 American Library Association annual meeting, she pointed out that teenagers are so wrapped up in what the psychologists have labelled the "adolescent identity crisis" that they simply do not have the time for, nor the interest in, sitting down and reading about the world in general. What they are looking for are books that will help them decide on who they are and where they fit into the scheme of things. Informative books they judge to be helpful include sex education books, some physical and mental health books of the *I'm Okay, You're Okay* type, selected how-to books, and biographies or true accounts of experiences teenagers can imagine themselves or their acquaintances having. Nearly all of the other information books published for teenagers are read under duress—only because teachers assign reports and research papers.

This is partly an exaggeration, but it does point to the tremendous challenge that authors face when they set out to write factual books that will be intriguing enough to entice young readers to pick them up even when there is no one forcing them to study. The adult who is going to be successful in encouraging the range of what teenagers read on their own is the teacher or librarian who is observant enough to notice, for example, which students avidly read science fiction, and is also knowledgeable and energetic enough to offer these same students Peter Nicholls' well-done, informative discussion of *The Science in Science Fiction*. In a similar way, a skilled adult will notice which students regularly read *Sports Illustrated* magazine and will offer these students William Jaspersohn's *Magazine:*

Behind the Scenes at Sports Illustrated. Because the book is so interesting, it may open an unexpected door for sports fans who hadn't previously given a thought to a possible career in journalism. At the very least, it will help them read their magazine with new appreciation.

Contemporary Influences on the Publishing of Informational Books

In the mid-1970s, James Haskins, a writer of informational books for young readers, conducted a study of the nonfiction written for older children and adolescents between 1950 and 1975. To his surprise, he found that he had not made just a partial study but had covered practically the whole development of nonfiction for young readers. Prior to the 1950s what was published for young readers was in the main either fiction (novels and short stories), poetry, or textbook material to be used in school. No one thought that young readers would be interested in factual books unless they were forced to study them as part of their school work.

One of the things that happened in the 1950s to change all this was that the Russians launched Sputnik, and we in America launched ourselves on a gigantic education explosion. We were in the midst of the Cold War and were sincerely frightened that Russia was scientifically and technologically ahead of us, and so we began to put new emphases on education and the learning of factual material. In 1961, Congress passed the National Defense Education Act, which gave millions of dollars to school libraries. At first, the money was specifically earmarked for the purchase of science and math books. These books were not textbooks but supplements to the curriculum to be used by students independently. Publishers stumbled over each other in trying to fill their catalogues with books that would not only qualify for purchase under the Act but would also excite young readers enough to make them take the books out or purchase them on their own.

Another change in society that contributed to the increased popularity of nonfiction is the knowledge explosion of the last few decades. Today there is simply more information to be shared between writer and reader. It is this fact, more than any other, that is responsible for the wide variety of books available.

It's probably more than a coincidence that the rise in popularity of nonfiction books paralleled the rise in the power and influence of the mass media. Television, radio, movies, newspapers, and magazines all communicate the same kinds of information to the general public as do the authors of books, but it is from books that people expect the most because the other media are more limited in the amount of space and time that they can devote to any one topic. And whatever is produced by the mass media must be of interest to a *mass* audience while it is individual readers who select books. Of course publishers want masses of individual readers to select their books, but still there is more room for experimentation and for controversial ideas in books than in the kinds of media which are supported by advertisers and therefore must attract an audience. Nevertheless book publishers look to the media for ways to increase their sales and general appeal.

◈ THE PEOPLE BEHIND THE BOOKS

OUIDA SEBESTYEN, Author

Far from Home
IOU's
Words by Heart

My son didn't become the reader I'd been or expected him to be. While fiction was read, written, and discussed all around him, he grew up using books to give him fast, exact information. I think he missed something enriching and important, but the thing is that thousands of busy, practical kids like him are going to need good books that tell them how-to or why-not. With luck, their awakened curiosity and enthusiasm will draw them on into general nonfiction (if it moves along at their personal RPM) and, who knows, maybe even those of us who write fiction will get a quick crack at them, especially if our books

happen to metamorphose into movies or TV dramas. So more of us may want to explore ways of expressing complex and abstract ideas in dramatic form as well as in print. Meanwhile, we'll happily go on writing fiction, fantasy, poetry, and all that wonderful slow stuff for young people whose temperament, ocular orientation, or other lucky circumstances make them traditional readers. We'll philosophically watch the sale of the safe, the perfect-for-packaging, and the attention-grabbers that make possible the publishing of the risks, the sleepers and the noble failures. I expect we'll go on writing for love and money, but mostly because trying to enlarge other lives enlarges ours. ◆

Far from Home. Little, Brown, 1980.
IOU's. Little, Brown, 1982.
Words by Heart. Little, Brown, 1979.

As the most pervasive of the media, television has a tremendous influence on book publishing. For example, obvious TV tie-ins include Carl Sagan's *Cosmos* based on his television series, David Attenborough's *Life on Earth: A Natural History* based on the BBC series, and David S. Reiss' *M*A*S*H: The Exclusive Inside Story of TV's Most Popular Show*. Less obvious TV tie-ins include books about those current events which are discussed regularly enough on television that authors are inspired to do research to answer the questions that cursory news reports don't have time or space to probe. Nigel Calder's *The Comet Is Coming* is this kind of a treatment of the 1985 appearance of Halley's Comet. Mary Shapiro's *A Picture History of the Brooklyn Bridge: With 167 Prints and Photographs* was published in honor of the centennial of the famous bridge, while Robert Ehringer's *Strike for Freedom: The Story of Lech Walesa and Polish Solidarity* examines the Polish workers' movement. David Wallechinsky's *The Complete Book of the Olympics* of course hit its peak popularity during the 1984 Olympics, but because of its wealth of fascinating details will probably continue to be read for decades.

The media often present only the surface facts of intriguing social issues. It's up to the authors to explore them further. One such area is ecology and appreciation for nature. The Sierra Club produces attractive books, for example, David Rains Wallace's *The Dark Range: A Naturalist's*

Night Notebook and *Idle Weeds: The Life of a Sandstone Ridge*, but always from a predictable slant. Charles E. Roth's *Then There Were None* is refreshing in that it treats the issue of possible extinction as a natural process to be understood—not helped along or encouraged, but at least viewed as part of a bigger picture. Laurence Pringle is a skilled and prolific author in this area with such books as *Lives at Stake: the Science and Politics of Environmental Health* and *Wolfman: Exploring the World of Wolves*. A much fuller book on wolves is Barry Holstun Lopez' *Of Wolves and Men*. Augusta Goldin's *Water: Too Much, Too Little, Too Polluted?* and Bjorn Berglund's *Noah's Ark is Stranded: The Message of African Ecology* are examples of books giving a worldwide perspective to the issue of ecology.

People's inhumanity to each other is another area in which books can provide a background for discussion and thought at a deeper level than can a television show or a news article, for example Margaret O. Hyde's *Cry Softly! The Story of Child Abuse*, Milton Meltzer's *The Terrorists*, and Robert Yeager's *Seasons of Shame: The New Violence in Sports*. An aspect of the arms race that isn't often thought about is explored in Robert Harris and Jeremy Paxman's *A Higher Form of Killing: The Secret Story of Chemical and Biological Warfare*.

Legal rights are spelled out for young readers in Jules Archer's *You and the Law* and *Who's Running Your Life?: A Look at Young People's Rights*. A more recent book is Sam and Beryl Epstein's *Kids in Court: The ACLU Defends Their Rights*.

The influence of television on format and design is hard to prove, but there's an obvious difference between the majority of informative books coming out today and those that were published twenty years ago. More of the current books are illustrated with numerous photographs, many in color, and they are organized and laid out in little chunks of information so that readers can browse, skim, and take rest breaks—comparable to taking time out for commercials—without losing their trains of thought.

Peter Matthiessen's *The Tree Where Man Was Born* resembles a well-done travelogue on Africa while John Phillips' *A Will to Survive: Israel: The Faces of Terror 1948, The Faces of Hope Today* is like a television documentary.

Two very personal books by photographer Jill Krementz, *How It Feels When a Parent Dies* and *How It Feels to Be Adopted* feature personal interviews with several young people. Krementz chose to present the accounts as if the young people are speaking directly to the reader. The well-done photographic portraits—which is what Krementz was famous for long before she became an author—give readers the feeling that they are watching television and listening while nearly twenty unique stories are told. In the adoption book, for example, fifteen-year-old Philip from a Jewish family confesses:

> ◇ Whenever I go to temple or when we celebrate the Sabbath on Friday night, I often sense that there's a Hebrew loyalty that my relatives have that I don't. Even though people tell me that my natural parents were Jewish, in my heart

I'm just not all that certain. I mean, how do I know that they were both really Jewish? How do I know that my real mother didn't fall in love with a Roman Catholic or something?[6]

Joey, age fourteen, was adopted by a Chicago priest when he was twelve. Joey explains:

◇ Father Clements thought it would be nice to invite me to his house for Christmas dinner, but when he asked me I said I had to think about it because I had a lot of other invitations from family and friends. I was lying because I had too much pride to let him think I didn't have any place to go. And it was my pride which actually impressed this priest and made him come back to see me again and again.[7]

A widespread interest in photography may be another outgrowth of the respect that people feel for the mass media. Martin W. Sandler's *The Story of American Photography: An Illustrated History for Young People* is the most highly recommended of recent books. Other good ones include Shirley Glubok's *The Art of Photography*, Eric Eriksenn and Els Sincebaugh's *Aventures in Closeup Photography: Rediscovering Familiar Environments Through Details*, Ruth Orkin's *More Pictures from My Window*, Lida Moser's *Career Photography: How to Be a Success as a Professional Photographer*, and less directly Beatrice Sieger's *An Eye on the World: Margaret Bourke-White, Photographer*.

Good photographs make readers interested in a subject; they put drama into Jaydie Putterman and Rosalynde LeSur's large format *Police* and they cast an adventurous spirit of wanderlust over Verne Huser and R. Valentine Atkinson's *River Camping: Touring by Canoe, Raft, Kayak, and Dory*. On a subject such as war they bring home the horror and leave readers with a humility over the frailty of human life. This is true whether it's a historical collection as in Jorge Lewinski's *The Camera at War: A History of War Photography from 1848 to the Present Day* or a contemporary collection as in George Esper and the Associated Press' *The Eyewitness History of the Vietnam War 1961–1975*.

Informational books purchased by school libraries are usually referred to as "books to support the curriculum." A more descriptive term would probably be "books to extend the curriculum." For the most part, these are not books that will help students who are not doing well in class.

It's the smartest science students who are going to profit from Horace Freeland Judson's *The Search for Solutions* which through interviews and historical accounts shows how scientists set out to creatively solve problems. The good language student, the one who may go into linguistics as a career, will be fascinated to read Francine Patterson and Eugene Linden's *The Education of Koko*. The book is the story of Koko's (a lowland gorilla) acquisition of sign language. And certainly the student who has a hard time understanding math even when there's a teacher there to help won't be able to read *Mathematics for the Million: How to Master the Magic of Numbers* and actually go from simple arithmetic to calculus as author Lancelot

Hogben promises. Nor is the poor math student likely to be the one to refer to *The Prentice-Hall Encyclopedia of Mathematics* edited by Beverly H. West and others even though it is supposed to be a straightforward explanation of frequently difficult concepts.

Budding artists will enjoy the *Looking at Art* series featuring *Faces* by Giles Waterfield and *People at Home* and *People at Work*, both by Patrick Conner. Ronald Parkinson, Head of Education at the Victoria and Albert Museum in London, was the consulting editor for the beautifully done series which was printed in Italy for Atheneum. In each book approximately thirty paintings are reproduced in full color. The formats are uncrowded and aesthetically pleasing and the thematic organization makes it so that pictures on opposing pages complement rather than detract from each other. Each painting is described briefly and interesting parts pointed out; then something is told about the artist. A sampling of the paintings featured in *People at Home* include Edgar Degas' "The Tub," Mary Cassatt's "Woman Bathing," Henri Matisse's "Conversation," and Horace Pippin's "The Domino Players."

Another good new book is *Meet Matisse* by Nelly Munthe. She focuses on the last part of Matisse's life when he was confined to his wheelchair but still insisted on working. It was then, when as he said, "My suitcases are packed and I am waiting for the train, but I do not know when it leaves," that he did his well-known cutouts. Munthe's goal throughout the book is to inspire and instruct readers in using Matisse's techniques to create their own striking cutouts.

Readers expect art books to be "picture books" and so there isn't the same degree of self-consciousness about a childish format that there is with story books. This means that publishers are quite right in printing "for all ages" on such interesting art books as the ones just described as well as on the *Self-Portrait Collection* which Addison-Wesley is producing. They have asked artists to write—and paint—their autobiographies. Highly recommended are *Self-Portrait: Margot Zemach*, *Self Portrait: Erik Blegvad*, and *Self-Portrait: Trina Schart Hyman*. Shirley Glubok's books are also highly recommended including *The Art of the New American Nation*, *The Art of the Plains Indians*, and *The Art of the Old West*.

Good history students will want to read the following books which present information that is too complicated, too detailed, too obscure, or too controversial to be included in the regular textbooks: Milton Meltzer's *The Jewish Americans: A History in Their Own Words*; Oscar and Lilian Handlin's *A Restless People: Americans in Rebellion,* 1770–1787; Jervis Anderson's *This Was Harlem: A Cultural Portrait, 1900–1950*; Francois Kersuady's *Churchill and DeGaulle*; Theodore Kazimiroff's *The Last Algonquin*; and Leonard Gross' *The Last Jews in Berlin* which is a collection of World War II stories about Jewish survivors and the non-Jews who made their survival possible.

Among the best of the Vietnam books is *Tim Page's Nam* which *School Library Journal* described as "A tough but honest book that captures the reality of the Vietnam War in brilliant photographs and descriptions from

◆ Readers expect art books to be "picture books" and so there isn't the same degree of self-consciousness about format as there is with fiction. Publishers are quite right in promoting the art books featured here as appropriate for all ages.

the men who served there." "Tough, horrifying, honest, and moving," is how the same journal described Al Santoli's *Everything We Had: An Oral History of the Vietnam War by Thirty-three Soldiers Who Fought It* when the editors put it on their 1981 best book list. Santoli, who served as an infantryman, took photos of most of the men he interviewed. He also recorded the time and place of service so that he could arrange everything chronologically as an illustration of the change and deterioration that went through the ranks between the beginning and the end of America's most unpopular war. James Kaufmann, writing about Santoli's book for the *Christian Science Monitor,* compared it to Mark Baker's *NAM:*

> ◇ [It] is probably a more representative oral history. The 33 soldiers he interviews range from "grunt" to admiral, from helicopter gunner to POW, from medic to interrogation officer. His subjects were in Vietnam as early as 1962, and as late as the mad dash out of Saigon in 1975. . . . The stories can be every bit as gruesome as those in *NAM,* but they are counterbalanced by more tales of compassion and heroism.[8]

A less controversial book on the subject is Don Lawson's *The United States in the Vietnam War* which is done as part of a Young People's History of American Wars Series. The emphasis in this book is on the underlying causes of the war and its tragic consequences.

Recent books about World War II go beyond the obvious historical facts, for example Daniel S. Davis' *Behind Barbed Wire: The Imprisonment of Japanese Americans during World War II* traces political, economic, and social factors that resulted in a shameful chapter in American history. Hasso G. Stachow's *If This Be Glory,* translated from German by J. Maxwell Brownjohn, raises questions about patriotism and courage through interviews with a former Nazi soldier. Robert Goldston's *Sinister Touches: The Secret War Against Hitler* shows how underground spies influenced the outcome of the war and A. J. P. Taylor's *The Origins of the Second World War* shows that the responsiblity for the war must be shared by both the Germans and the Allies.

A legitimate complaint often voiced about history books is that they focus on war and violence and leave out life as it really was for the majority

◆ **TABLE 8.2 Suggestions for Evaluating Informative Nonfiction**

A good piece of informative writing usually has:	A poor piece of informative writing may have:
A subject of interest to young readers, written about with zest. Information that is up-to-date and accurate.	Obsolete or inaccurate information and/or illustrations. Even one such occurrence causes the reader to lose faith in the rest of the book.
New information, or information organized in such as way as to present a different point of view than in previously available books.	Evidence of cutting-and-pasting in which the author merely reorganized previously prepared material without developing anything new in content or viewpoint.
A reading level, vocabulary, and tone of writing that are at a consistent level appropriate to the intended audience.	Inconsistencies in style or content, for example, college level vocabulary but a childish or cute style of writing.
An organization in which basic information is presented first so that chapters and sections build on each other.	An awkward mix of fiction and nonfiction techniques through which the author unsuccessfully tries to slip information in as an unnoticed part of the story.
An index and other aids to help readers look up facts if they want to return to the book for specific information or to glean ideas and facts without reading the entire book.	A reflection of out-of-date or socially unfair attitudes, for example, a history book that presents only the history of white upper-class males with a title and introduction that give the impression that it is a comprehensive history of the time period being covered.
Adequate documentation of the sources of information, including some original sources.	
Information to help interested students locate further readings on the subject.	A biased presentation in which only one side of a controversial issue is presented with little or no acknowledgement that many people hold different viewpoints.
In how-to books, clear and accurate directions including complete lists of the equipment and supplies needed in a project.	
Illustrations that add interest as well as clarity to the text.	In how-to books, frustrating directions that oversimplify and/or set up unrealistic expectations so that the reader is disappointed in the result.
A competent author with expertise in the subject matter.	

of people. As one of the counterbalances, authors have done several good books on women's history, including Joanna L. Stratton's *Pioneer Women: Voices from the Kansas Frontier*, Robert McHenry's *Famous American Women: A Biographical Dictionary from Colonial Times to Present*, Charlotte Streifer Rubenstein's *American Women Artists: from Early Indian Times to the Present*, and Bernice Selden's *The Mill Girls*. Linda Peavy and Ursula Smith's *Women Who Changed Things: Nine Lives that Made a Difference* and Diana C. Gleasner's *Breakthrough: Women in Science* might inspire young women.

An illustration of how quickly informative books change is the fact that in the earlier edition of this text we did not list a single book on computers. Today there are probably over a hundred that we could recommend for teenagers. They include such introductory books as Pat Conniffe's straightforward *The Computer Dictionary*, and Guy L. Steele's more playful *The*

Hacker's Dictionary: A Guide to the Computer Underworld. Some of the books are very specific. For example, Pocket Books puts out a series edited by *Consumer Guide* including *The User's Guide to Atari* and *The User's Guide to Commodore*, . . . *Texas Instruments*, . . . *Timex/Sinclair*, and Donald Spencer has written *Problem Solving with BASIC*.

More general books include Alfred Glossbrenner's *The Complete Handbook of Personal Computer Communications* and Henry Horenstein and Eliot Tarlin's *Computerwise: An Accessible Guide to What Personal Computers Can Do for You*. The practical how-to types of books for young readers will most likely be about personal computers because that is what teenagers have access to, but that doesn't mean that they aren't interested in learning about larger computers and about the theoretical bases of such. Margaret O. Hyde's *Computers That Think?: The Search for Artificial Intelligence* and Stan Augarten's *State of the Art: A Photographic History of the Integrated Circuit* are good for taking computer "whiz kids" beyond the basics. Michael Crichton, already known to young readers as the author of *The Andromeda Strain* and *The Great Train Robbery*, has written what is so far the best of the general information books, *Electronic Life: How to Think about Computers*. See "Computer Books for Young Adults" by Betty Carter in *English Journal* (November 1984) for a discussion of Crichton's book as well as guides to use in selecting other types of computer books.

There's no way in this chapter to give anything other than a sampling of the many books available as companion reading, or even replacement reading, for typical textbooks. In selecting academically oriented books, librarians should probably keep in mind the purpose for which teenagers read this kind of book. It differs from the books discussed below as leisure time reading. With books designed to communicate information, young readers who pick them up do not want to casually wander through a morass of facts and opinions. They want the material to be streamlined and to the point. They also want it to be indexed and organized in such a way that they can easily refer back to something they remember or can look up facts without reading the whole book. And since young readers lack the kind of background knowledge that most adults have, it is especially important that the basic information comes first so they won't be confused by unclear references.

◈ READING FOR ENTERTAINMENT

From the very beginning of life, babies are testing their limits. They want to know how much they can eat, how far they can reach, how loudly they can scream, and how much their parents will let them get away with. As the years go by and children grow into teenagers, they become more subtle and more sophisticated, but they are still interested in testing limits. The difference is that with young adults, their sphere of interest is now so much broader that it includes the whole world and even beyond. There is no way that they can personally test all the limits in which they are interested. Some would be too dangerous, some are mutually exclusive, some would take too long, and some cannot be entered into voluntarily. Because of these and other considerations, teenagers and adults turn to books that present the extremes of life's experiences.

Whatever is the biggest, the best, or the most bizarre is of interest. That is the basis of the *Ripley's Believe It or Not* series, as well as the *Guinness Book of World Records*. One librarian said that if she just had 100 copies of the latter title she could start a library by having students bring in books to trade for what she has found to be an all-time favorite. Part of the appeal of the Guinness book is that it is continually updated and many of the record setters are young. Of interest to less ambitious readers are the simplified versions, which have come out under such titles as the *Guinness Book of Amazing Achievements* and the *Guinness Illustrated Collection of World Records for Young People*. These books are about 100 pages long and their appearance is similar to the original except that only one event is told about on each illustrated page.

Because the nature of the subject matter makes this kind of book even more ephemeral than most, a large percentage of them come out only as inexpensive paperbacks, for example, Jeff Rovin's *Count Dracula's Vampire Quiz Book*, Al Jaffee's *The Ghoulish Book of Weird Records*, Bart Andrews' *TV Picture Quiz Book*, and The World Almanac's *Book of the Strange*.

An almost opposite approach to the inexpensive paperback is that taken by some publishers who make a big investment in oversize and beautifully illustrated hardcover or trade paperback books. Brian Froud's *The World of the Dark Crystal*, based on the film *The Dark Crystal*, Wil Huygen and Rien Poorevliet's *Gnomes*, and Peter Hogarth and Val Clery's *Dragons* exemplify the most successful of these kinds of books. Reprintings of comic strips are also done this way as in Garry Trudeau's *Doonesbury's Greatest Hits* and in Michael Uslan and Bruce Solomon's *Pow! Zap! Wham! Comic Book Trivia Quiz*. An advantage to this kind of book is that it is instant entertainment. People who have only a minute or two can open the books anywhere and read a complete discourse. The same is true for David Wallechinsky and Irving Wallace's *The People's Almanac* and *The People's Almanac II*. *The Book of Lists* by David Wallechinsky, Irving Wallace, and Amy Wallace is full of wonderful trivia such as the shoe sizes of twenty famous men, ten foods claimed to be aphrodisiacs, fifteen well-known love offerings, and fifteen famous events that happened in a bathtub.

Caroline Sutton's *How Do They Do That?: Wonders of the Modern World Explained* is more than the typical trivia book in that it gives accurate explanations ranging from a paragraph to two or three pages on such fascinating questions as "How do they get the stripes onto Stripe toothpaste?" "How does a Contac time-release capsule know when to release?" "How do they determine from the rubble the cause of a building's collapse?" and "How do they measure the ratings that reveal on Tuesday morning what Americans watched on TV Sunday evening?" Its sequel *How Did They Do That?* answers such questions as "How did they put out the San Francisco fire of 1906?" "How did they decide that blue was for boys, pink for girls?" and "How did 3M tape become Scotch?"

Trivia books can be amazingly specialized, for example William Neely and John S. F. McCormick, Jr.'s 505 *Automobile Questions Your Friends Can't Answer*; Rosemary Guiley's *Lovelines* which has articles, quizzes, and trivia about the world of romance fiction; Carole Potter's *Knock on Wood* which is an encyclopedia of superstitions, talismans, and charms; Jerome Agel's *America at Random: Questions and Answers* for history buffs; and Vernon Pizer's *Eat the Grapes Downward: An Uninhibited Romp through the Surprising World of Food*.

Many sports books fit into the leisure time reading category, especially photographic extravaganzas such as Robert Riger's *The Athlete* and anthologies of winners such as Michael Bartlett and Bob Gillen's *The Tennis Book* which is a history of tennis greats—both people and events. Robert A. Liston's *The Great Teams: Why They Win All the Time*, Wayne Coffey's *All-Pro's Greatest Football Players*, and *Sports Quotes* by Bob Abel and Mike Valenti list those notable sayings by players, coaches, writers, and spectators.

Books on subjects that aren't taught in school must be especially appealing to entice young readers to pick them up. The art work may be sufficient enticement as with David Macaulay's intricate drawings in *Pyramid*, *Cathedral*, *Underground*, *Mill* and the previously mentioned *Unbuilding*. Or it may be an unusual subject, for example Teresa Jordan's *Cowgirls: Women of the American West*, which is an oral history of thirty women who have succeeded either as rodeo contestants or as ranchers. Another unusual topic is that in John Keane's *Sherlock Bones: Tracer of Missing Pets*. Keane is an animal detective, who, in addition to offering some solid advice on locating missing pets, recounts some of his fascinating experiences.

Alvin Schwartz has made collections of amusing jokes, beliefs, and superstitions in American folklore. They are more interesting than jokes created by an author because they have really been believed by at least some people. Some of the titles of Schwartz's well-illustrated books are *Kickle Snifters and Other Fearsome Critters Collected from American Folklore*; *Witcracks: Jokes and Jests from American Folklore*; *Tomfoolery: Trickery and Foolery with Words Collected from American Folklore*; and *Cross Your Fingers, Spit in Your Hat: Superstitions and Other Beliefs*. His *Scary Stories to Tell in the Dark* will be especially appealing because teenagers will probably have heard various versions of several of the stories from their friends. They may get some new insights into how contemporary folklore works.

Kids who have grown up with model trains might be interested enough in railroads to pick up Stuart Leuthner's *The Railroaders*, Dee Brown's *Hear That Lonesome Whistle Blow: Railroads in the West*, and the simplified version *Lonesome Whistle: The Story of the First Transcontinental Railroad*.

Aspiring airplane pilots might browse through *The Armchair Aviator* edited by John Thorn or *Famous First Flights Across the Atlantic* by Frank J. Delear. Young people wanting to go into show business might pick up James Haskins' *Black Theater in America*, Ellen Switzer's *Dancers! Horizons in American Dance*, or Toni Bentley's *Winter Season: A Dancer's Journal*.

Musicians or music fans could be expected to be interested in *The*

THE PEOPLE BEHIND THE BOOKS

ALVIN SCHWARTZ, Author

Flapdoodle: Pure Nonsense from American Folklore

Scary Stories to Tell in the Dark

Unriddling: All Sorts of Riddles to Puzzle Your Guessery

Witcracks: Jokes and Jests from American Folklore

I plan to continue the writing and the compiling of books of folklore. I will go on exploring the folklore of humor and word play, fields rich enough to occupy me for years. But I also will begin exploring the other side of the coin: the folklore of the supernatural and the unknown.

Since more and more of us live in urban settings, more and more of the material I collect inevitably will reflect urban rather than rural experiences and values. Tales, riddles, games, ways of having a good time, ways of saying things and ways of doing things all will reflect this.

Based on experience, something else is sure. A large number of the "ordinary" people I interview—primarily young people and old people—will express themselves in the most remarkable ways. They will deal with prosaic subjects in lovely, spare, richly suggestive prose; tell the funniest stories imaginable; and engage in the wildest shenanigans with words. It is one of the dividends of my work. ◆

Rolling Stone Record Guide edited by Dave Marsh with John Swenson, Peter Goddard's two books *David Bowie: The Man Who Came Out of the Cool* and *The Who: The Farewell Tour,* and Tony Palmer's *All You Need is Love: The Story of Popular Music.* Michael Bane's *White Boy Singin' the Blues: the Black Roots of White Rock* was on the *School Library Journal's* 1982 best book list while Paul Griffiths' *A Guide to Electronic Music* was on the 1981 list.

◆ **ANIMAL BOOKS**

Anyone who recognizes Americans' fondness for their pets, who watched even one episode of the PBS series about Yorkshire veterinarian James Herriot, who saw the movie version of Farley Mowat's *Never Cry Wolf,* who has any knowledge of the lifelong work of naturalists, or who is aware of our national dedication to the world of nature and its inhabitants shouldn't be surprised at the abundance of reasonably intelligent and nonsentimentalized books about such subjects as veterinarians, zoos, horses, dogs, wolves, coyotes, and other animals. Nor should readers be surprised at the excellent adventure stories, the fantasies, and satires that use animals as characters. From a structural standpoint, such widely differing books are a mixed bag. But what they have in common is important. It is the pleasure as well as the information that they bring to readers.

James Herriot's four books introduce young people to a world they hardly know exists, a veterinarian's life in northern England. More important, the books are warm and funny stories about strange people, and sometimes even stranger animals. The first in the series, *All Creatures Great and Small* may be the most appealing, but once young readers are caught by that, they will probably go on to *All Things Bright and Beautiful*, *All Things Wise and Wonderful*, and *The Lord God Made Them All*. Another veterinarian book worth young adults' time is Louis J. Camuti's *All My Patients Are under the Bed: Memoirs of a Cat Doctor*.

David Taylor's *Zoo Vet: Adventures of a Wild Animal Doctor* is more exciting than most adventure novels; Taylor's *Going Wild: Adventures of a Zoo Vet* and *Next Panda, Please: Further Adventures of a Wildlife Vet* are equally absorbing.

Gerald Durrell, brother of the world-famous novelist Lawrence Durrell, has been something of a family misfit since he was young. His *The Amateur Naturalist*, *A Bevy of Beasts*, and *The Mockery Bird*—a very funny novel—are most pleasing. Other books about zoo collectors and zoo veterinarians include Sheldon Campbell's *Lifeboats to Ararat*, Desmond Morris' *Animal Days*, and Joan Embery's *My Wild World*. Two naturalists demand more than mere listing, Heinz Sielman's *Wilderness Expedition* and David Attenborough's *The Zoo Quest Expeditions*. Sielman provide more than 400 pages of magnificent color shots of nature at its most beautiful. Attenborough describes expeditions to Guyana, Borneo, and Paraguay, all filled with adventure and the fascination of animals.

Horse books have been popular for years, none more so than Enid Bagnold's *National Velvet*, but anyone who remembers it as a sentimental picture of a lovely horse needs to reread the book. It *is* about a horse and the Grand National, but even more it is about the maturation of a young woman and her drive to find her place in the universe. James Aldridge's *The Marvelous Mongolian* is a more conventional animal story about the natural desire of a wild horse brought to Wales to return to his home in Mongolia. The animals are brave but they do not become objects of pity to the reader, nor are they idealized nor anthropomorphic. Rumer Godden's *The Dark Horse* is based on fact. Some fifty years ago a fine racehorse was exiled from England and sent to race in India. Most of the humans in the book are also exiles in some way, and they and the horse ultimately, to no one's surprise, redeem themselves. A loving book.

Dog stories are even more common and equally popular. Fortunately, many of them deserve young adult readers. James Street's *Good-bye, My Lady*, Fred Gipson's *Old Yeller*, and Wilson Rawls' *Where the Red Fern Grows* have become classics in the field. More recent and just as good are Sheila Burnford's *The Incredible Journey* and *Bel Ria*. The first is not based on fact, which may surprise some readers, but its tale of an old Bull Terrier, a young Yellow Labrador, and a Siamese cat who made an epic journey home appeals to the mythic in all of us, and the animals are not sentimentalized. Dangerously close to sentimentalizing but always avoiding it, *Bel Ria* relates how a small trained dog in France during World War II affected the people who knew and loved him.

In W. E. Butterworth's *A Member of the Family*, a family discovers that inbreeding has led the family puppy to attack whenever one of the family appears to be threatened, and the dog must be destroyed. Characterizations of the family make this better than the reader might expect. Sonia Levitin's *Reigning Cats and Dogs* is about the life and death of a beloved old German Shepherd. Elizabeth Yates' *The Seventh One* tells of Tom and the seven dogs he has owned (or they have owned him) from his childhood through his seventies. Gavriil Troyepolsky's *Beem* is the heart-tugging story of a Golden Setter separated from his master and searching for his home. It is well-written and appealing, despite the possible overdose of sentimentality.

Two quite different kinds of dog books are Pat Feeley's *Best Friend* and Faith Sullivan's *Watch Dog*. The best friend is Beau, a German Shepherd, who chooses sides in a marriage, loves the wife and hates the husband, and makes the husband regret all his cruelties. As *Watch Dog* opens, Louise Andrews is waiting for her veterinarian husband to come home. A car crash occurs, the husband is killed, and the only survivor is an Irish Setter the husband is bringing home. Very slowly, the dog takes over the household, and before long, the wife (and readers) wonders if the husband's spirit has taken over the dog's body. A spooky book.

T. Ernesto Bethancourt's *The Dog Days of Arthur Cane* is a clever and convincing animal fantasy. Young Arthur foolishly offends an African friend, has a spell placed upon him, and wakes up one morning to find he has become a dog.

Perhaps the book that best describes our ambivalent love-cruelty to animals is Richard Adams' *The Plague Dogs*. A small Fox Terrier and a large mongrel are held in an animal experimentation station, endure unspeakable cruelties, escape, and are temporarily assisted by a fox. It is, as some critics have pointed out, a tirade, but it is also unquestionably effective.

The animal most frequently written about of late is the wolf. Readers of Farley Mowat's *Never Cry Wolf* will be aware of the many myths surrounding this animal, most of them unpleasant and untrue. Barry Lopez's *Of Wolves and Men* offers a wealth of information about wolves, their supposed legendary power and bloodthirstiness, and does much to dispel the myths. Michael W. Fox's *The Soul of the Wolf* offers more insights in a beautifully illustrated book. Roger Caras' *The Custer Wolf* tells of a fabled wolf in 1915 North Dakota and humanity's unjustified war against all wolves. Kathleen Kilgore's *The Wolfman of Beacon Hill* is both a story of an escaped white wolf who survives living in downtown Boston and a young, equally lost, fourteen-year-old boy.

R. D. Lawrence's *The North Runner* and *Secret of the Wolves* are among the best of all animal books, for Lawrence knows animals, and, perhaps more important, he knows himself and his place in their world. *The North Runner* is the story of a huge half-wolf sled dog that Lawrence saves from mistreatment. *Secret of the Wolves* shows the naturalist and his wife raising two orphaned wolf pups. Lawrence's later books are equally worth any reader's time, *The Zoo That Never Was* in which the author and his wife save injured animals and record their reactions to each other, *Voyage of the Stella* in which the author spends six months on a solitary cruise following the sudden death of his wife, and *The Ghost Walker* in which Lawrence spends ten months following a puma and recording its life. Lawrence is, unhappily, too little known. He deserves better.

Other animals have been subjects of books, all of them more exciting than the mass of straight adventure books. Joy Adamson's *Born Free: A Lioness in Two Worlds, Living Free, Forever Free, The Spotted Sphinx,* and *Pippa's Challenge* are likely already well-known studies of lions. Her more recent *Queen of Shaba*, the story of an African leopard is almost as good. Adamson's autobiography, *The Searching Spirit* is likely to appeal to most of her fans, though it will disappoint anyone looking for an understanding of the author.

Foxes have been the subject of Brian Carter's *A Black Fox Running*, a book in which readers virtually become foxes running for their lives, and Joyce Stranger's *The Fox at Drummers' Darkness*, in which the author tells of two tragedies, animal and human.

In Frank C. Craighead, Jr.'s *Track of the Grizzly*, the author and his brother studied the grizzly's world, three thousand square miles of Yellowstone National Park, from 1959 until 1971. A few among the many other animal books deserving readers are Allan W. Eckert's *Incident at Hawk's Hill* where a small boy wanders away from his prairie home and is befriended by a female badger, based on a true incident; Sterling North's *Rascal*, a true story about finding a young raccoon and making a pet of him; and two books by Farley Mowat, *The Dog Who Wouldn't Be*, a tale of a young boy and a dog in Canada, and *A Whale for the Killing*, in which a female whale is stranded in a cove in southern Newfoundland and is tormented and finally killed by "humans."

Cris Freddi's *Pork and Others* is a collection of short stories from various animals' points of view. The title character is a hedgehog who dies all too soon for the reader. Freddi is unafraid of bold honesty about his animals, and the lyrical accounts of their lives—and sometimes their deaths—is surprising and far more sensitive than most readers will expect.

A few novelists have deliberately anthropomorphized their animal characters to make comments about the human condition. John Donovan's *Family* tells of a number of apes, some born in captivity and a few captured and brought to this country, kept in a university for observation. Sasha hears that the humans are about to begin a new experiment and persuades three other apes to join him in a breakout. In nearby mountains, the apes reestablish the old ways until hunters kill two of them. The narrator of R. K. Narayan's *A Tiger for Malgudi* is Raja, a beautiful and strong tiger who frightens villagers, becomes the star of a circus, almost becomes a movie star, and receives wisdom from a master. The novel has violence, though readers may overlook much of it as they read the fabulous fable. It also has the grace and wit of a fine storyteller—Narayan is a major Indian novelist— who writes believably about animals lost in the mad world of humans.

◈ HOW-TO BOOKS

Part of learning about the world is learning how to do things. How-to books therefore fill an important need although very few of them ever find their way to best-book lists. This is not because there aren't good how-to books, but because how-to books appeal to such specific interests, for example, how to invest, how to play soccer, how to enamel jewelry, and how to get good marks on college entrance examinations. The more specific such a book is the more it will appeal to a specialized—and therefore limited—audience.

Authors of how-to books need to be extremely good writers. Even one ambiguous sentence can cause a project to fail. Directions that are hard to understand, failure to list all the supplies and tools that will be needed, and come-on statements that make projects look easier than they are set the stage for frustration. If there is no index to aid readers in finding what they need to know, or if the illustrations are inaccurate, then readers are apt to lose interest in the project and also to lose faith in such books.

Some libraries have given up stocking books on automobile and motorcycle repair because readers find them so useful that they never bring them back. *The Complete Motorcycle Book* by Lyle Kenyon Engel is one that is frequently stolen because it has easily read directions on repairing motorcycles and some appealing and sensible talk that counteracts the stereotype of motorcyclists as reckless speed-crazed menaces to society. A similarly appealing book is *All About Motorcycles: Selection, Care, Repair, and Safety* by Max Alth. Less technical how-to books such as Charles Coombs' series *Be a Winner in . . .* (Tennis, Basketball, and so forth) are more likely to be read and returned to the library since the athlete doesn't usually feel the need to have a book nearby for handy reference in the same way that the mechanic does.

Recent recommended how-to books include Gerald Durrell and Lee Durrell's *The Amateur Naturalist,* John Gardner's *The Art of Fiction: Notes on Craft for Young Writers,* and Elaine Costello's *Signing: How to Speak with Your Hands.*

One of the few how-to books to make it to several best book lists is Jean Young's *Woodstock Craftsman's Manual.* It comes in two volumes and includes directions for such crafts as quilting, wood carving, and making stained-glass windows. The topics for how-to books are almost unlimited. They range from something as simple as how to embroider your jeans to the moderately complex task of making your own shoes to the very complex task of building your own solar energy house. Some books that are not specifically designed as how-to books nevertheless may serve as inspirations and models for young readers. For example, amateur artists would probably get ideas from Elinor Lander Horwitz's *Contemporary American Folk Artists,* which presents the work of untrained sculptors, painters, and other artists. Among the most inspiring of the books of this type are *The Foxfire Books* edited by Eliot Wigginton, but written by teenagers. They were uninterested in school until an inspired teacher interested them in investigating and recording the everyday life around Rabun Gap, Georgia. The books show such varied skills as slaughtering hogs, reading weather signs, recording snake lore, and building log cabins.

In some cases how-to books open the door for high-school students who have never really gotten into books. They come to the library seeking a book telling them how to accomplish a specific task. Their interest may be caught by a display or by a book someone else is checking out. Gradually they begin to feel at home in the library and to return for other how-to books as well as other informational books and perhaps an occasional fiction title.

Motivated students will read how-to books that are far beyond their school-tested reading levels. Perhaps one of the reasons is that how-to books incorporate the principles of programmed learning. Readers are punished for their inattention or poor reading by failing in their project, but on the other hand, they gain an immediate reward for their good reading by achieving success in their goal.

With the how-to kind of sports books, obviously the first thing a reader looks for is the particular sport and so authors choose titles that practically shout out to potential readers: *The Skater's Handbook* by John Misha Petkevich, *Everybody's Hockey Book* by Stan and Shirley Fischler, *The Official Pompon Girl's Handbook* by Randy Neil, *The Complete Beginner's Guide to Gymnastics* by Edward F. Dolan, Jr., *Football Rules in Pictures* by Don Schiffler and Lud Duroska, *International Rugby* by Don Rutherford, *Calling the Play: A Beginner's Guide to Amateur Sports Officiating* by Edward F. Dolan, Jr., and *Treasury of Trick Shots in Pool and Billiards* by Robert Byrne.

The sports books that stand out from the crowd seem to be the ones that have a believable and likable personality behind them. They are inspirational as much as instructive, for example *Basketball My Way* by Nancy Lieberman with Myrna and Harvey Frommer. *Arnold: The Education of a Bodybuilder* by Arnold Schwarzenegger does for weight lifting what James Fixx's *The Complete Book of Running* did for running. A kind of sequel to Fixx's running book is *Jackpot* in which Fixx used excerpts from the personal journal which he kept between 1976 and 1981 to let readers know, sometimes humorously, how the success of his running book altered his lifestyle and his relationship with friends and family.

One thing to watch for in the how-to kind of sports book is whether there is any mention of the costs involved. It is almost cruel of an author to write a glowing account of a child star in tennis, gymnastics, skating, swimming, or dancing and leave young readers with the impression that all it takes is hard work. Those readers whose parents do not have time or money for transportation, lessons, entry fees, equipment, and clothes should be let in on the secret that there's more to how you play the game than meets the eye.

◈ MANAGING ONE'S LIFE: PHYSICAL AND MENTAL HEALTH, CAREERS, AND MONEY

A kind of how-to book deserving its own category is that of self-help, i.e., managing one's own life so as to be successful right now as well as in the future. This includes taking care of one's physical body. When young people go to the shelves of libraries in search of books about health it is most often in search of an answer to a specific problem, for example:

◇ Am I pregnant? Do I have diabetes? What's mononucleosis? How serious is scoliosis? Is being fat "really" unhealthy? What causes pimples? What happens if someone has Hodgkin's disease? My mother has breast cancer; is she going to die? Is anorexia nervosa just in a person's head? Why does my grandfather say such strange things? Will I be like that when I'm old? What will happen if I have V.D. and don't go to the doctor?

For answering such questions, readers will most likely go first to handy reference guides such as Linda de Wolfe Fritschle and Susan Rudnick's *Pocket Reference to Health Disorders* or for a more positive approach to Jane Brody's *The New York Times Personal Guide to Health.* Then from there, they will go to more specific books such as Lawrence M. Pray's *Journey of a Diabetic*, Jonathan Zizmor and Diane English's *The Doctor's Do-It-Yourself Guide to Clearer Skin*, or Marcia Millman's *Such a Pretty Face: Being Fat in America.*

If a book on the physical body is to attract readers who aren't looking for specific answers, the book needs to have some distinctive quality. It might be an especially attractive format or it might be a specialized approach as in the *Sports Medicine Book* by Gabe Mirkin, M.D., and Marshall Hoffman, which promises to present, "What every athlete, coach, trainer, and fitness buff needs to know about exercise, training, nutrition, drugs, injuries, environment, sex." Or it might be that the book is specifically aimed at teenagers as is Kathy McCoy's *The Teenage Body Book.* The amazing photographs in the books of Lennart Nilsson, including *Behold Man* and *A Child Is Born* make them appealing to readers of all ages. Fitness books that appeal to teenagers' desire to look their best include the best-selling *Jane Fonda's Workout Book* and Helane Royce's *Sportshape: Body Conditioning for Women and Men from the Daily Jogger to the Weekend Athlete.*

Going Vegetarian: A Guide for Teen-Agers by Sada Fretz is the kind of sensible well-written book that any age reader could profit from. The reason the author chose to aim her book toward teenagers is that because their growing bodies have certain nutritional needs, they may be in more danger than adults if they do not understand the intricacies of balancing their diets.

A decade ago, dozens of books on drugs were being published, but the flood has slowed to a trickle probably because there's not much left to say. A recent book that does a good job of being interesting and objective is Andrew Weil and Winifred Rosen's *Chocolate to Morphine: Understanding Mind-Active Drugs.* Another recommended book is the most recent edition of Margaret O. Hyde's *Mind Drugs* in which six experts discuss with the author particular drugs, patterns of behavior, alternatives to drug abuse, and the extent of the drug culture. In selecting books on drugs, adults should remember that most teenagers think and know more about drugs than do teachers and librarians and this results in a credibility gap. We therefore need to be extra careful to provide realistic books. Peter G. Hammond, writing in *School Library Journal*, said that after the National Coordinating Council on Drug Education, of which he was executive director, had studied some 1000 books and pamphlets and 300 drug abuse education films, they reached this conclusion:

> ◇ You can trust most contemporary pieces of drug information to be valid and relevant about as much as you can trust the drug sold by your friendly street pusher to be potent, safe, and unadulterated. In both cases vested interests abound: scientists and drug educators can be just as irrational about the dangers and benefits of drugs as can those who promote these chemicals to the youth culture. [9]

In the late 1960s and early 1970s there was a blitz of information on drugs, but Hammond says that information and education are not the same thing. One of the problems has been that everyone wants a pat answer, a quick and easy solution to a very complex problem. Sociologists and anthropologists know it is a temptation when studying any new culture to want to simplify matters by lumping everything together in one clear-cut picture. Such a one-dimensional presentation would make the drug culture so much easier to comprehend, but in reality it isn't that simple.

What is missing from many of the informational books about drugs is the human element, the feeling side of the story. This is corrected in the best of the fiction, but still another problem arises, and that is the issue of language. Realistic problem novels, for example *A Hero Ain't Nothin' But a Sandwich* and *Go Ask Alice* are frequently censored because the characters' language fails to meet "community standards." Even M. E. Kerr's *Dinky Hocker Shoots Smack* sometimes comes under attack because of its misleading title.

Richie by Thomas Thompson is a true story of the George Diener family and what happens when their teenage son begins taking puffs of his friends' marijuana cigarettes and then goes on to barbiturates. When Richie is on drugs, he becomes aggressive, and earns himself a police record as well as his father's hatred. In the midst of one bitter quarrel after Richie had had two automobile accidents in the same afternoon, George Diener shoots and kills his son. At the trial he is acquitted. The concluding pages of the book make a vivid statement about both drugs and the generation gap.

There are all kinds of books designed to help teenagers manage their mental health. They range from Andrea Boroff Eagan's *Why Am I So Miserable If These Are the Best Years of My Life?* also available in Spanish, to *Step Kids: A Survival Guide for Teenagers in Stepfamilies* by Ann Getzoff and Carolyn McClenahan. *The Teenage Survival Guide* by Kathy McCoy is filled with solid advice on a myriad of problems—school, family, health, etc. Some of the books use an encouraging almost cheerleader-like tone as reflected in Joyce L. Vedral's title *I Dare You: How to Get What You Want out of Life, A Guide for Teenagers*. Others combine spiritual guidance with mental health advice as does Lorraine Peterson's *If God Loves Me Why Can't I Get My Locker Open?* Some focus on specific problems that teenagers may be having with parents. For example, *The Kids' Book of Divorce: By, For and About Kids* was edited by Eric Rofes and based on the experiences of twenty kids between the ages of 11 and 14 who were part of a class at the Fayerweather Street School in Cambridge, Massachusetts. Richard Gardner's *A Boys' and Girls' Book About Divorce* has good information in it, but some librarians report that the size and the format make it seem too difficult for junior high readers while the words *boys* and *girls* keep high school students from approaching it.

The dust jacket of Judith S. Seixas' *Living with a Parent Who Drinks Too Much* states that perhaps as many as "20 million children live in homes where there is an alcoholic parent." The book gives advice on coping and includes names and addresses of places to go for help.

An excellent book that libraries should have on hand is aimed not at teenagers but at parents. It is *Talking With Your Teenager: A Book for Parents* by Ruth Bell and Leni Zeiger Wildflower. Following each of the seven sections, "What is Adolescence?," "Our Own Issues," "Communication," "The Changes of Puberty," "Emotional Health," "Sexuality," and "Substance Abuse," suggested readings include both fiction and nonfiction for teens as well as for parents.

Probably the mental health book most appreciated by young adults is Robert M. Pirsig's *Zen and the Art of Motorcycle Maintenance: An Inquiry into Values*. In this the author writes a gently persuasive book about the Zen approach to working on "the motorcycle that is yourself." The narrative that holds it all together is an account of a cross-country motorcycle trip that Pirsig took with his eleven-year-old son.

Part of managing one's life involves decision-making about jobs and work. Any young adult collection needs to have up-to-date books for college-bound students, for example, Richard Rosenberg and John D. Kelly's *Lovejoy's Preparation for the SAT*, Lawrence Graham's *Conquering College Life: How to Be a Winner in College*, and Edward Fiske's *Selective Guide to College* (updated regularly). Libraries also need a wide variety of "career education" books, for example, Ruth Mandel's *In the Running: The New Woman Candidate*, Peter Muller's *The Fast Track to the Top Jobs in Computer Careers* and *The Fast Track to the Top Jobs in Engineering Careers*, James Craig's *Graphic Design Career Guide*, and Peter MacGarr Rabinowitz's *Talking Medicine: America's Doctors Tell Their Stories*.

Today's readers want real people, not the old-fashioned Nurse Cherry Ames kind of career book. They want books that show the bad as well as the good side of different jobs, for example, Alan Jones and Keith Botsford's *Driving Ambition: A Bitingly Honest Look Inside the World of Grand Prix Motor Racing* by the 1980 Formula One World Champion Alan Jones and Gloria Skurzynski's *Safeguarding the Land: Women at Work in Parks, Forests, and Rangelands*. The success of Studs Terkel's *Working: People Talk about What They Do All Day and How They Feel about What They Do* is largely due to Terkel's skill in communicating the emotional side of people's jobs and how their work affects every aspect of their lives. Some parents have objected to use of the book in high school English classes ostensibly because of the language, but part of their discomfort may actually be due to the ambivalent or even negative feelings expressed about work.

The work ethic may be more important to Americans than to other people because of our frontier heritage and the value that was put on hard work. Folklorists point out that only frontier cultures such as those of the United States, Canada, and Australia have stories about such work heroes as John Henry, Paul Bunyan, Pecos Bill, and Old Stormalong. In other cultures, it is common for the heroes of the folktales to be the tricky individuals, the ones who manage to get out of work, but in the United States people are accorded social standing in relation to the jobs they hold, rather than their ancestry, religion, or wealth. Even the children of very wealthy parents prepare for and usually pursue a career. Work is considered an essential part of a meaningful life.

The work heroes of today are individuals whose jobs may be quite ordinary but who have found personal fulfillment through what they do. Readers are interested first in the person as a whole and second in the job as it relates to the person. The best examples of this kind of book are James Herriot's books mentioned earlier.

Presenting several individuals' stories that are in some way related is a common approach. In *Gifford on Courage* Frank Gifford put together ten short biographies of top athletes from various sports. Dozens of good books give the inside story of sports figures, and many of these are presented in Chapter 7 on heroes. One that isn't there is Ken Denlinger's and Len Shapiro's *Athletes for Sale,* an exposé of the devious ways that colleges go about getting and keeping top high-school athletes. A successful presentation of a career as part of a total life story is Larry Ferazani's *Rescue Squad,* which shows the emotional and physical costs of being on a fire department rescue squad. *Serpico* by Peter Maas and *Report from Engine Co. 82* by Dennis Smith are other good books about careers.

Another thing that young readers want in career books is a here-and-now immediacy. They can much better imagine themselves as medical students than as surgeons which is why they like Kenneth Klein's *Getting Better: A Medical Student's Story.* It was written from the journal that the author kept while he was studying at Harvard. Sheila Cole's *Working Kids on Working* presents accounts of 25 workers between the ages of 9 and 15. The jobs range from the highly glamorous type (model, dancer, musical prodigy) to the very ordinary (busboy, farmer, dishwasher). A concluding section "Working Kids and the Law" gives a history of child labor laws and answers questions such as "What should you do if you think your employer is not paying you as agreed?" and "Who has a right to the money a young person earns?"

Dan Fitzgibbon has written an appealing money-management book *All About Your Money* and so has Sylvia Porter, *Your Own Money.* Hers is for older teens and includes a section on investment strategies and financial planning. *The First Official Money Making Book for Kids* by Fred Shanaman with Anita Malnig outlines more than 175 ways for kids to start making money. Gloria D. Miklowitz and Madeleine Yates' *The Young Tycoons: Ten Success Stories* presents dramatic stories of young people between the ages of 10 and 20 who made substantial amounts of money, one as a florist, one as a deliverer of advertisements, and one as a photographer. The thing to be careful about with such wish-fulfilling books is that they don't make things look so easy that readers will think that with a little effort they too can become rich overnight, and then if it doesn't happen they lose faith in the printed word.

One more type of book that should be mentioned in relation to work is the general information book designed to provide knowledge, but not about any one particular job. For example, *Thursday's Daughters: The Story of Women Working in America* by Janet Harris tells about agricultural work, factory work, and professional work. *People Who Make Things: How American Craftsmen Live and Work* by Carolyn Meyer provides detailed descriptions as well as photographs of eight different skills including bookbinding, silversmithing, and quilting. *People and Spaces: A View of History Through Architecture* by Anita Abramovitz has only an indirect relationship to a career, but a young person may become interested in architecture as a result of reading it.

Career-related books are extremely important to young adults. They are at a stage in their lives when they must make decisions that will strongly influence not only how they will earn a living, but because the two are so closely intertwined, what life-styles they will have. Teachers and librarians should make a special effort to bring books of this type to the attention of all students. The more knowledge students have the better position they will be in to make the kinds of far-reaching decisions that society demands of its young adults.

◈ SEX EDUCATION BOOKS

We debated about whether sex education books should go in this chapter on informational books or in Chapter 11 where we discuss controversial issues. In a moment of optimism, we decided to disagree with the high school girl who complained that writers of sex education books "want to control us— not educate us," and include them here as providers of information.

The exploration of sexual matters in books for young readers is an especially sensitive area for the following reasons.

1. Young adults are physically mature, but they probably have had little intellectual and emotional preparation for making sex-related decisions.
2. Parents are anxious to protect their children from making sex-related decisions that might prove harmful.
3. Old restraints and patterns of behavior and attitudes are being questioned so that there is no one clear-cut model to follow.

You don't need a hairy chest to be tough.

◆ As shown by this illustration from *What's Happening to Me?* Peter Mayle's books give a light, even humorous tone to sex education.

4. Sex is such an important part of American culture and the mass media that young people are forced to think about and take stands on such controversial issues as homosexuality, premarital sex, violence in relation to sex, and the role of sex in love and family relationships.

5. Talking about sexual attitudes and beliefs with their teenage children may make parents uncomfortable especially if the father and the mother have different feelings and opinions. This means that many young people must get their information outside of the home.

It is true with all categories of books, but especially with sex education, that no one book can satisfy all readers. The entire collection must be evaluated and books provided for a wide range of interests, attitudes, beliefs, and life-styles. Those conservatives who criticize libraries for including books that present teenage sexual activity as the norm have a justified complaint if the library does not also have sex education books that present, or even promote, abstinence as a normal route for young people.

Certainly the authors of sex education books do not intend to promote promiscuity, but the fact that topics are being treated "nonjudgmentally" may give some readers that impression. It is similar to the quandry that the authors of one sex education book found themselves in when they did a chapter on abortion. They felt compelled to explain that simply because they were including a chapter on abortion, they were not advocating it as the "right" or "best" or "most liberated" decision to make. Instead, they chose to give it considerable space in their book because of its controversial nature and because information had been so unavailable in past years.

Among the most highly recommended sex education books are Lynda Madaras' *What's Happening to My Body? A Growing Up Guide for Mothers and Daughters*, Ruth Bell and others' *Changing Bodies, Changing Lives: A Book for Teens on Sex and Relationships*, Michael Carrera's *Sex: The Facts, The Acts and Your Feelings*, Alex and Jane Comfort's *The Facts of Love: Living, Loving, and Growing Up*, Eric W. Johnson's *Love and Sex in Plain Language* and its simplified form *Sex: Telling It Straight*, Sol Gordon and Roger Conant's *You! The Teenage Survival Book*, and Gary F. Kelly's *Learning about Sex: The Contemporary Guide for Young Adults*.

Materials dealing with sex are judged quite differently from books on less controversial topics. For example, in most subject areas books are given plus marks if they succeed in getting the reader emotionally involved, but with books about sex, many readers feel more comfortable with straightforward, "plumbing manuals"—the less emotional involvement the better. Other readers argue that it's the emotional part that children need to learn. Girls don't get pregnant because they don't know where babies come from. It's a much more complex matter.

Another example of how differently teachers, librarians, and critics treat sex-related materials is the way in which we ignore pornography as a reading interest of teenagers, especially boys. Most of us pretend not to know about pornography so that we won't have to analyze and evaluate it or talk with students about it. One of the few mentions of this kind of reading that has appeared in professional literature was a mid-1970s survey made by Julie Alm of the spare-time reading interests of high school students in Hawaii. In this survey, fourteen students listed *The Sensuous Woman* by "J" as their favorite book. This was the same number as listed John Steinbeck's *The Pearl*, John Knowles' *A Separate Peace*, and the *Bible*.

Tone seems extra important in books about sex because people come to them with their own ideas about appropriateness. Peter Mayle's books give a light, even humorous touch to the whole matter of sex. A surprised graduate student when he looked at them, exclaimed, "Why, I'd rather make fun of the flag than of sex." Mayle's book for children, *Where Did I Come From?* is read by teenagers because of the humor and the cartoonlike drawings. The two specifically for teenagers are *What's Happening to Me?* and *Will I Like It?*

When selecting sex education books, one of the things to watch for is whether or not sex is portrayed from only one viewpoint, either male or female. For example in *Where Did I Come From?* sexual intercourse is described from the traditional active man/passive woman stance:

> ◇ The man loves the woman. So he gives her a kiss. And she gives him a kiss. And they hug each other very tight. And after a while, the man's penis becomes stiff and hard, and much bigger than it usually is. It gets bigger because it has lots of work to do.

> By this time, the man wants to get as close to the woman as he can, because he's feeling very loving to her. And to get really close the best thing he can do is lie on top of her and put his penis inside her, into her vagina.[10]

While defenders will point out that Mayle's book is simplified so as to be readable by very young children, critics argue that because young children are so impressionable it's more important than ever that readers do not come away with the impression that sex is something done *to* women *by* men. Defenders also point out that in most sexual partnerships it is the male who initiates sexual activity, which brings up the old question of whether education is supposed to maintain the status quo or bring about "improvements." If the latter, who is to say what these improvements are?

The design and format of all books, but especially of books about such a sensitive subject as sex, send out their own messages. For example, the cover of *Changing Bodies, Changing Lives: A Book for Teens on Sex and Relationships* includes three photos of teenagers. One of them is a "romantic" couple; the other two are group shots of males and females, not necessarily paired off, but obviously enjoying each other's company as they listen to music and talk. The effect is to downplay the topic of sex, making sexuality seem like a normal, pleasant part of growing up.

The dust jackets to Wardell B. Pomeroy's two books on the same subject provide a stark contrast and show how an entirely different message can be sent out. The first big difference is that Pomeroy's books are segregated. He has *Boys and Sex: A Revised Edition of the Classic Book on Adolescent Sexuality* and *Girls and Sex: A Revised Edition of the Classic Book on Adolescent Female Sexuality.* For his qualifications, he lists "Ph.D." and "co-author of the Kinsey Reports and author of *Girls and Sex/Boys and Sex.*" Ruth Bell identifies herself as co-author of *Our Bodies, Ourselves* and *Ourselves and Our Children* and gives as collaborators members of the Teen-book Project. Pomeroy tried to aim his book at both parents and their children, but the clinical sounding subtitle will do little to attract teenagers. If they should find the books in their home libraries, they might read them, but the boldface print, the blatant title, and the colors of the dust jackets (bright purple and orange) will practically insure that no self-conscious teenager is going to check these books out of a library, unless the librarian has been perceptive enough to provide a plain brown wrapper.

The fact that Pomeroy treats boys in a separate book from girls is itself a controversial issue. In no other area, except perhaps athletics, is there such purposeful separation between boys and girls. Starting in the fourth grade, girls are taken off to see their first movie on menstruation and boys are left in the room to be given a talk by the coach. Some people believe that this kind of separation is quite appropriate, and in fact, has advantages sort of like the check-and-balance system practiced by the separate branches of the federal government. However, others believe that since sex is something participated in by males and females together, they should be taught the same sets of rules. If they understood each other a bit better, perhaps men

◆ The effect of the different photos on the cover of *Changing Bodies, Changing Lives* is to make sexuality seem like a normal, pleasant part of growing up.

and women wouldn't have so much trouble communicating and establishing fulfilling lifelong relationships.

In the early and mid-1970s, several books came out focusing on venereal diseases, for example, Sol Gordon's *Facts about VD for Today's Youth* and Eric W. Johnson's *VD* with its cover message, "Don't get scared, get smart." Today in what we consider a healthy development, the topic of STD (sexually transmitted diseases) is more likely to be incorporated into overall treatments that cover emotional as well as physical aspects of sexual activity. Also, books such as James E. Lieberman and Ellen Peck's *Sex and Birth Control: A Guide for the Young* and Andrea Balis' *What Are You Using?* present information on disease prevention along with birth control.

Preventing pregnancy and being pregnant are as different as Mark Twain said the lightning bug was from lightning. Once a girl is pregnant, there are so many aspects of the matter to be considered that it takes a whole book—or even several—to satisfy her need to collect information before she is ready to ponder and make her own decision about her and her baby's future. A book that was chosen for the 1983 YASD Best Books for Young Adults list is Arlene Kramer Richards and Irene Willis' *What to Do If You or Someone You Know Is Under 18 and Pregnant*. This is definitely written for teenagers, although it isn't cloying or written-down. The authors say such things as "If you are able to afford real maternity clothes, one of the most useful items is a pair of maternity pants in a dark color." Then it goes on to give advice about getting hand-me-down clothes or buying a winter coat from a thrift shop since it will be worn only one season. Such common sense suggestions are surprising only when contrasted to those in more typical books for newly expectant mothers. They advise buying so many things that one suspects the publishers are more interested in boosting the economy than in launching a new life.

In Paula McGuire's *It Won't Happen to Me: Teenagers Talk about Pregnancy*, fifteen girls from an assortment of social levels and ethnic groups tell how their lives have been changed by unplanned pregnancies. Sean Gresh's *Becoming a Father* is a welcome balance to all the attention that goes to the mother. It presents information on childbirth methods, care of the newborn, and the emotional changes that fathers are likely to undergo.

The mother who is thinking of giving her baby up for adoption should have access to Laurie Wishard and William Wishard's *Adoption: The Grafted Tree*, which besides providing basic information includes state-by-state adoption laws. Young people planning to raise their child would profit from Linda McDonald's *Everything You Need to Know about Babies*, Jeanne Warren Lindsay's *Teens Parenting*, Tracy Hotchner's *Pregnancy and Childbirth: The Complete Guide for a New Life*, and Sol Gordon and Myra Wollin's *Parenting: A Guide for Young People*.

Maria Corsaro and Carole Korzeniowsky have written *A Woman's Guide to Safe Abortion* which promises to provide "Everything you need to know about tests, costs, procedures, facilities, physical and emotional complications, and birth control." The abortion issue is also discussed as part of several of the already mentioned books.

The sex-related topic that many young adults are hesitant even to read about is homosexuality. Morton Hunt, who wrote the well-received *Young Person's Guide to Love*, did a more controversial book when he wrote *Gay: What You Should Know about Homosexuality*. The whole area of homosexuality presents a difficult problem, made more so by the fact that there are not many books treating it. Even if there were, students would probably shy away from reading many of them. Peer pressure is strong and young people seem to have an underlying fear that homosexuality is contagious. This means that each book that is read takes on a disproportionate level of importance. Even nonfiction books supposedly presenting information in an objective manner cannot be totally free of bias.

This was illustrated by John Cunningham's criticism of Morton Hunt's book. Cunningham pointed out that although it is common for sex education books to have a conversational style using the second person pronoun "you," in this book Hunt consistently uses the third person pronoun "them," which communicates that he does not intend "to put the gay reader at ease or to suggest that the book might be directed to gays." Cunningham further criticized Hunt's book because its tone is so different from his books about heterosexuality:

◇ Hunt clearly deplores what he terms "queer gays"—those that are obvious and refuse to blend into the heterosexual landscape. Anything from a flick of the wrist to a bitchy mood might be enough to qualify for this group. Flaming faggots, nellie queens, bull dikes, drags, leather numbers, hustlers and Saturday night cruisers all qualify. According to Hunt, "straight gays" find these people very objectionable; his implicit message is that the reader should also.[11]

As a direct result of his dissatisfaction with Hunt's book, as well as with others on the topic, Cunningham worked with Frances Hanckel to write *A Way of Love, A Way of Life: A Young Person's Introduction to What It Means to Be Gay*. Some of the chapter titles give the flavor of the book: "Sticks and Stones: Understanding Names and Terms about Homosexuality," "How to Tell If You're Gay," "Feeling Bad about It; Feeling Good about It," "Sex Isn't All Good News," and "A Dozen Gay Lives." Hanckel and Cunningham's book solved some of the problems that Cunningham had with Hunt's book, but it undoubtedly created other problems for other readers. Other books recommended by David E. Wilson writing in a November 1984 *English Journal* article, "The Open Library: YA Books for Gay Teens" include the fictional *Annie on My Mind* by Nancy Garden, *Independence Day* by B. A. Ecker, and *Dance on My Grave* by Aidan Chambers. For nonfiction he recommended *Young, Gay and Proud* edited by Sasha Alyson, *Reflections of a Rock Lobster* by Aaron Fricke, and *One Teenager in Ten* edited by Ann Heron.

With fiction that treats sexuality it is important for adults to help young readers realize that only one person's story is being told. Sometimes these stories may be quite atypical, but young readers have very little real-life experience to use for background comparisons. It's not that we want everything to be as typical as possible. Surely that would be a deadly approach, but there is an obligation for adults who are providing books for young readers to provide a variety and to encourage the reading of accurate and well-balanced informative nonfiction. Again, the reader's purpose must be considered. If it is basic information that the reader wants, then nonfiction is far superior because it can present a wider range of information in a clear and unambiguous way. But if it is an understanding of the emotional and physical aspects of one particular relationship, an honest piece of fiction does a better job. The important thing for adults to remember is that they should provide both kinds in conjunction with a listening ear and a willingness to discuss questions.

Because the area of sex is such a sensitive and personal one, this is probably the one area most in need of open discussion and exchanges of ideas. Schools and libraries need to seek community help in developing policies. Family values must be respected, but honest and accurate information must also be available for those who are seeking it. Charting a course along this delicate line is more than any one individual should be expected to do. People need to get together to work out the philosophy and policy that best fits their particular situation. But this cannot be done in ignorance. The general public may get away with objecting to or endorsing ideas and books that they have never really explored or read, but a professional working with books is obligated to find and study the latest, most authentic information and to bring that information to those who are helping to shape policies and practices. It is important to realize that such policies and practices will differ from group to group and from person to person. The more you understand about such differences the better able you will be to participate in book selection, discussion, and sometimes, defense.

◆ ACTIVITIES ◆

1. At the 1983 American Library Association annual convention, Patty Campbell listed the following as her favorite writers of informative nonfiction for young adults: Jules Archer, Melvin Berger, Edward Dolan, James Forman, Robert Goldston, James Haskins, Margaret Hyde, Robert Liston, Robert Loeb, Alvin Silverstein. Find two books by one of these authors and skim them. Make notes on the books, paying special attention to those qualities which might have influenced Campbell to judge this author a particularly good one.

2. Select a subject that is of interest to young adults or that they might study in school such as teenagers and the law, solar energy, microcomputers, consumerism, a possible career, nuclear energy, or any current controversy. Prepare an annotated bibliography of relevant books. Ask teachers, librarians, and young adults for recommendations. Look through publishers' catalogues and read reviews and advertisements in *School Library Journal, English Journal, Booklist,* and the *New York Times Book Review.* Depending on your topic, you should probably also look at offerings for the general public since young adults read many informative books offered as adult titles. Browse through or skim as many of the books as you can find in libraries or bookstores.

3. Read a new journalism book and then one on a similar subject that is written just for communicating information. Write a short paper in which you compare the two. Which book is better for which purpose? What different techniques did the authors use? Are the differences more of degree or of kind?

4. What appeal do animal stories have for children? For young adults? For adults? How do these appeals change as readers grow older? Read two or three animal stories mentioned in this chapter. Which would you recommend to what age levels? Why? After your students have read one or two animal stories either recommended by you or found by them, talk with them about the appeal (or nonappeal) of the books and what other students might enjoy them.

5. Find and read (or skim) three informational books on the same subject, for example, sex education, mental health, how to be a photographer, planning for a career, or using a computer. Write a comparison of the three. How did tone differ? What about point of view? Reading level? Amount of information? Format and design? If you were a high school librarian and had only enough money to purchase one of them, which one would it be? Why?

◆ NOTES ◆

[1]Alleen Pace Nilsen, "The House That Alice Built: An Interview with the Author Who Brought You *Go Ask Alice*," *School Library Journal* 25 (October 1979): 109–12.

[2]Jean Fritz, *Homesick: My Own Story* (New York: Putnam's, 1982), p. 9.

[3]Milton Meltzer, "Where Do All the Prizes Go? The Case for Nonfiction," *Horn Book Magazine* 52 (February 1975): 17–23.

[4]Meltzer, p. 23.

[5]George A. Woods, Personal correspondence to Alleen Pace Nilsen (summer 1978).

[6]Jill Krementz, *How It Feels to Be Adopted* (New York: Knopf, 1982), p. 67.

[7]Krementz, pp. 103–4.

[8]James Kaufmann, "Vietnam War Recalled in the Words of the Soldiers who Fought There," *Christian Science Monitor,* July 1, 1981, p. 17.

[9]Peter G. Hammond, "Turning Off: The Abuse of Drug Information," *School Library Journal* 19 (April 1973): 17–21.

[10]Peter Mayle, *Where Did I Come From?* (Secaucus, NJ: Lyle Stuart, 1973), pp. 14, 16.

[11]John Cunningham, "Growing Up Gay Male," *Voice of Youth Advocates* 1 (June 1978): 11–16.

◆ TITLES MENTIONED IN CHAPTER 8 ◆

For information on the availability of paperback editions of these titles, please consult the most recent edition of *Paperbound Books in Print*, published annually by R. R. Bowker Company.

Informational Books/The New Journalism

Alcott, Louisa May. *Little Women*. 1868

Ali Muhammad and Richard Durham. *The Greatest: My Own Story*. Random House, 1975.

Anderson, Jervis. *This Was Harlem: A Cultural Portrait, 1900–1950*. Farrar, 1982.

Angelou, Maya. *I Know Why the Caged Bird Sings*. Random House, 1970.

Anonymous. *Go Ask Alice*. Prentice-Hall, 1971.

Archer, Jules. *Who's Running Your Life?: A Look at Young People's Rights*. Harcourt Brace Jovanovich, 1979.

Attenborough, David. *Life on Earth: A Natural History*. Little, Brown, 1980.

Augarten, Stan. *State of the Art: A Photographic History of the Integrated Circuit*. Tichnor and Fields, 1983.

Baker, Mark. *NAM*. Morrow, 1981.

Bell, Ruth. *Changing Bodies, Changing Lives: A Book for Teens on Sex and Relationships*. Random House, 1980.

Bell, Ruth and Leni Zeiger Wildflower. *Talking with Your Teenager: A Book for Parents*. Random House, 1983.

Berglund, Bjorn. *Noah's Ark Is Stranded: The Message of African Ecology*. Delacorte, 1976.

Blegvad, Erik. *Self-Portrait: Erik Blegvad*. Addison-Wesley, 1979.

Boston Women's Health Book Collective. *Our Bodies, Ourselves: A Book by and for Women*. Rev. ed. Simon and Schuster, 1976.

Boswell, James. *Life of Samuel Johnson*. 1791.

Brancato, Robin. *Blinded by the Light*. Knopf, 1978.

————. *Winning*. Knopf, 1977.

Brown, Claude. *Manchild in the Promised Land*. Macmillan, 1965.

Brown, Dee. *Bury My Heart at Wounded Knee: An Indian History of the American West*. Holt, Rinehart and Winston, 1971.

Bugliosi, Vincent and Curt Gentry. *Helter Skelter*. Norton, 1974.

Calder, Nigel. *The Comet Is Coming*. Viking, 1981.

Capote, Truman. *In Cold Blood*. Random House, 1966.

Castaneda, Carlos. *Journey to Ixtlan*. Simon and Schuster, 1973.

Chambers, S. Allen. *Discovering Historical America: Mid-Atlantic States*. E. P. Dutton, 1983.

Chernin, Kim. *In My Mother's House: A Daughter's Story*. Ticknor and Fields, 1983.

Cleaver, Eldridge. *Soul on Ice*. McGraw-Hill, 1968.

Coniffe, Pat. *The Computer Dictionary*. Scholastic, 1983.

Conner, Patrick. *People at Home*. Atheneum, 1982.

————. *People at Work*. Atheneum, 1982.

Conroy, Pat. *The Water Is Wide*. Houghton Mifflin, 1972.

Consumer Guide. *The User's Guide to Atari/Commodore/Texas Instruments/Timex-Sinclair*. Pocket Books, 1983.

Crichton, Michael. *The Andromeda Strain*. Knopf, 1969.

————. *Electronic Life: How to Think about Computers*. Knopf, 1983.

————. *The Great Train Robbery*. Knopf, 1975.

Davis, Daniel S. *Behind Barbed Wire: The Imprisonment of Japanese Americans during World War II*. E. P. Dutton, 1982.

Dillard, Annie. *Pilgrim at Tinker Creek*. Harper & Row, 1974.

Doctorow, E. L. *Ragtime*. Random House, 1975.

Ehringer, Robert. *Strike for Freedom: The Story of Lech Walesa and Polish Solidarity.* Dodd, Mead, 1982.

Elder, Lauren. *And I Alone Survived.* E. P. Dutton, 1978.

Epstein, Sam and Beryl Epstein. *Kids in Court: The ACLU Defends Their Rights.* Four Winds, 1983.

Eriksenn, Eric and Els Sincebaugh. *Adventures in Closeup Photography: Rediscovering Familiar Environments through Details.* Amphoto/Watson-Guptil, 1983.

Esper, George and the Associated Press. *The Eyewitness History of the Vietnam War 1961–1975.* Villard Books, 1983.

Fritz, Jean. *Homesick: My Own Story.* Putnam's, 1982.

Gleasner, Diana C. *Breakthrough: Women in Science.* Walker, 1983.

Glossbrenner, Alfred. *The Complete Handbook of Personal Computer Communications.* St. Martin's, 1983.

Glubok, Shirley. *The Art of the New American Nation.* Macmillan, 1972.

————. *The Art of the Old West.* Macmillan, 1971.

————. *The Art of Photography.* Macmillan, 1977.

————. *The Art of the Plains Indians.* Macmillan, 1975.

Goldin, Augusta. *Water: Too Much, Too Little, Too Polluted?* Harcourt Brace Jovanovich, 1983.

Goldston, Robert. *Sinister Touches: The Secret War against Hitler.* Dial, 1982.

Graham, Robin. *Dove.* Harper & Row, 1972.

Greenberg, Harvey R. *Hanging In: What You Should Know about Psychotherapy.* Four Winds, 1982.

Griffin, John H. *Black Like Me.* Houghton Mifflin, 1977.

Gross, Leonard. *The Last Jews in Berlin.* Simon and Schuster, 1982.

Haley, Alex. *Roots.* Doubleday, 1976.

Handlin, Oscar and Lilian Handlin. *A Restless People: Americans in Rebellion, 1770–1787.* Anchor, 1982.

Hansberry, Lorraine. *A Raisin in the Sun.* Random House, 1969.

Harris, Robert and Jeremy Paxman. *A Higher Form of Killing: The Secret Story of Chemical and Biological Warfare.* Hill and Wang, 1983.

Harris, Thomas. *I'm Okay, You're Okay.* Harper & Row, 1969.

Hayden, Torey. *Murphy's Boy.* Putnam's, 1983.

————. *One Child.* Putnam's, 1980.

Herriot, James. *All Creatures Great and Small.* St. Martin's, 1972.

Highwater, Jamake. *The Sun, He Dies.* Lippincott, 1980.

Hogben, Lancelot. *Mathematics for the Million: How to Master the Magic of Numbers.* Norton, 1983.

Horenstein, Henry and Eliot Tarlin. *Computerwise: An Accessible Guide to What Personal Computers Can Do for You.* Vintage, 1983.

Huser, Verne and R. Valentine Atkinson, *River Camping: Touring by Canoe, Raft, Kayak, and Dory.* Dial, 1981.

Hyde, Margaret O. *Computers That Think?: The Search for Artificial Intelligence.* Enslow Publishers, 1982.

————. *Cry Softly! The Story of Child Abuse.* Westminster, 1980.

————. *Is the Cat Dreaming Your Dream?* McGraw-Hill, 1980.

Hyman, Trina Schart. *Self-Portrait: Trina Schart Hyman.* Addison-Wesley,1981.

Ipswitch, Elaine. *Scott Was Here.* Delacorte, 1979.

Jaspersohn, William. *Magazine: Behind the Scenes at Sports Illustrated.* Little, Brown, 1983.

Judson, Horace Freeland. *The Search for Solutions.* Holt, Rinehart and Winston, 1980.

Kaku, Michio and Jennifer Trainer. *Nuclear Power: Both Sides.* Norton, 1983.

Kazimiroff, Theodore. *The Last Algonquin.* Walker, 1982.

Kerr, M. E. *Me, Me, Me, Me, Me, Not a Novel.* Harper & Row, 1983.

Kersuady, Francois. *Churchill and DeGaulle.* Atheneum, 1983.

Krementz, Jill. *How It Feels to Be Adopted.* Knopf, 1982.

————. *How It Feels When a Parent Dies.* Knopf, 1981.

Lawson, Don. *The United States in the Vietnam War.* Crowell, 1981.

Leitner, Isabella. *Fragments of Isabella: A Memoir of Auschwitz.* Crowell, 1978.

Lewinski, Jorge. *The Camera at War: A History of War Photography from 1948 to the Present Day.* Simon and Schuster, 1980.

Lopez, Barry Holstun. *Of Wolves and Men.* Scribner's, 1978.

Lubin, Leonard. *The Elegant Beast.* Viking, 1981.

Lund, Doris. *Eric.* Harper & Row, 1974.

Maas, Peter, *Serpico.* Viking, 1973.

Macaulay, David. *Unbuilding.* Houghton Mifflin, 1980.

Matthiessen, Peter, *The Tree Where Man Was Born.* World pbk, 1983.

McClelland, Doug. *Hollywood on Ronald Reagan: Friends and Enemies Discuss Our President, the Actor.* Faber and Faber, 1983.

McCracken, Mary. *A Circle of Children.* Lippincott, 1973.

———. *City Kid.* Little, Brown, 1981.

———. *Lovey.* Little, Brown, 1981.

McHenry, Robert. *Famous American Women: A Biographical Dictionary from Colonial Times to Present.* Dover, 1983.

Meltzer, Milton. *The Jewish Americans: A History in Their Own Words.* Crowell, 1982.

———. *All Times, All Peoples: A World History of Slavery.* Harper & Row, 1980.

———. *Never to Forget: The Jews of the Holocaust.* Harper & Row, 1976.

———. *The Terrorists.* Harper & Row, 1983.

Momaday, N. Scott. *The Way to Rainy Mountain.* University of New Mexico Press, 1976.

Moore, Patrick. *The Unfolding Universe.* Crown, 1982.

Moser, Lida. *Career Photography: How to Be a Success as a Professional Photographer.* Prentice-Hall, 1983.

Munthe, Nelly. *Meet Matisse.* Little, Brown, 1983.

Nicholls, Peter. *The Science in Science Fiction.* Knopf, 1983.

O'Neill, Cherry Boone. *Starving for Attention.* Continuum, 1982.

Orkin, Ruth. *More Pictures from My Window.* Rizzoli, 1983.

Page, Tim. *Tim Page's Nam.* Knopf, 1983.

Paine, Tom. "Common Sense," in *The Writings of Thomas Paine,* 1792.

Patterson, Francine and Eugene Linden. *The Education of Koko.* Holt, Rinehart and Winston, 1981.

Peavy, Linda and Ursula Smith. *Women Who Changed Things: Nine Lives that Made a Difference.* Scribner's, 1983.

Peck, Richard. *Are You in the House Alone?* Viking, 1976.

Phillips, John. *A Will to Survive: Israel: The Faces of Terror 1948, The Faces of Hope Today.* Dial, 1977.

Powers, John. *The Last Catholic in America.* Bentley, 1981.

Pringle, Laurence. *Lives at Stake: the Science and Politics of Environmental Health.* Macmillan, 1980.

———. *Wolfman: Exploring the World of Wolves.* Scribner's, 1983.

Putterman, Jaydie and Rosalynde LeSur. *Police.* Holt, Rinehart and Winston, 1983.

Read, Piers Paul. *Alive.* Lippincott, 1974.

Reiss, David S. *M*A*S*H: The Exclusive Inside Story of TV's Most Popular Show.* Bobbs, Merrill, 1983.

Richards, Arlene Kramer and Irene Willis. *What to Do if You or Someone You Know Is under 18 and Pregnant.* Lothrop, 1983.

Robertson, Dougal. *Survive the Savage Sea.* G. K. Hall, 1974.

Roth, Charles E. *Then There Were None.* Addison-Wesley, 1977.

Rubenstein, Charlotte Streifer. *American Women Artists: From Early Indian Times to the Present.* G. K. Hall, 1982.

Ryden, Hope. *God's Dog.* Viking, 1979.

Sagan, Carl. *Cosmos.* Random House, 1983.

Sandler, Martin W. *The Story of American Photography: An Illustrated History for Young People.* Little, Brown, 1979.

Santoli, Al. *Everything We Had: An Oral History of the Vietnam War by Thirty-three Soldiers Who Fought It.* Random House, 1981.

Schlissel, Lillian. *Women's Diaries of the Westward Journey.* Schocken Books, 1983.

Schulke, Flip. *Martin Luther King, Jr.: A Documentary.* Norton, 1976.

Selden, Bernice. *The Mill Girls.* Atheneum, 1983.

Shapiro, Mary. *A Picture History of the Brooklyn Bridge: With 167 Prints and Photographs.* Dover, 1983.

Sieger, Beatrice. *An Eye on the World: Margaret Bourke-White, Photographer.* Warne, 1980.

Simon, Nissa. *Don't Worry, You're Normal: A Teenager's Guide to Self-Health.* Crowell, 1982.

Sparks, Beatrice. *Jay's Journal.* Times Books, 1979.

————. *Voices.* Times Books, 1978.

Spencer, Donald. *Problem Solving with BASIC.* Scribner's, 1983.

Stachow, Hasso G. *If This Be Glory.* Doubleday, 1982.

Steele, Guy L. *The Hacker's Dictionary: A Guide to the Computer Underworld.* Harper & Row, pbk., 1983.

Stratton, Joanna L. *Pioneer Women: Voices from the Kansas Frontier.* Simon and Schuster, 1981.

Stuart, Colin. *Shoot an Arrow to Stop the Wind.* Dial, 1969.

Switzer, Ellen. *Our Urban Planet.* Atheneum, 1980.

Taylor, A. J. P. *The Origins of the Second World War.* Atheneum, 1983.

Taylor, Theodore. *Battle in the Arctic Seas.* Harper & Row, 1976.

Terkel, Studs. *Working.* Pantheon, 1974.

Thoreau, Henry David. *Walden.* 1854.

Toffler, Alvin. *Future Shock.* Random House, 1970.

Wade, Graham. *The Shape of Music: An Introduction to Form in Classical Music.* Allison and Busby, 1981.

Wallace, David Rains. *The Dark Range: A Naturalist's Night Notebook.* Sierra, 1978.

————. *Idle Weeds: The Life of a Sandstone Ridge.* Sierra, 1980.

Wallechinsky, David. *The Complete Book of the Olympics.* Viking, 1984.

Waterfield, Giles. *Faces.* Atheneum, 1982.

West, Beverly H. et al., eds., *The Prentice-Hall Encyclopedia of Mathematics.* Prentice-Hall, 1982.

Wigginton, Eliot, ed. *The Foxfire Book.* Doubleday, 1972.

Williams, Margery. *The Velveteen Rabbit.* Doubleday, 1958. Written in 1922.

Wolfe, Tom. *The Right Stuff.* Farrar, Straus and Giroux, 1979.

Yeager, Robert. *Seasons of Shame: The New Violence in Sports.* McGraw-Hill, 1979.

Young, Jean. *The Woodstock Craftsman's Manual.* Praeger, 1972.

Zemach, Margot. *Self-Portrait: Margot Zemach.* Addison-Wesley, 1978.

Reading for Entertainment

Abel, Bob and Mike Valenti. *Sports Quotes.* Facts on File, 1983.

Agel, Jerome. *America at Random: Questions and Answers.* Arbor House, 1983.

Andrews, Bart. *TV Picture Quiz Book.* New American Library, 1979.

Bane, Michael. *White Boy Singin' the Blues: The Black Roots of White Rock.* Penguin, 1982.

Bartlett, Michael and Bob Gillen. *The Tennis Book.* Arbor House, 1983.

Bentley, Toni. *Winter Season: A Dancer's Journal.* Random House, 1982.

Brown, Dee. *Hear That Lonesome Whistle Blow: Railroads in the West.* Holt, Rinehart and Winston, 1977.

————. *Lonesome Whistle: The Story of the First Transcontinental Railroad.* Holt, Rinehart and Winston, 1980.

Coffey, Wayne. *All-Pro's Greatest Football Players.* Scholastic, 1983.

Delear, Frank J. *Famous First Flights Across the Atlantic.* Dodd, Mead, 1979.

Froud, Brian. *The World of the Dark Crystal.* Knopf, 1982.

Goddard, Peter. *David Bowie: The Man Who Came Out of the Cool.* Beaufort Books, 1983.

————. *The Who: The Farewell Tour.* Beaufort Books, 1983.

Griffiths, Paul. *A Guide to Electronic Music.* Thomas and Hudson, distributed by Norton, 1981.

Guiley, Rosemary. *Lovelines.* Facts on File, 1983.

Haskins, James. *Black Theater in America.* Crowell, 1982.

Hogarth, Peter and Val Clery. *Dragons.* Viking, 1979.

Huygen, Wil and Rien Poorevliet. *Gnomes.* Abrams, 1977.

Jaffee, Al. *The Ghoulish Book of Weird Records.* New American Library, 1979.

Jordan, Teresa. *Cowgirls: Women of the American West.* Doubleday, 1982.

Keane, John. *Sherlock Bones: Tracer of Missing Pets.* Lippincott, 1979.

Leuthner, Stuart. *The Railroaders.* Random House, 1983.

Liston, Robert A. *The Great Teams: Why They Win All the Time.* Doubleday, 1979.

Lubin, Leonard. *The Elegant Beast.* Viking, 1981.

Macaulay, David. *Cathedral.* Houghton Mifflin, 1973.

————. *Mill.* Houghton Mifflin, 1983.

————. *Pyramid.* Houghton Mifflin, 1975.

————. *Unbuilding.* Houghton Mifflin, 1980.

————. *Underground.* Houghton Mifflin, 1976.

Marsh, Dave and John Swenson, eds. *The Rolling Stone Record Guide.* Random House, 1980.

McWhirter, Norris and Ross McWhirter. *Guinness Book of Amazing Achievements.* Sterling, 1975.

————. *Guinness Book of World Records.* Bantam, 1981.

Neely, William and John S. F. McCormick, Jr. *505 Automobile Questions Your Friends Can't Answer.* Walker, 1984.

Palmer, Tony. *All You Need Is Love: The Story of Popular Music.* Penguin, 1977.

Pizer, Vernon. *Eat the Grapes Downward: An Uninhibited Romp Through the Surprising World of Food.* Dodd, Mead, 1983.

Potter, Carole. *Knock on Wood.* Beaufort, 1983.

Riger, Robert. *The Athlete.* Simon and Schuster, 1980.

Ripley, Robert. *Believe It or Not.* Warner, 1976.

The Rolling Stone. *The Rolling Stone Illustrated History of Rock and Roll.* Random House, 1976.

Rovin, Jeff. *Count Dracula's Vampire Quiz Book.* New American Library, 1979.

Schwartz, Alvin. *Cross Your Fingers, Spit in Your Hat: Superstitions and Other Beliefs.* Harper & Row, 1974.

————. *Flapdoodle: Pure Nonsense from American Folklore.* Harper & Row, 1980.

————. *Kickle Snifters and Other Fearsome Critters Collected from American Folklore.* Harper & Row, 1976.

————. *Scary Stories to Tell in the Dark.* Harper & Row, 1981.

————. *Tomfoolery: Trickery and Foolery with Words Collected from American Folklore.* Harper & Row, 1973.

————. *Unriddling: All Sorts of Riddles to Puzzle Your Guessery.* Lippincott, 1983.

Sutton, Caroline. *How Do They Do That?: Wonders of the Modern World Explained.* Morrow, 1981.

————. *How Did They Do That?: Wonders of the Far and Recent Past Explained.* Morrow, 1984.

Switzer, Ellen. *Dancers! Horizons in American Dance.* Atheneum, 1982.

Thorn, John, ed. *The Armchair Aviator.* Scribner's, 1983.

Trudeau, Gary. *Doonesbury's Greatest Hits.* Holt, Rinehart and Winston, 1978.

Uslan, Michael and Bruce Solomon. *Pow! Zap! Wham! Comic Book Trivia Quiz.* Morrow, 1977.

Wallechinsky, David and Irving Wallace. *The People's Almanac.* Doubleday, 1975.

————. *The People's Almanac II.* Morrow, 1978.

Wallechinsky, David, Irving Wallace, and Amy Wallace. *The Book of Lists.* Morrow, 1977.

The World Almanac. *Book of the Strange.* New American Library, 1982.

Animal Books

Adams, Richard. *The Plague Dogs.* Knopf, 1978.

Adamson, Joy. *Born Free: A Lioness in Two Worlds.* Pantheon, 1960.

————. *Forever Free.* Harcourt Brace Jovanovich, 1963.

————. *Living Free.* Harcourt Brace Jovanovich, 1961.

————. *Pippa's Challenge.* Harcourt Brace Jovanovich, 1972.

————. *Queen of Shaba: The Story of an African Leopard.* Harcourt Brace Jovanovich, 1980.

————. *The Searching Spirit.* Harcourt Brace Jovanovich, 1979.

————. *The Spotted Sphinx.* Harcourt Brace Jovanovich, 1969.

Aldridge, James. *The Marvelous Mongolian.* Little, Brown, 1974.

Attenborough, David. *The Zoo Quest Expeditions.* Penguin, 1982.

Bagnold, Enid. *National Velvet.* Morrow, 1935.

Bethancourt, T. Ernesto. *The Dog Days of Arthur Cane.* Holiday House, 1976.

Burnford, Sheila. *Bel Ria.* Little, Brown, 1975.

————. *The Incredible Journey*. Little, Brown, 1961.

Butterworth, W. E. *A Member of the Family*. Four Winds, 1983.

Campbell, Sheldon. *Lifeboats to Ararat*. Harper & Row, 1979.

Camuti, Louis J. and Marilyn and Haskel Frankel. *All My Patients Are under the Bed: Memories of a Cat Doctor*. Simon and Schuster, 1980.

Caras, Roger. *The Custer Wolf*. Holt, Rinehart and Winston, 1979.

Carter, Brian. *A Black Fox Running*. St. Martin's, 1982.

Craighead, Frank C., Jr. *Track of the Grizzly*. Sierra Club, 1979.

Donovan, John. *Family*. Harper & Row, 1976.

Durrell, Gerald. *The Amateur Naturalist*. Knopf, 1983.

————. *A Bevy of Beasts*. Simon and Schuster, 1973.

————. *The Mockery Bird*. Simon and Schuster, 1982.

Eckert, Allan W. *Incident at Hawk's Hill*. Little, Brown, 1971.

Embery, Joan. *My Wild World*. Delacorte, 1980.

Feeley, Pat. *Best Friend*. E. P. Dutton, 1977.

Fox, Michael W. *The Soul of the Wolf*. Little, Brown, 1980.

Freddi, Chris. *Pork and Others*. Knopf, 1981.

Gipson, Fred. *Old Yeller*. Harper & Row, 1956.

Godden, Rumer. *The Dark Horse*. Viking, 1981.

Herriot, James. *All Creatures Great and Small*. St. Martin's, 1972.

————. *All Things Bright and Beautiful*. St. Martin's, 1974.

————. *All Things Wise and Wonderful*. St. Martin's, 1977.

————. *The Lord God Made Them All*. St. Martin's, 1981.

Kilgore, Kathleen. *The Wolfman of Beacon Hill*. Little, Brown, 1982.

Lawrence, R. D. *The Ghost Walker*. Holt, Rinehart, and Winston, 1983.

————. *The North Runner*. Holt, Rinehart and Winston, 1979.

————. *Secret of the Wolves*. Holt, Rinehart, and Winston, 1980.

————. *Voyage of the Stella*. Holt, Rinehart, and Winston, 1982.

————. *The Zoo that Never Was*. Holt, Rinehart and Winston, 1981.

Levitin, Sonia. *Reigning Cats and Dogs*. Atheneum, 1978.

Lopez, Barry. *Of Wolves and Men*. Scribner's, 1978.

Morris, Desmond. *Animal Days*. Morrow, 1980.

Mowat, Farley. *The Dog Who Wouldn't Be*. Little, Brown, 1957.

————. *Never Cry Wolf*. Little, Brown, 1963.

————. *A Whale for the Killing*. Little, Brown, 1972.

Narayan, R. K. *A Tiger for Malgudi*. Viking, 1983.

North, Sterling. *Rascal: A Memoir of a Better Era*. E. P. Dutton, 1963.

Rawls, Wilson. *Where the Red Fern Grows*. Doubleday, 1961.

Sielman, Heinz. *Wilderness Expedition*. Franklin Watts, 1981.

Stranger, Joyce. *The Fox at Drummer's Darkness*. Farrar, Straus & Giroux, 1977.

Street, James. *Good-bye, My Lady*. Lippincott, 1954.

Sullivan, Faith. *Watch Dog*. McGraw-Hill, 1982.

Taylor, David. *Going Wild: Adventures of a Zoo Vet*. Stein and Day, 1981.

————. *Next Panda, Please! Further Adventures of a Wildlife Vet*. Lippincott, 1983.

————. *Zoo Vet: Adventures of a Wild Animal Doctor*. Lippincott, 1977.

Troyepolsky, Gavriil. *Beem*. Harper & Row, 1978.

Yates, Elizabeth. *The Seventh One*. Walker, 1978.

How-To Books

Alth, Max. *All About Motorcycles: Selection, Care, Repair, and Safety*. Hawthorne, 1975.

Byrne, Robert. *Treasury of Trick Shots in Pool and Billiards*. Harcourt Brace Jovanovich, 1983.

Coombs, Charles. *Be A Winner in (Tennis, Basketball, etc.)*. Morrow, 1973–1982.

Costello, Elaine. *Signing: How to Speak with Your Hands*. Bantam, 1983.

Dolan, Edward F. Jr. *Calling the Play: A Beginner's Guide to Amateur Sports Officiating*. Atheneum, 1982.

————. *The Complete Beginner's Guide to Gymnastics*. Doubleday, 1980.

Durrell, Gerald and Lee Durrell. *The Amateur Naturalist*. Knopf, 1983.

Engel, Lyle Kenyon. *The Complete Motorcycle Book*. Four Winds Press, 1974.

Fischler, Stan and Shirley Fischler. *Everybody's Hockey Book*. Scribner's, 1983.

Fixx, James. *The Complete Book of Running*. Random House, 1977.

———. *Jackpot*. Random House, 1982.

Gardner, John. *The Art of Fiction: Notes on Craft for Young Writers*. Knopf, 1984.

Horwitz, Elinor Lander. *Contemporary American Folk Artists*. Harper & Row, 1975.

Lieberman, Nancy with Myrna and Harvey Frommer. *Basketball My Way*. Scribner's, 1982.

Neil, Randy. *The Official Pompon Girl's Handbook*. St. Martin's, 1983.

Petkevich, John Misha. *The Skater's Handbook*. Scribner's, 1984.

Rutherford, Don. *International Rugby*. David and Charles, 1983.

Schiffler, Don and Lud Duroska. *Football Rules in Pictures*. Putnam's, 1983.

Schwarzenegger, Arnold. *Arnold: The Education of a Bodybuilder*. Simon and Schuster, 1977.

Wigginton, Eliot, ed. *The Foxfire Book*. Doubleday, 1972.

Young, Jean. *Woodstock Craftsman's Manual*. Praeger, 1972.

Managing One's Life: Physical and Mental Health, Careers, and Money

Abramovitz, Anita. *People and Spaces: A View of History Through Architecture*. Viking, 1979.

Anonymous. *Go Ask Alice*. Prentice-Hall, 1971.

Bell, Ruth and Leni Zeiger Wildflower. *Talking with Your Teenager: A Book for Parents*. Random House, 1983.

Brody, Jane. *The New York Times Personal Guide to Health*. Avon, 1983.

Childress, Alice. *A Hero Ain't Nothin' But a Sandwich*. Coward, 1973.

Cole, Sheila. *Working Kids on Working*. Lothrop, Lee and Shepard, 1980.

Craig, James. *Graphic Design Career Guide*. Watson-Guptil, 1983.

Denlinger, Ken and Len Shapiro. *Athletes for Sale*. Crowell, 1975.

Eagan, Andrea Boroff. *Why Am I So Miserable If These Are the Best Years of My Life*. Harcourt Brace Jovanovich, 1976.

Ferazani, Larry. *Rescue Squad*. Morrow, 1974.

Fiske, Edward. *Selective Guide to College*. Times Books, 1983.

Fitzgibbon, Dan. *All about Your Money*. Atheneum, 1984.

Fonda, Jane. *Jane Fonda's Workout Book*. Simon and Schuster, 1981.

Fretz, Sada. *Going Vegetarian: A Guide for Teenagers*. Morrow, 1983.

Fritschle, Linda de Wolfe and Susan Rudnick. *Pocket Reference to Health Disorders*. Littlefield, Adams, 1983.

Gardner, Richard. *A Boys' and Girls' Book about Divorce*. Bantam, 1971.

Getzoff, Ann and Carolyn McClenahan. *Stepkids: A Survival Guide for Teenagers in Stepfamilies*. Walker, 1984.

Gifford, Frank. *Gifford on Courage*. M. Evans, 1976.

Graham, Lawrence. *Conquering College Life: How to Be a Winner in College*. Pocket Books, 1983.

Harris, Janet. *Thursday's Daughters: The Story of Women Working in America*. Harper & Row, 1977.

Hyde, Margaret O. *Mind Drugs*. McGraw-Hill, 1981.

Jones, Alan and Keith Botsford. *Driving Ambition: A Bitingly Honest Look inside the World of Grand Prix Motor Racing by the 1980 Formula One World Champion Alan Jones*. Atheneum, 1981.

Kerr, M. E. *Dinky Hocker Shoots Smack*. Harper & Row, 1972.

Klein, Kenneth. *Getting Better: A Medical Student's Story*. Little, Brown, 1981.

Maas, Peter. *Serpico*. Viking, 1973.

Mandel, Ruth. *In the Running: The New Woman Candidate*. Beacon, 1983.

McCoy, Kathy. *The Teenager Body Book*. Wallaby, 1979.

———. *The Teenage Survival Guide*. Simon and Schuster, 1981.

Meyer, Carolyn. *People Who Make Things: How American Craftsmen Live and Work*. Atheneum, 1975.

Miklowitz, Gloria D. and Madeleine Yates. *The Young Tycoons: Ten Success Stories*. Harcourt Brace Jovanovich, 1981.

Millman, Marcia. *Such a Pretty Face: Being Fat in America.* Norton, 1980.

Mirkin, Gabe, M.D. and Marshall Hoffman. *Sports Medicine Book.* Little, Brown, 1978.

Muller, Peter. *The Fast Track to the Top Jobs in Computer Careers.* Putnam's, 1983.

————. *The Fast Track to the Top Jobs in Engineering Careers.* Putnam's, 1983.

Nilsson, Lennart. *Behold Man.* Little, Brown, 1974.

————. *A Child Is Born.* La Leche, 1983.

Peterson, Lorraine. *If God Loves Me Why Can't I Get My Locker Open.* Bethany House, 1980.

Pirsig, Robert M. *Zen and the Art of Motorcycle Maintenance: An Inquiry into Values.* Morrow, 1974.

Porter, Sylvia. *Your Own Money.* Avon, 1983.

Pray, Lawrence M. *Journey of a Diabetic.* Simon and Schuster, 1983.

Rabinowitz, Peter MacGarr. *Talking Medicine: America's Doctors Tell Their Stories.* New American Library, 1983.

Rofes, Eric, ed. *The Kids' Book of Divorce: By, For, and About Kids.* Random House, 1982.

Rosenberg, Richard and John D. Kelly. *Lovejoy's Preparation for the SAT.* Simon and Schuster, 1983.

Royce, Helane. *Sportshape: Body Conditioning for Women and Men from the Daily Jogger to the Weekend Athlete.* Arbor House, 1983.

Seixas, Judith S. *Living with a Parent Who Drinks Too Much.* Greenwillow, 1979.

Shanaman, Fred with Anita Malnig. *The First Official Money Making Book for Kids.* Bantam, 1983.

Skurzynski, Gloria. *Safeguarding the Land: Women at Work in Parks, Forests, and Rangelands.* Harcourt Brace Jovanovich, 1981.

Smith, Dennis. *Report from Engine Co. 82.* Dutton, 1972.

Terkel, Studs. *Working: People Talk about What They Do All Day and How They Feel about What They Do.* Pantheon, 1974.

Thompson, Thomas. *Richie.* Saturday Review Press, 1973.

Vedral, Joyce L. *I Dare You: How to Get What You Want out of Life, A Guide for Teenagers.* Holt, Rinehart and Winston, 1983.

Weil, Andrew and Winifred Rosen. *Chocolate to Morphine: Understanding Mind-Active Drugs.* Houghton Mifflin, 1983.

Zizmor, Jonathan and Diane English. *The Doctor's Do-It-Yourself Guide to Clearer Skin.* Lippincott, 1980.

Sex Education

Alyson, Sasha, ed. *Young, Gay and Proud.* Alyson Publications, 1980.

Balis, Andrea. *What Are You Using?* Doubleday, 1981.

Bell, Ruth. *Changing Bodies, Changing Lives.* Random House, 1980.

Boston Women's Health Book Collective. *Our Bodies, Ourselves,* rev. ed. Simon and Schuster, 1976.

————. *Ourselves and Our Children: A Book by and for Parents.* Random House, 1978.

Carrera, Michael. *Sex: The Facts, The Acts and Your Feelings.* Crown, 1981.

Chambers, Aidan. *Dance on My Grave.* Harper & Row, 1982.

Comfort, Alex and Jane Comfort. *The Facts of Love: Living, Loving, and Growing Up.* Crown, 1979.

Corsaro, Maria and Carole Korzeniowsky. *A Woman's Guide to Safe Abortion.* Holt, Rinehart and Winston, 1983.

Cunningham, John and Frances Hanckel. *A Way of Love, A Way of Life: A Young Person's Introduction to What It Means to Be Gay.* Lothrop, Lee and Shepard, 1979.

Ecker, B. A. *Independence Day.* Avon, 1983.

Fricke, Aaron. *Reflections of a Rock Lobster.* Alyson Publications, 1981.

Garden, Nancy. *Annie on My Mind.* Farrar, Straus & Giroux, 1982.

Gordon, Sol. *Facts about VD for Today's Youth.* John Day, 1973.

Gordon, Sol and Roger Conant. *You! The Teenage Survival Book.* Times Books, 1981.

Gordon, Sol and Myra Wollin. *Parenting: A Guide for Young People.* Oxford Press, 1975.

Gresh, Sean. *Becoming a Father.* New Century, 1980.

Heron, Ann, ed. *One Teenager in Ten.* Alyson Publications, 1983.

Hotchner, Tracy. *Pregnancy and Childbirth: The Complete Guide for a New Life.* Avon, 1979.

Hunt, Morton. *Gay: What You Should Know about Homosexuality*. Farrar, Straus & Giroux, 1977.

————. *Young Person's Guide to Love*. Farrar, Straus & Giroux, 1975.

"J." *The Sensuous Woman*. Lyle Stuart, 1970.

Johnson, Eric W. *Love and Sex in Plain Language*. Bantam, 1979.

————. *Sex: Telling It Straight*. Harper & Row, 1979.

————. *VD*. Lippincott, 1973.

Kelly, Gary F. *Learning about Sex: The Contemporary Guide for Young Adults*. Barron's Educational Series, 1978.

Knowles, John. *A Separate Peace*. Macmillan, 1960.

Lieberman, James E. and Ellen Peck. *Sex and Birth Control: A Guide for the Young*. Harper & Row, 1981.

Lindsay, Jeanne Warren. *Teens Parenting*. Morning Glory Press, 1981.

Madaras, Lynda. *What's Happening to My Body? A Growing Up Guide for Mothers and Daughters*. Newmarket, 1983.

Mayle, Peter. *What's Happening to Me?* Lyle Stuart, 1975.

————. *Where Did I Come From?* Lyle Stuart, 1973.

————. *Will I Like It?* Corwin, 1977.

McDonald, Linda. *Everything You Need to Know about Babies*. Oaklawn Press, 1978.

McGuire, Paula. *It Won't Happen to Me: Teenagers Talk about Pregnancy*. Delacorte, 1983.

Pomeroy, Wardell B. *Boys and Sex: A Revised Edition of the Classic Book on Adolescent Sexuality*. Delacorte, 1981.

————. *Girls and Sex: A Revised Edition of the Classic Book on Adolescent Female Sexuality*. Delacorte, 1981.

Richards, Arlene Kramer. *What to Do If You or Someone You Know Is Under 18 and Pregnant*. Lothrop, Lee and Shepard, 1983.

Steinbeck, John. *The Pearl*. Viking, 1947.

Wishard, Laurie and William Wishard. *Adoption: The Grafted Tree*. Cragmont, 1980.

POETRY, DRAMA, AND HUMOR

◈

OF LINES AND LAUGHS

The poetry, drama, and humor that young adults enjoy belongs less exclusively to them than do their reading choices in other genres. For example, when teenagers go to movies, the audience usually includes some children and many adults. And when teenagers watch television with their families, they often find themselves laughing at the same time that their parents laugh. The lyrics of popular songs, which are one form of poetry, are sung by people from ages 8 to 80, and when we examined the card catalogues of three different libraries to see how the books on the Honor Sampling were purchased and shelved, the only book we found in three different areas of the same library—children's, young adult, and adult—was a poetry collection, *Reflections on a Gift of Watermelon Pickle*.

Perhaps one of the reasons that these three genres tend to transcend age division is that they are social. Rather than being enjoyed in solitude as is a good mystery or a sad problem novel, poetry is better when it's read aloud—note the popularity of poetry readings. With humor, normal people laugh more when they are with others than they do when they are alone. And when someone is watching a dramatic presentation it's noticeably different to be part of a large, enthusiastic audience than to be by oneself in a car at a drive-in theater or home alone with the television set. It's because radio and television producers realize the social nature of both drama and humor that they arrange for studio audiences and sometimes dub in laughter and applause.

◇ POETRY

If poets are as honorable as Humpty Dumpty, who explained to Alice in *Through the Looking Glass*, "When I make a word do a lot of work like that, I always pay it extra," then they too will pay words extra because of the demands they place on them. Poets use words not only for their literal meanings, but also for figurative meanings, and they select and place them in their poems according to their sounds and the patterns that they make.

Almost everything we've said about literature in general could also be said about poetry. Poets use the same literary devices discussed in Chapter 2, only they do it more succinctly. One of the characteristics of poetry is its compactness. Poets do with words something similar to what manufacturers do with dehydrated food. They shrink bulky thoughts down to packageable sizes which they expect consumers to fluff back up. With dried food the consumer usually adds water. With poetry, the consumers have to add their own thoughts, ideas, memories, and images. This is why reading poetry is harder work than reading prose, but it can also be more rewarding because the reader is more involved.

Readers' appreciation for poetry develops in much the same way as their appreciation for prose. They begin with an unconscious delight in sounds— the repetition and rhythm of nursery rhymes, songs, and television commercials. Then they go on to the fun of riddles, puns, playground chants, and autograph rhymes. Researchers into child language development have found that many times children do not understand the dual meanings of the words that are keys to particular jokes or riddles, yet they take pleasure in hearing themselves recite joke patterns, and then when they learn enough about the world to catch onto the double meanings of what they are saying, their pleasure is increased.

In a study where children were asked to select from a long list those words that went well together, the younger children—those in the primary grades—matched *monsoon*, with *baboon* and *cocoon*. In contrast, the older children used meaning as their basis for selection. To go with *cocoon*, they chose the words *moth* and *butterfly*. This doesn't mean that the sounds of words were no longer important; it simply means that as the children matured and knew more about the world they could rely on more than sound.

Something similar can be observed in children's appreciation of poetry. Although it may be the sounds of the nursery rhymes which first appeal to them, very soon they get involved in such simple plots as those found in "This Little Piggie Went to Market," "Ring Around the Rosie," and "Pat-a-Cake, Pat-a-Cake." By the time children are in the middle grades, their favorite poems are those that tell stories, for example Robert Browning's "The Pied Piper of Hamelin," Henry Wadsworth Longfellow's "Hiawatha's Childhood" and "The Midnight Ride of Paul Revere," Robert Service's "The Cremation of Sam McGee," Alfred Noyes' "The Highwayman," Ernest L. Thayer's "Casey at the Bat," James Whitcomb Riley's "The Gobble-Uns'll Get You If You Don't Watch Out," and Edgar Allan Poe's "The Raven."

The next stage in development is taking pleasure in recognizing a kinship with a poet, finding someone who expresses a feeling or makes an observation that the reader has come close to but hasn't quite been able to put into words. Much of the "Pop" poetry that English teachers consider trite or overdone is appreciated by young readers in this stage. For example, a creative writing teacher criticized a student-written poem as being overly sentimental. She wrote on the paper, "This sounds like Rod McKuen." The student was thrilled at being compared to McKuen. The teacher didn't have the heart to explain that she had not intended the remark as a compliment.

Progressing from this stage, readers begin to identify with the poet as a writer. They understand and appreciate the skill with which the poet has achieved the desired effect. This understanding brings extra pleasure which is why English teachers are interested in helping students arrive at this level of poetic appreciation, but the teacher who tries to get there too fast runs the risk of leaving students behind.

Poet Eve Merriam believes that something like this has happened to most of the students who are turned off to poetry. They were made to feel dumb because they didn't catch onto every nuance of meaning or sound that their teacher saw, hence the experience was a negative one and they don't wish to repeat it. But fortunately, more teachers are realizing the damage that can be done by too early and too intensive a concentration on the "literary" aspects of poetry. They are providing students with a variety of poems and encouraging them to read first for pleasure and secondarily for literary analysis. They let students start where they are in their appreciation of poetry, whether it's with the humorous poems of Shel Silverstein in his *Where the Sidewalk Ends* and *The Light in the Attic*, the religious poems selected by Nancy Larrick in her *Tambourines! Tambourines to Glory! Prayers and Poems*, the wordplay poems of Eve Merriam in her *Rainbow Writing* and *Out Loud*, the almost militant poems in Maya Angelou's *And Still I Rise*, the almost classic poems in Edna St. Vincent Millay's *Poems Selected for Young People*, the "poetry of open space" selected by Nancy Larrick for her *Room for Me and a Mountain Lion*, or the contemporary poems selected by Richard Peck for his two collections *Sounds and Silences: Poetry for Now* and *Pictures That Storm Inside My Head: Poems for the Inner You*.

Poetry Written or Collected Specifically for Young Adults

We did not include poetry in the first edition of this book because we were convinced that people do not write poetry specifically for teenagers. There are such poets as David McCord and Aileen Fisher who search for topics especially appealing to and appropriate for children, but we didn't know anyone who did this for young adults. Then in 1982, Mel Glenn published *Class Dismissed! High School Poems* which made it to several best-book lists. Here was poetry with all the characteristics of the modern YA problem novel. Young protagonists from a variety of racial and socioeconomic backgrounds were using candid, first-person speech to discuss intense situations ranging from having a crush on a teacher, to quitting school, to getting

Danny Vargas

My father drinks, so I don't stay home much.
My teachers bore me, so I don't go to class much.
Baseball is my life,
My present and my future.
When I take the relay from Conti
And cut down the runner trying to score from first.
There's no thrill in the world that comes close.
Not even sex.
I have to scratch for everything,
Beating out grounders.
Dodging inside pitches.
Advancing the runner over to third.
I thought I was doin' fine
Until the coach threw me a nasty curve
That sent me sprawling to the dirt.
He said I couldn't play no more because
I had failed three subjects.
He asked me to turn in my uniform.
I refused and ran out of his office, crying.
Onto the field, to the batter's box,
To the only place I can call home.

25

caught shoplifting, and to getting stabbed. The titles of the poems are kids' names and each poem is illustrated with a photograph. The format was probably chosen to capitalize on the current popularity of "folk poetry," that is, the writing and sharing of original poems.

Although writing poetry specifically for a young adult audience is a recent development, collecting poems with special appeal to teenagers and packaging them for the high school market has a much longer history. A book that twenty years ago proved the potential success of this kind of venture was *Reflections on a Gift of Watermelon Pickle*, published first by Scott, Foresman in 1966 and later reprinted in various formats and issued on a record. Editors Steve Dunning, Edward Lueders, and Hugh L. Smith selected the poems by reading hundreds of both well known and new poems gleaned from poetry magazines to groups of teenagers and getting their reactions. But there was more to their success than just the individual poems. The title, taken from the concluding poem (see "Reflections on a Gift of Watermelon Pickle" and "Further Reflections on 'A Gift of Watermelon Pickle'" *English Journal*, April and September, 1983) was intriguing. The spacious design of the book with its watermelon green cover and reddish-pink endpapers highlighted the title poem, making the book memorable.

Dunning, Lueders, and Smith combined efforts to do a second book, *Some Haystacks Don't Even Have Any Needle and Other Complete Modern Poems*. Reviewers praised the book as highly, or even more highly than *Watermelon Pickle*, but probably only because they were now alert to the names of the anthologists. Lueders went on to do a third collection with the help of Primus St. John, *Zero Makes Me Hungry: A Collection of Poems for Today.* The books are both highly recommended, but neither one was quite as successful as *Watermelon Pickle,* which leads one to suspect that the anthologists used the first place winners in their initial book and then came back to the second and third choices for the later books.

Paul Janeczko, a high school English teacher in Auburn, Maine, is the newest anthologist to achieve a success comparable to that of the *Watermelon Pickle* book. Janeczko says that "Today I read poetry the way some people watch soap operas, work in their gardens, or follow the Red Sox: irrationally, compulsively, endlessly."[1] Out of this compulsion has come four anthologies. His first one, *Postcard Poems,* is filled with poems short enough to send to a friend on a postcard, for example, W. S. Merwin's "Separation":

> Your absence has gone through me
> Like thread through a needle.
> Everything I do is stitched with its color.[2]

Karl Shapiro's "Man on Wheels":

> Cars are wicked, poets think.
> Wrong as usual. Cars are part of man.
> Cars are biological.
> A man without a car is like a clam without a shell.
> Granted, machinery is hell,
> But carless man is careless and defenseless.
> Ford is skin of present animal.
> Automobile is shell.
> You get yourself a shell or else.[3]

Ralph Waldo Emerson's "Poet":

> To clothe the fiery thought
> In simple words succeeds,
> For still the draft of genius is
> To mask a King in weeds.

May Swenson's "Waking from a Nap on the Beach":

> Sounds like big
> rashers of bacon frying.
> I look up from where I'm lying
> expecting to see stripes
>
> red and white. My eyes drop shut,
> stunned by the sun.
> Now the foam is flame, the long
> troughs charcoal, but
>
> still it chuckles and sizzles, it
> burns and burns, it never gets done.
> The sea is that
> fat.[4]

And Richard Brautigan's "In a Cafe":

> I watched a man in a cafe fold a slice of bread
>   as if he were folding a birth certificate or looking
>   at the photograph of a dead lover.[5]

Janeczko's second book, *Dont forget to fly*, is interesting because of its cyclical organization with between two and five poems on similar subjects grouped together, for example, Constance Sharp's "I Show the Daffodils to the Retarded Kids," is grouped with Joyce Carol Oates' "Children Not Kept at Home," and Theodore Roethke's "My Dim-Wit Cousin." In all, there are forty groupings with subjects ranging from suicide to dressmaker's dummies, swimming, and Sunday. In *Strings: A Gathering of Family Poems*, Janeczko uses a similar kind of organization only going through members of the family: wives, husbands, grandparents, etc. and through places with special meanings for families such as kitchens—with "a slice of sun and a song," as well as one where a 1940s child playing under the table is filled with thoughts of Hitler, Roosevelt, and Joe Louis when the radio announcer begins "We interrupt this broadcast."

Janeczko's book which will probably be used in the most English classes is *Poetspeak: In Their Work, About Their Work*. Probably because of the success of his earlier anthologies, Janeczko was able to convince several poets to contribute more than their poems. Forty-four contributed their photographs, and more importantly, over sixty contributed notes ranging from a few sentences to a few pages telling how they happened to write the included poem, what it means to them, or some other interesting details about the writing of poetry. If all of the poems were accompanied by such an essay, it might be tedious, but as it is there is a good balance between prose and poetry. What makes *Poetspeak* ideal for either class or individual young adult reading is that the poems are dramatic enough to grab the reader's attention and still challenging enough to demand the reader's involvement. Also, the statements from the poets are reassuring to students who may think that every poem is some secret code to be unlocked.

Stanley Kunitz, as part of the explanation following his poem "The Portrait," wrote:

> ◇ . . . a poem demands of its readers that they must come out to meet it, at least as far as it comes out to meet them, so that *their* meaning may be added to its. A common fallacy is to think that a poem begins with a meaning which then gets dressed up in words. On the contrary, a poem is language surprised in the act of changing into meaning.[6]

Kunitz' poem, "The Portrait," is a good example of a poem that tells a story, but it's a more subtle or less common kind of story than the kinds students relate to when they're in the middle grades. High school students are beginning to enjoy the stories of the inner self, to see the intensity of the feelings of the two characters in this poem.

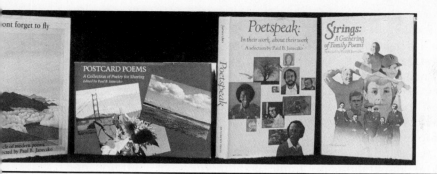

◆ Paul Janeczko, a high school English teacher in Maine, has achieved an unusual level of success with his anthologies, which include *Dont forget to fly: A cycle of modern poems, Postcard Poems: A Collection of Poetry for Sharing, Poetspeak: In Their Work, About Their Work,* and *Strings: A Gathering of Family Poems.*

The Portrait
by Stanley Kunitz

My mother never forgave my father
for killing himself,
especially at such an awkward time
and in a public park,
that spring
when I was waiting to be born.
She locked his name
in her deepest cabinet
and would not let him out,
though I could hear him thumping.
When I came down from the attic
with the pastel portrait in my hand
of a long-lipped stranger
with a brave moustache
and deep brown level eyes,
she ripped it into shreds
without a single word
and slapped me hard.
In my sixty-fourth year
I can feel my cheek
still burning.[7]

In reference to this particular poem, Kunitz only added his testament to its authenticity:

◇ I have nothing left to say except that more years than I want to count have passed, according to the relentless calendar, since my widowed mother and I acted out our wordless drama in the house on Providence Street in Worcester; and it might as well be yesterday. Memory is each man's poet-in-residence.[8]

The biggest controlling influence on the format and design of most poetry books is the theme that the collector has decided to pursue. The current trend in anthologizing is to select a topic and then find either a goodly number of poems or a number of good poems (depending on the standards of the anthologist) on a similar topic. Limiting themselves to either a particular topic or a particular poet gives anthologists a way to get a handle on what could be an overwhelming job of selection. It also makes designing and naming a book easier, but at the same time it handicaps the anthologist by restricting the raw material from which selections can be made. Some of the best poems are those that treat unique experiences or that explore hidden sides of life. These poems are appealing simply because they are on topics that are usually ignored. For example, Paul Janeczko could never have found enough good poems to make a whole book on such offbeat topics as amputation, insomnia, grandmothers, or gluttony, nor would readers have been interested in reading a hundred different poems on these rather limited subjects. Part of the enjoyment to be found in *Dont forget to fly* is the surprise of the topics and the originality with which two or three poets look at them from different angles.

Poetry appeals to the senses—sight as well as sound—and because of this its reading shouldn't be rushed. Books of poems need to be designed to give readers room to breathe. A book jam-packed with poems exudes a sense of urgency, a need to speed-read. The more successful anthologies have shown that collectors can sometimes do more by doing less. For example, the 35 poems in *Dusk to Dawn: Poems of the Night* collected by Helen Hill, Agnes Perkins, and Alethea Helbig probably get read more than do the 200 poems in *New Coasts and Strange Harbors* collected by Helen Hill and Agnes Perkins. Another example is *The Complete Poems of Paul Laurence Dunbar* where as many as five poems are crammed onto the small double-page spreads. This is an efficient book and a good reference tool for someone wanting to find a particular Dunbar poem, but it isn't a book that readers—teenage or adult—are likely to pick up for pleasure time browsing.

Fads and trends are just as likely to influence the reception of poetry as the reception of realistic fiction. And so it can be expected that as a follow-up to the popularity of the romance novels in the early 1980s, people would start producing collections of love poems. Lee Bennett Hopkins came out with the simplest and most obvious *Love and Kisses* in 1983. This was followed by Eve Merriam's *If Only I Could Tell You: Poems for Young Lovers and Dreamers* also in 1983, and Frances McCullough's *Love Is Like the Lion's Tooth* in 1984. The *Booklist* review praised its "depth, breadth, sophistication, and a lasting quality," which it said was a far cry from the innocuous innocence of other teenage love poems.[9]

Because readers come to poetry not so much for gathering information as for seeking a change of pace, a bit of pleasure through sharing with the poet such things as amusement in word play, a sudden recognition or insight, a recollection from childhood, or a time of emotional intensity, the design of the book needs to invite readers in. Random House did a good job with Maya Angelou's books. The relationship is shown between her autobiographies *I Know Why the Caged Bird Sings, Singin' and Swingin' and Gettin' Merry Like Christmas,* and *The Heart of a Woman* and her poetry

◆ Designer Janet Halverson did a good job of tying Maya Angelou's autobiographical books in with her poetry. Bold primary colors were used in several variations on a rainbowlike design. Shown here is Angelou's autobiographical *Singin' and Swingin' and Gettin' Merry Like Christmas* and her poetry collection *Oh Pray My Wings Are Gonna Fit Me Well.*

collections *Just Give Me a Cool Drink of Water 'fore I Diiie, Oh Pray My Wings Are Gonna Fit Me Well,* and *And Still I Rise* by using the same bright colors in a series of variations on a basic rainbowlike design.

Once readers get past the covers, the inside of a good poetry collection should also give them something to look at while they savor the poems. This may be photographs as in Lois Duncan's *From Spring to Spring,* splashes of color as in Edward Lueders and Primus St. John's *Zero Makes Me Hungry: A Collection of Poems for Today,* designs that extend the meanings of the poems as do the drawings in Eve Merriam's *Out Loud,* or simply adequate white space as in *Those Who Ride the Night Winds: Poems by Nikki Giovanni.*

A few select anthologies are so attractive that they would be worth their prices even if the poems were somehow accidentally left out. One of these is *Rainbows Are Made.* Lee Bennett Hopkins selected Carl Sandburg poems that he judged appropriate for an older audience than Sandburg's children's books *Early Moon* and *Wind Song.* Fritz Eichenberg did six wood engravings to use as the divider pages between the sections as well as a Carl Sandburg portrait for the cover. Each of the engravings illustrates a definition of poetry taken from Sandburg's introduction to his *Good Morning, America,* for example "Poetry is a series of explanations of life, fading off into horizons too swift for explanations," and "Poetry is a shuffling of boxes of illusions buckled with a strap of facts." Each definition gets its own full-size page of heavy, cream-colored paper opposite the engraving. The wide margins, ample spacing, rich brown endpapers, and the high-quality crafts-manship of both Eichenberg and Hopkins are appropriate matches for some of Sandburg's best poetry. Hopkins is currently working to prepare a similar collection for young adults of Emily Dickinson poems.

Even though poetry can usually be read and enjoyed by a much wider age range than prose, there is still a subtle dividing line between children's and young adult poetry. Teenagers will be amused by the humorous poetry in Jack Prelutsky's *Nightmares: Poems to Trouble Your Sleep,* Alvin Schwartz's *Tomfoolery: Trickery and Foolery with Words,* William Cole's collection *Beastly Boys and Ghastly Girls,* and some of the poems from Lewis Carroll's *Alice in Wonderland* and *Through the Looking Glass,* but they will be slightly insulted if offered serious children's poetry. It's the same old thing about their being offended if they should be taken to the children's department of a store to buy their clothes, but by themselves, they might wander into a children's department to buy a stuffed animal. Two poetry books that are clearly made for children but that teenagers might like in the same way that they like stuffed animals (probably because of a combination of nostalgia and basic attractiveness) are Susan Jeffers' picture book inter-pretations of Longfellow's *Hiawatha* and Robert Frost's *Stopping by Woods on a Snowy Evening.*

The freedom of choice is what's at issue, and the thing for book people to realize is that if a collection of poems is going to be marketed basically to high schools the designers should be aware of their audience's feeling that they have passed through childhood and are now young adults.

Helen Plotz is a good anthologist who has put together several collec-tions for Crowell, Macmillan, and Greenwillow. These books, for example, *Imagination's Other Place: Poems of Science and Mathematics* and *Eye's Delight: Poems of Art and Architecture* find their way into many young adult collections. However, it seems to us that some of the titles stand between the poems and a young adult audience. One example is the title *Saturday's Children: Poems of Work.* It makes an appropriate allusion to the old nursery rhyme about Monday's child being fair of face, Tuesday's child full of grace, etc., but without encouragement from a forceful teacher or li-brarian, not many young adults are going to pick up a book whose five-word title includes three words that for most teenagers have negative connota-tions: *children, poems,* and *work.* Another example is *Gladly Learn and Gladly Teach: Poems of the School Experience,* which seems to exude a sort of middle-aged, schoolmarm fustiness.

Some of the best anthologists are themselves poets: for example, Myra Cohn Livingston has put together several anthologies that are standard in young adult collections including *Poems of Christmas, O Frabjous Day! Poetry for Holidays and Special Occasions, What a Wonderful Bird the Frog Are: An Assortment of Humorous Poetry and Verse, One Little Room, an Everywhere: Poems of Love,* and *Why Am I Grown So Cold? Poems of the Unknowable.*

Poetry for Sophisticated Readers

Well-read, sophisticated young adults are ready to read and enjoy the same poetry that educated adults enjoy, but a few guiding principles might help teachers and librarians smooth the path to what they consider appropriate appreciation of the best poetry.

First, young adults, who simply haven't been around as long as adults and therefore haven't had time to pick up as much background information, will be more likely to understand the allusions made by contemporary as opposed to historical poets. It's not that we are recommending that anyone try to limit the poetry that young adults are exposed to. But we do think that they should first be offered the works of such modern poets as Donald Hall, Theodore Roethke, Marge Piercy, Joyce Carol Oates, Robert Penn Warren, Ted Hughes, Donald Justice, Denise Levertov, Maxine Kumin, James Dickey, Anne Sexton, Randall Jarrell, Nikki Giovanni, Eve Merriman, Karl Shapiro, May Swenson, X. J. Kennedy, Judith Hemschemeyer, William Stafford, John Updike, and Maya Angelou before they are offered the work of such historical poets as John Donne, Ben Jonson, John Milton, Samuel Butler, and John Dryden; such so-called modern poets as Robert Browning, Walt Whitman, Emily Dickinson, A. E. Housman, Gerard Manley Hopkins, and Rudyard Kipling; and even such almost contemporary poets as William Butler Yeats, Robert Frost, Carl Sandburg, William Carlos Williams, Wallace Stevens, Langston Hughes, D. H. Lawrence, Edna St. Vincent Millay, E. E. Cummings, Countee Cullen, and W. H. Auden.

A second guiding principle is that young adults will be better able to relate to poets who are presenting their own cultures. Certainly we are not asking for segregation of poetry by race, country, or ethnic background of the poet. But it stands to reason that an American teenager is going to be able to picture the Boston that Anne Sexton wrote about in "The Wedding Night" and the allusions both to Walt Whitman and to American life-styles that Allen Ginsberg wrote about in "A Supermarket in California" better than is an Australian or British teenager. Likewise, a native American teenager is going to be more ready to appreciate poetic renditions of ceremonial chants than is a child from white, middle-class suburbia. And the minority child who has grown up being forced to think about racial differences is in a better position than other readers to relate to Imamu Amiri Baraka's (LeRoi Jones) "Poem for Half White College Students" and Nikki Giovanni's "Ego Tripping." The power of literature is that it helps people transcend the circumstances that they happened to be born into, and so we highly recommend that students be offered poetry representing cultures and times different from their own, but adults who work with young readers need to realize that they will probably need to make a conscious effort to help even bright and sophisticated students transcend cultural barriers.

A third principle is to ease students into literary criticism through a biographical approach. Successful high school students are accustomed to reading biographies, but they probably haven't had much experience with literary criticism. Fortunately most biographies of poets, whether they are book length as is Neil Baldwin's *To All Gentleness, William Carlos Williams: The Doctor Poet,* chapter length as in Jean Gould's *American Women Poets: Pioneers of Modern Poetry,* or only a few paragraphs in length as in Paul Janeczko's *Poetspeak* include substantial doses of *explication de texte,* which can serve as an introduction to literary criticism.

A fourth principle is based on the fact that prose is much more like everyday language than poetry is. Young people therefore usually find it easier to read prose than poetry. Adults can help students bridge this gap by bringing to their attention poetry written by authors whose prose works they already feel comfortable with. For example, someone who has read Alice Walker's *The Color Purple* will probably be ready to appreciate the poems in her *Good Night Willie Lee, I'll See You in the Morning.* In a similar way, Ray Bradbury's science fiction fans may want to read his fifty-plus poems in *When Elephants Last in the Dooryard Bloomed* and students who have read Richard Brautigan's books may relate to his poetry, for example *June 30th, June 30th,* or *The Pill Versus the Springhill Mine Disaster.* On a less sophisticated level, students familiar with the work of YA writers Lois Duncan, Richard Peck, and R. R. Knudson may be interested in their collections of poetry.

The Writing and Reading Connection

Today there are hundreds of small poetry magazines published in the United States, and many of these include poems written by high school and college students. A class assignment that we have given for several years is to ask our college students to collect examples they like of ten different kinds of poems, for example a narrative or storytelling poem, a nonsense poem, a poem set to music, a humorous poem, a poem that describes an everyday happening, a concrete or visual poem, a haiku or cinquain, etc. One of the categories is an original, unpublished poem written by either the student or a roommate, friend, or family member. No student has ever complained about not being able to find a friendly poet willing to share.

Poets are looking for audiences. After a poetry reading on our campus by a nationally known poet, a man in the audience stood up to complain that he had been told by the editor of the local newspaper, who kept rejecting his poems, that there were too many people writing poems today. The poet looked thoughtful for a moment and then responded, "No, there just aren't enough people reading poems."

Poetry lovers all over are working to change this state of affairs. Don Mainprize, who teaches English at Houghton Lake High School in Michigan, made the following suggestions on increasing the writing, and indirectly the reading, of poetry in an article entitled "Ouchless Poetry":

◇ Have in-class readings by students.
◇ Read poetry to other classes. Have poets dress formally for the occasions, like the athletes who wear suits and ties the day they're going to do their thing.

◇ Hold full, voluntary, or selective assembly readings.

◇ Make classroom displays of poems and art. Volunteer to do the hallway display with creative writing.

◇ Choose or have students choose ten poems of the week for display (with names displayed or not, as the poet wishes).

◇ Hold a poetry open house for the public.

◇ Put a poem a day in the office bulletin.

◇ Have a poem chosen for each edition of the school paper.

◇ Get your radio station to air poems on its weekly school program.

◇ Send poems to the local newspaper. Our paper has given us three-quarters of a page for student poems.

◇ Enter poems in state and national contests. Publish a book of student poems. Our local press printed our collection, *Star, Stars, Stars* at a reduced rate. Money for the project came from student council earnings.

◇ At the earliest and best moment in the poetry unit, announce these end-of-the-year awards for the Honors Banquet: Poet Laureate, Most Improved Poet, Most Prolific Poet, Best-Anything-You-Can-Come-Up-With-Poet. These awards mean a lot more to kids than you think.[10]

Another good article worth looking up and reading is Jesse Hise's "Writing Poetry: More than a Frill" in the November 1980 *English Journal*. He begins with poetry patterns guaranteed to bring feelings of success and then goes on to show ways of breaking out of the patterns. Kenneth Koch's *Wishes, Lies, and Dreams*, and *Rose, Where Did You Get That Red?* are excellent in presenting poetry ideas or patterns and also some very enjoyable poetry written by students in the New York Public schools where Koch was a poet-in-residence. Alberta Turner, who teaches at Cleveland State University, advises making poetry writing spontaneous:

◇ Surprise the class. Don't call it poetry. Don't assign it ahead of time. Don't discuss the poetry in the literature book first. Trick them into letting their subconscious minds present them with concerns, feelings they haven't yet had time to formulate into verbal clichés. For instance, have them dump out their pockets and purses and list the things contained in order of increasing importance to themselves. Students may discover they're very cautious, others that they're dreamers, still others that they're light travelers.

I would discourage some of the time-honored ways of writing poetry in the classroom, the poems that fill traditional literary forms, such as limericks or haiku. Feeling doesn't occur first in such forms, and to force feeling into forms before it has expressed itself in unconscious impulse—chiefly images and emotional rhythms—may make the poems mechanical and/or trite. However, natural forms like questions and answers or counting-out chants or game tunes don't have that disadvantage. . . . I'd discourage assigning first drafts of poems for homework. The poem, unlike the essay, doesn't benefit from being planned. It needs to surprise the poet. It's the final editing that can be done at home.[11]

What the teachers have in mind is making young people comfortable with poetry so that their pleasure can be increased in reading as well as writing "throughout the year . . . not something we do to be 'creative' or to separate us from the normal writing [and reading] process."[12] Anyone who wants to accomplish this goal should have an ample supply of poetry books for readers to pick up and browse through whenever there's extra time as well as when class attention is specifically focused on poetry. These should include small magazines, local literary publications of your own and neighboring schools, and poetry anthologies from national presses.

Books that include poems written by young people may be especially appreciated by student writers. Richard Lewis has put together several such collections.

Poetry is a medium that lends itself to brief but intense encounters with strong emotions, hence when young people write poetry they are apt to write about things that upset or worry them—unfairnesses, hostilities, sexuality, disagreements with adults, etc. During the 1970s, two books that frequently found their way to lists of censored books were *the me nobody knows: children's voices from the ghetto* edited by Stephen M. Joseph and *Male and Female Under Eighteen* edited by Eve Merriam and Nancy Larrick. Both books contained poetry as well as short prose statements by young writers. They were criticized for "objectionable" words as well as for expressions of ideas thought to be inappropriate for young readers.

Another poetry book that during the 1970s was so controversial that it virtually disappeared from library shelves was Eve Merriam's parody *Inner City Mother Goose*. It was reissued by Bantam in 1984 and may serve as an inspiration for students to write parodies. Myra Cohn Livingston's less controversial collection of parodies *Speak Roughly to Your Little Boy* would also be good for this because it includes the original pieces along with parodies of them.

As a final note, we should point out that what we have presented in this section has been little more than a sampling of available poetry. Young readers are fortunate in having practically the whole world of poetry from which to choose. They are also fortunate in that poetry-loving adults are anxious to recruit young readers as poetry lovers and so they make an extra effort to design books that are particularly inviting because of their spaciousness and high-quality design and layout.

◈ DRAMA

Drama is another genre which was not included in the first edition of this text. Our decision not to include it was consistent with the decisions of many other critics working with literature for young adults, but obviously between 1980 and 1985 we changed our minds and decided we were guilty of contributing to the situation that Anthony L. Manna complained about when he labelled drama the "hidden genre." He examined several recent best-of-the-year lists compiled by such publications as *Booklist, School Library Journal,* and the *New York Times Book Review* and found only one play, Paul Zindel's *Let Me Hear You Whisper.* To prove that the exclusion wasn't because good drama isn't being written, he went on to recommend more than a dozen contemporary plays that would be excellent for reading in either junior or senior high school classrooms.[13]

In pondering Manna's point and trying to figure out why drama has been the "hidden genre" for young adults, we came up with the following reasons:

◇ Teenagers are not the ones buying the tickets to Broadway plays nor flying to London on theater tours. Therefore not many playwrights purposely set out to write plays that will appeal exclusively to a young adult audience.

◇ Scripts are harder for teachers to obtain than are books of poetry, information, and fiction. A much smaller number of plays are published by mass market or school oriented publishers. Occasionally a play will prove to be such good reading that it will be published in book form as was Ossie Davis' *Langston*, Joan Aiken's *Street*, and Paul Zindel's *The Effect of Gamma Rays on Man-in-the-Moon Marigolds*, but usually the plays that are published for general consumption are the classics that are used as college textbooks, for example, Pocket Book's *Four Tragedies*, which includes *Romeo and Juliet*, *Macbeth*, *Julius Caesar*, and *Hamlet*, or they are collections of either excerpted scenes or short plays as with Paul Kozelka's *Fifteen American One-Act Plays*. Teachers may not want to buy whole collections when they only want students to read one play. And since those companies specializing in publishing scripts do not advertise directly to schools, teachers may not realize that they can order reading scripts for about the same price as a quality paperback book (see the list of publishers at the end of this chapter). Teenagers miss out on the heritage of children's theater which encourages playwrights, producers, and actors to work with child drama. In even moderately sized communities there are usually community theater groups or college or university sponsored groups which produce plays for children. Parents either bring their children or the plays are brought directly to elementary or junior high schools. High school students are more likely to select their own live entertainment of athletic events or musical performances. Of course many high school students attend school-produced plays, but the discouraging news on this front is that fewer schools can afford the time and the money to produce such plays, and an ever increasing percentage of students leave school early in the day because of part-time employment and so are unable to participate in drama as an extracurricular activity.

◇ In 1939 when Dora V. Smith began the first adolescent literature class for future teachers at the University of Minnesota, she excluded drama from consideration, and as might be expected so did most of her students who went forth to spread the word about adolescent literature.

◇ Neither English teachers nor librarians have been trained in drama. They therefore are not likely to pick up plays for their own leisure time reading and hence find it more comfortable to leave the whole matter of plays to the drama teacher.

◇ Plays are written to be seen, not read. To translate words on a page into the imaginative experiences the playwright had in mind requires a kind of active involvement that demands a great deal from the reader. Young people may not be ready to bring this much to their reading and hence are not inclined to pick up plays for leisure time reading.

In spite of these factors—or maybe because of the last one—some teachers are bringing plays into their English classrooms. For a feature in *English Journal* (see "Our Readers Write," October 1984) we invited teachers to report on plays they had successfully used for classroom reading. That twenty-four teachers responded surprised us. A further surprise was that four of them suggested the same play, Reginald Rose's three-act television play *Twelve Angry Men*. It is the story of a jury making a decision on the future of a nineteen-year-old boy who is charged with murdering his father. Three out of the four teachers made some comment to the effect that they and their students affectionately called the play "Twelve Angry People" since girls as well as boys were assigned to read the parts. The following excerpts taken from the teachers' descriptions not only show why this particular play is successful in class but also can serve as guides when predicting the potential of other scripts for in-class reading.

◇ It calls for twelve continual parts, enough to satisfy all students who like to read aloud.

◇ It teaches practical lessons of value to students' lives.

◇ It may serve as a springboard for research and further discussion on how the judicial system works.

◇ It creates a forum for students to probe the psychology of group dynamics and peer behavior.

◇ It sparks student excitement from the beginning and sustains it throughout.

◇ It can be read in two-and-a-half class sessions.

◇ The "business" is minimal and can be easily carried out as students read from scripts.

◇ Pertinent questions can be asked when the jury recesses after Acts I and II.

◇ The setting is a hot, stuffy jury room—just like our classrooms in June.

◇ Students are attracted to the realism and they can relate to a motherless, slum youth of nineteen.

◇ The excellent characterization allows students to discover a kaleidoscope of lifelike personalities.

The influence of the mass media was seen in several teachers' explanations of why other plays worked in their classes. For example, one teacher explained that he goes back to the days of radio for Lucille Fletcher's *Sorry, Wrong Number*. Since "it was written to be heard and not seen, it is ideal for reading aloud." Another teacher said that because Gore Vidal's *Visit to a Small Planet* was written for television "the action was easy to visualize and the stage directions were simple enough to discuss as an important aspect of the drama itself." Television writer Rod Serling's *A Storm in Summer* was recommended for the way it relates an encounter between a ten-year-old Harlem boy and a bitter, sarcastic, Jewish delicatessen owner in upstate New York.

Suggested plays from the more standard lists included Thornton Wilder's *Our Town*, to be taught along with Edgar Lee Masters' *Spoon River Anthology*. Robert Bolt's *A Man for All Seasons* was recommended for its portrayal of one of the most famous periods of English history and also for its exploration of a hero. Comparisons can be drawn to works treating heroes of noble birth as in *Antigone* and *Hamlet* and heroes of ordinary birth as in *Death of a Salesman* and *The Stranger*. Oliver Goldsmith's *She Stoops to Conquer* was recommended for seniors of average as well as superior ability levels. "Despite its eighteenth-century origins, the dialogue is surprisingly modern, with very few words needing explanation . . . The characters are warm, human, and lovable; the humor, easy-going and readily accessible." Robinson Jeffers' translation of Euripedes' *Medea* was recommended as more accessible to average students than other Greek plays such as *Oedipus* and *Antigone*. Students readily understand jealousy and the desire for revenge. And the idea that Medea kills her children repels yet intrigues them, but by the end of the play they develop understanding and sympathy for her. George Bernard Shaw's *Arms and the Man* may help students view the almost daily news accounts about war from a different slant. A lighter, more frivolous play that also helps students gain a new perspective is John Patrick's *The Teahouse of the August Moon*, which was recommended for the light-hearted way that it pokes fun at American customs and values.

Jerome Lawrence and Robert E. Lee's *Inherit the Wind*, which is based on the Scopes trial, was recommended because of its relevance to the current controversy over creationism versus evolution and also because the lines are easy to read aloud and there is enough balance between sharp wit and high drama "to allow would-be actors the chance to step out as much as they wish." William Gibson's *The Miracle Worker* was recommended not only for the poignancy of the story of Helen Keller and Annie Sullivan, but also for its illustration of such dramatic devices as flashbacks, foreshadowing, symbolism, and dramatic license—when compared to such biographies as Nella Braddy's *Anne Sullivan Macy* and Helen Keller's *The Story of My Life*.

Junior high students can understand the lesson of faith in William Saroyan's short play, *The Oyster and the Pearl*. It's a good one-day reading to use as a companion piece to Ring Lardner's short story "Haircut" or Moss Hart and George S. Kaufman's play *You Can't Take It With You*. *Pygmalion* was recommended as a "turn-on" for students in basic skills English classes who "have reading, writing, and sometimes attitude problems about school." They have empathy for Eliza Doolittle because "she speaks the same way they do, and, as one student commented, 'Eliza probably don't spell too hot, either!' " *The Diary of Anne Frank,* "a roller coaster of emotions," is appreciated because "Anne Frank is someone who has lived, who has shared her experiences, and who has described them *while* she was a teenager and knew most about them."

The plays mentioned above are only a sampling which show the variety of drama that is being read and studied in English classes. Probably the key point about these plays is that most of them wouldn't have been picked up for leisure-time reading. A teacher's encouragement was needed to help students make the conceptual leap from reading words on a page to seeing images on the stage in the mind.

Reading a play is obviously different from seeing one produced. The only people who playwrights think of as readers are professionals—producers, actors, and directors—who peruse plays with an eye to transforming them from words on a page to an imaginative experience being brought to an audience from stage or screen. When we guide young people in reading plays we might encourage them to read from the perspective of a particular professional, for example, an advertiser of designer jeans marketed to teenagers and looking for a television play that will attract a young adult audience, a particular actress looking for a part that will enhance her reputation as a serious performer, a director looking for a movie that can be made at little expense, etc.

For further recommendations of plays that are good for classroom reading, refer to Anthony Manna's article in the October 1984 *English Journal* "Curtains Up on Contemporary Plays." You might also send to the Young Adult Services Division of the American Library Association, 50 E. Huron Street, Chicago, IL 60611 and ask for their 1984 publication *Outstanding Books for the College Bound* compiled by Mary Ann Paulin and Susan Berlin. The $5.95 book is a compilation of the brochures which the division used to publish. The divisions are fiction, nonfiction, biography, theater, and other performing arts.

Other books for teacher reference are listed in a bibliography at the end of this chapter. A bibliography of recommended plays is also appended to this chapter. It was compiled by Ric Alpers, a candidate for the MFA degree in Child Drama at Arizona State University. His goal in making the list was not only to pull together a representative sampling of good contemporary drama but also to select plays whose characters would be ones that young adults would be likely to identify with.

◈ DRAMA ON SCREEN

In today's world of mass communication, stage plays make up a small percentage of contemporary drama. Most of it appears on screen—either movies or television. And at least in the United States and probably in much of the rest of the world, both television and movies are very much youth

◈ THE PEOPLE BEHIND THE BOOKS

H. M. HOOVER, Author

Another Heaven, Another Earth
The Bell Tree
The Lost Star
The Rains of Eridan

The world of children's books remains a generally jolly place full of imagination, poetry, and bright pictures, talking animals, and children off on adventures. The world of teenage books is pretty grim. As with all fiction, that which is written for adolescents has its fads and fashions; topics considered salesworthy today are less than so tomorrow. We have had (what I hope is) a surfeit of Teenage Problem Books whose young hero or heroine is totally self-preoccupied and usually socially crippled by some overwhelming grief. Bless Paula

Danziger, Mary Rodgers, and all who put laughter into their books.

I suspect the appeal of humor, and of fantasy and science fiction will grow among younger readers; partly as a backlash to too much topical literature, partly because there is evidence of both imagination and timelessness in this writing—but mostly because it *entertains*. Being a teenager is tough enough for most of us without constantly reading of another's misery. I think young readers will, if given the choice, make writers return to their proper role, to telling a real story, to entertaining. ◆

Another Heaven, Another Earth. Viking, 1981.
The Bell Tree. Viking, 1982
The Lost Star. Viking, 1979.
The Rains of Eridan. Viking, 1977.

---

oriented. Few teenagers need teacher encouragement to watch. A teacher in one of our graduate classes complained—or perhaps just observed—that twenty years ago when he first started teaching, he could illustrate the points he was making with references to books. But today if he wants to make a comparison or give a second example that most of the class will understand he has to refer to such television shows as *Happy Days, Mork and Mindy, Three's Company, The Waltons, Welcome Back, Kotter,* or *Eight Is Enough.* The fact that these shows have all been cancelled and are shown only through syndication or as reruns probably means that by now this teacher has had to come up with an even more contemporary set of examples from similar shows. And although no one has labelled these shows, which are descendants of the earlier *Dobie Gillis* and *Leave It to Beaver,* "young adult" or "adolescent," they have the same characteristics as those that Maia Mertz and David England identified as belonging to modern adolescent literature.

1. Adolescent fiction will involve a youthful protagonist.
2. It often employs a point of view which presents the adolescent's interpretation of the events of the story.
3. It is characterized by directness of exposition, dialogue, and direct confrontation between principal characters.

4. It is characterized by such structural conventions as being generally brief, taking place over a limited period of time and in a limited number of locales, having few major characters, and resulting in a change or growth step for the young protagonist.

5. The main characters are highly independent in thought, action, and conflict resolution.

6. The protagonists reap the consequences of their actions and decisions.

7. The authors draw upon their sense of adolescent development and the concomitant attentions to the legitimate concerns of adolescents.

8. Adolescent fiction strives for relevance by attempting to mirror current societal attitudes and issues.

9. The stories most often include gradual, incremental, and ultimately incomplete "growth to awareness" on the part of the central character.

10. The books are hopeful.[14]

Some of the most popular movies also fit the above description, for example, *Breaking Away*, *Gregory's Girl*, *Diner*, and *Grease*. In such movies as *Flashdance*, *An Officer and A Gentleman*, *Ordinary People*, and *Terms of Endearment*, at least one of the main characters is a young adult. In a visual medium, youthful characters are especially appealing simply because of their physical attractiveness. A second reason for their appeal relates as much to books as to movies, that is, young people are at an age in life when their emotions are especially intense and when their life-styles are undergoing the kinds of changes that form the basis for interesting plots as they make decisions about leaving home, for example, or choosing a mate or the values they will live by for the rest of their lives.

The fact that the unlabelled "adolescent literature" on television and in movies enjoys a much broader and more appreciative audience than does the labelled "adolescent literature" in books makes us wonder if such authors as Sue Ellen Bridgers and Sylvia Engdahl don't have a point when they express ambivalence about their books being classified as "young adult." They have questioned whether it is this labelling that keeps adults from finding and reading their stories in the same way that adults go to movies and watch television shows with young protagonists.

In the early 1980s, YA lit made it to the big-time movies, not just to television specials as M. E. Kerr's *Dinky Hocker Shoots Smack*, Bette Greene's *Summer of My German Soldier*, Richard Peck's *Are You in the House Alone?* and Judy Blume's *Forever* had done in the '70s. In the summer of 1982, S. E. Hinton's *Tex* was released as a Walt Disney movie directed by Tim Hunter and starring Matt Dillon as Tex and Jim Metzler as big brother Mason. The following spring, Hinton's *The Outsiders* directed by Francis Ford Coppola was released, to be followed by *Rumble Fish*. Robert Cormier's *I Am the Cheese* came out the following summer.

One of the "myths" discussed in Chapter 1 was the idea that if kids see a film they won't read the book. Solid evidence has put this idea to rest, but nevertheless a kind of hostility lingers on with people fearing that movies and television are taking the place of books, that nonprint media is an enemy of print media. If this is so, then at least we book lovers can be comforted by the fact that some of our soldiers are now behind "the enemy lines." Paul Zindel has moved to Hollywood to be a screenwriter. S. E. Hinton moved up from being an advisor on *The Outsiders* to being a co-author of the script for *Rumble Fish*. Robert Cormier played a bit part in *I Am the Cheese*, and Madeleine L'Engle is writing a movie script for *A Wrinkle in Time*. We optimistically predict that this closer relationship between book and movie people will be mutually beneficial. One good thing that has already come out of the publicity surrounding the movies is that many people who knew nothing about books for teenagers now realize that there is such a thing as "YA lit." This has to be a plus when teachers and librarians seek funds from taxpayers, school boards, and library trustees.

On the negative side we must admit that the movies have not been totally successful. *I Am the Cheese* must have been a great disappointment to Robert Cormier, as well as to its financial backers. After a very short New York run, it was released to television where because of the distractions of interruptions for commercials and the generally less concentrated viewing of a home television audience as compared to a darkened theater audience, viewers had even a harder time getting involved in the complex story with its flash-forwards and its repetitious scenes of Adam (Robert Macnaughton of *E.T.* fame) riding his bicycle through the Vermont countryside.

Even though kids liked *The Outsiders* (see "A Boy's View of *Outsiders*," Todd Camhe, *Los Angeles Times Calendar*, April 3, 1983, pp. 18–19) and the week of its release it grossed five million dollars and was the biggest moneymaker in several large cities, adult reviewers competed to see who could be the most cleverly negative about it. Vincent Canby writing in the *New York Times* started his review with "It's as if someone had handed Verdi a copy of 'The Hardy Boys Attend a Rumble' and, holding a gun to the poor man's head, forced him to use it as a libretto."[15] David Denby, a reviewer for *New York Magazine*, labelled the movie "the cinematic equivalent of purple prose," while Peter Rainer, a reviewer for the *Los Angeles Herald Examiner*, called it a "gusty, overblown vacuum."[16]

Tex was much more successful. Richard Schickel writing in *Time Magazine* praised the new sophistication of Walt Disney studios and called the movie "modest, intelligent, and entirely engaging."[17] When movie critics Gene Siskel and Roger Ebert did a special TV program which aired September 3, 1983, about movies with young male protagonists, they cited *Tex* for being what the others only pretend to be—stories of growing up to be a man. They criticized the falseness of the male/female relationships shown in such movies as *Porky's*, *The Last American Virgin*, *Going All the Way*, *Spring Break*, *Homework*, *Class*, and *Private School*. In what they described as an epidemic of horny, teenage movies, they pointed out how the boys never risk a real relationship. There is always a wall—either real or figurative—between them and the women they lust after. What is missing in these "lust/hate" relationships is affection, friendship, and honesty. They praised the line in *Tex* where big brother Mace confesses to fifteen-year-old Tex that he's never had sexual intercourse. The implication is that probably most of his friends haven't either and that it's generally unwise to believe everything one hears in locker rooms. Siskel and Ebert thought this bit of honesty was worth all of the other movies put together.

This kind of discussion is intellectually stimulating for teenagers because it is about their generation and their medium. They can get much more involved when talking about mass media than when talking about the same kinds of things in relation to literature written fifty, a hundred, or two hundred years ago. In its finest moments, the modern mass media has brought to millions of people the best of our plays, poems, stories, and novels. Even at its worst, it has introduced people to literary traditions and certain symbols, and has raised their expectations. But there are other far-reaching effects of the mass media that will probably never be completely measured or understood. The best that teachers can hope to do is to make students aware of the potential for problems and get them to think about questions such as the following:

1. Do movies and television discourage reading by taking up too much time?
2. How is one's mental picture of life affected by the thousands of hours of viewing that most teenagers have experienced? For example, do people become desensitized to violence? Do people feel that their own lives are disappointing and boring when they are not as amusing as is a sit-com or as full of drama as is a soap opera?
3. Is television particularly damaging in the stereotypes that it presents, especially of women and minorities, and of male/female relationships?
4. If certain kinds of language and acts are commonplace in the media, don't books have to offer similar sensationalism?
5. Does watching television promote passivity and laziness when it comes to reading?

No one has answers to these questions, but perhaps some of the young people now in our schools will be the ones to find the answers, especially if they are helped to view movies and television at a level beyond that of simple pleasure. Because the mass media are such a powerful tool of socialization and shaper of tastes and expectations, sociological issues are part and parcel of literary discussions.

Because of the popularity of cable television, it's much easier today to assign students to see feature length films outside of class and then come to class prepared to discuss such things as whether a book is better than a movie, or just different. Students can compare the techniques that authors and screenwriters use to establish character, setting, and tone. The movie-maker goes about establishing setting in an entirely different way from the storyteller. What makes it easier? What harder? The movie-maker has an advantage over the writer when it comes to portraying action, but the writer has an advantage when it comes to revealing a character's inner thoughts. The storyteller writing from the omniscient viewpoint can simply tell what a character is thinking, but the screenwriter has to figure out some believable stage business to reveal the character's thoughts. The failure of *I Am the Cheese* as a movie relates to this because it is a story that basically happened inside Adam Farmer's head. Getting a camera inside anyone's head is not easy.

An especially important difference between characterization in a fully developed novel and in a shortened drama is that in the latter there is little or no room to show the relationship between the character's personality and the developments in the plot. Media critics have expressed concern over a generation growing up to think people have no control over their destinies. Things seem to happen *to* the characters, but not in any way *because of* their actions, attitudes, or beliefs. Searching out cause-and-effect relationships can be a revealing exercise from both a literary and a personal development viewpoint.

Books are typically adapted into plays, musicals, movies, or something for television as, for example, Rona Jaffe's *Mazes and Monsters* was made into a television special and Glendon Swarthout's *Bless the Beasts and Children* was adapted into a full-length movie. An adaptation has basically the same characters, plot, tone, and many of the words of the original piece. However, the printed story doesn't always come first. For example, Norma Klein's book *Sunshine* began as a tape-recorded diary made by a young mother dying of cancer as a legacy for her daughter. The diary was adapted for television where it appeared as a movie. Norma Klein used the television movie as a basis for a book, which she labelled "fiction." A brief television series also grew out of the story as did a full-length movie and a second book by Klein. At the point that Klein felt it appropriate to label her book "fiction," it probably became more appropriate to use the wording "inspired by" or "based on" rather than "adapted from."

Financial considerations have a greater influence on the production of television shows and movies than they do on books. A writer can create a story to appeal to a relatively small group of readers with particular interests and tastes, but a mass media piece must appeal to large numbers of people— the more, the better. That is why there are many more choices available in books than there are in visual entertainment. Because producing a movie is such a large task, it has to be done by a team of people rather than by one individual. Glendon Swarthout in talking about the movie version of his *Bless the Beasts and Children* spoke resignedly about the great part that luck plays in putting a film together. Writing the book was an individual artistic endeavor that he controlled with his own intellect, but once it got to the movie studios, literally hundreds of creative people had an input.

Joanna Greenberg said much the same thing when she spoke at the 1983 American Library Association convention about her experience with *I Never Promised You a Rose Garden*, which she wrote under the pseudonym Hannah Green. She compared selling the movie rights to her book to selling a well-loved car. You make the people who buy it promise to give it a good home and not to soup it up with headers and rainbow tape. They promise faithfully and even say you'll be invited to come and look it over occasionally. But then the buyer falls on hard times and has to sell the car to someone else. In a half-hearted way he passes on your requests, but of course he doesn't insist because he's anxious for the sale. The same thing happens again and again and eventually everyone forgets that you were the original owner. Years later you see your old car coming down the street. You hardly recognize it because it not only has headers and rainbow tape, it has a hood scoop, mag wheels, and a blower.

But regardless of the disappointment that authors might feel in the movie productions of their books, it is interesting to note that of the books on the Honor List that are still popular after a decade, a surprisingly large number have been made into movies, for example, *Mr. and Mrs. Bo Jo Jones, The Autobiography of Miss Jane Pittman, Go Ask Alice, Red Sky at Morning, The Andromeda Strain, Sounder, Where the Lilies Bloom, Alive, Watership Down, A Hero Ain't Nothin' But a Sandwich,* and *The Chosen.*

To help high school students understand the changes made in a book's plot it may be useful to divide a class into task forces of three or four students. Each group draws up a proposal "to sell" a book that the class has just finished reading to a movie producer. Their proposal should include why they think it would be a good movie, what approach should be taken, an outline of the major events and characters, and suggestions for where it should be filmed and who should play the parts.[18] A report from each group shared with the class will reveal some of the difficulties of getting total agreement on something as subjective as artistic creation.

Space precludes going into a full discussion of media that is prepared specifically for schools, but there are carry-overs from popular to school media. Sixteen millimeter films, sound recordings, filmstrips, and promotional posters are all commonly used in schools. The best of the sound recordings, such as those done by Caedmon (many of which feature the author as the reader), are also offered for sale outside of school markets, and some of the films are shortened versions of movies originally prepared for television or for theaters.

It is not as easy to make filmstrips of young adult books as it is of children's books. Young adult literature uses words, not pictures. One solution is to make filmstrips from the frames of movies. Another possibility is for artists to paint pictures, but many stories don't have enough action to support the sixty or seventy illustrations needed for a filmstrip. A third kind of filmstrip is made from a combination of book illustrations and photographs relating the book or books to the author. The result is a combination feature article and television interview with an author.

The length of visual presentations may be a problem because of expenses and because they must not be too long to be enjoyed in a single sitting. One philosophy is that it is better to present an uncut excerpt in the hope that the listener or viewer will be motivated to read the whole story. Another opinion is that it is better to present the whole story in shortened

◆ On March 21, 1980, Jo Ellen Misakian, librarian at the Lone Star K–8 school library in Fresno, California, mailed a copy of S. E. Hinton's *The Outsiders*, a cover letter asking that the book be turned into a movie, and a petition signed by seventh and eighth grade students to director Francis Ford Coppola. Coppola turned the letter over to his producer, Fred Roos, with instructions to "check it out." Three years later on March 17, 1983, Roos and five of the film's young stars (Front row: Darren Dalton, Leif Garrett, Patrick Swayze; back row: C. Thomas Howell and Ralph Macchio) paid an official visit to the Lone Star School Library to thank the students for suggesting the book. Star Matt Dillon arrived that night for the premiere showing. Seventy-five of those who signed the petition and were now sophomores at Sanger High School came back for the celebration. They cheered their own credit line given at the end of the movie.

Photo by Donald Peoples, Sanger High School. Courtesy of Jo Ellen Misakian.

form so that seeing the filmstrip substitutes for reading the book. Some pieces of this kind have been so simplified that the heart of the story gets lost. Many teachers and librarians are appalled at what seems like misrepresentation, but others argue that a great service is being performed, especially for reluctant readers who are introduced in a pleasurable way to the books about which their friends are talking. They get at least some of the value of the piece, and many of them are motivated to begin reading once they get a taste of current young adult literature.

There is a whole wealth of short films that are wonderful for class or library use. Each January, the Young Adult Services Division of the American Library Association releases a list of the fifteen or twenty films they judge to be the best of the previous year's productions. The *English Journal* regularly has articles recommending films for classroom use. The following would be worth looking up: "Short Stories on Film" (February 1984), and "Short Films Revisited" (January 1984), both by David Burmester, and "Our Readers Write: What's a good film you wish you owned so you could use it anytime you want? (January 1985)

Some books that libraries ought to have on hand for those young adults (and their teachers) whose interests in the media extend beyond simple viewing pleasure include such movie books as Pauline Kael's *5001 Nights at the Movies: A Guide from A to Z* and *Taking It All In*; Bosley Crowther's *Vintage Films: 50 Enduring Motion Pictures*; David Sohn's *Good Looking: Film Studies, Short Films and Filmmaking*; Fred H. Marcus' *Short Story/ Short Film*; Ron Johnson and Jan Bone's *Understanding the Film*; Phil Hardy's *The Western*; Leslie Halliwell's *The Filmgoer's Companion*; Arthur Knight's *The Liveliest Art: A Panoramic History of the Movies*; Danny Peary's *Cult Movies: The Classics, the Sleepers, the Weird, and the Wonder-*

ful; Edward Edelson's *Funny Men of the Movies*; Brian Garfield's *Western Films: A Complete Guide*; and William R. Meyer's *The Making of the Great Westerns*. Good books for television fans include *Great Television Plays* selected by William I. Kaufman and introduced by Ned E. Hoopes and *Great Television Plays*, Vol. 2 edited and introduced by Ned. E. Hoopes and Patricia Neale Gordon; Rose K. Goldsen's *The Show and Tell Machine: How Television Works and Works You Over*; Marie Winn's *The Plug-In Drug*; Tim Brooks and Earle Marsh's *The Complete Directory to Prime Time Network TV Shows 1946–Present*; and Vincent Terrace's *The Complete Encyclopedia of Television Programs 1947–1975*.

◈ THE DRAMA OF VIDEO GAMES AND MUSIC TELEVISION VIDEOS

In contrast to the kinds of drama we have just described as being appreciated by a wide age range, two kinds of screen drama belong almost exclusively to teenagers. These are the short dramas of video games and the longer, more symbolic dramas in the rock music videos prepared for television, such as the ones on MTV.

Many people might argue that these are neither drama nor literature, but if we accept the broad definition of literature as all writings in either prose or verse that are of an imaginative nature and reflect a particular culture, then both of these qualify as literature. They can be used to help students gain a broader view of literature and the interrelatedness of popular culture and literature "with a capital L."

As Susan Latta described her initial experience with MTV, "It was terribly annoying at first. Instead of music providing a background to listen to while I was occupied with something else, it had suddenly become a visual experience as well as an aural one. I realized that I was being forced to think about the music, its emotional impact, the lyrics, the imagery—in other words, its poetic qualities."[19]

Latta went on to recommend that English teachers use video music as "stepping stones to develop abilities that will help students in approaching literature and writing." She gave the following reasons for its potential success:

1. Near the top of any list of what teenagers are interested in will be music and television. Video music combines these two media into a new, exciting art form.
2. Music videos are easily available, either on cable television or as part of such syndicated programs as *Solid Gold*, *Top Ten*, and *Music Magazine*.
3. The videos are short, only three or four minutes, yet they are packed with imagery and symbolism which can serve as the basis for such thought-provoking questions as these based on Michael Jackson's *Billy Jean*:

◇ Who is Billy Jean? Why do we never see her? Who is the man in the trenchcoat? Is it Jackson himself as some viewers assert, and if it is, what is the meaning of this "alter ego"? Why was a shabby setting chosen, and in this setting, why is Jackson so fashionably dressed? What is the function of the fantasy elements? Why is a hobo's attire changed from rags to a tuxedo when Jackson throws a coin into his cup? What role does the cat, who suddenly changes into a dog at one point in the video, play? Is it symbolic of Billy Jean? How do the images of the video tie in with the song's lyrics which are ostensibly about a paternity suit?[20]

While the music videos are good for studying images and symbolism, video games are good raw material to look at in relation to theme and plot. Because they have to be so pared down, the plots are easily seen. In the first generation of video games, plots were little more than protagonist (the player) vs. another (the machine). The point of the games was to see how long the player could keep a ball in motion. In the second generation of games, plots were extended to protagonist vs. nature as when rocket ships were threatened by asteroids, and protagonist vs. society when players had to protect themselves from aliens. The makers of video games soon went beyond such basic plots to create a variety of protagonists in a variety of situations. We sent a class of college students to the basement of the Student Union and told them to play a video game and then come back with an analysis of plot and theme. Here are some of their statements:

◇ The plot of *Gamma-Goblins* is progressive and the theme is that life is a battle for survival. If one survives Wave A, there is the danger of being wiped out by Wave B, then by Wave C, and Wave D, etc.

◇ In most video games, players have to protect themselves. But in *Death Chase* the player is the attacker. You drive around the course searching for unwary pedestrians. When you run one down, a horrible scream is heard and a gravestone appears on the spot accompanied by vaguely funereal music. The moral seems to be "Get them before they get you." I'm ashamed to admit it was fun.

◇ In *Armor Attack* the theme is one of surviving as long as possible. This could be interpreted as a moral, "Do unto others before they do unto you."

◇ I was amused to find out that *Ms. Pac-Man* differs from *Pac-Man* in that the patterns are less predictable and that there are three intermission acts. In Act I Ms. Pac-Man meets Mr. Pac-Man, in Act II they marry, and in Act III children are born. Players who are good enough get to see all three acts.

◇ The theme of *Tempest* was one of survival—kill or be killed. The plot was episodic with various climactic levels experienced in increasing intensity up to an inevitable end.

◇ In *Donkey Kong*, a gorilla abducts a fair maiden, climbs to the top of what looks like several floors of a warehouse where he ties the maiden to a post. A man (the player) tries to climb the girders to get to the top and rescue the maiden, but the gorilla is throwing barrels down to crush him. The theme could be that love is a never-ending quest since the man can never get to the woman. I didn't see a donkey. Someone told me the name was supposed to be Monkey Kong (after King Kong), but the inventors were not English speakers and didn't realize they had made a spelling error.

◇ *Frogger* teaches the lesson that "Life is Hell" or that you should learn to get to your goal without getting in the way of others. The poor little frog stands on the curb forlornly gazing at his mission— to cross a busy street with five lanes of cars and trucks and then to cross a river with rows of logs, turtles, alligators, and other foes. He is safe only when he can hop into a home bay on the bank without touching any shrubs. Maybe the theme is that it pays to persevere or that success *is* possible if you try hard enough.

◇ When I played *Pac-Man*, it made me think of my life in school. My professors are Speedy, Shadow, Bashful, and Pokey, and they are out to get me. I try to avoid collisions with these professors as I struggle to get my assignments done, always moving quickly but cautiously. My reward when I turn in an assignment is like when Pac-Man eats an energy dot. I get to turn around and chase my professors for a little while, but it's just so they can spill more work on me. When I receive a good grade it's like when Pac-Man eats the cherry, orange, apple, and strawberry to receive more points. As the game progresses, Pac-Man's opponents move faster and so Pac-Man has to move faster too. This is like toward the end of the semester when we are swamped with a lot of work and pressured to finish.

◇ What I got out of the game *Centipede* is that after all life's challenges, it doesn't get any easier. There will always be obstacles in the way and once you get around one, there are more to overcome.

◇ *Jack and the Beanstalk* is based on the old folktale. The purpose is to maneuver your way through rows and rows of beanstalks while being hit with eggs and bluebirds. Then you must sneak past the giant to grab the magic harp and the goose that lays the golden eggs. If you succeed, you win a free chance to put poor Jack through his adventures again.

◇ The most expensive game (50¢ compared to 25¢) is *Dragon's Lair*. It is a computerized romantic quest complete with a sword buried in stone, castles to assault, chasms to cross, mountains to climb, dragons to slay, and a princess to be rescued. A player who is really expert can actually rescue the princess. This is the only game that has the possibility of a happy ending.

These comments about a sampling of video games illustrate both similarities and differences between their storylines and those found in the majority of books that are offered to young readers. Notice how pessimistic most of the games are, how they nearly all end in the defeat of the protagonist. Yet with books, the demand from parents has been that their children be given happy stories, ones in which the young reader is left with hope. Perhaps it's just that most adults, at least most educators, don't play video games and therefore do not know enough to criticize them for their pessimism and glorification of violence as well as their sometimes sexism, racism, and general hostility. However, teachers wishing to discuss such matters with their students would need to approach the task cautiously. Teenagers are extra sensitive to criticisms of "their culture," especially from outsiders.

Cynics might be suspicious of our motivation in suggesting that teachers bring the study of rock music, videos, and video games into the literature class. They might think that since we can't ban video games the way the government did in the Philippines, our plan for the United States is to make them an object of study in literature classes and thereby kill off their appeal.

That's certainly not our goal. Instead, we want some of the appeal of the games to transfer over to the study of literature. We want students to see that all of literature has common elements which appeal to something deep within the human psyche. This love of story is one of the things that sets humans apart. And of all the literature discussed in this book, drama is perhaps the most accessible. All one needs to do is to turn on the radio or television set, enter a theater, put on a record or tape, or for that matter enter a video game room. What all of these media do is to put a frame around a bit of life. People who do not have this kind of commercially prepared drama create it themselves through ceremony, dance, telling or acting out stories, or just plain old eavesdropping on their neighbors.

◈ HUMOR

Rafael Sabatini began his finest novel, *Scaramouche*, with a one-sentence characterization of his hero, "He was born with a gift of laughter and a sense that the world was mad." The ability to laugh at ourselves and the madness of the world is nature's kindest, most needed, gift to a perpetually beleagured humanity. The need seems even more deperate today, though probably every previous generation could have made the same claim, so we laugh at almost everything and anything. At a time when taxes and death and sex are serious matters indeed, they are also staples of humor. We laugh at taxes because they are plagues, and we must laugh at things that threaten us. We laugh at death because it is inevitable, and we must laugh at things that terrify us. We laugh at sex because it is an enigma, and we must laugh at things that bewilder us.

We are pleased when we find something, anything, to laugh at. We are even more pleased when we discover someone who consistently makes us laugh. As Steve Allen reminds us:

◇Without laughter, life on our planet would be intolerable. So important is laughter to us that humanity highly rewards members of one of the most unusual professions on earth, those who make a living by inducing laughter in others. This is very strange if you stop to think of it; that otherwise sane and responsible citizens should devote their professional energies to causing others to make sharp, explosive barking-like exhalations.[21]

Given their enforced world of school and an ever-demanding society, young people need laughter every bit as much as adults, maybe even more so.

What do young people find funny? Lance M. Gentile and Merna M. McMillen's article, "Humor and the Reading Program," offers a starting point. Their stages of children's and young adults' interests in humor, somewhat supplemented, are:

◇ Ages 10–11: literal humor, slapstick (e.g., "The Three Stooges"), laughing at accidents (banana-peel humor) and misbehavior, some-times mildly lewd jokes (usually called "dirty jokes"), and grossness.

◇ Ages 12–13: practical jokes, teasing, goofs, sarcasm, more lewd jokes, joke-riddles, sick jokes, elephant jokes, grape jokes, tongue-twisters, knock-knock jokes, moron jokes, TV blooper shows, and grossness piled upon grossness.

◇ Ages 14–15: more and more lewd jokes (some approaching a mature recognition of the humor inherent in sex), humor aimed at schools and parents and adults in authority, "Mork and Mindy" and their ilk, and grossness piled upon even greater grossness. Young adults may still prefer their own humor to their parents' humor, but they are increasingly catching on to adult humor and may prefer it to their own.

◇ Ages 16–up: more subtle humor, satire and parody now acceptable and maybe even preferable, witticisms (rather than last year's half-witticisms which they now detest in their younger brothers and sisters). Adult humor is increasingly part of their repertoire, partly because they are anxious to appear sophisticated, partly because they *are* growing up.[22]

Anyone who has worked with young people knows how important humor is to them. The humor may range from collections of "Peanut" comic strips to the sophistication of "Doonesbury" comics, from the poetry of limericks to Shel Silverstein's verses, from the gentle satire in Paula Danziger's novels to the more perceptive satire in Leonard Wibberley's *The Mouse That Roared* to the black humor in Joseph Heller's *Catch-22*, but humor of many kinds is essential to most young people.

Much humor cuts across age lines. Television's "M*A*S*H" was an extraordinarily popular network situation comedy which retains its popu-larity in syndication, mostly because different age groups could find differ-ent facets of the show they thought especially funny. That applies almost equally well to other TV shows like "Rocky and His Friends" and "The Roadrunner" cartoons and "Peanuts" specials and to that greatest of mod-ern inadvertent humorists, Howard Cosell.

Teachers and librarians need to know what humor is popular with what ages and what kinds of young people. The categories that follow and the titles in each may (or may not) amuse teenagers in a particular school at a particular time. Almost nothing is so transitory as humor, though a few titles and a few authors may seem nearly permanent. Teachers and librarians looking for the permanently popular in humor are looking for the nearly impossible.

Films, Television, and Comics

Young people delight in going to the movies, especially to watch horror films like *Halloween* or *Friday the 13th* and their spawnings or to catch something funny. What they find hysterically amusing—*Porky's* or *National Lampoon's Animal House* or *Splash*—adults may find childish or stupid, but some films appeal to adults and young people alike, albeit for different reasons. Fairly recent films like *Risky Business* or *Stripes* or *Airplane* have wider appeal to the young and the old. But then, to some adults' surprise, classic comedies like Harold Lloyd's *The Freshman* (1925), Charlie Chaplin's *The Gold Rush* (1925), Buster Keaton's *The General* (1927), and Stan Laurel and Oliver Hardy in almost anything (the short film, "Big Business," in 1929 is their finest film) often prove popular with young people.

Enduring TV sitcoms in syndication like "The Andy Griffith Show," "The Beverly Hillbillies," "Happy Days," "One Day at a Time," and "I Love Lucy" may win no prizes for sophistication, but they are consistently admired and laughed at by young people and older people (who presumably ought to know better and seldom do). But then more sophisticated shows also endure, "The Bob Newhart Show," "Barney Miller," "Soap," "Taxi," and "The Mary Tyler Moore Show." And for the aficionado, syndication has restored "Sergeant Bilko" and "Rocky and His Friends" (with the wonderful Boris Badenov and Dudley Do-Right and Snively Whiplash) to American homes.

No art form has brought more humor to Americans than the daily comic strip. If comics before World War II provided little that was more than the silly, with the exceptions of "Krazy Kat" and the surrealistic "Smokey Stover," today's comic strips offer humor of many sorts for almost any reader—"Hagar the Horrible," "The Wizard of Id," "Miss Peach," "Herman," "Andy Capp," "Drabble," and "Doonesbury." And many of these comics have been collected and bound into books, some of them exceptionally and deservedly popular with young people, Jim Davis' *Garfield Eats His Heart Out* appeals to the nastily sentimental in all of us. Jeff MacNelly's collections of "Shoe" cartoons are gentle and admirable satires. Charles Schulz's many "Peanuts" books are widely, sometimes extravagantly, popular with young readers. For more sophisticated and knowledgeable readers, Garry Trudeau's "Doonesbury" strips are available in book form. For those willing to look a bit harder, Walt Kelly's "Pogo" strips offer wonderful and warm and sometimes biting comments about humans through the mouths of immortals like Pogo the opossum, Porkypine the porcupine, Albert the alligator, Beauregard Buglebay the hounddog, Churchy La Femme the reformed pirate and turtle, and Ma'm'selle Hepzibah the skunk.

Comic books have usually found less favor with teachers and librarians, and *MAD Magazine* has too often been lumped together with adventure/thriller/sexy comic books. But since 1956 when Alfred E. Neuman beamed his idiotic smile from *MAD*'s cover, the magazine has been steadily popular with teenagers. If they often miss the point of satires or the parodies, young people have continued to find something to laugh at in *MAD*. Periodically, collections of *MAD* material appear in book form, usually but not always edited by Larry Siegel or William Gaines or Albert Feldstein, and these collections are treasured and quoted lovingly by the young, many of whom treasure the material because parents, teachers, and librarians claim to dislike it.

Children's Books and Wordplay

Good children's books are humorous, and the best are delights for both the children who hear them and the adults who read them aloud. Michael Bond's Paddington Bear books, especially *A Bear Called Paddington* and *Paddington at the Seaside*, retain their popularity, as do Beverly Cleary's books about a misunderstood mouse, *The Mouse and His Motorcycle* and *Runaway Ralph*. Cleary's books for slightly older children, *Ellen Tebbits* and *Henry Huggins* and *Henry and Beezus*, are hardly recent, but they continue to be read and enjoyed. Deborah and James Howe's delightful spoof about vampires, *Bunnicula: A Rabbit-Tale of Mystery*, amuses almost all readers. The finest of them all, Dr. Seuss (sometimes known as Theodor Seuss Geisel) received a special Pulitzer Prize in 1984, but several generations of children had given him a far more important, if less official, award as their favorite funny writer. *And to Think That I Saw It on Mulberry Street*, *The 500 Hats of Bartholomew Cubbins*, *Thidwick the Big-Hearted Moose*, *If I Ran the Circus*, and *How the Grinch Stole Christmas* are admired and, more important, read. Seuss' greatest work is *Horton Hatches the Egg*, a tale of true and faithful Horton the elephant and flighty Mazie who flits off, leaving Horton with her egg to hatch.

Some adults are driven by their own Protestant ethic to argue that as young people mature they should put away childish things—humor, for example—to become serious and dull (and pompous, just as these adults are). Growing up may mean that the type of humor most enjoyed may change, but humor remains a constant. Some books, surprisingly, remain almost as constant. Dr. Seuss' books, particularly, are often fondly remembered by secondary students, and these books might prove valuable in the secondary English class as examples of humor and wordplay. Imitations or emulations of Seuss are far more difficult than most students realize, and the humor is still capable of infecting older students than some teachers or librarians recognize.

Wordplay is popular with teenagers, a fact that teachers should encourage for that is what writing is all about, playing with words until they fall into place to make interesting sense. Two writers fascinated by wordplay and aiming at quite different audiences have consistently intrigued young adults. Alvin Schwartz's many books aimed at junior high students are as much fun as their titles would indicate, for example, *Chin Music: Tall Tales and Other Tales*; *Flapdoodle: Pure Nonsense from American Folklore*; *Tomfoolery: Trickery and Foolery with Words*; and *A Twister of Twists, A Tangle of Tongues*. More subtle and aimed at older students are the books of Willard R. Espy, but any high school student who enjoys fooling around with words will love *An Almanac of Words*; *Have a Word on Me: A Celebration of Language*; *Espygrams*; and *O Thou Improper, Thou Uncommon Noun*.

YA Novels and Humor

Librarians and teachers who have kept up-to-date with the best of YA fiction may wonder if much quality YA humor can be found. Certainly, few readers would associate humor with the compelling dramas of Robert Cormier, the historical novels of Rosemary Sutcliff or Scott O'Dell, the realism of Alice Childress, or the fantasies of Alan Garner. The high seriousness of these writers may have won them richly deserved applause by adult critics. Inadvertently, that may have cost them some young adult readers who prefer the light to the serious.

Few critics would place Paula Danziger's novels in the pantheon of YA fiction, yet Danziger is among the most popular writers for young adults. Her novels are, admittedly, loaded with puns and jokes and one-liners and visual humor, but they are far more than mere collections of laughs. *The Cat Ate My Gymsuit, There's a Bat in Bunk Five, The Pistachio Prescription, Can You Sue Your Parents for Malpractice?* and *The Divorce Express* remain favorites with junior high school students because they do not talk down to their readers, because they present real issues and real problems facing their readers, and because they do not pretend that there are easy answers to any problems. Danziger's inability to develop characters, particularly adults, and her willingness to toss glib comments around as if they were profound may annoy adults, but her humor is exactly what her readers want.

More successful by far for a slightly older audience is T. Ernesto Bethancourt's *The Dog Days of Arthur Cane*. Reduced to the simple plot of a young man who irritates an African student and is thereby turned into a mongrel dog, the novel sounds simple-minded, but it is not. Arthur wakes up one morning, finds that he is a quite different self, and tries to resolve the immediate problems (and eventually must solve some long-range problems or die).

◇ I tried to stand up. The tile on the bathroom floor was too slippery for my paws, and my toenails kept sliding in between the cracks. It was then that I realized that I was trying to stand up people style.

THE PEOPLE BEHIND THE BOOKS

PAULA DANZIGER, Author

**Can You Sue Your Parents for
 Malpractice?**
The Cat Ate My Gymsuit
The Divorce Express
There's a Bat in Bunk Five

As to the future of young adult literature, I've signed a multiple book contract with Dell and so my future is fine. Actually, I'm optimistic about the whole future of YA books. It's a writer's job to tell good stories with good characters. And when writers do that there will be readers. I got into this business while I was a high school reading and English teacher. It was a tough business. The last year I taught in junior high my slip fell down in class and two students crazy-glued the desks to the floor. The realization came that it was incredibly hard to be a good creative writer and a good creative teacher. Each was a full time commitment. I chose to go with the writing, but I write to the kids I once taught and to the ones who, I hope, still learn from what I write. The next generation of YA writers will be kids who've grown up on kids' books so the genre won't seem strange to them. This means these future writers won't have to worry about a lot of the things we worry about and they can concentrate on telling good stories. I'm looking forward to reading their books, and I hope they'll keep on reading mine. ◆

And he grows thirsty:

 ◇ Thinking that a drink of water would help, I went back into the bathroom. I looked up at a sink that seemed ten feet high. I could see my glass up there, but no way to reach it. But being a good sized dog, I could get up on my hind legs and get my head into the sink. After falling down a few times, I got my front paws hooked over the edge of the sink and my hind feet braced. The only problem was that the water wasn't running, and I couldn't turn it on.

And later, still unsatisfied:

 ◇ My thirst was worse now, if that was possible. And there was the john, with cool water in it. But I still couldn't bring myself to drink any.

And even later, even more unsatisfied:

 ◇ I won't lie to you about what I ended up doing. By the way, that blue stuff doesn't taste bad at all. Kind of like a raunchy Kool-Aid.

And all this in the first chapter.

 Of all YA novelists, M. E. Kerr is consistently the funniest though all her novels are essentially serious studies of young people caught up in emotional quandaries. If Kerr looks wryly at her young characters, she never lacks compassion for them or her readers.

 Dinky Hocker Shoots Smack, her first novel and the only one not told in first person, is filtered through the consciousness of fifteen-year-old library habitué Tucker Woolf, whose sketches remind his mother of a "depressing

THE PEOPLE BEHIND THE BOOKS

M. E. KERR, Author

Dinky Hocker Shoots Smack
Him She Loves?
Me, Me, Me, Me, Me, Not a Novel
What I Really Think of You

I *hope* I can woo young adults away from the boob tube and Pac Man not just with entertaining stories, but also with subject matter which will provoke concern and a questioning about this complicated and often unfair world we live in. I would like my readers to laugh, but also to think; to be introspective, but also to reach out . . . and I hope I can give them characters and situations which will inspire these reactions. Now that the young adult field seems to have grown up, I hope it will grow out and touch, and that I'll be contributing. ◆

Dinky Hocker Shoots Smack! Harper & Row, 1972.
Him She Loves? Harper & Row, 1984.
Me, Me, Me, Me, Me, Not a Novel. Harper & Row, 1983.
What I Really Think of You. Harper & Row, 1982.

Bosch." In advertising for a home for his cat Nader (named after Ralph Nader), Tucker meets Dinky, whose mother suffers for the ills of the world and ignores Dinky; Dinky's cousin Natalia, who is emotionally troubled and talks in rhymes; and P. John Knight, whose left-wing father has made P. John become right wing with a vengeance. Kerr's humor in this book, as in later ones, does not arise from one-liners or obvious jokes but from the characters themselves. She does not write down to her readers, dropping references to Nader, Bosch, Dostoevsky, and the Bible, among others, in her books. She assumes young adults can think and feel and laugh.

Her best and funniest book is *If I Love You, Am I Trapped Forever?* Alan Bennett, the narrator, lives in upstate New York with a grandfather and a mother deserted by Alan's father years before. Alan describes himself early in the book as "*The* most popular boy at Cayuta High. Very handsome. Very cool. Dynamite." His life and his love life with Leah are perfect in every way until Duncan Stein moves to town, and slowly Alan's life and world crumble. Whatever else Doomed (Alan's nickname for Duncan) is, he is untypical. No basketball, no school clubs, no going steady, nothing that makes him identifiable to Alan. But Doomed does gain notoriety with his underground newspaper, *Remote*, and creates a dating fad at Cayuta High—going steady is out and one-time-only dates become the in-thing.

Alan's puzzlement is obvious and understandable. Doomed plays by no rules Alan knows, nor is Doomed interested in Alan's friendship. When Alan and Doomed walk together from homeroom to English class, they have a short and pointed conversation:

◇ We were studying Alfred, Lord Tennyson's poem "In Memoriam" that week. The poem was a tribute to his friend, Arthur Hallan, who died suddenly of influenza when he was just twenty-two.

I said something to Doomed then about trying to make friends with him, and then I said, "Well, I guess we'll never be known as Tennyson and Hallam, will we, Stein?"

Stein said, "Croak and find out, why don't you?"

How hostile can you get?

If Kerr's later books have not lived up to the promise of her first two, they are all enjoyable.

Other YA novelists whose humor deserves attention are Richard Peck for his three amusing novels about the supernatural, *The Ghost Belonged to Me, Ghosts I Have Been*, and *The Dreadful Future of Blossom Culp* and Leon Garfield for several novels described in Chapter 5, especially *The Strange Affair of Adelaide Harris* and *The Night of the Comet*. Readers, adult or young adult, who think that Judy Blume has little, if any, sense of humor as shown in *Forever* and *Tiger Eyes* should read three of her books written for a much younger audience, *Blubber, Superfudge*, and *Tales of a Fourth Grade Nothing*. Why Blume's books for children are so funny and her books for young adults so deadly serious is something of a mystery. (Though there are some readers who regard *Forever* as one of the funniest books in the language.)

Humor and Poetry

Too many young adults, hardly enamored of poetry to begin with, assume that poetry and humor are mutually exclusive terms. Librarians and teachers can, of course, remind youngsters of the joys of the poetry in Lewis Carroll's *Alice in Wonderland* and *Through the Looking Glass*, remembering all the time that virtually all these poems are parodies of poetry doomed to nonexistence through the success of Carroll's work, or of the wonderful wit available by reading Gilbert and Sullivan's *The Pirates of Penzance* or *The Mikado* or *Iolanthe*, but the fun of reading Carroll or Gilbert and Sullivan are largely reserved for adults. Ernest Lawrence Thayer's "Casey at the Bat" and much of Ogden Nash will remain unfunny to many young adults.

Far funnier, because the authors are inherently serious writers writing for adults, are Dorothy Parker's poetry and Don Marquis' *archy and mehitabel*. Parker's cynicism and skepticism appeal to young people once they find her work. Marquis' archy is a gigantic cockroach with guts, a born writer who had a desperate drive to write. He approached the typewriter and then:

◇ would climb painfully upon the framework of the machine and cast himself with all his force upon a key, head downward, and his weight and the impact of the blow were just sufficient to operate the machine, one slow letter after another. He could not work the capital letters, and he had a great deal of difficulty operating the mechanism that shifts the paper so that a fresh line may be started. We never saw a cockroach work so hard or perspire so freely in all our lives before. After about an hour of this frightfully difficult literary labor he fell to the floor exhausted, and we saw him creep feebly into a nest of the poems which are always there in profusion.

So Marquis discovers archy's first literary effort, and he follows with other poems, all of them funny, though they are well over fifty years old: "the song of mehitabel," "the cockroach who had been to hell," "aesop revised by archy," "pete the parrot and shakespeare," and "freddy the rat perishes."

Two witty and funny modern poets deserve to be read by young adults. Shel Silverstein's *Where the Sidewalk Ends* and *A Light in the Attic* are filled with antic rhymes and silly ideas almost any reader would enjoy. His "Crowded Tub" describes a childhood experience common to many readers:

> There's too many kids in this tub.
> There's too many elbows to scrub.
> I just washed a behind
> That I'm sure wasn't mine,
> There's too many kids in this tub.[23]

Other poems from *A Light in the Attic* like "They've Put a Brassiere on the Camel," "Who Ordered the Broiled Face?" "Adventures of a Frisbee," "The Toad and the Kangaroo," and "Skin Stealer" illustrate Silverstein's skill, poetry that is sometimes silly, sometimes slapstick, sometimes thoughtful, sometimes all those at once.

Not better but presumably more sophisticated (and sometimes equally silly) are Piet Hein's poems which he calls *grooks*,[24] short aphoristic poems accompanied by a simple line drawing. Two grooks from his first collection illustrate the form:

> Living is
>   a thing you do
> now or never—
>   which do you?

> Man's a kind
>   of Missing Link,
> fondly thinking
>   he can think.

Other grooks are widely quoted by fans, and there are many:

> To make a name for learning
> when other roads are barred,
> take something very easy
> and make it very hard.

> Wisdom is
> the booby prize
> given when you've been
> unwise.

Those who always
know what's best
are
a universal pest.

Limericks, often assumed to be the funniest of poems and rarely so, can be found in abundance in Ray Allen Billington's *Limericks Historical and Hysterical, Plagiarized, Arranged, Annotated, and Some Written by Ray Allen Billington*. The collection is excellent and, surprisingly enough, often funny and sometimes even witty, but teachers and librarians are warned that the limericks are often bawdy and coarse and, of course, delightful. Perhaps more proper are the limericks by Morris Bishop, "Limericks Long after Lear" in *The Best of Bishop*,[25] witness these two innocent examples:

A ghoulish old fellow in Kent
Encrusted his wife in cement;
  He said with a sneer:
  "I was careful, my dear,
To follow your natural bent."

A joker who haunts Monticello
Is really a terrible fellow;
  In the midst of caresses
  He fills ladies' dresses
With garter snakes, ice cubes, and jell-o.

Gentle, Almost Nostalgic Humor

In the last fifteen years, several books of humor have appeared that are mildly mocking but clearly do not mean to hurt anyone, unless it is the authors as they reminisce on their ill-spent youth. Librarians and teachers will recognize that the type derives from Stephen Leacock, as in "My Financial Career," and Paul Rhymer who wrote so many warm and funny scripts for "Vic and Sade."

Garrison Keillor's "A Prairie Home Companion" on National Public Radio is consistently funny and warm about the people in the fictitious town of Lake Wobegon, Minnesota. The advertisements are amusing (Ralph's Pretty Good Grocery store and Powdermilk Biscuits, "made from the whole wheat that gives shy persons the strength to do what needs to be done") and Keillor's quiet charm make Lake Wobegon ("the town that time forgot and the decades cannot improve") come alive.

Keillor's humor comes across in the pages of *Happy To Be Here*, especially in a brief plea, "Shy Rights: Why Not Pretty Soon," which gently spoofs the noisier arguments advanced by other minority groups for their rights.

Better known, and for some young adults one of their peak reading experiences, is the work of Jean Shepherd. While Shepherd enthusiasts are fond of *In God We Trust, All Others Pay Cash, A Fistful of Fig Newtons*, and *The Ferrari in the Bedroom*, most readers agree that his funniest book is *Wanda Hickey's Night of Golden Memories and Other Disasters*.

Shepherd is clearly fond of his characters. While he certainly uncovers some of life's absurdities, there is no bitterness in his work. Shepherd relishes the golden memories, slightly painful and slightly exaggerated, of his own youth and his own youthful dreams.

The title story in *Wanda Hickey's Night . . .* begins as Shepherd remembers back on his junior prom, renting a white jacket formal, polishing up the old Ford V-8 convertible, and vainly pushing himself to ask Daphne Bigelow for the big date. ("Each time, I broke out in a fevered sweat and chickened out at the last instant.") In desperation, he asks the ever-present, ever-available Wanda Hickey to double-date with a friend.

Off to the Cherrywood Country Club to dance to Mickey Isley and his Magic Music Makers, our hero discovers that he soon develops a bad case of the sweats which soon leads to an even worse case of rash. Outside and ready for the big drink at the Red Rooster Roadhouse, he discovers that he has left the convertible top down and rain has poured, and the foursome, miserable and wet, drive off.

But the roadhouse proves no oasis of sanity. Proving his masculinity and sophistication, he orders triple shots of bourbon on the rocks and drinks up:

> ◇ Down it went—a screaming 90 proof rocket searing savagely down my gullet. For an instant, I sat stunned, unable to comprehend what had happened. Eyes watering copiously, I had the brief urge to sneeze, but my throat seemed to be paralyzed.

All during this, Wanda coos into his ear, "Isn't this romantic? Isn't this the most wonderful night in all our lives?"

Our hero, sure that the liquor had done its worst, proceeds to eat a meal of lamb chops, turnips, mashed potatoes, cole slaw, and strawberry shortcake, almost immediately followed by a trip to the restroom where he sees his meal a second time. Later he takes Wanda home, but he cannot bring himself to kiss her when he smells sauerkraut on her breath. He returns home to a sardonic, if mildly sympathetic, father who reassures his son that his head will "stop banging" in a couple of days, and an exhausted and strangely satisfied young man falls into bed.

Nora Ephron's *Crazy Salad* is stronger fare than either Keillor's or Shepherd's book, but many young women will laugh as they read "A Few Words about Breasts" and "On Never Having Been a Prom Queen."

Some Gentle Satires

One of the more widely used handbooks of literature opens its definition of satire this way:

> ◇ A literary manner which blends a critical attitude with humor and wit to the end that human institutions of humanity itself may be improved. The true satirist is conscious of the frailty of institutions of man's devising and attempts through laughter not so much to tear them down as to inspire a remodeling.[26]

Some teachers and librarians assume that satire must be vicious or biting in tone and content, but some effective satires are gentle, even loving.

Two newspaper columnists whose books sell by the millions are gentleness personified, though they have their astringent moments. Erma Bombeck's spoofs of motherhood and homemaking and children amuse a wide range of readers, but she is safely on the side of tradition and apple pie and all that the home represents. Conservatives love her because she writes about a world they know, a world that sometimes bores them. Liberals love her because she seems to make light of traditions. Her assumptions are safe ones, that readers know about growing up in a home that is warm and loving, if sometimes strange indeed. Young adults sometimes find her amusing—she writes about a world they certainly know—though they wonder why adults find her habit-forming, she so belabors the obvious in most columns. Still there are those clever one-liners (which often serve as titles for her collected columns), and her columns do serve as antidotes to the joyless worlds of Ann Landers and Abigail Van Buren.

Art Buchwald's world of Washington politics and scandal and intrigue is certainly less familiar to young people, but adults often find Buchwald's light spoofing of politicians a pleasant relief after the seriousness of the rest of the daily paper. Buchwald assumes readers know and care about the political world and the sins and oddities that bureaucracy is prone to. Young people curious about politics should read Buchwald. Teachers and librarians who care about wit and cleverness ought to alert other young people to the satisfactions of reading an often first-rate talent who cares about people and their frailties.

Three novelists write gentle and loving satires and deserve attention from teenagers. Stanley Kiesel's *The War between the Pitiful Teachers and the Splendid Kids* attacks the educational bureaucracy and bad teachers and much that good teachers and librarians deplore even more than young people do. Leonard Wibberley's Mouse series, *The Mouse That Roared*, *The Mouse on the Moon*, and *Beware of the Mouse*, poke the gentlest of fun at the pomposity and stupidity of the modern world. In *The Mouse That Roared*, the Duchy of Grand Fenwick, buried somewhere in Europe, is bankrupt. It declares war on the United States, knowing it will lose the war and thereby become eligible for assistance to rebuild the country. But Grand Fenwick, almost but not quite unbelievably, wins the war.

Jean Merrill's *The Pushcart War* is a classic among children's and young adult books, a gentle and most effective satire of war and human cupidity. Supposedly written in 1996, ten years after the end of the brief "Pushcart War," the novel is presented as straight, factual history, allowing the reader to see the humor and nobility and nastiness of humans as the war unfolds. The war begins as a truckdriver drives over and demolishes a pushcart while the pushcart owner is propelled into a pickle barrel. Soon the pushcart owners band together to fight back and the war is on. Noble figures like General Anna (formerly Old Anna), Maxie Hammerman, Morris the Florist, and Frank the Flower walk across history as do bad guys like Albert P. Mack (usually known simply as Mack, the truckdriver), Big Moe, Louis Livergreen, and Mayor Emmett P. Cudd. *The Pushcart War* is funny and wise and learned and utterly delightful for almost any reader, young adult or adult.

Richard Armour may have less appeal to young adults, but for a few sophisticated teenagers who like and know literature and history and who enjoy a good spoof of pompous writers about either literature or history, *Twisted Tales from Shakespeare, The Classics Reclassified, English Lit Relit, It All Started with Columbus,* and *It All Started with Eve* are essential books.

While young adults may not know the comedy of Bob Elliott and Ray Goulding, that should be remedied by teachers and librarians who care about wit and comedic style. *Write if You Get Work: The Best of Bob and Ray* and *From Approximately Coast to Coast . . . It's the Bob and Ray Show* offer sample scripts from their many shows. Especially good are the several episodes from "Garish Summit," their spoof of the "Dallas" and "Knots Landing" tripe, "Wally Ballou and the Cranberry Grower," a spoof of an inarticulate interviewer faced by a talentless giant of agriculture, and "Mary Backstayge, Noble Wife," a spoof of soap operas.

More Sophisticated Satire

Several writers, all of whom have written for the *New Yorker,* offer young adults the chance to sample somewhat more sophisticated, though still reasonably gentle, satire.

James Thurber's gentleness may be more apparent than real, but many of his short sketches and short stories have proved popular to the young. Nostalgic pieces like "The Night the Bed Fell" and "University Days" are accessible to young people, and "Fables for Our Time," especially "The Shrike and the Chipmunk," "The Owl Who Thought He Was God," and "The Unicorn in the Garden," are popular with many teenagers. His rewriting of history, "If Grant Had Been Drinking at Appomattox," is funny *if* readers know history just as "The Macbeth Murder Mystery" is funny *if* readers know the play. Thurber's three best short stories are, unhappily, often beyond the emotional understanding of young adults, but if readers can handle them, "The Secret Life of Walter Mitty," "The Catbird Seat," and "The Greatest Man in the World" are among the finest, most sophisticated, and least gentle satires.

E. B. White is far more gentle and likable than Thurber, though his adult material has less immediate appeal to the young. *The Second Tree from the Corner* is, simply put, one of the great works in American literature and why it goes largely unknown among so many teachers and librarians is one of life's great mysteries. White's poetry in that book is clever and amusing, especially "The Red Cow Is Dead" and "Song of the Queen Bee," and "The Retort Transcendental" is a wonderful parody of Thoreau taken too far. The finest short stories are "The Decline of Sport," a relatively funny satire on the inevitable decline in sports, and "The Morning of the Day They Did It," a less than amusing satire on the end of the world.

Two wonderfully witty men are probably doomed never to have wide appeal to young people, though some adults revere them and their work. Frank Sullivan's wit is most apparent in *The Night the Old Nostalgia Burned Down,* a collection of columns, largely from the *New Yorker,* about the

Cliché Expert who appears as a witness at court trials and spouts clichés of every profession. A bit more accessible and less dated is the sketch on "Dr. Arbuthnot's Academy" where people come to see if clichés are literally possible (a woman learns to tickle people pink, others learn how to rub people the wrong way, a woman in a kettle on a stove learns how to stew in her own juice, and an accountant learns how to add insult to injury). S. J. Perelman was once a writer for the Marx Brothers, and titles for several of his sketches in *The Most of S. J. Perelman* and *The Last Laugh* suggest the wackiness of Marx Brothers comedies: "Waiting for Santy," "Farewell, My Lovely Appetizer," "Rancors Aweigh," and "To Yearn Is Subhuman, to Forestall Divine." Young people fascinated by comic word play will love Perelman. Others are hereby warned.

Woody Allen is a favorite of young people, though many probably have trouble following his verbal play. His movies, especially *Annie Hall* and *Take the Money and Run*, are filled with wackiness and wisdom, more often than not strangely mixed, but Allen's books are far wittier and have far better one-liners than his films. *Getting Even* is typical Allen wit which assumes readers will know Freud and the Hasidic Jews and what college catalogues read like and more. *Without Feathers* and *Side Effects* assume intelligent and sophisticated readers. Allen is fascinated by God and death, and his books have wisdom and some wacky wit about both.

Peter De Vries is the apotheosis of *New Yorker* cleverness, and his novels have consistently appealed to a sophisticated audience sure that when they read a De Vries novel, they will receive humor and a gentle, slightly wry satire. *Reuben, Reuben* satirizes poetry and gullible people as poet Gowan McCland rambles through the chicken à la king poetry circuit. Better yet is *The Mackerel Plaza*, De Vries' most successful satire. Andrew Mackerel is a liberal minister of the People's Liberal Church, "the first split-level church in America" with a "small worship area at one end" and with a congregation that takes delight in questioning everything about religion.

Black Humor and Satire

So-called Black Humor uses irony and fantasy to ridicule the absurdities and bleakness of the human situation. Often savagely satirical, Black Humor virtually forces readers to laugh at the despair they feel when they are confronted by war, bureaucracies, social control, obsessive love—and obsessiveness generally—illogical political talk and propaganda, television, advertising, *the* bomb, and psychiatrists. If Black Humor has an obvious weakness, which goes largely happily ignored by most readers, it is an obsession with the theme which arises out of situations to illustrate the theme, rather than the most traditional method of beginning with a human situation involving believable characters and letting theme emerge. Douglas M. Davis' anthology, *The World of Black Humor*, has excerpts from writers like John Hawkes, J. P. Donleavy, Terry Southern, Joseph Heller, Thomas Pynchon, and John Barth and serves as a fine introduction to the genre.

Of the many writers plowing this field, two have proved popular with young people who enjoy iconoclastic literature. Ken Kesey's *One Flew over the Cuckoo's Nest* concerns Randal Patrick McMurphy's confinement to a mental hospital because he refuses to knuckle under to authority. He changes the lives of and brings hope to other patients despite the attempts of Nurse Ratchet to bring peace and conformity to the ward.

Perhaps even more popular is Joseph Heller's savage attack on war and wartime stupidity in *Catch-22*. Captain John Yossarian, bombardier in the 25th squadron based on a Mediterranean island near the end of World War II, wants no part of any more missions. He believes that if he can convince everyone that he is crazy, he will be freed of all combat duty. But Doc Daneeka points out a catch:

> ◇ "You mean there's a catch?"
>
> "Sure there's a catch," Doc Daneeka replied. "Catch-22. Anyone who wants to get out of combat duty isn't really crazy."
>
> There was only one catch and that was Catch-22, which specified that a concern for one's own safety in the face of dangers that were real and immediate was the process of a rational mind. Orr was crazy and could be grounded. All he had to do was ask; and as soon as he did, he would no longer be crazy and would have to fly more missions. Orr would be crazy to fly more missions and sane if he didn't, but if he was sane he had to fly them. If he flew them he was crazy and didn't have to; but if he didn't want to he was sane and had to. Yossarian was moved very deeply by the absolute simplicity of this clause of Catch-22 and let out a respectful whistle.
>
> "That's some catch, that Catch-22," he observed.
>
> "It's the best there is," Doc Daneeka agreed.

Heller's novel preceded the Vietnam War and the peace movement by several years, but because the book so perfectly pointed out the absurdity of a pointless war, *Catch-22* became something of a rallying point for protesters, just as it still rallies those who wonder about the military mind and bureaucracies gone mad in wartime.

Wacky British Humor and Parodies

"Monty Python's Flying Circus" has long been a favorite with many Americans, first as an imported television series, later as a series of movies—*Monty Python and the Holy Grail*, *Life of Brian*, and *Monty Python's The Meaning of Life*, and for fewer people, as recording artists—*Monty Python's Flying Circus*, *Another Monty Python Record*, *Monty Python's Previous Record*, and *Matching Tie and Handkerchief*. The British group provided much that was vulgar, a bit that was charming, and even more that was hysterically funny, and it added a catch-phrase to the language, "And now for something completely different."

Three members of Monty Python added further luster through two additional television shows, originally on British television but available in the United States, usually on PBS. John Cleese and his ex-wife Connie Booth's scripts for "Fawlty Towers" were exercises in pandemonium and general nasty and unrelieved humor. Michael Palin and Terry Jones developed a series of spoofs and parodies under the general title, "Ripping Yarns," among them such thrillers as "Across the Andes by Frog," "Murder at Moorstones Manor," "Curse of the Claw," "The Testing of Eric Olthwaite," and "Roger of the Raj." Unhappily, the scripts from "Fawlty Towers" are not in print. Happily, those from "Ripping Yarns" and its sequel, "More Ripping Yarns" are.

For readers curious about the origins of this sort of British comedy, Spike Milligan's "Goon Show Scripts" are not difficult to find on tape, and some of the best of the radio series—starring Milligan and Peter Sellers— can be found in print.

Because parody assumes readers' awareness of the work being satirized, gently or otherwise, some teachers and librarians assume that young adults would find parody difficult if not impossible. That may be true for the more esoteric sort of parody, usually of poetry, to be found in anthologies of parody, but some parodies are not merely within the grasp of young people, they are works young people would very much enjoy.

Some delightful parodies will probably appeal to the few. Will Jacobs and Gerard Jones' *The Beaver Papers: The Story of a Lost Season* imagines what would have happened had famous authors submitted scripts for "Leave It to Beaver" to save the show from cancellation, and the results include John Steinbeck's "The Beaver of Wrath," Samuel Beckett's "Waiting for Wally," Ingmar Bergman's "Cries and Beaver," and adaptations of classics like "Lady Cleaver's Beaver" and "The Brothers Beaver." Donald Ogden Stewart is almost forgotten, but his wonderful *A Parody Outline of History* parodies both history and literature in chapters like "Main Street: Plymouth Mass. in the Manner of Sinclair Lewis," "The Courtship of Miles Standish in the Manner of F. Scott Fitzgerald," and the two funniest chapters, "The Whisky Rebellion in the Bedtime Story Manner of Thornton W. Burgess" and "How Love Came to General Grant in the Manner of Harold Bell Wright."

Other parodies should prove easy for young adults. P. J. O'Rourke's *National Lampoon: Sunday Newspaper Parody* contains all the normal features of a Sunday paper, in this case the *Sunday Dacron Republican-Democrat* with parodies of various comic strips, columns by Merl Buchenwald and William F. Ducksward, strange obituaries, and even stranger ads. National Lampoon's *Off the Wall Street Journal* reproduces a newspaper that seems strangely like another newspaper with a frontpage headline reading, "Death and Taxes—A Special Report on How to Avoid Both." A bit more difficult is Jeff Greenfield's *Book of Books*, also from National Lampoon, offering tidbits from some current favorites, for example, Hans Stricker's *Get Out of Way or I'll Kill You* (or, *The Triumph of the Will Power*), *The Cooking of Provincial New Jersey*, and Delores Lash's *Love's Tormenting Itch*. And readers sick of self-improvement and self-fulfillment books should enjoy Joseph L. Troise's magnificent *Dare to Be Dull*, a self-help for those anxious to get out of the trendy rat race and back to being dull and invisible.

Two young adult novels are excellent parodies, although whether they will be read as parodies (or in the case of the first book, read at all) is unknown. John Rowe Townsend's *Kate and the Revolution* is set in the fictitious country of Essenheim. Heroine Kate and George, an English reporter, become entangled in a palace coup to overthrow Rudi, Crown Prince of Essenheim. Other characters in the Graustarkian tale of intrigue and derring-do are Dr. Stockhausen, a reactionary, Herman Schweiner, leader of the first coup, and Konrad Finken, leader of the second coup. When Kate and George visit Essenheim's national university, they find strange things going on as they talk to Klaus Klappdorf, Dean of the Faculty of Arts, Sciences, and Other Studies:

> ◇ A clutch of young people in dirty jeans, most with uncombed hair, emerged from a doorway they were passing. Beside the doorway was a placard that read PASSIVE RESISTANCE 102.
>
> "Is passive resistance taught as a course for credit?" asked George, startled.
>
> "To be sure!" Klaus replied happily. "As you may know, this university was founded only twelve years ago, when Herr Finkel decided that pickles were no longer a profitable business. When the university opened, we felt that we ought to have our own specialty, something this university could become known for. Something that wasn't done elsewhere. And we hit upon Studentship Studies."
>
> George looked up at Klaus with a dubious expression. Klaus, unaware of it, went on. "The young people who come to the University of Essenheim are students for four of the most formative years of their lives. What ought they to be studying? The answer is obvious, isn't it? They should be studying the thing that most concerns them, namely being a student. So"—he cleared his throat— "so we have established Studentship Studies, in the context of the interpersonal and transsocietal relationship structure that we seek to encourage through a meaningful, ongoing dialogue between the new generation and the world that surrounds it. The world of today."

Judie Angell's *Suds: A New Daytime Drama Brought to You* features Sue Sudley, orphaned when her parents, flying in separate planes, collided in midair. She comes to live with her aunt and uncle in Pallantine, Ohio. Readers who wonder about the likelihood of such a strange airplane accident will wonder even more as they meet the cast of stereotypes straight out of soap-operaland. Sue meets Storm Ryder, former football star but now paralyzed in a wheelchair; Dinah Deenie, video junkie; Joe Coffee, English teacher at Pallantine High and frustrated novelist; Joanna Coffee, Joe's wife and school bus driver and soon-to-be amnesia victim; Roger Gurney, Jr., Pallantine High's school newspaper editor; and assorted other dingalings. Sue saves the soul and cash of Dinah Deenie. And Sue prays that Storm will recover from his bout with paralysis, and he does. Near the end of the book as Sue has wrapped up most of the problems of the town and the universe, Storm has an accident. Dr. Proctor comes out of the hospital room:

> ◇ It's going to be all right," Dr. Proctor said. He was smiling faintly. "He's recovered consciousness and—"
>
> "And what," Will Ryder said, almost whispering.
>
> "And his left foot—*twitched*."

◆ *Suds* has a cast of wonderful stereotypes straight out of soap-opera-land.
From SUDS by Julie Angell. Copyright © 1983 by the Bradbury Press. Jacket painting by Jenny Rutherford. Reprinted by permission of Bradbury Press.

Anyone who watches soap operas—and that covers a major portion of young adults—and can still see the silliness in much of what passes for soap opera drama should love this book. So should adults.

Equally funny are two books about Miss Piggy. Jim Henson's *Miss Piggy's Guide to Life* is 113 pages of undiluted wisdom. Miss Piggy's eclectic diet (choose carefully from each diet whatever goodies are there and ignore the rest) and her advice to the lovelorn are particularly good. Asked what a woman should do if the man still wishes to see other women, Miss Piggy sensibly replies that she would "calmly, reasonably, and maturely explain to him that if he values his life, he should change his behavior." Henry Beard's *Miss Piggy's Treasury of Art Masterpieces from the Kermitage Collection* will likely appeal to fewer readers, but Muppet fans are insatiable.

Douglas Adams' trilogy, *The Hitchhiker's Guide to the Galaxy*, *The Restaurant at the End of the Universe*, and *Life, The Universe, and Everything*, began as BBC radio scripts, progressed to television scripts, and ultimately became three highly successful novels. The first, far and away the best of the lot, begins as Arthur Dent's house is due for demolishment to make way for a highway. He finds Ford Prefect, a somewhat strange friend and an apparently out of work actor, anxiously seeking a drink at a nearby pub. Ford seems hopelessly indifferent to Arthur's plight, mostly, as Ford tells Arthur, because the world will be destroyed in a few minutes to make way for a new galactic freeway. Soon, the pair are safe aboard a Vogon Construction Fleet Battleship only to find danger awaiting as the Vogon

◆ David Macaulay's *Motel of the Mysteries* is a spoof of scientific arrogance.

From MOTEL OF THE MYSTERIES by David Macaulay. Copyright © 1979 by David Macaulay. Reprinted by permission of Houghton Mifflin Company and The Hutchinson Publishing Group Ltd.

Commander of the ship orders them tossed out into space. Death appears likely, but they are picked up by a ship powered by Infinite Improbability Drive piloted by Zaphod Beetlebrox, a two-headed and three-armed ex-president of the Galaxy.

Improbabilities arise out of more improbabilities, but by this time, readers are caught up in the wild, and utterly unbelievable, adventures and the wildness of the tale and the characters, and the improbabilities are less important than the sheer enjoyment and humor of Adams' novel. And for those who wonder about reading the book, wisdom can be found. In what other book, recent or old, can readers learn that the answer "to life, the universe, and everything" is "forty-two."

Readers who have wondered about the apparent superhuman efforts of scientists to unravel the secrets of everything and anything will find David Macaulay's *Motel of the Mysteries* a wonderful spoof of scientific arrogance unmasked as wild guessing games. The book begins with the ominous description of the burial of the North American continent under tons of third- and fourth-class mail (caused by an accidental reduction in postal rates). Since 3850, scholars have wondered about the lost civilization, but it is left to forty-two-year-old Howard Carson to stumble and fall into a secret chamber. There he discovers "a gleaming secret seal" (DO NOT DISTURB) and "a plant that would not die." He enters the chamber and finds a body atop a "ceremonial platform" near a statue of the "deity WATT" and a container, "ICE," designed to "preserve, at least symbolically, the major internal organs of the deceased for eternity." Later he enters the inner chamber and there finds another body "in a highly polished white sarcophagus" behind translucent curtains. Near this body is a "sacred urn" and a "sacred parchment" holder and the "sacred collar" with a headband bearing a ceremonial chant, "Sanitized for Your Protection."

Macaulay's spoof should have wide appeal, and his drawings of Howard Carson playing savant and the many artifacts recovered from the two chambers add to the fun. Adults who have been to museums will particularly enjoy the concluding section of the book devoted to "Souvenirs and Quality Reproductions" from the Carson excavations now for sale.

The Humor of Death

Of all catastrophes, death is perhaps most feared. Perhaps for that reason, death is often the subject of humor. Charles Addams' macabre cartoons in the *New Yorker* have always been popular, and discovering humorous epitaphs on gravestones is almost an American industry. Fritz Spiegl's *A Small Book of Grave Humor*[27] has several examples that are funny to many readers and at least strange to those few who cannot regard anything about death as amusing:

Here lies	HERE
Poor Charlotte	LIES
Who died no harlot—	Lester Moore
But in her Virginity	Four slugs
Of the age of nineteen	From a 44
In this vicinity	No Les
Rare to be found	No More
or seen	

Humor about death goes back to the Greeks. In the mammoth collection of odds-and-ends verses called *The Greek Anthology*[28] can be found tributes to fallen heroes and conventional poems and some that seem strikingly unconventional. Dudley Fitts translates them in the following manner. A few are bitter:

"Epitaph of Dionysius of Tarsos"
At Sixty I, Dionysios of Tarsos, lie here,
Never having married:
    And I wish my father had not.

A few are satiric and amusing to us if not the object of scorn.

"On Marcus the Physician"
Yesterday Dr. Marcus went to see a statue of Zeus.
Though Zeus,
    and though marble,
We're burying the statue today.

"On Envious Diophon"
Diophon was crucified:
But seeing beside him another on a loftier cross,
He died of envy.

Mark Twain makes great fun of bad poetry about death in *The Adventures of Huckleberry Finn,* and he may have been inspired by Julia Moore, "The Sweet Singer of Michigan," who never lost an opportunity to write about the dead and the bereaved. Granted that she wrote in dead seriousness, her poetry can now be read only as amusing, or odd, verse. One of her major works concerned a little girl named Libbie:

> One morning in April, a short time ago,
>   Libbie was alive and gay;
> Her Savior called her, she had to go,
>   Ere the close of that pleasant day,
> While eating dinner, this dear little child
>   Was choked on a piece of beef.
> Doctors came, tried their skill awhile,
>   But none could give relief.

A contemporary of Julia Moore, Howard Heber Clark, who tilled the same poetic field, possibly helped to kill obituary verse with this tribute to little Willie:

> Willie had a purple monkey climbing on a yellow stick,
> And when he sucked the paint all off it made him deathly sick,
> And in his latest hours he clasped that monkey in his hand,
> And bade good-bye to earth and went into a better land.
>
> Oh! no more he'll shoot his sister with his little wooden gun;
> And no more he'll twist the pussy's tail and make her yowl, for fun.
> The pussy's tail now stands out straight; the gun is laid aside;
> The monkey doesn't jump around since little Willie died.[29]

If Clark's little Willie was presumably not meant for our laughter, a series of poems about another little Willie deliberately provoked laughter. Harry Graham, an English soldier in the Coldstream Guards who wrote under the penname, Col. D. Streamer, produced an enduring and much quoted masterpiece in 1902 with his *Ruthless Rhymes for Heartless Homes*[30] with poems like these:

> Billy, in one of his nice, new sashes,
> Fell in the fire and was burned to ashes.
> Now, although the room grows chilly,
> I haven't the heart to poke poor Billy.
>
> Making toast at the fireside,
> Nurse fell in the grate and died;
> And what makes it ten times worse,
> All the toast was burnt with nurse.
>
> Father heard his children scream,
> So he threw them in the stream,
> Saying, as he drowned the third,
> "Children should be seen, *not* heard."

So popular were these sadistic poems that papers printed new catastrophes by imitators, most—but not all—about Little Willie and his latest nastiness, and the form of poetry became known as "Little Willie" poems.[31] A few of the most popular imitations were these:

Willie poisoned Auntie's tea.
Auntie died in agony.
Uncle came and looked quite vexed.
"Really, Will," he said, "what next?"

Willie fell down the elevator—
Wasn't found till six days later.
Then the neighbors sniffed, "Gee whiz!
What a spoiled child Willie is."

Dr. Jones fell in the well,
And died without a moan.
He should have tended to the sick
And let the well alone.

Little Willie, mean as hell,
Drowned his sister in the well.
Mother said, while drawing water,
"Gee, it's hard to raise a daughter."

Death is hardly treated as serious in the early pages of Benjamin Lee's *It Can't Be Helped*. This too-often ignored, and very funny, English novel for young adults concerns young Max Orloff. His father has died, and Max and relatives gathered at the graveside. Max will long remember what followed as he stood there in his too-tight trousers:

◇ I was told to stand at the edge of the grave. It was astonishingly deep, hacked out of London clay, a large part of which I was on top of. I had no idea what I was supposed to do next. By a lucky chance, I found that, by leaving one leg a little way down the side of the small mountain of clay, dug out of the grave, I could take the strain off my crotch. I was soon to discover that being off balance could be disastrous. The service was not in English, so I could understand very little. A man who, although he also had the same shape nose as my relatives, behaved as if he was the manager of the graveyard, handed me a spade. I was astounded. It was a colossal pit and would take me, single-handed, about three days to fill it. I stood there helplessly, staring down into it. The same man bent toward my ear and muttered: "Throw a little earth on the coffin."

I took the spade. It was unexpectedly heavy. I lunged into the pile of dug-out earth and came up with an enormous spadeful, much more than I had intended. I could hardly lift it. Bracing all my muscles, which are not all that powerful, I swung it toward the grave. I knew I was going to fall in, on top of the coffin. It may seem funny to you, and immediately afterward it did to me. In fact, I laughed, which offended everyone.

None of the women had been allowed near the grave, but in the distance I could see my mother swearing to herself. It would not have been in English, but most of the relatives would have understood all right. I slowly toppled forward, holding out the spade at forty-five degrees, sliding down the hillock into the hole. The clay was sticky, so it happened in slow motion. I was about to disappear below ground level, wondering how a person ought to behave in his father's grave, when somebody grabbed my trousers from behind and hauled me back. The agony in my crotch was unbelievable. It was as if someone had stuck a knife in my balls. I let out a yell of pain, dropping the spade, which crashed down and bounced loudly on the lid of my father's coffin. The graveyard manager gave me a peculiar glance. One of the few relatives I had met before, Isadore Lansky, was trying to stop himself from laughing. Soon after, fortunately, the service ended. I did not think I had risen to the occasion, but then I seldom do.

The classic satiric novel about death is, of course, Evelyn Waugh's *The Loved One*, a wonderfully nasty assault on Americans and our customs of death. Dennis Barlow, English expatriate and one-time poet and now failed Hollywood writer, must arrange the funeral of an old friend. Dennis goes to Whispering Glades to see about the arrangements, and there he meets cosmetician Aimee Thanatogenos who introduces him to the euphemisms of death. Later, readers meet Mr. Joyboy, the person who puts the smiles on the bodies, or "loved ones."

The Ultimate in Humor

For some young adults, and for far more adults, the finest of all humorists was and is P. G. Wodehouse. This English writer of nearly one hundred novels created a fantasy world permanently locked somewhere vaguely in the 1920s and 1930s and featuring some highly unbelievable characters. But other writers as different politically and socially as Evelyn Waugh and George Orwell and Rudyard Kipling ardently admired Wodehouse and thought him a genius. So he is.

Wodehouse's best-known creations are the feeble-brain Bertie Wooster and his brilliant and snobbish butler, Jeeves. Readers who begin with some of the Jeeves short stories in *Very Good, Jeeves* (especially "Jeeves and the Song of Songs," "The Love That Purifies," and "Jeeves and the Impending Doom") or *Carry On, Jeeves* (particularly "Without the Option," "Jeeves and the Hard-Boiled Egg," and "Jeeves Takes Charge") may be puzzled by the comic opera world they find, but they will discover wit and charm and fun in abundance. Readers may then be prepared to move on to the Jeeves novels, for example, *The Inimitable Jeeves*, *The Mating Season*, *Jeeves and the Feudal Spirit*, *Stiff Upper Lip, Jeeves*, and *Much Obliged, Jeeves*.

Wodehouse enthusiasts may differ on the stories or novels they consider the funniest (some would vote for "Mulliner's Buck-U-Uppo" in *Meet Mr. Mulliner* while others would argue for "Uncle Fred Flits By" in *Young Men in Spats*), but almost anyone who has sampled Wodehouse will stay for other items on the menu.

The range of humor available to young adults is incredible. Mockery, heroism, naiveté, cynicism, stupidity, cruelty, mayhem, death, the quest, madness, nastiness, sexuality, insults, viciousness, innocence, tears, the macabre, bitterness, and laughter, laughter, laughter in abundance are easily found to meet the tastes of any reader. There is almost nothing we cannot and will not laugh at. Librarians and teachers who wonder if any humor for young adults deserves their attention need only to read in works as different as Dr. Seuss' *Horton Hatches the Egg,* Garrison Keillor's *Happy to Be Here,* M. E. Kerr's *If I Love You, Am I Trapped Forever?,* Bob Elliott and Ray Goulding's *Write if You Get Work* and *From Approximately Coast to Coast,* Frank Sullivan's *The Night the Old Nostalgia Burned Down,* Judie Angell's *Suds,* Douglas Adams' *The Hitchhiker's Guide to the Galaxy,* Benjamin Lee's *It Can't Be Helped,* or anything, absolutely anything, by P. G. Wodehouse to know better.

◆ **ACTIVITIES** ◆

1. Skim through a variety of poetry books and make a collection of ten different poems that you like and can imagine yourself sharing with young adults. Force yourself to look beyond the books and poets you already know. It might help you to do this if you try to find different types of poems, for example, a concrete poem (one whose shape helps communicate the meaning), lyrics to a song, a poem about someone's childhood, a militant or political poem, a love poem, an ethnic poem, a poem that rhymes, a poem written in a special format such as haiku or cinquain, a poem that tells a story, and a poem that celebrates some aspect of life unique to teenagers.

2. If you have the opportunity, view a movie either in a theater or on television that is based on a young adult novel. Make a list of differences between the book and the film. See if you can figure out why the changes were made. Was it to streamline the story, add visual excitement, make the story more broad-based in its appeal, or something else?

3. Read one of the plays recommended for YA's. List three aspects of the play that would probably appeal to young readers. If you see aspects that would make it unappealing to this age range, list those in a separate column.

4. Watch a rock music video on television. Make a list of the symbols that appear in it. Try to determine what they are symbolizing. Do you think that part of the appeal of music videos is that they leave something to be thought about? If so, list the questions you have in your mind about the video that you saw.

5. Read two of the books recommended in the section on humor and write a brief comparison of the humor. Did the authors rely on the same techniques? Was it humor that made you laugh aloud or smile quietly inside? Was word play part of it? How about funny situations?

◆ **NOTES** ◆

[1]Paul Janeczko, "Facets: Successful Authors Talk about Connections between Teaching and Writing," *English Journal* 73 (November 1984): 25.

[2]"Separation" by W. S. Merwin, from *The Moving Target* by W. S. Merwin.

[3]"Man on Wheels" by Karl Shapiro, from *Collected Poems 1940–1978* by Karl Shapiro.

[4]"Waking from a Nap on the Beach" by May Swenson, from *New & Selected Things Taking Place* by May Swenson.

[5]"In a Cafe" by Richard Brautigan; excerpted from *The Pill Versus the Springhill Mine Disaster* by Richard Brautigan.

[6]Stanley Kunitz in *Poetspeak: In Their Work, About Their Work,* edited by Paul B. Janeczko (New York: Bradbury Press, 1983), p. 74.

[7]"The Portrait" by Stanley Kunitz in *Poetspeak: In Their Work, About Their Work,* edited by Paul B. Janeczko.

[8]Kunitz, p. 75.

[9]Review of *Love Is Like the Lion's Tooth: An Anthology of Love Poems,* in *Booklist* 80 (April 1, 1984): 1107.

[10]Don Mainprize, "Ouchless Poetry," *English Journal* 71 (February 1982): 31–33.

[11]Alberta Turner, "Teaching Poetry Writing in Secondary School," *English Journal* 71 (September 1982): 53–56.

[12]Jesse Hise, "Writing Poery: More Than a Frill," *English Journal* 69 (November 1980): 19–22.

[13]Anthony L. Manna, "Curtains Up on Contemporary Plays," *English Journal* 73 (October 1984): 51–54.

[14]Maia Pank Mertz and David K. England, "The Legitimacy of American Adolescent Fiction," *School Library Journal* 30 (October 1983): 119–23.

[15]Vincent Canby, "Screen: 'Outsiders,' Teen-Age Violence," The *New York Times*, March 25, 1983, p. 18.

[16]Quoted in "Calendar Supplement," *Los Angeles Times*, April 3, 1983, p. 18.

[17]Richard Schickel, "Cinema: Antic Storms, Lopsided Charm," *TIME* 120 (October 11, 1982): 89.

[18]In 1980 librarian Jo Ellen Misakian and her students sent a petition and a copy of *The Outsiders* to Francis Ford Coppola. Three years later, these same students gathered to applaud the film and its final message: "The film *The Outsiders* is dedicated to the people who first suggested that it be made—librarian Jo Ellen Misakian and the students of the Lone Star School in Fresno, California."

[19]Susan Latta, "MTV and Video Music: A New Tool for the English Teacher," *English Journal* 73 (January 1984): 38–39.

[20]Latta, p. 39.

[20]Latta, p. 39.

[21]Steve Allen, *Funny People* (New York: Stein and Day, 1981), p. 1.

[22]Lance M. Gentile and Merna M. McMillan, "Humor and the Reading Program," *Journal of Reading* 21 (January 1978): 343–50.

[23]"Crowded Tub" by Shel Silverstein from *A Light in the Attic* by Shel Silverstein.

[24]"Grook Poems" by Piet Hien from *Grooks, Grooks 2, Grooks 3,* and *Grooks 5* by Piet Hein.

[25]Limericks by Morris Bishop from *Spilt Milk* by Morris Bishop.

[26]Willard Flint Thrall and Addison Hibbard, *A Handbook to Literature,* revised by C. Hugh Holman (New York: Odyssey, 1960), p. 436.

[27]Epitaphs by Fritz Spiegl from *A Small Book of Grave Humor* by Fritz Spiegl.

[28]Epitaphs from *Poems from the Greek Anthology,* translated by Dudley Fitts.

[29]Walter Blair's Edition of *The Sweet Singer of Michigan* (New York: Pascal Covici, 1928) is excellent on Clark and Moore. A deliciously funny article by Bradley Hayden, "In Memoriam Humor: Julia Moore and the Western Michigan Poets," *English Journal* 72 (September 1983): 22–28 is a good introduction to these wonderful nonpoets.

[30]From *Ruthless Rhymes for Heartless Homes* by Harry Graham (Col. D. Streamer).

[31]More anonymous "Little Willie" poems from *Poet's Handbook* by Clement Wood.

◆ Titles Mentioned in Chapter 9 ◆

For information on the availability of paperback editions of these titles, please consult the most recent edition of *Paperbound Books in Print,* published annually by R. R. Bowker Company.

Poetry

Angelou, Maya. *And Still I Rise*. Random House, 1978.

———. *Just Give Me a Cool Drink of Water 'fore I Diiie*. Random House,1971.

———. *Oh Pray My Wings Are Gonna Fit Me Well*. Random House, 1975.

Baldwin, Neil. *To All Gentleness: William Carlos Williams, The Doctor Poet*. Atheneum, 1984.

Bradbury, Ray. *When Elephants Last in the Dooryard Bloomed*. Knopf, 1973.

Brautigan, Richard. *June Thirtieth, June Thirtieth*. Delacorte, 1977.

———. *The Pill Versus the Springhill Mine Disaster*. Dell, 1969.

Cole, William, ed. *Beastly Boys and Ghastly Girls*. Collins/World, 1964.

Dunbar, Paul Laurence. *The Complete Poems of Paul Laurence Dunbar*. Dodd, Mead, 1913.

Duncan, Lois. *From Spring to Spring*. Westminster, 1982.

Dunning, Stephen, and others, eds. *Reflections on a Gift of Watermelon Pickle and Other Modern Verse*. Scott, Foresman, 1966.

————. *Some Haystacks Don't Even Have Any Needle: And Other Complete Modern Poems*. Lothrop, Lee & Shepard, 1969.

Frost, Robert. *Stopping by Woods on a Snowy Evening*. E. P. Dutton, 1978.

Giovanni, Nikki. *Those Who Ride the Night Winds*. Morrow, 1983.

Glenn, Mel. *Class Dismissed! High School Poems*. Clarion Books, 1982.

Gould, Jean. *American Women Poets: Pioneers of Modern Poetry*. Dodd, Mead, 1980.

Hill, Helen; Agnes Perkins, and Alethea Helbig, eds. *Dusk to Dawn: Poems of the Night*. Crowell, 1981.

Hill, Helen and Agnes Perkins, eds. *New Coasts and Strange Harbors*. Crowell, 1974.

Hopkins, Lee Bennett, ed. *Love and Kisses*. Houghton Mifflin, 1983.

Janeczko, Paul B., ed. *Dont forget to fly*. Bradbury, 1981.

————. *Poetspeak: In Their Work, About Their Work*. Bradbury, 1983.

————. *Postcard Poems: A Collection of Poetry for Sharing*. Bradbury, 1979.

————. *Strings: A Gathering of Family Poems*. Bradbury, 1984.

Joseph, Stephen M. *the me nobody knows*. Avon, 1969.

Koch, Kenneth. *Wishes, Lies and Dreams: Teaching Children to Write Poetry*. Chelsea House, 1970.

————. *Rose, Where Did You Get That Red?* Random House, 1974.

Larrick, Nancy, ed. *On City Streets: An Anthology of Poetry*. Lippincott, 1968.

————. *Room for Me and a Mountain Lion: Poetry of Open Space*. M. Evans, 1974.

————. *Tambourines! Tambourines to Glory! Prayers and Poems*. Westminster, 1982.

Livingston, Myra Cohn, ed. *O Frabjous Day! Poetry for Holidays and Special Occasions*. Atheneum, 1977.

————. *One Little Room, an Everywhere: Poems of Love*. Atheneum, 1975.

————. *Poems of Christmas*. Atheneum, 1980.

————. *Speak Roughly to Your Little Boy: A Collection of Parodies and Burlesques*. Harcourt Brace Jovanovich, 1971.

————. *What a Wonderful Bird the Frog Are: An Assortment of Humorous Poetry and Verse*. Harcourt Brace Jovanovich, 1973.

————. *Why Am I Grown So Cold? Poems of the Unknowable*. Atheneum, 1982.

Longfellow, Henry Wadsworth. *Hiawatha* (illustrated by Susan Jeffers). Dial, 1983.

Lueders, Ed and Primus St. John, eds. *Zero Makes Me Hungry: A Collection of Poems for Today*. Scott, Foresman, 1976.

McCullough, Frances, ed. *Love Is Like the Lion's Tooth: An Anthology of Love Poems*. Harper & Row, 1984.

Merriam, Eve. *If Only I Could Tell You: Poems for Young Lovers and Dreamers*. Knopf, 1983.

————. *Inner City Mother Goose*. Simon and Schuster, 1969.

————. *Out Loud*. Atheneum, 1973.

————. *Rainbow Writing*. Atheneum, 1976.

Merriam, Eve and Nancy Larrick, eds. *Male and Female Under Eighteen*. Avon, 1973.

Millay, Edna St. Vincent. *Poems: Selected for Young People*. Harper & Row, 1979.

Peck, Richard, ed. *Pictures That Storm inside My Head: Poems for the Inner You*. Avon, 1976.

————. *Sounds and Silences: Poetry for Now*. Dell, 1970.

Plotz, Helen, ed. *Eye's Delight: Poems of Art and Architecture*. Greenwillow, 1983.

————. *Gladly Learn and Gladly Teach: Poems of the School Experience*. Greenwillow, 1981.

————. *Imagination's Other Place: Poems of Science and Mathematics*. Crowell, 1955.

————. *Saturday's Children: Poems of Work*. Greenwillow, 1982.

Prelutsky, Jack. *Nightmares: Poems to Trouble Your Sleep*. Greenwillow, 1976.

Riley, James Whitcomb. *The Gobble-Uns'll Get You If You Don't Watch Out*. Lippincott, 1975.

Sandburg, Carl. *Rainbows Are Made: Poems by Carl Sandburg* (selected by Lee Bennett Hopkins). Harcourt Brace Jovanovich, 1982.

Schwartz, Alvin. *Tomfoolery: Trickery and Foolery with Words*. Lippincott, 1973.

Service, Robert W. *The Shooting of Dan McGrew and the Cremation of Sam McGee*. Young Scott, 1969.

Silverstein, Shel. *Where the Sidewalk Ends.* Harper & Row, 1974.

————. *The Light in the Attic.* Harper & Row, 1983.

Thayer, Ernest L. *Casey at the Bat.* Prentice-Hall, 1964. Written in 1888.

Walker, Alice. *Good Night Willie Lee, I'll See You In the Morning.* Dial, 1979.

Plays

Aiken, Joan. *Street.* Viking, 1978.

Bolt, Robert. *A Man for All Seasons.* Baker (also French), 1960.

Davis, Ossie. *Langston.* Delacorte, 1982.

Fletcher, Lucille. *Sorry, Wrong Number* in *Fifteen American One-Act Plays* edited by Paul Kozelka. Pocket Books, 1971.

Gibson, William. *The Miracle Worker.* Baker (also French), 1959.

Goldsmith, Oliver. *She Stoops to Conquer.* 1792.

Goodrich, Frances and Albert Hackett. *The Diary of Anne Frank.* Dramatists, 1956.

Hart, Moss and George S. Kaufman. *You Can't Take It With You.* Dramatists, 1936.

Kozelka, Paul. *Fifteen American One-Act Plays.* Pocket Books, 1971.

Lawrence, Jerome and Robert E. Lee. *Inherit the Wind.* Dramatists, 1955.

Patrick, John. *The Teahouse of the August Moon.* Dramatists, 1953.

Rose, Reginald. *Twelve Angry Men* in *Great Television Plays* selected by William I. Kaufman. Dell, 1969.

Saroyan, William. *The Oyster and the Pearl* in *America Reads—The United States* in *Literature* ed. by Walter Blair et al. Scott, Foresman, 1963.

Serling, Rod. *A Storm in Summer* in *Great Television Plays* Vol. 2 edited by Ned E. Hoopes and Patricia Neale Gordon. Dell, 1975.

Shaw, George Bernard. *Arms and the Man.* 1894.

————. *Pygmalion.* 1913.

Vidal, Gore. *Visit to a Small Planet.* In *Visit to a Small Planet and Other Television Plays* by Gore Vidal. Little, Brown, 1956.

Wilder, Thornton. *Our Town.* Baker (also Eldridge and French), 1938.

Zindel, Paul. *The Effect of Gamma Rays on Man-in-the-Moon Marigolds.* Harper & Row, 1971.

————. *Let Me Hear You Whisper.* Harper & Row, 1974.

Books on Movies and Television

Brooks, Tim and Earle Marsh. *The Complete Directory of Prime Time Network TV Shows 1946–Present.* Ballantine, 1979.

Crowther, Bosley. *Vintage Films: 50 Enduring Motion Pictures.* Putnam's, 1977.

Edelson, Edward. *Funny Men of the Movies.* Doubleday, 1976.

Garfield, Brian. *Western Films: A Complete Guide.* Rawson Associates, 1982.

Goldsen, Rose K. *The Show and Tell Machine: How Television Works and Works You Over.* Dial, 1977.

Halliwell, Leslie. *The Filmgoer's Companion.* Hill and Wang, 1977.

Hardy, Phil. *The Western.* Morrow, 1983.

Hoopes, Ned E. and Patricia Neale Gordon. *Great Television Plays* Vol. 2. Dell, 1975.

Johnson, Ron and Jan Bone. *Understanding the Film.* National Textbook, 1976.

Kael, Pauline. *5001 Nights at the Movies: A Guide from A to Z.* Holt, Rinehart and Winston, 1982.

————. *Taking It All In.* Holt, Rinehart and Winston, 1984.

Kaufman, William I, and Ned E. Hoopes. *Great Television Plays.* Dell, 1969.

Knight, Arthur. *The Liveliest Art: A Panoramic History of the Movies.* New American Library, 1979.

Marcus, Fred H. *Short Story/Short Film.* Prentice-Hall, 1977.

Meyer, William R. *The Making of the Great Westerns.* Arlington House, 1979.

Peary, Danny. *Cult Movies: The Classics, the Sleepers, the Weird, and the Wonderful.* Delacorte, 1981.

Sohn, David A. *Good Looking: Film Studies, Short Films and Filmmaking.* National Textbook, 1978.

Terrace, Vincent. *The Complete Encyclopedia of Television Programs 1947–1975,* Volumes I and II. A. S. Barnes, 1976.

Winn, Marie. *The Plug-In Drug.* Viking, 1977.

Humor

Adams, Douglas. *The Hitchhiker's Guide to the Galaxy.* Harmony, 1980.

————. *Life, the Universe and Everything.* Harmony, 1982.

————. *The Restaurant at the End of the Universe.* Harmony, 1982.

Allen, Steve. *Funny People.* Stein & Day, 1981.

Allen, Woody. *Four Films of Woody Allen.* Random House, 1982.

————. *Getting Even.* Random House, 1971.

————. *Side Effects.* Random House,1980.

————. *Without Feathers.* Random House, 1975.

Angell, Judie. *Suds.* Bradbury, 1983.

Armour, Richard. *The Classics Reclassified.* McGraw-Hill, 1960.

————. *English Lit Relit.* McGraw-Hill, 1969.

————. *It All Started with Columbus.* McGraw-Hill, 1953.

————. *It All Started with Eve.* McGraw-Hill, 1963.

————. *Twisted Tales from Shakespeare.* McGraw-Hill, 1957.

Beard, Henry, ed. *Miss Piggy's Treasury of Art Masterpieces from the Kermitage Collection.* Holt, Rinehart and Winston,1984.

Bethancourt, T. Ernesto. *The Dog Days of Arthur Cane.* Holiday House, 1976.

Billington, Ray Allen. *Limericks Historical and Hysterical, Plagiarized, Arranged, Annotated, and Some Written by Ray Allen Billington.* Norton, 1981.

Bishop, Morris. *The Best of Bishop.* Cornell University Press, 1980.

Blair, Walter, ed. *The Sweet Singer of Michigan.* Pascal Covici, 1928.

Blume, Judy. *Blubber.* Bradbury, 1974.

————. *Superfudge.* E. P. Dutton, 1980.

————. *Tales of a Fourth Grade Nothing.* E. P. Dutton, 1972.

Bond, Michael. *A Bear Called Paddington.* Houghton Mifflin, 1958.

————. *Paddington at the Seaside.* Random House, 1978.

Cleary, Beverly. *Ellen Tebbits.* Morrow, 1951.

————. *Henry and Beezus.* Morrow, 1952.

————. *Henry Huggins.* Morrow, 1950.

————. *The Mouse and the Motorcycle.* Morrow, 1965.

————. *Runaway Ralph.* Morrow, 1970.

Danziger, Paula. *Can You Sue Your Parents for Malpractice?* Delacorte, 1979.

————. *The Cat Ate My Gymsuit.* Delacorte, 1974.

————. *The Divorce Express.* Delacorte, 1982.

————. *The Pistachio Prescription.* Delacorte, 1978.

————. *There's a Bat in Bunk Five.* Delacorte, 1980.

Davis, Douglas M., ed. *The World of Black Humor.* E. P. Dutton, 1967.

Davis, Jim. *Garfield Eats His Heart Out.* Ballantine, 1983.

De Vries, Peter. *The Mackerel Plaza.* Little, Brown, 1958.

————. *Reuben, Reuben.* Little, Brown, 1964.

Elliott, Bob and Ray Goulding. *From Approximately Coast to Coast . . . It's the Bob and Ray Show.* Atheneum, 1983.

————. *Write if You Get Work: The Best of Bob and Ray.* Random House,1975.

Ephron, Nora. *Crazy Salad.* Knopf, 1975.

Espy, Willard R. *An Almanac of Words at Play.* Clarkson N. Potter, 1975.

————. *Another Almanac.* Clarkson N. Potter, 1980.

————. *Espygrams.* Clarkson N. Potter, 1981.

————. *Have a Word on Me: A Celebration of Language.* Simon and Schuster, 1981.

————. *O Thou Improper, Thou Uncommon Noun.* Clarkson N. Potter, 1978.

Fitts, Dudley, ed. and trans. *Poems from the Greek Anthology in English Paraphrase.* New Directions, 1956.

Graham, Harry. *More Ruthless Rhymes for Heartless Homes.* Putnam's, 1930.

————. *Ruthless Rhymes for Heartless Homes.* R. H. Russell, 1901.

Greenfield, Jeff. *Book of Books.* National Lampoon Magazine, 1979.

Hein, Piet. *Grooks.* Doubleday, 1969.

————. *Grooks 2.* Doubleday, 1969.

————. *Grooks 3.* Doubleday, 1970.

————. *Grooks 4.* Doubleday, 1972.

————. *Grooks 5.* Doubleday, 1973.

Heller, Joseph. *Catch-22.* Simon and Schuster, 1955.

Henson, Jim. *Miss Piggy's Guide to Life.* Knopf, 1981.

Howe, Deborah and James Howe. *Bunnicula: A Rabbit-Tale of Mystery.* Atheneum, 1979.

Jacobs, Will and Gerard Jones. *The Beaver Papers: The Story of a Lost Season.* Crown, 1983.

Keillor, Garrison. *Happy to Be Here*. Atheneum, 1982.

Kelly, Walt. *Beau Pogo*. Simon and Schuster, 1960.

Kerr, M. E. *Dinky Hocker Shoots Smack!* Harper & Row, 1972.

———. *If I Love You, Am I Trapped Forever?* Harper & Row, 1973.

Kesey, Ken. *One Flew Over the Cuckoo's Nest*. Viking, 1962.

Kiesel, Stanley. *The War between the Pitiful Teachers and the Splendid Kids*. E. P. Dutton, 1980.

Leacock, Stephen. *Laugh with Leacock*. Dodd, Mead, 1915.

Lee, Benjamin. *It Can't be Helped*. Farrar, Straus & Giroux, 1979.

Macaulay, David. *Motel of the Mysteries*. Houghton Mifflin, 1979.

Marquis, Don. *archy and mehitabel*. Doubleday, 1927.

Merrill, Jean. *The Pushcart War*. W. R. Scott, 1964.

Milligan, Spike. *The Goon Show Scripts*. St. Martin's, 1973.

O'Rourke, P. J., ed. *National Lampoon: Sunday Newspaper Parody*. National Lampoon Magazine, 1978.

Palin, Michael and Terry Jones. *More Ripping Yarns*. Pantheon, 1981.

———. *Ripping Yarns*. Pantheon, 1978.

Parker, Dorothy. *The Portable Dorothy Parker*. Viking, 1944.

Peck, Richard. *The Dreadful Future of Blossom Culp*. Viking, 1983.

———. *The Ghost Belonged to Me*. Viking, 1975.

———. *Ghosts I Have Been*. Viking, 1977.

Perelman, S. J. *The Last Laugh*. Simon and Schuster, 1981.

———. *The Most of S. J. Perelman*. Simon and Schuster, 1958.

Rhymer, Paul. *The Small House Half-way Up in the Next Block: Paul Rhymer's Vic and Sade*. McGraw-Hill, 1972.

———. *Vic and Sade: The Best Radio Plays of Paul Rhymer*. Seabury, 1976.

Schwartz, Alvin. *Chin Music: Tall Tales and Other Tales*. Lippincott, 1979.

———. *Flapdoodle: Pure Nonsense from American Folklore*. Lippincott, 1980.

———. *Tomfoolery: Trickery and Foolery with Words*. Lippincott, 1973.

———. *A Twister of Twists, a Tangle of Tongues*. Lippincott, 1972.

Seuss, Dr. (Theodor Seuss Geisel) *And to Think That I Saw It on Mulberry Street*. Vanguard, 1937.

———. *The 500 Hats of Bartholomew Cubbins*. Vanguard, 1938.

———. *Horton Hatches the Egg*. Random House, 1940.

———. *How the Grinch Stole Christmas*. Random House, 1957.

———. *If I Ran the Circus*. Random House, 1956.

———. *Thidwick the Big-Hearted Moose*. Random House, 1948.

Shepherd, Jean. *The Ferrari in the Bedroom*. Dodd, Mead, 1973.

———. *A Fistful of Fig Newtons*. Doubleday, 1982.

———. *In God We Trust, All Others Pay Cash*. Doubleday, 1976.

———. *Wanda Hickey's Night of Golden Memories and Other Disasters*. Doubleday, 1971.

Silverstein, Shel. *A Light in the Attic*. Harper & Row, 1981.

———. *Where the Sidewalk Ends*. Harper & Row, 1974.

Spiegl, Fritz. *A Small Book of Grave Humor*. Arco, 1973.

Stewart, Donald Ogden. *A Parody Outline of History*. Doran, 1921.

Sullivan, Frank. *The Night the Old Nostalgia Burned Down*. Little, Brown, 1953.

Thurber, James. *The Thurber Carnival*. Modern Library, 1957.

Townsend, John Rowe. *Kate and the Revolution*. Lippincott, 1983.

Troise, Joseph L. *Dare to Be Dull*. Bantam, 1983.

Waugh, Evelyn. *The Loved One*. Little, Brown, 1948.

White, E. B. *The Second Tree from the Corner*. Harper and Brothers, 1954.

Wibberley, Leonard. *Beware of the Mouse*. Putnam's, 1958.

———. *The Mouse on the Moon*. Morrow, 1962.

———. *The Mouse That Roared*. Little, Brown, 1955.

Wodehouse, P. G. *Carry on, Jeeves*. 1925; Penguin, 1975.

———. *The Inimitable Jeeves*. 1924; Penguin, 1975.

——————. *Jeeves and the Feudal Spirit*. 1954;
Penguin, 1975.

——————. *The Mating Season*. 1949; Har-Row
Perennial, 1983.

——————. *Meet Mr. Mulliner*. 1927; Penguin,
1981.

——————. *Much Obliged, Jeeves*. 1971; Penguin,
1982.

——————. *Mulliner Nights*. 1933; Penguin, 1975.

——————. *Stiff Upper Lip, Jeeves*. 1963; Penguin,
1976.

——————. *Very Good, Jeeves*. 1930; Penguin,
1975.

——————. *Young Men in Spats*. 1922; Penguin,
1981.

Anthologies of Humor

Jennings, Paul, ed. *The Book of Nonsense*. Ballantine, 1981.

Richler, Mordecai, ed. *The Best of Modern
Humor*. Knopf, 1983.

Untermeyer, Louis, ed. *A Treasury of Great
Humor*. McGraw-Hill, 1972.

White, E. B. and Katharine S., eds. *A Subtrea-
sury of American Humor*. Random House,
1941.

Anthologies of Parody

Baker, Robert A., ed. *A Stress Analysis of a
Strapless Evening Gown and Other Essays
from a Scientific Age*. Doubleday, 1969.

Falk, Robert P., ed. *American Literature in
Parody*. Twayne, 1955. Published by Grove
Press in paperback as *The Antic Muse*.

Lewis, D. B. Wyndham and Charles Lee, eds.
The Stuffed Owl: An Anthology of Bad Verse.
Coward-McCann, 1930.

Lowrey, Burling, ed. *Twentieth Century Parody:
American and British*. Harcourt, Brace, and
World, 1960.

MacDonald, Dwight, ed. *Parodies: An Anthology
from Chaucer to Beerbohm—And After*. Random House, 1960.

Scherr, George H., ed. *Best of the Journal of
Irreproducible Results*. Workman, 1984.

Zaranka, William, ed. *The Brand-X Anthology of
Poetry*, Burnt Norton Edition. Apple-Wood
Books, 1981.

◆ A Starter Collection of Drama for Teachers and Librarians ◆

The History of Drama:

Arnott, Peter. *The Theatre in Its Time: An
Introduction*. Little, Brown, 1981.

Brockett, Oscar. *History of the Theatre*, 4th ed.
Allyn and Bacon, 1981.

Cheney, Sheldon. *The Theatre: Three Thousand
Years of Drama, Acting, and Stagecraft*. Longmans, Green, 1952.

Encyclopedias of Drama:

Gassner, John and Edward Quinn, eds. *The
Reader's Encyclopedia of World Drama*.
Thomas Y. Crowell, 1969.

Hartnoll, Phyllis, ed. *Oxford Companion to the
Theatre*, 3rd ed. Oxford University Press, 1967.

Digests of Plays:

Guide to Play Selection, 3rd ed. National Council of Teachers of English, 1975. (Brief
summaries of many plays with a fine concluding bibliography.)

Shank, Theodore, ed. *A Digest of 500 Plays: Plot
Summaries and Production Notes*. Crowell-
Collier, 1963.

Hardback Anthologies of Drama:

Barnes, Clive, ed. *John Gassner's Best American
Plays—Seventh Series, 1967–73*. Crown, 1974.

Block, Haskell M. and Robert G. Shedd, eds.
Masters of Modern Drama. Random House,
1962.

Brockett, Oscar and Lenyth Brockett, eds. *Plays
for the Theatre: An Anthology of World
Drama*. Holt, Rinehart and Winston, 1979.

Cartmell, Van H. and Bennett Cerf, eds. *Famous
Plays of Crime and Detection*. Blakiston, 1946.

Cerf, Bennett, ed. *Sixteen Famous American
Plays*. Modern Library, 1941.

——————. *Sixteen Famous British Plays*. Modern
Library, 1942.

——————. *Sixteen Famous European Plays*. Modern Library, 1943.

——————. *Thirty Famous One-Act Plays*. Modern
Library, 1949.

Cerf, Bennett and Van H. Cartmell, eds. *SRO:
The Most Successful Plays on the American
Stage*. Doubleday, 1944.

Gassner, John, ed. *Best American Plays: 1918–58*.
Crown, 1961.

————. *Best Plays of the Modern American Theatre: Second Series, 1939–46*. Crown, 1947.

————. *Best American Plays: Third Series, 1945–51*. Crown, 1952.

————. *Best American Plays: Fourth Series, 1952–57*. Crown, 1958.

————. *Best American Plays: Fifth Series, 1958–63*. Crown, 1963.

————. *Best American Plays: Supplementary Volume, 1918–58*. Crown, 1961.

————. *Twenty Best European Plays on the American Stage*. Crown, 1957.

————. *Twenty Best Plays of the Modern American Theatre*. Crown, 1939.

————. *Twenty-Five Best Plays of the Modern American Theatre*. Crown, 1949.

Gassner, John and Clive Barnes, eds. *Best American Plays: Sixth Series, 1963–67*. Crown, 1971.

————. *Fifty Best Plays of the American Theatre: From 1787 to the Present*, 4 vols. Crown, 1970.

Gassner, John and Bernard Dukore, eds. *A Treasury of the Theatre: From Henrik Ibsen to Robert Lowell*, 4th ed. Simon and Schuster, 1970.

Gassner, John and Mollie Gassner, eds. *Best Plays of the Early American Theatre: From the Beginning to 1916*. Crown, 1967.

Moody, Richard, ed. *Dramas from the American Theatre, 1762–1909*. World, 1966.

Richards, Stanley, ed. *Ten Great Musicals of the American Theatre*. Chilton, 1973.

Paperback Anthologies of Drama:

Barnet, Sylva, Morton Berman, and William Burto, eds. *Eight Great Comedies*. Mentor Books, New American Library, 1958.

————. *Eight Great Tragedies*. Mentor Books, New American Library, 1957. (Two exceptional anthologies for the library or the classroom. Excellent selection of plays and some equally fine critical essays conclude each volume.)

Macgowan, Kenneth, ed. *Famous American Plays of the 1920s*. Dell, 1959.

Clurman, Harold, ed. *Famous American Plays of the 1930s*. Dell, 1959.

Hewes, Henry, ed. *Famous American Plays of the 1940s*. Dell, 1960.

Strasberg, Lee, ed. *Famous American Plays of the 1950s*. Dell, 1962.

Clurman, Harold, ed. *Famous American Plays of the 1960s*. Dell, 1972.

Hoffman, Ted, ed. *Famous American Plays of the 1970s*. Dell, 1981.

(For anyone interested in American theatre or teaching it, this is the best inexpensive set of books. *Street Scene, What Price Glory?, The Time of Your Life, Of Mice and Men, All My Sons, The Member of the Wedding, Camino Real, The Autumn Garden, Hogan's Goat, We Bombed in New Haven, Buried Child, Moonchildren* and others are here for a small price.)

◆ Fifty Plays for Young Adult Reading Selected and Annotated by Ric Alpers ◆

The Andersonville Trial by Saul Levitt (Dramatists 1960)
Drama; a dramatization of the trial of Henry Wirz, commander of the infamous Andersonville POW camp during the Civil War. A study of the moral issues involving conscience vs. authority.

The Apple Tree by Jerry Bock and Sheldon M. Harnick (Random House, 1967)
Musical; an adaptation of three stories, "The Diary of Adam and Eve" by Mark Twain, "The Lady or the Tiger" by Frank Stockton, and "Passionella" by Jules Feiffer.

The Arkansas Bear by Aurand Harris (Anchorage 1980)

Fantasy; the story deals with a young girl's ability to accept the approaching death of her grandfather by helping the World's Greatest Dancing Bear accept his own.

Arsenic and Old Lace by Joseph Kesselring (Dramatists 1941)
Comedy; a very funny piece of classic American Theater about two old ladies and their hobby.

The Bad Seed by Maxwell Anderson (Dramatists 1954)
Thriller; a theatrical horror story about a very naughty little girl. Stephen King would be proud.

Becket by Jean Anoulih (French 1959)

Drama; the story of Henry, King of England and his good friend Thomas à Becket whom he made Archbishop of Canterbury. A study of the nature of friendship vs. duty by one of the top dramatists in the world.

The Boy with Green Hair by F. Andrew Leslie (Dramatists 1961)
Fantasy; a story of the nature of prejudice about a boy whose hair suddenly turns green.

Butterflies Are Free by Leonard Gershe (French 1969)
Comedy; a touching story of a blind young man's coming of age.

The Butterfly by Bijan Mofid (Anchorage 1974)
Allegory; adapted from a Persian fable, it is the story of a butterfly who has been captured by a spider and is promised freedom if she will lure another insect into the web to take her place as the spider's dinner.

Carnival by Michael Stewart and Bob Merrill (Tams-Witmark 1961)
Musical; a story about love in which a young girl must choose between a charming, but shallow, magician and a crippled puppeteer who speaks through his puppets.

Celebration by Tom Jones and Harvey Schmidt (Drama Book Specialists 1973)
Musical; an allegory about the changing of the seasons as an orphan searches for the Garden of Peace.

The Chalk Garden by Enid Bagnold (French 1954)
Drama; reality is explored through a young girl's dealings with her eccentric grandmother and her governess with a mysterious past.

Children of a Lesser God by Mark Medoff (Dramatists 1980)
Drama; Tony Award winning play about the plight of the deaf focuses on the relationship between a deaf student and her hearing teacher.

The Children's Crusade by Paul Thompson (Dramatists 1975)
Drama; the story of the people and events that lead to the tragic children's crusade in thirteenth-century Europe. A wonderful examination of the generation gap.

Circus Home by Joanna Kraus (New Plays 1980)
Drama; the story of a young man affected by giantism and the home he finds in a circus. A marvelous treatment of prejudice against those who are different.

The Crucible by Arthur Miller (Dramatists 1952)
Drama; the classic play concerning the causes of the Salem Witch Hunt. Great historical drama as well as a comment on the nature of humanity.

The Crucifer of Blood by Paul Giovanni (French 1979)
Mystery; one of the many plays about Sherlock Holmes.

Dark of the Moon by Howard Richardson and William Berney (French 1945)
Drama; a haunting tale of love based on the folk song "Barbara Allen." Wonderful exploration of the nature of superstition.

David and Lisa by James Reach (French 1967)
Drama; probably the best play ever written about young emotionally disturbed teens and how they learn to cope with their problems.

The Diary of Anne Frank by Francis Goodrich and Albert Hackett (Dramatists 1956)
Drama; based on the book, a remarkable story of a young girl's coming of age during the Holocaust. Still powerful and moving.

Educating Rita by Willy Russell (French 1981)
Comedy; a life-affirming play about a young woman's determination to get an education.

The Effect of Gamma Rays on Man-in-the-Moon Marigolds by Paul Zindel (Dramatists 1970)
Drama; the Pulitzer Prize winning play that brought Paul Zindel to the attention of the world. A moving story of the damaging forms love can take but the ultimate outcome is that something good can still come of it.

The Elephant Man by Bernard Pomerance (French 1979)
Drama; the story of the tragically deformed John Merrick who was able to rise above his disabilities.

The Fantasticks by Tom Jones and Harvey Schmidt (Avon 1968)
Musical; two young people discovering the real meaning of love is explored in what may be the best musical ever written.

The Glass Menagerie by Tennessee Williams (Dramatists 1945)
Drama; an American Classic about a rebellious son, a shy daughter, and an overprotective mother.

The Great White Hope by Howard Sackler (French 1971)
Drama; Tony Award winning play based on the life of Jack Johnson, the first black Heavy-

weight Champion. A powerful play about racial prejudice.

Harvey by Mary Chase   (Dramatists 1944)
Comedy; a whimsical comedy about a charming tippler and his best friend, a six-foot rabbit.

Ice Wolf by Joanna Kraus   (New Plays 1963)
Drama; story of a light-skinned Eskimo shunned by her tribe. A powerful play about the nature of prejudice.

Indians by Arthur Kopit   (French 1969)
Drama; an indictment of the treatment of the Indian. A powerful drama that introduces many of the historical characters from the American West.

Inherit the Wind by Jerome Lawrence and Robert E. Lee   (Dramatists 1955)
Drama; based on the famous Scopes Monkey Trial, this play explores commitment to an ideal and the responsibilities and possible consequences of that commitment.

Johnny Belinda by Elmer Harris   (Dramatists 1940)
Drama; the story of a deaf girl diagnosed as retarded and the young doctor who helps her.

Liliom by Ferenc Molnar   (French 1908)
Fantasy; the play that the musical *Carousel* is based on. A charming tale of a rogue reformed by love.

The Lion in Winter by James Goldman   (French 1964)
Comedy-drama; the intrigues of the court of Henry II and Eleanor as they and their sons Richard, Geoffrey, and John plot and counterplot against each other.

A Man for All Seasons by Robert Bolt   (French 1960)
Drama; the story of Thomas More and his stand against Henry VIII's divorce. A strong treatment of a man's commitment to his own conscience.

The Miracle Worker by William Gibson   (French 1959)
Drama; the story of Helen Keller and her teacher Annie Sullivan. A paean to the human spirit.

Mister Roberts by Thomas Heggen and Joshua Logan   (Dramatists 1948)
Comedy-drama; a story of humanity and the few people that can make a difference in their own small way.

Once Upon a Mattress by Jay Thompson, Marshall Barer, and Dean Fuller. Music by Mary Rodgers and Lyrics by Marshall Barer.   (Rodgers and Hammerstein Library, 1959)
Musical; a very funny retelling of "The Princess and the Pea." A touching tale about love.

Our Town by Thornton Wilder   (French 1938)
Drama; the American classic that is a tribute to the small town and the value of life.

The Prime of Miss Jean Brodie by Jay Allen   (French 1968)
Drama; the story of the effects, both good and bad, that a teacher has on her young charges.

The Rainmaker by N. Richard Nash   (French 1954)
Comedy-drama; a play about dreams, both large and small, and the need to have them.

A Raisin in the Sun by Lorraine Hansberry   (French 1959)
Comedy-drama; the story of a black family's efforts to find a better way of life. A treatment of the importance of family.

1776 by Peter Stone and Sherman Edwards   (MTI 1969)
Musical; the story of the writing and signing of the Declaration of Independence, the Founding Fathers, and their struggles to start a new nation.

Step on a Crack by Susan Zeder   (Anchorage 1976)
Drama; the story of a young girl and her acceptance of a new mother. A topical and very real approach to the problems of stepparents.

Talley's Folly by Lanford Wilson   (Dramatists 1980)
Comedy; the courtship of Matt and Sally. A tribute to the power of love.

Tea and Sympathy by Robert Anderson   (French 1953)
Drama; a story about what the effects of rumor can be. A young boy is almost destroyed because he is different from his fellows.

A Thousand Clowns by Herb Gardner   (Baker's 1962)
Comedy; the story of a young boy raised by his unorthodox uncle. Explores the real meaning of the concept of family.

The Warrior's Husband by Julian Thompson   (French 1931)
Comedy; a retelling of the tenth labor of

Hercules—the stealing of the girdle of the
Amazon Queen. Very funny and witty.
Wiley and the Hairy Man by Susan
Zeder   (Anchorage 1978)
Fantasy; a wonderful telling of an American
folktale about how a young boy outsmarts the
magical Hairy Man.
You Can't Take It with You by Moss Hart and

George S. Kaufman   (Dramatists 1936)
Comedy; the original screwball comedy about
a very strange but loving family. A classic.
You're a Good Man, Charlie Brown by Clark
Gesner   (Tams-Witmark 1967)
Musical; the wit and wisdom of the Peanuts
gang. Covers a wide range of topics—first
love, homework, friendship.

◆ A Selected List of Play Publishers ◆

Anchorage Press
P.O. Box 8067
New Orleans, LA 70182

Baker's Plays
100 Chauncy Street
Boston, MA 02111

The Coach House Press, Inc.
53 West Jackson Boulevard
Chicago, IL 60604

The Dramatic Publishing Co.
4150 N. Milwaukee Avenue
Chicago, IL 60641

Dramatists Play Service, Inc.
440 Park Avenue South
New York, NY 10016

Music Theatre International
1350 Avenue of the Americas
New York, NY 10019

New Plays, Inc.
P.O. Box 273
Rowayton, CT 06853

Samuel French, Inc.
25 West 45th Street
New York, NY 10036
or
7623 Sunset Boulevard
Hollywood, CA 90046

Tams-Witmark
560 Lexington Avenue
New York, NY 10022

P·A·R·T T·H·R·E·E

ADULTS AND THE LITERATURE OF YOUNG ADULTS

USING AND PROMOTING BOOKS WITH YOUNG READERS

Chances are that you are studying adolescent literature because you expect to work, or are already working, in some situation that calls for you to bring young adults in touch with books. This chapter is divided into five sections, each centered around a professional role for adults who work with books and young readers: the librarian, the English teacher, the reading teacher, the social studies teacher, and the counselor or youth worker. These areas were chosen to give focus and organization to the information, but it should be realized that there is considerable overlap. Everyone working with young readers and books needs to be skilled in suggesting the right book for the right student or at least pointing someone in the right direction. When two people are talking honestly and openly about a book that they both enjoyed, there is no way to divide the conversation into such discrete categories as literary analysis, personal feelings, sociological implications, and evaluation of potential popularity. Librarians will find themselves discussing books as if they were classroom teachers. Teachers can adopt some of the promotional techniques that librarians use, and librarians can use some of the book discussion tactics that teachers use. In short, the organization of this chapter may make it appear that the work different professionals do with young readers and books is quite separate. But in reality, nearly all adults who work with young readers and books have much the same goals and share many of the same approaches.

All of us will meet wide-ranging differences in abilities and personalities, which implies great differences in interests. Those interests demand an alert and prepared adult who is aware of them, who can uncover them, and who knows an enormous number of titles to meet them. To an inexperienced person, the knowledge of books a librarian or teacher can call forth seems magical, but that repertoire of good books that students will like takes time, patience, and hard work to develop. Reading many young adult books comes with the territory for the professional, but so does reading professional books, magazines of all sorts, several newspapers, adult books and much, much more. The professional likes to read (or would not be a librarian or teacher), so that makes the job easier and more fun, but the professional reads beyond the areas that are personally enjoyable. For example, whether a professional likes science fiction or not, he or she must know titles of new science fiction. When young adults ask a teacher or librarian for another book like *The Martian Chronicles* (or *Forever* or *The Hitchhiker's Guide to the Galaxy* or *Crossings* or *The Color Purple*), they pay that person a sublime compliment. Woe unto the teacher or librarian who says, "I'm sorry, but I don't know anything about science fiction," or "Why don't you read something besides science fiction? Why not broaden your reading background just a bit?" Anything of that ilk kills interest and to do this to someone who is just beginning to try books is almost criminal and may very well turn someone away from reading.

In any given group, a teacher or librarian might find students like these and gradations between: Alice reads nothing at all (she did once but now that she has become a woman she has put away childish things); Brenda reads nothing because her reading skills are so poor she is virtually illiterate; Candy read a book once, her first book all the way through, and she hated it; Del reads magazines and an occasional sports biography if he's in an intellectual mood; Emily reads Harlequin romances; Fred reads all kinds of books as long as they're science fiction; George reads a few books but always classics ("He's going to college," his mother says proudly); Howie reads only religious books and has already warned the teacher about the Satanic powers in *Lord of the Flies* scheduled for class reading in two weeks; Imogene reads anything that is popular—Harold Robbins, best-sellers, novelizations of movies and television specials; Jon reads classics, football stories, mysteries, and everything else and refuses to be pigeonholed; Jean reads from the Great Books list and anything else a college suggests for its prospective students; and Lynn reads all the time, perhaps too much—she's bright but socially immature.

Serving the needs of such a diverse group is far from easy, but when the job is well done, it's a valuable contribution.

◈ **IN THE LIBRARY**

When discussing public libraries, it is often assumed that every library has a young adult librarian and a special section serving teenagers. Although this may be the ideal arrangement, certainly there are many libraries where this has never been the practice and many others where shrinking budgets are making young adult librarians endangered species. The February 1984 *VOYA* (*Voice of Youth Advocates*) addressed this problem from several viewpoints. In an editorial, Mary K. Chelton warned YA librarians that they had to be prepared to answer questions such as the following:

◆ The young adult section of the Tempe, Arizona, Public Library differs from the children's section not only in its basic furnishings, but also in its carousels of records, paperback books, and current magazines.
Courtesy of the Tempe, Arizona, Public Library.

◇ How many young adults reside in your library service area and what percentage of them have used the library at least once in the last year? Why—for schoolwork, personal reading, information, a program, etc.?

◇ Is there a demographic change occurring in your community such as a changing ratio of white to black or Hispanic; can you show a proportionate change in the percentage of those kids using the library?

◇ Does your budget allocation match the types of use young adults prefer?

◇ How does the proportion of the young adults using the library compare to the proportion of children and adults?

◇ How many titles were purchased by the Young Adult Department by format in the last month, quarter, or year?

◇ How many reference questions originated with young adults?

◇ To which adults in the community have you made yourself indispensable because of service to their adolescent children or clients? Have you made sure that their gratitude is on file in writing? Can you get to them if you need them? How are you assuring their ongoing involvement in the YA program?

Chelton recommended two publications of the American Library Association, *The Planning Process* and *Output Measures for Public Libraries*, warning that if young adult librarians ignore such advice and the work that it entails—even if it's in favor of reading the latest YA novel—they do so at their own peril.[1]

Two current events were behind the selection of VOYA's focus on young adult librarianship. One was the abolishing in 1983 of the position of

Coordinator of Young Adult Services in the Los Angeles City Library system and the other was a proposal being considered by the Atlanta and Fulton County Library to integrate Young Adult services into a "Young People's Program" in which the children's librarians would extend their work to include 13- to 15-year-olds. Anyone over 16 would be served as an adult. Several librarians were asked to respond to this proposal, and in doing so, they revealed both philosophical and pragmatic views. Excerpts from their statements can serve as a mini-introduction to YA librarianship and its relationship to the books that teenagers read.[2]

◇ On a temporary basis, teenagers can be persuaded to use the children's department but they go reluctantly and make it clear that they do not belong there. Physically, they should not be in children's rooms—their size, voices, and active natures can only be intimidating to children, and in any number, the teenagers may develop a "take over" attitude which will result in an unpleasant atmosphere with a resulting disservice to children.

> Ruth Rausen, Coordinator, Young Adult Services
> The New York Public Library

◇ The purpose of young adult services is to provide a transition from the children's collection to the resources of the total library with the aid of the young adult librarian. . . . A practical question which needs to be considered is who will be serving the children while the children's librarian accompanies the teenager venturing "into the larger adult collection." When "service" and "collection" are used synonymously, confusing conclusions result. . . . The young adult collection is a means to an end and as such is marked by flexibility to reflect current interests while also introducing new ones. The collection is small in comparison with children's and adult collections, but it does give visibility to a choice of materials that will help convince the young adult that reading can be enjoyed for its own sake.

> Julia M. Losinski, Young Adult Services Coordinator
> Prince George's County Memorial Library System

◇ [Successful YA librarians] have probably involved their young adult clientele in activities that help them participate in decision-making about YA services. . . . A frequently neglected area is periodicals directed at teens. Take a look at the newsstand. Even so-called "non-readers" are purchasing periodicals on media stars, hobbies, sports, music, and other youth interests.

There should be young adult collections that include fiction, poetry, sports, self-help books, sex information, drug information, etc. In short, collections developed by trained YA specialists who are able to keep up with the fads and continuing interests of youth. This is not likely to be the person who is also running programs for pre-schoolers, story hours for older children, reviewing children's books and all the other activities needed to provide good service to young children.

> Penelope S. Jeffrey, Young Adult Librarian
> Cuyahoga County Public Library, Ohio

◇ A shelf of books is not YA Services any more than the Reference Room is Reference Services. . . . Adequate Young Adult Services deal not only with those "safe" YA books that are easy to find, but also with adult materials of interest to young adults. These are often, by their very nature, controversial. It

THE PEOPLE BEHIND THE BOOKS

MARY K. CHELTON, Co-editor

Voice of Youth Advocates

I am delighted that the publishing industry has finally broken the umbilical cord with librarians and English teachers and managed to find a way to market and distribute young adult books in trade (as opposed to institutional) outlets. I would not, however, like to see the educational market totally eclipsed, because then there would be no place for the really special book or reader, nor anyone to be an advocate for either. Unfortunately, mass popular culture interests of adolescents suffered under the previous arrangement, and I hope there is now a balance between the quality and popularity ends of the publishing and reading spectrum.

I hope two things don't happen, the first being that bookstores come under censorship pressure and become as timid as many of us in the educational market are. There is already self-censorship in the distribution end of the publishing industry, and if a lot of litigation and citizen vigilantes started converging on bookstore owners, I doubt that they would have more intestinal fortitude than their

is not happenstance that many censorship cases involve books for young adults; books which explore life, sexuality, and conflict. . . . There are real differences between how one works with elementary age students and how one works with the high school age. The differences are as much in perception as in attitude.

Regina Minudri, Director of Library Services
Berkeley, California, Public Library

In a companion piece "And All for the Want of a Horseshoe-Nail: Dilemma of a Writer—And of Us All," author Adrienne Jones expressed her concern over "the plight of the writers whose novels are not written for the large 'popular' audience." The fate of the writers of the "serious," the "quality" books "who know at the outset that their audience is relatively small," is intimately connected with the fate of young adult librarians who purchase and promote such books as *To Kill a Mockingbird, Summer of My German Soldier, The Catcher in the Rye, After the First Death,* and *A Sound of Chariots.* Jones explained her concern:

> ◇ It is easy to see that, with the cutbacks in YA services, only the "popular" books may survive. As in TV fare, the rate of attrition will rise for the smaller audience production. Right now the light romance book holds sway—that formula novel of escape that, like candy, is all right in moderate amounts, but is deadly when it becomes the staple of diet. We do observe that popular taste in TV assures a long run for *The Dukes of Hazzard* and allows *The Paper Chase* to quickly disappear.[3]

As these people pointed out, it takes more than a shelf of books labeled YA to make up something that can honestly be called YA services. This section will discuss a few of those things as related to literature.

librarian/teacher counterparts. Secondly, I hope that bookstores do not further limit the definition of "young adult" or "adolescent literature" only to realistic teen novels and series books, continuing the exclusion of science fiction and mysteries, when it could be argued that both are the most generic forms of adolescent literature because of the onset of formal operations thinking processes in adolescence.

Having watched many publishing fads which die out with the next corporate merger, I would hate to see the new paperback YA lines go by the wayside, although I would like to see them designed better than a new sort of category book which doesn't quite come up to mass market packaging. Last of all, I hope the academics of the library and English education fields will engage in some unbiased, creative content/audience analysis research to discover why adolescents read what they read, in this case (at last) unencumbered by the prejudices of either their librarians or their English teachers. If research can supplant the current hand wringing going on in educational circles, we might finally see beyond the end of our collective nose. ◆

Most people working with books and young readers have come to accept the idea that there is no such thing as one sacred list of books that every student should read. The best that can be hoped for are agreeable matches between particular books and particular students. To bring about such matches, adults need to be acquainted with a wide range of books and with individual students. A commonly used technique in getting to know students is to ask them what books they have previously enjoyed and then to suggest something similar or something by the same author. An alternative is to ask young readers to describe the book they would most like if an author were going to write a book just for them, and then to suggest three or four books that contain elements they have mentioned.

Other people use written forms as reader interest surveys in which students write down their hobbies, the kinds of classes they are taking, what they want to do for a career, what books they have read, and the kinds of stories they most enjoy. The problem with such forms is that they are usually filled out and then stored in a drawer. No one has time to interpret them. However, one creative librarian who had access to a computer terminal designed a reader interest survey that could be answered on a computer card to which she added the students' reading test scores. She programmed the computer with one hundred of the best books she had read. All of the students got individual computer print-outs suggesting six books that they would probably like and that would be within their reading level. Her students were intrigued with the idea of getting their own print-outs, but that wasn't what made the program successful; that was only the attention getter. What made it work was that the librarian had read and personally reacted to each of the books that she had programmed into the machine and could talk knowledgeably to students about them. The print-out started conversations from which one-to-one relationships began to grow. She considered it well worth the effort because once the machinery was set in order, it could be done for hundreds of students almost as easily as for thirty.

The key to being able to recommend the right book to the right student is for adults to have such a large and varied reading background that they can personally act as a computer. Skilled teachers and librarians program their minds to draw relationships between what students tell or ask and what they remember about particular books. Experience sharpens this skill, and those librarians who make an effort consistently to read a few new books every month increase their repertoire of books rapidly. As an aid to memory, many people keep a card file of the books they read. They glance through it every few weeks to remind themselves of all the books they know. They also use it as a handy reference when a title or an author slips their minds.

Book Talks

With all of their other responsibilities, few librarians have as much opportunity as they would like to guide individual reading on a one-to-one basis. The next best thing is giving presentations or book talks to groups. In her highly recommended *Booktalk! Booktalking and School Visiting for Young Adult Audiences*, Joni Bodart defines a book talk "in the broadest terms" as "what you say to convince someone to read a book." She goes on to describe the act as:

> ◇ Sharing your enjoyment of a book with other people and convincing them that they would enjoy it too. . . . As a dramatic art, booktalking has something in common with storytelling, although in content it more nearly resembles an unfinished murder mystery—it doesn't say "who dunnit," but it makes you want to find out. . . . A good booktalk is enticing. It is a come-on. It is entertaining. And it is fun, for both the listener and the booktalker.[4]

Another advantage that Bodart mentions is that when a librarian comes to a classroom with a cartload of books and a set of interesting book talks, it lets students know "that somebody (an adult who is not a teacher) thinks that books are important, and is willing to visit their class to say so."[5]

In an article in *School Library Journal*, Mary K. Chelton added her testimony:

> ◇ The best young adult librarians I have known, whether they see their book selection role as one of expanding horizons and literary tastes or of just giving kids what they want (and most of us usually fall somewhere in between) have a "hidden agenda" for promoting the love of reading for pleasure, and have found book talks a superb way of doing that. . . . Once acquired, this skill can be adapted to floor work with individual readers, radio spots, booklist annotations, and class visits in the library or in the classroom. It can be combined with slide-tape, film, or musical presentations, and with outreach skills.[6]

The simplest kind of book talk may last only sixty seconds and consist of fewer than ten sentences. In giving it, the book talker has the obligation to let listeners know what to expect. For example, it would be unfair to present only the funniest moments in a serious book—a reader might check it out expecting a comedy. If a book is a love story, then some clue should be given, but care needs to be taken because emotional scenes read out loud and out of context can sound silly. The cover of a book often reveals its tone, which is one of the reasons for holding up a book while it is being talked about. If a presentation is being given to a large audience, it might be worth the time to make slides that can be flashed on a screen while the book talk is being given.

Book talks need to be carefully prepared ahead of time. It takes both concentration and skill to select the "heart" of a story. People who try to ad lib have the advantage of sounding spontaneous, but they also run the risk of using up all their time telling about one or two books or of getting bogged down in telling the whole story, which would defeat the purpose. Most young readers do not want to hear a ten- or fifteen-minute talk on one book, unless it is dramatic and used as a change of pace along with several shorter book talks. This whole procedure works well if the librarian comes to a class with a cart full of books ready to be checked out. Most of the class period can be devoted to the book talks with the last fifteen minutes saved as question and answer, browsing, and check-out time.

This kind of group presentation has the advantage of introducing students to the librarian, which is especially important with public librarians. When students go to the library already feeling acquainted, they are more at ease in initiating a one-to-one relationship, a valuable part of reading guidance. It also has the advantage of giving students more freedom in choosing books that really appeal to them. For example, if a student asks a librarian to recommend a good book, the librarian will probably not have time to tell the student about more than two or three books. The student usually feels an obligation to take one of these books whether or not it really sounds appealing. But when the librarian presents twenty or thirty different titles, then students have the advantage of being able to choose from a much larger offering. This also enables students to learn about and to select books that might cause them embarrassment if they were recommended on a personal basis. For example, if a girl is suspected of having lesbian leanings, it may not help the situation for the librarian to hand her Nancy Garden's *Annie on My Mind*. But if this were included among several books introduced to the class and the student chose it herself, then it might fill a real need. And the fact that the librarian had talked about it, showing that she had read it, opens the door for the girl to initiate a conversation if she so desires.

Another advantage to group presentations is that they are obviously more efficient. For example, if a social studies class is beginning a unit on World War II in which everyone in the class is going to have to read a novel having something to do with the war and also write a small research paper, then it makes sense for the librarian to give the basic information in one group presentation. Being efficient in the beginning will enable the librarian to spend time with individual students who have specific questions rather than making an almost identical presentation to thirty individuals.

Table 10.1 gives some suggestions that should increase one's chances for success with book talks. Mary K. Chelton's article served as a basis for this table.

Displays

Making displays is another effective way to promote books. Most young adults have some common needs though they might not admit them or even be aware of them. The sensitive adult who knows books can quietly alert students to titles and authors that might prove worthwhile. It can be done simply, indeed the simpler and less obvious the better, perhaps nothing more than a sign that says "Love John Wayne Films?—You'll Love These" (books on courage and facing death, though not identified in just that way), or "Did You Cry Over *Gone with the Wind?*" (books about love problems and divorce).

None of these simple gimmicks involves much work, but, more important, they do their job without the librarian seeming pushy or nosy. The point is to alert young adults to many titles on all kinds of themes. No book report is required and no one will know whether John checks out Howard Fast's *April Morning* because his father recently died or because he likes American history.

When it comes to promoting books, librarians should not be ashamed to borrow ideas from the world of commerce. After all, we are in a competitive business. We are competing directly for students' time and interest and indirectly for a share of the library budget and the taxpayers' dollars. As part of this competition, we should not overlook the benefits of having attractive, professional-looking displays and bulletin boards. They should give evidence that things are happening and they should help patrons develop positive attitudes toward books and reading.

Well-done displays draw attention to selected books and therefore make it more likely that they will be read. Even if there is no artwork connected with a display, it can still promote books simply by showing the front covers. Preparing displays can bring the same kind of personal satisfaction that comes from creatively decorating a room or painting a picture. People with negative feelings toward making displays have probably had bad experiences in which the results did not adequately compensate for the amount of time and effort expended. One way to correct this imbalance is to follow some general principles that help to increase the returns on a display while cutting down on the work. To help ensure a good design, go window shopping in the best stores—the ones that appeal to the young adults that you are wooing—and when you see a display that you like, adapt its features to your own purposes. Promote more than one book and have multiple copies available. Enthusiasm wanes if people have to put their names on a list and wait. Tie the displays into current happenings and take advantage of television and movie tie-ins with mini-displays including a poster and an advertisement supplemented by copies of whatever book is currently being featured.

◆ **TABLE 10.1   Do's and Don't's for Book Talking**

Do

1. Do prepare well. Either memorize your talks or practice them so much that you can easily maintain eye contact.

2. Do organize your books so that you can show them as you talk. To keep from getting confused, you might clip a note card with your talk on it to the back of each book.

3. When presenting excerpts, do make sure they are representative of the tone and style of the book.

4. Even though you might sometimes like to focus on one or two themes, do be sure, over the months you meet with any group, that you present a wide variety of books. Include informative books that young readers would probably like to know about but might be too embarrassed to ask for.

5. Do experiment with different formats, for example, a short movie, some poetry, or one longer presentation along with your regular book talks.

6. Do keep a record of which books you have introduced to which groups. This can be part of your evaluation when you compare before and after circulation figures on the titles you have talked about. Also, good record keeping will help you not to repeat yourself with a group.

7. Do be assertive in letting teachers know what you will and will not do. Perhaps distribute a printed policy statement explaining such things as how much lead time you need, the fact that the teacher is to remain with the group, and how willing you are to make the necessary preparation to do book talks on requested themes or topics.

Don't

1. Don't introduce books that you haven't read or books that you wouldn't personally recommend to a good friend as interesting.

2. Don't "gush" over the books. If it's a good book and you have done an adequate job of selecting what to tell, then it will sell itself.

3. Don't tell the whole story. When listeners beg for the ending, hand them the book. Your purpose is to get them to read.

4. Don't categorize books as to who should read them, for example, "This is a book you girls will like"; or show by the books you have brought to a particular school that you expect only Asian-Americans to read about Asian-Americans and only American Indians to read about American Indians, and so forth.

5. Don't give literary criticisms. You have already evaluated the books for your own purposes and if you did not think they were good, you would not be presenting them.

Use displays to get people into the library. Offer free bibliographies and have announcements of their availability made through local media. A display can also be an announcement of, and a follow-up to, a program or special event. For example, if an author is coming to speak, include a photograph and articles about the author along with all of his or her books. The same type of display could work for a hang-gliding demonstration, a talk on the Bermuda triangle, or on fashion modeling. Put your displays in high

◆ The very ordinary objects shown here—soda pop cans, pizza boxes, and cloth-sculptured pizzas—become out-of-the-ordinary when they are put into a display. In this table display, modern problem novels are promoted as "Slice of Life" books.

Courtesy of the Instructional Resources Library, Arizona State University, Tempe, Arizona.

traffic areas where everyone, not just those who already use the young adult collection, will see them.

Use interchangeable parts so that it isn't necessary to start from scratch each time. Coat hooks screwed into blocks of wood make good upright book holders as do drapery rod supports and the L-shaped metal doorstops available at hardware stores. These latter two are screwed into boards that either stand upright or lean against a wall. Standing boards are a good way to get some height into a display. Fruit baskets and crates from grocery stores can also be used as props. A wood stain is easy to apply and gives a finished effect. For making table displays, collect several sturdy cardboard cartons of various shapes and sizes. Tape them securely shut with strapping tape or plumber's tape and then sew cloth covers for them. Use the same cloth or coordinating colors so that they can be used together as mix-and-match stackable platforms. Books are much more attractive if they are put at different levels and at different distances from the viewers. Boxes that are not covered can still be used for this purpose if they are hidden beneath a tablecloth or drape.

Plain is better than figured cloth for table coverings and bulletin boards because books have their own designs. In displays featuring several books, the jackets are already competing with each other, and if they also have to compete with background patterns, then the display looks cluttered.

People lacking formal display areas and bulletin boards are fortunate in that they can make portable displays that can be set up in a variety of locations. The changing location is in itself an attention getter. A portable display can be as small as a foot-square sandwich board set in the middle of a table or as large as a camper's tent set up in the middle of the room and surrounded by books about camping, hiking, backpacking, ecology, and nature foods. If space is a problem, small bulletin boards can be hung from the ceiling or stood against pillars or walls. They can be covered on both sides with cloth sewed like a snug pillow case, or stretchy tubular cloth can be slipped on them. This also works well for long narrow boxes that can be wedged between the floor or a table and the ceiling using the spring mechanism borrowed from a pole lamp. Such hanging or standing displays can do double duty, for example, dividing the children's section from the young adult section or separating a reading corner with its casual furniture from the desks and tables set aside for study.

It's a good idea to give students a sense of ownership over the displays by involving them as much as possible. Students in woodworking, plastics, and home economics classes will sometimes be glad to help in making display equipment. Occasionally students working as library interns or helpers will enjoy the challenge of doing displays all by themselves. Art teachers are usually happy to work with librarians in order to have a place where student work can be attractively displayed. Students enjoy lending such things as family portraits or baby pictures to add interest to a display of genealogy books. They will collect items from the city dump for a display on recycling or ecology or bring in an overstuffed chair and a footstool as the focal point of a display of leisure time books. Whatever is interesting and different is the key to tying books in with real life. A very ordinary object—a kitchen sink, a moped, or a torn and dirty football jersey—is out of the ordinary when it appears on a bulletin board or a display table.

Also, don't overlook the possibility of tying commercial posters in with books. Remember the part that the poster message, "Don't disturb the universe," played in Cormier's *The Chocolate War*. The American Library Association continuously offers attractive posters, and within the last few years The Children's Book Council has become more sensitive to young adults and has begun to offer promotional material specifically aimed at teenagers, in addition to their standard material promoting children's reading.

Programs

Stores have special sales and events to get people into the marketplace where they will be tempted to buy something. In the same way ambitious librarians put on young adult programs to do something special for those who regularly use the library and, at the same time, to bring nonusers into the library. Opinions are divided on whether or not programs should necessarily be designed to promote the use of library materials, and on whether they should be educational rather than recreational. Without getting into a discussion of both viewpoints or a complete description of how to set up young adult programs, we can offer some advice from people whose libraries have been especially active in arranging programs:

1. Take a survey, or better, talk with your teenage clientele to see what their interests and desires are.
2. Avoid duplicating the kinds of activities that students do in school and in conjunction with other community agencies.
3. Include young adults in planning and actually putting on programs. The library can be a showcase for young adult talent.
4. Work with existing youth service agencies to cosponsor events, or plan them in conjunction with school programs so as to have the beginning of an audience and the nucleus of a support group.
5. Do a good job of publicizing the event. The publicity may even influence people unable to come so that they will feel more inclined to visit the library at some other time.
6. Have a casual setting planned for a relatively small group with extra chairs available in case more people come than you expect. Bustling around at the last minute to set up extra chairs gives an aura of success to a program that is much more desirable than having row upon row of empty chairs with a few people sitting here and there.

Among the kinds of programs commonly held are film programs, outdoor music concerts featuring local teenage bands, talent shows in a coffeehouse setting, chess tournaments, and contests in such areas as filmmaking and decorating blue jeans. Workshops are held in fields such as computer programming, photography, creative writing, bicycle repair, and all sorts of crafts ranging from macrame and embroidery to the silk-screening of T-shirts and posters. Another kind of program features guest speakers. In public libraries these are often on subjects that school librarians tend to shy away from such as self-defense and rape prevention, drug and birth control information, and an introduction to various hotlines and other agencies that help young adults. Large-scale workshops are sometimes held in libraries to which various schools bring their students. For example, in a town with three high schools, one big day on choosing careers may be planned at the community library. Guest speakers who could not give up three days of time are willing to make a single appearance; special exhibits and displays can be set up once rather than three times.

Regardless of the topic or format of a workshop or its main purpose, there are certain things that a librarian should do to reap full benefit from the effort that has gone into attracting extra visitors to the library. As librarians, our chief business is information and its retrieval, and today books are still the main carriers of information. Therefore it stands to reason that we will want to do whatever we can to encourage library visitors to become regular book users. The time of a program is the time to be sure that an attractive young adult display is out in full view of participants. If possible, hold the program so that it is in or very near the young adult book section. If space precludes this, plan the traffic pattern so that visitors at least see the young adult area. Perhaps refreshments could be served there.

When there is a group audience, it is a good time to pass out miniature bibliographies, perhaps printed on a bookmark. It's also a good time to sign up people for library cards. The program should be scheduled so that it ends at least a half-hour before the library closes. This way participants will have time to browse in the library rather than having to leave by the nearest exit because the building is being locked. Also, in the first ten or fifteen minutes, while the group is waiting for the latecomers to straggle in, the librarian could give a few book talks. Just as grocery and discount stores crowd the checkout areas with all kinds of tempting little items, it makes sense to place paperback book racks where they are equally tempting.

Some libraries have had success with book discussion groups in which teenagers serve as readers and critics. This usually works best if their evaluations can be publicized perhaps in a teen opinion magazine, through a display of books they recommend, on a bulletin board or in a set of file cards containing their reviews for others to look at, in a monthly column in a local newspaper, or through the periodic printing and distribution of annotated lists of favorites.

When an author is invited to speak, it is the host librarian's responsibility to begin several weeks in advance to be sure that people are reading the author's books. English and reading teachers should be notified so that they can devote some class time to the author's work. A panel of students who especially enjoyed the author's work might be set up to interact with the author at the end of the formal presentation. Another way to involve students, and perhaps teachers, would be to invite three or four to have lunch or dinner with the guest author. (Check this out first since some people prefer to be left alone before they are to speak.) If you are setting up an author's visit, it is usually best that you first write the publisher of the author's most recent book. State how much money, if any, you have available. Sometimes publishers will pay for the transportation of an author, but at your end you will usually need to pay at least for food and housing, and if possible, offer an honorarium. If you have no money, say so immediately, and then be patient, flexible, and grateful for whomever you get. What could happen is that an author will be scheduled to speak in or near your area and will come to you as an extra. Also it is highly possible that there are young adult authors living in your own state. The Children's Book Council (67 Irving Place, New York, NY 10003) has a geographical listing of authors. However, it should be considered only a beginning as not all authors are listed with them.

◈ IN ENGLISH CLASSES

Young adult literature has never been invited to sit at the head of the table in English classes. If included at all, it's more apt to be brought in only for a brief period during which it is treated either as a child who hasn't yet learned company manners or as a not-quite-respectable relative who is adored by youngsters but mistrusted by adults.

This latter attitude results in the kind of note that one frustrated librarian received from the English department head in her school:

◇ As for adolescent fiction, I'm generally indifferent to the stuff. I suppose it doesn't hurt students, but I wouldn't go out of my way to purchase or recommend it.

Nevertheless there is some evidence that attitudes are softening. Connie C. Epstein wrote to the English departments of the Ivy League and Seven Sister colleges and universities asking what they recommended for pre-college reading. Their responses leaned toward the expected classics, but also included such comments as this one from Arthur R. Gold, chair of the English department at Wellesley, "I'd have secondary school teachers weigh books on a scale and award letter grades for reading done by the pound." Other revealing statements included this one from Richard Johnson, director of freshman English at Mount Holyoke, "You can never quite be sure what will spark, and what will dull, a young reader's interest. . . . I therefore recommend a great diversity of works for a school library, and a certain eccentricity of taste." Peter M. Briggs, associate professor of English at Bryn Mawr wrote that "new directions in curricular thinking and simple proliferation of curricular options for high-school students have tended to erode whatever communal core of literary experience might have existed earlier."[7]

In doing research for her Ph.D. dissertation at the University of Houston in 1981, Barbara Samuels found that it was not fear of censorship, lack of funding, nor district or department requirements that kept English teachers from including young adult novels in their curriculum. Instead the following reasons were cited:

1. Teachers were unfamiliar with the genre and had not read many examples. Fewer than half of the 268 respondents to her national survey had taken a college class in young adult literature or even a course that included a unit on such novels.
2. Teachers believed that young adult novels were not sufficiently challenging in structure and style to be taught to average and above average high school students.
3. Teachers felt that as transmitters of culture, they were responsible for exposing students to time-tested classics of world literature.[8]

The solving of problem 1 will indirectly solve problems 2 and 3 because knowledgeable teachers can select those books for teaching that are worthy of class time and they can also use young adult books as bridges to studying respected modern literature as well as the classics.

Going back to the birthday cake theory discussed in Chapter 2, teachers need to keep in mind that lasting progress is necessarily slow and is accomplished in infinitely small steps. None of us want young people to get stuck on a reading level that is beneath their ability or emotional maturity, but it's unrealistic to think that we can prevent this simply by assigning "hard books" or classics. As Robert LeBlanc observed, high school students have to be gradually led to a love of fiction. "Unfortunately, many students are lost as lifelong readers by the abrupt shift from what they choose to read outside of school to what they are assigned to read in school. The jump from

Nancy Drew and the Hardy Boys to *Moby Dick* and *Crime and Punishment* leaves out adolescent literature which can serve as a bridge between these two very different kinds of reading experiences."⁹

For large numbers of junior and senior high school students it's already a giant leap to go from watching television or from skimming magazines and record jackets to reading "real books" by such authors as Virginia Hamilton, Mildred Lee, and Cynthia Voigt. The trick is in finding out just where students are and then in helping them to go a little bit further. For example, eighth-grade teacher Jan Hartman didn't suggest teaching *King Lear* to her students, but she did speak up for giving them something more challenging than what they would pick out to read on their own when she wrote a short piece entitled "Anne Frank vs. Pony Boy." She argued for teaching *The Diary of a Young Girl* by Anne Frank rather than *The Outsiders* by S. E. Hinton:

> ◇ In our school library, the most popular books checked out are *The Outsiders* and the Judy Blume titles. Wonderful, but we don't need to teach what students already know—we're there to teach what they don't know. And sad experience has taught that the "interesting, fun" novel takes on an insidious air when the beleaguered teacher suggests a composition on the "theme" or "characters." The cry sounds again, "It's boring!"
>
> Accept the refrain as aberrant behavior—normal. And teach them something important. Bruno Bettelheim points out that education is hard work and important. By stressing its importance and tackling difficult concepts we can only win.¹⁰

Pairing Books

A teaching method which is becoming increasingly popular is the pairing of significant young adult books with respected adult books. The idea isn't totally new. For example, one of Dell's long time best-sellers is a paperback edition of *Romeo and Juliet* along with the script from *West Side Story*. One reason that such pairing is successful is that as educational attitudes have moved away from the free thinking of the late '60s and early '70s into the "back to the basics" movement of the late '70s and now into the "push for excellence" philosophy of the '80s, teachers feel more anxious that young readers make observable progress. The pairing of books helps both students and their teachers feel this sense of progression. In "An English Teacher's Fantasy," Robert LeBlanc suggested pairing Sue Ellen Bridgers' *Home Before Dark* with John Steinbeck's *The Grapes of Wrath*; Mildred Taylor's *Roll of Thunder, Hear My Cry* with Harper Lee's *To Kill a Mockingbird*; and Irene Hunt's *Across Five Aprils* with Ernest Hemingway's *For Whom the Bell Tolls*. LeBlanc gave as his rationale for such pairings:

> ◇ These book teams have several advantages over teaching significant literature in isolation. The reader is hooked on the theme by reading the easily manageable adolescent novel first. The more difficult book has the advantage of being based on a familiar theme and is associated with the positive, successful experi-

ence of reading the young adult novel. The long term benefit for young readers is that they are more likely to make the connection between adolescent literature and its adult counterpart—the best seller [and then go on to become lifelong readers].[11]

Author Patricia Lee Gauch suggested in an article entitled " 'Good Stuff' in Adolescent Fiction" that teachers pair Mildred Taylor's *Roll of Thunder, Hear My Cry* with Maya Angelou's *I Know Why the Caged Bird Sings*; M. E. Kerr's *Gentlehands* with Elie Wiesel's *Night*; and Robert Cormier's *The Chocolate War* with Walter Van Tilburg Clark's *The Ox-Bow Incident*. She explained "This isn't 'babying kids into reading decent prose.' It's yoking 'good stuff' with 'good stuff,' to take advantage of the length and teen-centered subject of the younger book."[12]

Walter H. Johnson recommended a particularly interesting pairing of two stories based on the same event but written a century apart. The event was the discovery and rescue of a lone Indian woman from the Island of San Nicolas in 1853. She had lived there for eighteen years. The two stories are the "Ninth Sketch" in Herman Melville's *The Encantadas* and Scott O'Dell's *Island of the Blue Dolphins*. Melville moved his story, which was inspired by the wide publicity surrounding the finding of the woman, to the Galápagos islands and wrote a heavy tragedy full of symbolism. Most high school students would find it inaccessible, but after having read O'Dell's triumphant story of Karana written one hundred years later, they can be led to explore and appreciate what Herman Melville did with the same raw material.[13]

Susan Nugent recommends pairing for teaching literary concepts:

◇ Learning difficult concepts (such as point of view, symbolism or internal monologue) while reading difficult and often unfamiliar content prematurely places too many demands upon the student. Instead, adolescent literature allows the student to focus on the new concept, addressing that demand while reading about more familiar content. The point is that a difficult concept plus difficult content often results in frustration.[14]

She recommended Patricia McKillip's *The Night Gift* and Robert C. O'Brien's *Z for Zachariah* as good books for teaching the concept of setting as an integral part of plot before moving on to Nathaniel Hawthorne's *The Scarlet Letter*. Barbara Wersba's *Run Softly, Go Fast* and Maia Wojciechowska's *Don't Play Dead Before You Have To* are easy books (especially the latter one) to use in discussing literary style prior to going on to the more complex *The Catcher in the Rye*.

The idea of pairing could be extended beyond particular books to authors who have similarities in either their writing styles or in the themes they pursue. Units could begin with a significant author for young adults, continue on to a modern author for adults, and then finally to an established author. Table 10.2 illustrates some possible combinations with suggested thematic and literary focal points upon which teaching could be based.

◆ **TABLE 10.2 Teaching Relationships Between YA and Established Literature**

Significant Author for Young Adults	Significant Modern Author for Adults	Significant Established Author	Thematic Focus	Literary Focus
Katherine Paterson	Ann Tyler	Mark Twain	Personal Growth	Development of Character
Robert Cormier	James Baldwin	Henrik Ibsen	The Individual vs. the System	Development of Plot
Sue Ellen Bridgers	Flannery O'Connor	Jane Austen	Human Relationships	Exploration of Tone
Virginia Hamilton	John Steinbeck	The Brontës	Survival	Settings and Their Effects on Story
M. E. Kerr	Carson McCullers	D. H. Lawrence	Coming of Age	Style

Discussing Books

Nearly everyone agrees that discussing books is valuable. It enables students to exchange ideas, and to practice their persuasive techniques by arguing about and examining various interpretations. Another advantage of discussing a book is that, through verbalization, readers get a handle on their own thoughts. Their ideas and reactions intermingle with those of the author, which is one of the things that reading is all about.

Probably most adults who have worked with books and young readers remember having had some wonderful conversations about books, but they probably also remember having had some distinctly nondescript conversations in which students recited the plot of the story and then had nothing more to say. With a little planning and a modicum of skill, such negative experiences can be avoided or at least kept to a minimum.

Teachers know that one of their most valuable techniques is that of asking questions and responding carefully to student answers so that a genuine exchange of ideas occurs. If this takes place right after or during the reading of a piece of literature, then new information will be taken in, measured, evaluated, and integrated with the tentative conclusions already reached. To bring about this kind of "enlargement through talk," adults have to walk a middle ground between accepting just any comment that a student makes and having a prepared list of examination-type questions with one and only one acceptable answer. The best discussions resemble the kind of real-life conversations that good friends have when they've both read a new book and are anxious to share opinions and gain insights from each other.

The sense of equality necessary in this kind of discussion may be unsettling to teachers who are accustomed to arriving in class with either a lecture to be given or a set of dittos to be filled out. As Robert C. Small, Jr., wrote in "Teaching the Junior Novel," the generally accepted goal of a high-school literature program is to place the student in a position of incapacity while the teacher is elevated to that of translator. With most adult novels, students are at a tremendous disadvantage when they are asked to evaluate the accuracy with which an author has written about such concerns as marriage and divorce, ambition, greed, and hate. Even though these situations and feelings are related to teenage problems, they are not matters with which students have had experience. In contrast, when the subject of the book is a modern teenager, the balance of knowledge is changed. At least in the area of evaluating the characters, their problems, and the resolution of those problems, Small says "the students can justifiably be said to speak from a greater authority than their teacher."[15] But of course the teacher still has greater knowledge than the students in such matters as the development of plot, setting, characterization, theme, dialogue, and point of view and can use this knowledge to lead the students to worthwhile analysis and evaluation.

When students are at a stage in their intellectual development in which their primary interest is in finding themselves and their peers in the books they read, it stands to reason that an appropriate approach to use in talking about books would be that of subjective response. Suzanne Howell uses the following questions as a "bridge" for those who are "just finding the way to affective response."

1. What was your immediate (first) response to the story? What was your immediate (first) feeling about the story? What were your immediate (first) associations? (What did the story remind you of?) What were your immediate (first) ideas? (What ideas came to your mind?)
2. Does the story remind you of anything you've seen on TV, anything you've read before, and so forth?
3. Can you relate the story to anything in your own experience?
4. Can you relate any characters in the story to anyone you know?
5. What questions does the story raise in your mind?

It is Howell's experience that students do better in class discussion if they have first taken time to write down their responses. Otherwise, they tend to hide their feelings behind euphemisms or they resort to the objective kinds of analyses that they think most teachers really want. But as students become accustomed to the subjective response approach, they learn to trust their judgments and their feelings. Certainly some responses show more sensitivity than others, but no responses are "right" or "wrong," since each was triggered by something in the story. As classes work, there is a natural progression from subjective response to objective interpretation. As an example, Howell cites a discussion about Virginia Moriconi's short story "Simple Arithmetic," which is told through "letters to and from a boy whose

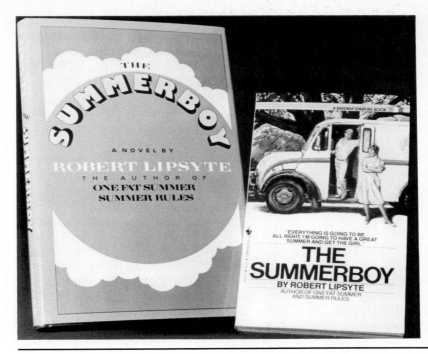

◆ A different cover and format may mean an entirely different audience for a book. Here the Bantam paperback edition is compared to the Harper & Row hardback edition of Robert Lipsyte's *The Summerboy*.

From THE SUMMERBOY by Robert Lipsyte. Copyright © 1982 by Robert M. Lipsyte. Jacket by Ellen Weiss. Jacket © 1982 by Harper & Row, Publishers. Reprinted by permission of Harper & Row, Publishers. From THE SUMMERBOY by Robert Lipsyte. Copyright © 1982 by Robert M. Lipsyte. Cover art © 1984 by John Thompson. Reprinted by permission of Darwin Bahm, Agent.

parents give him everything but love." The subjective response of nearly everyone in the class was that they hated Stephen's father. These are the steps through which the class discussion went:

◇ "I hated Stephen's father."
"Stephen's father is a cold person."
"Stephen's father is a cold, detached person, as shown by the fact that he corrects Stephen's spelling instead of dealing directly with his personal problems."
"The author reveals the character of Stephen's father indirectly through his tone and the style of his letters to Stephen."[16]

Larry Andrews is another teacher who recommends starting with the students' subjective responses and then working from there. He says:

◇ Any critical approach to any text must be considered in relation to the adolescent reader. It would be much easier for us to consider only the texts themselves, but we can't do that because of our simultaneous responsibilities to our students, to the texts they read, and their reponses to those texts.[17]

The disadvantage to be overcome, he feels, is that students typically have a superficial reaction consisting of little more than "I like it" or "I don't like it." These reactions may be based on only one aspect of the material, such as whether or not it had a happy ending or was about a subject that they like. Class discussions can encourage students to go beyond this initial response.

As one way to do this, he recommends the breakage technique in which the reading is broken into sections. At the end of a section, students express their response to a particular section and, based on these responses; they predict what will happen in the next section. By defending their predictions against others', students have to look more deeply at their responses; they have to see if their clues actually appear in the piece or whether they are so familiar with literary techniques and patterns that they are just making good guesses. As students try to agree on what will come next, they look carefully for the clues laid down by the author. Then as they read the rest of the piece to see how their ideas match the author's, they begin to see the difference between a quality piece of literature with its inevitable conclusion and the poorly written one in which an author cheated by relying on an unjustified coincidence or an unbelievable character to make the plot come out all right.

Another way to extend students' responses is to use semantic differentials. Prior to the discussion, students fill out a written form on which they rate different aspects of the piece. This encourages them to look beyond the one aspect they might have originally used to justify liking it or disliking it. It also enables them to speak in specifics rather than generalities. Thinking out their decisions and then explaining them forces students to take more than a cursory look at the text. The form should be varied throughout the year with different aspects being examined as they apply to a particular book. Concentrating on only a few aspects at a time will keep from spreading thinking and discussion too thin on any one book. If the exercise is repeated with other titles and other aspects, then by the end of a semester or a year, students will understand the wide range of elements that determines the success of the author/reader communication. An example of how such a form might look for Robert Lehrman's *Juggling* is given on page 391.

A practice that is becoming increasingly common in English classes is to concentrate on a theme rather than on a particular book. The teacher selects five to ten titles with a closely related theme and group members read one or more of them. When the group discussion is held, it centers on the common theme with readers of various books telling how the theme was developed in their particular books. Both small and large group discussions can be held.

The smaller the group doing the discussing, obviously the greater the number who get to talk. For example, when a class of thirty students spends a half-hour talking about a story, there will probably be time for a maximum of twenty well-developed comments. But if for half of the time the class were divided into five or six groups, then the number of comments offered by students could be increased to something like sixty or seventy. Worthwhile discussions do not happen automatically. Students must be trained and given guided practice. It's a good idea especially with inexperienced students for the teacher to get a discussion going in the class as a whole and then to offer suggestions or help in the continuation of the talk in the small groups. Students are apt to be more serious and to attend to the task at hand if they must come up with something to be shared with the group as a whole.

For a class to read different but related books has several advantages. It

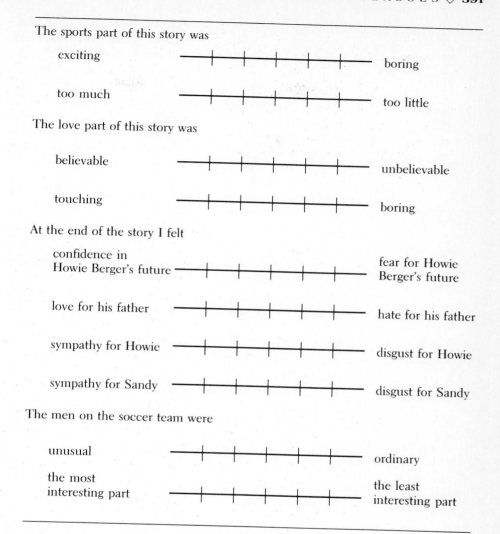

The sports part of this story was

exciting ——————— boring

too much ——————— too little

The love part of this story was

believable ——————— unbelievable

touching ——————— boring

At the end of the story I felt

confidence in Howie Berger's future ——————— fear for Howie Berger's future

love for his father ——————— hate for his father

sympathy for Howie ——————— disgust for Howie

sympathy for Sandy ——————— disgust for Sandy

The men on the soccer team were

unusual ——————— ordinary

the most interesting part ——————— the least interesting part

is easier to get four or five copies of a particular title than to get thirty. They can be borrowed from libraries and friends. Or if purchased with school funds, it seems to be a better use of money to acquire several different titles that will be available later for students to read individually. The books can also be at different reading levels with students self-selecting the one with which they feel most comfortable. And in this day of censorship, books that would perhaps cause public relations problems if they were assigned to a large group can be read and studied by a small number of students who make their own decisions on whether or not they want to read a particular title.

One of the things that teachers should remember in any kind of discussion is that when they question students, they must allow time for thinking.

When, for example, teachers ask students to explain the motivation of a character and then give them twelve seconds in which to do it, they force students to oversimplify.[18] Characters in literature are just as complex as those in real life and should be approached with equal respect.

The only questions that can be asked and answered in rapid fire order are those to which students already know the answers. At the beginning of a discussion these may serve to refresh memories and to ensure that the class is starting from the same factual base, but even very simple-sounding questions may have very complex answers. It sometimes helps if during a discussion, the questioning begins at a concrete or factual basis and then moves progressively toward the abstract. One such schema has been developed and recommended by Edward J. Gordon and Dwight L. Burton. It is printed here as it appeared in an article by Burton based on an earlier one by Gordon:[19]

1. Questions requiring students to remember facts in a selection. (What objects did the poet refer to? What happened in the story immediately after the storm?)

2. Questions that require students to prove or disprove a generalization someone else has made. One critic has said that _____ _____. Can you cite any examples from the novel to substantiate this? Or, the teacher may pose a hypothesis for the students to prove or disprove: This story is an attack upon

_____.

3. Questions that require students to derive their own generalizations. (What relationship do the coffee drinking scenes in the novel have to the central theme?) How does the poet make use of flower symbols? If there is little or no response to this question, the teacher needs to go back to simpler levels and build up to this level again: Where is a red rose referred to in the poem? Can you find any support for this interpretation: The rose symbolizes _____. Now what other flower symbols do you find?

4. Questions that require students to generalize about the relation of the total work to human experience. (What is the universal human problem dramatized in _____?)

5. Questions that require students to carry generalizations derived from the work into their own lives. (Is the kind of experience which this poem glorifies one that your friends value?)

Combining the Teaching of Writing with Literature

As Ted Hipple has pointed out, "In the contemporary secondary school English classroom, writing occupies center stage. It captures the attention of the public, gets the grants, even, in some instances, is tolerated by students." But, he went on to argue that writing has not, nor should not, replace the teaching of literature. "What is needed is a more effective blending of the study of literature and the teaching of writing."

He outlined three kinds of literature writing activities, all of which can be used with young adult books. The first is creative writing using YA literature as a model. He does not recommend assigning students to write the same amount as an adult author would; instead they focus on only a small part, perhaps a monologue or a dialogue. For example, Michelle in *The Bigger Book of Lydia* by Margaret Willey imagines a conversation that she plans to have with her mother. Students can be asked to write a new conversation between Michelle and her mother, one in which the mother does not respond in the way Michelle imagines she will.

Another idea is to assign students to write the beginning of a story, "those opening few sentences or paragraphs that set the scene and mood, introduce the central characters, and suggest the plot." Some students may get caught up in their creativity and go on to finish the story. But whether they write a whole story or only a beginning, they are likely to feel more successful in writing about their own feelings and experiences which is more often the kind of writing found in books by Robert Lipsyte, Paula Danziger, and Judy Blume than in books by Stephen Crane, Nathaniel Hawthorne, or Walt Whitman.

An alternative is to assign students to rewrite a small piece of a story or book. For example, students who don't like the ending of Katherine Paterson's *Bridge to Terabithia* can try writing a new ending. Students who think that Maureen Daly's *Seventeenth Summer* is outdated can rewrite a section to make it contemporary. Sections from books in which the physical setting is important, such as Wilson Rawls' *Where the Red Fern Grows* and Frank Bonham's *Durango Street*, can be rewritten with different settings, which may lead students to recognize the relationship between setting and plot. A similar exercise is to rewrite a small section changing the sex of a character or the ethnic group to which the character belongs. Additional incidents, conversations, or descriptions might also be written, for example, newspaper accounts of the events in Robert Cormier's *After the First Death* and M. E. Kerr's *Gentlehands*; "Dear Abby" letters or diary entries for any of the troubled teens in Hila Colman's or Norma Klein's books; and love letters between the characters in such books as Harry Mazer's *I Love You, Stupid!* Judy Blume's *Tiger Eyes*, and Robert Cormier's *The Bumblebee Flies Anyway*.

The second approach to teaching writing in relation to literature is writing about literature. This is the approach most commonly used. Students begin it in fourth grade when they write book reports and continue it throughout their schooling. In Hipple's words, the important thing for the teacher to remember is:

> ◇ Students aren't born critics, able to discuss the importance of Hardy's settings or Hemingway's characterizations without help. Teachers can provide students useful critical topics, can suggest criteria appropriate for judging specific pieces of literature, and can aid students in discovering what makes a piece of literature work. . . . Ideally, students should begin this kind of study with something specific to look for, a work's emotional effect and how that is wrought, its reflection of real life, its internal consistency, then examine the work in this light, and finally write about what they see. Their insights may be a bit shallow, but they will be theirs.[20]

THE PEOPLE BEHIND THE BOOKS

JUDY BLUME, Author

Are You There God? It's Me, Margaret
Deenie
Forever
Tiger Eyes

I need the freedom, the challenge, of dealing with all age groups. I expect to write novels about young people as well as adults. I expect to write about those subjects that are important to me. And what is especially important are human relationships. I hope to deal with the realities of life, to present characters and situations that will cause readers to think. I don't make moral judgments in my books. I would rather have my readers reach their own conclusions. I think our young people need to be better prepared for life. They need to learn to reason, they need to learn that there is more than one answer to most questions, they need to learn that they have choices and how to decide which ones will be best for them. Most of all they need to learn to think for themselves. To some people thinking for one-self is considered controversial. To me it is what life is all about! ◆

Are You There God? It's Me, Margaret. Bradbury, 1970.
Deenie. Bradbury, 1973.
Forever. Bradbury, 1975.
Tiger Eyes. Bradbury, 1981.

The third approach that Hipple suggests is writing in response to literature. The students write about their own feelings using "literature as a stimulus, a springboard, to what are often personal, affective kinds of writing." Since this kind of writing is to reflect students' own unique responses, then the teacher needs to allow considerable freedom. A list of options can be presented, but students should always be given the opportunity to ignore the teacher's suggestions and do something different.

Hipple suggested what he calls lit/comp units in which he takes "a small portion of a total work—one stanza from a poem, twenty lines or so from a play, a paragraph from a novel or short story" and uses this excerpt as the stimulus for a variety of writing activities. Here is an example of one such writing assignment based on the concluding lines of a popular poem. Similar lit/comp units could be created in relation to excerpts from many YA books:

The late great sportswriter Grantland Rice ended one of his poems with these lines:

"When the One Great Scorer comes
To write against your name,
He marks,—not that you won or lost—
But how you played the game."

Potential Writing Activities: Complete one or more of these.

1. Write a several paragraph essay that states your agreement or disagreement with Rice. Think of your own attitudes about

competition, be it in basketball or backgammon, football or frisbee. Think of Coach Vince Lombardi's famous line: "Winning isn't everything—it's the only thing." Do you want/have to win? Do your fellow players? Once you've thought through some ideas, jot them down on paper and try to shuffle them into some organizational pattern that seems logical and makes sense to you. Then write your essay.

2. Choose (or make up) a sports figure who lost a game or match after playing well. Try to write the athlete's diary entry for the day of the defeat, in which the athlete responds to Rice's poem.

3. Survey at least a dozen athletes in your school. Develop a list of questions you want to ask, keep track of the answers you get, and follow the survey with a short written report about what athletes in your school think about winning and losing and playing the game.

4. Imagine an athletic contest, a basketball game or football match, in which the home team, the team supported by the school newspaper for which you write, lost. Write the sports page entry for the game, letting your readers know how their team really played the game, even though it did lose. Or write the after-game locker room conversations.

5. Compose at least ten lines of free or rhymed verse about sports that gets at, if you choose, competition in athletics or in other walks of life—school grades, for example, or the business world.

6. Write your own journal entry that explores your own feelings about what Rice says.

7. Choose some other writing activity altogether and write a comment on the Rice question. Check with me if you have some doubts about what to choose or how to proceed.[21]

In summary, adolescent literature can be the raw material from which an English teacher fashions lessons to teach a great deal about literature. But we are certainly not recommending that all literature lessons be based on YA books, nor are we recommending that whenever students read books a literary lesson should be attached. What we are saying is that English classes need to be filled with balance and variety and that including young adult literature provides teachers with one more way to ensure this.

◈ IN THE READING CLASS

In one sense this section is superfluous because this whole book is devoted to the teaching and promoting of reading, but there are some things about the interests and responsibilities of teachers of reading that differ from those of English teachers or of librarians. One difference is that, except for remedial programs, the teaching of reading as an academic discipline in the high schools is a fairly recent development. The assumption used to be that normal students had received enough formal instruction in reading by the time they completed elementary school. They were then turned over to

English teachers who taught mostly literature, grammar, and composition. Certainly English teachers worked with reading skills, but they were not the primary focus. Today more and more states are passing laws setting minimal reading standards for high school graduation, and this has meant that reading has become almost a regular part of the high school curriculum. In some schools, all ninth-graders now take a reading class, while in other schools, it is only for those students who test one or two years below grade level. Depending on how long it takes them to pass the test, students may take basic reading classes for several semesters.

In the teaching profession the reluctant reader is nearly always stereotyped as a boy from the wrong side of town, someone S. E. Hinton would describe as an outsider, a greaser. Actually reluctant readers come in both male and female varieties and from all social and I.Q. levels. Many of them have fairly good reading skills; they simply don't like to read. Others are poor readers partly because they get so little practice. What these students have in common is that they have been disappointed in their past reading. The rewards of reading—what they received either emotionally or intellectually—have not come up to their expectations, which were based on how hard they worked to read the material. They have therefore come away feeling cheated.

The reading profession has recognized this problem and has attempted to solve it by lowering the price the student has to pay, that is by devising reading materials that are easier, that demand less effort from the student. These are the controlled vocabulary books commonly known as high-low books, meaning high interest, low vocabulary. They are moderately successful. One problem is that there isn't enough variety to appeal to everyone. A disproportionate number of them have been written to the stereotyped target audience of the young male from a motorcycle gang. The authors are rarely creative artists; they are educators who have many priorities that come before telling a good story. An alternative approach to encourage reluctant readers is to make the rewards greater rather than to reduce the effort. This is where the best adolescent literature comes into the picture. The rewards are often high enough to fully recompense supposedly reluctant teenage readers. And once these readers enjoy the satisfaction of receiving what they consider full pay for their work, then they are happy to play the reading game.

Young adult literature has a good chance of succeeding with the reluctant reader for the following reasons:

1. It is written specifically to be interesting to teenagers. It is geared to their age level and their interests.
2. It is usually shorter and more simply written than adult material, yet it has no stigma attached to it. It isn't written down to anyone nor does it look like a reading textbook.
3. There is so much of it—almost 800 new books published every year—that individual readers have a good chance of finding books that appeal to them.
4. As would be expected since they are the creations of some of the

best contemporary writers, the stories are more dramatic, better written, and easier to get involved in than are the controlled vocabulary books.

5. The language used in good adolescent literature is much more like the language that students are accustomed to hearing. In this day of mass media communication, a student who does not read widely may still have a fairly high degree of literary and language sophistication gained from watching television and movies.

Taking all of this into account, there are still some types of adolescent literature that will be enjoyed more than others by reluctant readers. In general, reluctant readers want the same things from the books they read that the rest of us want only they want them faster and in less space. If it's information they are looking for, they want it to be right there. If they are reading a book for thrills and chills, they want it to be really scary. And if it's for humor, they want it to be really funny. And if they're not sure about committing themselves for a large chunk of time, they want books in which they can get a feeling of accomplishment from reading short sections or even paragraphs. This helps explain the continuing popularity of the *Guinness Book of World Records*.

The push for higher reading scores has had the effect of opening the high school curriculum to reading classes for all students, not just those with low reading scores. For example, study skills courses are commonly given in which students are taught principles of skimming, reading for the main idea, and speed reading.

Another class that has been taught since the 1930s, but which enjoyed a new surge of popularity in the 1970s, is individualized reading. In this class, students spend most of their time reading books of their choice. The thinking behind the organization of such classes is that one of the chief reasons that out-of-school reading drops off so dramatically when children leave elementary school is that the social structure of high school students leaves them little time for reading. Classes go under such titles as Paperback Power, Paperback Reading, Contemporary Reading, Individualized Reading, and Personalized Reading. The following guidelines have been gleaned from several successful programs, most notably that of the one at Cedar Falls High School in Cedar Falls, Iowa, directed by Barbara Blow.[22]

1. Students can read any books they choose.
2. When students register for the course, a note goes home to parents explaining that the choice of books is up to the student and his or her parents. This is a friendly note, inviting parent participation, and quoting from parents of previous students who have enjoyed recommending books to their children and talking about reactions, and so on.
3. When students finish reading each book, they have a ten to fifteen minute individual conference in which they discuss the book with the teacher. The teacher makes suggestions for other books that the student will probably enjoy.

4. The teacher reads each book (or at least skims it) prior to the discussion. To enable teachers to build up a sufficiently large background of reading so that they can talk knowledgeably about the books, most programs have the same teacher handle several sections over an extended period of time. This contrasts with some unstructured (and usually unsuccessful) programs in which the course is seen more or less as a free reading study hall with little or no preparation required from the teacher.

5. The room is organized and students seated so as to minimize in-class visiting and make it easy to take the roll and locate students for conferences.

6. Teachers' aides handle such clerical tasks as taking the roll, scheduling conferences, recording grades, and checking out books so that the teacher (or teachers if it is team-taught) can concentrate entirely on student conferences.

7. Conferences are held in nearby offices or screened-off areas so that they will not disturb the students who are reading and so that the teacher's attention will not be divided between the class and the individual student.

8. Nearly all class time is reserved for reading. The exceptions are three or four days in a semester when the librarian gives book talks.

9. Although students are allowed to select their own books from any source, a special individualized paperback collection is made available to them. This includes multiple copies of popular books so that when enthusiasm about a book spreads from one student to another, copies will be available.

10. Lists of the books most frequently read by class members are distributed at regular intervals to serve as idea sources for further reading.

11. Students sign up a week in advance for conferences so that the teacher has time to read the book and so that the student has time to plan an approach. Some schools give students suggestions for organizing their discussion so that the student takes the initiative. Others are teacher-directed.

12. Grading is handled in various ways including credit for promptness and good attendance, numbers of pages read, quality of preparation for conferences, selection of "challenging" books, and so forth. Some teachers reported that it was necessary to be fairly stringent so that students understood that the class was serious and not just a study hall.

13. Some programs emphasize the keeping of a record card marking down the number of pages read each day. Students get a feeling of achievement as their number of pages steadily increases.

The kind of individualized reading program that is described here is not for the dysfunctional or disabled reader. It is for the average, or above-average, student who simply needs a chance to read and discuss books. In effect, it is one last try on the part of the school to instill in young people the habit of reading for pleasure. The student who lacks the skills for this kind of reading class or for a more standard class in literature needs expert help from a professional reading teacher. Preparing teachers for that kind of role is beyond the scope of this book.

◈ IN THE SOCIAL STUDIES CLASS

One of the great values and pleasures of literature is that it frees us to travel vicariously to other times and places. Movies, television, and photographs allow people to see other places, but literature has an added dimension. It allows the reader to share the thoughts of another person. It has been said that one never feels like a stranger in a country whose literature one has read. In today's jet age, distances are rapidly shrinking and it is more important than ever that people feel at home in other countries and with other cultures. People then begin to realize that members of the human race, regardless of where or how they live, have more similarities than differences.

Historical fiction, fiction set in other countries, fiction about members of ethnic groups in the United States, and well-written informative books should all be part of high-school social studies classes. When Lawrence Yep wrote *Dragonwings*, he fictionalized the true story of a Chinese immigrant in California who made a flying machine in 1909 that flew for twenty minutes. Yep explained in an afterword that very little was actually known about the man because "Like the other Chinese who came to America, he remains a shadowy figure. Of the hundreds of thousands of Chinese who flocked to these shores we know next to nothing." What Yep wanted to do with his story was to change at least a few of these people from "statistical fodder" into real people with "fears and hopes, joys and sorrows like the rest of us."

This is what good literature can do for any mass of social facts, figures, and statistics. Esther Forbes' *Johnny Tremain* breathes life into a study of the American Revolution. Irene Hunt's *Across Five Aprils* does the same thing for the Civil War, and Anne Frank's *The Diary of a Young Girl*, Johanna Reiss' *The Upstairs Room*, and Nathaniel Benchley's *Bright Candles* do it for World War II. In thinking about history, these books come immediately to mind because it is the wars that have been covered in traditional history textbooks. But within recent years, critics have been vociferous in their objection to the glorification of violence and war in histories and the lack of information about the contributions of women and minorities. Such critics are asking for an enlarged view of history that will teach how everybody lived, not just soldiers and statesmen, not just the winners, but ordinary people at home. What was happening in all the years when people were not fighting wars?

It may be in answering these questions that literature can make its biggest contribution to the social studies class. A book with the power of Robert Newton Peck's *A Day No Pigs Would Die* gives readers a feel for rural Vermont life in the 1920s. Anne Stallworth's *This Time Next Year* shows what the Depression did to farm families, and Jessamyn West's *The Massacre at Fall Creek* makes readers think of what it meant in 1824 to have to change one's thinking on something so basic as whether or not it is murder to kill an Indian.

However, it is important for readers to realize that no one book can tell them everything about what every person in a particular group thinks and feels. Many different books need to be read, always keeping in mind the fact that each book presents only one perspective. Stereotypes exist in people's minds for two reasons. One is that the same attitudes are repeated over and over so that they become the predominant image in the reader's mind. Another is that an individual may have had only one exposure to a particular race, group, or country. For example, a young reader who knows nothing about Africa and then reads D. R. Sherman's *The Lion's Paw*, about a young Bushman caught in a conflict between white hunters and his and a lion's needs, can hardly be said to have developed an understanding of a whole continent and its people. Nevertheless, the reader will have caught a reflection from a multifaceted jewel and will perhaps have become intrigued enough to go on and look for other reflections. Similarly, a reader who finishes Chaim Potok's *The Chosen* doesn't know everything about Hasidic Jews, but he or she knows a lot more than before, including the fact that there are groups within groups.

By reading widely and sharing their findings, social studies class members can lead each other to go beyond stereotypes. They will begin to realize that every person is a unique blend of characteristics even though that person may be a member of a particular group.

◈ IN CLARIFYING HUMAN RELATIONS AND VALUES

Workers with church and civic youth groups, teachers of classes in human relations, and professional counselors working with young adults have all found that adolescent literature can be a useful tool in the work they do. When talking about using books for the general purposes of helping students understand their own and other people's feelings and behavior, we sometimes use the term "bibliotherapy." But it is a word that goes in and out of fashion, at least in reference to the informal kind of work that most teachers and librarians do with young adults. Its technical meaning is the use of books by professionally trained psychologists and psychiatrists in working with people who are mentally ill. It is because of this association with illness that many "book" people reject the term. Their reasoning is that if a young adult is mentally ill and in need of some kind of therapy, then the therapy should be coming from someone trained in that field rather than from someone trained in the book business or in teaching and guiding normal and healthy young adults.

BRING ON THE BOOKS!

Book Week · November 12-18, 1984

◆ Within the last few years, The Children's Book Council has become more aware of the different needs of young adult librarians and has begun to offer promotional material specifically aimed at teenagers, as is this 1984 Book Week poster printed from a hand-tinted photograph by Ken Robbins. For information on current offerings send a stamped, self-addressed envelope to CBC, 67 Irving Place, New York, NY 10003.

1984 Book Week Poster courtesy of The Children's Book Council, Inc.

However, most people agree that normal and healthy young adults can benefit psychologically from reading and talking about the problems of fictional characters. They get the kinds of insights that are reflected in the following comments collected from students by Ina Ewing, a teacher at Maryvale High School in Arizona:

◇ The book [Judy Blume's] *Forever* shows a girl making a hard decision. Every girl has to make that decision at one time or other and so Kathy is like a lot of girls I know. My friends don't talk about it though, so it's good to read about someone else's decision. I think it helps.

[In reference to John Neufeld's *Lisa, Bright and Dark*] I guess if you're going crazy you should try to get help from doctors yourself. Is that possible? Can you just walk into a hospital or someplace like that and ask for help? I'll have to check it out.

[Also in reference to *Lisa, Bright and Dark*] I never realized that even kids our age have big enough problems to go crazy. I always thought the ones who went nuts were the ones who were taking dope. I would sure try to help a friend of mine though who thought she was going crazy. It must be scary.

[In reference to Paul Zindel's *The Pigman*] When my grandma died my grandpa came to live with us. It was a big bother because I had to move into a room with my brother. Now I'm glad that he has a place to stay so he won't be so lonely.

[In reference to Paula Danziger's *The Cat Ate My Gym Suit*] I think that this book says that you should listen to your parents but I also think it says that you should stand up for what you believe in. This book made it seem so easy to stick

to a cause. I would be so afraid like Marcy was. She was shy at first. That's me.
Well then when she really believed in something it was easy not to be so shy. I
could maybe find a cause.

[In reference to Ann Head's *Mr. and Mrs. Bo Jo Jones*] I liked the way the book
told the side of a couple that makes it when they get married. Most books tell
you that if a girl and guy have to get married, it won't last. Even though they had
their share of problems, they made their marriage work in the end. It shows that
sometimes pregnancy occurs because love is strong in spite of everything else.[23]

All teenagers have problems of one type or another, and simply finding
out that other people have them too provides some comfort. We are reassured to know that our fears and doubts have been experienced by others.
We feel more confident when we read about people successfully coping with
problems that we may have in the future. Notice that of the six student
comments given here, only one refers to an actual event. The others are
conjectures about things that might happen.

David A. Williams, a communications professor at the University of
Arizona, said in a newspaper interview that he would die happy if he could
"prove that a positive correlation exists between the rise in anxiety in the
country and the decline of pleasure reading." Research done during the
1950s and 1960s has shown that anxiety is directly related to a poor concept
of oneself. "It seems to me," he says, "that the human being's major
concern in life is to determine what it means to be a human being." The
paradox is that before people can see themselves, they have to get outside of
themselves and look at the whole spectrum of human experience to see
where they fit in. He points out that, "When we are feeling anxious it is
usually because we have a narrow perspective which sees only what it wants
to see." Someone who is anxiety-ridden, paranoiac, or resentful selects from
life's experiences things to validate those feelings. For people like this,
reading can put things back into perspective. "When we read about others
who have suffered similar anxieties, we don't feel so cut off and, although
the world doesn't change, we change the way we look at it."[24]

Books put things back into perspective because they talk about the
human experience in ways that everyday language cannot. Some of the
human truths that most concern us are very difficult to talk about. We do
not share our feelings with others because we think we are the only ones
who feel this way. Reading brings us back to an awareness of our com-
monality with other human beings and opens up avenues of communication that successful discussion leaders tap into.

However, it is important for adults to be careful in guiding students to
read and talk about personal problems. No one should be forced to participate in such a discussion nor should a special effort be made to relate stories
to the exact problem that a group member is having. In fact, it would
probably be best to avoid matching up particular problems with particular
students. When someone is in the midst of a crisis, chances are good that he
or she does not want to read and talk about someone else in a similar
predicament. As a general rule, one will probably get the most from such a
discussion before and/or after—rather than during—a time of actual crisis.

THE PEOPLE BEHIND THE BOOKS

MADELEINE L'ENGLE, Author

A Ring of Endless Light
A Swiftly Tilting Planet
A Wind in the Door
A Wrinkle in Time

Like most storytellers, my stories reflect my own response to what is happening in the world around me. In my case, I respond very strongly to what is happening in the world of astrophysics, quantum mechanics and cellular biology, since these exciting new sciences are dealing with the nature of being.

As more and more people become aware of the new trends which science has taken, the general thinking is going to be influenced, and teenagers are, I believe, the most eagerly excited and fearless in their response to new ideas.

During the next few years what we do about the world and keeping the peace, which also means keeping the world, is of the utmost importance, and that is bound to be reflected in the work of most storytellers, particularly those who listen to what is going on around them, in the lives of people all over the planet and who listen to young people.

Right now, I am deeply involved in writing the screenplay for a major movie of *A Wrinkle in Time*, and that surely is going to change my approach to my newest works of fiction. I think it will make them more human, more open and more realistic. ◆

A Ring of Endless Light. Farrar, Straus & Giroux, 1980.
A Swiftly Tilting Planet. Farrar, Straus & Giroux, 1978.
A Wind in the Door. Farrar, Straus & Giroux, 1976.
A Wrinkle in Time. Farrar, Straus & Giroux, 1962.

The kinds of groups in which such discussions are usually held are clubs, church groups, classes on marriage and human relations, counseling sessions, and "rap" sessions at crisis centers and various institutions to which young people are sent. Since these groups are often the kind where membership changes from meeting to meeting and there are no pressures for participants to do outside reading as "homework," a leader will probably be disappointed or frustrated if the discussion is planned around the expectation that everyone will have read the book. A more realistic plan is for the leader to give a summary of the book and a ten to twenty minute prepared reading of the part of the book that best delineates the problem or the topic for discussion.

Plan to use fairly well-known books so that the chances will be greater that someone in the group will have read the book or at least heard of it and therefore feel inclined to help get the discussion started, perhaps by filling in some of the background. Using popular books will also make it easier for students whose appetites have been whetted to find the book and read it on their own. In an adult group of professionals, the same purpose would be accomplished by reading a case study that would then be discussed. But case studies are written for trained adults who know how to fill in the missing details and how to interpret the symptoms. Teenagers are not psychologists, nor are they social workers or philosophers. Literature may be as close as

◆ **TABLE 10.3   Classification of Moral Judgment into Levels and Stages of Development**

Levels	Stages of Development
Level I. Preconventional	Stage 1: Obedience and punishment orientation
	Stage 2: Naively egoistic orientation
Level II. Conventional	Stage 3: Good-boy orientation
	Stage 4: Authority and social-order maintaining orientation
Level III. Postconventional	Stage 5: Contractual legalistic orientation
	Stage 6: Conscience or principle orientation

SOURCE: Adapted from Lawrence Kohlberg, "Stage and Sequence: the Cognitive Developmental Approach to Socialization," from Goslin, ed., HANDBOOK OF SOCIALIZATION THEORY AND RESEARCH, copyright © 1969 by Houghton Mifflin Company.

they will ever come to discussing the kinds of problems dealt with in these fields. And the oral presentation of a well-written fictional account has the advantage of being entertaining and emotionally moving in ways that factual case studies could not be.

What follows the oral presentation can be extremely varied depending on the nature of the group, the leader's personality, and what the purpose or the goal of the discussion is. The literature provides the group—both teenagers and adults—with a common experience presented through the neutral (as far as the group is concerned) eyes of the author. This common experience can then serve as the focus for discussion. Pressures and tensions are relieved because everyone is talking in the third person about the characters in the book, although in reality many of the comments will be about first-person problems.

The theory developed by Lawrence Kohlberg and his associates about how moral problems are solved is relevant to this discussion. According to Kohlberg's theory, which was developed at Harvard University during the 1960s, moral judgment is not something that can be intellectually taught. Rather it develops with experience and age, and the interesting thing that Kohlberg's studies uncovered is that there is an invariant sequence in its development. Longitudinal studies conducted in many different cultures have shown that young people between the ages of ten and twenty-five go through six stages of development in their attempts to solve moral problems. People sometimes become fixated at one of these stages, for example, an adult operating at the second stage, that of immediate reciprocity, sort of a you-be-nice-to-me and I'll-be-nice-to-you approach. Typically, however, people continue to progress through the stages, which are grouped into three levels. Table 10.3 shows these levels and stages. It is taken from one of the few articles that has been written on the relationship between books and the behaviors involved in moral judgment, "Moral Development and Literature for Adolescents" by Peter Scharf.

In Scharf's article he makes the point that the way a reader responds to a particular story will depend on the stage of moral judgment that he or she has reached. For example, at age thirteen a reader is apt to respond to

◆ **TABLE 10.4   The Powers and Limitations of YA Literature**

What literature can do:	What literature cannot do:
1. It can provide a common experience or a way in which a teenager and an adult can focus their attention on the same subject.	1. It cannot cure someone's emotional illness.
2. It can then serve as a discussion topic and a way to relieve embarrassment by enabling people to talk in the third person about problems with which they are concerned.	2. It cannot guarantee that readers will behave in socially approved ways.
3. It can give young readers confidence that, should they meet particular problems, they will be able to solve them.	3. It cannot directly solve readers' problems.
4. It can increase a young person's understanding of the world and the many ways that individuals find their places in it.	
5. It can comfort and reassure young adult readers by showing them that they are not the only ones who have fears and doubts.	
6. It can give adults as well as teenagers insights into adolescent psychology and values.	

Dostoevsky's *Crime and Punishment* as a mystery, but at age twenty the same reader would be more likely to look at it as a complex study of human morals. Great literature has an impact at almost any age, but naturally students will respond the most to that which fits the particular level at which they are struggling to make sense of the world. At the beginning levels (early teens), readers are reassured to read books in which there are definite rules and clear-cut examples of right and wrong. As readers move into the conventional or middle levels, they are interested in literature that focuses on social expectations. According to Scharf, this literature:

◇ stimulates a sense of moral conventionality by praising "appropriate" social attitudes. Often protagonists will represent heroic values which are reflected and emulated by young readers. Villains are often portrayed as "unfeeling" or "cruel" in often one-dimensional, somewhat stereotyped ways. Good literature of this type presents a coherent moral universe in which good and evil are polarized and defined. This provides a platform of social conventions upon which the early adolescent can differentiate his group's social ideology from other philosophies. While this type of literature may seem "corny" or "sentimental" to adults, it is a necessary stage toward the learning of more complex personal moral philosophies.[25]

As students become confident at this level and feel that they understand the expectations of society, they begin tentatively to explore and question these expectations. It is at this stage that many young people reject the conventional moral order and seek to set up or to find a more satisfactory social order. Scharf wrote:

◇Needless to say, this questioning is disturbing to many adults, including librarians. They fail to see that such a rejection of conventional societal truth is a critical step in the adolescent's defining for himself an autonomous value base.[26]

Because many young adults are in the stage of rebellion and questioning, Holden Caulfield in Salinger's *The Catcher in the Rye* speaks forcefully to them. As people mature, they gradually pass through this stage of rebellion and are not so concerned with society and its expectations. Instead they develop their own internal system by which they make moral judgments. This final stage is distinct from both early adolescent conformity and the relativism and nihilism of middle adolescence. Scharf thinks that books and libraries have a unique role in providing readers with the range of material that they need to reflect upon in developing their own set of inner values.

In conclusion, literature can in no way solve someone's problems. But it can serve as a stimulus to thought, and it can open channels of communication. It can serve as a conversation topic while rapport and understanding grow between an adult and a teenager or among the members of a group. And reading widely about all kinds of problems and all kinds of solutions will help to keep young people involved in thinking about moral issues.

Table 10.4 (p. 405) shows what young adult literature can and cannot do when it is used as a tool to teach about human relations and values.

This chapter has shown that using and promoting books with young readers is a shared opportunity and responsibility. It belongs not only to librarians and English and reading teachers but to everyone who works closely with young people and wants to understand them better. It can serve as a medium through which to open communication with young adults about their concerns.

We specifically focused on librarians, teachers, and youth workers or counselors, but we could also have mentioned many others, including parents. Contrary to the impression given by the mass media (adolescent fiction included), many parents serve in the roles described here, that is, teacher, counselor, conversation partner, and reading friend.

◆ ACTIVITIES ◆

1. Prepare a display of young adult books for a school or public library. Include a take-home bibliography, perhaps in the form of a bookmark or some other creative souvenir of the display. Most librarians would be pleased to have your volunteer services. If it is not practical for you to set up an actual display, think up five different ideas. Write down the basic idea, a brief description, and list at least ten books that you would feature in each display.

2. Read two of the books that are recommended for "pairing" in English classes. Make yourself a list of teaching notes in which you jot down similarities in either plot or literary techniques. Tell how you would use the books in a classroom.

3. Using Ted Hipple's lit/comp unit on the con-

cluding lines of Grantland Rice's poem as a model, choose a popular piece of YA writing and draw up a lit/comp assignment sheet.

4. Plan an informal discussion dealing with some affective area of young adult life, for example, social pressure, alienation, friendship, love, or discouragement. Prepare a reading from an adolescent novel that you will use to set the stage for the discussion. List several questions and ideas that you might use throughout the discussion.

5. Design a reader interest survey that you could have students fill out as part of getting acquainted at the start of a new school year. Design it so that it will take fewer than ten minutes for students to fill out and so that you can use it as the basis for an individual conference in which you would suggest books. You might have students list such things as their hobbies, the kinds of books they like, the last book they read, a book they did not like, the television shows they watch, and the movie they have enjoyed the most within the last year.

◆ NOTES ◆

[1] Mary K. Chelton, "Editorial," *VOYA* 6 (February 1984): 310, 315.

[2] Dorothy M. Broderick, "Whose Job Is It Anyway?" *VOYA* 6 (February 1984): 320–26.

[3] Adrienne Jones, "And All for the Want of a Horseshoe-Nail," *VOYA* 6 (February 1984): 316–18, 327.

[4] Joni Bodart, *Booktalk! Booktalking and School Visiting for Young Adult Audiences* (New York: H. W. Wilson, 1980), pp. 2–3.

[5] Bodart, p. 2.

[6] Mary K. Chelton, "Booktalking: You Can Do It," *School Library Journal* 22 (April 1976): 39–43.

[7] Connie C. Epstein, "The Well-Read College-Bound Student," *School Library Journal* 30 (February 1984): 32–35.

[8] Barbara G. Samuels, "Young Adult Novels in the Classroom?" *English Journal* 72 (April 1983): 86–88.

[9] Robert LeBlanc, "An English Teacher's Fantasy," *English Journal* 69 (October 1980): 35–36.

[10] Jan Hartman, "Anne Frank vs. Pony Boy," *English Journal* 73 (March 1984): 90.

[11] LeBlanc, 35–36.

[12] Patricia Lee Gauch, " 'Good Stuff' in Adolescent Fiction," *Top of the News* 40 (Winter 1984): 125–29.

[13] Walter H. Johnson, "A Stepping Stone to Melville," *English Journal* 73 (April 1984): 69–70.

[14] Susan Nugent, "Adolescent Literature: A Transition into a Future of Reading," *English Journal* 73 (November 1984): 35–37.

[15] Robert C. Small, "Teaching the Junior Novel," *English Journal* 61 (February 1972): 222–29.

[16] Suzanne Howell, "Unlocking the Box: An Experiment in Literary Response," *English Journal* 66 (February 1977): 37–42.

[17] Larry Andrews, "Responses to Literature: Enlarging the Range," *English Journal* 66 (February 1977): 60–62.

[18] This is what James Hoetker found in "better" schools with "better" staff. Teachers were asking five questions per minute. "Teacher Questioning Behavior in Nine Junior High School English Classes," *Research in the Teaching of English* 2 (Fall 1968): 99–106.

[19] Edward J. Gordon, "Levels of Teaching and Testing," *English Journal* 44 (September 1955): 330–34; and Dwight L. Burton, "Well, Where Are We in Teaching Literature?" *English Journal* 63 (February 1974): 28–33.

[20] Ted Hipple, "Writing and Literature," *English Journal* 73 (February 1984): 50–53.

[21] Hipple, p. 53.

[22] Barbara Blow, "Individualized Reading," *Arizona English Bulletin* 18 (April 1976): 151–53.

[23] Ina Ewing, "The Psychological Benefits of Young Adult Literature," unpublished paper, Arizona State University Department of Educational Technology and Library Science, spring semester, 1978.

[24] "Feeling Uptight, Anxious? Try Reading, UA Prof Says," *Tempe Daily News*, December 15, 1977.

[25] Peter Scharf, "Moral Development and Literature for Adolescents," *Top of the News* 33 (Winter 1977): 131–36.

[26] Scharf, 131–36.

◆ TITLES MENTIONED IN CHAPTER 10 ◆

For information on the availability of paperback editions of these titles, please consult the most recent edition of *Paperbound Books in Print*, published by R. R. Bowker Company.

In the Library
Adams, Douglas. *The Hitchhiker's Guide to the Galaxy.* Crown, 1980.

Blume, Judy. *Forever.* Bradbury, 1975.

Bodart, Joni. *Booktalk! Booktalking and School Visiting for Young Adult Audiences.* H. W. Wilson, 1980.

Bradbury, Ray. *The Martian Chronicles.* Doubleday, 1958.

Fast, Howard. *April Morning.* Crown, 1961.

Garden, Nancy. *Annie on My Mind.* Farrar, Straus & Giroux, 1982.

Golding, William. *Lord of the Flies.* Coward, 1955.

Greene, Bette. *Summer of My German Soldier.* Dial, 1973.

Hunter, Mollie. *A Sound of Chariots.* Harper & Row, 1972.

Lee, Harper. *To Kill a Mockingbird.* Lippincott, 1960.

Mitchell, Margaret. *Gone with the Wind.* Macmillan, 1936.

Salinger, J. D. *The Catcher in the Rye.* Little, Brown, 1951.

Steele, Danielle. *Crossings.* Delacorte, 1982.

Walker, Alice. *The Color Purple.* Harcourt Brace Jovanovich, 1982.

In English and Reading Classrooms
Angelou, Maya. *I Know Why the Caged Bird Sings.* Random House, 1970.

Blume, Judy. *Tiger Eyes.* Bradbury, 1981.

Bonham, Frank. *Durango Street.* Dutton, 1967.

Bridgers, Sue Ellen. *Home Before Dark.* Knopf, 1976.

Clark, Walter Van Tilburg. *The Ox-Bow Incident.* Peter Smith, 1940.

Cormier, Robert. *After the First Death.* Pantheon, 1979.

———. *The Bumblebee Flies Anyway.* Pantheon, 1983.

Daly, Maureen. *Seventeenth Summer.* Dodd, Mead, 1942.

Dostoevsky, Feodor. *Crime and Punishment.* 1866.

Frank, Anne. *Diary of a Young Girl.* Doubleday, 1967.

Hawthorne, Nathaniel. *The Scarlet Letter.* 1850.

Hemingway, Ernest. *For Whom the Bell Tolls.* Scribner's, 1940.

Hinton, S. E. *The Outsiders.* Viking, 1967.

Hunt, Irene. *Across Five Aprils.* Follett, 1964.

Kerr, M. E. *Gentlehands.* Harper & Row, 1978.

Lee, Harper. *To Kill a Mockingbird.* Lippincott, 1960.

Lehrman, Robert. *Juggling.* Harper & Row, 1982.

McKillip, Patricia. *The Night Gift.* Atheneum, 1976.

McWhirter, Norris. *Guinness Book of World Records,* 18th ed. Bantam, 1980.

Mazer, Harry. *I Love You, Stupid!* Crowell, 1981.

Melville, Herman. *The Encantadas,* in *Piazza Tales.* 1856.

———. *Moby Dick.* 1851.

O'Brien, Robert C. *Z for Zachariah.* Atheneum, 1975.

O'Dell, Scott. *Island of the Blue Dolphins.* Houghton Mifflin, 1960.

Paterson, Katherine. *Bridge to Terabithia.* Crowell, 1977.

Rawls, Wilson. *Where the Red Fern Grows.* Doubleday, 1974.

Salinger, J. D. *The Catcher in the Rye.* Little, Brown, 1951.

Steinbeck, John. *The Grapes of Wrath.* Viking, 1939.

Taylor, Mildred. *Roll of Thunder, Hear My Cry.* Dial, 1976.

Wersba, Barbara. *Run Softly, Go Fast.* Atheneum, 1970.

Wiesel, Elie. *Night.* Farrar, Straus & Giroux, 1960.

Willey, Margaret. *The Bigger Book of Lydia.* Harper & Row, 1983.

Wojciechowska, Maia. *Don't Play Dead Before You Have To.* Harper & Row, 1970.

In Social Studies and Human Relations Groups
Benchley, Nathaniel. *Bright Candles.* Harper & Row, 1974.

Blume, Judy. *Forever.* Bradbury, 1975.

Danziger, Paula. *The Cat Ate My Gym Suit.* Delacorte, 1974.

Dostoevsky, Feodor. *Crime and Punishment.* 1866.

Forbes, Esther. *Johnny Tremain.* Houghton Mifflin, 1943.

Frank, Anne. *Diary of a Young Girl.* Doubleday, 1967.

Hawthorne, Nathaniel. *The Scarlet Letter,* 1850.

Head, Ann. *Mr. and Mrs. Bo Jo Jones.* Putnam's, 1967.

Hunt, Irene. *Across Five Aprils.* Follett, 1964.

Neufeld, John. *Lisa, Bright and Dark.* Phillips, 1969.

Peck, Robert Newton. *A Day No Pigs Would Die.* Knopf, 1972.

Potok, Chaim. *The Chosen.* Simon and Schuster, 1967.

Reiss, Johanna. *The Upstairs Room.* Crowell, 1972.

Salinger, J. D. *The Catcher in the Rye.* Little, Brown, 1951.

Sherman, D. R. *The Lion's Paw.* Doubleday, 1975.

Stallworth, Anne. *This Time Next Year.* Vanguard, 1972.

West, Jessamyn. *The Massacre at Fall Creek.* Harcourt Brace Jovanovich, 1975.

Yep, Lawrence. *Dragonwings.* Harper & Row, 1976.

ISSUES AND CONCERNS FOR ADULTS

For those of us who work with young adults and their reading materials, our lot is one of controversy. At the most basic level many well-meaning book lovers think there should be no such field as YA literature. They went from reading children's books directly into reading adult books and they don't see why all of today's teenagers can't or won't do the same thing. On other fronts, people argue about book selection based on the relative values of literary quality (what Patty Campbell has called the "kiss of death")[1] and popularity (what Lillian Shapiro has called "the drugstore approach")[2] Questions arise about how to build good collections of ethnically related books or books reflecting religious values. We wonder about the influence of big business on educational practices and about the mass media and what it is doing to kids and books. Censorship is such a problem that it's treated in a chapter of its own following this one, and the controversial nature of sex-related books is discussed in Chapter 8.

As teachers and librarians, we need to be alert to such matters and to be sensitive to the necessity of understanding many viewpoints. We must also realize that as professionals, it is part of our job to investigate and to develop our own personal philosophies. Some of the issues mentioned in this chapter are long-term problems that will be solved only gradually, if at all. Others are not really problems; they are simply signs of healthy growth. Some questions, however, demand that each of us take a stand. In the library or classroom, our daily activities will be affected by the decisions that we make whether or not we are aware of the underlying issues. We can't fully discuss all the opinions that are held on the issues mentioned in this chapter, much less all the other issues that might be talked about. But we hope this chapter will be enough to convince you that you are entering a dynamic field where thinking for oneself is not only desirable, it's a necessity.

◈ EVALUATION, YES! BUT ACCORDING TO WHOSE STANDARDS AND FOR WHAT PURPOSES?

For all of us working with books and young people, skilled evaluation is a primary function. It is not always the same kind of evaluation, nor should it be. People select books for different purposes and evaluate them according to different criteria, but we should understand the reasoning and the value system behind the choices that are made, whether these choices are our own or those of a critic or reviewer.

Evaluation criteria fall into three general categories: literary quality, reader interest or popularity, and social or political philosophy. However, these criteria overlap somewhat and their purposes interweave. Nearly everyone wants to be able to predict which books will be successful, but each person's definition of success may be quite different.

Traditionally, most critics have been expected to review books on the basis of literary merit, but this doesn't always satisfy the needs of librarians and teachers strapped with shrinking budgets and demands that they turn kids onto reading. They need to know if recommendations are being made on the basis of potential popularity, life expectancy of the piece and literary quality, or on what the book teaches and the example it sets. These three are closely related, yet they are not one and the same. There are subtle differences and it is hard for reviewers to communicate these. A critic may review a book positively because of its literary quality, which a librarian or teacher interprets as a prediction of popularity. The book is purchased and put on the shelf where it is ignored by teenagers. The purchaser feels cheated and loses confidence in the reviewing source.

Or the opposite happens. A reviewer makes positive comments about the high interest level of something like *Go Ask Alice* and when teachers or librarians read it, they are disappointed in a lack of literary quality and style. This results in the kind of frustration that Lillian L. Shapiro expressed in an article for *School Library Journal*. She decried using popularity as a major evaluation criteria. "Who's in charge?" she asked and then went on to caution:

> ◇ If the measuring stick for the selection of materials for children and young adults is simply "what they want," let us remember that under those conditions there is no need for a trained cadre of reading advisers. Let us remember also that what we want at any age is not always healthful; sometimes it may save one's life to listen to those whose expertise—doctors, parents, teachers—could make a difference in the road taken.

In making a plea for selection based on "discriminating judgment" and "sensitivity" she proposed that young adult librarians consider the books from university presses that relate to young people's interests:

> ◇ These are not easy reading but are all the materials libraries offer supposed to be? Is it not the very *raison d'être* of our profession to call to the attention of our young patrons those titles they would never find themselves?

As a concluding point, she wrote:

> ◇ Response to popular demand then turns libraries into what one librarian calls a drugstore collection. I would think the drugstore and the library serve different purposes. If this is not so, then why have professional personnel in one and not the other?[3]

A different opinion holds that it takes a great deal of skill and training to pick out potentially popular books, and that the person who can do this is as necessary as—or perhaps in young adult service more necessary than—the person who can analyze the literary qualities of a book. No matter how good a book is, it won't become popular unless young adults are given a chance to read it. In most cases this means that it must be brought to the attention of library and school personnel so that it will be purchased and made available. The University of Iowa's Books for Young Adults Program, which was begun in 1972 under the direction of G. Robert Carlsen, is based on the goal of predicting popularity. Graduate students take review copies of new books to individualized reading classes in the Iowa City area and get three or four students to read each new book and serve as critics. Individualized conferences are held with the sample readers whose opinions are then used to draw up an annual listing of the books that have proven themselves to be the most popular. Since 1973 this list has been published at the end of each year in the *English Journal*.

The disagreement over whether literary quality or popularity should be the yardstick of selection is reflected in how this listing has changed over the years. It was initially entitled the "Books for Young Adults Honor Listing," but by 1975 the title had changed to the "BYA Book Poll" because the students' selections didn't always qualify according to adult literary standards of "honorable." The new title was chosen to lessen the chances for confusion and to make clear the purpose of the program. However, that year three of the books were cited as "Honor Books," meeting the "criteria of literary quality, adolescent interest, and significant themes": *If Beale Street Could Talk* by James Baldwin, *A Cry of Angels* by Jeff Fields, and *House of Stairs* by William Sleator. By 1977, there was no mention of "Honor." Instead three books, *Ordinary People* by Judith Guest, *The Seeker* by William Alan Bales, and *The Shepherd* by Frederick Forsyth were "Recommended for Teaching." In 1978 no books were given special designation. When Carlsen was questioned about this, he said that the adult staff responsible for drawing up the final list did not feel they could personally endorse any of the students' choices as "great literature."

Another example of the growing awareness that popularity and literary quality may not be the same thing is the evaluation code shown in Table 11.1 devised by Mary K. Chelton and Dorothy M. Broderick for their publication *Voice of Youth Advocates* (VOYA). Each review of a teen or adult title is preceded by a *Q* number indicating quality and a *P* number indicating popularity.

The editors suggest that one use for such a clearly outlined code is to help librarians analyze their buying patterns. Those who lean heavily to-

◆ **TABLE 11.1 *VOYA* Evaluation Code**

Quality	Popularity
5Q: Hard to imagine it being better written.	5P: Every young adult was dying to read it yesterday.
4Q: Better than most, marred only by occasional lapses.	4P: Broad general young adult interest.
3Q: Readable without serious defects.	3P: Will appeal without pushing.
2Q: A little better editing or work by the author would have made it 3Q.	2P: For the young adult reader with a special interest in the subject.
1Q: Hard to understand how it got published.	1P: No young adult will read unless forced to for assignments.

ward either quality or popularity will see their biases and be able to strike a more appropriate balance.

Patty Campbell reported in the Winter 1979 issue of *Top of the News:*

◇ Not so long ago the YA librarians of Los Angeles Public Library engaged in a modest brouhaha about the phrase "literary quality." It had come time to revise the form used to evaluate young adult books, and there was a contingent that felt that LQ should be added to CV (current value), Pop (popular), RV (replacement value), etc., as one of the criteria for analyzing a book's appeal to YAs. "Not so!" cried the others. Literary quality, they argued, was not only not in it, it was completely out of it, the kiss of death. As the majority, of course, they prevailed. When the children's librarians heard about it they were horrified.[4]

She went on to explain that although the decision was something of an overreaction since what the librarians probably had in mind was a self-conscious posturing kind of "literary quality," the story does point up a basic difference between the reviewing of children's and young adult books. Children are essentially passive and uncritical observers of society who are engaged in soaking up the data about the world around them. It is the role of the librarian to provide them with the very best of that data. But teenagers have passed through this stage. They are in the process of sorting out the data, deciding which of it they are going to reject, and which they are going to adopt as their own. Campbell commented:

◇ This process is maddening to adults, but absolutely necessary if young adults are not going to end up puddings on legs. Remember always that the basic YA question is "Who am I, and what am I going to do about it?" In the turmoil of adolescence, the young adult no longer has much patience for new factual data, for the classics, for anything that doesn't bear on the answer to The Question.

It is her opinion that reviewers of books for young adults must first ask the question, "Will the kids think it's good?" Then, only after "discussing relevance and format, may the question of literary value be considered."

A quite different set of criteria from either popularity or literary quality is that of social or political values. The Council on Interracial Books for children has been very open about their belief that books should "become a tool for the conscious promotion of human values that lead to greater human liberation."[5] The organization provides a checklist to use in evaluating books to see whether they perpetuate or counterbalance old stereotypes either through omission or commission. The checklist includes the categories of racism, sexism, elitism, materialism, individualism, ageism, conformism, escapism, positive vs. negative images of females and minorities, cultural authenticity, and the level of inspiration toward positive action. It is expected that reviews in the *Interracial Books for Children Bulletin* will focus on such matters.

However, most reviewers—whether or not they realize it—are influenced by their personal feelings towards how a book treats social issues. For example, Sue Ellen Bridgers' *Notes for Another Life* was highly recommended and praised in *Horn Book Magazine*, the *New York Times Book Review*, and the *Bulletin of the Center for Children's Books*, but when Janet French reviewed the book for *School Library Journal* she wrote:

> ◇ The blurb suggests that this is "a family chronicle for all ages." It would have been more accurate to describe it as a propaganda vehicle for female domesticity. Good women subordinate their talents and yearnings to the home and their children; all other paths lead to havoc. For a riveting story of four deserted children, lead readers instead to Cynthia Voigt's marvelous upbeat *Homecoming*."[6]

This review was written in such a way that readers can easily recognize that the reviewer's opinion was shaped by her disagreement with the plot. For a reviewer to use this as the basis for a negative recommendation is perfectly justifiable *if* the situation is made clear. The problem comes when reviewers reject books on the bases of such social issues but don't admit to themselves, much less to their readers, that their feelings have been influenced by whether a story sharpens or dulls whatever personal axe they happen to be grinding at the moment.

Differences of opinion are natural. It is not possible or even desirable for all critics and reviewers to agree on the criteria they will use for evaluating books. But just as teachers and librarians explore their own reasoning, so must reviewers analyze their feelings and communicate the principles that underlie their personal reactions. With this kind of information and their own deductions about a writer's biases, people can interpret recommendations and make use of them in ways appropriate to their own needs.

◈ WRITING ABOUT AND CRITIQUING YOUNG ADULT LITERATURE

The writing about and critiquing of young adult literature is not so much an issue as it is an area of concern. Three kinds of concerns will be discussed in this section. (1) What different types of writing meet specific needs, and how can they do it best? (2) Should reviews of young adult books be less promotional and more critical? (3) Is the current writing and scholarship in the field aimed too much at the uses of literature rather than at the analysis of the literature itself? Evaluation, which we have already discussed, underlies nearly all writing about books. Even when someone is simply making notes to serve as a reminder of the contents of a book, that person is making an evaluation and concluding that the book is one worth remembering.

Note Cards

It is important to understand that the kind of writing that is done will differ considerably depending on the purpose of the writer. The type of writing we will be doing most often is that of making note cards on our reading. College students in adolescent and children's literature classes sometimes look at this activity as little more than a teacher-imposed duty that they will be only too glad to leave behind once the class is finished. But in reality, making notes is probably going to be a lifelong activity for anyone who works professionally with books. Most librarians and teachers make note cards as a continuous record of the books they have read and can personally recommend. They use the cards to jog their memories when they compile book lists, when students ask for "a good book," and when they plan teaching units and promotional activities. A story is told about a library that caught fire. The librarian grabbed her card file, and only then did she run to warn the patrons.

The comments put on note cards vary according to the needs of the writer. Most people include the publisher and date, a short summary of the story, and perhaps an evaluative comment. It is usually wise to write down the characters' names and other details that make this book different from others. After this basic information, the writer might add a few comments suggesting future uses of the book. For example, if the book were Alice Childress' *A Hero Ain't Nothin' But a Sandwich*, a librarian who planned on introducing the book to patrons might make out the card in the form of a book talk and might also include information about the movie. An English teacher might note that it would be a good book for illustrating a literary principle of point of view. A reading teacher might note that it is short and easy reading except that the use of black dialect would perhaps cause problems for less skilled readers. A youth worker might make a note about the potential of the book as a catalyst to get kids talking about what they think adults should do in situations like Benjie's, and whether or not the responsibility belongs to Benjie rather than to those around him. In a community where books are judged as appropriate for school study on the basis of their topic and such things as "perfect" grammar and happy endings, someone might note that it would be desirable to share the book with other professionals and adult friends of the library in order to develop community support for its use. Positive reviews and honors won might also be helpful information. The sample card that follows was prepared by a student in an adolescent literature class who was planning to be an English teacher.

```
A Hero Ain't Nothin' But a Sandwich by Alice Childress.
Coward, McCann & Geoghegan, 1973, Avon paperback.

     The best part of this drug-related book is that
it shows people really trying.  A family rallies
around thirteen-year-old Benjie.  The dad is just
living with the family, but he proves himself to be
a real father.  The story is told from several view-
points--one chapter at a time.  This makes it good
for showing that not all people who live in a ghetto
feel and act the same.  It's open-ended with the
reader being left to wonder whether or not Benjie
shows up for drug counseling.  Realistic, black
dialogue adds to the authenticity.  I liked it.
Could be used as a read-aloud introduction to a unit
on drugs.
```

Annotations

Annotations are similar to note cards but they are usually written for someone else to see rather than for the writer's own use. And since they are usually a part of an annotated bibliography or list on which space is at a premium, writers must make efficient use of every word. It is not easy to communicate the plot and tone of a book as well as a recommendation in only one or two sentences. Nor is it easy to make annotations into interesting reading. You might help yourself by resolving never to begin an annotation with "This book . . . " The two sample annotations below are for Virginia Hamilton's *Sweet Whispers, Brother Rush*. The first is from *School Library Journal*, December 1982, and the second appeared in *Booklist*, March 15, 1983. (To save space, the bibliographical information given on the lists is not reprinted here.)

◇ Poetic, many-layered novel of 14-year-old Teresa's devotion to her retarded and doomed brother Dab. A strong story of hope and power of love.

Fourteen-year-old Tree learns a lot about her family and the interconnections between their past and present tragedies from Brother Rush, her uncle's ghost.

Notice how both writers communicated the age of the protagonist, the fact that it was a family story, and, through the use of "doomed" and "tragedies," that it was a fairly heavy or serious book. The writers also hinted at mystery and intrigue, the first one through such words as "Poetic, many-layered . . . hope and the power of love" and the second one through the reference to "Brother Rush, her uncle's ghost."

Reviews

Another kind of writing about adolescent literature commonly done by librarians and teachers is the writing of reviews for local and national circulation newspapers, magazines, and journals. The practice of having books reviewed on a part-time and usually volunteer basis is more a part of the juvenile than the adult book world. Probably fewer than two dozen people in the United States are full-time reviewers of juvenile books, but hundreds of people do it on a part-time basis. One day you may be one of these reviewers.

A problem in the reviewing of juvenile books is that more books are published than there is room in the media for reviewing. Major reviewing sources for young adult books include the *ALAN Review, Booklist, Bulletin of the Center for Children's Books, English Journal, Horn Book Magazine, Kirkus Reviews, New York Times Book Review, Publishers Weekly, School Library Journal,* and *VOYA.* But in addition to these, dozens of national publications carry occasional review articles, and many library systems sponsor reviewing groups whose work is published either locally or through such nationally distributed publications as *Book Waves* from the Bay Area (Northern California) Young Adult Librarians and *Books for the Teen Age* from the Young Adult Services Office of the New York Public Library. And some teachers of children's and young adult literature work with their students to write regular review columns for local newspapers.

When publishers send out their new books, the review editors glance through them and select the ones that they judge to be of the greatest potential interest to their readers. The company that sends books to the largest number of publications has the greatest chance of having them reviewed. And the authors who have already established names for themselves will probably have their books reviewed before newcomers will.

The fact that juvenile books are reviewed mostly by librarians and teachers working on a part-time basis is one of the reasons that the distribution of juvenile books is so different from that of adult books. Before an adult book is released, prepublication copies are distributed to the major reviewing sources, book clubs, and moviemakers. By the time the book actually arrives in bookstores, it is not unusual for excerpts to have been featured and for reviews to have appeared in national publications. It might also have been selected as a book-club offering and been sold to a moviemaker and paperback publisher.

Things do not work this fast with juvenile books. There are delays at each step. Quite often completed books, not prepublication galleys, are sent out to reviewing journals. Several weeks can pass before the editors decide whether or not to review a particular title, and if so, to whom it should be assigned. The reviewer is given between a month and six weeks in which to write the review, and it is fitted into the magazine as space permits. Sometimes it may appear within a month or two, but, in other cases, a much longer time elapses. If a reviewer takes the book to young adults and has them read and react to it, the whole process will be slowed down by many more months. The Books for Young Adults program at the University of Iowa is one of the few evaluation groups that has attempted to do its work by using individualized reading classes in local schools. Systematically incorporating the opinions of young readers is something more reviewers probably should do, but the benefit has to be weighed against the time lost.

Because of these delays in the reviewing process, young adult books get

◆ For ordering information on these publications, all of which devote considerable space to young adult literature, See Appendix B, "Book Selection Guides."

off to a slower start than do adult books, but, once launched, they stay around longer. Teachers work them into classroom units, librarians promote them, and paperback book clubs keep selling them for years.

The fact that adolescent literature is a part of the massive business of public education undoubtedly contributes to its long life span. Children continue to grow older and to advance in their reading skill and taste so that every year there is a whole new set of students ready to read A *Separate Peace, The Catcher in the Rye,* and even *The Outsiders.* As a result, reviews, articles, and papers continue to cover particular titles years after their original publication dates.

The field of juvenile reviewing is sometimes criticized for being too laudatory. When reviewers are writing for audiences who are not totally committed to the idea of buying books for children, the general public, for instance, a desire to "sell" literature may keep them from being as critical as they would be of adult books. Many editors feel that since they can bring only a limited number of books to the attention of their readers, it makes sense to write about the ones that they think are the best, so of course they are complimentary.

There are as many reviewing styles as there are journals and individual reviewers. But nearly all reviews contain complete bibliographical information including number of pages and prices, the intended age level, a summary statement of the contents, and some hint of the quality of the book as evaluated by the reviewer.

The Winter 1979 issue of *Top of the News* had as its feature topic "Reviews, Reviewing, and the Review Media." Editor Audrey Eaglen solicited comments from people working in different roles with books and young readers. The question she asked them was, "What Makes a Good Review?" Author-illustrator Rosemary Wells said, "an intelligent review . . . is never obsequious, if it is favorable. It is never flip, if it is unfavorable. It never quotes from a front flap." School librarian Katherine Haylman wants reviewers to tell her of "any clever device or intriguing aspect of the book which could be used to pique the interest of a group and 'sell' the book." And she thinks reviewers should inform potential buyers "if there is a potentially controversial issue in the book, be it strong language, explicit sex, violence, or whatever." She doesn't want to know this so she can avoid buying the book, but so that she can plan and prepare and thereby deal with a conflict should it arise.

Dorothy Broderick, an editor and educator, wants comments on the attractiveness of the cover illustration: "While we might feel that no one should judge a book by its cover," she says, "the truth is that everyone does." Author Walter Dean Myers wants every review to "contain a clear-cut commitment as to recommendation or nonrecommendation." He doesn't have the time to read every book published, and he is hoping that some literate person will help him decide where he should invest his valuable reading hours.

Patty Campbell, a young adult librarian and review editor, wants to know first "if a book has magic for YA's." She wants "to be alerted to format faults: does the size and shape make it look like a baby book? . . . Is the word 'children' used anywhere on the dust jacket?" And if there is going to be a film or television tie-in, she wants to know who's starring in it and exactly when it's going to be released.

The reviewer must decide what information is most important for the particular book being reviewed and for the particular audience for which the review is being written. Writing reviews is a skill that improves with practice and effort. A good way to begin developing this skill is to study several reviews of the same book as they appear in different publications. Note the essentials that seem to be the same in each review and then compare the information that is different. See if you can explain the differences in light of the source's reading audience.

For the person reading reviews, one of the biggest problems is that they all run together and begin sounding the same. To keep this from happening, reviewers need to approach their task with the same creative spirit with which authors write books. They need to think of new ways of putting across the point that a book is highly recommended or that it has some unique quality that readers should watch for as in these three excerpts of reviews which were written by authors reviewing books of other authors. Granted, authors probably have had more practice in working with words and therefore their skill is greater than that of most reviewers, but they probably also try harder because they know how important it is to do something to make a review stand out, to give the reader something by which to remember the book.

This first excerpt is taken from a review of Alice Childress' *Rainbow Jordan* written by Anne Tyler for the *New York Times Book Review*:

◇ Rainbow is so appealing that she could carry this book on her own, but she doesn't have to. There's Miss Josie, who gives us her clearer view to balance what Rainbow tells us. . . . And there's the mother herself—short-tempered, inconsistent, sometimes physically abusive, not much of a mother at all, really. Seen through Rainbow's adoring eyes, she's at least someone we can understand. ("Life is complicated," Rainbow says, "I love her even now while I'm putting her down.") In fact, Rainbow's story moves us not because of her random beatings or financial hardships, but because Rainbow needs her mother so desperately that she will endlessly rationalize, condone, overlook, forgive. She is a heartbreakingly sturdy character, and *Rainbow Jordan* is a beautiful book.[7]

This excerpt about Judy Blume's *Tiger Eyes* is taken from an article Robert Lipsyte published in *Nation*:

◇ It is her finest book—ambitious, absorbing, smoothly written, emotionally engaging and subtly political. It is also a lesson on how the conventions of the genre can best be put to use. . . . *Tiger Eyes* never falters, never slides into melodrama or preachment. Blume is a crisp and often funny stylist . . . unafraid of emotion. And she offers no final answers. No one in *Tiger Eyes* changes forever, or emerges sadder but wiser, or even learns her lesson well. Rather a girl and her mother weather a crisis.[8]

Katherine Paterson made these comments about Virginia Hamilton's *Sweet Whispers, Brother Rush* as part of an article she wrote for the *New York Times Book Review*:

◇ There are those who say that Virginia Hamilton is a great writer but that her books are hard to get into. This one is not. It fairly reaches out the first page to grab you, and once it's got you, it sets you spinning deeper and deeper into its story. Needless to say, this is not a conventional ghost story. In fact, the function of the ghost in this book is to provide 14-year-old Tree Pratt with a place from which to view her world. . . . In this book everyone we meet, including the ghost, is wonderfully human. . . . The language too is of Miss Hamilton's own special kind, which uses the speech forms of the young to enhance rather than restrict the music of the book.[9]

Scholarly and Pedagogical Articles

A fourth kind of writing about young adult books is made up of articles or papers that go into more depth than is possible in reviews. Since most reviewers of juvenile books have little hope of coming out with a "scoop" or of being the first one to pass judgment on a new book, they focus on deeper treatments or on tying several books together. Dorothy Matthews analyzed the writing about adolescent literature that appeared in professional journals over a five-year period.[10] She categorized the writing into three types. First are those articles that focus on the subjective responses of readers to particular books, such as reader surveys, lists of popular titles, and reviews written from the point of view of how the book is likely to affect young readers. Articles of this kind are primarily descriptive.

The second type is also descriptive and consists of pedagogical articles giving teachers lists of books that fit together for teaching units, ideas for book promotion, and techniques for teaching reading, social studies, or English. They may include brief comments on the literary qualities of the novels, but, again, the writer's primary intention is to be informative.

The third kind of writing is that restricted to the books themselves. It is in this group that Matthews thinks hope lies for the development of a body of lasting scholarly knowledge that will be taken seriously by the academic community. These papers include discussions of adolescent literature as a genre, historical background of the field, relationships between authors and their work, patterns that appear in junior novels, and themes and underlying issues. More of this kind of literary analysis is being done as authors write books serious enough to support it. Examples of some of these articles are included in Appendix C, "Some Outstanding Books and Articles about Young Adult Literature." Also, a look into a recent edition of *Dissertation Abstracts International* will show an increasing number of dissertations being written on young adult literature. However, the majority of topics deal more with social or pedagogical issues than with literary ones, for example, *The Image of the Puerto Rican in Ethnic Literature for Young Adults: A Cross-Cultural Perspective* by Joyce Freundlich at Rutgers University (1980); *Effects of Three Approaches to Teaching Poetry to Sixth Grade Students* by Bernard Paul Folta at Purdue University (1979); and *A Content Analysis of Selected Adolescent Novels Dealing with Divorce, Separation, and Desertion Published Between January 1970 and May 1979,* by Richard Gifford at the University of Colorado at Boulder (1980).

Another indication of a growing body of literary criticism dealing with books for young readers is the recent increase in publishing markets for both pedagogical and literary articles about children's and adolescent literature; for example, *Children's Literature in Education: An International Quarterly, Children's Literature,* the *ALAN Review,* and *VOYA* (*Voice of Youth Advocates*). Within the last decade these journals have joined the other well-established journals listed in Appendix B. Another first is the 1985 publication of a series of books about popular young adult authors including Judy Blume, M. E. Kerr, and Robert Cormier. The biographies are a new addition to the Twayne series of literary criticism published by the G. K. Hall company.

In summary, writing about young adult books falls into four categories: notecards for personal use, annotations, reviews, and scholarly or pedagogical writing. Most of you will be involved in the first kind, that is, making notecards for your own use. But some of you will also be making annotations, writing reviews, and doing scholarly or pedagogical analyses. This latter kind of writing and critiquing can be especially intriguing because significant changes have occurred within recent years and relatively few scholars have worked with young adult literature. This means there is ample opporunity for original research and observation. The field as a whole will grow strong as a result of serious and competent criticism and analysis.

◈ ETHNIC BOOKS: QUESTIONS ON CENSORSHIP, OVERGENERALIZATION, AUTHENTICITY, AND PROMOTION

A few years ago a student in a suburban Arizona high school borrowed from her school library the book, *The Me Nobody Knows* which is a collection of poems written by inner-city kids. The girl left it on the coffee table. Her parents picked it up and were shocked at some of the words in the book and at the sexual implications of one of the poems. They happened to live next door to a state legislator, and so they took the book over to their neighbor with the plea that he do something about it. He took it to the state capital and proposed a bill to ban the book from the shelves of any public school library.

While the legislators debated the merits of the book, the eighteen-year-old female pages were dismissed from the legislative chamber so they wouldn't be embarrassed (or have their morals contaminated) when the poem was read aloud. Of course there was considerable publicity about the matter which embarrassed the principal of the school. Resolving not to let himself or his school in for this kind of humiliation a second time, he instructed the librarian to take from the shelves all the books that contained swear words or other "suggestive" language. She spent the better part of two weeks "weeding" her collection and stacking books on the floor. By the time she had finished, the legislators had also finished. The proposed bill was defeated, and the publicity had died down. The principal came to the library to see how the librarian was doing, and he was appalled to see how many books were stacked on the floor. Both he and the librarian were even more appalled to realize that if they discarded the books, they would virtually destroy any semblance of ethnic representation in what had been a well-balanced collection. The librarian spent the next week putting the books back on the shelves.

Similar incidents have happened all over the country, only most of them didn't have this moderately happy ending. As Spencer G. Shaw said in a speech at the 1983 American Library Association meeting:

> ◇ Once again, a threatening wind is sweeping across the land, causing the pendulum of ethnic and cultural progress to swing back as the forces of conservatism and bigotry seek to corrode the democratic ideal. For the past several years there has been a noticeable decrease in books that portray ethnic and cultural minority groups as other subjects are becoming the concern of publishers. In addition, the wave of "social consciousness" has been supplanted by a more dangerous, negative phenomenon—*censorship*.[11]

Chapter 12 looks at the whole issue of censorship, so here we will just point out how differences in life-styles and language use may cause white, middle-class readers to look more critically at books with ethnic group settings, or it may be that simple prejudice is at work. Assigning definite cause-and-effect relationships is not possible, but one clear fact is that on any list of censored books a disproportionate number treat the experiences of minority group members, for example, Sharon Bell Mathis' *Teacup Full of Roses*, Claude Brown's *Manchild in the Promised Land*, Alice Childress' A

Hero Ain't Nothin' But a Sandwich, William Armstrong's *Sounder*, Gordon Parks' *The Learning Tree*, Eldridge Cleaver's *Soul on Ice*, Richard Wright's *Native Son*, Oliver LaFarge's *Laughing Boy*, and Piri Thomas' *Down These Mean Streets*.

A related problem, which in fact may contribute to censorship, is that of stereotyping. Al Muller has made the point that black novels today are stereotyped negatively to the same degree that young adult novels in general used to be stereotyped positively:

> ◇ The majority of black Americans are not pushers, pimps, or prostitutes. Not all black Americans live in ghettos. But, to a large extent, a composite of the above statements is the new "black image" presented (constructed?) by the popular media and, to an extent, adopted by the YA novel.[12]

Walter Dean Myers, who writes about "good, lovable kids" in such books as *Fast Sam, Cool Clyde, & Stuff, It Ain't All for Nothing*, and *The Young Landlords* has said that "Editors are often hampered by preconceived attitudes arising from their (typically) white, middle-class backgrounds." These editors tend to view books by black authors in terms of "the ghetto child." Myers grew up in Harlem four blocks from where Claude Brown grew up, but obviously the two men came from different families and had different experiences and as a result have different outlooks on life. People are individuals, first, and then only secondarily members of a group.

It is the grossest kind of overgeneralizing for teachers, librarians, and reviewers to present books to kids and to discuss them as if any single book represents THE black point of view or THE Asian-American point of view, etc. Instead we need to be constantly looking for ways to help young readers go beyond the stereotypes. In John Patrick's play *The Teahouse of the August Moon*, one of the lines that gets a big laugh from the white middle-class American audience is about all Americans looking alike. The audience laughs because the tables are turned on an old joke, and they get a glimpse of how ridiculous it is to think of any group of individuals being carbon copies of one another.

Helping students to realize this and to apply it in their thoughts and their dealings with other people is not quite so simple. People may be grouped together on such bases as their sex, their age, their color, the origin of their last names, the neighborhood they live in, the language or dialect they speak, or the religion to which they subscribe, but there is constant shifting among people and the groups to which they belong. Naturally there are some similarities among group members, but the correlation is far from perfect. For example, Native Americans are often treated as one group, but when Europeans first landed on the American continent there were more than thirty distinct nations whose members spoke perhaps a thousand different languages. During the past 400 years these peoples have had certain common experiences—losing their lands, being forced to move to reservations, having to adapt their beliefs and life styles to a technological society. These experiences may have affected their attitudes in similar ways, but still it is a gross overgeneralization to write about American Indians as though they were one people holding the same religious and cultural values.

Perhaps for the sake of efficiency, history and social studies textbooks have to lump people together and talk about them according to the characteristics of the majority in the group, but good literature can counterbalance these generalizations and show the individual perspective. When students have read enough to go beyond the stereotypes with at least one group, then they will be more aware that the study of people as groups needs to be filled in with individual portrayals.

Other areas of disagreement about ethnically related books include questions of authenticity, idealism versus realism, and the degree to which differences should be stressed or minimized. Jamake Highwater, author of *Anpao, an American Indian Odyssey, The Sun He Dies,* and *Many Smokes, Many Moons: A Chronology of American Indian History through Indian Art* plants himself in the camp of those who favor stressing the differences:

> ◇ In the process of trying to unify the world we must be exceedingly careful not to destroy the diversity of the many cultures of man that give human life meaning, focus, and vitality. . . .
>
> Today we are beginning to look into the ideas of groups outside the dominant culture, and we are finding different kinds of "truth" that make the world we live in far bigger than we ever dreamed it could be—for the greatest distance between people is not geographical space but culture.[13]

In contrast, Lorenz Graham, author of *North Town; South Town, John Brown: A Cry for Freedom,* and *Son of the Boat* wants to build on similarities. He is quoted in Anne Commire's *Something About the Author* saying, "My personal problem with publishers has been the difference between my images and theirs. Publishers have told me that my characters, African and Negro, are 'too much like white people.' And I say, 'If you look closely you will see that people are people.' "[14]

As shown by Janet Lunn's review of Kevin Major's *Far from Shore,* the issue of "differentness" is not restricted to discussions of particular races. Major's book is set in Newfoundland and Lunn wrote:

> ◇ His picture of life in Newfoundland is bright and sharp, not, thank God, that salty picaresque pastiche we mainlanders so often get to chuckle indulgently over.[15]

As a reaction against misinformation and writers who hurriedly seized on whatever ethnic interest seemed to be selling at the moment, many ethnic group members began asking that only people in their group write about them. Although there are understandable reasons for this feeling, such a restriction would be one way of saying that it is impossible for us to understand one another. Also, much of the drama lies in the developing relationships between and among groups, and if authors were restricted to writing only about their own groups, we couldn't have any cross-cultural stories.

Besides, if we analyze our reactions to what we read, we will see that there are many things that transcend ethnic or group identification. For example, Scott O'Dell's *Sing Down the Moon* is the story of the Navajos' forced march from Canyon de Chelly to Fort Sumner, New Mexico, in 1864. If sex or race is the most important thing in group identification, then

Anglo readers should identify with Kit Carson and his "Long Knives," who are the soldiers driving the group on the tragic long walk. Students with Spanish surnames should identify with the Spanish slavers who steal Bright Morning and sell her as a slave. Male readers should identify with Bright Morning's young husband who gives up after the group arrives at its destination. But none of these things happen. Nearly everyone who reads the book identifies with Bright Morning, the young Navajo girl whose story is being told.

The negative light in which O'Dell places all the groups except the Navajos brings up another problem in ethnic literature. If each book is written strictly from the viewpoint of one group, then the tendency might be to build up that group at the expense of others. It is part of our literary heritage for there to be a "good guy" and a "bad guy." The result of being overly conscious of races or of other groups is that readers tend to classify the bad guys and the good guys according to their group rather than by their individual characteristics. To a large extent, this is what brings about stereotyping.

In the 1960s when the civil rights movement caused people to look seriously at books for young readers, what they found was very disturbing. Rather than enriching and extending young readers' views of the world and the people around them, many of the books reinforced prejudices and relied heavily on negative stereotypes. This was more apparent in juvenile than in adult books for several reasons. First, books for young people are often illustrated with either drawings or photographs, and, when nearly all of the people in the illustrations are white, it makes it more difficult for nonwhite readers to identify with the characters and to imagine that the books are about them and their friends. Second, juvenile books tend to be condensed. With less space in which to develop characters, authors are forced to develop background characters as efficiently as possible. One way to be efficient is to use stereotypes that people already recognize, for example, the stoic Indian, the happy black, the dumb blonde, the insensitive jock, and so forth, down the line through many other demeaning and offensive overgeneralizations. When positive portrayals were made of blacks, Indians, Asians, and other minority group members, the stories were most often historical or in some faraway place. The characters were written about as "foreigners," not as Americans. A third contributing factor is that much of what young people read is from the popular culture which is even less likely than school materials to have been created with care and thought being given to the presentation of minority members. As Australian writer Ivan Southall said in the 1974 May Hill Arbuthnot Honor Lecture at the University of Washington:

> ◇ From our English comics we learned the fundamental truths of life: for instance, people with yellow skins were inscrutable and cunning, people with brown skins were childlike and apt to run amok, people with black skins were savages but, if tamed, made useful carriers of heavy loads on great expeditions of discovery by Englishmen. It was in order for black people to be pictured without clothes; after all, they didn't know what clothes were and didn't count, somehow. [16]

THE PEOPLE BEHIND THE BOOKS

LAWRENCE YEP, Author

Dragon Wings
Liar, Liar
Sea Glass
The Mark Twain Murders

Probably the reason that much of my writing has found its way to a teenage audience is that I'm always pursuing the theme of being an outsider—an alien—and many teenagers feel they're aliens. As a Chinese child growing up in a black neighborhood, I served as the all-purpose Asian. When we played war, I was the Japanese who got killed; then when the Korean war came along, I was a North Korean communist. This sense of being the odd-one-out, is probably what made me relate to the Narnia and the Oz books. They were about loneliness and kids in alien societies learning to adjust to foreign cultures. I could understand these a lot better than the stories in our readers where every house had a front lawn and no one's front door was ever locked. When I went to high school, I really began to feel like an outsider. I lost my grammar school

Part of the solution to this problem was simply to pay more attention to members of minority groups. An illustration is the fact that in all the years between 1922 and 1969 only three winners of the Newbery Award—Elizabeth Yates' *Amos Fortune, Free Man* (1951), Joseph Krumgold's *. . . and Now Miguel* (1954), and Scott O'Dell's *Island of the Blue Dolphins* (1961)—featured nonwhite American protagonists. But during the 1970s, five out of the ten winners featured members of nonwhite minority groups—William Armstrong's *Sounder* (1970), Jean Craighead George's *Julie of the Wolves* (1973), Paula Fox's *The Slave Dancer* (1974), Virginia Hamilton's *M. C. Higgins the Great* (1975), and Mildred Taylor's *Roll of Thunder, Hear My Cry* (1977). Honor books included two Jewish stories, *Our Eddie* by Sulamith Ish-Kishor (1970) and *The Upstairs Room* by Johanna Reiss (1973); three Indian books, *Sing Down the Moon* by Scott O'Dell (1971), *Annie and the Old One* by Miska Miles (1972), and *Anpao, An American Indian Odyssey* by Jamake Highwater (1978); a Chinese story, *Dragon Wings* by Laurence Yep (1976); and two more books about blacks, *The Planet of Junior Brown* by Virginia Hamilton (1972) and *The Hundred Penny Box* by Sharon Bell Mathis (1976).

The trends reflected here can be seen as well on various other book lists from the 1970s. Besides the obvious increase in numbers of minority related books, it is important to notice the variety and also how as the decade went by the percentage of books written by authors who were themselves members of the groups steadily increased. But by the end of the decade and now into the mid-1980s there has been a slowing down. Part of the reason is financial. Because of the recession, publishers took fewer risks and went more into mass marketing, as discussed in the following section. Also, once schools and libraries had purchased a few of the new prize-winners, many of friends because they all went into basketball while I went into science fiction. Then every morning I would get on a bus and ride into Chinatown where I attended Catholic school. My family didn't speak Chinese so I was put in the dumbbell Chinese class. I resented that, but what I resented more was that all the dirty jokes and the snide remarks were told in Chinese so the Sisters wouldn't understand them. I couldn't understand them either.

At first it was only through science fiction that I could treat the theme of the outsider, but then I began to do historical fiction and finally contemporary fiction. *Sea Glass* is my most autobiographical novel, but I can't always write that close to home because it requires me to take a razor blade and cut through my defenses. I'm bleeding when I finish, and I have to take time off by writing fantasy or something only marginally related to my Chinese heritage such as *The Mark Twain Murders.* ◆

Dragon Wings. Harper & Row, 1975.
Liar, Liar. Morrow, 1983.
Sea Glass. Harper & Row, 1979.
The Mark Twain Murders. Four Winds, 1982.

them settled back into a kind of color-coded selection policy purchasing books about blacks, for example, only if their clientele included many blacks. Arguments run hot and heavy on this issue. Walter Dean Myers has compared it "to not purchasing Dickens' novels because there are no nineteenth-century English children in the schools."

Related to this is the tendency on the part of professional adults to recommend books to young readers based on some physical attribute such as physical disability, place of residence, etc. This is inappropriate because the ties that develop between characters, authors, and readers are most often based on internal things. Students are easily offended. Someone from a minority family that has struggled to rise may be either crushed or resentful if given a book about a ghetto family with the implication that "It's about people just like you and your family." Adults have no right to make such decisions for young readers. Instead they have an obligation to offer opportunities for readers to discover for themselves the similarities and differences between their lives and the lives they are reading about.

This means that a wide range of books about all ethnic groups needs to be available to all students. As writers dig deeper into cultural and ethnic backgrounds, they are producing some very good historical fiction exploring previously forgotten backgrounds, for example, Rose Sobel's *Woman Chief*, Fred Uhlman's *Reunion*, Jeanne Wakatsuki Houston and James D. Houston's *Farewell to Manzanar*, Dorothy M. Johnson's *Buffalo Woman*, Toni Morrison's *Sula*, and Brenda Wilkinson's *Ludell*.

In books like these, the difference in life-style between the characters and modern teenage readers is likely to be extreme, but while reading the books, students may find that deep down there is a great deal they have in common. On the other hand, they may share very little with other characters even though they belong to the same cultural background. Either way, though, readers will develop a feeling of respect for the contributions of a particular group and they will have broadened their horizons at least a bit. They will also have come closer to the realization that every person is an individual.

Today, because of the tremendous variety of books available, this is an easier lesson to learn than it used to be. The best new books with ethnic group settings concentrate first on the individuals and then on their backgrounds. The setting is a part of the story, but it is not the whole story. There has been a swing away from the heavy-handed efforts that were made in the beginning years of consciousness-raising about minorities. In the early 1970s a writer could often be guaranteed library sales simply by featuring someone from a group about which there was a shortage of reading material. Today that is not enough. There are so many books about different ethnic groups that readers can pick and choose. The poorly written books are falling by the wayside because readers are demanding more sophistication and a better integration of ethnic stories with literary merit. But just because there are many ethnically related books does not mean that they no longer need to be written. There is always room for good books featuring protagonists from different groups. Good literature is one of the few places left in modern life where the uniqueness of the individual is celebrated, while at the same time the common threads that bind all people together are revealed.

◇ RELIGIOUS THEMES IN YOUNG ADULT BOOKS

Historical books of a religious nature such as Lloyd Douglas' *The Robe*, Scott O'Dell's *The Hawk That Dare Not Hunt by Day*, Elizabeth George Speare's *Bronze Bow*, and Jessamyn West's *Friendly Persuasion* are acceptable in almost any school or public library where it is assumed that the authors' intentions were to recreate a time and place in history that in some way was especially interesting or inspirational. People have a similar attitude toward other books that have acquired the status of almost classics in the popular culture sense, for example Margaret Craven's *I Heard the Owl Call My Name*, Catherine Marshall's *A Man Called Peter*, and William Barrett's *Lilies of the Field*.

But with hundreds of other books being published by Christian presses today, it's not so easy to figure out whether the goal is to raise (or calm) religious doubts, bring about a spiritual experience, encourage young readers to think critically, give guidance in decision making, proselytize for a particular church, or simply earn money for the author and publisher.

Mainstream book publishers along with public schools and libraries have traditionally shied away from children's and young adult books that included an emphasis on religious experience or thought. One reason was the fear of mixing church and state while another was the fact that neither authors nor publishers wanted to run the financial risk of cutting into potential markets by offending readers whose beliefs differed from their own.

But in the late 1970s and early 1980s there was evidence of an increased—or at least more visible—interest in religion, for example, President Jimmy Carter's sister was an evangelical healer and many of his associates were "Born Again" Christians. President Reagan campaigned for prayer in the public schools and for tax breaks for parents who chose to send their children to private schools, most of which were religiously affiliated. In the mass media, newspapers and magazines gave more space to religious matters and network television featured evangelists exhorting audiences to return to old fashioned values. Cable stations provided round-the-clock religious programming, and while the standard publishers were struggling against inflation and a depressed economy, religious publishers flourished. Christian bookstores moved into the big time. Patty Campbell described her visit to the Lighthouse Bookstore in Glendale, California:

> ◇ I was unprepared for the big, modern store and the bright, attractive displays of new books, all shelved face out to show handsome covers. Somehow I had expected something a bit more—well, amateurish. Bookselling has come a long way since my days as a church librarian.[17]

The sales figures on some of the religious best-sellers are truly amazing. For example, Lorraine Peterson's 1980 book for teenagers *If God Loves Me Why Can't I Get My Locker Open?* went into its eighth printing in January of 1983, which means that more than a quarter of a million have been sold.

For people just getting acquainted with the Christian press, the big surprise is the variety. There are Christian adventure and mystery stories (*Gopher Hole Treasure Hunt* by Ralph Bartholomew, *Breaker, Breaker 37: A CB Mystery* by Ron Wilson, and the *Jodi* series by Virginia Work); futuristic works (*Checkpoint* by Roy Huron); Biblical romance (*Two from Galilee* by Marjorie Holmes, *Until the Day Break* by Sallie Bell, and *In Shady Groves* by Yvonne Lehman); western romance and adventure (*Love's Long Journey* series by Janette Oke, *The Giant Trunk Mystery* and *The Mystery Man of Horseshoe Bend* by Linda Boorman, and the *Pioneer Family Adventure* series by Sandy Dengler); guides to mental and physical health (*When Someone Really Loves You* by Carolyn E. Phillips, *Free to Be Thin* by Marie Chapian and Neva Coyle, and *Fun to Be Fit* by Marie Chapian); realistic problem novels (*Lisa* by Betty Shaffer, *Caught in the Middle* by Ann Schraff, and *Blessing Deer* by Lois Henderson); persuasive nonfiction (*Satan's Music Exposed* by Lowell Hart, and *The Legacy of John Lennon: Charming or Harming a Generation?* by David A. Noebel); and inspirational biographies and autobiographies (*Lulu* by Lulu Roman, *Never Quit* by Glenn Cunningham, *Debby Boone So Far* by Debby Boone with Dennis Baker, *Hold Me Tight* by Beth Jameson, and *Joni* by Joni Eareckson).

With all this variety, why don't librarians simply make out a purchase order and go shopping? The first reason is that there's a problem in using public funds to purchase sectarian promotional material. Even though there's a tremendous range in the degree to which a hard sell approach is used, underlying all such books is the authors' desire to increase the faith of readers. And as Kathy Piehl wrote:

> ◇ Publishing houses that specialize in such books often have a "built-in" market. Many are affiliated with a single denomination or a group of churches with similar teachings. Consequently, the books contain assumptions about faith and life that may be unfamiliar to the general public. This emphasis on a particular religious viewpoint is expected by their regular customers, but it may limit the book's sales elsewhere. [18]

A second problem is one of fairness. The discussion here has centered on the Christian press because at the present time it happens to be the most active, but as visible as Christian fundamentalist religions have recently become, they still represent the beliefs of only a percentage of readers. Besides those who are Jewish, Muslim, Buddhist, Hindu, animistic, agnostic, aetheistic, etc., there are millions of people who believe in Christianity but who disagree with the approach, the life-styles, or the doctrines that particular groups promote. In a pluralistic society, public institutions need to be especially sensitive about overgeneralizing on something which is as unique to each individual as are religious beliefs. Also the aggressive kinds of conversion tactics used by some fundamentalist religions include large doses of polemics against those groups who are in competition for the same potential converts. We are not saying that teachers and librarians should avoid purchasing controversial books, but we are saying that they need to be aware of both the explicit and implicit messages in what they offer to young readers and to strive for balance.

A third question relates to the skill of the authors and others concerned with such matters as format, illustration, and book promotion. Many of the books on the shelves of religious bookstores are simply poorly written and poorly packaged. The didactic message is the author's first priority and such things as characterization, dialogue, suspense, and originality take a back seat. There is a striking difference in the literary quality of Phyllis Naylor's *A String of Chances* published by Atheneum and her *Never Born a Hero* published by Augsburg. Perhaps Naylor received more and better editorial guidance from the larger publisher. Or perhaps the difference is caused by the fact that the latter book is made up of very short stories suitable for daily inspirational reading by young teens. Because of the brevity, there simply isn't room for the kind of characterization that makes readers care what happens. And collections of inspirational stories also suffer from the fact that there's very little suspense because readers realize that they all have to end on the side of righteousness. Even as fine a writer as Katherine Paterson is less successful in her *Angels and Other Strangers*, which is a collection of stories about Christmas blessings, than she is in *Jacob Have I Loved* and *The Great Gilly Hopkins*, which both include less predictable religious references.

On the other side of the issue a variety of thoughtful critics have begun to encourage libraries to provide young readers with more books that touch on religious matters, for example, Dean Hughes wrote:

◆ Religious publishing flourished in the 1980s and Christian bookstores moved into the big time. Shown here is the teen section of the Carpenter's Village in Tempe, Arizona.

Courtesy of Carpenter's Village Bookstore, Tempe, Arizona.

◇ Writers need to confront religion directly as an important integral part of maturation. We need to be careful that, in effect, we do not say to young people that they *should* be most concerned about pimples and clothes and dates and football games—or even sex. Part of being human is addressing oneself to questions about justice, creation, morality, and the existence of divinity.[19]

James M. Brewbaker took a second look at the reading list he had prepared for his graduate class in adolescent literature when one of the teachers in the class articulated the group's question about the reading list:

◇ I like these books. I really do. My students read them, and I want my children to read them, too. What bothers me is that all of them I've read, taken together, teach, between the lines, that religion is not very important, that a handicap or divorce or rape or even a parent's death can be dealt with in purely secular terms. That's not the way it is for most people, at least not for me, and I don't think it's that way for high school kids either.[20]

The Reverend Martin E. Marty, who teaches the history of modern Christianity at the University of Chicago, made a similar point in an article for *TV Guide,* "We Need More Religion in Our Sitcoms," which, he says, "center on precisely those aspects of life where Americans engage in and honor faith. These include family and leisure, work and play, home and friendship"—the same topics dealt with in much Young Adult literature. Rev. Marty wrote:

◇ Look at it this way: maybe the absence of believers in sitcoms is what is bizarre. Studies show that nine out of 10 Americans believe in God and almost seven out of 10 belong to a church or synagogue. Three out of 10 attend worship services at least once a week, far more than attend sporting events. It is artificial, almost eerie, to see characters like George and Louise Jefferson of *The Jeffersons*, Arthur (the Fonz) Fonzarelli of *Happy Days* or Klinger's Korean war bride Soon-Lee of *AfterM*A*S*H* cut off from their roots and the religion that would very likely be a large part of their lives in real life.[21]

From another corner the voices of political conservatives were heard, many of whom were associated with religious groups. They complained that while they paid their share of taxes, they were doubly punished by school and public librarians who refused to take "offensive" books off the shelves and at the same time refused to purchase the books the groups liked. At the 1981 Arizona State Library conference, Shirley Whitlock, president of the local Eagle Forum, got sympathy from the audience by telling how she had donated new copies of several books to the Mesa Public library. When she returned a few weeks later to look for the books on the shelves, she was horrified to find that they had been rejected by the acquisitions staff and given to the Friends of the Library who sold them for twenty-five cents each.

It's a challenge for librarians and teachers to please all sides on this issue. Many feel they could do better if they had more to choose from. As one librarian plaintively remarked at the 1983 ALA Young Adult Services pre-conference workshop in Los Angeles, "What we need is a Christian version of *The Chosen*." But at least librarians can be comforted by the fact that there is much available today, for example, literature dealing with issues of good and evil from an ecumenical Christian viewpoint as in Susan Cooper's *The Grey King* series, and Madeleine L'Engle's books about the Murry family and Lloyd Alexander's and J. R. R. Tolkien's fantasies. Katherine Paterson, who has attended theological school and also has served as a Christian missionary, includes both implicit and explicit religious references in her books. Judy Blume's best-selling book is still *Are You There, God? It's Me, Margaret*. In spite of the attention given to the onset of menstruation as a rite of passage, the major problem in growing up that Margaret faces is religious in nature—should she join a Christian church like her mother's parents or should she go to Jewish temple like her father's parents?

In Fran Arrick's *Tunnel Vision*, religion comes into the picture as Anthony Hamil's friends and family try to console themselves over his suicide. And Arrick's *God's Radar* is about Roxie Cable and her family's adjustments to the religious elements of the small southern town to which they have moved. Gloria D. Miklowitz' *The Love Bombers* and Robin Brancato's *Blinded by the Light* are fictional explorations of cults and what they offer young people. Robert Cormier's *The Chocolate War* (see Chapter 3) is heavily influenced by religion, while Alice Childress' *Rainbow Jordan* has several references to religious people and beliefs.

M. E. Kerr is one of the few popular Young Adult writers who has consistently included elements of religion in her books. For example, *Is That You, Miss Blue?* is the ironic story of a very religious teacher who is asked to resign her job in a church sponsored school because her faith makes the other teachers and some of the students uncomfortable. *Little Little* features a young dwarf who under his slogan of "scheme" has become a successful evangelist preacher. And *What I Really Think of You* is a different sort of love story between the son of a rich evangelist and the daughter of a struggling pentecostal preacher. In her autobiographical *Me, Me, Me, Me, Me*, Kerr wrote:

> ◇ While I came from a religious background (with one aunt who was a Roman Catholic nun) and attended an Episcopal boarding school, I always seemed to have a quarrel with organized religion.
>
> I suppose the reason was simply that I always had a quarrel with authority of any kind.
>
> Religion still fascinates me, whether it's a book by Paul Tillich, a local church service, a seder I'm invited to by Jewish friends, a talk with a Moonie on the street, a Billy Graham appearance, or one of the Sunday-morning TV preachers. I don't yet "believe"—and some of what I see I love or hate, but I'm rarely indifferent, which leaves me more involved than not.[22]

Kerr's ambivalent feelings come out in her writing. For example in *Little Little*, which is narrated by a misshapen dwarf named Sidney Cinnamon, Sidney tells about a time when he and some of the other handicapped kids who lived at Miss Lakes (commonly referred to as *Mistakes*) went to hear a tent preacher:

> ◇ The evangelist was asking people to testify as to what the Lord had done for them. People began getting up and shouting out they'd been changed or transformed overnight. Then there was a lull in the proceedings . . . then Wheels' voice (Wheels has no legs). He raised himself as high as he could on his board, and he yelled, "You was asking what the Lord done for me! So I'll tell you! He just blamed near ruint me!"

Kerr's *What I Really Think of You* was simultaneously criticized for "copping out" with a "spiritual" ending and for "taking cheap shots at religion." What some people interpreted as "cheap shots" were incidents and comments that other readers responded to as "healthy skepticism" about the connections between religion and money. In the spiritual ending, Opal Ringer, the P.K. (preacher's kid), finds herself speaking in tongues and enjoying a celebrity status when television cameras roll into her father's church to film her. Throughout the rest of the book she was terribly embarrassed at the "strangeness" of her family. She hated being a "have-not" living among "haves," and she was humiliated when some of the affluent kids from her high school came to her father's shabby little church acting as if they were on a field trip.

The real power of the book is its portrayal of Opal's ambivalent feelings. One of our graduate students grew up in a family much like Opal's. She has a brother who is now a famous—and as she's quick to add very wealthy—evangelist. She swears by the authenticity of Kerr's presentation of the

◆ M. E. Kerr is one of the few popular young adult writers who has consistently included elements of religion in her books. Shown here is her recent *What I Really Think of You* and her 1975 book *Is That You, Miss Blue?*
    From WHAT I REALLY THINK OF YOU by M. E. Kerr. Copyright © 1982 by M. E. Kerr. Jacket by Robert Blake.   From IS THAT YOU, MISS BLUE? by M. E. Kerr. Copyright © 1975 by M. E. Kerr. Jacket by Leslie Bauman. Reprinted by permission of Harper & Row, Publishers.

preacher's family and the girl's feelings, at least in the first nine-tenths of the book. She was less pleased with the ending, but she couldn't honestly tell whether her reaction was due to a literary disappointment in that Kerr failed to make the conclusion ring true or whether she felt uncomfortable simply because Opal's early life closely resembled her own and reading the book gave her such a strong feeling of "What if?" that she couldn't be objective about it. She wanted Opal's choice to be the same as her own.

The kind of confusion experienced by a well-read, sophisticated adult must be all the stronger for young people when they come across books that touch their deepest religious feelings. Adults working with young readers need to be extra sensitive to the potential problem because it's easy to blur the line between criticizing the literary skill with which an author presents an experience and criticizing the experience itself. This can be especially troublesome when discussing the many books in which a misguided life is set right by an end-of-the-book conversion. An extreme example of such books are those written by John Benton and sold in Christian bookstores. They have girl's names (*Debbie, Patti, Sheila, Carmen*, etc.) and are sold to give financial support to the Walter Hoving Home for delinquent girls. Patty Campbell described her reaction to *Carmen* as one of astonishment:

◇ Here from the people who gave us such shocked opposition to *Steffie Can't Come Out to Play*, was a book that surpassed in sordid detail any realistic Young Adult novel I had ever read. A young girl runs away from her brutal, alcoholic father to a life as a junkie and prostitute. True, there is no explicit sex, only hints and suggestions for the imagination to fill in. Also, there are no four-letter words. But there *are* lingering, loving descriptions of the joys of shooting up with heroin; there are enthusiastic scenes of beatings, muggings, knife fights, razor slashings. . . . The life of the hooker is made to seem attractive and exciting, with hard drugs the ecstatic reward for a night's work. In the very last chapter, Carmen gets saved by David Wilkerson's Teen Challenge, but this is tame stuff compared to what went before.[23]

Even though most books of this type are more subtle than the John Benton ones, the sudden "miraculous" change of heart is endemic to the genre, and before we are too harsh with these books, we need to realize that in the process of building up literary sophistication we may be tearing down religious faith.

In summary, here are the challenges facing teachers, librarians, authors, and publishers as they prepare and select books with religious overtones to be offered to young readers:

◇ Recognizing authors' intentions and the underlying assumptions of particular books.

◇ Using the above knowledge to make sound decisions about book purchases so that public funds are not used to promote particular belief systems at the expense of others.

◇ Purchasing enough books with religious references that the total collection offers a representative view of the role that religion fills in society.

◇ Seeking out and supporting those authors and publishers who have treated religious motifs with honesty and respect at the same time that they demanded high literary quality.

◇ Helping parents and other critics understand that a variety of religiously oriented books are needed. Religious doubts are part of the maturation process and reading about the doubts that others have or the imperfections of organized religion will not necessarily destroy one's own faith.

◇ Learning to distinguish in our book discussions between criticizing the subject matter of a book and criticizing the way the author handles that subject matter.

◈ ORIGINAL PAPERBACKS AND OTHER NEW WRINKLES IN THE BOOK BUSINESS

Probably the most significant long-range change that is occurring to books in this decade is the coming of age of the original YA paperback. It's directly responsible for getting big business involved in YA books and it is bringing about a revolution in marketing. As Tom Stanley, Avon's manager of marketing, said in 1982:

◇ Book people are just beginners who need to take lessons from those who sell clothes, movies, and records. We would never expect teenagers to look for their clothes in the children's departments of stores. They go to the youth boutiques, yet we continue to send them to the children's sections for their books. We've got to realize that the teenage market is an offshoot of adult rather than children's books and treat it accordingly.[24]

THE PEOPLE BEHIND THE BOOKS

BARBARA S. BATES, Editor

The Westminster Press

Religious books for young adults proliferate from denominational presses and from general publishers who cater to specific religious audiences, from Jewish to Catholic, from fundamentalist to liberal. Authors of these books are usually preachers or educators first, writers second, and they write with specific purpose. The results are therefore apt to be too didactic for the general teenage reader and not appropriate for school or public libraries.

The only religious titles found in recommended library lists are books on holidays, from Christmas to Yom Kippur, and a few fictionalized Bible stories.

Nondenominational literature for youth from these sources features two types of books, biographies of sports stars or entertainers professing their faith or describing their conversion, and collections of emotional poetry with profuse art or photographs. Since youth is rebellious and resents didacticism, most general publishers find that young adults can be better reached through the vicarious experience of fiction. Moral and ethical truths

Traditionally, books for leisure time reading had been sold to school and public libraries or through school book clubs to teenagers themselves. Either way, there was a professionally trained adult acting as a buffer between publishers and young readers. But now the mass market paperback houses are bypassing these traditional school and library sources of review and evaluation and going directly to teenagers through bookstores located in shopping malls. According to an article in the *Philadelphia Inquirer*, bookstore sales to teenagers tripled between 1980 and 1983.[25]

The change in marketing has similarities to what happened back in the 1950s to books for young children. Parents used to be told not to "interfere" by teaching their children to read. That was the school's business. But then the Russians launched Sputnik which triggered an education explosion in the United States. Rudolf Flesch wrote his best-selling *Why Johnny Can't Read*, Congress passed the National Defense Education Act providing money for libraries to purchase supplemental reading books, and Random House, with the help of Dr. Seuss, launched its series of easy-to-read books written under strict vocabulary control. In general, literary critics were not pleased with the controlled vocabulary books, comparing them, for example, to rice pudding without any raisins. The idea of taking a list of words and then trying to find a story that could be told with these particular words rather than taking a story and then trying to find the best words to tell that story was revolutionary. But just as revolutionary was the way the books were sold. The publishers bypassed schools and libraries and mass marketed the books directly to the parents of the intended readers. The eventual result was good for everyone. More children owned and read books, they went on to read more complex books, and the extra money brought in by and demonstrations of faith and love, come through as implicit values in a book where story and characters come first. Such novels, written with creativity, conviction, and the impact of reality, make their spiritual mark and often win major secular awards. But these are not explicitly "religious books."

After five years of research, we decided to move away from our traditionally secular stance and try to bring to religious books for youth the literary talent, national recognition, and enduring values of the very best in secular writing. We asked outstanding authors, "What would you like to say to young people about faith?" These writers were given free rein as to type of work, style, and expression, so that they could speak from the heart. We invited them to express conflict, search, or conviction, as they pleased. We think creativity and spontaneity will fuse and produce a new level of religious literature that no amount of purposeful assignment or prescription could ever reach.

The receptivity of readers and reviewers in every area shows that the need is there. It is both my hope and my prediction for the future that publishers will be able to bring young people the very best in religious writing. ◆

---

these increased sales attracted better writers to the field resulting in more and better books for both home and school use.

Perhaps the direct marketing of fiction to teenagers will have an equally happy ending, but many people are doubtful. On the negative side, educators feel a bit hurt that in the overall picture their views are going to be less important. For example, at the 1983 workshop put on by the Young Adult Services Division of the American Library Association, George Nicholson, editor of Delacorte and Dell, shocked the audience by saying, "For the first time in my 23 years in the business, we don't need librarians to review and buy our books." He went on to explain that B. Dalton has 1,000 stores throughout the country supplied by a central office. In a single visit to the buyer, his company sold 7,500 copies of Stephen Tchudi's *The Burg-O-Rama Man*.

Once Nicholson had the audience's attention, he went on to make amends by pointing out some of the benefits that will accrue to all of us through the increased interest of the bookstores in the teenage market. For example, he explained that what first got the bookstores' attention was the success of the teen romances. However, Dell did not start a romance line. Instead they went through their catalogues and selected particular books to identify with a golden locket and the imprint "Laurel Leaf Young Love." Although the books were "serious works of fiction" rather than the typical romances, their sales nevertheless doubled. Nicholson explained "That golden locket was like the Good Housekeeping seal of approval. Because of it, the books got to the right place in the store, and they stayed alive."

A few months later in an interview, Nicholson expressed optimism that we will "inch forward" even with frivolous books. "Tonally today's romances

THE PEOPLE BEHIND THE BOOKS

GEORGE NICHOLSON, Editor

Delacorte and Dell Publishing Company

One of the big changes I see in our future is a different way of writing author's contracts. A different kind of pay structure will be needed as we cross over between hardback and paperback and the reissuing of books every five or six years. Hardbacks won't be so important to the next generation of authors because they grew up with positive feelings toward paperbacks.

Another change is that today we're treating writers as professionals who have careers and are interested in making money. Ten years ago nearly everyone I worked with had to have a supplemental means of support. Now I work with people who make $100,000 a year on their writing. I would estimate between 25 and 30 YA writers make substantial sums of money.

When writers come to us we don't look on them as one-book authors. I like to pluck out several ideas and give a two- or a four-book contract so as to take advantage of the investment we make in an author—both editorially and with publicity. There's never enough money to fully promote single books. This is why we are less interested in obtaining books

are very different from those of the 1940s." Another positive note from him was that although publishers who never gave the young adult market a thought until this decade are now doing books for teens, those who survive will have to be the ones with the background experience, the ones who are knowledgeable enough to come to teachers and librarians and use what they know about kids and books. And of course library and school sales will remain the foundation of the industry.[26]

Few people would argue with the statement that money is power or that the field of young adult literature could use some powerful friends when it comes to such issues as censorship, allocations of school and library funds, and promotion of reading as a worthwhile activity. More money in the business will undoubtedly attract better talent. Increased sales will mean more and perhaps better independent reading (because it will be self-chosen), and when the general public recognizes young adult literature as a field of its own perhaps we won't have so much trouble getting library positions reserved for YA specialists.

On the negative side, critics fear that minorities will be ignored because they aren't the big spenders in shopping mall bookstores. Another fear is that everything will be watered down to suit mass tastes, comparable to most television programming. But there are some crucial differences which are that one person at a time reads a book while television is usually viewed by a group. And even with cable television, the number of channels from which a viewer can choose is limited, while with books there can be thousands of choices. Also television is paid for by advertisers while readers pay the production costs of books.

from the outside. We've developed our own writers who aren't ashamed to talk to us about writing something "to order." For example, we saw the television pilot "Square Pegs," and we talked with Marjorie Sharmat about writing a companion set for the TV series. The television show was cancelled, but the books are going strong, 250,000 copies have been sold. Ten years ago we were feisty and literary in a way that was false. Today we aren't so self-conscious. We realize that an author's inspiration can come from lots of different places. After all, Sinclair Lewis wrote plots for Jack London and Theodore Dreiser is known to have bought some of his plots. I would be uncomfortable with a writer who lived only on other people's ideas—that's a hack vs. an author, but I'm glad our people aren't ashamed to talk about the business end of publishing, because even frivolous books need not be badly written.

Our traditional approach to young adult literature has been to think of one particular audience. This is a mistake. There are dozens of audiences. We estimate 125,000 hardcore readers of occult books. Five thousand of these belong to our fan club, a third of them boys, while the traditional YA audience is virtually all girls. ◆

In spite of these differences, it will probably be well for those of us who specialize in young adults and their reading to think of ourselves as an advocacy group for teenagers who will keep reminding publishers that there is no such thing as *one* young adult audience. There are dozens of such audiences all needing their own kinds of books. An illustration of the influence that publishers can have on a book is what happened with Lloyd Alexander's *Prydain* series. When Dell first published it in paperback, they commissioned Evaline Ness to do the drawings and they promoted the books as children's literature by using large type and lots of space and by advertising the fact that *The High King* had won the Newbery Award. A few years later, they reissued the books packaged as mythical, hero tales for older readers, and then in a later edition they packaged them as fantasy. Each edition was successful, but with an entirely different group of readers.

A special challenge for people in our business is to make sure that each generation of teenagers is offered a balanced array of reading materials. The nature of big business is to follow trends. What starts out as a good idea by one company is soon followed by all the companies so that what ends up at the corner drugstore or the shopping mall bookstore is most likely a lopsided collection. In the '70s it was mostly grim, problem novels, in the early '80s it was the romances followed by occult books. By now there is probably some other fad. What this means is that librarians and teachers need to work extra hard at providing the kinds of books that aren't the current trend setters. It would be unfortunate if young people missed out on developing the reading habit simply because the books that happened to be handy during three or four key years weren't a kind that appealed to them.

Another business related issue is that of support for conference speakers. Major publishers receive hundreds of requests for lending financial support to organizations by paying some or all of the expenses of authors who are invited as guest speakers. This makes for the most popular sessions at many conferences, but it is nevertheless a custom that is fraught with problems. The convention planners, the publishers, and the author probably feel equally awkward as they dicker about who will pay for what and how much the honorarium should be. If the publishers foot the bill, they quite understandably feel that this is a promotional tour and that they should have some say as to who they will send. A prerequisite is usually that a new book is being launched. Lillian N. Gerhardt criticized the practice as creating a "fan-club mentality" among teachers and librarians:

> ◇ [which] is nurtured by their professional associations, whose leaders continue to choose programs for conferences larded with popular authors present at their publishers' expense. This does not constitute continuing education for librarianship; it's too seldom more than just pleasant, ladies' club fare. It produces claques, not critics, sales, not selectivity. That's why the publishers pick up the tab.[27]

To a lesser extent similar questions arise about free copies of books that are sent to potential reviewers, invitations to convention dinners, and the whole business of courting judges for prizes and awards. Are such honors earned or purchased through clever public relations?

Before we get too critical, we need to remind ourselves that publishers are trying to accomplish the same thing we are, which is to have kids read. We should be grateful for an ally who will help kids connect their school world with the "real" world. Their approaches range from the paperback romances written about in Chapter 4 to Dell's occult series called "Twilight" and Bantam's "Dark Forces," which is advertised as its own "Demonically Good Occult Series." Avon took a broader approach with its "Flare" imprint and the slogan, "Avon's doing it *all* with FLARE!" The word and a picture of a small flame is used on its entire teen line regardless of genre, but at the top of the covers such identifiers are printed as "Flare Novel," "Flare Biography," "Flare Science Fiction," "Flare Nonfiction," "Flare Fantasy," and "Flare Mystery." Included in the Flare line are paperback editions of such well known and respected books as Katherine Paterson's *Jacob Have I Loved*, Virginia Hamilton's *Justice and Her Brothers*, Alice Childress' *Rainbow Jordan*, and Jill Paton Walsh's *Unleaving*. But also included are original books commissioned for the Flare series. On a 1983 promotional poster, 21 out of 68 featured books were identified as "Original." This is a significant change from only five or six years ago when most of the paperback houses limited themselves to doing reprints.

Among the 21 "original" books featured on the Avon poster was Norma Fox Mazer's *Taking Terri Mueller*, a well-written story of a young teen who, in a custody battle, had been kidnapped at age five and raised by her father. She was told that her mother had died, but gradually Terri begins to discover that something is amiss in the way her father manages their lives, and she eventually seeks for and finds her mother.

We asked Norma Mazer to compare writing an original paperback with the more traditional process:

◇ Production time was faster than with a hardcover, which I found exciting. Of course, a paperback doesn't have the solidity of a hardcover and for someone brought up on hardcovers that is a minus. But that goes with the terrain, obviously. I would say that my only substantive complaint is that reviewers apparently are still not taking paperback originals as seriously as hardcover books. *Taking Terri Mueller* did not get reviewed as extensively as my other books have been. *School Library Journal* and *Booklist* took note, took it seriously, but that's about it as far as the usual YA reviewing media. I look on this as snobbish and elitist; however, I think that, inevitably, reviewers will have to consider paperback originals exactly like other books. Why not? It's not the paper and print that's at issue, but the contents. Avon, of course, is a mass market house, but I was not pressured in any way to write a genre book. [Mazer probably used the term *genre book* as a euphemism for *formula fiction* lest she insult the rest of her editor's line.], a market book, or to tone down how and what I wanted to write . . . I wrote the book I wanted to write, exactly the way I would have written it if it were going to be published in hard cover.[28]

Even without the reviews, Mazer's book sold more copies faster than any of her previous books. And in a reversal of the usual pattern, William Morrow published *Taking Terri Mueller* as a hardback in the spring of 1983. Nevertheless, the frustration that she expressed about the lack of critical attention it received when first published is understandable. Arguing with her point that "It's not the paper and print that's at issue, but the contents," would be like arguing against apple pie and motherhood. But the problem is not so easy to solve. Granted, snobbishness and elitism—which might alternately be described as "tradition"—are involved, but so are other more practical matters, one of which is the previously discussed lack of review space for young adult books. A reviewer who is faced with a stack of twenty books, time to read only ten books, and space to print only five reviews, obviously has to make some choices.

Reviewers facing piles of books act much like people do when they are holding the daily mail and trying to decide which letters to open first. Initially, they look for names of loved ones or friends. Failing to find either and not knowing what's inside any of the letters, they make judgments, almost subconsciously, based on outside appearances and how much money the sender has invested. Telegrams and special delivery letters probably get opened before first class mail, which in turn gets opened before third class mail. Letters written on elegant, creamy stationery are likely to be opened before those on plain, white paper. And if the mail that is opened first proves interesting enough, the receiver may not bother to open the junk mail.

Reviewers treat paperbacks like third class mail, not only because it's obvious that less money has been invested, but also because reviewers have learned from experience that statistically their chances of finding gold are higher in the hardbacks than in the original paperbacks. Many of the original paperbacks are formula fiction, written to be sold to kids who want another book exactly like the one they just finished. For adult reviewers, reading and writing about such books is not very challenging. Since formula books run together in readers' minds (and why shouldn't they since they're written according to company laid out guidelines?), then it would be futile to take one of these books and try to write the kind of critical review that could be written about such unique and complex books as Sue Ellen Bridgers' *Notes for Another Life*, Mildred Lee's *The People Therein*, and Terry Davis' *Vision Quest*.

As Norma Mazer pointed out, not all original paperbacks are formula fiction, but the reviewer faced with a pile of books doesn't know which ones are and which ones aren't. Nor does the reviewer know which ones are going to be published on a long-term basis and which ones will be released for only a few months and then withdrawn to make room for other titles. As far as school and library personnel are concerned—and these are the people who do most of the evaluation of YA literature—it's inefficient to waste time reading, much less writing reviews of, books that may be unavailable within six months or a year. A reasonable expectation would be for reviewers to know the different lines and the policies of the different companies and therefore be able to predict which books are going to be sponsored as "educational" and therefore published over a long term basis rather than mass marketed through magazine distributors and therefore available only briefly. But going back to the analogy of paperbacks being treated as third class mail, reviewers have established many priorities before that of learning the intricacies of marketing by the different companies each with its own practices and policies. A further complication is that within each company there are different lines—again with different policies. For example, on the front of the Fawcett junior/senior high school catalogue, the *Juniper, Crest, Premier, Gold Medal*, and *Columbine* lines are all listed. The Pocket Books high school catalogue lists *Archway, Timescape, Washington Square Press, Pocket Books*, and *First Love from Silhouette*.

These factors conspire to discourage the established reviewing sources from paying serious attention to paperbacks. It doesn't matter so much with those that are reprints because they have already been reviewed in their hardback editions, but for the quality books that are now coming out as original paperbacks, it indeed matters. Finding ways to evaluate and promote such books is one of the challenges that needs to be met in this decade in which the relationship between hard and soft cover books is undoubtedly going to grow closer.

◆ ACTIVITIES ◆

1. Read one of the books in the Honor Sampling and write a review of it. *After* you finish writing your review, find two published reviews of the same book. Photocopy them and then make a comparison of what you wrote and what is in the published reviews. You might color-code the three, for example, marking in red all evaluation comments, high-lighting in yellow the summaries of plot, underlining pedagogical suggestions, marking in green the reviewer's interpretive statements, etc. Comparing your review to a professionally written one should help you become a better reviewer.

2. If you belong to a particular ethnic group or live in an out-of-the-way place that has been

featured in a book, then read the book and criticize it from an insider's viewpoint. Look carefully at the accuracy of the details that make the book specific to one group or locale. Do you feel differently about a book when it features your group than when it features some other group? If so, in what ways?

3. Read two of the books mentioned in the section about religion. Compare the treatment that the authors give to the religious aspects of the stories. Can you tell what purposes the authors had when they included the religious aspects in their stories? If so, compare their approaches. Which was the more successful of the two books from a literary standpoint? From a promotion of faith standpoint? From an appeal-to-the-reader standpoint?

4. Visit three places in your town or neighborhood where books are for sale. Check out how books are marketed to young adults. Is there a special section, shelf, or display for teenagers? If so, in what kind of an establishment was it? Report on the differences and see if you can explain them. How are paperbacks marketed? Are hardbacks marketed the same?

◆ NOTES ◆

[1]Patty Campbell, "Only Puddings Like the Kiss of Death: Reviewing the YA Book," *Top of the News* 35 (Winter 1979): 161–62.

[2]Lillian L. Shapiro, "Quality or Popularity? Selection Criteria for YAs," *School Library Journal* 24 (May 1978): 23–27.

[3]Shapiro, 23–27.

[4]Campbell, 161–62.

[5]*Human and Anti-Human Values* (New York: Council on Interracial Books for Children, 1976), p. 4.

[6]Janet French, *School Library Journal* 28 (September 1981): 133.

[7]Anne Tyler, "Looking for Mom," *New York Times Book Review*, April 26, 1981, p. 52.

[8]Robert Lipsyte, "A Bridge of Words," *Nation* 233 (November 21, 1981): 551.

[9]Katherine Paterson, "Family Visions," *New York Times Book Review*, November 14, 1982, p. 41.

[10]Dorothy Matthews, "Writing About Adolescent Literature: Current Approaches and Future Directions," *Arizona English Bulletin* 18 (April 1976): 216–19.

[11]Spencer G. Shaw, "Legacies for Youth: Ethnic and Cultural Diversity in Books," *School Library Journal* 39 (December 1983): 17–21.

[12]Al Muller, "Some Thoughts on the Black Y.A. Novel," *ALAN Newsletter* 5 (Winter 1978): 13.

[13]Jamake Highwater, *Many Smokes, Many Moons* (Philadelphia: Lippincott, 1978), pp. 13–14.

[14]Anne Commire, *Something about the Author* Vol. 2 (Detroit: Gale Research, 1971), pp. 122–23.

[15]Janet Lunn, *Books in Canada* 9 (December 1980): 21.

[16]Ivan Southall "Real Adventure Belongs to Us." in *A Journey of Discovery on Writing for Children* (New York: Macmillan, 1976), p. 69.

[17]Patty Campbell, "The Young Adult Perplex," *Wilson Library Bulletin* 56 (April 1982): 612–13, 638.

[18]Kathy Piehl, "Bait/Rebait: Books with Religious Themes," *English Journal* 70 (December 1981): 14–17.

[19]Dean Hughes, "Bait/Rebait: Books with Religious Themes," *English Journal* 70 (December 1981): 14–17.

[20]James M. Brewbaker, "Are You There, Margaret? It's Me, God—Religious Contexts in Recent Adolescent Fiction," *English Journal* 72 (September 1983): 82–86.

[21]Martin E. Marty, "We Need More Religion in Our Sitcoms," *TV Guide* 31 (December 24–30, 1983): 2–6.

[22]M. E. Kerr, *Me, Me, Me, Me, Me: Not a Novel.* (New York: Harper & Row, 1983), pp. 111–12.

[23]Campbell, 612–13.

[24]Personal Interview with Tom Stanley, November 29, 1982.

[25]Sue Chastain, "Teens Find Love in the Pulp Racks," *Philadelphia Inquirer*, November, 22, 1982, D-1, 4.

[26]Personal Interview with George Nicholson, November 18, 1983.

[27]Lillian N. Gerhardt, "Selectors vs. Cheerleaders," *School Library Journal* 29 (August 1983): 2.

[28]Personal correspondence with Norma Fox Mazer, November 30, 1982.

◆ **TITLES MENTIONED IN CHAPTER 11** ◆

For information on the availability of paperback editions of these titles, please consult the most recent edition of *Paperbound Books in Print*, published annually by R. R. Bowker Company.

Evaluating and Critiquing

Anonymous. *Go Ask Alice*. Prentice-Hall, 1971.

Baldwin, James. *If Beale Street Could Talk*. Doubleday, 1974.

Bales, William Alan. *The Seeker*. McGraw-Hill, 1976.

Blume, Judy. *Tiger Eyes*. Bradbury, 1981.

Bridgers, Sue Ellen. *Notes for Another Life*. Knopf, 1981.

Childress, Alice. *A Hero Ain't Nothin' But a Sandwich*. Coward, McCann & Geoghegan, 1973.

————. *Rainbow Jordan*. Putnam's, 1981.

Fields, Jeff. *A Cry of Angels*. Atheneum, 1974.

Forsyth, Frederick. *The Shepherd*. Atheneum, 1975.

Guest, Judith. *Ordinary People*. Viking, 1976.

Hamilton, Virginia. *Sweet Whispers, Brother Rush*. Putnam's, 1982.

Hinton, S. E. *The Outsiders*. Viking, 1967.

Knowles, John. *A Separate Peace*. Macmillan, 1960.

Salinger, J. D. *The Catcher in the Rye*. Little, Brown, 1951.

Sleator, William. *House of Stairs*. E. P. Dutton, 1974.

Voigt, Cynthia. *Homecoming*. Atheneum, 1981.

Ethnic Settings

Armstrong, William. *Sounder*. Harper & Row, 1969.

Brown, Claude. *Manchild in the Promised Land*. Macmillan, 1965.

Childress, Alice. *A Hero Ain't Nothin' But a Sandwich*. Coward, McCann & Geoghegan, 1973.

————. *Rainbow Jordan*. Putnam's, 1981.

Cleaver, Eldridge. *Soul on Ice*. McGraw-Hill, 1968.

Fox, Paula. *The Slave Dancer*. Bradbury, 1973.

George, Jean Craighead. *Julie of the Wolves*. Harper & Row, 1972.

Graham, Lorenz. *John Brown: A Cry for Freedom*. Harper & Row, 1980.

————. *North Town; South Town*. Crowell, 1965.

————. *Song of the Boat*. Crowell, 1975.

Hamilton, Virginia. *M. C. Higgins the Great*. Macmillan, 1974.

————. *The Planet of Junior Brown*. Macmillan, 1971.

————. *Sweet Whispers, Brother Rush*. Putnam's, 1982.

Highwater, Jamake. *Anpao, an American Indian Odyssey*. Harper & Row, 1977.

————. *Many Smokes, Many Moons, A Chronology of American Indian History through Indian Art*. Lippincott, 1978.

Houston, Jeanne Wakatsuki and James D. Houston. *Farewell to Manzanar*. Houghton Mifflin, 1973.

Ish-Kishor, Sulamith. *Our Eddie*. Pantheon, 1969.

Johnson, Dorothy M. *Buffalo Woman*. Dodd, Mead, 1977.

Joseph, Stephen M., ed. *the me nobody knows*. Avon, 1969.

Krumgold, Joseph. *. . . and Now Miguel*. Harper & Row, 1953.

LaFarge, Oliver. *Laughing Boy*. Houghton Mifflin, 1929.

Major, Kevin. *Far from Shore*. Delacorte, 1981.

Mathis, Sharon Bell. *The Hundred Penny Box*. Viking, 1975.

————. *Teacup Full of Roses*. Viking, 1975.

Miles, Miska. *Annie and the Old One*. Little, Brown, 1971.

Morrison, Toni. *Sula*. Knopf, 1973.

Myers, Walter Dean. *Fast Sam, Cool Clyde, & Stuff*. Viking, 1975,

————. *It Ain't All for Nothing*. Viking, 1978.

————. *The Young Landlords*. Viking, 1979.

O'Dell, Scott. *The Hawk that Dare Not Hunt by Day*. Houghton Mifflin, 1975.

————. *Island of the Blue Dolphins*. Houghton Mifflin, 1960.

————. *Sing Down the Moon*. Houghton Mifflin, 1970.

Parks, Gordon. *The Learning Tree*. Harper & Row, 1963.

Reiss, Johanna. *The Upstairs Room*. Harper & Row, 1972.

Sobel, Rose. *Woman Chief*. Dial, 1976.

Taylor, Mildred. *Roll of Thunder, Hear My Cry*. Dial, 1976.

Thomas, Piri. *Down These Mean Streets*. Knopf, 1967.

Uhlman, Fred. *Reunion*. Farrar, Straus & Giroux, 1977.

Wilkinson, Brenda. *Ludell*. Harper & Row, 1975.

Wright, Richard. *Native Son*. Harper & Row, 1969.

Yates, Elizabeth. *Amos Fortune, Free Man*. E. P. Dutton, 1967.

Yep, Laurence. *Dragon Wings*. Harper & Row, 1977.

Religious Themes

Arrick, Fran. *God's Radar*. Bradbury, 1983.

————. *Steffie Can't Come Out to Play*. Bradbury, 1978.

————. *Tunnel Vision*. Bradbury, 1980.

Barrett, William. *Lilies of the Field*. Popular Library, 1962.

Bartholomew, Ralph. *Gopher Hole Treasure Hunt*. Victor, 1977.

Benton, John. *Carmen*. Revell, 1974.

Blume, Judy. *Are You There, God? It's Me, Margaret*. Bradbury, 1970.

Boone, Debby, with Dennis Baker. *Debby Boone So Far*. Jove, 1982.

Boorman, Linda. *The Giant Trunk Mystery*. Victor, 1981.

————. *The Mystery Man of Horseshoe Bend*. Victor, 1980.

Brancato, Robin. *Blinded by the Light*. Knopf, 1978.

Chapian, Marie. *Fun to Be Fit*. Revell, 1982.

Chapian, Marie and Neva Coyle. *Free to Be Thin*. Bethany House, 1979.

Cooper, Susan. *The Grey King* series. Atheneum, 1973–1977.

Cormier, Robert. *The Chocolate War*. Pantheon, 1974.

Craven, Margaret. *I Heard the Owl Call My Name*. Doubleday, 1973.

Cunningham, Glenn. *Never Quit*. Chosen Books/Zondervan, 1981.

Dengler, Sandy. *Pioneer Family Adventure* series. Moody, 1979–1983.

Douglas, Lloyd. *The Robe*. Houghton Mifflin, 1942.

Eareckson, Joni. *Joni*. World Wide, 1977.

Hart, Lowell. *Satan's Music Exposed*. Kirban, 1980.

Henderson, Lois. *Blessing Deer*. Cook, 1980.

Holmes, Marjorie. *Two from Galilee*. Revell, 1972.

Jameson, Beth. *Hold Me Tight*. Revell, 1980.

Kerr, M. E. *Is That You, Miss Blue?* Harper & Row, 1975.

————. *Little Little*. Harper & Row, 1981.

————. *Me, Me, Me, Me, Me*. Harper & Row, 1983.

————. *What I Really Think of You*. Harper & Row, 1982.

Lehman, Yvonne. *In Shady Groves*. Zondervan, 1983.

Marshall, Catherine. *A Man Called Peter*. McGraw-Hill, 1951.

Miklowitz, Gloria D. *The Love Bombers*. Delacorte, 1980.

Naylor, Phyllis. *Never Born a Hero*. Augsburg, 1982.

————. *A String of Chances*. Atheneum, 1982.

Noebel, David A. *The Legacy of John Lennon: Charming or Harming a Generation?* Nelson, 1982.

O'Dell, Scott. *The Hawk That Dare Not Hunt by Day*. Houghton Mifflin, 1975.

Oke, Janette. *Love's Long Journey*. Bethany House, 1982.

Paterson, Katherine. *Angels and Other Strangers*. Crowell, 1979.

————. *The Great Gilly Hopkins*. Crowell, 1978.

————. *Jacob Have I Loved*. Crowell, 1980.

Peterson, Lorraine. *If God Loves Me Why Can't I Get My Locker Open?* Bethany House, 1980.

Phillips, Carolyn E. *When Someone Really Loves You*. Regal, 1983.

Potok, Chaim. *The Chosen*. Simon and Schuster, 1967.

Roman, Lulu. *Lulu*. Revell, 1978.

Schraff, Anne E. *Caught in the Middle*. Baker, 1981.

Shaffer, Betty. *Lisa*. Bethany House, 1982.

Speare, Elizabeth George. *Bronze Bow*. Houghton Mifflin, 1973.

West, Jessamyn. *Friendly Persuasion*. Harcourt Brace Jovanovich, 1956.

Wilson, Ron. *Breaker, Breaker 37: A CB Mystery.* Cook, 1979.

Work, Virginia. *Jodi* series. Moody, 1980–1983.

Paperbacks and Marketing Practices

Alexander, Lloyd. *The High King.* Holt, Rinehart and Winston, 1968.

Bridgers, Sue Ellen. *Notes for Another Life.* Knopf, 1981.

Childress, Alice. *Rainbow Jordan.* Putnam's, 1981.

Davis, Terry. *Vision Quest.* Viking, 1979.

Hamilton, Virginia. *Justice and Her Brothers.* Greenwillow, 1978.

Lee, Mildred. *The People Therein.* Houghton Mifflin, 1980.

Mazer, Norma Fox. *Taking Terri Mueller.* Avon, 1981; Morrow, 1983.

Paterson, Katherine. *Jacob Have I Loved.* Crowell, 1980.

Tchudi, Stephen. *The Burg-O-Rama Man.* Delacorte, 1983.

Walsh, Jill Paton. *Unleaving.* Avon, 1977.

CENSORSHIP

OF WORRYING AND WONDERING

Whether they like it or not, librarians and English teachers know that censorship is very much a part of their professional lives. Indeed, comments about censorship of all kinds appear with almost nauseating regularity in the daily press. In the first few months of 1984 alone, these stories appeared. On February 6, Jack Anderson devoted his column to an $800,000 U.S. Justice Department proposal, through the Office of Juvenile Justice and Delinquency Prevention, to investigate the biological, hormonal, and neurological responses of young people as they read magazines like *Playboy*, *Penthouse*, and *Hustler* and watch pornographic films. The study presumably aims at determining whether early exposure to pornography will lead the juveniles into criminal activity. The February 21 *Arizona Republic* scathingly attacked that notion in an editorial, "Science or Prurience?" On February 15, *The New York Times* headlined, "Reagan to Relent on Secrecy Pledge," on the President's decision to suspend a national security order that would have imposed lifelong censorship on more than 128,000 government officials. The Cox News Service for February 13 had a long release about cities and groups attempting to ban certain channels on cable TV to eliminate what they considered pornographic. And newspapers carried lengthy stories in mid-March about the list of banned speakers ineligible to represent the United States overseas.

English teachers and librarians are painfully aware that book banning has become extremely serious—some would call it epidemic—in the last ten or so years. As Colin Campbell wrote:

◇ A censorial spirit is at work in the United States, and for the past year or so it has focused more and more on books. Efforts to remove certain titles from school and public libraries, from paperback racks and bookstores, from the eyes of adults as well as children, have increased measurably.[1]

The American Library Association has been on record against censorship since the 1920s, but its strongest statement first appeared in 1939 as the Library Bill of Rights. The document has periodically been tightened and strengthened, and the latest version, that of January 23, 1980, can be found in the *Intellectual Freedom Manual*, 2nd ed. The entire *Intellectual Freedom Manual* is filled with provocative ideas and helpful suggestions and should be required reading for librarians and English teachers alike. The National Council of Teachers of English was a bit later entering the battle, but the first edition in 1962 of *The Students' Right to Read* set forth NCTE's position and contained a widely used form for complaints, "Citizen's Request for Reconsideration of a Book." The 1972 edition expanded and updated the earlier edition. In 1982, the complaint form was amended to read "Citizen's Request for Reconsideration of a Work," and a complementary publication, *The Students' Right to Know* by Lee Burress and Edward B. Jenkinson, elaborated on NCTE's position toward education and censorship.

◈ A BRIEF HISTORY OF CENSORSHIP

Some English teachers and librarians apparently believe the censorship of young adult reading began with the publication of J. D. Salinger's *The Catcher in the Rye*. But censorship goes far back in history. Plato believed in censorship. In *The Republic*, he argued that banishing poets and dramatists from his perfect state was essential for the moral good of the young. Writers often told lies about the gods, he maintained, but even when their stories were true, writers sometimes made the gods appear responsible for the evils and misfortunes of mortals. Plato reasoned that fiction was potentially emotionally disturbing to the young. Plato's call for moral censorship to protect the young is echoed by many censors today.

In *The Leviathan* in 1615, Thomas Hobbes justified the other basic case for censorship. Humanity was, in Hobbes' view, inherently selfish, venal, brutish, and contentious. Strife was inevitably humanity's fate unless the State established and enforced order. Hobbes acknowledged the right of subjects to refuse to obey a ruler's orders if he did not protect his people, but in all cases the sovereign had not merely the right but the duty to censor anything for the good of the State.

Between Plato and Hobbes and thereafter, history offers a multitude of examples of censorship for moral or political good—the Emperor Chi Huang Ti burned Confucius' *Analects* in 211 B.C.; Julius Caesar burned much of the Library of Alexandria in 48–47 B.C.; English officials publicly burned copies of William Tyndale's translation of the Bible in 1525; the Catholic Index of Forbidden Works was published in 1555; Prime Minister

Walpole forced passage of a Licensing Act in 1737 which required that every English play be examined and approved before production, and on and on and on.

America's premier censor, though hardly its last, appeared in the early 1870s. Anthony Comstock came from a religious family, and before he was eighteen, he had raided a saloon to drive out the devil and the drinkers. In June 1871, Comstock was so outraged by repeated violations of Sunday Closing Laws by saloons in his neighborhood that he reported them to the police. They ignored him which taught him a good lesson about the futility of fighting city hall alone. Armed with the Lord's help and his own determination, Comstock secured the help of three prominent men and founded the Society for the Suppression of Vice in New York in 1872, and he was off and running. The following year he went to Washington, D.C., to urge passage of a federal statute against obscenity and abortion and contraceptive devices. That same year, he was commissioned a Special Agent of the Postmaster General, all without salary until 1906.

With the new law and Comstock's zeal and energy, he confiscated and destroyed "bad" literature and imprisoned evil authors and publishers almost beyond belief. By 1914, he had caused the arraignment of 3,697 people with 2,740 convicted or pleading guilty, total fines of $237,134.30, and prison sentences totaling 565 years, 11 months, and 20 days. In his last year of life, 1915, Comstock added another 176 arrests and 140 convictions. He also caused fifteen suicides.[2]

His most famous book was *Traps for the Young* (1883). By traps, Comstock meant the devil's work for young people—light literature, newspaper advertisements, saloons, literature obtained through the mail, quack medicine, contraceptives, gambling, playing pool, free love and anyone who advocated it, and artistic works (fine arts, classics of literature, photographic reproductions of art). Comstock was convinced that any young person who shot pool or smoked or chewed tobacco or drank or read dime novels or did anything else he disapproved of (and that catalogue was long indeed) was doomed to hell and to a life of crime and degradation.

Librarians, as may be seen in "Fiction and Libraries" in Chapter 13 of this book, were more frequently pro-censorship than anti-censorship. As Arthur E. Bostwick wrote in 1910:

> ◇ In the exercise of his duties in book selection it is unavoidable that the librarian should act in some degree as a censor of literature. It has been pointed out that no library can buy every title that is published, and that we should discriminate by picking out what is best instead of by excluding what is bad.[3]

Mark Twain's encounters with late nineteenth-century censors are described in Chapter 13, but he was hardly the only major writer of his time to come under attack. Stephen Crane's *The Red Badge of Courage* was attacked for lacking integrity and being inaccurate. At the sixth session of the American Library Association in 1896, a discussion of *The Red Badge of Courage* and whether it should be included in a list of ALA recommended books brought forth comments that revealed more about the commentors than about the book:

◇ Mr. Larned: "What of Crane's *Red Badge of Courage*?"

A. L. Peck: "It abounds in profanity. I never could see why it should be given into the hands of a boy."

G. M. Jones: "This *Red Badge of Courage* is a very good illustration of the weakness of the criticism of our literary papers. The critics in our literary papers are praising this book as being a true picture of war. The fact is, I imagine, that the criticisms are written by young men who know nothing about war, just as Mr. Crane himself knows nothing about war. Gen. McClurg, of Chicago, and Col. Nourse, of Massachusetts, both say that the story is not true to the life of the soldier. An article in the *Independent*, or perhaps the *Outlook*, says that no such profanity as given in the book was common in the army among the soldiers. Mr. Crane has since published two other books on New York life which are simply vulgar books. I consider the *Red Badge of Courage* a vulgar book, and nothing but vulgar."[4]

It is more difficult to know how much censorship occurred in English classes of the nineteenth century since the major journal for English teachers, the *English Journal*, did not begin until 1912, but a few items may suggest that English teachers endured or perhaps encouraged censorship at the time. Until 1864, Oberlin College would not allow Shakespeare to be studied in mixed classes. That Shakespeare was apparently of questionable value can be seen by an editorial in 1893 lauding students of Oakland High School who objected to using an unexpurgated edition of *Hamlet*:

◇ All honor to the modest and sensible youths and maidens of the Oakland High School who revolted against studying an unexpurgated edition of *Hamlet*! The indecencies of Shakespeare in the complete edition are brutal. They are more than indelicacies, they are indecencies. They are no part of Shakespeare's thought, have no connection with the play, and can be eliminated with as little jar as could the oaths of a modern slugger. Indeed, Shakespeare's vulgarity was, to all intents and purposes, profanity, scattered promiscuously through the lines with no more meaning than so many oaths.[5]

An editorial writer in 1890 quoted from a contemporary account in the *Congregationalist* about books some young people had been reading:

◇ In this series of papers we purposely avoid all mention of some thoroughly bad books chosen by our young friends. We remember hearing the principal of a young ladies' seminary, in trying to express her strong disapproval of a certain book, say impulsively to the pupils, "I think I should expel a girl if I found her reading such a work." Before the week closed no less than three copies were in surreptitious circulation. There is something in human nature which craves that which is prohibited. Just so surely as we gave the titles of books worthy of condemnation, some youth would thirst instantly for a knowledge of their contents.[6]

Would that present-day censors could recognize what this critic obviously recognized, that merely mentioning an objectionable title creates new readers by the hundreds.

And one last incident a few years later: An English teacher reported on her use of *Treasure Island* with a junior high school class. Of the students who were enthusiastic, one student well on her way to becoming a literary censor wrote:

◇ *Treasure Island* should be read, firstly, because it is by a famous author, secondly, most people like it and, thirdly, because it is considered a classic.

Two other students objected. A boy wrote:

◇ I like a cleaner story. In this story there is too much bloodshed, drinking, and swearing.

A girl, however, pointed out the evil nature of the story and the nefarious and inevitable consequences of reading Stevenson's awful book:

◇ This story full of murder, fighting, and wiping blood off of knives is not suitable for boys and girls to read and if these kinds of books were not written there would not be so many boys go wrong. I don't think there should be any more books written like it, because it don't learn you anything and nowadays we should read books that do us some good.[7]

A modern censor could not have said it better.

◈ AND WHAT IS THE STATE OF CLASSROOM AND LIBRARY CENSORSHIP TODAY?

Censorship was hardly a major concern of English teachers or school librarians (though it certainly was for public librarians) until recently. Before World War II, it rarely surfaced in schools although John Steinbeck's *The Grapes of Wrath* and *Of Mice and Men* caused some furor in newspapers, and when students began to read the books, the furor reached the schools. After World War II, Norman Mailer's *The Naked and the Dead* and J. D. Salinger's *The Catcher in the Rye* and other books "indicative of a permissive, lax, immoral society," as one censor noted, caught the eyes of adults and young adults alike. Granted, most objections were aimed at the writers and bookstores that stocked them. Few high school teachers would use or high school librarians would stock anything objectionable for several years, but teachers were now aware that they needed to be more careful about books they allowed students to read for extra credit or book reports. Two events changed the mild worry into genuine concern.

Paperback books seemed to offer little of intellectual or pedagogical value to teachers before World War II. Even after the war, many teachers blithely assumed paperbacks had not changed, and given the often lurid covers, teachers seemed to have a point, though it was more superficial than real. Administrators and parents continued to object even after the Bible and Plato's *Dialogues* and *Four Tragedies of Shakespeare* proved to teachers and librarians that paperbacks had merit. Students discovered even earlier that paperbacks were handy to stick in a purse or back pocket, and paperback titles were appealing, not stodgy as were most textbooks. So paperbacks came to schools, censors notwithstanding, and these cheap and ubiquitous books created problems galore for teachers.

Perhaps as important, young adult books until about 1967 were generally safe, pure, and simplistic, devoid of the reality that young people daily faced—violence, pregnancy, premarital sex, profanity, drinking, smoking, abortion, runaways, alienation, the generation gap, suicide, death, preju-dice, poverty, class distinctions, drugs, divorce, and on and on. Sports and going to the prom and getting the car for the big Friday night date loomed large as the major problems of young adult life in too many of these novels. Young people read them for fun, knowing that they were nothing more than escape reading with little relationship to reality or to anything of signifi-cance. Then in 1967, Ann Head's *Mr. and Mrs. Bo Jo Jones* and S. E. Hinton's *The Outsiders* appeared and young adult literature changed and could not go back to the good-old-pure days. Paul Zindel's *The Pigman* followed in 1968, and while all YA books that followed were hardly great or honest, a surprising number were. English teachers and librarians who had accepted the possibility of censorship with adult authors popular with the young—Steinbeck, Fitzgerald, Heller, Hemingway, for example—now learned that the once safe young adult novel was no longer safe, and censorship attacks soon began. Head's and Hinton's and Zindel's books were denounced, but so were young adult novels as good as Robert Lipsyte's *The Contender* (1967), A. E. Johnson's *A Blues I Can Whistle* (1969), John Donovan's *I'll Get There. It Better Be Worth the Trip* (1969), Jean Renvoize's *A Wild Thing* (1971), and that was merely the beginning.

Surveys of the state of censorship since 1963 indicate that censorship is either getting worse or fewer teachers and librarians are willing to lie quietly while the censor trods over them. Lee Burress' pioneer study, "How Cen-sorship Affects the School," in October 1963 was only the first of these surveys. Nyla H. Ahrens' doctoral study in 1965 was the first national survey. State surveys of Arizona censorship conditions appeared in the February 1969 and February 1975 *Arizona English Bulletin*. National stud-ies appeared ever more often: L. B. Woods' "The Most Censored Materials in the U.S." in the November 1, 1978, *Library Journal*, Burress' "A Brief Report of the 1977 NCTE Survey" in James Davis' *Dealing with Censorship*, and the much anticipated and disappointing *Limiting What Students Shall Read* in 1981. The 1982 survey of high school librarians by Burress, not yet in print though summarized in several news accounts, found that 34 percent of the librarians reported a challenge to at least one book as compared to 30 percent in his 1977 survey.

The most recent state study, "Censorship in North Carolina Public Schools," by the North Carolina Unit of People for the American Way polled 2,461 teachers, administrators, and librarians in that state and found 243 censorship attempts since 1980. Twenty-five percent of schools reported some form of censorship or attempted censorship. More details can be found in the January 1984 *Newsletter on Intellectual Freedom* published by the American Library Association. The *Newsletter* is without question the best source of material on censorship and should be known and read by English teachers and librarians and anyone who cares about the freedom to read.

But surveys often make for dull reading and say all too little about the individual besieged by censors—parents, ministers, organized groups, ad-ministrators, other teachers or librarians, or that mysterious telephone

◆ Comments about censorship of all kinds appear with almost nauseating regularity in the daily press as is shown by this collection of articles.

caller. Reports of incidents, taken from newspaper clippings or the *Newsletter on Intellectual Freedom*, at least hint at the emotional and pedagogical problems faced by real teachers and librarians. In the summaries of censorship incidents (some might more properly be called wars) below, note the books under attack, the announced reasons for the attacks, the sources of attacks, the disposition of the cases, and the geographical spread of the attacks. These represent only a tiny fraction of attacks in the last fifteen years.

1. *April 1971, Phoenix, Arizona. Love Story* was no longer allowed for sale in the Camelback High School bookstore after a parent complained about the four-letter words. The associate principal was quoted in local newspapers as saying, "We don't wish to have any controversial books in the bookstore or the library. *Love Story* will probably be a classic in five years, but for the time being, it will not be sold in Camelback."[8]

2. *March 1972, Dallas, Texas.* Two school trustees attacked *The Catcher in the Rye.* One said, "I think high school-age people are just too young, not stable enough, to handle this kind of material. . . . I think it's kind of silly to teach our youngsters living at home not to use profanity and then have the school encourage them to read books containing such material. To me, that is endorsement and I don't think public schools should be endorsing something like that."[9]

3. *May 1972, Old Town, Maine.* Members of the local school committee objected to *Manchild in the Promised Land* in an

elective course, "The Nature of Prejudice," because, as they said, there were no blacks in Old Town so prejudice was not that much of a problem. By a 4-3 vote, the committee banned the book from the schoolrooms immediately and from the school library after the close of the term.[10]

4. *1973, Pinellas County, Florida.* The Citizens Commission on Education asked the board of education to remove Eric Partridge's *Dictionary of Slang and Unconventional English* from the library. The chairman of the group linked the book's presence to the 696 suspensions for student profanity during that school year.[11]

5. *June 1973, Boston, Massachusetts.* The Boston Patrolmen's Association denounced Eve Merriam's *The Inner City Mother Goose* as "anti-police, anti-law and order, and anti-government" and demanded its removal from Boston library shelves. The city council refused, 8-1, to ban the book. In August, a city councilman took a copy out on permanent loan and said, "I don't call that education when a book like that is subject to the reading of little boys and girls."[12]

6. *November 1973, Drake, North Dakota.* Three dozen copies of *Slaughterhouse-Five* are burned in the school incinerator by order of the school board. A minister called the book "profane" and "obscene" and the "tool of the devil." The school superintendent noted, "That's the way we get rid of all our trash." At a hearing about the book, the board brought in a town policeman who testified that Vonnegut's book was "filthy" although he admitted he didn't know the name of the book and admitted he had not read it. The teacher in question was fired, sued, and won his case (but not restitution to the job) in June 1975.[13]

7. *1974, Wild Rose, Wisconsin.* An administrator banned Dee Brown's *Bury My Heart at Wounded Knee* though he had never read the book, but he had heard a radio review which led him to believe the book was "slanted." He talked the matter over with an English teacher who didn't agree, but the administrator would not relent. "If there's a possibility that something might be controversial, then why not eliminate it," he said.[14]

8. *March 1975, Littleton, Colorado.* A mother attacked an anthology of poetry, *Beastly Boys and Ghastly Girls*, because the book had "no redeeming social value." She also attacked *Go Ask Alice* because it had "filthy, rotten, crappy, dirty, garbage language."[15]

9. *April 1975, Randolph, New York.* Almost 150 books were removed from the district high school library to determine whether they were fit reading and submitted to a parental group demanding more say in educational policy. The list included *Soul on Ice, A Clockwork Orange,* Benchley's *Jaws,* Friedan's *The Feminine Mystique,* Kerr's *Dinky Hocker Shoots Smack,* Ellison's *Invisible Man,* Swarthout's *Bless the Beasts and Children,* Zindel's *The*

Pigman, and Vonnegut's *Breakfast of Champions*, the latter because "It blunts their senses toward sex, which should be revered." One parent, a defender of the books, remarked, "If you raise your child right at home, he is going to know how to accept the books he reads away from home. Sooner or later he is going to face life and would be better suited to face the world knowing what's in it."[16]

10. *November 1975, Logan County, Kentucky.* The school board banned *Go Ask Alice*. The superintendent said that the "school system was not censoring any book [but wanted to get this one off the shelves] to keep it out of the hands of small children who might be affected by its graphic, blunt language." A board member agreed the book was obscene but "did not want to make an issue out of the matter and would keep it quiet" if possible.[17]

11. *March 1976, Island Trees, New York.* In the start of what became in 1982 *the* major court battle about the right of school boards to ban books over student protests, the Island Trees School Board ordered these books removed—*Black Boy, Slaughterhouse-Five, The Naked Ape, Laughing Boy, Go Ask Alice, A Hero Ain't Nothin' But a Sandwich, Down These Mean Streets,* and *The Fixer*. The ban was later lifted on *Laughing Boy* and partially so on *Black Boy*.[18]

12. *April 1977, Eldon, Missouri.* By a 6-0 vote, the school board banned *The American Heritage Dictionary* because it included too many four-letter words. A Missouri Highway Patrol trooper had been offended by "39 objectionable words." According to the trooper, "If people learn words like that, it ought to be where you and I learned them—in the streets and in the gutter." The *St. Louis Post-Dispatch* began its article on the Eldon matter, "I'm rough," admitted a construction worker at Eldon's South Side Bar. "I've used all kinds of language. But not at home, and not in front of my daughter. That's what these damned bars are for."[19]

13. *August 1978, Issaquah, Washington.* The school board voted 3-1 to ban *The Catcher in the Rye* from high school classes after an objector told the board she had counted "785 profanities." The book, she said, "brainwashes students" and "is part of an overall communist plot in which a lot of people are used and may not even be aware of it." In June 1979, the board returned the book to the classroom.[20]

14. *August 1981, Yelm, Washington.* A parent requested that Zeffirelli's film of *Romeo and Juliet* not be shown as part of the high school English curriculum because his daughter had complained after seeing the film. He was disturbed by the bedroom scene, calling it "flat immoral nudity," and added, "I don't think adults should see that kind of thing."[21]

15. *November 1981, Vero Beach, Florida.* School Superintendent James Burns had nine pages cut from Time-Life *Great Cities'* chapter on Paris (the section showed nightlife and some nude dancers) in the middle school-junior high school library. When the school librarian and others objected, Burns said that a review committee was not needed since reviews are for borderline cases, and this was clearly inappropriate material.[22]

16. *July 1982, Fresno, California.* Three mothers, all members of a group called Family IMPACT (Interested Monitoring Persons Against Contemporary Textbooks), told the State Curriculum Commission that some new elementary reading texts were "primers for rebellion" because the books taught children to lie, cheat, and steal. The books also contained "an overwhelming stress on death, killing, and violence." One of the mothers said, "I cannot communicate with my oldest boy" and blamed textbooks for his dropping out of school. Another of the three found soft-porn in some text illustrations. She found a picture of a rabbit yawning at a crocodile offensive because "the far leg on the bunny starts in the center of his tummy. It appears subliminally to represent a different part of the body." Two months later, the same women objected to a Holt, Rinehart and Winston book, once more because of "subtle subliminal" art, this time a girl wearing what the mother called a "transparent skirt." The mother told the Holt representative that her group studies textbooks with "high-powered magnifying glasses." A new member of the State Curriculum Commission told the Holt representative to remove the material. "Why run the risk of offending some well-intentioned people?" The Holt representative went along with the suggestion, saying, "I agreed with him completely. I'd rather do that than have a controversy at a public meeting. When you're publishing a book, if there's something that is controversial, it's better to take it out."[23]

17. *January 1983, Montgomery, Alabama.* Four members of the state textbook committee filed a minority report asking for the rejection of approximately one hundred works approved for use in Alabama schools. Among the works objected to were Anne Frank's *The Diary of a Young Girl* ("a real downer"), Maya Angelou's *I Know Why the Caged Bird Sings* ("preached hatred and bitterness against whites"), and Ibsen's *A Doll's House* (feminist propaganda).[24]

18. *December 1983, Howard, Wisconsin.* After one parent objected to Judy Blume's *Forever* in the high school library, a five-person committee was created and the book was removed from the shelves pending a committee report. The parent said, "I just feel that it demoralizes marital sex. If it had pictures, you could put it in the adult bookstore."[25]

◈ SOME ASSUMPTIONS ABOUT CENSORSHIP AND CENSORS

Given the censorship attacks of the last thirteen years, we can make the following assumptions about censorship.

First, any work is potentially censorable by someone, someplace, sometime, for some reason. Nothing is permanently safe from censorship, not even books most teachers and librarians would regard as far removed from censorial eyes—not *Hamlet* or *Julius Caesar* or *Silas Marner* or *Treasure Island,* or anything else.

Second, the newer the work, the more likely it is to come under attack.

Third, censorship is capricious and arbitrary. Two teachers bearing much the same reputation and credentials and years of experience and using the same work will not necessarily be equally free from attack (or equally likely to be attacked). Some schools in conservative areas go free from censorship problems even though teachers may use controversial books. Other schools in relatively liberal areas may come under the censor's gun.

Fourth, censorship spreads a ripple of fear. The closer the censorship, the greater the likelihood of its effect on other teachers. But if the newspaper coverage of the incident has been extensive, the greater the likelihood that schools many miles away may feel the effect. Administrators may gently (or loudly) let their teachers know it is time to be traditional or safe in whatever the teachers choose for the coming year.

Fifth, censorship does not come only from people outside the school. Administrators, other teachers or librarians, or the school board may initiate an incident. That often surprises some English teachers or librarians. It should not.

Sixth, censorship is for too many educators like cancer or a highway accident. It happens only to other people. Most incidents happen to people who know "it couldn't happen to me." It did and it will.

Seventh, schools without clear and established and school board-approved policies and procedures for handling censorship are accidents waiting to happen. Every school should develop a policy and a procedure which helps both educators and objectors when an incident arises. The aim of both policy and procedures should be to ensure that everyone has a fair hearing, not to stall or frustrate anyone.

Eighth, if one book is removed from a classroom or library, no book is any longer safe. If a censor succeeds in getting one book out, every other person in the community who objects to another book should, in courtesy, be granted the same privilege. When everyone has walked out of the library carrying all those objectionable books, nothing of any consequence will be left no matter how many books remain. Some books are certain to offend some people and be ardently defended by others. Indeed, every library will have books offensive to someone, maybe everyone. After all, ideas do offend many people.

Ninth, educators and parents should, ideally, coexist to help each other for the good of the young, but the clash of parents with some educators appears to be sadly inevitable. Some people would prefer to see young adults *educated* which means allowing them to think and wonder about ideas and to consider the consequences of those ideas. Others would prefer to see young people *indoctrinated* into certain community or family values or beliefs or traditions and to eschew anything controversial. With so little in common between these two philosophies of schooling, disagreement is not only natural but certain.

Educators should be aware that not everyone who objects to a book is necessarily a censor. Most parents are sincerely concerned about the welfare of their children, but making a special effort to go to school to make a complaint is likely to make them feel resentful or nervous or angry. If taking time from work were not enough reason to feel irritated, many parents have a built-in ambivalent love-hate feeling about schools. Maybe they had a miserable time with a teacher when they were young. They may worry about being talked down to by a much younger teacher or librarian. They may wonder if anyone will take them or their complaint seriously.

Unfair as it doubtlessly seems, educators will need to be considerate and reasonable and to listen more than talk for the first few minutes. Once objectors calm down and recognize that the teacher or librarian might just possibly be human, then and only then will the educator learn what is really troubling the parents. Everyone may learn, sometimes to the teachers' surprise, that no one wants to ban anything, but parents do wonder *why* the teacher is using the book or *why* the librarian recommended it to their child. They may want their child to read something else but agree that they have no wish to control the reading of anyone else. If that is true, the problem is easier to handle, not always easy but certainly easier.

But sometimes the objectors really are censors, and they have no desire to talk and reason, only to condemn. For these people, we can make the following assumptions.

Censors seem unwilling to accept the fact that the more they attack a book, the greater the publicity and likelihood that more young adults will read the offensive book. In their messianic drive to eliminate a book, censors create a wider and wider circle of readers. In some cases with older or more obscure works, they revive something that has been virtually dead for years. If *Romeo and Juliet* once went largely ignored by young adults before Zeffirelli's film, censors have now replaced the film as a motivation to read the play.

Censors will not believe that in trying desperately to keep young people pure and innocent they often expose those young people to the very thing the censors abhor. Several years ago, a group violently objected to a scholarly dictionary which contained some "offensive" words. Worried that others might not believe all those degrading, evil, pernicious words were so easily found in one work, censors compiled a sort of digest of "The Best Dirty Words in ⎯⎯⎯⎯," duplicated the list, and disseminated it to anyone curious, including the very students censors claimed to be protecting. More than one censor has read the "offensive" parts of a book aloud at a school board meeting to prove his points while young students raptly listened.

Censors often have a simplistic belief that there is an easily established and absolute relationship between books and deeds. A bad book, however, defined, produces bad actions. What one reads, one immediately imitates. To read profane language automatically leads to young people swearing. Presumably, nonreading youngsters who swear must eagerly await more literate fellows to instruct them in the art of the profane. To read about seduction is to wish to seduce or to be seduced (though it is possible the wish may precede the book). To read about crime is to wish to commit that crime, or at the very least something vaguely anti-social. Anthony Comstock loved to visit boys in jail because when he asked what led them into the world of crime, they told him exactly what he wanted to hear (as they knew full well), that dime novels and drinking and shooting pool were *the* sources of all their present misery. J. Edgar Hoover was also a true believer in the one-to-one relationship between bad material and criminal acts.

Sociologists and psychologists and educators know that only rarely is there a simple explanation for a complex act. What makes young people delinquent? Perhaps bad reading. Perhaps violence on television. Perhaps home life, friends, acquaintances, school experiences, parents, teachers, religion, jobs, or any number of other variables, all interrelated. Perhaps no one cause is individually responsible. Censors like simplistic, easy, satisfying, lazy answers to tough questions. That puts them one up on teachers and librarians. Censors do not need to think to react or to believe.

Censors believe that whatever material the school provides is an index to what the school or the teachers or the librarians believe. If the school library has copies of Heller's *Catch-22* and Plato's *Dialogues* and one teacher recommends Orwell's *1984* and another teaches *The Adventures of Huckleberry Finn*, the librarian and the teachers and the school must approve of bloodshed and homosexuality and socialism and drugs and slavery and much, much more that is objectionable.

Censors seem to have limited, if any, faith in the ability of young adults to read and think. Censors wonder if young people can handle controversial, suspect books like Huxley's *Brave New World* or Salinger's *The Catcher in the Rye*, the young are so innocent and pure and untainted by contact with reality. That may have been what caused one censor who objected to Ann Head's *Mr. and Mrs. Bo Jo Jones* and Paul Zindel's *The Pigman* to announce to an audience, "Teenagers are too young to learn about pregnancy."

A related act of censorial faith is the assumption that whatever a teacher says is automatically believed and accepted by students. If a teacher assigns something to be read by tomorrow, by tomorrow that something will be read and believed. Young people asked to read a short story will always read carefully, heed precisely whatever point the story or the author seems to be

THE PEOPLE BEHIND THE BOOKS

ROBERT LIPSYTE, Author

Assignment: Sports
The Contender
Jock and Jill
One Fat Summer

Once, YA books could get by as superficial excapist mindwash, but now that television offers junk food for the head, YA books have not only the responsibility (which they always had and often refused to assume) but the desperate need, if they wish to survive, to engage young people on a deeper level, on a searching, helpful, option-expanding level. For example, this current rage for "realistic sexuality"—Well, there's too much sexuality, unexplained, teasing sexuality in the culture as is. We don't need to know that boys and girls have sex. If YA literature is to be worthwhile, to be necessary, it must go beyond to expose more questions (young people often need the right questions more than answers) about relationships between girls and boys, about the possibility of relationships that don't put sexual pressure on boys and girls, about ways of diffusing the terrible pressures of "scoring" for boys, of losing or keeping virginity for girls, honest ways of looking at sex, through characters we can identify with and who entertain us, and perhaps coming to the radical conclusion that sex is at once less

making, and then go and do likewise. Many a teacher would be happy if even 50 percent of the class read anything during a given week, much less everything and that carefully.

Censors seem to have no sense of humor, or at least none is exhibited at times of censorial stress. Having none, they dislike and distrust any literature that is ironic or satiric or humorous, regarding all as time-wasters.

Censors alternately love and hate English teachers and librarians. Censors would appear to hate what educators use, but censors would also appear to approve of great literature, particularly the classics. Being essentially nonreaders, they know little about literature but that it must be uplifting and noble and fine. They may claim to have read the uplifting when they were young, "back when schools knew what they were doing," but they often cannot remember titles; when they do their comments suggest the book was read in an emasculated child's edition. Censors assume that classics have no objectionable words or actions or ideas. So much for *Crime and Punishment, Oedipus Rex, Hamlet, Madame Bovary, Anna Karenina,* and most other classics. For censors, the real virtue of great literature is that it is old, dusty, dull, and hard to read, in other words, good for young people.

Censors care little what others believe. Censors are ordained by God to root out evil, and they are divinely inspired to know the truth. Where teachers and librarians may flounder searching for the truth, censors need not fumble for they *know.* They are sincerely unable to understand that others may regard the censors' arrogance as sacrilegious, but they rarely important than the deodorant makers would have us believe, yet more intrinsic a part of our lives than books up to now have told us. And abortion and birth control and loving and considerate sexual technique must eventually be dealt with, too, again in a way that is a part of the story being told—rather than the story being the candy-coating for a "problem" book that can move off the shelf. Gay sex must be treated as honestly as hetero-sex. Beyond sex, into sex roles, into job vs. family, into making money, into political involvement, YA books must also be ready to offer a view of the world that is uncompromising in realism, but also hopeful of improvement—and willing to leave unanswered, un-pat, major questions. The

world is going to get more complicated, not less, and young people are going to have more available information and more chances for physical and emotional encounters. If YA literature is going to be in their knapsack as they march up the electronic grid road then the entire community of interest here—writers, editors, publishers, teachers, and librarians— are going to have to be willing to admit we don't know the answers any better than the readers do, but we might have an idea what the most important questions are. ◆

Assignment: Sports. Harper & Row, 1970 and 1984.
The Contender. Harper & Row, 1967.
Jock and Jill. Harper & Row, 1982.
One Fat Summer. Harper & Row, 1977.

worry since they represent the side of morality. One censor counts for any number of other parents. When Judy Blume's *Deenie* was removed from an elementary library in the Cotati-Rohnert Park School District, California, in October 1982, a trustee said that a number of parents from a nearby college wanted the book retained, but "the real down-to-earth parents who have lived in the district for quite awhile didn't want it,"[26] and that was clearly that. No one counted the votes, but no one needed to. Orwell knew what he was talking about when he wrote, "All animals are equal but some are more equal than others." Censors would agree with Orwell's comment if not his ironic intention.

Finally, censors use language carelessly or sloppily. Sometimes they cannot possibly mean what they say. The administrator who said, "We don't wish to have any controversial books in the bookstore or the library," either did not understand what the word *controversial* meant or he was speaking gibberish (the native tongue of embarrassed administrators talking to reporters who think they may have a juicy story here). Three adjectives are likely to pop up in the censors' description of objectionable works: *filthy, obscene,* or *vulgar* along with favored intensifiers like *unbelievably, unquestionably,* and *hopelessly* though a few censors favor oxymoronic expressions like *pure garbage* or *pure evil.* Not one of the adjectives is likely to be defined operationally by censors who assume that *filth* is *unquestionably filth,* and everyone shares their definition. Talking with censors is, thus, often difficult, which may disturb others while it is often a matter of sublime indifference to the censors. If talking is difficult, communicating with them is usually nigh unto impossible.

◈ ATTACKS ON MATERIALS

Who Are the Censors?

There are three reasonably distinct kinds of censors and pressure groups: (1) those from the right, the conservatives; (2) those from the left, the liberals; and (3) an amorphous band of educators and publishers and editors and distributors who most other educators might assume would be opposed to censorship. The first two groups operate from different guiding principles, or so one would assume. But it is sometimes easy for educators to be confused whether the attack stems from the right or the left, the coercive methods, the censorial rhetoric, and the messianic fervor seem so similar. The third group is unorganized and functions on a personal, ad hoc, case-by-case approach, though people in the group are more likely than not to feel sympathetic to the conservative case for censorship.

There are an incredible number of small censorship or pressure groups on the right who continue to *worry* educators (worry in the sense of alarm *and* harass). Many are better known for their acronyms which often sound folksy or clever, for example, *Save Our Schools* (SOS); *People of America Responding to Educational Needs of Today's Society* (PARENTS); *Citizens United for Responsible Education* (CURE); *Let's Improve Today's Education* (LITE); *American Christians in Education* (ACE); and everyone's favorite, *Let Our Values Emerge* (LOVE). Probably the most powerful, far beyond the state boundary implied by the title, is *Parents of New York— United* (PONY-U). Chapter 9 in Ed Jenkinson's *Censors in the Classroom: The Mind Benders* summarizes quite well the major groups, big or small.

With few exceptions, these groups seem united in announcing that they want to protect young people from insidious forces that threaten the schools, to remove any vestiges of sex education and secular humanism from classes or libraries, to put God back into public schools, and to restore traditional values to education. Very few announce openly that they favor censorship of books or teaching materials, though individual members of the groups may so proclaim. Indeed, what is particularly heartening about the groups is that many of them maintain that they are anti-censorship, though occasionally a public slip occurs. The president of the Utah chapter of Citizens for Decency was quoted as saying:

> ◇ I am opposed to censorship. We are not a censorship organization. But there are limits to the First Amendment. People have the right to see what they want on television, but that has nothing to do with the right to exhibit pornography on television. We're not stopping anyone from buying books and magazines or going to the movies they want. They just can't do it in Utah. Let them go to Nevada. Nobody there cares.[27]

Whether anyone from Nevada with a similar anti-censorial attitude responded with a suggestion that people from Nevada seeking cheap thrills should go to Utah is unknown. Something similar to the above comment came from the Rev. Ricky Pfeil. Wheeler, Texas, apparently has its moral problems with objectionable movies like *Porky's* and *Flashdance* and *E.T.*

(Pfeil's argument against the latter film, "The film's an attempt to show something supernatural and it's not God. There's only one other power that's supernatural and that's Satan.") The good minister also is against censorship, as he said:

◇ You know, I am not for censorship. People have a right to see what they want or read what they want, but I'd just as soon they go to Los Angeles to get a copy of *Playboy* magazine. I'm responsible for here. Evil left unchecked will go rampant. God tells me what to do. [28]

Given the doublespeak of Ms. Brimhall and the Rev. Pfeil, readers will admire the honesty and the original Constitutional interpretation of the Rev. Vincent Strigas, co-leader of the Mesa (Arizona) Decency Coalition. Slashing merrily away at magazines that threatened the "moral fiber" of residents, the Rev. Strigas answered complaints about his approach:

◇ Some people are saying that we are in violation of First Amendment rights. I do not think that the First Amendment protects people [who sell] pornographic materials. The Constitution protects only the freedom to do what's right. [29]

Surely there is no ambiguity in that message.

Two highly vocal and nationally visible conservative groups have worried educators for several years. If the Eagle Forum and the Moral Majority *seemed* pro-censorship until recently, teachers and librarians can now turn to other opponents, for both organizations have announced that they, too, are not in favor of censorship. In the November 1981 issue of the Eagle Forum's *Phyllis Schlafly Report*, the leader of the group castigated librarians for buying a "tremendous quantity of pornographic and trashy fiction" and for not stocking "conservative, pro-family, and patriotic" books. Judith Krug agreed that behind Schlafly's strident rhetoric there lay a valid point, that as the American Library Association had said for years:

◇ Books should be readily available to the general public and to students on all sides of controversial issues of public importance. But often they are not. [30]

Krug noted that these principles are uncontestably valid and should apply to all book selection in a library. Readers can only assume that fairness and balance are the hallmarks of the Eagle Forum's attitude toward both libraries and education, and the day when individuals (or units) of the group attempted to censor books lies safely in the past.

Members of the Moral Majority once seemed even more anxious to monitor and censor books, but if Cal Thomas, Vice President for Communications of the Virginia-based group, is correct, that day is gone. In *Book Burning*, Thomas argued that today's most pervasive censorship came from liberals who would not publish or review or stock conservative books. On April 14, 1983, the Rev. Jerry Falwell, founder and president of Moral Majority, Inc., said of the campaign to get more conservative books before the public:

◇ This is not a campaign to take any book off the shelf of any library. Rather it is a campaign to get books containing conservative and traditional moral views and philosophies on the shelves. [31]

Librarians must have breathed a sigh of relief after those words. They could only assume that "any book" and "any library" must include school libraries as well as public libraries.

But educators might be forgiven for harboring memories of recent times when members of the Moral Majority seemed more intent on censorship than reasoned argument. The Rev. George A. Zarris, Chair of the Illinois Moral Majority, was quoted in a UPI dispatch for December 14, 1980, as saying:

> ◇ I don't believe in censorship, but there is some stuff that is just so far out, you have to ban it. . . . I would think moral-minded people might object to books that are philosophically alien to what they believe. If they have the books and feel like burning them, fine. [32]

And the Rev. Falwell's "Confidential" letter to millions of people on January 1, 1981, contained this brief paragraph hardly calculated to reassure educators that the Moral Majority was on their side:

> ◇ If you find obscene books, films, or other such material being used by our young people in schools, please advise us right away.

The Rev. H. Lamarr Mooneyham, Chair of the North Carolina Moral Majority, launched a campaign in March 1981 to remove library books and texts he deemed unfit for public schools, books that were:

> ◇ anti-family, anti-God, anti-Bible, and pro all that other stuff. . . . Really atheistic humanism is what it is and we're concerned about it. [33]

A month later, the Rev. Mooneyham released a twenty-eight page review of materials and cited four books in particular as offensive—J. D. Salinger's *The Catcher in the Rye*, Gordon Parks' *The Learning Tree*, Judy Blume's *Forever*, and Thomas Altman's *Kiss Daddy Goodbye*:

> ◇ Filled with explicit sex and violence, it is little wonder that the teen-age pregnancy rate as well as public school crime is at an all-time high. [34]

And in December 1980 and February 1981, Michael Farris, Executive Director and General Legal Counsel of the Washington State Moral Majority, filed two suits. The first was against a school district for its use of Parks' *The Learning Tree* in its school curriculum. The second was against the Washington State Library and demanded that it release the names of all "public schools and public school employees" who had borrowed a short film, "Achieving Sexual Maturity." [35]

But those were in the bad old days of long ago, and as the Rev. Falwell said, "This is not a campaign to take any book off the shelf of any library."

Best known of all censors in America today are Mel and Norma Gabler who operate a small but powerful company out of their Longview, Texas, home. Educational Research Analysts came about when the Gablers found a vast difference between their son's American history text and ones they remembered. Norma Gabler appeared before the State Board of Education in 1962 and went largely ignored. Upset, she came home and did her spadework on offensive textbooks. (Most texts seem to be offensive to the

Gablers until they help writers and publishers to correct the material and remove secular humanism and anything that might prove offensive to Christians or any proponents of traditional values.) Now Educational Research Analysts cranks out thousands of pages of textbook analyses and reviews to aid any school or school board in selecting the best, the most proper, and the most accurate texts by the Gablers' standards. Readers who wish to know more about the Gablers or their organization should read William Martin's "The Guardians Who Slumbereth Not," a model of fair play reporting by a writer who does not agree with the Gablers on fundamental points but who clearly likes and admires their openness and caring.

Whatever else conservative groups may agree or disagree on, they seem united in opposing secular humanism and the teaching of evolution.

Secular humanism is both too large and too fuzzy to handle adequately in a few paragraphs (or even a short chapter). Briefly, if inexactly, conservatives appear to define secular humanism as any teaching material which denies the existence of (or ridicules the worth of) absolute values of right and wrong. Secular humanism is said to be negative, anti-God, anti-American, anti-phonics, and anti-afterlife and pro-permissive, pro-sexual freedom, pro-situation ethics, pro-socialism, and pro-one worldism. Conservatives hopelessly intolerant about secular humanism often have problems explaining what the term means to outsiders, or even insiders, usually defining the presumably philosophical term operationally and offering little more than additional examples of the horror that secular humanism implies. Such was the case when secular humanism reared its ugly head at a meeting of the Utah Association of Women:

> ◇One woman says with disgust that two recent school board members didn't know what secular humanism was; thus they weren't qualified to run for office. Lots of "tsks" run through the group until a young woman visitor apologizes for her ignorance and asks, Just what is secular humanism? There is an awkward silence. No one gives a definition, but finally they urge her to attend a UAW workshop on the subject. Later in the meeting, during a discussion of unemployment a vice-president says, "Our young people are only taught to do things that give them pleasure. That's secular humanism."[36]

Librarians and teachers curious to learn more about secular humanism (and that should include all educators since they are likely to hear the term used more and more or come under attack for espousing it) should read the documents which started all the fuss. The first *Humanist Manifesto* appeared in 1933 and was signed by thirty-four intellectuals, *Humanist Manifesto II* in 1973 signed by 114 intellectuals, among them Isaac Asimov, John Ciardi, Richard Kostelanetz, Lord Ritchie-Calder, and B. F. Skinner. Robert Primack and David Aspy's "The Roots of Humanism,"[37] Ben Brodinsky's "The New Right: The Movement and Its Impact" (note the responses from conservatives that follow the article),[38] and Robert T. Rhode's "Is Secular Humanism the Religion of the Public Schools?"[39] present one point of view. Conservative views can be found in Alan Stang's "Why Secular Humanists Are Making War on the Religious Right,"[40] Tim LaHaye's *The Battle for the Mind*,[41] and two books by the most persuasive of new right authors, Onalee McGraw, *Family Choice in Education: The New Imperative*[42] and *Secular Humanism and the Schools: The Issue Whose Time Has Come.*[43]

Evolution has always been a sore point with religious conservatives, particularly in the past few years when they have rallied behind scientific creationism, demanding it be taught along with evolution as another theory. The conservative viewpoint may be found by reading LaHaye's and McGraw's books above as well as by listening to Jerry Falwell's "Old Time Gospel Hour." The scientific community's position can be found in Dorothy Nelkin's *Science Textbook Controversies and the Politics of Equal Time*[44] and Chris McGowan's *In the Beginning . . . A Scientist Shows Why Creationists Are Wrong.*[45]

Fortunately for educators already concerned about the many pressure groups from the right, only one pressure group from the left need concern them, but that one group is worrisome. The Council on Interracial Books for Children was formed in 1965 to change the all-white world of children's books and to promote literature which more accurately portrayed minorities or reflected the goals of a multiracial, multiethnic society. They offer meetings and publications to expedite their goals, but for most teachers, the CIBC is best known for its often excellent *Bulletin*.

No humane person would disagree with the CIBC's goals. And, as it has maintained over the years, the CIBC does not censor teaching or library materials. It has, however, perhaps inadvertently, perhaps arrogantly, been guilty of coercing educators into not purchasing or stocking or using books offensive to the CIBC or its reviewers. Its printed articles have attacked Paula Fox's *The Slave Dancer*, Ouida Sebestyen's *Words by Heart*, and Harper Lee's *To Kill a Mockingbird* and, by implication, have criticized those who stocked or taught these books.

The CIBC has argued that *evaluation* is hardly identical with *censorship*, and no one would dispute an organization or journal's right to criticize or lambast any book with which it disagreed for whatever reason. But the CIBC and the *Bulletin* are unable to see any distinction between *Bulletin* reviews and reviews appearing in the *New York Times Book Review*, the *Horn Book Magazine*, *School Library Journal*, or *Voice of Youth Advocates*, not a difference in quality but in kind. *Bulletin* reviews are, whether the CIBC accepts it or not, a call for censorship based on social awareness. If book reviewer X reviews a YA book in any national publication except for the CIBC *Bulletin*, readers may disagree with the reviewer's opinion, but in any case readers will decide on their own whether they wish to buy or reject the book. Differences in taste are so commonplace that almost no one would attack someone else for choosing or not choosing to purchase on literary merit or personal taste. And, as anyone knows who reads many reviews of the same book, literary merit is an inexact term used to justify personal judgments.

But literary merit does not loom large in the reviews in CIBC's *Bulletin*. Replacing it are terms like *racist*, *sexist*, *handicappist*, and *ageist*, all of them personal judgments, none of them objective though doubtless all are used sincerely and, in the case of a favorite author gone awry, sometimes sadly. If librarians purchase or teachers use a book attacked in the *Bulletin*, those educators had better be prepared to defend it against the true believer who will often assume the worst about them, that they are racists or sexists or worse. In most cases, it is less troublesome simply to avoid buying or using any book which has aroused the ire of the CIBC or a CIBC reviewer. The CIBC carries greater weight with librarians and teachers and school officials than it apparently is willing to recognize, and it is hardly a secret—save perhaps to the CIBC—that it is regarded by many as a censor. And supporters of the CIBC are almost certain to assume the worst about anyone who dares to criticize the organization, witness the letters to the editor that followed Lillian Gerhardt's editorial, "The Would-be Censors of the Left" in the November 1976 *School Library Journal* or Nat Hentoff's article, "Any Writer Who Follows Anyone Else's Guidelines Ought to Be in Advertising" a year later in the same magazine.

The case for the racist-free library is carried to its absurd and dangerous conclusion by Bettye I. Latimer in "Telegraphing Messages to Children about Minorities." After defining censorship as: "the actual destruction of a book through banning, exiling, or burning it, so that no one has access to it,"[46] Latimer proclaims that she is "strongly opposed to censorship for adult readers, since adults are responsible for their own values," but that apparently does not hold true for young people:

> ◇I am *not* suggesting censorship for books that are racist-oriented. I *am* suggesting that we remove these books to archives. This will permit scholars and researchers to have access to them. Since old racist books have no use in constructing healthy images for today's children, they need to be put in cold storage. As for contemporary racist books, educational institutions ought to stop purchasing and thereby stop subsidizing publishers for being racist.
>
> Finally, I would like to see librarians, teachers, and reading coordinators reeducate themselves to the social values which books pass on to children. I invite them to learn to use antiracist criteria in evaluating and assessing books.

Amidst all the noble sentiments in these words, some people will sense a hint of liberal censorship or pressure at work. All censors, whatever their religious or sociological biases, *know* what is good and bad in books and are only too willing to *help* the rest of us fumbling mortals learn what to keep and what to exile (or put in the archives).

The third kind of censorship or pressure group comes from within the schools, teachers or librarians or school officials who either censor materials themselves or support others who do. Sometimes these educators do so fearing reprisals if they do not. Sometimes because they fear being noticed, preferring anonymity at all costs. Sometimes because they are fearful of dealing with reality in literature. Sometimes because they regard themselves as highly moral and opposed to whatever they label immoral in literature. Sometimes because they prize (or so they claim) literary merit and the classics above all other literature, and refuse to consider teaching or recommending anything recent or second-rate however they define those terms.

THE PEOPLE BEHIND THE BOOKS

NAT HENTOFF, Author

The Day They Came to Arrest the Book
The First Freedom
Jazz Country
This School Is Driving Me Crazy

The fun for me—and, I hope, for the reader—is the story and the people in it. The unpredictability of both. That's why I most like to write fiction, for readers of any age, because I keep getting surprised. By what's in me.

I expect to keep on writing about the age of self-discovery—for that's what adolescence will continue to be no matter what technology accompanies it. An age of testing the values of the grown-ups (!) at home and at school. And testing one's own values—against the herd-like pressures of one's peers. A theme that never dulls, because what the author remembers learning in those years about one's very self, keeps reverberating for decades. ◆

The Day They Came to Arrest the Book. Delacorte, 1982.
The First Freedom. Delacorte, 1980.
Jazz Country. Harper & Row, 1976.
This School Is Driving Me Crazy. Delacorte, 1975.

Fear permeates many of these people, though this may be masked as fear of or kowtowing to anyone in authority. A survey of late 1960s Arizona censorship conditions among teachers uncovered three such specimens:

◇ I would not recommend any book any parent might object to.

◇ The Board of Education knows what parents in our area want their children to read. If teachers don't feel they can teach what the parents approve, they should move on.

◇ The English teacher is hired by the school board which represents the public. The public, therefore, has the right to ask any English teacher to avoid using any material repugnant to any parent or student.[47]

Lest readers assume that Arizona is unique in certifying these nonprofessionals, note these two Connecticut English Department Chairs quoted in Diane Shugert's "Censorship in Connecticut" in the Spring 1978 *Connecticut English Journal*:

◇ At this level, I don't feel it's [censorship] a problem. We don't deal with controversial material, at least not in English class.

◇ We have no problems at all in my department. The teachers order books directly and don't clear them with me or with a committee. But *I* receive the shipments. Copies of books that I think to be inappropriate simply disappear from the book room.[48]

In a letter to the book review editor of the *School Library Journal*, a librarian told how she had been approached by a parent objecting to words in Alice Childress' *A Hero Ain't Nothin' But a Sandwich*. The librarian particularly objected to the book's listing among the "Best Books of the Year for 1973." She wrote:

> ◇ Our school strongly recommends you remove this book from your list as profanity at the junior high level is not appropriate in a library book. [49]

More recently, the book was the subject of a school hearing when two Arizona mothers argued, "Most kids don't have the maturity to handle this." A junior high school principal agreed when he said, "I would like to see it banned altogether. That kind of language is not acceptable. I don't want any book on the shelf that would result in a student being disciplined if he used that language. Otherwise, our disciplinary policy will go out the window."

The December 1973 *School Library Journal* carried an article by Mary F. Poole objecting to Johanna Reiss' *The Upstairs Room*:

> ◇ The book proved to be a well-told account of a truly horrible situation. It is peopled with well delineated characters, who are in truth, "people with weaknesses and strengths," an aim of the author which was accomplished quite well: so the more than 50 irreverent expletives and the use of one four-letter word in the book are mere baggage or are used for their shock appeal, their monetary value, out of unconcern for the name of God, or to prove that the author is not a prude. Take your choice. [50]

The moral question of whether an author can make a valid moral or psychological point with "strong language," a not untypical euphemism in such cases, raged in letters in the following issues.

Similarly, Patty Campbell's "The YA Perplex" column in the December 1978 *Wilson Library Bulletin* led to increased letters as Campbell noted, "Judging from the letters to the editors in various library publications, obscene language rings alarm bells for most librarians"[51] and proceeded to review three possibly controversial novels, Fran Arrick's *Steffie Can't Come Out to Play*, Kin Platt's *The Doomsday Gang*, and Sandra Scoppettone's *Happy Endings Are All Alike*. Sure enough, controversy produced letters, the best or most typical from an admitted self-censoring high school librarian. After announcing that he had played football and coached for eleven years—proving, one can assume, that he was a real man, not a wimp—he added:

> ◇ I have a philosophy of what it should be like within the walls and pages (especially pages) of a library. Two different worlds? You bet.
> Do I want our teens to see a sugarcoated world through rose-colored glasses? Why not? Is there anything wrong with reading about the good things that happen? . . . Is it wrong for a character of fiction to say "gosh darn" instead of "damn it"?
> In my library censorship lives, and I'm not ashamed or afraid to say it, either. I have books like *The Boy Who Could Made Himself Disappear* on my shelves, but these are few and far between. To all you so-called liberal librarians out there in city or country schools now condemning this letter, I say to you: "The kids of today are great! Do you want to help give them a boost or a bust?"[52]

And at least one book distributor was only too willing to help librarians precensor books. The Follett Library Book Company of Crystal Lake, Illinois (not to be confused with Follett Publishing Company in Chicago), has for several years marked titles with a pink card *if* three or more customers had objected to the vocabulary or illustrations or subject matter of a book. The cards read:

> ◇ Some of our customers have informed us of their opinion that the content or vocabulary of this book is inappropriate for young readers. Before distributing this book, you may wish to examine it to assure yourself that the subject matter and vocabulary meet your standards.[53]

Publishers, too, have been guilty of rewriting texts or asking authors to delete certain words to make books or texts more palatable to highly moral librarians or communities. "Expurgation Practices of School Book Clubs" in the December 1983 *Voice of Youth Advocates* and Gayle Keresey's "School Book Club Expurgation Practices" in the Winter 1984 *Top of the News* uncovered censorship practices in Scholastic Book Club selections, as titles were changed and deletions of offensive words or ideas occurred between the hardback edition and its publication in a paperback club edition.

What Do the Censors Censor?

The answer to that question is easy—almost anything. Books, films, magazines, anything that might be enjoyed by someone is likely to feel some censor's scorn and moral wrath.

Some works, however, are more likely to be attacked. Judging from state and national surveys of censorship conditions, these works are almost certain to be objected to last year, this year, next year, and for years to come.

> ◇ J. D. Salinger's *The Catcher in the Rye* (seemingly on every censor's hit list and leading every survey but one as the most widely censored book in America)
> ◇ *Go Ask Alice* (the only close rival to *Catcher* on hit lists)
> ◇ Steinbecks' *Of Mice and Men* and *The Grapes of Wrath*
> ◇ Joseph Heller's *Catch-22*
> ◇ Aldous Huxley's *Brave New World*
> ◇ William Golding's *Lord of the Flies*
> ◇ Harper Lee's *To Kill a Mockingbird*
> ◇ Kurt Vonnegut's *Slaughterhouse-Five*
> ◇ Judy Blume's *Forever*

Slightly behind these ten golden favorites come these adult novels widely read by young adults:

> ◇ Ken Kesey's *One Flew over the Cuckoo's Nest*, Ernest Hemingway's *The Sun Also Rises* and *For Whom the Bell Tolls* and *A Farewell to Arms*, F. Scott Fitzgerald's *The Great Gatsby*, Eve Merriam's *The Inner City Mother Goose*, Claude Brown's *Manchild in the Promised Land*, Gordon Parks' *The Learning Tree*, George Orwell's *1984* and *Animal Farm*, Jerzy Kosinski's *The Painted Bird*, Mark Twain's *The Adventures of Huckleberry Finn*, and Alexandre Solzhenitsyn's *One Day in the Life of Ivan Denisovich*.

Along with these come young adult novels:

◇ Judy Blume's *Deenie* and *Are You There, God? It's Me, Margaret*, Robert Cormier's *The Chocolate War* and *After the First Death*, Paula Fox's *The Slave Dancer*, Alice Childress' *A Hero Ain't Nothin' but a Sandwich*, Johanna Reiss' *The Upstairs Room*, Rosa Guy's *Ruby*, M. E. Kerr's *Dinky Hocker Shoots Smack*, S. E. Hinton's *The Outsiders*, Paul Zindel's *The Pigman* and *My Darling, My Hamburger*, and Norma Klein's *Mom, the Wolfman and Me*.

And who could forget favorites like *The American Heritage Dictionary* and *Romeo and Juliet* and *Othello* and *The Merchant of Venice*? Or short stories (and films) like Shirley Jackson's "The Lottery" or Ambrose Bierce's "An Occurrence at Owl Creek Bridge"? Or modern plays like Thornton Wilder's *Our Town* or Tennessee Williams' *The Glass Menagerie* or *Summer and Smoke* or Arthur Miller's *Death of a Salesman* or *All My Sons*?

Readers surprised to discover an obvious censorial title not on the list above should feel free to add whatever they wish. Anyone who wishes to expand the list (easy and probably necessary for some) should casually read any issue of the *Newsletter on Intellectual Freedom* or skim through James E. Davis' *Dealing with Censorship* or any other book on censorship. The list of objectionable works could go on and on and on and on.

Why Do the Censors Censor What They Do?

That is a far more important and far more complex question than merely asking what do censors censor. Unfortunately for readers who want simple answers and an easy to remember list of reasons, the next paragraphs will certainly be disappointing.

In "Censorship in the 1970s: Some Ways to Handle It When It Comes (and It Will)" in early 1974, Donelson listed eight different kinds of materials which get censored. Those which censors (1) deem offensive because of sex (usually calling it "filth" or "risque" or "indecent"); (2) see as an attack on the American dream or the country ("un-American" or "pro-commie"); (3) label peacenik or pacifistic—remember the Vietnam war had not yet become unpopular with the masses; (4) consider irreligious or against religion or, specifically, un-Christian; (5) believe promote racial harmony or stress civil rights or the civil rights movements ("biased on social issues" or "do young people have to see all that ugliness?"); (6) regard as offensive in language ("profane" or "unfit for human ears"); (7) identify as drug books, pro or con ("kids wouldn't hear about or use drugs if it weren't for these books"); and (8) regard as presenting inappropriate adolescent behavior and therefore likely to cause other young people to act inappropriately.[54]

Then Ed Jenkinson added more in "Dirty Dictionaries, Obscene Nursery Rhymes and Burned Books" in James E. Davis' *Dealing with Censorship*; adding fourteen in all, such as young adult novels, works of "questionable" writers, literature about or by homosexuals, role playing, texts lacking proper rules of grammar, sexist stereotypes, and sex education.

Presumably that was that. Not so. Jenkinson added even more—the new list totaled twenty-three reasons for censoring—in *Censors in the Class-*

◆ As the issue of censorship invaded the general public consciousness, authors began including it in the plots of books written for young readers. The books shown here all include some aspects of censorship in their plots.

room: *The Mind Benders*. New to the list were materials that defamed historical personalities, assignments that invaded the privacy of young people, secular humanism, nudity, values clarification, pagan cultures and life styles, and behavior modification.

More was to come, by Jenkinson alone. His 1979 *Publishers Weekly* article[55] contained a list of forty targets of the censors, new among them being sociology, anthropology, the humanities generally (if secular humanism is bad, so then must be humanism or anything that sounds like humanism, and that easily extends to humanities), ecology, world government, world history if it mentions the United Nations, basal readers lacking phonics, basal readers with many pictures or drawings, situation ethics, violence, and books that do not promote the Protestant ethic or do not promote patriotism.

And in the last effort to expand his ever widening list, Jenkinson listed sixty-seven censorial objections in the May 1980 *Missouri English Bulletin*[56] adding these to the list: "Soviet propaganda," citizenship classes, uncaptioned pictures in any text but especially history texts, black dialects, science fiction, concrete poetry, world literature in translation, psychodrama, magazines that have ads for alcohol or contraceptives, songs in basal readers or history texts, cartoons in textbooks, texts that refer to the United States as a democracy rather than a republic, and "depressing thoughts." The last of the objections is truly depressing, apparently for censors and educators alike.

Teachers and librarians should remember that the announced objection may not always be the real objection. Censors have been known to attack Huxley's *Brave New World* or Orwell's *1984* for their sexual references only for others to discover that the real objection was to the frightening political attitudes the author displayed (or was thought to display). An attack on the language in John Howard Griffin's *Black Like Me* was only a subterfuge for one censor's hatred of blacks (and any minority group) as an investigation disclosed.

The underlying reasons for the announced reasons often are more significant than teachers or librarians may suspect. Parents worried about the moral climate facing their children are painfully aware that they apparently cannot change the material on television nor can they successfully fight the movies offered by local theatres nor can they do away with local "adult" bookstores. Whom then can they fight? What can they change? An easy answer—attack teachers and librarians and local schools to do away with materials that censors do not like.

Inflation, depressions, recessions, rising taxes, threats of nuclear war, gas prices, rising food costs, all these depress most of us most of the time. But there is little we can do to attack the gigantic problems spurred on by who knows what or whom. Either we give up or, in the case of censors, we strike back at the only vulnerable element in most communities, the schools. And why not attack schools, what with the rising militancy of teachers and the massive public criticism of schools' performances on SAT or ACT tests? Why not indeed? And censors attack.

◈ SOME COURT DECISIONS WORTH KNOWING ABOUT

Legal battles and court decisions often seem abstract and dull and irrelevant to practical matters for too many educators, but several court decisions have been significant and have affected thousands of educators who hardly knew the battles had taken place, much less their disposition. A brief run-through of two kinds of decisions, those involving attempts to define obscenity and its supposed influence on readers and viewers and those directly involving schools and school libraries, may be helpful to readers. The problem of extralegal battles will conclude this section.

Court Decisions About Obscenity and Attempting to Define Obscenity

Since censors frequently bandy the word *obscene* about in attacking books, teachers and librarians should know something about the history of courts vainly attempting to define the term.

While it was hardly the first decision involving obscenity, the first decision announcing a definition of and a test for obscenity came about in an English case in 1868. *The Queen v. Hicklin* (L.R. 3 Q.B. 360) concerned an ironmonger who was also an ardent anti-papist. He sold copies of *The Confessional Unmasked: Showing the Depravity of the Romish Priesthood, the Iniquity of the Confessional and the Questions Put to Females in Confession*, and though the Court agreed that his heart was pure, his publication was not. Judge Cockburn announced a test of obscenity which was to persist in British law for nearly a century and in American law until the 1930s:

> ◇ I think the test of obscenity is this, whether the tendency of the matter charged as obscenity is to deprave and corrupt those whose minds are open to such immoral influences, and into whose hands a publication of this sort may fall.

Clearly, but not exclusively, Cockburn was attempting to protect young people.

In 1913 in *United States v. Kennerly* (209 F. 119), Judge Learned Hand ruled against the defendant since his publication clearly fell under the limits of the Hicklin test, but he added:

◇ I hope it is not improper for me to say that the rule as laid down, however consonant it may be with mid-Victorian morals, does not seem to me to answer to the understanding and morality of the present time, as conveyed by the words, "obscene, lewd, or lascivious." I question whether in the end men will regard that as obscene which is honestly relevant to the adequate expression of innocent ideas, and whether they will not believe that truth and beauty are too precious to society at large to be mutilated in the interest of those most likely to pervert them to base uses.

Then in 1933 and 1934, two decisions (5 F. supp. 182 and 72 F. 2d 705) overturned much of the Hicklin test. James Joyce's *Ulysses* had been regarded as obscene by most legal authorities since its publication, largely for Molly Bloom's soliloquy. The novel was stopped by Customs officials and tried before Judge John M. Woolsey of the Federal District Court for Southern New York. Woolsey found the book "sincere and honest" and "not dirt for dirt's sake" and ruled that in matters determining what is obscene, the work *must* be judged as a whole, not on the basis of its parts. An appeal to the Federal Circuit Court of Appeals in 1934 led to Judge Learned Hand's upholding Woolsey's decision.

In 1957 in *Butler v. Michigan* (352 U.S. 380), Butler challenged a Michigan statute which tested obscenity in terms of its effect on young people, arguing that this restricted adult reading to that fit only for children. Mr. Justice Frankfurter agreed, and wrote:

◇ The State insists that, by thus quarantining the general reading public against books not too rugged for grown men and women in order to shield juvenile innocence, it is exercising its power to promote the general welfare. Surely, this is to burn the house to roast the pig. . . . The incidence of this enactment [the Michigan statute] is to reduce the adult population of Michigan to reading only what is fit for children.

Frankfurter agreed with Butler and declared the Michigan statute unconstitutional.

Later in 1957 in *Roth v. United States* (354 U.S. 476), the U.S. Supreme Court announced that obscenity was not protected by the Constitution, for "implicit in the history of the First Amendment is the rejection of obscenity as utterly without redeeming social importance." (That phrase, "without redeeming social importance" was to cause problems for several years thereafter.) Reading for the majority, Justice Brennan added a new definition of obscenity:

◇ Obscene material is material which deals with sex in a manner appealing to prurient interest.

And a new test:

◇ whether to the average person, applying contemporary community standards, the dominant theme of the material taken as a whole appeals to prurient interest.

Roth rejected the Hicklin test (already in patches) as "unconstitutionally restrictive of the freedoms of speech and press."

Jacobellis v. Ohio (84 S. Ct. 1676) in 1964 further refined the *Roth* test when Justice Brennan announced that the "contemporary community" standard referred to national standards, not local standards though Chief Justice Warren angrily dissented, arguing that community standards meant local and nothing more.

In 1966 in *Memoirs v. Attorney General of Massachusetts* (86 S. Ct. 975) Justice Brennan further elaborated on the *Roth* test:

> ◇ Under this definition, as elaborated in subsequent cases, three elements must coalesce: it must be established that (a) the dominant theme of the material taken as a whole appeals to a prurient interest in sex; (b) the material is patently offensive because it affronts contemporary community standards relating to the description or representation of sexual matters; and (c) the material is utterly without redeeming social value.

The *Ginsberg v. New York* (390 U.S. 692) decision in 1968 did not develop or alter the definition of obscenity, but it did introduce the concept of variable obscenity and caused some concern for librarians and English teachers. Ginsberg, who operated a stationery store and luncheonette, had sold "girlie" magazines to a sixteen-year-old boy in violation of a New York statute which declared illegal the sale of anything "which depicts nudity" and "was harmful" to anyone under seventeen years of age. Ginsberg maintained that New York State was without power to draw the line at the age of seventeen. The Court dismissed his argument, sustained the New York statute, and wrote:

> ◇ The well-being of its children is of course a subject within the State's constitutional power to regulate.

The Court futher noted, in lines that proved worrisome to anyone dealing in literature, classic or modern or what-have-you:

> ◇ To be sure, there is no lack of "studies" which purport to demonstrate that obscenity is or is not "a basic factor in impairing the ethical and moral development of . . . youth and a clear and present danger to the people of the state." But the growing consensus of commentators is that "while these studies all agree that a casual link has not been demonstrated, they are equally agreed that a causal link has not been disproved either."

Those words were lovingly quoted by censors across the nation, though few of them bothered to read the citations in the decision which suggested the dangers of assuming too much either way about the matter.

Then in 1973, five decisions were announced by the Court. The most important, *Miller v. California* (413 U.S. 15) and *Paris Adult Theatre II v. Slaton* (413 U.S. 49), enunciated a new (or more refined) test, one designed to remove all ambiguities from past tests and to endure. That the test proved as ambiguous and as difficult to enforce and understand as previous tests should come as no surprise to readers. After attacking the 1957 *Roth* test, the majority decision read by Chief Justice Burger in *Miller* provided this three-pronged test of obscenity:

> ◇ The basic guidelines for the trier of fact must be: (a) whether "the average person, applying contemporary community standards" would find that the work, taken as a whole, appeals to the prurient interest; (b) whether the work depicts or describes in a patently offensive way, sexual conduct specifically defined by the applicable state law; and (c) whether the work taken as a whole lacks serious literary, artistic, political or scientific value.

To guide state legislatures with "a few plain examples of what a state statute could define for regulation under the second part (b) of the standard announced in this opinion," the Court provided these:

> ◇ (a) Patently offensive representations or descriptions of ultimate sexual acts, normal or perverted, actual or simulated.
> (b) Patently offensive representations or descriptions of masturbation, excretory functions, and lewd exhibition of the genitals.

After this so-called "Miller catalogue," Burger announced that "contemporary community standards" meant state standards, not national standards.

Paris Adult Theatre II repeated and underscored *Miller* and added more worrisome words about the dangers of obscenity and what it can lead to. Chief Justice Burger, again, for the majority:

> ◇ But, it is argued, there is no scientific data which conclusively demonstrates that exposure to obscene material adversely affects men and woman or their society. It is urged on behalf of the petitioner that, absent such a demonstration, any kind of state regulation is "impermissible." We reject this argument. It is not for us to resolve empirical uncertainties underlying state legislation, save in the exceptional case where that legislation plainly impinges upon rights protected by the Constitution itself. . . . Although there is no conclusive proof of any connection between antisocial behavior and obscene material, the legislature of Georgia could quite reasonably determine that such a connection does or might exist.

In other words, no proof exists that obscenity does (or does not) lead to any certain antisocial actions (or nonactions), yet state legislatures can assume or guess that such a relationship may exist and pass legislation to that effect.

Justice Brennan dissented, noting that the dangers to "protected speech are very grave" and adding that the decision would not halt further cases before the Court:

> ◇ The problem is that one cannot say with certainty that material is obscene until at least five members of this Court, applying inevitably obscure standards, have pronounced it so.

To few observers' surprise, Brennan's prophecy proved correct.

On January 13, 1972, police in Albany, Georgia, seized the film *Carnal Knowledge* (starring Jack Nicholson) and charged the manager with violating a state statute against distributing obscene material. He was convicted in the Superior Court and the decision was affirmed by a divided vote in the Georgia State Supreme Court. In 1974, the U.S. Supreme Court announced its decision in *Jenkins v. the State of Georgia* (94 S. Ct. 2750), Justice Rehnquist reading the unanimous decision to reverse the Georgia Supreme Court opinion. Although *Carnal Knowledge* had been declared obscene by state standards and though it had a scene showing simulated masturbation, Rehnquist stated that "juries do not have unbridled discretion" in determining obscenity and that *Carnal Knowledge* had nothing which fell "within either of the two examples given in *Miller*."

The history of litigation and court decisions about obscenity and its definition are hardly models of clarity or consistency. Anyone interested in more details of this frustrating but fascinating story should read that marvelous book by Felice Flanery Lewis, *Literature, Obscenity and Law*.

Court Decisions About Teaching and School Libraries

If the implications of court decisions about obscenity are a bit vague, decisions about teaching and school libraries are not notably better. Courts are notoriously leery of decisions involving schools and libraries, but a few decisions, not unsurprisingly ambiguous, are worth noting about school libraries.

The U.S. Supreme Court had ruled in *Tinker v. the Des Moines (Iowa) School District* (393 U.S. 503) in 1969:

> ◇ First Amendment rights, applied in light of the special characteristics of the school environment, are available to teachers and students. It can hardly be argued that either students or teachers shed their constitutional rights to freedom of speech or expression at the schoolhouse gate.

But the Courts, federal or state, seemed unwilling to extend those rights to the school library in *Presidents Council, District 25 v. Community School Board No. 25* (457 F. 2d 289) in 1972. A New York City School Board voted 5-3 in 1971 to remove all copies of Piri Thomas' *Down These Mean Streets* from junior high libraries because of its offensive nature and language. The U.S. Court of Appeals, Second Circuit, held for the school board. The book, so the Court decided, had dubious literary or educational merit, and since the state had delegated the selection of school materials to local school boards and there was no evidence of basic constitutional impingement by the board, the Court saw no merit in the opposing view.

Presidents Council was cited for several years thereafter as the definitive decision, but since it was not a Supreme Court decision, it served as precedent only for judges so inclined. A different decision prevailed in *Minarcini v. Strongsville (Ohio) City School District* (541 F. 2d 577) in 1977. The school board refused to allow a teacher to use Heller's *Catch-22* or Vonnegut's *God Bless You, Mr. Rosewater*, ordered Vonnegut's *Cat's Cradle* and Heller's novel removed from the library, and proclaimed that students and teachers were not to discuss these books in class. The U.S. District Court found for the school board, but on appeal to the U.S. Circuit Court of Appeals, the three-member panel reversed the lower court. Judge Edwards focused on the main issues of the case in eloquent words widely quoted and much admired by school librarians:

◇ A library is a storehouse of knowledge. When created for a public school it is an important privilege created by the state for the benefit of the students in the school. That privilege is not subject to being withdrawn by succeeding school boards whose members might desire to "winnow" the library for books the content of which occasioned their displeasure or disapproval. Of course, a copy of a book may wear out. Some books may become obsolete. Shelf space alone may at some point require some selection of books to be retained and books to be disposed of. No such rationale is involved in this case.

The opinion of the Court that library books gained a tenure of sorts and could not easily be culled by a school board was at odds with the parallel U.S. Circuit Court in *Presidents Council*, but again, the Ohio decision served as precedent only if judges in other Federal District Courts (or Federal Appeals Courts) so wished to use it.

A year later in *Right to Read Defense Committee of Chelsea (Massachusetts) v. School Committee of the City of Chelsea* (454 F. Supp. 703) in the U.S. District Court for Massachusetts, another decision supported the rights of students and libraries. The librarian of Chelsea High School ordered and made available a paperback anthology, *Male and Female under 18*, containing a poem by a student, "The City to the Young Girl," which had, as the judge wrote, "street language." A parent felt the language was "offensive" and called the board chairman who happened also to be the editor of the local paper. The chairman-editor concluded that the poem was "filthy" and contained "offensive" language and should be removed from the library. He scheduled an emergency meeting of the school committee to consider the subject of "objectionable, salacious and obscene material being made available in books of the High School Library" and wrote an article for his newspaper about the matter concluding with these words:

◇ Quite frankly, I want a complete review of how it was possible for such garbage to even get on bookshelves where 14-year-old high school—ninth graders—could obtain them.

The superintendent urged caution and noted that the book could not be removed from the library without a formal review, but the chair was adamant. When the librarian argued that the poem was not obscene, the chair-editor wrote in his newspaper:

◇ [I am] shocked and extremely disappointed to have our high school librarian claim there is nothing lewd, lascivious, filthy, suggestive, licentious, pornographic or obscene about this particular poem in this book of many poems.

The school committee claimed "an unconstrained authority to remove books from the shelves of the school library." While the judge agreed that "local authorities are, and must continue to be, the principal policy makers in the public schools," he was more swayed by the reasoning in *Minarcini* than in *Presidents Council*. He wrote:

◇ The Committee was under no obligation to purchase *Male and Female* for the High School Library, but it did. . . . The Committee claims an absolute right to remove *City* from the shelves of the school library. It has no such right, and compelling policy considerations argue against any public authority having such an unreviewable power of censorship. There is more at issue here than the poem *City*. If this work may be removed by a committee hostile to its language and theme, then the precedent is set for removal of any other work. The prospect of successive school committees "sanitizing" the school library of views divergent from its own is alarming, whether they do it book by book or one page at a time.

What is at stake here is the right to read and be exposed to controversial thoughts and language—a valuable right subject to First Amendment protection.

What may prove to be the most significant decision about school libraries began in September 1975 when three members of the Island Trees (New York) School Board attended a conference sponsored by the conservative Parents of New York—United (PONY-U). After examining lists of books deemed "objectionable" by PONY-U, the three returned home, checked their district's school libraries, and found several suspect works—Bernard Malamud's *The Fixer*, Vonnegut's *Slaughterhouse-Five*, Desmond Morris' *The Naked Ape*, Piri Thomas' *Down These Mean Streets*, Langston Hughes edition of *Best Short Stories of Negro Writers*, Oliver LaFarge's *Laughing Boy*, Richard Wright's *Black Boy*, Alice Childress' *A Hero Ain't Nothin' But a Sandwich*, Eldridge Cleaver's *Soul on Ice*, and *Go Ask Alice*. In February 1976, the board gave "unofficial direction" that the books be removed from the library and delivered to the board for their reading.

Once the word got out, the board issued a press release attempting to justify its actions, calling the books "anti-American, anti-Christian, anti-Semitic, and just plain filthy" and argued:

> ◇ It is our duty, our moral obligation, to protect the children in our schools from this moral danger as surely as from physical or medical dangers.

When the board appointed a review committee—four members of the school staff and four parents—they politely listened to the report suggesting that five books should be returned to the shelves, two should be removed (*The Naked Ape* and *Down These Mean Streets*), and ignored their own chosen committee. (The board did return one book to the shelves, *Laughing Boy*, and placed *Black Boy* on a restricted shelf available only with parental permission.) Stephen Pico, a student, and others brought suit against the board claiming that their rights under the First Amendment had been denied by the board.

The U.S. District Court heard the case in 1979 and granted a summary judgment to the board. The Court held that the state had vested school boards with broad discretion to formulate educational policy, and the selection or rejection of books was clearly within their power. The Court found no merit in the First Amendment claims of Pico et al. A three-judge panel of the U.S. Court of Appeals for the Second Circuit (638 F. 2d 404) reversed the District Court's decision 2-1 and remanded the case for trial. The case then, though not directly, wended its way to the U.S. Supreme Court, the first such ever to be heard at that level.

In a strange and badly fragmented decision—and for that reason it is unclear just how certainly it will serve as precedent—Justice Brennan delivered the plurality (*not* majority) opinion in *Board of Education, Island Trees Union Free School District v. Pico* (102 S. Ct. 2799). He immediately emphasized the "limited nature" of the question before the court, for "precedents have long recognized certain constitutional limits upon the power of the State to control even the curriculum and classroom," and he further noted that *Island Trees* did not involve textbooks "or indeed any books that Island Trees students would be required to read." The case concerned only the removal, not the acquisition, of library books. He concluded the first section of his opinion by pointing out that the case concerned two questions:

> ◇ First, Does the First Amendment impose *any* limitations upon the discretion of petitioners to remove library books from the Island Trees High School and Junior High School? Second, If so, do the affidavits and other evidentiary materials before the District Court, construed most favorably to respondents, raise a genuine issue of fact whether petitioners might have exceeded those limitations?

Brennan proceeded to find for Pico (and ultimately for the library and the books):

> ◇ . . . . we think that the First Amendment rights of students may be directly and sharply implicated by the removal of books from the shelves of a school library.
>
> Petitioners emphasize the inculcative function of secondary education, and argue that they must be allowed *unfettered* discretion "to transmit community values" through the Island Trees schools. But that sweeping claim overlooks the unique role of the school library. . . . Petitioners might well defend their claim of absolute discretion in matters of *curriculum* by reliance upon their duty to inculcate community values. But we think that petitioners' reliance upon that duty is misplaced where, as here, they attempt to extend their claim of absolute discretion beyond the compulsory environment of the classroom, into the school library and the regime of voluntary inquiry that there holds sway.
>
> Petitioners rightly possess significant discretion to determine the content of their school libraries. But that discretion may not be exercised in a narrowly partisan or political manner. . . . Our Constitution does not permit the official suppression of ideas. Thus whether petitioners' removal of books from their school libraries denied respondents their First Amendment rights depends upon the motivation behind petitioners' actions. If petitioners *intended* by their removal decision to deny respondents access to ideas with which petitioners disagreed, and if this intent was the decisive factor in petitioners' decision, then petitioners have exercised their discretion in violation of the Constitution.

Four pages follow before Justice Blackmun's generally concurring opinion and Justices Burger, Rehnquist, Powell, and O'Connor offered their stinging dissents, but it is clear that school librarians won something, though precisely what and how much will need to be resolved by future court decisions.

It is equally clear that secondary teachers lost something in *Island Trees*. In an understandable ploy, the American Library Association, the New

York Library Association, and the Freedom to Read Foundation submitted an *Amicus Curiae* brief which sought to distinguish between the functions of the school classroom and the school library, a distinction that worked to the advantage of the school librarian but certainly not to that of the classroom teacher. Apparently, Brennan bought the argument as readers will see comparing Brennan's words with those from the brief below:

> ◇ This case, however, is about a library, not a school's curriculum. This is an extremely important distinction for the evaluation of the First Amendment interests at stake here.
>
> The school board below banned books from a library. Thus, this case does not present an issue concerning the board's control of curriculum, i.e., what is taught in the classroom. We freely concede that the school board has the right and duty to supervise the general content of the school's course of study.

Whether these words will cause serious disagreements between teachers and librarians remains to be seen. Certainly, that phrase, "we freely concede," has rankled a number of English teachers who recognized that *Island Trees* was a serious setback for intellectual freedom in the classroom.

Extralegal Decisions

Most censorship episodes do not result in legal hearings and court decisions. Teachers or librarians come under attack and unofficial rumor-mongering charges are lodged because someone objects and labels the offending work "obscene" or "filthy" or "pornographic." The case is heard in the court of public opinion, sometimes before the school board, with few legal niceties prevailing. The censors (and too often the school board) almost never operate under any definitions of obscenity that a court would recognize, but their interpretations of the issues are operationally effective for their purposes. The book may not always be judged as a whole book (though individual parts may be juicily analyzed), and the entire procedure may be arbitrary and capricious. With all its inherent sloppiness, the trial is speedier than a court hearing. The decision, once announced, rapidly disposes of the offending book and frequently the teacher or librarian to boot, a variation of old fashioned Western justice at work. Extralegal trials need not be cluttered with trivia like accuracy or reasoning or fairness or justice. Many of the eighteen censorship incidents described earlier in this chapter were handled extralegally.

Why would librarians or teachers allow their books and teaching materials to be so treated? Court cases cost money, lots of money, and unless a particular case is likely to create precedent, many lawyers would discourage educators from going to the courts. Court cases, even more important, cause friction among the community and—surprising to many neophyte teachers and librarians—cause almost equal friction among a school's faculty. A teacher or librarian who assumes that all fellow teachers will support a case for academic freedom or intellectual freedom is a fool. Many educators, to misuse the word, will have little sympathy for troublemakers or their causes. Others will be frightened at the prospect of possibly antagonizing their superiors. Others will "know their place" in the universe. Others are morally offended by anything stronger than "darn" and may regard most of modern literature (and old literature) as inherently immoral and therefore objectionable for high school students' use. Others will find additional or different reasons aplenty for staying out of the fray. And that, more likely than not, is the reason most censorship episodes do not turn into court cases.

◈ WHAT TO DO BEFORE AND AFTER THE CENSORS ARRIVE

Certain steps should be taken by librarians and teachers, preferably acting in concert, to prepare for censorship.

Before the Censors Arrive

Teachers and librarians should have some knowledge about the history of censorship and why citizens would wish to censor. They should keep up-to-date with censorship problems and court decisions and what books are coming under attack for what reason. That means they should read the *Newsletter on Intellectual Freedom, School Library Journal, English Journal, Wilson Library Bulletin, Top of the News,* and *Voice of Youth Advocates* along with other articles cited in the bibliography that concludes each issue of the *Newsletter.* A lot of work? Of course, but better than facing a censor totally ignorant of the world of censorship. Laziness and unprofessionalism are always easier than handling any job professionally.

They should develop clear and succinct statements, devoid of any educational or library or literary jargon, on why they teach literature or stock books. These statements ought to be made easily available to the public, partly to demonstrate educators' literacy—always an impressive beginning for an argument—and to make parents feel that someone intelligent works in the school, partly because teachers and librarians have a duty to communicate to the public what is going on and why it goes on.

They need to develop and publicize procedures for book selection, in the library or the classroom. Most parents have not the foggiest notion how educators go about selecting books, more or less assuming it comes about through sticking pins through a book catalogue. It might be wise to consider asking some parents to assist teachers and librarians in selection, partly to let parents learn how difficult the matter is, partly to use their ideas (which might prove surprisingly helpful).

They need to develop procedures for handling censorship should it occur. The National Council of Teachers of English monographs *The Students' Right to Read* and *The Students' Right to Know* should prove

◆ Some materials are essential for librarians and teachers who want to keep up-to-date on censorship.

helpful as should the American Library Association's *Intellectual Freedom Manual,* both for general principles and specific suggestions. Whether adopted from any of these sources or created afresh, the procedure should include a form to be completed by anyone who objects to any teaching material or library book, and a clearly defined way in which the matter will be handled after completion of the form (Will it go to a committee? How many are on the committee? Are people outside the school on the committee? How many teachers? Administrators?). The procedural rules must be openly available for anyone to consult, the procedures must apply to everyone (no exceptions should be allowed, no matter whether the complainant is the local drunk or the school board president), every complainant must be treated courteously and promptly, and the procedures must be approved by the school board. If the board does not approve the procedures, they have no legal standing. If the school board is not periodically reminded of the procedures—say, every couple of years—it may forget its obligation. Given the fact that many school boards will change membership slightly in three or four years and may change its entire composition within five or six, teachers and librarians should take it upon themselves to remind the board, else an entirely new board may wonder why it should support something it neither created nor particularly approves of.

Teachers who assign long works (other than texts) for common reading

THE PEOPLE BEHIND THE BOOKS

HARRY MAZER, Author

The Island Keeper
I Love You, Stupid
The Last Mission
The War on Villa Street

Realistic fiction for the young reader is under attack and so are its authors. For a decade there has been an exciting expansion of children's literature. "Forbidden" subjects were dealt with—sex, broken homes, violence, death. Like Pandora's box, once the lid was off more and more of what was hidden came to light. It was an exhilarating time for writers and I think for readers as well.

Now the lid is being pushed down by those who want pretty fictions, a return to a make-believe world. The call is out for safe books, light fiction, romances, pure entertainment.

And in the background, conglomerates, those crocodiles of business, with their narrow concerns for profit, are gobbling up publishing companies. We are seeing more nonbook books produced and marketed as products. It's not a good time for books, authors or readers.

I feel that I'm riding a dark wave. Sense tells me that things are not likely to improve soon, yet I think the need for realistic fiction is greater than ever. The world is not getting saner, calmer or more peaceful. Young readers need real books to make sense of the world, to validate their experience. So while there is little to crow about I remain hopefully committed to the realistic direction of adolescent fiction. ◆

The Island Keeper. Delacorte, 1981.
I Love You, Stupid. Harper & Row, 1981.
The Last Mission. Delacorte, 1979.
The War on Villa Street. Delacorte, 1978.

should write rationales, statements aimed at parents but open to anyone explaining why the teacher chose *1984* or *Silas Marner* or *Manchild in the Promised Land* or *Hamlet* for class reading and discussion. Rationales should answer the following though they should be written as informal essays, not answers to essay tests: (1) Why would the teacher use this book with this class at this time? (2) What specific objectives—not couched in behavioral terms unless the teachers are anxious to alienate parents— literary or pedagogical, is the teacher aiming at? (3) How will this book meet those objectives? (4) What problems of style, tone, theme, or subject matter exist and how will the teacher face them? Answering those questions should force teachers to take a fresh look at the book and think more carefully about the possibilities and problems inherent in the book. Rationales are *not* designed to protect the teacher by showing careful advance preparation before teaching, although clearly such rationales would be valuable should censorship strike. Rather, rationales should be written for public information easily available to the public as part of the professional responsibility of teachers. Diane Shugert offers a number of sample rationales in the Fall 1983 *Connecticut English Journal* and in "How to Write a Rationale in Defense of a Book" in James Davis' *Dealing with Censorship*.

Educators should woo the public to gain support for intellectual and academic freedom. Any community will have its readers and former teachers interested in students' freedom to read. Finding them ahead of time is part of teachers and librarians' jobs. Waiting until censorship strikes is too late. Pat Scales' ideas about working with parents in the November 1983 *Calendar* (distributed by the Children's Book Council) are most helpful. Scales was talking to a parent who helped in Scales' school library and who had picked up copies of Maureen Daly's *Seventeenth Summer* and Ann Head's *Mr. and Mrs. Bo Jo Jones* and wondered about students reading books with such provocative covers. Scales asked the mother to read the books before forming an opinion. From that experience came a program called "Communicate Through Literature" with monthly meetings to discuss with parents the reading that young adults do.

Educators should know censors' arguments, and they should prepare for the possible conflict almost as if they were preparing for a college debate. To know the opponents and their arguments is to assure educators of few surprises, though a few may occur no matter how extensive the preparation.

Finally, teachers and librarians should know the organizations that may be the most helpful should censorship strike. Diane Shugert's "A Body of Well-Instructed Men and Women: Organizations Active for Intellectual Freedom" in James Davis' *Dealing with Censorship* has a long list of such groups.

After the Censors Arrive

Teachers and librarians should begin by refusing to panic, easier said than done but essential. Censors always have one advantage. They can determine the time and the place for the attack. No matter how well prepared the teacher or the librarian, only the censor can say *when*. If educators have prepared, reasoned calm is essential for them, or they may say or do something they will later regret.

Educators should not be too surprised or appalled to discover that not all their fellow teachers or librarians will rush in with immediate support. If teachers and librarians will assume they represent the entire cause by themselves, they are far better off and considerably less likely to be instantly disillusioned.

Educators ought to urge the potential censors to talk first to the teacher or librarian in question before completing the complaint form, not to stall the objectors but to assure everyone of fair play all around. Teachers or librarians may discover what others have before, that objectors sometimes simply want to be heard and their complaints treated with dignity and dispatch. Sometimes, teachers and librarians may even be able to talk calmly—once the need to battle has died down—with the objectors and to reason with them, which is not exactly the same as convincing them that the teachers or librarians are necessarily right. The objectors may even see why the offending work was assigned or recommended, sometimes even seeing the difficulty in choosing a book for a class or an individual. Many teachers and librarians, though by no means all, agree that if parents ask that their child not be required to read a certain book, educators must agree to find a substitute book. If a substitute book is to be found and if it is to meet a different fate than the first book, parents must help in selecting the new book. Most objectors are deadly serious about their children's education, and they will understand why the substitute book should not be easier or shorter (thus rewarding the student) or harder and longer (thus unduly punishing the student). Finding another book approximately as long and as difficult as the original choice is no easy matter, but parents who demand substitutes must help, lest the teacher offend once more.

Librarians and teachers must treat objectors with every possible courtesy, though courtesy may not always be what educators first consider. Objectors should be expected to complete the school's forms detailing the objection, but the forms should be easily accessible and politely distributed. The complaint form should *never* be used to stall objectors. If it is so long that objectors get discouraged, the school may win one battle, but it will have produced one disgruntled citizen, and at school bond time, one irritated citizen and friends are quite enough to harm the cause of education.

Last, a committee (spelled out in detail prior to the censorship) meets to look at and discuss the complaint. After considering the problem though before arriving at a decision, the committee must meet with the teacher or librarian in question *and* the objectors to hear their cases. The committee will then make its decision and forward it to the highest administrator in the school who will forward it to the superintendent who will forward it to the school board. That body, already aware of the policy and procedures much earlier adopted to handle such matters, will consider this objection and make its decision, probably after at least one open meeting.

In no case and at no level should the actions of the educators or administrators or the school board be viewed as pro forma but rather thoughtfully considered actions to resolve a problem, not to create newer and bigger ones. Objectors should feel that they have been listened to and courtesy has been extended them at all levels and all stages.

We believe that the school—classroom or library—must be a center of intellectual ferment in the community. This does not imply that schools should be radical, just that they should be one place where freedom to think and inquire is protected, where ideas of all sorts can be considered, analyzed, investigated, discussed, and their consequences thought through. We believe librarians and English teachers must protect these freedoms, not merely in the abstract but in the practical day-by-day world of the school and library. To protect those freedoms we must fight censorship, for without them no education worthy of the name is possible.

◆ ACTIVITIES ◆

1. Using the advice and the examples in Diane Shugert's "How to Write a Rationale in Defense of a Book" in James E. Davis' *Dealing with Censorship*, write a two or three page, typed rationale for a work (novel or play or biography) you believe deserves to be taught in an English class. Direct your words to parents and avoid jargon.

2. Read one of the recent young adult novels about censorship, for example, Barbara Corcoran's *Strike* (Atheneum, 1983); Nat Hentoff's *The Day They Came to Arrest the Book* (Delacorte, 1982); Norma Howe's *God, the Universe, and Hot Fudge Sundaes* (Houghton Mifflin, 1984); Betty Miles' *Maudie and the Dirty Book* (Knopf, 1980); and John Neufeld's *A Small Civil War* (Fawcett Juniper, 1982). Analyze the book in terms of the likelihood of such censorship and the believability of the situation and the issues and people presented. Is the work a novel or a sociological commentary?

3. Select a court case summarized in this chapter. Read the entire case, background, legal opinions, and decision, and analyze the implications of the case and the decision for literature, for readers, and for education. Seek out background articles insofar as they are available in your library.

4. Select one book that has come under attack. Then browse through back issues of the *Newsletter on Intellectual Freedom* seeking other examples of censorship of this work. Write a brief paper explaining where and how and why the book has come under attack and what its probable future is for its use in English classes or libraries. (Hint: the *Newsletter* lists on the second page of each issue the books currently under attack.)

5. Skim through the past two years of the *Newsletter on Intellectual Freedom* to find the books most frequently under attack. List the twenty most likely to be watched by censors. Then check that list with the holdings of five or ten local high school libraries. Write a brief essay describing what you find.

6. If a censorship group operates in your area, interview the head of the group. Cautiously and politely, try to determine what kinds of materials the group objects to and why and what their past and present activities have been. If that is not possible, choose a censorship group and read as widely as possible about it, its aims and methods and accomplishments. Evaluate the group and its work in a brief essay.

◆ NOTES ◆

[1]Colin Campbell, "Book Banning in America," *New York Times Book Review*, December 20, 1981, p. 1.

[2]Comstock's life and work have been the subject of many books and articles. Heywood Broun and Margaret Leech's *Anthony Comstock: Roundsman of the Lord* (New York: Albert and Charles Boni, 1927) is amusing and nasty and still worth reading. A brief overview of Comstock's life can be found in Robert Bremner's introduction to the reprinting of *Traps for the Young* (Cambridge: Harvard University Press, 1967), pp. vii–xxxi. See also Paul S. Boyer's *Purity in Print: the Vice-Society Movement and Book Censorship in America* (New York: Charles Scribner's Sons, 1968) and Robert W. Haney's *Comstockery in America: Patterns of Censorship and Control* (Boston: Beacon Press, 1960).

[3]Arthur E. Bostwick, *The American Public Library* (New York: Appleton, 1910), pp. 130–31.

[4]*Library Journal* 21 (December 1896): 144.

[5]"Unexpurgated Shakespeare," *Journal of Education* 37 (April 13, 1883): 232.

[6]"What Books Do They Read?" *Common School Education* 4 (April 1890): 146–47.

[7]Evaline Harrington, "Why *Treasure Island?*" *English Journal* 9 (May 1920): 267–68.

[8]"Book Store Bans *Love Story*," "Teen Ga-

zette," *Phoenix Gazette*, April 3, 1971, p. 2.

9*Newsletter on Intellectual Freedom* 21 (July 1972): 105–106.

10*Newsletter on Intellectual Freedom* 21 (July 1972): 116.

11*Newsletter on Intellectual Freedom* 23 (May 1974): 32.

12*Newsletter on Intellectual Freedom* 22 (November 1973): 135.

13Widely reported. For a firsthand account by the teacher attacked, see Bruce Severy, "Scenario of Bookburning," *Arizona English Bulletin* 17 (February 1975): 68–74.

14*Newsletter on Intellectual Freedom* 23 (November 1974): 145.

15*Denver Post*, March 21, 1975.

16*Buffalo (New York) Courier-Express*, April 27, 1975. See also *Newsletter on Intellectual Freedom* 24 (May 1975): 75 and 24 (July 1975): 103.

17*Logan Leader* (Russellville, Logan County, Kentucky), November 10, 1975, p. 1.

18Widely reported. See *Newsletter on Intellectual Freedom* 25 (May 1976): 61–62.

19*Newsletter on Intellectual Freedom* 26 (July 1977): 101 and *St. Louis Post-Dispatch*, May 29, 1977, pp. 1, 5.

20*Newsletter on Intellectual Freedom* 27 (November 1978): 138, 144.

21*Newsletter on Intellectual Freedom* 30 (November 1981): 163.

22*Newsletter on Intellectual Freedom* 31 (March 1982): 43.

23William Trombley, "School Texts Called 'Primers for Rebellion,'" *Los Angeles Times*, July 30, 1982, pp. I-3, 22 and William Trombley, "Fresno Group Gets Textbooks Changed," *Los Angeles Times*, September 9, 1982, pp. II-1, 7.

24*Newsletter on Intellectual Freedom* 32 (March 1983): 39.

25*Newsletter on Intellectual Freedom* 33 (March 1984): 39.

26*San Francisco Examiner*, October 8, 1982, p. B-4.

27Louise Kingsbury and Lance Gurwell, "The Sin Fighters: Grappling with Gomorrah at the Grass Roots," *Utah Holiday* 12 (April 1983): 46.

28Lee Grant, "Shoot-out in Texas," Calendar section, *Los Angeles Times*, December 25, 1983, p. 21.

29*Phoenix Gazette*, June 10, 1981, p. SE-6.

30"Editorial," *Newsletter on Intellectual Freedom* 31 (January 1982): 4.

31*Newsletter on Intellectual Freedom* 32 (July 1983): 103.

32*Arizona Republic*, December 14, 1980, p. J-1.

33*Newsletter on Intellectual Freedom* 30 (March 1981): 29.

34*Newsletter on Intellectual Freedom* 30 (July 1981): 112.

35Sue Fontaine, "Dismissal with Prejudice," *Library Journal* 106 (June 15, 1981): 1273–77.

36Kingsbury and Gurwell, p. 52.

37*Educational Leadership* 37 (December 1980): 224–26.

38*Phi Delta Kappan* 64 (October 1982): 87–94; the responses are on pp. 94–98.

39In James E. Davis, editor, *Dealing with Censorship* (Urbana, Illinois: National Council of Teachers of English, 1979), pp. 117–124.

40*American Opinion* 25 (November 1982): 7–12, 71–78.

41(Old Tappan, New Jersey: Fleming H. Revell, 1980).

42(Washington, D. C.: The Heritage Foundation, 1978).

43(Washington, D.C.: The Heritage Foundation, 1976).

44(Cambridge: M.I.T. Press, 1977).

45(Buffalo: Prometheus Books, 1984).

46Bettye I. Latimer, "Telegraphing Messages to Children About Minorities," *Reading Teacher* 30 (November 1976): 155.

47*Arizona English Bulletin* 11 (February 1969): 37.

48Diane Shugert, "Censorship in Connecticut," *Connecticut English Journal* 9 (Spring 1978): 59–61.

49*School Library Journal* 21 (December 1974): 34.

50"The Upstairs Room: Room for Controversy," *School Library Journal* 20 (December 1973): 67.

51*Wilson Library Bulletin* 53 (December 1978): 340.

52*Wilson Library Bulletin* 53 (February 1979): 421.

53*Publishers Weekly* 215 (April 30, 1979): 24.

54Ken Donelson, "Censorship in the 1970s: Some Ways to Handle It When It Comes (and It Will)," *English Journal* 63 (February 1974): 47–51.

55"Protest Groups Exert Strong Impact," *Publishers Weekly* 216 (October 29, 1979): 42–44.

56"Sixty-Seven Targets of the Textbook Protesters," *Missouri English Bulletin* 38 (May 1980): 27–32.

◆ A STARTER BIBLIOGRAPHY ON CENSORSHIP ◆

Bibliographical Sources

McCoy, Ralph E. *Freedom of the Press: An Annotated Bibliography.* Southern Illinois University Press, 1968.

————. *Freedom of the Press: A Bibliocyclopedia Ten-Year Supplement.* Southern Illinois University Press, 1979.

Newsletter on Intellectual Freedom. A bi-monthly edited by Judith F. Krug with a sizable bibliography at the end of each issue. Available from the American Library Association, 50 East Huron Street, Chicago, Illinois 60611.

Books

Ahrens, Nyla H. *Censorship and the Teaching of English: A Questionnaire Survey of a Selected Sample of Secondary Teachers of English.* Dissertation, Teachers College, Columbia University, 1965.

Bosmajian, Haig A., ed. *Censorship: Libraries and the Law.* Neal-Schuman, 1983.

Boyer, Paul S. *Purity in Print: The Vice-Society and Book Censorship in America.* Charles Scribner's Sons, 1968.

Burress, Lee and Edward B. Jenkinson. *The Students' Right to Know.* National Council of Teachers of English, 1982.

Carrier, Esther Jane. *Fiction in Public Libraries, 1876–1900.* Scarecrow Press, 1965.

Censorship: 500 Years of Conflict. Oxford University Press, 1984. A marvelous collection.

Censorship Litigation and the Schools. American Library Association, 1983.

Cline, Victor B., ed. *Where Do You Draw the Line?* Brigham Young University Press, 1974.

Clor, Harry M. *Obscenity and Public Morality.* University of Chicago Press, 1969.

Daily, Jay E. *The Anatomy of Censorship.* Marcel Dekker, 1973.

Davis, James E., ed. *Dealing with Censorship.* National Council of Teachers of English, 1979.

DeGrazia, Edward, ed. *Censorship Landmarks.* R. R. Bowker, 1969. Censorship cases reprinted from 1663 through 1968. A basic source.

Downs, Robert B., ed. *The First Freedom.* American Library Association, 1960.

Ernst, Morris L. and Alan U. Schwartz. *Censorship: The Search for the Obscene.* Macmillan, 1964.

Fiske, Marjorie. *Book Selection and Censorship: A Study of School and Public Libraries in California.* University of California Press, 1968.

Geller, Evelyn. *Forbidden Books in American Public Libraries, 1876–1939: A Study in Cultural Change.* Greenwood Press, 1984.

Haight, Anne Lyons. *Banned Books*, 4th ed. R. R. Bowker, 1978.

Haney, Robert W. *Comstockery in America: Patterns of Censorship and Control.* Beacon Press, 1960.

Hefley, James C. *Textbooks on Trial.* Victor Books, 1976. A defense of Mel and Norma Gabler and their work.

Hentoff, Nat. *The First Freedom: The Tumultuous History of Free Speech in America.* Delacorte, 1980.

Intellectual Freedom Manual, 2nd ed. American Library Association, 1983. Basic for all the help it provides.

Jenkinson, Edward B. *Censors in the Classroom: The Mind Benders.* Southern Illinois University Press, 1979.

Kuh, Richard H. *Foolish Figleaves? Pornography in—and out of—Court.* Macmillan, 1967.

Lewis, Felice Flanery. *Literature, Obscenity and Law.* Southern Illinois University Press, 1976. The book on literature and its battles with various courts.

Limiting What Students Shall Read: Books and Other Learning Materials in Our Public Schools—How They Are Selected and How They Are Removed. Association of American Publishers, American Library Association, and Association for Supervision and Curriculum Development, 1981.

Nelkin, Dorothy. *Science Textbook Controversies and the Politics of Equal Time.* MIT Press, 1977.

Oboler, Eli M., ed. *Censorship and Education.* H. W. Wilson, 1981.

O'Neil, Robert M. *Classrooms in the Crossfire: The Rights and Interests of Students, Parents, Teachers, Administrators, Librarians and the Community.* Indiana University Press, 1981.

Rembar, Charles. *The End of Obscenity.* Random House, 1968.

Schauer, Frederick F. *The Law of Obscenity.* Bureau of National Affairs, 1976.

The Students' Right to Read. National Council of

Teachers of English, 1982.

Thomas, Cal. *Book Burning*. Crossway Books, 1983.

Thomas, Donald. *A Long Time Burning: The History of Literary Censorship in England*. Frederick A. Praeger, 1969.

Articles

"Are Libraries Fair? Pre-Selection Censorship in a Time of Resurgent Conservatism." *Newsletter on Intellectual Freedom* 31 (September 1982): 151, 181–88. Comments by Cal Thomas, Vice-President of the Moral Majority, and Nat Hentoff, *Village Voice* columnist and author of *The First Freedom*.

Arons, Stephen. "Book Burning in the Heartland." *Saturday Review* 9 (July 21, 1979): 24–29.

Asheim, Lester. "Not Censorship, But Selection." *Wilson Library Bulletin* 28 (September 1953): 63–67.

––––––––. "Selection and Censorship: A Reappraisal." *Wilson Library Bulletin* 58 (November 1983): 180–84.

Berninghausen, David K. "Antithesis in Librarianship: Social Responsibility vs. *The Library Bill of Rights*." *Library Journal* 97 (November 15, 1972): 3675–81.

––––––––. "Toward an Intellectual Freedom Theory for Users of Libraries." *Drexel Library Quarterly* 18 (Winter 1982): 57–81.

Booth, Wayne C. "Censorship and the Values of Fiction." *English Journal* 53 (March 1964): 155–64.

Bostwick, Arthur E. "The Librarian as Censor." *Library Journal* 33 (July 1908): 257–64.

Boyle, Robert (S.J.). "Literature and Pornography." *Catholic World* 193 (August 1961): 295–302.

Bradley, Julia Turnquist. "Censoring the School Library: Do Students Have the Right to Read?" *Connecticut Law Review* 10 (Spring 1978): 747–75.

Briley, Dorothy. "Are Editors Guilty of Precensorship?" *School Library Journal* 29 (October 1982): 114–15.

Broderick, Dorothy. "Censorship—Reevaluated." *School Library Journal* 18 (November 1971): 30–32.

Brodinsky, Ben. "The New Right: The Movement and Its Impact." *Phi Delta Kappan* 64 (October 1982): 87–94. See also the responses following Brodinsky's article by Onalee McGraw, Mel and Norma Gabler, and others.

Bryant, Gene. "The New Right and Intellectual Freedom." *Tennessee Librarian* 33 (Summer 1981): 19–24.

Bundy, Mary Lee and Teresa Stakem. "Librarians and Intellectual Freedom: Are Opinions Changing?" *Wilson Library Bulletin* 56 (April 1982): 584–89.

Burger, Robert H. "The Kanawha County Textbook Controversies: A Study of Communication and Power." *Library Quarterly* 48 (April 1978): 143–62.

Burress, Lee A. "How Censorship Affects the School." Wisconsin Council of Teachers of English, *Special Bulletin No. 8*. October 1963, 1–23.

Campbell, Colin. "Book Banning in America." *New York Times Book Review*, December 20, 1981, pp. 1, 16–18.

"Censorship: Don't Let It Become an Issue in Your Schools." *Language Arts* 55 (February 1978): 230–42.

Donelson, Kenneth L. "Shoddy and Pernicious Books and Youthful Piety: Literary and Moral Censorship, Then and Now." *Library Quarterly* 51 (January 1981): 4–19.

Edwards, Margaret A. "Mrs. Grundy, Go Home." *Wilson Library Bulletin* 33 (December 1958): 304–305.

Eudy, Lisa L. "The Influence of the Moral Majority on Public Library Censorship." *Southeastern Libraries* 31 (Fall 1981): 97–101.

"Expurgation Practices of School Book Clubs." *Voice of Youth Advocates* 6 (December 1983): 268–69.

FitzGerald, Frances. "A Disagreement in Baileyville." *New Yorker* 59 (January 16, 1984): 47–90.

Geller, Evelyn. "Intellectual Freedom: Eternal Principles or Unanticipated Consequences?" *Library Journal* 99 (May 15, 1974): 1364–67.

––––––––. "The Librarian as Censor," *Library Journal* 101 (June 1, 1976): 1255–58.

Glatthorn, Allan A. "Censorship and the Classroom Teacher." *English Journal* 66 (February 1977): 12–15.

Goldstein, S. R. "Asserted Constitutional Rights of Public School Teachers to Determine What They Teach." *University of Pennsylvania Law Review* 124 (June 1976): 1293–1357.

Groves, Cy. "Book Censorship: Six Misunderstandings." *Alberta English '71* 11 (Fall 1971): 5–7.

Harvey, James A. "Acting for Children?" *School Library Journal* 20 (February 1973): 26–29.

Hentoff, Nat. "Any Writer Who Follows Anyone Else's Guidelines Ought to Be in Advertising." *School Library Journal* 24 (November 1977): 27–29.

————. "Censorship in the Schools." *Learning* 9 (March 1981): 78–81.

————. "When Nice People Burn Books." *Progressive* 47 (February 1983): 42–44.

Hillocks, George, Jr. "Books and Bombs: Ideological Conflicts and the School—A Case Study of the Kanawha County Book Protest." *School Review* 86 (August 1978): 632–54.

Hirschoff, Mary-Michelle Upson. "Parents and the Public School Curriculum: Is There a Right to Have One's Child Excused from Objectionable Instruction?" *Southern California Law Review* 50 (1977): 871–959.

Janeczko, Paul. "How Students Can Help Educate the Censors." *Arizona English Bulletin* 17 (February 1975): 78–80.

Kamhi, Michelle Marder. "Censorship vs. Selection—Choosing the Books Our Children Shall Read." *Educational Leadership* 39 (December 1981): 211–15.

Keresey, Gayle. "School Book Club Expurgation Practices." *Top of the News* 40 (Winter 1984): 131–38.

Kingsbury, Louise and Lance Gurwell. "The Sin Fighters: Grappling with Gomorrah at the Grass Roots." *Utah Holiday* 12 (April 1983): 42–61.

Kneer, Leo B. and Clement Stacey. "Censorship: A Publisher's View." *Arizona English Bulletin* 17 (February 1975): 102–106.

Krislov, Samuel. "From Ginzburg to Ginsberg: The Unhurried Children's Hour in Obscenity Litigation" in Philip B. Kurland, ed., *The Supreme Court Review, 1968.* University of Chicago Press, 1968, pp. 153–97.

Martin, William. "The Guardians Who Slumbereth Not." *Texas Monthly* 10 (November 1982): 145–50.

Niccolai, F. R. "Right to Read and School Library Censorship." *Journal of Law and Education* 10 (January 1981): 23–26.

Nocera, Joseph. "The Big Book-Banning Brawl." *New Republic* 187 (September 13, 1982): 20, 22–25.

O'Malley, William J. (S.J.) "How to Teach 'Dirty' Books in High School." *Media and Methods* 4 (November 1967): 6–11.

O'Neil, Robert M. "Libraries, Liberties and the First Amendment." *University of Cincinnati Law Review* 42 (1973): 209–52.

Orleans, Jeffrey H. "What Johnny Can't Read: 'First Amendment Rights' in the Classroom." *Journal of Law and Education* 10 (January 1981): 1–15.

"Rationales for Commonly Challenged Taught Books." *Connecticut English Journal* 15 (Fall 1983): entire issue.

Reed, Michael. "What Johnny Can't Read: School Boards and the First Amendment." *University of Pittsburgh Law Review* 42 (Spring 1981): 653–67.

Rodgers, Harrell R., Jr. "Censorship Campaigns in Eighteen Cities: An Impact Analysis." *American Politics Quarterly* 2 (October 1976): 371–92.

Rush, Betsy. "Weeding and Censorship: Treading a Fine Line." *School Library Journal* 21 (November 1974): 42–43.

Serebnick, Judith. "Book Reviews and the Selection of Potentially Controversial Books in Public Libraries." *Library Quarterly* 51 (October 1981): 390–409.

————. "The 1973 Court Rulings on Obscenity: Have they Made a Difference?" *Wilson Library Bulletin* 50 (December 1975): 304–10.

————. "Self-Censorship by Librarians: An Analysis of Checklist-Based Research." *Drexel Library Quarterly* 18 (Winter 1982): 35–56.

Small, Robert C., Jr. "Censorship and English: Some Things We Don't Seem to Think About Very Often (But Should)." *Focus* 3 (Fall 1976): 18–24.

Stielow, Frederick J. "Censorship in the Early Professionalization of American Libraries, 1876 to 1929." *Journal of Library History* 18 (Winter 1983): 37–54.

Taylor, Kenneth I. "Are School Censorship Cases Really Increasing?" *School Library Media Quarterly* 11 (Fall 1982): 26–34.

Watson, Jerry J. and Bill C. Snider. "Educating the Potential Self-Censor." *School Media Quarterly* 9 (Summer 1981): 272–76.

West, Celeste. "The Secret Garden of Censorship: Ourselves." *Library Journal* 108 (September 1, 1983): 1651–53.

Whaley, Elizabeth Gates. "What Happens When You Put the Manchild in the Promised Land? An Experiment with Censorship." *English Journal* 63 (May 1974): 61–65.

Williams, Patrick and J. T. Pearce. "Common Sense and Censorship: A Call for Revision." *Library Journal* 98 (September 1, 1973): 2401–2402.

Woods, L. B. "The Most Censored Materials in the U.S." *Library Journal* 103 (November 1, 1978): 2170–73.

P·A·R·T F·O·U·R

LESSONS FROM THE PAST

1 8 0 0 - 1 9 0 0

◈

A CENTURY OF PURITY WITH A FEW PASSIONS

Prior to 1800, literature read by children and young adults consisted largely of a few religious novels and many pietistic tracts. They advanced the belief that the young were merely small adults who must, like larger adults, accept the brevity of mortal life and God's judgment soon to come.

By 1800, the United States was no longer a vision but a real and stable country. The attitude toward young people gradually changed during the first half of the nineteenth century for several reasons—our rapid national expansion in territory and population, widespread immigration, and the slow but certain evolution from agrarian to urban society. Developments in medical knowledge led to a decrease in infant mortality and longer life expectancy, which, along with slowly evolving changes in life-style, encouraged a more secular education and reduced the need for children to begin working at the age of thirteen or fourteen. The parental duty to prepare small adults for death slowly became an equally intense parental duty to prepare young people for the role of patriotic and Christian adults.

The newer literature remained pious and somber, but it increasingly hinted at the possibility of humanity's experiencing a satisfying life here on earth. One could participate in responsibilities, work, family life, and even some joy before death. Books continued to reflect adult ideas and fashions, but of this world, not merely the next.

It was a time of change, an early version of Toffler's "future shock" with cultural changes everywhere. Society moved, often without noticing, from a simple to a far more complex society.

The abolitionist movement and the eventual legal emancipation of black people and the women's suffrage movement began our moral commitment to social consciousness. The westward expansion, the rise and decline of Indian wars in the West, and the growth of railroad transportation drastically changed the country. The Industrial Revolution along with the growth of the cities produced an urbanized society. Giants of industry appeared, and others lurked over the horizon. Cities had not yet produced anyone like a Boss Tweed, but corruption and slums were well on their way. Education became more popular and more accessible, not yet mass education, but education available to more people. The public library became an important part of many towns.

The Protestant ethic rode high. If God put mortals on earth to work hard to suit His purpose, it followed that there was nothing evil but much potential good in working hard for material success. Material success, so the argument went, implied wealth to advance God's plan on earth, and that easily led to idealism about and exaltation of successful businessmen. The rise of men not necessarily of the best families but successful in the hard world of business fostered the spirit of democracy. Could anything be more democratic than the steady rise to conspicuous wealth of bright, energetic, and Christian young men?

Literature written specifically for young adults reflected the Protestant ethic and the need for hard work to assure happiness and wealth. Protagonists in Horatio Alger's novels were so desperately imbued with the Protestant ethic that they risked becoming crashing bores, but Alger's novels provided ideals and impetus for thousands of young men and women. There were no limits to the future of the young man willing to strive, for to strive was to succeed, or so went the popular belief.

Literature aimed at young women, and most adult women, emphasized home and family responsibilities, for women were expected to find solace and satisfaction in love, husband, children, and home. However, in some books there were subtle hints, some not so subtle, that women had brains and feelings along with responsibilities.

More literature was written for young adults than ever before. An increasingly secularized society produced writers aware that love, adventure, work, and recreation existed in the real world of young people, and that these could provide useful themes in books. A new kind of novel began to appear aimed somewhat less obviously at moralizing and instructing and more at interesting the young adult. If moral lessons were still there, they were less direct, less immediate, less heavenly. Getting ahead in life, possibly even enjoying some aspects of life, became a central theme.

It was a changing time, an exciting time, a dangerous time to be alive. Life changed and literature changed and neither could go back to the simplicity of an earlier day. Some wept over the change, some worried over it, but most accepted its inevitability.

◈ **MORAL WRITERS AND MORAL BOOKS**

While major writers, notably eighteenth-century novelists Henry Fielding, Tobias Smollett, and Laurence Sterne, were ignored and despised for their lack of obvious moral tone, other writers of the eighteenth and early nineteenth century became staples for the young.

Hannah More and her many tracts, especially *Repository Tracts* (1795–98) with its "The Shepherd of Salisbury Plain," *Moral Sketches* (1819), and *Coelebs in Search of a Wife* (1809), became a necessary, sometimes soporific, but certainly moralistic part of every young person's reading. Almost equally popular was Maria Edgeworth whose *The Parent's Assistant* (1796), *Moral Tales for Young People* (1801), *Harry and Lucy* (1801), *Popular Tales* (1804), *Rosamund* (1821), *Frank* (1822), and *Harry and Lucy Concluded* (1825) sold well though none had the least literary merit compared to her *Castle Rackrent* (1800) for adults. Thomas Day remained popular for years through his edifying and moralizing *The History of Sanford and Merton* (1783, 1786, 1789), one of the great exercises of literary persiflage of its time or any other time. Mason Locke Weems, better known as Parson Weems, published his popular if inaccurate and sugar-coated *A History of the Life and Death, Virtues and Exploits, of General George Washington* (1800), later altered to *The Life of Washington the Great* (1806), and finally altered to *The Life of George Washington* (1808).

But three books led all the rest in number of readers. John Bunyan's *The Pilgrim's Progress from This World to That Which Is to Come* (Part I, 1678; Part II, also 1678) was predictably popular, a religiously symbolic account of Christian, who flees his doomed city and journeys to the Celestial City. Pleased as adults could be with the pious lessons, Christian's travails through the Slough of Despond, the Valley of Humiliation, the Valley of the Shadow of Death, Vanity Fair, and the Country of Beulah could easily be read by young people as melodrama and adventure. Religious, perhaps, but also exciting, a fictional ambiguity pleasing to both young and old and insuring the steady popularity of the book. Part II, in which Christian's wife, Christiana, flees the city with similar adventures, was never quite so popular.

Daniel Defoe was close behind Bunyan in popularity, not of course for *Moll Flanders* (1722) or *Roxanna* (1724), but for *The Life and Strange Surprising Adventures of Robinson Crusoe* (1719) based on the true story of Alexander Selkirk, marooned in 1704 at his own request on the uninhabited island of Juan Fernandez until his rescue in 1709. The life was strange, the adventures of Crusoe were surprising, and the book proved a permanent addition to libraries of both young and old, probably because the book was ostentatiously sermonistic and demonstrated that a civilized white person could defeat a hostile environment and ignorant savages. Crusoe's ability to survive, to find a purpose for his existence, and to discover God everywhere pleased many while the numerous, practical details about housebuilding and gardening endeared him to others.

The third book remains something of an enigma. Jonathan Swift was hardly a model writer for pious young people. His *A Tale of Tub* (1704) and his often scatological poetry and prose made him an unlikely candidate for literary sainthood in early nineteenth-century America. *Gulliver's Travels* (1726) seemed as unlikely to gain admittance to American homes, but the book is such that it can be read by the young (usually in expurgated and emasculated editions) as a fantasy and by adults as misanthropic satire. Even then it remains puzzling that Lemuel Gulliver's travels to Lilliput and Brobdingnag did not merely escape attack but were highly praised. Presumably, young people did not realize how Gulliver put out the fire in the Queen's palace in Book I nor were they aware of some of the unpleasant aspects of Book II, much less the voyage to the land of the Houyhnhnms with its indictment of humans as Yahoos for their filth and evil.

These three books must have seemed refreshing indeed for young readers compared to two writers who wrote specifically for young people, Samuel Goodrich and Jacob Abbott.

Under the pen name Peter Parley, Goodrich wrote 170 books from 1827 through 1850, selling more than seven million copies. He revealed in his 1856 autobiography, *Recollections of a Lifetime, or Men and Things I Have Seen*, that as a child he had disliked fairy stories and Mother Goose rhymes because they were frightening and untrue. He liked *Robinson Crusoe* as an honest and moral book, but he loved Hannah More's "The Shepherd of Salisbury Plain" in *Repository Tracts* and later vowed to write American books emulating her work. His fiction proved to be every bit as compelling as Hannah More's, just as surely as it was moral.

In 1827, he published his first book, *The Tales of Peter Parley about America*. Parley, an old man who is the focal point of this and the remainder of the series, tells stories of New England and its history to admiring children who gather to hear him ramble on and on. In the next four years, Goodrich produced eleven other Peter Parleys, all emphasizing the American view of life and history.

Abbott studied for the Congregational ministry and later served as professor of mathematics and natural philosophy at Amherst and as a minister in Roxbury, Massachusetts. In 200 or more books, Abbott set out with a vengeance to plant seeds of morality and education in the vineyard of childhood. Most famous were his twenty-eight Rollo books beginning in 1834. The title of the 1838 *Rollo at Work, or The Way for a Boy to Learn to Be Industrious* sounds the tenor and tone of the series. Only slightly less priggish than the Peter Parley books, they remain sticky and stilted, staggering in terms of what Abbott believed boys were intended to be—all serious, all decent, kind, and thoughtful, all perfect or at least easily perfectible, all unlike any real boy this side of fiction. *Rollo at School* (1839) continues to mine this strain, but later books taking Rollo abroad (some unkind American readers maintained that that was where he should stay) are more entertaining since they force Rollo and Abbott to look for new territories and ideas. *Rollo on the Atlantic* (1853), *Rollo in London* (1855), *Rollo in Rome* (1858), and their ilk made Rollo seem a veritable boy Baedeker, but their sugar-coated geography lessons in the midst of a saccharin plot made them palatable and even popular.

The world had changed by the 1860s and young adults were being exposed (or exposing themselves) to far more secular literature. Morality was paraded forth in the guise of sentimentalism and melodrama, but whether the morality was real or superficial was a question in the minds of many parents, educators, and clergymen. Young adults read first and worried about the morality of the literature second just as people have done throughout history.

◆ DOMESTIC NOVELS

In 1855, Nathaniel Hawthorne wrote his publisher bitterly lamenting the state of American literature:

> ◇ America is now wholly given over to a d--d mob of scribbling women, and I should have no chance of success while the public taste is occupied with their trash—and should be ashamed of myself if I did succeed. What is the mystery of these innumerable editions of *The Lamplighter,* and other books neither better nor worse?—worse they could not be, and better they need not be, when they sell by the 10,000?[1]

The trash was the domestic novel, the best-selling literature from 1850 through the 1870s. Born out of a belief that humanity was redeemable, the domestic novel preached morality; woman's submission to man; the value of cultural, social, and political conservatism; a religion of the heart and the Bible; and the glories of suffering.

Many domestic novels concern a young girl, usually orphaned and placed in the home of a relative or other benefactor, who soon meets a darkly handsome young man with dark shadows lurking in his past, a man not easily trusted but one eventually worth redeeming and loving. Melodramatic devices were commonplace—mysterious deaths, illnesses, sobbing women, malevolent men, instinctive benevolence, strange figures, forged letters, disappearing wills, frightened virgins, and somnambulism and trances—each novelist finding it necessary to provide greater thrills than her previous novel or that of any previous novelist. Domestic novels provided moral lessons in the midst of gothic thrills, but they soon created heroines with a love-hate feeling about men, ambivalently frightening, erotic, and attractive to female readers and puzzling if not appalling to male readers.

Heroines differed more in name than in characteristics. Uniformly submissive to—yet distrustful of—their betters and men, they were self-sacrificing and self-denying beyond belief, interested in the primacy of the family unit and a happy marriage as the goal of all decent women. They abhorred sin generally, but particularly divorce, alcohol, tobacco, and adultery.

Domestic novels were a product of the religious sentiment of the time, the espousal of traditional virtues, and the anxieties and frustrations of women trying to find a role in a changing society. These novels became weapons against a male-dominated society and the first American glimmer of feminist literature.

The promise and problems of domestic novels are apparent in the writings of Susan Warner, creator of the genre, and Augusta Jane Evans Wilson, whose *St. Elmo* was one of the all-time best-sellers.

Writing under the pen name of Elizabeth Wetherell, Susan Warner produced more than twenty novels. *The Wide, Wide World* (1850), her best-known novel, was claimed in the 1890s as one of the four most widely read books in England along with the Bible, *Pilgrim's Progress*, and *Uncle Tom's Cabin*, and was still read in the early 1900s. An abridged edition was published in England in 1911, and an abridged and illustrated edition was published by the University of London Press in 1950.

Her manuscript was at first rejected by several New York publishers. George Putnam was also ready to send it back but decided to ask his mother to read it. The next morning she said, "If you never publish another book, George, publish this." Putnam followed her advice, and the book was out in time to attract the Christmas trade. Sales were slow at first, though critical praise was high, but sales picked up and the first edition sold out in four months. Translations into French, German, Swedish, and Italian followed. English sales exceeded those of any previous American novel, and, by 1852, *The Wide, Wide World* was in its fourteenth printing.

The author's life paralleled that of her heroine, Ellen Montgomery. Warner's father was pathetically unable to provide, and the household was barren, bitter, and deadly serious. Ellen's family life is not so penurious, but her mother dies early and her father is consumed with serious business matters and determines to leave Ellen with Aunt Fortune Emerson. The aunt is not gladdened by the news and a mutual distaste develops. Ellen, to her aunt's displeasure, forms a firm, if platonic, friendship with Mr. Van Brunt, Fortune Emerson's intended, and an even more significant friendship with Miss Alice, daughter of the local minister, who showers Ellen with pity and piety and all that Ellen cannot find in her aunt's home. Unhappily for Alice, but happily for the moral good of the reader, Alice is doomed—she is too good for this world—and in a deathbed scene highly admired by readers old and young, Alice dies. She is followed by her brother John, a divinity student, who replaces Alice's sermons with his own. Later, Ellen's father dies, and tears flow before and after. In this first of many lachrymose domestic novels, Ellen cries at every turn: she "almost shrieked," "answered with a gush of tears," "burst into tears," "sobbed," "mingled bitter tears with eager prayers," "drew long, sobbing sighs," "watered the rock with tears," and "burst into violent grief." Warner's novel taught morality, the dangers of self-righteousness, and the virtues of submission and religion. Despite its weepy and moralistic nature—perhaps because of it—it was incredibly successful. E. Douglas Branch called it, "The greatest achievement of any of the lady novelists."[2]

Augusta Jane Evans Wilson may well have been the most popular writer of the domestic school for her *St. Elmo* (1867). No other novel so literally touched the American landscape—thirteen towns were named or renamed St. Elmo, as were hotels, railway coaches, steamboats, one kind of punch, and a brand of cigars. Every home seemed to have a copy. Edition after edition was printed, and some indication of the number of copies sold may

◆ Despite its weepy and moralistic nature, *The Wide, Wide World* (1850) was incredibly successful.

be gauged by a notice in a special edition of *St. Elmo* that it was "limited to 100,000 copies." Only *Uncle Tom's Cabin* exceeded it in sales, and Wilson was more than once called by her admirers, the American Brontë. Men and women publicly testified that their lives had been permanently changed for the better by reading the book.

Edna Earl, heroine of *St. Elmo* and the daughter of a village blacksmith, is orphaned by the death of her father and bereft at the death of her grandfather. Rescued from a train wreck by snobbish and wealthy Mrs. Murray who sets out to raise Edna as her daughter, she finds herself in the same house with St. Elmo Murray, her benefactor's son, an evil and self-centered man who has not only killed another in a duel but has a well-deserved reputation as a seducer. St. Elmo takes one look at Edna and leaves home for four years. Pastor Allan Hammond becomes Edna's friend and teacher. When St. Elmo returns, Edna has Greek, Latin, Sanskrit, Chaldee, Hebrew, and Arabic firmly in hand. Fascinated by Edna, if not by her learning, St. Elmo falls in love, but she despises and rejects him. Edna turns to writing and becomes a successful novelist. The once arrogant and thwarted St. Elmo continues his courtship but is always rejected until he becomes a Christian and finally a minister. They marry, another wicked man reformed by a good woman; another woman proves her innate superiority to man.

◈ DIME NOVELS

Dime novels were as popular as domestic novels (and condemned as strongly) but with quite a different audience. James Fenimore Cooper's *Leatherstocking Tales* and some adventure writing of the early nineteenth century, tales of Indians, pirates, and mysteries, influenced the subject matter of dime novelists. But it was left to Boston publisher Maturin Murray Ballou to set the physical (and to some degree the emotional) pattern. His sensational novels were usually fifty pages, eight-and-a-half inches by five inches, often illustrated with a lurid hand-colored wood-cut. With wild tales by writers like Edward S. Ellis and Ned Buntline (soon to be staple writers of dime novels), they were a bargain at twenty-five cents.

Beadle and Adams Appear on the Scene

In 1858, Erastus Beadle and his brother Irwin, successful publishers of sheet music in Buffalo, moved to New York City, and with Robert Adams, formed the company of Beadle and Adams, destined for years to be the most successful purveyors of dime novels.

In June 1860, Beadle and Adams published Mrs. Ann S. Stephens' *Malaeska: The Indian Wife of the White Hunter*, probably with the help of Orville J. Victor, the resident editorial genius who guided many dime novels to success. Mrs. Stephens had originally published her novel in 1839 in *The Ladies' Companion*, which she edited, but the reprinting made Beadle and Adams famous and guaranteed her future employment as a dime novelist. Published in a salmon-colored wrapper, *Malaeska* was given the spectacular promotion readers soon associated with Beadle and Adams. On June 7, 1860, an advertisement appeared in the *New York Tribune*:

BOOKS FOR THE MILLIONS

A dollar Book for a dime!
128 pages complete, only ten cents! ! !
MALAESKA
The
Indian Wife of the White Hunter
by Mrs. Ann Stephens
Irwin P. Beadle and Co., Publishers

Curious readers buying the six by four inches, 128-page book may have been uncertain about just what they were getting, but what they got was good enough, and 65,000 copies were sold.

A bald plot summary makes the first dime novel appear incredibly melodramatic and crude. Malaeska marries a white hunter who, when he is dying, tells his Indian wife to take their child from the wilds of upper New York state to his wealthy parents in New York City. The parents accept the child, and Malaeska remains, for a time, known to him as his nurse. She tries to kidnap the boy to take him home but fails and goes back alone to the woods and her tribe. Her son, not knowing his parents, grows up hating Indians. Later, Malaeska identifies herself to him, and he commits suicide. She dies the next day on her husband's grave. Melodramatic it may have been, but it was also fast-moving, thrilling, exotic—all for ten cents. Mass literature, priced for the masses, had arrived.

Other successes followed, but the eighth dime novel topped all previous efforts after an intriguing promotional campaign. On October 1, 1860, the *New York Tribune* carried this simple and intriguing ad, sans company, sans price, sans author:

> ◇ Seth Jones is from New Hampshire.
> Seth Jones understands the redskins.
> Seth Jones answers a question.
> Seth Jones strikes a trail.
> Seth Jones makes a good roast.
> Seth Jones writes a letter.
> Seth Jones objects to sparking.
> Seth Jones is in his element.
> Seth Jones takes an observation.
> Seth Jones can't express himself.

On October 2, 1860, the *New York Tribune* carried another ad, still not listing the company involved.

> ◇ Seth Jones; or, The Captives of the Frontier.
> For sale at all the news depots.

Seth Jones was published that day to 60,000 readers. At least 500,000 copies were sold over the years in the United States alone, and it was translated into ten languages. Contrary to later journals, which damned dime novels often without reading them, contemporary reviews were good, even at times enthusiastic. Four years after the publication of *Seth Jones*, reviewer William Everett wrote:

> ◇ Mr. E. S. Ellis' *Seth Jones* and *Trail Hunters* are good, very good. Mr. Ellis' novels are favorites and deserve to be. He shows variety and originality in his characters; and his Indians are human beings, and not fancy pieces.[3]

This book was not the first by Edward S. Ellis, who had written for Ballou, but *Seth Jones* made him famous and insured his financial success even after he stopped writing dime novels and turned to writing what turned out to be an incredible number of boys' books. *Seth Jones* takes place near the close of the eighteenth century. Seth, once a scout in the Revolutionary War, comes to Alfred Haverland's clearing in western New York state to announce the nearby Indians are ready for the warpath. In the attack, Haverland's sixteen-year-old daughter, Ina, is captured, and Seth, along with Ina's sweetheart, goes off on the rescue. At the end of the story Seth is revealed as aristocratic Eugene Morton in search of his lost fiancée. A double wedding, Seth and his love, Ina and hers, concludes the book.

Seth Jones would not have been enough to maintain Beadle and Adams' success by itself, but it served as a prototype, and dime novels numbering about 600 from this publisher alone reaffirmed the success of *Seth Jones*. Beadle and Adams revolutionized some aspects of the publishing trade. They spent more money on advertising than other companies, they made advertising pay and made it respectable, and they knew how to merchandise their products.

◆ *Seth Jones*, published in 1860, served as a prototype for other dime novels.

Other Companies Get into the Act

Beadle and Adams did not long monopolize the field. Success breeds competition as surely as it breeds success, and in 1863 Irwin Beadle left the firm accompanied by foreman George Munro to establish a rival publishing house. Beadle lasted only a short time, but for almost thirty years Munro's ten-cent novels were Beadle and Adams' chief competition. Other serious competition came from Norman Munro, George's brother, who started his firm in 1870, first using the name of Ornum (Munro spelled backward) and later, when the brothers became bitter enemies, using the family name. The entry of Frank Tousey into the market in 1878 was even more serious, and the competition of Street and Smith, beginning eleven years later, was the roughest of all. Street and Smith eventually became *the* dime novel company. Companies vied for public favor by producing rival fictional characters, George Munro's fictional detective "Old Sleuth" competing with Norman Munro's "Old Cap Collier," Frank Tousey's "Old King Brady," and Street and Smith's "Nick Carter." Beadle and Adams never developed a successful detective character and lost out in this limited field and finally in the broader market. By 1900, only two companies remained, Tousey and Street and Smith.

Dime Novel Characteristics

From 1860 until approximately 1875, dime novels cost ten cents, ran about 100 pages in small format (about seven by five inches), and were aimed at adults. By 1875, publishers discovered that boys were the most avid readers. Thereafter, publishers concentrated on the younger audience, dropping the price to a nickel (though the public continued to call them dime novels, mostly out of habit) and cutting costs. The result was a nickel (or half-dime) novel of sixteen or thirty-two pages, usually part of a series and featuring one fictional hero, Diamond Dick, Fred Fearnot, Buffalo Bill, or some other equally fascinating and impossible character. The cover portrayed in lurid black and white (color came later) an heroic act of derring-do or a villainous performance of darkest evil.

Plots and Conventions of the Dime Novel

Action-packed dime novels grabbed the reader's imagination from the first lines. Fast paced throughout with cliffhanging chapter endings and imaginative, if often farfetched, thrills and chills, each surpassing the previous adventure, dime novels celebrated mystery, suspense, and the thrill of the chase. The prose was purple, the vocabulary seemed erudite, and literary allusions were common, but boys were not fooled. Dime novels were superior to anything else on the market, more readable than classics, more imaginative than other popular literature.

Daring Davy, the Young Bear Killer, or The Trail of the Border Wolf by Harry St. George (pen name for the prolific writer of dime novels and later boys' series books, St. George Rathbone), published as number 108 in Beadle's Half Dime Library on August 19, 1879, illustrated the *in medias res* opening so common to dime novels, the promised action, the purple prose, and the erudite vocabulary, all in the first brief paragraphs of the first chapter:

> ◇ "Then Davy Crockett must die!"
> The man who gave utterance to this emphatic sentence stood in the middle of a dilapidated old cabin that was almost entirely hidden in the heart of a dense forest. Giant trees grew all around it, their branches drooping so as to almost conceal the log hut from view.
> Outside the night breeze swept down the forest aisle, rustling the leaves in the passage and carrying many of them with it to the ground. The fair moon had wheeled up in the eastern heavens, and Jupiter was leading the march of the planets across the firmament. Now and then the melancholy howl of a wolf could be heard, sounding dismally through the silence of the night, and once a panther lent its shrill scream to awaken the echoes of the glen beyond, for the woods of old Tennessee were full of savage game at this early day.
> The scene inside the cabin was certainly wild enough to have pleased the most exacting.
> Four men stood around a rickety table with drawn knives. The man who had just uttered that sentence of death was a perfect giant in point of size. He was known in the backwoods as Hercules Dan, and had been a hunter and trapper, living on what he could shoot and steal.
> Two of the others possessed ill-favored faces, while the last did not condescend to show his features, which were completely hidden under a heavy hat, and a rough scarf which he had wound around his neck and the lower half of his face.

Six paragraphs into the tale and already we have threats, implied violence soon to become real, death, poetic writing (or what passed for it), and mystery. The remainder of the roughly 40,000-word novel (three columns of tiny print to the page) was no anticlimax.

Stock characters in dime novels included the hero's closest friend, weaker but almost as decent; an older person who moved about spouting tiresome but supposedly wise sayings; and a comic black man, the butt of all humor, frequently superstitious but always servile and loyal, occasionally surprising the reader by proving far wiser and more courageous than anyone would then have suspected.

Formulaic writing and stock characters were predictable and common, for dime novels never pretended to be great literature, and their use of standard characters, settings, and situations made readers comfortable. Today's situation comedies, westerns, or mysteries on television do the same as they ease viewers into a relaxed state of expectation by providing elements, situations, and plot twists that have become satisfyingly traditional. Dime novels provided what dime novel readers wanted and demanded, rapid beginnings, implied and realized violence, periodic cliffhangers, contrived and fast endings, strained but possible coincidences, good versus evil, vengeance, purity, love, and the sanctity of marriage, all for a nickel.

Beyond the excitement, they provided morality. Virtue victorious and villainy vanquished were the watchwords of dime novels. Thrills, of course, but morality had to be there too, and not just to make them acceptable to parents. Erastus Beadle sincerely believed that books should represent sound moral values, and the strict rules he imposed on his writers insured adventure and morality as this memo to his staff reveals:

> ◇ So much is said, and justly, against a considerable number of papers and libraries now on the market, that we beg leave to repeat the following announcement and long-standing instructions to all contributors;
>
> Authors who write for our consideration will bear in mind that—
> We prohibit all things offensive to good taste in expression and incident—
> We prohibit subjects or characters that carry an immoral taint—
> We prohibit the repetition of any occurrence which, though true, is yet better untold—
> We prohibit what cannot be read with satisfaction by every right-minded person—old and young alike—
> We require your best work—
> We require unquestioned originality—
> We require pronounced strength of plot and high dramatic interest of story—
> We require grace and precision of narrative, and correctness in composition.
> Authors must be familiar with characters and places which they introduce and not attempt to write in fields of which they have no intimate knowledge.[4]

Some Dime Novel Types and Authors

Printed in editions running between 35,000 and 70,000 copies, depending on authors' reputations and the popularity of a particular series, dime novels sold by the millions. Beadle and Adams sold four million in 1865 only five years after the genre began. And Bragin notes:

> ◇ Publishers never revealed their sales, but we estimate that the Tip Top Weekly Merriwell stories had a circulation up to a million copies weekly. We base this

estimate on a talk we had with Mr. Harry Wolff, who stated that the Tousey story paper *Happy Days*, had circulation of 500,000 copies weekly, and that was, to use his words, "small potatoes," compared with the Street and Smith output.[5]

Many early dime novels were set in the West of the 1840s and 1850s, and some were set in an even earlier "west," for example, upper New York state in *Malaeska*. But with the opening of the West beyond the Mississippi River, the dime novel found a topic of insatiable interest. Fictional characters like Deadwood Dick, the James Boys, Pawnee Bill, Diamond Dick, and the Young Wild West were introduced, and lengthy series developed around them. Real people like Buffalo Bill, Wild Bill Hickok, and the James Brothers might not have been able to recognize themselves in the fiction written about them since their exploits were mixed only occasionally with something bordering on the truth. Readers cared little in the midst of the heroic exploits.

Rivaling the popularity of the western dime novel was the detective story with such fictional heroes as Nick Carter, Old King Brady, Old Sleuth, Young Sleuth, and Cap Collier. Best known of the writers of detective dime novels was Frederic Van Rensselaer Dey who wrote most of the Nick Carter novels. A dignified man, he was pleased with the success of Nick Carter—he wrote more than a thousand of them—because they were clean: "I never wrote one that could not have been read aloud to a Bible class."[6]

Two other kinds of dime novels that had many fans were sports novels, with heroes like Frank Merriwell and Fred Fearnot, and science fiction novels featuring Frank Reade, Frank Reade, Jr., Jack Wright, and Tom Edison, Jr.

Objections to Dime Novels and Objections to the Objections

By the 1870s, schoolteachers, librarians, writers, and politicians were taking notice of dime novels, first attacking the sensationalism, sentimentality, and distance from reality, and later attacking the alleged power of dime novels to corrupt morals and to turn the young toward crime. In 1878, William Sumner itemized beliefs promoted by dime novels and argued their potential corruptive influence, especially since dime novels were inexpensive and ubiquitous.[7] And in 1896 Theodore C. Burgess argued for stronger laws and more vigorous enforcement of laws already on the books to stave off the dime novel menace:

> ◇ We have a law against the sale of that which is obscene, and it is worthy of consideration whether a law should not go one step farther—not a long one—and include such papers as the *Police Gazette* and those other forms of degrading literature known as the dime novel.[8]

A politician, either for the sake of morality or votes, tried to get such a bill through the New York Assembly in 1883. Part of the Honorable Abel Goddard's bill read:

> ◇ Any person who shall sell, loan, or give to any minor under sixteen years of age any dime novel or book of fiction, without first obtaining the written

consent of the parent or guardian of such minor, shall be deemed guilty of a misdemeanor, punishable by imprisonment or by a fine not exceeding $50.[9]

One newspaper noted ironically that the bill would prohibit giving a copy of *Pilgrim's Progress* to a minor without first getting permission, and the length of the sentence, being indeterminant, might range from a few days to life if the judge were of the same persuasion as Goddard.[10]

Both librarians and schoolteachers discovered to their horror that dime novels were widely read by young people, revealing their own naiveté and ignorance about young people. Tales of the horror teachers and librarians felt when they uncovered dime novel addicts among the young were staples of the *Library Journal* and educational journals of the day.[11]

Then critics found startling proof that dime novels created juvenile delinquents. The *Literary News* for May 1884 told of four youngsters in Milwaukee who organized a gang after reading some dime novels. Frustrated in their plan to move west, the gang set fires about the city.[12] The 1883 *New York Herald* warned:

> ◇ Pernicious stories of the "dime novel" class continue to do their mischievous work. The latest recorded victim was a New London boy, aged fourteen, who shot himself during a period of mental aberration caused by reading dime novels.[13]

Dime novels also had defenders. William Everett, writing in the prestigious *North American Review* in 1864, found them "unobjectionable morally, whatever fault be found with their literary style and composition. They do not even obscurely pander to vice, or excite the passions."[14] Writing in the *Library Journal* fifteen years later, Thomas Wentworth Higginson hardly overpraised dime novels, but his words were far more perceptive and honest than most other commentators' of the time:

> ◇ I have turned over hundreds of dime novels in such places [book stalls] within a year or two, without finding a single word of indecency; they are overly sensational, and, so far as they deal with thieves and house-breakers, demoralizing; but they are not impure.[15]

Death of the Dime Novel

The end of the dime novel cannot be attributed to any one factor. By 1900, Indian wars were over and with that came the end of the contemporary western heroes. Dime novel detectives had been replaced by stories and books about Sherlock Holmes. If they didn't care for Holmes, readers could turn to the many detectives in the growing pulp magazine industry. Series books were now commonplace. The popular getting-ahead-in-life stories begun by Horatio Alger and continued by series books had few parallels in dime novels. The growing number of young people spending more years in school led to a demand for more realistic school and sports stories.

And so a pervasive, ubiquitous literature passed away. Many adults saw nothing in dime novels beyond potential harm and evil. Young adults knew better. Dime novels allowed them to people their lives with exciting characters doing fascinating things in a mildly realistic but mostly wildly romantic world. Of all literature written between 1860 and 1900, dime novels were probably the most widely read by young people seeking escape from an otherwise dull existence.

◈ OTHER PAPERBACK BOOKS

Dime novels produced one significant offspring: the early paperback novel series costing a dime or less.

In 1864 Boston publisher James Redpath announced a series of dime books of high quality, each running from 96 to 124 pages, including Alcott's *On Picket Duty and Other Tales*, Balzac's *The Vendetta*, Swift's *Gulliver's Travels*, and Hugo's *Battle of Waterloo*.

By the 1870s attacks on the dime novel were common, and Chicago's Donnelly and Lloyd began its Lakeside Library with contemporary and classic books far superior, they argued, to sensational dime novels. Their high moral tone would have been more impressive had not most of their library been books pirated from England and the continent. Beadle and Adams retaliated by starting their Fireside Library, and soon Frank Leslie began his Home Library. Later George Munro published his Seaside Library (the first three titles were Mrs. Wood's *East Lynne*, Mulock's *John Halifax, Gentleman*, and Brontë's *Jane Eyre*), and Harper and Brothers began its Franklin Square Library. Paperback libraries cost little. Publishers needed to develop a stable of writers to create dime novel libraries, but Frank Tousey was able to save money by "borrowing" many, if not all, stories from his paperback series.

By 1877, fourteen libraries of inexpensive paperbacks offered many titles (George Munro alone reprinted almost 500 titles) and increasingly good literature. Beadle's Waverly Library included novels by Mrs. Southworth and Mrs. Stephens, hardly the greatest literature, but it also published Dumas' *Camille*, Reade's *Peg Woffington*, Porter's *Thaddeus of Warsaw*, Goldsmith's *The Vicar of Wakefield*, and Bulwer-Lytton's *Leila*. Equally impressive, each novel in the Waverly Library cost only five cents from a newsdealer or six cents by mail.

◈ THE POPULAR STORY WEEKLY

American weekly magazines containing large amounts of fiction began in 1837 when depression-hit publishers needed cheaper methods of producing books. They devised a scheme for printing books as newspapers, in many ways like modern Sunday supplements, on which they paid no taxes and which qualified for cheaper postage rates. Newspapers, irritated by what they considered unfair competition, started printing their own fiction supplements, at first for fifty cents, then twenty-five cents, and then six and one-quarter cents. By 1843, the Post Office Department changed the rules charging book rates for supplements as well as for books and newspapers, but the cheap fiction supplements were then well established.

In 1855, Francis S. Street and Francis S. Smith took over the *New York Weekly Dispatch,* and by 1857 they doubled the circulation with Smith's *The Vestmaker's Apprentice, or the Vampyres of Society,* a tale of villainy and virtue set against a background of greed, filth, and wickedness in New York City. Two years later, Street and Smith bought the *New York Weekly* outright for $40,000 though they had less than $100 between them. Within five years they paid off the debt. Their advertising methods teased the audience with hints of stories to come. To create interest for the forthcoming *Lillian the Wanderer, or The Perils of Beauty,* they announced:

> ◇ The heroine is a noble-souled and pure, but unfortunate orphan-girl, who is forced by circumstances to leave her home in Europe and come to this country. Upon arriving here, she falls into the clutches of some soulless ruffians, and her sufferings and narrow escapes from a fate worse than death are graphically sketched by the author. In the course of the Story, the reader is introduced both into the miserable hovel of poverty and into the mansion of luxury and wealth, and a clearer insight is had into all classes of society. The Story is written in the Author's best style and cannot fail to create a great sensation.[16]

Street and Smith published sea tales, adventures, and tales of suspense, but the most popular were about love and its tribulations. Mary Kyle Dallas' *Neglected Warnings, or The Trials of a Public School Teacher* was doubtlessly well calculated to keep readers in suspense but was equally calculated to make schoolteachers question Street and Smith's sanity in running the story which they claimed:

> ◇ . . . will touch a sympathetic chord in the bosom of every reader, male or female. For who is not, either directly or indirectly, interested in those noble institutions, our public schools?[17]

The heroine was not perhaps a typical schoolteacher, for at different times she lay unconscious in the snow dressed only in her nightclothes, was locked in a church, had a friend who was buried alive and rose from his coffin at night, was rescued from a burning ship, and was married only to see her husband arrested for murder during the wedding ceremony.

As with the dime novel, critics found fault with the popular story weekly, especially the sensational stories and the glorification of impossible lives that readers could dream about but never approach. Critics worried that a maid or a working girl in a mill might waste time dreaming about a better life and the perfect man. In truth, popular story weeklies, like dime novels, provided escape literature to cheer up drab people leading drab lives. There was and is nothing wrong with that, critics to the contrary.

◈ TWO MAJORS FOR MINORS: ALCOTT AND ALGER

Louisa May Alcott and Horatio Alger, Jr., were the first writers for young adults to gain national attention. Both wrote *Bildungsroman,* a novel of a young person growing from childhood to maturity. The similarity between the two stops almost as it begins. Alcott wrote about happy families. Alger wrote about broken homes. Alcott's novels were sometimes harsh but always honest. Alger's novels were romantic fantasies. Alcott's novels continue to be read for good reason. Except for the historian or the Alger buff, Alger's novels lie virtually forgotten.

The second daughter of visionary Amos Bronson Alcott, Louisa May Alcott lived her youth near Concord and Boston with a practical mother and a father who was brilliant, generous, improvident, and impractical.

After publishing *Hospital Sketches* (1863) based on her work in a Union hospital, she turned to writing thrillers, solely, she maintained, for money. Then, after an abortive effort to create dime novels, she wrote *Little Women*, her most enduring work. The reigning young adults' author of the time was Oliver Optic, the pen name of William T. Adams, and Boston publishers Roberts Brothers were eager to find a story for young adults that might offer competition to Optic's stories published by rival Boston publisher Lee and Shepard. Roberts' representative, Thomas Niles, had once told Alcott, "Stick to your teaching. You can't write," but as a publisher he had requested permission to reprint the successful *Hospital Sketches*. In September 1866 Niles suggested she write a girls' book, and in May 1868 he gently reminded her.

She sent a manuscript off to Niles who thought early parts of it dull, but other readers disagreed, and the first part of *Little Women: Meg, Jo, Beth, and Amy. The Story of Their Lives. A Girl's Book* was published on September 30, 1868, with three illustrations and a frontispiece at $1.50 a copy. Slightly more than a month earlier, Alcott had read the proofs:

> ◇ August 26th—Proof of the whole book came. It reads better than I expected. Not a bit sensational, but simple and true, for we really lived most of it; and if it succeeds that will be the reason for it. Mr. N. likes it better now, and says some girls who have read the manuscripts say it is "splendid!" As it is for them, they are the best critics, so I should be satisfied.[18]

Little Women was well received by reviewers and sales were good here and in England. By early November 1868, she had begun work on the second part, and *Little Women or Meg, Jo, Beth and Amy. Part Second* was published on April 14, 1869.

The book was certainly the Alcott family story, the major difference being that an impractical and therefore unsympathetic father is replaced by an absent and therefore heroic father now on duty with the Union Army. The March family survive happily without him, reminiscent of Alcott's thrillers in which women revenge themselves on men or prove them unnecessary.

The novel has vitality, joy, real life, and love generally devoid of sentimentality, a wistful portrait of a life Alcott wished she could have lived. The Civil War background is subtle, pervasive but rarely spoken, better expressing the loneliness and never ending quality of war than many war novels for all their suffering, death, pain, and horror. Aimed at young adults, *Little Women* has maintained steady popularity with them and with younger children. Adults reread it to gain a sense of where they were when they were young.

Her later books were well received and remain favorites of many young adults: *An Old-Fashioned Girl* (1870), *Little Men* (1871), *Eight Cousins* (1875), *Rose in Bloom* (1876), *Under the Lilacs* (1878), *Jack and Jill* (1880), and *Jo's Boys* (1886). None, however, were as successful as *Little Women*.

Son of an unctuous Unitarian clergyman who made the boy's childhood a nightmare of guilt and frustration, Horatio Alger spent his youth studying and becoming known as "Holy Horatio." After graduation from Harvard at eighteen, Alger vacillated, entering and then leaving Harvard Divinity School, writing for the *Boston Transcript*, and teaching at a boys' school. Ordained a Unitarian minister in 1864, he served a Brewster, Massachusetts, church only to leave two years later under a cloud of scandal, effectively hushed up at the time.[19] Already the author of seven books, Alger moved to New York City and began to write full time.

That same year he sent *Ragged Dick, or Street Life in New York* to Oliver Optic's *Student and Schoolmate*, a goody-goody magazine for moral boys and girls. Optic knew salable pap when he saw it, and he bought Alger's work for the January 1867 issue. Published in 1867 or 1868 in hardback, *Ragged Dick* was the first of many successes for Alger and publisher A. K. Loring in Boston and remains Alger's most readable novel, probably because it was the first from the mold that soon became predictably moldy.

The plot, as in most Alger books, consisted of semiconnected episodes illustrating a boy's first steps toward maturity, respectability, and affluence. Ragged Dick, a young bootblack, sleeps "in a wooden box half full of straw." Grubby but not dirty, he smokes and gambles occasionally, but the reader immediately recognizes his essential goodness. On his way to work, he meets Mr. Greyson who gives him a quarter for a shine, says he cannot wait for change, and asks Dick to bring the fifteen cents to his office. Dick is the only one surprised, for Greyson sees in Dick what Alger assumes readers see, inherent honesty and nobility. A few minutes later, Dick overhears Mr. Whitney talking to his nephew Frank, who is in need of a guide. Dick volunteers, to no one's surprise (except that of the reader who wonders why anyone would choose a totally unknown bootblack with whom to entrust his nephew). Mr. Whitney accepts, and the boys set out on a nine-chapter tour of the city, a handbook to the sights, sounds, and dangers of New York City.[20]

After Frank and Dick temporarily part, Dick vows a course of self-improvement with Frank as his model. When he returns the fifteen cents change to Mr. Greyson, the much-impressed Greyson asks Dick to attend the church where he teaches Sunday School. That same day, Dick befriends better-educated Henry Fosdick who, in return for sharing Dick's room, agrees to tutor him. He and Fosdick go to church and meet Greyson and his wife and their daughter, Ida, whom Dick clearly likes. Dick and Henry move steadily upward in the world, saving a bit each week and becoming more respectable every day. The novel, although wooden in style and episodically plotted, has touches of reality till this point. Alger, apparently unwilling or unable to move Dick slowly up the ladder of respectability, puts pluck aside and adds the infamous luck that characterized his novels. Dick and Fosdick find themselves on a ferry, a little boy falls overboard, and Dick, ignoring personal danger, follows the child into the water and saves him. A grateful father rewards Dick with new clothing and a job at ten dollars a week, a princely sum for the time. As the book closes, Alger cannot resist the temptation to gild the moral lily and at the same time sell a copy of the sequel:

> ◇ Here ends the story of Ragged Dick. As Fosdick said, he is Ragged Dick no longer. He has taken a step upward, and is determined to mount still higher. There are fresh adventures in store for him, and for others who have been introduced in these pages. Those who have felt interested in his early life will find his history continued in a new volume, forming the second half of the series, to be called,—

Fame and Fortune:
or,
The Progress of Richard Hunter.

Some readers inaccurately label Alger's books "rags to riches," but the hero rarely achieves riches though he does find himself at the book's end on the lower rungs of the ladder of success. "Rags to respectability" would be a more accurate statement about Alger's work.

Alger wrote at least 119 novels, many of them popular until the early 1900s, selling altogether between sixteen million and seventeen million copies. Typically revealing titles were *Luck and Pluck, or John Oakley's Inheritance* (1869), *Sink or Swim, or Harry Raymond's Resolve* (1870), *Bound to Rise, or Harry Walton's Motto* (1873), *Risen from the Ranks, or Harry Walton's Success* (1874), *Do and Dare, or A Brave Boy's Fight for Fortune* (1884), and *Struggling Upward, or Luke Larkin's Luck* (1890).

◈ OTHER EARLY SERIES WRITERS

The Boston publishing firm of Lee and Shepard established the format for young adult series. To the distress of teachers, librarians, and some parents, the series became *the* method of publishing most young adult novels, though it became far more sophisticated in Edward Stratemeyer's hands nearly forty years later. If sales are any index, readers delighted in Lee and Shepard's series just as they delighted in other series from other publishing houses. *Publishers' Trade List* for 1887 contained sixteen pages listing 440 authors and 900 books under the Lee and Shepard logo. Series books clearly sold very well.

Four series writers were especially popular: Harry Castlemon, Oliver Optic, Martha Finley, and Susan Coolidge.

Under the pen name of Harry Castlemon, Charles Austin Fosdick wrote his first novel, *Frank the Young Naturalist* (1864), while in the Navy. Admiral David B. Porter agreed to read it and suggested Castlemon submit it to Cincinnati publisher Robert W. Carrol who answered with a $150 check, a letter of praise, and a recommendation that the author follow up with a series of five more books featuring Frank. Castlemon's career was off. He received $200 each for the remainder of the series, *Frank on a Gunboat* (1864), *Frank in the Woods* (1865), *Frank Before Vicksburg* (1865), *Frank on the Lower Mississippi* (1867), and *Frank on the Prairie* (1868), all under the "Gunboat Series" title. Other series followed.

Castlemon's approach was pragmatic. "Boys don't like fine writing. What they want is adventure, and the more of it you can get into 250 pages of manuscript, the better fellow you are."[21]

Typical of Castlemon's work is *Frank at Don Carlos' Ranch* (1871), second in the "Rocky Mountain Series." Archie, Frank's friend, stands before a large oil painting. Something about the painting catches Archie's eye, he touches it, and a mysterious door opens. Archie's words and Castlemon's comment are the essence of Castlemon's style and the moral tone of his books:

> ◇ "Now I'd like to know what this means," thought he, pressing the knob harder than before. "This thing must be attached to a spring, because it comes back when I let go of it. Well—by—gracious!"
>
> It was very seldom indeed that Archie used any slang words, but sometimes, when he was greatly excited or astonished, he did like other boys—forgot all the good resolutions he had made regarding this bad habit.

Castlemon's popularity had dimmed by 1900, but a Philadelphia librarian in 1925 woefully admitted that Castlemon's novels were still read.[22]

Oliver Optic, pen name of William Taylor Adams, was a prolific writer, producing more than 100 books for young people under the Lee and Shepard banner. *The Boat Club* (1855), his first book and the first volume of the six book "Boat Club Series," ran through sixty editions and set a pattern for such series to follow as "The Army and Navy Series," "The Lake Shore Series," "The Onward and Upward Series," "The Great Western Series," "The Blue and the Gray Afloat Series," and "The Blue and the Gray on Land Series."

Kilgour maintains that Optic created mass-production writing for young people which led librarians and teachers to attack Optic as they criticized few other authors.[23] Some irritation may have stemmed from Optic's sales—he was a best-seller during his lifetime and afterwards—but adults never forgave him his fantastic plots and wooden dialogue.

If Optic is remembered at all today, it is for his quarrel with Louisa May Alcott who attacked his books in her *Eight Cousins* (1875). In Chapter 8, Alcott describes four young men on a rainy Sunday afternoon reading and smoking. Mother appears and has nothing good to say about their choice of reading material, the sensational and unrealistic plots and the language. Optic saw the attack when the episode was first published in the August 1875 *St. Nicholas*. He defended himself in his *Oliver Optic's Magazine* for September 1875 by implying that Alcott may have borrowed the title for *Eight Cousins* from Amanda Douglas' *Seven Daughters*, published in his magazine, and by arguing that she mixed titles and plots and wildly exaggerated the stories. Optic concluded:

◇ Ah, Louisa, you are very smart, and you have become rich. Your success mocks that of the juvenile heroes you despise. Even the author of "Dick Dauntless" and "Sam Soaker," whoever he may be would not dare to write up a heroine who rose so rapidly from poverty and obscurity to riches and fame as you did; but in view of the wholesale perversion of the truth as we have pointed out, we must ask you to adopt the motto you recommend for others—"Be honest and you will be happy," instead of the one you seem to have chosen: "Be smart and you will be rich."[24]

Attacks by reviewers, teachers, librarians, and even Alcott did not carry the day, for as late as 1900 Lee and Shepard's catalogue advertised 123 Oliver Optic novels.

Martha Farquharson Finley wrote the "Elsie Dinsmore" series, probably the most popular series of its time. In twenty-eight volumes, the series carried Elsie through life from childhood to grandmotherhood. A favorite with young women and a girl critics loved to hate, Elsie is persistently and nauseatingly docile, pious, sincere, lachrymose, virtuous, humble, timid, ignorant, and good.

Published in 1867 and running to an amazing number of editions after that, *Elsie Dinsmore* opens with virtuous and Christian Elsie awaiting the return of her beloved but long-absent father. Elsie has continual problems with her cold and indifferent father, Finley's way of demonstrating that children must love parents, no matter how blind the love must be, and that girls must love God and Jesus above all, no matter what the pressures. And if Elsie needs her love or faith tried, her father is unquestionably trying.

The most widely quoted episode, by those who loved or hated the book, occurs one Sunday when father asks Elsie to perform at the piano for guests. Elsie pleads, always in a pious and respectful tone, that the Sabbath forbids secular music, but father demands she remain at the piano until she is willing to play. Several hours pass while Elsie sits playing the martyr but never the piano. Then Elsie feels a pain and suddenly falls. A guest rushes to Elsie:

◇ "A light! quick, quick, a light!" he cried, raising Elsie's insensible form in his arms; "the child has fainted."
One of the others, instantly snatching a lamp from a distant table, brought it near, and the increased light showed Elsie's little face, ghastly as that of a corpse, while a stream of blood was flowing from a wound in the temple, made by striking against some sharp corner of the furniture as she fell.

Seconds later, her soft eyes open and her first words are:

◇ "Dear papa, are you angry with me?"

Next morning, a temporarily remorseful father visits Elsie:

◇ "Elsie, do you know that you were very near being killed last night?"
"No, papa, was I?" she asked with an awestruck countenance.
"Yes, the doctor says if that wound had been made half an inch nearer your eye—I should have been childless."

◆ Elsie Dinsmore is persistently and nauseatingly docile, pious, sincere, lachrymose, virtuous, humble, timid, ignorant, and good.

His voice trembled almost too much for utterance as he finished his sentence, and he strained her to his heart with a deep sigh of thankfulness for her escape.

Piety reigns equally in *Elsie's Girlhood* (1872), in which Elsie incessantly cries, faints, loves, and prays; *Elsie's Motherhood* (1876); *Elsie's Children* (1877); *Elsie's Widowhood* (1880)—Elsie's husband was probably killed because he was an obstacle in plots; *Christmas with Grandma Elsie* (1888); and *Elsie in the South* (1899). Elsie moves from childhood to marriage to widowhood affirming the joys of fainting and crying, the American Dream fulfilled through piety, morality, and prayer.[25]

Susan Coolidge, pen name of Sarah Chauncey Woolsey, wrote fewer books than other series writers. Only one of her series found wide favor, but it once rivalled Alcott's books. It is still published in England and reads well even today. *What Katy Did* (1872) features tomboy Katy Carr, her widowed doctor-father, and three sisters and two brothers. *What Katy Did at School* (1873) carries sixteen-year-old Katy on to boarding school where her escapades keep her in trouble. *What Katy Did Next* (1886) takes Katy off to Europe and a young naval officer. *Clover* (1888) and *In the Valley* (1891) conclude the series.

Coolidge's heroine resembles Alcott's Jo March in several ways. She is stubborn and sometimes willful but essentially good, loving, and caring. Katy is almost as attractive as Jo and sometimes more believable in her pranks. In 1978, the Public Broadcasting System produced six episodes of Katy's life, condensing too much too fast but proving that Coolidge's books deserve reading today, perhaps even a revival.

◈ THE LITERATURE OF THE BAD BOY

Beginning with Thomas Bailey Aldrich's *The Story of a Bad Boy* in 1870, a literature developed around bad boys, flesh and blood, imperfect boys, tough on the outside and able to survive troubles in a brutal world.

The books were, except for Twain's, nostalgic books about old times, harking back to a golden age that had never been. Sometimes cruel and frequently confusing boyishness with barbarism, they were ultimately patronizing and backward-looking and, with the exception of Twain's, doomed to a relatively short life.

Thomas Bailey Aldrich's reputation rests on *The Story of a Bad Boy*. Serialized in *Our Young Folks*, January to December 1869, and published as a book a year later, Aldrich's part-novel, part-autobiography became an immediate success with critics and readers. William Dean Howells began his review in the *Atlantic*:

> ◇ Mr. Aldrich has done a new thing in—we use the phrase with some gasps of reluctance, it is so threadbare and so near meaning nothing—American literature. We might go much farther without overpraising his pleasant book, and call it an absolute novelty, on the whole. No one else seems to have thought of telling the story of a boy's life, with so great desire to show what a boy's life is, and so little purpose of teaching what it should be; certainly no one else has thought of doing this for the life of an American boy.[26]

Aldrich's book was a novelty, but more important, it told the story of a boy as he was, or might be, not as he should have been. The book marked the beginning of realistic literature about boys, just as Alcott's *Little Women* had served the cause of young women only two years before.

The Story of a Bad Boy begins in New Orleans where Tom lives with his parents, though he is soon forced to return North where he will live with his grandfather. The part that stays with readers concerns Tom's gang, The Centipedes, the snowball fights, picnics, pranks of all sorts, and the girls whom members of the gang love. Aldrich illustrates with singular accuracy the social and moral values of the time, but other than Tom, the book falls back on stereotyped characterizations.

Newspaperman, writer, humorist, and later Governor of Wisconsin, George Wilbur Peck began writing about "Peck's Bad Boy" in *Peck's Sun*, his Milwaukee newspaper-family humor magazine, in 1882 and published *Peck's Bad Boy and His Pa* a year later. The crude jokes go beyond cruelty and the dialect becomes outlandish in later sequels.

Peck's Bad Boy and His Pa devotes separate chapters to the Bad Boy's pranks, often played on his father though the Boy does not discriminate. Two episodes convey the book's spirit. In Chapter 11, the Boy douses his father's handkerchief with rum and wraps it around playing cards. Pa attends a prayer meeting where the preacher asks him to tell about his recent reformation. When Pa speaks, breaking into tears and taking out his handkerchief, cards fly and fumes spread. In Chapter 30, Pa comes home drunk. The Boy pretends to take him to a dissecting room where the Boy and his friends act as if they will cut him up as Pa wakes up and is horrified.

◈ THE PEOPLE BEHIND THE BOOKS

FELICE HOLMAN, Author

Slake's Limbo
The Murderer
The Wild Children

I don't think I *try* to, but what I seem to write about is "coping" and "surviving." And, while I am not strong on theorizing—believing that as soon as we start chiseling in stone, the erosion process sets in—I guess I dare say that those are the things that are the least common denominators, what life is about. Yes, life *is* about having fun (and no fun); it is about divorce (and marriage); it is about homosexuality (and hetero); it is about druggies (and clean-livers). But all this shifts in real life, and what the story seems really to be is less what *happens* to us than how we handle it, how we cope, how we survive. And that is what I have been writing about. Now, anyhow. Who knows about tomorrow!◆

Slake's Limbo. Scribner's, 1974.
The Murderer. Scribner's, 1978.
The Wild Children. Scribner's, 1983.

Peck had no subtlety, but his humor brought him readers far beyond any other writer of bad boy literature excepting Twain.

Mark Twain was the capstone of both bad boys' literature and nineteenth-century literature generally. *The Adventures of Tom Sawyer* (1876) and *The Adventures of Huckleberry Finn* (1884) took the bad boy theme far beyond Aldrich or Peck. Humor, sometimes savage adventure, and other conventions of the bad boy books can be found in Twain, but compassion is mixed with cynicism, and there is none of the condescension or simplistic nostalgia of earlier bad boy books. As many critics have noted, *Huck Finn*, and to a lesser degree *Tom Sawyer*, are books young and old can read over and over on quite different levels, young adults for adventure and perhaps more, adults for insight and perhaps more.

Twain's problems with the censor are well known. Before *Huck Finn* was published in hardback, the February 1885 *Century Magazine* published extracts but not all that Twain submitted. *Century* editor Richard Watson Gilder apparently found some material too harsh or too coarse and left out the preacher's harangue at the camp meeting and the lynching of Colonel Sherburn.[27]

After the publication of *Huck Finn*, the Concord (Massachusetts) Library banned the book as trashy, vicious, and unfit to be placed next to books by Emerson or Thoreau. Louisa May Alcott said, "If Mr. Clemens cannot think of something better to tell our pure-minded lads and lasses, he had best stop writing for them," a comment Twain felt would sell an additional 25,000 copies. The Concord Library was not alone in damning the book. *The Springfield Republican* wrote in 1885, "They [*Tom Sawyer* and *Huck Finn*] are no better in tone than the dime novels which flood the blood-and-thunder reading population. . . . Their moral tone is low, and their perusal cannot be anything less than harmful."[28] And the *St. Louis Republican* surveying the reading of young people in 1889 concluded its comments with:

> ◇ This also proves that there is growing up in this country a standard juvenile literature which is healthy and hopeful. There were but few lists containing books of a harmful tendency. It is not much to say that the books of the *Tom Sawyer* and *Huckleberry Finn* order were the worst mentioned.[29]

The Brooklyn Public Library excluded both books from their children's room as "bad examples for ingenuous youth" in 1905. Asa Don Dickinson, Librarian of Brooklyn College, pleaded that Twain's books be put back on the shelves, but "It was no use. The good ladies assured me in effect that Huck was a deceitful boy."[30] Dickinson sent an apologetic letter to Twain and received this reply:

> ◇ Dear Sir:
>
> I am greatly troubled by what you say. I wrote *Tom Sawyer* and *Huck Finn* for adults exclusively, and it always distresses me when I find that boys and girls have been allowed access to them. The mind that becomes soiled in youth can never again be washed clean; I know this by my own experience and to this day I cherish an unappeasable bitterness against the unfaithful guardians of my young life, who not only permitted but compelled me to read an unexpurgated Bible through before I was 15 years old. None can do that and ever draw a clean sweet breath again this side of the grave. Ask that young lady—she will tell you so.
>
> Most honestly do I wish I could say a softening word or two in defence of Huck's character, since you wish it, but really in my opinion it is no better than God's (in the Ahab chapter and 97 others) and those of Solomon, David, Satan, and the rest of the sacred brotherhood.
>
> If there is an unexpurgated in the Children's Department, won't you please help that young woman remove Huck and Tom from that questionable companionship?[31]

◈ WRITERS OF ADVENTURE TALES

Many important writers for young adults did not write series books. Most wrote fiction, for surveys reported that young adults liked fiction more than other literary genres, the favorites being adventure with boys, adventure and love stories with girls.[32] And tales of adventure, many of them first-rate, were easily found.

The past was a continual source of adventure. George Alfred Henty acquired a fascination for and knowledge of foreign countries and their history as a newspaper reporter, and his eighty or so historical-adventure tales read well even today once readers overcome some dated nineteenth-century diction. Of special worth are *Beric, The Briton: A Story of the Roman Invasion* (1893), *When London Burned: A Story of the Plague and the Fire* (1895), and *Winning His Spurs: A Tale of the Crusades* (1892), but Henty is readable in most of his books. John Bennett is best remembered for *Master Skylark: A Story of Shakespeare's Time* (1897), a delightful account of young Nick Attwood, a golden-voiced boy singer involved in more than his share of adventure. Howard Pyle was known as an illustrator of young people's books as well as a writer, and *The Merry Adventures of Robin Hood* (1883) is still read. Even better were *Otto of the Silver Hand* (1888), set in medieval Germany, and *Men of Iron* (1892), a marvelously effective and exciting story of villainy and feudal rights in fifteenth-century England.

Piracy and smuggling have always appealed to our sense of adventure. John Meade Falkner's *Moonfleet* (1898) captivated readers with its story of smuggling in Dorset, England, buried vaults, and a diamond with a curse. Only Robert Louis Stevenson, master of the genre, surpassed Falkner. Stevenson's *Kidnapped* (1886) is a thriller with few faults, but *Treasure Island* (1883) is a jewel among adventure stories, popular then and no less popular now.

Adventures among boys was the theme of three once-popular, now badly underrated writers. Robert Michael Ballantyne is probably best known for *The Coral Island* (1858) since William Golding's *Lord of the Flies* (1955) parallels the earlier book and mentions it. *The Young Fur Traders* (1856) and *The Gorilla Hunters* (1861) were almost equally popular during the author's lifetime. Noah Brooks wrote biographies of Lincoln and a superb story of boys going west across the plains, *The Boy Emigrants* (1876). Best of the three was Kirk Munroe. Two of his excellent novels are *The Flamingo Feather* (1887), about early days in Florida, and *Derrick Sterling* (1888), about a young miner working his way up in life, Alger-like in theme but Dickensian in flavor.

The new adventure tales of mystery and detection were handled by the master, Arthur Conan Doyle, whose *Adventures of Sherlock Holmes* (1891) were first published for a delighted *Strand Magazine* audience. Later tales proved equally popular.

Even more exotic adventure was the province of Jules Verne, whose science fiction and adventure tales *Twenty Thousand Leagues Under the Sea* (1872), *From the Earth to the Moon* (1873), and *Around the World in Eighty Days* (1874) delighted and confounded adult and young adult readers for many years.

◈ THE DEVELOPMENT OF THE AMERICAN PUBLIC LIBRARY

Today, we too easily assume that the public library has always played an important role in American educational and cultural life. In fact, its development from colonial time to the founding of the American Library Association in 1876 was as rocky and slow as it was inevitable.

In 1731, Benjamin Franklin suggested to the Junto, a middle-class social and literary club in Philadelphia, that members bring their books to the club so other members might enjoy them. Franklin's suggestion led to the forming of the Philadelphia Library Company, America's first subscription library. Other such libraries soon followed, for example, the Library of the Carpenters' Club in Philadelphia in 1736 and the Proprietors' Library in Pomfret, Connecticut, in 1737.

These libraries were hardly free public libraries, but they made more books accessible to more people than ever before. They also made clear in their founding statements the moral purpose of a library. The constitution of the Salisbury, Connecticut, Social Library announced its purpose as "The promotion of Virtue, Education, and Learning, and . . . the discouragement of Vice and Immorality."[33] The articles of association of the Social Library in Castine, Maine, in 1801 provided even greater detail on the democratic and moral values of the library:

> ◇ It is proposed by persons whose names are hereby subjoined, to establish a social library in this town. It is greatly to be lamented that excellent abilities are not infrequently doomed to obscurity by reason of poverty; that the rich purchase almost everything but books; and that reading has become so unfashionable an amusement in what we are pleased to call this enlightened age and country. To remedy these evils; to excite a fondness for books; to afford the most rational and profitable amusement; to prevent idleness and immorality; to promote the diffusion of useful knowledge, piety, and virtue, at an expense which small pecuniary abilities can afford, we are induced to associate for the above purposes.[34]

In 1826, New York Governor DeWitt Clinton urged that school district libraries be established, in effect using school buildings for libraries for people nearby. By 1838, $55,000 was annually appropriated for these libraries. Horace Mann advocated similar libraries for Massachussetts, and similar legislation passed in Connecticut in 1839, Rhode Island and Iowa in 1840, Indiana in 1841, and other states soon followed. Proponents of school district libraries recognized that schools and the availability of many books for school use were mutually beneficial, but the concept failed for several practical reasons:

> ◇ They usually consisted of text books, general works, and a smattering of inspirational literature, with little attention paid to their selection. The majority were above the reading level and beyond the interests of all but the most advanced students, and though they were theoretically available to the adults of the community, they were not widely used.[35]

A much more promising approach came in October 1847 when Boston Mayor Josiah Quincy, Jr., suggested that the state legislature be petitioned for permission to levy a tax so that the city could establish a free public library open to all citizens. The petition was granted the following year, and thereafter Boston was to spend $5,000 annually to support its library. On March 20, 1854, the Boston Public Library opened its doors to readers and six weeks later to borrowers.

THE PEOPLE BEHIND THE BOOKS

PATRICIA J. CAMPBELL,
Author and Editor

Columnist, "The Young Adult Perplex,"
Wilson Library Bulletin
Sex Education Books for Young Adults
Passing the Hat
Robert Cormier: a Biocritical Study

The future—I don't believe in it. Never have. *Now* always seems to me to be all there is, and I'm always pleasantly surprised when some more comes after. Someone once told me, not kindly, that such an outlook is typically adolescent. I chose to consider it a compliment.

So what I guess will happen in the future of YA literature is that we'll just keep on keeping on. Librarians and teachers will push what they think is the right stuff, and kids will absolutely love some of it and firmly ignore the rest. And on the side they'll go on reading junk of their very own choosing that meets their needs and appalls those of us who consider ourselves the guardians of literary quality.

The bad news is that computer recreations will probably permanently seduce away some potential readers, but the good news is that more and better YA books will be published now that the book industry has discovered the megabucks to be had from the YA market. (As soon as they finish chasing every YA reading fad hither and yon, that is, to the detriment of the development of the good stuff.) We teachers and librarians long ago discovered that with YA literature you have to tread the tightrope of quality and appeal, and you fall on your backside if you lean too far in either direction. And *that's* not going to change. ◆

Sex Education Books for Young Adults. R. R. Bowker, 1979.
Passing the Hat. Delacorte, 1981.
Robert Cormier: A Biocritical Study. G. K. Hall, 1985.

Other states followed. In 1849, New Hampshire passed the first general library law, and in 1851, the Massachusetts legislature made the 1848 Boston act applicable to all cities and towns in the state. Maine followed in 1854, followed by a deluge of states after the Civil War. By 1863, there were a thousand public libraries in the country and by 1875, two thousand public libraries with at least a thousand books each in their collections.

The first major report on the developing public library came in an 1876 document from the U.S. Bureau of Education. Part I, "Public Libraries in the United States of America, their History, Condition, and Management" contained 1,187 pages with reports and comments and analyses from various prominent librarians plus statistics on 3,649 public libraries with holdings of 300 volumes or more.

That same year marks the beginning of the modern library movement. Melvil Dewey, then assistant librarian in the Amherst College library, was largely responsible for the October 4, 1876, conference of librarians which formed the American Library Association the third day of the meeting. The first issue of the *American Library Journal* appeared that same year (it became the *Library Journal* the following year), the world's first professional journal for librarians—England's *The Library Chronicle* began in 1884 and Germany's *Centralblatt für Bibliothekswesen* in 1889. While there had been an abortive conference in 1853, the 1876 meeting promised continuity the earlier meeting lacked.[36]

In 1884, Columbia College furthered the public library movement when it established the first school of Library Economy (later to be Library Science) under the leadership of Melvil Dewey. The school opened January 5, 1887, offering a three-month course. Shortly, the course was extended to two years.

Excellent as the public libraries were then, they grew immeasurably in number of libraries and individual holdings through the impetus of Andrew Carnegie's philanthropy. A Scottish immigrant to the United States, Carnegie left millions of dollars for the creation of public libraries across America. He began in 1881 with a gift to Pittsburgh where his steelworkers lived, and by 1920, his money had provided funds to build more than 2,500 other public libraries.[37]

Problems and Lamentations of the Public Librarian

Some common problems then still remain problems for librarians today. At the 1876 meeting, a Mr. Walters asked if there were any way to prevent people from stealing books. A Mr. Vickers replied that he knew of only one effective method, "which was to keep a man standing over each book with a club (laughter)."[38] Four years later, the *Library Journal* devoted three and a half columns to the "Capture of a Notorious Book-Thief"[39] with enough details to make the case sound like something out of Sherlock Holmes.

Proof that the library contained what some readers considered dangerous or immoral material came in 1894 when a Los Angeles librarian brought suit for libel against a local minister. Apparently the library had earlier purchased some French books, a local newspaper had attacked the books, and the minister followed up with a sermon in which he prayed for the soul of the librarian in these words:

> ◇ O Lord, vouchsafe thy saving grace to the librarian of the Los Angeles City Library, and cleanse her of all sin, and make her a woman worthy of her office.

The librarian, understandably, was unhappy with the publicity and filed suit.[40]

Fiction and Libraries

The growth of public libraries presented opportunities for pleasure and education of the masses, but arguments about the purposes of the libraries arose almost as fast as the buildings themselves. William Poole listed three common objections to the public library in the October 1876 *American Library Journal*: the normal dread of taxes; the more philosophical belief that government had no rights except to protect people and property, that is no right to tax anyone to build and stock a public library; and concern over the kinds of books libraries might buy and circulate.[41] In this third class of objection, Poole touched upon a controversy that would rage for years, that is, whether a public library is established to provide assistance for scholars or pleasure for the masses. Poole believed that a library existed for the entire community or else there was no justification for a general tax.

Poole's words did not quiet critics who argued that the library's sole *raison d'être* was educational. Waving the banner of American purity in his hands, W. M. Stevenson maintained:

> ◇ If the public library is not first and foremost an education institution, it has no right to exist. If it exists for mere entertainment, and for a low order of entertainment at that, it is simply a socialistic institution.[42]

Many librarians agreed.

The problem lay almost exclusively with fiction. Librarians, appalled by what they considered cheap, sensational, *pernicious* (a favorite word, much overused to describe the horror they felt) trash, anointed themselves to bring the unwashed masses to literary, if not personal, salvation.

But the debate over fiction and its propriety had begun much earlier.

Early Attacks on Fiction

The English novel originated by Richardson in his supposedly moral *Pamela* (1740) and continued by the more realistic, honest, and moral novels of Fielding led to some opposition in England but considerably more in America. Moral qualms became even stronger following the Revolutionary War, partly because of chauvinism but mostly from pietistic reasons, as novel reading became widespread and approached a national craze. Minor American authors warned youth of the dangers of the novel-reading habit. The Rev. Enos Hitchcock, a novelist now forgotten for good reason, wrote to young women in his *Memoirs of the Bloomsgrove Family* (1790):

> ◇ Nothing can have a worse effect on our sex, than a free use of these writings which are the offspring of our modern novelists. Their only tendency is to excite romantic notions, while they keep the mind void of ideas, and the heart destitute of sentiment.[43]

Later novelists, perhaps to please moralists and defend themselves from potential attack and perhaps because they themselves wondered about the propriety and inherent decency of novels and novel reading, found occasion, paradoxically, to attack novel reading in their own novels. In the first domestic novel, Susan Warner's *The Wide, Wide World*, lachrymose heroine Ellen Montgomery is forbidden to read *Blackwood's Magazine* since it contains fiction.

Fiction Can Be Dangerous If Taken Internally

The second session of the 1876 American Library Association meeting in Philadelphia was devoted to "Novel-Reading." Controversy rose immediately, symptomatic of an argument to rage for years. A librarian announced that his rules permitted no novels in the library. His factory-worker patrons might ask for them, but he recommended other books and was able to keep patrons without supplying novels. To laughter, he said he never read novels so he "could not say what their effect really was."[44]

His sublimely ridiculous and condescending attitude toward library patrons was echoed by others. Librarians worried that catering to popular taste was dangerous, for "by supplying such books, a library fosters the taste that craves them, and it increases the demand."[45]

Laymen joined in. Thomas De Witt Talmage, a colorful and exceptionally popular Brooklyn Presbyterian minister, frequently wrote and spoke on the dangers of the novel habit. He regarded novels, with but rare exceptions, as tools of Satan and perversity in print:

> ◇ A man who gives himself up to the indiscriminate reading of novels will be nervous, inane, and a nuisance. He will be fit neither for the store, nor the shop, nor the field. A woman who gives herself up to the indiscriminate reading of novels will be unfitted for the duties of wife, mother, sister, daughter. There she is, hair disheveled, countenance vacant, cheeks pale, hands trembling, bursting into tears at midnight over the fate of some unfortunate lover; in the daytime when she ought to be busy, staring by the half hour at nothing; biting her finger nails into the quick. . . . I could tell you of a comrade that was great-hearted, noble, and generous. He was studying for an honorable profession, but he had an infidel book in his trunk, and he said to me one day: "De Witt, would you like to read it?" I said: "Yes, I would." I took the book and read it only for a few minutes. I was really startled with what I saw there, and I handed the book back to him and said: "You had better destroy that book." No, he kept it. He read it, he re-read it. After awhile he gave up religion as a myth. He gave up God as a nonentity. He gave up the *Bible* as a fable. He gave up the Church of Christ as a useless institution. He gave up good morals as being unnecessarily stringent. I have heard of him but twice in many years. The time before the last I heard of him he was a confirmed inebriate. The last I heard of him he was coming out of an insane asylum—in body, mind and soul an awful wreck. I believe that infidel book killed him for two worlds.[46]

Fiction and Young Adults

Librarians particularly worried about fiction's effect on young adults. No doubt they envied the plan devised by the Massachusetts Board of Education in 1840 providing leisure reading for young people but carefully excluding all fiction from its lists. Librarians, generally, had no easy way out, for most of their libraries had fiction. The problem was how to control it and restrict its use among young adults.

Poole argued in 1876 that the problem lay with parents who must regulate the reading of young people. But in the same volume of the *American Library Journal*, William Kite lamented the dangers novels presented to young adults, and library literature did not relinquish the theme for some time. Green posed the question, at least a bit tongue in cheek, "Is it proper to have sensational novels and highly spiced stories for the young in public libraries?" and then answered "They do good two ways. They keep men and women and boys from worse reading. . . . They give young persons a taste for reading." James Mascarene Hubbarb warred with trustees of the Boston Public Library for years over the corruptive fiction he wanted removed. *Library Journal* authors worried about the young adult fiction question while the battle raged and even after 1900 when the war was over and fiction had become available to young adults in most libraries.

Teachers worried almost as much as librarians. A principal of a large endowed academy was approvingly quoted by a librarian for having said:

> ◇ The voracious devouring of fiction commonly indulged in by patrons of the public library, especially the young, is extremely pernicious and mentally unwholesome.[47]

Similar complaints led some librarians to limit the number of books young adults could take out at one time. When Caroline M. Hewins surveyed library conditions in 1893, she found:

> ◇ 90 libraries allow them [young people] to change a book every day; one (subscription) gives them a dozen a day if they wish. 15 limit them to 2, and 3 to 3 a week, and 15 to only 1. Several librarians in libraries where children are allowed a book a day express their disapproval of the custom and one has entered into an engagement with her young readers to take 1 book in every 4 from some other class than fiction.[48]

A gradual change from piety to morality led to literature that was more subtly if still surely didactic by 1900. Literature read by young adults, whether adult works or those written specifically for young adults—and the latter made great strides in quantity and quality—reflected the increasing freedom of writers. The development of inexpensive and ubiquitous dime novels, the popular story weeklies, and paperback libraries, along with more expensive but equally ubiquitous domestic novels, created a mass market of readers and led to an expanded national literacy. The rise of the public library permitted easier access to a greater quantity of literature just as it raised problems about the purpose of the library, especially for young adults. Series books, for better or worse, began. Expansion of literature written for young adults, and especially series books, lay only a few years away.

◆ ACTIVITIES ◆

1. Locate a Domestic Novel (most university libraries have copies of books by Susan Warner or Augusta Jane Evans Wilson and secondhand bookstores often have copies, so many were printed when they were popular). Read the first few pages and skim a few pages throughout the book. What kinds of style, diction, plot devices, and formula conventions were used? What parallels can you find in Domestic Novels and present-day Gothics and Harlequin Romances? What made the Domestic Novel so popular at the time?

2. Read a dime novel to get a feeling for the style, diction, and conventions. Why do you suppose they were so popular, especially with boys? Choose a currently popular adventure novel (or an adventure movie or an adventure series on TV) and compare the conventions and excitement of the dime novel with the current favorites. What similarities exist? What differences? What dime novel conventions persist in modern adventure literature?

3. Trying very hard to stay awake (no easy task this), read one of Horatio Alger's novels.

(Several have been reprinted and they are not difficult to find in secondhand bookstores.) What elements of Alger's books made him popular with readers? If you were asked to write a brief introduction to a modern reissue of an Alger novel, what would you say to the reader about Alger's life, style, message, readability, and popularity?

4. Select one of the series novels popular with young people a hundred years ago, for example, a novel by Castlemon, Optic, Finley, or Coolidge. Read and analyze what the book tells you about its contemporary readers and their beliefs and values. Would this book be readable by a young adult today? Why or why not?

5. Select one of these nonseries boys' books— Thomas Bailey Aldrich's *The Story of a Bad Boy*, John Bennett's *Master Skylark*, Howard Pyle's *Men of Iron*, John Meade Falkner's *Moonfleet*, Robert Ballantyne's *The Coral Is-land*, or Kirk Munroe's *The Flamingo Feather*—and read it. What are the conventions of boys' adventure tales of the time? What moral values does the author assume and preach or teach? Does the book deserve reprinting and reading today?

6. Read Evelyn Geller's "The Librarian as Censor" in the June 1, 1976, *Library Journal* as background. Then read several articles in the early issues of *Library Journal* prior to 1900 on restricting the reading of fiction for young adults. Why do you suppose the restrictions applied almost exclusively to fiction? What arguments parallel modern-day censors? What arguments seem dated? Skim through a few issues of the *Newsletter on Intellectual Freedom* to note the objections sounded today about controversial fiction for young adults. Are the comments and arguments of censors in the *Newsletter* reminiscent of those in early issues of *Library Journal*?

◆ NOTES ◆

[1]Caroline Ticknor, *Hawthorne and His Publisher* (Boston: Houghton Mifflin, 1913), p. 141.

[2]E. Douglas Branch, *The Sentimental Years, 1836–1860* (New York: Appleton, 1934), p. 131.

[3]William Everett, "Beadle's Dime Novels," *North American Review* 9 (July 1864): 308.

[4]Quentin Reynolds, *The Fiction Factory, or From Pulp Row to Quality Street* (New York: Random House, 1955), pp. 74–75.

[5]Charles Bragin, *Bibliography: Dime Novels 1860–1964* (New York: Privately printed, 1964), p. 2.

[6]Frederic Van Rensselaer Dey, "How I Wrote a Thousand 'Nick Carter' Novels," *American Magazine* 89 (February 1920): 19.

[7]William Sumner, "What Our Boys Are Reading," *Scribner's Monthly* 15 (March 1878): 681–85.

[8]Theodore C. Burgess, "Means of Leading Boys from the Dime Novel to Better Literature," *Library Journal* 21 (April 1896): 147.

[9]*Publisher's Weekly* 23 (April 28, 1883): 500.

[10]*Publisher's Weekly* 23 (April 28, 1883): 500.

[11]See especially Burgess; Clement C. Young, "The Public Library and the Public School," *Library Journal* 21 (March 1896): 140–44; Arthur P. Irving, "Home Reading of School Children," *Pedagogical Seminary* 7 (April 1900): 138–40; "The Pawtucket Free Library and the Dime Novel," *Library Journal* 10 (May 1885): 105; and Ellen M. Cox, "What Can Be Done to Help a Boy to Like Good Books after He Has Fallen into the 'Dime Novel Habit'?" *Library Journal* 20 (April 1895): 118–19.

[12]Quoted in Esther Jane Carrier, *Fiction in Public Libraries, 1876–1900* (Metuchen, NJ: Scarecrow Press, 1965), p. 186.

[13]Quoted in *Library Journal* 8 (March–April 1883): 57.

[14]Everett, p. 308.

[15]T. W. Higginson, "Address," *Library Journal* 4 (September–October 1879): 359.

[16]Mary Noel, *Villains Galore . . . The Heyday of the Popular Story Weekly* (New York: Macmillan, 1954), p. 111.

[17]Noel, pp. 112–13.

[18]Ednah D. Cheney, ed., *Louisa May Alcott: Her Life, Letters, and Journals* (Boston: Little, Brown, 1901), p. 199.

[19]Edwin P. Hoyt, *Horatio's Boys: The Life and the Works of Horatio Alger, Jr.* (Radnor, Pennsylvania: Chilton, 1974), pp. 1–6.

[20]See Eric Monkkonen, "Socializing the New Urbanites: Horatio Alger, Jr.'s Guidebooks," *Journal of Popular Culture* 11 (Summer 1977): 77–87,

for a fine discussion of *Ragged Dick* as guidebook and handbook.

[21]Jacob Blanck, *Harry Castlemon, Boys' Own Author* (New York: R. R. Bowker, 1941), pp. 5–6.

[22]Samuel Scoville, Jr., "Rescue, Robbers, and Escapes," *Forum* 74 (July 1925): 86.

[23]Raymond L. Kilgour, *Lee and Shepard: Publishers for the People* (Hamden, Connecticut: Shoe String Press, 1965), p. 270.

[24]Oliver Optic, "Sensational Books," *Oliver Optic's Magazine* 18 (September 1875): 718. For an account of the quarrel, see Gene Gleason, "What Ever Happened to Oliver Optic?" *Wilson Library Bulletin* 49 (May 1975): 647–50.

[25]For a somewhat different point of view, see Jacqueline Jackson and Philip Kendall, "What Makes a Bad Book Good: Elsie Dinsmore" in Francelia Butler, ed., *Children's Literature: Annual of the Modern Language Association Group on Children's Literature and the Children's Literature Association* 7 (1978): 45–67.

[26]*Atlantic* 25 (January 1870): 124.

[27]Robert Berkelman, "Mrs. Grundy and Richard Watson Gilder," *American Quarterly* 4 (Spring 1952): 66–72.

[28]Quoted in *Critic* 3 (March 28, 1885): 155.

[29]*Library Journal* 14 (November 18, 1889): 445.

[30]Asa Don Dickinson, "Huckleberry Finn Is Fifty Years Old—Yes; But Is He Respectable?" *Wilson Bulletin* 10 (November 1935): 183.

[31]Dickinson, 183.

[32]For examples, see *Library Journal* 8 (March–April 1883): 49–50, and Royal W. Bullock, "Some Observations on Children's Reading," *NEA Journal of Proceedings and Addresses, 1897* (Chicago: University of Chicago Press, 1897), pp. 1015–21.

[33]Jesse H. Shera, *Foundations of the Public Library: The Origins of the Public Library Movement in New England, 1629–1885.* (Chicago: University of Chicago Press, 1949), p. 238.

[34]Joseph Leroy Harrison, "The Public Library Movement in the United States," *New England Magazine*, new series 10 (August 1894): 710.

[35]Elmer D. Johnson, *History of Libraries in the Western World*, 2nd ed. (Metuchen, N.J.: Scarecrow Press, 1970), p. 358.

[36]A brief summary of the 1853 and 1876 library conventions can be found in Sister Gabriella Margeath, "Library Conventions of 1853, 1876, and 1877," *Journal of Library History* 8 (April 1973): 52–69.

[37]See George Bobinski, *Carnegie Libraries: Their History and Impact on American Library Development* (Chicago: American Library Association, 1967).

[38]*American Library Journal* 1 (November 30, 1876): 109.

[39]S. S. Green, "Capture of a Notorious Book-Thief," *Library Journal* 5 (February 1880): 48–49.

[40]"The Los Angeles Library Libel Suit," *Library Journal* 19 (October 1894): 340.

[41]William F. Poole, "Some Popular Objections to Public Libraries," *American Library Journal* 1 (October 1876): 48–49.

[42]W. M. Stevenson, "Weeding Out Fiction in the Carnegie Free Library of Allegheny, Pa.," *Library Journal* 22 (March 1897): 135.

[43]Quoted in Tremaine McDowell, "Sensibility in the Eighteenth-Century American Novel," *Studies in Philology* 24 (July 1927): 395.

[44]"Novel Reading," *American Library Journal* 1 (October 1876): 98.

[45]George T. Clark, "Improper Books," *Library Journal* 20 (December 1895): 34.

[46]T. De Witt Talmage, *Social Dynamite, or The Wickedness of Modern Society* (Chicago: Standard Publishing Co., 1888), quoted in Neil Harris, ed., *The Land of Contrasts, 1880–1901* (New York: George Braziller, 1970), pp. 275, 278–79.

[47]"Monthly Reports from Public Librarians upon the Reading of Minors: A Suggestion," *Library Journal* 24 (August 1899): 479.

[48]Caroline M. Hewins, "Report on the Reading of the Young," *Library Journal* 18 (July 1893): 252.

◆ TITLES MENTIONED IN CHAPTER 13 ◆

Abbott, Jacob. *Rollo at School.* 1839.

————. *Rollo at Work, or, The Way for a Boy to Learn to Be Industrious.* 1838.

————. *Rollo in London.* 1855.

————. *Rollo in Rome.* 1858.

————. *Rollo on the Atlantic.* 1853.

Alcott, Louisa May. *Eight Cousins.* 1875.

————. *Hospital Sketches.* 1863.

————. *Jack and Jill.* 1880.

————. *Jo's Boys.* 1886.

_____. *Little Men.* 1871.

_____. *Little Women: Meg, Jo, Beth, and Amy. The Story of Their Lives. A Girl's Book.* 1868.

_____. *Little Women, or Meg, Jo, Beth and Amy. Part Second.* 1869.

_____. *An Old-Fashioned Girl.* 1870.

_____. *On Picket Duty and Other Tales.* 1864.

_____. *Rose in Bloom.* 1876.

_____. *Under the Lilacs.* 1878.

Aldrich, Thomas Bailey. *The Story of a Bad Boy.* 1870.

Alger, Horatio. *Bound to Rise, Or, Harry Walton's Motto.* 1873.

_____. *Do and Dare, Or, A Brave Boy's Fight for Fortune.* 1884.

_____. *Fame and Fortune, Or, The Progress of Richard Hunter.* 1868.

_____. *Luck and Pluck, Or, John Oakley's Inheritance.* 1869.

_____. *Ragged Dick, Or, Street Life in New York.* 1867.

_____. *Risen from the Ranks, Or, Harry Walton's Success.* 1874.

_____. *Sink or Swim, Or, Harry Raymond's Resolve.* 1870.

_____. *Struggling Upward, Or, Luke Larkin's Luck.* 1890.

Ballantyne, Robert Michael. *The Coral Island.* 1858.

_____. *The Gorilla Hunters.* 1861.

_____. *The Young Fur Traders.* 1856.

Bennett, John. *Master Skylark; A Story of Shakespeare's Time.* 1897.

Brontë, Charlotte. *Jane Eyre.* 1847.

Brooks, Noah. *The Boy Emigrants.* 1876.

Bunyan, John. *The Pilgrim's Progress from This World to That Which Is to Come.* 1678.

Castlemon, Harry. (real name: Charles Austin Fosdick). *Frank at Don Carlos' Ranch.* 1871.

_____. *Frank Before Vicksburg.* 1865.

_____. *Frank in the Woods.* 1865.

_____. *Frank on a Gunboat.* 1864.

_____. *Frank on the Lower Mississippi.* 1867.

_____. *Frank on the Prairie.* 1868.

_____. *Frank the Young Naturalist.* 1864.

Coolidge, Susan (real name: Sarah Chauncey Woolsey). *Clover.* 1888.

_____. *In the Valley.* 1891.

_____. *What Katy Did.* 1872.

_____. *What Katy Did at School.* 1873.

_____. *What Katy Did Next.* 1886.

Dallas, Mary Kyle. *Neglected Warning, or, The Trials of a Public School Teacher.* n.d.

Day, Thomas. *The History of Sanford and Merton.* 1783, 1786, and 1789.

Defoe, Daniel. *The Life and Strange Surprising Adventures of Robinson Crusoe.* 1719.

_____. *Moll Flanders.* 1722.

_____. *Roxanna.* 1724.

Dey, Frederic Van Rensselaer. "Nick Carter" Series.

Doyle, Arthur Conan. *The Adventures of Sherlock Holmes.* 1891.

Edgeworth, Maria. *Castle Rackrent.* 1800.

_____. *Frank.* 1822.

_____. *Harry and Lucy.* 1801.

_____. *Harry and Lucy Concluded.* 1825.

_____. *Moral Tales for Young People.* 1801.

_____. *The Parent's Assistant.* 1796.

_____. *Popular Tales.* 1804.

_____. *Rosamund.* 1821.

Ellis, Edward S. *Seth Jones.* 1860.

_____. *Trail Hunters.* 1862.

Falkner, John Meade. *Moonfleet.* 1898.

Finley, Martha (real name: Martha Farquharson). *Christmas with Grandma Elsie.* 1888.

_____. *Elsie Dinsmore.* 1867.

_____. *Elsie in the South.* 1899.

_____. *Elsie's Children.* 1877.

_____. *Elsie's Girlhood.* 1872.

_____. *Elsie's Motherhood.* 1876.

_____. *Elsie's Widowhood.* 1880.

Golding, William. *Lord of the Flies.* Putnam's, 1955.

Henty, George Alfred. *Beric, The Briton. A Story of the Roman Invasion.* 1893.

_____. *When London Burned. A Story of the Plague and the Fire.* 1895.

_____. *Winning His Spurs. A Tale of the Crusades.* 1892.

More, Hannah. *Coelebs in Search of a Wife.* 1809.

_____. *Moral Sketches.* 1819.

_____. *Repository Tracts.* 1795–1798.

Mulock, Dinah Maria. *John Halifax, Gentleman.* 1857.

Munroe, Kirk. *Derrick Sterling.* 1888.

_____. *The Flamingo Feather.* 1887.

Optic, Oliver (real name: William Taylor Adams). *The Boat Club.* 1855.

Parley, Peter (real name: Samuel Goodrich). *Recollections of a Lifetime, or Men and Things I Have Seen.* 1856.

————. *The Tales of Peter Parley about America.* 1827.

Peck, George Wilbur. *Peck's Bad Boy and His Pa.* 1883.

Porter, Jane. *Thaddeus of Warsaw.* 1803.

Pyle, Howard. *Men of Iron.* 1892.

————. *The Merry Adventures of Robin Hood.* 1883.

————. *Otto of the Silver Hand.* 1888.

St. George, Harry (real name: St. George Rathbone). *Daring Davy, The Young Bear Killer; Or, The Trail of the Border Wolf.* 1879.

Smith, Francis S. *The Vestmaker's Apprentice; Or, The Vampyres of Society.* 1857.

Stephens, Ann S. *Malaeska: The Indian Wife of the White Hunter.* 1860.

Stevenson, Robert Louis. *Kidnapped.* 1886.

————. *Treasure Island.* 1883.

Stowe, Harriet Beecher. *Uncle Tom's Cabin.* 1852.

Swift, Jonathan. *Gulliver's Travels.* 1726.

————. *A Tale of a Tub.* 1704.

Twain, Mark (real name: Samuel Clemens). *The Adventures of Huckleberry Finn.* 1884.

————. *The Adventures of Tom Sawyer.* 1876.

Verne, Jules. *Around the World in Eighty Days.* 1874.

————. *From the Earth to the Moon.* 1873.

————. *Twenty Thousand Leagues under the Sea.* 1872.

Weems, Mason Locke. *The Life of George Washington.* 1808.

————. *The Life of Washington the Great.* 1806.

————. *A History of the Life and Death, Virtues and Exploits, of General George Washington.* 1800.

Wetherell, Elizabeth (real name: Susan Warner). *The Wide, Wide World.* 1850.

Wilson, Augusta Jane Evans. *St. Elmo.* 1867.

Wood, Mrs. Henry. *East Lynne.* 1861.

◆ SOME SUGGESTED READINGS ◆

General Comments on Literature 1800–1900:

Blanck, Jacob. *Peter Parley to Penrod: A Bibliographical Description of the Best Loved American Juvenile Books.* New York: R. R. Bowker, 1938.

————. "A Twentieth-Century Look at Nineteenth-Century Children's Books" in *Bibliophile in the Nursery,* ed. William Targ. Cleveland: World, 1957, pp. 427–51.

Crandall, John C. "Patriotism and Humanitarian Reform in Children's Literature, 1825–1860." *American Quarterly* 21 (Spring 1969): 3–22.

Gorham, Deborah. *The Victorian Girl and the Feminine Ideal.* Bloomington: Indiana University Press, 1982.

Kiefer, Monica. *American Children through Their Books, 1700–1835.* Philadelphia: University of Pennsylvania Press, 1948.

MacLeod, Anne Scott. "Children's Literature and American Culture 1820–1860" in James H. Fraser, ed., *Society and Children's Literature* (Papers Presented at a Symposium Sponsored by the School of Library Science Simmons College, 1976). Boston: David R. Godine, 1978, pp. 13–31.

————. *A Moral Tale: Children's Fiction and American Culture 1820–1860.* Hamden, Connecticut: Archon Books, 1975.

Oggel, L. Terry. "The Background of the Images of Childhood in American Literature." *Western Humanities Review* 33 (Autumn 1979): 281–97.

Rayward, W. Boyd. "What Shall They Read? A Historical Perspective." *Wilson Library Bulletin* 51 (October 1976): 146–53.

Sloane, William. *Children's Books in England and America in the Seventeenth Century.* New York: Columbia University Press, 1955.

Wishy, Bernard. *The Child and the Republic: The Dawn of Modern American Child Nurture.* Philadelphia: University of Pennsylvania Press, 1968.

General Comments on Literature 1850–1900:

Ashford, Richard K. "Tomboys & Saints: Girls' Stories of the Late Nineteenth Century." *School Library Journal* 26 (January 1980): 23–28.

Avery, Gillian. *Childhood's Pattern: A Study of the Heroes and Heroines of Children's Fiction,*

1770–1950. London: Hodder and Stoughton, 1975.

Branch, E. Douglas. *The Sentimental Years, 1836–1860*. New York: Appleton, 1934.

Bratton, J. S. *The Impact of Victorian Children's Fiction*. London: Croom Helm, 1981; Totowa, New Jersey: Barnes and Noble, 1981.

Cadogan, Mary, and Patricia Craig. *You're a Brick, Angela! A New Look at Girls' Fiction from 1839 to 1975*. London: Victor Gollancz, 1976.

Campbell, Patricia J. *Sex Education Books for Young Adults, 1892–1979*. New York: R. R. Bowker, 1979.

Cowie, Alexander. *The Rise of the American Novel*. New York: American, 1948.

Cruse, Amy. *The Victorians and Their Reading*. Boston: Houghton Mifflin, 1935. First published in England as *The Victorians and Their Books*.

Darling, Richard. *The Rise of Children's Book Reviewing in America, 1865–1881*. R. R. Bowker, 1968.

Ellis, Alec. *A History of Children's Reading and Literature*. Oxford: Pergamon Press, 1968.

Petter, Henri. *The Early American Novel*. Columbus: Ohio State University Press,1971.

Van Doren, Carl. *The American Novel*. New York: Macmillan, 1929.

The Domestic Novel:

Brown, Herbert Ross. *The Sentimental Novel in America, 1789–1860*. Durham: North Carolina University Press, 1940.

Hofstadter, Beatrice K. "Popular Culture and the Romantic Heroine." *American Scholar* 30 (Winter 1960–61): 98

Papashvily, Helen Waite. *All the Happy Endings: A Study of the Domestic Novel in America, The Women Who Wrote It, The Women Who Read It, in the Nineteenth Century*. New York: Harper & Row, 1956.

Pattee, Fred Lewis. *The Feminist Fifties*. New York: Appleton, 1940.

Susan Warner:

Denman, Frank. "How to Drive the Sheriff from the Homestead Door." *New York Times Book Review*, December 24, 1944, p. 8.

Jordan, Alice M. "Susan Warner and Her *Wide Wide World*." *Horn Book Magazine* 10 (September 1934): 287–93.

Warner, Anna B. *Susan Warner*. New York: G. P. Putnam's Sons, 1904.

Augusta Jane Wilson:

Calkins, Ernest Elmo. "St. Elmo, or, Names for a Best Seller." *Saturday Review of Literature* 21 (December 16, 1939): 3.

Fidler, William Perry. *Augusta Evans Wilson 1835–1900*. University, Alabama: University of Alabama Press, 1951.

Maurice, Arthur Bartlett. "Best Sellers of Yesterday: Augusta Jane Evans' *St. Elmo*." *Bookman* 31 (March 1910): 35–42.

Dime Novels (General):

Admari, Ralph. "Ballou: The Father of the Dime Novel." *American Book Collector* 4 (September–October 1933): 121–29.

Curti, Merle. "Dime Novels and the American Tradition." *Yale Review* 26 (June 1937): 761–68.

Dey, Frederic Van Rensselaer. "How I Wrote a Thousand 'Nick Carter' Novels." *American Magazine* 89 (February 1920): 19.

Jenks, George C. "Dime Novel Makers." *Bookman* 20 (October 1904): 108–14.

Johannsen, Albert. *The House of Beadle and Adams and Its Dime and Nickel Novels: The Story of a Vanished Literature*. 3 Volumes. Norman: University of Oklahoma Press, 1950, 1962. A basic work.

Jones, Daryl. *The Dime Novel Western*. Bowling Green, Ohio: Bowling Green University Popular Press, 1978.

Leithead, J. Edward. "The Anatomy of Dime Novels: No. 1—Nick Carter." *Dime Novel Roundup* 33 (September 15, 1964): 76–79; and 33 (October 15, 1964): 84–89. From his vast reading and collecting, Leithead wrote prolifically about dime novels in *Dime Novel Roundup*, the best source of information about the subject, and *American Book Collector* until his death in 1970.

Pearson, Edmund. *Dime Novels, or Following an Old Trail in Popular Literature*. Port Washington, New York: Kennikat Press, 1968. First published in 1929.

Reynolds, Quentin. *The Fiction Factory, or From Pulp Row to Quality Street*. New York: Random House, 1955. On Street and Smith.

Smith, Henry Nash. *Virgin Land: The American*

West as Symbol and Myth. Cambridge: Harvard University Press, 1950.

Turner, E. S. *Boys Will Be Boys*, 3rd ed. London: Michael Joseph, 1978. Primarily on English Penny Dreadfuls, but Chapter 10 is excellent on the American Frank Reade series.

Dime Novels (Objections to and Objections to the Objections):

Bishop, W. H. "Story-Paper Literature." *Atlantic* 44 (September 1879): 383–93.

Burgess, Theodore C. "Means of Leading Boys from the Dime Novel to Better Literature." *Library Journal* 21 (April 1896): 144–47.

Comstock, Anthony. *Traps for the Young*, ed. Robert Bremner. Cambridge: Harvard University Press, 1967. First published in 1883.

Cox, Ellen M. "What Can Be Done to Help a Boy to Like Good Books after He Has Fallen into the 'Dime Novel Habit'?" *Library Journal* 20 (April 1895): 118–19.

Harvey, Charles M. "The Dime Novel in American Life." *Atlantic* 100 (July 1907): 37–45.

Sumner, William. "What Our Boys Are Reading." *Scribner's Monthly* 15 (March 1878): 681–85.

Thurber, James. "Thix" in *The Beast in Me and Other Animals*. New York: Harcourt, Brace, World, 1948.

Popular Story Weeklies:

Bishop, W. H. "Story-Paper Literature." *Atlantic* 44 (September 1879): 383–93.

Noel, Mary. *Villains Galore . . . The Heyday of the Popular Story Weekly*. New York: Macmillan, 1954.

Louisa May Alcott:

Cheney, Ednah D., ed. *Louisa May Alcott: Her Life, Letters and Journals*. Boston: Little, Brown, 1901.

Morrow, Honoré Willsie. *Father of Little Women*. Boston: Little, Brown, 1927.

Payne, Alma J. "Louisa May Alcott (1832–1888)." *American Literary Realism, 1870–1910* 6 (Winter 1973): 23–43. Excellent bibliographical material.

Salyer, Sandford. *Marmee: The Mother of Little Women*. Norman: University of Oklahoma Press, 1949.

Saxton, Martha. *Louisa May: A Modern Biography of Louisa May Alcott*. Boston: Houghton Mifflin, 1977.

Stern, Madeleine. *Louisa May Alcott*. Norman: University of Oklahoma Press, 1950. The most readable and satisfying of all the Alcott biographies.

Horatio Alger, Jr.:

Alger, Horatio, Jr. "Writing Stories for Boys." *Writer* 9 (March 1896): 36–37.

Cawelti, John G. *Apostles of the Self-Made Man*. Chicago: University of Chicago Press, 1965, pp. 101–23.

Enslin, Morton. "Horatio Alger, Jr., after Seventy Years." *Dime Novel Roundup* 39 (April 15, 1970): 40–45; and 39 (May 15, 1970): 50–55.

Falk, Robert. "Notes on the 'Higher Criticism' of Horatio Alger, Jr." *Arizona Quarterly* 19 (Summer 1963): 151–67.

Holland, Norman. "Hobbling with Horatio, or the Uses of Literature." *Hudson Review* 12 (Winter 1959–60): 549–57.

Hoyt, Edwin P. *Horatio's Boys: The Life and Works of Horatio Alger*. Radnor, Pennsylvania: Chilton, 1974.

Seelye, John. "Who Was Horatio? The Alger Myth and American Scholarship." *American Quarterly* 17 (Winter 1965): 749–56.

Weiss, Richard. "Horatio Alger, Jr., and the Response to Industrialism" in *The Age of Industrialism in America: Essays in Social Structure and Cultural Values*, ed. Frederic Cople Jahner. New York: Free Press, 1968, pp. 304–16.

Wohl, R. Richard. "The 'Rags to Riches Story': An Episode of Secular Idealism" in *Class, Status, and Power: Social Stratification in Comparative Perspective*, ed. Reinhard Bendix and Seymour Martin Lipset, 2nd ed. New York: Free Press, 1966, pp. 501–6.

Early Series Writers:

Harry Castlemon

Blanck, Jacob. *Harry Castlemon, Boys' Own Author: An Appreciation and Bibliography*. New York: R. R. Bowker, 1941.

Castlemon, Harry. "How to Write Stories for Boys." *Writer* 9 (January 1896): 4–5.

Martha Finley

Brown, Janet. *The Saga of Elsie Dinsmore*. Buffalo: University of Buffalo Press, 1945.

Jackson, Jacqueline and Philip Kendall. "What Makes a Bad Book Good: Elsie Dinsmore" in Francelia Butler, ed., *Children's Literature: Annual of the Modern Language Association Group on Children's Literature and the Children's Literature Association* 7 (1978): 45–67.

Literature of the Bad Boy:

Geller, Evelyn. "Tom Sawyer, Tom Bailey, and the Bad-Boy Genre." *Wilson Library Bulletin* 51 (November 1976): 245–50.

Hunter, Jim. "Mark Twain and the Boy-Book in 19th-Century America." *College English* 24 (March 1963): 430–38.

Trensky, Anne. "The Bad Boy in Nineteenth-Century American Fiction." *Georgia Review* 27 (Winter 1973): 503–17.

Libraries:

Development of Libraries in America

Ditzion, Sidney. *Arsenals of a Democratic Culture: A Social History of the American Public Library Movement in New England and the Middle States from 1850 to 1900.* Chicago: American Library Association, 1947.

Harris, Michael H., and Donald G. Davis, Jr. *American Library History: A Bibliography.* Austin: University of Texas Press, 1978.

Margeath, Sister Gabriella. "Library Conventions of 1853, 1876, and 1877." *Journal of Library History* 8 (April 1973): 52–69.

Shera, Jesse H. *Foundations of the Public Library: The Origins of the Public Library Movement in New England, 1629–1885.* Chicago: University of Chicago Press, 1949.

————. "The Literature of American Library History" in Jesse H. Shera, ed., *Knowing Books and Men. Knowing Computers, Too.* Littleton, Colorado: Libraries Unlimited, 1973, pp. 124–61.

Thompson, C. Seymour. *Evolution of the American Public Library, 1653–1876.* Washington, D.C.: Scarecrow Press, 1952.

The Problem of Fiction

Carrier, Esther Jane. *Fiction in Public Libraries, 1876–1900.* New York: Scarecrow Press, 1965.

Crane, the Rev. J. T. *Popular Amusements.* Cincinnati: Cranston and Stowe, 1869. See esp. 121–52 on "Novels and Novel-Reading."

Garrison, Dee. *Apostles of Culture: The Public Librarian and American Society, 1876–1920.* New York: The Free Press, 1979, Chapters 4 and 5.

Geller, Evelyn. "The Librarian as Censor." *Library Journal* 101 (June 1, 1976): 1255–58.

Orians, G. Harrison. "Censure of Fiction in American Romances and Magazines 1789–1810." *PMLA* 52 (March 1937): 195–214.

Poole, William F. "Some Popular Objections to Public Libraries." *American Library Journal* 1 (October 1876): 45–51.

Taylor, John Tinnon. *Early Opposition to the English Novel: The Popular Reaction from 1760 to 1830.* New York: King's Crown Press, 1943.

Restricting Fiction from Young Adults

Cohen, Max. "The Librarian as Educator, and Not a Cheap-John." *Library Journal* 13 (December 1888): 366–67.

Jones, Richard. "The Moral and Literary Responsibilities of Librarians in Selecting Books for a Public Library." *NEA Journal of Proceedings and Addresses,*1897. Chicago: University of Chicago Press, 1897, pp. 1025–28.

Kite, William. "Fiction in Public Libraries." *American Library Journal* 1 (February 1877): 277–79.

Stevenson, W. M. "Weeding Out Fiction in the Carnegie Free Library of Allegheny, Pa." *Library Journal* 22 (March 1897): 133–35.

Young, Clement C. "The Public Library and the Public School." *Library Journal* 21 (April 1896): 140–44.

Loosening Restrictions on Young Adults

Cole, George Watson. "Fiction in Libraries: A Plea for the Masses." *Library Journal* 19 (December 1894): 18–21.

Geller, Evelyn. *Forbidden Books in American Public Libraries, 1876–1939: A Study in Cultural Change.* Westport, Connecticut: Greenwood Press, 1984.

Green, S. S. "Sensational Fiction in Public Libraries." *Library Journal* 4 (September–October 1879): 345–55.

Hardy, George E. "The School Library a Factor in Education." *Library Journal* 14 (August 1889): 343–47.

Higginson, T. W. "Address." *Library Journal* 4 (September–October 1879): 357–59.

1900-1940

❖

FROM THE SAFETY OF ROMANCE TO THE BEGINNING OF REALISM

The first forty years of the twentieth century were times of change and challenge, aspiration mixed with frustration. The western frontier disappeared, and the country changed from an agrarian society to an urban one. It was a time of ragtime and jazz, the Armory Show in New York and the Ashcan School of Art, and the growing popularity of college football. World War I brought certainty that it would end all wars. It led to the League of Nations and indirectly to women's suffrage. The specter of communism appeared, movies became a popular art form, and Sacco and Vanzetti were on trial. The labor movement grew along with Ford's production lines and cars, cars, cars: in 1900 only 13,824 cars were registered throughout the country; by 1919 there were more than 6,500,000; by 1929, more than 23,000,000. President Hoover came along, then the Wall Street crash of 1929 and the Great Depression. By 1938, three million young people from sixteen through twenty-five were out of school and unemployed, and a quarter of a million boys were on the road. Franklin Delano Roosevelt introduced the "New Deal," and we watched the rise of Nazi Germany. When the end of the Depression seemed almost in sight, the New York World's Fair of 1939 became our optimistic metaphor for the coming of a newer, better, happier, and more secure world. World War II lay just over the horizon, apparent to some, ignored by most.

These forty years saw literary and pedagogical changes, among them new ways of assessing reading interests of young adults and the rise of

English teaching as a discipline. There were further developments in series books, "junior" or "juvenile" divisions were started in publishing houses, and pulps and comics began. Fashions changed in the kinds of books read by young adults, just as they changed in everything else.

◈ READING INTEREST STUDIES

Before 1900, librarians and English teachers published little about reading interests of young people. Many adults, intent on telling the young what to read, had scant interest in finding out what young adults cared to read. English teaching was a relatively new discipline—English was not given the time and attention accorded Latin and other school subjects until late in the nineteenth century—and teachers faced pressure from colleges to prepare the young for study and weighty matters. Recreational reading seemed vaguely time wasting, if not downright wicked. With the exception of a few articles like True's "What My Pupils Read,"[1] reading interests went largely unexplored. But after publication of the Vostrovsky study,[2] the first significant reading interest investigation, came the deluge. Simple and unsophisticated and naive they may have been, but they were honest attempts to find what young adults liked. From brief two- or three-page articles to books of several hundred pages, reading interest studies ranged from simple, direct status quo reports to complex analyses of what young adults liked and why. Sometimes a wounded librarian or teacher would wax indignant about the dullness of the young and their lamentably mediocre tastes. Most reading interest studies, however, provided modern English teachers and librarians with helpful information that could be put to use in the classroom or library.

Findings of Reading Interest Studies

Generally, studies revealed that young adults read far more fiction than any other genre. They read books written specifically for them, series books from Stratemeyer's Literary Syndicate such as Tom Swift, Nancy Drew, Hardy Boys, Baseball Joe, and Ruth Fielding, and non-Stratemeyer series like Boys of Bob's Hill, Frank Merriwell, Roy Blakely, and Campfire Girls. They read adolescent books by Barbour, Heyliger, Pease, Terhune, Montgomery, Alcott, O'Brien, Seaman, and Altsheler. They read classics by Dickens, Scott, and Shakespeare. They read modern best-sellers by Wright, Grey, Churchill, Curwood, Webster, Tarkington, McCutcheon, and many, many more.

In effect, they read many of the same writers and books reported in Irving Harlow Hart's "The Most Popular Authors of Fiction between 1900 and 1925,"[3] and they read best-sellers selected by the Book-of-the-Month Club when it began in 1926 and the Literary Guild when it began a year later.

Some Reactions

Some investigators and readers reacted predictably and emotionally to reading interest studies. English teacher Alfred M. Hitchcock voiced fears that education and the reading public were hurtling steadily downward:

> ◇ Books, magazines, journals are written to catch the multitudes—the multitudes who are not very keenly intellectual, nor gifted with imagination, nor trained to appreciate artistic form—the easy-going, pleasure-seeking, not over-ambitious, somewhat unmoral multitudes. There are notable exceptions, it is true; yet one cannot avoid the suspicion that many writers are content to give the public what the public wants, not what it needs. Reading the truly popular literature of the hour, in the manner in which it is commonly read by the young, can hardly be called an intellectual exercise. It does not challenge the mind; it does not invite the imagination. Too often it feeds the passions rather than the higher emotions. The youth who reads gets little; his moral and intellectual fiber is not strengthened.[4]

Reactions led some critics to bombast and wild metaphors, comparing reading to eating and arguing that "A continual diet of one type of book is likely permanently to injure the taste."[5] The "you-are-what-you-eat-and-you-are-what-you-read" metaphor became increasingly tiresome in articles by librarians and teachers over the years.

The argument over the possible harm that might come from series books, or popular literature sometimes labeled "subliterature," has raged for years, and the end is unlikely to precede the millennium. In the lengthy *Winnetka Graded Book List*, partly concerned with the reading of junior-high students, Washburne and Vogel did not list all books reported; "Books that were definitely trashy or unsuitable for children, even though widely read, have not been included in this list."[6] Enough people were apparently curious about the trashy or unsuitable books to lead the authors to add two supplements.[7] Predictably, *Elsie Dinsmore* was among the damned, but so were Edgar Rice Burroughs' *Tarzan of the Apes*, Eleanor Porter's *Pollyanna*, Gene Stratton Porter's *Freckles* and *A Girl of the Limberlost*, Zane Grey's westerns, and books from the Ruth Fielding and Tom Swift series. No surprises there, but surprises did pop up. Many popular girls' mysteries by Augusta Huill Seaman were excluded from the original list, but other of her titles, seemingly no better or worse, were approved or recommended. Strangely, Mark Twain's *Tom Sawyer Abroad* was among the unwashed and disapproved. So was Mary Roberts Rinehart's *The Circular Staircase*. Arthur Conan Doyle's *The Adventures of Sherlock Holmes* was recommended, but *The Hound of the Baskervilles* was not acceptable. Such puzzlements must have disturbed readers looking for that most impossible of tools, a list applicable to all teachers, schools, libraries, and students.

Other critics seemed less concerned about the souls of the young even if trash were part of the diet. Critic and English professor William Lyon Phelps argued that reading some relatively poor literature was not only not harmful but almost inevitable for most young readers:

> ◇ I do not believe the majority of these very school teachers and other cultivated mature readers began in early youth by reading great books exclusively; I think they read Jack Harkaway, an Old Sleuth, and the works of Oliver Optic and Horatio Alger. From these enchanters they learned a thing of tremendous importance—the delight of reading. Once a taste for reading is formed, it can be improved. But it is improbable that boys and girls who have never cared to read a good story will later enjoy stories by good artists.[8]

In a book aimed at future English teachers, Reed Smith agreed with Phelps and no doubt horrified some librarians and English teachers:

> ◇ It is better for a boy to read Nick Carter or Frank Merriwell than not to read at all; and it is much better for him to read *Tarzan of the Apes* and *The Shepherd of the Hills* and like them than to read *Vanity Fair* and *Moby Dick* and hate them.[9]

Girls' Books and Boys' Books

Teachers and librarians frequently commented that girls' books, particularly up to the middle 1930s, were inferior to boys' books. Franklin T. Baker wrote that girls' books of 1908 were "numerous and . . . often painfully weak" lacking "invention, action, humor"[10] with the obvious exception of Alcott. Two years later Clara Whitehill Hunt agreed that many girls' books were empty, insipid, and mediocre.[11] As late as 1935, a writer could still object to the dearth of good fiction for girls. Reviewing some interesting nonfiction for boys, Julia Carter broke in with what appeared to be an exasperated obiter dictum:

> ◇ Will someone please tell me why we expect the *boys* to know these things and still plan for the girls to be mid-Victorian, and consider them hoydens beyond reclaiming, when instead of shrieking and running like true daughters of Eve, they are interested in snakes and can light a fire with two matches?[12]

Yet only two years later, writers like Caroline Dale Snedeker, Cornelia Meigs, Jeanette Eaton, Mabel Robinson, and Elizabeth Forman Lewis were producing enough quality girls' literature to encourage Alice M. Jordan to write:

> ◇ There was a time not long ago when the boys had the lion's share in the yearly production of books intended for young people. So writers were urged to give us more stories in which girls could see themselves in recognizable relationship to the world of their own time, forgetting perhaps that human nature does not change and the vital things are universal. Yet, none the less, the girls had a real cause to plead and right valiantly the writers have responded.[13]

Critics believed then, as they continued to do for years thereafter, that girls would read boys' books but boys would never read girls' books. One accepted boys' books as "more sincere, vigorous, wholesome, and free from affectation."[14] Boys' books consistently outsold girls' books—publishers could count on that—until the first Nancy Drews appeared on the market. At least part of the problem of stereotyping girls' and boys' books lay with stereotypes of boys' and girls' roles as expressed by two writers. Clara Vostrovsky, author of the first significant reading interest study, went back

⬥ THE PEOPLE BEHIND THE BOOKS

PAULA FOX, Author

Blowfish Live in the Sea
One-Eyed Cat
A Place Apart
The Slave Dancer

When I was a child, there was no special category in literature for adolescents. There were splendid books for children—a range that could include the work of a Victorian lady, Mrs. Molesworth, as well as the work of Robert Louis Stevenson—and then one came to the books the grown-ups read. I'm inclined to think that good books transcend special categories, and that although categories may focus attention on a special group, they also impose arbitrary limitations. I've known adolescents who read novels about heroes of football with the same intensity with which they read Dickens or D. H. Lawrence. Such eclecticism, I think, is the mark of real readers. Adolescence is not, after all, a thing apart from the rest of our lives; its difficulties and delights reflect back to the earlier days of childhood as much as they prefigure the days of adulthood. ◆

Blowfish Live in the Sea. Bradbury, 1970.
One-Eyed Cat. Bradbury, 1984.
A Place Apart. Farrar, Straus, Giroux, 1980.
The Slave Dancer. Bradbury, 1973.

---

to ancient times for her stereotypes suggesting that it was "probable" that the differences in reading interests between boys and girls lay "in the history of the race."[15] Psychologist G. Stanley Hall predicated reading interests of girls and boys on psychological differences:

> ◇ Boys love adventure, girls sentiment. . . . Girls love to read stories about girls which boys eschew, girls, however, caring much more to read about boys than boys to read about girls. Books dealing with domestic life and with young children in them girls have almost entirely to themselves. Boys, on the other hand, excel in love of humor, rollicking fun, abandon, rough horse-play, and tales of wild escapades. Girls are less averse to reading what boys like than boys are to reading what girls like. A book popular with boys would attract some girls, while one read by most girls would repel a boy in the middle teens. The reading interests of high-school girls are far more humanistic, cultural and general, and that of boys is more practical, vocational, and even special.[16]

The simple truth, perhaps too obvious and discomforting to be palatable to some parents, English teachers, and librarians, was that boys' books were generally far superior to girls' books. That had nothing to do with the sexual or psychological nature of boys or girls, but rather with the way authors treated their audience. Many authors insisted on making their girls good and domestic and dull (if a heroine were allowed some freedom to roam outside the house, she soon regretted it or grew up, whichever came first), perhaps because they thought parents and librarians wanted books that way. Boys were allowed outside the house to find work and responsibilities, of course, but also to find adventure and excitement in their books. Of course, boys rarely read girls' books, but girls did not necessarily like the books any better. One girl, not fitting the Vostrovsky or Hall stereotypes, preferred *Captains Courageous* to a girls' book because it had "so much more pep."[17] And she was right; it did.

Motion Pictures and Books

From the time motion pictures became a popular medium, librarians and teachers debated the value of films and worried that they would lead people, especially young adults, away from books. As early as 1918, one writer argued that motion pictures were more powerful and created more vivid impressions on the young than books, but he also felt movies would lead to "an increased demand for fiction dealing with the stories exhibited."[18] Eleven years later, Cleveland librarian Marilla Waite Freeman pointed out the number of potential library tie-ins with current movies like *The Covered Wagon, Ben-Hur, Scaramouche, Show Boat,* and *Seventh Heaven.*[19] Another acknowledged a fact many librarians and teachers had come to accept, "A motion picture production may send the circulation of the book from a little more than nothing to a million or more a year."[20] By 1940, Hollywood's influence on young adults' reading interests and tastes was acknowledged, accepted, and often praised for the good it could do for books, libraries, and classroom:

> ◇ Hollywood has a tremendous influence on reading tastes of youth today. Comprehensive surveys made in all libraries indicate that good movies made from books definitely stimulate reading of the book. Release of motion pictures made from books will often have immediate effect in the school library. Dust is blown off some of the older volumes, or books classified as "too dry," "not interesting," and they are removed from the shelf for reading and re-reading. There is often renewed interest in the classics. Such books as Dickens, *Tale of Two Cities*; Wyss, *Swiss Family Robinson*; Brontë, *Wuthering Heights*; Austen, *Pride and Prejudice*; Roberts, *Northwest Passage*; Kipling, *The Light That Failed*; Du Maurier's *Rebecca*; Fields' *All This, And Heaven Too* have been put in steady circulation.[21]

◈ THE DEVELOPING AND CHANGING ENGLISH CLASSROOM

By 1900, the library played a significant role in helping young adults find reading materials. Although many librarians reflected the traditional belief that classics should be the major reading of youth, other librarians helped young adults to find a variety of materials they liked, not trash, but certainly popular books.

That would have rarely been true of English teachers, saddled as they were with responsibility for preparing young adults for college. College entrance examinations virtually forced secondary school English teachers to feed their students a steady diet of great literature, not because great books were necessarily enjoyable or satisfying but because college exams were predicated on a study of the classics. High schools then hardly touched the masses of young adults, enrolling a mere one of twenty-five young people. They were regarded by most college teachers and many secondary teachers as preparatory schools, institutions to prepare students not for life but for college. The chances of students' discovering much joy and excitement in literature or in finding contemporary books in English classes were minimal.

The attention paid to poetry and nonfiction prose was hardly surprising, but some teachers argued for the use of the often ignored novel in the classroom. An Illinois committee surveying English teachers found novels all too rarely used, recommended their use, and then added a warning:

> ◇ The novel is conspicuous by its absence. The literary history of the Nine-teenth Century shows no names more remarkable than those of Scott, Dickens, Thackeray, and Eliot, to say nothing of Hawthorne, Cooper, and Cable. These men are celebrated for fiction. The novel has become a factor in our life. It is instructive and propagandist; it teaches psychology; preaches a new religion, or attacks the old; gives lessons in sociology; reforms old abuses; satirizes new follies; and continually retells the old but ever new story of human life. It forms the greater part of our reading, if library statistics are to be trusted, and certainly is most potent in its influence on human conduct. It therefore belongs in the English course of the high school. Perhaps one is enough; certainly five seems too large a number.[22]

Unhappily, the study of literature was often reserved for the senior year, as William E. Mead lamented in *The Academy* (a journal that is far and away the best source of information about English teaching prior to the *English Journal*):

> ◇ Most high schools give but a single year to literature, and that at the end of the course. To leave the average boy to the forlorn hope of reaching the last year of the high school before giving him an insight into literature is practically to condemn him for life to a taste for third-rate prose and third-rate poetry. He may pick up a knowledge of literature by himself, but we need not expect him to be very grateful to his teachers.[23]

College Entrance Examinations Ride High

Early entrance exams for college simply required some proof of writing proficiency, but in 1869 and 1870, Harvard began using Milton's *Comus* and Shakespeare's *Julius Caesar* as alternative books for the examination. Four years later Harvard required a short composition based on a question about one of the following: Shakespeare's *The Tempest, Julius Caesar,* and *The Merchant of Venice,* Goldsmith's *The Vicar of Wakefield,* or Scott's *Ivanhoe* and *The Lay of the Last Minstrel.*

In 1894, the prestigious Committee of Ten on Secondary School Stud-ies presented its report, and English became an accepted discipline in the schools, if not yet as respectable as Latin. Chaired by controversial Harvard president Charles W. Eliot, the Committee was appointed by the National Education Association in July 1892 and met later that year to determine the nature, limits, and methods appropriate to many subject matters in second-ary school.[24] Samuel Thurber of The Boston Girls' High School was unable to promote his belief that a high school curriculum should consist almost entirely of elective courses, but as chairman of the English Conference, his report both liberalized and dignified the study of English. Thurber wrote that one of the chief objectives of English teaching was to "cultivate a taste for reading, to give the pupil some acquaintance with good literature, and to furnish him with the means of extending that acquaintance."[25] Thurber and his committee urged that English be studied five hours a week for four years. Further, the English Conference urged uniform college entrance examinations be established throughout the country.

The result was the publication of book lists, mainly classics, to be the basis of entrance examinations. Plays and books such as Shakespeare's *Twelfth Night* and *As You Like It*, Milton's Books I and II from *Paradise Lost*, Scott's *The Abbott* and *Marmion*, Thackeray's *English Humorists*, Irving's *Bracebridge Hall*, or Dobson's *Eighteenth Century Essays* virtually became the English curriculum as teachers, inevitably concerned with their students' entry into college, increasingly adapted the English curriculum to fit the list. Not all teachers believed that the enjoyment of reading had anything to do with teaching English, and those who did were given little leeway in their choice of classroom books. Thurber worried about teaching literature too mature for young adults and the inevitable dichotomy between school reading and voluntary reading or real reading, that "dismal gulf" between the study of literature and reading outside the school:

> ◇ Not a month ago I saw a boy of fourteen pass through a similar experience. I had just taken from a class *The Lady of the Lake* and put into their hands Stevenson's *Treasure Island*. At the close of the hour an astonished, excited voice said to me: "I—I've read this book!" "Well, and what of that?" "Why, I didn't know we studied *this kind of a book* in school."[26]

Thurber's point was well taken. Teachers labored under the responsibility for preparing students to pass college entrance exams. Their responsibility did not extend to encouraging students to enjoy reading or to extend reading beyond the required text.

But Hitchcock likely presented *the* widely held point of view at the time about literature and college entrance examinations when he wrote:

> ◇ To say that with one or two exceptions the present college requirements are all absurdly inappropriate is hardly respectful to the college professors, and the hundreds of high-school teachers who sanction them. It may take years of experimenting to find the best way of presenting the *Conciliation Speech* and Milton's lyrics; it certainly requires more skill to handle the Milton lyrics than it does to play with the works of G. A. Henty. Not only must pupils work; teachers must work too.
>
> Those who recommended the abolishment of the present college requirements, and the substitution of much easier and inferior classics to be studied in a wholly agreeable way, show very little faith in the ability of the average teacher to make his work profitable, and still less faith in the hardihood of the average pupil. A love for literature which can be blighted by the *Conciliation Speech* or the *Essay on Milton* is hardly worth coddling.[27]

The National Council of Teachers of English (NCTE) Begins

Out of the growing protest about college entrance exams, a group of English teachers attending a National Education Association English Table formed a Committee on College Entrance Requirements in English to assess the problem through a national survey of English teachers. The Committee uncovered a not unexpected hostility to colleges presumptuous enough to try to control the secondary English curriculum through the guise of entrance examinations. John M. Coulter, a professor at the University of Chicago, tried to sound that alarm to college professors, without much success:

> ◇ The high school exists primarily for its own sake; and secondarily as a preparatory school for college. This means that when the high-school interest and the college interest come into conflict, the college interest must yield. It also means that the function of a preparatory school must be performed only in so far as it does not interfere with the more fundamental purpose of the high school itself. It also means that independent dictation by colleges, either directly or indirectly, must be changed to adaptation to what the high school can do or ought to do, as determined by the high schools themselves. The high school must be regarded as an autonomous, not subordinate, institution.[28]

Some irate teachers recognized that the problem of college control would hardly be the last issue to face English teachers and formed the nucleus of the National Council of Teachers of English. The First Annual Meeting in Chicago on December 1 and 2, 1911, was largely devoted to resentment about actions of the National Conference on Uniform Entrance Requirements, particularly because that body had representatives from twelve colleges, two academies, and only two public high schools (principals, not English teachers). Wilbur W. Hatfield, soon to edit the *English Journal* and then at Farragut High School in Chicago, relayed instructions from the Illinois Association of Teachers of English on two responsibilities NCTE should recommend:

> ◇ 1. To include in its list for class reading, study, or whatever you choose to call it, some books of the last ten years. Our present custom of using only old books in the classroom leaves the pupil with no acquaintance with the literature of the present day, from which he is sure to choose his reading after graduation.
> 2. To appoint a committee to compile a list of comparatively recent books suitable for home reading by the pupils.[29]

Later Actions of English Teachers

James Fleming Hosic's 1917 report on the *Reorganization of English in Secondary Schools*, part of a larger report on reorganization of all subject matter fields and all published under the aegis of the U.S. Bureau of Education, looked at books and teaching ways that must have seemed muddle-headed, perverted, or perverse to traditionalists. Looking at literature for the tenth, eleventh, and twelfth grades, Hosic chose works that pleased many, puzzled others, and alienated some:

◇ The literature lesson should broaden, deepen, and enrich the imaginative and emotional life of the student. Literature is primarily a revelation and an interpretation of life; it pictures from century to century the growth of the human spirit. It should be the constant aim of the English teacher to lead pupils so to read that they find their own lives imaged in this larger life, and attain slowly, from a clearer appreciation of human nature, a deeper and truer understanding of human nature. . . . It should be the aim of the English teacher to make [reading] an unfailing resource and joy in the lives of all.[30]

To encourage this, Hosic provided several pages listing books for study and general reading. Classics were included but so were modern works such as Churchill's *Richard Carvel*, Jackson's *Ramona*, London's *Martin Eden*, Norris' *The Pit*, and Wister's *The Virginian* for the tenth grade; Allen's *The Kentucky Cardinal*, Farnol's *The Broad Highway*, Kipling's *The Light That Failed*, and Johnston's *To Have and To Hold* for the eleventh grade; and Galsworthy's *Justice*, Synge's *Riders to the Sea*, and Deland's *The Awakening of Helena Richie* for the twelfth grade. Teachers terrified by the contemporary reality reflected in these books—and perhaps equally terrified by the possibility of throwing out age-old lesson plans and tests on classics—had little to fear. In many schools, nothing changed.

Dora V. Smith reported in 1933 that the most widely studied full-length works in secondary schools were classics. *Silas Marner* led the list followed by *Julius Caesar, Idylls of the King, A Tale of Two Cities,* and *Lady of the Lake*.[31] Most such required books were taught at interminable length, teachers seemingly smitten by what came to be known as the "intensive" method, four to six weeks—sometimes even more—of detailed examination per work while horrified or bored students vowed never to read anything once they escaped high school. Another study offered proof that the "intensive" method produced no better test results and considerably more apathy toward literature than the "extensive" method in which students read assigned works faster. The latter gave them time for many other works and they enjoyed literature far more.[32] This research had a negligible effect on most classroom teachers as did most other significant research.

However, the work of two college professors in the 1930s influenced more English teachers. A 1936 study by Lou LaBrant on the value of free reading at the Ohio State University Laboratory School revealed that students with easy access to different kinds of books and some guidance read more, enjoyed what they read, and moved upward in literary sophistication and taste.[33] Earlier, Dora V. Smith found English teachers knew next to nothing about books written for adolescents. She corrected the situation at the University of Minnesota, establishing the first course in adolescent literature.[34] Later, she wrote:

◇ We must provide teachers who know books first-hand and recognize their place in the lives of boys and girls. It is fair neither to young people nor to their teachers to send out from our colleges and universities men and women trained alone in Chaucer and Milton and Browning to compete with Zane Grey, Robert W. Chambers, and Ethel M. Dell. At the University of Minnesota we have instituted a course in adolescent literature which aims to supplement the necessary training in the classics given by the English department with this broader knowledge of good books, old and new, for boys and girls and for intelligent, cultured men and women—books not commonly judged worthy of academic consideration.[35]

◈ THE SCHOOL LIBRARY

The development of the school library was almost as slow and convoluted as the development of the public library. In 1823, Brooklyn's Apprentice Library Association established a Youth Library where "Boys over twelve were allowed . . . as were girls whose access to the library was limited to one hour an afternoon, once a week."[36] And in 1853, Milwaukee School Commissioner Increase A. Lapham provided for a library open Saturday afternoons and recommended that schools spend $10.00 a year for books. Rules for the Milwaukee library were clear and more than a bit reminiscent of rules in some school and public libraries until the 1940s.

> ◇(1) Only children over ten years old, their parents, teachers, and school commissioner could withdraw books; (2) books might be withdrawn between 2:00 p.m. and sunset on Saturdays and kept for one week; (3) withdrawals were limited to one book per person; and (4) fines were to be assessed for overdue or damaged books.[37]

Writers in the early years of the *Library Journal* paid considerable attention to working out good relations between the public library and the schools. Samuel Swett Green of the Worcester, Massachusetts, Free Public Library wrote:

> ◇Teachers and librarians are co-educators.
> Librarians should cultivate friendly relations with teachers and let them understand that they are ready to afford them any available facilities for using books and getting them information, and to join them in endeavors to make the books of the library serviceable to their scholars.[38]

Writers in the late 1890s National Education Association's *Journal of Proceedings and Addresses* were equally concerned and a Committee on Relations of Public Libraries to Public Schools Report in 1899 announced:

> ◇The library must be regarded as an important and necessary part of the system of public education.
> The teachers of a town should know the public library, what it contains, and what use the pupils can make of it. The librarian must know the school, its work, its needs, and what he can do to meet them.[39]

In that same publication in the previous year, two administrators had written about the school library itself, not merely the relation between the school and the public library—Alfred Bayliss, State Superintendent of public instruction for Illinois, on "The Function of the School Superintendents in Procuring Libraries for, and Their Proper Use in, the Public Schools"[40] and Richard Hardy, Superintendent, Ishpeming, Michigan, "The Use of the School Library."[41]

The ambiguity persisted for some time thereafter. Should the school

NORMA FOX MAZER, Author

Dear Bill, Remember Me?

Someone to Love

Summer Girls, Love Boys and Other Short Stories

Taking Terri Mueller

I'm going to keep on writing books that are about and for the young, not just because the land of the young is the land of energy, enthusiasm, confusion, hope, despair, love, optimism, faith, and belief but also because I've never become completely convinced that my passport to that country has been stamped invalid. Every time I write a book about a young person, I sneak back in. What astounding good luck!

Books for the young are, I hope, getting tougher, realer, and truer. We're told the world is shrinking—yes and no. While it shrinks, it expands. Now we know not only what goes on in Syracuse, in New York, in the United States, in Canada, Mexico, England, France, and Hungary, but also in China, Ethiopia, and South Africa. The world is big, bigger, bigger than ever: hard, confusing, difficult, demanding. Lies won't do. The truth will help. I don't mean political truths, but the truth about people, human beings, how they live, what they feel, how they love, what they want—the truth about the human condition, if you will. It's the news of this truth which fiction has the power to bring us most accurately. ◆

Dear Bill, Remember Me? Delacorte, 1976.
Someone to Love. Delacorte, 1983.
Summer Girls, Love Boys and Other Short Stories. Delacorte, 1982.
Taking Terri Mueller. Avon, 1981.

---

depend on the public library or should the school establish its own library within the confines of the school? In 1896, Melvil Dewey recommended to the NEA that it form a library department (as it had for other subject disciplines) since the library was as much a part of the educational system as the classroom. The previous year, a branch of the Cleveland, Ohio, Public Library was established within Central High School, and in 1899, a branch of the Newark, New Jersey, Public Library was placed in a local high school.

As long as separate high school libraries remained what most of them became, dumping grounds for donated books and old or discarded textbooks, they had little chance for local appropriation, and they lacked direction or focus. But as more teachers required more reading than merely the textbook, and as education under the leadership of John Dewey and James Fleming Hosic and Samuel Thurber gradually changed the thinking of educators, a need for a variety of books easily accessible to students became apparent.

In 1900, Mary Kingston became the first library school graduate appointed to a high school library (Erasmus Hall High School, Brooklyn). Mary E. Hall, librarian at Girls' High School in Brooklyn, argued in 1912 the need for many more professionally trained librarians in high school libraries:

◇ (1) The aims and ideals of the new high school mean we must stop pretending that high school is entirely college preparatory. "It realizes that for the great majority of pupils it must be a preparation for life." (2) Modern methods of teaching demand that a textbook is not enough. "The efficient teacher to-day uses books, magazines, daily paper, pictures, and lantern slides to supplement the textbook." (3) Reading guidance is easier for the school librarian than the public librarian. "The school librarian has the teacher always close at hand and can know the problems of these teachers in their work with pupils."[42]

Though there was no deluge in appointments to high schools of professionally trained librarians after Mary Kingston's appointment in 1900, the promise and excitement of the high school library was obvious to the believers.

◇ The high school librarian who spends her days year in and year out in this library feels each day the fascination and wonder of it all. To have as your visitors each day, from 500 to 700 boys and girls of all nationalities and all stations in life, to see them come eagerly crowding in 100 or more every 40 minutes, and to realize that for four years of the most important years of their lives it is the opportunity of the library to have a real and lasting influence upon each individual boy and girl, gives the librarian a feeling that her calling is one of high privilege and great responsibility.[43]

In 1916, C. C. Certain began standardizing high school libraries across the country as head of an NEA committee. He discovered conditions so mixed, from deplorable (mostly) to good (rarely) that his committee decided to establish a list of minimum essentials for high schools of various sizes. The report divided schools into four different classes (high schools with 500–3000 enrollment; high schools with 200–500 enrollment; high schools enrolling fewer than 100; and junior high schools) and specified the housing and equipment, the librarians' qualifications, the educational work of the library, the selection and care of books, and the annual appropriations for each of the four classes.[44]

The report, adopted by the NEA in 1918, for the first time allowed high schools to compare their libraries with comparable high school libraries and to determine what was needed to bring them up to standard. How that was to be accomplished was, of course, left up to local personnel and administrators.

Two reports by the U.S. Office of Education, in 1923 and 1929, indicate the growth of high school libraries. The 1923 report found only 947 school libraries with more than 3000 volumes, and they were largely in the northeastern part of the country. Six years later, the report found 1,982 school libraries with holdings of more than 3000 volumes, and the libraries were more equally spread over the country, New York having 211 such libraries and California with 191.[45]

The unspectacular, if steady, growth of high school libraries slowed down drastically during the Depression. In 1934, Charlotte H. Clark and Louise P. Latimer argued that the high school library was incredibly costly and unnecessarily duplicated the work of the public library in an article that answered the title, "The Taxpayer and Reading for Young People: Would a 'Library in Every School' Justify the Cost?"[46]

And five years before the 1945 American Library Association's publication of *School Libraries for Today and Tomorrow*, which established modern guidelines for developing school libraries, a letter from a school principal made clear that no matter what the ALA or NCTE or NEA or any group wished, school librarians and school libraries remained low on the list of priorities of too many schools. The principal wrote:

> ◇ The Southern Association requires that we have a librarian next year. I should like to have a person who can teach one class in algebra, one in English, one in American history, and one in French, coach basketball, direct the glee club, take care of the library, and type my letters. Salary, $75.00 a month.[47]

◈ EDWARD STRATEMEYER'S LITERARY SYNDICATE

Whatever disagreements librarians and English teachers may have had over the years about books suitable for young adults, they ineffectively bonded together and loudly opposed the books produced by Edward Stratemeyer and his numerous writers. Stratemeyer founded the most successful industry ever built around adolescent reading. Sometime in 1886, he took time off from working for his stepbrother and wrote an 18,000-word serial, *Victor Horton's Idea*, on brown wrapping paper and mailed it to *Golden Days*, a Philadelphia weekly boys' magazine. A check for seventy-five dollars arrived shortly, and Stratemeyer's success story was underway. By 1893 Stratemeyer was editing *Good News*, Street and Smith's boys' weekly, building circulation to more than 200,000. In addition to editing a few other boys' magazines, his work at Street and Smith made his name known to the public, particularly young adults. Even more important, he came to know staff writers such as William T. Adams, Edward S. Ellis, and Horatio Alger, Jr. When Optic and Alger died leaving some uncompleted manuscripts, Stratemeyer was asked to finish the last three Optic novels, and he completed (or possibly wrote from scratch) at least eleven and possibly as many as eighteen Alger novels.

His first hardback book published under his own name was *Richard Dare's Venture, or Striking Out for Himself* (1894), first in a series he titled "Bound to Succeed." By the close of 1897, Stratemeyer had six series and sixteen hardcover books in print.

A major breakthrough came in 1898. After Stratemeyer sent a manuscript about two boys on a battleship to Lothrop and Shepard, one of the most successful publishers of young adult fiction, Admiral Dewey won his great victory in Manila Bay, and a Lothrop reader asked Stratemeyer to place the boys at the scene of Dewey's victory. He rewrote and returned the book shortly, and *Under Dewey at Manila, or, The War Fortunes of a Castaway* hit the streets in time to capitalize on all the publicity. Not one to miss an opportunity, Stratemeyer used the same characters in his next books, all published from 1898 to 1901 under the series title "Old Glory." Using the same characters in contemporary battles in the Orient, Strat-

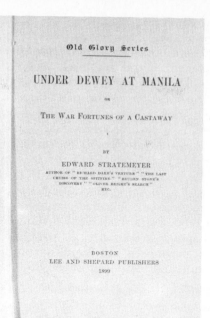

Old Glory Series

UNDER DEWEY AT MANILA

OR

THE WAR FORTUNES OF A CASTAWAY

BY

EDWARD STRATEMEYER
AUTHOR OF "RICHARD DARE'S VENTURE," "THE LAST
CRUISE OF THE SPITFIRE," "REUBEN STONE'S
DISCOVERY," "OLIVER BRIGHT'S SEARCH,"
ETC.

BOSTON
LEE AND SHEPARD PUBLISHERS
1899

◆ Stratemeyer's *Under Dewey at Manila* capitalized on all the publicity of the Spanish-American War.

emeyer created another series called "Soldiers of Fortune," published from 1900 through 1906.

By this time Stratemeyer had turned to full-time writing and was being wooed by the major publishers of his day, notably Grosset & Dunlap and Cupples & Leon, for his formula for writing appealed to young adults. For a time he turned to stories of school life and sports, the "Lakeport" series (1904–1912), the "Dave Porter" series (1905–1919), and the most successful of his early series, the "Rover Boys" (thirty books from 1899 to 1926), books so popular they sold in Canada, Australia, and England, were translated into German and Czechoslovakian, and somewhere between five or six million copies were sold across the world.

But Stratemeyer aspired to greater things. Some time between 1906 and 1910, he approached both his publishers suggesting they reduce the price of his books to fifty cents. The publishers may have been shocked to find an author willing to sell his books for less money, but, as they soon realized, mass production of fifty-centers increased their revenue and Stratemeyer's royalties almost geometrically.

But an even greater breakthrough came, at roughly the same time, when he evolved the idea of his Literary Syndicate, perhaps modeled loosely after Alexandre Dumas' fiction factory in which Dumas and sixty or more anonymous assistants produced 277 books. Stratemeyer was aware that he could create plots and series faster than he could possibly write them. Details of the Stratemeyer Syndicate are fuzzy, but the general outline is clear. Stratemeyer advertised for writers who needed money and sent them sketches of settings and characters along with a chapter-by-chapter outline of the plot. Writers had a few weeks to fill in the outlines, and when the copy arrived, Stratemeyer tightened the prose and checked for discrepancies with earlier volumes of the series. Then the manuscript was off to the printer and checks went out to the writers, from fifty to one hundred dollars depending upon the writer and the importance of the series.

Possibly we may never know all the Syndicate authors. Stratemeyer wrote the books appearing under his own name and presumably those under the pen names Arthur M. Winfield or Captain Ralph Bonehill. Leslie McFarlane wrote the first twenty-six Hardy Boys and three of the Dana Girls, Howard Garis (better known for his "Uncle Wiggily" stories) wrote the first thirty-five Tom Swift books, and Harriet Adams, Stratemeyer's daughter, may have written the Dana Girls and the Nancy Drew books, though that common assumption has been challenged.[48]

Stratemeyer books had common formulaic elements that held readers through book after book. The first lines promised adventure, and the rest of the chapters delivered thrills page after page. Andrew Svenson, Harriet Adams' partner in the Syndicate until his death, summarized both the technique and the power of the Stratemeyer Syndicate books:

> ◇ The trick in writing children's books is to set up danger, mystery and excitement on page one. Force the kid to turn the page. I've written page one as many as 20 times. Then in the middle of each chapter there's a dramatic point of excitement and, at the chapter's end, a cliffhanger.[49]

Readers of books featuring Baseball Joe, Tom Swift, the Hardy Boys, or Nancy Drew will remember that heart-stopping, chapter-ending sentence, "Watch out, Joe!" (or Tom, or Frank, or Nancy). Heroes and heroines were trustworthy, resilient, strong, courageous, and likable. Perhaps most important, they proved the equal, if not the superior, of adults. It is no accident that Nancy Drew, the most successful of all the many Stratemeyer Syndicate protagonists, represents a catalogue of characteristics her young readers most admired, the most significant being her love of mysteries, her independence, her popularity, and her ability to solve puzzles totally befuddling adult characters.

The use of hooks typified most series books. Early in the opening chapters in any but the initial volumes of a series, a hook to the previous volume or volumes would appear. In the last paragraph or two of the last chapter, another hook would be thrown out to attract readers to the next volume:

> ◇ As Helen relaxed from her recent adventures, she thought to herself, "How peaceful it will be to spend a few weeks at the farm just enjoying myself." Helen could not forsee that in only a few weeks she would find a mysterious bracelet and be caught up again in a mystery that would puzzle her and amaze her friends.

Finally, roughly halfway through the second chapter of many series books, action was suspended to summarize the preceding volumes, no great problem in the second or third volume, but as series ran to many volumes, summaries became highly compressed and almost frantic. In *Ruth Fielding and Her Greatest Triumph, or Saving Her Company from Disaster* (1933), the twenty-ninth of the series, the author "Alice B. Emerson" wrote a page-and-a-half of breathless summary:

◇ Ruth's life was not unlike a thrilling moving picture scenario. As the reader learns in the first volume of the series, *Ruth Fielding at the Red Mill*, the girl came as an orphan to live at the picturesque red mill of old Jabez Potter and Aunt Alvirah Boggs, his faithful housekeeper. There she had grown up, and learned to know Helen Cameron and her brother Tom, and had met Chess Copley.

In time Ruth listened to Tom's insistent plea that they become engaged, while Helen gave her promise to Chess. Yet neither girl was to think seriously of marriage for years to come, and with college days intervening, good times and exciting adventures were always at hand.

During her college days Ruth had shown marked ability as a scenario writer and moving picture actress. Eager to "try her wings," she had induced Mr. Hammond, president of the Alectron Film Corporation, to give her a real opportunity. Her first venture was a marked success and after that she organized her own film company, with Tom as the efficient treasurer.

Marriage had not terminated Ruth's career, for Tom was a sensible husband and proud of his wife's renown and prestige. Helen, not to be outdone by her chum, had become the wife of Chess Copley. While her interests had not centered in business, she too had discovered that marriage by no means spelled the end of adventure.

At the birth of Baby June, Ruth had given up her moving picture work, but only for a short time. The discovery that a rival company was endeavoring to exploit an inexperienced actress and make the public believe it was Ruth Fielding, had brought her back to Hollywood. For a time her reputation had been threatened and many persons had believed that Ruth Fielding was no longer the great actress she once had been. Her attempt to discover the identity of her strange "twin" and outwit the men who had plotted her downfall, is related in the book, *Ruth Fielding and Her Double*.

If all that weren't enough to outline the life of this truly remarkable young woman, the summary ignores the many mysteries Ruth solved, her work in the Red Cross and on the front lines of World War I, and her trips across the country.

Attacks on Stratemeyer were soon in coming. Librarian Caroline M. Hewins criticized both Stratemeyer's books and the journals that praised his output:

◇ Stratemeyer is an author who mixes "would" and "should," has the phraseology of a country newspaper, as when he calls a supper "an elegant affair" and a girl "a fashionable miss," and follows Oliver Optic closely in his plots and conversations. [50]

Most librarians supported Hewins, but the effect of librarians' attacks hardly affected Stratemeyer's sales. A far more stinging and effective attack came in 1913. Chief Boy Scout executive James E. West was disturbed by the deluge of what he thought inferior books and urged the Library Commission of the Boy Scouts of America to establish a carefully selected and recommended library to protect young men. Not long afterward, Chief Scout Librarian Franklin K. Mathiews urged Grosset & Dunlap to make better books available in fifty-cent editions—to compete with Stratemeyer—and on November 1, 1913, the first list appeared in a Boy Scout publication, "Safety First Week."

But that was not enough to satisfy Mathiews. In 1914, Mathiews wrote his most famous article under the sensational title, "Blowing Out the Boy's Brains," a loud and vituperative attack, sometimes accurate but often unfair. Mathiews' most famous sentence was widely quoted: "I wish I could label each one of these books: 'Explosives! Guaranteed to Blow Your Boy's Brains Out.' "[51] The attack was mildly successful for the moment though how much harm it did to Stratemeyer's sales is open to question. Stratemeyer went on to sell more millions of books. When he died in 1930, his two daughters ran the Syndicate and daughter Harriet Adams continued it till her death in 1982. But the Syndicate persists, presumably forever.

Grosset & Dunlap and Cupples & Leon, Stratemeyer's publishers, were only two of the many publishers of series books. Henry Altemus, M. A. Donahue, Barse & Hopkins, A. L. Chatterton, Reilly & Lee, Street and Smith, and Sully & Kleintiech ground them out. But so did quality publishers of adult books: Appleton-Century; Crowell; Dodd & Mead; Farrar & Rinehart; Harper & Brothers; Holt; Houghton Mifflin; Lippincott; Little, Brown; McKay; Putnam; and Scribner. Later, five publishers—Goldsmith, Saalfield, Whitman, Winston, and World—reprinted many of the more popular series.

Series covered everything young adults care about from adventure to scouting, the circus, Indians, mysteries, prehistoric times, science fiction, and every war in which we have been involved. Thousands of volumes were printed and millions of copies sold.

Series books were inevitably moral. Whatever parents, teachers, or librarians might have objected to about the unrealistic elements of the books or the poor literary quality, they would have agreed that the books were clearly on the side of good and right, if simplistically and unrealistically so. Series books—and many adult books as well—repeatedly underlined the same themes. Sports produced truly manly men. Foreigners were not to be trusted. School, education, and life should be taken seriously. The outdoor life was healthy, physically and psychologically. Good manners and courtesy were essential for moving ahead. Work in and of itself was a positive good and would advance one in life. Anyone could defeat adversity, any adversity, *if* that person had a good heart and soul. The good side (ours and God's) always won in war. Evil and good were clearly and easily distinguishable. And good always triumphed over evil (at least by the final chapter).

◈ THE COMING OF THE "JUNIOR" OR "JUVENILE" NOVEL

Though countless books had been published and widely read by young adults for years, the term "junior" or "juvenile" was first applied to young adult literature during the early 1930s.

◆ In *Let the Hurricane Roar*, Rose Wilder Lane made readers care about two likable young adults living a tough life in a hostile world.

Rose Wilder Lane's novel *Let the Hurricane Roar* had been marketed by Longmans, Green, and Company as an adult novel. A full-page blurb on the front cover of the February 11, 1933, *Publishers Weekly* bannered THE BOOK THAT MAKES YOU PROUD TO BE AN AMERICAN! and quoted an unnamed reader, presumably an adult, saying, "Honestly, it makes me ashamed of cussing about hard times and taxes." The tenor of the ad and ones to follow suggest an adult novel likely to be popular with young adults as well. It had been the same with the earlier serialization of the novel in the *Saturday Evening Post,* and also with the many favorable reviews. But, sometime later in 1933, Longmans, Green began to push the novel as the first of their series of "Junior Books," as they termed them.

That the company wanted to attract young adults to Lane's novel is not difficult to understand. Daughter of Laura Ingalls Wilder, Lane wrote of a threatening frontier world she had known in a compelling manner certain to win readers and admirers among young adults. *Let the Hurricane Roar* tells of newly married David and Molly and their life on the hard Dakota plains. David works as a railroad hand for a time, Molly waits for her baby to arrive, and both strive for independence and the security of owning their own fifty-acre homestead. When they reach that dream and the baby is born, all looks well, but David overextends his credit, grasshoppers destroy the wheat crop, and no employment can be found nearby. David heads East to find work and later breaks his leg, leaving Molly isolated on the Dakota plains for a winter. Neighbors flee the area, and Molly battles loneliness, blizzards, and wolves before David returns. In summary, *Let the Hurricane Roar* sounds melodramatic, but it is not. In a short, quiet, and loving work, Lane made readers care about two likable young adults living a tough life in a hostile environment. The book's popularity is attested to by its twenty-six printings between 1933 and 1958 and a recent reissue in paperback under the title *Young Pioneers.*

The development of publishing house divisions to handle books lying in limbo between children's and adults' books grew after *Let the Hurricane Roar,* though authors of the time were sometimes unaware of the "junior" or "juvenile" branches as John R. Tunis was when he tried to market *Iron Duke* in 1934 and 1935. After sending the manuscript to Harcourt, Tunis was invited into the president's office. Mr. Harcourt clearly did not want to talk about the book, but instead took the startled author directly to the head of the Juvenile Department. He explained that Harcourt wanted to publish the book as a juvenile, much to Tunis' bewilderment and dismay, since he had no idea what a "juvenile" book was. Thirty years later he still had no respect for the term. "That odious term juvenile is the product of a merchandising age."[52]

◈ PULPS AND COMICS AND STUFF

Hardcover books had four rivals for young adult readership during the first forty years of the twentieth century: pulp magazines, comic strips, comic books, and Big-Little Books. All four were disliked and attacked by many teachers, librarians, and parents, and all were widely read by young adults.

Pulp Magazines

Frank Munsey began his magazine *Argosy* in 1891 for adults, but it proved popular with young and old alike. By 1903, Street and Smith had begun publishing *Popular Magazine* aimed at rivaling *Argosy* but rapidly developed a stable of pulp magazines (so-called because of the high fiber content used in the cheap paper) for specialized interests—*Detective Story, Western Story, Love Story, Sports Story* and *Sea Stories.* Other pulps followed: *Top-Notch, Flying Aces, Real Love, Battle Stories, True Love, Spy Stories, All-Western, Ranch Romances, Sweetheart Stories,* and *Lariat,* producing some popular heroes like Clarence E. Mulford's Hopalong Cassidy, Walter Gibson's The Shadow, Richard Wormser's Nick Carter, and Lester Dent's Doc Savage. Long after the death of pulp fiction, writer Jack Smalley explained the two basics of all pulp stories, "All you needed to sell a story to the pulps was a good title and an arresting lead paragraph."[53]

Pulps were often ridiculed, usually by people who never read them. Two recent collections of pulp stories suggest a higher quality of writing than is usually suspected. *The Fantastic Pulps*[54] included stories by Stephen Crane, Jack London, Upton Sinclair, Sinclair Lewis, Dashiell Hammett, MacKinlay Kantor, and Ray Bradbury, among others. *Hard-Boiled Detective: Stories from "Black Mask Magazine," 1920–1951*[55] features such writers as Dashiell Hammett, Raymond Chandler, Erle Stanley Gardner, and George Harmon Coxe.

Comic Strips

When James Swinnerton began his "Little Bears" in 1892 in the *San Francisco Examiner*, he surely was unaware that he had created an art form soon to be emulated by other artists and read by people of all ages. A year later, bitter rivals Joseph Pulitzer of the *New York World* and William Randolph Hearst of the *New York Journal* were feuding, as usual. Pulitzer purchased a four-color rotary press to reprint artworks in his Sunday supplement. The rotary press did not work well, but the Sunday editor suggested it would work for comic art, so Pulitzer went to Richard F. Outcault who created a comic strip, "Down in Hogan's Alley." One character stood out in all the slum scenes, a strange-looking boy with an oriental face, a bald head, and only one tooth. Due to a freakish printing accident, the boy appeared in bright yellow and thus was born on February 16, 1896, the best remembered early comic strip, "The Yellow Kid." A year later, Rudolph Dirks began "The Katzenjammer Kids," and comic strips were here to stay.

By 1900, the comic strip formula was established—dialogue was contained in balloons, strips had sequential narratives, from one drawing to the next, but generally developed only one joke, and they presented a continuity from day to day or week to week that readers could depend on.

Winsor McCay's "Little Nemo in Slumberland," the most innovative of the early strips, pictured surrealistic but magnificently drawn dreams of a six-year-old boy. In 1911, the greatest of all comic strips began, George Herriman's "Krazy Kat." Herriman's work set an imposing and almost impossible to surpass standard of creativity, whimsy, and humor for other writers. Krazy was a strange, androgynous creature hated by Ignatz Mouse who threw brick after brick at Krazy only to be caught by Offisser B. Pupp.

George McManus' "Bringing Up Father" in 1913 brought Maggie and Jiggs to the nation as the first domestic comic strip. Later popular comic strips were Fontaine Fox's "Toonerville Folks" (1913), Sydney Fisher's "The Gumps" (1917), Frank King's "Gasoline Alley" (1919)—the first comic strip to advance characters chronologically and still one of the great comic strips—Harold Gray's "Little Orphan Annie" (1924), Philip Newlan and Richard Calkins' "Buck Rogers" (1929), Chic Young's "Blondie" (1930), Chester Gould's "Dick Tracy" (1931), Martha Orr's "Apple Mary" (1932)—in 1940 called "Mary Worth's Family" and in 1944 simply "Mary Worth"—Alex Raymond's magnificently drawn "Flash Gordon" (1934), Al Capp's "Li'l Abner" (1934), Bill Holman's wacky "Smokey Stover" (1935), Jerry Siegel and Joe Shuster's "Superman" (1938), and Walt Kelly's loving contribution to American folklore and culture, "Pogo" (1949).

Comic Books

Comic books began as an offshoot of comic strips. A collection of "The Yellow Kid" strips was published in March 1897, and reprints of other comic strips were offered at least through the early 1920s. In 1922, a reprint magazine, *Comic Monthly*, began, each month given to reprints of a different comic strip, and in 1929, George Delacorte published thirteen issues of *The Funnies,* the first four-color comic books.

In 1933, 10,000 copies of *Funnies on Parade* were published by Eastern Color Printing Company in New York and distributed as a premium by Procter & Gamble. Later that same year, M. C. Gaines convinced Eastern that other companies could use the gimmick for premiums, and Eastern printed *Famous Funnies: A Carnival of Comics,* reprints of Sunday color comics, in quantities of more than 100,000. Sure of success, Gaines asked Eastern to print 35,000 copies of *Famous Funnies, Series 1,* a sixty-four page book that sold for ten cents in chain stores.

National Periodical Publications' *New Fun* (after the first issue, entitled *More Fun*) in 1935 was the first comic book to publish original material, not merely reprints. Later that year Walt Disney began his *Mickey Mouse Magazine* (in 1940 to become *Walt Disney's Comics and Stories*), a combination of reprinted and original material.

Detective Comics in 1937 was the first themed nonreprint comic book. Published by National Periodical Publications, the company soon became known in the trade as DC Comics. DC's *Action Comics* opened in June 1938 with a character soon to become part of American mythology, "Superman," who began as one of several strips but was soon given his own separate publication. Later comic heroes included Batman, who appeared first in DC's *Detective Comics #27* in 1939. The Sub-Mariner and the Human Torch debuted in Marvel Comics that same year, Captain Marvel started in Fawcett's *Whiz Comics* in 1940, and Wonder Woman first appeared in DC's *All-Star Comics #8* a year later.

By the close of 1941, over 160 comic book titles were distributed monthly selling more than twelve million copies. A year later *Crime Does Not Pay* brought realistic crime stories to readers. In 1950 William M. Gaines, son of M. C. Gaines, began realistic crime horror comics, *Crypt of Terror, The Vault of Horror, Weird Science,* and *Two-Fisted Tales.*

The suspicion of parents, teachers, librarians, and other critics that comic books had a potentially evil influence on the young led to formation of a U.S. Senate Subcommittee, chaired by Estes Kefauver, to investigate detrimental effects of comic books. It also led to an investigation by psychologist Frederic Wertham resulting in a bitter attack on crime, horror, and hero comics:

> ◇ Slowly, and at first reluctantly, I have come to the conclusion that this chronic stimulation, temptation, and seduction by comic books, both their content and their alluring advertisements of knives and guns, are contributing factors to many children's maladjustment.
>
> All comic books with their words and expletives in balloons are bad for reading, but not every comic book is bad for children's minds and emotions. The trouble is that "good" comic books are snowed under by those which glorify violence, crime and sadism.
>
> At no time, up to the present, has a single child ever told me as an excuse for a delinquency or a misbehavior that comic books were to blame. Nor do I nor my associates ever question a child in such a way as to suggest that to him. If I find a child with fever, I do not ask him "What is the cause of your fever? Do you have

measles?" I examine him and make my own diagnosis. It is our clinical judgment, in all kinds of behavior disorders and personality difficulties of children, that comic books do play a part.[56]

After the Senate Subcommittee Report[57] and the furor surrounding Wertham's impassioned book, publishers, fearful of pressures to come, staved off some of the fury by creating a Comics Code Authority banning profanity, nudity, excessive violence and horror, portrayal of crime as attractive, and disrespect for established authority. The Code also recommended less slang and better grammar in comics. Presumably, critics, teachers, librarians, and parents were pacified. Few young people probably noticed anything very different in the comics, and things soon were back to normal.

Big-Little Books

Less significant than pulps, comic strips, or comic books, Big-Little Books still were widely read (and today bring a nice sum for sound copies). Published originally by Whitman in cardboard covers, they normally had one page of text facing a full-page illustration. Sizes varied from approximately three inches by three inches to those slightly larger. Selling for ten cents and usually featuring a new adventure of a popular comic strip or movie hero, they appealed both to those who liked comic books and those presumably a little more literate. The first Big-Little Book, *The Adventures of Dick Tracy*, was printed in 1932, and hundreds followed based on comic strips such as "Flash Gordon," "Skippy," "Terry and the Pirates," "Moon Mullins," or "Apple Mary"; on movies, movie characters, or actors such as "Our Gang," "Donald Duck," Gene Autry, Jackie Cooper, or Johnny Mack Brown; and other sources such as *The Three Musketeers*, *Tom Swift and His Magnetic Silencer*, or Edgar Bergen and Charlie McCarthy.

◈ THE LITTLE BLUE BOOKS

All too little has been written about the work of Emanuel Haldeman-Julius and his incredible and influential library of Little Blue Books. Basing his operation in Girard, Kansas, Haldeman-Julius sold roughly five hundred million copies from his library of about two thousand titles, many purchased by young adults with—or without—parental permission. Although he lived in the heart of the Bible belt and was always controversial, he gained the respect of many midwesterners earnestly—sometimes desperately—seeking education. A rationalist and an atheist, he had an ingrained belief in the educational perfectibility of humanity if people had inexpensive good books readily available. Haldeman-Julius began battling ignorance, superstition, and misunderstanding by publishing a library of small, paperbound books at twenty-five cents each. He soon discovered enough interested readers to drop the price to fifteen cents, then ten cents, and finally five cents, selling them in bulk by mail. Two-page ads in newspapers and magazines such as *Saturday Evening Post*, *Popular Mechanics*, *Ladies Home Journal*, and the

New York Times Book Review brought him first orders and repeat business. The blue-covered books dealt with an incredible variety of subjects. The scope of these five-cent books was without parallel in American publishing. Using that amazing nickel, one could purchase titles as different as Poe's *The Fall of the House of Usher,* Darrow's *Debate on Capital Punishment, The Diary of Samuel Pepys,* Doyle's *Sherlock Holmes Problem Stories,* Verne's *Five Weeks in a Balloon, Nature Poems of Wordsworth, An Encyclopedia of Sex, Famous $12,000 Prize-Winning Tongue-Twisters,* and Haldeman-Julius' own *The Art of Reading.* He even published Will Durant's *The Story of Philosophy* (1926) in a dozen or so booklets. A mixed but impressive bag.

Haldeman-Julius' contribution to American education was profound. He made books and education available for thousands of Americans denied more than a few years of formal education.

◈ A FEW BOOKS YOUNG ADULTS LIKED

Books popular with young adults fall into six reasonably discrete categories, each a mixture of good (or adequate) and bad (or dismal) books. Some deserve reading today; others deserve the interment already decently provided.

And a Little Child Shall Lead Them (Though God Knows Where)

Among the most popular books prior to World War I were those featuring a small child, usually a girl, who significantly changed people around her. At their best, they showed an intriguing youngster humanizing sterile or cold people. At their worst (and they often were) they featured a child rapturously happy and miraculously even-dispositioned who infected an entire household—or perhaps a community—with her messianic drive to improve the world through cheer and gladness.

The type began promisingly with Kate Douglas Wiggin's *Rebecca of Sunnybrook Farm* (1904). Nothing Wiggin wrote surpassed Rebecca, which sold more than a million and a quarter copies between 1904 and 1975. Living in a small town during the 1870s, the optimistic heroine is handed over to two maiden aunts while her parents cope with a large family. She is educated despite her imperfections, high spirits, and rebelliousness, and at the close of the book seems cheerfully on her way upward to a better life. Wiggin's book preaches acceptance of the status quo, not surprising for the time, but the heroine gets herself into believable scrapes, the book does not overly sentimentalize either itself or the world, and humor is more common than sadness or preaching. The book deserved its success, just as it deserves reading today.

Anne of Green Gables (1908) by Lucy Maud Montgomery was a worthy successor. As in Wiggin's book, Anne travels to an alien society. Here, a childless couple who wants to adopt a boy gets Anne by mistake. Anne changes the couple for the better, but they also change her, and Anne's delightfully developed character goes far to remedy any defects in the book. Docile as she tries to be (and occasionally succeeds), she is alive, charming, and impulsive. When the book ends, Anne is believably ready to take on responsibilities.

Wiggin and Montgomery generally managed to skirt the sea of sentimentalism, that fatal syrupy deep beloved by bad writers. Occasionally, Rebecca and Anne waded out dangerously far, but their common sense, their impulsiveness, their love of laughter, and their ability to laugh at themselves saved them and brought them back to shore. After them came the disaster: authors and characters so enamored of humanity, so convinced that all people were redeemable, so stickily and uncomplainingly sweet and good that they drowned in goodness while readers either drowned with them or gagged.

Jean Webster's *Daddy-Long-Legs* (1912) was sticky enough in its picture of a college girl who falls in love with her benefactor. Gene Stratton Porter was worse in her *Freckles* (1904), *A Girl of the Limberlost* (1909), *Laddie* (1913), and *Michael O'Halloran* (1915) where sentiment is all and coincidence and a good heart solve every problem.

But it was left to Eleanor Porter to write the genre's magnum opus and destroy it with *Pollyanna* (1913). *Pollyanna* is usually remembered as a children's book, but it began as a popular adult novel, eighth among bestsellers in 1913 and second in 1914. So sickeningly sweet is the heroine that countless adults and young people could rightfully credit her with their diabetes. Orphaned Pollyanna comes to the house of rich Aunt Polly, who scorns her. Lovely but wholesome Pollyanna plays her "glad game," befuddling Nancy, the maid. Nancy asks Pollyanna to explain the game:

> ◇ "Why, it's a game. Father taught it to me, and it's lovely," rejoined Pollyanna. "We've played it always, ever since I was a little, little girl. I told the Ladies' Aid, and they played it—some of them."
> "What is it? I ain't much on games, though."
> Pollyanna laughed again, but she sighed, too: and in the gathering twilight her face looked thin and wistful.
> "Why, we began it on some crutches that came in a missionary barrel."
> "*Crutches!*"
> "Yes. You see I'd wanted a doll, and father had written them so; but when the barrel came the lady wrote that there hadn't any dolls come in, but the little crutches had. So she sent 'em along as they might come in handy for some child, sometime. And that's when we began it."
> "Well, I must say I can't see any game about that," declared Nancy, almost irritably.
> "Oh, yes; the game was to find something about everything to be glad about— no matter what 'twas," rejoined Pollyanna, earnestly. "And we began right then—on the crutches."
> "Well, goodness me! I can't see anythin' ter be glad about—gettin' a pair of crutches when you wanted a doll!"
> Pollyanna clapped her hands.
> "There is—there is," she crowed. "But I couldn't see it either, Nancy, at first," she added, with quick honesty. "Father had to tell it to me."
> "Well, then, suppose *you* tell *me*," almost snapped Nancy.

"Goosey! Why, just be glad because you *don't—need—'em!*" exulted Pollyanna, triumphantly. "You see it's just as easy—when you know how!"

To the loathing of sensible people, the "Glad Game" raged across the country. But Pollyanna does more than laugh at personal misfortunes. She reunites once-happy and now miserable lovers and friends, saves Aunt Polly from a loveless life, eliminates gloom for miles around, rescues the miserable, and gladdens everybody, just everybody.

Hearth, Home, and Responsibility (with Bits of Sin)

Stories of motherhood and true love were popular with young adults and adults. At times, little hints (and sometimes broad brushstrokes) of sin, redeemed or otherwise, made the stories more palatable.

Alice Hegan Rice could easily have created an ocean of treacle in *Mrs. Wiggs of the Cabbage Patch* (1901), but instead she portrayed an optimistic family led by an indomitable mother in the midst of a Louisville slum without making either seem unbelievable. Her publisher doubted the book would sell and printed only 2000 copies for the first edition. Once they were rapidly picked up, he admitted his guess was wrong and began turning out 40,000 copies a month. The book was a best-seller and remains in print today.

Several writers were unable to keep large doses of sentimentalism and goodness from their books, though no rival for sweetness arose to challenge Gene Stratton Porter or Eleanor Porter. John Fox, Jr., wrote of his beloved Cumberland Mountains and the coming of civilization and machines in *The Little Shepherd of Kingdom Come* (1903) and *The Trail of the Lonesome Pine* (1908). Harold Bell Wright moved to the Ozarks in search of better health and found interesting people, God, and a deep relief in muscular Christianity. He began preaching in a schoolhouse and spent the next twelve years moving from pastorate to pastorate. *The Shepherd of the Hills* (1907) and *The Calling of Dan Matthews* (1909) made money by attacking the hypocrisy of formalized religion, especially in big cities. By then Wright had left the pulpit for full-time writing, and later books were consistent best-sellers endorsed by ministers and attacked by literary critics. The first printing of *The Winning of Barbara Worth* (1911) ran to 175,000 copies and the printing of *Their Yesterdays* (1912) was even larger. *When a Man's a Man* (1916) and *The Re-creation of Brian Keith* (1919) are typically Wright, strong on theme and sermonistic to a fault. Brief bits of plot and stereotyped characters are manipulated to ensure that readers understand Wright's point about God and the church.

Simple love stories were popular. Grace Livingston Hill sold more than four million copies in a lifetime writing such novels as *The Girl from Montana* (1907), *Exit Betty* (1920), and *Rainbow Cottage* (1934). Prolific English novelist Florence Barclay produced a best-seller in America with *The Rosary* (1910) in which an incredible but plain young woman has faith in her blind sweetheart and sings the popular song of the time, "The Rosary," to help him onward and upward.

If the sanctity of the home and the love of God sold well, sin was equally attractive. In 1907, Elinor Glynn published *Three Weeks*, portraying the queen of a mythical European country who forgets her husband and duties for a glorious three weeks' sex romp with a handsome Englishman. Readers realized that it was nothing more than romanticized pornography, the love scenes on the tigerskin rug justified their feelings, and sales and libidos rose. What the book lacked in psychological probing, it compensated for with pages of physical probing. Just as sin-laden and equally popular was *The Sheik* (1921) by Edith Maude Hull. The abduction of self-centered Diana Mayo by the sensual Sheik and his rough treatment of her excited millions. The film version starring Rudolph Valentino was superior to the book. For many readers, young and old, these books broke conventions long overdue for destruction, and they were widely if covertly read.

Moving Westward

The closing of the West heightened interest in an exciting, almost magic, era. A few writers, aiming specifically at young adults, knew the West so well that they became touchstones for authenticity in other writers. George Bird Grinnell wrote *Pawnee Hero Stories and Folk Tales* (1889) and *By Cheyenne Campfires* (1926) and established an honest and generally unsentimentalized portrait of Indian life. Both he and Charles A. Eastman often appeared on reading interest studies as boys' favorites. Eastman's autobiography, *Indian Boyhood* (1902), was justifiably praised for its sense of time and place. Joseph Altsheler wrote more conventional adventure tales of the West, often lapsing into melodrama, but he was for some time a favorite for *The Young Trailers* (1907), *The Last of the Chiefs* (1909), and *The Horsemen of the Plains* (1910).

Far more sentimental but much more popular was Will James' *Smoky, The Cowhorse* (1926), originally published as an adult novel, soon read by thousands of young adults, and twice filmed to appreciative audiences. The story of a colt befriended by a cowboy, the horse's kidnapping and mistreatment, and the eventual reuniting of horse and man is still a tearjerker of the highest order.

The best written and most sensitive western of the time for young people was Laura Adams Armer's *Waterless Mountain* (1931). Unfortunately, the slow-moving, almost nonexistent plot about a young Navajo boy training to become a Medicine Priest was too mystical and mythical for young readers, and enthusiastic librarians and teachers had little success getting teenagers to read the novel.

The first great writer to focus on the West and its mystique of violence and danger mixed with open spaces and freedom was Owen Wister, whose *The Virginian: A Horseman of the Plains* (1902) provided a model of colloquial speech and romantic and melodramatic adventure for novels to follow. "When you call me that, *smile!*" was endlessly quoted by boys for years thereafter. Andy Adams was a far more trustworthy guide to the West in *The Log of a Cowboy: A Narrative of the Old Trail Days* (1903), but the public was clearly more interested in thrills and spills than it was in accuracy. Zane Grey fulfilled whatever need the public had with his incredibly romantic pictures of life in the older days of the West in *The Spirit of the Border* (1906), and *The Wanderer of the Wasteland* (1923). The best of his books—certainly the most-remembered and probably the epitome of the overly romanticized western—was *Riders of the Purple Sage* (1912) filled with classic elements: the mysterious hero, the innocent heroine, evil villains, and the open land. Criticized as Grey has been by librarians and teachers—who seem in general to have read little or nothing of his work—he was and is read, and his books stay in print. Anyone who wishes to know what the western dream was must read Grey.

Rah Rah for the School and Fair Play

With more young adults attending school and with the steadily rising popularity of sports—especially college football and professional baseball—more school-sports stories appeared. For many teachers and professors then and now, academic excellence and sports are mutually exclusive terms. Some people worried that football was too rough; many that it would distract from studies. We associate the term "football fever" with modern times, but it was used near the turn of the century when one educator fretted about sports:

> ◇ I noticed two years ago, when the football fever was raging, that it was generally believed that a college's success in football drew students to it, and that some schools thought it necessary to make football a leading feature in their "fit for college."[58]

William Gilbert Patten was not the first writer of sports novels, but he was the first to introduce a regular, almost mythic, sports character soon recognized throughout America—Frank Merriwell. In 1895, Ormond Smith (of Street and Smith) urged Patten, one of his stable of dime novelists, to write a school and sports series with lots of adventure. Under the pen name of Burt L. Standish, Patten created heroic Frank Merriwell and in two weeks wrote a story that appeared as "Frank Makes a Foe" in *Tip Top Weekly* in 1896. Circulation boomed and Patten and Frank Merriwell were hits. Several hundred stories about Frank followed, and Patten later combined a number of them into hardback books. A natural leader, an incredible boxer, an expert duelist, an exemplary baseball player, and an all-round great guy, Frank is also decent, heroic, modest, and everything a mother could wish for in a son. One episode near the end of *Frank Merriwell at Yale* (1903) illustrates Frank's charisma and charm in turning bad guys into good guys. A boxer-hood-bad-guy tries unsuccessfully to waylay Frank; later, he recognizes Frank's greatness when our hero quietly asks the boxer to go straight:

> ◇ I t'ink ye're right, an' I'm going ter try ter do it. I allus did hate ter work, but if I kin get any kind of a job I'm going ter try it once more. I don't know w'y it is, but jes' being wid youse makes me want ter do der square t'ing.

Although they did not create any heroes as well known as Frank Merriwell, three much better writers stand out for their more realistic sports books.

Owen Johnson wrote for adults, but *The Varmint* (1910) and *The Tennessee Shad* (1911), about sports and pranks at Lawrenceville School, were widely read by boys. *Stover at Yale* (1911) is about sports, but more significant to Johnson was his attack on Yale's problems—snobbery, social clubs, fraternities, senior societies, and anti-intellectualism.

Ralph Henry Barbour wrote an incredible number of fine books, beginning with *The Half-Back* (1899), presenting believable boys in believable situations at school playing the sports of different seasons. Dated as his books are by rule changes, they are still readable. Rarest of all for the time, Barbour presented few villains. His books became repetitious over the years as he used the same formula—a boy attending school and learning who and what he might become through sports—but the formula was Barbour's invention. His theme was stated in the dedication to *The Half-Back*: "To Every American Boy Who Loves Honest, Manly Sports." He steadfastly and sincerely believed that sports presented opportunities and challenges for every boy, a belief predicated on three acts of faith: schools must have school spirit, school spirit comes from sports, and sports must be amateur and free of any taint of commercialism or professionalism. He reflected the philosophy of Walter Camp, father of football and author of several sports novels—*Danny Fists* (1913) is his best—who wrote:

◇ If you are enough of a man to be a good athlete, and some one asks you to use that athletic ability on their behalf, don't take money for it, or anything that amounts to pay.

You don't want your boy "hired" by any one. If he plays, he plays as a gentleman, and not as a professional; he plays for victory, not for money; and whatever bruises he may have in the flesh, his heart is right, and he can look you in the eye as a gentleman should. [59]

To Barbour, sports were significant in a boy's life, but they were a part of life, not all of it. He would never have understood Knute Rockne's words, "After the Church, football is the best thing we have." Barbour's concern about encroaching professionalism in school and college football is illustrated in *The Spirit of the School* (1907). A young, likable boy, who happens also to be a good athlete, is paid to attend Beechcroft. The coach does not approve but he does nothing about the boy or the situation. A few members of the football squad know, but when others find out, dissension arises. A vote is taken and the amateur spirit is restored to the academy with Barbour's complete approval.

Barbour's best book is *The Crimson Sweater* (1907), first of a four-volume "Ferry Hill" series. While the plot is not unlike his other books, there is more humor and it introduces his most delightful girl, Harry (or Harriet), sprightly and alive and fun and highly competitive with boys.

William Heyliger followed in the same pattern with *Bartley: Freshman Pitcher* (1911). But Barbour's concerns were sports and school, whereas

The final game between Ferry Hill and Hammond.

The
Crimson Sweater

By
Ralph Henry Barbour

"Author of "The Half-Back," "For the
Honor of the School," etc.

With Illustrations
By C. M. Relyea

New York
The Century Co.
1907

◆ *The Crimson Sweater* introduces Ralph Henry Barbour's most delightful girl, Harriet (called Harry), who is sprightly and highly competitive with boys.

Heyliger wrote more varied books: school and sports stories in his "St. Mary's" series, "Fairview High" series, and "Lansing" series; and ground-breaking vocational stories in *High Benton* (1919), *High Benton, Worker* (1921), *Dan's Tomorrow* (1922), *Steve Merrill, Engineer* (1935), *You're on the Air* (1941), and *Top Lineman* (1943).

School stories for girls never had a similar number of readers, but some had loyal readers, and a few deserve reading even today. Laura Elizabeth Richards was best known for *Peggy* (1899) in which a poor girl goes to school and becomes a hero in basketball. Marjorie Hill Allee deserved attention for *Jane's Island* (1931) with its portrait of the biological laboratories and scientists at Woods Hole and its sense of place and its delight in scientific exploration. Even better was *The Great Tradition* (1937), set at the University of Chicago, which successfully mixed romances, college life, and the spirit of scientific adventure.

Best of them all was Mabel Louise Robinson's *Bright Island* (1937) for its story of spunky Thankful Curtis who was raised on a small island off the coast of Maine and later attends school on the mainland. *Bright Island* maintains a charm and warmth rare among books and deserves readers today.

Strange Deeds and Far Lands

Young adults, then and now, read tales of adventures as avidly as adults. No other literary genre has been so persistently successful with readers.

The public's fancy near the turn of the century was taken by a craze for adventure-romance set in imaginary countries: Anthony Hope, pen name of Anthony Hope Hawkins, created the passion for never-never lands in *The Prisoner of Zenda* (1894) loosely modeled after Robert Louis Stevenson's *Prince Otto* (1885). Englishman Rudolph Rassendyl, hunting in Ruritania at a crucial time, learns that he closely resembles King Rupert. Rassendyl agrees to foil the machinations of evil plotters, falls in love with the lovely Princess Flavia, but does his duty and nobly leaves the country alone having done his all. Twenty-six printings within the year established his popularity with Americans.

American author George McCutcheon pushed the tale of the mythical kingdom to its limits. In *Graustark: The Story of a Love Behind a Throne* (1901) romance is all, adventures are thrilling beyond real life, and Americans cannot be defeated by anyone. Twenty-nine-year-old American Grenfell Lorry falls in love with lovely Miss Guggenslocker, despite her name. He finds she is, in reality, Princess Yetive of Graustark, and learns that plots against her are brewing. Graustark's debt must be paid by her marriage to the prince of a neighboring country. Lorry foils plots, battles enemies, and wins the princess. Told he cannot marry Yetive since he is only a commoner, he says:

> ◇ I am not a prince, as you are saying over and over again to yourself. Every born American may become the ruler of the greatest nation in the world—the United States. His home is his kingdom; his wife, his mothers, his sisters are his queens and his princesses; his fellow citizens are his admiring subjects if he is wise and good. In my land you will find the poor man climbing to the highest pinnacle, side by side with the rich man. . . . We recognize little as impossible. Until death destroys this power to love and to hope I must say to you that I shall not consider the Princess Yetive beyond my reach.

And he marries her. Five sequels followed, none as successful as the original but all more than merely respectable sellers.

As the day of adventure fantasy waned, other authors turned to more conventional themes of adventure, notably survival against great odds. John Buchan produced his most enduring work in *The Thirty-Nine Steps* (1915), the tale of an innocent, naive, and not especially bright young man caught in a world of spying and intrigue. Alfred Hitchcock's 1935 film (and two later ones by other directors) helped to maintain the popularity of a book solidly entrenched as a classic of adventure literature.

Survival at sea against nature and fellow man was the theme of Charles Nordhoff and James Norman Hall in several books, notably the Mutiny trilogy about Captain William Bligh, Fletcher Christian, the mutineers, and those loyal to their king in *Mutiny on the Bounty* (1932), *Men Against the Sea* (1934), and *Pitcairn's Island* (1934).

That same sense of the sea, its beauty, its deadliness, and its boredom, pervades many books by Howard Pease, especially those about Tod Moran. *The Tattooed Man* (1926), *The Ship Without a Crew* (1934), *The Black Tanker* (1941), and *Heart of Danger* (1947) were widely read for their excitement and Pease's love of the sea.

More realistic than Pease, but a bit less popular, were Commander Edward Ellsberg's stories of sea adventure. *Ocean Gold* (1935) provided thrills as Philip Ramsey went after gold on a Spanish galleon sunk centuries before. Ellsberg's one book that retains excitement and is not dated is *Hell on Ice* (1938), a re-creation of an 1879 expedition in search of the North Pole. The almost unbelievable episodes of humans reacting to disaster after disaster are told in horrifying detail. A book worth reading today.

Rarest of all adventure writers is the one who creates a popular myth as Edgar Rice Burroughs did in *Tarzan of the Apes* (1914). Tarzan was rarely treated with any courtesy by teachers or librarians, but the ape-man myth attracted readers in vast numbers. *Tarzan* sold more than thirty-five million copies in the 1920s and 1930s. The sequels added more sales, and the many movies starring several different Tarzans made the character and its author household names.

Reality Can Sell

Although other types of books usually outsold realistic portrayals of the state of humanity, some books critical of society and its institutions sold well.

Margaret Deland broke new ground in her appraisal of a young minister seeking truth and struggling against his Calvinist background in *John Ward, Preacher* (1888). Slightly more sentimental, but even more popular, was her study of a woman living in sin yet seeking salvation for a young orphan in *The Awakening of Helena Richie* (1906).

Booth Tarkington, best known to young adults for *Penrod* (1914) and the condescending *Seventeen* (1902), produced a number of best-selling portraits of humanity, warts and all. Good as *The Turmoil* (1915) and *The Midlands* (1924) are, his most enduring (and oddly endearing) books of middle-America have proved to be *The Magnificent Ambersons* (1918), a picture of the fall of a young man, and *Alice Adams* (1921), the tale of a dangerous dreamer. Different as the two books are, both show Tarkington analyzing the American dream and questioning its reality.

Later iconoclastic writers proved equally popular with young adults. Sinclair Lewis destroyed the myth of the purity of small towns in *Main Street* (1921), the myths about small-town businessmen in *Babbitt* (1922), and the myths about small-minded evangelists in *Elmer Gantry* (1927), but he did not destroy his readers' faith in the process. What he did was challenge readers to think and convince them that an unexamined idea or belief was seductive and potentially dangerous.

What Lewis began, John Steinbeck carried forward for many readers. Lewis attacked people and ideas while Steinbeck attacked institutions and society; Lewis despised people, but Steinbeck loved his fellows. Steinbeck may be, as it has been claimed, less a writer than a social propagandist, but, given the social conditions of the 1930s, Steinbeck brought—and continues to bring—a needed voice to social issues. The number of his books that remain popular because of parallel social conditions today (it is difficult for young adults to read Steinbeck purely as a critical social historian) is impressive. *Tortilla Flat* (1935); *In Dubious Battle* (1936), surely his best book; and *The Red Pony* (1937) are sympathetic depictions of loneliness and the importance of family loyalty just as much as they are studies of social ills, past and present.

Few writers of the time turned to racial issues. Du Bose Heyward's *Porgy* (1925) is probably better known in the George Gershwin opera, *Porgy and Bess*, but both that book and *Mamba's Daughters* (1929) portrayed blacks pushed about by whites and poverty, yet able to keep their dignity. Joseph Gollomb, unfortunately largely forgotten today, wrote four books about a large racially troubled city high school, *That Year at Lincoln High* (1918), *Working Through at Lincoln High* (1923), *Up at City High* (1945), and *Tiger at City High* (1946).

Elizabeth Foreman Lewis deserves to be remembered for her honest and compassionate portraits of life in China, which she knew at first hand as a missionary. She won the Newbery Award for her 1932 *Young Fu of the Upper Yangtze* and its picture of an ambitious young apprentice to a coppersmith, but readers who care about integrity and good writing will find almost equal rewards in *Ho-Ming, a Girl of New China* (1934) and *To Beat a Tiger* (1956).

Young adult literature and books read by young adults underwent many changes from 1900 to 1940. Teachers and librarians took more interest in assessing types and titles of books read by young adults. The Stratemeyer Syndicate turned the creation of series stories from a small-scale operation into a major industry. If teachers and librarians heartily disapproved of Stratemeyer's series and other series, young adults read them avidly, though by 1940 most series books were dead except for the lively Hardy Boys and the even healthier Nancy Drew. Publishers added "Junior" or "Juvenile" divisions. Fiction of the time moved slowly and sometimes clumsily from the innocence of *Pollyanna* and *Graustark* to serious and nonromanticized books. Life seemed relatively sure, easy, simple, and safe in 1900; the First World War and the Depression dispelled that myth. When the Depression of the 1930s was ending, World War II and a very different world were just over the horizon, and a different kind of literature was soon to appear for young adults.

◆ ACTIVITIES ◆

1. The argument that boys will not read girls' books but that girls will read boys' books raged in the period from 1900 to 1940, just as it continues today. Select a few contemporary novels popular with girls and a few popular with boys. Read carefully to determine the sexist appeal of each group, *if* a sexist appeal exists. Interview both boys and girls to determine the truth of the claim that boys and girls read inherently different books, or the counterclaim that no such distinction exists.

2. People continue to argue, as they did from 1900 to 1940, that films detract from reading, that moviegoers are often nonreaders. How true is the assertion? How would you go about determining the truth (or falsity) of the claim? How would you go about counteracting it *if* the claim proved true?

3. Read some articles in the early issues of the *English Journal, Academy, Library Journal,* or *Horn Book Magazine.* What was it like to be a librarian or an English teacher in those "good

old days"? What professional problems did librarians or English teachers have then that were different from those now? Similar to those today? What kinds of books seemed to be popular then among young adults? What was the attitude of teachers or librarians to popular materials?

4. Do the claims of teachers in the 1910s that college entrance requirements mandated the English curriculum remain true for the 1980s? Read some of the current criticisms of English teaching, A *Nation at Risk* for example, and analyze the effect of the document on the present and future college prep curriculum. Who should determine the curriculum of the college bound? Why? How? What of the non-college bound?

5. Read one of the more popular books aimed at young adults in the period covered by this chapter (Wiggin's *Rebecca of Sunnybrook Farm*, Montgomery's *Anne of Green Gables*, Altsheler's *The Last of the Chiefs*, James' *Smoky, the Cowhorse*, Barbour's *The Crimson*

Sweater, Johnson's *Stover at Yale*, Richards' *Peggy*, Allee's *The Great Tradition*, or Robinson's *Bright Island*). What values are taught/preached by the author? How does the book differ from a book on the same general subject likely to be popular today? If this work were reissued, what are its chances for wide readership among young adults?

6. Read one of the Stratemeyer Literary Syndicate books still popular, a Nancy Drew or a Hardy Boys mystery. What assumptions about adult and young adult values are inherent in the book? What ingredients or assumptions made the book popular and keep it popular even today? Why do you suppose some teachers and librarians have criticized the two series, even keeping them out of classes and libraries? If possible, interview some teachers and librarians to determine their attitudes as adults toward the books (and their attitudes, as young people, to the books long ago). Talk to a few young adults to find what their reactions to the books were and are.

◆ NOTES ◆

[1]M. P. True, "What My Pupils Read," *Education* 14 (October 1893): 99–102.

[2]Clara Vostrovsky, "A Study of Children's Reading Tastes," *Pedagogical Seminary* 6 (December 1899): 523–35.

[3]*Publishers Weekly* 107 (February 21, 1925): 619–22.

[4]Alfred M. Hitchcock, "The Relation of the Picture Play to Literature," *English Journal* 4 (May 1915): 296.

[5]Montrose J. Moses, "Dietary Laws of Children's Books," *Bookman* 51 (July 1920): 590.

[6]Carleton Washburne and Mabel Vogel, *Winnetka Graded Book List* (Chicago: American Library Association, 1926), p. 5.

[7]Carleton Washburne and Mabel Vogel, "Supplement to the Winnetka Graded Book List," *Elementary English Review* 4 (February 1927): 47–52; and 4 (March 1927): 66–73.

[8]William Lyon Phelps, "The Virtues of the Second-Rate," *English Journal* 16 (January 1927): 13–14.

[9]Reed Smith, *The Teaching of Literature in the High School* (New York: American, 1935), p. 7.

[10]Franklin T. Baker, A *Bibliography of Children's Reading* (New York: Teachers College, Columbia University, 1908), pp. 6–7.

[11]Clara Whitehill Hunt, "Good and Bad Taste in Girls' Reading," *Ladies' Home Journal* 27 (April 1910): 52.

[12]Julia Carter, "Let's Talk about Boys and Books," *Wilson Bulletin for Librarians* 9 (April 1935): 418.

[13]Alice M. Jordan, "A Gallery of Girls," *Horn Book Magazine* 13 (September 1937): 276.

[14]Hannah Logosa, "Elements in Reading Guidance," *Public Libraries* 27 (March 1922): 147.

[15]Vostrovsky, p. 535.

[16]G. Stanley Hall, "Children's Reading: As a Factor in Their Education," *Library Journal* 33 (April 1908): 124–25.

[17]Fannie M. Clark, "Teaching Children to Choose," *English Journal* 9 (March 1920): 142.

[18]Orrin C. Cocker, "Motion Pictures and Reading Habits," *Library Journal* 43 (February 1918): 68.

[19]Marilla Waite Freeman, "Tying Up with the Movies: Why? When? How?" *Library Journal* 54 (June 15, 1929): 519–24.

[20]Robert Luther Duffus, *Books: Their Place in a Democracy* (Boston: Houghton Mifflin, 1930), p. 117.

[21]Louise Dinwiddie, "Best Sellers and Modern Youth," *Library Journal* 65 (November 15, 1940): 958–59.

[22]W. H. Ray et al., "English in the High School," *Academy* 4 (May 1889): 187.

[23]William E. Mead, "A Ten Years' Course in Literature," *Academy* 2 (March 1887): 55.

[24]*Report of the Committee of Ten on Secondary School Studies* (New York: American, 1894). For details about conditions leading to the Committee of Ten's formation, the committee's deliberations, and its influence see two excellent studies, Edward A. Krug, *The Shaping of the American High School* (New York: Harper & Row, 1964) and Theodore R. Sizer, *Secondary Schools at the Turn of the Century* (New Haven: Yale University Press, 1964).

[25]Samuel Thurber, "Report of English Conference" in *Report of The Committee of Ten on Secondary School Studies* (New York: Appleton, 1894), p. 86. Thurber was both a brilliant teacher and writer whose comments, especially in *School Review* and *Academy*, deserve attention today.

[26]Samuel Thurber, "Voluntary Reading in the Classical High School from the Pupil's Point of View," *School Review* 13 (February 1905): 170.

[27]Alfred M. Hitchcock in the discussion following a reading of Lilian B. Miner, "Voluntary Reading in the English High School," *School Review* 13 (February 1905): 188–89.

[28]J. M. Coulter, "What the University Expects of the Secondary School," *School Review* 17 (February 1909): 73.

[29]Wilbur W. Hatfield, "Modern Literature for High School Use," *English Journal* 1 (January 1912): 52.

[30]*Reorganization of English in Secondary Schools*, Department of the Interior, Bureau of Education, Bulletin 1917, no. 2 (Washington: Government Printing Office, 1917), p. 63.

[31]Dora V. Smith, *Instruction in English*, Bulletin, 1932, no. 17. National Survey of Secondary Education, Monograph no. 20 (Washington: Government Printing Office, 1933).

[32]Nancy Gillmore Coryell, *An Evaluation of Extensive and Intensive Teaching of Literature: A Year's Experiment in the Eleventh Grade*, Teachers College, Columbia University, Contributions to Education, no. 275 (New York: Teachers College, Columbia University, 1927).

[33]Lou LaBrant, *An Evaluation of the Free Reading Program in Grades Ten, Eleven, and Twelve for the Class of 1935*. The Ohio State University School, Contributions to Education No. 2 (Columbus: Ohio State University, 1936). See also Lou LaBrant, "The Content of a Free Reading Program," *Educational Research Bulletin* 16 (February 17, 1937): 29–34.

[34]Dora V. Smith, "Extensive Reading in Junior High School: A Survey of Teacher Preparation," *English Journal* 19 (June 1930): 449–62.

[35]Dora V. Smith, "American Youth and English," *English Journal* 26 (February 1937): 111.

[36]Manuel D. Lopez, "Children's Libraries: Nineteenth Century American Origins," *Journal of Library History* 11 (October 1976): 317.

[37]Graham P. Hawks, "A Nineteenth–Century School Library: Early Years in Milwaukee," *Journal of Library History* 12 (Fall 1977): 361.

[38]S. Swett Green, "Libraries and School," *Library Journal* 16 (December 1891): 22. Other representative articles concerned with the relationship include Mellen Chamberlain, "Public Libraries and Public School," *Library Journal* 5 (November–December 1880): 299–302; W. E. Foster, "The School and the Library: Their Mutual Relations," *Library Journal* 4 (September–October 1879): 319–41; and Mrs. J. H. Resor, "The Boy and the Book, or The Public Library a Necessity," *Public Libraries* 2 (June 1897): 282–85.

[39]"The Report of the Committee on Relations of Public Libraries to Public Schools," *NEA Journal of Proceedings and Addresses of the 38th Annual Meeting* (Chicago: University of Chicago Press, 1899), p. 455.

[40]*NEA Journal of Proceedings and Addresses of the 37th Annual Meeting* (Chicago: University of Chicago Press, 1898), pp. 1136–42.

[41]*NEA Journal . . . 37th Annual Meeting*, pp. 1007–09.

[42]Mary E. Hall, "The Possibilities of the High School Library," *ALA Bulletin* 6 (July 1912): 261–63.

[43]Mary E. Hall, "The Development of the Modern High School Library," *Library Journal* 40 (September 1915): 627.

[44]"A Standard High-School Library Organization for Accredited Secondary Schools of Different Sizes," *Educational Administration and Supervision* 3 (June 1917): 317–38.

[45]Elmer D. Johnson, *History of Libraries in the Western World*, 2nd ed. (Metuchen, New Jersey: Scarecrow Press, 1970), p. 389.

[46]*Library Journal* 59 (January 1, 1934): 9–15.

[47]Louis Shores, "The Public School Library," *Educational Forum* 4 (May 1940): 373.

[48]Geoffrey S. Lapin in "Carolyn Keene, Pseud.," *Yellowback Library* 3 (July/August 1983): 3–5. This article argues that Mildred Wirt wrote numbers 1–7, 11–25, and 30 of the Nancy Drew series while Walter Karig (best known for his 1947 satire *Zotz*) wrote numbers 8–10.

[49]Quoted by Ed Zuckerman, "The Great Hardy Boys' Whodunit," *Rolling Stone*, September 9, 1976, p. 39.

[50]Caroline M. Hewins, "Book Reviews, Book Lists, and Articles on Children's Reading: Are They of Practical Value to the Children's Librarian?" *Library Journal* 26 (August 1901): 58. Attacks on series books, especially Stratemeyer's books, persisted thereafter in library literature. Mary E. S. Root prepared a list of series books not to be circulated by public librarians, "Not to Be Circulated," *Wilson Bulletin for Librarians* 3 (January 1929): 446, including books by Alger, Finley, Castlemon, Ellis, Optic, and others, the others being heavily Stratemeyer. Two months later, Ernest F. Ayres responded, "Not to Be Circulated?" *Wilson Bulletin for Librarians* 3 (March 1929): 528–29, objecting to the cavalier treatment accorded old favorites and sarcastically adding, "Why worry about censorship so long as we have librarians?" Attacks continue today. Some librarians and English teachers to the contrary, the Syndicate clearly is winning, and students seem to be pleased.

[51]Franklin K. Mathiews, "Blowing Out the Boy's Brains," *Outlook* 108 (November 18, 1914): 653.

[52]John Tunis, "What Is a Juvenile Book?" *Horn Book Magazine* 44 (June 1968): 307.

[53]Jack Smalley, "Amazing Confessions of a Pulpeteer," *Westways* (June 1974): 20.

[54]Peter Haining, ed., *The Fantastic Pulps* (New York: Vintage Books, 1975).

[55]Herbert Ruhn, ed., *The Hard-Boiled Detectives: Stories from "Black Mask Magazine" 1920–1951* (New York: Vintage Books, 1977).

[56]Frederic Wertham, *Seduction of the Innocent* (New York: Holt, Rinehart and Winston, 1954), p. 10.

[57]*Comic Books and Juvenile Delinquency*, Interim Report of the Committee on the Judiciary (Washington, D.C.: Government Printing Office, 1955).

[58]E. L. Godkin, "The Illiteracy of American Boys," *Educational Review* 13 (January 1897): 6.

[59]Walter Camp, *Book of College Sports* (New York: Century, 1893), pp. 2–3.

◆ **TITLES MENTIONED IN CHAPTER 14** ◆

Adams, Andy. *The Log of a Cowboy: A Narrative of the Old Trail Days*. 1903.
Allee, Marjorie Hill. *The Great Tradition*. 1937.
———. *Jane's Island*. 1931.
Allen, James Lane. *The Kentucky Cardinal*. 1894.
Altsheler, Joseph. *The Horsemen of the Plains*. 1910.
———. *The Last of the Chiefs*. 1909.
———. *The Young Trailers*. 1907.
Appleton, Victor (Stratemeyer Syndicate pseudonym). Tom Swift series 1910–1935.
Armer, Laura Adams. *Waterless Mountain*. 1931.
Barbour, Ralph Henry. *The Crimson Sweater*. 1906.
———. *The Half-Back*. 1899.
———. *The Spirit of the School*. 1907.
Barclay, Florence. *The Rosary*. 1910.
Buchan, John. *The Thirty-Nine Steps*. 1915.
Burroughs, Edgar Rice. *Tarzan of the Apes*. 1914.
Burton, Charles Pierce. Boys of Bob's Hill series. 1905–1939.
Camp, Walter. *Danny Fists*. 1913.
Chadwick, Lester (Stratemeyer Syndicate pseudonym). Baseball Joe series. 1912–1928.
Churchill, Winston. *Richard Carvel*. 1899.
Deland, Margaret. *The Awakening of Helena Richie*. 1906.
———. *John Ward, Preacher*. 1888.

Dixon, Franklin W. (Stratemeyer Syndicate pseudonym). The Hardy Boys series. 1927–

Doyle, Arthur Conan. *The Adventures of Sherlock Holmes.* 1891.

————. *The Hound of the Baskervilles.* 1902.

Durant, Will. *The Story of Philosophy.* 1926.

Eastman, Charles A. *Indian Boyhood.* 1902.

Ellsberg, Edward. *Hell on Ice.* 1938.

————. *Ocean Gold.* 1935.

Emerson, Alice B. (Stratemeyer Syndicate pseudonym). *Ruth Fielding and Her Double.* 1932.

————. *Ruth Fielding and Her Greatest Triumph, Or, Saving Her Company from Disaster.* 1933.

————. *Ruth Fielding at the Red Mill.* 1913.

Farnol, Jeffrey. *The Broad Highway.* 1910.

Finley, Martha Farquharson. Elsie Dinsmore series. 1867–1905.

Fitzhugh, Percy Kees. Roy Blakely series. 1920–1931.

Fox, John. *The Calling of Dan Matthews.* 1909.

————. *The Little Shepherd of Kingdom Come.* 1903.

————. *The Trail of the Lonesome Pine.* 1908.

Frey, Hildegarde G. Campfire Girl series. 1916–1920.

Galsworthy, John. *Justice.* 1910.

Glynn, Elinor. *Three Weeks.* 1907.

Gollomb, Joseph. *That Year at Lincoln High.* 1918.

————. *Tiger at City High.* 1946.

————. *Up at City High.* 1945.

————. *Working Through at Lincoln High.* 1923.

Grey, Zane. *Riders of the Purple Sage.* 1912.

————. *The Spirit of the Border.* 1906.

————. *The Wanderer of the Wasteland.* 1923.

Grinnell, George Bird. *By Cheyenne Campfires.* 1926.

————. *Pawnee Hero Stories and Folk Tales.* 1889.

Heyliger, William. *Bartley: Freshman Pitcher.* 1911.

————. *Dan's Tomorrow.* 1922.

————. *Fairview High School Series.* 1916–1918.

————. *High Benton.* 1919.

————. *High Benton, Worker.* 1921.

————. *Lansing series.* 1912–1927.

————. *St. Mary's series.* 1911–1915.

————. *Steve Merrill, Engineer.* 1935.

————. *Top Lineman.* 1943.

————. *You're on the Air.* 1941.

Heyward, Du Bose. *Mamba's Daughters.* 1929.

————. *Porgy.* 1925.

Hill, Grace Livingston. *Exit Betty.* 1920.

————. *The Girl from Montana.* 1907.

————. *Rainbow Cottage.* 1934.

Hope, Anthony (real name Anthony Hope Hawkins). *The Prisoner of Zenda.* 1894.

Hull, Edith Maude. *The Sheik.* 1921.

Jackson, Helen Hunt. *Ramona.* 1884.

James, Will. *Smoky, the Cowhorse.* 1926.

Johnson, Owen. *Stover at Yale.* 1911.

————. *The Tennessee Shad.* 1911.

————. *The Varmint.* 1910.

Johnston, Mary. *To Have and To Hold.* 1900.

Keene, Carolyn (Stratemeyer Syndicate pseudonym). Dana Girls series. 1934–

————. Nancy Drew series. 1930–

Kipling, Rudyard. *Captains Courageous.* 1897.

————. *The Light That Failed.* 1890.

Lane, Rose Wilder. *Let the Hurricane Roar.* 1933.

————. *The Young Pioneers* (reissue of *Let the Hurricane Roar*). 1976.

Lewis, Elizabeth Foreman. *Young Fu of the Upper Yangtze.* 1932.

————. *Ho-Ming, A Girl of New China.* 1934.

————. *To Beat a Tiger.* 1956.

Lewis, Sinclair. *Babbitt.* 1922.

————. *Elmer Gantry.* 1927.

————. *Main Street.* 1921.

London, Jack. *Martin Eden.* 1909.

McCutcheon, George. *Graustark: The Story of a Love Behind a Throne.* 1901.

Montgomery, Lucy Maud. *Anne of Green Gables.* 1908.

Nordhoff, Charles and James Norman Hall. *Men Against the Sea.* 1934.

————. *The Mutiny on the Bounty.* 1932.

————. *Pitcairn's Island.* 1934.

Norris, Frank. *The Pit.* 1903.

Pease, Howard. *The Black Tanker.* 1941.

————. *Heart of Danger.* 1947.

————. *The Ship without a Crew.* 1934.

————. *The Tattooed Man.* 1926.

Porter, Eleanor. *Pollyanna.* 1913.

Porter, Gene Stratton. *Freckles.* 1904.

————. *A Girl of the Limberlost.* 1909.

————. *Laddie.* 1913.

————. *Michael O'Halloran.* 1915.

Rice, Alice Hegan. *Mrs. Wiggs of the Cabbage Patch.* 1901.

Richards, Laura Elizabeth. *Peggy.* 1899.

Rinehart, Mary Roberts. *The Circular Staircase.* 1908.

Robinson, Mabel Louise. *Bright Island.* 1937.

Scott, Sir Walter. *The Abbott.* 1820.

————. *Ivanhoe.* 1819.

————. *The Lay of the Last Minstrel.* 1805.

————. *Marmion.* 1808.

Standish, Burt L. (real name: William Gilbert Patten). Frank Merriwell series. 1901–1911.

————. *Frank Merriwell at Yale.* 1903.

Steinbeck, John. *In Dubious Battle.* 1936.

————. *The Red Pony.* 1937.

————. *Tortilla Flat.* 1935.

Stevenson, Robert Louis. *Prince Otto.* 1885.

————. *Treasure Island.* 1883.

Stratemeyer, Edward. Bound to Succeed series. 1895–1899.

————. Dave Porter series. 1905–1919.

————. Lakeport series. 1904–1912.

————. Old Glory series. 1898–1901.

————. *Richard Dare's Venture, Or, Striking Out for Himself.* 1894.

————. Rover Boys series. 1899–1926.

————. Soldiers of Fortune series. 1900–1906.

————. *Under Dewey at Manila, Or, The War Fortunes of a Castaway.* 1898.

————. *Victor Horton's Idea.* 1886.

Synge, John Millington. *Riders to the Sea.* 1904.

Tarkington, Booth. *Alice Adams.* 1921.

————. *The Magnificent Ambersons.* 1918.

————. *The Midlands.* 1924.

————. *Penrod.* 1914.

————. *Seventeen.* 1902.

————. *The Turmoil.* 1915.

Tunis, John R. *Iron Duke.* 1938.

Twain, Mark (real name: Samuel Clemens). *Tom Sawyer Abroad.* 1894.

Webster, Jean. *Daddy-Long-Legs.* 1912.

Wiggin, Kate Douglas. *Rebecca of Sunnybrook Farm.* 1904.

Wister, Owen. *The Virginian: A Horseman of the Plains.* 1902.

Wright, Harold Bell. *The Re-Creation of Brian Keith.* 1919.

————. *The Shepherd of the Hills.* 1907.

————. *The Calling of Dan Matthews.* 1909.

————. *Their Yesterdays.* 1912.

————. *When a Man's a Man.* 1916.

————. *The Winning of Barbara Worth.* 1911.

◆ SOME SUGGESTED READINGS ◆

General Comments on Literature 1900–1940:

Greene, Suzanne Ellery. *Books for Pleasure: Popular Fiction 1914–1945.* Bowling Green, Ohio: Bowling Green University Popular Press, 1974.

Hackett, Alice Payne, and James Henry Burke. *80 Years of Best Sellers, 1895–1975.* New York: R. R. Bowker, 1977.

Hart, Irving Harlow. "Best Sellers in Fiction during the First Quarter of the Twentieth Century." *Publishers Weekly* 107 (February 14, 1925): 525–27.

Hart, James D. *The Popular Book: A History of America's Literary Taste.* Berkeley: University of California Press, 1950.

Mott, Frank Luther. *Golden Multitudes: The Story of the Best Seller in the United States.* New York: Macmillan, 1950.

Sample, Hazel. *Pitfalls for Readers of Fiction.*

Chicago: National Council of Teachers of English, 1940.

Reading Interest Studies:

Anderson, Roxanna E. "A Preliminary Study of the Reading Tastes of High School Pupils." *Pedogogical Seminary* 19 (December 1912): 438–60.

Belson, Danylu, chairman. "The Reading Interests of Boys." *Elementary English Review* 3 (November 1926): 292–96.

"Books Boys Like Best." *Publishers Weekly* 88 (October 23, 1915): 1315–45.

Brink, William G. "Reading Interests of High School Pupils." *School Review* 47 (October 1939): 613–21.

Charters, W. W. "What's Happened to Boys' Favorites?" *Library Journal* 74 (October 15,

1949): 1577. An especially intriguing article as it sums up five surveys, all in *Library Journal*, in 1907, 1917, 1927, 1937, and finally, 1949.

Eaton, H. T. "What High School Students Like to Read." *Education* 43 (December 1922): 204–9.

Jordan, Arthur Melville. *Children's Interests in Reading.* 2nd ed. Chapel Hill: University of North Carolina Press, 1926.

Low, Florence B. "The Reading of the Modern Girl." *Nineteenth Century* 59 (February 1906): 278–87.

Popkin, Zelda. "The Finer Things in Life." *Harper's Magazine* 164 (April 1932): 602–11.

Scoggin, Margaret C. "Do Young People Want Books?" *Wilson Bulletin for Librarians* 11 (September 1936): 17.

Smith, Franklin Orin. "Pupils Voluntary Reading." *Pedagogical Seminary* 14 (June 1907): 209–22.

Terman, Lewis M., and Margaret Lima. *Children's Reading: A Guide for Parents and Teachers.* New York: Appleton, 1927.

Vostrovsky, Clara. "A Study of Children's Reading Tastes." *Pedagogical Seminary* 6 (December 1899): 523–35.

Waples, Douglas, and Ralph D. Tyler. *What People Want to Read About: A Study of Group Interests and a Survey of Problems in Adult Reading.* Chicago: American Library Association, 1931.

Washburne, Carleton, and Mabel Vogel. *Winnetka Graded Book List.* Chicago: American Library Association, 1926.

————. "Supplement to the Winnetka Graded Book List." *Elementary English Review* 4 (February 1927): 47–52; and 4 (March 1927): 66–73.

Young Adult Literature:

Cadogan, Mary, and Patricia Craig. *You're a Brick, Angela! A New Look at Girls' Fiction from 1839 to 1975.* London: Gollancz, 1976.

Coryell, Hubert V. "Boys, Books and Bait." *Wilson Bulletin* 2 (April–May–June 1926): 539–46.

Lerman, Leo. "An Industry within an Industry." *Saturday Review of Literature* 24 (November 8, 1941): 3–7.

Mearns, Hughes. "Bo Peep, Old Woman, and Slow Mandy: Being Three Theories of Read-

ing." *New Republic* 48 (November 10, 1926): 344–46.

Smith, Dora V. "American Youth and English." *English Journal* 26 (February 1937): 99–113.

————. "Extensive Reading in Junior High School: A Survey of Teacher Preparation." *English Journal* 19 (June 1930): 449–62.

English Teaching:

Cole, William Morse. "The Vital in Teaching Secondary English." *School Review* 14 (September 1906): 469–83.

Hatfield, Wilbur W., ed. *An Experience Curriculum in English.* New York: Appleton, 1935.

Hosic, James Fleming, chairman. *Reorganization of English in Secondary Schools.* Department of the Interior, Bureau of Education, Bulletin 1917, no. 2. Washington: Government Printing Office, 1917.

Smith, Dora V. *Evaluating Instruction in Secondary School English.* Chicago: National Council of Teachers of English, 1941.

Thurber, Samuel. "Report of the English Conference" in *Report of the Committee of Ten on Secondary School Studies.* New York: American, 1894, pp. 86–95.

————. "Voluntary Reading in the Classical High School." *School Review* 13 (February 1905): 168–79.

American Education:

Burstall, Sara A. *Impressions of American Education in 1908.* London: Longmans, Green, 1909. A comparison of American and English educational systems by a Head Mistress of a girls' school in England.

Cremin, Lawrence A. *American Education: The Colonial Experience, 1607–1783.* New York: Harper & Row, 1970.

————. *American Education: The National Experience, 1783–1876.* New York: Harper & Row, 1980.

————. *The Transformation of the School: Progressivism in American Education, 1876–1957.* New York: Alfred A. Knopf, 1961. All 3 are basic sources.

Inglis, Alexander James. *The Rise of the High School in Massachusetts.* Columbia University Contributions to Education, no. 45. New York: Teachers College, Columbia University, 1911. Excellent source material.

Krug, Edward A. *The Shaping of the American High School, 1880–1920*. Madison: University of Wisconsin Press, 1964.

————. *The Shaping of the American High School, 1920–1941*. Madison: University of Wisconsin Press, 1972.

College Entrance Requirements:

Applebee, Arthur N. *Tradition and Reform in the Teaching of English: A History*. Urbana, Illinois: National Council of Teachers of English, 1974.

Crowe, John M., Mrs. E. K. Broadus, and James Fleming Hosic. "Report of the Conference Committee on High-School English." *School Review* 17 (February 1909): 85–88.

Eaton, the Reverend Arthur Wentworth. *College Requirements in English, Entrance Examinations (Examination Papers for 1893 and 1894)*. Boston: Ginn, 1894.

Hays, Edna. *College Entrance Requirements in English: Their Effects on the High Schools— An Historical Survey*. New York: Teachers College, Columbia University, 1936.

Hosic, James Fleming. "A Brief Chapter of Educational History Together with a Summary of the Facts So Far Obtained by a Committee on the National Education Association and a List of References." *English Journal* 1 (February 1912): 95–121.

Scott, Fred Newton. "College-Entrance Requirements in English." *School Review* 9 (June 1901): 365–78.

Stout, John Elbert. *The Development of High-School Curriculum in the North Central States from 1860 to 1918*. Chicago: University of Chicago Press, 1921.

Thomas, Charles Swain, ed. *Examining the Examination in English: A Report on the College Entrance Requirements*. Harvard Studies in Education, no. 17. Cambridge: Harvard University Press, 1931, pp. 1–15.

Free Reading:

LaBrant, Lou. "The Content of a Free Reading Program." *Educational Research Bulletin* 16 (February 17, 1937): 29–34.

————. *An Evaluation of the Free Reading Program in Grades Ten, Eleven, and Twelve for the Class of 1935, the Ohio State University School*. Contributions to Education No. 2. Columbus: Ohio State University Press, 1936.

The School Library:

Cecil, Henry L., and Willard A. Heaps. *School Library Services in the United States: An Interpretive Survey*. New York: H. W. Wilson, 1940.

Fargo, Lucille. *The Library in the School*. Chicago: American Library Association, 1930 (revised several times).

Gambee, Budd L. "An 'Alien Body': Relationships between the Public Library and the Public Schools, 1876–1920" in *Ball State University Library Science Lectures*, First Series. Muncie, Indiana: Ball State University, 1973, pp. 1–23.

Heller, Frieda M., and Lou LaBrant, *The Librarian and the Teacher of English*. Chicago: American Library Association, 1938.

Logasa, Hannah. *The High School Library: Its Function in Education*. New York: Appleton, 1928.

School Libraries for Today and Tomorrow, Functions and Standards. Chicago: American Library Association, 1945.

Shapiro, Lillian A. *Serving Youth: Communication and Commitment in the High School Library*. New York: R. R. Bowker, 1975.

The Stratemeyer Literary Syndicate:

Abrahamson, Richard F. "They're Reading the Series Books, So Let's Use Them; or Who Is Shaun Cassidy?" *Journal of Reading* 22 (March 1979): 523–30.

Dizer, John T., Jr. "Fortune and the Syndicate." *Boys' Book Collector* 2 (Fall 1970): 146–53; and 2 (Winter 1970): 78–86.

————. *Tom Swift and Company: Boys' Books by Stratemeyer and Others*. Jefferson, North Carolina: McFarland, 1982.

"For It Was Indeed He." *Fortune* 9 (April 1934): 86.

Johnson, Deidre. *Stratemeyer Pseudonyms and Series Books: An Annotated Checklist of Stratemeyer and Stratemeyer Syndicate Publications*. Westport, Connecticut: Greenwood Press, 1980.

Kuskin, Karla. "Nancy Drew and Friends." *New York Times Book Review*. May 4, 1975, pp. 20–21.

Mason, Bobbie Ann. *The Girl Sleuth: A Feminist Guide.* Old Westbury, New York: Feminist Press, 1975.

McFarlane, Leslie. *Ghost of the Hardy Boys: An Autobiography of Leslie McFarlane.* New York: Two Continents Publishing Group, 1976.

Prager, Arthur. "Edward Stratemeyer and His Book Machine." *Saturday Review* 54 (July 10, 1971): 15.

————. "The Secret of Nancy Drew—Pushing Forty and Going Strong." *Saturday Review* 52 (January 25, 1969): 18.

Zuckerman, Ed. "The Great Hardy Boys' Whodunit." *Rolling Stone,* September 9, 1976, pp. 37–40.

Mathiews and Stratemeyer:

Mathiews, Franklin K. "Blowing Out the Boy's Brains." *Outlook* 108 (November 18, 1914): 652–54.

————. "The Influence of the Boy Scout Movement in Directing the Reading of Boys." *Bulletin of the American Library Association* 8 (January 1914): 223–28.

————. "Why Boys Read 'Blood and Thunder' Tales." *Elementary English Review* 2 (October 1925): 280–82.

Melcher, Frederic. "The Story of 'Book Week.'" *Elementary English Review* 7 (October 1930): 191.

Series Books:

Deane, Paul C. "The Persistence of Uncle Tom: An Examination of the Image of the Negro in Children's Fiction Series." *Journal of Negro Education* 37 (Spring 1968): 140–45.

Dizer, John T., Jr. "Boys' Books and the American Dream." *Dime Novel Roundup* 37 (February 15, 1968): 12–17; and 37 (March 15, 1968): 29–31.

Follett, Wilson. "Junior Model." *Bookman* 70 (September 1929): 11–14. An attack on boys' series books.

Garis, Roger. *My Father Was Uncle Wiggily.* New York: McGraw-Hill, 1966.

Girls' Series Books: A Checklist of Hardback Books Published 1900–1975. Minneapolis: Children's Literature Research Collections, University of Minnesota Library, 1978. A most handy research help.

Hudson, Harry K. *A Bibliography of Hard-Cover Boys' Books.* Rev. ed. Tampa, Florida: Data Print, 1977. The prototype for the *Girls' Series Books* listed above and *the basic book* in studying series books.

Kilgour, Raymond L. *Lee and Shepard: Publishers for the People.* Hamden, Connecticut: Shoe String Press, 1965.

MacDonald, J. Frederick. "The 'Foreigner' in Juvenile Series Books, 1900–1945." *Journal of Popular Culture* 8 (Winter 1974): 534–48.

Prager, Arthur. *Rascals at Large, or The Clue in the Old Nostalgia.* New York: Doubleday, 1971.

Root, Mary E. "Not to Be Circulated." *Wilson Bulletin for Librarians* 3 (January 1929): 446. See the response by Ernest F. Ayres, "Not to Be Circulated?" *Wilson Bulletin for Librarians* 3 (March 1929): 528–29.

Scoggin, Margaret C. "Junior Books for the Stepping-Stone Reader." *Wilson Bulletin for Librarians* 9 (December 1934): 209–11.

Soderbergh, Peter A. "Bibliographical Essay: The Negro in Juvenile Series Books, 1899–1930." *Journal of Negro History* 58 (April 1973): 179–82.

Yost, Edna. "The Fifty-Cent Juveniles." *Publishers Weekly* 121 (June 18, 1932): 2405–8.

————. "Who Wrote the Fifty-Cent Juveniles?" *Publishers Weekly* 123 (May 20, 1933): 1595–98.

Pulps:

Goulart, Ron. *An Informal History of the Pulp Magazine.* New Rochelle, NY: Arlington House, 1972.

Wilkinson, Richard Hill. "Whatever Happened to the Pulps?" *Saturday Review* 45 (February 10, 1962): 60.

Comics and Comic Books:

Couperie, Pierre. *A History of the Comic Strip.* New York: Crown, 1968.

Daniels, Les. *Comix: A History of Comic Books in America.* New York: Outerbridge and Dienstfrey, 1971.

Robinson, Jerry. *The Comics: An Illustrated History of Comic Strip Art.* New York: G. P. Putnam's Sons, 1974.

Wertham, Frederic. *Seduction of the Innocent.* New York: Holt, Rinehart and Winston, 1954.

Haldeman-Julius and His Little Blue Books:

Herder, Dale M. "Haldeman-Julius, the Little Blue Books, and the Theory of Popular Culture." *Journal of Popular Culture* 4 (Spring 1971): 881–91.

————. "The Little Blue Books as Popular Culture: E. Haldeman-Julius' Methodology" in Russell B. Nye (ed.), *New Dimensions in Popular Culture*. Bowling Green, Ohio: Bowling Green University Popular Press, 1972, pp. 31–42.

Mordell, Albert. *The World of Haldeman-Julius*. New York: Twayne, 1960.

1940-1966

❖

FROM CERTAINTY TO UNCERTAINTY IN LIFE AND LITERATURE COURTESY OF FUTURE SHOCK

Nineteen-forty began uncertainly as we moved from the Depression into a prewar economy and employment market. Our involvement in World War II began with heavy losses in the Pacific, the draft, and Gold Star mothers, and proceeded to victory at Iwo Jima, North Africa, and Omaha Beach. From a hatred of Communism before 1941 we moved to a temporary brotherhood during World War II. Then came Yalta, the Iron Curtain, blacklisting, and Senator McCarthy. We went from the A-Bomb to the H-Bomb to germ warfare to napalm. First our idols were John Wayne, Clark Gable, and Loretta Young, then youthful idols such as Marilyn Monroe and James Dean. We became increasingly permissive sexually—or so it seemed to many people. Music went from "Your Hit Parade" to folk music to rock and roll to the Beatles and the Rolling Stones, and Dick Clark beamed on from his "American Bandstand" every year. We entertained ourselves with radio drama, then Milton Berle and "I Love Lucy," and on to "Studio One," "See It Now," and "The Defenders." We went from "Li'l Abner" to "Pogo," and from Bob Hope to Mort Sahl. Among the problems of the time were school integration, racial unrest, the civil rights movement, riots in the streets, and women's rights. We went from violence to more violence, with the assassinations of John Kennedy and Malcolm X. The economy swung from inflation to recession and back again. We started World War II with the nation united; then we went to the Korean War with the nation unsure; we ended with the Vietnam War with an increasingly divided nation. The twenty-five years between 1940 and 1965 revealed a country separated by gaps of all kinds: generational, racial, technological, cultural, and economic.

◈ MORE READING INTEREST STUDIES

By 1940, reading interest studies were fixtures in educational journals, and increasingly they did not merely report findings but they interpreted results and questioned the kind of literature used in the schools. In 1946, George W. Norvell briefly reported in his long-range study, "Our data shows clearly that much literary material being used in our schools is too mature, too subtle, too erudite to permit its enjoyment by the majority of secondary-school pupils."[1] In his preliminary work and his book-length report, Norvell arrived at six implications for secondary schools: (1) Assigned material should be enjoyable to young adults; (2) "In addition to the study in common, there [should] be much wide reading through which young people may enjoy the materials which appeal to them individually"; (3) Teachers should refrain from choosing materials to please themselves and place the students' interests first; (4) Three-fourths of the selections currently used should be replaced by more interesting materials; (5) New programs should find materials to interest boys usually bored by the present curricula; and (6) "To increase reading skill, promote the reading habit, and produce a generation of book-lovers, there is no factor so powerful as interest."[2]

Others supported Novell's contention that young adults' choices of voluntary reading rarely overlapped books widely respected by more traditional English teachers. In 1947 Marie Rankin surveyed eight public libraries in Illinois, Ohio, and New York to discover the most consistently popular books with adolescents. Helen Boylston's *Sue Barton, Senior Nurse*, led the list; others from the top ten were probably not known to many English teachers.[3] Twelve years later, Stephen Dunning surveyed fourteen school and public librarians asking them to report on junior novels popular with students. Librarians listed the top ten as Maureen Daly's *Seventeenth Summer*, Henry Gregor Felsen's *Hot Rod*, Betty Cavanna's *Going On Sixteen*, Rosamund Du Jardin's *Double Date*, Walter Farley's *Black Stallion*, Sally Benson's *Junior Miss*, Mary Stolz's *The Sea Gulls Woke Me*, Rosamund Du Jardin's *Wait For Marcy*, James Summers' *Prom Trouble*, and John Tunis' *All-American*.[4]

Fiction consistently ranked high with young adults as any sampling of reading interest surveys reveals.

Near the height of the outpouring of published studies, Jacob W. Getzels assessed the value of reading interest surveys and found most of them wanting in "precision of *definition*, rigor of *theory*, and depth of *analysis*."[5] He was, of course, right. Most reports were limited to a small sample from a few schools—often only one school—and little was done except to ask students what they liked to read. From a scientific point of view, most were hopelessly deficient.

But the studies had value. They gave librarians and teachers insight into books young adults liked, and, by extrapolation, books they might like. They suggested which tastes were current and which were changing, which books were being read and which were losing popularity. More important yet, they gave insights into young adults and their interests, not just in reading but in other areas as well, and that suggested all sorts of activities in schools and libraries to attract recalcitrant readers. They brought hope to librarians and teachers that no matter how reluctant readers were in school, somewhere out there somebody was reading, a hope that—as any librarian or teacher knows on Friday afternoon or the day after Christmas vacation—needs constant rekindling.

These surveys need to be made every year by English teachers and librarians to assess—or reassess—where students are. Few of these surveys will be published, but they can be helpful locally.

G. Robert Carlsen summarized the reading interests discovered up to 1954 and argued that books could help to fulfill three broad areas of young adult needs:

◇ Young people need assurance of the status of human beings. With the end of childhood, children are painfully stirred by a desire to find that they as individuals are important creations of God, capable of infinite development.

A second area of need in the developing adolescent is for assurance of his own normality. Young people need to test their reactions, to experiment with them to find out whether or not they are normal human beings; but they do not want to reveal their own abnormality to others—if abnormality it is—by asking direct questions.

A third need of young people that seems to govern their reading choices, particularly in the later period, is a need for role-playing. With the developing of their personality through adolescence, they come to a semi-integrated picture of themselves as human beings. They want to test this picture of themselves in the many kinds of roles that it is possible for a human being to play and through testing to see what roles they may fit into and what roles are uncongenial.[6]

Dwight L. Burton reminded English teachers that their goal was to bring young adults into contact with books—good books and mediocre books and classics, books of all kinds—and that doing that would demand some significant changes in the traditional curriculum:

◇ If we are to prove that there is always a book for every student, then we must drop our concern with teaching any certain book. We must concern ourselves with any book, however ephemeral, which in any way can rekindle a flagging spirit or provide meaning for a searching mind. We need not worry about whether or not we are teaching "good" literature.[7]

◈ HAVIGHURST'S DEVELOPMENTAL TASKS

The work of Robert J. Havighurst at the University of Chicago was helpful to teachers and librarians in both reading interests and bibliotherapy. Havighurst maintained that at various stages in life (infancy and early childhood, middle childhood, adolescence, adulthood, and old age) certain tasks are imposed by society upon each of us. Havighurst did not argue that the tasks were good or bad, only that they existed, and a person unable or unwilling to perform the tasks at roughly the appropriate time would be rejected or ostracized, or, worse yet, pitied by society.

He first listed five adolescent tasks and later expanded them to ten:

1. Achieving new and more mature relations with age-mates of both sexes.
2. Achieving a masculine or feminine social role.
3. Accepting one's physique and using the body effectively.
4. Achieving emotional independence of parents and other adults.
5. Achieving assurance of economic independence.
6. Selecting and preparing for an occupation.
7. Preparing for marriage and family life.
8. Developing intellectual skills and concepts necessary for civic competence.
9. Desiring and achieving socially responsible behavior.
10. Acquiring a set of values and an ethical system as a guide to behavior.[8]

Implications for helping young adults find books illustrating or illuminating the ten developmental tasks were obvious. Some misguided librarians and English teachers tried desperately to fit students into developmental tasks independent of who or what or where they were. But Havighurst could not forestall fools—no one can achieve that most impossible of tasks—and good librarians and teachers found much in Havighurst to help them.

◈ BIBLIOTHERAPY COMES TO THE SCHOOLS

In writing his account of the use of books as part of his treatment for psychiatric patients in 1929, Dr. G. O. Ireland used the term *bibliotherapy*,[9] a new term for librarians and English teachers. The word soon caught on, and by the late 1930s and early 1940s articles dealing with bibliotherapy became almost commonplace. A 1939 author asked, "Can There Be a Science of Bibliotherapy?"[10] and was answered a year later:

◇ The science of bibliotherapy is still in its infancy, yet public libraries are featuring readers' advisory services, and hospital libraries are on the increase. All school librarians who practice individual reading guidance are participating, perhaps unconsciously, in a program of bibliotherapy.[11]

By the 1950s, bibliotherapy was firmly entrenched in the schools. Philosophically, it was related to and justified by Aristotle's *Poetics* and the theory of emotional release through catharsis, a theory with remarkably little support except for unverifiable personal testimonials.

One clear and easy application of bibliotherapy was the free reading program (sometimes too clear and too easy for the inept amateur psychologist/English teacher who, finding a new book in which the protagonist had acne, sought out the acne-ridden kid in class saying, "You must read this— it's about you." Not, incidentally, an apocryphal story). Lou LaBrant, popularizer of free reading, sounded both a recommendation and a warning when she wrote:

> ◇ Certainly I can make a much wiser selection of offerings if I understand the potential reader. . . . The first step has been taken when we have some assurance that the book or short selection which we recommend or teach will have a hearing; that it will come within the understanding of the young reader because it deals with problems with which he is conversant and that it will hold some appeal to him because he, like the author of the piece, is concerned with a certain aspect of living.
>
> This does not mean, as some have interpreted, that a young reader will enjoy only literature which answers his questions, tells him what is to be done. It is true, however, that young and old tend to choose literature, whether they seek solutions or escape, which offers characters or situations with which they can find a degree of identification.[12]

With all the problems inherent in some uses of bibliotherapy, few would argue with Frank Ross' appraisal of its contemporary potential and danger:

> ◇ This kind of fitting the book to the reader has always been the librarian's creed. . . . The teacher probably can do it better because he knows his students better sometimes than the parents do. One caution should be kept in mind. . . . Only after weeks of observing the student in his class performance, in his compositions, and in his conferences should anyone begin bibliotherapy.[13]

◈ THE RISE OF PAPERBACKS

Some young adult readers might assume paperbound books have always been with us. But, despite the success of dime novels and libraries of paperbacks in the late 1800s, paperbacks as we know them first entered the mass market in 1938 when Pocket Books offered Pearl Buck's *The Good Earth* as a sample volume in mail-order tests. In the spring of 1939, a staff artist created the first sketch of Gertrude the Kangaroo with a book in her paws and another in her pouch. It became Pocket Books' trademark. A few months later, the company issued ten titles in 10,000 copy editions, most of them remaining best-sellers for years: James Hilton's *Lost Horizon*, Dorothea Brande's *Wake Up and Live*, William Shakespeare's *Five Great Tragedies*, Thorne Smith's *Topper*, Agatha Christie's *The Murder of Roger Ackroyd*, Dorothy Parker's *Enough Rope*, Emily Brontë's *Wuthering Heights*, Samuel Butler's *The Way of All Flesh*, Thornton Wilder's *The Bridge of San Luis Rey*, and Felix Salten's *Bambi*. *The Good Earth* became the eleventh title. By the close of 1939, Pocket Books had published twenty-four other titles that sold more than one and a half million copies. In 1940, the company published fifty-three more titles selling more than four-and-a-half-million copies. Success for paperbacks was assured.

Avon began publishing in 1941, Penguin (in the United States) entered in 1942, and Bantam, New American Library, Ballantine, Dell, and Popular Library began publishing in 1943. By 1951, sales had reached 230 million paperbacks annually.

Phenomenal as the growth was, paperbacks were slow to appear in schools although a look at an early edition of Bowker's *Paperbound Books in Print* reveals an incredible number of titles available in areas from philosophy to adolescent books. That did not prevent some librarians from complaining that paperbacks did not belong in libraries because they were difficult to catalogue and attractive to steal. It did not prevent some teachers and principals from maintaining that paperback covers were lurid and the contents little more than pornography. They sometimes removed paperbacks from libraries or students and tore the paperbacks apart enthusiastically. In 1969 (and later in some schools) paperbacks were as serious a disciplinary matter as pornography:

> ◇ "I'd rather be caught with Lady Chatterley in hardcover than *Hot Rod* in paperback," a precocious high school junior in New York City told me earlier this year. "Hard covers get you one detention, but paperbacks get you two or three," he explained.
>
> Curriculum change is painfully slow in inner city schools where change is most needed. But even in the ghetto, changing perceptions of paperback books are making this high school junior's report a rare phenomenon. It seems that paperbacks are beginning to make the education scene. Having served its fifty years in educational purgatory, the paperback is becoming an acceptable "innovation" which, I suppose, means that it is no longer a true innovation.[14]

The innovation was overdue. Students had long before discovered the value of paperbacks. Paperbacks were ubiquitous, comfortably sized, and inexpensive, and students bought their own libraries while some teachers and librarians wondered where all their customers had gone. Part of the early enthusiasm for paperbacks and acceptance in the schools came from the creation of the Scholastic Book Clubs and the many editions of the Readers' Choice Catalogues. As Grosset and Dunlap, Tempo Books, Pyramid Publications, and Archway Books competed with Scholastic, schools opened paperback bookstores for sales to excited secondary students. Later, Dell's Yearling and Mayflower books would become the major suppliers of books written specifically for young adults, but by 1966 paperbacks were very much a part of young adults' lives, a point amply demonstrated by Daniel Fader's brilliant *Hooked on Books*.[15]

There is no apparent end for paperback possibilities in the young adult market. Enthusiastically assessing the growth by 1977, Ray Waiters noted that reader enjoyment and literacy itself depends upon the success of the paperback industry:

◇ The mass-market houses aren't alone in hoping that their crusade will succeed. After all, if Americans don't learn to read and enjoy books when they're young, what future is there for writers, publishers, booksellers, librarians—and book review editors?[16]

◈ CHANGES AND GROWTH IN YOUNG ADULT LITERATURE

In 1941, Leo Lerman surveyed the growth of juvenile literature defined as "books upon every conceivable subject for boys and girls ranging in age from six months to eighteen years," from 1920 to 1940. Noting that during that twenty year span, 14,536 juvenile books had been printed, Lerman concluded, "Children's books have become big business—an industry within an industry."[17] Lerman might have been surprised by the growth of young adult literature in the years that followed, particularly with the development of paperback books.

More important than mere quantity, the quality of young adult literature rose steadily, if at times hesitatingly and uncertainly, from 1941 to 1965. Series books, so popular from 1900 to 1940, died out—except for Stratemeyer Syndicate stalwarts Nancy Drew, the Hardy Boys, and one new series, Tom Swift, Jr.—killed by increasing reader sophistication and the wartime scarcity of paper. Their replacements were not always great advances, but young adult books did improve steadily.

Much young adult literature of the 1940s and 1950s celebrated those wonderful high school years. Books seemed at times to concentrate on concerns with dating, parties, class rings, working on the school newspaper, preparing for the school prom, senior year, the popular crowd (or learning to avoid it), and teen romance devoid of realities like sex. That accounted for titles such as *Boy Trouble, Girl Trouble, Prom Trouble, Teacher Trouble, Practically Fifteen, Going on Sixteen, Almost Seventeen, A Girl for Michael, A Boy for Debbie, A Touchdown for Harold, A Horse for Sheila.* Books often sounded alike, looked alike, and read alike, but they were unquestionably popular.

Plots were usually simple, simplistic, and too often simple-minded. One or two characters might be slightly developed, but other characters were merely sketched or tossed in as stock figures or stereotypes. Major characters faced a dilemma (joining a school sorority, playing football unfairly, joining the popular crowd, going to an all-night dance), adult figures stood by hoping the protagonists would come through morally unscathed, and after a bit of hesitation or uncertainty, the morals of the community and the goodness of young adults were reaffirmed. Books dealt almost exclusively with white, middle-class values and morality. Endings were almost uniformly happy and bright, and readers could be certain that neither their morality nor their intelligence would be challenged.

Taboos may never have been written down, but they were clear to readers and writers. Certain things were not to be mentioned—obscenity,

THE PEOPLE BEHIND THE BOOKS

AUDREY B. EAGLEN,
Librarian and Editor

Cuyahoga County, Ohio, Librarian
Former editor of Top of the News and
president of American Library
Association Young Adult Services
Division

Back in Olden Times (1972, to be exact), Natalie Babbitt wrote in an article in *Horn Book Magazine* that "Teenagers do not need a fiction of their own: they are quite ready to move into the world of adult fiction," a statement which is as silly as it is unequivocal—

especially coming from Ms. Babbitt, who herself writes books for the teenage audience. According to her, we can assume that once a 13-year-old has read all there is to read of Mary Poppins, he or she is ready for Henry Miller and Jackie Collins, or is capable of making the leap from Encyclopedia Brown to *Encyclopaedia Britannica* with nary a second thought.

The implications are that those magic four letters—TEEN—automatically confer adult status on the individual (which everything from common sense to common law refutes) and that all young people are exactly alike. Certainly there are 13-year-olds who go di-

profanity, suicide, sexuality, sensuality, homosexuality, protests against anything significant, social or racial injustice, or the ambivalent feelings of cruelty and compassion inherent in young adults and all real people. Some things could be mentioned, but rarely, and introduced by implication rather than direct statement and only then as bad examples for thoughtful, decent young adults: pregnancy, early marriage, drugs, smoking, alcohol, school dropouts, divorce, alienation of young adults. Consequently, YA books were generally innocuous and pervaded by a saccharine didacticism. They taught good, adult-determined attitudes: life is rewarding for the diligent worker and difficult for the slacker; a virtuous life is not merely its own reward but leads to a richer life here on earth; serious dilemmas deserve serious attention by adults who would then tell young adults how to handle the problems but not to think for themselves till later; fast driving kills, fast marriages do not last, fast money is evil money, fast actions will surely be regretted, and fast dates are dangerous. Good boys and girls must accept adult and societal rules as good and just without question; young people would survive all those funny preoccupations and worries of adolescence and emerge as thoughtful, serious adults.

Despite all those unwritten rules, some writers transcended the taboos and qualifications even in the 1940s and 1950s. Truth did reign in a number of books by writers Florence Crannell Means, John Tunis, Maureen Daly, Esther Forbes, Henry Gregor Felsen, Paul Annixter, and Mary Stolz.

Reviewing young adult literature in 1960, Stanley B. Kegler and Stephen Dunning could write: "Books written for adolescents are improving in quality. Books of acceptable quality have largely replaced poorly written and rectly to adult books, and probably even some elevens and twelves who do too, but the fact remains as librarians know that the chasm between the library's Children's Room and its often forbidding (even to a lot of grownups) Adult Collection is a formidable one, not easily bridged. And the reason is simple. Teenagers have questions, about themselves, others, the world, sexuality, acne, death, dating, parents, God, and a lot more things. The answers to those big questions may be in adult books, but not in ways that are accessible and comprehensible to young people. While reading *Are You There God? It's Me Margaret*, girls can readily understand and identify with Mar-

garet's problem with her breasts (or the lack of them). Such reassurance is not likely to come from reading *Madame Bovary* or *The Scarlet Letter*. And the boy who is suffering from peer pressure will find insights in *The Chocolate War* and *The Outsiders* that are simply inaccessible in adult fiction.

That is why young adult fiction has become a viable and admirable body of literature in its own right and why librarians will continue to buy it, publishers will continue to publish it, and kids will continue to read it. ◆

---

mediocre books."[18] Three years later, they queried editors of young adult books and found taboos still operating if lessening: "There are few house rules regarding taboos—other than those dictated by 'good taste and common sense.'" One editor responded:

> ◇ I see very little change in taboos in the past ten years. There are franker discussions of the problems of sex in nonfiction.

Another wrote:

> ◇ I think the number of narrow-minded taboos—smoking, drinking, swearing, etc.—have diminished. A creative author works best in "responsible" freedom. If an author is serious and responsible, and if we are, and if we together work within the areas of honest good taste, it is difficult to see how we can offend.[19]

By the middle of the 1960s many, though hardly all, taboos had disappeared as unwritten restrictions. Most authors learned that in young adult literature, as in all literature, good books do not set out deliberately to break taboos although some bad books seem to try to do so. Good books take up life and real problems and follow characters and emotions as they wend their way through reality, touching on or breaking their taboos where necessary. A few authors seemed deliberately to court taboo subjects, notably Jeanette Eyerly with *Drop-Out* (1963), her dropout and early marriage novel; *A Girl Like Me* (1966), her pregnancy novel; *Radigan Cares* (1970), her political novel; and *Bonnie Jo, Go Home* (1972), her abortion novel. Indeed that led to legitimate criticism of some writers for writing a "drug" novel or a "suicide" novel or a "pregnancy" novel. What William Rose Benét wrote about children's books in 1941 remains a persistent problem for writers of young adult books today. "You don't write for children anymore. You consult Gallup polls as to what they like, and compile statistics as to how they react."[20] Similarly, some adolescent novels have fixed on an apparently popular theme, a social or emotional ill for example, and are not novels about people but about things. That may increase sales, but it diminishes their chances of survival. Good books focus on people with problems. Bad books focus on problems that seem incidentally to involve people.

As young adult literature moved into the middle and late 1960s, novels presented more complex plots with better developed human beings enmeshed in real problems with no easy ways out. More use of sophisticated literary techniques, particularly in point of view, led to more honest and realistic literature. Happy endings were not precluded, but they were not required. More humor was apparent, not mere sophomoric silliness. Fewer taboos intruded, but good books remained very much on the side of angels, their didacticism more subtle and sometimes entirely missed by unsophisticated readers. Themes were more mature and complex as almost every subject area opened up for inquiry: alienation, death, loneliness, society's values, mental health, and illness, both physical and social. Novels reflected the increasing sophistication of readers and the complexity of the time. Most important, reality entered the world of books, just as it had always been a part of young adults' lives.

◈ NINE OUTSTANDING WRITERS FOR YOUNG ADULTS

Of authors popular with young adults, nine stand out for their psychological perception and exceptional writing talent.

Florence Crannell Means

Means was popular in the 1930s, and her popularity held up well into the 1940s and later. *A Candle in the Mist* (1931), about a young orphan boy who traveled with a family to Minnesota in 1871, mixed history with suspense and revealed a talented writer, but later books revealed even more talent. *Tangled Waters* (1936), the story of a fifteen-year-old Navajo girl on her Arizona reservation, was her first successful effort at characterizing a minority. Her first black adolescent appears in *Shuttered Windows* (1938). Sixteen-year-old Harriet Freeman grows up in Minneapolis and then chooses to live for a year with her great-grandmother on an island off the South Carolina coast. Formulaic as the plot is and paternalistic as the tone is by today's standards, the book conveyed a sense of worth and dignity about black people rare in young adult or adult literature for that time. *The Moved Outers* (1945), a story of Japanese-Americans forced into relocation camps during World War II, may appear dated and mild by today's standards, but it still has power. Means was unable to avoid drawing the too-

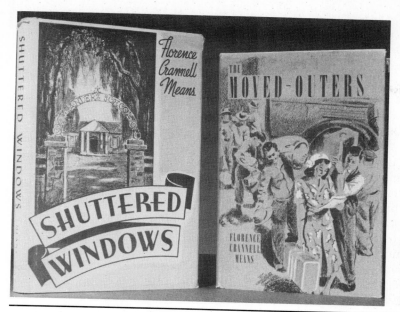

◆ Florence Crannell Means' books such as *Shuttered Windows* and *The Moved-Outers* hold mirrors up to prejudice.

From SHUTTERED WINDOWS by Florence Crannell Means. Copyright 1938; Copyright © renewed 1966 by Florence Crannell Means. From THE MOVED-OUTERS by Florence Crannell Means. Copyright 1945; Copyright © renewed 1972 by Florence Crannell Means. Reprinted by permission of Houghton Mifflin Company.

obvious moral about the danger of an increasingly totalitarian America, but her heart was in the right place. Her message was more powerful at the time than we now can realize, given the rabid anti-Japanese climate persisting even after World War II.

Later books, *Tolliver* (1963), *It Takes All Kinds* (1964), and *Our Cup Is Broken* (1969), are worth reading and establish Means as an important writer, one worth reading and even studying for the mirror she holds up to prejudice.

John Tunis

Newspaperman John Tunis published his first young adult novel, *Iron Duke*, in 1938. After four years of athletics at a small high school, Jim Wellington (the Iron Duke) wants desperately to enter the athletic big time at Harvard. His efforts are, at first, realistically unsuccessful, but the book is really a character study involving athletics, not just another sports story. What his first book promises, *All-American* (1942) delivers. The novel may be dated by changes that have taken place in football and in society, but it is a remarkable work for its time. Ronald Perry plays football for the Academy team and is partially responsible for injuring a local high school opponent in a crucial game. His Academy friends don't worry about the incident, but Perry cannot live with his guilt at the Academy. He leaves to go where he finds he is even less wanted, the local high school. There he learns some important lessons about racism and reality. The football team slowly accepts him, but after a successful season, an invitation to a postseason game in the

ALL-AMERICAN

threw him off his stride as Ronny came running up. The whole play was clear before him. Keith with one arm out, stumbling in the mud; Mike and Dave rushing in hard to fall on him so that if he wasn't knocked out he'd at least know he'd been hit. It made Ronald furious. He closed in, determined not to permit them to get away with it, to block off Dave anyway. He did block him off, and as he did so Mike accidentally slipped and hit him on the chin with the full force of his fist.

He saw stars. When he came to they were standing around in the mud. Doc Roberts was leaning over, wiping his face and holding smelling salts under his nose.

"I'm ok, Doc." He rose unsteadily, feeling dizzy, tried to step out a little, managed to trot a few steps. "I'm ok." But he was not ok, and he was mad clean through. This had to end. One thing or the other. They'd have to quit and play ball—or he would.

"C'm here, gang. This way. Look. This has gotta stop. It's gotta stop or I quit. If you guys don't lay off that bird, I'll leave the field, here, right now, and I'll tell Coach why. C'mon, gang, what say, gang, let's go. Let's forget that stuff. Let's get together, let's play against that crowd there, not against each other."

"You're dead right, Ronald!" Jim Stacey, adjusting his headgear, stepped in toward the center. "Listen, you guys, lay off that fella from now on and play ball. I've

190

◆ Published in 1942, John R. Tunis' *All-American* was a radical novel for young adults.
   Illustration by Hans Walleen from ALL-AMERICAN; Copyright 1942 by John R. Tunis; renewed 1970 by Lucy R. Tunis. Reprinted by permission of Harcourt Brace Jovanovich, Inc.

South requires that a black athlete stay home. Perry leads a quiet and tentative revolt, joined by a few of his teammates. To his surprise, he finds that things can change when people care. *All-American* seems somewhat paternalistic now, but for the time and the society then, it was a remarkable, even radical novel for young adults.

Yea! Wildcats (1944) eloquently mixes basketball with incipient totalitarianism in a small town. Its sequel, *A City for Lincoln* (1945), is also nominally a basketball story, but Tunis' liberal inclinations and didacticism led to a study of American politics, one of his least successful novels for young adults and one of his most intriguing for adults. Another successful account of basketball mania, *Go, Team, Go!* (1954), is a fine novel about public pressure on a coach who cares about more than merely winning. *Silence Over Dunkerque* (1962) contains nothing remotely athletic, but it is a good straightforward picture of the horrors and cruelty of war. Tunis' greatest book appeared in 1967. *His Enemy, His Friend* is a brilliant fusion of war and its aftermath and sports. A German soldier during World War II is forced to order the execution of some townspeople. Years later, the son of one of those executed opposes the soldier's team in a soccer match.

Tunis occasionally let his moral outrage and sensitivity carry him away, but at his best he wrote the finest sports stories since Ralph Henry Barbour. Tunis knew the power of athletic glory for good and for evil, and he knew what locker rooms smell like. His vision of the physical and moral aspects of athletics is impressive and endures with readers even after plots can no longer be remembered.

Maureen Daly

Daly published only one novel for young adults, but unlike almost all other young adult novels of its time, it endures. *Seventeenth Summer* (1942) is about shy, unnoticed Angie Morrow and her love for Jack Duluth in the summer before she is to set off for college. Very little happens in the novel, but very little happens during any one summer in most of our lives. Angie falls in love, she dates, and her relationship with Jack leads to misunderstandings and frustrations, mostly sexual. And at the close of the book, she and Jack part, sadly, as most first lovers do.

But it is not the plot so much as certain aspects of the story that make *Seventeenth Summer* different. In addition to portraying a young boy and girl sensitively and honestly, Daly shows a society in which drinking beer and even smoking will not inevitably lead to damnation, not even for young adults. At one point, Jack takes Angie to a roadhouse where they see a male pianist with painted fingernails. Angie innocently asks Jack to explain, and Jack stutters, looks embarrassed, and offers no satisfactory answer, but the reader recognizes what Angie does not.

Some critics, librarians, and English teachers are deeply, personally offended by Angie's innocence. They maintain that she could never have been *that* innocent, *that* naive, gullible, and unsuspecting. Innocence and sophistication are difficult to define at best. Some sophisticated young adults even today, more than forty years after Angie, wear a veneer of worldliness that, if penetrated even the tiniest bit, reveals a frightened innocent.

Possibly, say the accusers, but even so, Angie certainly wasn't typical of her time, not even of that 1942 world where good was good and bad was bad and never the twain could meet. Other girls of the time, so the reasoning goes, weren't all that innocent. They would have been aware of the physical implications (and consequences) of love, even first love.

But Daly never claimed Angie was typical—only the critics claim that. Angie was an individual, not a representative of seventeen-year-old girls in 1942. Writers, at least serious writers, create individuals out of the masses, not to represent the masses. And Angie is an individual.

Esther Forbes

Primarily a historian, in fact winner of the Pulitzer Prize for history in 1942 for *Paul Revere and the World He Lived In*, Forbes wrote one still-popular novel for young adults. *Johnny Tremain* (1943) sets fourteen-year-old Johnny in pre-Revolutionary War times. A cocky apprentice to a silversmith and clearly a young genius in the making, Johnny cripples his hand. Partly because of that and partly because of the fervor of the time, he becomes involved with patriots Sam Adams, John Hancock, and Paul Revere. The spirit of time is well captured by historian Forbes, but readers who care little about history can still find an engrossing and exciting tale about Johnny, his injury, his friends, and war.

Forbes did not write again for young adults, but the number of readers who continue to enjoy *Johnny Tremain* is wide indeed.

Henry Gregor Felsen

Felsen began writing for young adults with several World War II books, *Navy Diver* (1942), *Submarine Sailor* (1943), *He's in the Coast Guard Now* (1943), and *Pilots All* (1944). His first three major books concern short, fat Bertie in *Bertie Comes Through* (1947), *Bertie Takes Care* (1948), and *Bertie Makes a Break* (1949). Probably read by young adults because Bertie's troubles have hilarious results, the books are still a fascinating study of adolescent failure.

After a singularly dull stab at a vocational novel, *Davey Logan, Intern* (1950), Felsen wrote *Two and the Town* (1952) about a young couple forced to marry because the girl is pregnant. Old-hat today but fifteen years ahead of its time then, the book could safely have been placed in the hands of any young adult by any parent as a sure warning of the consequences of "doing it," for Felsen preached endlessly and was mercilessly moral to the boy and girl. With all that, *Two and the Town* broke ground in young adult literature by treating pregnancy honestly and seriously. What the reactions of young adults or parents might have been is largely conjectural, for many librarians skirted the issue of censorship by not buying the book. Contemporary reviewers recognized that the book might cause trouble. One began:

> ◇ Many libraries will not buy this, and others will treat it with kid gloves, but we need it. Factual pamphlets and books treating sex miss the emotions of error and repair that this book, written for and about youth, presents.[21]

Felsen's fame came with publication of *Hot Rod* (1950), and two other similar books, *Street Rod* (1953) and *Crash Club* (1958). *Hot Rod* is still in print and still widely read, though its didacticism is strong, particularly in the scene near the end in which accident victims are buried. Despite this, the story of Bud Crayne, his fondness for speeding, and his comeuppance and eventual salvation at the hands of Patrolman Ted O'Day had wide appeal. Few writers so intently didactic have been so widely read. Presumably, young adults learned long ago how to endure the moral lessons of their elders and still survive.

Paul Annixter

Under the Annixter pen name, Howard A. Sturtzel wrote many novels, often with his wife Jane Sturtzel, but his most exceptional book is *Swiftwater* (1950), a remarkable tale of excitement, symbolism, and ecology mixed with, alas, some stereotyped characters. Cam Calloway feels a kinship with the wild geese near his Maine farm, and his feelings and his love are emulated by his son Bucky. Something of a footloose wanderer, Cam dreams more than he acts. Bucky is both dreamer and actor, and his drive to find roots for himself and his mother and to establish a wild game preserve for his beloved geese becomes the heart of the novel. Much has been made of the early scenes between Bucky and the wolverine, with the animal symbolizing evil, perhaps too much so. However, individual chapters of the novel are excellent short stories in their own right, and the whole novel is a most convincing, honest, and well-written novel for young adults. Its wide readership is deserved whether it is enjoyed as an adventure story, an initiation story, or as an early ecological manifesto.

Jack Bennett

South African journalist Bennett wrote three novels for young adults, two of them among the best of the time. In *Jamie* (1963), set on a large South African farm, Jamie wants to be like his father. The opportunity to become a man comes early when Jamie's father is killed by a maddened water buffalo. Jamie vows to kill the animal, and that vow becomes almost a mania.

Mister Fisherman (1965) may remind readers of Theodore Taylor's *The Cay*, but Bennett's story of a young white boy helped by an old black fisherman to survive at sea is a better book.

Bennett's third novel, *The Hawk Alone* (1965), is an excellent study of white hunter Gord Vance. Vance had done everything and had shot everything. When he discovers he has outlived his time, that he is no longer a man, only a myth and a legend, Vance realizes that his hunting days are over. He knows he serves no valuable function, not even for himself, and he decides that suicide is the answer. Realistic, insightful, and extraordinarily well written, *The Hawk Alone* deserves far more readers than it ever received.

James Summers

Popular as Summers' books were at the time they were written, Summers is almost a forgotten writer. Capable of writing charming fluff such as *Girl Trouble* (1953), *Trouble on the Run* (1956), and *Off the Beam* (1956), he could also write sensitive novels. *Operation ABC* (1955) is almost a case study of a football hero, apparently successful in everything, who literally cannot read and fears college because he would be unmasked as a fraud. *The Wonderful Time* (1957) shows a nineteen-year-old returning to high school after a stretch in the Army, trying desperately to fit into a world that is no longer his. *The Shelter Trap* (1962) is about some gifted students who decide to live for a short time in a fallout shelter. *The Iron Doors Between* (1968) features Vic Shan recently released from a California State Reformatory with a future as uncertain as his past. *You Can't Make It by Bus* (1969) is about an intelligent Chicano high school student in an American society that will not accept him as a first-class citizen.

Summers has a wonderful ability to capture American youth, but his chief asset as a writer is also his major liability: his incredible ear for young adult jargon. Unhappily, by the time any of his books is published, the jargon is not merely dated but dead.

His two best books are *Ring Around Her Finger* (1957), a study of a young marriage told from the boy's point of view, and *The Limit of Love* (1959), a remarkable delineation of a sexual love affair. Ronnie Jordan knows she has missed two periods, and boyfriend Lee Hansen worries and blames Ronnie for ruining his life. In the weeks that follow, the mess leaves them emotionally bankrupt and no longer in love, but Lee remains a boy while Ronnie emerges as a real woman ready to face problems and her own responsibilities. *The Limit of Love* is now dated, but it was a book far ahead of its time. Many schools would not purchase it because of its picture of two nice kids sexually involved by an author who does not blame either one.

Mary Stolz

Stolz is, simply put, our most consistently artistic writer for young adults. Richard S. Alm spoke for teachers and librarians when he wrote that Stolz is "versatile and most skilled . . . [and] writes not for the masses who worship Sue Barton but for the rarer adolescent."[22] She joined the literary scene with her first novel, *To Tell Your Love* (1950), an introspective and moving portrait of a young girl waiting vainly all summer for a phone call from the boy she loves.

Later books fulfill the promise of her first novel. *The Sea Gulls Woke Me* (1951) deals with a protected girl and a domineering mother; *In a Mirror* (1953), and its sequel *The Day and the Way We Met* (1956), tells of girls in a lower-middle class environment; and *Rosemary* (1955) is about a college town and a local girl who cannot go to college.

Her two finest works are *Pray Love, Remember* (1954), a remarkable story of popular, lovely, and cold Dody Jenks who does not like her family or herself, and *A Love, or a Season* (1964) in which love between Harry and Nan threatens to get out of hand and become too passionate before they can handle it or themselves. Readers today may find *A Love, or a Season* a bit naive, but some girls presumably still have serious doubts about capriciously hopping into bed, no matter how intense the love may seem.

◈ BOOKS POPULAR WITH YOUNG ADULTS

Reading of young adults fell loosely into six areas, some containing many popular titles, some only a few.

Career Books March On

Fiction allowing, even encouraging, young adults to examine careers was hardly new in the 1940s. Francis Rolt-Wheeler wrote twenty volumes of career fiction beginning with *The Boy with the U.S. Survey* in 1909 and ending with *The Boy with the U.S. Aviators* in 1929.

Emma Bugbee was not the first to write career novels, but her five books about young newspaper reporter Peggy Foster begin the deluge in the 1930s

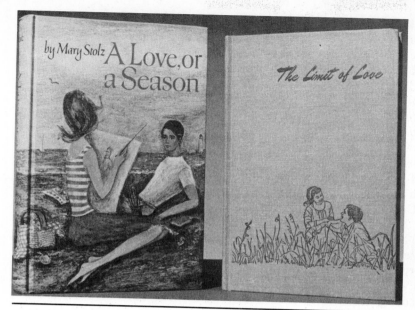

◆ Mary Stolz' *A Love, or a Season* and James Summers' *The Limit of Love* were books far ahead of their time.

From A LOVE, OR A SEASON by Mary Stolz. Copyright © 1954, 1964 by Mary Stolz. Reprinted by permission of Harper & Row, Publishers. From THE LIMIT OF LOVE by James L. Summers. Copyright © 1959 by James L. Summers. Reprinted by permission of The Westminster Press.

which carried on until the 1950s. Bugbee was a reporter for 55 years, first with the *New York Tribune* (later the *New York Herald-Tribune*), and *Peggy Covers the News* (1936) and its four sequels realistically conveyed the ambivalent excitement and boredom of getting and writing the news. Events do seem telescoped and thrills and success come too easily to Peggy—problems that increased as career novels multiplied—but the picture of a young woman breaking into a male-dominated profession served a purpose for its time.

Almost every job was covered by vocational books sugar-coated with fiction—librarianship by Lucile Fargo's *Marian Martha* (1936) and Mary Provines' *Bright Heritage* (1939), fashion designing by Adele de Leeuw's *Gay Design* (1942), and Christie Harris' *You Have to Draw the Line Somewhere* (1964), secretarial work by Blanche Gibbs and Georgiana Adams' *Shirley Clayton, Secretary* (1941) and Harriet Carr's *Confidential Secretary* (1958), television work by Dorothy McFadden's *Lynn Decker: TV Apprentice* (1953) and Ruth Milne's *TV Girl Friday* (1957), and on and on. Hardly an occupation escaped the eagle eyes of publishers and writers eager to ensure that every young adult, of whatever vocational persuasion, should have at least one novel about his or her field. Presumably no author penned any book-length fiction about garbage collectors or hangmen, but had any youngster expressed an interest in those fields, some author prompted by a publisher would have churned out *Robert Gimstock: Sanitation Expert* or *Hanging Them High with Harold*.

Without question, books about nursing led popularity polls with girls, and Helen Dore Boylston was the most popular of the writers. Her Sue Barton series ran to seven volumes from *Sue Barton, Student Nurse* (1936) to *Sue Barton, Staff Nurse* (1952) and is still readable, albeit dated. Curiously, Sue Barton seems more popular today in Great Britain. Boylston's chief rival, in a field where authors' names generally meant little and changed as publishers sought another vocational interest, was Helen Wells, whose Cherry Ames nursing series ran to twenty volumes and whose Vicki Barr flight stewardess series ran to thirteen books.

Lucille G. Rosenheim's *Kathie, The New Teacher* (1949), mediocre as it is, reveals both the strengths and weaknesses of vocational novels. Kathie Kerber, new seventh-grade teacher at Hillcrest, meets in one year all the problems and prejudices that a teacher with bad luck would perhaps meet in the first ten years of teaching. She encounters romance, intolerant students, a sneak thief, the town skinflint, sentimental parents, and much more. Everything comes too fast and easily and impossible problems are rapidly disposed of because Kathie cares and has a good heart. Still, the book may have given some readers an idea of what teaching is all about, although a bit melodramatically.

Whatever freshness the vocational novel may once have had, by the late 1940s it was a formula and little more. Four or five characters were certain to appear: a decent and attractive, if sometimes shy, hero/heroine just graduating from high school or college and needing a job desperately; one or two friends of different temperaments—two men if the book was directed at girls since romance was doomed to raise its head; a villain or at the very least a crotchety older person who puts temporary obstacles in the professional path of the protagonist; and an older and wiser person who helps the protagonist to advance. Early in the book the insecure hero/heroine suffers a mixture of major and minor setbacks, but, undaunted, the protagonist wins the final battle and a place in her or his profession. The novel passes rapidly and lightly over the job's daily grind, focusing instead on the high points, the excitement and events that make any job potentially, if rarely, dramatic. Many vocational books were widely read for that drama, although it certainly distorted the accuracy of information provided.

Adventure and Suspense

There was no diminution of interest in adventure or suspense though the interest was largely fulfilled by various kinds of war books until the late 1940s.

Young adult war literature at first tended to be nonfiction such as Carl Mann's *He's in the Signal Corps Now* (1943) or Betty Peckham's *Women in Aviation* (1945), or it consisted of military-vocational novels such as Martha Johnson's *Ann Bartlett, Navy Nurse* (1941) or Elizabeth Lansing's *Nancy Naylor, Flight Nurse* (1944).

True stories about battles and survivors were ultimately more popular. Richard Tregaskis was widely popular for the blood, death, and heroism of *Guadalcanal Diary* (1943), but by far the most respected and beloved of war reporters was Ernie Pyle whose *Here Is Your War* (1943), *Brave Men* (1944), and the posthumous *Last Chapter* (1946) won admirers for his journalistic skills and personal courage. Two accounts of heroism are still read today, not as museum pieces, but as exciting and effectively told accounts of men caught in war who find depths of courage and personal values within themselves that they might not otherwise have believed. They are Robert Trumbull's *The Raft* (1942) about three Navy fliers forced down in the Pacific, and Quentin Reynolds' *70,000 to One* (1946) about an American airman on a small Pacific island with 70,000 Japanese troops.

Of the many novels published about World War II, something more than mere bravado and jingoism could be found in John Hersey's *A Bell for Adano* (1944), John Horne Burns' sadly neglected but masterful *The Gallery* (1947), Norman Mailer's *The Naked and the Dead* (1948), and James Jones' *From Here to Eternity* (1951), though his *The Pistol* (1959) and *The Thin Red Line* (1962) are better novels. Herman Wouk's *The Caine Mutiny* (1951) proved more popular though (or perhaps because) it was little more than a proestablishment paean to blind conformity.

Perhaps as a reaction to the realities of war, the most popular series of books for both adults and young adults during the 1950s and 1960s centered about the fascinating James Bond, Agent 007. In *From Russia with Love* (1951), *Casino Royale* (1954), *Dr. No* (1959), *Goldfinger* (1959), *Thunderball* (1961), *You Only Live Twice* (1964), and *The Man with the Golden Gun* (1965), Ian Fleming caught the mood of the time, eager for escapist excitement tinged with what appeared to be realities. Cardboard sexist figure or not, Bond captured readers' imaginations and proved even more popular in film form.

Three historical novels full of adventure and growing up appealed to some young adults. Elizabeth Janet Gray's *Adam of the Road* (1942) revealed the color and music of the Middle Ages, as young Adam Quartermain became a minstrel. Marchette Chute's *The Innocent Wayfaring* (1943) covered only four days in June 1370 as Anne runs away from her convent school to join a band of strolling players. Chute's *The Wonderful Winter* (1954) was equally successful in conveying a sense of time. Young Sir Robert Wakefield, treated like a child at home, runs off to London to become an actor in Shakespeare's company.

Love, Romance, Passion, and Sex

Interest in tender feelings persisted, though the moments grew less tender and more tempestuous early in this period.

Writers for young adults contributed several fine romances. Margaret E. Bell wrote of an earlier, more innocent, time in Alaska in *Love Is Forever* (1954) about a young and often troubled marriage. Vivian Breck, pen name of Vivian Breckenfield, wrote a fine adventure story in *High Trail* (1948) and a superior study of young marriage in *Maggie* (1954). One of the most popular books, and one still read and most readable, is Benedict and Nancy Freedman's *Mrs. Mike* (1947), the story of Mike Flannigan and Kate O'Fallen who marry and move to the dangers of the northern Canadian wilderness. Mary Medearis' *Big Doc's Girl* (1942) is an authentic picture of love and a young girl forced by her father's death to change her life.

Perhaps the ideal romance of the time was *Green Dolphin Street* (1944) by Elizabeth Goudge, a writer who had long produced sensitive studies of small-town life in England but nothing approaching a best seller in America. *Green Dolphin Street* had everything working for it—a young and handsome man in love with one of a pair of sisters. He leaves and writes home his wishes, but the wrong sister accepts. The true love, apparently thwarted by his unfaithfulness, becomes a nun. Passion, love, and adventure are all handled well by a first-rate writer.

Kathleen Winsor was also one of a kind, though what one and what kind was widely debated. When her *Forever Amber* (1944) appeared, parents worried, censors paled, and young adults smiled. Winsor's book was hardly the first to be banned in Boston, but her publisher was adept at turning what appeared to be a defeat into a major victory, gloriously announcing in papers far and wide that the contents were indeed too shocking for Bostonians but not too strong for other cities. City fathers in many towns urged that it be banned, but most readers were only curious, not salacious, and *Forever Amber* sold more than a million and a half copies in three years. Generally, young adults ignored the fuss and read the book.

The uproar that greeted Amber and her affairs was much the same as the one that awaited Grace Metalious and *Peyton Place* (1956). Again parents and community leaders did not keep young people from reading the book avidly for all its unraveling of family scandals and multitudinous affairs in a small New England town. Nine million copies sold the first year, and a sequel, *Return to Peyton Place* (1959), a movie, and a television series ensured that virtually every young adult in the United States knew the book. A few brave English teachers acknowledged its existence, but many principals feared morality would deteriorate in their schools should even one copy of *Peyton Place* be found. The world survived.

Teachers were less sure morality could survive the onslaught that followed only a few years later in the form of Irving Wallace and books like *The Chapman Report* (1960), which capitalized on the Kinsey report, *The Prize* (1962), and *The Man* (1964). But worse was yet to come, though some young adults would have said better, with the appearance of Harold Robbins, pen name of Harold Rubins, and *The Carpetbaggers* (1961), and *The Adventurers* (1966), two potboilers and sexual thrillers Robbins wrote when his best book, *A Stone for Danny Fisher* (1952), went almost unnoticed.

Society's Problems

Young adults, especially in the last year or two of high school, have often been receptive to books about human dilemmas stemming from the ways society functions or malfunctions. Society changed rapidly and drastically from 1940 through 1966, and malfunctions seemed almost the norm and the human consequences deeply disturbing.

Of increasing concern to many young adults was their growing awareness that the democracy announced in our Constitution was more preached than practiced. As the censorship applied to John Steinbeck's *The Grapes of Wrath* (1939) and *Of Mice and Men* (1937) lessened—though it never entirely disappeared—young readers read of the plight of migrant workers and learned that all was not well with our country.

Many were deeply bothered by Alan Paton's stories of racial struggles in South Africa, *Cry the Beloved Country* (1948), and Paton's most mature study of love in the midst of injustice, *Too Late the Phalarope* (1953). Still more were touched by the sentiment and passion of Harper Lee's *To Kill a Mockingbird* (1960). Viewed as dated and patronizing by some critics today, *Mockingbird* was for many young adults the first book they had read about racial problems in the South, a book that gave them a hero in the gentle but strong Atticus Finch and some understanding of the American dream gone sour. For some, Lee's novel served as a sympathetic introduction to black people.

Literature about blacks was not difficult to find before World War II, but literature by blacks was another matter. After 1945, black literature became easier to find. Perhaps the war itself, which spotlighted Hitler's fervent belief in racism, contributed to the growing awareness of the state of blacks and the rise of black writing. Perhaps the GI Bill of Rights after the war helped as some blacks were allowed education hitherto denied them for economic reasons. Whatever the exact causes, blacks increasingly and rightfully became literary and moral forces to be reckoned with and young adults often took notice.

Richard Wright and his books served as bitter prototypes for much black literature. *Native Son* (1940) shocked some blacks and many whites with the stored-up anger of Bigger Thomas, and *Black Boy* (1945) was both Wright's autobiography and his denouncement of America.

The greatest black novel, and one of the greatest novels of any kind of the last fifty years, is *Invisible Man* (1952) by Ralph Ellison. Existential in tone, *Invisible Man* is at different times bawdy (the incest scenes remind readers of Faulkner without being derivative), moving, frightening, but always stunning and breathtaking. Ellison begins by describing the black as the figuratively invisible man:

> ◇ I am an invisible man. No, I am not a spook like those who haunted Edgar Allan Poe; nor am I one of your Hollywood-movie ectoplasms. I am a man of substance, of flesh and bone, fiber and liquids—and I might even be said to possess a mind. I am invisible, understand, simply because people refuse to see me. Like the bodiless heads you see sometimes in circus sideshows, it is as though I have been surrounded by mirrors of hard, distorting glass. When they approach me they see only my surroundings, themselves, or figments of their imagination—indeed, everything and anything except me.

Invisible Man remains Ellison's only novel. His collection of essays, *Shadow and Act* (1964), is significant for any young adults who care about good prose or about understanding Ellison's ideas.

Several white writers were popular with young adults for their statements about racial dilemmas. Lillian Smith was attacked for her novel *Strange Fruit* (1944), the story of a marriage of a black and a white. A court decision banning the book temporarily made a few reactionaries happy, but the book's national reception and sales were good enough to distress racists.

John Howard Griffin suffered some censorship for his novel *The Devil Rides Outside* (1952) though less than he experienced with his popular and sometimes reviled *Black Like Me* (1961), his account of temporarily becoming black, traveling through much of the South, and suffering indignities common to blacks. Griffin's books may have become dated, though not so much as some think, but accusations of some blacks that *Black Like Me* was paternalistic seem ill-advised and revisionist. David Westheimer developed a sweet-sour romance between a pregnant white girl and a young black lawyer in trouble with the law in *My Sweet Charlie* (1965).

Three black nonfiction writers remain popular. Claude Brown painted a stark picture of black ghetto life in *Manchild in the Promised Land* (1965), and, despite anguished cries from many parents about the "filth" in the book, Brown's book appears to have a permanent place in the literature of oppression and freedom. Malcolm X and Alex Haley, the latter better known for *Roots*, painted a no more attractive picture in *The Autobiography of Malcolm X* (1965). The most enduring work may prove to be Eldridge Cleaver's *Soul on Ice* (1968), an impassioned plea by a black man in prison, in a prison of concrete and a prison of the mind, who wrote to save himself.

Writings about blacks aimed at young adults were not long in coming. They were, at first, simplistic books either encouraging young blacks to cooperate with whites since whites had the power or portraying kind whites taking young blacks into tow and getting them started on the right path. Typical were novels by Jesse Jackson: *Call Me Charley* (1945), *Anchor Man* (1947), *Charley Starts from Scratch* (1958), and *Tessie* (1968). Catherine Marshall's *Julie's Heritage* (1957) differentiated so little between whites and blacks that it was hard for readers to recognize Julie as a black with somewhat different problems.

Lorenz Graham brought realistic black characters to young adult literature. If *South Town* (1958) with its characters seeking a better life in the North seems dated today, *North Town* (1965) is still believable as it moves the Williams family and son David, the major character, into conflict with both whites and blacks. *Whose Town?* (1969) brings David more problems as he sees his best friend shot by a white man. Graham's books probed for answers but did not provide any easy ones.

Nat Hentoff has written good topical books that quickly become dated, for example his story of Vietnam and draft resistance, *I'm Really Dragged but Nothing Gets Me Down* (1968), and his somewhat lesser study of radical teachers and high school revolutions, *In the Country of Ourselves* (1971). His first novel for young adults was a superb story of a white boy trying to break into the black world of jazz, *Jazz Country* (1965). It is an unusual topic, and perhaps neither blacks nor whites are comfortable with the themes or the characters, which is sad because Hentoff is a remarkable, compassionate, and honest writer. *Jazz Country* is a major work.

Of the nonfiction writings for young adults about blacks, Shirley Graham has provided several good biographies: *There Was Once a Slave: The Heroic Story of Frederick Douglass* (1947), probably her best book; *Your Most Humble Servant: The Story of Benjamin Banneker* (1949), her most intriguingly different story; *The Story of Phillis Wheatley: Poetess of the Ameri-*

can Revolution (1949); and *Booker T. Washington: Educator of Hand, Head, and Heart* (1955). Elizabeth Yates won applause for *Amos Fortune, Free Man* (1950) and the Newbery Prize a year later, but her account of a slave who gained freedom in 1801 and fought the rest of his life for freedom for other blacks has been attacked by some black groups as paternalistic, a word much overused by black critics who assume that any white writer is inherently incapable of writing about blacks.

Personal Problems and Initiation Novels

Intrigued and concerned as many young adults were about social issues and dilemmas, something far more immediate constantly pressed in upon them—their own personal need to survive in an often unfriendly world. As one youngster said, "What do they mean, 'What am I going to do when I grow up?' First I have to survive and that's a problem with school and parents and my girl friend."

Survival was hardly the theme of many popular writers for girls. The watchword for Janet Lambert was acceptance. She preached the·doctrine of happiness, sentimentalism, and acceptance in *Star-Spangled Summer* (1941), in which the lonely daughter of a millionaire spends a summer on an army post finding herself and ennobling those around her, much as Pollyanna did years before.

After Lambert there was a deluge of girls' books detailing their emotional traumas but almost entirely ignoring their physical concerns. Betty Cavanna wrote many romances of youth engaged in dating and early love, but they contained nothing remotely resembling passion. Her characters were stereotypes and her plots repetitious, but *Going on Sixteen* (1946) remained popular for years. *Paintbox Summer* (1949) about an art colony and two loves for one girl was her best book, melodramatic and a bit flossy but still effective at times. Far worse was Rosamund Du Jardin whose books have interchangeable titles, incredibly undramatic or unbelievable plots, and wooden dialogue. Nevertheless, books such as *Practically Seventeen* (1949), *Wait for Marcy* (1950), and *Double Feature* (1953) were avidly read. Typical of Du Jardin's books is *Senior Prom* (1957), which finds Marcy struggling to decide whether to date noble but poor Rick or flashy but rich Bruce for that most important activity, the senior dance. Marcy is also worried about befriending an old man others have warned her against. She proves true to her trust and her essential goodness by deciding to date Rick (Bruce dates another in desperation and has a bad car accident, presumably in retribution) and to befriend the old man (who soon dies, willing her $15,000).

Superior to the earlier authors, Anne Emery certainly preached acceptance of the status quo, especially acceptance of parental rules, but she offered better books that proved popular with young adult women. With an exception here or there, her books eschew real controversy yet they appear to focus on real social concerns: *Going Steady* (1950), *Sorority Girl* (1952), and her best book *Married on Wednesday* (1957).

At the same time conventional girls' books appeared, Mina Lewiton dealt with far more suspect, even controversial, topics. *The Divided Heart* (1947) was an early study of the effect of divorce on a young woman, and *A Cup of Courage* (1948) was an honest and groundbreaking account of alcoholism and its destruction of a family. Later, Zoa Sherburne proved more enduring with her portrait of alcohol's effect in *Jennifer* (1959), though her best and most likely to last book is *Too Bad About the Haines Girl* (1967), a superb novel about pregnancy, honest and straightforward without being unduly preachy.

But something far more significant and enduring appeared during the same years that the personal problem novel seemed supreme. The *Bildungsroman*, a novel about the initiation, maturation, and education of a young adult, grew in appeal. The number of such books, most of them originally published for adults but soon read by young adults, appearing from 1940 onward was prodigious.

One of the first, now nearly forgotten, was Dan Wickenden's *Walk Like a Mortal* (1940). Seventeen-year-old Gabe McKenzie learns that he will never achieve his longed-for excellence in athletics, and he accepts his excellence in journalism as a substitute. His neurotic mother and dull father are verging on separation and Gabe must accept the fact of his own conflicting loyalties. Girls found an equally appealing and honest book in Betty Smith's *A Tree Grows in Brooklyn* (1943).

But no book won the young adult favor or the adult opposition that J. D. Salinger's *The Catcher in the Rye* (1951) did. Still the most widely censored book in American schools, and still hated by people who assume that a disliked word (*that* word) corrupts an entire book, *Catcher* has been avidly read ever since it became a selection of the Book-of-the-Month Club. Holden Caulfield may indeed be what so many have accused him of being, vulgar and cynical and capable of seeing only the phonies around him, but he is also loyal and loving to those he sees as good or innocent. His struggle to preserve innocence leads him to the brink of a mental breakdown. *Catcher* is many things, literary, profane, sensitive, cynical. For many young adults it is the most honest and human story they know about someone they recognize—even in themselves—a young man caught between childhood and maturity and unsure which way to go. Whether *Catcher* is a masterpiece like James Joyce's *Portrait of the Artist as a Young Man* depends on subjective judgment, but there is no question that Salinger's book captured—and continues to capture—the hearts and minds of countless young adults as no other book has.

Most teachers and librarians would have predicted just as long a life for John Knowles' *A Separate Peace* (1961) and William Golding's *Lord of the Flies* (1955), but fame and longevity are sometime things, and despite many articles in *English Journal* about the literary and pedagogical worth of both books, they seem to be in a state of decline. Knowles' account of Gene Forrester and his close friend raised fascinating questions about loyalty, friendship, and responsibility. Golding's book, pessimistic as it is, had great appeal for young adults with its story of young English boys stranded on a desert island and learning that civilization can too easily degenerate into barbarism. Though some facets of the book appear at first to resemble clichés out of some badly written imitation of *Treasure Island*, the bloodlust and horrifying realities soon involve readers. It may be a gloomy picture but it is an honest and possible vision, disturbingly so.

Sports and Cars

Sports stories continued to be popular with some young adults, though aside from John Tunis no writer of any great talent appeared between 1940 and 1966.

Nonfiction was not yet as popular as it would later become, but one of the best books of the time was the autobiography of Boston Red Sox outfielder Jim Piersall, *Fear Strikes Out* (1955), telling about his life as an athlete and his mental breakdown. Almost equally worthwhile was Roy Campanella's *It's Good to Be Alive* (1959) dealing with his life as a catcher and his adjustment to a tragic and almost fatal car accident.

Occasionally, a good sports book appeared, but, oddly enough, the few quality books were rarely about popular sports like football, baseball, or basketball. Bob Allison's *The Kid Who Batted 1.000* (1951) is about baseball, but more than that, it is a genuinely amusing story of a young man with only one athletic talent, the ability to foul off pitch after pitch. Philip Harkins' *Knockout* (1950) and Frank O'Rourke's *The Last Round* (1956) were fine novels about boxing, though neither found a large number of fans.

Two authors were the best of the crop. John F. Carson's basketball novels convey a love of the game and an understanding of the power of athletics for good or evil. They are *Floorburns* (1957), *The Coach Nobody Liked* (1960), and *Hotshot* (1961). C. H. Frick, pen name of Constance Frick Irwin, used clever plot twists to make her sports novels different. *Five Against the Odds* (1955) features a basketball player stricken with polio, *Patch* (1957) is about a runner who loves running for its own sake, not because it may lead to winning anything, and *The Comeback Guy* (1961) focuses on a too-popular, too-successful young man who gets his comeuppance and works his way back to self-respect through sports.

More popular at the time than sports stories were car books, especially hot rod stories. Henry Gregor Felsen led all the rest with *Hot Rod* (1949), but also popular were Philip Harkins' *Road Race* (1953) and William Gault's *Thunder Road* (1952) and *Road Race Rookie* (1962).

◇ THE RISE OF CRITICISM OF YOUNG ADULT LITERATURE

Today, we take criticism of young adult literature for granted in journals such as the *ALAN Review*, *Top of the News*, *School Library Journal*, *English Journal*, *Wilson Library Bulletin*, *Horn Book Magazine*, *Children's Literature in Education*, *The Lion and the Unicorn*, and *Interracial Books for Children Bulletin*, but it developed slowly. In the 1940s, journals provided little information and less criticism of young adult literature, excepting book lists, book reviews, and occasional references to a few authors or titles in articles on reading interests or raising young peoples' literary tastes. A teacher and author as gifted as Dwight L. Burton could devote considerable

THE PEOPLE BEHIND THE BOOKS

W. GEIGER ELLIS,
Professor and Editor

Professor, University of Georgia
Former Editor of the ALAN Review

During the past couple of decades, YA literature has grown, sometimes painfully, as is the case with adolescents themselves. Two manifestations of this growth are significant. First, the range of subjects has expanded to the same breadth found in literature for adults. The period of "shocking realism" has passed, and the challenge to authors now is to create artistic works worthy of their audience.

Improved literary quality of *some* YA books is the second part of this growth. In the future I believe there will be an increasing number of books of quality. Because the YA market is lucrative, authors and publishers will continue to be drawn to this market. Books of quality are sure to be part of the increased volume. But unfortunately, the new-found freedom which makes increased quality possible also brings a corresponding similarity in books absolutely lacking in quality. The current publishers' goldmine is the teen romance. Inspired by great financial success at the adult level, publishers have turned to a more youthful audience which is ever ready to be titillated by the trite. This kind of fantasy literature—for that is what it is—will always have some appeal, whether we like it or not. It is now experiencing a periodic revival, to be replaced eventually by some other insipid offering.

In keeping with my belief that it is more productive to praise the positive than to damn the negative, I would rather be inspired by the belief that in future years we can expect even more outstanding literature for young people. ◆

space in 1947 to the worth of Daly's *Seventeenth Summer* or Wickenden's *Walk Like a Mortal*, but Burton's perceptive comments were more appreciative than critical.[23] Given the times and the attitude of many teachers and librarians, appreciation or even recognition may have been more important than criticism.

Four years later, Burton wrote the first criticism of young adult novels, again concerned with Daly and Wickenden, but this time injecting criticism along with appreciation and commenting on more titles, among them Paul Annixter's *Swiftwater*, Betty Cavanna's *Going on Sixteen*, and Madeleine L'Engle's *The Small Rain*.[24] Concluding his article, Burton identified the qualities of the good young adult novel and prophesied its potential and future:

> ◇ The good novel for the adolescent reader has attributes no different from any good novel. It must be technically masterful, and it must present a significant synthesis of human experience. Because of the nature of adolescence itself, the good novel for the adolescent should be full in true invention and imagination. It must free itself of Pollyannaism or the Tarkington-Henry Aldrich-Corliss Archer tradition and maintain a clear vision of the adolescent as a person of complexity, individuality, and dignity. The novel for the adolescent presents a ready field for the mature artist.[25]

In 1955 Richard S. Alm provided even greater critical coverage of the young adult novel.[26] He agreed with critics that many writers presented "a sugar-puff story of what adolescents should do and should believe rather than what adolescents may or will do and believe," but he argued that if writers like Janet Lambert and Helen Boylston wrote airy exercises in superficialism, other writers provided young adults with books of greater psychological accuracy and literary merit. Not only did Alm cite specific authors and titles he found good, for example, Maureen Daly's *Seventeenth Summer*, Henry Gregor Felsen's *Two and the Town*, Mildred Walker's *Winter Wheat*, Mary Stolz's *To Tell Your Love*, and Esther Forbes' *Johnny Tremain*, he painted their strengths and weaknesses in clear strokes and concluded by offering teachers some questions that might be useful in analyzing the merit of young adult novels.

A year later, Emma L. Patterson began her fine study of the origin of young adult novels, "The junior novel has become an established institution."[27] Her command of history, her knowledge of trends in young adult novels, her awareness of shortcomings and virtues of the novels, and her understanding of the place of young adult novels in schools and libraries made her article essential reading for librarians and teachers.

But, despite the leadership of Burton, Alm, and Patterson, helpful criticism of young adult literature was slow in coming. But biting criticism of the worst of young adult novels was soon forthcoming. Only a few months after Patterson's article, Frank G. Jennings' "Literature for Adolescents— Pap or Protein?"[28] appeared. The title was unambiguous, but if any reader had doubts about where Jennings stood, the doubt was removed with the first sentence, "The stuff of adolescent literature, for the most part, is mealy-mouthed, gutless, and pointless." The remainder of the article added little to that point, and if Jennings did overstate his case, Burton, Alm, Patterson, and other sensible supporters would have agreed that much young adult literature, like much adult literature, was second-rate or worse. Jennings' article was not the first broadside attack, and it certainly would not be the last.[29]

Much of the literature written for young adults from 1940 through 1966 goes largely and legitimately ignored today. Books by once popular writers like Janet Lambert, Jesse Jackson, or Margaret Bell gather dust.

But some writers for young adults between 1940 and 1966 are still read, perhaps by an audience younger than originally intended, but often by readers as old as their first ones. Mary Stolz is still read, but then so are Maureen Daly and Esther Forbes.

More important than mere longevity is the effect these authors had on books appearing after 1966. Readers before then could not have anticipated S. E. Hinton's *The Outsiders* or Paul Zindel's *The Pigman*, which were to appear in only a year or two, much less Isabelle Holland's *The Man Without a Face*, Norma Klein's *Mom, The Wolfman and Me*, Rosa Guy's *Ruby*, or Robert Cormier's *The Chocolate War*, all to be published soon afterward. But the iconoclastic, taboo-breaking novels today would not have been possible had it not been for earlier novels that slowly broke ground and prepared readers, teachers, and librarians (and even some parents) for contemporary novels. Society's changes, of course, inevitably lead to changes in literature, but changes in young adult literature can be attributed in large part to authors like Tunis, Means, Annixter, Daly, and Stolz.

◆ ACTIVITIES ◆

1. Read a few of the reading interest studies cited in this chapter. What are their strengths (and weaknesses) for an English teacher or librarian? How would you go about constructing a reading interest inventory of your class or classes or school that would benefit you the most? What value would the study have for other educators in your school? Devise such an inventory and give it to students. What might you have guessed would be true of students before the inventory? What turned out to be true?

2. Some people have argued that Havighurst's developmental tasks are now dated, sexist, and elitist. Reread the section on developmental tasks in this chapter and read some of Havighurst's original words in *Human Development and Education* (New York: Longmans, Green, 1953). Do you feel the critics are correct? Why? Why not? What are the initiation rites our contemporary society demands that young adults undergo? How do we (or teachers or parents or librarians) know that? Have they changed since Havighurst listed his developmental tasks? How so?

3. Read an article or two on bibliotherapy in classrooms or libraries today. What are the values (and problems) inherent in bibliotherapy? What contemporary books would be most useful for contemporary students? How can we get those books to those students without hurting or insulting them?

4. Read a novel by one of the outstanding authors of this period, for example, John Tunis' *All-American*, Maureen Daly's *Seventeenth Summer*, Florence Crannell Means'

Shuttered Windows, Henry Gregor Felsen's *Two and the Town*, Esther Forbes' *Johnny Tremain*, or Mary Stolz's *Pray Love, Remember*. Review the book in terms of the audience of its time and a contemporary audience. What values were obviously dear to the author? Are those values equally germane to young adults today?

5. Read a novel paralleling the one you read in Activity #4. For example, if you read Tunis' *All-American*, read Richard Blessing's *A Passing Season* or Chris Crutcher's *Running Loose*. If Daly or Stolz, read one of Norma Fox Mazer's books. If Forbes, read a historical novel by Rosemary Sutcliff or James and Christopher Collier. If Means, read a novel by Alice Childress or Mildred Taylor. If Felsen, read Paul Zindel's *My Darling, My Hamburger*. Compare and contrast the values in the 1940s and 1950s books with those in the 1970s and 1980s. What values have endured? What have changed? In what ways?

6. Note the taboos about young adult literature cited in this chapter. What taboos have dropped by the wayside? What taboos endure? What people want taboos presented in young adult books? Why? Are there taboos about contemporary young adult literature? Skim through articles (and letters to the editor) in *School Library Journal, Top of the News, English Journal, Voice of Youth Advocates, Wilson Library Bulletin, Horn Book Magazine,* and *Newsletter on Intellectual Freedom* to note what some people believe are (or should be) taboos in young adult literature.

◆ NOTES ◆

[1]George W. Norvell, "Some Results of a Twelve-Year Study of Children's Reading Interests," *English Journal* 35 (December 1946): 532.

[2]Norvell, "Some Results . . . " p. 536.

[3]Marie Rankin, *Children's Interests in Library Books of Fiction*, Teachers College, Columbia University, Contributions to Education, no. 906 (New York: Teachers College, Columbia Univ., 1947).

[4]Stephen Dunning, "The Most Popular Junior Novels," *Junior Libraries* 5 (December 15, 1959): 7–9.

[5]Jacob W. Getzels, "The Nature of Reading Interests: Psychological Aspects" in *Developing Permanent Interests in Reading*, ed. Helen M. Robinson, Supplementary Education Monographs, no. 84, December 1956 (Chicago: University of Chicago Press, 1956), p. 5.

[6]Robert Carlsen, "Behind Reading Interests," *English Journal* 43 (January 1954): 7–10.

[7]Dwight L. Burton, "There's Always a Book for You," *English Journal* 38 (September 1949): 374.

[8]Robert J. Havighurst, *Human Development and Education* (New York: Longmans, Green, 1953), pp. 111–56.

[9]G. O. Ireland, "Bibliotherapy: The Use of Books as a Form of Treatment in a Neuropsychiatric Hospital," *Library Journal* 54 (December 1, 1929): 972–74.

[10]Alice I. Bryan, "Can There Be a Science of Bibliotherapy?" *Library Journal* 64 (October 15, 1939): 773–76.

[11]William A. Heaps, "Bibliotherapy and the School Librarian," *Library Journal* 65 (October 1, 1940): 789.

[12]Lou LaBrant, "Diversifying the Matter," *English Journal* 40 (March 1951): 135.

[13]Frank Ross, "Bibliotherapy," *Media and Methods* 5 (January 1969): 36.

[14]S. Alan Cohen, "Paperbacks in the Classroom," *Journal of Reading* 12 (January 1969): 295.

[15]Daniel Fader, *Hooked on Books* (New York: Berkley, 1966), revised as *Hooked on Books: Program and Proof* in 1968, and updated in 1976 as *The New Hooked on Books.*

[16]Ray Waiters, "Paperback Talk," *New York Times Book Review*, November 13, 1977, p. 90.

[17]Leo Lerman, "An Industry Within an Industry," *Saturday Review of Literature* 24 (November 8, 1941): 3.

[18]Stanley B. Kegler and Stephen Dunning, "Junior Book Roundup—Literature for the Adolescent, 1960," *English Journal* 50 (May 1961): 369.

[19]Stanley B. Kegler and Stephen Dunning, "Junior Book Roundup," *English Journal* 53 (May 1964): 392.

[20]"Children's Books," *Saturday Review of Literature* 24 (November 8, 1941): 12.

[21]*Library Journal* 77 (July 1952): 1216.

[22]Richard S. Alm, "The Glitter and the Gold," *English Journal* 44 (September 1955): 320.

[23]Dwight L. Burton, "Books to Meet Students' Personal Needs," *English Journal* 36 (November 1947): 469–73. See also G. Robert Carlsen, "Literature and Emotional Maturity," *English Journal* 38 (March 1949): 130–38, and Isabel V. Eno, "Books for Children from Broken Homes," *English Journal* 38 (October 1949): 457–58 for similar articles.

[24]Dwight L. Burton, "The Novel for the Adolescent," *English Journal* 40 (September 1951): 363–69.

[25]Burton, "The Novel . . . " p. 369.

[26]Richard S. Alm, "The Glitter and the Gold," *English Journal* 44 (September 1955): 315.

[27]Emma L. Paterson, "The Junior Novels and How They Grew," *English Journal* 45 (October 1956): 381.

[28]*English Journal* 45 (December 1956): 526–31.

[29]See for examples, Alice Krahn, "Case Against the Junior Novel," *Top of the News* 17 (May 1961): 19–22; Esther Millett, "We Don't Even Call Those Books!" *Top of the News* 20 (October 1963): 45–47; and Harvey R. Granite, "The Uses and Abuses of Junior Literature," *Clearing House* 42 (February 1968): 337–40.

◆ TITLES MENTIONED IN CHAPTER 15 ◆

For information on the availability of paperback editions of these titles, please consult the most recent edition of *Paperbound Books in Print*, published annually by R. R. Bowker Company.

Allson, Bob and F. E. Hill. *The Kid Who Batted 1.000.* Doubleday, 1951.

Annixter, Paul. *Swiftwater.* A. A. Wyn, 1950.

Bell, Margaret Elizabeth. *Love Is Forever.* Morrow, 1954.

Bennett, Jack. *The Hawk Alone.* Little, Brown, 1965.

——————. *Jamie.* Little, Brown, 1963.

——————. *Mister Fisherman.* Little, Brown, 1965.

Benson, Sally. *Junior Miss.* Doubleday, 1947.

Boylston, Helen Dore. *Sue Barton, Senior Nurse.* John Lane, 1950.

——————. *Sue Barton, Staff Nurse.* Little, Brown, 1952.

————. *Sue Barton, Student Nurse*. Little, Brown, 1936.

Brande, Dorothea. *Wake Up and Live*. World, 1941.

Breck, Vivian. *High Trail*. Doubleday, 1948.

————. *Maggie*. Doubleday, 1954.

Brown, Claude. *Manchild in the Promised Land*. Macmillan, 1965.

Buck, Pearl S. *The Good Earth*. John Day, 1931.

Bugbee, Emma. *Peggy Covers the News*. Dodd, Mead, 1936.

Burns, John Horne. *The Gallery*. Harper & Row, 1947.

Campanella, Roy. *It's Good to Be Alive*. Little, Brown, 1959.

Carr, Harriet. *Confidential Secretary*. Macmillan, 1958.

Carson, John F. *The Coach Nobody Liked*. Farrar, Straus, Giroux, 1960.

————. *Floorburns*. Farrar, Straus, Giroux, 1957.

————. *Hotshot*. Farrar, Straus, Giroux, 1961.

Cavanna, Betty. *Going on Sixteen*. Ryerson, 1946.

————. *Paintbox Summer*. Presbyterian Board of Christian Education, 1949.

Christie, Agatha. *The Murder of Roger Ackroyd*. Grossett & Dunlap, 1940.

Chute, Marchette. *The Innocent Wayfaring*. Scribner's, 1943.

————. *The Wonderful Winter*. E. P. Dutton, 1954.

Cleaver, Eldridge. *Soul on Ice*. McGraw-Hill, 1968.

Daly, Maureen. *Seventeenth Summer*. Dodd, Mead, 1942.

De Leeuw, Adele Louise. *Gay Design*. Macmillan, 1942.

Du Jardin, Rosamund. *Double Feature*. Longmans, 1953.

————. *Practically Seventeen*. Longmans, 1949.

————. *Senior Prom*. Lippincott, 1957.

————. *Wait for Marcy*. Longmans, 1950.

Ellison, Ralph. *Invisible Man*. Random House, 1952.

————. *Shadow and Act*. Random House, 1964.

Emery, Anne. *Going Steady*. Westminster, 1950.

————. *Married on Wednesday*. Ryerson, 1957.

————. *Sorority Girl*. Westminster, 1952.

Eyerly, Jeanette. *Bonnie Jo, Go Home*. Lippincott, 1972.

————. *Drop-Out*. Lippincott, 1963.

————. *A Girl Like Me*. Lippincott, 1966.

————. *Radigan Cares*. Lippincott, 1970.

Fargo, Lucile Foster. *Marian Martha*. Dodd, Mead, 1936.

Farley, Walter. *Black Stallion*. Random House, 1944.

Felsen, Henry Gregor. *Bertie Comes Through*. E. P. Dutton, 1947.

————. *Bertie Makes a Break*. E. P. Dutton, 1949.

————. *Bertie Takes Care*. E. P. Dutton, 1948.

————. *Crash Club*. Random House, 1958.

————. *Davey Logan, Intern*. E. P. Dutton, 1950.

————. *He's in the Coast Guard Now*. Mac-Bride, 1943.

————. *Hot Rod*. E. P. Dutton, 1950.

————. *Navy Diver*. E. P. Dutton, 1942.

————. *Pilots All*. Harper & Row, 1944.

————. *Street Rod*. Random House, 1953.

————. *Submarine Sailor*. E. P. Dutton, 1943.

————. *Two and the Town*. Scribner's, 1952.

Fleming, Ian. *Casino Royale*. Macmillan, 1954.

————. *Dr. No*. Macmillan, 1958.

————. *From Russia with Love*. Macmillan, 1957.

————. *Goldfinger*. Macmillan, 1959.

————. *The Man with the Golden Gun*. New American Library, 1965.

————. *Thunderball*. Viking, 1961.

————. *You Only Live Twice*. Clarke, Irwin, 1964.

Forbes, Esther. *Johnny Tremain*. Houghton Mifflin, 1943.

————. *Paul Revere and the World He Lived In*. Houghton Mifflin, 1942.

Freedman, Benedict and Nancy. *Mrs. Mike*. Coward, McCann & Geoghegan, 1947.

Frick, Constance H. *The Comeback Guy*. Harcourt Brace Jovanovich, 1961.

————. *Five Against the Odds*. Harcourt Brace Jovanovich, 1955.

————. *Patch*. Harcourt Brace Jovanovich, 1957.

Gault, William, *Thunder Road*. E. P. Dutton, 1952.

————. *Road Race Rookie*. E. P. Dutton, 1962.

Gibbs, Blanche L. and Georgiana Adams. *Shirley Clayton, Secretary*. Dodd, Mead, 1941.

Golding, William. *Lord of the Flies*. Coward, McCann & Geoghegan, 1955.

Goudge, Elizabeth. *Green Dolphin Street*. Coward, McCann & Geoghegan, 1944.

Graham, Lorenz. *North Town*. Crowell, 1965.

————. *South Town*. Follett, 1958.

————. *Whose Town?* Crowell, 1969.

Graham, Shirley. *Booker T. Washington: Educator of Hand, Head, and Heart*. Julian Messner, 1955.

————. *The Story of Phillis Wheatley: Poetess of the American Revolution*. Julian Messner, 1949.

————. *There Was Once a Slave: The Heroic Story of Frederick Douglass*. Julian Messner, 1947.

————. *Your Most Humble Servant: The Story of Benjamin Banneker*. Julian Messner, 1949.

Gray, Elizabeth Janet. *Adam of the Road*. Viking, 1942.

Griffin, John Howard. *Black Like Me*. Houghton Mifflin, 1961.

————. *The Devil Rides Outside*. William Collins Sons, 1952.

Harkins, Philip. *Knockout*. Holiday House, 1950.

————. *Road Race*. Crowell, 1953.

Harris, Christie. *You Have to Draw the Line Somewhere*. Atheneum, 1964.

Hentoff, Nat. *I'm Really Dragged but Nothing Gets Me Down*. Simon and Schuster, 1968.

————. *In the Country of Ourselves*. Simon and Schuster 1971.

————. *Jazz Country*. Harper & Row, 1965.

Hersey, John Richard. *A Bell for Adano*. Knopf, 1944.

Hilton, James. *Lost Horizon*. Grosset & Dunlap, 1933.

Jackson, Jesse. *Anchor Man*. Harper & Row, 1947.

————. *Call Me Charley*. Harper & Row, 1945.

————. *Charley Starts from Scratch*. Harper & Row, 1958.

————. *Tessie*. Harper & Row, 1968.

Johnson, Martha. *Ann Bartlett, Navy Nurse*. Crowell, 1941.

Jones, James. *From Here to Eternity*. Scribner's, 1951.

————. *The Pistol*. Scribner's, 1959.

————. *The Thin Red Line*. Scribner's, 1962.

Knowles, John. *A Separate Peace*. Macmillan, 1960.

Lambert, Janet. *Star-Spangled Summer*. E. P. Dutton, 1941.

Lansing, Elizabeth. *Nancy Naylor, Flight Nurse*. Crowell, 1944.

Lee, Harper. *To Kill a Mockingbird*. Lippincott, 1960.

L'Engle, Madeleine. *The Small Rain*. Vanguard, 1945.

Lewiton, Mina. *A Cup of Courage*. McKay, 1948.

————. *The Divided Heart*. McKay, 1947.

Mailer, Norman. *The Naked and the Dead*. Clarke, Irwin, 1948.

Malcolm X. and Alex Haley. *The Autobiography of Malcolm X*. Grove, 1965.

Mann, Carl. *He's in the Signal Corps Now*. McBride, 1943.

Marshall, Catherine. *Julie's Heritage*. Longmans, 1957.

McFadden, Dorothy. *Lynn Decker: TV Apprentice*. Dodd, Mead, 1953.

Means, Florence Crannell. *A Candle in the Mist*. Houghton Mifflin, 1931.

————. *It Takes All Kinds*. Houghton Mifflin, 1964.

————. *The Moved Outers*. Houghton Mifflin, 1945.

————. *Our Cup Is Broken*. Houghton Mifflin, 1969.

————. *Shuttered Windows*. Houghton Mifflin, 1938.

————. *Tangled Waters: A Navajo Story*. Houghton Mifflin, 1936.

————. *Tolliver*. Houghton Mifflin, 1963.

Medearis, Mary. *Big Doc's Girl*. Lippincott, 1942.

Metalious, Grace. *Peyton Place*. Julian Messner, 1956.

————. *Return to Peyton Place*. Julian Messner, 1959.

Milne, Ruth. *TV Girl Friday*. Little, Brown, 1957.

O'Rourke, Frank. *The Last Round*. Morrow, 1956.

Parker, Dorothy. *Enough Rope*. Sun Dial, 1940.

Paton, Alan. *Cry the Beloved Country*. Scribner's, 1948.

————. *Too Late the Phalarope*. Scribner's, 1953.

Peckham, Betty. *Women in Aviation*. Thomas Nelson, 1945.

Piersall, James Anthony and Albert Hirshberg. *Fear Strikes Out*. Little, Brown, 1955.

Provines, Mary Virginia. *Bright Heritage*. Longmans, 1939.

Pyle, Ernie. *Brave Men*. Holt, Rinehart and Winston, 1944.

————. *Here Is Your War*. Holt, Rinehart and Winston, 1943.

————. *Last Chapter*. Holt, Rinehart and Winston, 1946.

Reynolds, Quentin James. *70,000 to One.* Random House, 1946.

Robbins, Harold. *The Adventurers.* Simon and Schuster, 1966.

————. *The Carpetbaggers.* Simon and Schuster, 1961.

————. *A Stone for Danny Fisher.* Knopf, 1952.

Rolt-Wheeler, Francis William. *The Boy with the U.S. Aviators.* Lothrop, Lee & Shepard, 1929.

Rosenheim, Lucille G. *Kathie, the New Teacher.* Julian Messner, 1949.

Salinger, J. D. *The Catcher in the Rye.* Little, Brown, 1951.

Sherburne, Zoa. *Jennifer.* Morrow, 1959.

————. *Too Bad about the Haines Girl.* Morrow, 1967.

Smith, Betty. *A Tree Grows in Brooklyn.* Harper & Row, 1943.

Smith, Lillian. *Strange Fruit.* Reynal, 1944.

Smith, Thorne. *Topper.* Sun Dial, 1942.

Steinbeck, John. *The Grapes of Wrath.* Viking, 1939.

————. *Of Mice and Men.* Viking, 1937.

Stolz, Mary Slattery. *The Day and the Way We Met.* Harper & Row, 1956.

————. *In a Mirror.* Harper & Row, 1953.

————. *A Love, or a Season.* Harper & Row, 1964.

————. *Pray Love, Remember.* Harper & Row, 1954.

————. *Rosemary.* Harper & Row, 1955.

————. *The Sea Gulls Woke Me.* Harper & Row, 1951.

————. *To Tell Your Love.* Harper & Row, 1950.

Summers, James. *Girl Trouble.* Westminster, 1953.

————. *The Iron Doors Between.* Westminster, 1968.

————. *The Limit of Love.* Ryerson, 1959.

————. *Off the Beam.* Westminster, 1956.

————. *Operation ABC.* Westminster, 1955.

————. *Prom Trouble.* Ryerson, 1954.

————. *Ring Around Her Finger.* Westminster, 1957.

————. *The Shelter Trap.* Westminster, 1962.

————. *Trouble on the Run.* Ryerson, 1956.

————. *The Wonderful Time.* Ryerson, 1957.

————. *You Can't Make It by Bus.* Westminster, 1969.

Tregaskis, Richard William. *Guadalcanal Diary.* Random House, 1943.

Trumbull, Robert. *The Raft.* Holt, Rinehart and Winston, 1942.

Tunis, John R. *All-American.* Harcourt, Brace, 1942.

————. *A City for Lincoln.* Harcourt, Brace, 1945.

————. *Go, Team, Go!* Morrow, 1954.

————. *His Enemy, His Friend.* Morrow, 1967.

————. *Iron Duke.* Harcourt, Brace, 1938.

————. *Silence over Dunkerque.* Morrow, 1962.

————. *Yea! Wildcats.* Harcourt, Brace, 1944.

Wallace, Irving. *The Chapman Report.* Simon and Schuster, 1960.

————. *The Man.* Simon and Schuster, 1964.

————. *The Prize.* Simon and Schuster, 1962.

Westheimer, David. *My Sweet Charlie.* Doubleday, 1965.

Wickenden, Dan. *Walk Like a Mortal.* Morrow, 1940.

Wilder, Thornton. *The Bridge of San Luis Rey.* Harper & Row, 1927.

Winsor, Kathleen. *Forever Amber.* Macmillan, 1944.

Wouk, Herman. *The Caine Mutiny.* Doubleday, 1951.

Wright, Richard. *Black Boy.* Harper & Row, 1945.

————. *Native Son.* Harper & Row, 1940.

Yates, Elizabeth. *Amos Fortune, Free Man.* Aladdin, 1950.

◆ SOME SUGGESTED READINGS ◆

General Comments on Literature, 1940–1966:

Alm, Richard. "The Glitter and the Gold." *English Journal* 44 (September 1955): 315–22.

Burton, Dwight. *Literature Study in the High Schools.* 3rd ed. New York: Holt, Rinehart and Winston, 1970.

————. "The Novel for the Adolescent." *English Journal* 40 (September 1951): 363–69.

Carlsen, G. Robert. "Forty Years with Books and Teen-Age Readers." *Arizona English Bulletin* 18 (April 1976): 1–5.

Davis, James E. "Recent Trends in Fiction for Adolescents." *English Journal* 56 (May 1967): 720–24.

Edwards, Margaret A. "The Rise of Teen-Age Reading." *Saturday Review* 37 (November 13, 1954): 88.

Epstein, Jason. "Good Bunnies Always Obey: Books for American Children." *Commentary* 35 (February 1963): 112–22.

Hackett, Alice Payne and James Henry Burke. *80 Years of Best Sellers, 1895–1975*. New York: R. R. Bowker, 1977.

Hart, James D. *The Popular Book: A History of America's Literary Taste*. Berkeley: University of California Press, 1950.

Hentoff, Nat. "Getting Inside Jazz Country." *Horn Book Magazine* 42 (October 1966): 528–32.

Jennings, Frank G. "Literature for Adolescents—Pap or Protein?" *English Journal* 45 (December 1951): 526–31.

Johnson, James William. "The Adolescent Hero: A Trend in Modern Fiction." *Twentieth Century Literature* 5 (April 1959): 3–11.

Nordstrom, Ursula. "Honesty in Teenage Novels." *Top of the News* 21 (November 1964): 35–38.

Rosenblatt, Louise M. *Literature as Exploration*. 3rd ed. New York: Noble and Noble, 1977.

Rosenheim, Edward W., Jr. "Children's Reading and Adults' Values" in *A Critical Approach to Children's Literature*. Sara Innis Fenwick, ed. Chicago: University of Chicago Press, 1967, pp. 3–14.

Sample, Hazel. *Pitfalls for Readers of Fiction*. Chicago: National Council of Teachers of English, 1940.

Reading Interest Studies:

Anderson, Esther M. "A Study of Leisure-Time Reading of Pupils in Junior High School." *Elementary School Journal* 48 (January 1948): 258–67.

Anderson, Scarvia B. *Between the Grimms and "The Group": Literature in American High Schools*. Princeton: Educational Testing Service, 1964.

Barbe, Walter. "A Study of the Reading of Gifted High-School Students." *Educational Administration and Supervision* 38 (March 1952): 148–54.

Broehl, Frances. "New Influences in the Field of Recreational Reading." *English Journal* 30 (April 1941): 281–86.

Carlsen, G. Robert. "Behind Reading Interests." *English Journal* 43 (January 1954): 7–12.

————. "For Everything There Is a Season." *Top of the News* 21 (January 1967): 103–10.

Dunning, Stephen. "The Most Popular Junior Novels." *Junior Libraries* 5 (December 1959): 7–9.

Edwards, Margaret A. "A Time When It's Best to Read and Let Read." *Wilson Library Bulletin* 35 (September 1960): 43–45.

Getzels, Jacob W. "The Nature of Reading Interests: Psychological Aspects" in *Developing Permanent Interest in Reading*. Helen M. Robinson, ed. Supplementary Education Monographs, no. 84. Chicago: University of Chicago Press, 1956, pp. 5–9.

Lapides, Linda P. "Unassigned Reading: Teen-Age Testimonies I and II: A Decade of Teen-Age Reading in Baltimore, 1960–1970." *Top of the News* 27 (April 1971): 278–91.

Nelms, Ben F. "Reading for Pleasure in Junior High School." *English Journal* 55 (September 1966: 676–81.

Norvell, George W. *The Reading Interests of Young People*. Boston: D. C. Heath, 1950.

————. "Some Results of a Twelve-Year Study of Children's Reading Interests." *English Journal* 35 (December 1946)): 531–36.

Petitt, Dorothy. "A Search for Self-Definition: The Picture of Life in the Novel for the Adolescent." *English Journal* 49 (December 1960): 616–26.

Plotz, Helen. "The Rising Generation of Readers." *New York Times Magazine*, August 5, 1956, p. 44.

Rankin, Marie. *Children's Interests in Library Books of Fiction*. Teachers College, Columbia University Contributions to Education, no. 906. New York: Teachers College Press, 1947.

Scanlan, William J. "One Hundred Most Popular Books of Children's Fiction Selected by Children." *Elementary English* 25 (February 1948): 83–97.

Scoggin, Margaret C. "Young People's Reading Interests Not Materially Changed in Wartime." *Library Journal* 68 (September 15,1943): 703–6.

Soares, Anthony T. "Salient Elements of Recreational Reading of Junior High School Students." *Elementary English* 40 (December 1963): 843–45.

Havighurst's Developmental Tasks:

Brooks, Alice. "Integrating Books and Reading with Havighurst's Developmental Tasks." *School Review* 58 (April 1950): 211–19.

Havighurst, Robert J. *Developmental Tasks and Education.* New York: Longmans, Green, 1948.

―――. *Human Development and Education.* New York: Longmans, Green, 1953.

Johnson, Gladys B. "Books and the Five Adolescent Tasks." *Library Journal* 68 (May 1, 1943): 350–52.

Bibliotherapy:

Beatty, William K. "A Historical Review of Bibliotherapy." *Library Trends* 11 (October 1962): 106–17.

Bryan, Alice I. "Can There Be a Science of Bibliotherapy?" *Library Journal* 64 (October 15, 1939): 773–76.

Darling, Richard L. "Mental Hygiene and Books: Bibliotherapy as Used with Children and Adolescents." *Wilson Library Bulletin* 32 (December 1957): 293–96.

Dreyer, Sharon Spredemann. *The Bookfinder: A Guide to Children's Literature about the Needs and Problems of Youth Aged 12–15.* Circle Pines, Minnesota: American Guidance Service,1977.

Elser, Helen. "Bibliotherapy in Practice." *Library Trends* 30 (Spring 1982): 647–59.

Heaps, Willard A. "Bibliotherapy and the School Librarian." *Library Journal* 65 (October 1, 1940): 789–92.

Jackson, Evalene P. "Bibliotherapy and Reading Guidance: A Tentative Approach to Theory." *Library Trends* 11 (October 1962): 118–26.

Lindeman, Barbara and M. Kling. "Bibliotherapy: Definitions, Uses, and Studies." *Journal of School Psychology* 7 (1968–69): 34–41.

Newton, Eunice S. "Bibliotherapy in the Development of Minority Group Self-Concept." *Journal of Negro Education* 38 (Summer 1969): 257–65.

Riggs, Corinne W., ed. *Bibliotherapy: An Annotated Bibliography.* Newark, Delaware: International Reading Association, 1971.

Russell, David H. and Caroline Shrodes. "Contributions of Research in Bibliotherapy to the Language Arts Program." *School Review* 58 (September 1950): 335–42; and 58 (October 1950): 411–20.

Warner, Lucy. "The Myth of Bibliotherapy." *School Library Journal* 27 (October 1980): 107–11.

Paperbacks:

Butman, Alexander; Donald Reis; and David Sohn, eds. *Paperbacks in the Schools.* New York: Bantam, 1963.

Davis, Kenneth C. *Two-Bit Culture: The Paperbacking of America.* Boston: Houghton Mifflin, 1984.

Enoch, Kurt. "The Paper-Bound Book: Twentieth-Century Publishing Phenomenon." *Library Quarterly* 24 (July 1954): 211–25.

Fader, Daniel. *The New Hooked on Books.* New York: Berkley, 1976.

Lewis, Freeman. "The Future of Paper-Bound Books." *Bulletin of the New York Public Library* 57 (October 1953): 506–15.

―――. "Paper-Bound Books in America." *Bulletin of the New York Public Library* 57 (February 1953): 55–75.

Schick, Frank L. *The Paperbound Book in America: The History of Paperbacks and Their European Background.* New York: R. R. Bowker, 1958.

Career Books:

Edwards, Anne. "Teen-Age Career Girls." *English Journal* 42 (November 1953): 437–42.

Forrester, Gertrude. *Occupational Literature: An Annotated Bibliography.* New York: H. W. Wilson, 1971.

Haebich, Kathryn A., ed. *Vocations in Biography and Fiction.* Chicago: American Library Association, 1962.

Ives, Vernon. "Careers for Sale: $2.00 List." *Horn Book Magazine* 19 (March-April 1943): 107–12.

Splaver, Sarah. "The Career Novel." *Personnel and Guidance Journal* 31 (March 1953): 371–72.

HONOR SAMPLING

Title and Author	Hardbound Publisher	Publishing Division	Paperback Publisher	ALA	SLJ	EJ	NYT	Ad. Lit. Prof.	Genre	Sex	Age	Number of Pages	TV	Movie	Ethnic Group
1983															
Beyond the Divide Kathryn Lasky	Macmillan	J		•		•	•		Historical Fiction	F	teens	254			
The Bumblebee Flies Anyway Robert Cormier	Pantheon	J	Dell	•	•	•			Realistic Fiction	M/F	teens	211			
A Gathering of Old Men Ernest J. Gaines	Knopf	A	Vintage	•		•		•	Realistic Fiction	M	elderly	214			Black
Poetspeak: In Their Work, About Their Work Paul Janeczko, ed.	Bradbury	J		•	•	•	•	•	Poetry			224			
The Sign of the Beaver Elizabeth Speare	Houghton Mifflin	J	Dell	•	•	•	•		Historical Fiction	M	young teens	144			Indian/ Anglo
Solitary Blue Cynthia Vogel	Atheneum	J		•	•	•		•	Realistic Fiction	M	7–18	182			
The Tempering Gloria Skurzynski	Clarion	J		•	•	•			Historical Fiction	M	teens	178			
The Wild Children Felice Holman	Scribner	J				•		•	Historical Fiction	M	teens	151			Set in 1920s Russia

Title and Author	Hardbound Publisher	Publishing Division	Paperback Publisher	ALA	SLJ	EJ	NYT	Ad. Lit. Prof.	Genre	Protagonist Sex	Age	Number of Pages	TV	Movie	Ethnic Group
1982															
Annie on My Mind Nancy Garden	Farrar, Straus & Giroux	J	Farrar, Straus & Giroux	•					Realistic Fiction	F	18	186			
The Blue Sword Robin McKinley	Greenwillow	J	Berkley	•		•			Fantasy	F	late teens	272			
Class Dismissed! High School Poems Mel Glenn	Clarion	J		•		•		•	Poetry	F/M	teens	96			
The Darkangel Meredith Ann Pierce	Atlantic	J		•	•	•	•	•	Fantasy	F	early teens	223			
A Formal Feeling Zibby Oneal	Viking	J	Fawcett	•	•	•		•	Realistic Fiction	F	16	162			
Homesick Jean Fritz	Putnam	J	Putnam	•	•				Auto-biography Fiction	F	10–12	163			Set in China
A Midnight Clear William Wharton	Knopf	A	Ballantine	•	•	•			Realistic Fiction	M	early 20s	241			
Sweet Whispers, Brother Rush Virginia Hamilton	Philomel	J	Avon	•	•		•	•	Occult	F	14	224			Black
1981															
The Battle Horse Harry Kullman	Bradbury	J		•	•	•		•	Realistic Historical Fiction	M	14	183			Set in 1930s Stockholm
Dont forget to fly Paul Janeczko, ed.	Bradbury	J		•	•	•			Poetry			144			
Let the Circle Be Unbroken Mildred D. Taylor	Dial	J	Bantam	•	•	•		•	Realistic Historical Fiction	F	16	394			Black
Little Little M. E. Kerr	Harper & Row	J	Bantam	•	•	•		•	Humor Realistic Fiction	F	18	183			

Title / Author	Pub. (HC)	A/J	Pub. (PB)							Genre	M/F	Age	Page		Notes
Mazes and Monsters Rona Jaffe	Delacorte	A	Dell	•			•	•	•	Realistic Fiction	M/F	16–20	329	•	
Notes for Another Life Sue Ellen Bridgers	Knopf	J	Bantam	•		•	•	•	•	Realistic Fiction	M/F	13–16	252		
Pack of Wolves Vasil Bykov	Crowell	J		•		•	•	•	•	Historical Fiction	M	mixed	181		Translated from Russian
Rainbow Jordan Alice Childress	Coward McCann	J	Avon	•	•	•	•	•	•	Realistic Fiction	F	14	142		Black
Stranger with My Face Lois Duncan	Little, Brown	J	Dell	•	•	•	•	•	•	Occult	F	17	250		
Tiger Eyes Judy Blume	Bradbury	J	Dell	•		•	•	•	•	Realistic Fiction	F	15	206		Mexican-American New Mex.
Westmark Lloyd Alexander	Dutton	J	Dell	•		•	•	•	•	Historical Fiction	M	16	184		
1980															
The Beginning Place Ursula K. Le Guin	Harper & Row	J	Bantam	•		•	•	•	•	Fantasy	M/F	early 20s	183		
Jacob Have I Loved Katherine Paterson	Crowell	J	Avon	•		•	•	•	•	Realistic Historical Fiction	F	teens	216		Chesapeake Bay island
A Matter of Feeling Janine Boissard	Little, Brown	A	Fawcett	•		•	•	•	•	Realistic Fiction	F	17	214		Translated from French
One Child Torey Hayden	Putnam	A	Avon	•		•	•	•	•	New Journalism	F	6	251		
The Pigman's Legacy Paul Zindel	Harper & Row	J	Bantam	•		•	•	•	•	Realistic Fiction	M/F	17	183		
The Quartzsite Trip William Hogan	Atheneum	A	Avon	•		•	•	•	•	Realistic Fiction	M/F	17–18	307		
When No One Was Looking Rosemary Wells	Dial	J				•	•	•	•	Realistic Fiction	F	14	218		
1979															
After the First Death Robert Cormier	Pantheon	J	Avon	•		•	•	•	•	Suspense	M	13	233		
All Together Now Sue Ellen Bridgers	Knopf	J	Bantam	•	•	•	•	•	•	Realistic Fiction	F	12	238		

Title and Author	Hardbound Publisher	Publishing Division	Paperback Publisher	ALA	SLJ	BL	NYT	Ad. Lit. Prof.	Genre	Sex	Age (teens & early 20s)	Number of Pages	TV	Movie	Ethnic Group
Birdy William Wharton	Knopf	A	Avon	•		•	•	•	Realistic Fiction	M		310			
The Disappearance Rosa Guy	Delacorte	J	Dell	•	•	•	•	•	Realistic Fiction	M	16	246			Black
The Last Mission Harry Mazer	Delacorte	J	Dell	•	•	•		•	Suspense	M	16	182			
Tex S. E. Hinton	Delacorte	J	Dell	•	•	•	•	•	Realistic Fiction	M	15	194		•	
Words by Heart Ouida Sebestyen	Little, Brown	J	Bantam	•	•	•	•	•	Historical Fiction	F	12	162			
1978															
Beauty: A Retelling of the Story of Beauty and the Beast Robin McKinley	Harper & Row	J		•		•			Fantasy	F	15	247			
The Book of the Dun Cow Walter Wangerin, Jr.	Harper & Row	J	Pocket Books		•	•		•	Fantasy	M	—	255			
Dreamsnake Vonda N. McIntyre	Houghton Mifflin	A	Dell	•	•	•		•	Science Fiction	F	teen	313			
Father Figure Richard Peck	Viking	J	NAL	•		•			Realistic Fiction	M	17	192	•		
Gentlehands M. E. Kerr	Harper & Row	J	Bantam	•	•	•	•		Realistic Fiction	M	16	183			German Jewish
1977															
Hard Feelings Don Bredes	Atheneum	A	Bantam	•	•	•			Realistic Fiction	M	16	377			
I Am the Cheese Robert Cormier	Knopf	J	Dell	•	•	•	•	•	Realistic Fiction	M	14	233		•	
I'll Love You When You're More Like Me M. E. Kerr	Harper & Row	J	Dell		•	•			Realistic Fiction	M/F	17	183			

Title / Author	Publisher	Level	Paperback	Genre	M/F	Age	Pages	Group
Ludell & Willie Brenda Wilkinson	Harper & Row	J	Bantam	Realistic Fiction	F	16	181	Black
One Fat Summer Robert Lipsyte	Harper & Row	J	Bantam	Realistic Fiction	M	16	150	
Trial Valley Vera and Bill Cleaver	Lippincott	J	Bantam	Realistic Fiction	F	17	158	Rural Isolated
Winning Robin Brancato	Knopf	J	Bantam	Realistic Fiction	M	17	211	
1976								
Are You in the House Alone? Richard Peck	Viking	J	Dell	Realistic Fiction	F	16	156	
Dear Bill, Remember Me? Norma Fox Mazer	Delacorte	J	Dell	Real Short Stories	F	teen-age	195	
The Distant Summer Sarah Patterson	Simon & Schuster	A	Pocket Books	Historical Fiction Romance	F	16	153	
Home Before Dark Sue Ellen Bridgers	Knopf	J	Bantam	Realistic Fiction	F	14	176	Migrant Workers
Never to Forget Milton Meltzer	Harper & Row	J	Dell	New Journalism			217	Jewish
Ordinary People Judith Guest	Viking	A	Ballantine	Realistic Fiction	M	17	263	
Pardon Me, You're Stepping on My Eyeball Paul Zindel	Harper & Row	J	Bantam	Realistic Fiction	M/F	17	262	
Roots Alex Haley	Doubleday	A	Dell	New J. Family History	M/F	mixed	587	Black
Tunes for a Small Harmonica Barbara Wersba	Harper & Row	J	Dell	Realistic Fiction Humor	F	16	178	
Very Far Away from Anywhere Else Ursula Le Guin	Atheneum	J	Bantam	Realistic Fiction	M	17	89	

Title and Author	Hardbound Publisher	Publishing Division	Paperback Publisher	ALA	SLJ	BL	NYT	Ad. Lit. Prof.	Genre	Protagonist Sex	Age	Number of Pages	Media Edition TV	Movie	Ethnic Group
1975															
Dragonwings Laurence Yep	Harper & Row	J	Harper & Row	•	•	•			Historical Fiction	M	12	248			Chinese American
Feral Berton Roueche	Harper & Row	A	Avon	•	•	•	•		Horror Fiction	M/F	20s	137			
Is That You Miss Blue? M. E. Kerr	Harper & Row	J	Dell	•	•	•			Realistic Fiction	F	14	170			
The Lion's Paw D. R. Sherman	Doubleday	A		•	•	•	•	•	Realistic Fiction	M	16	233			African Native
The Massacre at Fall Creek Jessamyn West	Harper & Row	A	Fawcett	•		•			Historical Fiction	M/F	adult, teen	373			Native American
Rumble Fish S. E. Hinton	Delacorte	J	Dell	•	•	•			Realistic Fiction	M	14	122			
Z for Zachariah Robert C. O'Brien	Atheneum	J	Dell	•	•	•	•	•	Science Fiction	F	16	249			
1974															
The Chocolate War Robert Cormier	Pantheon	J	Dell	•	•	•		•	Realistic Fiction	M	14	253			
House of Stairs William Sleator	Dutton	J	Avon	•	•	•		•	Science Fiction	M/F	teens	166			
If Beale Street Could Talk James Baldwin	Dial	A	NAL	•				•	Realistic Fiction	F	19	197			Black
M. C. Higgins, the Great Virginia Hamilton	Macmillan	J	Dell	•	•	•			Realistic Fiction	M	13	278			Black
Watership Down Richard Adams	Macmillan	A	Avon	•	•	•		•	Fantasy	M	—	429		•	
1973															
A Day No Pigs Would Die Robert Newton Peck	Knopf	J	Dell	•	•	•		•	Historical Fiction	M	13	159			

Title / Author	Publisher	Level	Paperback							Genre	Sex	Age	Pages		Group
The Friends — Rosa Guy	Holt	J	Bantam				•	•	•	Realistic Fiction	F	14	203		West Indian Black
A Hero Ain't Nothin' But a Sandwich — Alice Childress	Coward, McCann	J	Avon			•	•	•	•	Realistic Fiction	M	13	126		Black
The Slave Dancer — Paula Fox	Bradbury	J	Dell			•	•	•	•	Historical Fiction	M	13	176		Black
Summer of My German Soldier — Bette Greene	Dial	J	Bantam				•	•	•	Historical Fiction	F	14	199	•	Jewish
1972															
Deathwatch — Robb White	Doubleday	J	Dell		•	•	•	•	•	Suspense Fiction	M	early 20s	228		
Dinky Hocker Shoots Smack! — M. E. Kerr	Harper & Row	J	Dell		•	•	•	•	•	Humor Realistic Fiction	F	16	198	•	
Dove — Robin L. Graham	Harper & Row	A	Bantam			•	•	•	•	Non-Fiction	M	16	199	•	
The Man Without a Face — Isabelle Holland	Lippincott	J	Bantam		•	•	•	•	•	Realistic Fiction	M	16	248		
My Name Is Asher Lev — Chaim Potok	Knopf	A	Fawcett		•	•	•	•	•	Realistic Fiction	M	early 20s	369		Jewish
Report from Engine Co. 82 — Dennis E. Smith	McCall	A			•		•	•	•	New Journalism	M	20s 30s	215		
Soul Catcher — Frank Herbert	Putnam	A	Berkley		•		•	•	•	Suspense Fiction	M	early 20s	250		Native American
Sticks and Stones — Lynn Hall	Follett	J	Dell		•		•	•	•	Realistic Fiction	M	16	220		
Teacup Full of Roses — Sharon Bell Mathis	Viking	J	Avon		•		•	•	•	Realistic Fiction	M	17	125		Black
1971															
The Autobiography of Miss Jane Pittman — Ernest Gaines	Dial	A	Bantam		•		•	•	•	Historical Fiction	F	life-time	245	•	Black
The Bell Jar — Sylvia Plath	Harper & Row	A	Bantam		•		•	•	•	Realistic Fiction	F	19	296	•	Black

Title and Author	Hardbound Publisher	Publishing Division	Paperback Publisher	ALA	SLJ	EJ	NYT	Ad. Lit. Prof.	Genre	Protagonist Sex	Age	Number of Pages	TV	Movie	Ethnic Group
Go Ask Alice / Anonymous	Prentice-Hall	J	Avon	•					Nonfiction	F	16	159	•		
His Own Where / June Jordan	Crowell	J	Dell	•	•	•	•		Realistic Fiction	M/F	15	89			Black
Wild in the World / John Donovan	Harper & Row	J	Avon	•	•	•	•	•	Realistic Fiction	M	17	94			Rural Isolated
1970															
Bless the Beasts and Children / Glendon Swarthout	Doubleday	A	Pocket Books	•	•	•			Realistic Fiction	M	young teens	205		•	
I Know Why the Caged Bird Sings / Maya Angelou	Random House	A	Bantam	•	•	•		•	Biography	F	childhood	281		•	Black
Love Story / Erich Segal	Harper & Row	A	Avon	•	•	•		•	Realistic Fiction	M/F	early 20s	131			
Run Softly, Go Fast / Barbara Wersba	Atheneum	J	Bantam	•	•	•		•	Realistic Fiction	M	19	169			
1969															
I'll Get There. It Better Be Worth the Trip / John Donovan	Harper & Row	J		•	•	•	•	•	Realistic Fiction	M	13	189			
My Darling, My Hamburger / Paul Zindel	Harper & Row	J	Bantam	•	•	•		•	Realistic Fiction	M/F	17/18	168			
Sounder / William H. Armstrong	Harper & Row	J	Harper & Row	•	•	•	•	•	Historical Fiction	M	14	116		•	Rural Black
Where the Lilies Bloom / Vera and Bill Cleaver	Lippincott	J	NAL	•	•	•	•	•	Realistic Fiction	F	14	174		•	Isolated Rural

1968

Title / Author	Publisher	J/A	Genre	M/F	Age	Pages	Setting/Group
The Pigman Paul Zindel	Harper & Row	J	Realistic Fiction	M/F	16	182	
Red Sky at Morning Richard Bradford	Lippincott	A	Realistic Fiction	M	17	256	Mexican American
Soul on Ice Eldridge Cleaver	McGraw-Hill	A	New Journalism	M	20s	210	Black
True Grit Charles Portis	Simon & Schuster	A	Historical Fiction	F	14	215	1880s Arkansas

1967

Title / Author	Publisher	J/A	Genre	M/F	Age	Pages	Setting/Group
The Chosen Chaim Potok	Simon & Schuster	A	Realistic Fiction	M	teen	284	Jewish
Mr. and Mrs. Bo Jo Jones Ann Head	Putnam NAL Signet	A	Realistic Fiction	F	18	253	
The Outsiders S. E. Hinton	Viking	J	Realistic Fiction	M	14	156	
Reflections on a Gift of Watermelon Pickle Stephen Dunning and others	Scott, Foresman	J	Poetry	M/F	mixed	160	

BOOK SELECTION GUIDES

The sources listed below are designed to aid professionals in the selection and evaluation of books and other materials for young adults. An attempt was made to include sources with widely varying emphases. However, in addition to these sources—most of which appear at regular intervals—many specialized lists are prepared by committees and individuals in response to current and/or local needs. Readers are advised to check on the availability of such lists with librarians and teachers. For purposes of comparison, the 1984 prices are included, but readers should expect that many of them will have risen because of inflation.

The ALAN Review. Assembly on Literature for Adolescents, National Council of Teachers of English $10.00 for three issues. Order from William Subick, NCTE, 1111 Kenyon Rd., Urbana, IL 61801.

> This publication has appeared three times a year since 1973. It is currently edited by Arthea (Charlie) Reed of the University of North Carolina and is unique in being devoted entirely to adolescent literature. Each issue contains "Clip and File" reviews of approximately twenty new hardbacks or paperbacks and includes two or three feature articles, news announcements, and occasional reviews of professional books.

Book Bait: Detailed Notes on Adult Books Popular with Young People. Ed. Eleanor Walker. 3rd ed., 1979. $5.00
American Library Association, 50 E. Huron Street, Chicago, IL 60611.

> A useful bibliography for bridging the gap between young adult and adult novels, this listing contains one hundred books with extensive annotations that include plot summaries, discussions of appeal to teenagers, hints for book talks, and suggested titles for use as follow-ups. Arrangement is alphabetical by author; subject and title indexes are appended.

Booklist. American Library Assocation, 50 E. Huron St., Chicago, IL 60611. $40.00 for twenty-three issues.

> The size of the reviews varies from twenty-word annotations to three-hundred-word essays. "Books for Young Adults" (ages fourteen through eighteen) is a regular feature. Occasionally, books in both the children's and adult sections are

also marked YA. A review constitutes a recommendation for library purchase. Stars are given to books of high literary quality. Multimedia materials are also reviewed and a special section highlights books that have both a high interest potential for teenagers and a lower-than-average reading level. An early spring issue includes the annual "Best Books for Young Adults" list drawn up by the ALA Young Adult Services Division.

Books for the Teen Age: 1984. Ed. Office of Young Adult Services. $5.00 per copy. New York Public Library, Fifth Ave. and 42nd St., Rm. 58, New York, NY 10018.

This sixty-four-page guide with minimal annotations is updated yearly and is thus an outstanding source of current titles which have been "tested and tried with teen age readers." Grouping is by subject; title and author indexes are included.

Books for You: A Booklist for Senior High Students. Ed. Robert C. Small, Jr. Rev. ed., 1982. National Council of Teachers of English, 1111 Kenyon Rd., Urbana, IL 61801. $6.75.

Nearly 1,400 books are listed and described in this bibliography intended to help students find "pleasurable reading." Annotations consist of one or two sentence summaries. "Frank" or "Offensive" language is noted, as are additional titles of similar interest and appeal. Titles are grouped by subject or theme; title and author indexes are appended. The book is prepared by an ongoing committee in NCTE with a new edition appearing every six or seven years. Don Gallo of Central Connecticut State College is editing the next edition. Since all books in this edition appeared between the beginning of 1976 and 1982, the 1976 edition of *Books for You* is worth holding onto for the information it has on earlier books.

Bulletin of the Center for Children's Books. Ed. Zena Sutherland. The University of Chicago Graduate Library School, University of Chicago Press, 5801 S. Ellis Ave., Chicago, IL 60637. $22.00 yearly.

This monthly (except August) journal reviews approximately sixty new books for children and young adults each issue. Though there is a time lag between the publication date and the appearance of a review, the *Bulletin* includes both recommended and not recommended titles. Since it is under the editorship of a single individual, the consistency of the reviews can be depended upon. Listed on the back cover are books, articles, and bibliographies of current interest to teachers, parents, and librarians.

Children's Literature in Education: An International Quarterly. Agathon Press, Inc., 49 Sheridan Avenue, Albany, NY 12210. Individuals, $13.50 per year, institutions, $22.50.

Directed by a United Kingdom Editorial Committee and a United States Editor (currently Anita Moss from the University of North Carolina at Charlotte) and Editorial Board, this quarterly journal is one of the best sources for scholarly criticism. The editors show a preference for substantive analysis rather than pedagogical advice or quick once-overs. A goodly proportion of the articles are about YA authors and their works.

English Journal. National Council of Teachers of English, 1111 Kenyon Rd., Urbana, IL 61801. $30.00 for eight issues, which includes membership in NCTE.

> Aimed at high school English teachers, nearly every issue contains something about new books of interest to teenage readers. Reviews, articles about young adult literature in the classroom, interviews with successful authors, and a yearly "Young Adult Book Poll" are among the regular features.

High Interest–Easy Reading for Junior and Senior High School Students. Ed. Marian E. White. 3rd ed., 1979. National Council of Teachers of English, 1111 Kenyon Rd., Urbana, IL 61801. $3.85.

> Grouped by subject, this listing is aimed at reluctant young adult readers rather than at parents or teachers. Criteria for inclusion are high interest, easy reading, and literary quality. The annotations are written in the form of miniature book talks; author and title indexes are appended.

Horn Book Magazine. The Horn Book, Inc., Park Square Building, 31 St. James Avenue, Boston, MA 02116. $23.00 for six issues.

> This magazine has been devoted to the critical analysis of children's literature since 1924. Reviews are approximately two hundred words long and in a typical issue seven or eight adolescent novels will be reviewed under the heading of "Stories for Older Readers." "Outlook Tower" highlights current adult books of interest to high school readers. Popular appeal takes a back seat to literary quality in the selection of titles for review. Feature articles are frequently of interest to teachers and librarians working with young adults.

Interracial Books for Children Bulletin. Council on Interracial Books for Children, 1841 Broadway, New York, NY 10023. Institutions $15.00, individuals $10.00 for eight issues.

> Nearly all reviews and articles in this twenty-five page bulletin are written for the purpose of examining the relationship between social issues and how these are treated or reflected in current fiction, nonfiction, and curriculum materials.

Journal of Reading. International Reading Association, Box 8139, Newark, DE 19711. $25.00 for nine issues, which includes membership in The International Reading Association.

> The audience for this journal is high school reading teachers. Although most of the articles are reports on research in the teaching of reading, some articles focus on reading interests and literature. Also included are reviews of new young adult books written by association members.

Junior High School Library Catalog. Eds. Richard H. Isaacson and Gary L. Bogart. 4th ed. H. W. Wilson Company, 950 University Ave., Bronx, NY 10452. $62.00.

> Designed as a suggested basic book collection for junior high school libraries, this volume is divided into two major parts. The first includes an annotated listing by Dewey Decimal Number for nonfiction, author's last name for fiction, and author's/editor's last name for story collections. The second part relists all

books alphabetically by author, title, and subject. Cumulated every five years with yearly supplements, this is an outstanding reference tool for junior high school librarians.

Kirkus Reviews. Kirkus Service, Inc., 200 Park Avenue South, New York, NY 10003. $185.00.

Although this is one of the most expensive sources, it is also one of the most complete and up-to-date. Reviews are approximately two hundred words long, and a section is devoted to young adult books.

Kliatt Paperbook Book Guide. 425 Watertown St., Newton, MA 02158. $27.00 for three issues with five interim supplements.

Because teenagers prefer to read paperbacks, this source serves a real need. It attempts to review all paperbacks (originals, reprints, and reissues) recommended for readers ages twelve through nineteen. A code identifies books as appropriate for advanced students, general young adult readers, junior high students, students with low reading abilities, and emotionally mature readers who can handle "explicit sex, excessive violence and/or obscenity." Reviews are arranged by subject. A title index and a directory of cooperating publishers are included.

New York Times Book Review. New York Times Co., 229 W. 43rd St., New York, NY 10036. 52 issues, $22.00.

The currency of the reviews makes this an especially valuable source. Most weeks there is a section featuring children's books, many of which are suitable for teenagers. Of special interest are a fall and spring issue devoted almost exclusively to children's books—the fall issue usually includes a roundup of the "best books" of the year. Editor George A. Woods has a good record for predicting the popularity of books.

Reading Ladders for Human Relations. Ed. Eileen Tway. 6th ed., 1981. American Council on Education and National Council of Teachers of English, 1111 Kenyon Rd., Urbana, IL 61801. $9.95.

This 398-page bibliography, ranging from picture books to mature novels, is of particular use to the young adult specialist because it focuses on five categories of interest to junior and senior high school readers: Growing into Self, Relating to Wide Individual Differences, Interacting in Groups, Appreciating Different Cultures, and Coping in a Changing World. Junior, senior, and mature books are listed separately within these categories. Annotations are written with an eye toward the human relations aspect of each book. Author and title indexes are appended; the introductory section addresses various topics relating to young people and books.

School Library Journal. R. R. Bowker Company, 1180 Avenue of the Americas, New York, NY 10036. $38.00.

The most comprehensive of the review media, *SLJ* reviews both recommended and not recommended books. Reviews are written by a panel of four hundred librarians who are sent books particularly appropriate to their interests and backgrounds. Starred reviews signify exceptionally good books. Books of interest to teenagers will appear in the children's listings identified by grade levels (5–up, 6–8, 9–12, etc.) if they come from the juvenile division of a publisher or in a special young adult listing if they come from the adult division of a publisher.

Senior High School Library Catalog. Ed. Gary L. Bogart. 12th ed. H. W. Wilson Company, 950 University Ave., Bronx, NY 10452. $70.00.

Using the same format as the *Junior High School Library Catalog* (see above), this lists some books appropriate for both junior and senior high school collections as well as those aimed specifically at readers in grades ten through twelve. Like its companion volume, it is cumulated every five years with yearly supplements and is an invaluable aid for anyone involved in the building of a high-school library collection.

Top of the News. Joint publication of the Association for Library Service to Children and the Young Adult Services Division of the American Library Association, 50 E. Huron St., Chicago, IL 60611. Included in the dues of ALSC and YASD members; nonmembers pay $15.00 for four issues.

Although the journal does not have room to review juvenile books on a regular basis, feature articles are often of interest to young adult librarians. Also of interest is the "Added Entries" column in which professional publications are reviewed.

Voice of Youth Advocates (VOYA). Ed. Dorothy M. Broderick and Mary K. Chelton. P.O. Box 6569, University, AL 35486. $16.50 for six issues.

One of the aims of this publication, founded in 1978, is "to change the traditional linking of young adult services with children's librarianship and shift the focus to its connection with adult services." Feature articles are especially good because they present viewpoints not commonly considered. About one-fourth of the journal is devoted to reviews in the following categories: pamphlets, mysteries, science-fiction, audiovisual, adult and teenage fiction and nonfiction, and professional books.

Wilson Library Bulletin. H. W. Wilson Co., 1950 University Avenue, Bronx, NY 19452. $14.00 for ten issues.

Although the focus of the *Wilson Library Bulletin* is much broader than young adult librarianship, "The Young Adult Perplex," edited by Patty Campbell, is a regular feature that reviews current books. "Cine-Opsis," edited by Jana Varlejs, is also helpful in reviewing media of interest to young adults.

Your Reading: A Booklist for Junior High and Middle School Students. Ed. Jane Christensen (1984). National Council of Teachers of English, 1111 Kenyon Rd., Urbana, IL 61801. $12.00.

Over 3,000 books published since 1975 are described in this new edition compiled by the Committee on the Junior High and Middle School Booklist. The book is designed for student use, and the annotations are written to capture student interest. Categories of books range from adventure stories to the supernatural and include books about youngsters dealing with physical handicaps, emotional problems, and the death of a parent or friend. Nonfiction books include biography, fine arts, history, hobbies and crafts, sciences, and sports. Author and title indexes and a directory of publishers are provided.

SOME OUTSTANDING BOOKS AND ARTICLES ABOUT YOUNG ADULT LITERATURE

The list below represents our personal choices. We followed the ground rules of the first edition, and that may explain, if not justify, why some works were included or excluded.

1. Books or articles were primarily on young adult literature, not on the psychology of the young, cultural milieu, literary history, or literary criticism. If we had wanted to include the last, we'd have chosen Eudora Welty's *The Eye of the Story* and left it at that. Since we didn't, we won't.

2. Books or articles had to cover more than just one author. No matter how good the articles were on Virginia Hamilton or Alan Garner or Judy Blume (and some were very good indeed), we ignored them in favor of articles with wider implications.

3. Books or articles had to excite us. No doubt some readers will find us culpable for our tastes in including this or ignoring that. So be it.

4. No books or articles were included to fit into some category otherwise ignored. We make no claims that the list below is balanced to have the proper number of this or that kind of book or article, whether it would be on censorship or minority literature or feminist literature. We chose what we did because we believed in them.

5. No books or articles by Nilsen or Donelson appear below. Readers may continue to assume either that we believe none of our work belongs under the rubric "outstanding" or that we are modest to a fault.

◆ **BOOKS** ◆

Histories of Young Adult Literature

Avery, Gillian. *Childhood's Pattern: A Study of the Heroes and Heroines of Children's Fiction 1770–1950*. London: Hodder and Stoughton, 1975.

Bingham, Jane and Grayce Scholt. *Fifteen Centuries of Children's Literature: An Annotated Chronology of British and American Works in Historical Context*. Westport, CT: Greenwood Press, 1980.

Bratton, J. S. *The Impact of Victorian Children's Fiction*. London: Croom Helm, 1981; Totowa, New Jersey: Barnes and Noble, 1981.

Cadogan, Mary and Patricia Craig. *You're a Brick, Angela! A New Look at Girls' Fiction from 1839 to 1975*. London: Victor Gollancz, 1976. A delightful and witty view of girl's books and social history.

Campbell, Patricia J. *Sex Education Books for Young Adults, 1892–1979*. New York: R. R. Bowker, 1979. Accurate, critical, and often very funny.

Crouch, Marcus. *The Nesbit Tradition: The Children's Novel in England 1945–1970*. London: Ernest Benn, 1972.

————. *Treasure Seekers and Borrowers: Children's Books in Britain 1900–1960*. London: Library Association, 1962.

Darling, Richard. *The Rise of Children's Book Reviewing in America, 1865–1881*. New York: R. R. Bowker, 1968. Impressive and scholarly study of early children's and YA books, book reviewing, and reviewers.

Darton, F. J. Harvey. *Children's Books in England: Five Centuries of Social Use*, 2nd ed. Cambridge: Cambridge University Press, 1958. First published in 1932 and still a basic source.

Ellis, Alec. *A History of Children's Reading and Literature*. Oxford: Pergamon Press, 1968. Children's and YA books from 1740 to 1965.

Eyre, Frank. *British Children's Books in the Twentieth Century*. New York: E. P. Dutton, 1973.

Fraser, James H., ed. *Society and Children's Literature* (papers from the 1976 Simmons College School of Library Science Symposium). Boston: David R. Godine, 1978. Especially good are papers by Anne Scott MacLeod, R. Gordon Kelly, and Fred Erisman.

Girls' Series Books: A Checklist of Hardback Books Published 1900–1975. Minneapolis: Children's Literature Research Collections, University of Minnesota Library, 1978. Not as thorough as Hudson (see below) but most helpful in working with series books.

Howarth, Patrick. *Play Up and Play the Game: The Heroes of Popular Fiction*. London: Eyre Methuen, 1973. On nineteenth-century popular boys' books.

Hudson, Harry K. *A Bibliography of Hard-Cover Boys' Books*, rev. ed. Tampa, FL: Data Print, 1977. An outstanding checklist of boys' series books, mostly of this century.

Kiefer, Monica. *American Children through Their Books, 1700–1835*. Philadelphia: University of Pennsylvania Press, 1948.

Kilgour, Raymond L. *Lee & Shepard: Publishers for the People*. Hamden, CT: Shoe String Press, 1965. A history of a major publisher of boys' series books in the nineteenth and twentieth centuries.

MacLeod, Anne Scott. *A Moral Tale: Children's Fiction and American Culture, 1820–1860*. Hamden, CT: Archon Books, 1975.

Mason, Bobbie Ann. *The Girl Sleuth: A Feminist Guide*. Old Westbury, NY: Feminist Press, 1975. Perceptive and witty comments about girls' series books, especially Nancy Drew.

Meigs, Cornelia, et al. *A Critical History of Children's Literature*, rev. ed. New York: Macmillan, 1969. An encyclopedic study of children's literature, often including YA books, from ancient times onward.

Sloane, William. *Children's Books in England and America in the Seventeenth Century*. New York: Columbia University Press, 1955.

Thwaite, Mary E. *From Primer to Pleasure: An Introduction to the History of Children's Books in England from the Invention of Printing to 1914 with an Outline of Some Developments in Other Countries*. Boston: Horn Book, 1972. First published in England in 1963.

Townsend, John Rowe. *Written for Children: An Outline of English-Language Children's Liter-*

Brief annotations are given for works where titles are not self-explanatory.

ature, rev. ed. Philadelphia: Lippincott, 1983. The most readable history, albeit more English than American.

Criticism of Young Adult Literature

Broderick, Dorothy M. *Images of the Black in Children's Fiction*. New York: R. R. Bowker, 1973. Racism and YA literature.

Chambers, Aidan. *The Reluctant Reader*. London: Pergamon Press, 1969. One of the great books about YA literature. Sympathetic and helpful ideas about bringing books to the hard-to-get-to reader.

Children's Literature Review. Detroit: Gale Research Company, 1976. A continuing series and a basic source of material.

Contemporary Literary Criticism. Detroit: Gale Research Company, 1973. A continuing series with essential source material.

Dixon, Bob. *Catching Them Young: Political Ideas in Children's Fiction*. London: Pluto Press, 1977.

————. *Catching Them Young: Sex, Race and Class in Children's Fiction*. London: Pluto Press, 1977.

Egoff, Sheila A. *Thursday's Child: Trends and Patterns in Contemporary Children's Literature*. Chicago: American Library Association, 1981. Without qualification, the most important book in the field in the last fifteen years.

Hazard, Paul. *Books, Children and Men*. Trans. Marguerite Mitchell. Boston: Horn Book, 1944. Nominally about children and literature but really about readers of any kind at any age with clear implications for young adults.

Hearne, Betsy and Marilyn Kaye, eds. *Celebrating Children's Books: Essays on Children's Literature in Honor of Zena Sutherland*. New York: Lothrop, Lee and Shepard, 1981. Papers by Lloyd Alexander, Robert Cormier, Virginia Hamilton, John Donovan, John Rowe Townsend, David Macaulay, and others.

Inglis, Fred. *The Promise of Happiness: Value and Meaning in Children's Fiction*. Cambridge: Cambridge University Press, 1981.

Lukens, Rebecca. *A Critical Handbook of Children's Literature*. Glenview, IL: Scott, Foresman, 1976. Criteria and aspects of children's literature easily applicable to YA literature.

MacCann, Donnarae and Gloria Woodward, eds. *The Black American in Books for Children: Readings on Racism*. Metuchen, NJ: Scarecrow Press, 1972.

Probst, Robert. *Adolescent Literature: Response and Analysis*. Columbus, OH: Charles E. Merrill, 1984. Outstanding discussions of reader response and literary analysis.

Salmon, Edward. *Juvenile Literature as It Is*. London: Henry J. Drane, 1888. Sympathetic and forward-looking views on the values of children's and YA literature. Undeservedly neglected.

Sloan, Glenna Davis. *The Child as Critic*. New York: Teachers College Press, 1975. Application of Northrop Frye's critical theories to children's and YA literature.

Stanford, Barbara Dodds and Karima Amin, eds. *Black Literature for High School Students*. Urbana, IL: National Council of Teachers of English, 1978.

Stensland, Anna Lee. *Literature by and About the American Indian: An Annotated Bibliography*, 2nd ed. Urbana, IL: National Council of Teachers of English, 1979.

Sutherland, Zena, ed. *The Arbuthnot Lectures, 1970–1979*. Chicago: American Library Association, 1980. Talks by John Rowe Townsend, Ivan Southall, Jean Fritz, and Sheila Egoff, among others.

Libraries and Young Adult Literature

Bodart, Joni. *Booktalk! Booktalking and School Visiting for Young Adult Audiences*. New York: H. W. Wilson, 1980.

Carrier, Esther Jane. *Fiction in Public Libraries, 1876–1900*. New York: Scarecrow Press, 1965. The "fiction question" and YA literature.

Edwards, Margaret A. *The Fair Garden and the Swarm of Beasts: The Library and the Young Adult*, rev. ed. New York: Hawthorn, 1974. The problems and joys of being a YA librarian.

Marshall, Margaret R. *Libraries and Literature for Teenagers*. London: Andre Deutsch, 1975.

English Classrooms and Young Adult Literature

Burton, Dwight L. *Literature Study in the High Schools*, 3rd ed. New York: Holt, 1970. For many English teachers, *the* book that introduced them to YA literature.

Carlsen, G. Robert. *Books and the Teen-Age Reader*, 2nd ed. New York: Harper & Row, 1980.

Fader, Daniel. *The New Hooked on Books*. New York: Berkley, 1976. First published in 1966 as *Hooked on Books* and revised in 1968, Fader's book probably led more English teachers to take YA books seriously than any other source.

Reed, Arthea J. S. *Reaching Adolescents: The Young Adult and the School*. New York: Holt, Rinehart and Winston, 1984.

Sample, Hazel. *Pitfalls for Readers of Fiction*. Chicago: National Council of Teachers of English, 1940. Too little known, unfortunately, since it has many insights into reading popular fiction and the dangers thereof.

"Young Adult Literature," entire issue of the November 1984 *English Journal*. Especially good for articles by G. Robert Carlsen, Don Gallo, Ellen Kolba, and Janice Hartwick Dressel.

Authors of Young Adult Literature

Cech, John, ed. *American Writers for Children, 1900–1960. Dictionary of Literary Biography*, Volume Twenty-Two. Detroit: Gale Research Company, 1983.

Commire, Anne, ed. *Something About the Author*. Detroit: Gale Research Company, 1971. A continuing series about many authors, their lives and their books. An indispensable source of help.

_____. *Yesterday's Authors of Books for Children*. Detroit: Gale Research Company, 1977. Authors who died prior to 1961. Extremely useful.

Haviland, Virginia, ed. *The Openhearted Audience: Ten Authors Talk About Writing for Children*. Washington, DC: Library of Congress, 1980. Talks by Joan Aiken, Ivan Southall, Virginia Hamilton, and others.

Jones, Cornelia and Olivia R. Way. *British Children's Authors: Interviews at Home*. Chicago: American Library Association, 1976. Interviews with Nina Bawden, Alan Garner, Allan Campbell McLean, K. M. Peyton, Rosemary Sutcliff, Barbara Willard, and others.

Kirkpatrick, D. L., ed. *Twentieth-Century Children's Writers*. New York: St. Martin's Press,

1978. A mammoth (1507 page) index of authors listing biographical and bibliographical details along with critical assessments.

Rees, David. *The Marble in the Water: Essays on Contemporary Writers of Fiction for Children and Young Adults*. Boston: Horn Book, 1980. Essays on Penelope Farmer, Alan Garner, Ursula Le Guin, Mildred Taylor, and others.

Sarkissian, Adele, ed. *Writers for Young Adults: Biographies Master Index*. Detroit: Gale Research Company, 1984. A handy help in locating information about YA authors.

Townsend, John Rowe. *A Sense of Story: Essays on Contemporary Writers for Children*. Philadelphia: Lippincott, 1971. Essays on John Christopher, Paula Fox, Leon Garfield, Scott O'Dell, K. M. Peyton, Patricia Wrightson, and others.

Weiss, M. Jerry, ed. *From Writers to Students: The Pleasures and Pains of Writing*. Newark, DE: International Reading Association, 1979. Interviews with Judy Blume, Vera and Bill Cleaver, Mollie Hunter, M. E. Kerr, Norma and Harry Mazer, Laurence Yep, and others.

Wintle, Justin and Emma Fisher, eds. *The Pied Pipers: Interviews with the Influential Creators of Children's Literature*. New York: Paddington Press, 1974. Interviews with Scott O'Dell, Leon Garfield, Judy Blume, Lloyd Alexander, Alan Garner, K. M. Peyton, and others.

Books of Readings About Young Adult Literature

Egoff, Sheila, G. T. Stubbs, and L. F. Ashley, eds. *Only Connect: Readings in Children's Literature*, 2nd ed. New York: Oxford University Press, 1980. Significant articles by Edward W. Rosenheim, John Rowe Townsend, Donnarae MacCann, C. S. Lewis, Rosemary Sutcliff, and others.

Fox, Geoff, et al., eds. *Writers, Critics, and Children: Articles from Children's Literature in Education*. New York: Agathon Press, 1976. Articles from an important journal by Nina Bawden, Peter Dickinson, Myles McDowell, Edward Blishen, and others.

Haviland, Virginia, ed. *Children and Literature: Views and Reviews*. Glenview, IL: Scott,

Foresman, 1973. Articles by Hester Burton, Frank Eyre, Peter Dickinson, Sylvia Engdahl, and others.

Salway, Lance, ed. *A Peculiar Gift: Nineteenth Century Writings on Books for Children.* London: Kestrel, 1976. Articles and excerpts from books about children's and YA British literature from authors such as Edward Salmon and Joseph Conrad.

Varlejs, Jana, ed. *Young Adult Literature in the Seventies: A Selection of Readings.* Metuchen, NJ: Scarecrow Press, 1978. Articles by G. Robert Carlsen, Dorothy Broderick, Mary Chelton, Linda Lapides, Lou Willett Stanek, and others.

◆ PERIODICALS ◆

History and Young Adult Literature

Ashford, Richard K. "Tomboys and Saints: Girls' Stories of the Late Nineteenth Century." *School Library Journal* 26 (January 1980): 23–38.

Cantwell, Robert. "A Sneering Laugh with the Bases Loaded." *Sports Illustrated* 16 (April 23, 1962): 67–70, 73–76. Baseball novels for boys—especially novels by Barbour and Heyliger.

Carlsen, G. Robert. "Forty Years with Books and Teen-Age Readers." *Arizona English Bulletin* 18 (April 1976): 1–5. From 1939 to 1976 in YA literature.

Crandall, John C. "Patriotism and Humanitarian Reform in Children's Literature, 1825–1860." *American Quarterly* 21 (Spring 1969): 3–22. An excellent overview of children's and YA books and periodicals before Alcott.

Edwards, Margaret A. "The Rise of Teen-Age Reading." *Saturday Review of Literature* 37 (November 13, 1954): 88–89, 95. The state of YA literature in the 1930s and 1940s and what it led to.

Evans, Walter. "The All-American Boys: A Study of Boys' Sports Fiction." *Journal of Popular Culture* 6 (Summer 1972): 104–21. Formulas underlying boys' school sports books, notably Barbour and series books.

"For It Was Indeed He." *Fortune* 9 (April 1934): 86–89, 193–94, 204, 206, 208–9. An important, influential, and biased article on Stratemeyer's Literary Syndicate.

Geller, Evelyn. "The Librarian as Censor." *Library Journal* 101 (June 1, 1976): 1255–58. Social control as censorship in late nineteenth-century library selection.

————. "Tom Sawyer, Tom Bailey, and the Bad-Boy Genre." *Wilson Library Bulletin* 51 (November 1976): 245–50.

Hutchinson, Margaret. "Fifty Years of Young Adult Reading, 1921–1971." *Top of the News* 29 (November 1973): 24–53. A "survey (of) the field of young adult reading for the last fifty years by examining articles indexed in *Library Literature* from its inception in 1921." Admirable.

Lapides, Linda F. "A Decade of Teen-Age Reading in Baltimore, 1960–1970." *Top of the News* 27 (April 1971): 278–91. YA favorites over ten years.

Kelly, R. Gordon. "American Children's Literature: An Historiographical Review." *American Literary Realism, 1870–1910* 6 (Spring 1973): 89–107.

Morrison, Lillian, "Fifty Years of 'Books for the Teen Age.'" *School Library Journal* 26 (December 1979): 44–50.

Radner, Rebecca. "You're Being Paged Loudly in the Kitchen: Teen-Age Literature of the Forties and Fifties." *Journal of Popular Culture* 11 (Spring 1978): 789–99. Ways in which Maureen Daly and other YA novelists of the 1940s influenced young women, not always for the best.

Repplier, Agnes. "Little Pharisees in Fiction." *Scribner's Magazine* 20 (December 1896): 718–24. Assessment of the didactic and embarrassingly joyless tone of the "goody-goody" girls' school of fiction.

Trensky, Anne. "The Bad Boy in Nineteenth-Century American Fiction." *Georgia Review* 27 (Winter 1973): 503–17.

Vostrovsky, Clara. "A Study of Children's Reading Tastes." *Pedagogical Seminary* 6 (December 1899): 523–35. A pioneer effort at a statistical account of the kinds of books young people read.

Criticism and Young Adult Literature

Abrahamson, Jane. "Still Playing It Safe: Restricted Realism in Teen Novels." *School Library Journal* 22 (May 1976): 38–39.

Brewbaker, James M. "Are You There, Margaret? It's Me, God—Religious Contexts in Recent Adolescent Fiction." *English Journal* 72 (September 1983): 82–86.

Burton, Hester. "The Writing of Historical Novels." *Horn Book Magazine* 45 (June 1969): 271–77.

Carlsen, G. Robert. "For Everything There Is a Season." *Top of the News* 21 (January 1965): 103–10. Stages in reading growth and reading tastes.

————. "The Interest Rate Is Rising." *English Journal* 59 (May 1970): 655–59. YA literature, the nature of literature, and the reality of YA readers.

Davis, James E. "Recent Trends in Fiction for Adolescents." *English Journal* 56 (May 1967): 720–24.

Early, Margaret J. "Stages of Growth in Literary Appreciation." *English Journal* 49 (March 1960): 161–67. A seminal article.

Edwards, Margaret A. "A Time When It's Best to Read and Let Read." *Wilson Library Bulletin* 35 (September 1960): 43–47. Myths of buying books for young adults demolished.

Engdahl, Sylvia. "Do Teenage Novels Fill a Need?" *English Journal* 64 (February 1975): 48–52. Justification and criteria for the best YA novels.

Green, Samuel S. "Sensational Fiction in Public Libraries." *Library Journal* 4 (September-October 1879): 345–55. All the usual warnings about dime novels and other sensational fiction coupled with some extraordinary forward-looking and intelligent comments about young adults and books. The entire issue for September-October is worth reading, especially for T. W. Higginson's "Address," pp. 357–59, William P. Atkinson's "Address," pp. 359–62, and Mellen Chamberlain's "Address," pp. 362–66.

Hanckel, Frances and John Cunningham. "Can Young Gays Find Happiness in YA Books?" *Wilson Library Bulletin* 50 (March 1976): 528–34. An argument for more authenticity and less preachiness in YA books about gays.

Hentoff, Nat. "Fiction for Teen-Agers." *Wilson Library Bulletin* 43 (November 1968): 261–64. Worries about the shortcomings of YA fiction.

————. "Tell It as Is." *New York Times Book Review*, May 7, 1967, pp. 3, 51.

Hinton, Susan. "Teen-Agers Are for Real." *New York Times Book Review*, August 27, 1967, pp. 26–29. Brief and excellent, "must" reading.

Hipps, G. Melvin. "Adolescent Literature: Once More to the Defense." *Virginia English Bulletin* 23 (Spring 1973): 44–50. One of the most intelligent arguments for YA books.

Janeczko, Paul B. "Seven Myths About Adolescent Literature." *Arizona English Bulletin* 18 (April 1976): 11–12.

Kraus, W. Keith. "Cinderella in Trouble: Still Dreaming and Losing." *School Library Journal* 21 (January 1975): 18–22. Pregnancy in YA novels from Felsen's *Two and the Town* (1952) to Neufeld's *For All the Wrong Reasons* (1973).

————. "From Steppin' Stebbins to Soul Brothers: Racial Strife in Adolescent Literature." *Arizona English Bulletin* 18 (April 1976): 154–60.

Martinec, Barbara. "Popular—But Not Just a Part of the Crowd: Implications of Formula Fiction for Teenagers." *English Journal* 60 (March 1971): 339–44. Formulaic elements in six YA novelists. Provocative.

Matthews, Dorothy. "An Adolescent's Glimpse of the Faces of Eve: A Study of the Images of Women in Selected Popular Junior Novels." *Illinois English Bulletin* 60 (May 1973): 1–14.

————. "Writing About Adolescent Literature: Current Approaches and Future Directions." *Arizona English Bulletin* 18 (April 1976): 216–19.

McDowell, Myles. "Fiction for Children and Adults: Some Essential Differences." *Children's Literature in Education* 4 (March 1973): 48–63.

Meltzer, Milton, "Where Do All the Prizes Go? The Case for Nonfiction." *Horn Book Magazine* 52 (February 1976): 17–23.

Merla, Patrick. " 'What Is Real?' Asked the Rabbit One Day." *Saturday Review* 55 (November 4,

1972): 43–49. The rise of YA realism and adult fantasy.

Mertz, Maia Pank and David A. England. "The Legitimacy of American Adolescent Fiction." *School Library Journal* 30 (October 1983): 119–23.

Neufeld, John. "The Thought, Not Necessarily the Deed: Sex in Some of Today's Juvenile Novels." *Wilson Library Bulletin* 46 (October 1971): 147–52. Urges that YA novels need the "whole kid," sex, warts, and dirty jokes as well as naiveté and freedom.

Peck, Richard. "In the Country of Teenage Fiction." *American Libraries* 4 (April 1973): 204–7. Concerns about YA needs and YA books.

————. "Some Thoughts on Adolescent Literature." *News from ALAN* 3 (September-October 1975): 4–7. The "discernible traits" of YA novels.

Pollack, Pamela D. "The Business of Popularity: The Surge of Teenage Paperbacks." *School Library Journal* 28 (November 1981): 25–28. Changes in paperback practices, especially the development of YA romances.

Popkin, Zelda F. "The Finer Things in Life." *Harpers* 164 (April 1932): 602–11. The contrast between what young adults like to read and what parents and other adults want them to read.

"Romance Series for Young Readers: A Report to Educators and Parents in Concert with the National Education Association." *Interracial Books for Children Bulletin* 12 (Numbers 4 & 5, 1981): 4–31. Hard-sell comments that teenage romances are sexist trash.

Root, Sheldon L. "The New Realism—Some Personal Reflections." *Language Arts* 54 (January 1977): 19–24. What the new realism brought to children's and YA books and the criteria by which it needs to be evaluated.

Silver, Linda R. "Criticism, Reviewing, and the Library Review Media." *Top of the News* 35 (Winter 1979): 123–30. On reviewing YA books. The entire issue is excellent, especially for Rosemary Weber's "The Reviewing of Children's and Young Adult Books in 1977," pp. 131–37; Melvin H. Rosenberg's "Thinking Poor: The Nonlibrary Review Media," pp. 138–42; "What Makes a Good Review? Ten Experts Speak," pp. 146–52; and Patty Camp-

bell's "Only Puddings Like the Kiss of Death: Reviewing the YA Book," pp. 161–62.

Stanek, Lou Willett. "Adults and Adolescents: Ambivalence and Ambiguity." *School Library Journal* 20 (February 1974): 21–25. Comments on the "innocent youth" myth; analyzes several YA novels.

————. "The Junior Novel: A Stylistic Study." *Elementary English* 51 (October 1974): 947–53. A pioneer study of YA novels.

————. "The Maturation of the Junior Novel: From Gestation to the Pill." *School Library Journal* 19 (December 1972): 34–39. Fiction formulas and the YA novel on pregnancy.

Stein, Ruth. "From Happiness to Hopelessness: A Decade of Adolescent Girls." *Arizona English Bulletin* 18 (April 1976): 144–50.

Sutton, Roger. "The Critical Myth: Realistic YA Novels." *School Library Journal* 29 (November 1982): 33–35.

Townsend, John Rowe. "Didacticism in Modern Dress." *Horn Book Magazine* 43 (April 1967): 159–64. Argues that nineteenth-century didacticism is remarkably like the didacticism in modern YA novels. A fine article.

————. "Standards of Criticism for Children's Literature." *Top of the News* 27 (June 1971): 373–87.

Unsworth, Robert. "Holden Caulfield, Where Are You?" *School Library Journal* 23 (January 1977): 40–41. A plea for more books about males by males.

Wigutoff, Sharon. "Junior Fiction: A Feminist Critique." *The Lion and the Unicorn* 5 (1981): 4–18.

Using Young Adult Literature in Classrooms and Libraries

Chelton, Mary K. "Booktalking: You Can Do It." *School Library Journal* 22 (April 1976): 39–43. A rationale for and some ways to give booktalks.

Hipps, G. Melvin. "Adolescent Literature and Values Clarification: A Warning." *Wisconsin English Journal* 20 (January 1978): 5–9.

Mearns, Hughes. "Bo Peep, Old Woman, and Slow Mandy: Being Three Theories of Reading." *New Republic* 48 (November 10, 192[6]): 344–46. Witty and profound; deserves rea[d] every year.

Nelms, Ben F. "Reading for Pleasure in Jun[

High School." *English Journal* 55 (September 1966): 676–81.

Peck, Richard. "Ten Questions to Ask About a Novel." *ALAN Newsletter* 5 (Spring 1978): 1, 7.

Scharf, Peter. "Moral Development and Literature for Adolescents." *Top of the News* 33 (Winter 1977): 131–36. Application of Lawrence Kohlberg's six stages of moral judgment to YA books.

Scoggin, Margaret C. "Do Young People Want Books?" *Wilson Bulletin for Librarians* 11 (September 1936): 17–20, 24.

Shontz, Marilyn Louise. "Selected Research Related to Children's and Young Adult Services in Public Libraries." *Top of the News* 38 (Winter 1982): 125–42. Contains an excellent list of sources.

Small, Robert C., Jr. "The Junior Novel and the Art of Literature." *English Journal* 66 (October 1977): 56–59. Using YA novels to teach aspects of the art of the novel.

_____. "Teaching the Junior Novel." *English Journal* 61 (February 1972): 222–29.

Thurber, Samuel. "Voluntary Reading in the Classical High School from the Pupil's Point of View." *School Review* 13 (February 1905): 168–79. A marvelous modern article, no matter what the date, from the best writer and thinker of the time on teaching English. Anything by Thurber is worth reading.

Acknowledgments

CHAPTER 1 (p. 20) From an interview with Leon Garfield by Justin Wintle from THE PIED PIPERS: INTERVIEWS WITH THE INFLUENTIAL CREATORS OF CHILDREN'S LITERATURE by Justin Wintle and Emma Fisher. Copyright © 1973 and 1974 by Justin Wintle. Reprinted by permission of Paddington Press Ltd. (p. 27) From MR. AND MRS. BO JO JONES by Ann Head. Copyright © 1967 by Ann Head. Jacket art by Paul Bacon. Reprinted by permission of G. P. Putnam's Sons. From THE CHOSEN by Chaim Potok. Copyright © 1967 by Chaim Potok. Jacket design by Paul Bacon. Reprinted by permission of Simon and Schuster. From THE OUTSIDERS by S. E. Hinton. Copyright © 1967 by S. E. Hinton. Reprinted by permission of Dell Publishing Co., Inc. From THE PIGMAN by Paul Zindel. Copyright © 1968 by Paul Zindel. Reprinted by permission of Dell Publishing Co., Inc.

CHAPTER 2 (pp. 42–43) From "Finally Only the Love of the Art" by Donald Hall. *The New York Times Book Review*, January 16, 1983. Copyright © 1983 by The New York Times Company. Reprinted by permission. (p. 62) From an introduction to LORD OF THE FLIES by E. M. Forster. Copyright © 1962 by Coward-McCann, Inc. Reprinted by permission of the Putnam Publishing Group. (p. 68) From JUSTICE AND HER BROTHERS by Virginia Hamilton. Copyright © 1978 by Virginia Hamilton. Jacket painting by James McMullan. Back cover photo of Virginia Hamilton from WILLIE BEA AND THE TIME THE MARTIANS LANDED by Cox Studios. Reprinted by permission of Greenwillow Books, a division of William Morrow & Company, Inc. From A LITTLE LOVE by Virginia Hamilton. Copyright © 1984 by Virginia Hamilton. Jacket illustration by Leo and Diane Dillon © 1984. Reprinted by permission of Philomel Books, a division of The Putnam Publishing Group. (p. 69) From "Sentimental Education" by Harold Brodkey. Reprinted by permission of International Creative Management. First published in *The New Yorker*. Copyright © 1958 by Harold Brodkey.

CHAPTER 3 (p. 78) From "Bait/Rebait: Literature Isn't Supposed to Be Realistic" by G. Robert Carlsen from ENGLISH JOURNAL, January 1981, Vol. 70. Copyright © 1981 by National Council of Teachers of English. Reprinted by permission of the National Council of Teachers of English. (p. 80) Reprinted by permission of the American Library Association from the "May Hill Arbuthnot Honor Lecture: Beyond the Garden Wall" by Sheila Egoff, from TOP OF THE NEWS, Spring 1979, p. 264. Copyright © 1979 by the American Library Association. (p. 85) From THE CHOCOLATE WAR by Robert Cormier. Copyright © 1974 by Robert Cormier. From I AM THE CHEESE by Robert Cormier. Copyright © 1977 by Robert Cormier. From AFTER THE FIRST DEATH by Robert Cormier. Copyright © 1979 by Robert Cormier. From THE BUMBLEBEE FLIES ANYWAY by Robert Cormier. Copyright © 1983 by Robert Cormier. Jacket art by Norman Walker. Reprinted by permission of Pantheon Books, a Division of Random House, Inc. (p. 104) From "1983 Books for Young Adults Poll" by Elizabeth A. Belden et al. from ENGLISH JOURNAL, December 1983, Vol. 72, No. 8. Copyright © 1983 by National Council of Teachers of English. Reprinted by permission of the National Council of Teachers of English. (p. 106) From review by Jean Fritz of "Up in Seth's Room" by Norma Fox Mazer from *The New York Times Book Review*, January 20, 1980. Copyright © 1980 by The New York Times Company. Reprinted by permission.

CHAPTER 4 (p. 124) Covers of PLEASE LET ME IN by Patti Beckman, KATE HERSELF by Helen Erskine, NEW BOY IN TOWN by Dorothy Francis, FLOWERS FOR LISA by Veronica Ladd, SERENADE by Adrienne Marceau, and GIRL IN THE ROUGH by Josephine Wunach reprinted by permission of Harlequin Books. (p. 126) From "The Business of Popularity: The Surge of Teenage Paperbacks" by Pamela D. Pollack. Reprinted with permission from *School Library Journal*, November 1981. Copyright © 1981 R. R. Bowker Co./A Xerox Corporation. (p. 130)

"Holden Caulfield, Where Are You?" by Robert Unsworth. Reprinted with permission from *School Library Journal*, January 1977. R. R. Bowker Co./A Xerox Corporation. (pp. 130–31) From "Bringing Boys' Books Home" by Hazel Rochman. Reprinted with permission from *School Library Journal*, August 1983. Copyright © 1983 R. R. Bowker Co./A Xerox Corporation.

CHAPTER 5 (p. 160) From THE STRANGE AFFAIR OF ADELAIDE HARRIS by Leon Garfield. Copyright © 1971 by Leon Garfield. Illustrated by Fritz Wegner; illustrations Copyright © 1971 by Longman Young Books. Reprinted by permission of Pantheon Books, a division of Random House, Inc. Cover of THE EAGLE OF THE NINTH by Rosemary Sutcliff. Copyright 1954 by Oxford University Press, London. Reprinted by permission of Oxford University Press, London. (p. 164) From THE ROAD TO MANY A WONDER by David Wagoner. Copyright © 1974 by David Wagoner. Jacket design by Janet Halverson. Reprinted by permission of Farrar, Straus & Giroux, Inc. Reprinted with permission of Macmillan Publishing Company from BEYOND THE DIVIDE by Kathryn Lasky. Jacket illustration by Judy Clifford. Jacket illustration Copyright © 1983 by Macmillan Publishing Company.

CHAPTER 6 (p. 174) From PROFILES OF THE FUTURE by Arthur C. Clarke. Copyright © 1984 by Arthur C. Clarke. Reprinted by permission of Holt, Rinehart and Winston, Publishers, and Scott Meredith Literary Agency, Inc. (p. 176) "Ray Guns and Rocket Ships" by Robert A. Heinlein. Reprinted, with permission from *The Library Journal*, July 1953, Vol. 78, No. 13. R. R. Bowker Co./A Xerox Corporation. Copyright 1953 by Xerox Corporation. (p. 178) From "Runaround" by Isaac Asimov. Copyright 1942 by Street & Smith Publications Inc. Copyright © 1970 by Isaac Asimov. Reprinted by permission of the author. (p. 179) Illustration from HAVE SPACESUIT—WILL TRAVEL by Robert A. Heinlein. Copyright © 1958 by Robert A. Heinlein. Used by permission of Charles Scribner's Sons. From 2010: ODYSSEY TWO by Arthur C. Clarke. Copyright © 1982 by Serendib BV. Cover painting by Michael Whelan. Jacket design by Gary Friedman. Reprinted by permission of Ballantine Books, a Division of Random House, Inc. From THE BEST OF ISAAC ASIMOV by Isaac Asimov. Copyright © 1973 by Isaac Asimov; Copyright © 1973 by Sphere Books Ltd. Jacket Design by Richard Mantel. Reprinted by permission of Doubleday, Inc. (p. 189) Ursula K. Le Guin, illustrated from THE FARTHEST SHORE. Copyright © 1972 Ursula K. Le Guin. Used by permission of Atheneum Publishers. From THE WHITE DRAGON by Anne McCaffrey. Copyright © 1978 by Anne McCaffrey. Cover painting by Michael Whelan. Jacket design by Don R. Smith/James Ramage. A Del Rey Book. Reprinted by permission of Ballantine Books, a Division of Random House, Inc.

CHAPTER 7 (p. 223) From ROLL OF THUNDER, HEAR MY CRY by Mildred D. Taylor. Copyright © 1976 by Mildred D. Taylor. Jacket art and design by Jerry Pinkney. From LET THE CIRCLE BE UNBROKEN by Mildred D. Taylor. Copyright © 1981 by Mildred D. Taylor. Jacket painting and design © 1981 by Wendell Minor. Reprinted by permission of The Dial Press. (p. 227) From "Athletes Chasing After Their Potential" by Jonathan Goodman, *Los Angeles Times*, September 6, 1983. Copyright © 1984 Los Angeles Times. Reprinted by permission. (p. 230) From A PASSING SEASON by Richard Blessing. Copyright © 1982 by Richard Blessing. Jacket painting by Richard Sparks. A PASSING SEASON is published by Little, Brown and Company and is available for $12.45. From RUNNING LOOSE by Chris Crutcher. Copyright © 1983 by Chris Crutcher. Jacket painting by Derek James. Reprinted by permission of Greenwillow Books, a division of William Morrow & Company. (pp. 234, 244) Excerpt from CHILDREN OF WAR by Roger Rosenblatt. Copyright © 1983 by Roger Rosenblatt. Reprinted by permission of Doubleday & Company, Inc. (p. 237) From "The Haunting Spectre of Teen-Age Suicide" by Jane E. Brody, *The New York Times*, March 4, 1984. Copyright © 1984 by The New York Times Company. Reprinted by permission.

CHAPTER 8 (p. 275) From MEET MATISSE by Nelly Munthe. Copyright © 1983 by Nelly Munthe. MEET MATISSE is published by Little, Brown and Company and is available for $12.45. Cover illustration from ANNO'S FLEA MARKET by Mitsumasa Anno. Copyright © 1984 by Mitsumasa Anno. Reprinted by permission of Philomel Books, and Japan Foreign-Rights Centre (JFC). (p. 287) "Turning Off: The Abuse of Drug Information" by Peter G. Hammond. Reprinted with permission from *School Library Journal*, April 1973. R. R. Bowker Co./A Xerox Corporation. (p. 291) From WHAT'S HAPPENING TO ME? by Peter Mayle. Copyright © 1975 by Peter Mayle. Illustrations by Arthur Robins. Reprinted by permission of Lyle Stuart, Inc. (p. 294) From CHANGING BODIES, CHANGING LIVES by Ruth Bell et al. Copyright © 1980 by Ruth Bell. Photographs by John Launois/Black Star, Peter Vadnai/Editorial Photocolor Archives, and Dan Nelkin. Jacket design by Richard Adelson. Reprinted by permission of Random House, Inc.

CHAPTER 9 (p. 311) W. S. Merwin, "Separation" from THE MOVING TARGET. Copyright © 1963 by W. S. Merwin. Reprinted with the permission of Atheneum Publishers and David Higham Associates Limited. "Man on Wheels" by Karl Shapiro. Copyright © 1968 by Karl Shapiro. Reprinted from COLLECTED POEMS 1940–1978 by Karl Shapiro, by permission of Random House, Inc. "Waking From a Nap on the Beach" from NEW & SELECTED THINGS TAKING PLACE by May Swenson. Copyright © 1966 by May Swenson. First appeared in *The Saturday Review*. By permission of Little, Brown and Company in association with the Atlantic Monthly Press. (p. 312) "In a Cafe" excerpted from the book THE PILL VERSUS THE SPRINGHILL MINE DISASTER by Richard Brautigan. Copyright © 1968 by Richard Brautigan. Reprinted by permission of Delacorte Press/Seymour Lawrence and Sterling Lord Agency. (p. 313) From DON'T FORGET TO FLY by Paul B. Janeczko, ed. Copyright © 1981 by Paul Janeczko. Jacket design by Neil Waldman. From POSTCARD POEMS by Paul B. Janeczko, ed. Copyright © 1979 by Paul Janeczko. Jacket photographs by Robert Verrone. From POETSPEAK: IN THEIR WORK, ABOUT THEIR WORK by Paul B. Janeczko, ed. Copyright © 1983 by Paul B. Janeczko. Jacket painting by Neil Waldman. Copyright © 1983 by Bradbury Press. From STRINGS: A GATHERING OF FAMILY POEMS by Paul B. Janeczko, ed. Copyright © 1984 by Paul B. Janeczko. Jacket painting by Neil Waldman. Copyright © 1984 by Bradbury Press. Reprinted by permission of Bradbury Press. "The Portrait" from THE POEMS OF STANLEY KUNITZ 1928–1978. Copyright © 1971 by Stanley Kunitz. Reprinted by permission of Little, Brown and Company in Association with the Atlantic Monthly Press. From Comments by Stanley Kunitz on his poem "The Portrait." Reprinted by permission of Stanley Kunitz. (p. 315) From SINGIN' AND SWINGIN' AND GETTIN' MERRY LIKE CHRISTMAS by Maya Angelou. Copyright © 1976 by Maya Angelou. Jacket design by Janet Halverson. From OH PRAY MY WINGS ARE GONNA FIT ME WELL by Maya Angelou. Copyright © 1975 by Maya Angelou. Jacket design by Janet Halverson. Reprinted by permission of Random House, Inc. (p. 318) From "Ouchless Poetry" by Don Mainprize from ENGLISH JOURNAL, February 1982, Vol. 71, No. 2. Copyright © 1983 by National Council of Teachers of English. Reprinted by permission of the National Council of Teachers of English. (p. 319) From "Teaching Poetry Writing in Secondary School" by Alberta Turner from ENGLISH JOURNAL, September 1982, Vol. 71. Copyright © 1982 by National Council of Teachers of English. Reprinted by permission of the National Council of Teachers of English. (p. 325) From "The Legitimacy of American Adolescent Fiction" by Maia Pank Mertz and David A. England. Reprinted with permission from *School Library Journal*, October 1983. Copyright © 1983 R. R. Bowker Co./A Xerox Corporation. (pp. 343–44) Piet Hein, GROOKS, 1966, pp. 33 and 53 and GROOKS 2, 1968, p. 33, Garden City: Doubleday and Company. GROOKS 3, 1970, p. 19 and GROOKS 5, 1972, p. 14, Canada: General Publishing Co., Ltd.; New York: Doubleday and

Company; London: Hodder and Stoughton Limited; Copenhagen: Borgens Forlag; Oxford: Blackwell & Mott, Ltd. (p. 344) Reprinted by the permission of The Putnam Publishing Group from SPILT MILK by Morris Bishop. Copyright 1942; renewed 1969 by Morris Bishop. (p. 354) From A SMALL BOOK OF GRAVE HUMOR by Fritz Spiegl. Copyright © 1971 by Fritz Spiegl. Reprinted by permission of Pan Books. Dudley Fitts, POEMS FROM THE GREEK ANTHOLOGY. Copyright © 1956 by New Directions Publishing Corporation. Reprinted by permission of New Directions.

CHAPTER 10 (pp. 372–74) From VOICE OF YOUTH ADVOCATES, February 1984. Copyright © 1984 by Voice of Youth Advocates, Inc. Reprinted by permission. (pp. 376, 379) Adapted from "Booktalking: You Can Do It: by Mary K. Chelton. Reprinted with permission of Mary K. Chelton from *School Library Journal*, April 1976. R. R. Bowker Co./A Xerox Corporation. (p. 385) From "Anne Frank vs. Pony Boy" by Jan Hartman from ENGLISH JOURNAL, March 1984, Vol. 72, No. 7. Copyright © 1984 by National Council of Teachers of English. Reprinted by permission of the National Council of Teachers of English. (pp. 388–89) From "Unlocking the Box: An Experiment in Literary Response" by Suzanne Howell, from ENGLISH JOURNAL, February 1977, Vol. 66, No. 2. Copyright © 1977 by the National Council of Teachers of English. Reprinted by permission of the publisher and the author. (p. 389) From "Responses to Literature: Enlarging the Range" by Larry Andrews, from ENGLISH JOURNAL, February 1977, Vol. 66, No. 2. Copyright © 1977 by the National Council of Teachers of English. Reprinted by permission of the publisher and the author. (p. 392) From "Well, Where Are We in Teaching Literature?" by Dwight L. Burton, from ENGLISH JOURNAL, February 1974, Vol. 63, No. 2. Copyright © 1974 by National Council of Teachers of English. Reprinted by permission of the publisher and the author. (pp. 393–95) From "Writing and Literature" by Ted Hipple from ENGLISH JOURNAL, February 1984, Vol. 73, No. 2. Copyright © 1984 by National Council of Teachers of English. Reprinted by permission of the National Council of Teachers of English. (pp. 397–98) Adapted from "Individualized Reading" by Barbara Blow, from *Arizona English Bulletin*, Vol. 18, No. 3, April 1976. Reprinted by permission of the author and the Arizona English Teachers Association. (pp. 404–5) Reprinted by permission of the American Library Association from "Moral Development and Literature for Adolescents," by Peter Scharf, TOP OF THE NEWS, Winter 1977, p. 134 and Table 1.

CHAPTER 11 (p. 411) "Quality or Popularity? Selection Criteria for YAs" by Lillian L. Shapiro. Reprinted, with permission, from *School Library Journal*, May 1978, Vol. 24, No. 9. R. R. Bowker Co./A Xerox Corporation. (p. 413) From an editorial by Mary K. Chelton from VOICE OR YOUTH ADVOCATES, Vol. 1, No. 2, June 1978. Reprinted by permission. From "Only Puddings Like the Kiss of Death: Reviewing the YA Book" by Patty Campbell from TOP OF THE NEWS, Winter 1979, Vol. 35, No. 2. Reprinted by permission of the American Library Association. (p. 420) From Anne Tyler's review of "Rainbow Jordan" by Alice Childress, *The New York Times Book Review*, April 26, 1981. Copyright © 1981 by The New York Times Company. Reprinted by permission. From "A Bridge of Words" by Robert Lipsyte, a review of TIGER EYES by Judy Blume, *The Nation*, November 21, 1981. Copyright © 1981 Nation Magazine, The Nation Associates. Reprinted by permission. From Katherine Paterson's review of "Sweet Whispers, Brother Rush" by Virginia Hamilton, *The New York Times Book Review*, November 14, 1982. Copyright © 1982 by The New York Times Company. Reprinted by permission. (p. 423) "Some Thoughts on the Black YA Novel," by Al Muller from ALAN Newsletter, Assembly on Literature for Adolescents—NCTE, Vol. 5, No. 2, Winter 1978. Reprinted by permission. (pp. 430–31) from "Bait" by Dean Hughes; from "Rebait" by Kathy Piehl from ENGLISH JOURNAL, December 1981, Vol. 70, No. 8. Copyright © 1981 by National Council of Teachers of English. Reprinted by permission of the National Council of

Teachers of English. (**p. 441**) Excerpts from a letter to Alleen Pace Nilsen, November 30, 1982 by Norma Fox Mazer; comments reprinted by permission of Norma Fox Mazer.

CHAPTER 12 (**p. 472**) From THE FIRST FREEDOM by Nat Hentoff. Copyright © 1980 by Namar Productions, Ltd. Jacket design copyright © 1980 by Mike Stromberg. Reprinted by permission of Delacorte Press. From DEALING WITH CENSORSHIP by James Davis, ed. Copyright © 1979 by the National Council of Teachers of English. From THE STUDENTS' RIGHT TO READ by Kenneth L. Donelson and THE STUDENTS' RIGHT TO KNOW by Lee Burress and Edward B. Jenkinson. Copyright © 1982 by the National Council of Teachers of English. Reprinted by permission of the National Council of Teachers of English. From CENSORS IN THE CLASSROOM by Edward B. Jenkinson. Copyright © 1979 by Southern Illinois University Press. Reprinted by permission of Southern Illinois University Press. (**p. 483**) From GOD, THE UNIVERSE, AND HOT FUDGE SUNDAES by Norma Howe. Copyright © 1984 by Norma Howe. Jacket painting © 1984 by Ted Lewin. Reprinted by permission of Houghton Mifflin Company. From THE DAY THEY CAME TO ARREST THE BOOK by Nat Hentoff. Copyright © 1982 by Marnate Productions, Inc. Jacket illustration copyright © 1982 by Allan Manham. Reprinted by permission of Delacorte Press. Jacket painting from the cover of STRIKE! by Barbara Corcoran (Atheneum Publishers) reproduced by permission of the artist Michael Garland. From A MATTER OF PRINCIPLE by Susan Beth Pfeffer. Copyright © 1982 by Susan Beth Pfeffer. Jacket illustration copyright © 1982 by Gordon Johnson. Jacket design copyright © 1982 by Richard Oriolo. Reprinted by permission of Delacorte Press.

CHAPTER 13 (**p. 515**) From GRANDMOTHER ELSIE and ELSIE'S WIDOWHOOD by Martha Finley. Copyright 1910 by Charles B. Finley. Reprinted by permission of Dodd, Mead and Company.

CHAPTER 14 (**p. 536**) From "The Virtues of the Second-Rate" by William Lyon Phelps, from ENGLISH JOURNAL, January 1927, Vol. 16, No. 1. Copyright 1927 by the National Council of Teachers of English. Reprinted by permission of the publisher and the author. "A Gallery of Girls" by Alice M. Jordan. Reprinted from *Horn Book Magazine* (September–October 1937). Copyright 1937 by The Horn Book, Inc. (**p. 538**) "Best Sellers and Modern Youth" by Louise Dinwiddie. Reprinted, with permission, from *The Library Journal*, November 15, 1940, Vol. 65. R. R. Bowker Co./A Xerox Corporation. (**p. 551**) Cover from LET THE HURRICANE ROAR by Rose Wilder Lane. Copyright 1933, renewed 1960 by Rose Wilder Lane. Reproduced by permission of Roger Lea Macbride. LET THE HURRICANE ROAR will be republished by Harper & Row, Publishers, Inc. in 1985.

CHAPTER 15 (**p. 577**) From "Behind Reading Interests" by G. R. Carlsen from ENGLISH JOURNAL, January 1954, Vol. 43, No. 1. Copyright © 1954 by the National Council of Teachers of English. Reprinted by permission of the publisher and the author. (**p. 578**) "Bibliotherapy and the School Librarian" by Willard A. Heaps. Reprinted, with permission, from *The Library Journal*, October 1, 1940. R. R. Bowker Co./A Xerox Corporation. (**p. 579**) From "Diversifying the Matter" by Lou LaBrant from THE ENGLISH JOURNAL, March 1951, Vol. 40, No. 3. Copyright © 1951 by the National Council of Teachers of English. Reprinted by permission of the publisher and the author. From "Bibliotherapy" by Frank Ross from MEDIA & METHODS, January 1969, Vol. 5, No. 5. Copyright © 1969 Media and Methods Institute, Inc. Reprinted by permission. (**p. 580**) From "Paperbacks in the Classroom" by S. Alan Cohen from *Journal of Reading*, Vol. 12, No. 4, January 1969. Reprinted with permission of S. Alan Cohen and the International Reading Association. (**p. 581**) From "Paperback Talk" by Ray Walters, from *The New York Times Book Review*, November 13, 1977. © 1977 by The New York Times Company. Reprinted by permission. (**p. 583**) From "Junior Book Roundup" by Stanley B. Kegler and Stephen Dunning from ENGLISH JOURNAL, May 1964, Vol. 53, No. 5. Copyright © 1964 by the National Council of Teachers of English. Reprinted by permission of the publisher and the author.

Subject Index

Index of Critics and Commentators

Author and Title Index

Also Available from
Scott, Foresman and Company
Good Year Books

Good Year Books are reproducible resource and activity books for teachers and parents of students in preschool through grade 12. Written by experienced educators, Good Year Books are filled with class-tested ideas, teaching strategies and methods, and fun-to-do activities for every basic curriculum area. They also contain enrichment materials and activities that help extend a child's learning experiences beyond the classroom.

Good Year Books address many educational needs in both formal and informal settings. They have been used widely in preservice teacher training courses, as a resource for practicing teachers to enhance their own professional growth, and by interested adults as a source of sound, valuable activities for home, summer camp, Scout meetings, and the like.

Good Year Books are available through your local college or university bookstore, independent or chain booksellers, and school supply and educational dealers. For a complete catalog of Good Year Books, write:

Good Year Books
Department PPG-T
1900 East Lake Avenue
Glenview, Illinois 60025